THE
CRITERION
JOURNAL ON INNOVATION

VOL. 6		2020

Monopoly, Innovation, and Due Process:
FTC v. Qualcomm and the Imperative to Destroy

*J. Gregory Sidak**

* A.B. 1977, A.M., J.D. 1981, Stanford University. Chairman, Criterion Economics, Washington, D.C.
Email: jgsidak@criterioneconomics.com. Copyright 2020 by J. Gregory Sidak. All rights reserved.
For Richard Posner—scholar, jurist, mentor, friend.

INTRODUCTION

During the fire of Rome in 64 A.D., Nero reputedly burned the Palatine Hill so that he could buy its charred estates at distressed prices and enlarge his palace, the Domus Aurea.[1] In a deposition conducted 1,955 years later, a lawyer, representing a plaintiff class seeking $15 billion in antitrust treble damages from Qualcomm,[2] asked a former Qualcomm executive the following question. Patent licensing "is responsible for a majority of Qualcomm's profits," so, "if a judge came along and . . . slashed Qualcomm's royalty rate, that would destroy a great deal of the value of Qualcomm's business model; correct?"[3]

---

[1] Suetonius wrote that Nero "set fire to the city so openly that several ex-consuls did not venture to lay hands on his chamberlains although they caught them on their estates with tow and fire-brands, while some granaries near the Golden House [the Domus Aurea], whose room he particularly desired, were demolished by engines of war and then set on fire, because their walls were of stone." C. SUETONIUS TRANQUILLUS, THE LIVES OF THE TWELVE CAESARS, THE LIFE OF NERO 38.1 (A.D. 121). *See also* Silvia Donati, *Nero's Party House on Rome's Palatine Hill to Reopen*, ITALY MAG., Apr. 10, 2018 ("New openings on the Palatine Hill, where Nero had his imperial palace, the Domus Aurea, will allow visitors to get a further glimpse into the life of the last Roman emperor of the Julio-Claudian dynasty, who ruled Rome from 54 to 68 AD, believed by many to be responsible for the fire that destroyed Rome in 64 AD. . . . The fire that broke out at the Circus [Maximus] between 18 and 19 July, 64 d. C., changed everything, including the imperial residence, which was rebuilt and extended for about 80 hectares: the Domus Aurea, which covered parts of the slopes of the Palatine, Esquiline, Oppian and Caelian hills, a complex that could compete with the great dynastic palaces of the Mediterranean, and conveyed a message of lavishness and magnificence.").

[2] *See* Opening Brief of Defendant-Appellant Qualcomm Incorporated at 10, Stromberg v. Qualcomm Inc., No. 19-15159 (9th Cir. June 3, 2019) ("Because the class is so massive, plaintiffs' damages claim is approximately $5 billion before any statutory trebling."); Class Action Complaint for Violations of Federal and State Antitrust Laws, State Unfair Competition Laws, and the Common Law of Unjust Enrichment at 65, Stromberg v. Qualcomm Inc., No. 5:17-cv-00304 (N.D. Cal. Jan. 20, 2017) ("Plaintiffs and members of the Damages Class in each of the above jurisdictions seek damages (including statutory damages where applicable), to be trebled or otherwise increased as permitted by a particular jurisdiction's antitrust law."); *see also* Notice of Appearance of Rio S. Pierce at 2, *In re* Qualcomm Antitrust Litig., No. 17-md-02773-LHK (N.D. Cal. June 16, 2017), ECF No. 81 ("TO ALL PARTIES AND THEIR COUNSEL OF RECORD: PLEASE TAKE NOTICE that Rio S. Pierce of the law firm Hagens Berman Sobol Shapiro LLP hereby enters his appearance in this action on behalf of Direct Purchaser Plaintiffs."); Civil Minutes at 1, *In re* Qualcomm Antitrust Litig., No. 17-md.-02773-LHK (N.D. Cal. May 24, 2018), ECF No. 483 ("Attorney for MDL Plaintiffs: Rio Pierce").

[3] Videotaped Deposition of Eric Reifschneider (Vol. 2) at 319:10–12, 319:16–20, FTC v. Qualcomm Inc., No. 5:17-cv-00220-LHK (N.D. Cal. Feb. 22, 2018) (deposition examination conducted by Rio Pierce, Hagens Berman Sobol Shapiro LLP), *exhibit to* Federal Trade Commission's Submission of January 4[, 2019,] Testimony by Deposition, FTC v. Qualcomm Inc., No. 5:17-cv-00220-LHK (N.D. Cal. Jan. 7, 2019), ECF No. 1161-1 [hereinafter Deposition of Eric Reifschneider (Vol. 2)].

The lawyer's question shared none of what motivates the virtuous contest that Joseph Schumpeter famously named "creative destruction."[4] Instead, the lawyer's question seemed to outline, perhaps with inadvertent candor, a plan of destruction devoid of any increment of creative contribution. The lawyer's question suggested a rapacious imperative to destroy, evidently motivated by the prospect of appropriating, amid that imperious destruction, some small remnant of the enormous value that had been created over years by the extraordinary skill, foresight, and perseverance of those who had built Qualcomm. The lawyer's question suggested a war being waged on innovation by avarice. Perverting antitrust law would be the eristic means to an end.

On May 21, 2019, Judge Lucy Koh of the U.S. District Court for the Northern District of California issued her findings of fact and conclusions of law in the bench trial in *Federal Trade Commission v. Qualcomm Inc.*[5] and entered judgment in favor of the FTC.[6] Argued on February 13, 2020 on appeal to the Ninth Circuit, *FTC v. Qualcomm* was the government's most consequential monopolization case since *Microsoft.*[7] And its most overtly political. The FTC wanted a fundamental transformation. Judge Koh obliged. She did not mention in her findings of fact and conclusions of law that a class action, also pending before her, was seeking $15 billion in treble damages from Qualcomm on the same theories of liability as those that the FTC had just litigated in pursuit of its desired permanent, worldwide injunction.

On August 11, 2020, the three-judge panel hearing Qualcomm's appeal to the Ninth Circuit issued its unanimous opinion (1) reversing Judge Koh's judgment on every question of law on which Qualcomm had appealed, (2) vacating her permanent, worldwide injunction, and (3) vacating her grant to the FTC before trial of partial summary judgment:

> *First*, Qualcomm's practice of licensing its SEPs exclusively at the OEM level does not amount to anticompetitive conduct in violation of § 2, as Qualcomm is under no antitrust duty to license rival chip suppliers. To the extent Qualcomm has breached any of its FRAND commitments, a conclusion we need not and do not reach, the remedy for such a breach lies in contract and patent law. *Second*, Qualcomm's patent-licensing royalties and "no license, no chips" policy do not impose an anticompetitive surcharge on rivals' modem chip sales. Instead, these aspects of Qualcomm's business model are "chip-supplier neutral" and do not undermine competition in the

---

[4] Joseph Schumpeter, Capitalism, Socialism and Democracy 81 (Kessinger Publishing 2ᵈ ed. 2010) (1947).

[5] 411 F. Supp. 3d 658 (N.D. Cal. 2019).

[6] Judgment, FTC v. Qualcomm Inc., No. 5:17-cv-00220-LHK (N.D. Cal. May 21, 2019) ("On May 21, 2019, the Court entered its Findings of Fact and Conclusions of Law, and found that Defendant violated the Federal Trade Commission Act. ECF No. 1490. Accordingly, the Clerk shall enter judgment in favor of Plaintiff. The Clerk shall close the file. IT IS SO ORDERED.").

[7] United States v. Microsoft Corp., 253 F.3d 34 (D.C. Cir. 2001) (en banc) (per curiam).

relevant antitrust markets. *Third*, Qualcomm's 2011 and 2013 agreements with Apple have not had the actual or practical effect of substantially foreclosing competition in the CDMA modem chip market. Furthermore, because these agreements were terminated years ago by Apple itself, there is nothing to be enjoined.

We therefore **REVERSE** the district court's judgment and **VACATE** its injunction as well as its partial grant of summary judgment.[8]

The Ninth Circuit resoundingly condemned the imperative to destroy embodied in the prosecution of *FTC v. Qualcomm* and its follow-on litigation.

Had the Ninth Circuit affirmed Judge Koh, counsel for the plaintiff class litigating against Qualcomm could have been expected to claim that every principle of issue preclusion worked to its advantage. Indeed, it is telling that the question about a judge's power to destroy the value of Qualcomm's business model—though it was asked by a lawyer representing a class in parallel litigation—appeared in the videotaped deposition testimony of the very first witness whom the FTC called to testify in its case-in-chief in *FTC v. Qualcomm*.

Many articles, white papers, and *amicus* briefs have already been written about *FTC v. Qualcomm*, as befits a case of such significance. Most of those writings discuss the issues at the level of policy or theory. Abstractions fly back and forth like a shuttlecock in a game of badminton. Virtually none of these commentators digs into the actual evidentiary record of the case. As a consequence, little of the public commentary on *FTC v. Qualcomm* discerns and engages, at the level of proof rather than theory, the basis for Judge Koh's findings of fact and conclusions of law.

The same observation pertains to the three-judge panel's opinion issued on August 11, 2020 in Qualcomm's appeal to the Ninth Circuit. The three-judge panel concluded, as a matter of law, and without explicitly reviewing any of Judge Koh's findings of fact under any level of appellate scrutiny, that the FTC had failed at trial to produce preponderant evidence that Qualcomm had violated either section 1 or section 2 of the Sherman Act. That is, accepting (for purposes of Qualcomm's appeal) Judge Koh's findings of fact as absolutely correct, the Ninth Circuit found that Judge Koh's conclusions of law, which of course were predicated on her findings of fact that almost uniformly favored the FTC, were clearly erroneous. Thus, the Ninth Circuit did not scrutinize the evidentiary basis for Judge Koh's findings of fact, nor did it perform substantial incremental fact finding of its own. It did not mention the testimony of a single witness. It did not evaluate whether Judge Koh had

---

[8] FTC v. Qualcomm Inc., No. 19-16122, 2020 WL 4591476, at *21–22 (9th Cir. Aug. 11, 2020) (emphasis in original) (boldface in original).

abused her discretion as a federal judge. And it did not examine whether a deprivation of liberty or property without due process of law had occurred.

We shall see that the Ninth Circuit's opinion on Judge Koh's conclusions of law and mixed questions of law and fact, as opposed to its opinion on the evidentiary basis for her findings of fact alone, was the tip of the iceberg. My approach in this article is qualitatively different. I conduct in 774 pages a *de novo* review of the publicly available trial record in *FTC v. Qualcomm*. I have done so in part to demonstrate to any jurist interested in the question that the task is entirely possible to accomplish, and in part to show why due process of law requires it. I have read in their entirety the 11 volumes of the public (redacted) trial transcript containing the testimony of the 27 witnesses who testified at trial, as well as the public (redacted) deposition designations of the 22 other witnesses whose testimony the parties replayed by video at trial. My analysis reveals Judge Koh's errors of fact concerning monopoly, innovation, and due process—as well as her errors of law, many but not all of which the Ninth Circuit identified.

Table 1 reports the 24 main law firms that (1) defended the witnesses who testified at trial or (2) intervened in the case for other purposes, most notably to file sealing motions so as to maintain the confidentiality of documentary evidence (particularly individual bilateral license agreements, supply agreements, or other commercial contracts to which the clients of these law firms were parties). The law firms appearing in *FTC v. Qualcomm* were as of 2019 among the largest and most prestigious firms in the United States.

I have also reviewed the significant pretrial rulings in *FTC v. Qualcomm*, including such portions of expert reports as the parties made publicly available in connection with their associated motions practice before trial. This article does not rely on any confidential business information, any nonpublic information, or any privileged communications.

In the past, I have served as a consultant to and a testifying expert economic witness for Qualcomm. I was disclosed as a potential expert economic witness for Qualcomm in *FTC v. Qualcomm*. However, Qualcomm ultimately did not use me in either a testifying or consulting capacity in the case, I did not execute the protective order in the case, and I performed no professional services for Qualcomm in connection with the case. Neither Qualcomm nor any other client, intermediary, or third party has requested, commissioned, funded, or exercised editorial control over this article. The views expressed here are solely my own.

Table 1. Affiliations and Law Firms of Witnesses Who Testified (Either in Person or by Videotaped Deposition) in *FTC v. Qualcomm*

Company	Law Firm(s)
Apple	Boies Schiller Flexner
Bain & Company	McDermott Will & Emery
BlackBerry	Sullivan & Cromwell
Broadcom	Perkins Coie
Ericsson	Baker Botts
Huawei	Sidley Austin
Intel	Munger, Tolles & Olson
	Wilmer Cutler Pickering Hale and Dorr
InterDigital	Wilson Sonsini Goodrich & Rosati
Lenovo	K&L Gates
LG Electronics	Eimer Stahl
	Wright, L'Estrange & Ergastolo
MediaTek	Boies Schiller Flexner
Motorola	K&L Gates
Nokia	Alston & Bird
Pegatron	Gibson, Dunn & Crutcher
Qualcomm	Cravath, Swaine & Moore
	Keker, Van Nest & Peters
	Morgan, Lewis & Bockius
	Norton Rose Fulbright
	Quinn Emanuel Urquhart & Sullivan
Samsung	O'Melveny & Myers
Texas Instruments	Winston & Strawn
Wistron	Gibson, Dunn & Crutcher

A. *Mobile Communications and Standard-Essential Patents*

As of June 2020, there were 6.1 billion mobile broadband subscriptions globally.[9] Qualcomm helped as much as any other company to make that achievement possible. It is an American company, based in San Diego,

---

[9] ERICSSON, ERICSSON MOBILITY REPORT 34 (June 2020), https://www.ericsson.com/49da93/assets/local/mobility-report/documents/2020/june2020-ericsson-mobility-report.pdf.

California, that has 37,000 employees[10] and a portfolio of more than 140,000 patents and patent applications worldwide.[11] Qualcomm has developed and commercialized "foundational technologies and products used in mobile devices and other wireless products."[12] It holds and licenses one of the leading intellectual property portfolios for wireless communication technologies.[13] Its portfolio includes both standard-essential patents (SEPs) and implementation patents (or non-SEPs).[14] SEPs are patents essential to practice industry standards, such as the fourth-generation (4G) Long-Term Evolution (LTE) standard or the fifth-generation (5G) standard that will enable the mobile connectivity between machines (including vehicles, smart meters, medical devices, home appliances, and many others) that, in turn, will support the Internet of Things (IoT).

With more than 300 licensees, Qualcomm's portfolio is "the most widely and extensively licensed in the [wireless] industry."[15] Qualcomm also has developed and supplied application-specific integrated circuits (ASICs) to original equipment manufacturers (OEMs), such as manufacturers of mobile phones and other devices, tablets, laptops, routers, and infrastructure equipment.[16] Qualcomm has licensed its patents through its Qualcomm Technology Licensing (QTL) business unit, and it has developed and supplied ASICs through its separate Qualcomm CDMA Technologies (QCT) business unit.[17] CDMA stands for Code Division Multiple Access, a mobile-communications technology invented by Qualcomm and adopted by the Telecommunications Industry Association (TIA) for the cdmaOne second-generation (2G) wireless standard.[18]

A baseband processor modem—commonly called simply a "modem"—is a particular kind of ASIC.[19] Other names for a modem are a "baseband," a "digital baseband," a "modem chip," or a "cellular baseband."[20] A modem

---

[10] Qualcomm Inc., Annual Report for the Period Ending September 29, 2019 (SEC Form 10-K), at 16 (filed Nov. 6, 2019) [hereinafter 2019 Qualcomm 10-K].

[11] *About Qualcomm*, QUALCOMM (Aug. 2020), https://investor.qualcomm.com/about-qualcomm/overview.

[12] 2019 Qualcomm 10-K, *supra* note 10, at 43.

[13] *Id.* at 11.

[14] *Id.*

[15] *Id.*

[16] *Id.* at 9.

[17] *Id.* at 9–13.

[18] FTC v. Qualcomm Inc., 411 F. Supp. 3d 658, 671 (N.D. Cal. 2019).

[19] *Id.* at 674 n.4.

[20] *See, e.g.*, Brian Klug, *The State of Qualcomm's Modems—WTR1605 and MDM9x25*, ANANDTECH, Jan. 4, 2013, https://www.anandtech.com/show/6541/the-state-of-qualcomms-modems-wtr1605-and-mdm9x25 ("Finally we have the baseband, which effectively functions as the controller for power amplifiers, switches, and transceiver and handles all the demodulation of received I/Q data and modulation for transmission. In addition the baseband worries about the layers above physical required to get the phone online, for example signaling required for the particular air interface. I've seen people refer to this as digital baseband, baseband processor, and modem interchangeably, it's the same part they're referring to."); Gary Sims, *Smartphones Use a Second CPU and Second Operating System in Their Baseband Modems*, ANDROID AUTHORITY,

"modulate[s] and demodulate[s] the information at the transmitter and receiver block respectively in order to transmit the information signal reliably through the propagating medium."[21] Put simply, a modem processes information received from the user's device (such as a voice call or data transfer) and prepares it for transmission *to* the wireless network. It also processes information received *from* the wireless network. Thus, a modem enables the communication between an end user's mobile handset and a carrier's base station (which, in turn, provides access to the carrier's core network). Modems are essential to smartphones, and they are used in other electronic devices, including tablets, wearable devices, and, increasingly, in wirelessly connected devices designed for use in the IoT.[22]

The majority of modems intended for use in smartphones are sold as either a part of a "System on a Chip" (SoC) (also called a "chip" or "chipset"), which integrates the baseband processor modem with an applications processor,[23] or as a standalone (or discrete) baseband processor modem, also called a "slim modem" or a "thin modem,"[24] which does not combine the baseband processor modem with an applications processor. Instead, a thin modem contains only a baseband processor modem and a radio frequency (RF) transceiver.[25] Inside a smartphone, a thin modem "require[s] an additional applications processor to perform tasks such as graphics and image processing to provide a better user experience."[26] As Judge Koh noted in her findings of fact and conclusions of law, Apple uses the latter configuration in its smartphones; it "buys thin modems from external modem chip suppliers

---

Nov. 18, 2013, https://www.androidauthority.com/smartphones-have-a-second-os-317800/; *Why Qualcomm Remains the No. 1 Player in Cellular Baseband*, FORBES, July 11, 2014.

    Judge Koh twice stated: "ASIC is another term for modem chip." *FTC v. Qualcomm*, 411 F. Supp. 3d at 753, 760. Similarly, near the beginning of her findings of fact and conclusions of law, she stated that another term for a modem chip is an "application specific integrated circuit[] ('ASIC[]')." *Id.* at 674 n.4. But that definition is imprecise. A modem is an ASIC, but not all ASICs are modems. Videotaped Deposition of Eric Reifschneider (Vol. 1) at 30:2–9, FTC v. Qualcomm Inc., No. 5:17-cv-00220-LHK (N.D. Cal. Feb. 22, 2018), *exhibit to* Federal Trade Commission's Submission of January 4[, 2019,] Testimony by Deposition, FTC v. Qualcomm Inc., No. 5:17-cv-00220-LHK (N.D. Cal. Jan. 7, 2019), ECF No. 1161-1 [hereinafter Deposition of Eric Reifschneider (Vol. 1)]. An ASIC is a synonym for a modem chip only in the limited sense that the documents and testimony in evidence intended that meaning. Cars and trucks are vehicles, but whether "vehicle" means "truck" depends on the context and is not unconditionally true. The instances of potential ambiguity on this point in Judge Koh's findings of fact and conclusions of law were numerous. Before first asserting at page 753 in the body of her findings of fact and conclusions of law (rather than in her footnotes) that "ASIC is another term for modem chip," Judge Koh had already referred without elaboration to an ASIC or ASICs 29 times. *FTC v. Qualcomm*, 411 F. Supp. 3d at 673, 699, 700 (four times), 706 (four times), 722 (three times), 723, 724, 744 (four times), 745 (twice), 747 (six times), 748 (twice).

    [21] SAJAL KUMAR DAS, MOBILE TERMINAL RECEIVER DESIGN 9 (John Wiley & Sons 2017).

    [22] *Id.* at 1–2, 350–51.

    [23] *See, e.g.*, Transcript of Proceedings (Volume 7) at 1361:6–17, FTC v. Qualcomm Inc., No. 5:17-cv-00220-LHK (N.D. Cal. Jan. 18, 2019) (Testimony of James Thompson (CTO, Qualcomm)).

    [24] *Id.* at 1378:14.

    [25] *Id.* at 1378:4–14.

    [26] STRATEGY ANALYTICS, BASEBAND MARKET SHARE TRACKER Q3 2017: QUALCOMM GAINS SHARE tab 5 (2018).

and internally develops application processors, which include the multimedia capability necessary for smartphones."[27]

B. *The FTC's Case Against Qualcomm*

On January 17, 2017, the FTC filed a complaint in the U.S. District Court for the Northern District of California in which it alleged that Qualcomm had violated federal antitrust law.[28] For reasons that will become clear in Part I, it is hard to imagine that the FTC would have brought this case against Qualcomm if Qualcomm's principal rival modem manufacturer were not Intel, and if the principal OEM manufacturing smartphones were not Apple.

The FTC's complaint asserted that Qualcomm possessed monopoly power in two alleged product markets: (1) the CDMA modem market and (2) the "premium" LTE modem market.[29] The complaint then focused on three of Qualcomm's alleged practices: (1) "Qualcomm withholds its baseband processors unless a customer accepts a license to standard-essential patents on terms preferred by Qualcomm, including elevated royalties that the customer must pay when using competitors' processors ('no license-no chips')," [30] (2) "Qualcomm has consistently refused to license its cellular standard-essential patents to its competitors, in violation of Qualcomm's FRAND commitments" (that is, Qualcomm's contractual commitments to several standard-setting organizations (SSOs) to offer to license its cellular SEPs on fair, reasonable, and nondiscriminatory (FRAND) terms),[31] and (3) Qualcomm executed two agreements to supply the leading U.S. smartphone OEM—Apple—with modems, subject to allegedly unlawful exclusivity provisions.[32]

The FTC alleged that these three practices enabled Qualcomm to charge "elevated royalties that apply to baseband processors supplied by [Qualcomm's] competitors."[33] Those "elevated royalties," the FTC alleged, imposed a "tax"[34] on the "all-in price" of rivals' modems, thereby, "increas[ing] the all-in cost to an OEM of using a competitor's" modem.[35] (The "all-in price"

---

[27] FTC v. Qualcomm Inc., 411 F. Supp. 3d 658, 674 (N.D. Cal. 2019) (citing Transcript of Proceedings (Volume 7) at 1378:7–14, FTC v. Qualcomm Inc., No. 5:17-cv-00220-LHK (N.D. Cal. Jan. 18, 2019) (Testimony of James Thompson (CTO, Qualcomm))).

[28] Federal Trade Commission's Complaint for Equitable Relief (Public Redacted Version), FTC v. Qualcomm Inc., No. 5:17-cv-00220-LHK, 2017 WL 242848 (N.D. Cal. Jan. 17, 2017) [hereinafter FTC Complaint, 2017 WL 242848].

[29] *Id.* at 9–12; *see also id.* at 28–29.

[30] *Id.* at 2.

[31] *Id.* at 3.

[32] *Id.*

[33] *Id.*

[34] The word "tax" (or its variants) appeared 14 times in the FTC's complaint to describe one allegedly anticompetitive effect of Qualcomm's conduct. *Id.* at 2, 3 (twice), 19 (twice), 20 (five times), 24 (twice), 28, 30.

[35] *Id.* at 20.

that an OEM purchasing a modem allegedly paid was supposedly the sum of the prices of (1) a bare (unlicensed) modem sold by a rival manufacturer and (2) "any patent royalties that the OEM must pay to use that processor in a handset," including an exhaustive license to Qualcomm's cellular SEPs.)[36] Qualcomm's "tax" (the FTC alleged) reduced competition from those rival modem manufacturers and harmed competition in each of the two asserted relevant product markets.[37] Although the FTC's complaint focused on the allegation that Qualcomm had unlawfully monopolized two global product markets—conduct which section 2 of the Sherman Act prohibits[38]—the FTC also alleged that Qualcomm's agreements with some OEMs were agreements in restraint of trade[39] violating section 1 of the Sherman Act.[40]

Qualcomm—represented by Cravath, Swaine & Moore and other law firms—filed a motion to dismiss in which it argued that the FTC's complaint did not "plead facts supporting the basic elements of an antitrust claim" and did "not allege a plausible antitrust theory."[41] Qualcomm said that, in presenting its royalty "surcharge" and modem "tax" theory, the FTC conceded that OEMs pay the same royalty "surcharge" and the same modem "tax" on every handset, irrespective of whether the handset uses a Qualcomm modem or a non-Qualcomm modem.[42] Qualcomm then observed that such a "chip-neutral" royalty "surcharge" and modem "tax" "cannot create any incentive or disincentive for the handset maker to purchase any particular firm's modem chip."[43] "Whether the royalties are 'elevated' or not," Qualcomm reasoned, "customers face no discriminatory penalty (or 'tax') for the purchase of competitors' modem chips."[44] Qualcomm added that, in the absence of any allegation of a discriminatory licensing practice, the FTC's theory "boils down to a claim that Qualcomm charges 'too much' for royalties and 'too little' for chips, thereby 'squeezing' the margin that Qualcomm's chip-making rivals can make on their own chip sales."[45] But, as Qualcomm observed, the Supreme Court in *linkLine* abolished the price squeeze as a theory of antitrust liability in the United States.[46] Qualcomm said:

---

[36] *Id.*

[37] *Id.* at 19–21.

[38] 15 U.S.C. § 2.

[39] *See* FTC Complaint, 2017 WL 242848, *supra* note 28, at 31.

[40] 15 U.S.C. § 1.

[41] Defendant Qualcomm Incorporated's Motion to Dismiss and Memorandum of Points and Authorities in Support (Redacted Version) at 1, FTC v. Qualcomm Inc., No. 5:17-cv-00220-LHK, 2017 WL 4678941 (N.D. Cal. Apr. 3, 2017) [hereinafter Qualcomm's Motion to Dismiss, 2017 WL 4678941].

[42] *Id.*

[43] *Id.*

[44] *Id.*

[45] *Id.* at 2.

[46] *Id.* (citing Pacific Bell Tel. Co. v. linkLine Commc'ns, Inc., 555 U.S. 438 (2009)).

As the Court made clear in *linkLine*, a vertically integrated firm such as Qualcomm has no independent duty under the Sherman Act to ensure that the price it charges for upstream inputs (here, royalties) is low enough, and the price it charges for downstream products (here, modem chips) is high enough, so as to leave a "fair" or "adequate" profit margin for its downstream competitors (here, other chip suppliers).[47]

In other words, Qualcomm reasoned that, even if the facts alleged by the FTC were true, they would not support a finding of unlawful behavior.[48] On June 26, 2017, Judge Koh denied Qualcomm's motion to dismiss and permitted the case to proceed to discovery and trial.[49]

On October 15, 2018, contrary to the common practice of judges to encourage settlement negotiations, Judge Koh also denied without explanation a joint administrative motion filed by the FTC and Qualcomm that requested that she defer her ruling on the FTC's motion for partial summary judgment.[50] The parties had jointly represented that "deferral of a ruling would facilitate the Parties' ongoing discussions concerning the potential settlement of th[e] litigation."[51]

Three weeks later, on November 6, 2018, Judge Koh ruled on the FTC's motion for partial summary judgment on the issue of whether the commitment to offer licenses to its cellular SEPs on reasonable and nondiscriminatory (RAND) terms that Qualcomm had made to two standard-setting organizations—the Telecommunications Industry Association (TIA) and the Alliance for Telecommunications Industry Solutions (ATIS)—obligated Qualcomm to offer exhaustive licenses to its cellular SEPs to rival modem manufacturers.[52] Qualcomm had argued that the commitments that it made to the two SSOs created only a duty to offer an exhaustive license to its cellular SEPs to *OEMs*, an obligation with which Qualcomm had always complied. The FTC, in contrast, had contended that Qualcomm must offer an exhaustive license to its cellular SEPs to rival modem manufacturers also.

---

[47] *Id.*

[48] *Id.* at 12–13.

[49] Order Denying Motion to Dismiss (Redacted), FTC v. Qualcomm Inc., No. 5:17-cv-00220-LHK, 2017 WL 2774406, at *25 (N.D. Cal. June 26, 2017) [hereinafter Order Denying Motion to Dismiss, 2017 WL 2774406].

[50] Order Denying Joint Administrative Motion to Defer the Court's Ruling on the FTC's Motion for Partial Summary Judgment at 1, FTC v. Qualcomm Inc., No. 5:17-cv-00220-LHK (N.D. Cal. Oct. 15, 2018) ("The parties' joint administrative motion to defer the Court's ruling on the Federal Trade Commission's motion for partial summary judgment is DENIED. IT IS SO ORDERED.").

[51] Joint Administrative Motion to Defer the Court's Ruling on the FTC's Motion for Partial Summary Judgment at 1, FTC v. Qualcomm Inc., No. 5:17-cv-00220-LHK (N.D. Cal. Oct. 15, 2018).

[52] Order Granting FTC's Motion for Partial Summary Judgment, FTC v. Qualcomm Inc., No. 5:17-cv-00220-LHK, 2018 WL 5848999, at *1 (N.D. Cal. Nov. 6, 2018) [hereinafter Order Granting FTC's Motion for Partial Summary Judgment on Qualcomm's Contractual Duties Pursuant to the Contracts with ATIS and the TIA, 2018 WL 5848999].

Judge Koh found that no genuine dispute existed as to any material fact and granted the FTC's motion for partial summary judgment.[53] In other words, Judge Koh found that the respective RAND commitments that Qualcomm had made to the TIA and ATIS had created for Qualcomm a contractual duty to offer an exhaustive license to its cellular SEPs to rival modem manufacturers. The case proceeded to trial in January 2019.

C. *Judge Koh's Apparent Resources, Patience, Attention, and Temperament at Trial in January 2019*

Judge Lucy Koh was appointed to the U.S. District Court for the Northern District of California in 2010,[54] after serving as a judge on the Superior Court of California for Santa Clara County from 2008 to 2010.[55] From 2002 to 2008, she was a partner with the law firm McDermott Will & Emery in Menlo Park, California, and, from 2000 to 2002, she was a senior associate at the law firm Wilson Sonsini Goodrich & Rosati in Palo Alto, California. Between 1993 and 2000, Judge Koh worked for the U.S. Senate Committee on the Judiciary, for the U.S. Department of Justice, as a Special Assistant to the Deputy Attorney General, and as an Assistant U.S. Attorney in the Office of the U.S. Attorney for the Central District of California.[56] Judge Koh graduated from Harvard Law School in 1993 and from Harvard College in 1990 with a concentration in social studies.[57]

Starting on December 22, 2018 and continuing through the entire period of the trial in *FTC v. Qualcomm*, a partial government shutdown was in effect because Congress and President Trump could not agree on appropriations legislation and enact a continuing resolution.[58] However, any concern over the continued funding of the federal courts would affect the continuity (and possible suspension) of the trial in *FTC v. Qualcomm*, not its duration.

The trial in *FTC v. Qualcomm* began on Friday, January 4, 2019. After little more than an hour on the morning of the first day of trial, Judge Koh remarked following some confusion over the introduction into evidence of a portion of videotaped deposition testimony, "You know, we're on a tight timeframe to get this case tried in ten days."[59] Why? Judge Koh was presiding over the most significant government monopolization case since *Microsoft*, so why the

---

[53] *Id.* at *1, *4–5.

[54] *District Judge Lucy H. Koh*, UNITED STATES DISTRICT COURT: NORTHERN DISTRICT OF CALIFORNIA, https://www.cand.uscourts.gov/judges/koh-lucy-h-lhk/.

[55] *Id.*

[56] *Id.*

[57] *Id.*; *The Honorable Lucy H. Koh*, TRELLIS LEGAL INTELLIGENCE, https://trellis.law/judge/lucy.h.koh.

[58] *See, e.g.*, Julie Hirschfeld Davis & Emily Cochrane, *Government Shuts Down as Talks Fail to Break Impasse*, N.Y. TIMES, Dec. 21, 2018.

[59] Transcript of Proceedings (Volume 1) at 52:15–16, FTC v. Qualcomm Inc., No. 5:17-cv-00220-LHK (N.D. Cal. Jan. 4, 2019).

rush? The bench trial in *Microsoft* lasted 76 days.[60] At the conclusion of the trial in *FTC v. Qualcomm*, Judge Koh remarked that "there may not even be any funding for the Court" to write its findings of fact and conclusions of law "because I think we've exhausted the funds that we have to continue operating without a continuing resolution."[61] Judge Koh also lamented on various occasions the manifold constraints on her time and on the time of the small team assisting her. Those comments invite the question: Did Qualcomm receive all the process that it was due?

1. *The Apparent Constraints on Judge Koh's Time and Institutional Resources*

The scarcity of Judge Koh's time, the limited size of the staff assisting her, the limited size and seating and availability of the courtroom, and the limited federal funding to run the trial and perform her duties were themes that would permeate her transcribed comments from the very beginning of trial.[62]

---

[60] United States v. Microsoft Corp., 253 F.3d 34, 47 (D.C. Cir. 2001) (en banc) (per curiam) ("After a 76–day bench trial, the District Court issued its Findings of Fact.").

[61] Transcript of Proceedings (Volume 11) at 2182:25–2183:2, FTC v. Qualcomm Inc., No. 5:17-cv-00220-LHK (N.D. Cal. Jan. 29, 2019).

[62] Judge Koh repeatedly interrupted the examination of witnesses to ask that those already in the courtroom make room to squeeze in more observers. How much did this recurring distraction of crowd control divert Judge Koh's attention from weightier concerns during the trial? *See, e.g.*, Transcript of Proceedings (Volume 1) at 46:22–24, FTC v. Qualcomm Inc., No. 5:17-cv-00220-LHK (N.D. Cal. Jan. 4, 2019) ("Can we make room for the gentleman in the back, please. If someone could scoot further over? Thank you. Sorry it's a little bit tight in here."); Transcript of Proceedings (Volume 4) at 764:11–13, FTC v. Qualcomm Inc., No. 5:17-cv-00220-LHK (N.D. Cal. Jan. 11, 2019) ("The Court: I'm sorry to interrupt you. Could people please make room. We have people standing in the back. Can you make room?"); Transcript of Proceedings (Volume 6) at 1153:3–5, FTC v. Qualcomm Inc., No. 5:17-cv-00220-LHK (N.D. Cal. Jan. 15, 2019) ("The Court: I'm sorry to interrupt. Would all please make room so people don't have to stand in the back? If you could squeeze in? Thank you."); *id.* at 1155:21–23 ("The Court: I'm sorry to interrupt. We have more people standing in the back. Would you please make room? If you could please squeeze in towards the walls. Thank you."); *id.* at 1189:23–25 ("The Court: Can you all scoot in so we can accommodate someone standing in the back? Thank you."); *id.* at 1231:19–22 ("The Court: I'm sorry to interrupt you. Could you all please make room for people standing in the back? Thank you. Sorry to interrupt."); Transcript of Proceedings (Volume 11) at 2098:13–20, FTC v. Qualcomm Inc., No. 5:17-cv-00220-LHK (N.D. Cal. Jan. 29, 2019) ("The Court: We can fit one more person up here, and one more person up there on [sic] the front row. I don't think anyone should sit in front of the screen, right, because we'll be using that? So there are two seats up here. How many more seats do we need? So go ahead and take a seat. Can everyone please squeeze in[?] Please take a seat. Let's see how much room we have. How many more seats do we need?"); *id.* at 2099:11–2100:16 ("The Court: . . . How many more seats do we need? How many more people are out there? Anyone else? The Marshal: One, two. The Court: Two. Okay. I don't want to interfere with the people who are presenting. Is this enough space for whoever is presenting? Mr. Van Nest: Yes, your honor, it's fine. The Court: Is that okay? Mr. Van Nest: Fine. The Court: All right. Because we could put another two chairs over here, if it's getting too tight over there. How many more? Let's bring in two more chairs. It looks like we only need two more. Let's bring in three, just in case. (Pause in proceedings.) The Court: How many more seats could your team use? The Marshal: There's nobody outside. Mr. Van Nest: Everyone is in, your honor. The Court: Okay. Is everyone—it's—it's only, what, 1:33. We may get more people. So let's go ahead and bring that chair in, please. Could we have more of your team come into the well so that if someone comes in late, they can squeeze into a seat? Mr. Van Nest: Sure. (Pause in proceedings.) The Court: It looks like there's room on the front row, so if we could slide in, please. (Pause in proceedings.)"). Day 10 was the final day of witness testimony in the trial in *FTC v. Qualcomm*. Closing arguments would be held the following day, which

Expressions of these concerns—along with ruling on motions to seal certain confidential business documents, which Judge Koh came to describe by the sixth day of trial as a "nightmare process"[63]—preoccupied her remarks from the bench.

The multitude of sealing motions that so irritated Judge Koh was something beyond Qualcomm's control; it was instead the direct result of how the FTC had framed its complaint and constructed its order of proof. Judge Koh appeared to blame Qualcomm for the burden of the sealing motions. Yet, the existence and number of those motions reflected the inherent complexity of the litigation, which was far more attributable to the FTC than Qualcomm and which, in any event, Judge Koh appeared to have underestimated.

On the afternoon of the first day of trial, Judge Koh remarked, concerning her need to rule on high-priority objections and third-party motions to seal:

> [W]e are trying to keep other civil and criminal cases going. I have other court Wednesday morning and afternoon this [upcoming] week and Thursday afternoon. So it's a little bit challenging.[64]

As we shall see, at times Judge Koh's focus on quotidian concerns seemed to come at the cost of her being less engaged in the substantive relevance and probative value of the testimony she was hearing in *FTC v. Qualcomm*—considering that she rather than a jury was sitting as the finder of fact. An experienced appellate judge or trial lawyer reading the transcript of *FTC v. Qualcomm* in light of the circumstances might get the impression that Judge Koh was approaching the task more as if she were functioning as an administrative law judge than a federal district judge—working against the clock to compile a record accepting the FTC's novel theory of the case, and summarizing the agency's witnesses and documentary evidence, more or less at face value, which Judge Koh would then adopt as her own findings of fact and conclusions of law to forward to the Ninth Circuit so that she could then redirect her scarce time to the Sisyphean tasks of presiding over criminal sentencings and Social Security appeals.

Statements by Judge Koh having the atmospherics of impatience and overwork accumulated in the transcript. And as more trial days passed with

---

prompted Judge Koh to instruct the parties on which limited seating they could occupy: "The Court: . . . So tomorrow, the second row on both sides of the courtroom will be for media, so I'm going to ask if you would please not have your teams sit there. Okay? They'll have to move back. The . . . first row is for the parties and your counsel. The second row is for media, and then everything after that is a free-for-all, so sit wherever you'd like." Transcript of Proceedings (Volume 10) at 2094:2–8, FTC v. Qualcomm Inc., No. 5:17-cv-00220-LHK (N.D. Cal. Jan. 28, 2019).

[63] Transcript of Proceedings (Volume 6) at 1340:1, FTC v. Qualcomm Inc., No. 5:17-cv-00220-LHK (N.D. Cal. Jan. 15, 2019).

[64] Transcript of Proceedings (Volume 1) at 79:7–10, FTC v. Qualcomm Inc., No. 5:17-cv-00220-LHK (N.D. Cal. Jan. 4, 2019).

an apparent absence of her greater engagement from the bench on more substantive questions of fact or law, a sophisticated trial lawyer or judge reading the transcript might be drawn to perceive a kind of detachment and might begin to ask whether Judge Koh, by squeezing a bench trial as complex and consequential as *FTC v. Qualcomm* into 10 days, had exercised her case-management discretion prudently and was giving Qualcomm all the process it was due.

2. *Reading Judge Koh's Derogatory Statements Toward Qualcomm's Lawyer in Light of the Code of Conduct for United States Judges*

Between 9:04 and 9:15 a.m. on the second day of trial, Monday, January 7, 2019, a colloquy between Judge Koh and Qualcomm's counsel, Robert Van Nest, on sealing motions became contentious. Judge Koh then made a series of startling statements that implicated her duties under the Code of Conduct for United States Judges.[65] Judge Koh appeared to imply that Qualcomm had retained too many lawyers for the case, and she then accused Mr. Van Nest of "churning":

> How many law firms do you have in this case? Five? You have Norton, Rose, Fulbright, right? You've got Quinn, Emanuel; you've got Morgan, Lewis & Bockius; you've got Keker Van Nest; you've got Cravath, Swaine [&] Moore. How many firms are representing Qualcomm? . . . *How many lawyers do you have working on this trial? How many? I want the full number, not just who's here in court. Are you guys at the Fairmont or are you at the Marriott? How many lawyers do you have churning on this case?*[66]

Perhaps Judge Koh's remark was an attempt at humor that fell flat. At this point, we have as the official record only the printed transcript, which indicates when laughter erupted in the courtroom on several occasions. The transcription of the quoted portion of the colloquy between Judge Koh and Mr. Van Nest does not contain any such indication of levity. Judge Koh's remarks to Mr. Van Nest were reminiscent of a four-week patent-infringement case between Apple and Samsung in which, the *New York Times* reported, she told William Lee, the leader of WilmerHale's intellectual property litigation practice, that he must be "smoking crack" to think it possible to call as many rebuttal witnesses as he was disclosing to Judge Koh.[67] The same *New York*

---

[65] CODE OF CONDUCT FOR UNITED STATES JUDGES Canon 2A (Mar. 20, 2014).

[66] Transcript of Proceedings (Volume 2) at 167:25–168:4, 168:14–17, FTC v. Qualcomm Inc., No. 5:17-cv-00220-LHK (N.D. Cal. Jan. 7, 2019) (emphasis added).

[67] *See* Brian X. Chen, *Meet Lucy H. Koh, a Silicon Valley Judge*, N.Y. TIMES, Mar. 30, 2014 ("The monthlong trial between Apple and Samsung Electronics was nearing an end when Apple's lawyer presented an unwanted gift to the judge: a 75-page list of potential witnesses. The judge, Lucy H. Koh, minced no words. 'Unless you're smoking crack, you know these witnesses aren't going to be called when you have less than four hours,' Judge Koh said to Apple's lawyers after jurors had cleared out of the room.").

Times story reported that, in earlier patent litigation between Apple and Samsung, Judge Koh had remarked: "I don't trust what any lawyer tells me in this courtroom."[68]

If humor was not her intended effect when accusing Mr. Van Nest of "churning," then what was Judge Koh's purpose in uttering those particular words to him? How would Mr. Van Nest's decision to sleep at the Fairmont rather than the Marriott (if that were in fact his decision) have any tendency to make the existence of any fact that was of consequence to the determination of the action more or less probable, or any particular interpretation and application of controlling legal authority more or less cogent, than it would be without Judge Koh's knowing Mr. Van Nest's hotel arrangements?

We can ask, more pointedly, the same of Judge Koh's accusation of Mr. Van Nest's "churning." The *Merriam-Webster Dictionary* explains that one definition of the verb "to churn" is "to make (the account of a client) excessively active by frequent purchases and sales primarily in order to generate commissions."[69] In the world of attorney-client relationships, "churning" has a narrower but equally derogatory connotation, which, Professor Ronald Rotunda explained, is based on a lawyer's having undertaken unnecessary tasks for which she has billed her client on an hourly basis:

> If a lawyer says that she spent two hours reading a case and she spent only one, it is almost impossible to catch that, unless she brags about it to her colleagues or on her Facebook page. Other lawyers may not overbill, but engage in unnecessary work, known as churning the bill. In an email to other lawyers at the firm, one lawyer wrote, "Now Vince has random people working full time on random research projects in standard 'churn that bill, baby!' mode." The email came to light after a fee dispute. The three lawyers on these emails have since left the firm, which settled the fee dispute.[70]

What did Judge Koh intend to convey by her comment in open court about the number of lawyers that Mr. Van Nest supposedly had "churning" on *FTC v. Qualcomm*? Was she accusing Mr. Van Nest of overbilling Qualcomm, and was she thus insinuating that she therefore would not trust his advocacy at trial? In the first two minutes of the first day of trial, Friday, January 4, 2019, Mr. Van Nest had announced to Judge Koh, "And our representative from Qualcomm for trial is Mark Snyder, Your Honor, the head of Qualcomm's litigation, who's sitting right here."[71] The trial transcript indicates that Mr. Snyder was indeed present on the second day of trial, Monday, January 7,

---

[68] *Id.* ("In the first Apple-Samsung patent trial, when Apple bid to block testimony from a Samsung witness, she said: 'I don't trust what any lawyer tells me in this courtroom. I want to see actual papers.'").

[69] *Churn*, MERRIAM-WEBSTER DICTIONARY, https://www.merriam-webster.com/dictionary/churn.

[70] Ronald D. Rotunda, *The Problem of Inflating Billable Hours*, VERDICT, Nov. 17, 2014.

[71] Transcript of Proceedings (Volume 1) at 5:24–6:1, FTC v. Qualcomm Inc., No. 5:17-cv-00220-LHK (N.D. Cal. Jan. 4, 2019).

2019, when Judge Koh made her disparaging remarks about Mr. Van Nest in the first minutes of the opening hour.[72] At that point, only David Wise, Qualcomm's Senior Vice President of Finance and Treasurer, had given live (as opposed to videotaped) testimony at trial, after having been called as a witness by the FTC.

Canon 2A of the Code of Conduct for United States Judges provides that a judge "should act at all times in a manner that promotes public confidence in the integrity and impartiality of the judiciary."[73] The commentary to Canon 2A further provides: "Public confidence in the judiciary is eroded by irresponsible or improper conduct by judges. A judge must avoid all impropriety and appearance of impropriety."[74] In turn, the commentary to Canon 2A explains that "[a]n appearance of impropriety occurs when reasonable minds, with knowledge of all the relevant circumstances disclosed by a reasonable inquiry, would conclude that the judge's . . . impartiality [or] temperament . . . to serve as a judge is impaired."[75] From these general rules and statements of purpose descend more specific imperatives: "A judge should be patient, dignified, respectful, and courteous to litigants, jurors, witnesses, lawyers, and others with whom the judge deals in an official capacity."[76] In particular, a federal judge's "duty to be respectful includes the responsibility to avoid comment or behavior that could reasonably be interpreted as harassment, prejudice or bias."[77] And Canon 3A(2) provides that a judge "should maintain . . . decorum in all judicial proceedings."[78]

In response to a question posed by Senator Jeff Sessions during her confirmation to the Northern District of California in 2010, Judge Koh herself wrote that "judges should treat parties and counsel with dignity and respect."[79] And in response to a question posed by Senator Chuck Grassley in connection with her nomination to the Ninth Circuit in 2016, Judge Koh wrote that "the Code of Conduct for United States Judges[] inform[s] my view of the judicial role today."[80] Yet, there is no evidence in the trial tran-

---

[72] Transcript of Proceedings (Volume 2) at 161, FTC v. Qualcomm Inc., No. 5:17-cv-00220-LHK (N.D. Cal. Jan. 7, 2019) ("Also present: Mark Snyder").

[73] CODE OF CONDUCT FOR UNITED STATES JUDGES, *supra* note 65, Canon 2A.

[74] *Id.* cmt. Canon 2A.

[75] *Id.* Canon 2A.

[76] *Id.* Canon 3A(3).

[77] *Id.* cmt. Canon 3A(3).

[78] *Id.* Canon 3A(2).

[79] Responses of Lucy H. Koh, Nominee to the U.S. District Court for the Northern District of California to the Written Questions of Senator Jeff Sessions 3 (Feb. 22, 2010), https://www.judiciary.senate.gov/imo/media/doc/LucyKoh-QFRs.pdf.

[80] Senator Chuck Grassley Questions for the Record: Lucy Haeran Koh Nominee, United States Court of Appeals for the Ninth Circuit 1 (Aug. 22, 2016), https://www.judiciary.senate.gov/imo/media/doc/Koh%20Responses%20to%20QFRs.pdf. The "Document Properties" of this PDF report "Mehler, Lauren (Judiciary-Rep)" as the "Author" of the PDF. *Id.* ("Document Properties"). One "Lauren Mehler" was reportedly counsel to the Senate Judiciary Committee during the 114th Congress during 2015 and 2016. OFFICIAL CONGRESSIONAL DIRECTORY 114TH CONGRESS, 2015-2016, CONVENED JANUARY 2015, at 380 (Gov't Prtg. Office 2016).

script of *FTC v. Qualcomm* that Judge Koh ever apologized to Mr. Van Nest for her accusation, in front of Mr. Van Nest's client and a courtroom full of Mr. Van Nest's professional peers, that he was "churning" the case.

It is possible that Judge Koh's remarks to Mr. Van Nest on the second day of trial in *FTC v. Qualcomm* might have appeared to someone present in the courtroom—and might continue to appear to someone now reading the trial transcript—to have been impatient or undignified or disrespectful or discourteous. But is it also possible that those same remarks "could reasonably be interpreted" by others as indicating potential prejudice or bias?[81]

3. *Judge Koh's Decision to Forgo Further Submissions on Facts or Law*

At the end of the third day of trial, on Tuesday, January 8, 2019, Judge Koh confirmed that the trial would not resume until Friday of that week:

> We'll resume on Friday at 9:00. No trial tomorrow. I'm having a full criminal calendar in here tomorrow, so I recommend that you take everything out of the court[.][82]

Shortly after 9:05 a.m. on the fourth day of trial, Friday, January 11, 2019, Judge Koh again emphasized her busy caseload:

> You know, during these breaks, you know, I'm granting motions to compel arbitration, denying motions to remand, vacating Social Security appeals, sentencing criminal defendants. This is not my only case. So, you know, we did seven sealing orders yesterday.[83]

A few minutes later, Judge Koh again emphasized the competing demands on her limited time and staffing:

> I'm going to ask you all, we have a tiny team here. We're keeping all of our other civil and criminal aces [sic] going. This is not the only case we're working on right now.[84]

These words are not reassuring for litigants in a case as consequential as *FTC v. Qualcomm* to hear on a daily basis from their judge in a bench trial in federal district court. The drip-drip-drip of these comments might convey to some readers of the trial transcript the impression that it is a nuisance for a federal

---

[81] CODE OF CONDUCT FOR UNITED STATES JUDGES, *supra* note 65, cmt. Canon 3A(3).

[82] Transcript of Proceedings (Volume 3) at 630:5–8, FTC v. Qualcomm Inc., No. 5:17-cv-00220-LHK (N.D. Cal. Jan. 8, 2019).

[83] Transcript of Proceedings (Volume 4) at 645:20–25, FTC v. Qualcomm Inc., No. 5:17-cv-00220-LHK (N.D. Cal. Jan. 11, 2019).

[84] *See id.* at 648:4–7.

judge to be asked to focus his or her attention and energy with the intensity that an historic government monopolization case demands.

At the end of the fourth day of trial, Friday, January 11, 2019, Judge Koh discussed with counsel in open court the format for closing arguments to be held on February 1, 2019. She instructed the parties to produce a joint chart:

> So what I would prefer is if you could come up with a joint proposed chart that you will then populate with your evidence. . . . I just want page and exhibit cites, and then I just want deposition date, page, and line cites. . . . So you have at least two weeks maybe to figure out the format.[85]

Such a chart is understandably very helpful to the finder of fact. In her next colloquy with counsel, however, Judge Koh made it clear that she did not want to read any more *analysis* of the relevant facts or law:

> The Court: But I'd like us to get agreement on the format, and I'll approve it, and that's what you'll populate, and we'll have page limits. So you've already briefed findings of fact and conclusions of law in about 221 pages. So I feel like I am—
>
> Ms. Milici [for the FTC]: Ours is shorter.
>
> The Court: I'm sorry?
>
> Ms. Milici: Ours is shorter.
>
> The Court: Well, you're still 68 pages. I agree they're [Qualcomm's memorandum is] 153 [pages]. But I can't take any more briefing on findings of fact and conclusions of law. It's too long. All right? I want this to be tight.[86]

It does not inspire public confidence in the quality of justice for a federal judge to call 221 pages of briefing on the facts and law of an historic government antitrust case as complex as *FTC v. Qualcomm* "too long" and then to announce that she "can't take any more." Moreover, Judge Koh made those disconcerting remarks in open court *before Qualcomm had even begun to put on its defense*.

On January 15, 2019, after Qualcomm had put on only two witnesses in its defense, Judge Koh reversed her instruction from Day 4. She no longer wanted even the proposed evidentiary chart:

> So I won't need the chart. I'll just have the one hour of closing arguments. I've, you know, been reviewing and re-reviewing what you've already filed and I think that's—I think it's sufficient, your [proposed] findings of fact

---

85   *Id.* at 851:22–24, 852:5–6, 853:16–17.
86   *Id.* at 853:19–854:5.

and conclusions of law. It pretty much tracks a lot of—it pretty much tracks all the evidence that's been coming in, so I think that will be sufficient.[87]

By this comment it might have appeared to some present in the courtroom (or thereafter it might appear to some readers of the trial transcript) that, by Tuesday, January 15, 2019, Judge Koh had already made up her mind on the merits of *FTC v. Qualcomm*.

4. Judge Koh's Apparent Confusion About Patent Exhaustion

Whatever Judge Koh's motivation for dispensing with additional written closing submissions from the parties, it appeared from her comments in open court on Friday, January 18, 2019, that she would have greatly benefited from receiving those submissions. As we shall examine at some length in Part III, the goal of avoiding patent exhaustion apparently motivated Qualcomm (1) to offer exhaustive licenses to its cellular SEPs only to OEMs and (2) to sell Qualcomm modems only to *licensed* OEMs, so as to preserve its revenue stream from exhaustively licensing its cellular SEPs. Judge Koh called those actions by Qualcomm anticompetitive.

On Friday, January 18, 2019, Judge Koh created the appearance, through the confusion inherent in her questions to a Qualcomm witness concerning the doctrine of patent exhaustion, that she had an incomplete understanding of the doctrine's full ramifications for component-level licensing of patents:

> The Court: Can I ask a question? I'm sorry to interrupt. You're saying no one licenses at the chip level, so you're saying all the chip licenses are not exhaustive. But according to you, there are none. So I guess I'm not willing [sic] following. You're saying device level licenses are exhaustive. Chip level licenses are not, no one does. But you're also saying no one licenses at the chip level anyway. So then there's nobody that does a nonexhaustive license according to what you're saying? Isn't that right? . . . So who does the chip licenses then? . . . You said it's common that essential patent holders don't grant licenses to chips exhaustively. So what were you referring to? Are there licenses—are there such licenses? I'm just looking at your testimony. . . . I think I might be confused.[88]

Perhaps Judge Koh's confusion arose from a misunderstanding of the doctrine of patent exhaustion.

Although in 2008 the Supreme Court held that courts must interpret every commercial agreement called a "license" to be exhaustive, the Federal

---

[87] Transcript of Proceedings (Volume 6) at 1342:2–8, FTC v. Qualcomm Inc., No. 5:17-cv-00220-LHK (N.D. Cal. Jan. 15, 2019).

[88] Transcript of Proceedings (Volume 7) at 1436:9–18, 1436:21, 1437:3–7, 1437:11, FTC v. Qualcomm Inc., No. 5:17-cv-00220-LHK (N.D. Cal. Jan. 18, 2019).

Circuit had held during approximately the two preceding decades that the counterparties could agree upon a *nonexhaustive* "license" if those counterparties intended the agreement to convey only a nonexhaustive subset of the rights conferred on the patent holder by the grant of a patent. Consequently, a commercial agreement called a "license" before 2008 was thought by the parties and American courts to be capable of being nonexhaustive. After 2008, a commercial agreement called a "license" was thought by the parties and American courts to be *incapable* of being nonexhaustive.

Put simply, "license" did not necessarily denote "exhaustive license" in American patent law before 2008. Thus, to paraphrase Judge Koh, it was true both that "no one [after 2008] licenses at the chip level," because such licenses after 2008 would necessarily be interpreted to be exhaustive, and that "all the chip [']licenses['] [before 2008] are not exhaustive."

Put differently, without additional context, one cannot properly impute the meaning "exhaustive license" to any instance in which the counterparties to a commercial agreement before 2008 invoked the word "license." Indeed, Qualcomm and various rival modem manufacturers before 2008 agreed to enter *nonexhaustive* "licenses."

The critical importance to *FTC v. Qualcomm* of the distinction between an exhaustive license and a nonexhaustive "license" (before 2008) cannot be overstated. The distinction was essential to understanding *FTC v. Qualcomm*. Yet, it was absent from Judge Koh's findings of fact and conclusions of law. This critical distinction appears to have been the reason that Judge Koh admitted during trial on January 18, 2019 that she was confused about the relevance of patent exhaustion to the proper resolution of the antitrust claims asserted in *FTC v. Qualcomm*.

Without a rigorous understanding of the legal and economic ramifications of patent exhaustion, Judge Koh could not have begun to analyze reliably whether Qualcomm's licensing practices designed to avert patent exhaustion served a legitimate business purpose and thus provided Qualcomm a defense to the antitrust claims alleged in *FTC v. Qualcomm*. As we shall see in Part III, Judge Koh's admission of her possible confusion was the harbinger of the superficial discussion of patent exhaustion that appeared four months later in her findings of fact and conclusions of law in *FTC v. Qualcomm*. In particular, she concluded that Qualcomm acted anticompetitively when it continued to pursue the more "lucrative" strategy of choosing to offer exhaustive licenses to its SEPs only to OEMs.[89]

To the contrary, substantial evidence indicated that the doctrine of patent exhaustion, concern about multi-level licensing, and the cognitive dissonance of trying to apply a seemingly high royalty rate to a small royalty

---

[89] FTC v. Qualcomm Inc., 411 F. Supp. 3d 658, 756 (N.D. Cal. 2019).

base (at the component level) motivated Qualcomm's business decision. When it subsequently reversed Judge Koh, the Ninth Circuit found that the FTC was wrong that Qualcomm's decision to offer exhaustive licenses to its cellular SEPs exclusively to OEMs harmed competition among rival modem manufacturers by inhibiting entry, and the court further found that the FTC had given "inadequate weight to Qualcomm's reasonable, procompetitive justification that licensing at the OEM and chip-supplier levels simultaneously would require the company to engage in 'multi-level licensing,' leading to inefficiencies and less profit."[90] The incremental burden to Judge Koh of receiving additional briefing on the question of patent exhaustion would have been nil. The incremental benefit to Qualcomm from Judge Koh's achieving greater clarity on the law and economics of patent exhaustion would have been substantial, because it would have flipped the outcome of the case.

In addition to foreshadowing the confusion immanent in her findings of fact and conclusions of law of May 21, 2019, Judge Koh's apparent admission of confusion while hearing testimony on January 18, 2019 explained her failure to define the word "license" in her order granting the FTC's motion for partial summary judgment on November 6, 2018. Interpreting contracts between Qualcomm and each of two SSOs, she concluded that Qualcomm was obligated by contract to offer "licenses" to its cellular SEPs to rival modem manufacturers.

Yet, Judge Koh never defined a "license." Her order granting the FTC's motion for partial summary judgment apparently took as given that the verb "to license" always denotes "to license on an exhaustive basis," and that the noun "license" always denotes an "exhaustive license," even though the two intellectual property rights (IPR) policies that Judge Koh purported to interpret predated 2008. Her failure to address that fundamental matter of contract interpretation harks back to the famous question that Judge Henry Friendly posed, "[W]hat is chicken?"[91] There is no reason to believe that Qualcomm (or either of the SSOs in question, for that matter) understood the word "license" in its agreements with SSOs preceding 2008 necessarily to denote an "exhaustive license." To the contrary, Qualcomm at the time was granting what it and its counterparties apparently thought were *nonexhaustive* "licenses" to rival modem manufacturers.

Among its other legal ramifications for the merits of *FTC v. Qualcomm*, Judge Koh's anachronistic reading of the word "license" was legal error that

---

90 FTC v. Qualcomm Inc., No. 19-16122, 2020 WL 4591476, at *13 (9th Cir. Aug. 11, 2020).

91 Frigaliment Importing Co. v. B.N.S. Int'l Sales Corp., 190 F. Supp. 116, 117 (S.D.N.Y. 1960) (Friendly, J.) ("The issue is, what is chicken? Plaintiff says 'chicken' means a young chicken, suitable for broiling and frying. Defendant says 'chicken' means any bird of that genus that meets contract specifications on weight and quality, including what it calls 'stewing chicken' and plaintiff pejoratively terms 'fowl'. . . . I have concluded that plaintiff has not sustained its burden of persuasion that the contract used 'chicken' in the narrower sense.").

at a minimum meant that she could not have properly granted the FTC's motion for partial summary judgment.

5.   *Was Qualcomm Blameworthy for Pursuing Its Preferred Strategy to Defend Against the FTC's Allegations?*

Day 7 of trial presented another oddity. Considering Judge Koh's recurrent warnings about the limited amount of time allotted for the trial in *FTC v. Qualcomm*, one might have thought that she would respect a party's decision in the thick of trial to jettison one of its planned witnesses—in this instance, Michael Hartogs, a former Senior Vice President of Qualcomm who left the company in 2012 after 12 years.[92] Yet, when Mr. Van Nest, "in the interest of time,"[93] did so on behalf of Qualcomm, Judge Koh said that she found Qualcomm's decision "a bit odd"[94] and intimated that he should stick to his original plan to call Mr. Hartogs.[95]

Judge Koh's conduct appeared from the transcript then to turn quarrelsome. Just a moment after the next witness was sworn in, Judge Koh interrupted to scold Mr. Van Nest for burdening the court with "a lot of evidentiary objections and sealing motions"[96] and to praise the FTC for "show[ing] a lot of professional courtesy" because "their witness list was right on, they called witnesses they were going to call, they fully disclosed them, [and] they called them in the same order."[97]

Judge Koh's assertion that Qualcomm wanted to call far too many witnesses in the limited number of trial hours allowed was puzzling. Qualcomm was a defendant in a government monopolization case, appearing in a bench trial before a judge who had already granted the FTC partial summary judgment on the contractual interpretation of Qualcomm's FRAND (actually, RAND) obligations. Judge Koh's annoyance might have appeared to some as tending to confirm that she had underestimated the logistical burdens that she had created for herself and her staff by trying to shoehorn into only 10 days a monopolization trial imbued with byzantine complexity by the FTC's novel theory of liability. From her colloquy with Mr. Van Nest it might have

---

[92] Transcript of Proceedings (Volume 7) at 1530:3–1531:12, FTC v. Qualcomm Inc., No. 5:17-cv-00220-LHK (N.D. Cal. Jan. 18, 2019).

[93] *Id.* at 1530:3.

[94] *Id.* at 1530:12.

[95] *Id.* at 1530:3–20 ("Mr. Van Nest [for Qualcomm]: Your Honor, in the interest of time, we're going to skip—pass over Mr. Hartogs. The Court: Okay. Mr. Van Nest: And release him and move on to Mr. Chen. The Court: Okay. Are you not going to call Mr. Hartogs at all? Mr. Van Nest: We are not going to call Mr. Hartogs at all. The Court: Okay. I think that's a bit odd. Mr. Van Nest: We're on a pretty stiff time clock and some of our witnesses today have been longer than we anticipated and just in the interests of time[] I haven't got the time budget. So we advised the FTC that we would not be calling Mr. Hartogs, and we're calling Mr. Chen. I'm not trying to move him [Mr. Hartogs] in the order. I'm dropping him out.").

[96] *Id.* at 1531:24–25.

[97] *Id.* at 1532:3–6.

appeared to some that Judge Koh believed that Qualcomm should be blamed for its supposed inability to compress its defense during this complicated trial into the arbitrarily constrained schedule.

Was Judge Koh blaming Qualcomm for the amount of evidence that it sought to introduce? She remarked that the set of witness binders supplied to her by counsel "takes up almost a full wall"[98] and that "we don't have room in the clerk's office for all those binders."[99] These complaints might strike some readers of the trial transcript as petty and dyspeptic. Yet again, Judge Koh belabored the point in what might seem from the transcript to be an expression of pique:

> [T]he clerk's office is really, really—has very confined space, and so we don't want your witness binders going down there. *And it's really unnecessary because all of your witness binders* include *way more exhibits than what you actually introduced.* So we just don't need copies and copies and copies. We just don't are [sic] room, unfortunately. . . . [T]he binders take up space, and we don't have the space and otherwise the clerk's office will pay for space. And as you know, *we're running out of money next Friday.* So please *don't keep burdening us with more and more binders.* What we need is as light as possible and taking up as minimal space as possible.[100]

Was Qualcomm really being given all the process it was due if Judge Koh was instructing its lawyers to tailor their witness binder submissions to the arbitrary constraint of the size of the office occupied by the clerk of the court? Judge Koh said in open court that she and her staff felt "burdened" by the witness binders.[101] Did other aspects of the litigation cause them to feel burdened? Did that sense of burden engender resentment?

6. *Wi-Fi in the Courtroom and the Value of Cellular Broadband*

Shortly before 9:35 a.m. on the eighth day of trial, Tuesday, January 22, 2019, Judge Koh exclaimed, near the end of the direct examination of Professor Jeffrey Andrews, a professor of electrical engineering at the University of Texas who was testifying as expert witness for Qualcomm's defense:

> The Court: . . . What was the question? Can you repeat the question, please[?] Unfortunately, my Realtime has stopped. Has your Realtime stopped?

---

[98] *Id.* at 1557: 25.

[99] *Id.* at 1558:4–5.

[100] *Id.* at 1559:7–13, 1559:25–1560:6 (emphasis added).

[101] At the end of the ninth day of trial, Judge Koh remarked, "I think the order is going to take some time just because the quantity of evidence that's been introduced is voluminous and the legal issues are complex." Transcript of Proceedings (Volume 9) at 2026:4–6, FTC v. Qualcomm Inc., No. 5:17-cv-00220-LHK (N.D. Cal. Jan. 25, 2019).

Mr. Van Nest: Yes, Your Honor.

The Court: Does everyone in the room have their cell phones off? If you don't, I'm going to just have everyone leave the room because we need the Realtime. Okay. Let's do it. It's 9:35.

(Pause in proceedings.)

The Court: I'm going to have everyone leave the room, and just have the parties here. We need to have the Wi-Fi, and if there are too many phones on the system, then we can't have Realtime.[102]

By 9:39 a.m., the cross examination of Professor Andrews had begun with questioning by J. Alexander Ansaldo for the FTC. Intimating that Qualcomm's patents were overrated, Mr. Ansaldo actually asked as his third cross-examination question, "And users that have LTE enabled phones that also have Wi-Fi can use the Wi-Fi for data transmission; is that correct?"[103] To which Professor Andrews replied, "Assuming they're connected to a Wi-Fi access point that works, yes."[104] Moments later, at 9:43 a.m., Judge Koh announced in apparent exasperation:

Let's take a couple minute break to see if we can get the Realtime restored. If we can get it restored, I'll invite everyone back. But if it shuts down again, I'm just going to excuse everyone for the rest of the day, because I'm sorry, but I need the transcript. Okay. Let's take a couple minute break just to see if we can get this resolved. Thank you.

(Recess from 9:43 a.m. until 9:49 a.m.)

The Court: All right. Welcome back. Please take a seat. Now, we have a collective action problem with this all the time. Everyone thinks I need my device, other people can turn theirs off. So the way I'm going to solve this collective action problem is there will be collective consequences. I'm going to ask you one more time, if you can, please turn off your devices. If this shuts down again, the rest of the day I'm just going to ask everyone to step outside and I'm only going to have the parties can [sic] stay. So there will be collective consequences if you don't turn off your devices. I'm sorry, but I need the transcript. *Especially with something technical, I really need the transcript. So it was a real handicap not to have this during the last witness [Professor Jeffrey Andrews], who was speaking very fast.* So I'm going to ask one last time, please turn off your devices. I will ask everyone to leave if this shuts down again. So call your next witness, please.[105]

---

[102] Transcript of Proceedings (Volume 8) at 1613:12–1614:2, FTC v. Qualcomm Inc., No. 5:17-cv-00220-LHK (N.D. Cal. Jan. 25, 2019).

[103] *Id.* at 1615:5–6.

[104] *Id.* at 1615:7–8 (Testimony of Jeffrey Andrews (University of Texas)).

[105] *Id.* at 1618:21–1619:25 (emphasis added).

Judge Koh was of course *not* complaining about cellphones in her courtroom consuming bandwidth on licensed spectrum with their uploads and downloads of cellular data. Rather, she was complaining about *Wi-Fi congestion*: too many persons in the courtroom were using their cellphones or laptops to connect to the court's Wi-Fi network. The resulting congestion was evidently consuming all the bandwidth in the unlicensed spectrum over which the Wi-Fi network operates, and consequently that congestion was interfering with the ability of Judge Koh and others in the courtroom to receive by Wi-Fi the court reporter's real-time text transcription of Professor Andrews' testimony.[106]

The irony of the situation was evidently lost on the FTC's lawyer, Mr. Ansaldo, who had been trying to prove the mediocrity of Qualcomm's patent portfolio during his cross examination of Professor Andrews. The irony was also evidently lost on Judge Koh. From the trial transcript, it appears that both Mr. Ansaldo and Judge Koh seemed oblivious to the fact that Qualcomm's innovations for expanding the capacity of cellular data transmission had provided a solution to the problem of too little unlicensed bandwidth in the courtroom and the resulting debilitating effect of congestion on real-time applications that depend exclusively on the capacity of Wi-Fi networks.

In effect, by her expression of frustration with her malfunctioning Realtime transcription system, Judge Koh was unwittingly providing a testimonial to the exceptional value of Qualcomm's patented contributions to cellular data communications.

7.   *Was Judge Koh's Eventual Opinion Attentive to the Testimony Presented at Trial?*

As we shall see, the result of Judge Koh's approach to trying *FTC v. Qualcomm* was an opinion that was credulous and superficial on both the facts and law. Perhaps the fact that Judge Koh and her team were being stretched in too many directions manifested itself in the quality of the findings of fact and conclusions of law that resulted.

Judge Koh's findings of fact and conclusions of law in *FTC v. Qualcomm* are so redundant that an experienced judge or trial lawyer cannot read the opinion without experiencing *déjà vu*. The same expurgated draft of a PowerPoint slide entitled, "Strategy Recommendations," from a 2009

---

[106] *See, e.g.*, Dawn Houghton, *Easily Connect to Your Court Reporter's Realtime Transcription*, O'BRIEN & BAILS, Nov. 14, 2014, http://www.obrienandbails.com/easily-connect-to-your-court-reporters-realtime-transcription/ ("[R]ealtime transcription is a system . . . whereby the spoken word is recorded by the court reporter and delivered as text on a computer screen within a few seconds of the words being spoken."). To "[c]onnect to the court reporter's wireless network," one must first "[v]erify that [one's] computer is WiFi enabled." *Id.*

internal Qualcomm presentation appeared as an image embedded into the text of Judge Koh's findings of fact and conclusions of law on *four* different pages.[107] The same paragraph discussing the permissible scope of the permanent, worldwide injunction that Judge Koh intended to order appears twice, almost verbatim, within the span of six pages.[108] Another puzzling example of Judge Koh's repetition concerned her discussion of Qualcomm's settlement of its legal disputes with Samsung: three times she inserted the same passage of nearly 500 words, almost verbatim.[109]

Why? Repeating the same evidence, reprising the same locution time after time, did not make that evidence any more probative. Perhaps the repetition

---

[107] FTC v. Qualcomm Inc., 411 F. Supp. 3d 658, 745, 761, 799, 811 (N.D. Cal. 2019) (all pages reproducing CX5809-041). I will discuss in detail in Part VIII.B the precise nature of Judge Koh's expurgation of CX5809-041 and its substantive relevance to her findings of fact and conclusions of law on anticompetitive intent.

[108] *Id.* at 812–13; *id.* at 819.

[109] *See id.* at 709, 814–15, 823. I reproduce the first of those three passages that Judge Koh repeated, nearly verbatim, not to divert attention to a discussion of Qualcomm's settlement agreement with Samsung (to which we shall return later), but simply to document the extent to which Judge Koh's findings of fact and conclusions of law were inexplicably repetitious. Judge Koh wrote:

> Qualcomm paid Samsung $100 million to extinguish Samsung's antitrust claims and to silence Samsung. In the Settlement Agreement, Samsung specifically releases claims based on the following:
>
>> any claim of coercion or other similar claims regarding the negotiation, execution, or terms of this Settlement Agreement, the 2018 Amendment, the CMCPCA, and/or the Collaboration Agreement . . .
>>
>> any patent licensing conduct of Qualcomm or any of its Affiliates or (b) any conduct of Qualcomm or any of its Affiliates in the Private and Regulatory Action . . . [and]
>>
>> any claim that Qualcomm's Existing Practices violate any antitrust, competition, or similar laws of any state or territory of the United States (including federal law), Korea, or any other country or any jurisdiction, or any principle of common or civil law to similar effect including any claim based on or arising from findings or conclusions articulated in . . . (4) the ultimate decisions, settlement agreements or other dispositions of any of the cases brought against Qualcomm (or that contain counterclaims against Qualcomm) by the U.S. Federal Trade Commission ("U.S. F.T.C.") (*FTC v. Qualcomm Incorporated*, Case No. 5:17-CV-00220-LHK (N.D. Cal.)) . . .
>
> Further, in the Settlement Agreement, Samsung agreed to withdraw from participation in this action and others:
>
>> Samsung will promptly take all actions reasonably required to withdraw all pending or accepted applications for intervention, or any other forms of substantive participation (except for any participation, including discovery or deposition, to the extent required by law), in any of the Private or Regulatory Actions and any other proceedings involving claims that Qualcomm's Existing Practices violate antitrust, competition, or similar laws. . . . [and]
>>
>> Samsung will withdraw from all existing Common Interest Agreements and all other similar agreements in which the general purpose is to share information and communications under some form of protection against disclosure (collectively, the "CIAs") between Samsung or any of its Affiliates and any third party that pertains to any of the Private and Regulatory Actions or any other proceedings or collaboration by third parties involving claims or potential claims that Qualcomm's Existing Practices violate antitrust, competition, contract, or similar laws or undertakings.
>
> Moreover, Samsung promised to make the following statement to the KFTC: "[I]n any statement Samsung provides to the KFTC regarding Qualcomm's compliance with the KFTC 2017 Orders, Samsung agrees that it shall confirm that it has resolved its disputes with

was inadvertent. Conspicuous repetition might signal that a committee drafted the document and that Judge Koh did not exercise close enough scrutiny to discern whether the assemblage of siloed parts fit together coherently before she released that document as a judicial order having the force of law. That possibility invites a sophisticated reader to ask more serious questions about Judge Koh's substantive analysis of facts and law. If so much conspicuous redundancy in an opinion could escape the notice of Judge Koh and her "tiny team,"[110] then how confident can we be that the citations to the record—or the citations to the ostensibly controlling authority—were accurate, complete, and reliable? I will address that question in detail in the pages that follow. Alternatively, if the repetition in *FTC v. Qualcomm* was intentional, what was its purpose? Anaphora is a device common in literature, but not legal opinions. Would the Ninth Circuit tolerate a brief containing such repetition? Would the Supreme Court?[111]

D. *Professor Carl Shapiro's Role as the FTC's Expert Economic Witness*

Professor Carl Shapiro of the University of California, Berkeley and the Charles River Associates (CRA) consultancy was the FTC's expert economic witness at trial.[112] The publicly available portions of his testimony in *FTC v. Qualcomm* consist of at least (1) the oral testimony that he gave at trial on two separate days, January 15 and 28, 2019,[113] (2) the redacted demonstrative exhibits to which he referred in his direct testimony at trial on January 14, 2019,[114] and (3) the redacted fragments of two of his expert reports filed by the FTC as exhibits to certain pretrial motions in 2018.[115] Professor Shapiro's

---

Qualcomm and the resolution of such dispute satisfies Samsung's demands made under the KFTC 2017 Orders."

Id. at 709 (alterations in original) (citations omitted) (first quoting JX0122-050 to -052; then quoting JX0122-056; and then quoting JX0122-055).

[110] Transcript of Proceedings (Volume 4) at 648:5, FTC v. Qualcomm Inc., No. 5:17-cv-00220-LHK (N.D. Cal. Jan. 11, 2019).

[111] *Cf.* FED. R. APP. P. 28(a)(6) ("The appellant's brief must contain . . . a *concise* statement of the case setting out the facts relevant to the issues submitted for review[.]") (emphasis added).

[112] Yet, as we shall see, CRA did not assist Professor Shapiro in *FTC v. Qualcomm*.

[113] Transcript of Proceedings (Volume 6) at 1117:2–1250:17, FTC v. Qualcomm Inc., No. 5:17-cv-00220-LHK (N.D. Cal. Jan. 15, 2019) (Testimony of Carl Shapiro); Transcript of Proceedings (Volume 10) at 2031:5–2090:2, FTC v. Qualcomm Inc., No. 5:17-cv-00220-LHK (N.D. Cal. Jan. 28, 2019) (Testimony of Carl Shapiro).

[114] Shapiro Demonstratives (Redacted Version), FTC v. Qualcomm Inc., No. 5:17-cv-00220-LHK (N.D. Cal. Jan. 14, 2019) [hereinafter Shapiro Demonstratives].

[115] Fragments of Professor Shapiro's initial expert report appear primarily in two filings. The two fragments are substantially similar, except that their redactions differ. Expert Report of Carl Shapiro (Public Version), FTC v. Qualcomm Inc., No. 5:17-cv-00220-LHK (N.D. Cal. May 24, 2018), *Exhibit 4 to* Federal Trade Commission's Notice of Motion and Motion to Exclude Expert Testimony of Dr. Edward A. Snyder, and Memorandum in Support (Redacted Version), FTC v. Qualcomm Inc., No. 5:17-cv-00220-LHK (N.D. Cal. Aug. 30, 2018), ECF No. 788-2; Expert Report of Carl Shapiro (Public Version), FTC v. Qualcomm Inc., No. 5:17-cv-00220-LHK (N.D. Cal. May 24, 2018), *Exhibit 4 to* Federal Trade Commission's Notice of Motion and Motion to Exclude Expert Testimony of Dr. Edward A. Snyder, and Memorandum

testimony seemed to adopt without alteration much of the bespoke terminology that the FTC had used in its complaint to describe Qualcomm's allegedly anticompetitive conduct.

In his initial expert report, Professor Shapiro opined that CDMA modems and "premium" LTE modems constituted two relevant antitrust markets in which Qualcomm possessed monopoly power.[116] He also opined on the combined effect that Qualcomm's practices had on competition. Professor Shapiro opined that Qualcomm's practice of selling modems only to licensed OEMs permitted Qualcomm to negotiate "unreasonably high royalties for its cellular SEPs, notwithstanding Qualcomm's [FRAND] commitment."[117] (It is unclear whether Professor Shapiro opined that Qualcomm had engaged in "patent holdup," a theory of harm that he had championed for years,[118] and which the FTC mentioned in filings early in the litigation,[119] but which he appeared not to mention in his trial testimony in *FTC v. Qualcomm*.) Professor Shapiro also opined and subsequently testified that Qualcomm's allegedly "unreasonably high" royalty "surcharge" on an exhaustive license to its cellular SEPs allegedly became a "tax" on the "all-in price" that OEMs paid for rivals' modems, which in turn supposedly reduced the demand for the modems of those rivals, reduced their profit margins, and limited their resources to invest in innovation.[120] Professor Shapiro opined in his initial

---

in Support (Redacted Version), FTC v. Qualcomm Inc., No. 5:17-cv-00220-LHK (N.D. Cal. Dec. 21, 2018), ECF No. 1042-2 [hereinafter collectively Initial Expert Report of Carl Shapiro in *FTC v. Qualcomm*]. The cover page and a single unredacted page of Professor Shapiro's rebuttal expert report appear in another filing. Rebuttal Report of Carl Shapiro (Public Version) at 92, FTC v. Qualcomm Inc., No. 5:17-cv-00220-LHK (N.D. Cal. July 26, 2018), *Exhibit 6 to* Federal Trade Commission's Notice of Motion and Motion to Exclude Expert Testimony of Dr. Edward A. Snyder, and Memorandum in Support (Redacted Version), FTC v. Qualcomm Inc., No. 5:17-cv-00220-LHK (N.D. Cal. Aug. 30, 2018), ECF No. 788-2 [hereinafter Rebuttal Expert Report of Carl Shapiro in *FTC v. Qualcomm*]. As I will explain later in greater detail, there is no indication that any portion of Professor Shapiro's expert reports was moved into evidence.

[116] Initial Expert Report of Carl Shapiro in *FTC v. Qualcomm*, *supra* note 115, at 3.

[117] *Id.*

[118] *See* Mark A. Lemley & Carl Shapiro, *Patent Holdup and Royalty Stacking*, 85 Tex. L. Rev. 1991 (2007); Mark A. Lemley & Carl Shapiro, *A Simple Approach to Setting Reasonable Royalties for Standard-Essential Patents*, 28 Berkeley Tech. L.J. 1135 (2013). For critiques of Professor Shapiro's patent-holdup conjecture, see J. Gregory Sidak, *Is Patent Holdup a Hoax?*, 3 Criterion J. on Innovation 401 (2018); J. Gregory Sidak, *Mandating Final-Offer Arbitration of FRAND Royalties for Standard-Essential Patents*, 18 Stan. Tech. L. Rev. 1 (2015).

[119] *See* FTC Complaint, 2017 WL 242848, *supra* note 28, at 12 ("To address this 'hold-up' risk, SSOs often require patent holders to disclose their patents and commit to license standard-essential patents ('SEPs') on fair, reasonable, and non-discriminatory ('FRAND') terms. Absent such requirements, a patent holder might be able to parlay the standardization of its technology into a monopoly in standard-compliant products."); Order Denying Motion to Dismiss, 2017 WL 2774406, *supra* note 49, at *2 ("Importantly, before incorporating a technology into a standard, SSOs 'often require patent holders to disclose their patents and commit to license [SEPs] on fair, reasonable, and nondiscriminatory ("FRAND") terms.' 'Absent such requirements, a patent holder might be able to parlay the standardization of its technology into a monopoly in standard-compliant products.'") (alteration in original) (citation omitted) (quoting FTC Complaint, 2017 WL 242848, *supra* note 28, at 12).

[120] Initial Expert Report of Carl Shapiro in *FTC v. Qualcomm*, *supra* note 115, at 114–15; *see also* Transcript of Proceedings (Volume 6) at 1137:18–1139:2, FTC v. Qualcomm Inc., No. 5:17-cv-00220-LHK (N.D. Cal. Jan. 15, 2019) (Testimony of Carl Shapiro).

expert report and subsequently testified at trial that Qualcomm's refusal to license its cellular SEPs exhaustively to rival modem manufacturers exacerbated the alleged harm to competition.[121] He also testified that the supposed exclusivity of the modem supply agreements that Qualcomm executed with Apple further weakened the competitiveness of rival modem manufacturers—in particular, Intel, by limiting Intel's ability to work with Apple.[122] In short, it was Professor Shapiro's expert economic opinion and testimony that Qualcomm's practices harmed competition in two relevant product markets by undermining the abilities of Qualcomm's rivals to compete with it in the supply of modems to OEMs.

E.	*What Patents Did Qualcomm License, and What Were the Supposedly "Unreasonably High" Royalties Actually Paid for an Exhaustive License to Qualcomm's Portfolio of Cellular SEPs?*

Professor Shapiro's opinions were based on a theoretical bargaining model that did not analyze the actual royalties that Qualcomm charged OEMs for an exhaustive license to its portfolio of cellular SEPs. In other words, Professor Shapiro never examined what royalty OEMs actually paid for an exhaustive license to Qualcomm's cellular SEPs or what precise price would be a reasonable royalty for an exhaustive license to Qualcomm's portfolio of cellular SEPs (or what range of prices would constitute a range of reasonable royalties).

1.	*The Relative Shares of Cellular SEPs, Non-Cellular SEPs, and Non-SEPs in Qualcomm's Patent Portfolio*

Professor Shapiro's opinion appeared to disregard the vast number of SEPs and non-SEPs that Qualcomm licensed. Liren Chen, Senior Vice President and Legal Counsel for QTL and himself the recipient of 130 patents and pending patent applications owned by Qualcomm,[123] testified at trial that, as

---

[121] Initial Expert Report of Carl Shapiro in *FTC v. Qualcomm*, *supra* note 115, at 121; Transcript of Proceedings (Volume 6) at 1120:3–10, FTC v. Qualcomm Inc., No. 5:17-cv-00220-LHK (N.D. Cal. Jan. 15, 2019) (Testimony of Carl Shapiro).

[122] Transcript of Proceedings (Volume 6) at 1121:12–16, FTC v. Qualcomm Inc., No. 5:17-cv-00220-LHK (N.D. Cal. Jan. 15, 2019) (Testimony of Carl Shapiro).

[123] Transcript of Proceedings (Volume 7) at 1535:7–13, FTC v. Qualcomm Inc., No. 5:17-cv-00220-LHK (N.D. Cal. Jan. 18, 2019) (Testimony of Liren Chen (Senior Vice President and Legal Counsel, QTL)). For an example of one of Mr. Chen's patents, see Adaptive Quality of Service Policy for Dynamic Networks, U.S. Patent No. 8,867,390, at [57] (filed Apr. 30, 2012) (issued Aug. 23, 2012) ("Abstract: A close-loop quality of service system is provided that collects real-time network performance indicators at the physical, data link and network layers. Using those indicators, the system dynamically controls the network traffic in order to achieve improved performance according to the priority and policy defined by a data user or system/network administrator. Several features of this quality of service system includes (1) dynamic maximum bandwidth reallocation, (2) dynamic maximum packet sizing, (3) adaptive policing, and/or (4) real-time link status feedbacks to make more efficient use of available bandwidth and adjust to transmission requirements.").

of March 2018, Qualcomm held about 140,000 granted patents and pending patent applications.[124] He further testified that, at an earlier point in time when Qualcomm had only 120,000 granted patents and pending applications, the portfolio's breakdown by technology area was 20 percent cellular SEPs, 14 to 15 percent non-cellular SEPs, and 65 to 66 percent non-SEPs.[125] Mr. Chen gave no testimony stating or implying that this breakdown was materially different for Qualcomm's portfolio as of the close of fact discovery in March 2018. In other words, Qualcomm's patent portfolio as of March 2018 appeared to include about 80,000 granted patents and pending patent applications that Qualcomm had *not* declared essential to any standard.[126]

Mr. Chen testified that Qualcomm offers *all* of its patent portfolio for licensing:

> Q. And which of these categories of patents does Qualcomm present during licensing discussions?
>
> A. We typically present all of them.
>
> Q. Why is that?
>
> A. Because Qualcomm is a system innovator. We are very often known for creating technology in [the] cellular space. We actually conduct very broad R&D and technology development in many different areas. And all those technology [sic] are relevant, and they're very important for the overall working together of the system for a smartphone user. So we try to present all the information about our patents because they are delivering value to our licensees together. . . . Qualcomm has a lot of ongoing R&D that keep[s] generating new I.P. that keep[s] getting added to our portfolio. . . . [W]hen we negotiate with [a] licensee, we are trying to generally negotiate a longer term deal that's five to ten years long. . . . So I want[] the licensee to have a clear understanding of how Qualcomm keep[s] on getting inventions into the portfolio and, therefore, access to the technology.[127]

Mr. Chen testified that, for more than 20 years, Qualcomm's portfolio had grown at more than a 30-percent compound annual growth rate.[128] He testified that, on average, Qualcomm received a net addition of "35 granted patents" into its portfolio "per day worldwide."[129] Qualcomm computed net

---

[124] Transcript of Proceedings (Volume 7) at 1540:14–17, FTC v. Qualcomm Inc., No. 5:17-cv-00220-LHK (N.D. Cal. Jan. 18, 2019) (Testimony of Liren Chen (Senior Vice President and Legal Counsel, QTL)).

[125] *Id.* at 1538:5–15.

[126] *Id.* at 1552:16–17.

[127] *Id.* at 1538:23–1539:10, 1539:24–25, 1540:3–7; *see also id.* at 1554:23–1555:3 ("Q. And does Qualcomm make the three categories of patents that we've talked about, the standard essential, the cellular standard essential, the non-cellular and beyond cellular essential patents and the implementation patents available to licensees? A. Yes, we do.").

[128] *Id.* at 1540:8–11.

[129] *Id.* at 1540:23–24.

additions to its portfolio by "counting . . . newly granted patents" and then subtracting any "patent that has expired."[130]

2.   *What Creates Value in a Smartphone? Apple's Design Patents Versus Qualcomm's Foundational Cellular SEPs*

In contrast to investing, as Qualcomm did, in the kind of basic R&D necessary to produce breakthrough cellular technologies, Apple applied its resources and talents differently—and to great effect. Apple's COO Jeff Williams memorably testified at trial in *FTC v. Qualcomm* in January 2019 that "Apple spends a lot of time making its products *really beautiful*."[131]

In particular, in 2011, Apple sued Samsung for allegedly infringing three of Apple's design patents relating to the physical design of a smartphone and smartphone screen.[132] A jury initially awarded Apple $399 million in damages—the entire profit that Samsung had earned from the sale of the allegedly infringing devices.[133] The three design patents at issue in *Apple v. Samsung* were "the D618,677 patent, covering a black rectangular front face with rounded corners, the D593,087 patent, covering a rectangular front face with rounded corners and a raised rim, and the D604,305 patent, covering a grid of 16 colorful icons on a black screen."[134] None of the three patents in suit included an abstract, as they all concerned strictly the physical appearance—the "ornamental design"—of a smartphone, not how a smartphone operates.[135]

As we shall see shortly, Apple's three design patents claiming the invention of curved edges and colorful icons for a smartphone are a far cry from Qualcomm's foundational SEPs concerning, for example, carrier aggregation or the physical uplink control channel or base station acquisition or the single-carrier frequency-division multiple access waveform.

Judge Koh presided over *Apple v. Samsung*. Her orders on motions filed in the case appear to have been more impressive works of judicial craftsmanship than her findings of fact and conclusions of law in *FTC v. Qualcomm*, perhaps because there is a material difference between ruling on motions in connection with a jury trial, on the one hand, and sitting as finder of fact

---

[130] *Id.* at 1540:25–1541:2.

[131] Transcript of Proceedings (Volume 5) at 869:25–870:1, FTC v. Qualcomm Inc., No. 5:17-cv-00220-LHK (N.D. Cal. Jan. 14, 2019) (Testimony of Jeff Williams (COO, Apple)) (emphasis added).

[132] *See* Samsung Elecs. Co. v. Apple, Inc., 137 S. Ct. 429, 433 (2016).

[133] *Id.*

[134] *Id.*

[135] *See* U.S. Patent No. D618,677, at [57] (filed June 29, 2010) ("The ornamental design of an electronic device, as shown and described."); U.S. Patent No. D593,087, at [57] (filed May 26, 2009) ("The ornamental design of an electronic device, substantially as shown and described."); U.S. Patent No. D604,305, at [57] (filed Nov. 17, 2009) ("The ornamental design for a graphical user interface for a display screen or portion thereof, as shown and described.").

responsible for producing reasoned findings of fact and conclusions of law in a bench trial, on the other hand.[136]

On appeal, the Supreme Court unanimously remanded *Apple v. Samsung* to the Federal Circuit on the grounds that, pursuant to 35 U.S.C. § 289, "the relevant 'article of manufacture'" for purposes of awarding damages for the infringement of a design patent need not "always be the end product sold to the consumer" but "can also be a component of that product."[137] The Federal Circuit in turn remanded the case to Judge Koh to determine (1) whether to hold a new damages trial and, before holding any such trial, (2) the proper test for identifying the relevant "article of manufacture" for purposes of 35 U.S.C. § 289.[138]

On remand, Judge Koh issued two orders complying with the Federal Circuit's opinion remanding the case.[139] The jury in the second damages trial awarded Apple $533 million in damages for Samsung's infringement of Apple's three design patents, even though Samsung had prevailed in its appeal to the Supreme Court of the $399 million damages award that the first jury trial had produced.[140] Apple and Samsung notified Judge Koh on June 27, 2018 that they had settled their dispute and had agreed to drop all claims in the case, and Judge Koh dismissed the case that very day.[141]

If Apple is a company built on panache and marketing and a portfolio of precious design patents, then Qualcomm is a company built on engineering and research and technological innovation. How does one compare the value bestowed by a beautiful appearance with the value created from a technological innovation like carrier aggregation—without which the fetching iPhone would be substantially less productive and versatile? If a jury found that Samsung's infringement of three design patents for a smartphone entitled

---

[136] *See, e.g.*, Apple, Inc. v. Samsung Elecs. Co., 920 F. Supp. 2d 1079 (N.D. Cal. 2013) (Koh, J.) (Order of January 29, 2013, Granting in Part and Denying in Part Samsung's Motion for Judgment as a Matter of Law); *Apple v. Samsung*, 920 F. Supp. 2d at 1139–42 (analyzing the ETSI FRAND contract and concluding that, "[r]egarding FRAND obligations, Samsung's licensing behavior could only give rise to Sherman Act liability if it constituted anticompetitive behavior"); Apple, Inc. v. Samsung Elecs. Co., 926 F. Supp. 2d 1100 (N.D. Cal. 2013) (Koh, J.) (Order of March 1, 2013, Regarding Damages), *aff'd in part and rev'd in part*, 786 F.3d 983 (Fed. Cir. 2015) (Prost, C.J.), *rev'd*, Samsung Elecs. Co. v. Apple Inc., 137 S. Ct. 429 (2016) (8-0 decision) (Sotomayor, J.); *see also* Apple, Inc. v. Samsung Elecs. Co., No. 12-CV-00630-LHK, 2014 WL 794328 (N.D. Cal. Feb. 25, 2014) (Koh, J.) (Order Granting in Part and Denying in Part Motions to Exclude Certain Expert Opinions).

[137] *Samsung v. Apple*, 137 S. Ct. at 434 (quoting 35 U.S.C. § 289); *see also* Ronald J. Mann, *Design Patent Damages After* Samsung v. Apple, 1 CRITERION J. ON INNOVATION 197, 197–99 (2016).

[138] Apple Inc. v. Samsung Elecs. Co., 678 F. App'x 1012, 1013–14 (Fed. Cir. 2017) (per curiam).

[139] *See* Apple Inc. v. Samsung Elecs. Co., No. 11-CV-01846-LHK, 2017 WL 3232424 (N.D. Cal. July 28, 2017) (Koh, J.) (Order Regarding Waiver of Article of Manufacture Issue and New Trial on Design Patent Damages); Apple Inc. v. Samsung Elecs. Co., No. 11-CV-01846-LHK, 2017 WL 4776443 (N.D. Cal. Oct. 22, 2017) (Koh, J.) (Order Requiring New Trial on Design Patent Damages).

[140] Jury Verdict, Apple Inc. v. Samsung Elecs. Co., No. 11-cv-01846-LHK (N.D. Cal. May 24, 2018), ECF No. 3761.

[141] *See* Joint Notice of Settlement and Stipulation of Dismissal with Prejudice at 2, Apple Inc. v. Samsung Elecs. Co., No. 11-cv-01846-LHK (N.D. Cal. June 27, 2018), ECF No. 3835; Order of Dismissal, Apple Inc. v. Samsung Elecs. Co., No. 11-cv-01846-LHK (N.D. Cal. June 27, 2018), ECF No. 3836.

Apple to damages of upwards of half a billion dollars, what must an exhaustive license to all of Qualcomm's thousands of foundational cellular SEPs be worth?

Next, we shall see that the public record offered important insights into the royalties that OEMs actually paid for a license to Qualcomm's patent portfolio.

3.   *The $7.50 Royalty Per iPhone That Apple Actually Paid to Qualcomm*

Qualcomm calls its patent license a Subscriber Unit License Agreement, or SULA.[142] "With a SULA," Judge Koh explained, "an OEM may sell handsets that practice Qualcomm's patents without fear of an infringement suit from Qualcomm."[143] The FTC and Qualcomm stipulated that, "in a typical SULA, Qualcomm receives consideration in the form of a running royalty rate calculated as a percentage of the licensee's *wholesale* net selling price of the end-user device (minus applicable deductions), subject to royalty caps."[144] Evidently, Qualcomm typically charged up to a $20 royalty per handset, calculated by multiplying (1) a royalty rate of 5 percent[145] by (2) a royalty base equal to the wholesale price of a handset (capped at $400).[146] Qualcomm apparently charged different royalty rates for handsets implementing different combinations of patented technologies. For example, using a royalty base capped at $400, Qualcomm historically charged a 5-percent royalty rate for an exhaustive license to its CDMA portfolio and a 4-percent royalty rate for an exhaustive license to its LTE portfolio.[147]

Judge Koh found that some of Qualcomm's licensees paid substantially less than $20 per handset. For example, Apple's Chief Operating Officer, Jeff Williams, testified at trial that the company paid only a net royalty of $7.50 per handset after Qualcomm had paid Apple its negotiated rebates (at a time when Apple was paying $30 for each (unlicensed) modem sourced solely from

---

[142] FTC v. Qualcomm Inc., 411 F. Supp. 3d 658, 673 (N.D. Cal. 2019).

[143] *Id.* (citing Transcript of Proceedings (Volume 7) at 1426:2–10, FTC v. Qualcomm Inc., No. 5:17-cv-00220-LHK (N.D. Cal. Jan. 18, 2019) (Testimony of Fabian Gonell (Legal Counsel and Senior Vice President, Licensing Strategy, Qualcomm Technology Licensing))).

[144] *Id.* (emphasis added) (citing Joint Stipulation Regarding Undisputed Facts at 10, FTC v. Qualcomm Inc., No. 5:17-cv-00220-LHK (N.D. Cal. Jan. 16, 2019) [hereinafter Joint Stipulation Regarding Undisputed Facts]).

[145] *Id.*

[146] *Id.*; Transcript of Proceedings (Volume 9) at 1979:16–23, FTC v. Qualcomm Inc., No. 5:17-cv-00220-LHK (N.D. Cal. Jan. 25, 2019) (Testimony of Alex Rogers (President, Qualcomm Technology Licensing)). Qualcomm's royalty caps apparently were not entirely uniform. For example, beginning in 2004, Qualcomm capped Samsung's royalty at $20 per handset. *FTC v. Qualcomm*, 411 F. Supp. 3d at 707. Qualcomm's royalty rates apparently were not entirely uniform either. For example, Judge Koh reported that, under certain conditions beginning in or around 2003, Huawei owed Qualcomm a royalty rate of as much as 7 percent, which, when applied to a royalty base capped at $500, produced a royalty cap of $35 per handset. *FTC v. Qualcomm*, 411 F. Supp. 3d at 710.

[147] *FTC v. Qualcomm*, 411 F. Supp. 3d at 673.

Qualcomm).[148] He testified that Apple understood that $7.50 per unit "was the average price everyone was paying"[149] Qualcomm—presumably for an exhaustive license to Qualcomm's entire patent portfolio.

When testifying about the post-rebate $7.50 per iPhone that Apple agreed to pay Qualcomm, Mr. Williams elaborated on the iPhone's design and manufacture: "We [Apple] design our products, and we design the processes that make our products, but the final assembly for almost all of our products are [sic] done by other companies who employ the labor and do the actual final assembly. We call them contract manufacturers."[150] He testified that "Apple's contract manufacturers ha[d] direct license agreements with Qualcomm,"[151] and that Apple "ended up reimbursing the contract manufacturers"[152] the royalty amount that those contract manufacturers paid Qualcomm, which was "5 percent of the cost of the phone."[153] Mr. Williams further testified that the royalty amount (in dollars) that the contract manufacturers paid Qualcomm was "in the teens," or "anywhere from, you know, $12 to $20 range,"[154] which would indicate that the transfer price for an iPhone from the contract manufacturers to Apple was between $240 and $400. Qualcomm then rebated to Apple the difference between the "$12 to $20" per iPhone that Apple had reimbursed its contract manufacturers and the $7.50 per iPhone that Apple had agreed to pay on net to Qualcomm.

In regard to the scope of Qualcomm's licenses to Apple's contract manufacturers, in various places in her findings of fact and conclusions of law, Judge Koh said that Apple paid the rebated per-unit royalty of $7.50 to Qualcomm for an "indirect patent license agreement"[155] to Qualcomm's patent portfolio, including its non-SEPs.[156] Judge Koh described the arrangement between Qualcomm and Apple's contract manufacturers, on the one hand, and Apple and its contract manufacturers, on the other hand:

> The [2007] MIA [Marketing Incentive Agreement] lowered Apple's royalty payments to Qualcomm through a rebate structure. Apple does

---

148   Transcript of Proceedings (Volume 5) at 870:13–23, FTC v. Qualcomm Inc., No. 5:17-cv-00220-LHK (N.D. Cal. Jan. 14, 2019) (Testimony of Jeff Williams (COO, Apple)), *cited in FTC v. Qualcomm*, 411 F. Supp. 3d at 725 ("Q. So back to the marketing incentive agreement. Under the rebate arrangement that you ultimately put in place with Qualcomm in 2007, what was the net royalty paid to Qualcomm through this arrangement? A. [$]7.50. So the contract manufacturers paid the 5 percent, and then Qualcomm rebated us down to the [$]7.50. Q. And how did the parties arrive at the $7.50 figure? A. We originally proposed 5 percent of the cost of the baseband chip, which is $30, so we originally proposed a dollar 50 [that is, $1.50]. We flew down to San Diego and proposed that. That was rejected.").

149   *Id.* at 871:14.

150   *Id.* at 868:15–19.

151   *Id.* at 868:20–21.

152   *Id.* at 869:4–5.

153   *Id.* at 869:1–2; *accord id.* at 869:3–4.

154   *Id.* at 869:7–8.

155   *FTC v. Qualcomm*, 411 F. Supp. 3d at 724.

156   *Id.* at 725, 727, 730, 732.

not manufacture handsets itself but instead uses contract manufacturers, including Pegatron and Wistron, to manufacture handsets. These contract manufacturers pay Qualcomm a 5% running royalty rate on the manufacturers' handset selling price. Then, according to Jeff Williams (Apple COO), Apple reimburses the contract manufacturers: "Qualcomm had a standard agreement with contract manufacturers and the contract manufacturers paid Qualcomm, and we reimburse the contract manufacturers." In the MIA, Qualcomm agreed to provide Apple royalty rebates on each handset to reduce Apple's royalty payments: "For each Apple Phone purchased by Apple or an Apple Authorized Purchaser during the Term, Qualcomm agrees to pay a Marketing Incentive (defined below) to Apple." According to Jeff Williams, the MIA rebated Apple's royalty payments to a total of $7.50 per handset.[157]

Qualcomm's license to Apple's contract manufacturers thus appeared to be exhaustive with respect to Qualcomm's entire patent portfolio (as opposed to merely its cellular SEPs). As we shall see in Part E.5 to the Introduction, the reference by both Mr. Williams and Judge Koh to a "5-percent" royalty rate supports that inference because Qualcomm specified a "5-percent" royalty rate for an exhaustive license to its entire patent portfolio. Consequently, Apple's "indirect license" also appears to have been exhaustive with respect to Qualcomm's entire patent portfolio.

In Judge Koh's words, Apple considered even $7.50 per smartphone to be an "excessive" royalty to pay Qualcomm for an exhaustive license to its enabling standardized cellular technology used in a $1000 iPhone.[158] As we shall see in Part I.A.6, even the $7.50 royalty per iPhone that Apple eventually paid Qualcomm was substantially less than the $20 royalty cap per handset that Qualcomm agreed to accept from Chinese OEMs following an investigation into Qualcomm's licensing practices in China. That is, the government of the People's Republic of China, which appeared to act as the leader of a buyers' cartel so as jointly (rather than bilaterally) to negotiate with Qualcomm on behalf of all Chinese OEMs, agreed that Chinese OEMs would pay Qualcomm a royalty not to exceed $20 per handset. That agreed-upon amount was more than twice as much per handset as what Apple agreed to pay Qualcomm (and more than an order of magnitude greater than the $1.50 per iPhone that Apple had first offered to pay).

---

[157] *Id.* at 724–25 (citations omitted) (first quoting Transcript of Proceedings (Volume 5) at 868:5–7, FTC v. Qualcomm Inc., No. 5:17-cv-00220-LHK (N.D. Cal. Jan. 14, 2019) (Testimony of Jeff Williams (COO, Apple)); and then quoting JX0040-002) (first citing Joint Stipulation Regarding Undisputed Facts, *supra* note 144, at 4; then citing JX0042-014 to -015 (Wistron SULA); and then citing Transcript of Proceedings (Volume 5) at 870:17–18, FTC v. Qualcomm Inc., No. 5:17-cv-00220-LHK (N.D. Cal. Jan. 14, 2019) (Testimony of Jeff Williams (COO, Apple))).

[158] *Id.* at 725 ("Apple viewed the $7.50 per handset royalty payment . . . as excessive.").

Mr. Williams, in response to the question, "What do you think of [$7.50] in terms of its fairness for Apple—for Qualcomm's I.P.?", testified: "I thought it was too high. We had started to learn about other rates and it was excessive. *Qualcomm charges us more than everybody else put together*."[159] Mr. Williams' testimony appeared to indicate that Apple paid a cumulative royalty no greater than $15 per iPhone. Thus, through Mr. Williams' sworn testimony in *FTC v. Qualcomm*, Apple appeared to reaffirm the position that $15 per iPhone would have been an "excessive" royalty to pay for *all* of the intellectual property required to make the iPhone.

4.   The Conjecture, Propagated by Qualcomm's Detractors, of a $120 Per Unit Aggregate Royalty

Coincidentally (and presumably inadvertently), Mr. Williams' testimony about Apple's royalty payments debunked the long-advanced conjecture that the cumulative royalty payments for SEPs practiced in a smartphone were excessive and justified intervention on competition law grounds by enforcement agencies or regulators. In particular, a 2014 unpublished paper by Ann Armstrong of Intel and Joseph Mueller and Timothy Syrett of WilmerHale had estimated "potential patent royalties in excess of $120 on a hypothetical $400 smartphone,"[160] or 30 percent of the price of the hypothetical smartphone. In 2007, Professors Mark Lemley and Carl Shapiro had claimed that "stacked royalties" could be as high as 40 percent of the total price of a smartphone.[161] Those conjectures diverged by roughly an order of magnitude from Mr. Williams' testimony at trial in *FTC v. Qualcomm* in January 2019 that Qualcomm's $7.50 royalty accounted for more than half of all the royalties that Apple was paying on each iPhone.[162]

Nevertheless, some antitrust enforcers had credulously endorsed the conjecture that the cumulative payments for SEPs practiced in a smartphone were so high as to justify government intervention. In a speech delivered in November 2016, the European Commissioner for Competition, Margrethe Vestager, mentioned (without identification or citation) "[o]ne recent study" claiming "that 120 dollars of the cost of each smartphone comes from paying royalties for the patents it contains."[163] Yet, even at the time of Commissioner

---

[159] Transcript of Proceedings (Volume 5) at 871:2–6, FTC v. Qualcomm Inc., No. 5:17-cv-00220-LHK (N.D. Cal. Jan. 14, 2019) (Testimony of Jeff Williams (COO, Apple)) (emphasis added).

[160] Ann Armstrong, Joseph Mueller & Timothy Syrett, The Smartphone Royalty Stack: Surveying Royalty Demands for the Components Within Modern Smartphones 2 (May 29, 2014) (unpublished manuscript), https://www.wilmerhale.com/en/insights/publications/the-smartphone-royalty-stack.

[161] *See* Lemley & Shapiro, *Patent Holdup and Royalty Stacking, supra* note 118, at 2026.

[162] *See supra* note 159 and accompanying text.

[163] Margrethe Vestager, Commissioner for Competition, European Commission, Protecting Consumers from Exploitation (Nov. 21, 2016), https://wayback.archive-it.org/12090/20191129221154/https://ec.europa.eu/commission/commissioners/2014-2019/vestager/announcements/protecting-consumers-exploitation_en.

Vestager's speech, empirical studies relying solely on publicly disclosed financial data contradicted the $120 conjecture and instead estimated that the cumulative royalty payment for SEPs practiced in a smartphone was between $20 and $25 per smartphone.[164] In January 2019, Mr. Williams in effect confirmed by his sworn trial testimony in *FTC v. Qualcomm* that those empirical studies were actually high, when he testified that Apple's cumulative royalty payment was less than or equal to $15 per iPhone.

5. *Qualcomm's Clarification and Reduction of Its Royalties in November 2017*

In November 2017, 10 months after the FTC had filed its complaint in *FTC v. Qualcomm*, Qualcomm clarified the royalty rates that it expected to apply "on a worldwide basis to a license for Original Equipment Manufacturer (OEM) branded mobile handsets that implement the 5G NR [New Radio] standard, up to and including release 15 of the 3GPP [3ʳᵈ Generation Partnership Project] specifications."[165] Table 2 reports those royalty rates.

Alex Rogers, President of QTL, testified that when Qualcomm says "multimode, that means that for a device that practices 3G standards and 4G standards and in this case the first release of 5G, that device would be fully licensed under the SEP only license agreement at 3.25 percent."[166] In addition, he clarified during his testimony that all of those rates applied to a royalty base that was subject to a cap, which Qualcomm had reduced as of January 2018 from $500 to $400,[167] such that the maximum royalty per handset that a licensee could pay would equal $20 (that is, 5 percent of $400). Thus, the Qualcomm royalty amounts at stake were in the low tens of dollars per handset (or, in the case of Apple, $7.50 per iPhone). Notably,

---

[164] *See, e.g.*, Keith Mallinson, *Cumulative Mobile-SEP Royalty Payments No More Than Around 5% of Mobile Handset Revenues* 6, WISEHARBOR (2015), http://www.wiseharbor.com/pdfs/Mallinson%20on%20cumulative%20mobile%20SEP%20royalties%20for%20IP%20Finance%202015Aug19.pdf.   Subsequent research confirmed these results or found that cumulative royalty payments per smartphone were even lower. *See* J. Gregory Sidak, *What Aggregate Royalty Do Manufacturers of Mobile Phones Pay to License Standard-Essential Patents?*, 1 CRITERION J. ON INNOVATION 701 (2016); Alexander Galetovic & Stephen Haber, *Innovation Under Threat? An Assessment of the Evidence for Patent Holdup and Royalty Stacking in SEP-Intensive, IT Industries*, CPI ANTITRUST CHRON., Sept. 2016, at 1, 2; Alexander Galetovic & Stephen Haber, *The Fallacies of Patent-Holdup Theory*, 13 J. COMPETITION L. & ECON. 1, 23–26 (2017); Alexander Galetovic, Stephen Haber & Lew Zaretzki, *An Estimate of the Average Cumulative Royalty Yield in the World Mobile Phone Industry: Theory, Measurement and Results*, 42 TELECOMM. POL'Y 263, 271–72 (2018).

[165] Qualcomm Inc., Qualcomm 5G NR [New Radio] Royalty Terms Statement (Nov. 19, 2017) [hereinafter Qualcomm 5G Royalty Terms Statement], https://www.qualcomm.com/media/documents/files/qualcomm-5g-nr-royalty-terms-statement.pdf.

[166] Transcript of Proceedings (Volume 9) at 1979:11–15, FTC v. Qualcomm Inc., No. 5:17-cv-00220-LHK (N.D. Cal. Jan. 25, 2019) (Testimony of Alex Rogers (President, Qualcomm Technology Licensing)).

[167] *Id.* at 1979:16–23 ("Q. Are these rates all subject to a cap? A. Yes, they are. Q. What is the cap? A. So at the time, the rates would be applied to the net selling price of a device. At the time the cap for the device was $500. That was in November of 2017. But at the present time, as of January 2018, the cap was reduced from $500 to $400."), *cited in FTC v. Qualcomm*, 411 F. Supp. 3d at 673 ("Qualcomm has capped the maximum royalty base or net selling price of the handset at $400.").

although Mr. Williams of Apple testified that the company had offered to pay Qualcomm a royalty of $1.50 per iPhone,[168] he never clearly stated whether Apple considered the "excessive" amount of royalty that it ultimately paid to Qualcomm to be the entire difference between the $7.50 it ultimately agreed to pay and its $1.50 offer (that is, $6), or some other amount.

Table 2. Royalty Rates Announced by Qualcomm
in November 2017 for Handsets Implementing
Various Configurations of Technologies

	Cellular SEPs Only	Entire Patent Portfolio
Single-Mode (5G) Handset	2.275%	4%
Multimode (3G/4G/5G) Handset	3.25%	5%

Source: Qualcomm 5G Royalty Terms Statement, *supra* note 165; *see also* Transcript of Proceedings (Volume 9) at 1978:17–1979:15, FTC v. Qualcomm Inc., No. 5:17-cv-00220-LHK (N.D. Cal. Jan. 25, 2019) (Testimony of Alex Rogers (President, Qualcomm Technology Licensing)).
Note: As of January 2018, these rates applied to a royalty base capped at $400 per handset. Transcript of Proceedings (Volume 9) at 1979:16–23, FTC v. Qualcomm Inc., No. 5:17-cv-00220-LHK (N.D. Cal. Jan. 25, 2019) (Testimony of Alex Rogers (President, Qualcomm Technology Licensing)).

F.   *Were the Empirically Testable Hypotheses Concerning Harm to Competition in the Modem Industry Substantiated or Refuted?*

When a monopolist engages in exclusionary conduct, economists would predict one or more of the following outcomes: higher quality-adjusted prices, reduced output, or less innovation.[169] Judge Koh did not report evidence-based findings on any of those indicators of competitive harm, either in her market for CDMA modems or in her market for "premium" LTE modems. She did not empirically substantiate her findings of fact concerning

---

[168]   *See supra* note 148.
[169]   *See, e.g.*, PAUL A. SAMUELSON & WILLIAM D. NORDHAUS, ECONOMICS 199–200, 649 (Irwin McGraw-Hill 19th ed. 2010); *see also* Fishman v. Estate of Wirtz, 807 F.2d 520, 563 (7th Cir. 1986) (Easterbrook, J., dissenting) ("In 1972 Chicago had one professional basketball team, playing at the Stadium. In 1973 Chicago had one professional basketball team, playing at the Stadium. The district court found the team to be a natural monopoly and the Stadium to be an 'essential facility', so no matter who owned the Bulls, Chicago was doomed to have one professional basketball team, playing at the Stadium. The change of ownership in July 1972 did not alter the structure of the market or the potential for new entry. *It did not reduce the quantity produced, increase the price charged, or affect the quality supplied.* There is no claim of consumers' injury, actual or potential, now or in the future. For their role in this non-event, the defendants have been ordered to pay more than $12 million under the Sherman Act.") (emphasis added); Brooke Grp. Ltd. v. Brown & Williamson Tobacco Corp., 509 U.S. 209, 237 (1993) ("Where . . . output is expanding at the same time prices are increasing, rising prices are equally consistent with growing product demand."), *quoted in* FTC v. Qualcomm Inc., No. 19-16122, 2020 WL 4591476, at *9 (9th Cir. Aug. 11, 2020) (alteration in original).

harm to competition. Judge Koh's findings of harm to competition instead rested entirely on her *a priori* arguments, which might or might not be found eventually to be false. If her *a priori* arguments were correct, then they would imply various economic hypotheses, which should be found to be consistent with empirical observation.

Yet, Judge Koh did not approach her fact-finding duties in the bench trial in *FTC v. Qualcomm* with this kind of epistemological discipline. She did not examine any rival's revenue or R&D investments or acquisitions. Nor did Judge Koh examine evidence about competition in her relevant product markets, which would have obligated her to examine hard evidence of prices, output levels, and entry. Quality-adjusted prices of modems fell and output rose when Qualcomm allegedly possessed and exploited market power in Judge Koh's two modem markets.

A comprehensive analysis of the empirical data from the modem industry exceeds the scope of this article. Yet, even limited industry data disproved Judge Koh's conclusion that Qualcomm's challenged practices harmed competition.

1.   Did the Quality-Adjusted Price of Modems Increase?

Economic theory predicts that lessened competition can elevate *quality-adjusted* prices. But of course a price increase alone does not indicate that competition has been harmed. The Supreme Court explained in *Leegin* in 2007, for example, that a firm can take many actions that increase both price and quality without harming competition.[170] Thus, if Qualcomm's licensing practices had been truly anticompetitive, as Judge Koh found, one would expect the prices of modems, adjusted for increases in quality, to have risen during the period when Qualcomm allegedly engaged in the exclusionary conduct. Yet, the data showed otherwise.

Data reported by Strategy Analytics, a market research firm, show that the average selling price (ASP) of CDMA modems fell each year between 2008 and 2015, the time period during which Judge Koh found that Qualcomm had a monopoly in the market for CDMA modems.[171] Figure 1 shows the ASP of CDMA modems from 2008 through 2015.

---

[170] Leegin Creative Leather Prods., Inc. v. PSKS, Inc., 551 U.S. 877, 896–97 (2007) ("Many decisions a manufacturer makes and carries out through concerted action can lead to higher prices. A manufacturer might, for example, contract with different suppliers to obtain better inputs that improve product quality. . . . Yet no one would think these actions violate the Sherman Act because they lead to higher prices. . . . The manufacturer strives to improve its product quality or to promote its brand because it believes this conduct will lead to increased demand despite higher prices.").

[171] Judge Koh found that Qualcomm had monopoly power in the market for CDMA modems from 2006 through 2015. FTC v. Qualcomm Inc., 411 F. Supp. 3d 658, 685, 691 (N.D. Cal. 2019). However, the Strategy Analytics data do not include the ASP for CDMA modems between 2006 and 2007. Consequently, I restrict my analysis to the period from 2008 through 2015.

Figure 1. Average Selling Price of CDMA
Modems Sold Globally, 2008–2015

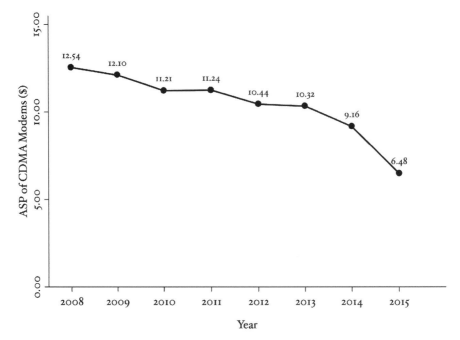

Source: STRATEGY ANALYTICS, BASEBAND MARKET SHARE TRACKER 2017: INTEL, HISILICON AND SAMSUNG REGISTER DOUBLE-DIGIT LTE SHIPMENT GROWTH tab 4c ("CDMA") (2018).

Figure 1 shows that between 2008 and 2015 the ASP of CDMA modems decreased in every year except one. That single exception was 2011, when the ASP increased by 0.3 percent.[172] In 2015, the ASP of a CDMA modem was 48.3 percent lower than it had been in 2008.[173]

Strategy Analytics data also show that the ASP for LTE modems decreased from 2012 to 2016.[174] After U.S. network operators deployed LTE networks in 2012 and handset manufacturers widely adopted LTE baseband processors,[175]

---

[172] That is, (11.24 − 11.21) ÷ 11.21 = 0.0027.

[173] That is, (6.48 − 12.54) ÷ 12.54 = −0.4833. Figure 1 does not adjust for inflation, and therefore it understates the extent of the decline in quality-adjusted prices.

[174] STRATEGY ANALYTICS, BASEBAND MARKET SHARE TRACKER 2017: INTEL, HISILICON AND SAMSUNG REGISTER DOUBLE-DIGIT LTE SHIPMENT GROWTH, *supra* sources cited in Figure 1, tab 4e ("LTE").

[175] *See, e.g.*, Press Release, Sprint Nextel Corp., Sprint Announces First Major Markets to Receive 4G LTE in 2012 (Jan. 5, 2012), https://newsroom.sprint.com/sprint-announces-first-major-markets-to-receive-4g-lte-in-2012.htm; Press Release, Verizon Communications Inc., What the Mobile Internet Meant to 2012 (Dec. 19, 2012), https://www.verizon.com/about/news/vzw/2012/12/2012-year-of-the-mobile; Press Release, T-Mobile USA Inc., T-Mobile Network Advancements Enrich Customer Experience with Nationwide HD Voice and Enhanced 4G Coverage in New Metro Areas (Jan. 7, 2013), https://www.t-mobile.com/news/t-mobile-network-advancements-enrich-customer-experience-with-hd; Press Release, AT&T Corp., AT&T 4G LTE Now Covers More Than 225 Million People (July 17, 2013), https://about.att.com/newsroom/att4gltenowcoversmorethan225millionpeople.html.

the ASP of LTE modems fell each year from 2012 to 2016. Figure 2 shows the ASP of LTE modems from 2012 through 2016.

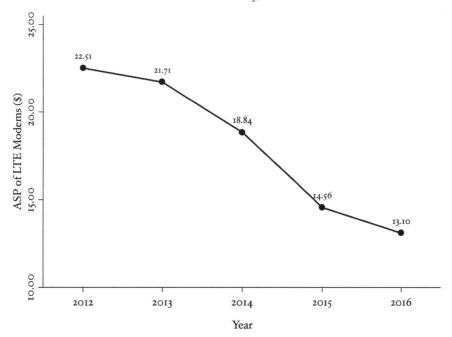

Figure 2. Average Selling Price of LTE
Modems Sold Globally, 2012–2016

Source: STRATEGY ANALYTICS, BASEBAND MARKET SHARE TRACKER 2017: INTEL, HISILICON AND SAMSUNG REGISTER DOUBLE-DIGIT LTE SHIPMENT GROWTH, *supra* sources cited in Figure 1, tab 4e ("LTE").

Figure 2 shows that in 2016 the ASP of LTE modems was 41.8 percent lower than it was in 2012.[176] (The data commercially provided by Strategy Analytics do not include the ASP for "premium" LTE modems, which tends to confirm that that categorization was predicated on arbitrary terminology adopted by Judge Koh and the FTC but not used by Strategy Analytics in its industry analysis.[177])

Similarly, the empirical evidence does not support the claim of decreased quality in modems during the period of Qualcomm's alleged monopoly. Qualcomm reported in 2016 that the peak download speed supported in its modems was less than 10.2 Mbps in 2008, whereas the download speed of

---

[176] That is, $(13.10 - 22.51) \div 22.51 = -0.4180$. Again, this figure does not control for inflation and thus understates the extent of the decline in quality-adjusted prices.

[177] We shall see in Part XI that Judge Koh identified a subset of LTE modems as a relevant product market, not on the basis of any properly defined characteristics of the modems, but instead solely on the basis of the price of the handsets that use each modem.

its modems had increased to 100 Mbps by 2012 and to 600 Mbps by 2016.[178] That evidence indicates that the quality of modems had increased from 2008 to 2016.

If a product's performance increases while its nominal price falls, then obviously the product's quality-adjusted price has fallen by an even greater proportion. Evidence of decreasing ASPs for CDMA and LTE modems therefore disproved, rather than supported, the first testable hypothesis that would naturally follow from Judge Koh's finding that Qualcomm engaged in exclusionary practices that harmed competition in what she defined as the relevant markets for two kinds of modems.

2.   Did the Output of Modems Decrease?

When a monopolist engages in an exclusionary practice, one would predict that reduced output subsequently would be observed.[179] Yet, evidence from the modem industry showed that the output of LTE modems *increased* during the period when Judge Koh found that Qualcomm had excluded rival modem manufacturers. Table 3 reports manufacturers' unit sales of LTE modems sold globally from 2012 through 2016.

Table 3 shows that in 2012 there were 146.4 million LTE modems sold in the world. By 2016, nearly 1.5 billion LTE modems were sold, an increase of more than 905 percent.[180] Table 3 also shows that, between 2012 and 2016, new companies entered the industry and increased its total output. In 2012, only three companies (Qualcomm, Samsung, and GCT) sold more than one million LTE modems. In 2016, the unit sales of 10 companies (Qualcomm, MediaTek, Samsung, Spreadtrum, Intel, HiSilicon, Altair, Sequans, Leadcore, and Marvell) exceeded that threshold.

---

[178]   QUALCOMM, DELIVERING ON THE LTE ADVANCED PROMISE 8 (2016), https://www.qualcomm.com/media/documents/files/delivering-on-the-lte-advanced-promise.pdf.

[179]   *See, e.g.*, SAMUELSON & NORDHAUS, ECONOMICS, *supra* note 169, at 199–200; DENNIS W. CARLTON & JEFFREY M. PERLOFF, MODERN INDUSTRIAL ORGANIZATION 88–92 (Pearson 4th ed. 2005).

[180]   That is, $(1472.3 - 146.4) \div 146.4 = 9.0567$.

Table 3. Manufacturers' Unit Sales of LTE
Modems Sold Globally, 2012–2016 (Millions of Units)

Manufacturer	2012	2013	2014	2015	2016
Qualcomm	131.2	296.4	518.3	707.9	763.8
MediaTek	–	–	32.1	163.0	353.9
Samsung	8.7	10.7	13.4	87.8	118.5
Spreadtrum	0.0	0.1	2.9	15.0	90.7
Intel	–	3.2	12.4	15.3	60.9
HiSilicon	0.0	1.4	23.2	40.0	70.5
Altair	0.0	1.0	3.7	4.7	4.4
Sequans	0.0	0.2	1.4	2.6	3.7
Leadcore	–	–	0.1	20.4	2.1
GCT	1.7	2.4	1.3	0.9	0.6
Marvell	–	0.7	28.7	31.6	3.1
Others	4.7	1.0	2.3	0.2	0.1
Total	146.4	317.1	639.6	1089.4	1472.3

Source: Strategy Analytics, Baseband Market Share Tracker 2017: Intel, HiSilicon and Samsung Register Double-Digit LTE Shipment Growth, *supra* sources cited in Figure 1, tab 4e ("LTE").
Note: Table 3 reports the top 11 manufacturers that have the highest average unit sales of LTE modems from 2012 through 2016.

The empirical evidence also shows that Qualcomm's competitors increased their collective output more rapidly than Qualcomm increased its output. Table 4 reports manufacturers' shares of LTE modems sold globally from 2012 through 2016.

Table 4 shows that MediaTek—a Taiwanese fabless semiconductor company—entered the market in 2014 and, by 2016, supplied the second-highest share of LTE modems sold globally (24.0 percent). Other new entrants—such as HiSilicon, Intel, and Spreadtrum—similarly increased their shares of sales from 2013 to 2016. Specifically, HiSilicon's share of sales increased from 0.4 percent in 2013 to 4.8 percent in 2016, Intel's share of sales increased from 1.0 percent in 2013 to 4.1 percent in 2016, and Spreadtrum's share of sales increased from zero percent in 2013 to 6.2 percent in 2016. From 2013 to 2016, Qualcomm's share of LTE modem sales fell every year, from 93.5 percent in 2013 to 51.9 percent in 2016.

TABLE 4. MANUFACTURERS' SHARES OF LTE
MODEMS SOLD GLOBALLY, 2012–2016

Manufacturer	2012	2013	2014	2015	2016
Qualcomm	89.7%	93.5%	81.0%	65.0%	51.9%
MediaTek	–	–	5.0%	15.0%	24.0%
Samsung	5.9%	3.4%	2.1%	8.1%	8.0%
Spreadtrum	0.0%	0.0%	0.4%	1.4%	6.2%
Intel	–	1.0%	1.9%	1.4%	4.1%
HiSilicon	0.0%	0.4%	3.6%	3.7%	4.8%
Leadcore	–	–	0.0%	1.9%	0.1%
GCT	1.1%	0.7%	0.2%	0.1%	0.0%
Marvell	–	0.2%	4.5%	2.9%	0.2%
Others	3.2%	0.7%	1.1%	0.7%	0.6%
Total Units (in millions)	146.4	317.1	639.6	1089.4	1472.3

Source: STRATEGY ANALYTICS, BASEBAND MARKET SHARE TRACKER 2017: INTEL, HISILICON AND SAMSUNG REGISTER DOUBLE-DIGIT LTE SHIPMENT GROWTH, *supra* sources cited in Figure 1, tab 4e ("LTE").

Note: Table 4 reports the manufacturers whose shares of LTE modems has ever exceeded 1 percent in any year from 2012 to 2016. The shares are measured as a percentage of LTE modems unit sales.

In sum, empirical evidence disproved rather than supported Judge Koh's conclusion that Qualcomm's practices harmed competition in what she defined as the two relevant markets for modems. During the period in which Qualcomm allegedly engaged in anticompetitive conduct, prices for modems in fact fell, output of modems in fact rose, and the quality of modems in fact improved. Those outcomes are not what one would predict for markets in which a monopolist is supposedly engaging in practices that Judge Koh said would "'tend[] to destroy competition itself.'"[181]

G. *Judge Koh's Findings of Fact and Conclusions of Law in May 2019*

On May 2, 2019, while awaiting Judge Koh's findings of fact and conclusions of law following the January 2019 trial in *FTC v. Qualcomm*, the Antitrust Division of the Department of Justice took the unusual step of intervening in the FTC's case by filing a Statement of Interest requesting that Judge Koh

---

[181] FTC v. Qualcomm Inc., 411 F. Supp. 3d 658, 803 (N.D. Cal. 2019) (alteration in original) (quoting Spectrum Sports, Inc. v. McQuillan, 506 U.S. 447, 458 (1993)).

"permit additional briefing and schedule an evidentiary hearing" on remedies if she were to find Qualcomm liable.[182] Judge Koh did not respond.

On May 21, 2019, having never acknowledged the Antitrust Division's Statement of Interest, Judge Koh issued her findings of fact and conclusions of law in *FTC v. Qualcomm*.[183] The opinion embraced virtually every material argument that the FTC had raised in its complaint and that Professor Shapiro had presented in his trial testimony. Judge Koh found that Qualcomm had a monopoly both in a relevant antitrust product market consisting of CDMA modems and in a relevant antitrust product market consisting of "premium" LTE modems.[184] She found that, "[i]n combination, Qualcomm's licensing practices have strangled competition in the CDMA and premium LTE modem chip markets for years, and harmed rivals, OEMs, and end consumers in the process."[185]

Upon finding violations of both section 1 and section 2 of the Sherman Act (and therefore a violation of section 5 of the FTC Act),[186] Judge Koh issued a permanent, worldwide injunction that imposed on Qualcomm (1) an obligation to renegotiate the license agreements that Qualcomm had previously executed with OEMs, (2) a prohibition against Qualcomm's limiting the sale of its modems to licensed OEMs, and (3) an obligation to offer exhaustive licenses to its cellular SEPs to rival modem manufacturers.[187] In practical economic effect, Judge Koh's permanent, worldwide injunction would compel Qualcomm to raise the price of its modems and lower the royalties for an exhaustive license to its cellular SEPs. The Supreme Court of course long ago recognized that rate setting (an anterior component of which is rate design, which is what Judge Koh's permanent, worldwide injunction in effect dictated to Qualcomm) is inherently legislative in character. Justice Oliver Wendell Holmes wrote for the Supreme Court in 1908 in *Prentis v. Atlantic Coast Line Co.*:

> A judicial inquiry investigates, declares, and enforces liabilities as they stand
> on present or past facts and under laws supposed already to exist. That is
> its purpose and end. Legislation, on the other hand, looks to the future and
> changes existing conditions by making a new rule, to be applied thereafter

---

[182] Statement of Interest of the United States of America at 3, FTC v. Qualcomm Inc., No. 5:17-cv-00220-LHK (N.D. Cal. May 2, 2019), ECF No. 1487 [hereinafter Statement of Interest of the United States Concerning Remedies].

[183] *FTC v. Qualcomm*, 411 F. Supp. 3d 658.

[184] *Id.* at 683–95.

[185] *Id.* at 812.

[186] *Id.* ("Qualcomm's practices violate § 1 and § 2 of the Sherman Act, and . . . Qualcomm is liable under the FTC Act, as 'unfair methods of competition' under the FTC Act include 'violations of the Sherman Act.'") (quoting FTC v. Cement Inst., 333 U.S. 683, 693–94 (1948)).

[187] *Id.* at 818; *see also* FTC v. Qualcomm Inc., No. 19-16122, 2020 WL 4591476, at *5 (9ᵗʰ Cir. Aug. 11, 2020) ("The district court ordered a permanent, worldwide injunction prohibiting Qualcomm's core business practices.") (citing *FTC v. Qualcomm*, 411 F. Supp. 3d at 820–24).

to all or some part of those subject to its power. The establishment of a rate is the making of a rule for the future, and therefore is an act legislative, not judicial, in kind.[188]

Judge Koh's permanent, worldwide injunction thus raised fundamental questions concerning the separation of power that her findings of fact and conclusions of law never recognized, much less answered.

Qualcomm appealed the decision and, in August 2019, persuaded the Ninth Circuit to stay enforcement of Judge Koh's permanent, worldwide injunction pending its decision on the merits of Qualcomm's appeal.[189] The Ninth Circuit held oral argument on February 13, 2020, before a panel consisting of Circuit Judges Johnnie B. Robinson and Consuelo Callahan and, sitting by designation, District Judge Stephen Murphy III of the Eastern District of Michigan.[190] The Antitrust Division received five minutes of Qualcomm's time to argue as *amicus curiae* in support of reversal.[191]

H. The Ninth Circuit's Reversal of Judge Koh's Judgment and Its Vacatur of Both Her Permanent, Worldwide Injunction and Her Grant to the FTC of Partial Summary Judgment

On August 11, 2020, the three-judge panel that had heard Qualcomm's appeal in the Ninth Circuit reversed Judge Koh's judgment and vacated both her permanent, worldwide injunction and her grant to the FTC of partial summary judgment.[192] In framing its opinion, the Ninth Circuit remarked: "This case asks us to draw the line between *anti*competitive behavior, which is illegal under federal antitrust law, and *hyper*competitive behavior, which is not."[193] The Ninth Circuit "h[e]ld that the district court went beyond the scope of the Sherman Act."[194]

---

[188] 211 U.S. 210, 226 (1908).

[189] FTC v. Qualcomm Inc., 935 F.3d 752, 755–57 (9th Cir. 2019) (per curiam) (granting Qualcomm's motion to stay in part Judge Koh's injunction).

[190] Oral Argument, FTC v. Qualcomm Inc., No. 19-16122 (9th Cir. Feb. 13, 2020), https://www.ca9.uscourts.gov/media/view_video.php?pk_vid=0000017078. On March 16, 2020, the Ninth Circuit curtailed certain of its operations after the coronavirus pandemic struck the United States around the beginning of 2020. *See* Order (9th Cir. Mar. 16, 2020), http://cdn.ca9.uscourts.gov/datastore/general/2020/03/16/building_closure_order.pdf ("The Center for Disease Control and Prevention as well as a host of Federal, State and Local officials have warned the public to take precautions due to the COVID-19 pandemic. Chief among the recommended precautions is to limit person to person interactions."); Press Release, U.S. Court of Appeals for the Ninth Circuit, COVID-19 Notice (as of 3/26/20) (Mar. 16, 2020), http://cdn.ca9.uscourts.gov/datastore/general/2020/03/16/COVID-19%20Notice.pdf. It was unclear whether those operational changes delayed the three-judge panel's eventual issuance of its opinion, on August 11, 2020, in the appeal of *FTC v. Qualcomm*.

[191] Oral Argument, FTC v. Qualcomm Inc., No. 19-16122 (9th Cir. Feb. 13, 2020), https://www.ca9.uscourts.gov/media/view_video.php?pk_vid=0000017078.

[192] FTC v. Qualcomm Inc., No. 19-16122, 2020 WL 4591476, at *22 (9th Cir. Aug. 11, 2020).

[193] *Id.* at *2 (emphasis in original).

[194] *Id.*

The Ninth Circuit summarized Judge Koh's findings of fact and conclusions of law as follows:

> The district court's decision consists of essentially five mixed findings of fact and law: (1) Qualcomm's "no license, no chips" policy amounts to "anticompetitive conduct against OEMs" and an "anticompetitive practice[] in patent license negotiations"; (2) Qualcomm's refusal to license rival chipmakers violates both its FRAND commitments and an antitrust duty to deal under § 2 of the Sherman Act; (3) Qualcomm's "exclusive deals" with Apple "foreclosed a 'substantial share' of the modem chip market" in violation of both Sherman Act provisions; (4) Qualcomm's royalty rates are "unreasonably high" because they are improperly based on its market share and handset price instead of the value of its patents; and (5) Qualcomm's royalties, in conjunction with its "no license, no chips" policy, "impose an artificial and anticompetitive surcharge" on its rivals' sales, "increas[ing] the effective price of rivals' modem chips" and resulting in anticompetitive exclusivity. "Collectively," the district court found, these policies and practices "create insurmountable and artificial barriers for Qualcomm's rivals, and thus do not further competition on the merits."[195]

The Ninth Circuit emphatically rejected the FTC's royalty "surcharge" and modem "tax" theory, as well as Judge Koh's conclusion of law embracing it:

> We hold that the district court's "anticompetitive surcharge" theory fails to state a cogent theory of anticompetitive harm. Instead, it is premised on a misunderstanding of Federal Circuit law pertaining to the calculation of patent damages, it incorrectly conflates antitrust liability and patent law liability, and it improperly considers "anticompetitive harms to OEMs" that fall outside the relevant antitrust markets.[196]

The Ninth Circuit further held that, "even if we were to accept the district court's conclusion that Qualcomm's royalty rates are unreasonable, we conclude that the district court's surcharging theory still fails as a matter of law and logic."[197]

As a matter of law, the Ninth Circuit appeared to reject the tax-incidence reasoning of the FTC and Judge Koh that an allegedly "unreasonably high" royalty paid by an OEM for an exhaustive license to Qualcomm's cellular SEPs would produce antitrust harm in Judge Koh's two relevant markets for modems rather than merely the markets in which OEMs sold mobile devices:

---

[195] *Id.* at *6 (alterations in original) (citations omitted) (footnote omitted) (quoting FTC v. Qualcomm Inc., 411 F. Supp. 3d 658, 697–98, 751–62, 766, 771–92, 797 (N.D. Cal. 2019)).
[196] *Id.* at *15.
[197] *Id.*

[E]ven assuming that a deviation between licensing royalty rates and a patent portfolio's "fair value" could amount to "anticompetitive harm" in the antitrust sense, the primary harms the district court identified here were to the OEMs who agreed to pay Qualcomm's royalty rates—that is, Qualcomm's *customers*, not its *competitors*. These harms were thus located outside the "areas of effective competition"—the markets for CDMA and premium LTE modem chips—and had no direct impact on competition in those markets.[198]

The Ninth Circuit also "decline[d] to adopt a theory of antitrust liability that would presume anticompetitive conduct any time a company could not prove that the 'fair value' of its SEP portfolios corresponds to the prices the market appears willing to pay for those SEPs in the form of licensing royalty rates."[199] The Ninth Circuit was of course ruling in Qualcomm's favor on this point; yet, it bears emphasis that it never would be plausible as a matter of due process to recognize a theory of unilateral antitrust liability that would presume anticompetitive conduct and then impose on the defendant the burden to prove its innocence.

The Ninth Circuit said that whether "Qualcomm is contractually obligated via its SSO commitments to license rival chip suppliers [is] a conclusion we need not and do not reach,"[200] and it purported to remand that question for trial.[201] Yet, the Ninth Circuit did not say on what statutory authority (or procedural or jurisdictional basis) the FTC could continue to litigate that question of pure contract interpretation, considering that the Ninth Circuit also found that the FTC had never "satisfactorily explain[ed] how Qualcomm's alleged breach of this contractual commitment *itself* impairs the opportunities of rivals."[202] Nor did the Ninth Circuit specify whether to remand that question to Judge Koh or to a different trial judge altogether.

Finally, the Ninth Circuit concluded that Qualcomm's 2011 and 2013 agreements with Apple were not unlawful exclusive dealing agreements because they "did not have the actual or practical effect of substantially foreclosing competition in the CDMA modem chip market"—and, in any event, "because these agreements were terminated years ago by Apple itself, there is nothing to be enjoined."[203]

Although the Ninth Circuit's outcome was sound, its opinion barely scratched the surface of the imperative to destroy that was on display in *FTC v. Qualcomm*.

---

[198]   *Id.* at *17 (emphasis in original) (quoting Rambus Inc. v. FTC, 522 F.3d 456, 464 (D.C. Cir. 2008)).
[199]   *Id.* at *16.
[200]   *Id.* at *13.
[201]   *Id.* at *6.
[202]   *Id.* at *13 (emphasis in original).
[203]   *Id.* at *21.

I. Two Dimensions of Judicial Misadventure

Judge Koh's findings of fact and conclusions of law contained material errors of fact, economics, and law. The opinion lacked the rigor that one would expect to find in a judgment that so emphatically reprehended a leading U.S. innovator and so peremptorily ignored that its permanent, worldwide injunction might produce unintended consequences graver than the ostensible harm to be corrected. To borrow a phrase from Justice Brett Kavanaugh, Judge Koh's findings of fact and conclusions of law in *FTC v. Qualcomm* "seem[] a relic of a bygone era when antitrust law was divorced from basic economic principles."[204]

Others have already questioned as a matter of theory or doctrine the soundness, rigor, and wisdom of Judge Koh's findings of fact and conclusions of law.[205] Most of the published criticism of Judge's Koh's findings of fact and conclusions of law in *FTC v. Qualcomm* understandably focused on questions of antitrust law. But her findings of fact and conclusions of law actually transgressed two separate strands of the law—not solely the Supreme Court's antitrust jurisprudence, but also the Constitution's promise of due process of law.

---

[204] FTC v. Whole Foods Mkt., Inc., 548 F.3d 1029, 1063 (D.C. Cir. 2008) (Kavanaugh, J., dissenting).

[205] *See, e.g.*, Joshua D. Wright & John M. Yun, *Use and Abuse of Bargaining Models in Antitrust*, 68 KAN. L. REV. 1055 (2020); Richard A. Epstein, *Judge Koh's Monopolization Mania: Her Novel Antitrust Assault Against Qualcomm Is an Abuse of Antitrust Theory*, 98 NEB. L. REV. 241 (2019); Lindsey M. Edwards, Douglas H. Ginsburg & Joshua D. Wright, *Section 2 Mangled: FTC v Qualcomm on the Duty to Deal, Price Squeezes, and Exclusive Dealing*, 8 J. ANTITRUST ENFORCEMENT 335 (2020); Richard Epstein, *Judge Koh Is No 5G Wiz*, HOOVER INSTITUTION (May 28, 2019); Jonathan M. Barnett, *FTC v. Qualcomm: A Case of Regulatory Capture?*, TRUTH ON THE MARKET (July 18, 2019); Dirk Auer, *In FTC v. Qualcomm, Judge Koh Gets Lost in the Weeds*, TRUTH ON THE MARKET (Aug. 28, 2019); Christine Wilson, *A Court's Dangerous Antitrust Overreach*, WALL ST. J., May 28, 2019; Matthew Spitzer, *FTC v. Qualcomm: Origins and Problems*, COMPETITION POL'Y INT'L, Oct. 2019; Erik Hovenkamp, *FTC v. Qualcomm, Antitrust, and Intellectual Property*, REGULATORY REV. (June 11, 2019) (agreeing with Judge Koh on the findings about exclusive dealing, but finding her conclusion about a duty to deal "precarious"); Unopposed Motion of Ericsson, Inc. to File Brief as Amicus Curiae in Support of Qualcomm's Motion for a Partial Stay Pending Appeal, FTC v. Qualcomm Inc., No. 19-16122 (9ᵗʰ Cir. July 15, 2019); Motion of the Honorable Paul R. Michel (Ret.) for Leave to File *Amicus Curiae* Brief in Support of Qualcomm Incorporated's Motion for Partial Stay of the Injunction, FTC v. Qualcomm Inc., No. 19-16122 (9ᵗʰ Cir. July 15, 2019); United States' Statement of Interest Concerning Qualcomm's Motion for Partial Stay of Injunction Pending Appeal, FTC v. Qualcomm Inc., No. 19-16122, 2019 WL 3306496, at *12 (9ᵗʰ Cir. July 16, 2019) [hereinafter United States' Statement of Interest Concerning Partial Stay, 2019 WL 3306496]; Brief of *Amicus Curiae* Cause of Action Institute in Support of Defendant-Appellant Qualcomm Incorporated, FTC v. Qualcomm Inc., No. 19-16122 (9ᵗʰ Cir. Aug. 30, 2019); Brief of *Amici Curiae* Antitrust and Patent Law Professors, Economists, and Scholars in Support of Appellant and Reversal, FTC v. Qualcomm Inc., No. 19-16122 (9ᵗʰ Cir. Aug. 30, 2019); Brief of the United States of America as Amicus Curiae in Support of Appellant and Vacatur, FTC v. Qualcomm Inc., No. 19-16122 (9ᵗʰ Cir. Aug. 30, 2019); Brief of Amicus Curiae Alliance of U.S. Startups & Inventors for Jobs ("USIJ") in Support of Appellant Qualcomm Incorporated, FTC v. Qualcomm Inc., No. 19-16122 (9ᵗʰ Cir. Aug. 30, 2019); Brief of *Amici Curiae* International Center for Law & Economics and Scholars of Law and Economics in Support of Appellant and Reversal, FTC v. Qualcomm Inc., No. 19-16122 (9ᵗʰ Cir. Aug. 30, 2019). *But see* Herbert Hovenkamp, *FRAND and Antitrust*, 105 CORNELL L. REV. (forthcoming 2020) (manuscript at 108–09) (examining the circumstances in which a violation of a FRAND commitment constitutes an antitrust violation and praising Judge Koh for addressing claims about unlawful exclusive dealing and a refusal to license "largely without reference to standard setting or FRAND").

Each strand of judicial misadventure justified reversing Judge Koh's judgment and vacating both her permanent, worldwide injunction and her grant to the FTC of partial summary judgment, rather than remanding the case for a new trial. But, if I turn out to be incorrect and the Ninth Circuit (if it decides to rehear *FTC v. Qualcomm en banc*) or the Supreme Court determines that some remand to the district court is necessary, then, for reasons that I will explain, it would serve the interests of justice to remand in light of Federal Rule of Civil Procedure 52(a)(1) the unresolved portions of the case to a different district judge.

1.   *Due Process, Discretion, and the Quality of Justice*

The first of the two categories of judicial misadventure evident in *FTC v. Qualcomm* concerns Judge Koh's exercise of discretion in her findings of fact. It is of course well-established that a reviewing court typically defers to a district judge's findings of fact in a bench trial, particularly findings on the credibility of a witness.[206] But broad deference from an appellate court is not license for the trial judge to exercise discretion over fact finding in a mystifying manner. Typically the Courts of Appeals do not need to reverse a judge's findings of fact. Yet, Judge Koh's findings of fact in *FTC v. Qualcomm* are the outlier.

On the question of the boundaries of judicial discretion, Judge Richard Posner has observed: "In fields . . . in which economic analysis is an accepted tool of judicial decision making, judicial discretion is curtailed by an analytic method distinct from the methods of legalism but not necessarily any less effective in generating outcomes felt as objective, as dictated by methodology rather than left to free choice."[207] If one accepts Judge Posner's observation that it is proper for economic analysis to circumscribe judicial discretion in a case presenting explicitly economic questions of fact—as any government monopolization case surely would—then Judge Koh's oblique exercise of fact-finding discretion, particularly in suppressing vast amounts of material expert economic testimony, was erroneous and arbitrary. That conclusion holds with greater force when we see, as we will in the following pages, that some of that suppressed testimony was materially exculpatory.

More fundamentally, Judge Koh's findings of fact in *FTC v. Qualcomm* might prompt an experienced appellate judge or trial lawyer to ask whether there is a problem here with the quality of justice. Litigation solely over an equitable remedy of course occurs in a bench trial, during which there is no

---

[206]   Fed. R. Civ. P. 52(a)(6).
[207]   Richard A. Posner, How Judges Think 87 (Harvard Univ. Press 2008). By "legalism," Judge Posner means deciding cases "by applying preexisting rules." *Id.* at 7.

Seventh Amendment right to a jury.[208] Juries in complex commercial litigation are often portrayed as unsophisticated and gullible. Yet, were it present, a jury would produce the salutary effect of preventing the findings of fact from being groomed by the judge in a manner that excluded materially exculpatory evidence and gave negligible weight to the defendant's witnesses for reasons that unfairly impugned their reputations. Recognition of that vulnerability compels one to ask whether, in her exercise of discretion over fact finding in the bench trial in *FTC v. Qualcomm*, Judge Koh gave Qualcomm all the process that it was due.

The Due Process Clause of the Fifth Amendment provides: "No person shall . . . be deprived of life, liberty, or property, without due process of law[.]"[209] In its early examination of the meaning of "due process of law" in *Murray's Lessee*, the Supreme Court observed in 1856: "The Constitution contains no description of those processes which it was intended to allow or forbid. It does not even declare what principles are to be applied to ascertain whether it be due process."[210] Over the following century, the Court at least was able to say unambiguously that "[a] fair trial in a fair tribunal is a basic requirement of due process."[211] But the need remained for a framework for determining when the process given in a trial is fair enough to achieve the level of process that is due in the circumstances. The Court needed to put meat on the bones of its statement in 1972 that "due process is flexible and calls for such procedural protections as the particular situation demands."[212]

Finally, in 1976, the Court announced in *Mathews v. Eldridge* a kind of unified field theory of due process:

> [I]dentification of the specific dictates of due process generally requires consideration of three distinct factors: First, the private interest that will be affected by the official action; second, the risk of an erroneous deprivation of such interest through the procedures used, and the probable value, if any, of additional or substitute procedural safeguards; and finally, the Government's interest, including the function involved and the fiscal and administrative

---

[208] *See* TCL Commc'n Tech. Holdings Ltd. v. Telefonaktiebolaget LM Ericsson, 943 F.3d 1360, 1371–72 (Fed. Cir. 2019).

[209] U.S. Const. amend. V.

[210] Murray's Lessee v. Hoboken Land & Improvement Co., 59 U.S. (18 How.) 272, 276 (1856); *see also* Michael Stokes Paulsen, Steven Gow Calabresi, Michael W. McConnell, Samuel L. Bray & William Baude, The Constitution of the United States 1476–80 (Foundation Press 3ᵈ ed. 2017); Nathan S. Chapman & Michael W. McConnell, *Due Process as Separation of Powers*, 121 Yale L.J. 1672 (2012).

[211] *In re* Murchison, 349 U.S. 133, 136 (1955), *quoted in* Caperton v. A.T. Massey Coal Co., 556 U.S. 868, 876 (2009) (Kennedy, J.); *see also* Erwin Chemerinsky, Constitutional Law: Principles and Policies 596–97 (Wolters Kluwer 4ᵗʰ ed. 2011).

[212] Morrissey v. Brewer, 408 U.S. 471, 481 (1972); *accord* Mathews v. Eldridge, 424 U.S. 319, 334 (1976); *see also* Cafeteria Workers v. McElroy, 367 U.S. 886, 895 (1961) ("'Due process,' unlike some legal rules, is not a technical conception with a fixed content unrelated to time, place and circumstances.'") (quoting Joint Anti-Fascist Refugee Comm. v. McGrath, 341 U.S. 123, 162 (1951)).

burdens that the additional or substitute procedural requirement would entail.[213]

Judge Posner has crisply restated the principle: "in deciding how much process is due to someone complaining that the government has deprived him of property the courts should consider the value of the property, the probability of erroneous deprivation because the particular procedural safeguard sought was omitted, and the cost of the safeguard."[214] As we shall see, Judge Koh's materially incomplete findings of fact in *FTC v. Qualcomm* embody a deprivation of a procedural safeguard due Qualcomm which, had it been afforded (at insignificant cost to either the court or the FTC), would have required Judge Koh to rule in Qualcomm's favor on the novel legal theory that was the centerpiece of the FTC's case.[215]

a.   Why Did Judge Koh Ignore Testimony Establishing the Breadth of Qualcomm's Foundational Innovations?

Trial testimony establishing the breadth of Qualcomm's foundational technical contributions to wireless communications technologies, including to the 5G standard, went largely unmentioned in Judge Koh's findings of fact and conclusions of law. The FTC argued, and Judge Koh agreed, that Qualcomm was washed up. They both damned Qualcomm with faint praise for having invented CDMA, but they then proceeded to contend that Qualcomm's subsequent contributions to mobile communication technologies had been mediocre, such that the royalties that Qualcomm continued to charge for a

---

[213] *Mathews v. Eldridge*, 424 U.S. at 335 (citing Goldberg v. Kelly, 397 U.S. 254, 263–71 (1970)). For an early application of this test by Judge Posner, see Sutton v. City of Milwaukee, 672 F.2d 644, 645–46 (7ᵗʰ Cir. 1982) (Posner, J.) (applying *Mathews v. Eldridge* and noting that Judge Henry Friendly anticipated it in Frost v. Weinberger, 515 F.2d 57, 66 (2ᵈ Cir. 1975) (Friendly, J.)) ("The [Supreme] Court's decisions can be fairly summarized as holding that the required degree of procedural safeguards varies directly with the importance of the private interest affected and the need for and usefulness of the particular safeguard in the given circumstances and inversely with the burden and any other adverse consequences of affording it.")).

[214] RICHARD A. POSNER, ECONOMIC ANALYSIS OF LAW 773–74 (Wolters Kluwer 9ᵗʰ ed. 2014). Judge Posner of course was analogizing this tradeoff of marginal costs and expected marginal benefits to Judge Learned Hand's famous formula for defining negligence. *See id.* at 191–92 (discussing United States v. Carroll Towing Co., 159 F.2d 169, 173 (2ᵈ Cir. 1947) (Hand, J.)). In his fourth month on the Seventh Circuit, Judge Posner extended this reasoning to the Due Process Clause in his opinion for the court in *Sutton*, 672 F.2d at 645–46, which was issued March 18, 1982. Two months later, Judge Posner was assigned the opinion in a negligence case in admiralty (like *Carroll Towing*), for which the controlling law—federal common law— gave him *carte blanche* to issue, on May 28, 1982, a law-and-economics paean to the Hand Formula for negligence. United States Fidelity & Guaranty Co. v. Jadranska Slobodna Plovidba, 683 F.2d 1022, 1026 (7ᵗʰ Cir. 1982).

[215] *See* CHEMERINSKY, CONSTITUTIONAL LAW: PRINCIPLES AND POLICIES, *supra* note 211, at 619 ("A review of the cases concerning what procedures are required reveals that everything depends on context and the Court's perception of it. This seems inevitable under the *Mathews* three-part balancing test, which accords enormous discretion in weighing such diverse interests as the importance of the interest to the individual, *the ability of additional procedures to increase the accuracy of the fact-finding*, and the government's interest in administrative efficiency.") (emphasis added).

license to its portfolio of cellular SEPs were in some undefined sense excessive and unjustified—as expressed in their chorus of "unreasonably high" royalties for an exhaustive license to Qualcomm's cellular SEPs.

Qualcomm directly refuted these slurs of technological mediocrity through the testimony of two witnesses whom it called in its defense. The FTC did not put on testimony attempting to rebut either witness.

Qualcomm called as an expert witness in its defense Jeffrey Andrews, a professor of electrical and computer engineering at the University of Texas who received his Ph.D. in electrical engineering from Stanford, had worked as an engineer at both Qualcomm (to develop CDMA systems) and Intel in the 1990s, and had been the named inventor on patents related to cellular networks and smartphone connectivity.[216] Professor Andrews received the Frederick Terman Award from the American Society of Engineering Educators and the Kiyo Tomiyasu Award from the IEEE—both awards recognizing outstanding contributions in engineering by someone under the age of 45.[217]

Professor Andrews found that "34 patents that Qualcomm holds made very fundamental contributions to cellular standards, 3G, 4G, which is LTE, as well as 5G, and that these patents are over a wide ranging and very important set of topics that enable data communication over cellular networks."[218] Professor Andrews testified that Qualcomm had made foundational contributions to wireless communications technologies including the waveform known as single-carrier frequency-division multiple access (SC-FDMA),[219] the system known as the physical uplink control channel (PUCCH),[220] the procedure known as base station acquisition,[221] carrier aggregation,[222] cellular

---

[216] *See* Transcript of Proceedings (Volume 8) at 1589:10, 1590:2–13, FTC v. Qualcomm Inc., No. 5:17-cv-00220-LHK (N.D. Cal. Jan. 22, 2019) (Testimony of Jeffrey Andrews (University of Texas)). For an example of one of Professor Andrews' patents, see Interference Management and Decentralized Channel Access Schemes in Hotspot-Aided Cellular Networks, U.S. Patent No. 9,078,138, at [57] (filed Nov. 20, 2008) ("Abstract: A system and method are provided wherein one or more femtocell base stations are deployed within a range of a cellular base station and utilize substantially the same frequency band as the cellular base station. Each femtocell base station may be configured to employ one or more interference avoidance techniques such that coexistence between the cellular and the corresponding femtocell base station is enabled. The interference avoidance techniques employed may include use of randomized time or frequency hopping; randomly selecting a predetermined number, or identifying one or more unutilized, frequency subchannels for signal transmission; using two or more transmit and two or more receive antennas; nulling one or more transmissions in a direction of a nearby cellular base station user; handing off at least one cellular user to one of the femtocell base stations and vice versa; and/or reducing the transmission power of at least one femtocell base station.").

[217] *See* Transcript of Proceedings (Volume 8) at 1591:11–1592:1, FTC v. Qualcomm Inc., No. 5:17-cv-00220-LHK (N.D. Cal. Jan. 22, 2019) (Testimony of Jeffrey Andrews (University of Texas)).

[218] *Id.* at 1592:22–1593:1.

[219] *Id.* at 1597:25–1600:2.

[220] *Id.* at 1602:18–1603:16.

[221] *Id.* at 1603:17–1604:22.

[222] *Id.* at 1604:23–1607:16.

communication in unlicensed spectrum,[223] and cellular networks known as heterogeneous networks (HetNets).[224]

Qualcomm also called Dr. Durga Malladi, Senior Vice President and General Manager of 4G and 5G at Qualcomm, who testified at length about Qualcomm's innovations and how the company approaches the process of innovation.[225] He testified that Qualcomm's wireless research concentrated not merely on modems but on "end-to-end system design" that encompassed all elements of cellular communications[226]—an approach to problem solving in wireless R&D that, Dr. Malladi testified, was "quite unique."[227] Qualcomm's R&D agenda did not have a "fixed timeframe," but rather focused on solutions to "long-term problems," which in some cases required "close to a decade" of work before those solutions had commercial applications.[228] Qualcomm also proved the value of the commercial application of its foundational technologies through field demonstrations,[229] in the spirit of its mantra, "If it's not tested, it doesn't work."[230] Dr. Malladi testified that Qualcomm was active in standards development,[231] and he explained that standards are not stagnant even after commercial deployment:

> There's no such thing as a one and done deal. It's not like 4G was done or LTE was done in 2008 and that's pretty much it. Every 18 to 24 months, give or take, there's usually a new release of the technology, so new features get added and . . . sometimes they're bug fixes from a previous feature, but new features keep getting added.[232]

Dr. Malladi also testified about Qualcomm's innovations after CDMA, including contributions to carrier aggregation,[233] cellular communications in

---

[223] *Id.* at 1607:17–1608:20.

[224] *Id.* at 1608:21–1611:12.

[225] Transcript of Proceedings (Volume 6) at 1303:6–8, FTC v. Qualcomm Inc., No. 5:17-cv-00220-LHK (N.D. Cal. Jan. 15, 2019) (Testimony of Durga Malladi (Senior Vice President and General Manager of 4G and 5G, Qualcomm)). For an example of one of Dr. Malladi's patents, see Systems and Methods for Improving Channel Estimation, U.S. Patent No. 8,615,200, at [57] (filed Sept. 23, 2010) (issued Dec. 24, 2013) ("Abstract: A method for improving channel estimation in a wireless communication system is disclosed. A wireless signal that includes a plurality of multipath components is received. N channel estimates are then obtained, where N is any positive integer greater than one. Each channel estimate of the N channel estimates corresponds to a different multipath component of the plurality of multipath components. The effects of interference between the plurality of multipath components on the N channel estimates is then reduced.").

[226] *See* Transcript of Proceedings (Volume 6) at 1304:18–1305:20, FTC v. Qualcomm Inc., No. 5:17-cv-00220-LHK (N.D. Cal. Jan. 15, 2019) (Testimony of Durga Malladi (Senior Vice President and General Manager of 4G and 5G, Qualcomm)).

[227] *Id.* at 1311:15.

[228] *Id.* at 1305:21–1306:6.

[229] *See id.* at 1308:11–1309:9.

[230] *See id.* at 1307:25–1308:1.

[231] *See id.* at 1310:7–1311:17, 1313:13–1314:8, 1315:2–1316:1, 1316:21–1320:14.

[232] *Id.* at 1320:19–25.

[233] *See id.* at 1321:6–1324:6.

unlicensed spectrum,[234] and millimeter wave technology,[235] which tended to disprove Judge Koh's finding of fact that the royalties that Qualcomm continued to charge for an exhaustive license to its portfolio of cellular SEPs were "unreasonably high" because Qualcomm supposedly had not made important technical contributions to cellular standards after CDMA.

These witnesses understood from firsthand experience the R&D process for cellular communications and the successful creation of commercially valuable technical innovation, for they had been awarded *hundreds* of patents for their inventions. Judge Koh made no mention of this aspect of their testimony anywhere in her findings of fact and conclusions of law in *FTC v. Qualcomm*. Instead, she mentioned these witnesses only to fault them for not having provided any testimony that the royalty that Qualcomm charged for an exhaustive license to its portfolio of cellular SEPs was reasonable. With equal cogency, Judge Koh could have faulted these witnesses for having failed to cure cancer.

b. Suppression of Professor Shapiro's Expert Economic Testimony at Trial

Without relying on the affirmative testimony of *any* expert economic witness, Judge Koh made critical findings on economic questions of fact that fall squarely outside a layman's competence—such as the definition of the relevant market, or the determination whether the royalties that Qualcomm charged for a license to its portfolio of cellular SEPs were "unreasonably high." (With few exceptions, Judge Koh cited the testimony of an expert economic witness only when she sought to make a finding of fact adverse to the party proffering that witness.) It is not clear why one should suppose that Judge Koh had the expertise in applied microeconomics and industrial organization to make valid findings of fact on complex economic questions by relying solely on her own instincts rather than weighing the informed testimony of the parties' economic experts.

Most notably, Judge Koh's findings of fact and conclusions of law conspicuously and materially omitted any reference to the FTC's premier economic witness, Professor Shapiro. Shortly after Judge Koh issued her findings of fact and conclusions of law, *Forbes* quoted Professor Fiona Scott Morton of Yale University and Charles River Associates, who opined that, although "Carl Shapiro was not mentioned by name[,] . . . the court adopted his economic opinions throughout the decision."[236] Professor Scott Morton added:

---

[234] *See id.* at 1324:18–1329:19.
[235] *See id.* at 1329:20–1332:19.
[236] *No License, No Chips? No Dice: Dissecting Judge Koh's Opinion in FTC v. Qualcomm*, FORBES, June 10, 2019 (quoting Professor Fiona Scott Morton).

The court cites Professor Greg Mankiw's economics textbook for an explanation of the tax on rivals; the court carries out a hypothetical monopolist test to determine Qualcomm has market power. *These are economic concepts that the judge learned from the FTC economist.* It is very difficult, in my view, to get to the right answer in an antitrust case without good economics. . . . And for a witness, having the court simply adopt your words, rather than quoting you, is fantastic. A total win. *The strength of the government's witness shows up in the narrative connecting the 233 pages of facts.*[237]

Notwithstanding the fact that the single instance in Judge Koh's findings of fact and conclusions of law in which she purported to apply economic reasoning—and cited an economics textbook—contained elementary mistakes (as we shall see), I have no reason to dispute Professor Scott Morton's opinion that Judge Koh "learned" key "economic concepts" for the first time from Professor Shapiro and that his influence permeated Judge Koh's lengthy "narrative connecting" the facts of *FTC v. Qualcomm*. But Professor Scott Morton's assessment leaves unsolved the mystery of why Judge Koh did not give Professor Shapiro proper credit for his tutelage.

Judge Koh did not mention Professor Shapiro's name once in her findings of fact and conclusions of law, even though he was the only witness to testify twice in *FTC v. Qualcomm* and despite the fact that the trial transcript contains more pages of his testimony than the testimony of any other witness. Professor Shapiro's testimony covers a total of 192 pages of the transcript, none of which was under seal.[238] The next-closest witness in terms of length of transcribed testimony was Fabian Gonell of Qualcomm, at 109 pages.[239] Judge Koh had complained at trial that Qualcomm was calling too many witnesses (and consequently was forced to cut at least one from testifying), yet she did not complain about the FTC's devoting large portions of two days of trial testimony to Professor Shapiro, whom Judge Koh did not once acknowledge in her findings of fact and conclusions of law.

A different judge might have considered it the wiser exercise of discretion—more respectful of Qualcomm's right to due process of law—to cite the testimony of Professor Shapiro if indeed it so infused the judge's understanding of the essential economic concepts as to enable the judge to give legal meaning to "233 pages of facts." Justice Stephen Breyer and Professors Richard Stewart, Cass Sunstein, and Matthew Spitzer wrote in

---

[237] *Id.* (quoting Professor Fiona Scott Morton) (emphasis added).

[238] Transcript of Proceedings (Volume 6) at 1117:2–1250:17, FTC v. Qualcomm Inc., No. 5:17-cv-00220-LHK (N.D. Cal. Jan. 15, 2019) (Testimony of Carl Shapiro); Transcript of Proceedings (Volume 10) at 2031:5–2090:2, FTC v. Qualcomm Inc., No. 5:17-cv-00220-LHK (N.D. Cal. Jan. 28, 2019) (Testimony of Carl Shapiro).

[239] Transcript of Proceedings (Volume 7) at 1393:4–1502:1, FTC v. Qualcomm Inc., No. 5:17-cv-00220-LHK (N.D. Cal. Jan. 18, 2019) (Testimony of Fabian Gonell (Legal Counsel and Senior Vice President, Licensing Strategy, Qualcomm Technology Licensing)).

their casebook on administrative law in 1999 that, in administrative adjudication, "[j]udges characteristically approach the question of how much process is due in terms of the extent to which an administrative proceeding must adopt the panoply of procedural formalities found in court trials."[240]

And precisely what are those specific procedural formalities found in court trials? Justice Breyer and his colleagues observed that Judge Henry Friendly of the Second Circuit, widely considered the foremost appellate judge of his day,[241] made a list of 10 "ingredients of judicial due process," which started with "[a]n unbiased tribunal" and ended with the "[r]equirement that the tribunal prepare a record of the evidence presented" and the "[r]equirement that the tribunal prepare written findings of fact and reasons for its decision."[242] When scrutinized according to Judge Friendly's venerated checklist of the elements of due process, Judge Koh's findings of fact and conclusions of law in *FTC v. Qualcomm* are wanting: Professor Shapiro presented copious amounts of expert economic testimony of seemingly great potential relevance and probative value in *FTC v. Qualcomm*, and although Judge Koh did receive that testimony into evidence at trial, she nonetheless declined to weigh that evidence in her findings of fact and conclusions of law or explain the extent to which it informed her reasoned decision on findings of fact and conclusions of law.

    c.   Suppression of Materially Exculpatory Portions of Professor Shapiro's Trial Testimony—the Brady *Rule Analogy for Bench Trials*

One possible explanation for why Judge Koh did not mention Professor Shapiro in her findings of fact and conclusions of law in *FTC v. Qualcomm* is that Professor Scott Morton might have been only half-correct: correct

---

[240] Stephen G. Breyer, Richard B. Stewart, Cass R. Sunstein & Matthew L. Spitzer, Administrative Law and Regulatory Policy: Problems, Text, and Cases 691 (Aspen Law & Business 4th ed. 1999). According to Professor Adrian Vermeule of Harvard Law School, the process of defining due process has acquired in practice a kind of circularity, in which it has become curiously necessary to read administrative law decisions about the extent of process provided by administrative agencies to intuit what the Due Process Clause requires in a trial before an Article III court. *See* Adrian Vermeule, *Deference and Due Process*, 129 Harv. L. Rev. 1890, 1891 (2016) ("[A]gencies themselves are now the primary frontline expositors and appliers of the *Mathews* test. Administrative constitutionalism has already come to the Due Process Clause.") (discussing Mathews v. Eldridge, 424 U.S. 319 (1976)).

[241] *See, e.g.*, Jon O. Newman, *From Learned Hand to Henry Friendly*, N.Y. Times, Mar. 24, 1986, at A18 ("In the 40's and 50's the foremost appellate judge was Learned Hand, who also served on the Second Circuit. In the 60's and 70's that mantle belonged to Judge Friendly.").

[242] Breyer, Stewart, Sunstein & Spitzer, Administrative Law and Regulatory Policy, *supra* note 240, at 691–92 (discussing Henry J. Friendly, *"Some Kind of Hearing,"* 123 U. Pa. L. Rev. 1267 (1975)); *see also* Vermeule, *Deference and Due Process, supra* note 240, at 1896–97 ("As to adjudicative action by agencies, . . . due process requires," among other elements, "an impartial decisionmaker, but the [Supreme] Court takes a narrow view of what counts as impartiality; pecuniary interest in the decision at hand is disqualifying, but there is no general due process prohibition on institutions that combine legislative, executive, and adjudicative functions and thus 'judge in their own cause.'") (citations omitted).

to infer that Professor Shapiro materially influenced Judge Koh's findings of fact and conclusions of law, but incorrect to infer that Professor Shapiro's testimony was "[a] total win" for either him or the FTC. Perhaps Judge Koh found Professor Shapiro's conclusions attractive but his testimony not reliable enough to cite in her findings of fact and conclusions of law.

In that case, it would be understandable if the omission of any reference to Professor Shapiro puzzles readers of her findings of fact and conclusions of law, including readers at the Ninth Circuit and the Supreme Court, considering that Judge Koh *did* explicitly report in her findings of fact and conclusions of law (1) her assessment that all three of Qualcomm's expert economic witnesses were unreliable and (2) her explanation for refusing to rely on their testimony at all in reaching her findings.²⁴³ A reader confined to Judge Koh's reported findings of fact and conclusions of law would be left to wonder why Judge Koh did not mention Professor Shapiro's testimony to support her findings concerning economic questions of fact, since those findings closely resembled his testimony at trial, as we shall see. That is why it is so critical for the Ninth Circuit and the Supreme Court to read in its entirety the transcript of Professor Shapiro's trial testimony in *FTC v. Qualcomm*.

A sophisticated jurist reading that transcript would immediately see that Professor Shapiro's expert economic testimony had been demolished on cross examination. His admissions on cross examination (and, oddly, even his admissions on direct examination by the FTC) were so devastating for the FTC's case that it is staggering that Judge Koh did not acknowledge in her findings of fact and conclusions of law that Professor Shapiro actually *undermined* the FTC's proof of its case-in-chief and its rebuttal case. One could easily imagine the Ninth Circuit or the Supreme Court getting queasy over the fact that Judge Koh did not report in her findings of fact and conclusions of law that *Professor Shapiro's testimony actually was materially exculpatory for Qualcomm* because it tended to refute, rather than prove, the FTC's novel theory of antitrust liability based on a supposedly anticompetitive royalty "surcharge" and modem "tax."

By analogy, the *Brady* Rule holds, with respect to the Due Process Clause of the Fourteenth Amendment, that "the suppression by the prosecution of evidence favorable to an accused upon request violates due process where the evidence is material either to guilt or to punishment, irrespective of the good faith or bad faith of the prosecution."²⁴⁴ "Impeachment evidence," the

---

²⁴³ *See* FTC v. Qualcomm Inc., 411 F. Supp. 3d 658, 676–80 (N.D. Cal. 2019); *see also id.* at 786, 805.

²⁴⁴ Brady v. Maryland, 373 U.S. 83, 87 (1963) (Douglas, J., announced by Brennan, J.); *see also* Cynthia E. Jones, *A Reason to Doubt: The Suppression of Evidence and the Inference of Innocence*, 100 J. CRIM. L. & CRIMINOLOGY 415, 473–74 (2010) ("Prosecutors have not performed well as the stewards of exculpatory evidence but have remained steadfast in their resistance to any external restrictions on their ability to control whether and when *Brady* evidence is disclosed to the defense."). The Supreme Court conventionally uses the word "suppression" in its *Brady* rule cases to denote the prosecution's material nondisclosure

Supreme Court subsequently made clear, "falls within the *Brady* rule."[245] *Brady* of course concerned a criminal prosecution rather than a civil one, although it is not obvious why that distinction should matter. And a judge of course is not a prosecutor, unless the judge sits in an inquisitorial system of justice rather than an adversarial one.[246] Although "[j]udges assume th[e] role [of inquisitor] in some countries, . . . Article III gives no prosecutorial or inquisitorial power to federal judges."[247] Yet, as we shall see, Judge Koh's findings of fact and conclusions of law give off an inquisitorial *odeur*—for example, through her aggressive findings that Qualcomm's witnesses lacked credibility or reliability.

In any event, the due process analogy to *Brady* is plainly not the only source, much less the first source, of an obligation for Judge Koh to have discussed the exculpatory significance of Professor Shapiro's entirely unmentioned expert economic testimony for the FTC. Federal Rule of Civil Procedure 52(a)(1) requires that, "[i]n an action tried on the facts without a jury . . . , the court *must* find the facts specially[.]"[248] My point is simply that *FTC v. Qualcomm* neatly illustrates how a violation of Rule 52(a)(1) can escalate into a serious deprivation of due process if the special findings of fact that the judge neglected to make following a bench trial would have materially exculpated the defendant. In Qualcomm's case, they would.

Consequently, Judge Koh's findings of fact and conclusions of law in *FTC v. Qualcomm* invite the Ninth Circuit (should it choose to rehear the case

---

of exculpatory evidence, and I follow that convention in this article. In a different context in criminal procedure, a defendant can move to suppress inculpatory evidence, so as to exclude from the evidentiary record facts obtained through unconstitutional means. *See* FED. R. CRIM. P. 12(b)(3)(C); Hudson v. Michigan, 547 U.S. 586, 590–91 (2006) (Scalia, J.) ("In *Weeks v. United States*, we adopted the federal exclusionary rule for evidence that was unlawfully seized from a home without a warrant in violation of the Fourth Amendment. We began applying the same rule to the States, through the Fourteenth Amendment, in *Mapp v. Ohio*. Suppression of evidence, however, has always been our last resort, not our first impulse.") (citations omitted) (first citing Weeks v. United States, 232 U.S. 383 (1914); and then citing Mapp v. Ohio, 367 U.S. 643 (1961)); *see also* United States v. Leon, 468 U.S. 897, 908–09 (1984) ("The Court has, to be sure, not seriously questioned, 'in the absence of a more efficacious sanction, the continued application of the rule to suppress evidence from the [prosecution's] case where a Fourth Amendment violation has been substantial and deliberate . . . .' Nevertheless, the balancing approach that has evolved in various contexts—including criminal trials—'forcefully suggest[s] that the exclusionary rule be more generally modified to permit the introduction of evidence obtained in the reasonable good-faith belief that a search or seizure was in accord with the Fourth Amendment.'") (alterations in original) (citations omitted) (first quoting Franks v. Delaware, 438 U.S. 154, 171 (1978); and then quoting Illinois v. Gates, 462 U.S. 213, 255 (1983) (White, J., concurring in the judgment)).

245 United States v. Bagley, 473 U.S. 667, 676 (1985).

246 On the salient differences between judges in the adversarial system versus the inquisitorial system, see POSNER, ECONOMIC ANALYSIS OF LAW, *supra* note 214, at 724–25, 839. Judge Posner observes that the inquisitorial judge "takes the lead in gathering evidence and framing the issues and the lawyers play a subordinate role—more than *kibitzers* but less than principals in the litigation process." *Id.* at 725 (emphasis in original). *Cf. In re* United States, 345 F.3d 450, 453 (7th Cir. 2003) (Posner, J.) ("The judge . . . is playing U.S. Attorney. It is no doubt a position that he could fill with distinction, but it is occupied by another person.").

247 *In re* Flynn, 961 F.3d 1215, 1227 (D.C. Cir. 2020) (Rao, J.), *vacated as moot, reh'g en banc granted per curiam*, No. 20-5143, 2020 WL 4355389 (D.C. Cir. July 30, 2020).

248 FED. R. CIV. P. 52(a)(1) (emphasis added).

en banc) and the Supreme Court to consider *sua sponte* the following question, apparently one of first impression:

> Does a federal judge presiding as the finder of fact in a civil bench trial in a government antitrust case have a duty under the Due Process Clause of the Fifth Amendment to facilitate appellate review of the trial court's findings of fact and conclusions of law by specially reporting, in the court's written opinion, the existence of materially exculpatory testimony given by the government's expert economic witness, and to make special findings of fact in that written opinion as to how the materially exculpatory testimony affects the court's conclusions of law (or equity) concerning liability or remedies or both?

In answering this question, one should be mindful that the Supreme Court has said, when construing *Brady*, that, "[f]or though the attorney for the sovereign must prosecute the accused with earnestness and vigor, he must always be faithful to his client's overriding interest that 'justice shall be done.' He is the 'servant of the law, the twofold aim of which is that guilt shall not escape or innocence suffer.'"[249] *FTC v. Qualcomm* compels us to ask, Is a federal district judge any less a servant of the law, any less interested that justice be done, any less committed to ensuring that innocence not suffer?

FTC v. Qualcomm illustrates why there needs to be a *Brady* Rule for judicial findings of fact in bench trials. It might understandably trouble the Ninth Circuit and the Supreme Court on due process grounds that Judge Koh did not acknowledge a word of Professor Shapiro's testimony; that she did not state whether she was excluding his testimony (or had decided to give it no weight) for lack of credibility or for lack of reliability or for some other reason recognized in the Federal Rules of Evidence; and that she excluded from her findings of fact and conclusions of law any mention that significant portions of Professor Shapiro's testimony for the FTC materially exculpated Qualcomm. Even if that were the sole respect in which the findings of fact and conclusions of law in *FTC v. Qualcomm* were less than forthcoming, an appellate court might ask, What was Judge Koh thinking?

Yet, there was more.

d. *The Absence of Findings of Fact on Professor Nevo's Probative Testimony Rebutting Professor Shapiro's Theory of the Royalty "Surcharge" and the Modem "Tax"*

In addition to suppressing any reporting of the materially exculpatory implications of Professor Shapiro's testimony, Judge Koh discredited in its

---

[249] United States v. Agurs, 427 U.S. 97, 110–11 (1976) (quoting Berger v. United States, 295 U.S. 78, 88 (1935)).

entirety the testimony of Professor Aviv Nevo, an expert economic witness for Qualcomm, supposedly because he failed to present opinions on the allegedly anticompetitive effects of Qualcomm's challenged actions. That is, Judge Koh deemed *none* of Professor Nevo's testimony to be reliable because, she explained, Professor Nevo did not testify about the allegedly anticompetitive effects of Qualcomm's challenged conduct, which of course was a question on which the *FTC* bore the burden of production and the burden of persuasion.

Again, it is critical to read Professor Nevo's trial testimony closely, because Judge Koh's wholesale discrediting of Professor Nevo as unreliable was absolutely necessary to support her findings of fact and conclusions of law that Qualcomm committed the alleged antitrust violations. Professor Nevo testified that his "assignment consisted of three parts."[250] One was "to evaluate the FTC's allegations that Qualcomm uses its market power in certain chip markets to obtain supra-FRAND royalty rates" from OEMs.[251] A second was "to assess the pro-competitive and business justifications for Qualcomm's practices."[252] And the third, and arguably most important, was "to evaluate the FTC's claim that Qualcomm's alleged supra-FRAND rates acts [sic] as a tax that harms competition."[253]

Pursuant to this last part of his assignment, Professor Nevo expressly testified at trial why Professor Shapiro's royalty "surcharge" and modem "tax" theory of antitrust liability was fallacious on economic grounds. Specifically, Professor Nevo explained that the alleged royalty "surcharge" and modem "tax" (if they even existed—which they did not, as we shall see) were not imposed asymmetrically on rival modem manufacturers; that is, Qualcomm would impose the same royalty "surcharge" and modem "tax" on its *own* modems sold to OEMs.[254] Even Professor Shapiro made this admission at trial. During his direct examination by Rajesh James of the FTC on January 28, 2019, Professor Shapiro testified that "of course the OEM pays the royalty and the surcharge regardless of which chip they buy. That's not in dispute."[255]

That admission was momentous. The Ninth Circuit directly seized upon this central fallacy of the FTC's "tax" theory of antitrust liability: "Qualcomm's practices, taken together, are 'chip supplier neutral'—that is, OEMs are required to pay a per-unit licensing royalty to Qualcomm for its

---

[250] Transcript of Proceedings (Volume 9) at 1863:18, FTC v. Qualcomm Inc., No. 5:17-cv-00220-LHK (N.D. Cal. Jan. 25, 2019) (Testimony of Aviv Nevo).

[251] *Id.* at 1863:19–21.

[252] *Id.* at 1863:25–1864:2.

[253] *Id.* at 1863:22–24.

[254] *Id.* at 1892:3–8.

[255] Transcript of Proceedings (Volume 10) at 2057:19–21, FTC v. Qualcomm Inc., No. 5:17-cv-00220-LHK (N.D. Cal. Jan. 28, 2019) (Testimony of Carl Shapiro).

patent portfolios regardless of which company they choose to source their chips from."[256] To the contrary, by rejecting all of Professor Nevo's testimony, Judge Koh's findings of fact and conclusions of law suppressed any evidence that the royalty "surcharge" and modem "tax" theory—which Judge Koh expressly adopted as her own reasoning, as Professor Scott Morton astutely observed—had been thoroughly debunked, not only in the trial testimony of Professor Nevo, but also in Professor Shapiro's own sworn admissions at trial under both direct examination and cross examination.

e.   *The Consequences of Legal Rules for Future Economic Behavior*

One motif to which we shall periodically return is Oliver Wendell Holmes' definition of the law: "The prophecies of what the courts will do in fact, and nothing more pretentious, are what I mean by the law."[257] The content of the law is what economists would call a rational expectation. In expounding on the task of judging, which is the task of revealing "what the courts will do in fact," Judge Frank Easterbrook has elaborated on Holmes' definition:

> The nature of litigation invites judges to treat the parties' circumstances as fixed and to apportion gains and losses. Often the application of legal rules requires no more than that. By the time the judges see the case, it may be too late for the parties to do anything in response to a decision.[258]

Judge Easterbrook explained how the tendency to rely on analysis of *ex post* outcomes rather than *ex ante* incentives cuts across many fields of law. We will see how, in *FTC v. Qualcomm*, that tendency is apparent in the FTC's contentions, in Professor Shapiro's testimony, and in Judge Koh's findings of fact and conclusions of law. Judge Easterbrook explained:

> Once ships have collided, the court may see nothing to do except tote up the losses and order each shipowner to pay half (the rule in admiralty). Once a manufacturer has fired a dealer, causing the dealer to lose profits, it may appear best to require the deep-pocket firm to make whole the loss. Once a firm possesses a patent and tries to extract royalties, it may seem wise to restrict the devices available to that end; the royalties lead to less use of the invention and consequent social loss, while restricting the collection of royalties has no visible social costs. Once a firm makes a tender offer for the stock of another, the investors in the target can gain if a court stops the bid long enough for an auction to develop. A party who has agreed in advance to arbitrate a dispute may contend that the particular dispute in question

---

[256] FTC v. Qualcomm Inc., No. 19-16122, 2020 WL 4591476, at *4 (9ᵗʰ Cir. Aug. 11, 2020).
[257] Oliver Wendell Holmes, *The Path of the Law*, 10 Harv. L. Rev. 457, 461 (1897).
[258] Frank H. Easterbrook, *The Supreme Court 1983 Term-Foreword: The Court and the Economic System*, 98 Harv. L. Rev. 4, 10 (1984).

nonetheless should be resolved by a court; he seeks relief from the adverse consequences of his choice. Similar situations are common in commercial litigation, and the tendency to take the situation as given and divide the gains or losses is common too.[259]

Judges instead should view litigation, Judge Easterbrook admonished, as something akin to a repeated game so as to appreciate the dynamic economic consequences of reaching a particular decision in a particular case:

> When judges take the positions of the parties as given, however, they forfeit any opportunity to create gains through the formulation of the legal rule. The principles laid down today will influence whether similar parties will be in similar situations tomorrow. Indeed, judges who look at cases merely as occasions for the fair apportionment of gains and losses almost invariably ensure that there will be fewer gains and more losses tomorrow.[260]

He applied that insight to different areas of law:

> When a court divides the damages between shipowners, it sends the message that one may as well be careless; it is costly to take care, yet the careful and the careless are treated alike. When a court restricts the patent holder's ability to collect royalties, it reduces the rewards anticipated from patents and thus the incentive for other people to invent. When a court declines to enforce the arbitration agreement, it makes others situated similarly to the one who avoided arbitration worse off. These people no longer can strike one kind of bargain; because they cannot agree to arbitrate, they cannot receive any compensation for their forbearance. A right that cannot be the subject of bargaining is worth less, just as eagle feathers that cannot be sold are worth less to their owners.[261]

Judge Easterbrook emphasized that it is essential for judges to consider the future when they create information through the act of deciding cases:

> Often, discovering the correct balance between promised rewards and realized ones is exceptionally difficult. In the patent case, for example, it may be impossible to discover the "right" system of rules that gives incentives to invent yet preserves the optimal use of things that already have been invented. There is a great tension between optimal creation and optimal use of information.[262]

---

[259] *Id.*
[260] *Id.* at 10–11.
[261] *Id.* at 11 (footnote omitted).
[262] *Id.* (footnote omitted).

The apparent response of the FTC, Professor Shapiro, and Judge Koh to the line of reasoning epitomized by Judge Easterbrook's commentary is that they *are* supposedly looking to the future—at least their own peculiar vision of it. Yet, as we shall now see, that vision relies on a specious utopian depiction of the counterfactual state of the world.

f. Reliance on a Utopian Counterfactual Conditional to Denigrate, as Market Failures, the Market Successes Actually Observed in the Presence of Qualcomm's Challenged Practices

Professor Shapiro's testimony (which ultimately pervaded Judge Koh's findings of fact and conclusions of law) exposed a profound epistemological divide in how to approach monopolization law and, more generally, in how to use economic analysis to inform litigation and public policy debates. In his attempt to rebut Professor Nevo's testimony—that, during the relevant time period the prices of modems decreased, their output expanded, and their quality increased—Professor Shapiro argued that he could envision an alternative state of the world in which, in the absence of Qualcomm's challenged conduct, prices of modems fell *even more*, output increased *even more*, and quality improved *even more*.

I will call Professor Shapiro's epistemological device the *utopian counterfactual conditional*. It is a familiar device in literature, history, and political theory. Rhetorically, the utopian counterfactual conditional is supposed to be the showstopper, like the end of history. We are expected to feel suitably humbled to glimpse into the world of what might have been, which only the expert's clairvoyance can reliably reveal to less perceptive beings. (One can also posit a dystopian counterfactual conditional. When Jimmy Stewart's character in *It's a Wonderful Life* or Ebenezer Scrooge peers into the counterfactual conditional world, it is courtesy of the literary device of an angel or a spirit empowered to foretell the misery that will befall others unless the protagonist immediately changes his life's course in the real world.)

We are also expected to accept that the utopian counterfactual conditional is plausible—or even absolutely true—merely because some personage has invoked it. Consequently, we are expected to accept that the utopian counterfactual conditional should trump any objective knowledge to the contrary that has been constructed from facts observed in the real world.

Here Professor Shapiro describes his utopian counterfactual conditional in his own words:

> As I . . . discuss above in Section III, Professor Nevo appears to believe that because mobile phone sales have increased and prices have fallen, the conduct at issue could not have had any anticompetitive effects. He states:

> In recent years, handset prices have fallen while sales and quality have increased dramatically. There has been significant entry and expansion among OEMs and modem chip makers. As a result, consumers have enjoyed lower prices, higher quality, and increased variety. The evidence shows that the cellular industry is healthy, competitive, and driven by innovation. In this section, I present economic evidence that demonstrates these facts and show that they are not consistent with the FTC and Professor Shapiro's claim that the cellular industry suffers from reduced competition and innovation.

Professor Nevo's logic here is transparently faulty. The evidence he puts forward regarding cellular handset prices and quality does not demonstrate an absence of anticompetitive effects. Professor Nevo has not addressed the relevant comparison: *competitive conditions with vs. without Qualcomm's no-license/no-chips policy*. Industries that are growing and where technology is advancing are certainly not immune from antitrust problems. To suggest otherwise is antithetical to a long history of antitrust enforcement in technology-driven industries in the United States, from the *Standard Oil* case in 1911 to the *Microsoft* case 20 years ago. A central danger in such industries is that a powerful incumbent will stifle competition and retard innovation in an effort to protect its position. These effects can arise in the context of ongoing innovation. The current case fits that general pattern.[263]

In Professor Shapiro's opinion, evidence of lower prices, increased output, and higher quality do not contradict the finding that Qualcomm's licensing practices harmed competition. What is the limiting principle to his line of reasoning? What prevents Professor Shapiro from arguing that the proper standard for evaluating competitive effects in any near-perfect world should be the counterfactual conditional of a more perfect world?

The counterfactual conditional was named by philosopher Nelson Goodman in 1947.[264] Economists have since recognized that they also use, particularly in empirical work, this epistemological tool of the "imaginary . . . alternative[] to actual history" that "would have happened . . . if, contrary to fact, some present condition were changed."[265] That use of the counterfactual

---

[263] Rebuttal Expert Report of Carl Shapiro in *FTC v. Qualcomm*, *supra* note 115, at 92 (emphasis in original) (quoting paragraph 225 of Professor Nevo's expert report, which does not appear to be publicly available).

[264] *See* Nelson Goodman, *The Problem of Counterfactual Conditionals*, 44 J. PHIL. 113, 113 (1947).

[265] Deirdre McCloskey, *Counterfactuals*, *in* 1 THE NEW PALGRAVE: A DICTIONARY OF ECONOMICS 701, 701 (John Eatwell, Murray Millgate & Peter Newman eds., Macmillan 1ˢᵗ ed. 1987); *see also* WILLIAM H. GREENE, ECONOMETRIC ANALYSIS 55 (Pearson 7ᵗʰ ed. 2012) (describing a "hypothetical (*counterfactual*) circumstance") (emphasis in original); JEFFREY M. WOOLDRIDGE, INTRODUCTORY ECONOMETRICS: A MODERN APPROACH 799 (Cengage 7ᵗʰ ed. 2020) (defining counterfactual reasoning as "[a] method of policy evaluation in which we imagine an identical observation (individual, firm, country, etc.) under two different states of the world (e.g. with a policy and without a policy)").

conditional by economists in turn has elicited among them the further recognition of two common problems: vagueness and absurdity.[266]

Professor Shapiro's utopian counterfactual conditional suffered from both problems. It was vague because it implicitly truncated the distribution of possible outcomes in the counterfactual conditional world. To the extent that Professor Shapiro considered only hypothetical outcomes that would have been superior to those experienced in the real world, he ignored the opposite tail of the probability distribution of possible counterfactual conditional outcomes. Professor Shapiro's utopian counterfactual conditional was also absurd because it was pure speculation to suppose that prices could have been even lower, output could have been even greater, and quality could have been even better than what the real world had achieved in the presence of Qualcomm's challenged licensing practices. Philosophers have facetiously noted that, "[i]f kangaroos had no tails, they would topple over."[267] Are we to believe that, but for Qualcomm's licensing practices, mobile broadband subscriptions and smartphone sales would have already outnumbered the Earth's human inhabitants? Or that the smartphone would have been commercially introduced a decade or two earlier? Or that a more advanced standard for mobile communications would have been deployed sooner? Or, in the absence of Qualcomm's challenged licensing practices, would there be only half as many mobile broadband subscriptions today, such that mobile communications would figuratively "topple over," like a kangaroo without a tail?

Professor Shapiro's reasoning leads to a dead end in the real world. His utopian counterfactual conditional world can never be known with sufficient clarity to be used as evidence probative of a violation of law. To restate a question asked above, what if the counterfactual conditional state of affairs delivered something worse than what the real world has already dealt us?[268] To

---

[266] McCloskey, *Counterfactuals, supra* note 265, at 701.

[267] DAVID K. LEWIS, COUNTERFACTUALS 1 (Wiley-Blackwell 2ᵈ ed. 2001), *quoted in* 1 KEN BINMORE, GAME THEORY AND THE SOCIAL CONTRACT: PLAYING FAIR 221 (MIT Press 1994); *see also* CHRISTOPHER PRENDERGAST, COUNTERFACTUALS: PATHS OF THE MIGHT HAVE BEEN 3, 56 (Bloomsbury 2019) ("If huge numbers of unemployable counterfactuals lounge about in La La Land, very many do productive work in an impressive range of disciplines," yet, "unless also well managed, 'commonplace assumptions', . . . often function less as a disciplining constraint on the counterfactual imagining of alternatives than as the framework for what we lazily take for granted."); Ken Binmore, *Fairness*, 4 CRITERION J. ON INNOVATION 533, 537 (2019) (describing an absurd counterfactual as a "fanciful notion[] from the golden age of the poets"). Ken Binmore disagrees with David Lewis's "suggest[ion] that the default choice of a possible world in which a counterfactual holds should be that which is closest to the actual world," reasoning that "[s]uch a criterion does not seem . . . to be very useful *for game-theoretic purposes* because it is usually far from clear what the 'closest' ought to mean" and that "[t]he 'actual world' of game theory is not the imperfect habitat of our everyday experience." 1 BINMORE, GAME THEORY AND THE SOCIAL CONTRACT: PLAYING FAIR, *supra*, at 221 (emphasis added). Nevertheless, I would argue as a matter of legal reasoning that, when a judge is analyzing liability in the "imperfect habitat" of an antitrust case brought by the government (rather than when an economist is performing game-theoretic analysis), the relevant counterfactual conditional clearly should resemble the actual world as much as possible.

[268] *See* Goodman, *The Problem of Counterfactual Conditionals, supra* note 264, at 117.

compare a real-world market outcome with "what would have happened" if Qualcomm had not engaged in its challenged licensing practices is to ignore the law of unintended consequences and to fall prey to a logical fallacy that is reminiscent of what Harold Demsetz famously dubbed the "Nirvana Fallacy."[269]

By what standard of proof should one judge the plausibility of the supposedly brighter world that never was? Must the alleged monopolist prove the negative—that there was no rosier counterfactual conditional world that could have eventuated, even though the world that did eventuate delivered impressive measures of economic performance and advancement of consumer well-being? If the answer to this question is yes, what exactly is the antitrust offense? An unlawful restraint of trade? Or is it a failure to meet the five-year plan of a central economic planner posing as an antitrust enforcer intervening in a technologically dynamic market?

---

[269] *See* Harold Demsetz, *Information and Efficiency: Another Viewpoint*, 12 J.L. & ECON. 1, 1 (1969). Nobel laureate Gary Becker restated the Nirvana Fallacy (though without explicitly using Demsetz's distinctive label) with emphasis on its practical significance for policymakers:

> When an industry in the private sector is not performing efficiently or effectively, there is said to be "market failure." The recommendation by economists and others typically is then for government actions to combat such failure, such as taxes to help reduce pollution. The diagnosis of market failure may be accurate, but the call for government involvement may be naïve and inappropriate.
>
> The reason is that actual governments do not necessarily do what economists and others want them to do because there is "government failure" as well as market failure. Before recommending government actions to correct market failures, one should consider whether actual government policies would worsen rather than improve private sector outcomes. *Since many factors often make for considerable government failure, considering such failure is crucial and not just a theoretical fine point.*

Gary Becker, *Market Failure Compared to Government Failure*, BECKER-POSNER BLOG (Sept. 18, 2011) (emphasis added). Writing in 2014, Judge Posner provided the following account of the Nirvana Fallacy:

> Well do I remember hearing, when I first came to University of Chicago in 1969, the expression "Nirvana Fallacy," used to describe the belief then dominant in the economics profession that market failures could and should be rectified by government intervention, assumed to be apolitical and effectively costless. The belief was unsound; government failure is commonplace, partly because of politics, partly because of the intrinsic difficulty of many of the tasks that are given to government to perform.
>
> The critics of the Nirvana Fallacy did not deny the existence of market failures; they just wanted the costs of such failures to be balanced against the cost of government intervention before deciding whether to recommend government intervention.

POSNER, ECONOMIC ANALYSIS OF LAW, *supra* note 214, at 626. To be sure, following the financial crisis of 2008, Judge Posner became more supportive of government intervention in financial markets. *See id.* at 620–28. He criticized "conservative economists . . . [who] began to regard markets as Nirvana—as self-regulating—and thus to regard virtually any form of government regulation as superfluous, costly, and inefficient." *Id.* at 626. Yet, whether one agrees or disagrees with Judge Posner's critique of the Nirvana Fallacy after the financial crisis of 2008, his argument is distinguishable from whether, in enforcing the antitrust laws, the FTC and the Antitrust Division should prosecute, and a judge should decide, monopolization cases in technologically dynamic industries by using utopian counterfactual conditionals of the kind that Professor Shapiro, the FTC, and Judge Koh all explicitly or implicitly used in *FTC v. Qualcomm.*

g.   *Repudiation of* Grinnell

The Supreme Court articulated in *Grinnell* its now well-known requirement that "[t]he offense of monopoly under [§] 2 of the Sherman Act has two elements: (1) the possession of monopoly power in the relevant market and (2) the willful acquisition or maintenance of that power as distinguished from growth or development as a consequence of a superior product, business acumen, or historic accident."[270] This language gets quoted with far greater frequency than it gets parsed.

A generation before Justice William O. Douglas penned this famous phrase for the Court in *Grinnell*, Judge Learned Hand of course had coined a similar phrase in *Alcoa*: "A single producer may be the survivor out of a group of active competitors, merely by virtue of his superior skill, foresight and industry."[271] Although much that was said in *Alcoa* is no longer considered as authoritative today as it was in 1945, this particular passage has aged well and still can be read profitably alongside *Grinnell* and its more recent restatements by the Supreme Court in *Trinko* and other contemporary monopolization cases. Two sentences later in *Alcoa*, Judge Hand remarked even more enduringly: "The successful competitor, having been urged to compete, must not be turned upon when he wins."[272] This observation of course framed what Robert Bork later called the antitrust paradox.

Does *Grinnell*'s phrase "as distinguished from growth or development as a consequence of a superior product, business acumen, or historic accident" merely mean that a monopolist has an affirmative defense if it can prove the existence of one or more of these three things? Or does the phrase mean that, as part of its case-in-chief, the plaintiff—here, the FTC—must prove the *absence* of *all three* of these things? The answers to these questions influence (1) the allocation of the burden of production, (2) whether a disjunctive or conjunctive proposition of fact must be proven (or disproven) to carry that burden once it has been allocated, and (3) when (if at all) the burden of production shifts to the adverse party.

Judge Koh cited *Grinnell*'s "business acumen" passage three times in her findings of fact and conclusions of law in *FTC v. Qualcomm*.[273] But she did not ask these questions, much less answer them.

---

270   United States v. Grinnell Corp., 384 U.S. 563, 570–71 (1966).
271   United States v. Aluminum Co. of Am., 148 F.2d 416, 430 (2ᵈ Cir. 1945).
272   *Id.*
273   FTC v. Qualcomm Inc., 411 F. Supp. 3d 658, 681, 682, 696 (N.D. Cal. 2019).

b.   Reversal of the Burden of Production, the Burden of Persuasion, and the Presumption of Innocence

Fortunately, the foundational principles of American antitrust jurisprudence provide clear guidance for assessing the truth or falsity of assertions that bear on these questions of what might have been. The plaintiff bears the burden to prove that a challenged practice has anticompetitive effects in the relevant market. The Supreme Court has long recognized this principle and most recently reaffirmed it in 2018 in *Ohio v. American Express Co.*[274] It was thus the FTC's burden to prove that Qualcomm's challenged practices had anticompetitive effects in the market for "premium" LTE modems and the market for CDMA modems.

More specifically, the FTC had both (1) the burden to produce evidence to support its claim that Qualcomm's challenged practices had an anticompetitive effect in the relevant markets and (2) the burden of persuasion, which is the burden to prove the merits of its claim according to some specified quantum of proof, such as a preponderance of evidence. Besides advancing theoretical conjectures, the FTC evidently offered no empirical evidence about harm to competition, such as higher prices, lower output, or reduced innovation, for Judge Koh did not identify any such analysis in her findings of fact and conclusions of law. If anything, as we saw in Part F to the Introduction, publicly available information showed that prices decreased and output increased. The argument advanced by both the FTC and Professor Shapiro—that they could imagine a utopian counterfactual conditional that would be more magnificent than what we actually observed in the modem industry—could not suffice to carry the FTC's burden of proof.

The Federal Rules of Evidence exhibit similar principles of general applicability to prevent the admission into evidence of expert testimony that falls prey to the Nirvana Fallacy or the fallacy of the utopian counterfactual conditional. To be validated in a scientific sense, a given conjecture must survive attempts at falsification, just as the scientific method demands of any theory. This process of conjecture and refutation is, Sir Karl Popper taught us, how we recognize a genuine contribution to objective knowledge.[275] It is not some pedantic proposition to debate over drinks at the faculty club; it is instead the Supreme Court's stated epistemological foundation for deciding whether ostensibly "expert" testimony is admissible evidence under Federal

[274] 138 S. Ct. 2274, 2284 (2018); *see also* NYNEX Corp. v. Discon, Inc., 525 U.S. 128, 135 (1998) ("We conclude no boycott-related *per se* rule applies and that the *plaintiff* here must allege and prove harm, not just to a single competitor, but to the competitive process, *i.e.,* to competition itself.") (first and third emphases in original) (second emphasis added).

[275] *See* KARL R. POPPER, CONJECTURES AND REFUTATIONS: THE GROWTH OF SCIENTIFIC KNOWLEDGE (Routledge 5th ed. 1989); KARL R. POPPER, OBJECTIVE KNOWLEDGE: AN EVOLUTIONARY APPROACH (Oxford Univ. Press rev. ed. 1979).

Rule of Evidence 702.[276] The expert witness is permitted to testify only to the extent that his expert insights will help the finder of fact; he is not invited into the courtroom to reign over it as its philosopher king.

Yet, Professor Shapiro and Judge Koh evidently ignored those basic principles. Judge Koh discredited Qualcomm's expert economic witnesses in part because she found that they did not attempt to rebut Professor Shapiro's utopian counterfactual conditional in which prices would have been even lower, output would have expanded even more, and quality would have been even better. The effect of that discreditation by Judge Koh was to eliminate or denigrate evidence of how, in the less-than-utopian real world, prices had actually fallen, output had actually expanded, and quality had actually increased.

Instead, Judge Koh's evidentiary ruling in essence required Qualcomm to proceed from either of two untenable propositions. Qualcomm could concede liability (because, to refute the plaintiff's *prima facie* case, it was not enough under Professor Shapiro's utopian counterfactual conditional for Qualcomm to prove that prices decreased, output expanded, and quality increased), and it then could hope for the best on the question of remedies. Alternatively, Qualcomm could profess its innocence but proceed in the recognition that a defendant in a government monopolization is, as a practical matter, presumed guilty rather than innocent. Under either alternative, Judge Koh's new *de facto* standard of liability would make it impossible for an accused monopolist to satisfy its burden of persuasion.

Professor Shapiro's idiosyncratic view that a utopian counterfactual conditional was the relevant one for a court to use was unworkable. It did not reflect the law. It relied on an epistemological fallacy. And it reflected an approach that economists have long recognized is preposterous and nonfalsifiable. Yet, it also corresponded to how Judge Koh approached fact finding in *FTC v. Qualcomm*, even though she did not ever acknowledge Professor Shapiro by name.

---

[276] *See* Daubert v. Merrell Dow Pharm., Inc., 509 U.S. 579, 591–93 (1993) (construing Fed. R. Evid. 702). The Court has emphasized that, to be helpful to the finder of fact, and thus to be admissible as evidence in a federal court proceeding, an expert's testimony must rely on the scientific method, *id.* at 591, which the Court clearly understood to be the process of conjecture and attempts at empirical refutation that Popper outlined in his famous writings on objective knowledge. *Id.* at 593 ("'[T]he criterion of the scientific status of a theory is its falsifiability, or refutability, or testability.'") (alteration in original) (emphasis omitted) (quoting Popper, Conjectures and Refutations: The Growth of Scientific Knowledge, *supra* note 275, at 37); *see also* J. Gregory Sidak, *Court-Appointed Neutral Economic Experts*, 9 J. Competition L. & Econ. 359, 384–86 (2013) (analyzing the epistemological foundation of *Daubert* and its progeny).

> *i.   Why the Multiple Links in the Chain of Causation for Professor Shapiro's Theory of Anticompetitive Harm Made It Improbable That a Preponderance of the Evidence Ultimately Supported Judge Koh's Finding of Liability*

Besides the FTC's failure to satisfy its burden of production, it was improbable as a matter of economic analysis that a preponderance of the evidence ultimately supported Judge Koh's finding of liability. Economic theory distinguishes between partial equilibrium analysis and general equilibrium analysis. Any student in Econ 1 learns this lesson. Changes in one market lead to changes in almost all other markets, but the greatest effects will tend to occur in related markets. Thus, it is an economically fallacious argument to string together a series of *ceteris paribus* arguments in related markets and ignore the interaction of the markets and the effects of one change in one market on behaviors and outcomes in the other markets. One can trace the intellectual provenance of this insight to Alfred Marshall's seminal treatise, *Principles of Economics*:

> The forces to be dealt with are however so numerous, that it is best to take a few at a time: and to work out a number of partial solutions. . . . Thus we begin by isolating the primary relations of supply, demand and price in regards to a particular commodity. We reduce to inaction all other forces by the phrase "other things being equal": we do not suppose that they are inert, but for the time being we ignore their activity. . . . In the second stage more forces are released from the hypothetical slumber that had been imposed on them.
>
> The element of time is a chief cause of those difficulties in economic investigations which make it necessary for a man with limited powers to go step by step; breaking up a complex question, studying one bit at a time, and at last combining his partial solutions into a more or less complete solution of the whole riddle. In breaking it up, he segregates those disturbing causes, whose wanderings happen to be inconvenient, for the time in a pound called *Ceteris Paribus*. The study of some groups of tendencies is isolated by the assumption *other things being equal* . . . . With each step more things can be let out of the pound.[277]

We can extend Marshall's insights to the economic analysis of legal disputes, and in particular Professor Shapiro's ornate, multi-step theory of supposed anticompetitive harm from Qualcomm's business practices.

---

[277] ALFRED MARSHALL, PRINCIPLES OF ECONOMICS: AN INTRODUCTORY ANALYSIS, at xiv–xv, 366 (Macmillan 8th ed. 1920) (alterations in original) (emphasis in original), *quoted in* Peter Kriesler, *Partial Equilibrium Analysis*, *in* 4 POST-KEYNESIAN ESSAYS FROM DOWN UNDER: ESSAYS ON THEORY 33, 33–34 (Joseph Halevi, G.C. Harcourt, Peter Kriesler & J. W. Nevile eds., Springer 2016); *see also* Peter Kriesler, *Partial Equilibrium Analysis*, *in* INTERNATIONAL ENCYCLOPEDIA OF THE SOCIAL SCIENCES 151, 151–53 (Macmillan Reference 2d ed. 2008).

Professor Shapiro's theory of anticompetitive harm fits somewhere between a partial equilibrium approach (ignoring, for example, the strategic reaction of Qualcomm's OEMs or of its rival modem manufacturers or of potential entrants) and a general equilibrium approach (hypothesizing, for example, some effects on competitors, customers, and end consumers over an extended period of time). It is important to note the probabilistic implications of moving from partial equilibrium predictions to general equilibrium predictions concerning the response to some economic perturbation. As the hypothesis becomes more richly detailed, it adds more links to the chain of causation. If each link in the chain has a probability of occurrence (or of being true) that is independent of the probabilities of occurrence (or truth) associated with each of the other links in the chain of causation, then the probability of the ultimate effect being predicted will equal the multiplicative product of all the independent probabilities in the chain.

The law of evidence imposes the threshold probability for imposing legal liability for an alleged offense. In civil cases, such as *FTC v. Qualcomm*, the applicable burden of persuasion is a preponderance of the evidence, which for ease of exposition we can define to be 51 percent. So viewed, a preponderance of the evidence is just a scintilla more than the evidence being in equipoise. Whether in the real world finders of fact demand some greater level of certitude under the preponderance-of-the-evidence standard is a debate, undertaken by others, that need not detain us because it does not alter the logic and intuition that we seek to elucidate here.[278]

We can solve for the probability threshold that each link in the chain must have met, in Judge Koh's estimation, for the FTC to have been able to prove to her by a preponderance of the evidence that the overall chain of causation on which the agency rested its theory of anticompetitive harm was true. In doing so, we will assume for ease of computation (and in a manner that indulges Professor Shapiro's theory, the FTC's arguments, and Judge Koh's findings) that every one of these independent probabilities is equal and exceeds 51 percent. Obviously, if *any* link the chain of causation is less than 50 percent likely to be true, the entire causal narrative of anticompetitive harm falls below equipoise and cannot possibly support a finding of liability by a preponderance of the evidence—since, as I explained above, the ultimate probability that the causal chain is true equals the multiplicative product of all the independent probabilities in the chain.

Let us assume that Professor Shapiro's causal chain can be summarized as consisting of the following six links (the precise number, whether it is five or seven, does not detract from the insight to be gleaned from the exercise):

---

[278] Judge Posner, for example, doubts as a positive matter that judges and juries treat the preponderance-of-the-evidence standard as requiring just a sliver more than a 50-percent likelihood of truth. *See* POSNER, ECONOMIC ANALYSIS OF LAW, *supra* note 214, at 848–49.

(1) OEMs paid an "unreasonably high" royalty for an exhaustive license to Qualcomm's cellular SEPs,

(2) the increment of the royalty that was "unreasonably high" (which was the per-device amount by which the "unreasonably high" royalty paid for an exhaustive license to Qualcomm's cellular SEPs exceeded the upper bound on a reasonable royalty bilaterally negotiated pursuant to a FRAND or RAND obligation) acted as a royalty "surcharge" on an exhaustive license to its cellular SEPs that allegedly became a "tax" on the "all-in price" that OEMs paid for rivals' modems in the two supposedly relevant markets for modems (which we will generously assume constitute monopolies),

(3) OEMs paying the royalty "surcharge" and modem "tax" reduced the quantity purchased of (or amount paid for) rivals' modems (or perhaps both),

(4) the profit margins of rival modem manufacturers fell,

(5) rival modem manufacturers, who are assumed to rely exclusively on funding from their net free cash flow from operations to finance their R&D investments, reduced their investments in modem R&D, and

(6) the decrement of modem R&D investments by rival modem manufacturers that proximately flowed from Qualcomm's "unreasonably high" royalty for an exhaustive license to its cellular SEPs reduced the output of the R&D investments in modems by rival modem manufacturers to such an extent that rival modem manufacturers could no longer offer OEMs modems that were technologically advanced enough to compete profitably against Qualcomm's modems for adoption by OEMs in new generations of smartphones or other mobile devices.

Under the preponderance-of-the-evidence standard of proof, the minimum probability of truth p of each of the n causal links in Professor Shapiro's narrative that is needed for the entire narrative to be proven true is $p^n = 0.51$. Taking logarithms—and giving n the value of 6, because that is the number of discrete causal links in Professor Shapiro's narrative of the competitive harm from Qualcomm's conduct—we have $6 \log p = \log 0.51$, which solves to $p = 0.8938$ In other words, for Professor Shapiro's entire narrative of competitive harm to be at least 51 percent likely to be true, every one of the six independent links in his chain of causation would need to be at least 89.38 percent likely to be true.

Even if some of the probabilities of Professor Shapiro's causal links had been dependent, the likelihood of the links collectively satisfying the preponderance-of-the-evidence standard was low. For example, even if one were to assume that four of the six conditional probabilities equaled 1, and if the remaining two conditional probabilities had been equal to 0.70, the joint probability of all six conditional probabilities obtaining would have fallen below the preponderance-of-the-evidence standard. Moreover, to argue that the probability of any single causal link obtaining equaled 1 would have been tantamount to arguing that the additional facts to be proven made no marginal contribution to making the answer to the ultimate question of fact more likely to be true, such that those conditionally certain events would have had no probative value as evidence. In his expert report, Professor Shapiro foresaw the difficulty of establishing causation in *FTC v. Qualcomm*.[279] We shall see in greater detail in Part IV why Professor Shapiro's analysis could not have been capable of proving, by a preponderance of the evidence, that Qualcomm's actions caused any actual harm to the competitive process.

Judge Koh did not even make any economic finding of fact identifying actual harm to the competitive process. The principal harm to the competitive process that she seemed to identify was the supposed "exit" by rival modem manufacturers. Yet, she never established the proper counterfactual conditional to consider. In particular, she did not analyze the probability of what she called "exit" as a risk inherent in the natural functioning of the markets in question. Consequently, because she did not appear to examine any evidence that Qualcomm's actions materially increased that risk of "exit" in the proper counterfactual conditional, how did she conclude that the FTC satisfied its burden of persuasion? Judge Koh's findings of fact and conclusions of law seemed to simplify the FTC's burden of persuasion by taking as given that the probability of harm to the competitive process, although unproven, was equal to 1.

2. *The Application of Erroneous Antitrust Principles*

Apart from these due process deficiencies, a second instance of judicial misadventure in Judge Koh's findings of fact and conclusions of law is that she misapplied or ignored controlling Supreme Court precedent on the law of monopolization.

a. *Judge Koh's Failure to Apply the Supreme Court's Controlling Precedent on Monopolization*

The centerpiece of Judge Koh's findings of fact and conclusions of law in *FTC v. Qualcomm* was her novel ruling that Qualcomm's licensing practice was unlawful because it allegedly imposed on OEMs a royalty "surcharge" on an exhaustive license to Qualcomm's cellular SEPs that allegedly became a "tax" on the "all-in price" that OEMs paid for rivals' modems, supposedly raising the "all-in cost" to OEMs of purchasing modems from Qualcomm's

---

[279] Initial Expert Report of Carl Shapiro in *FTC v. Qualcomm*, *supra* note 115, at 115 ("While it is difficult to isolate the effect of Qualcomm's conduct on its modem chip rivals, we do know, as discussed above in Section VIII.C, that Texas Instruments, Broadcom, Marvell, Nvidia, and ST-Ericsson all stopped selling modem chips between 2012 and 2015.") (internal citation omitted).

rivals, which in turn supposedly reduced rivals' profit margins and under-mined their ability to compete.[280] Yet, her findings of fact were strikingly obscure on a critical fact, which Professor Shapiro had admitted at trial and to which Professor Nevo had precisely testified. That fact was that the supposed royalty "surcharge" and modem "tax" were symmetric as between Qualcomm's own modem sales and the sales of rival modems. One can get an idea of what Judge Koh was apparently trying to say in her findings of fact and conclusions of law only by reading directly the trial testimony on this point given by Professors Shapiro and Nevo, which Judge Koh declined to acknowledge even existed.

In turn, that key economic fact (that the supposed royalty "surcharge" and modem "tax" were symmetric) meant that the novel theory of antitrust liabil-ity advanced by the FTC and embraced by Judge Koh collapsed to a simple allegation of a margin squeeze. Judge Koh never should have permitted the FTC's royalty "surcharge" and modem "tax" theory of antitrust liability to survive a motion to dismiss under *Twombly*,[281] because the Supreme Court in *linkLine* explicitly held in 2009 that a firm has no duty to price its products in a way that "preserves its rivals' profit margins."[282] Judge Koh misapplied that unambiguous statement of controlling law.

Similarly, Judge Koh invoked the Court's 1985 decision in *Aspen Skiing*[283] to support her conclusion that Qualcomm's refusal to license its cellular SEPs exhaustively to rival modem manufacturers violated the Sherman Act.[284] But the Court emphasized in 2004 in *Trinko* that *Aspen Skiing* is "at or near the outer boundary of § 2 liability," and the Court reiterated that it had been "very cautious" in creating exceptions to the general rule in American antitrust jurisprudence that a firm—even a monopolist—has no duty to cooperate with its rivals.[285]

Remarkably, in its briefs on appeal and in its oral argument at the Ninth Circuit, the FTC took the position that, although Judge Koh correctly found liability, her finding was predicated on an erroneous interpretation of *Aspen Skiing* that the FTC had never advocated. If accurate, the FTC's representa-tion would cast doubt on Judge Koh's attentiveness to the questions of law being presented for her decision over the course of two years of enormously

---

[280] FTC v. Qualcomm Inc., 411 F. Supp. 3d 658, 790 (N.D. Cal. 2019) ("Qualcomm imposes an artificial surcharge on all sales of its rivals' modem chips. The surcharge increases the effective price of rivals' modem chips, reduces rivals' margins, and results in exclusivity.").

[281] Bell Atl. Corp. v. Twombly, 550 U.S. 544 (2007).

[282] Pacific Bell Tel. Co. v. linkLine Commc'ns, Inc., 555 U.S. 438, 452 (2009).

[283] Aspen Skiing Co. v. Aspen Highlands Skiing Corp., 472 U.S. 585 (1985).

[284] *FTC v. Qualcomm*, 411 F. Supp. 3d at 758–62 (construing *Aspen Skiing*).

[285] Verizon Commc'ns Inc. v. Law Offices of Curtis V. Trinko, LLP, 540 U.S. 398, 409 (2004) (construing *Aspen Skiing*); *see also id.* at 408 ("We have been very cautious in recognizing such exceptions, because of the uncertain virtue of forced sharing and the difficulty of identifying and remedying anticompetitive conduct by a single firm.").

costly litigation. After all, as we saw earlier in the Introduction, Judge Koh repeatedly complained (particularly to Qualcomm's lawyers) that they were burdening her with too many sealing motions, too many pages of merits briefing, too much preparation for witnesses who wound up not being called to testify at the last minute, and too many binders of trial exhibits. Yet, here was the FTC now telling the Ninth Circuit that Judge Koh regrettably had made a huge amount of unnecessary work for herself by deciding an antitrust claim that the agency actually never pleaded. A federal district judge is of course jurisdictionally constrained by Article III to decide only cases or controversies; to issue findings of fact and conclusions of law on a question that the government subsequently claims that it never raised suggests one material difference between a judge's role in an adversarial system of justice and a judge's role in an inquisitorial system of justice.

On brief, the FTC said that at trial it did "not argue that Qualcomm has a duty to deal with its rivals under the heightened *Aspen/Trinko* standard."[286] And at oral argument before the Ninth Circuit, the following collo-quy prompted stammering from the FTC's otherwise eloquent appellate advocate, Brian Fletcher:

> Circuit Judge Consuelo Callahan: Well, but you're conceding that [Judge Koh's reliance on *Aspen Skiing* to find that Qualcomm had a duty to deal] was wrong; not only [that Judge Koh found] more than she had to, but that it was wrong.
>
> Brian Fletcher, Counsel for the FTC: That—that—that's right. We don't think the *Aspen* standard applies.[287]

At the time of his oral argument, Mr. Fletcher was a Visiting Clinical Professor of Law in the Supreme Court Litigation Clinic at Stanford Law School. He was formerly an Assistant to the Solicitor General of the United States, an appellate and Supreme Court litigator at WilmerHale, a law clerk to Justice Ruth Bader Ginsburg and Circuit Judge Merrick Garland, President of the *Harvard Law Review*, and recipient of the Fay Diploma at Harvard Law School.[288] He evidently appeared as special counsel to the FTC on its answering brief to the Ninth Circuit, but not in district court before Judge Koh, and not as a lawyer employed by the FTC.[289] Put differently, it might appear to

---

[286] Brief of the Federal Trade Commission at 30, FTC v. Qualcomm Inc., No. 19-16122 (9th Cir. Nov. 22, 2019) [hereinafter FTC Brief to the Ninth Circuit].

[287] Oral Argument at 41:53–42:01, FTC v. Qualcomm Inc., No. 19-16122 (9th Cir. Feb. 13, 2020), https://www.ca9.uscourts.gov/media/view_video.php?pk_vid=0000017078; *see also* FTC v. Qualcomm Inc., No. 19-16122, 2020 WL 4591476, at *13 (9th Cir. Aug. 11, 2020) (remarking that the FTC had "[c]onced[ed] error in the district court's conclusion that Qualcomm is subject to an antitrust duty to deal under *Aspen Skiing*").

[288] *See Brian Fletcher*, STANFORD LAW SCHOOL, https://law.stanford.edu/directory/brian-fletcher/.

[289] FTC Brief to the Ninth Circuit, *supra* note 286.

some observers that the FTC's unambiguous repudiation of the *Aspen Skiing* theory of liability in *FTC v. Qualcomm* coincided with the commencement of Mr. Fletcher's public involvement in the case before the Ninth Circuit. How might the litigating of *FTC v. Qualcomm* have advanced differently if the FTC had sought Mr. Fletcher's counsel sooner?

Mr. Fletcher seemed to be telling the Ninth Circuit as diplomatically as possible to go ahead and reverse on the *Aspen Skiing* finding because Judge Koh, ignoring the Supreme Court's call for caution, had erroneously imposed on Qualcomm an expansive antitrust duty to deal, notwithstanding that the relationships between Qualcomm and rival modem manufacturers in *FTC v. Qualcomm* differed materially in their economic character from the relationship between the access seeker and its competitor in *Aspen Skiing.*[290] Mr. Fletcher seemed to be telegraphing to the Ninth Circuit that the FTC well understood that there was no chance that the current Supreme Court would ever affirm Judge Koh's findings of fact and conclusions of law predicated on an *Aspen Skiing* duty-to-deal theory of liability.

In *Aspen Skiing*, the Court found that, although ending an existing course of dealing with a rival might be a legitimate business decision, the jury could reasonably conclude on the facts of the case that the termination of that course of dealing was not justified by "any normal business purpose" but instead was motivated by the monopolist's desire to reduce competition.[291] In contrast, in *FTC v. Qualcomm*, Judge Koh explicitly found that Qualcomm's practice of not exhaustively licensing its patents to rival modem manufacturers was motivated by the firm's desire to *increase* its patent-licensing revenue[292]—a normal and lawful business objective of any patent holder, and certainly not by itself evidence of anticompetitive intent. She even found that other SEP holders that did not compete in the modem industry (and therefore would not have had any plausible interest in harming competition among modem manufacturers) had followed the same licensing practice as Qualcomm's.[293] Yet, Judge Koh instead found that anticompetitive malice motivated Qualcomm's choice of the level of production at which to offer exhaustive licenses to its cellular SEPs.

If we credit Mr. Fletcher's statements in oral argument to the Ninth Circuit, Judge Koh's findings on *Aspen Skiing* were an unconstitutional advisory opinion: The FTC never argued the legal theory, and obviously Qualcomm did not; so there was no case or controversy with respect to the *Aspen Skiing* argument. Judge Koh reached the question by an inquisitorial assertion of federal jurisdiction that she did not have.

---

[290] *FTC v. Qualcomm*, 411 F. Supp. 3d at 759–62 (construing *Aspen Skiing*, 472 U.S. at 602).
[291] *Aspen Skiing*, 472 U.S. at 608.
[292] *FTC v. Qualcomm*, 411 F. Supp. 3d at 753.
[293] *Id.* at 754–55.

  b. *The Lack of Substantial Evidence Supporting a Finding of Liability Even Under Judge Koh's Mistaken Statement of the Applicable Antitrust Principles*

Suppose that one ignored Judge Koh's failure to apply binding Supreme Court precedent. Even then, her findings of fact and conclusions of law would not support her ruling that Qualcomm's licensing practices were unlawful. The FTC's theory of harm would require, at the very least, evidence (1) that Qualcomm's royalties for its portfolio of cellular SEPs were "unreasonably high" and (2) that the "unreasonably high" royalty "surcharge" imposed a "tax" on OEMs' purchases solely of rivals' modems that thereby harmed competition. Yet, the evidence that Judge Koh summarized in her findings of fact and conclusions of law did not support either of those two findings of fact.

  Judge Koh stated 85 times in her findings of fact and conclusions of law that the royalties that Qualcomm charged for an exhaustive license to its portfolio of cellular SEPs were "unreasonably high."[294] Yet, she did not once rely on *any* economic analysis to support that inherently economic finding of fact.[295] The evidence that Judge Koh summarized in her findings of fact and conclusions of law did not show what a reasonable royalty would be for an exhaustive license to Qualcomm's portfolio of cellular SEPs—or by how much, if at all, the royalty that OEMs actually paid to Qualcomm for such a license supposedly exceeded that reasonable royalty. In other words, Judge Koh did not identify any empirical evidence to support her finding of fact that Qualcomm was charging an "unreasonably high" royalty "surcharge" for an exhaustive license to its portfolio of cellular SEPs that allegedly became a "tax" on the "all-in price" that OEMs paid for rivals' modems (though supposedly *not* on modems that Qualcomm itself sold to OEMs).

  Judge Koh's findings about the effects that such an alleged royalty "surcharge" and modem "tax" had on competition were also conspicuously incurious. At the very outset of litigation in *FTC v. Qualcomm*, Commissioner Maureen Ohlhausen, who alone dissented in the 2–1 vote by the FTC's commissioners to file a complaint against Qualcomm, focused like a laser on the logical defect in the FTC's royalty "surcharge" and modem "tax" theory of antitrust liability in January 2017:

   The core theory of the complaint is that Qualcomm uses its alleged chipset monopoly to force its customers—smartphone manufacturers

---

[294] *Id.* at 698 (twice), 707, 710, 713, 714, 716, 717, 719, 744 (twice), 751, 754 (twice), 757, 760, 761, 762, 773 (six times), 774 (three times), 775 (twice), 776 (twice), 778 (twice), 780 (three times), 784, 785, 786 (seven times), 788 (twice), 789 (twice), 790 (eight times), 791, 792 (twice), 794 (three times), 795 (five times), 796 (twice), 797 (three times), 798, 800, 809 (three times), 810 (twice), 811, 819, 820, 821.
[295] *Id.* at 773–90.

(OEMs)—to pay unreasonably high royalties to license FRAND-encumbered patents that are essential to practicing CDMA and LTE cellular-communications standards. Because OEMs have to pay those royalties regardless of which chipset manufacturers they purchase from, the alleged effect is to squeeze the margins of Qualcomm's competitors in chipsets. Qualcomm allegedly implements that strategy through its "no license – no chips" policy and refusal to license its chipset-maker rivals. *The fundamental element of this theory is a royalty overcharge.* If Qualcomm charges reasonable royalties for its patents, then there is no anticompetitive "tax"—the complaint's nomenclature for a price squeeze—but only the procompetitive monetization of legitimate patent rights. *Importantly, there is no suggestion that Qualcomm charges higher royalties to OEMs that buy non-Qualcomm chipsets.* Hence, the complaint's taxation theory requires that Qualcomm charge OEMs unreasonably high royalties.

Rather than allege that Qualcomm charges above-FRAND royalties, the complaint dances around that essential element. It alleges that Qualcomm's practices disrupt license challenges and bargaining in the shadow of law, and that the ensuing royalties are "elevated." *But the complaint fails to allege that Qualcomm charges more than a reasonable royalty.* That pleading failure is no accident; it speaks to the dearth of evidence in this case. Although the complaint frames its price-squeeze claim as a "tax", *it overlooks the fact that reasonable royalties are not an exclusionary tax, even if paid by competitors.* And it includes no allegation of below-cost pricing (presumably of chipsets) by Qualcomm, even if one infers an antitrust duty to deal with chipset manufacturers.[296]

Judge Koh's findings of fact and conclusions of law did not mention Commissioner Ohlhausen or her dissent even once. Considering the murkiness of the royalty "surcharge" and modem "tax" conjecture when the FTC filed its complaint, as succinctly documented in Commissioner Ohlhausen's dissent, did two years and presumably several hundreds of millions of dollars spent on discovery, legal advocacy, and expert economic testimony do anything to make the FTC's explanation of its conjecture any clearer and any more plausible?[297] Judge Koh did not explain in her findings of fact and conclusions of law how, in theory, the alleged royalty "surcharge" and modem "tax" (assuming that they existed) were capable as a matter of law of harming competition among modem manufacturers.

---

[296] Dissenting Statement of Commissioner Maureen K. Ohlhausen at 1–2, *In re* Qualcomm, Inc., File No. 141-0199, 2017 WL 410340 (F.T.C. Jan. 17, 2017) (emphasis added) (footnote omitted) (citing Pacific Bell Tel. Co. v. linkLine Commc'ns, Inc., 555 U.S. 438, 451–52 (2009)). Commissioner Ohlhausen was a Republican appointee. The two majority votes were from Chairwoman Edith Ramirez and Commissioner Terrell McSweeny, both Democrat appointees.

[297] Qualcomm's litigation costs in its fiscal year 2018 exceeded $1.5 million per day. *See* Qualcomm Inc., Annual Report for the Fiscal Year Ended September 30, 2018 (SEC Form 10-K), at 44 (filed Nov. 7, 2018) [hereinafter 2018 Qualcomm 10-K] ("[Qualcomm encountered] $325 million in higher litigation costs, with total litigation costs of $554 million and $229 million in fiscal 2018 and fiscal 2017, respectively.").

Judge Koh also did not identify any empirical evidence that would tend to support her conclusion that the alleged royalty "surcharge" and modem "tax" harmed competition in practice. She found that Qualcomm's licensing practices harmed competition in the supposedly relevant product markets for CDMA modem chips and "premium" LTE modem chips.[298] But Judge Koh never analyzed any *empirical evidence* on competition in her defined markets. She found that some modem manufacturers "exited" the industry, but she never found that those companies competed in what she defined as the relevant markets, much less that the proximate cause of their "exit" was Qualcomm's allegedly anticompetitive conduct rather than some extraneous force or factor (such as the inferior products or lesser business acumen of Qualcomm's rivals).

Furthermore, publicly available information from the modem industry contradicted Judge Koh's conclusion about harm to competition. Evidence showed that prices for modems had decreased, output had increased, and quality had improved during the period when Qualcomm was allegedly engaging in anticompetitive practices. Evidence also showed that new companies had been able to enter the modem business and had gained a significant market share. This evidence was not what one would expect to observe in a market in which a firm's conduct had supposedly "strangled competition in the CDMA and premium LTE modem chip markets for years."[299]

J.   The Structure of the Analysis That Follows

In this article, I examine the many errors of commission and omission in Judge Koh's findings of fact and conclusions of law in *FTC v. Qualcomm*. I focus my analysis primarily on her conclusion that Qualcomm violated section 2 of the Sherman Act. As Judge Koh acknowledged, quoting the same language from *Grinnell* that we examined earlier, to establish that the challenged conduct violates section 2, the Supreme Court requires proof of two elements: (1) the defendant possesses monopoly power in the relevant market and (2) "'the willful acquisition or maintenance of that power' through exclusionary conduct 'as distinguished from growth or development as a consequence of a superior product, business acumen, or historic accident.'"[300] Judge Koh did not establish the presence of either of these two elements of a section 2 violation. Implicit in the second element is the further requirement of proof that the challenged conduct harmed consumers or competition, by which

---

[298] *FTC v. Qualcomm*, 411 F. Supp. 3d at 803–07.
[299] *Id.* at 812.
[300] *Id.* at 681 (quoting United States v. Grinnell Corp., 384 U.S. 563, 570–71 (1966)).

courts mean not harm to individual competitors but harm to the competitive process.[301]

In Part I of this article, I discuss the political economy of *FTC v. Qualcomm*, including what was alleged in court filings in the public domain about the role that Apple, one of the major implementers of industry standards in mobile communications and a large buyer of modems, reportedly played in the FTC's decision to sue Qualcomm in January 2017.

In Part II, I analyze Judge Koh's misunderstanding and denigration of Qualcomm for its innovative and unique business model. I examine the trial testimony of Alex Rogers, President of Qualcomm Technology Licensing (QTL). Although Mr. Rogers' testimony served as an important factual predicate for the case, Judge Koh largely ignored it in her findings of fact and conclusions of law. I thus reproduce key passages of that testimony, which explained in detail the innovative and unique qualities of Qualcomm's dual business model of licensing a portfolio of 140,000 patents and patent applications and of selling modems. I explain why the trial testimony of Richard Donaldson, the FTC's expert witness on patent licensing, was uninformative and irrelevant. In particular, Qualcomm's decision not to emulate the business model that Texas Instruments, Mr. Donaldson's employer from 1969 to 2000, followed in or before 2000 was irrelevant to whether Qualcomm violated antitrust law. Finally, I examine how, in contrast to the seminal insights of Ronald Coase and other eminent economists, Judge Koh's "imperative" view of the nature of the firm myopically presumed that no procompetitive rationale could plausibly have motivated the institutional structure of production upon which Qualcomm had settled.

In Part III, I analyze how the Supreme Court's refinement of the judicially created doctrine of patent exhaustion materially affected Qualcomm's licensing practices. The practical economic effect of this doctrinal change was to diminish the alienability of U.S. patent rights. Qualcomm's apparent business motivation to avoid patent exhaustion explained why Qualcomm both (1) sold its modems only to *licensed* OEMs and (2) never intentionally licensed its cellular SEPs *exhaustively* to rival modem manufacturers. Qualcomm in fact had never offered exhaustive licenses to its cellular SEPs to rival modem manufacturers. After a decision by the Supreme Court in 2008 that abrogated approximately two decades of Federal Circuit law holding the opposite, it became evident that, under U.S. law, Qualcomm's sale of a modem or its grant of any contractual agreement labeled a "license" would exhaust Qualcomm's patent rights, even if the counterparties believed that "license" to be nonexhaustive. Consequently, Qualcomm could not seek patent royalties for both the modems sold and the downstream mobile devices licensed.

---

[301] *See, e.g.*, NYNEX Corp. v. Discon, Inc., 525 U.S. 128, 135 (1998); United States v. Microsoft Corp., 253 F.3d 34, 59 (D.C. Cir. 2001) (en banc) (per curiam).

So, Qualcomm and its rival modem manufacturers restructured certain agreements—some of which the counterparties previously had called *nonexhaustive* "licenses"—as covenants, so as to continue to grant those rival modem manufacturers freedom to operate while preserving Qualcomm's ability to license exhaustively (and to collect royalties from) OEMs. Judge Koh did not draw the critical distinction between (1) the exhaustive licenses to its portfolio of cellular SEPs that Qualcomm offered to OEMs and (2) what were thought before 2008 to be nonexhaustive "licenses" to its cellular SEPs that Qualcomm offered to rival modem manufacturers.

In Part IV, I examine in detail the expert economic opinions that Professor Shapiro (1) disclosed in the redacted versions of two expert reports that he produced on behalf of the FTC and (2) expressed in his live (case-in-chief and rebuttal) testimony on two days in January 2019 at the bench trial in *FTC v. Qualcomm*. Professor Shapiro testified that his expert economic opinion in *FTC v. Qualcomm* depended on the premise that Qualcomm was charging OEMs an "unreasonably high" royalty "surcharge" on an exhaustive license to its cellular SEPs that allegedly became a "tax" on the "all-in price" that OEMs paid for rivals' modems. That was a factual premise that Professor Shapiro merely *assumed* existed, that he testified that he made no attempt to quantify, and that he ultimately defended on the last day of witness testimony by analogizing Qualcomm's licensing practices—evidently for the first time in his disclosure of ostensibly expert economic opinions in the case—to an accused cheater's placement of rocks in his rivals' kayaks in a boat race down a river. Professor Shapiro also assumed that the alleged royalty "surcharge" and modem "tax" harmed competition in his two relevant product markets (for CDMA modems and "premium" LTE modems), although he did not examine any empirical evidence to verify that assumption. He asked the court instead to trust the predictions of his theoretical bargaining model, despite the fact that he admitted that those predictions contradicted evidence of what had actually occurred in the real world. Finally Professor Shapiro made the key admission that the alleged royalty "surcharge" and modem "tax" would apply *symmetrically* to a Qualcomm modem and to the modem of a rival, such that an OEM would pay Qualcomm the same royalty for an exhaustive license to its cellular SEPs, regardless of the brand of modem that the OEM chose to purchase.

In Part V, I examine Judge Koh's peculiar omission of any discussion of Professor Shapiro's expert economic testimony for the FTC. Professor Shapiro gave substantially more pages of transcribed trial testimony than any other witness in *FTC v. Qualcomm*, yet Judge Koh did not mention him once in her findings of fact and conclusions of law. That omission is material because Judge Koh's findings of fact and conclusions of law closely resemble Professor Shapiro's testimony. Consequently, her lack of attribution invites one to ask whether any of her conclusions of law rest on findings of fact that she did not report in her May 2019 opinion. An appellate court reviewing Judge Koh's findings of fact might find them insufficiently transparent to support her conclusions of law. Consequently, it appears at a minimum that Judge Koh violated Federal Rule of Civil Procedure 52(a)(1) by failing, after conducting her bench trial in *FTC v. Qualcomm*, to make special findings of fact concerning Professor Shapiro's testimony. The consequences of that shortcoming as a matter of due process of law are serious. Judge Koh's suppression of Professor Shapiro's testimony, and even more her failure to acknowledge and weigh his testimony as evidence materially tending to exculpate Qualcomm, violated the Due Process Clause of the Fifth Amendment to the U.S. Constitution as interpreted by the Supreme Court in *Mathews v. Eldridge*.

In Part VI, I analyze how Judge Koh violated the Supreme Court's burden-shifting framework in *American Express* and thus denied Qualcomm due process of law by reversing the burden of proof. It is a well-recognized principle of American antitrust law that the plaintiff, whether a private party or the government, bears the burden of proving (that is, it bears both the burden of production and the burden of persuasion) that the challenged conduct has an anticompetitive effect in the relevant market. The FTC offered no evidence that would suffice to satisfy its initial burden of production, much less its burden of persuasion amounting to a preponderance of the evidence. The FTC's failure of proof meant that Judge Koh's finding of liability necessarily was predicated on her having required Qualcomm to prove the *negative* of the first step in the Supreme Court's three-step burden-sharing framework. That inversion of *American Express* and earlier Supreme Court precedent was clearly an erroneous application of law. Judge Koh then seemed to say that *American Express* did not require her to weigh Qualcomm's evidence of a "procompetitive rationale" after the burden of production had supposedly shifted to Qualcomm, if she could instead peremptorily classify that evidence as "pretextual," which she did with respect to every production of evidence that Qualcomm had made in support of its affirmative defense. Judge Koh concluded in the exiguity of a single sentence that the anticompetitive harm from Qualcomm's alleged conduct was so great that *nothing* that Qualcomm could produce as evidence would suffice to carry its burden of persuasion on the existence of a procompetitive rationale. In practical effect, Judge Koh announced her own novel rule of *per se* illegality.

In Part VII, I explain that Judge Koh did not perform any rigorous economic analysis to determine whether the royalties that OEMs paid for an exhaustive license to Qualcomm's portfolio of cellular SEPs were "unreasonably high," as she repeatedly asserted. Professor Shapiro himself admitted in sworn trial testimony that, in the absence of proof that Qualcomm's royalty for an exhaustive license to its cellular SEPs was "unreasonably high," there could be no basis for concluding that Qualcomm's licensing practices had imposed a "tax" on rival modems that, in turn, had supposedly reduced the profit margins on, and unit sales of, those rival modems. But even if one were to assume (contrary to the evidence that Judge Koh identified) that Qualcomm's royalty for an exhaustive license to its cellular SEPs was "unreasonably high," it would still be unclear how those royalties would harm Qualcomm's rivals. Finally, even if Qualcomm's rivals were harmed, Qualcomm's conduct *still* would not violate the Sherman Act. The Supreme Court unambiguously held in *linkLine* that a firm does not have a duty to price its products so as to maintain the profit margins of its rivals.

In Part VIII, I examine why, as a matter of law, evidence of anticompetitive intent is insufficient to prove that Qualcomm's licensing practices had an anticompetitive effect. In any case to which the rule of reason applies, a plaintiff may not prove antitrust liability without independently proving an anticompetitive effect. Evidence of anticompetitive intent is not a substitute for evidence of anticompetitive effect. Judge Koh's unconvincing findings concerning Qualcomm's allegedly anticompetitive intent were predicated on (1) a slide presentation identifying antitrust litigation as a risk, (2) the expurgated version of a single slide taken from a draft strategy presentation, and (3) the existence of enforcement actions that foreign antitrust enforcement agencies had brought against Qualcomm under more invasive antitrust principles and lesser procedural safeguards than American law recognizes.

In Part IX, I analyze Judge Koh's decision to give no weight to the trial testimony of many of Qualcomm's fact witnesses or any of its expert economic witnesses. On the basis of erroneous factual predicates, Judge Koh summarily dismissed as "made-for-litigation" the trial testimony of Nokia's and Ericsson's corporate representatives and suppressed that testimony from her findings of fact and conclusions of law. She impugned the reputations of Qualcomm's witnesses and other third-party witnesses whose testimony, if credited, would have made her findings of fact and conclusions of law untenable. Although a judge in a bench trial has broad discretion in weighing evidence, Judge Koh's reasoning for completely ignoring the testimony of most of Qualcomm's witnesses was scant, unconvincing, and an immoderate exercise of discretion. Her decision to give no weight to the trial testimony of most of Qualcomm's witnesses had important practical implications, as it eliminated from the factual record (and confounded appellate review of) evidence that was critical to assessing the plausibility of the FTC's theory of harm and to evaluating Qualcomm's procompetitive rationale for its licensing practices.

In Part X, I explain that Judge Koh erroneously granted the FTC's motion for summary judgment as to whether the RAND commitment that Qualcomm made to two standard-setting organizations, the TIA and ATIS, created for Qualcomm a contractual duty to offer an exhaustive license to its cellular SEPs to rival modem manufacturers. The evidence that Judge Koh identified indicates that, at the very least, the parties had a genuine dispute of material fact regarding the proper interpretation of those two contracts, such that the issue was not suitable for judgment as a matter of law and instead should have proceeded to trial.

In Part XI, I examine Judge Koh's conclusion that Qualcomm had a monopoly in the CDMA modem market and in the "premium" LTE modem market. Judge Koh did not correctly define the relevant product markets and did not accurately assess Qualcomm's market power in those markets. She ignored, among other things, that, to maintain its market position, Qualcomm continuously needed to make significant investments in research and development (R&D). Judge Koh herself found that Qualcomm needed to offer significant price discounts on modems to win contracts with OEMs, including Apple, to supply them with modems. Those practices were consistent with the characteristics of a "design win" market that was contestable—not a market over which a monopolist exerted what Judge Koh believed to be a stranglehold.

In Part XII, I analyze Judge Koh's conclusion that Qualcomm engaged in anticompetitive conduct. Some of Qualcomm's challenged practices could not possibly have constituted unlawful behavior, even if for sake of argument one were to accept Judge Koh's findings of fact at face value. For example, Qualcomm's alleged use of its monopoly power in the asserted product markets for CDMA modems and "premium" LTE modems to cause OEMs to pay supposedly "unreasonably high" royalties for exhaustive licenses to Qualcomm's cellular SEPs is not even actionable conduct under the Sherman Act. The Supreme Court has made clear that the Sherman Act does not condemn a monopolist merely for charging high prices.[302] Other challenged practices, such as a monopolist's refusal to deal with a competitor, could theoretically violate the Sherman Act in exceptional circumstances. Yet, Judge Koh's conclusion that Qualcomm had an antitrust duty to offer an exhaustive license to its cellular SEPs to rival modem manufacturers lacked any support in either the facts of the case or the Supreme Court's antitrust jurisprudence. During oral argument before the Ninth Circuit, the FTC's outside counsel represented to the court that the FTC had never made any argument predicated solely on the supposed authority of *Aspen Skiing*.

In Part XIII, I evaluate Judge Koh's conclusion that Qualcomm engaged in anticompetitive exclusive dealing when giving Apple price discounts in the form of certain loyalty payments. Under Supreme Court precedent, an exclusive dealing agreement might be unlawful if it harmed competition.

---

[302] Verizon Commc'ns Inc. v. Law Offices of Curtis V. Trinko, LLP, 540 U.S. 398, 407 (2004) (citing United States v. Grinnell Corp., 384 U.S. 563, 570–71 (1966)).

Yet, Judge Koh never determined what portion of the market Qualcomm's allegedly exclusive agreements with Apple affected. Consequently, she had no factual basis for determining whether those agreements were even capable of harming the competitive process.

In Part XIV, I examine Judge Koh's finding that Qualcomm harmed competition by diminishing investment in R&D by rival modem manufacturers. That finding ignored substantial evidence that Qualcomm's R&D investment was much more productive than the R&D investment of rival modem manufacturers, including Intel.

In Part XV, I examine the ways in which Judge Koh misunderstood the economic causes and consequences of "exit." In particular, she did not identify and analyze whether testimony by OEMs and rival modem manufacturers concerning "exit" connoted the transfer of productive assets to their highest-value use within the industry (an economic principle that I call *transcendent* exit), rather than the extinguishment of those assets and their removal from the industry (an economic principle that I call *existential* exit). Trial testimony given by Intel's chief strategy officer indicated that Intel's testimony about "exit" was not reliable. That testimony incorrectly predicted that Intel's dynamic capabilities and productive assets would cease to exist in the event of Intel's "exit" from the modem industry, and that Intel's investment in 5G would vanish. Neither of those predictions eventuated when Intel "exited" the business of selling modems to Apple in July 2019, two months after Judge Koh issued her findings of fact and conclusions of law in *FTC v. Qualcomm*. Instead, Apple *entered* the modem industry by virtue of its acquisition of Intel's modem business.

In Part XVI, I explain that each of Judge Koh's findings that led her to conclude, ominously, that Qualcomm's challenged practices "'tend[] to destroy competition itself'"[303] rested solely on *a priori* conjectures that found no support in the factual record that she described in her findings of fact and conclusions of law. Judge Koh rejected the proposition that the FTC bore the burden of production and the burden of persuasion to prove a reasonably proximate causal nexus between Qualcomm's supposedly anticompetitive acts and the supposed harm that its rivals experienced. She did not examine the information necessary to determine whether any empirical evidence supported the FTC's theoretical conjecture that Qualcomm's practices had harmed competition, a conjecture that she was willing to accept as true solely on *a priori* grounds. Judge Koh disregarded preponderant evidence establishing the superiority of Qualcomm's modems and relied instead on the lamentations of rival modem manufacturers to conclude that Qualcomm's acts "promoted" the "exit" of certain rivals from the industry or produced

---

[303] *FTC v. Qualcomm*, 411 F. Supp. 3d at 803 (alteration in original) (quoting Spectrum Sports, Inc. v. McQuillan, 506 U.S. 447, 458 (1993)).

some other anticompetitive effect. In particular, the trial testimony of Intel's chief strategy officer and the trial testimony of a partner at Bain & Company (Intel's management consultant) provided substantial evidence that the inferior business acumen of Intel's modem business proximately caused its failure, as of March 2018, ever to have been profitable. Yet, without disaggregating the causal significance of Intel's apparently inferior business acumen from the supposed effect of Qualcomm's allegedly anticompetitive conduct, Judge Koh summarily imputed to Qualcomm responsibility for Intel's poor performance. Her findings of fact and conclusions of law exemplified the competitor-protection view of antitrust law—and, in its extreme form, unveiled an "Intel-welfare" standard—rather than the consumer-welfare standard that modern antitrust law considers its guiding principle. Judge Koh condemned Qualcomm's lawful right to modify its business model as economic circumstances dictated.

In Part XVII, I examine Judge Koh's finding of fact that Qualcomm killed the WiMAX standard, which she treated as an independent factual basis for finding that Qualcomm had violated the Sherman Act. Judge Koh's analysis of this issue consisted of only 425 words and was not a remotely plausible finding of fact or conclusion of law.

In Part XVIII, I explain how Judge Koh lowered the evidentiary bar in a manner that would help the FTC prove its case. She found that some (ill-defined) *combination* of Qualcomm's individually lawful practices had an anticompetitive effect in her relevant product markets and was therefore unlawful. Interpreting a 1992 decision by the Ninth Circuit in a price-squeeze case, Judge Koh reasoned that it was relevant to her conclusion of law to examine Qualcomm's allegedly anticompetitive practices on a collective basis. That reasoning contradicted the Supreme Court's 2009 decision in *linkLine*, which specified that, if no practice individually violates the Sherman Act, then a court cannot "alchemize" from some combination of lawful practices a novel violation of antitrust law. Judge Koh's theory of combinatorial liability rested on the totality-of-the-circumstances test, which jurists have decried as an evidentiary crutch, and which, as applied to *FTC v. Qualcomm*, was unconstitutionally vague as a matter of due process because the test so magnified Judge Koh's discretion as to make the Sherman Act's command opaque.

In Part XIX, I explain that Judge Koh's conclusion that Qualcomm coerced Apple and other large OEMs in their purchases of modems and their exhaustive licensing of Qualcomm's portfolio of cellular SEPs strains credulity when one considers the existence of the market for corporate control that exists for Qualcomm, a publicly traded firm. The market for corporate control constrains the ability of a publicly traded supplier to exercise monopoly power over a customer. The customer can mitigate such harm through the unsolicited acquisition of enough voting equity in the supplier to realign the incentives of the supplier's management with the customer's interests. If the harm to competition that the FTC alleged and Judge Koh found had been genuinely palpable, Apple and other OEMs could have swiftly acquired voting control of Qualcomm and ended its alleged exploitation of monopoly power. Those sophisticated companies, with enormous market capitalization and access to funds, did not so do. The most plausible inference to draw from that absence of mitigation is obvious.

In Part XX, I examine whether Judge Koh's issuance of a permanent, worldwide injunction was clearly erroneous because she applied the wrong legal test. I next ask whether it was a wise exercise of discretion for Judge Koh to have excluded post-discovery evidence of the diminution of Qualcomm's alleged market power and, following her bench trial, to have declined to hold a separate evidentiary hearing on the economic effects of the FTC's requested permanent, worldwide injunction before issuing her own.

I. The Political Economy of *FTC v. Qualcomm*

Before examining Judge Koh's findings of fact and conclusions of law in *FTC v. Qualcomm*, it is worth pausing to ask how the FTC's complaint came to be. Why was the FTC investigating Qualcomm? Why was the FTC not investigating one or more of Qualcomm's detractors for possible violations of the Sherman Act? Those questions potentially became answerable when certain court records were publicly docketed in *FTC v. Qualcomm* and in subsequent, related cases.

One source of public records was the case that Apple initiated against Qualcomm three days after the FTC filed its complaint in *FTC v. Qualcomm*. Apple's wide-ranging complaint, filed in the U.S. District Court for the Southern District of California, sought (among other remedies) damages for breach of contract, a declaratory judgment that Apple had not infringed certain of Qualcomm's patents (or, in the alternative, a declaratory judgment of a FRAND royalty for those patents), and various forms of injunctive relief relating to Qualcomm's alleged monopolization and other matters.[304] Apple explained on January 20, 2017 in *Apple v. Qualcomm* what had motivated it to file its complaint:

> Apple is bringing this Complaint now, in light of the FTC filing a lawsuit against Qualcomm on January 17, 2017, because Apple is identified as a key purchaser of Qualcomm chipsets in the FTC complaint, and Qualcomm

---

[304] Redacted Complaint for Damages, Declaratory Judgment and Injunctive Relief at 95–97, Apple Inc. v. Qualcomm Inc., No. 3:17-cv-00108-GPC (S.D. Cal. Jan. 20, 2017); *accord* Redacted First Amended Complaint for Damages, Declaratory Judgment and Injunctive Relief at 156–58, Apple Inc. v. Qualcomm Inc., No. 3:17-cv-00108-GPC (S.D. Cal. June 20, 2017).

has demonstrated its willingness to retaliate swiftly against Apple when it believes agency or other actions are contrary to its interests.[305]

Many other complaints (filed by Apple, Qualcomm, and other parties) followed in various fora in the United States.

By 2018, Qualcomm and Apple had become involved in such a complex concatenation of legal disputes that Judge Dana Sabraw of the U.S. District Court for the Southern District of California commented in a pretrial order: "This case is but a single wave in a tsunami of litigation between the parties over alleged patent infringement and antitrust violations."[306] Within the United States, those disputes included two patent-infringement investigations at the U.S. International Trade Commission (ITC) initiated by Qualcomm,[307] seven private litigations in federal or state courts in California initiated by or against Apple or Qualcomm or other third parties,[308] and the Federal Trade Commission's monopolization case against Qualcomm before Judge Koh.[309] Although a complete analysis of Qualcomm's dispute with Apple exceeds the scope of this article, some of the public records in those cases shed light on the origin of the FTC's case against Qualcomm.

A. Did Apple Seek to Devalue Qualcomm?

Did Apple induce the FTC to investigate Qualcomm? Did Apple, acting alone or in concert with others, seek to devalue Qualcomm and its intellectual property? Judge Koh did not address those questions. Other federal judges came closer to answering those questions.

---

[305] Redacted Complaint for Damages, Declaratory Judgment and Injunctive Relief ¶ 221, at 57, Apple Inc. v. Qualcomm Inc., No. 3:17-cv-00108-GPC (S.D. Cal. Jan. 20, 2017); *accord* Redacted First Amended Complaint for Damages, Declaratory Judgment and Injunctive Relief ¶ 260, at 73, Apple Inc. v. Qualcomm Inc., No. 3:17-cv-00108-GPC (S.D. Cal. June 20, 2017).

[306] Order Granting Qualcomm's Motion to Sever at 1, Qualcomm Inc. v. Apple Inc., No. 3:17-cv-01375 (S.D. Cal. Mar. 2, 2018).

[307] *See* Complaint, Certain Mobile Electronic Devices and Radio Frequency and Processing Components Thereof, Inv. No. 337-TA-1065 (USITC July 7, 2017); Complaint, Certain Mobile Electronic Devices and Radio Frequency and Processing Components Thereof (II), Inv. No. 337-TA-1093 (USITC Nov. 30, 2017).

[308] *See* Redacted Complaint for Damages, Declaratory Judgement and Injunctive Relief, Apple Inc. v. Qualcomm Inc., No. 3:17-cv-00108-GPC (S.D. Cal. Jan. 20, 2017); Complaint for Patent Infringement, Qualcomm Inc. v. Apple Inc., No. 3:17-cv-01375 (S.D. Cal. July 6, 2017); Plaintiffs' Consolidated Class Action Complaint and Demand for Jury Trial, *In re* Qualcomm Antitrust Litig., No. 5:17-md-02773 (N.D. Cal. July 11, 2017); Complaint for Breach of Contract, Qualcomm Inc. v. Apple Inc., No. 37-2017-00041389 (Cal. Super. Ct. Oct. 31, 2017); Complaint for Patent Infringement, Qualcomm Inc. v. Apple Inc., No. 3:17-cv-02398 (S.D. Cal. Nov. 29, 2017); Complaint for Patent Infringement, Qualcomm Inc. v. Apple Inc., No. 3:17-cv-02402 (S.D. Cal. Nov. 29, 2017); Complaint for Patent Infringement, Qualcomm Inc. v. Apple Inc., No. 3:17-cv-02403 (S.D. Cal. Nov. 29, 2017).

[309] *See* FTC Complaint, 2017 WL 242848, *supra* note 28; Order Reassigning Case, FTC v. Qualcomm Inc., No. 5:17-cv-00220-HRL (N.D. Cal. Jan. 26, 2017).

*1. Judge Curiel's Ruling That It Was a Triable Question of Fact for the Jury
Whether Apple Induced the FTC's Informal Investigation of Qualcomm*

In his order denying Apple's motion for summary judgment in a separate lawsuit that Qualcomm filed against Apple, *In re Qualcomm Litigation*, Judge Gonzalo P. Curiel of the U.S. District Court for the Southern District of California reported the following facts on March 12, 2019 concerning Apple's efforts to "educate" the FTC:

> It is undisputed that the FTC initiated an informal investigation of Qualcomm in September of 2014 . . . , and as part of this investigation, the FTC asked Apple to provide information about Qualcomm. . . .
>
> Qualcomm alleges that in August 2012, Apple suggested to the FTC [Redacted] that they should investigate Qualcomm's licensing practices. There is no dispute that on August 9, 2012, Apple met with the FTC [Redacted] "to educate" [Redacted] "on the scope and value of a cellular standard" within iPhones. Apple's goal was to "have the FTC [Redacted] influence the industry in the way it computes royalties for standard essential patents." Apple stated at the meeting "that royalty payment should not be based on the sale price of the device." Moreover, Apple stated that "some chipset suppliers (e.g. Qualcomm) seek royalties even when purchasing the supplier's chipset."
>
> According to the SEC Form 10-K that Qualcomm filed on September 17, 2014, the FTC had notified Qualcomm that the agency was conducting an investigation of Qualcomm relating to Section 5 of the Federal Trade Commission Act. The FTC notified Qualcomm that it was investigating conduct under antitrust and unfair competition laws related to standard essential patents, pricing, and contract prices with respect to baseband processors and related products.
>
> On October 27, 2014, the FTC emailed Apple "as part of [its] non-public investigation to determine whether" Qualcomm has engaged in unfair methods of competition "through licensing practices related to cellular chipset patents, including potential breach of any FRAND commitments." The FTC asked Apple to discuss "[Redacted][.]" On November 6, 2014, the FTC emailed Apple, reaffirming that the FTC is conducting an investigation to determine whether Qualcomm is violating the FTCA "[Redacted]." The FTC asked Apple to submit any request, proposal, or agreement with Qualcomm "[Redacted][.]" Apple responded to the FTC's requests on November 18, 2014. Apple asserted that Qualcomm charges for its chipsets and its patents, including those patents allegedly embodied in its chipset. Apple also asserted that Qualcomm [Redacted], and that Qualcomm seeks to avoid its FRAND commitments by mixing SEPs and non-SEPs.
>
> In a complaint filed in the Northern District of California on January 17, 2017, the FTC sought injunctive relief, claimed that Qualcomm has unlawfully maintained a monopoly in baseband processors, alleged that Qualcomm has

a "no license-no chips policy," and that Qualcomm had violated its FRAND commitments. The FTC referenced some of Qualcomm's negotiations and agreements with Apple.[310]

Following that lengthy recitation of facts and allegations, Judge Curiel concluded:

> [D]rawing all inferences from the evidence in favor of Qualcomm, the trier of fact could reasonably infer that Apple induced the investigation based upon the information disclosed by Apple in 2012 and the scope of the FTC investigation. In the meeting, Apple [Redacted]. *Apple's specific goal was to have the FTC influence the way the industry computes royalties for SEPs. In other words, Apple intended for the FTC to investigate Qualcomm's licensing practices, and the FTC did in fact do that.* The FTC's investigation was to determine whether Qualcomm violated the FTC Act through its licensing practices related to cellular chipset patents, which was the topic Apple raised to the FTC. Moreover, the FTC asked Apple to [Redacted]. A trier of fact could find that the scope of this investigation was correlated to Apple's 2012 proffer to the FTC. . . .
>
> [I]t was not unreasonable for the FTC to take time to perform its due diligence before launching an investigation into a company as large as Qualcomm, especially given the highly technical patent licensing issues with multi-billion dollar implications. After the meeting, Apple [Redacted][.] [Redacted][.][311]

Judge Curiel found as follows with respect to Qualcomm's claim that Apple's 2012 meetings induced the FTC to investigate Qualcomm: "The Court finds that Qualcomm has created a genuine dispute of material fact that Apple's 2012 actions induced the FTC informal investigation."[312]

2. *Common Interest Agreements Involving Apple, Intel, and the FTC*

Long before Judge Koh presided over the bench trial in *FTC v. Qualcomm*, it had become publicly known through court filings that Apple had entered into a common interest agreement with the FTC.[313] Pursuant to a common

---

[310] Order on Apple's Motion for Summary Judgment at 8–9, *In re* Qualcomm Litig., No. 3:17-cv-00108-GPC (S.D. Cal. Mar. 12, 2019), ECF No. 1029 (citations omitted) (quoting numerous motions and exhibits) [hereinafter Order on Apple's Motion for Summary Judgment].

[311] *Id.* at 11–12 (emphasis added). The *Financial Times* reported in December 2019 that Apple had urged the European Commission to take actions against "patent abuses" concerning the licensing of SEPs for use in telematics control units (TCUs) in automobiles. *See* Javier Espinoza & Tim Bradshaw, *Apple, Cisco, Daimler and BMW Complain to Brussels Over Patents*, Fin. Times, Dec. 17, 2019.

[312] Order on Apple's Motion for Summary Judgment, *supra* note 310, at 12.

[313] *See* Transcript of Official Electronic Sound Recording of Proceedings at 26:17–27:7, FTC v. Qualcomm Inc., No. 5:17-cv-00220-LHK (N.D. Cal. Aug. 31, 2017) ("[Qualcomm's lawyer Gary] Bornstein: . . . Apple is not a traditional third party. And Your Honor [Magistrate Judge Nathanael Cousins] made the point, or at least raised the question about how that matters. . . . Apple has been not only a complainant at the FTC,

interest agreement, "[i]f two or more clients with a common interest in a litigated or nonlitigated matter are represented by separate lawyers and they agree to exchange information concerning the matter, a communication of any such client that otherwise qualifies as privileged . . . that relates to the matter is privileged as against third persons."[314] Parties to such an agreement can coordinate their litigation strategies while benefiting from the same privileged communications that clients share with their attorneys.[315] According to Magistrate Judge Nathanael Cousins, to whom Judge Koh had delegated the task of presiding over a hearing on August 31, 2017 that concerned a discovery dispute in *FTC v. Qualcomm*:

> There could be an argument that because of the FTC proceeding, that in some ways [the] FTC is standing in the shoes or is fighting Apple's fight on its behalf, and that maybe that should be different from a usual case, and that Qualcomm therefore shouldn't be as reasonable as it might be in some case where Apple had absolutely no interest in the proceedings and was an innocent third party or uninvolved third party. *Here, Apple is not an uninvolved, uninterested third party, but has a strong commercial interest in the proceeding.*[316]

---

but as you see in the papers, Apple has a common interest agreement now with the FTC, and has a . . . common interest agreement with the consumer [class action] plaintiffs. They have linked arms and they're litigating hand in hand against Qualcomm. And so to plead . . . complete innocence and third party I think is not a fair reflection of the state of affairs.").

[314] Restatement (Third) of the Law Governing Lawyers § 76 (Am. Law Inst. 2000); *see also* United States v. BDO Seidman, LLP, 492 F.3d 806, 815–16 (7th Cir. 2007) ("Although occasionally termed a privilege itself, the common interest doctrine is really an exception to the rule that no privilege attaches to communications between a client and an attorney in the presence of a third person. In effect, the common interest doctrine extends the attorney-client privilege to otherwise non-confidential communications in limited circumstances. For that reason, the common interest doctrine only will apply where the parties undertake a joint effort with respect to a common legal interest, and the doctrine is limited strictly to those communications made to further an ongoing enterprise.") (citing Robinson v. Texas Auto. Dealers Ass'n, 214 F.R.D. 432, 443 (E.D. Tex. 2003); United States v. Evans, 113 F.3d 1457, 1467 (7th Cir. 1997)); *In re* Pacific Pictures Corp., 679 F.3d 1121, 1129 (9th Cir. 2012) ("Rather than a separate privilege, the 'common interest' or 'joint defense' rule is an exception to ordinary waiver rules designed to allow attorneys for different clients pursuing a common legal strategy to communicate with each other. However, a shared desire to see the same outcome in a legal matter is insufficient to bring a communication between two parties within this exception. Instead, the parties must make the communication in pursuit of a joint strategy in accordance with some form of agreement—whether written or unwritten.") (citations omitted).

[315] Restatement (Third) of the Law Governing Lawyers § 76 (Am. Law Inst. 2000); *see also* 1 Paul R. Rice, Attorney-Client Privilege in the United States § 4:35 (Thomson Reuters 2012) (stating that parties to a common interest agreement "may communicate among themselves and with [their] separate attorneys on matters of common legal interest, for the purpose of preparing a joint strategy, and the attorney-client privilege will protect those communications to the same extent as it would communications between each client and his own attorney") (footnotes omitted); Irving Scher & Scott Martin, 1 Antitrust Adviser § 4:34 (Thomson Reuters 5th ed. 2017) ("Courts generally recognize the common interest doctrine for otherwise privileged materials in situations where parties (1) have a common legal interest and (2) exchange information pursuant to that common legal interest. In other words, (1) the communications must be made in the course of a joint defense, and (2) the communications must be made to further that joint defense effort. *The common interests must be legal, rather than commercial.*") (emphasis added) (footnotes omitted).

[316] Transcript of Official Electronic Sound Recording of Proceedings at 13:10–18, FTC v. Qualcomm Inc., No. 5:17-cv-00220-LHK (N.D. Cal. Aug. 31, 2017) (emphasis added).

It had likewise become publicly known long before Judge Koh's bench trial in *FTC v. Qualcomm* began that Intel (Qualcomm's principal rival in supplying modems to Apple) had entered into a common interest agreement with Apple.[317] Qualcomm argued that "Intel is anything but a disinterested third party [in *FTC v. Qualcomm*]. *Intel actively challenged Qualcomm's conduct in these actions, submitting advocacy materials to the FTC* and an *amicus curiae* brief to the Court."[318]

---

[317] Defendant Qualcomm Incorporated's and Non-Party Intel Corp.'s Joint Discovery Statement at 3, FTC v. Qualcomm Inc., No. 5:17-cv-00220-LHK (N.D. Cal. Jan. 30, 2018) ("Intel has a common interest agreement with Apple, and Apple has a common interest agreement with the FTC."). Notably, Wilmer Cutler Pickering Hale and Dorr LLP (WilmerHale) jointly represented *both* Apple and Intel in the 1065 Investigation before the U.S. International Trade Commission (ITC), which Qualcomm filed against Apple. *See* Open Sessions Hearing Transcript at 9:5–9, Certain Mobile Electronic Devices and Radio Frequency and Processing Components Thereof, Inv. No. 337-TA-1065 (USITC June 15, 2018) ("I am Bill Lee from Wilmer Hale, and with me at counsel table are Ruffin Cordell, Nina Tallon and Joe Mueller. With us in the courtroom from Apple are Noreen Krall and Ryan Moran, and with us from Intel are Ben Ostapuck and Kim Schmidt."). Qualcomm filed its complaint in the 1065 Investigation on July 7, 2017, slightly less than six months after the FTC had filed its complaint in *FTC v. Qualcomm*. *See* FTC Complaint, 2017 WL 242848, *supra* note 28; Complaint, Certain Mobile Electronic Devices and Radio Frequency and Processing Components Thereof, Inv. No. 337-TA-1065 (USITC July 7, 2017). The 1065 Investigation went to hearing before an administrative law judge (ALJ) on June 18, 2018, before Judge Koh's bench trial in *FTC v. Qualcomm* commenced on January 4, 2019. *See* Open Sessions Hearing Transcript (Revised & Corrected), Certain Mobile Electronic Devices and Radio Frequency and Processing Components Thereof, Inv. No. 337-TA-1065 (USITC June 18, 2018); Transcript of Proceedings (Volume 1), FTC v. Qualcomm Inc., No. 5:17-cv-00220-LHK (N.D. Cal. Jan. 4, 2019). In the 1065 Investigation, Mr. Lee of WilmerHale referred to his clients as "Apple/Intel." Open Sessions Hearing Transcript at 74:16, Certain Mobile Electronic Devices and Radio Frequency and Processing Components Thereof, Inv. No. 337-TA-1065 (USITC June 15, 2018).

As of the date of trial in *FTC v. Qualcomm*, Apple had been a longstanding client of WilmerHale, and of Bill Lee in particular, on patent litigation. *See, e.g.*, Jenna Greene, *Litigation Leaders: Wilmer's Howard Shapiro on 'Classic Trial Lawyering,' Suing the Government and Lateral All-Stars* 2, Am. Lawyer, May 14, 2019, https://www.wilmerhale.com/-/media/d66ef47cd9084566bffc6cc69bce9931.pdf ("I'd also have to point to our final victory in the patent war between Apple and Samsung. In May 2018, a jury ordered Samsung to pay Apple $539 million for infringing on its patents, and in June the parties settled, bringing an end to the long-running litigation, which was a major accomplishment for our team. The case began in 2010 and we did six trials and 14 appeals, all the way through the U.S. Supreme Court. In Apple-Samsung, our team, led by Bill Lee, litigated 59 cases in 14 countries.") (boldface suppressed) (quoting Howard Shapiro, Chair of WilmerHale's litigation practice).

WilmerHale also provided joint representation of both Apple and Intel again in the 1093 Investigation before the ITC, which Qualcomm filed against Apple. *See* Notice of Limited Appearance on Behalf of Non-Party Intel Corporation, Certain Mobile Electronic Devices and Radio Frequency and Processing Components Thereof (II), Inv. No. 337-TA-1093 (USITC Mar. 12, 2018); Open Sessions Hearing Transcript (Revised and Corrected) at 22:11–17, Certain Mobile Electronic Devices and Radio Frequency and Processing Components Thereof (II), Inv. No. 337-TA-1093 (USITC Sept. 17, 2018) ("Judge McNamara[.] Okay, very good. Thank you, Mr. Nelson. Mr. Lee[.] It's also fine from our side, Your Honor. Judge McNamara[.] Very good, Mr. Lee. Thank you. I really appreciate that. How about Intel? Mr. Lee[.] Fine as well, Your Honor."). Again, Qualcomm filed its complaint in the 1093 Investigation on November 30, 2017, 10 months after the FTC had filed its complaint in *FTC v. Qualcomm*. *See* Complaint, Certain Mobile Electronic Devices and Radio Frequency and Processing Components Thereof, Inv. No. 337-TA-1093 (USITC Nov. 30, 2017). The 1093 Investigation went to hearing before an ALJ on September 17, 2018, before Judge Koh's bench trial in *FTC v. Qualcomm* began. *See* Open Sessions Hearing Transcript (Revised and Corrected), Certain Mobile Electronic Devices and Radio Frequency and Processing Components Thereof (II), Inv. No. 337-TA-1093 (USITC Sept. 17, 2018).

[318] Defendant Qualcomm Incorporated's and Non-Party Intel Corp.'s Joint Discovery Statement at 3, FTC v. Qualcomm Inc., No. 5:17-cv-00220-LHK (N.D. Cal. Jan. 30, 2018) (emphasis added); *see also id.* ("Intel has argued to this Court that it is 'Qualcomm's only remaining competitor in the premium LTE chipset market' and that 'any harm to Intel's premium chipset business will have profound anticompet-

3.   *Did Apple Business Records Disclosed in Litigation Reveal a Strategy to Devalue Qualcomm's SEPs?*

On April 16, 2019, Qualcomm displayed various records apparently created by Apple to a San Diego jury during Qualcomm's opening statement in its trial against Apple before Judge Curiel, and those records comported with Judge Curiel's observations in his order denying Apple's motion summary judgment, decided a month earlier.[319] By coincidence—or perhaps not—Judge Curiel's jury trial ended immediately following the lawyers' opening statements, when Apple's settlement with Qualcomm was announced.[320] That settlement produced for Qualcomm the third in a triumvirate of commercial agreements with Apple, Huawei, and Samsung, which as of 2019 were the world's three largest smartphone OEMs.[321]

On April 16, 2019, Qualcomm's stock price rose 23 percent (or $15.8 billion) relative to its level immediately before announcement of the settlement between Apple and Qualcomm;[322] the stock rose a total of nearly 40 percent (or $27.3 billion) over three trading days.[323] (By comparison, about one month

---

itive effects on the market as a whole.' Qualcomm should be able to explore these allegations with each of the Intel Deponents. Intel is cooperating with the other parties, and limiting deposition length will prejudice Qualcomm.") (quoting Non-Party Intel Corporation's Motion and Memorandum of Points and Authorities in Support of Its Motion for Entry of Supplemental Protective Order at 7, FTC v. Qualcomm Inc., No. 5:17-cv-00220-LHK (N.D. Cal. May 23, 2017), ECF No. 110).

[319]   *See* Qualcomm—Opening Statement, *In re* Qualcomm Litig. at 12, No. 3:17-cv-0108-GPC (S.D. Cal. Apr. 16, 2019) [hereinafter Qualcomm Opening Statement in *In re Qualcomm*]. Although a number of these records were marked "Apple Proprietary & Confidential" and "Apple Highly Confidential—Attorneys' Eyes Only," they nonetheless entered the public domain by their having been included in the publicly available slide deck accompanying Qualcomm's opening statement, which was recorded in the trial transcript. *See* Transcript of Jury Trial (Volume 2) at 300:24–349:19, *In re* Qualcomm Litig., No. 17-cv-0108-GPC (S.D. Cal. Apr. 16, 2019) (Curiel, J.).

[320]   *See* Transcript of Jury Trial (Volume 2) at 352:22–353:10, *In re* Qualcomm Litig., No. 17-cv-0108-GPC (S.D. Cal. Apr. 16, 2019) (Curiel, J.).

[321]   *See* Press Release, Apple Inc., Qualcomm and Apple Agree to Drop All Litigation (Apr. 16, 2019), https://www.apple.com/newsroom/2019/04/qualcomm-and-apple-agree-to-drop-all-litigation/; Qualcomm Inc., Quarterly Report for the Quarterly Period Ended March 31, 2019 (SEC Form 10-Q), at 35 (filed May 1, 2019) ("QTL revenues in the second quarter of fiscal 2019 included $150 million of royalties due under an interim agreement with Huawei. This represents a minimum, non-refundable amount for royalties due for the second quarter of fiscal 2019 by Huawei while negotiations continue. This payment does not reflect the full amount of royalties due under the underlying license agreement."); Qualcomm Inc., Quarterly Report for the Quarterly Period Ended June 28, 2020 (SEC Form 10-Q), at 21 (filed July 29, 2020) ("In July 2020, [Qualcomm] entered into a settlement agreement with Huawei to resolve our prior dispute related to our license agreement that expired on December 31, 2019. [Qualcomm] also entered into a new long-term, global patent license agreement, including a cross license granting back rights to certain of Huawei's patents, covering sales beginning January 1, 2020."); Press Release, Qualcomm Inc., Qualcomm and Samsung Amend Long-Term Cross-License Agreement (Jan. 31, 2018), https://www.qualcomm.com/news/releases/2018/01/31/qualcomm-and-samsung-amend-long-term-cross-license-agreement.

[322]   Ian King & Mark Gurman, *Apple, Qualcomm Reach Courthouse-Steps Settlement to Suits*, BLOOMBERG, Apr. 16, 2019. At the close of trading on April 16, 2019, Qualcomm's stock had gained $12.99 per share over its value at that day's start of trading. *See Qualcomm Incorporated*, YAHOO! FINANCE, https://finance.yahoo.com/chart/QCOM. Combined with 1,215,698,926 outstanding shares, this share-price increase resulted in a gain to shareholders of $15.8 billion. *See* Qualcomm Inc., Quarterly Report for the Quarterly Period Ended March 31, 2019 (SEC Form 10-Q), at 1 (filed May 1, 2019).

[323]   Mike Freeman, *In the End, Apple-Qualcomm Settlement Came Down to 5G*, SAN DIEGO UNION-TRIBUNE, Apr. 21, 2019 ("Since the deal was announced Tuesday, [April 16, 2019,] Qualcomm's shares have soared

later, by May 24, 2019, which was the third trading day following Judge Koh's issuance of her findings of fact and conclusions of law in *FTC v. Qualcomm*, Qualcomm's stock price had fallen nearly 15 percent (or $14 billion) relative to its level immediately before Judge Koh issued her findings of fact and conclusions of law.[324])

One Apple slide deck that Qualcomm presented in its opening statement on April 16, 2019 in Judge Curiel's jury trial, entitled "Qualcomm Royalty Reduction PoR," presumably referring to Apple's "plan of record," contained a slide, dated June 26, 2016, which stated: "Goal: Reduce Apple's Net Royalty to Qualcomm."[325] Another Apple slide, entitled "Reshaping FRAND—Licensing, Litigation & Competition Law," specified three prongs: "Devalue SEPs," "Limit Injunctions," and "Resolve Efficiently."[326] The following four bullet points appeared in the "Devalue SEPs" category:

- Base = derived from smallest priceable component (i.e., baseband)

- Rate = no higher than adjusted pro-rata share of SEPs

- Control for quality, over-declaration & royalty stacking

- Build favorable, arms-length "comp" licenses[.][327]

Four other slides appeared to describe how Apple would go about "[c]reating [e]vidence [and s]avings" pursuant to its plan of record to devalue SEPs, including, in Apple's words, to (1) "leverage our purchasing power," (2) "captur[e] IP value with purchase power," (3) "*selectively filter* this pipeline to identify the most desirable deals," and (4) "*use as evidence . . .* as a comparable in disputes with others."[328] Elsewhere in Apple's apparent plan of record, on a slide entitled "PoR—Create Leverage by Building Pressure Three Ways," three bullet points appeared:

---

nearly 40 percent."). At the close of trading on April 18, 2019, Qualcomm's stock had gained $22.43 per share over its value at the start of trading on April 16, 2019. *See Qualcomm Incorporated*, YAHOO! FINANCE, https://finance.yahoo.com/chart/QCOM. Combined with 1,215,698,926 outstanding shares, this share-price increase resulted in a gain to shareholders of $27.27 billion. *See* Qualcomm Inc., Quarterly Report for the Quarterly Period Ended March 31, 2019 (SEC Form 10-Q), at 1 (filed May 1, 2019).

[324] At the close of trading on May 24, 2019, Qualcomm's stock had fallen $11.54 per share below its value at the close of business on May 21, 2019. *See Qualcomm Incorporated*, YAHOO! FINANCE, https://finance.yahoo.com/chart/QCOM. Combined with a reported 1,215,657,726 shares, this share-price decrease resulted in a loss of approximately $14.03 billion. *See* Quarterly Report for the Quarterly Period Ended June 30, 2019 (SEC Form 10-Q), at 1 (filed July 31, 2019).

[325] Qualcomm Opening Statement in *In re Qualcomm*, *supra* note 319, at 6 (quoting DTX09321).

[326] *Id.* at 7 (quoting DTX09313). I do not know whether the Apple slide deck was alluding to the title of an article that I published in 2015—J. Gregory Sidak, *The Antitrust Division's Devaluation of Standard-Essential Patents*, 104 GEO. L.J. ONLINE 48 (2015)—which criticized the solicitude of the Antitrust Division during the Obama administration to the policy advocacy of certain large implementers to diminish the legal protection, and hence the economic value, of SEPs.

[327] Qualcomm Opening Statement in *In re Qualcomm*, *supra* note 319, at 7 (quoting DTX09313).

[328] *Id.* at 8 (emphasis in original) (fifth alteration in original) (quoting DTX09352).

- Hurt Qualcomm Financially

- Put Qualcomm's Licensing Model at Risk

- Drive Qualcomm to engage Apple on a Level [].[329]

The same Apple slide deck specified other "Future Scenarios," including that (1) Apple's contract manufacturers might "stop[] paying royalties to Qualcomm," "[i]ndependently or triggered by Apple," (2) Apple might "sue[] Qualcomm," perhaps alleging an "antitrust violation or patent infringement," and (3) Apple might impose "[c]ommercial pressure against Qualcomm (switching to Intel[)]."[330] Apple evidently also considered a plan of "non-payment of royalties by CMs [contract manufacturers]," and noted that it would be "[b]eneficial to wait to provoke a patent fight until after the end of 2016," when certain existing contractual agreements between Apple and Qualcomm were due to "expire."[331] Apple evidently recommended that its new statement of work with Qualcomm "ensure that [its] supply commitment is not conditioned on CMs paying royalties."[332] In other words, Apple apparently sought to include—and succeeded in including—a provision in its subsequent supply agreement with Qualcomm to ensure that Qualcomm's agreement to supply modems to Apple would "apply irrespective of whether or not the Authorized Purchaser," which in this case appeared to be the licensed contract manufacturer producing iPhones for Apple, "has made or continues to make royalty payments for licensing of Qualcomm's patents."[333]

Indeed, an email from one of Apple's contract manufacturers that appeared to be dated April 27, 2017, stated that Apple had "recently formally requested [it] to stop the royalty payment to [Q]ualcomm."[334] If true, that instruction from Apple would appear on its face to have breached Apple's agreement with Qualcomm, which in relevant part specified that "Apple shall not knowingly take (or continue taking) any action against or make any demand of any Qualcomm Licensee that prevents, restricts, or discourages such Qualcomm Licensee from which it purchases Apple Devices from complying fully with the terms of such Qualcomm Licensee's QC License Agreement"[335]—except that the relevant agreement had expired at the end

---

[329] *Id.* at 12 (quoting DTX09321). A text box obscured the text following the word "Level" in Apple's third bullet point, which perhaps referred to a "Level Playing Field."

[330] *Id.* at 15 (quoting DTX09317).

[331] *Id.* at 17A (quoting DTX09317), 38 (quoting DTX09317). Apple used (and continues to use) contract manufacturers, including Pegatron and Wistron, to make its iPhones. *See* FTC v. Qualcomm Inc., 411 F. Supp. 3d 658, 724 (N.D. Cal. 2019).

[332] Qualcomm Opening Statement in *In re Qualcomm, supra* note 319, at 38 (quoting DTX09317).

[333] *Id.* at 39 (quoting JTX009).

[334] *Id.* at 4 (quoting DTX01470).

[335] *Id.* at 2 (quoting JTX007). The agreements in question were evidently the Business Cooperation and Patent Agreement (BCPA), effective as of January 1, 2013, and the First Amendment to Transition Agreement (FATA), effective as of January 1, 2013. *See id.* at 38; *FTC v. Qualcomm*, 411 F. Supp. 3d at 732.

of 2016.[336] In addition, Apple appeared to exercise corporate control over the contract manufacturers' decisions that concerned litigation. One provision of Apple's agreements with certain contract manufacturers specified that the contract manufacturer would

> not settle any such claim or allegation, or make any admissions of liability or admissions relevant to the claim or allegation (related to the Goods), or take any other action that [the contract manufacturer] knows or should reasonably know will harm Apple's position(s) with respect to the claim or allegation, without Apple's prior written permission.[337]

Perhaps Apple's observation that it would be "[b]eneficial to wait to provoke a patent fight until after the end of 2016"[338] explains why Apple waited until after the agreements expired at the end of 2016 to "formally request[]"[339] that its contract manufacturers cease paying Qualcomm royalties.

Qualcomm's litigation expenditures mounted in fiscal year 2017 (when Apple and the FTC filed their actions against Qualcomm) and exceeded half a billion dollars in fiscal year 2018 alone.[340] Figure 3 shows Qualcomm's annual litigation expenses in millions of 2019 dollars over the six years from fiscal year 2014 to fiscal year 2019. Over that period, it appears that Qualcomm spent $1.5 billion (in September 2019 dollars) on litigation costs. Presumably not all of those litigation costs concerned Qualcomm's dispute with the FTC or its constellation of disputes with Apple, but surely a large share did.

As they review *FTC v. Qualcomm*, the Ninth Circuit (should it decide to rehear the case *en banc*) and the Supreme Court might incidentally ask themselves, What if Apple's management had not devoted its attention and resources to generating PowerPoint presentations on how Apple could "Hurt Qualcomm Financially"?[341] How much more innovation might have resulted if the $554 million that Qualcomm was compelled to spend on litigation *in 2018 alone*, rather than being spent to defend a licensing model that Apple evidently had decided to put "at risk,"[342] could have been invested in R&D instead?

---

[336] Qualcomm Opening Statement in *In re Qualcomm, supra* note 319, at 38 (quoting DTX09317).
[337] *Id.* at 5 (quoting DTX01193, DTX01194, DTX01195, DTX02588).
[338] *Id.* at 17A (quoting DTX09317), 38 (quoting DTX09317).
[339] *Id.* at 4 (quoting DTX01470).
[340] *See supra* note 297.
[341] Qualcomm Opening Statement in *In re Qualcomm, supra* note 319, at 12 (quoting DTX09321).
[342] *Id.* The $544 million in 2018 is equivalent to $563.5 million in 2019 dollars, as Figure 3 shows.

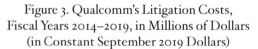

Figure 3. Qualcomm's Litigation Costs,
Fiscal Years 2014–2019, in Millions of Dollars
(in Constant September 2019 Dollars)

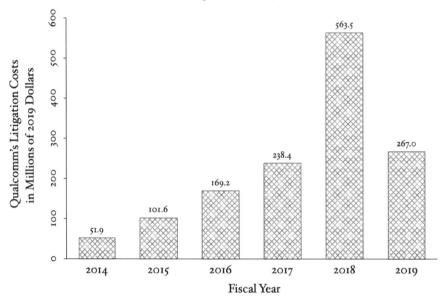

Sources: 2019 Qualcomm 10-K, *supra* note 10, at 45 ("$287 million in lower professional fees and costs, primarily driven by Broadcom's withdrawn takeover proposal in fiscal 2018 and our then proposed acquisition of NXP Semiconductors N.V. (NXP) in fiscal 2018"); *id.* ("$325 million in higher litigation costs, with total litigation costs of $554 million and $229 million in fiscal 2018 and fiscal 2017, respectively"); Qualcomm Inc., Annual Report for the Fiscal Year Ended September 24, 2017 (SEC Form 10-K), at 42 (filed Nov. 1, 2017) [hereinafter 2017 Qualcomm 10-K] ("The dollar increase in selling, general and administrative expenses in fiscal 2017 was primarily attributable to increases of $136 million in professional services fees, primarily related to third-party acquisition and integration services resulting from the proposed acquisition of NXP, $70 million in costs related to litigation and other legal matters and $33 million in employee-related expenses, primarily related to our recently formed RF360 Holdings joint venture, which closed in February 2017. The dollar increase in selling, general and administrative expenses in fiscal 2016 was primarily attributable to increases of $65 million in costs related to litigation and other legal matters, $39 million in employee-related expenses and $27 million in depreciation and amortization expense."); Qualcomm Inc., Annual Report for the Fiscal Year Ended September 27, 2015 (SEC Form 10-K), at 39 (filed Nov. 4, 2015) [hereinafter 2015 Qualcomm 10-K] ("The dollar increase in selling, general and administrative expenses in fiscal 2015 was primarily attributable to increases of $73 million in selling and marketing expenses and $46 million in costs related to litigation and other legal matters.").

Notes: Qualcomm's litigation costs during fiscal year 2019 can be calculated by: $554 M – $287 M = $267 M. Qualcomm's litigation costs during fiscal year 2016 can be calculated by: $229 M – $70 M = $159 M. Qualcomm's litigation costs during fiscal year 2015 can be calculated by: $159 M – $65 M = $94 M. Qualcomm's litigation costs during fiscal year 2014 can be calculated by: $94 M – $46 M = $48 M. I express Qualcomm's litigation costs in September 2019 U.S. dollars because Qualcomm specified in its annual reports that each fiscal year between 2013 and 2019 ended in September. I adjust amounts for years other than 2019 on the basis of the Historical Consumer Price Index for All Urban Consumers (CPI-U), which is provided by the Bureau of Labor Statistics (BLS). *CPI for All Urban Consumers (CPI-U): All Items in U.S. City Average, All Urban Consumers, Seasonally Adjusted*, Bureau of Labor Statistics (2020), https://beta.bls.gov/dataViewer/view/timeseries/CUSR0000SA0.

4. *Litigation by Qualcomm Alleging That Apple Misappropriated Qualcomm's Technology to Help Establish Intel as a Second Supplier of Modems to Apple*

In yet another case, filed in California state court by Quinn Emanuel, Jones Day, and Cravath, Swaine & Moore on behalf of Qualcomm against Apple on November 1, 2017, Qualcomm alleged:

> Apple long ago devised a plan to improve the performance of non-Qualcomm chipset solutions, including Intel's, by stealing Qualcomm's technology and using it to establish a second source of chipsets in order to pressure Qualcomm in business negotiations over chipset supply and pricing, and ultimately to divert Qualcomm's Apple-based business to Intel, from which Apple could extract more favorable terms.[343]

Qualcomm further contended in its first amended complaint:

> Apple developed and carried out an intricate plan, beginning at least several years [before September 24, 2018] and continuing through the present, to steal vast swaths of Qualcomm's confidential information and trade secrets and to use the information and technology to improve the performance of non-Qualcomm chipset solutions and, in conjunction, the performance of iPhones based on such non-Qualcomm chipset solutions.[344]

In particular, Qualcomm alleged:

> Apple engineers working to incorporate Intel chipsets into Apple devices . . . , after becoming aware of certain performance deficiencies with Intel's chipset solutions, repeatedly accessed, used, and provided to Intel engineers Qualcomm software and confidential information, including source code, for the purpose of improving the performance of Intel's chipset solutions.[345]

Qualcomm's complaint continued:

> On information and belief, this unauthorized access, use, and disclosure was independently initiated by Apple on some occasions and affirmatively requested by Intel on others, beginning at least several years ago and continuing through the present [that is, September 24, 2018]. Further, Apple engineers repeatedly used Qualcomm's software development tools and

---

[343] First Amended Complaint for Breach of Contract and Trade Secret Misappropriation (Civil Code § 3426, *et seq.*) ¶ 14, at 6, Qualcomm Inc. v. Apple Inc., No. 37-2017-00041389 (Cal. Super. Ct. Sept. 24, 2018).

[344] *Id.* ¶ 29, at 11.

[345] *Id.* ¶ 30, at 12.

related highly confidential files to open and process Qualcomm log files to provide to Intel, again for the purpose of improving Intel's chipset solutions. Intel engineers even complained to Apple engineers about being unable to open Qualcomm log files, which Apple had provided to Intel, for lack of the appropriate Qualcomm tools. In response, Apple engineers routinely used Qualcomm tools to create post-processed log files, which they then sent to Intel engineers to use in improving Intel's chipset solutions. . . .

On information and belief, Apple created and executed this scheme in part to reduce its cost of goods and increase its commercial leverage over Qualcomm, but at the cost to Qualcomm of its valuable trade secrets and Apple-based business.[346]

No mention of any of these allegations appeared in Judge Koh's findings of fact and conclusions of law in *FTC v. Qualcomm*.

Although, as noted above, Apple and Qualcomm settled all litigation between them on April 16, 2019, they did not publicly disclose whether their mutual settlement and release extended to any claims that Qualcomm might be able to assert against Intel individually.

5. *Did Apple, Acting Alone or in Concert with Competitors or Other Firms, Induce Foreign Agencies to Investigate Qualcomm?*

Judge Curiel's summary judgment order publicly discussed Qualcomm's allegations that Apple solicited foreign companies (including its largest competitor, Samsung) and foreign governments to take actions that would tend to harm Qualcomm financially. In Judge Curiel's words, Qualcomm alleged (1) that "Apple induced Samsung to suggest to the KFTC ('Korean Fair Trade Commission') that it should broaden its investigation into Qualcomm, made untrue statements to the KFTC and other government agencies about Qualcomm, and urged the KFTC to impose extraterritorial, worldwide remedies against Qualcomm,"[347] (2) that "Apple induced the Contract Manufacturers ('CMs')," which manufactured iPhones for Apple, "to reduce royalty payments to Qualcomm, interfered with audit procedures, and directed the CMs to misstate the selling price of the devices they sell to Apple,"[348] and (3) that Apple "induc[ed] governmental agencies to attack Qualcomm's business."[349] If proven to be true, these alleged acts could have

---

[346] *Id.* ¶¶ 30–31, at 12.
[347] Order on Apple's Motion for Summary Judgment, *supra* note 310, at 3.
[348] *Id.*
[349] *Id.* at 3–4; *see also* Korea Fair Trade Commission, Hearing Before Full Commission, *In re* Alleged Abuse of Market Dominance of Qualcomm Incorporated, Case No. 2015Sigam2118, Decision No. 2017-0-25 (Jan. 20, 2017), *Exhibit FF to* Apple Inc.'s Notice of Motion and Motion for Summary Judgment on BCPA Counterclaims (Counterclaims VI, VII, VIII, IX), *In re* Qualcomm Litig., No. 3:17-cv-00108-GPC (S.D. Cal. Sept. 1, 2018) [hereinafter Apple's Motion Concerning BCPA Counterclaims], ECF No. 602-37;

established certain elements of various civil or criminal violations of the laws of the United States.

The Petition Clause of the First Amendment to the Constitution provides that "Congress shall make no law . . . abridging . . . the right of the people . . . to petition the Government for a redress of grievances."[350] The *Noerr-Pennington* doctrine of course has created a long line of cases immunizing from antitrust liability someone who unilaterally exercises his First Amendment right to petition the government for a redress of grievances, including a private actor's sincere (as opposed to sham) attempt to petition government to crush its competitors, subjugate its suppliers or customers, or otherwise rid it of noxious detractors in the marketplace.[351]

The Petition Clause is one of the rare passages in the Constitution that speaks of "the Government" rather than some more specific branch or officer.[352] The Framers of the Bill of Rights specifically replaced "the Legislature" with "the Government."[353] And when they did so, they chose to refer to "*the* Government," not "*a* Government" or simply "Government." The *Noerr-Pennington* doctrine thus can properly read the Petition Clause only to immunize from antitrust liability the petitioning of "the Government" *of the United States (or of one of the states)* "for a redress of grievances"—not the petitioning of a foreign government, such as Korea, including a foreign government's antitrust enforcement agency, such as the KFTC. And certainly nothing in the *Noerr-Pennington* doctrine immunizes an American firm from antitrust liability under the Sherman Act (or any other civil or criminal statute of the United States) for harm caused to another firm by the act of making untrue statements to a foreign enforcement agency. To the sensibilities of some, Qualcomm's allegations if true might incidentally make the FTC appear more incurious and obsequious than a government enforcement agency needs to be.

This limitation on *Noerr-Pennington* immunity is significant, for the ease with which one can flagellate an American multinational corporation before a foreign antitrust authority can corrode the rule of law *within* the United States. It is tempting for American companies (or perhaps even American antitrust enforcers) to encourage foreign agencies to prosecute

---

Apple's Response to KFTC Request, Views on Qualcomm's Abuse of Dominance (Redacted Version), *Exhibit N to* Apple's Motion Concerning BCPA Counterclaims, *supra*, ECF No. 602-19.

[350] U.S. Const. amend. I.

[351] *See* Eastern R.R. Presidents Conference v. Noerr Motor Freight, Inc., 365 U.S. 127 (1961); United Mine Workers of Am. v. Pennington, 381 U.S. 657 (1965); California Motor Transp. Co. v. Trucking Unlimited, 404 U.S. 508 (1972).

[352] *See* Benjamin Plener Cover, *The First Amendment Right to a Remedy*, 50 U.C. Davis L. Rev. 1741, 1775 & n.118 (2017). "The Petition Clause is the only provision in the Bill of Rights to use the term 'Government,' and the only provision in the entire [C]onstitution to refer to the 'Government' as opposed to the 'Government of the United States.'" *Id.* at 1775 n.118.

[353] *See id.* at 1775–77 (analyzing the drafting history of the Petition Clause).

American multinationals under more parsimonious standards of due process and more invasive theories of antitrust liability than American law would ever permit. Often the business practice being investigated is one that the American multinational employs in every country throughout the world and cannot feasibly vary from one nation to another. Consequently, the practical economic effect of the prosecution of the American multinational by the foreign antitrust authority can be to produce a result having extraterritorial effect throughout the world—even in the United States, where the conduct might be unquestionably lawful.

President Obama's Antitrust Division well understood this dynamic. Encouraged by several Silicon Valley giants, the Division aggressively sought to suppress the price that those companies needed to pay to use U.S. patents that are essential to manufacturing smartphones and other mobile devices.[354] The Division's problem, however, was that under no legitimate understanding of American antitrust law had the patent owners done anything remotely unlawful.

So the Antitrust Division pivoted from being an enforcer of U.S. antitrust law to being a global industrial planner that favored the business model of users of standard-essential patents and disfavored the business model of companies that offered, as Qualcomm did, to license their portfolios of such patents. The Division then concocted and disseminated soft law in the form of speeches and business review letters that favored the economic interests of the Silicon Valley giants.[355] Such edicts circle the globe in a mouse click and abet antitrust enforcers in Korea and China, as well as Europe.[356] Just as Henry II asked in the presence of his barons, "Will no one rid me of this troublesome priest?," an American antitrust enforcement agency that believes that the ends justify the means might be tempted to express to its

---

[354] *See* Business Review Letter from Hon. Renata B. Hesse, Acting Assistant Attorney Gen., U.S. Dep't of Justice, to Michael A. Lindsay, Esq., Dorsey & Whitney, L.L.P. (Feb. 2, 2015) [hereinafter 2015 IEEE Business Review Letter], http://www.justice.gov/sites/default/files/opa/press-releases/attachments/2015/02/02/ieee_business_review_letter.pdf; Renata Hesse, Deputy Assistant Attorney Gen., U.S. Dep't of Justice, IP, Antitrust and Looking Back on the Last Four Years: Remarks Presented at the Global Competition Review 2nd Annual Antitrust Law Leaders Forum 17 (Feb. 8, 2013), http://www.justice.gov/atr/public/speeches/292573.pdf; Renata Hesse, Deputy Assistant Attorney Gen., U.S. Dep't of Justice, Six "Small" Proposals for SSOs Before Lunch: Remarks as Prepared for the ITU-T Patent Roundtable 5 (Oct. 10, 2012), http://www.justice.gov/atr/public/speeches/287855.pdf.

[355] *See* Sidak, *The Antitrust Division's Devaluation of Standard-Essential Patents*, *supra* note 326; J. Gregory Sidak, *Testing for Bias to Suppress Royalties for Standard-Essential Patents*, 1 CRITERION J. ON INNOVATION 301 (2016); J. Gregory Sidak, *The Tempting of American Antitrust Law: An Open Letter to President Trump*, 2 CRITERION J. ON INNOVATION 201 (2017).

[356] *See* J. Gregory Sidak, *How Commissioner Vestager's Mistaken Views on Standard-Essential Patents Illustrate Why President Trump Needs a Unified Policy on Antitrust and Innovation*, 1 CRITERION J. ON INNOVATION 721 (2016).

confrères in Europe and Asia its exasperation that American law denies it the muscle to get the job done.[357]

6. The Relationship of the NDRC's Rectification Plan in China to Qualcomm's November 2017 Announcement of Rates for Its 5G Patents and the Reduction of Its Rates for Patents Reading on Earlier Standards

Judge Koh observed that the National Development and Reform Commission (NDRC), an antitrust enforcement agency of the People's Republic of China, had investigated Qualcomm.[358] She cited the investigation as evidence that Qualcomm had been a recurrent target of foreign antitrust investigations.[359] Yet, Judge Koh did not mention that Alex Rogers, the President of Qualcomm Technology Licensing (QTL), testified in detail at trial in *FTC v. Qualcomm* how Qualcomm's "rectification plan" with the NDRC had in fact become the template for Qualcomm's November 2017 rate announcement, which we examined in Part E to the Introduction. On direct examination by Mr. Van Nest during Qualcomm's presentation of its defense, Mr. Rogers testified:

> Q. Now, how did you arrive at this offer in late 2017? What was the genesis of it?
>
> A. So we developed this licensing framework in China following the resolution of the NDRC action in China in February of 2015. In February of 2015 when we resolved the NDRC action, there was a rectification plan that was put in place whereby . . . Qualcomm's licensing program in China would proceed under certain terms and conditions. And the program that we developed in China was essentially according to the same licensing

---

[357] Because of these concerns, I urged President Trump, in an open letter published on the day of his inauguration, to issue an executive order to the following effect and to exercise his appointment power in a complementary manner:

> By executive order, you should instruct your administration that no official of the U.S. government may aid a foreign antitrust authority (1) that seeks to prosecute an American company doing business in its jurisdiction on a theory of "abuse of dominance" that would be unlikely to withstand a motion to dismiss if instead pleaded under U.S. antitrust law in an American court or (2) that employs investigatory or judicial procedures that lack the fundamental fairness that American justice requires.
>
> Finally, you should appoint to the Antitrust Division and the FTC only persons who are willing to bear the burden of proving in federal court that the interpretation of antitrust principles that they espouse deserves to be called the law of the United States.

Sidak, *The Tempting of American Antitrust Law: An Open Letter to President Trump, supra* note 355, at 204.

[358] FTC v. Qualcomm Inc., 411 F. Supp. 3d 658, 673 (N.D. Cal. 2019) ("Qualcomm has been forced to alter certain royalty rates and licensing practices after a 2014 investigation of Qualcomm's business practices by China's National Development and Reform Commission ('NDRC'), the government entity responsible for antitrust. The NDRC issued a 'rectification plan,' which requires Qualcomm to offer SEP-only licenses to Qualcomm's China patents at specified rates.") (citations omitted).

[359] *Id.* at 676 ("Accordingly, Qualcomm's licensing practices have been the subject of government investigations in the United States since at least 2014 and in Asia and Europe since at least 2009.").

framework I just described. It was 3 and a quarter percent for multimode devices, 3G, 4G branded devices, through a particular release of 4G at that point in time, release 11. And then we built a licensing program in China based on those terms, and as of November 2017 when we announced our 5G rate, we had built that licensing program up to about 150 agreements by that point in time. And so we took that same licensing program and simply extended it to apply the same rates inside of China and outside of China, and also included additional technologies, that is, the later releases of 4G and the first release of 5G.

Q. Okay. Let's back up just a little bit, Mr. Rogers. Tell the Court, what is the NDRC?

A. So the NDRC is the agency in China that is responsible, at least was at that time, responsible for . . . essentially managing the anti monopoly law in China, at least the parts of it that applied. So the NDRC was the agency that essentially conducted the investigation of Qualcomm's licensing program in China.

Q. Now, you mentioned the rectification plan came into being in 2015. What is the rectification plan?

A. So when that investigation concluded, it concluded with a plan that essentially was the plan under which Qualcomm's licensing program would proceed in China. And the rectification plan is the name of that plan. And essentially the rectification plan set the terms and the restrictions under which . . . Qualcomm could license in China, and it applied to our Chinese cellular . . . standard essential patents, and it applied to devices made . . . and sold for use in China.

Q. Did the plan apply outside of China?

A. No, it did not. But the . . . licenses that were available under that plan, which we call Chinese patent license agreements, CPLA's, were made available to everybody in the world for devices made and sold for use in China.

Q. Now, you may have told us this, but as of March of 2018, how many licensees had signed up for the CPLA as you described?

A. Well, as of November of 2017, . . . we had at least 150 agreements. And so by March of 2018, we had a significant additional number. I couldn't tell you if it's over 200 by that point in time.

Q. Now, did any company that was eligible for a CPLA SEP license elect to keep their existing full portfolio license in place?

A. Yes.

Q. How many companies did that?

A. I don't know the exact number, but there were a significant number of companies that did elect to keep their full portfolio license. There were companies from Korea, Japan, [and] Taiwan that chose to keep their full portfolio licenses.[360]

Remarkably, despite Judge Koh's preoccupation in *FTC v. Qualcomm* with Qualcomm's choice to sell its modems only to licensed OEMs and not to offer exhaustive licenses to its cellular SEPs to rival modem manufacturers, the NDRC's rectification plan did not require Qualcomm to offer exhaustive licenses to its cellular SEPs at the component level, and it also did not interfere with Qualcomm's choice to sell its modems only to licensed OEMs:

Q. Now, under the rectification plan, does the plan require Qualcomm to license at the component level?

A. No, it does not.

Q. Does the plan allow Qualcomm to license at the handset level?

A. Yes, it does.

Q. And with respect to Qualcomm's policy of selling chips only to licensed OEM's, does the plan allow for that?

A. Yes, it does. The plan expressly states that Qualcomm can sell chips only to licensed OEM's consistent with the terms set forth in the rectification plan.

Q. What does that mean?

A. So in other words, we were permitted under this plan to essentially offer the licensing terms under the rectification plan and sell only to . . . customers who were licensed under those terms.

Q. Now, were the license negotiations that you had pursuant to the rectification plan, were they conducted under the supervision of the NDRC in China?

A. Yes, they were.

Q. And did you have reporting obligations as well?

A. Yes, we did.

Q. Can you describe to the Court what action you took in that regard?

A. So I would regularly visit with the NDRC following the rectification plan to brief the NDRC case team on the status of the licensing program as it rolled out after February of 2015. And in addition, we would regularly

---

360 Transcript of Proceedings (Volume 9) at 1980:10–1982:22, FTC v. Qualcomm Inc., No. 5:17-cv-00220-LHK (N.D. Cal. Jan. 25, 2019) (Testimony of Alex Rogers (President, Qualcomm Technology Licensing)).

provide the NDRC with copies of the license agreements that were signed under the rectification plan. The NDRC would also independently talk to licensees and talk to us about their conversations with licensees, and in one meeting in Shenzhen, the NDRC called a large meeting with Qualcomm and probably about 30 or so manufacturers to talk about the rectification plan and the licensing that would occur after the rectification plan.

Q. Now, did the plan require Qualcomm to make this offer available globally or worldwide?

A. No. The . . . rectification plan and the licensing terms that were set forth under the rectification plan, you can think of it as jurisdictionally limited to China. Again, the offer was made to everybody, any licensee round the world, but it was made with respect to Qualcomm's Chinese standard essential patents and to devices made and sold for us in China.[361]

Judge Koh did not appear to consider whether, explicitly or in practical terms, the government of the People's Republic of China had stepped into the shoes of Chinese OEMs to negotiate royalties for exhaustive licenses to Qualcomm's cellular SEPs (collectively, rather than individually on bilateral terms) with Qualcomm on behalf of every Chinese OEM, such that the PRC operated as a state-sponsored rate regulator leading a buyers' cartel for a geographic market consisting of China, where one-fifth of the world's population lives. That activity could be characterized as monopsonistic, to the extent that the state negotiated on behalf of an entire industry to ensure that every firm in the industry paid the same suppressed price for an exhaustive license to Qualcomm's cellular SEPs.

Yet, if this interpretation of the facts is correct, it bears emphasis that even the putative monopsonist for all of China did not seek to drive the price of an exhaustive license to Qualcomm's portfolio of cellular SEPs down to zero. As Mr. Rogers testified, Qualcomm extended the licensing terms that it had granted to 150 licensees pursuant to the NDRC's rectification plan to apply the same rates outside China, and (as of November 2017) Qualcomm had also included the later releases of 4G and the first release of 5G in that same price. And, as we saw in Part E to the Introduction, the effect of Qualcomm's extending those terms to all prospective OEM licensees would be to grant a license to its entire patent portfolio to an OEM in exchange for a royalty not to exceed $20 per device.

Recall also from Part E to the Introduction that Apple had expressed a willingness to pay a royalty in the amount of $1.50 per device for an exhaustive license to Qualcomm's (entire) patent portfolio (not strictly its cellular SEPs), which appeared to differ by more than one order of magnitude from the royalty for Qualcomm's portfolio of cellular SEPs that emerged from

---

[361] *Id.* at 1982:23–1984:17.

the NDRC's rectification plan. To be precise, Apple's offer to Qualcomm was 7.5 percent of the price cap that the NDRC agreed that Chinese OEMs would pay Qualcomm. Did the vast difference between what Apple offered to pay for an exhaustive license to Qualcomm's entire patent portfolio and what the Chinese government actually agreed that Chinese OEMs would pay for an exhaustive license to Qualcomm's portfolio of cellular SEPs indicate a lack of concern on Apple's part about paying Qualcomm a high enough royalty to sustain its continued investment in R&D for future technologies in mobile communications and adjacent fields?

Judge Koh appeared to be oblivious to the relevance and substantial probative weight of these facts concerning what Chinese OEMs actually paid Qualcomm and the substantially lesser amount that Apple had actually proposed to pay Qualcomm. Instead, she mistakenly appeared to have found the NDRC's investigation into Qualcomm to be evidence probative of Qualcomm's anticompetitive intent toward rival modem manufacturers—despite Mr. Rogers' unrebutted testimony that the NDRC did not disturb Qualcomm's business practices of licensing its patents exhaustively only at the device level and selling its modems only to licensed OEMs.

7. *Apple's 2016 Proposal to Qualcomm to Arbitrate the Validity, Infringement, and Essentiality of Every One of Qualcomm's Thousands of Cellular SEPs*

During the cross examination of Mr. Rogers, the FTC's lawyer, Daniel Matheson, asked about a proposal for arbitration between Apple and Qualcomm. Quoting an unidentified document used to refresh Mr. Rogers' recollection, Mr. Matheson said that, on April 18, 2016, Apple sent Qualcomm a proposal to arbitrate "whether each party's cellular SEPs are essential and infringed and not otherwise invalid, unenforceable, licensed, exhaustive," and the like.[362] The transcript suggests that Mr. Matheson's framing of his questions—which evidently were intended to establish the undisputed fact that Apple and Qualcomm could not agree to arbitrate—elicited from Mr. Rogers a series of responses that were ultimately ambiguous on their face:

> Q. Now, the parties never ended up arbitrating; right?
>
> A. We did not arbitrate.
>
> Q. Qualcomm did not accept the terms on which Apple proposed arbitration to Qualcomm; correct?

---

[362] *Id*, at 2001:24–2002:1.

A. Qualcomm proposed terms for an arbitration under Google MMI [Motorola Mobility] generally, and Apple didn't accept those, so we couldn't come to a mutual agreement on terms for an arbitration.

Q. Okay. My question was about the terms that Apple proposed to Qualcomm. Now, Apple wanted to arbitrate whether Qualcomm's patents are actually valid and actually infringed by the devices Apple sells, and Qualcomm would not arbitrate under those conditions; right?

A. That's correct. That's false.[363]

It is unclear what Mr. Rogers meant by the last of these answers. Perhaps he meant that it was correct that "Apple wanted to arbitrate whether Qualcomm's patents are actually valid and actually infringed by the devices Apple sells," but that it was false that "Qualcomm would not arbitrate under those conditions" in the sense that Qualcomm in fact had made a counteroffer to arbitrate according to a different methodology.

In any event, Mr. Rogers had the opportunity on redirect examination to provide an unambiguous explanation of what he meant and why he found Apple's arbitration proposal to have been pointless. Mr. Van Nest asked Mr. Rogers:

Q. . . . Why didn't Qualcomm accept Apple's arbitration proposal?

A. So it's really simple. Apple had an arbitration proposal that no human being could actually complete, or no sets of arbitrators could actually complete within a reasonable timeframe. They insisted that every SEP, a claim from every SEP[,] be evaluated for essentiality[,] validity, infringement, on a detailed basis for thousands upon thousands of SEPs. For example, in this case [*FTC v. Qualcomm*] both sides are allotted 50 hours. That arbitration would take both sides to have 1,000 hours. It just simply wasn't practical. So what we said to Apple was, look, we're happy to do patent-by-patent analysis, but let's put it to the arbitrators as to what actually makes sense because we don't think an arbitration panel will agree to your proposal. So we'll present to the arbitrators the way a patent portfolio license ought to be arbitrated, and you present it to the arbitrators the way you think a portfolio license will be arbitrated, neither side will tell the other side what to do, and the arbitrator will decide what to do. That's reflected later in the letter as I informed counsel.

Q. And now the parties are litigating in court around the world, Apple and Qualcomm?

A. Yes, we are.[364]

---

363 *Id.* at 2000:18–2001:6.
364 *Id.* at 2016:25–2017:23.

Not a single sentence in Judge Koh's findings of fact and conclusions of law in *FTC v. Qualcomm* discusses Apple's proposal to arbitrate or Qualcomm's counterproposal to arbitrate.

B. *Consulting or Testifying Engagements for Apple, Intel, and the FTC*

Professor Shapiro's redacted expert report in *FTC v. Qualcomm* disclosed that he was being assisted not by Charles River Associates, but by a different economic consultancy, Bates White.[365] Why? With interruptions for service in government, Professor Shapiro has been for more than two decades CRA's premier authority on antitrust matters, a "senior consultant" to the firm.[366] Such a position, in which a distinguished university professor typically is under exclusive contract as an independent contractor to (rather than an employee of) the economic consulting firm, sometimes permits the senior economist to undertake projects supported by a rival economic consulting firm if the first consulting firm would have a conflict in undertaking the work. Yet, CRA economists and senior consultants have publicly supported lines of economic argumentation that favor implementers and disfavor SEP holders.[367] So it would seem surprising that CRA would have a conflict in supporting Professor Shapiro's testimony on behalf of the FTC in its case

---

[365] Initial Expert Report of Carl Shapiro in *FTC v. Qualcomm, supra* note 115, at 2.

[366] *See* Transcript of Bench Trial (Afternoon Session) at 2349:8–2350:17, United States v. AT&T Inc., No. 1:17-cv-02511-RJL (D.D.C. Apr. 11, 2018) ("The Court [Senior Judge Richard J. Leon]: Hold on a second. How many are on this team [of yours]? The Witness [Professor Carl Shapiro]: Well, I would say there's three or four people at Bates White who I'm really thinking of when I say that. And then there's— we work together with the economists at the [A]ntitrust [D]ivision, who also are reviewing information, and we talk with them. [Q.] So the [A]ntitrust [D]ivision staff helps to helps [sic] you write and prepare your expert report? [A.] No. [Q.] Is that what you're saying? [A.] No, that's not what I'm saying, Your Honor. [Q.] Okay, let's be clear about that. [A.] When we have questions about, the data would come in and be provided to Justice Department, and then we would get it from them so we wouldn't actually communicate with them. [Q.] But the actual analysis of the data and modeling and all that, that's you and your team, right? [A.] Yes, sir. [Q.] And the team is you and three or four other people? [A.] Yes, sir. [Q.] And this Bates and White, is that a company in—near Berkeley as in San Francisco— [A.] No, it's a consulting company here, they're based here in Washington, D.C. Keith Waeher is the lead person helping me there, he's one of the partners there. [Q.] Keith Waeher. Do they have offices in San Francisco? [Q.] No, I don't believe so, no. No. [Q.] So you deal with them here? [A.] *I usually work with a different consulting company actually, but in this case I'm working them* [sic].") (emphasis added); *see also Carl Shapiro*, CHARLES RIVER ASSOCIATES, http://www.crai.com/expert/carl-shapiro. Professor Shapiro, after the first of his two stints as Deputy Assistant Attorney General for Economic Analysis (chief economist) at the Antitrust Division of the U.S. Department of Justice, co-founded the Tilden Group with Michael Katz, another Berkeley economics professor, which they sold two years later, in 1998, to CRA for $9.6 million in cash and common stock. Charles River Associates Inc., Annual Report for the Fiscal Year Ended November 28, 1998 (SEC Form 10-K), at 4 (filed Feb. 23, 1999).

[367] *See, e.g.,* PIERRE RÉGIBEAU, RAPHAËL DE CONINCK & HANS ZENGER, TRANSPARENCY, PREDICTABILITY, AND EFFICIENCY OF SSO-BASED STANDARDIZATION AND SEP LICENSING: A REPORT FOR THE EUROPEAN COMMISSION (Charles River Associates 2016); J. Gregory Sidak, *Does the International Trade Commission Facilitate Patent Holdup?*, 1 CRITERION J. ON INNOVATION 601 (2016) (discussing *International Trade Commission (ITC) Patent Litigation: Hearing Before the H. Comm. On the Judiciary Subcomm. On Courts, Intellectual Prop., & the Internet*, 114th Cong. (2016) (written testimony of Fiona M. Scott Morton, Professor, Yale University School of Management), https://republicans-judiciary.house.gov/wp-content/uploads/2016/04/04.14.16-Scott-Morton-Testimony.pdf).

against Qualcomm, such that Professor Shapiro would need to secure alternative case support from a different consultancy.

A small detail like this one sometimes can be revealing. One possible answer is that CRA was not intellectually adverse to the FTC's complaint against Qualcomm at all. Instead, CRA might already have been advising a client interested in the FTC's investigation of Qualcomm. Several months after the FTC had filed its complaint against Qualcomm on January 17, 2017, Qualcomm of course formally became adverse to both Apple and Intel in two contemporaneous investigations before the ITC, the 1065 Investigation[368] and the 1093 Investigation.[369]

In each of those two investigations before the ITC, Apple's affirmative defense to its alleged violation of section 337 of the Tariff Act of 1930[370] (on grounds of its alleged infringement of certain non-SEPs belonging to Qualcomm) consisted partly of allegations that the requested relief (an exclusion order barring importation of infringing iPhones) would allegedly enable Qualcomm to acquire or maintain a monopoly over the modem industry in the United States. Administrative Law Judge Thomas Pender in the 1065 Investigation summarized Apple's affirmative defense as follows:

> Apple alleges the relevant market for this investigation is for supply to third parties (the "merchant market") of premium baseband chipsets (currently premium LTE baseband chipsets and eventually 5G baseband chipsets), and that Qualcomm and Intel are the only suppliers to that market in the United States.
>
> . . . .
>
> Apple alleges that if Intel exits the market for premium LTE baseband chipsets, Qualcomm's monopoly would be reinstated. Apple insists there are no other suppliers that would fill the competitive void left by Intel.[371]

Administrative Law Judge MaryJoan McNamara in the 1093 Investigation summarized Apple's affirmative defense as follows:

> Apple, with Intel, have argued from the outset of this Investigation that if an exclusion order without tailoring issues, Intel will be forced to leave the

---

[368] *See* Complaint, Certain Mobile Electronic Devices and Radio Frequency and Processing Components Thereof, Inv. No. 337-TA-1065 (USITC July 7, 2017); Initial Determination and Recommended Determination (Public Version), Certain Mobile Electronic Devices and Radio Frequency and Processing Components Thereof, Inv. No. 337-TA-1065, slip op. at 191 (USITC Oct. 29, 2018) (Pender, ALJ) [hereinafter 337-TA-1065 Redacted Final Initial Determination].

[369] *See* Complaint, Certain Mobile Electronic Devices and Radio Frequency and Processing Components Thereof (II), Inv. No. 337-TA-1093 (USITC Nov. 30, 2017); Analysis and Findings with Respect to the Public Interest, and Recommendation on Remedy and Bond (Redacted Public Version), Certain Mobile Electronic Devices and Radio Frequency and Processing Components Thereof (II), Inv. No. 337-TA-1093 (USITC Apr. 16, 2019) (McNamara, ALJ) [hereinafter 337-TA-1093 Redacted Public Interest Findings].

[370] 19 U.S.C. § 1337.

[371] 337-TA-1065 Redacted Final Initial Determination, *supra* note 368, at 128, 142.

United States "premium" baseband chip market which, in turn, would leave Qualcomm as the only major player left—or as a monopolist—in that market in the United States.[372]

Apple's monopolization arguments in those two ITC investigations closely resembled arguments that the FTC made, and testimony that Professor Shapiro gave, to Judge Koh in *FTC v. Qualcomm*. In those two ITC investigations, Apple's premier expert economic witness was Professor Fiona Scott Morton of Yale University and Charles River Associates, who had been one of Professor Shapiro's co-authors in recent years on policy issues concerning patents and antitrust.[373] Professor Scott Morton publicly testified in the 1065 Investigation in June 2018 that she had previously consulted to both Apple and Intel.[374]

Professor Shapiro also disclosed a client relationship with Intel that apparently existed sometime between November 2015 and November 2018. In a disclosure statement dated November 2018 and lodged with the American Economic Association in connection with the publication of an article in the *Journal of Economic Perspectives*,[375] Professor Shapiro disclosed that he had "received significant fees as a consultant and/or expert witness *during the past three years* from a number of parties for [his] work on mergers and/or other antitrust issues addressed in [his] article," including Intel.[376]

---

[372] 337-TA-1093 Redacted Public Interest Findings, *supra* note 369, at 18.

[373] *See, e.g.*, Giulio Federico, Fiona Scott Morton & Carl Shapiro, *Antitrust and Innovation: Welcoming and Protecting Disruption*, *in* 20 INNOVATION POLICY AND THE ECONOMY 125 (Josh Lerner & Scott Stern eds., Univ. of Chicago Press 2020); Fiona Scott Morton & Carl Shapiro, *Patent Assertions: Are We Any Closer to Aligning Reward to Contribution?*, *in* 16 INNOVATION POLICY AND THE ECONOMY 89 (Josh Lerner & Scott Stern eds., Univ. of Chicago Press 2016); Fiona M. Scott Morton & Carl Shapiro, *Strategic Patent Acquisitions*, 79 ANTITRUST L.J. 463 (2014).

[374] Open Sessions Hearing Transcript (Revised & Corrected) at 1279:24–1281:2, Certain Mobile Electronic Devices and Radio Frequency and Processing Components Thereof, Inv. No. 337-TA-1065 (USITC June 25, 2018) (Testimony of Fiona Scott Morton) ("Q[.] This is not the first matter in which you have worked on behalf of Apple; is that right? A[.] That's correct. Q[.] And you've worked for Apple in connection with a litigation that's pending in the Northern District of California; is that correct? A[.] I think it's the Southern District of California, but yes . . . . Q[.] You've worked with Apple in connection with litigation pending in the Southern District of California; correct? A[.] I have. Q[.] And you've done work for Apple on other matters, but you can't disclose the particulars of those matters; is that right? A[.] That's right. Q[.] And you've also worked for Intel; is that correct? In the past? A[.] Very briefly, yes. Q[.] Now . . . in this case, you were engaged by Apple to speak to public interest issues; is that right? A[.] That's correct."). In July 2020, Bloomberg reported Professor Scott Morton to have said in June 2020, "'I've done a lot of work for Apple[.]'" David McLaughlin, *Star Critic of Big Tech Has Side Gig Working for Amazon, Apple*, BLOOMBERG, July 17, 2020 (quoting *CEPR Applied IO Policy Panel: What Should IO Economists Be Working on in Tech? (11 June 2020)*, YOUTUBE (June 12, 2020), https://www.youtube.com/watch?v=CWkovwBoGnY).

[375] Carl Shapiro, *Protecting Competition in the American Economy: Merger Control, Tech Titans, Labor Markets*, 33 J. ECON. PERSP., Summer 2019, at 69.

[376] Carl Shapiro, Protecting Competition in an Economy with Superstar Firms: Disclosure Statement (Nov. 2018), https://www.aeaweb.org/doi/10.1257/jep.33.3.69.ds (emphasis added). Professor Shapiro served as Intel's expert economic witness in the FTC's 1999 monopolization case against the company. *See, e.g.*, *Taking the Stand at Antitrust II*, WIRED, Feb. 22, 1999. He subsequently wrote about that experience in Carl Shapiro, *Technology Cross-Licensing Practices: FTC v. Intel (1999)*, *in* THE ANTITRUST REVOLUTION:

C.   *The Relevance to the Political Economy of* FTC v. Qualcomm *of the IEEE's Amendment of Its Bylaws in 2015 to Suppress RAND Royalties to SEP Holders*

Apple's apparent plan to "[d]evalue SEPs" and to "reshape[] FRAND" through "[l]icensing, [l]itigation & [c]ompetition [l]aw,"[377] which came to light in Qualcomm's opening argument at trial in *In re Qualcomm Litigation*, was reminiscent of the action taken in 2015 by the Institute of Electrical and Electronics Engineers (IEEE) to amend its bylaws to regulate the calculation of FRAND royalties for SEPs. Apple was one of the firms that publicly urged the IEEE to amend its bylaws.

1.   *The IEEE's 2015 Bylaw Amendments and the Antitrust Division's Devaluation of Standard-Essential Patents*

The IEEE is an SSO whose 802.11 Wi-Fi standard, universally used in cell-phones and other mobile devices, incorporates technologies owned by many different holders of SEPs. The IEEE's Patent Policy specifies the conditions under which an SEP holder voluntarily commits to offer licenses to its SEPs on RAND terms. Before 2015, the IEEE (like other SSOs) took no position on how to calculate a RAND royalty for SEPs. In February 2015, the IEEE reversed its longstanding Patent Policy and became the first SSO to regulate the calculation of RAND royalties.

The IEEE made that transformative change with the encouragement and blessing of the Obama administration's Antitrust Division, which several years earlier had begun urging SSOs to amend their bylaws to suppress the FRAND or RAND royalties that implementers pay to use SEPs. In a speech in October 2012 to another leading SSO for technologies used in mobile devices, the International Telecommunication Union (ITU), Deputy Assistant Attorney General Renata Hesse said that an SEP holder might "engag[e] in . . . patent hold-up, . . . obtaining an unjustifiably higher price for its invention than would have been possible before the standard was set."[378] She urged SSOs to adopt policies that she said would (1) identify SEPs that a patent holder has declined to commit to license on RAND terms, (2) clarify the binding nature of the SSO's licensing commitments, (3) prohibit an SEP holder from demanding its licensee to cross-license implementation patents, (4) limit an SEP holder's right to seek an injunction against a potential licensee, (5) set guidelines for determining RAND licensing terms, and

---

ECONOMICS, COMPETITION, AND POLICY 350 (John E. Kwoka, Jr. & Lawrence J. White eds., Oxford Univ. Press 4th ed. 2004).

[377]   Qualcomm Opening Statement in *In re Qualcomm, supra* note 319, at 7 (quoting DTX09313).

[378]   Hesse, Six "Small" Proposals for SSOs Before Lunch, *supra* note 354, at 5.

(6) increase the certainty that patents declared to be standard-essential are essential in fact.[379]

The Patent Committee of the IEEE's Standards Board embraced this advice. It appointed an *ad hoc* committee that drafted proposed amendments to the IEEE's bylaws that mirrored Ms. Hesse's recommendations.[380] The stated purpose of the amendments was to reduce the risk of patent holdup and royalty stacking by "provid[ing] greater clarity on issues that have divided SEP owners and standards implementers in recent years."[381] In substance, however, the amendments that the committee actually drafted, and thus the amendments that the IEEE ultimately ratified, transcended mere "clarification" of policy.[382] The actual amendments broadened the binding provisions of the IEEE's RAND commitment, diminished the SEP holder's ability to enforce its patent rights, and suppressed the royalties that the SEP holder may charge a licensee.[383] The amendments mandated, among other things, that a RAND royalty exclude any value attributable to the standard, and they restricted an SEP holder's right to seek an injunction against an unlicensed implementer.[384] Consequently, "clarity" and "clarification" were euphemisms for truncating the upper range of the distribution of bilaterally negotiated RAND royalties for SEPs.

Before ratifying these bylaw amendments, the IEEE sought, in September 2014, a business review letter from the Antitrust Division confirming that the amendments would "compl[y] with all applicable antitrust and competition laws."[385] The IEEE further sought assurance that the Division "would not bring action against IEEE under any antitrust theory."[386] Although the Division "is not authorized to give advisory opinions to private parties,"[387] it is "willing in certain circumstances to review proposed business conduct

---

[379] *Id.* at 9–10.

[380] Letter from Michael A. Lindsay, Esq., Dorsey & Whitney, L.L.P., to Hon. William J. Baer, Assistant Attorney Gen., U.S. Dep't of Justice 13 (Sept. 30, 2014) [hereinafter IEEE Business Review Letter Request], http://www.justice.gov/atr/public/busreview/request-letters/311483.pdf.

[381] *Id.* at 15; *see id.* at 16–17 ("When a SEP owner can seek a Prohibitive Order [either an injunction from a court or an exclusion order from the U.S. International Trade Commission] without any limitation, the negotiation can become a negotiation over the cost to the implementer of being excluded from implementing the standard, rather than the value that the particular SEP contributes to the implementation.").

[382] *See, e.g.,* IEEE-SA Standards Board Patent Committee, IEEE-SA Patent Policy: Draft Comments, cmt. 37, at 15 (Mar. 4, 2014) [hereinafter IEEE-SA Patent Policy: Draft Comments, Second Round], http://grouper.ieee.org/groups/pp-dialog/drafts_comments/PatCom_sort_by_commentID_040314.pdf (comment of Dina Kallay (Director for IP and Competition, Ericsson)).

[383] *See* Sidak, *Testing for Bias to Suppress Royalties for Standard-Essential Patents, supra* note 355, at 303, 319–22; *see also* IEEE-SA Patent Policy: Draft Comments, Second Round, *supra* note 382; Don Clark, *Patent Holders Fear Weaker Tech Role,* WALL St. J., Feb. 9, 2015; Ryan Davis, *Patent Owners Take Hit with Standard-Setting Body's Rules,* Law360, Feb. 9, 2015. I provide a comprehensive analysis of the 2015 IEEE bylaw amendments in Sidak, *The Antitrust Division's Devaluation of Standard-Essential Patents, supra* note 326, at 56–60.

[384] *See* Sidak, *Testing for Bias to Suppress Royalties for Standard-Essential Patents, supra* note 355, at 301, 320.

[385] IEEE Business Review Letter Request, *supra* note 380, at 17.

[386] *Id.* at 19.

[387] 28 C.F.R. § 50.6.

and state its enforcement intentions."[388] A party requesting a business review letter has "an affirmative obligation to make full and true disclosure with respect to the business conduct for which review is requested."[389]

The IEEE's Standards Board recommended that the IEEE's Board of Governors approve the amendments contingent on obtaining a "favorable Business Review Letter."[390] In its request to the Antitrust Division, the IEEE said that it was seeking a business review letter because some of the IEEE's stakeholders had expressed antitrust concerns over the proposed amendments and other stakeholders had asked the IEEE to seek such a letter.[391] Strictly speaking, "the issuance of such a letter is not to be represented to mean that the Division believes that there are no anticompetitive consequences warranting agency consideration."[392]

On Monday morning, February 2, 2015, a patent law blog posted a letter dated January 30, 2015 that executives from Apple, Cisco, Intel, Microsoft, and other companies reportedly sent to the IEEE's leadership, endorsing the proposed amendments.[393] BJ Watrous, Vice President and Chief IP Counsel at Apple, was one prominent signatory. Ira Blumberg, Vice President of Intellectual Property at Lenovo, and the FTC's second witness in its affirmative case in *FTC v. Qualcomm*, was another signatory. An Intel representative also signed the letter. Although six professors—economists Richard Gilbert and Fiona Scott Morton, and lawyers Michael Carrier, Jorge Contreras, Mark Lemley, and Daryl Lim—also signed the letter,[394] these scholars said nothing about how the proposed amendments, to the extent that they effected collective action among buyers, could facilitate their potential suppression of the prices they paid for technology inputs.

Later on February 2, 2015, the Antitrust Division released its business review letter, signed by Ms. Hesse, declining to challenge the IEEE's

---

[388] *Id.*

[389] *Id.* § 50.6(5).

[390] IEEE Business Review Letter Request, *supra* note 380, at 14–15.

[391] *Id.* at 17.

[392] 28 C.F.R. § 50.6(7)(a).

[393] Letter from Ira Blumberg, Vice President of Intellectual Prop., Lenovo Grp. Ltd., et al. to Howard E. Michel, President & CEO, IEEE, and Bruce Kraemer, President, IEEE-SA & Dir., IEEE (Jan. 30, 2015) [hereinafter Letter from Ira Blumberg to the IEEE], http://comparativepatentremedies.blogspot.com/2015/02/letter-in-support-of-proposed-ieee-sa.html. For critical reactions to the IEEE business review letter, see Roy E. Hoffinger, *The 2015 DOJ IEEE Business Review Letter: The Triumph of Industrial Policy Preferences Over Law and Evidence*, CPI ANTITRUST CHRON., Mar. 2015, at 7 ("[T]he outcome of the [IEEE patent policy revisions in 2015] was thoroughly in line with the public and litigation positions of the major licensees [of patents essential to the IEEE's standards]."); Ron D. Katznelson, *Perilous Deviations from FRAND Harmony—Operational Pitfalls of the 2015 IEEE Patent Policy*, 2015 IEEE 9ᵀᴴ INTERNATIONAL CONFERENCE ON STANDARDIZATION AND INNOVATION IN INFORMATION TECHNOLOGY (SIIT) 1 (2015); Sidak, *Testing for Bias to Suppress Royalties for Standard-Essential Patents*, *supra* note 355, at 314–16, 319–22; Sidak, *The Antitrust Division's Devaluation of Standard-Essential Patents*, *supra* note 326. The companies signing the letter were Apple, Cisco Systems, D-Link Systems, Dell, Hewlett-Packard Española, Intel, Juniper Networks, Kingston Technology, Lenovo, Microsoft, Samsung, Sceptre, Sierra Wireless, and Verizon. Letter from Ira Blumberg to the IEEE, *supra*, at 2–4.

[394] Letter from Ira Blumberg to the IEEE, *supra* note 393, at 2–4.

proposed amendments to its bylaws.[395] Ms. Hesse said that the amendments had "the potential to benefit competition and consumers" and were likely to "facilitat[e] licensing negotiations, mitigat[e] [patent] hold up and royalty stacking, and promot[e] competition among technologies for inclusion in standards."[396] Further, the Antitrust Division did not find the amendments likely to result in anticompetitive harm because, in Ms. Hesse's assessment, "licensing rates . . . are [still] determined through bilateral negotiations, the [amendments] are not out of step with the direction of current U.S. law interpreting [F]RAND commitments[,] . . . and patent holders can avoid" the amendments by refusing to submit a Letter of Assurance (LOA) or "can depart to other SSOs."[397] The Antitrust Division said that, even if the amendments did generate anticompetitive repercussions, the "potential procompetitive benefits" of the bylaw amendments would "likely outweigh those harms."[398]

Lest anyone get the wrong impression, Ms. Hesse said in her letter that "the U.S. government does not dictate patent policy choices to private SSOs,"[399] and that "[i]t is not the [Antitrust Division's] role to assess whether [the] IEEE's policy choices are right for [the] IEEE as a[n SSO]."[400] Six days after receiving Ms. Hesse's positive business review letter, the IEEE's Board of Directors ratified the bylaw amendments.[401]

In a letter to Ms. Hesse on January 28, 2015, I had expressed concern that the IEEE's proposed bylaw amendments posed a serious risk of violating section 1 of the Sherman Act by facilitating tacit or explicit collusion among implementers to suppress the royalties they pay for SEPs. I explained that the amendments would weaken patent rights, reduce incentives to invest in standard-essential technology, and thereby harm innovation and long-term consumer welfare.[402] Ms. Hesse's business review letter of February 2, 2015 did not acknowledge receipt of my letter, much less explain why my concerns did not merit the Antitrust Division's attention in its analysis of the IEEE's proposed amendments to its bylaws.

The Antitrust Division under the administration of President Trump all but repudiated Ms. Hesse's business review letter to the IEEE. Assistant

---

[395] 2015 IEEE Business Review Letter, *supra* note 354. Ms. Hesse signed the business review letter in her capacity as Acting Assistant Attorney General because Assistant Attorney General William J. Baer had recused himself from the matter.

[396] *Id.* at 16.

[397] *Id.* at 8.

[398] *Id.* at 16.

[399] *Id.* at 10.

[400] *Id.* at 1.

[401] Press Release, IEEE, IEEE Statement Regarding Updating of Its Standards-Related Patent Policy (Feb. 8, 2015).

[402] Letter from J. Gregory Sidak, Chairman, Criterion Economics, to Hon. Renata Hesse, Deputy Assistant Attorney Gen., U.S. Dep't of Justice (Jan. 28, 2015) [hereinafter Sidak's Letter to Hesse], http://www.criterioneconomics.com/proposed-ieee-bylaw-amendments-affecting-frand-licensing-of-seps.html.

Attorney General Delrahim said in November 2017 that "this letter should never be cited for the proposition that what IEEE did is required, or that a patent holder who seeks an injunction is somehow in violation of the antitrust laws."[403] This reversal of policy upset many academics and former antitrust enforcement officials, who subsequently expressed their longing for a continuation of the Obama administration's policy pronouncements on the patent-holdup conjecture that favored implementers over SEP holders.[404]

2. *The Established Law on Monopsony and Collusive Oligopsony*

Ex ante collective action that is privately undertaken in an SSO to counteract potential patent holdup might facilitate, if not serve as an outright façade for, horizontal price fixing by oligopsonists of the patented input. The Supreme Court has called horizontal agreements among competitors the "supreme evil" of antitrust.[405] It is also well established in antitrust jurisprudence that the rule of *per se* illegality applies to competitor exchanges of contemporaneous

---

[403] Makan Delrahim, Assistant Attorney Gen., Antitrust Div., U.S. Dep't of Justice, Remarks as Prepared for the LeadershIP Conference: The Long Run: Maximizing Innovation Incentives Through Advocacy and Enforcement 9 (Apr. 10, 2018), https://www.justice.gov/opa/speech/assistant-attorney-general-makan-delrahim-delivers-keynote-address-leadership-conference; *see also* Douglas H. Ginsburg, *Judge Douglas Ginsburg Interviews Makan Delrahim on Intellectual Property and Antitrust*, CPI Antitrust Chron., June 2018, at 1; David J. Teece, *Pivoting Toward Schumpeter: Makan Delrahim and the Recasting of U.S. Antitrust Towards Innovation, Competitiveness, and Growth*, 32 Antitrust, Summer 2018, at 32, 32 (2018) ("Assistant Attorney General Makan Delrahim . . . has signaled a subtle but important shift in antitrust policy in the United States, particularly where intellectual property and competition policy issues interact or appear to collide. . . . [I]f he is to be believed, we are henceforth not going to be waylaid by economic theory alone."); Economic Report of the President 225 (2020) ("The DOJ has emphasized the need to avoid rigid presumptions in the intellectual property area that could deter innovation. In particular, it has cautioned against the misapplication of antitrust laws, which carry the specter of treble damages, to commercial disputes involving the exercise of patent rights. In December 2017, the DOJ withdrew its support from its 2013 joint policy statement with the Patent and Trademark Office on remedies associated with standard essential patents, because the statement had been construed to suggest that the antitrust laws should limit patent holders from seeking injunctions or exclusionary remedies to defend their intellectual property rights. The DOJ's work in this area ensures that there are strong incentives to invest in developing technologies, and thus fostering dynamic competition.").

[404] *See, e.g.*, Letter from Michael A. Carrier, Prof., Rutgers L. Sch., et al. to Makan Delrahim, Assistant Attorney Gen., Antitrust Div., U.S. Dep't of Justice (May 17, 2018), https://patentlyo.com/media/2018/05/DOJ-patent-holdup-letter.pdf ("We, 77 former government enforcement officials and professors of law, economics, and business, write to express concern with recent speeches [Mr. Delrahim] [] made that we do not believe are consistent with the broad bipartisan legal and economic consensus that has existed for over a decade regarding standard setting."). Timothy Muris (former chairman of the FTC and senior counsel to Sidley), Douglas Melamed, and Fiona Scott Morton were among the letter's signatories. *Id.*; *see also* Terrell McSweeny, Comm'r, Fed. Trade Comm'n, Holding the Line on Patent Holdup: Why Antitrust Enforcement Matters 1 (Mar. 21, 2018) ("It would be unfortunate if the antitrust agencies were to unlearn the lessons of over 15 years of scholarship and bipartisan study and question their longstanding support for combatting holdup based on vague concerns about over-deterrence.").

[405] Verizon Commc'ns Inc. v. Law Offices of Curtis V. Trinko, LLP, 540 U.S. 398, 408 (2004); *see also* American Needle, Inc. v. Nat'l Football League, 560 U.S. 183, 190–91 (2010) ("In § 1 Congress 'treated concerted behavior more strictly than unilateral behavior,' because, unlike independent action, '[c]oncerted activity inherently is fraught with anticompetitive risk' insofar as it 'deprives the marketplace of independent centers of decisionmaking that competition assumes and demands.'") (second alteration in original) (first quoting Copperweld Corp. v. Indep. Tube Corp., 467 U.S. 752, 768 (1984); and then quoting *id.* at 768–79).

or forward-looking information on pricing. It is not obvious why a more lenient rule should apply when competing buyers of a patented input discuss the price that they believe the patented input should fetch now or in the future. It is also not obvious why policies of antitrust prosecutorial discretion should favor licensees of patented technologies over licensors.

A monopsony is a market in which a single firm purchases the entire market supply of the good—typically, but not necessarily, the supply of an input used to make an end product sold to consumers.[406] A monopsonist by definition influences the market price for the inputs that it exclusively purchases. Consequently, it can profitably reduce the price that it pays for an input, in turn reducing the quantity supplied of that input. For an input supplier with an upward-sloping supply curve, monopsony results in a lower market price for the input and a lower equilibrium quantity than would occur in a market in which buyers lacked market power.

An oligopsony is a market in which each of several firms purchases a substantial share of the market supply for an input.[407] In a market with a small number of buyers, perfect collusion with respect to the firms' purchases of a given input would result in the same equilibrium prices and quantities as if the market were a monopsony.[408] The welfare losses from monopsony and oligopsonistic collusion may be less familiar in antitrust law than are the welfare losses from monopoly and cartels, and monopsony and oligopsony might never be mentioned in a typical antitrust course.[409] Nonetheless, the Supreme Court long ago held, in *Mandeville Island Farms v. American Crystal Sugar Co.*, that oligopsonistic collusion is *per se* unlawful under the Sherman Act: "It is clear that the agreement is the sort of combination condemned by the Act, even though the price-fixing was by purchasers, and the persons

---

[406] *See, e.g.,* CARLTON & PERLOFF, MODERN INDUSTRIAL ORGANIZATION, *supra* note 179, at 107; ROGER D. BLAIR & JEFFREY L. HARRISON, MONOPSONY: ANTITRUST LAW AND ECONOMICS 73–75 (1993); Roger D. Blair & Jeffrey L. Harrison, *Antitrust Policy and Monopsony*, 76 CORNELL L. REV. 297 (1991); Roger G. Noll, *Buyer Power and Antitrust: "Buyer Power" and Economic Policy*, 72 ANTITRUST L.J. 589 (2005).

[407] *See* Roger D. Blair & Christine Piette Durrance, *The Economics of Monopsony, in* 1 ABA SECTION OF ANTITRUST LAW, ISSUES IN COMPETITION LAW AND POLICY 393 (AM. BAR ASS'N 2008); James M. Dowd, *Oligopsony Power: Antitrust Injury and Collusive Buyer Practices in Input Markets*, 76 B.U. L. REV. 1075, 1084 (1996). The most incisive analysis of the law on monopsony and collusive oligopsony is by Gregory Werden, formerly of the Antitrust Division. *See* Gregory J. Werden, *Monopsony and the Sherman Act: Consumer Welfare in a New Light*, 74 ANTITRUST L.J. 707 (2007).

[408] In a detailed survey of the legislative history of the Sherman Act and the subsequent case law, Werden concludes that "the Congress responsible for the Sherman Act and the courts that have interpreted it were far from indifferent to the plight of sellers exploited by buyer cartels or monopsonies." Werden, *Monopsony and the Sherman Act: Consumer Welfare in a New Light, supra* note 407, at 708.

[409] Werden found that, "[d]uring 1997–2006, the Department of Justice brought sixty-nine criminal cases against buyer cartels, all of which involved collusion among bidders in auctions." *Id.* at 716. Moreover, he found that "[b]uyer cartel cases constituted 20 percent of total criminal Sherman Act cases during the period." *Id.* at 716 n.42. Monopsony cases routinely are litigated in federal district court. *See, e.g.,* Campfield v. State Farm Mut. Auto. Ins. Co., 532 F.3d 1111 (10th Cir. 2008); Omnicare, Inc. v. UnitedHealth Grp., Inc., 524 F. Supp. 2d 1031 (N.D. Ill. 2007).

specially injured under the treble damage claim are sellers, not customers or consumers."[410]

Lower courts—including the Ninth Circuit and the Northern District of California—have similarly recognized that horizontal collusion has always been of gravest concern to antitrust law, no less when buyers rather than sellers collude. Citing *Mandeville Island Farms*, Judge Posner wrote in 1984 in *Vogel v. American Society of Appraisers* that "buyer cartels, the object of which is to force the prices that suppliers charge the members of the cartel below the competitive level, are illegal per se."[411] He explained that, "[j]ust as a sellers' cartel enables the charging of monopoly prices, a buyers' cartel enables the charging of monopsony prices."[412]

The Ninth Circuit echoed this message in 2000. In *Knevelbaard Dairies v. Kraft Foods, Inc.*, the Ninth Circuit rejected the argument by the buyers, a group of cheese makers, that the harm caused to the input suppliers (dairies) by horizontal collusion over the purchase price of the input was not a cognizable antitrust injury:

> They say, in substance, that a conspiracy to depress prices would not harm consumers but benefit them, because reduced milk acquisition costs would mean lower cheese manufacturing costs and, therefore, lower prices for cheese products. They contend that "the alleged conduct actually increased competition in the milk market," and that "injury from selling at lower, more competitive prices is simply not enough."
>
> The fallacy of this argument becomes clear when we recall that the central purpose of the antitrust laws, state and federal, is to preserve

---

[410] 334 U.S. 219, 235 (1948). The Court's most recent monopsony case, Weyerhaeuser Co. v. Ross-Simmons Hardwood Lumber Co., 549 U.S. 312, 320 (2007), was really a predation case in which overbuying of the input was allegedly the method by which to harm the monopsonist's competitors in the downstream market. *See id.* at 321 ("The reduction in input prices will lead to 'a significant cost saving that more than offsets the profit[s] that would have been earned on the output.' If all goes as planned, the predatory bidder will reap monopsonistic profits that will offset any losses suffered in bidding up input prices.") (quoting Steven C. Salop, *Anticompetitive Overbuying by Power Buyers*, 72 ANTITRUST L.J. 669, 672 (2005)). Nonetheless, *Weyerhaeuser* contains the following relevant observation: "The kinship between monopoly and monopsony suggests that similar legal standards should apply to claims of monopolization and to claims of monopsonization." *Id.* at 322. Analogously, horizontal fixing of input prices should be treated the same as horizontal fixing of output prices. *See, e.g.*, O'Bannon v. Nat'l Collegiate Athletic Ass'n, 7 F. Supp. 3d 955, 991 (N.D. Cal. 2014) ("[I]f proven, [a price-fixing agreement among buyers] would violate § 1 of the Sherman Act just as a price-fixing agreement among sellers would. . . . The Supreme Court has noted that the 'kinship between monopoly and monopsony suggests that similar legal standards should apply to claims of monopolization and to claims of monopsonization.'") (quoting *Weyerhaeuser*, 549 U.S. at 322).

[411] 744 F.2d 598, 601 (7th Cir. 1984); *see also* International Outsourcing Servs., L.L.C. v. Blistex, Inc., 420 F. Supp. 2d 860, 864 (N.D. Ill. 2006) ("[A] 'buyers' cartel' . . . occurs when a group of buyers band together in order to fix a maximum price (below competitive levels) that they will pay for an item. Buyers' cartels engaged in price fixing have been held to be illegal under the Sherman Act even though their goal is to lower the price of the input.").

[412] *Vogel*, 744 F.2d at 601; *see also* Omnicare, Inc. v. UnitedHealth Grp., Inc., 629 F.3d 697, 705 (7th Cir. 2011) ("Ordinarily, price-fixing agreements exist between sellers who collude to set their prices above or below prevailing market prices. But buyers may also violate § 1 by forming what is sometimes known as a 'buyers' cartel.'").

competition. It is competition—not the collusive fixing of prices at levels either low or high—that these statutes recognize as vital to the public interest. The Supreme Court's references to the goals of achieving "the lowest prices, the highest quality and the greatest material progress," and of "assur[ing] customers the benefits of price competition," do not mean that conspiracies among buyers to depress acquisition prices are tolerated. . . .

When horizontal price fixing causes buyers to pay more, or sellers to receive less, than the prices that would prevail in a market free of the unlawful trade restraint, antitrust injury occurs. . . .

. . . .

["]Most courts understand that a buying cartel's low buying prices are illegal and bring antitrust injury and standing to the victimized suppliers. Clearly mistaken is the occasional court that considers low buying prices pro-competitive or that thinks sellers receiving illegally low prices do not suffer antitrust injury.["][413]

The Second Circuit embraced similar reasoning in 2001.[414] Other circuits have followed.[415]

Herbert Hovenkamp has similarly endorsed the conclusion that *per se* illegality is appropriate for a buyer cartel, such as the cartel of local sugar refiners purchasing sugar beets in *Mandeville Island Farms*: "[I]n this case there is literally no injury to consumers, who are the main concern of the antitrust laws; the injury is to the farmer/producers who are forced to accept lower profits and to make inefficient substitutions to other products."[416] Note, however, that Hovenkamp's analysis of *Mandeville Island Farms* considers only static efficiency effects on consumer welfare. He implicitly assumes, and might or might not be correct, that there is no technological innovation in the production of sugar beets that might be forfeited by tolerating the lower input prices that a monopsony or a collusive oligopsony pays sellers.

---

[413] 232 F.3d 979, 986–89 (9th Cir. 2000) (first alteration in original) (citations omitted) (third quoting Northern Pac. Ry. v. United States, 356 U.S. 1, 4 (1958); fourth quoting Associated Gen. Contractors v. Cal. State Council of Carpenters, 459 U.S. 519, 538 (1983); and fifth quoting 2 PHILLIP E. AREEDA & HERBERT HOVENKAMP, ANTITRUST LAW ¶ 375(b), at 297 (Little Brown rev. ed. 1995)). The Ninth Circuit was applying California's Cartwright Act in *Knevelbaard Dairies*, but it relied on federal antitrust precedents to interpret that state antitrust law.

[414] Todd v. Exxon Corp., 275 F.3d 191, 201 (2d Cir. 2001) ("[A] horizontal conspiracy among buyers to stifle competition is as unlawful as one among sellers.").

[415] *See, e.g.*, West Penn Allegheny Health Sys., Inc. v. UPMC, 627 F.3d 85, 104 (3d Cir. 2010); Quality Auto Painting Ctr. of Roselle, Inc. v. State Farm Indem. Co., 917 F.3d 1249, 1277–78 (11th Cir. 2019).

[416] 12 PHILLIP E. AREEDA & HERBERT HOVENKAMP, ANTITRUST LAW ¶ 2011(b)(1) (Wolters Kluwer 4th ed. 2020). Hovenkamp has further observed: "The 'deadweight' loss is equal to that produced by the orthodox sellers' cartel, except that those experiencing the losses are growers rather than consumers." *Id.*

D. The Direct Implications of Donald Trump's Election as President for the FTC's Prosecution of Qualcomm

To understand the peculiar political context of *FTC v. Qualcomm*, it is useful to note first that President Obama's nomination of Judge Koh for elevation to the Ninth Circuit died in the Senate when the 114th Congress adjourned on January 3, 2017—13 days before the FTC filed its complaint and 17 days before President Trump's inauguration.[417] If Hillary Clinton had been elected President in 2016, Judge Koh might not have presided over *FTC v. Qualcomm* because she would instead be sitting on the Ninth Circuit, if not in Justice Brett Kavanaugh's seat on the Supreme Court.[418] Instead, *FTC v. Qualcomm* landed on Judge Koh's desk at the U.S. District Court for the Northern District of California.

Although Judge Koh's nomination to the Ninth Circuit did not survive Donald Trump's election as President, the FTC's policy preferences from the Obama era did, despite there being a new Republican majority among the commissioners. FTC Chairman Joseph Simons was confirmed on April 26, 2018 and took office on May 1, 2018.[419] The next day, May 2, 2018, Chairman Simons was joined in office by three other new commissioners (two Democrats and one Republican) who had also been confirmed on April 26, 2018.[420]

Yet, six months after taking office, and less than three weeks after Judge Koh had denied the parties' joint administrative request that she defer her ruling on the FTC's motion for partial summary judgment in *FTC v. Qualcomm*

---

[417] *See* Press Release, White House, Office of the Press Sec'y, President Obama Nominates Judge Lucy Haeran Koh to Serve on the United States Court of Appeals (Feb. 25, 2016) ("Today, President Obama nominated Judge Lucy Haeran Koh to serve on the United States Court of Appeals for the Ninth Circuit."), https://obamawhitehouse.archives.gov/the-press-office/2016/02/25/president-obama-nominates-judge-lucy-haeran-koh-serve-united-states; 163 CONG. REC. S1 (daily ed. Jan. 3, 2017) (documenting the U.S. Senate's adjournment for the 115th Congress and the official expiration of Judge Koh's nomination); FTC Complaint, 2017 WL 242848, *supra* note 28. Judge Koh's nomination, and the subsequent failure of the Senate to schedule a vote to confirm her, elicited law review articles urging her appointment to the Ninth Circuit. *See* Carl Tobias, *Nominate Judge Koh to the Ninth Circuit Again*, 74 WASH. & LEE L. REV. ONLINE 64 (2017); Carl Tobias, *Confirm Judge Koh for the Ninth Circuit*, 73 WASH. & LEE L. REV. ONLINE 449 (2016).

[418] Lydia Wheeler, *Clinton's Court Shortlist Emerges*, HILL, July 30, 2016 (identifying Judge Koh as having been on Hillary Clinton's short list of possible nominees for the Supreme Court); *see also* Tracy Mitrano, *Judge Lucy H. Koh for the Supreme Court*, INSIDE HIGHER ED (Feb. 14, 2016), https://www.insidehighered.com/blogs/law-policy-and-it/judge-lucy-h-koh-supreme-court ("Associate Justice Antonin Scalia was a towering intellect and a spoiled child, and, by all accounts, a loving husband and father. Condolences to his family. President Obama is going to nominate a candidate for the Senate to confirm. . . . United States District Judge for the North District of California Lucy H. Koh should be President Obama's nominee. Yes, she is young. And yes, she is a district not appellate court judge. But Judge Koh more than any other justice represents what this country needs to map law to technology at the highest levels of the judiciary. . . . If not literally, she is intellectually a student of [Harvard Law School Professor Lawrence] Lessig.").

[419] Press Release, Federal Trade Commission, Joseph Simons Sworn in as Chairman of the FTC (May 1, 2018), https://www.ftc.gov/news-events/press-releases/2018/05/joseph-simons-sworn-chairman-ftc.

[420] Press Release, Federal Trade Commission, Phillips, Slaughter, and Chopra Sworn in as FTC Commissioners (May 2, 2018), https://www.ftc.gov/news-events/press-releases/2018/05/phillips-slaughter-chopra-sworn-ftc-commissioners.

so as to facilitate settlement negotiations, Chairman Simons announced that he had recused himself from the case and thus restored the same deadlock that had permitted the case to be superintended by the agency's (supposedly nonpolitical) career employees since Chairwoman Edith Ramirez had resigned, effective February 10, 2017,[421] and precipitated a 1–1 deadlock at the FTC between Commissioner Ohlhausen (a Republican) and Commissioner Terrell McSweeney (a Democrat).[422] Chairman Simons had previously been a partner at the Paul Weiss law firm and evidently had represented Qualcomm (although there was no indication from media reports that his representation related to *FTC v. Qualcomm*).

Chairman Simons' recusal left the FTC with two Democrats and two Republicans, whose apparent disagreement over *FTC v. Qualcomm* disabled them from directing the FTC staff to change course in the ongoing litigation. Any change in the FTC's strategy or objective in the litigation required a majority vote, and sentiment toward the litigation evidently continued to be divided along party lines. Bloomberg reported that the 2–2 split consequently meant that "no action [could] be taken by the commission," such that the Democrats had "more leverage to shape the outcome of the case."[423] Consequently, the Democrat commissioners reportedly could "push for specific settlement conditions or keep the matter in litigation."[424]

The voting deadlocks between the FTC's Republican and Democrat commissioners turned *FTC v. Qualcomm* into the *Flying Dutchman* of antitrust, a ghost ship lacking anyone at the helm whom the President had nominated and the Senate had confirmed to exercise the powers of an FTC commissioner. Was it unconstitutional that no principal officer exercised those powers? In *Lucia v. SEC*, the Supreme Court held in 2018 that an administrative hearing tainted by a violation of the Appointments Clause[425] is null and void; so are all the rulings arising from that tainted hearing.[426] The derelic-

---

[421] *See* Tony Romm, *FTC Chair Ramirez to Step Down Next Month*, POLITICO, Jan. 13, 2017; *see also id.* ("Ramirez, a Harvard Law School classmate of President Barack Obama, joined the FTC as a commissioner in 2010, and Obama designated her chairwoman three years later.").

[422] Alexei Alexis, *FTC Chair Simons Recuses from Qualcomm Antitrust Case (1)*, BLOOMBERG, Nov. 2, 2018; *see also* Romm, *FTC Chair Ramirez to Step Down Next Month*, *supra* note 421. Commissioner McSweeny previously served as an adviser to Vice President Biden, as well as his Deputy Chief of Staff and Policy Director while he served in the Senate. *Terrell McSweeny, Former Commissioner*, FED. TRADE COMM'N, https://www.ftc.gov/about-ftc/biographies/terrell-mcsweeny. The effective month of Chairman Simons' recusal from *FTC v. Qualcomm* evidently was May 2018, because a spokesman for the FTC subsequently said that Chairman "Simons' two-year recusal expired in May" 2020, three months before the Ninth Circuit reversed Judge Koh's judgment in *FTC v. Qualcomm*. Victoria Graham, *FTC's Simons No Longer Recused in Qualcomm Antitrust Case*, BLOOMBERG, Aug. 14, 2020.

[423] Alexis, *FTC Chair Simons Recuses from Qualcomm Antitrust Case (1)*, *supra* note 422.

[424] *Id.*

[425] U.S. CONST. art. II, § 2, cl. 2.

[426] Lucia v. SEC, 138 S. Ct. 2044, 2055 (2018). In Edmond v. United States, 520 U.S. 651, 660 (1997), the Court reiterated that "the Appointments Clause was designed to ensure public accountability for both the making of a bad appointment and the rejection of a good one." This concern of public accountability arises with respect to Executive Branch agencies. *See* Free Enterprise Fund v. Pub. Co. Accounting Oversight

tion in that case was the delegation, by the commissioners of the Securities and Exchange Commission to their chief administrative law judge, of their statutory responsibility to appoint the agency's remaining administrative law judges. Why would the Court find the diminution of transparency and accountability surrounding the FTC's prosecutorial discretion and policy objectives in *FTC v. Qualcomm* any less troubling and consequential than what transpired at the SEC in *Lucia* regarding the appointment of ALJs?

The lack of transparency and accountability concerning who at the FTC has been and will be the real decisionmaker concerning *FTC v. Qualcomm* has practical and immediate significance for how the law of monopolization will evolve. The Trump administration so opposed the FTC's case against Qualcomm that the Antitrust Division intervened in the appeal before the Ninth Circuit and, at oral argument on February 13, 2020, the Antitrust Division received five minutes to argue—in direct opposition to the FTC—for reversal on Qualcomm's behalf.[427] The *Financial Times* reported: "'This is not just unusual, it's more directly confrontational than anything I've ever seen,' said Bill Baer, a fellow at the Brookings Institution who has headed competition enforcement under Democratic presidents at both the DoJ and the FTC."[428]

II. Is Qualcomm Innovative and Unique?

Every race has its winner. By the time of Judge Koh's bench trial in *FTC v. Qualcomm*, Qualcomm had long since distinguished itself as unique among

---

Bd., 561 U.S. 477, 499 (2010) (Roberts, C.J.) ("Our Constitution was adopted to enable the people to govern themselves, through their elected leaders. The growth of the Executive Branch, which now wields vast power and touches almost every aspect of daily life, heightens the concern that it may slip from the Executive's control, and thus from that of the people."); Seila Law LLC v. Consumer Fin. Prot. Bureau, 140 S. Ct. 2183, 2218 (2020) (Thomas, J., concurring in part and dissenting in part) ("Accountability . . . plays a central role in our constitutional structure."); Elena Kagan, *Presidential Administration*, 114 Harv. L. Rev. 2245, 2332 (2001) ("The lines of responsibility should be stark and clear, so that the exercise of power can be comprehensible, transparent to the gaze of the citizen subject to it."). Why should transparency and public accountability be any less necessary in an independent agency like the FTC?

[427] *See* Brent Kendall & Asa Fitch, *Qualcomm Appeal of Monopoly Decision Appears to Resonate with Court*, Wall St. J., Feb. 13, 2020.

[428] Kadhim Shubber, *US Regulators Face Off in Court Tussle Over Qualcomm*, Fin. Times, Feb. 9, 2020. Professor Shapiro similarly stated in June 2020:

> I think it's really a shame how bad relations are now between the FTC and DOJ. [The] DOJ going in to court to try to, on the side of Qualcomm, I testified for the FTC in Qualcomm, so I was involved in that case, to have the DOJ go into court and say, the FTC got it wrong in a major antitrust intellectual property case is breathtaking . . . because the DOJ's arguments are nonsense here, as they are in a number of other, most of the areas, what Makan Delrahim's been saying about antitrust and intellectual property is specious[.]

Thomas M. Lenard, Scott Walsten & Josh Wright, *"Carl Shapiro and Josh Wright Debate Antitrust and Competition Policy" (Two Think Minimum)*, Tech. Pol'y Inst. (June 15, 2020), https://techpolicyinstitute.org/2020/06/15/carl-shaprio-and-josh-wright-debate-antitrust-and-competition-policy-two-think-minimum/.

its peers. It consistently achieved a high productivity of investment in R&D that outpaced its rivals, and it produced modems that surpassed its rivals' modems in technical performance. The Ninth Circuit clearly intuited this dual business model:

> Qualcomm is no one-trick pony. The company also manufactures and sells cellular modem chips, the hardware that enables cellular devices to practice CDMA and premium LTE technologies and thereby communicate with each other across cellular networks. This makes Qualcomm somewhat unique in the broader cellular services industry.[429]

The Ninth Circuit also observed that, "[l]ike its licensing business, Qualcomm's modem chip business has been very successful."[430] Qualcomm's successful pursuit of a dual business model of innovation and product development epitomized David Teece's classic observation on how a firm might need to extend the boundaries of its activities if it is to profit from its technological innovation.[431]

Yet, the FTC's allegations and Judge Koh's findings of fact and conclusions of law treated Qualcomm's extraordinary accomplishments as something to scorn and punish rather than something to admire and applaud. In Australia, there is a saying that "the tall poppy gets cut down." In Japan, it is said that "the nail that sticks up gets hammered down." The evidence that the FTC presented in *FTC v. Qualcomm* sounded like Silicon Valley's own version of this centuries-old expression of envy and resentment toward one who possesses the skill to win the race again and again.

Before turning to the analysis of the legal dispute between the FTC and Qualcomm, it is worth taking a step back to and ask several questions. What is Qualcomm? What role has it played in American innovation? Why had its products become so widespread among the major smartphone OEMs? Testimony presented during the trial in *FTC v. Qualcomm* provided answers to these questions. Judge Koh scarcely mentioned that testimony in her findings of fact and conclusions of law.

---

[429] FTC v. Qualcomm Inc., No. 19-16122, 2020 WL 4591476, at *3 (9th Cir. Aug. 11, 2020) (footnote omitted).

[430] *Id.*

[431] David J. Teece, *Profiting from Technological Innovation: Implications for Integration, Collaboration, Licensing and Public Policy*, 15 Res. Pol'y 285, 302 (1986) ("Practically all forms of technological know-how must be embedded in goods and services to yield value to the consumer. . . . In a world of tight appropriability and zero transactions cost—the world of neoclassical trade theory—it is a matter of indifference whether an innovating firm has an in-house manufacturing capability, domestic or foreign. It can simply engage in arms-length contracting (patent licensing, know-how licensing, co-production, etc.) for the sale of the output of the activity in which it has a comparative advantage (in this case R&D) and will maximize returns by specializing in what it does best. However, in a regime of weak appropriability, and especially where the requisite manufacturing assets are specialized to the innovation, which is often the case, participation in manufacturing may be necessary if an innovator is to appropriate the rents from its innovation.").

A. Alex Rogers' Testimony Explaining Why Qualcomm's Business Model Was Innovative and Unique

During the trial, Qualcomm's final live (as opposed to videotaped) witness in its defense case was Alex Rogers, the President of QTL, who testified on January 25, 2019.[432] He provided extensive information about Qualcomm's business and its licensing practices. His testimony explained why Qualcomm's business model was both innovative and unique.

1. Mr. Rogers' Testimony on QTL's Relation to Qualcomm and Its Chip Business

Mr. Rogers testified that, as QTL's President, he had "general supervisory responsibilities over the management of the entire business, the license agreements, [and] the P&L [profit and loss] of the business,"[433] including participating in developing new licensing programs and managing existing license programs.[434] He began his testimony by explaining the relationship between QTL and QCT:

> Q. Can you tell us how QTL is related to QCT, the chip business?
>
> A. So QTL is the technology licensing arm of Qualcomm, and it's a separate business that's run with separate managers from QCT. We have separate accounting, separate P&L. And so QCT has its own set of management. QTL has its own set of management. We're two separate businesses within the same corporate structure.
>
> Q. And, Mr. Rogers, do you personally have any responsibility for QCT or the chip business?
>
> A. I do not.[435]

Mr. Rogers then explained QTL's operations in greater detail:

> Q. At a high level, how would you describe the business of QTL?
>
> A. . . . QTL is the commercialization arm of Qualcomm's research and development activities. . . . Qualcomm is essentially a technology development company, and we develop essential technologies for cellular systems. We conduct research and development that leads to the innovations that lead to the development of the cellular systems. We take this technology development, this R&D, and we push it into the industry primarily through

---

[432] Transcript of Proceedings (Volume 9) at 1970:3–8, FTC v. Qualcomm Inc., No. 5:17-cv-00220-LHK (N.D. Cal. Jan. 25, 2019) (Testimony of Alex Rogers (President, Qualcomm Technology Licensing)).

[433] *Id.* at 1971:6–8.

[434] *Id.* at 1971:9–14.

[435] *Id.* at 1971:15–25.

standards organizations. And then we also patent the innovations associated with that systemwide development activity and other activities. And then QTL takes the output of that, the intellectual property, the patent portfolio, and we license that for licensing revenue, and then we put that revenue back into research and development and technology and innovation.[436]

Thus, as Mr. Rogers explained, one might regard QTL as the business executive handling the affairs of Qualcomm, the inventor and innovator. Mr. Rogers testified how QTL licenses its technologies to third parties:

Q. And as of March of 2018, can you describe for us, just in general, the types of licenses that QTL offered to licensees?

A. So generally we offer portfolio wide licenses that include cellular standard essential patent licenses, as well as patents related to other standards outside of cellular, as well as non-essential patents. So our portfolio wide licensing program is at a certain rate, 5 percent. And then in addition to that, we also offer cellular standard essential portfolio licenses, that is, SEP only licenses as well.

Q. And are those SEP licenses relevant to more than one generation of the cellular standards?

A. Yes. Those licenses will cover 2G, 3G, 4G, and now 5G.

Q. Now, does QTL offer any other services to licensees?

A. Yes, we do. We fund a group within Qualcomm called ESG, Engineering Services Group, and that group actually offers services to carriers, infrastructure equipment manufacturers, handset and device manufacturers to help them implement new technologies. But in addition, QTL also has a small group of engineers and we work with . . . licensees to help them understand new technologies, to help them improve aspects of their products and bring them to market. And we also fund different labs in different places around the world, including the U.S., China, Taiwan, [and] India, where we help licensees essentially develop technologies for their products and help them bring them to market.[437]

Mr. Rogers also explained that Qualcomm licenses its patent portfolio to companies that use Qualcomm's modems as well as to those that do not:

Q. And these engineering services, are they available to licensees who don't purchase any Qualcomm chips?

A. Yes. You just need to be a licensee.

Q. And what is the benefit of this program to QTL?

---

[436] *Id.* at 1972:1–16.
[437] *Id.* at 1972:17–1973:19.

A. Well, the more that we can help licensees bring product[s] to market, particularly more quickly, and products that will be successful, the better off we are as a licensing business. In addition, we want to bring new companies to market. We want to bring smaller, startup companies that want to get into the market. We want to help them succeed in getting their products into the market successfully.[438]

Mr. Rogers next testified that he personally participated in licensing negotiations on behalf of QTL, and he explained how such negotiations typically proceed:

Q. Mr. Rogers, have you personally participated in licensing negotiations on behalf of QTL?

A. Yes, I have.

Q. In general terms, can you describe how QTL approaches licensing negotiations?

A. So negotiations are different depending on the licensee. We have certain terms that we offer. But once you get into a licensing negotiation, a lot depends on what the licensee is interested in, and the give and take between Qualcomm and the licensee. So it depends on the product that they're interested in, the scope of the license that they may be interested in, and other factors that affect their business.[439]

Mr. Rogers testified that QTL assembles an entire team for a license negotiation, which can take years to complete:

Q. Does QTL typically negotiate in teams?

A. Yes. We have licensing managers, and that set of folks is led by our General Manager, John Han . . . [,] and we also have lawyers within QTL that get involved in the licensing discussions, and sometimes some of our engineers within QTL will get involved in the licensing discussions as well.

Q. And how about on the licensee's side? How are their teams typically formed?

A. So they're typically represented by the same types of folks with the same types of expertise. They'll have business people involved, they'll have inhouse lawyers involved, they may have engineering folks involved as well. And sometimes they may also have outside counsel involved.

Q. How long do negotiations for licensing agreements typically last?

---

438   *Id.* at 1973:20–1974:5.
439   *Id.* at 1974:6–18.

A. So they can last, it's . . . varied. They can be weeks, which would be very quick. But they can last for months, and some can even last for years.[440]

Mr. Rogers' testimony then turned to whether and why licensees ask to renegotiate existing licenses with QTL:

Q. Now, from time to time do licensees ask QTL to renegotiate existing licenses?

A. Yes, they do.

Q. What circumstances would occasion that?

A. So they may have a change in their business, they may have stopped selling products, they may want to add certain products that are unlicensed, they may want to renegotiate the scope of a particular license. There are any variety of factors that can cause a licensee to want to renegotiate a license.

Q. What leverage, if any, are licensees able to exert over Qualcomm in these licensing negotiations[?]

A. I think the most typical would be either to stop paying or to threaten to stop paying.[441]

Mr. Rogers then gave specific examples of Qualcomm licensees that had stopped paying royalties and had used that withholding of payment as a tool to gain bargaining power in the negotiation with Qualcomm:

Q. And in your time as the President of QTL, have licensees done exactly that?

A. Yes, they have. When I first took over as Interim General Manager in the 2016 timeframe, there were a number of licensees in China, for example, that had stopped paying under their existing agreements. And in addition, Apple has recently caused its contract manufacturers to stop paying. And we have another licensee that is a fairly significant licensee that has stopped paying for some period of time and is now in a partial pay situation.

Q. And when that happens, do negotiations typically continue?

A. Yes. When that happens, negotiations do continue.

Q. And in any of these instances that you mentioned, did Qualcomm interrupt chip supply or threaten to interrupt chip supply to the licensees?

A. No.[442]

---

[440] *Id.* at 1974:19–1975:11.
[441] *Id.* at 1975:12–25.
[442] *Id.* at 1976:1–17.

Thus, it was Mr. Rogers' sworn testimony at trial that, during his tenure as President of QTL, when certain existing licensees had failed to pay patent royalties due to QTL, QCT did not interrupt or threaten to interrupt chip supply to those licensees.

2. *The Absence of Simultaneity Between an OEM's Negotiations for an Exhaustive License to Qualcomm's Cellular SEPs and the OEM's Negotiations for a Modem Supply Agreement with Qualcomm*

Mr. Rogers testified about the differences between the negotiation of an exhaustive license to Qualcomm's portfolio of cellular SEPs and a supply agreement for the purchase of Qualcomm's modem. He explained that Qualcomm does not negotiate with a given OEM for an exhaustive license to Qualcomm's cellular SEPs as frequently as Qualcomm negotiates agreements to supply the same OEM with Qualcomm modems:

> Q. Mr. Rogers, how often are licensing agreements and chip sale agreements negotiated at the same time?
>
> A. So these agreements are negotiated according to what I would call a different pace of play. So it's actually pretty rare that that would overlap. On the licensing side, we negotiate agreements that are going to last for years. On the chip side, they have a very fast pace of play where they go through their purchase order and their pricing at a much more rapid pace. So these don't typically overlap.[443]

As we shall see, although Qualcomm's exhaustive license agreements for its cellular SEPs typically last for 5 or 10 years, its supply agreements for Qualcomm modems are negotiated on shorter intervals.

We shall see that great economic significance attaches to the fact, established here in Mr. Rogers' unrebutted trial testimony, that Qualcomm and a given OEM typically would not negotiate an exhaustive license to cellular SEPs and a modem supply agreement simultaneously. That fact would play an important role in debunking the plausibility of the FTC's (and Professor Shapiro's) royalty "surcharge" and modem "tax" theory of anticompetitive harm. It simply bears emphasis at this early point in our examination of Judge Koh's findings of fact and conclusions of law in *FTC v. Qualcomm* that the factual testimony on this topic was unambiguous. It was clearly explained in the testimony of Mr. Rogers and never refuted by any other witness.

Yet, Judge Koh ignored this highly probative testimony by Mr. Rogers. She ruled his testimony inconsistent with other evidence in the case. Thus,

---

[443] *Id.* at 1976:18–1977:3.

Judge Koh evidently believed that none of Mr. Rogers' testimony deserved her consideration.

   3. *Mr. Rogers Testified That QTL Interpreted Qualcomm's FRAND Obligation Consistently with the IPR Policy of the European Telecommunications Standards Institute (ETSI)*

At trial, Mr. Rogers also testified about Qualcomm's interpretation of the FRAND and RAND commitments that it had made to various SSOs. In particular, he testified about the FRAND commitment contained in the IPR Policy of the European Telecommunications Standards Institute (ETSI):

> Q. I want to talk with you for just a minute about FRAND. Has Qualcomm made FRAND commitments to various standard setting organizations?
>
> A. Yes, we have.
>
> Q. And when you consider QTL's FRAND obligations in the context of the cellular standard setting, do you have a particular I.P. policy in mind?
>
> A. Yes. I typically look to the ETSI IPR Policy.
>
> Q. And why is that?
>
> A. Well, from my perspective, and I think from Qualcomm's perspective, the ETSI standard setting organization is the primary organization for cellular standards activities within 3GPP. And in addition, the ETSI IPR Policy is, from my perspective, kind of the central IPR Policy for FRAND commitments for cellular standard essential patents.[444]

Mr. Rogers then testified in greater detail regarding Qualcomm's FRAND commitment to ETSI and why, in his opinion, Qualcomm's licensing practice complied with ETSI's IPR Policy:

> Q. And based on your understanding of ETSI's policies, are QTL's licensing practices consistent with those obligations?
>
> A. Yes, they are.
>
> Q. How so?
>
> A. Well, we license at the equipment level, so, for example, that would be a smartphone or a handset. And we license on fair and reasonable terms, and we license on non-discriminatory terms. And so in our view, our licensing practices are consistent with ETSI's IPR Policy.
>
> Q. How does Qualcomm make its standard essential patented technology available to other chip makers?

---

[444] *Id.* at 1977:4–1977:19.

A. So we don't license at the component level, which is not required under the ETSI IPR Policy. But the way the technology is made available is we work on underlying technology[] that finds its way into the specifications that then become standardized. And then basically everybody in the industry has access to that. Those standards are published, anybody can access those specifications. And Qualcomm doesn't do anything with respect to component manufacturers to in any way preclude that access.[445]

Mr. Rogers emphasized that Qualcomm licenses its FRAND-committed cellular SEPs to OEMs. Although Qualcomm does not offer exhaustive licenses to its cellular SEPs to component manufacturers, component manufacturers remain free to access the standard's specifications.

4. *Qualcomm Publicly Announced Its 5G Royalty Rates Before 3GPP Had Adopted the 5G Standard*

As we shall examine in detail in Part IV.B, Professor Shapiro testified that a FRAND royalty for a portfolio of SEPs should equal the royalty that an SEP holder and an OEM would have negotiated *before* the standard's adoption. One can dispute the theoretical validity and the real-world practicality of Professor Shapiro's assertion about the proper methodology for calculating a FRAND royalty, and I have done so at great length in articles and expert economic testimony over a number of years.[446] But I suspend my disbelief of Professor Shapiro's assertion for the time being to show that Mr. Rogers' testimony at trial provided facts which, when plugged into Professor Shapiro's preferred method for calculating a FRAND royalty, actually disproved Professor Shapiro's contention that Qualcomm was charging OEMs rates for exhaustive licenses to its portfolio of cellular SEPs that exceeded the ceiling of the FRAND range.

Consistent with Professor Shapiro's definition of a FRAND royalty, Mr. Rogers testified that Qualcomm announced, *before* 3GPP adopted the technical specification for 5G, the royalty that Qualcomm expected to collect from OEMs for an exhaustive license to its portfolio of 5G cellular SEPs:

---

[445] *Id.* at 1977:20–1978:16.
[446] *See* J. Gregory Sidak, *The Meaning of FRAND, Part I: Royalties*, 9 J. Competition L. & Econ. 931, 968–88 (2013); J. Gregory Sidak & Jeremy O. Skog, *Hedonic Prices and Patent Royalties*, 2 Criterion J. on Innovation 601, 670–73 (2017); J. Gregory Sidak, *Misconceptions Concerning the Use of Hedonic Prices to Determine FRAND or RAND Royalties for Standard-Essential Patents*, 4 Criterion J. on Innovation 501, 504–15 (2019); *see also* Sidak, *Is Patent Holdup a Hoax?*, *supra* note 118; J. Gregory Sidak, *Tournaments and FRAND Royalties*, 1 Criterion J. on Innovation 101 (2016); J. Gregory Sidak, *Patent Holdup and Oligopsonistic Collusion in Standard-Setting Organizations*, 5 J. Competition L. & Econ. 123 (2009); J. Gregory Sidak, *Holdup, Royalty Stacking, and the Presumption of Injunctive Relief for Patent Infringement: A Reply to Lemley and Shapiro*, 92 Minn. L. Rev. 714 (2008).

Q. Now, at the time that the [Qualcomm's] 5G [SEP-licensing] program was announced in November of 2017, had the technical specification for 5G been finalized?

A. No, not yet.

Q. When did that happen?

A. That happened in December of 2017.

Q. And had the standard been adopted by 3GPP by that time?

A. Not by that time.

Q. Did that happen sometime after March of 2018?

A. It happened after the beginning of 2018. I'm not sure if it was before or after March.[447]

Judge Koh did not acknowledge this highly probative passage from Mr. Rogers' trial testimony in her findings of fact and conclusions of law.

5.   *Mr. Rogers' Testimony of Qualcomm's Expectations as of the Cutoff of Fact Discovery in March 2018 Concerning Competition in 5G Modems*

On redirect examination by Mr. Van Nest, Mr. Rogers testified as to Qualcomm's expectations in March 2018 of the competition that it would face from rival manufacturers of 5G modems:

Q. Mr. Rogers, as of March of 2018 were you expecting competition in 5G?

A. Yes, sir.

Q. What companies did Qualcomm believe would be competing for 5G?

A. Huawei had already announced a 5G chip I think in the prior month at [the] Mobile World Congress; Samsung had announced a 5G chip; Intel had a 5G project; MediaTek had a 5G chip project as well.

Q. Did you actually attend the 2018 Mobile World Congress in January?

A. I think it was in February.

Q. Did you attend?

A. Yes, I did.

Q. What did you see there?

A. I saw the head of the mobile department of Huawei holding up a 5G chip and talking about the 5G chip capabilities of Huawei.

---

447 Transcript of Proceedings (Volume 9) at 1984:18–1985:3, FTC v. Qualcomm Inc., No. 5:17-cv-00220-LHK (N.D. Cal. Jan. 25, 2019) (Testimony of Alex Rogers (President, Qualcomm Technology Licensing)).

Q. Could we have CX 8196 on the screen, and page 121. It's in your binder, but we have it here. Could we go to the bottom of the page. . . . With reference to the bottom result, 5G Chipset Competitive Landscape, can you tell us what is recorded there?

A. Yeah. It's Samsung and HiSilicon, that's the division or the company that belongs to Huawei that makes chips, [which are] expected to compete with QCT. And then it refers to Intel and MediaTek lagging on time to market, but obviously they're preparing 5G chips as well.[448]

Thus, Mr. Rogers testified that, as of March 2018, Qualcomm expected Huawei, Samsung, Intel, and MediaTek to be rival 5G modem suppliers.

6. *Qualcomm's License Negotiation with Samsung Leading to Their 2018 Amended Agreement*

At trial, Mr. Rogers also testified on direct examination about Qualcomm's negotiations with Samsung, lasting from 2016 to 2018, to amend their longstanding license. He further testified about the relationship to those negotiations of the investigation of Qualcomm by the Korea Fair Trade Commission (KFTC). As we saw earlier, Qualcomm had alleged in litigation in the U.S. District Court for the Southern District of California that Apple had helped to orchestrate the KFTC's investigation.[449] Mr. Rogers began by explaining the nature of the Samsung negotiation:

Q. Let's turn to talk briefly about Samsung. Did Samsung have a license agreement with Qualcomm when you were promoted into your current role?

A. Yes, it did.

Q. And did you become familiar with that license agreement?

A. Generally, yes.

Q. Have there been discussions with Samsung regarding amending that agreement since you took over at QTL?

A. Yes.

Q. When did you get involved in those?

A. So I would have been involved in the Samsung discussions probably going back to 2016, but certainly involved in 2017 into the beginning of 2018.[450]

---

[448] *Id.* at 2015:21–2016:24 (discussing CX8196).

[449] *See supra* note 349 and accompanying text.

[450] Transcript of Proceedings (Volume 9) at 1985:4–16, FTC v. Qualcomm Inc., No. 5:17-cv-00220-LHK (N.D. Cal. Jan. 25, 2019) (Testimony of Alex Rogers (President, Qualcomm Technology Licensing)).

Mr. Rogers then testified about his personal involvement in the negotiations, the other negotiators from both Qualcomm and Samsung, and the duration of the negotiations:

> Q. And did you personally participate in the discussions?
>
> A. Yes, I did.
>
> Q. Who represented QTL?
>
> A. So myself, Derek Aberle when he was there was involved, John Han, the General Manager of QTL, was very much involved. We also had some attorneys within QTL and licensing managers involved in those discussions as well, and also folks from the engineering side within QTL as well.
>
> Q. So it sounds like this was a pretty big group?
>
> A. Yes.
>
> Q. Who was representing Samsung?
>
> A. So Samsung was represented primarily by Dr. Ahn, who's the EVP, Executive Vice-President, of their licensing group[,] . . . [a]nd also by Injung Lee, who was second in charge. Samsung also had a number of inhouse attorneys involved, and I think also some, some engineers as well.
>
> Q. And over what period of time did these negotiations take place?
>
> A. As I said, I think these negotiations were ongoing beginning at least in 2016, all through 2017, and then into the beginning of 2018.[451]

Mr. Rogers explained that the negotiations resulted in the successful amendment of an agreement between Qualcomm and Samsung that had first begun in 1993. Among other things, the 2018 amendment reduced the cap on the royalty base for handsets from $500 to $400 and expanded the scope of Samsung's cross license of intellectual property rights to Qualcomm:

> Q. And was this [negotiation] to amend an existing Samsung agreement?
>
> A. Yes. It was an amendment to an agreement that was first entered into in 1993, and then amended again at least as of 2009, and then this was an amendment to that existing agreement.
>
> Q. And I take it these negotiations arrived ultimately at an agreement, or a series of agreements?
>
> A. Yes, it did.
>
> Q. And did you amend the existing patent license agreement?

---

451 *Id.* at 1985:17–1986:13.

A. Yes. We amended the agreement between Qualcomm and Samsung. The fundamental terms of the agreement remained in place, the royalty rate, for example, the license from Qualcomm to Samsung remained in place. But we amended other aspects of the agreement. One of the things that we did was we reduced the [royalty base] cap associated with the license from $500 to $400 for handsets. We also increased the scope of the rights that we got back from Samsung to their intellectual property for our products.

Q. And had there been an existing cross-license in the . . . agreement that was being amended?

A. Yes. We already had a cross-license from Samsung, and we increased the scope of that cross-license through a particularly complicated mechanism that essentially gave us rights to [a] significant new number of patents that they had.

Q. And did Qualcomm pay separate consideration for that expanded scope of rights?

A. Yes, we did.[452]

Mr. Rogers testified that the negotiation over the 2018 amended agreement also resolved various disputes between Qualcomm and Samsung pursuant to a mutual settlement and release that the parties executed simultaneously with their amendment:

Q. Now, as part of the discussion you had with Samsung, were there other disputes addressed?

A. Yes. There were a number of other disputes between Qualcomm and Samsung that were addressed and resolved as part of this overall negotiation.

Q. And what claims did Qualcomm have vis-à-vis Samsung?

A. So Samsung . . . has a large fab and Samsung was making Qualcomm chipset products, and we had some concerns because Samsung also has a competing chipset business. And we had some concerns about information exchange between the fab and the chipset business and between the fab and some of our customers. We raised those concerns, and those concerns were addressed as part of the overall resolution.

Q. And did Samsung—

A. There was also some, I think, overdue payment concerns, or under due payment concerns that were addressed.

Q. All right. And did Samsung have disputes of its own related to Qualcomm?

---

452 *Id.* at 1986:14–1987:15.

A. Yeah, Samsung had disputes relating to Qualcomm's license agreements that were part of the matters associated with the KFTC, and Samsung had some concerns about whether it was being treated fairly with respect to Apple.

Q. With respect to Apple?

A. Yes.

Q. Now, how were these disputes resolved?

A. So everything was resolved in a mutual settlement and release agreement that was entered into at the same time as the amended license agreement.

Q. And did Qualcomm pay Samsung separate consideration as part of that agreement?

A. We did.[453]

Mr. Rogers testified that the 2018 amendment of the Qualcomm-Samsung agreement also addressed component-level licensing of Qualcomm's patents. The amendment did so not by authorizing Samsung to take an exhaustive license to Qualcomm's cellular SEPs at the component level, but instead by conferring on Samsung the right to receive from Qualcomm a FRAND offer at the component level if Qualcomm were to attempt to assert its cellular SEPs against Samsung's modem business:

Q. Now, did the agreement or series of agreements address component level licensing as well?

A. Yes, there was a particular agreement that we entered into that addressed the question of component level licensing, but it wasn't itself a component level license. It was essentially a contractual assurance with respect to . . . Samsung's component business.

Q. And what was the assurance that Qualcomm gave?

A. So Samsung has a cellular baseband business that they make primarily for their own use, and Qualcomm gave Samsung an assurance that should Qualcomm ever seek to assert its cellular SEPs against that component business, against those components, we would first make Samsung an offer on fair, reasonable, and non-discriminatory terms.[454]

Mr. Gonell of Qualcomm elsewhere testified that it would contravene Qualcomm's commercial interests to assert its cellular SEPs against a rival modem manufacturer (such as Samsung) because Qualcomm did not seek to grant exhaustive licenses to its cellular SEPs to rival modem manufacturers:

---

453 *Id.* at 1987:16–1988:21.
454 *Id.* at 1988:22–1989:10.

Q. . . . Are there any other reasons why you believe it would not be in Qualcomm's commercial interest to assert cellular SEPs against other modem chip suppliers?

A. Yes. because it's counter to the foundational device-level licensing of our licensing program. If you assert against a chip supplier a cellular essential patent, you need to be prepared to license those patents to the chip maker. And for all the reasons I explained why multi level licensing is inefficient, we don't want to do it and if you assert, that's what you're signing on to. You're signing on to multi level licensing.[455]

Mr. Gonell explained why, in principle, Qualcomm would have no incentive to assert its cellular SEPs against rival modem manufacturers. Instead, Qualcomm executed nonexhaustive covenants or assurances, such as the agreement with Samsung that Mr. Rogers described, to enable rival modem manufacturers to achieve freedom to operate.

Mr. Rogers testified that Qualcomm informed the KFTC of the provision in its agreement with Samsung regarding component-level licensing, as Qualcomm did with respect to all of the series of agreements into which it and Samsung entered in 2018:

Q. Now, did you present this body of agreements to the Korea[] Fair Trade Commission?

A. Yes, we did.

Q. Why did you do that?

A. Well, the KFTC matter had concluded, it was on appeal, and we wanted to make sure that the KFTC was aware that we had reached this set of agreements and that they were fully informed.

Q. So was the entire series of agreements provided to the government?

A. Yes, and we basically gave them an overview.

Q. And did the KFTC express an objection to any provision of the agreements?

A. No.

Mr. Van Nest: Pass the witness, your honor.[456]

Judge Koh did not mention in her findings of fact and conclusions of law that Qualcomm gave the KFTC this opportunity to review the substantive terms

---

455 Transcript of Proceedings (Volume 7) at 1450:9–20, FTC v. Qualcomm Inc., No. 5:17-cv-00220-LHK (N.D. Cal. Jan. 18, 2019) (Testimony of Fabian Gonell (Legal Counsel and Senior Vice President, Licensing Strategy, Qualcomm Technology Licensing)).

456 Transcript of Proceedings (Volume 9) at 1989:11–25, FTC v. Qualcomm Inc., No. 5:17-cv-00220-LHK (N.D. Cal. Jan. 25, 2019) (Testimony of Alex Rogers (President, Qualcomm Technology Licensing)).

of the series of 2018 agreements with Samsung, including the provisions of that series of agreements relevant to potential component-level licensing of Qualcomm's cellular SEPs.

B. *Was the Testimony of the FTC's Licensing Expert, Richard Donaldson, Probative Evidence in* FTC v. Qualcomm?

The FTC during its case-in-chief put on expert testimony by Richard Donaldson, a patent licensing consultant who had retired from Texas Instruments after working "for thirty-one years as a licensing executive and patent attorney, retiring in 2000 as Senior Vice President and General Patent Counsel."[457] The apparent purpose of Mr. Donaldson's testimony was to rebut anticipatorily Mr. Rogers' expected defense testimony and the proposition that the uniqueness of Qualcomm's licensing model for monetizing its patents had salutary effects. Mr. Donaldson summarized his testimony as follows:

> Q. Mr. Donaldson, what are the core opinions that you offer in this case?
>
> A. I think primarily I've looked at license negotiations that Qualcomm entered into, considered the type of negotiations these were, and have concluded that they were very atypical. And they were atypical from normal patent license agreements because Qualcomm had a policy that they called "no license, no chips," and giving the criticality of the chips that Qualcomm possessed, this gave them tremendous bargaining power in the license negotiations and resulted in what I believe are some very atypical license terms that companies agreed to because of this "no license, no chips policy." A second opinion I would offer is that chip level licensing is a viable way of licensing in this industry. It's something that I did during my career at Texas Instruments. We licensed exhaustively chips at the component level and sold products exhaustively at that level. And I had a separate licensing program directed purely to the end items, like computers, and these were successful and they were—they were—those specific issues in trying to implement them.[458]

Mr. Donaldson provided compelling testimony that Qualcomm in January 2019 had a business model for monetizing its patent portfolio that differed materially from the business model that Texas Instruments used at some point between 1969 and 2000. So what?

---

[457] Redacted Expert Report of Richard Donaldson ¶ 2, at 1, FTC v. Qualcomm Inc., No. 5:17-cv-00220-LHK (N.D. Cal. May 24, 2018), ECF No. 1273 [hereinafter Redacted Initial Expert Report of Richard Donaldson].

[458] *See* Transcript of Proceedings (Volume 5) at 962:17–963:12, FTC v. Qualcomm Inc., No. 5:17-cv-00220-LHK (N.D. Cal. Jan. 14, 2019) (Testimony of Richard Donaldson).

Judge Koh found Mr. Donaldson's testimony to be reliable, but she did not explain why his testimony was the least bit relevant under the Federal Rules of Evidence.[459] Why was Mr. Donaldson's licensing experience at Texas Instruments from 1969 to 2000[460]—years before (as we shall see in Part III) the Supreme Court began revisiting the doctrine of patent exhaustion in 2008—evidence probative of any disputed material fact in *FTC v. Qualcomm*? To what extent was the FTC passing off Mr. Donaldson's percipient testimony concerning Texas Instruments as expert testimony that purported to draw broader conclusions based on more than Mr. Donaldson's career at a single company before the Supreme Court began its revisitation of the doctrine of patent exhaustion?

Moreover, Mr. Donaldson admitted on cross examination that Texas Instruments had a business strategy (at some undefined period between 1969 and 2000) concerning SEPs that was entirely dissimilar to Qualcomm's business strategy and to Qualcomm's evident belief that cellular SEPs are exceptionally valuable:

> Q. You don't know if a percentage of TI's patents were standard essential patents; right?
>
> A. I don't, because *we intentionally . . . made the decision not to seek standard essential patents because of our understanding of their not being valuable*, and we intentionally published, like, the fancy publications instead of seeking patents.[461]

Mr. Donaldson admitted that, unlike Qualcomm, Texas Instruments during his 31 years of service with the company did not own thousands of SEPs:

> Q. . . . So you have no reason to believe that TI had thousands and thousands of standard essential patents like Qualcomm has; right?
>
> A. No. I know for a fact they did not at the time I was there.[462]

As a matter of antitrust law, it is not clear why Mr. Donaldson's testimony that Qualcomm's licenses were "atypical" was legally relevant because section 2 of the Sherman Act does not seal even a monopolist's business model in a time capsule. And there is no reason to believe that Qualcomm's decision not to copy the business model that Texas Instruments followed in or before 2000 amounted to a violation of antitrust law, as the FTC's proffer of Mr. Donaldson's testimony awkwardly implied.

459   FTC v. Qualcomm Inc., 411 F. Supp. 3d 658, 788 (N.D. Cal. 2019).
460   Redacted Initial Expert Report of Richard Donaldson, *supra* note 457, app. A, at 2–4.
461   Transcript of Proceedings (Volume 5) at 982:5–7, 982:17–21, FTC v. Qualcomm Inc., No. 5:17-cv-00220-LHK (N.D. Cal. Jan. 14, 2019) (Testimony of Richard Donaldson) (emphasis added).
462   *Id.* at 982:23–983:2.

C. Business Innovation: Judge Koh Versus the Nature of the Firm

Economists speak of production occurring with "the firm."[463] Qualcomm is a firm. So is Apple. So is Intel. What defines the institutional structure of production? What shall be the boundaries of the firm and its modes of contracting with third parties?

1. Objective Knowledge and the Evolutionary View of the Firm

One view is that the nature of the firm is consciously devised by human ingenuity, that it defines how individuals and organizations shall interact with one another, and that the authority of the person who dictates that institutional structure of production imparts efficacy to what results. We can call this view the "imperative" theory of the nature of the firm, because of its obvious similarities to the imperative theory of law.[464]

A different view is that the nature of the firm continually evolves, that it reflects and summarizes information that has been revealed over decades regarding the optimal ordering of relationships among producers, consumers, and owners of the factors of production. On this evolutionary view of the firm, the worth of a business model arises from objective knowledge that the particular structure in question is superior to all other known means of ordering a specific kind of relationship or transaction. This view of the firm is associated with the works of a community of distinguished economists—including Armen Alchian and Harold Demsetz[465] and Nobel laureates Ronald Coase,[466] George Stigler,[467] and Friedrich Hayek.[468] For example, Stigler argued that the optimum scale of a firm in an industry could be inferred

---

[463] Nobel laureate Ronald Coase provided the canonical explanation. *See* Ronald H. Coase, *The Nature of the Firm*, 4 ECONOMICA (n.s.) 386, 404–05 (1937). Harold Demsetz later made additional contributions of significance. *See* Harold Demsetz, *The Theory of the Firm Revisited*, 4 J.L. ECON. & ORG. 141, 142–43 (1988); Harold Demsetz, *The Structure of Ownership and the Theory of the Firm*, 26 J.L. & ECON. 375, 377–78 (1983).

[464] A market, which the firm and its rivals populate, does not judge the "legitimacy" of a particular model for the institutional structure of production, but rather its efficiency or efficacy, for which I use "merit" or "worth" as a shorthand. Regarding the imperative theory of law and its claim to "legitimacy," Thomas Hobbes wrote that "the law is a command." THOMAS HOBBES, LEVIATHAN ch. 26, ¶ 8, at 187 (Cambridge Univ. Press 1991) (1651). He asserted that "all laws, written and unwritten, have their authority and force from the will of the commonwealth." *Id.* ch. 26, ¶ 6, at 186. This view of law was embraced by John Austin, JOHN AUSTIN, THE PROVINCE OF JURISPRUDENCE DETERMINED (Wilfrid E. Rumble ed., Cambridge Univ. Press 1995) (1832), and is epitomized by the famous remark of Oliver Wendell Holmes, "The prophecies of what the courts will do in fact, and nothing more pretentious, are what I mean by the law." Holmes, *The Path of the Law*, *supra* note 257, at 461. H.L.A. Hart called this perspective the "imperative theory" of law, for which "the key to the understanding of law is to be found in the simple notion of an order backed by threats." H.L.A. HART, THE CONCEPT OF LAW 16 (Clarendon Press 1961).

[465] Armen A. Alchian & Harold Demsetz, *Production, Information Costs, and Economic Organization*, 62 AM. ECON. REV. 777 (1972).

[466] Coase, *The Nature of the Firm*, *supra* note 463. Coase eloquently revisited these themes in his 1991 Nobel Prize lecture. *See* R.H. Coase, *The Institutional Structure of Production*, 82 AM. ECON. REV. 713 (1992).

[467] George J. Stigler, *The Economies of Scale*, 1 J.L. & ECON. 54 (1958).

[468] Hayek's voluminous writings are summarized in FRIEDRICH A. HAYEK, THE FATAL CONCEIT: THE ERRORS OF SOCIALISM (W.W. Bartley III ed., Univ. of Chicago Press 1988). His seminal work,

from what he called "the survivor principle," whose "fundamental postulate is that the competition of different sizes of firms sifts out the more efficient enterprises."[469]

The difference between the two views of the nature of the firm is illustrated by the following example. Two persons inspect a chart showing all of the jobs and lines of reporting in a factory. The first person sees a consciously devised network of authority. The second person sees the same chart as the summation of a vast quantity of knowledge. To the second observer, the hierarchy within the factory reveals the knowledge that has been gleaned from years of experience, in which alternative and less productive hierarchies have been tried and rejected or, if not rejected, have caused the companies that have continued to adhere to them to wither. Thus, to the second person, the worth of the management chart does not lie in the fact that the chief executive officer or the board of directors has the authority to draw and redraw the chart however it likes, but rather in the objective inferiority of all predecessors to this particular ordering of management responsibilities and its accompanying institutional structure of production. If a superior ordering subsequently becomes known, then even this present management chart will cease to have worth for the second observer, regardless of how uninterrupted the reign of authority of the board or CEO who imposed this ordering.

2. *What Makes a Particular Business Model Succeed?*

It has been my professional experience—foreshadowed roughly 40 years earlier in conversations that I was privileged as a young man to have had with Stigler, Richard Posner, William Baxter, and others on the role of industrial organization in antitrust law—that a firm that has developed a uniquely successful method of doing business often has great difficulty explaining in plain English why its business model has succeeded. Indeed, in a real-world experience consistent with Stigler's survivor principle, a client decades later engaged me to determine *why*, as an economic matter, it had been so consistently profitable and how it could stay that way. If the answer to this question were obvious to every firm, there would be far less demand for the handsomely compensated services of McKinsey, Bain, and the Boston Consulting Group.

In short, a firm might select a particular institutional structure of production for any one of a number of reasons, including those identified in famous

---

Friedrich A. Hayek, *The Use of Knowledge in Society*, 35 AM. ECON. REV. 519 (1945), of course has much broader implications than strictly the theory of the firm.

[469] Stigler, *The Economies of Scale, supra* note 467, at 55. In retrospect, one can see how seamlessly Stigler's survivor principle played off Judge Learned Hand's remark in *Alcoa* that "[a] single producer may be the survivor out of a group of active competitors." United States v. Aluminum Co. of Am., 148 F.2d 416, 430 (2ᵈ Cir. 1945).

monopolization cases—such as business acumen or historic accident[470] or superior skill, foresight, and industry.[471] But the firm perseveres in that particular definition of its boundaries because doing so remains more profitable than its metamorphosing into any other identifiable institutional structure of production.

3. *The FTC's and Judge Koh's "Imperative" View of the Firm*

The FTC and Judge Koh evidently believed that the principal function of Qualcomm's modem business was to exploit short-term switching costs once an OEM had committed to using Qualcomm as a modem supplier for a particular design-win contract. They would have us believe that an OEM's short-term dependence on Qualcomm modems for a given release of smartphone enabled Qualcomm to get the OEM to enter into an exhaustive license to Qualcomm's cellular SEPs more readily than it otherwise would; that that dependence on Qualcomm's modems enabled Qualcomm to charge the OEM an "unreasonably high" royalty for an exhaustive license to those cellular SEPs, greater than what Qualcomm otherwise could have charged; and that that dependence on Qualcomm's modems enabled Qualcomm to insulate itself from litigation by that OEM, which otherwise would have contended in court that Qualcomm's royalty for an exhaustive license to its cellular SEPs violated its relevant FRAND or RAND obligation (or that Qualcomm's cellular SEPs were invalid and therefore commercially worthless).

That narrative presumed that no procompetitive rationale could plausibly have motivated Qualcomm's particular mode of contracting, which both Qualcomm and the FTC agreed Qualcomm had uniquely developed and uniquely practiced continuously for several decades (though some individual features of Qualcomm's business model—notably, exhaustive licensing of its cellular SEPs at the device level rather than the component level—were also practiced by Nokia, Ericsson, and other owners of significant portfolios of SEPs for mobile communications).

4. *Economies of Scope Between Basic Research and Product Development*

While testifying at trial on why Qualcomm in December 2015 rejected the proposal to spin off its licensing business (QTL) from its modem business (QCT), David Wise, Qualcomm's Senior Vice President of Finance and Treasurer, offered several insights that help to explain Qualcomm's unique success:

---

[470] United States v. Grinnell Corp., 384 U.S. 563, 571 (1966).
[471] *Alcoa*, 148 F.2d at 430.

> Qualcomm has been successful in getting its technologies adopted into the standards bodies by the fact that we have the combined capabilities of QCT and QTL and we're able to invest and develop good technology and able to demonstrate that the technology functions[.] [W]e develop live systems to be able to show and demonstrate our innovations can perform as promised. And we, through QCT, have a large ability to implement the standards on the device side through chips, which positions us as a very good partner for infrastructure vendors and other important parties in the standards bodies that allow us to have good partnerships and success in getting folks to . . . adopt our technology.[472]

An economist hearing this testimony would recognize that Mr. Wise was describing something profound. In this passage, he was explaining from a business executive's perspective, and in a business executive's lexicon, the existence of economies of scope between basic research and product development.

One can put his insights into a more formal economic argument: by committing itself to producing and selling its own modem, which commercially embodied the basic technology that Qualcomm had committed to the standard, Qualcomm could credibly signal to OEMs that it believed its portfolio of cellular SEPs was indeed hugely valuable and consequently worthy of being licensed exhaustively to OEMs on the terms that Qualcomm offered. By making modems itself, Qualcomm made additional sunk investments complementary to its basic technology. Qualcomm thereby put its money where its mouth was. It had skin in the game. This account is a more nuanced economic explanation of Qualcomm's enduring success than is the convoluted web of conjectures that Professor Shapiro, the FTC, and Judge Koh offered.

This alternative explanation for the uniqueness and durability of Qualcomm's licensing practices rests entirely on an efficiency rationale for defining the boundaries of Qualcomm as a firm. It is consistent with the outcomes of two separate studies conducted by or on behalf of Qualcomm's senior management—Project Berlin in October 2007 and Project Phoenix in October 2015—on the question of whether Qualcomm would increase shareholder value if it were to divest its modem business from its technology-licensing business.[473] Both studies advised against a spinoff. It

---

[472] Transcript of Proceedings (Volume 1) at 116:3–15, FTC v. Qualcomm Inc., No. 5:17-cv-00220-LHK (N.D. Cal. Jan. 4, 2019) (Testimony of David Wise (Senior Vice President of Finance and Treasurer, Qualcomm)).

[473] *See id.* at 103:19–104:12, 104:13–105:19; Videotaped Deposition of Paul Jacobs (Qualcomm CEO) at 218:15–219:8, FTC v. Qualcomm Inc., No. 5:17-cv-00220-LHK (N.D. Cal. Mar. 17, 2018), *exhibit to* Federal Trade Commission's Submission of January 4[, 2019,] Testimony By Deposition, FTC v. Qualcomm Inc., No. 5:17-cv-00220-LHK (N.D. Cal. Jan. 7, 2019), ECF No. 1161.

appears that Project Phoenix was specifically studied at the urging of an activist investor who held a position in Qualcomm stock, Jana Partners.[474]

5. *Whether All That Is Not Permitted Is Forbidden*

A fundamental question of antitrust policy is whether all that is not forbidden is permitted, or whether all that is not permitted is forbidden. In the words of Ronald Coase, the field of industrial organization has evolved in such a manner that,

> if an economist finds something—a business practice of one sort or another—that he does not understand, he looks for a monopoly explanation. And as in this field we are very ignorant, the number of ununderstandable practices tends to be rather large, and the reliance on a monopoly explanation, frequent. . . . [T]he association of the study of industrial organization with antitrust policy has created a disposition to search for monopolistic explanations for all business practices whose justification is not obvious to the meanest intelligence.[475]

Qualcomm engaged in unique, original, and useful "business innovation"[476] in developing the practice of selling modems only to licensed OEMs and the practice of exhaustively licensing its cellular SEPs at the device level rather than the component level.

Unlike Judge Koh, the Ninth Circuit, citing *American Express*, observed that a firm's "unique business model" can "*increase*[] competition . . . by forcing rivals . . . to adapt and innovate, which . . . ultimately benefit[s] consumers by 'increas[ing] the quality and quantity of . . . transactions.'"[477] The Ninth Circuit recognized what Judge Koh could not see: that "what appeared at first to be *anti*competitive—[the use of a] unique business model . . . —was actually *pro*competitive and innovative."[478]

---

[474] Transcript of Proceedings (Volume 1) at 104:23–105:12, FTC v. Qualcomm Inc., No. 5:17-cv-00220-LHK (N.D. Cal. Jan. 4, 2019) (Testimony of David Wise (Senior Vice President of Finance and Treasurer, Qualcomm)) ("Q. Now, JANA Partners is an activist fund that took a position in Qualcomm prior to Project Phoenix; right? A. Correct. Q. And their thesis was that by separating QCT and QTL, they might create more shareholder value; right? A. Correct. Q. If you turn your attention to the bottom e-mail on this page from Scott Ostfeld, he was at JANA Partners according to the e-mail address; is that fair? A. That's right. Q. Okay. He writes, we wanted to share feedback on Qualcomm and the relationship between QCT/QTL from a former long-time executive of Ericsson. Do you see that, sir? A. Yes.").

[475] Ronald H. Coase, *Industrial Organization: A Proposal for Research*, *in* 3 Economic Research: Retrospect and Prospect: Policy Issues and Research Opportunities in Industrial Organization 59, 67, 68 (Victor R. Fuchs ed., Nat'l Bur. Econ. Res. 1972), *quoted in* Geoffrey A. Manne & Joshua D. Wright, *Innovation and the Limits of Antitrust*, 6 J. Competition L. & Econ. 153, 165 (2010).

[476] Manne & Wright, *Innovation and the Limits of Antitrust*, *supra* note 475, at 183; *see id.* at 183–86.

[477] FTC v. Qualcomm Inc., No. 19-16122, 2020 WL 4591476, at *8 (9th Cir. Aug. 11, 2020) (sixth alteration in original) (emphasis in original) (quoting Ohio v. Am. Express Co., 138 S. Ct. 2274, 2290 (2018)).

[478] *Id.* (emphasis in original).

That Professor Shapiro and the FTC and Judge Koh to the contrary of the Ninth Circuit evidently viewed Qualcomm's business model with revulsion—and that a plaintiff class action attorney evidently dreamt that a judge might "c[o]me along and . . . destroy a great deal of the value of Qualcomm's business model"[479]—simply tended to confirm Coase's observation that industrial organization theory has done its fair share of harm to antitrust jurisprudence.

The FTC looked skeptically on a method of doing business that seemed mysterious to the agency. So, the government's view in *FTC v. Qualcomm* was that Qualcomm had the burden of proving that its unique success did not result from unlawful behavior. And heaven forbid that Qualcomm's institutional structure of production was something original or even ingenious. Or that it enabled Qualcomm to earn positive economic profit. Or that it had not been successfully copied by any other firm, including Intel. The FTC's motto seemed to be, "The limit of my discernment is the proof of your culpability." Why did the FTC base its actions upon such a stultifying conception of innovation and competition?

III. Patent Exhaustion and Qualcomm's Apparent Business Purpose for Not Offering Exhaustive Licenses to Its Cellular SEPs to Rival Modem Manufacturers

Besides the political economy of the case, a second layer of factual palimpsest in *FTC v. Qualcomm*—Qualcomm's apparent business purpose for not offering licenses to its cellular SEPs to rival modem manufacturers, which was to avoid patent exhaustion—is an important factual predicate for understanding the case.

A. Patent Exhaustion

Qualcomm's apparent business motivation to avoid patent exhaustion completely explained why Qualcomm both (1) sold its modems only to *licensed* OEMs and (2) never intentionally *exhaustively* licensed its cellular SEPs to rival modem manufacturers. Yet, Judge Koh denounced as "anticompetitive conduct" Qualcomm's refusal "to sell its modem chips exhaustively and to sell modem chips to an OEM until the OEM signs a separate patent license agreement."[480] Why?

---

479 Deposition of Eric Reifschneider (Vol. 2), *supra* note 3, at 319:17–20.
480 FTC v. Qualcomm Inc., 411 F. Supp. 3d 658, 743 (N.D. Cal. 2019).

1.   Distinguishing a Nonexhaustive "License" Before Quanta *from an Exhaustive License After* Quanta

As we saw in Part C.4 to the Introduction, Judge Koh stated in open court that she "might be confused"[481] about patent exhaustion. A bit of history could have removed her apparent confusion. In 2008 in *Quanta*,[482] the Supreme Court held that *every* patent agreement called a "license" is exhaustive, even if its counterparties intended the agreement to convey only a nonexhaustive subset of the rights conferred on the patent holder by the grant of a patent.[483] What Judge Koh never acknowledged in her findings of fact and conclusions of law was that, for the approximately two decades before the Supreme Court's decision in *Quanta*, during which Qualcomm had made FRAND and RAND commitments to various SSOs and had begun to offer licenses to its cellular SEPs, the Federal Circuit had consistently held just the opposite—that counterparties *could* negotiate *nonexhaustive* "licenses." Tellingly, although Judge Koh cited *Quanta* in her brief discussion of patent exhaustion in her findings of fact and conclusions of law, she did not cite any other case law that would have indicated that the doctrine of patent exhaustion had materially evolved during the period of time when Qualcomm allegedly had monopoly power. Put simply, it was extremely important for Judge Koh to recognize that the use of the word "license" before 2008 did not necessarily imply "exhaustive license." It did not appear from her findings of fact and conclusions of law that Judge Koh discerned that difference.

Indeed, before 2008, Qualcomm had granted what it and its counterparties apparently agreed were narrow, nonexhaustive "licenses" to rival modem manufacturers. The apparently intended effect of those nonexhaustive "licenses" was to grant to Qualcomm and to its rivals freedom to operate. Around the time of *Quanta*, instead of granting a nonexhaustive "license," Qualcomm began to grant a covenant not to sue to rival modem manufacturers. Later, after the Federal Circuit declared, pursuant to *Quanta*, that even a covenant not to sue would (like a nonexhaustive "license") trigger patent exhaustion, Qualcomm began to grant rival modem manufacturers a covenant to sue *last*. The effect of the covenant to sue last was to grant Qualcomm's rivals substantially the same freedom to operate as a nonexhaustive "license," but without Qualcomm's exhausting its patent rights with respect to its rivals' modems.

As we shall see, Judge Koh in her findings of fact and conclusions of law appeared to commit legal error by equating a "license" to an "exhaustive

---

[481] Transcript of Proceedings (Volume 7) at 1437:11, FTC v. Qualcomm Inc., No. 5:17-cv-00220-LHK (N.D. Cal. Jan. 18, 2019).
[482] Quanta Comput., Inc. v. LG Elecs., Inc., 553 U.S. 617 (2008).
[483] *Id.* at 635–38.

license." Her failure to distinguish what (before 2008) were thought to be nonexhaustive "licenses" from exhaustive licenses appeared to lead Judge Koh erroneously to conclude that "Qualcomm *stopped licensing rivals* because doing so could jeopardize Qualcomm's ability to charge unreasonably high royalty rates to OEMs."[484] Setting to one side that the FTC never proved that the royalties that Qualcomm charged OEMs for an exhaustive license to its cellular SEPs were "unreasonably high," it was incoherent as a matter of fact and law for Judge Koh to conclude that "Qualcomm stopped licensing rivals." Substantial evidence showed that Qualcomm had *never* intentionally licensed its cellular SEPs to its rivals on an exhaustive basis. Even the FTC emphasized in its pretrial filings that Qualcomm had never licensed its cellular SEPs to its rivals exhaustively, even though Qualcomm had referred to nonexhaustive certain patent-related agreements (that predated *Quanta*) with its rivals as "licenses."[485]

---

[484] *FTC v. Qualcomm*, 411 F. Supp. 3d at 754 (emphasis added).

[485] Federal Trade Commission's Reply in Support of Partial Summary Judgment on Qualcomm's Standard Essential Patent Licensing Commitments at 11, FTC v. Qualcomm Inc., No. 5:17-cv-00220-LHK (N.D. Cal. Oct. 4, 2018), ECF No. 893 [hereinafter FTC's Reply in Support of Partial Summary Judgment] ("*Until at least 2007, Qualcomm widely publicized its practice of entering patent-related agreements with competing modem chip companies relating to cellular SEPs*. Although *these agreements were not exhaustive licenses*, Qualcomm listed these agreements on its website under the heading 'Licensing,' with a sub-heading for 'Component Related Products,' that identified a number of prominent modem chip companies, such as Infineon and Texas Instruments.") (emphasis added) (footnotes omitted); Federal Trade Commission's Motion for Partial Summary Judgment on Qualcomm's Standard Essential Patent Licensing Commitments and Memorandum of Points and Authorities in Support at 6, FTC v. Qualcomm Inc., No. 5:17-cv-00220-LHK (N.D. Cal. Aug. 30, 2018) [hereinafter FTC's Motion for Partial Summary Judgment] ("The President of Qualcomm's licensing business testified: 'At the current time, we don't license our portfolio to baseband chip manufacturers.' This has been Qualcomm's long-standing practice. As Qualcomm stated in response to an FTC investigative demand: 'Qualcomm has never granted exhaustive licenses under its patents with respect to modem chipsets.'") (first quoting Deposition of Alex Rogers at 112:7–11, FTC v. Qualcomm Inc., No. 5:17-cv-00220-LHK (N.D. Cal. Feb. 22, 2018), *Exhibit 16 to* FTC's Motion for Partial Summary Judgment, *supra* (filed under seal); and then quoting Qualcomm's Response to FTC Civil Investigative Demand Specification 7(c) (June 30, 2016)); *id.* at 6 n.15 ("'Admitted that Qualcomm has never exhaustively licensed its patents that it has disclosed as potentially essential to Cellular Communications Standards to any other chipset component manufacturer'") (quoting Qualcomm's Responses and Objections to Plaintiffs' First Set of Requests for Admission, No. 135 (Apr. 10, 2018)); *id.* at 6 n.17 ("'Qualcomm does not separately grant exhaustive licenses for the manufacture, assembly, importation[,] use or sale of Baseband Processor Chipsets.'") (quoting Qualcomm's Response to Apple's Special Interrogatory No. 15, at 14 (Mar. 10, 2018)); *id.* ("Qualcomm has in the past signed patent-related agreements with certain modem-chip sellers, but these agreements were not licenses. . . . Among other things, these agreements differed from conventional license agreements in that they purported to be 'non-exhaustive,' meaning that Qualcomm reserved the right to sue the customers of such counterparties for infringement of Qualcomm SEPs based on the use of the counterparties' modem-chip products.") (citations omitted); *id.* ("'When requested, Qualcomm has been willing to negotiate for non-exhaustive patent agreements with Baseband Processor Chipsets manufacturers . . . .'") (quoting Qualcomm's Response to Apple's Special Interrogatory No. 15, at 14 (Mar. 10, 2018)). Apart from the quoted excerpts from the deposition of Alex Rogers, Qualcomm's response to the FTC's civil investigative demand specification, requests for admission, and Apple's special interrogatory, these sources do not otherwise appear to be publicly available. *See* Plaintiff Federal Trade Commission's Pretrial Proposed Findings of Fact and Conclusions of Law (Redacted Version) ¶ 225, at 31, FTC v. Qualcomm Inc., No. 5:17-cv-00220-LHK (N.D. Cal. Dec. 6, 2018) [hereinafter FTC's Proposed Findings of Fact and Conclusions of Law] ("Qualcomm has a policy of not making exhaustive licenses for its cellular SEPs available to competing modem chip suppliers.").

2. *The Rationale for Avoiding Patent Exhaustion*

Why was avoiding patent exhaustion so important to Qualcomm and its business model? Recall that Qualcomm was "unique" in the industry because it had (1) a valuable portfolio of 140,000 patents (including cellular SEPs, non-cellular SEPs, and non-SEPs) and patent applications and (2) modems that were widely deployed in handsets. Recall also that it was Qualcomm's position that every device equipped with a cellular modem (sold either by Qualcomm or by one of its rivals) practiced Qualcomm's cellular SEPs. Qualcomm's practice was to sell its modems to OEMs at a price that *excluded* the price of an exhaustive license to Qualcomm's cellular SEPs. Rival modem manufacturers likewise sold their modems to OEMs at a price that excluded the price of an exhaustive license to Qualcomm's cellular SEPs. Instead, OEMs directly contracted with Qualcomm for an exhaustive license to practice its cellular SEPs in the manufacture and sale of smartphones.

Qualcomm's dual businesses (of selling licenses to its cellular SEPs and of selling modems) thus encountered possible patent exhaustion in two ways. First, by law, Qualcomm's sale of a modem would exhaust Qualcomm's patent rights in that modem. Consequently, patent exhaustion prevented Qualcomm from first selling an unlicensed modem to an OEM and thereafter licensing its cellular SEPs to that same OEM. Qualcomm avoided that problem by selling its modems only to *licensed* OEMs. Judge Koh considered that conduct anticompetitive.

Second, after *Quanta* and its progeny, *any* agreement styled as a "license" or "covenant not to sue" would exhaust Qualcomm's patent rights in the licensed or covenanted item. In particular, after *Quanta*, an exhaustively licensed rival's sale of a modem to an OEM would exhaust Qualcomm's patent rights in the modem sold, such that Qualcomm could not seek a patent royalty from the OEM purchasing the modem for use in the OEM's mobile device. In practice, therefore, Qualcomm could choose to license its cellular SEPs exhaustively at only one of two (but not both) levels of the supply chain: (1) the component level (that is, to a rival modem manufacturer like MediaTek) or (2) the device level (that is, to an OEM like HTC). Compelled to choose between those two mutually exclusive models of contracting, Qualcomm of course continued to offer exhaustive licenses to its cellular SEPs to OEMs. A licensed OEM selling a modem-equipped device could choose to purchase a modem for its device either from Qualcomm or from a rival modem manufacturer. The licensed OEM would pay Qualcomm the same amount of royalty on a Qualcomm-equipped smartphone as on a non-Qualcomm-equipped smartphone (assuming that the OEM set the same wholesale price for both smartphones).

Qualcomm did not choose the alternative option, which would have been to change its course of dealing and license its cellular SEPs exhaustively at the component level (that is, to rival modem manufacturers). Consider the following numerical example. Recall from Part E.5 to the Introduction that Qualcomm eventually capped the royalty for an exhaustive license to its portfolio of cellular SEPs at 3.25 percent of $400 (or $13) per device. That same $13 per device, charged to a rival modem manufacturer, might have equaled or exceeded the rival's price of its unlicensed modem, such that the price that a rival would need to pay Qualcomm for an exhaustive license to its cellular SEPs, as a percentage of the cost to the rival of producing a modem, could approach or exceed 100 percent of the price of the bare modem (that is, a modem not already bundled with the required permission to use the patents that it practices).

As we shall see, Qualcomm executives testified in effect that the cognitive dissonance that would arise from applying such a seemingly high royalty rate to such a small royalty base would make it impractical from a business perspective for Qualcomm to offer exhaustive licenses to its cellular SEPs at the component level. Rival modem manufacturers would argue (nonsensically) that the same 3.25-percent royalty rate applied to a device at the OEM level for an exhaustive license to Qualcomm's cellular SEPs should apply to the rival's price for a bare modem. Multiplying 3.25 percent by the price of a bare modem would produce a total royalty at least one order of magnitude less than the exhaustive royalty that Qualcomm had collected for decades from OEMs. Moreover, to offer exhaustive licenses to its cellular SEPs at the component level would have been unwise for Qualcomm from a litigation perspective, because juries, and even courts (and perhaps even Judge Koh) could fall prey to the cognitive dissonance that would disincline one to apply a seemingly high royalty rate to a small royalty base.

Yet, Judge Koh did not examine these questions. Instead, she concluded in her findings of fact and conclusions of law that Qualcomm's business decision to offer exhaustive licenses to its cellular SEPs only to OEMs was anticompetitive.

The crux of the confusion about patent exhaustion in Judge Koh's findings of fact and conclusions of law appeared to arise from the fact that Qualcomm had granted to rival modem manufacturers *nonexhaustive* "licenses" to its cellular SEPs before *Quanta*, which (as we shall see) did not confer on rivals the right to *use* Qualcomm's cellular SEPs, in exchange for a royalty per item of 3 percent of the price of the bare modem. Judge Koh's elision of the critical distinction between a nonexhaustive "license" before *Quanta* and an exhaustive license after *Quanta* appeared to lead her mistakenly to portray 3 percent of the price of a bare modem (which would amount to $0.30 on a $10 modem) as a reasonable royalty for an *exhaustive* license to Qualcomm's portfolio of cellular SEPs. A royalty of $0.30 per item for a nonexhaustive "license" is 2.3 percent of Qualcomm's $13 cap on a royalty for an exhaustive license to its portfolio of cellular SEPs.

Hence, Judge Koh appeared erroneously to infer that the royalties that OEMs paid Qualcomm for its cellular SEPs were "unreasonably high." Judge Koh thus appeared to fall prey to the very cognitive dissonance that Qualcomm executives foresaw would make it impossible as a practical matter to offer exhaustive licenses to its cellular SEPs at the component level.

3.   *Qualcomm's July 2012 Meeting with the Internal Revenue Service*

Judge Koh's apparent confusion over patent exhaustion was especially perplexing because, as we shall see, she accorded great prominence in her findings of fact and conclusions of law to the recording of a meeting that Qualcomm executives had with representatives of the Internal Revenue Service (IRS) in July 2012. In that meeting, Qualcomm executives—and in particular Eric Reifschneider, then QTL Senior Vice President and General Manager—extensively described Qualcomm's motivation in its licensing practices to avoid patent exhaustion, as well as the history of the doctrine of patent exhaustion. Considering Judge Koh's predilection for evidence that was not "made for litigation," the evidence of the IRS meeting—which was produced in 2012, more than four years before the FTC filed its complaint against Qualcomm—corroborated Qualcomm's extensive testimony at trial about the economic significance of patent exhaustion for its business model.

Judge Koh said in open court that she intended to listen to the audio recording of the July 2012 IRS meeting because it had "piqued [her] curiosity."[486] After explaining that she "drive[s a] long distance"[487] on her commute, Judge Koh also represented to the parties that she would "prefer to have a DVD"[488] of the audio recording so that she "could listen to it as [she was] driving to and from work."[489] Considering the substantial evidentiary significance of the IRS conference to understanding why Qualcomm had a legitimate business need to structure its licenses, contracts, and other commercial arrangements to navigate the evolving case law on patent exhaustion, a different judge might have chosen to review the transcript of the IRS conference in a setting more conducive to quiet contemplation (a judge's chambers during business hours, for example), rather than try to digest the audio recording while distracted by rush-hour traffic in Silicon Valley. Again, was Judge Koh's listening to the audio recording of a key piece of evidence while driving on

---

[486] Transcript of Proceedings (Volume 7) at 1575:8, FTC v. Qualcomm Inc., No. 5:17-cv-00220-LHK (N.D. Cal. Jan. 18, 2019).

[487] *Id.* at 1576:2.

[488] *Id.* at 1576:11–12.

[489] *Id.* at 1576:12–13.

the freeway all the process to which Qualcomm was due in a bench trial for a government monopolization case seeking to dismantle the business model that Qualcomm had so methodically created?

Judge Koh seemed incognizant of the relevance of patent exhaustion to the FTC's theories of antitrust liability. In particular, as we shall see in Part IX, Judge Koh's explanation in her findings of fact and conclusions of law for why she found certain Qualcomm witnesses not to be credible was irreconcilable with Qualcomm's consistent explanation of its apparent need to avoid exhaustive licensing of its cellular SEPs at the component level. In addition, as we shall see in Part XII.B, Judge Koh found that Qualcomm had an antitrust duty to offer exhaustive license to its cellular SEPs to rival modem manufacturers pursuant to *Aspen Skiing* because Qualcomm supposedly had "*previously licensed*" its rivals but voluntarily terminated that practice."[490] Yet, Judge Koh elided the critical distinction between an exhaustive license and the nonexhaustive "licenses" that Qualcomm sought to grant rival modem manufacturers before 2008. That critical distinction exposes as false the proposition that Qualcomm ever exhaustively licensed its cellular SEPs to rival modem manufacturers, such that Qualcomm might have had a duty supposedly to *continue* licensing its rivals exhaustively. Judge Koh's permanent, worldwide injunction was flawed for the same reason.

Before turning to those flaws and to a brief historical account of patent exhaustion in U.S. patent law, let us first expose the FTC's disingenuous argument that, despite the extensive evidence to the contrary, Qualcomm's avoidance of patent exhaustion was not a legitimate business justification for its practices of not offering exhaustive licenses to its cellular SEPs at the component level and instead selling its modems only to licensed OEMs, because (according to the FTC's fallacious reasoning) Qualcomm could supposedly have achieved the same results by simultaneously licensing at both the component level and the device level. That legal proposition, we have already seen, was incorrect.

B. Did the FTC Have Any Basis to Contend That the Avoidance of Patent Exhaustion Was Not a Legitimate Business Justification for Qualcomm's Licensing Practices?

During her opening statement at trial on January 4, 2019 on behalf of the FTC, attorney Jennifer Milici asserted that "[i]t is not procompetitive to avoid the doctrine of patent exhaustion."[491] It was not a slip of the tongue. Again, in her closing argument on January 29, 2019, Ms. Milici asserted that

---

[490] FTC v. Qualcomm Inc., 411 F. Supp. 3d 658, 760 (N.D. Cal. 2019) (emphasis added).

[491] Transcript of Proceedings (Volume 1) at 10:14–15, FTC v. Qualcomm Inc., No. 5:17-cv-00220-LHK (N.D. Cal. Jan. 4, 2019) (opening statement of Jennifer Milici for the FTC).

"avoiding exhaustion is not a valid business justification."[492] She argued that Qualcomm's "exhaustion defense boils down to a desire to avoid the risk of negotiating in the shadow of the law" and "is not cognizable as an antitrust defense."[493]

Ms. Milici's argument tended to contradict the jurisprudential insight in the Supreme Court's famous decision in *Gregory v. Helvering*, which affirmed Judge Learned Hand's "no business purpose" test, whose reasoning (albeit in the context of tax law) sounded like the argument for why avoiding patent exhaustion does not contradict antitrust law.[494] Judge Hand reasoned: "Any one may so arrange his affairs that his taxes shall be as low as possible; he is not bound to choose that pattern which will best pay the Treasury; there is not even a patriotic duty to increase one's taxes."[495] A generalized restatement of Judge Hand's reasoning might be the following: it is not a violation of the law to find a way to mitigate the burden of some principle of public law, and a firm—even a monopolist—has no duty to pursue the less propitious of two lawful ways of conducting business.

1. Is a Firm's Unilateral Conduct Intended to Minimize the Applicability of the Doctrine of Patent Exhaustion Unlawful?

The apparent purpose of Qualcomm's licensing practice was to maximize profit by maximizing royalty income. In sworn testimony and in company documents predating the FTC's lawsuit, Qualcomm executives consistently cited the doctrine of patent exhaustion as the company's principal motivation for not offering to rival modem manufacturers licenses to make, use, and sell items practicing the claimed inventions of Qualcomm's cellular SEPs. Granting such licenses, Qualcomm explained, could make its collection of royalties from OEMs difficult or impossible.

That outcome would not benefit either Qualcomm or the IRS, which we can safely presume would like to collect as much revenue as possible for the public treasury from taxing Qualcomm's corporate income from the licensing of its patent portfolio. A firm's unilateral actions intended to minimize the applicability of the doctrine of patent exhaustion, so as to increase its profits, does not violate any law—including federal tax law and federal antitrust law. For the FTC to contend that Qualcomm's avoidance of patent exhaustion was an illegitimate business purpose, unavailable as an efficiency defense to monopolization, was preposterous.

---

[492] Transcript of Proceedings (Volume 11) at 2131:23–24, FTC v. Qualcomm Inc., No. 5:17-cv-00220-LHK (N.D. Cal. Jan. 29, 2019) (closing argument of Jennifer Milici for the FTC).

[493] *Id.* at 2132:2–4, 2132:5–6.

[494] 293 U.S. 465 (1935).

[495] Helvering v. Gregory, 69 F.2d 809, 810 (2ᵈ Cir. 1934) (Hand, J.).

2.   *Did Any Controlling Authority Support the FTC's Argument?*

In its pretrial and posttrial briefs, the FTC did not cite any controlling authority for that proposition, and the authority that the agency did cite was unpersuasive. Perhaps the clearest statement of the FTC's argument appeared in three related allegations in its complaint—that (1) "Qualcomm's practices are not reasonably necessary to accomplish any significant procompetitive benefits," (2) "the anticompetitive harm from those practices outweighs any procompetitive benefits," and (3) "Qualcomm could reasonably achieve any procompetitive goals through less restrictive alternatives."[496] (Notice how the FTC took the liberty of raising the bar for Qualcomm by demanding that it prove that the procompetitive benefits be "significant.") In regard to the FTC's third allegation, the "less restrictive alternative" that the FTC apparently envisioned was Qualcomm's exhaustive licensing of its cellular SEPs to *both* OEMs and rival modem manufacturers. Yet, substantial evidence indicated that patent exhaustion prevented Qualcomm from licensing at both (rather than only one) of those two levels of the supply chain. Contrary to the FTC's misunderstanding of the law and the facts, there was no evidence that Qualcomm could have avoided patent exhaustion through "less restrictive alternatives."

The legal arguments predicating the FTC's first allegation and second allegation are harder to detect in the docketed pretrial and posttrial filings. The passage most closely resembling a legal argument appeared in the FTC's opposition at the Ninth Circuit to Qualcomm's motion for a partial stay of Judge Koh's permanent injunction, pending the appeal.[497] In a parenthetical quotation appended to a citation to *McWane, Inc. v. FTC*,[498] an Eleventh Circuit case that quoted *Microsoft*,[499] the FTC asserted that "profitability "'is not an unlawful end, but neither is it a procompetitive justification.'""[500] Yet, the FTC added an essential, unquoted word as the subject of the otherwise quoted sentence—"profitability." Neither *Microsoft* nor *McWane* referred explicitly to "profitability."[501] The FTC's supposed controlling legal authority

---

[496] FTC Complaint, 2017 WL 242848, *supra* note 28, at 30.

[497] [Corrected] Opposition of the Federal Trade Commission to Motion for Partial Stay Pending Appeal at 14–15, FTC v. Qualcomm Inc., No. 19-16122 (9th Cir. July 18, 2019) [hereinafter FTC's Opposition to Motion for Partial Stay Pending Appeal].

[498] 783 F.3d 814 (11th Cir. 2015).

[499] United States v. Microsoft Corp., 253 F.3d 34 (D.C. Cir. 2001) (en banc) (per curiam). The FTC erroneously referred to "251 F.3d 34" as the citation for *Microsoft*. FTC's Opposition to Motion for Partial Stay Pending Appeal, *supra* note 497, at 15.

[500] FTC's Opposition to Motion for Partial Stay Pending Appeal, *supra* note 497, at 15 (quoting *McWane*, 783 F.3d at 841 (quoting *Microsoft*, 253 F.3d at 71)).

[501] *Microsoft*, 253 F.3d at 71 ("Plaintiffs having demonstrated a harm to competition, the burden falls upon Microsoft to defend its exclusive dealing contracts with IAPs [Internet Access Providers] by providing a procompetitive justification for them. *Significantly, Microsoft's only explanation for its exclusive dealing is that it wants to keep developers focused upon its APIs [Application Programming Interfaces]—which is to say, it wants to preserve its power in the operating system market. That is not an unlawful end, but neither is it a procompetitive*

for its allegation that the avoidance of patent exhaustion was an illegitimate business justification was in fact no authority at all.

Moreover, the FTC's antipathy toward the pursuit of profit is directly contrary to the Supreme Court's understanding that the prospect of earning profit is what fuels the engine of competition. If the Court in *Trinko* had the self-confidence in 2004 to conclude unapologetically that "[t]he opportunity to charge monopoly prices—at least for a short period—is what attracts 'business acumen' in the first place" because "it induces risk taking that produces innovation and economic growth,"[502] it obviously has overcome any social embarrassment in defending the pursuit of profit. The Court, not the FTC, says what the law is; and it is telling that the FTC in 2019 considered profit a dirty word.

C. *The Supreme Court's Refinement of the Doctrine of Patent Exhaustion*

On July 27, 2012, Qualcomm executives met with representatives of the IRS in an audio-recorded meeting (which was later transcribed) to explain Qualcomm's "third-party licensing[,] and how the royalty rates work."[503] Remarkably, Judge Koh never explained in her findings of fact and conclusions of law *why* the IRS had asked Qualcomm's senior management to meet with the agency's staff to explain, in a recorded conversation, the company's licensing practices. Obviously, it is not the responsibility of the IRS to enforce the antitrust laws. Yet, it is of course common in vertically integrated firms to encounter transfer-pricing questions, particularly with respect to

---

justification for the specific means here in question, namely exclusive dealing contracts with IAPs. Accordingly, we affirm the District Court's decision holding that Microsoft's exclusive contracts with IAPs are exclusionary devices, in violation of § 2 of the Sherman Act.") (citation omitted); *McWane*, 83 F.3d at 841 ("McWane says that the Full Support Program was necessary to retain enough sales to keep its domestic foundry afloat. The Commission rightly rejected this argument; as other courts have recognized, such a goal is 'not an unlawful end, but neither is it a procompetitive justification.'") (quoting *Microsoft*, 253 F.3d at 71).

502 Verizon Commc'ns Inc. v. Law Offices of Curtis V. Trinko, LLP, 540 U.S. 398, 407 (2004) (quoting United States v. Grinnell Corp., 384 U.S. 563, 571 (1966)).

503 Transcript of Meeting Between Qualcomm and the Internal Revenue Service at 6:7 (July 27, 2012), *Exhibit A to* Joint Notice Regarding CX6786-R, FTC v. Qualcomm Inc., No. 5:17-CV-0220-LHK (N.D. Cal. Jan. 28, 2019), ECF No. 1455-1 [hereinafter IRS Transcript]; *see also id.* at 2:15–25 ("For those of you who don't know me, I'm Howard Schneck. And I am director of tax dealing with the IRS. I think maybe I'll just start with a quick agenda, and then maybe we can go around the room and just introduce ourselves to everyone. So the purpose of the meeting as you all know is to talk about the royalty. And the [Internal Revenue S]ervice has wanted to ask questions of our QTL executives. So Mariko Killion, who is the IRS economist, will conduct those interviews. And then we want to follow up that with trying to get some agreement on both sides on the facts in the case."); *id.* at 5:5–16 ([Ms. Mariko Killion, IRS Economist.] [T]he original request of mine was to speak to someone who could tell us something about how your third-party licensing and how the royalty rates work, and how that relates to how this CDMA technology was quickly adopted in the market, now it's one of the most dominant technology [sic] when it comes to the cell phone network protocol. So basically just wanted to get an idea of where that idea came from, and how that evolved over time. And I understand the royalty right [sic], especially with the third-party licensee chipmakers are now down to zero. So that sort of history and background, you know, we just wanted to hear about that."). It appears from the transcript that one or more participants in the conference attended telephonically. *See, e.g.*, IRS Transcript, *supra*, at 2:1–11.

intangible property, and it is conceivable that such questions might implicate where taxable corporate income is realized within an overall business organization, including in what tax jurisdiction.[504] Judge Koh did not give readers of her findings of fact and conclusions of law even this much of an explanation for the existence of this unusual piece of documentary evidence, which she treated as highly probative.

Describing in detail the skein of case law on patent exhaustion and its relevance to Qualcomm's business practices, Qualcomm represented to the IRS that it had *always* licensed its cellular SEPs exhaustively at the OEM level and that it had *always* declined to offer exhaustive licenses to its cellular SEPs to rival modem manufacturers. Qualcomm's nonexhaustive agreements with rival modem manufacturers merely enabled those manufacturers to achieve freedom to operate.

Refinements in the Supreme Court's explication of the doctrine of patent exhaustion (also known, primarily in copyright law, as the first-sale doctrine), between the time when Qualcomm began granting licenses to its patented cellular technology in the 1990s and the date of Qualcomm's meeting with the IRS in July 2012, evidently motivated Qualcomm to modify the nature (but not the effect) of its agreements with rival modem manufacturers. Qualcomm explained in detail to the IRS how the Supreme Court's judicial revelation of the doctrine of patent exhaustion had induced Qualcomm to grant freedom to operate to rival modem manufacturers (and to obtain freedom to operate from them) through different commercial means at different points in time throughout the history of Qualcomm's patent-licensing program. Qualcomm avoided the risk that a judge might rule that Qualcomm could not collect royalties from OEMs on devices that practiced Qualcomm's claimed inventions but were equipped with non-Qualcomm modems.

At the very least, the inferences that Judge Koh purported to derive from the recording of Qualcomm's meeting with the IRS were unreliable because they lacked any explanation by her of the essential context of the meeting. The way in which Judge Koh reported her findings produced a misleading impression of the facts of the case and the state of the law on patent exhaustion. In particular, in three cases decided between 2008 and

---

[504] *See* 26 U.S.C. § 482 ("In any case of two or more organizations, trades, or businesses (whether or not incorporated, whether or not organized in the United States, and whether or not affiliated) owned or controlled directly or indirectly by the same interests, the Secretary may distribute, apportion, or allocate gross income, deductions, credits, or allowances between or among such organizations, trades, or businesses, if he determines that such distribution, apportionment, or allocation is necessary in order to prevent evasion of taxes or clearly to reflect the income of any of such organizations, trades, or businesses. In the case of any transfer (or license) of intangible property (within the meaning of section 367(d)(4)), the income with respect to such transfer or license shall be commensurate with the income attributable to the intangible. For purposes of this section, the Secretary shall require the valuation of transfers of intangible property (including intangible property transferred with other property or services) on an aggregate basis or the valuation of such a transfer on the basis of the realistic alternatives to such a transfer, if the Secretary determines that such basis is the most reliable means of valuation of such transfers.").

2017, the Supreme Court revealed that Federal Circuit law decided between 1992 and 2006 contravened the doctrine of patent exhaustion. Qualcomm, operating in the shadow of Federal Circuit precedent in the 1990s, had by contract "licensed" a narrow bundle of patent rights to rival modem manufacturers without granting them exhaustive licenses to its cellular SEPs. Yet, in the 2000s, new court decisions on patent exhaustion evidently induced Qualcomm to convey substantially the same intended bundle of patent rights by different commercial means, so as to avoid triggering patent exhaustion. Importantly, (1) the avoidance of patent exhaustion and (2) the cognitive dissonance of trying to apply a seemingly high royalty rate to a relatively small royalty base together apparently induced Qualcomm to continue to grant exhaustive licenses to its cellular SEPs to OEMs only.

1.   The Supreme Court's Adumbration of the Doctrine of Patent Exhaustion

The word "exhaust" and its variants appear 46 times in Judge Koh's findings of fact and conclusions of law in *FTC v. Qualcomm*.[505] Yet, she cited only one Supreme Court case defining the doctrine of patent exhaustion, *Quanta Computer v. LG Electronics*: "Under the doctrine of patent exhaustion, 'the initial authorized sale of a patented item terminates all patent rights to that item.'"[506] Judge Koh made the law sound so simple.

---

[505] FTC v. Qualcomm Inc., 411 F. Supp. 3d 658, 678, 698 (four times), 710, 712, 723, 726 (three times), 727 (twice) (first quoting CX8261-004 (Qualcomm slide deck presented to Tony Blevins (Vice President of Procurement, Apple))), 732, 743, 748 (twice) (citing CX7580-001 (email from Steve Altman)) (quoting Deposition of Nanfen Yu (General Counsel, Huawei) at 133:14–15, FTC v. Qualcomm Inc., No. 5:17-cv-00220-LHK (N.D. Cal. Mar. 14, 2018), *attachment to* Federal Trade Commission's Submission of Trial Testimony That Occurred on January 7[, 2019], FTC v. Qualcomm Inc., No. 5:17-cv-00220-LHK (N.D. Cal. Jan. 8, 2019), ECF No. 1185-1), 749 (twice) (first quoting CX8285-001 (Email from Marv Blecker, President, Qualcomm Technology Licensing, to Derek Aberle, President, Qualcomm (June 2012)); and then quoting CX5179-001 (Email from Eric Reifschneider, Senior Vice President and General Manager, Qualcomm Technology Licensing, to Derek Aberle, President, Qualcomm, and Fabian Gonell, Legal Counsel and Senior Vice President, Licensing Strategy, Qualcomm Technology Licensing (Oct. 2015))), 750 (quoting CX5179-001 (Email from Eric Reifschneider, Senior Vice President and General Manager, Qualcomm Technology Licensing, to Derek Aberle, President, Qualcomm, and Fabian Gonell, Legal Counsel and Senior Vice President, Licensing Strategy, Qualcomm Technology Licensing (Oct. 2015))), 753 (quoting Transcript of Proceedings (Volume 7) at 1494:4–9, FTC v. Qualcomm Inc., No. 5:17-cv-00220-LHK (N.D. Cal. Jan. 18, 2019) (Testimony of Fabian Gonell (Legal Counsel and Senior Vice President, Licensing Strategy, Qualcomm Technology Licensing))), 754 (quoting IRS Transcript, *supra* note 503, at 26:6–12 (Eric Reifschneider (Senior Vice President and General Manager, Qualcomm Technology Licensing))), 755, 761 (three times) (first quoting IRS Transcript, *supra* note 503, at 26:6–12 (Eric Reifschneider (Senior Vice President and General Manager, Qualcomm Technology Licensing))), 777 (three times), 778 (three times) (third quoting Deposition of Eric Reifschneider (Vol. 1), *supra* note 20, 30:15–20), 796 (quoting IRS Transcript, *supra* note 503, at 26:6–12 (Eric Reifschneider (Senior Vice President and General Manager, Qualcomm Technology Licensing))), 797, 805, 807 (twice) (second quoting CX6548-002 (May 2012 slide deck prepared by Fabian Gonell (QTL Legal Counsel and Senior Vice President, Licensing Strategy))), 809 (four times) (second quoting CX6974-070 (July 2012 Qualcomm presentation to the Qualcomm Board of Directors); and fourth quoting Deposition of Eric Reifschneider (Vol. 1), *supra* note 20, at 30:15–20), 813, 815 (quoting CX6998-011 (2012 QTL strategic plan presentation)), 818, 820, 821 (N.D. Cal. 2019).

[506] *Id.* at 698 (quoting Quanta Comput., Inc. v. LG Elecs., Inc., 553 U.S. 617, 625 (2008)).

Yet, she ignored that, when the Court decided *Quanta* in 2008, it over-turned more than a decade of Federal Circuit law that had held that an initial authorized sale of a patented item did not necessarily exhaust all patent rights to that item. The Supreme Court's adumbration of the doctrine of patent exhaustion is a paragon for Oliver Wendell Holmes' definition of the law: "The prophecies of what the courts will do in fact, and nothing more pretentious, are what I mean by the law."[507] In the Holmesian sense, the "law" of patent exhaustion is our rational expectation of how the Supreme Court will decide the next case it hears on the subject. Thus, the critical context concerning the doctrine of patent exhaustion explains why Qualcomm and its counterparties chose, at various points in time, to employ different commercial means to achieve substantially the same intended voluntary exchange of rights and obligations.

2. *The Origin of the Patent Exhaustion Defense*

Patent exhaustion is an affirmative defense to a patentee's claim for patent infringement.[508] In 1852, the Supreme Court announced the doctrine of patent exhaustion in *Bloomer v. McQuewan*,[509] when it said that, "when the machine passes to the hands of the purchaser, it is no longer within the limits of the [patent] monopoly."[510] After *Bloomer*, and before the 21st century, the Court reiterated the doctrine of patent exhaustion,[511] but it seemed to hold open the possibility that the doctrine of patent exhaustion did not definitively prohibit a patent holder from imposing (and enforcing) post-sale restrictions on a patented article.[512] At least since 1966, when William Baxter of Stanford Law School published his ambitious article in the *Yale Law Journal* concerning

---

[507] Holmes, *The Path of the Law*, *supra* note 257, at 461.

[508] *See, e.g.*, ExcelStor Tech., Inc. v. Papst Licensing GMBH & Co. KG, 541 F.3d 1373, 1376 (Fed. Cir. 2008).

[509] 55 U.S. (14 How.) 539 (1852).

[510] *Id.* at 549. *But cf.* Wentong Zhang, *Exhausting Patents*, 63 UCLA L. Rev. 122, 129–30 & nn.22–25 (2016) (arguing that the decision in *Bloomer* might have been predicated not on the common law but on statutory text, such that crediting *Bloomer* as being the origin in U.S. law of the doctrine of patent exhaustion might be inaccurate).

[511] *See, e.g.*, United States v. Univis Lens, Co., 316 U.S. 241, 250 (1942) ("[S]ale of [a patented item] exhausts the monopoly in that article and the patentee may not thereafter, by virtue of his patent, control the use or disposition of the article."); Motion Picture Patents Co. v. Universal Film Mfg. Co., 243 U.S. 502, 516 (1917) ("[T]he right to vend is exhausted by a single, unconditional sale, the article sold being thereby carried outside the monopoly of the patent law and rendered free of every restriction which the vendor may attempt to put upon it.").

[512] *See, e.g.*, Mitchell v. Hawley, 83 U.S. (16 Wall.) 544, 547 (1872) ("[A] patentee, when he has himself constructed a machine and sold it *without any conditions*, or authorized another to construct, sell, and deliver it, or to construct and use and operate it, *without any conditions*, and the consideration has been paid to him for the thing patented, the rule is well established that the patentee must be understood to have parted to that extent with all his exclusive right, and that he ceases to have any interest whatever in the patented machine so sold and delivered or authorized to be constructed and operated.") (emphasis added).

economic analysis of the patent monopoly,[513] it had been understood in the Holmesian sense that, "since the courts have treated the 'first sale' rule as one of metaphysics rather than of the purposeful implementation of social objectives, it is difficult to predict results in any given case."[514]

3. *The Federal Circuit's Decision in* Quanta

During the 1990s, the Federal Circuit indicated that, in certain circumstances, a patent holder could enforce through patent law a restriction of the scope of the bundle of patent rights granted to the buyer following the sale of a patented item.[515] Thus, during the 1990s it appeared on the basis of the Federal Circuit's interpretation of Supreme Court precedent that a patent holder could avoid patent exhaustion by imposing post-sale restrictions on the scope of the patent rights granted to a buyer of an item practicing a claimed invention. Yet, in three cases from 2008 to 2017—*Quanta*[516] in 2008, *Bowman v. Monsanto*[517] in 2013, and *Impression Products v. Lexmark*[518] in 2017—

---

[513] William F. Baxter, *Legal Restrictions on Exploitation of the Patent Monopoly: An Economic Analysis*, 76 YALE L.J. 267, 348 (1966). Baxter traced the definitive analysis of the origins of the first-sale doctrine (which is the analogue in copyright law to the doctrine of patent exhaustion) to Zechariah Chafee's equally respected study on equitable servitudes on chattels. *See* Zechariah Chafee, Jr., *Equitable Servitudes on Chattels*, 41 HARV. L. REV. 945 (1928), *cited in* Baxter, *Legal Restrictions on Exploitation of the Patent Monopoly: An Economic Analysis, supra*, at 348 & n.110.

[514] Baxter, *Legal Restrictions on Exploitation of the Patent Monopoly: An Economic Analysis, supra* note 513, at 348 (footnote omitted) (citing Adams v. Burke, 84 U.S. (17 Wall.) 453, 456 (1873)); *see Adams*, 84 U.S. at 456 ("In the essential nature of things, when the patentee sells a machine . . . whose sole value is in its use . . . he parts with the right to restrict that use. The article passes without the limit of the monopoly."); *see also* Kirtsaeng v. John Wiley & Sons, Inc., 568 U.S. 519, 538 (2013) ("The 'first sale' doctrine is a common-law doctrine with an impeccable historic pedigree. In the early 17th century Lord Coke explained the common law's refusal to permit restraints on the alienation of chattels. Referring to Littleton, who wrote in the 15th century, . . . Lord Coke wrote: '[If] a man be possessed of . . . a horse, or of any other chattel . . . and give or sell his whole interest . . . therein upon condition that the Donee or Vendee shall not alien[ate] the same, the [condition] is voi[d], because his whole interest . . . is out of him, so as he hath no possibilit[y] of a Reverter, and it is against Trade and Traffi[c], and bargaining and contracting betwee[n] man and man: and it is within the reason of our Author that it should ouster him of all power given to him.' A law that permits a copyright holder to control the resale or other disposition of a chattel once sold is similarly 'against Trade and Traffi[c], and bargaining and contracting.' With these last few words, Coke emphasizes the importance of leaving buyers of goods free to compete with each other when reselling or otherwise disposing of those goods. American law too has generally thought that competition, including freedom to resell, can work to the advantage of the consumer.") (alterations in original) (citations omitted) (quoting 1 EDWARD COKE, INSTITUTES OF THE LAWS OF ENGLAND § 360, at 223 (1628)).

[515] *See, e.g.*, B. Braun Med. Inc. v. Abbott Labs., 124 F.3d 1419, 1426 (Fed. Cir. 1997) (citing Mallinckrodt, Inc. v. Medipart, Inc., 976 F.2d 700, 708 (Fed. Cir. 1992)).

[516] Quanta Comput., Inc. v. LG Elecs., Inc., 553 U.S. 617 (2008).

[517] Bowman v. Monsanto Co., 569 U.S. 278 (2013).

[518] Impression Prods. v. Lexmark Int'l, Inc., 137 S. Ct. 1523 (2017); *see also* Ronald J. Mann, *Patent Exhaustion After* Impression Products, 2 CRITERION J. ON INNOVATION 39, 43 (2017) ("[A]s with so many areas of the Federal Circuit's jurisprudence, the Supreme Court has stayed its hand from considering this problem [of patent exhaustion] for a generation, leaving the high-tech community to develop increasingly intricate patterns of contracting, all premised on the enforceability of regimes of post-sale patent enforcement. . . . In the end, though, the opinion [in *Impression Products*] shows a Supreme Court persuaded that the Federal Circuit did not merely err in some detail or nuance, but was as fundamentally misguided as it was when it came up with the venue rules discarded just a week earlier in *TC Heartland LLC v. Kraft Foods Group Brands, LLC*.") (citing TC Heartland LLC v. Kraft Foods Grp. Brands LLC, 137 S. Ct. 1514 (2017)).

the Supreme Court substantially restricted a patent holder's ability to avoid triggering patent exhaustion.

Quanta was particularly important because it was the first case since 1942 in which the Supreme Court analyzed patent exhaustion at length. The case was also important because the timeline of the case's progression through federal district court, the Federal Circuit, and the Supreme Court aligns with the period during which Qualcomm was negotiating commercial agreements that sought to avoid patent exhaustion.

In September 2000, LG Electronics (LGE) granted a patent license to Intel, which produced microprocessors and chipsets for sale to computer OEMs.[519] The LGE-Intel license "expressly disclaim[ed] any implied license" to computer OEMs that purchased Intel's microprocessors and chipsets.[520] Thereafter in 2001, LGE sued a number of computer OEMs that had purchased Intel's microprocessors and chipsets (including Quanta Computer) for patent infringement.[521] A number of the defendants moved "for summary judgment that a cross license agreement between Plaintiff LG Electronics (LGE) and Intel precludes LGE from seeking damages for infringement from Defendants."[522] Citing Supreme Court precedent, in 2002, Judge Claudia Wilken of the U.S. District Court for the Northern District of California, granted the defendants' motion for summary judgment on grounds of patent exhaustion:

> The question presented is whether the express disclaimer of the grant [by LGE] of an implied license [to the defendants] was effective. However, under the patent exhaustion doctrine as articulated in *Univis Lens*, LGE may not enforce its patents against purchasers of Intel microprocessor and chipsets who use those devices for their intended and sole purpose.[523]

Judge Wilken's conclusion was predicated on a 1942 Supreme Court case, *United States v. Univis Lens Co.*,[524] which said that a patentee's unconditional sale of a patented item rendered unenforceable in patent law any postsale restrictions on that sale.[525] In contrast, the more recent Federal Circuit law on patent exhaustion announced in the 1990s tended to favor the

---

[519] LG Elecs., Inc. v. Asustek Comput., Inc., Nos. C 01-00326 CW, C 01-01375 CW, C 01-01594 CW, C 01-02187 CW, C 01-01552 CW, 2002 WL 31996860, at *2 (N.D. Cal. Aug. 20, 2002). After receiving additional briefing and oral argument, Judge Wilken issued a second order in the same case that reached substantially the same conclusion concerning the same issue of patent exhaustion. *See* LG Elecs., Inc. v. Asustek Comput., Inc., 248 F. Supp. 2d 912, 914 (N.D. Cal. 2003).

[520] *LG v. Asustek*, 248 F. Supp. 2d at 914.

[521] *Id.* at 913.

[522] *LG v. Asustek*, 2002 WL 31996860, at *1.

[523] *Id.* at *14 (citing United States v. Univis Lens Co., 316 U.S. 241 (1942)).

[524] 316 U.S. 241 (1942).

[525] *Id.* at 250 ("[S]ale of [a patented item] exhausts the monopoly in that article and the patentee may not thereafter, by virtue of his patent, control the use or disposition of the article.").

enforceability of those same restrictions flowing from certain *conditional* sales.[526]

Deciding LGE's appeal in 2006, the Federal Circuit reversed Judge Wilken's finding that LGE's licenses triggered patent exhaustion.[527] Citing Supreme Court precedent and Federal Circuit precedent, the court explained its understanding of the doctrine of patent exhaustion:

> It is axiomatic that the patent exhaustion doctrine, commonly referred to as the first sale doctrine, is triggered by an unconditional sale. "[A]n *unconditional* sale of a patented device exhausts the patentee's right to control the purchaser's use of the device thereafter. The theory behind this rule is that in such a transaction, the patentee has bargained for, and received, an amount equal to the full value of the goods. *This exhaustion doctrine, however, does not apply to an expressly conditional sale or license.* In such a transaction, it is more reasonable to infer that the parties negotiated a price that reflects only the value of the 'use' rights conferred by the patentee."[528]

Reasoning that the LGE-Intel license contained an express condition on the sale or license of the patented items, the Federal Circuit concluded that the doctrine of patent exhaustion did not prohibit LGE from asserting infringement claims against the defendants, who had purchased Intel's microprocessors and chipsets for use in their computers.[529] The Federal Circuit thus reiterated its precedent developed during the 1990s and appeared to reject Judge Wilken's articulation of the doctrine of patent exhaustion.

4. *Patent Exhaustion After* Quanta

In *Quanta*, a unanimous Supreme Court in 2008 reversed the decision of the Federal Circuit and abrogated that court's precedent of the 1990s concerning patent exhaustion. The Supreme Court held that "[t]he authorized sale of an article that substantially embodies a patent exhausts the patent holder's rights and prevents the patent holder from invoking patent law to control postsale use of the article."[530] In 2013 in *Bowman*, the Court further said that, "by 'exhaust[ing] the [patentee's] monopoly' in that item, the sale confers on the purchaser, or any subsequent owner, 'the right to use [or] sell' the thing

---

[526] *See, e.g.*, B. Braun Med. Inc. v. Abbott Labs., 124 F.3d 1419, 1426 (Fed. Cir. 1997) ("[E]xpress conditions accompanying the sale or license of a patented product are generally upheld."); Mallinckrodt, Inc. v. Medipart, Inc., 976 F.2d 700, 703 (Fed. Cir. 1992) ("[N]ot all restrictions on the use of patented goods are unenforceable.").

[527] LG Elecs., Inc. v. Bizcom Elecs., Inc., 453 F.3d 1364 (Fed. Cir. 2006).

[528] *Id.* at 1369–70 (alteration in original) (first emphasis in original) (second emphasis added) (quoting *Braun*, 124 F.3d at 1426 (citing *Mallinckrodt*, 976 F.2d at 708)) (citing Mitchell v. Hawley, 83 U.S. (16 Wall.) 544, 547 (1873)).

[529] *Id.* at 1370.

[530] Quanta Comput., Inc. v. LG Elecs., Inc., 553 U.S. 617, 638 (2008).

as he sees fit."[531] In 2017 in *Impression Products*, the Court reiterated that "a patentee's decision to sell a product exhausts all of its patent rights in that item, regardless of any restrictions the patentee purports to impose or the location of the sale."[532] Quoting *Quanta*, the Court in *Impression Products* confirmed that, "if there were any lingering doubt that patent exhaustion applies even when a sale is subject to an express, otherwise lawful restriction, our recent decision in *Quanta Computer, Inc. v. LG Electronics, Inc.* settled the matter. . . . [W]e held that the patentee could not bring an infringement suit because the 'authorized sale . . . took its products outside the scope of the patent monopoly.'"[533] Consequently, the Supreme Court held, contrary to the rulings of the Federal Circuit, that patent exhaustion *does* apply to an expressly conditional sale or license.

Notably, the Supreme Court in *Impression Products* distinguished the effect of a license to a patented item from the effect of the sale of a patented item:

> A patentee can impose restrictions on licensees because a license does not implicate the same concerns about restraints on alienation as a sale. Patent exhaustion reflects the principle that, when an item passes into commerce, it should not be shaded by a legal cloud on title as it moves through the marketplace. But a license is not about passing title to a product, it is about changing the contours of the patentee's monopoly: The patentee agrees not to exclude a licensee from making or selling the patented invention, expanding the club of authorized producers and sellers. Because the patentee is exchanging rights, not goods, it is free to relinquish only a portion of the bundle of patent protections.[534]

Although a patent holder *can* impose on a licensee restrictions that are enforceable (pursuant to patent law) against that licensee, the Court explained that a licensee's subsequent sale to the purchaser of a licensed item—whether or not the patent holder authorized such a sale under the terms of the license— would preclude the patent holder from enforcing its patent rights *against the purchaser*:

> A patentee's authority to limit *licensees* does not, as the Federal Circuit thought, mean that patentees can use licensees to impose post-sale restrictions on *purchasers* that are enforceable through the patent laws. So long as a licensee complies with the license when selling an item, the patentee has, in effect, authorized the sale. *That licensee's sale is treated, for purposes of patent exhaustion, as if the patentee made the sale itself.* The result: The sale exhausts

---

[531] Bowman v. Monsanto Co., 569 U.S. 278, 283 (2013) (alterations in original) (quoting United States v. Univis Lens Co., 316 U.S. 241, 249–50 (1942)).

[532] Impression Prods. v. Lexmark Int'l, Inc., 137 S. Ct. 1523, 1529 (2017).

[533] *Id.* at 1533 (third alteration in original) (quoting *Quanta*, 553 U.S. at 638).

[534] *Id.* at 1534 (citing United States v. General Elec. Co., 272 U.S. 476, 489–90 (1926)).

the patentee's rights in that item. *A license may require the licensee to impose a restriction on purchasers . . . . But if the licensee does so[,] . . . the sale nonetheless exhausts all patent rights in the item sold.* The purchasers might not comply with the restriction, but the only recourse for the licensee is through contract law, just as if the patentee itself sold the item with a restriction.[535]

The concern that Qualcomm expressed to the IRS in July 2012, and which (Qualcomm represented) it had foreseen since the 2000s, was prescient. As the Supreme Court announced in 2017, "[o]nce a patentee decides to sell—whether on its own *or through a licensee*—that sale exhausts [the patentee's] patent rights, regardless of any post-sale restrictions the patentee purports to impose, either directly or through a license."[536]

The patentee in *FTC v. Qualcomm* was of course Qualcomm. *Impression Products* absolutely confuted the conjecture of the FTC, of Professor Shapiro, and of Judge Koh that Qualcomm could begin to license its cellular SEPs exhaustively to rival modem manufacturers and yet continue to license the same portfolio of cellular SEPs to OEMs. *Impression Products* indicated that the sale of a modem by a rival modem manufacturer that was a licensee of Qualcomm's portfolio of cellular SEPs would exhaust Qualcomm's patent rights in the modem. Patent exhaustion would result "regardless of any post-sale restrictions [Qualcomm] purport[ed] to impose, either directly or through a license,"[537] because the rival modem manufacturer's sale of a modem would be "treated, for purposes of patent exhaustion, as if [Qualcomm] made the sale itself."[538]

Thus, had Qualcomm granted what it thought was a nonexhaustive "license" to a rival modem manufacturer, the Court's 2017 decision in *Impression Products* would have prohibited Qualcomm's bringing a patent-infringement case against an infringing (or non-paying) OEM that had purchased that rival's modem—even if Qualcomm had not authorized the rival's modem sales to that OEM. To paraphrase the Court in *Impression Products*, Qualcomm's patent rights do not "stick remora-like"[539] to a modem "as it flows through the market."[540]

And so, as of 2008, and with greater clarity as of 2017, the Supreme Court appeared to have revealed that the doctrine of patent exhaustion prohibits the enforcement, through an infringement action brought pursuant to patent law, of post-sale restrictions on a patent holder's patent rights with

---

[535] *Id.* at 1534–35 (third and fourth emphases added) (first citing Hobbie v. Jennison, 149 U.S. 355, 362–63 (1893); and then citing Motion Picture Patents Co. v. Universal Film Mfg. Co., 243 U.S. 502, 506–07, 516 (1917)).

[536] *Id.* at 1535 (emphasis added).

[537] *Id.*

[538] *Id.*

[539] *Id.* at 1538.

[540] *Id.*

respect to a patent-practicing item. The past and present senior executives of Qualcomm clearly explained to the IRS in July 2012—and to Judge Koh at trial—how Qualcomm had the foresight to discern this evolving business risk. Moreover, Qualcomm's senior management had the presence of mind to *act* on that discernment by refining the company's business model. Their foresight animated the evolving structure of Qualcomm's contracts with OEMs and with rival modem manufacturers. Their conduct reified business acumen. Judge Koh considered it evidence of monopolization.

D. *Did the Supreme Court's Refinement of the Doctrine of Patent Exhaustion Affect How Qualcomm Structured Its Commercial Agreements with Rival Modem Manufacturers?*

When Qualcomm first began licensing its patented technology in the 1990s,[541] Qualcomm earned approximately 95 percent of its total annual royalty revenue from OEMs.[542] Qualcomm also granted to certain rival modem manufacturers narrow, nonexhaustive patent "license[s] to make and sell but not use"[543] certain of Qualcomm's claimed inventions, in exchange for a modest royalty that comprised approximately 1 percent of Qualcomm's total annual royalty revenue at the time.[544]

As Marv Blecker (then QTL Senior Vice President) explained to the IRS in July 2012, Qualcomm "clearly stated" in its nonexhaustive "licenses" with rival modem manufacturers (called ASIC companies or suppliers) that

> *the licensee has no right to use the patents in the chips that it's selling, and its customers have no right to use the patents in the chips that it's selling,* so we said[,] . . . and this was all in the contract, that it's a nonexhaustive license and that the customer has to have a patent license from Qualcomm in order to use those chips that it's buying from the ASIC company.[545]

---

[541] *See, e.g.*, Transcript of Proceedings (Volume 2) at 179:20–180:1, FTC v. Qualcomm Inc., No. 5:17-cv-00220-LHK (N.D. Cal. Jan. 7, 2019) (Testimony of Steven Altman (former President, Qualcomm)) ("Q. So at the time you joined Qualcomm, Qualcomm had not yet licensed its CDMA technology to others for use in cellular communications; is that right? A. That's correct. Q. It's fair to say you negotiated Qualcomm's first CDMA related patent licenses with AT&T and with Motorola? A. Yes."); *id.* at 182:8–11 ("Q. It's a true statement that in 1990, Qualcomm gave Motorola a license to make CDMA compliant ASICs; isn't that right? Isn't that right? A. Yes."). For purposes of this excerpt of trial testimony, ASICs were being treated as equivalent to modems.

[542] IRS Transcript, *supra* note 503, at 32:6–13 ("Mr. [Marv] Blecker: And when ninety-five percent of the royalties come from manufacturers of these things [mobile devices], and I don't know what the percentage was when we were collecting royalties, but it had to be well less than one percent came from component suppliers. . . . You don't want to fight to preserve the component royalty and risk ninety-five percent of your royalty.").

[543] *Id.* at 23:4 (Marv Blecker (Senior Vice President, Qualcomm Technology Licensing)).

[544] *Id.* at 32:6–13.

[545] *Id.* at 23:7–13 (emphasis added).

Mr. Blecker elaborated on the postsale restrictions that Qualcomm's nonexhaustive "licenses" contractually imposed on rival modem manufacturers:

> [O]ur initial approach was that we would license ASIC suppliers to make and sell but not to use, and that we would reserve the use right for their customers and license them in a separate license agreement. This was our way of saying[,] okay, all of the rights have not been exhausted by this sale and that we are entitled to still collect from the ASIC supplier's customer. That was our initial approach. . . [that] we started using in 1990. And we charged a royalty for that. We charged the ASIC person a royalty, and we charged their customer a royalty. . . . And [the idea was that] if we partition the rights, we have the ability to charge for each of the rights that we're licensing. So if we partition them to . . . two different entities, we could charge each of those entities for its [respective] rights that it's getting.[546]

Thus, early in the history of Qualcomm's licensing business, in addition to receiving royalty payments from OEMs, Qualcomm also received royalty payments from rival modem manufacturers.[547] Qualcomm earned the vast majority of its patent-licensing revenues from OEMs that implemented either Qualcomm modems or non-Qualcomm modems in mobile devices (as well as from infrastructure manufacturers whose equipment also practiced Qualcomm's claimed inventions). As we have seen, the Federal Circuit during the 1990s indicated that such royalties from rival modem manufacturers would be best understood as capturing the value only of the narrow bundle of rights that a patentee intended to grant to the licensee.[548]

In the July 2012 meeting with the IRS, Mr. Reifschneider (then QTL Senior Vice President and General Manager) explained how the law of patent exhaustion, as revealed during the 2000s, had required Qualcomm to revise its agreements with rival modem manufacturers to grant them the same intended bundle of rights but to do so in a manner that would enable Qualcomm to avoid any risk of patent exhaustion:

---

[546] *Id.* at 27:1–7, 27:9–12, 27:19–23.

[547] *See id.* at 13–22 ("Mr. [Fabian] Gonell: . . . [T]he ASIC agreements are . . . an exception to . . . [Qualcomm's] royalty structure staying the same . . . from time immemorial. The ASIC structure, at one point there were royalties charged. The standard form for ASIC[s] was a license, and royalties were charged. That was a limited license, but royalties were charged, and that changed some years ago so that it is now no longer a license and there are no royalties charged."). The Ninth Circuit's three-judge panel in *FTC v. Qualcomm* properly recognized that, "[p]reviously, in the 1990s, Qualcomm provided 'non-exhaustive licenses' to rival chip suppliers, charging a royalty rate on their chipset sales," and that, "[a]ccording to Qualcomm, these were actually 'non-exhaustive, royalty-bearing agreements with chipmakers that explicitly did not grant rights to the chipmaker's [OEM] customers.'" FTC v. Qualcomm Inc., No. 19-16122, 2020 WL 4591476 at *4 n.7 (9th Cir. Aug. 11, 2020) (third alteration in original) (first quoting FTC v. Qualcomm Inc., 411 F. Supp. 3d 658, 673, 754 (N.D. Cal. 2019); and then quoting Opening Brief for Appellant Qualcomm Incorporated at 45, FTC v. Qualcomm Inc., No. 19-16122 (9th Cir. Aug. 23, 2019)); *see also id.* at *12.

[548] *See supra note* 528 and accompanying text.

Mr. Reifschneider: Some of the [agreements used to achieve patent peace with rival modem manufacturers] flat out do not work, we know that now [in July 2012], but . . . things that ten, fifteen years ago people thought maybe would work in terms of avoiding exhaustion . . . we now know don't work, or we think there's a very good chance they don't work, and so you try different things. But *the concern all along has been that, . . . if we license somebody to make a chip, and that chip contains the inventions in our patents, when they sell that chip to somebody who's going to put the chip in a cell phone, . . . the licensee's sale of that chip will exhaust our rights in our patents and then we won't be able to collect a royalty on that patent from the guy who makes the cell phone.* And that would be a very bad thing, because we collect a royalty on a cell phone that's based on the price of the cell phone, and that's a lot higher than the price of a chip. *So given a choice, you're always going to want to collect a royalty on the cell phone, not on the chip.* And that's, in fact, what we do.[549]

Mr. Reifschneider's explanation is an essential fact whose profound significance to *FTC v. Qualcomm* Judge Koh remarkably did not seem to recognize. The revelation over time by the Federal Circuit and the Supreme Court of the metes and bounds of the doctrine of patent exhaustion clearly appeared, on the basis of Mr. Reifschneider's sworn testimony, to have motivated Qualcomm to revise its agreements with rival modem manufacturers. Qualcomm apparently sought to (1) continue to preserve patent peace with those manufacturers while (2) mitigating the risk that a court would find those agreements to constitute exhaustive licenses that could prevent Qualcomm from continuing to collect royalty payments from OEMs.

The potential consequence to Qualcomm of a court's finding that Qualcomm had, contrary to its intention, exhaustively licensed one or more rival modem manufacturers would be to forgo the royalties that Qualcomm expected to earn from the sale by OEMs of devices containing a non-Qualcomm modem—even though those devices practiced Qualcomm's claimed inventions and Qualcomm did not receive a reasonable royalty to which it was entitled on those devices merely from its having licensed rival modem manufacturers.

On cross examination during the FTC's case-in-chief, Finbarr Moynihan—the General Manager of MediaTek, a rival modem manufacturer—testified that he understood Qualcomm's business motivation to avoid patent exhaustion in the licensing of its patents. He communicated that understanding by email on March 6, 2014 to his colleagues at MediaTek:

---

[549] IRS Transcript, *supra* note 503, at 26:1–18 (emphasis added); *see also* Transcript of Proceedings (Volume 2) at 299:24, 300:5–7, FTC v. Qualcomm Inc., No. 5:17-cv-00220-LHK (N.D. Cal. Jan. 7, 2019) (Testimony of Derek Aberle (former President, Qualcomm)) (indicating that the case law on patent exhaustion was "evolving," such that Qualcomm grew "concerned that the structure we were proposing to [Samsung] actually would not hold up and be non-exhaustive," owing to that new case law).

Q. . . . [Y]ou wrote . . . , "A few years ago there was some lawsuits, I recall the key case was involving LG, Intel and Quantum [sic], that established the concept of patent exhaustion, i.e., if the IPR is licensed at the chipset and it became exhausted, then the IPR holder can no longer claim royalties from anyone else in the chain." Do you see that?

A. Yes, I do.

Q. And then you wrote, "I believe these rulings caused many of the IPR holders to rework their license agreements and policies and in my experience they now go out of their way to make it absolutely clear that they are not licensing to the chipset company." That statement accurately reflects your understanding of the industry in 2014; correct?

A. Correct.

Q. And then you wrote, "For example I worked on the MPA agreement with Nokia and there is language in there written over and over that nothing in the agreements gives MediaTek any rights to the Nokia IPR." And then you added, "But it is extremely important for them that their IPR is not seen to be licensed to the chipset companies." That accurately reflects the position that Nokia took in their negotiations with you; correct?

A. Yeah. I'm being dramatic, yes.[550]

Mr. Moynihan's testimony thus confirmed a competitor's understanding that, in revising its nonexhaustive "license" agreements with modem manufacturers, Qualcomm sought to avoid patent exhaustion. Moreover, Mr. Moynihan testified, this same objective was evident in the licensing policies of "many of the IPR holders," including Nokia.[551]

E. *Did* Quanta *and Subsequent Federal Circuit Precedent Affect How Qualcomm Achieved Patent Peace with Rival Modem Manufacturers?*

When *Quanta* began to wend its way through the Federal Circuit to the Supreme Court during the 2000s, and it became evident to Qualcomm's management that any kind of license issued to a rival modem manufacturer might trigger patent exhaustion,[552] Qualcomm began to grant a rival modem manufacturer a covenant not to sue rather than a license. Mr. Reifschneider

---

[550] Transcript of Proceedings (Volume 2) at 360:22–361:22, FTC v. Qualcomm Inc., No. 5:17-cv-00220-LHK (N.D. Cal. Jan. 7, 2019) (Testimony of Finbarr Moynihan (General Manager, MediaTek)) (quoting from QX219, an internal MediaTek email chain from March 6, 2014).

[551] *Id.* at 361:5–6; *see also id.* at 361:13–22.

[552] *See* IRS Transcript, *supra* note 503, at 31:3–8 ("[Mr. Eric Reifschneider.] [T]here's been a . . . general trend, certainly over the last ten years [preceding 2012], in the case law on patents generally, . . . to make things harder for patentees, not easier for licensors. And— [Mr. Marv Blecker.] But in particular with regards to exhaustion issues.").

explained to the IRS in July 2012 that, because of the threat of patent exhaustion, Qualcomm had

> gotten to the point where we decided you know what? We're not even going to try to collect license fees and royalties from guys who make chips. We'd just as soon not have any agreement with them at all. We will just leave them alone as long as they leave us alone, and we will concentrate our licensing program and our licensing negotiations on the guys who make the cell phones and the base stations and the test equipment, because that's where the real money is, so to speak.
>
> Now, there are times when other chip suppliers will come to us and say we're worried you might sue us for patent infringement, and we'd like to have an agreement with you where that won't happen. And for various reasons . . . including the fact that when you participate in a standard setting process, . . . and you contribute your technology to the standard, as part of that you often have to make commitments that you will . . . make that technology available to people who want to make products that practice the standard.
>
> And so . . . we would take the position that that doesn't mean you have to grant a license . . . to everybody at every step in the supply chain. But . . . to tell somebody no, we're sorry, we won't enter any kind of agreement with you at all, and, yes, in theory . . . you have to just live with this risk that we could sue you for patent infringement, it's not a great . . . position to be in in terms of defending yourself against . . . claims that you've broken those promises to make the technology available.
>
>   . . . .
>
> So, . . . when pressed, although it's not our preference, . . . we have over the last—I don't know how many years it is—been willing to enter into agreements with other chip companies, where at first . . . the approach was just to give them a covenant not to sue, a promise that we wouldn't sue them for infringement.[553]

At another point during the IRS conference call in July 2012, Mr. Reifschneider explained:

> [T]here was a period of time when a lot of people involved in patent licensing felt that there was a difference between granting a license versus granting a promise, a covenant not to sue for infringement, in that a license would authorize the licensee to make a sale, and therefore trigger patent exhaustion, whereas a promise not to sue for infringement wouldn't. And so the way to get around patent exhaustion was rather than grant a license, grant a promise or a covenant not to sue. And so we tried that.[554]

---

[553] *Id.* at 32:14–33:17, 33:25–34:5.
[554] *Id.* at 29:2–11.

In short, there was substantial evidence in the record in *FTC v. Qualcomm* indicating that the Supreme Court's decision in *Quanta* motivated Qualcomm to restructure its agreements with rival modem manufacturers as covenants not to sue, in the belief that such agreements would continue to enable Qualcomm to offer modem manufacturers a commercial means to achieve freedom to operate with Qualcomm (without those modem manufacturers paying Qualcomm any royalty), but without triggering exhaustion of Qualcomm's patents.

Yet, the law evolved further, such that Qualcomm's need to adapt continued. In April 2009, following the Supreme Court's decision in *Quanta*, the Federal Circuit concluded that even an unconditional covenant not to sue was tantamount to an exhaustive agreement. In *TransCore, LP v. Electronic Transaction Consultants Corp.*,[555] the Federal Circuit held that "an unconditional covenant not to sue authorizes sales by the covenantee for purposes of patent exhaustion."[556] Consequently, as Mr. Reifschneider explained to the IRS in July 2012, Qualcomm needed to update its standard practice, so as to grant rival modem manufacturers a covenant to sue *last*:

> [Mr. Reifschneider.] [A]fter a Federal Circuit decision called *TransCore*, we started to think well, even [a covenant not to sue] doesn't work to avoid patent exhaustion. . . .
>
> And so then we shifted to, and this is what we currently do [as of July 2012], an agreement where the promise we give to the chip company is that we will not sue them for patent infringement until and unless we have sued their customers and exhausted our remedies to collect royalties and damages from their customers, and only if we've done that and won on the merits but been unable to collect for some reason, like the customer's bankrupt, or judgment proof in some country where we can't get at their assets, or whatever the case may be, can we then sue the chip company? . . . [I] don't think there's any case I'm aware of . . . where a court has decided whether that works or not in terms of triggering patent exhaustion, but that's what we do now.
>
> And the thinking behind it is . . . we're not licensing you. We're not giving you an absolute promise we'll never sue you, because the Federal Circuit in *TransCore* would . . . say that that's the equivalent of a license. That's also authorizing them to sell . . . . We're just saying before we sue you, we're going to go try to get our royalty here. And we're free to make that choice. . . . [W]e're free to . . . collect our royalties on our patents at whatever step in the supply chain we want. That's, I think, become clear over the many decades of case law in this area as well.[557]

---

[555] 563 F.3d 1271 (Fed. Cir. 2009).
[556] *Id.* at 1274.
[557] IRS Transcript, *supra* note 503, at 34:6–8, 35:12–36:11.

Mr. Blecker similarly explained to the IRS that this arrangement was intended to achieve the same avoidance of patent exhaustion as were Qualcomm's prior commercial agreements:

> [W]e do have some protections in those agreements where if they're found to be exhaustive, or if the other party claims they're exhaustive, we generally have rights to terminate the agreements or to sit down and replace whatever provision is found to be exhaustive with a new provision that preserves the intent of the parties that they not be exhaustive. So they do have some remedies within themselves because the intent of both parties was that they not be exhaustive, that their customers would be required to pay royalties.[558]

Thus, there was substantial evidence in the record in *FTC v. Qualcomm* that "the fear of the risk of patent exhaustion"[559] and the emerging understanding of what agreements could trigger patent exhaustion animated Qualcomm's choice of the optimal kind of commercial agreement to achieve patent peace with rival modem manufacturers. Indeed, there was no testimony or documentary evidence in *FTC v. Qualcomm* that Qualcomm had ever licensed its cellular SEPs *exhaustively* to any rival modem manufacturer.

F. Why Was Offering Exhaustive Licenses Only to OEMs More Lucrative for Qualcomm Than Offering Exhaustive Licenses to Rival Modem Manufacturers?

Some, if not many, of Qualcomm's claimed inventions are embodied not in the modem but in the system enabling mobile communications.[560] A reasonable per-unit royalty payable to Qualcomm for an exhaustive license to its cellular SEPs therefore might well exceed the price of an unlicensed modem. Qualcomm executives considered it impractical to recover from rival modem manufacturers a reasonable royalty for an exhaustive license to its cellular SEPs:

> Mr. Blecker: [I]f I would [compute the] average royalty on all the handsets that we collect royalties on—I don't remember what it is anymore, I used to know the number—but if . . . it were ten dollars, for example, you couldn't

---

[558] *Id.* at 40:10–19 (Marv Blecker (Senior Vice President, Qualcomm Technology Licensing)).

[559] *Id.* at 48:1–2 (Eric Reifschneider (Senior Vice President and General Manager, Qualcomm Technology Licensing)).

[560] *See, e.g.*, Transcript of Proceedings (Volume 6) at 1304:18–1306:12, FTC v. Qualcomm Inc., No. 5:17-cv-00220-LHK (N.D. Cal. Jan. 15, 2019) (Testimony of Durga Malladi (Senior Vice President and General Manager of 4G and 5G, Qualcomm)). On direct examination during the FTC's case-in-chief, Professor Shapiro acknowledged this point but ignored, implausibly, that no OEM would request an exhaustive license from Qualcomm for its cellular SEPs once Qualcomm had been enjoined to offer exhaustive licensing at the component level. *See id.* at 1126:13–1127:1 (Testimony of Carl Shapiro).

charge a ten-dollar royalty on a chipset that cost five dollars, or six dollars, or seven dollars.

Mr. Gonell: Theoretically you could. . . but as a practical matter you can't. As a practical matter it's hard.

Mr. Blecker: Yeah, and it would be hard to convince a court that that was a fair royalty also.[561]

Put differently, although it would have been theoretically possible to draft a patent-license agreement that specified a royalty rate for Qualcomm's cellular SEPs that equaled or exceeded 100 percent of a royalty base consisting of the price of a bare (unlicensed) modem, at least as early as July 2012 Qualcomm executives manifestly deemed that theoretical possibility to be commercially infeasible. The cognitive dissonance produced by applying a seemingly high royalty rate to a relatively small royalty base (here, the price of the modem, exclusive of Qualcomm's intellectual property) would have been difficult to overcome when negotiating a patent license with a prospective licensee. And even a court might fall prey to that same cognitive bias and misunderstand the agreement's legitimate purpose.

It is impossible to reconcile Judge Koh's recitation of facts in *FTC v. Qualcomm* with the transcript of Qualcomm's July 2012 meeting with the IRS. Quoting the very same statements by Mr. Blecker to the IRS that I have quoted above, Judge Koh found that Mr. "Blecker said that Qualcomm could not charge *unreasonably high royalty rates* if Qualcomm licensed rival modem chip suppliers."[562] Perhaps Judge Koh misunderstood the context of Mr. Blecker's statement to the IRS, which followed directly from the antecedent discussion of patent exhaustion. Nothing in Mr. Becker's discussion indicated that Qualcomm sought to recover an *unreasonable* royalty. Nor, as we shall see, did the FTC ever prove that Qualcomm's royalties exceeded a reasonable level.

G. *Which of Judge Koh's Conclusions Were Predicated on Her Legally Erroneous Depiction of Patent Exhaustion?*

Throughout her findings of fact and conclusions of law, and in her explanation of her rationale for imposing her permanent, worldwide injunction on Qualcomm, Judge Koh relied on her finding that it was "anticompetitive conduct under the Sherman Act" for Qualcomm to "requir[e] OEMs to sign a separate license before buying modem chips"[563] and to "refus[e] to license

---

[561] IRS Transcript, *supra* note 503, at 73:10–21.
[562] FTC v. Qualcomm Inc., 411 F. Supp. 3d 658, 757 (N.D. Cal. 2019) (emphasis added).
[563] *Id.* at 820.

rival modem chip suppliers" Qualcomm's cellular SEPs exhaustively.[564] As we have seen, Qualcomm articulated compelling justifications for those business practices.

Yet, Judge Koh interpreted Qualcomm's avoidance of patent exhaustion as anticompetitive. Her findings of fact were contrary to substantial evidence, and her conclusions of law were clearly erroneous. Those errors were not harmless. Judge Koh's specious interpretation of the facts and law materially affected the outcome of *FTC v. Qualcomm*.

1. *Did Judge Koh Make Credibility Determinations on the Basis of Qualcomm's Refusal to Sell Modems to Unlicensed OEMs and Its Refusal to Offer Exhaustive Licenses to Its Cellular SEPs to Rival Modem Manufacturers?*

Judge Koh concluded that "Qualcomm's [j]ustifications for its [r]efusal to [l]icense [r]ivals [we]re [p]retextual."[565] She found that, at trial, "Qualcomm offer[ed] self-serving and pretextual justifications for Qualcomm's refusal to license modem chip suppliers."[566] Judge Koh said that "Qualcomm's own recorded statements to the IRS show that Qualcomm *used to license rival modem chip suppliers*, and that Qualcomm stopped licensing rivals *because it is more lucrative to license only OEMs*."[567] She added that "[n]owhere in QTL's long discussion with the IRS did any QTL executive raise concerns about multi-level licensing."[568] Judge Koh concluded that

> Fabian Gonell's (QTL Legal Counsel and Senior Vice President, Licensing Strategy) own recorded statements to the IRS, a U.S. government agency, contradict Gonell's trial claim that Qualcomm refuses to license rivals to avoid multi-level licensing. Rather, Gonell told the IRS in 2012 that Qualcomm stopped licensing its rivals because licensing only OEMs is more lucrative: "But having—having to choose between one or the other then you're right, obviously the handset is humongously more . . . lucrative for a bunch of—a bunch of reasons." Thus, Gonell's trial testimony was not credible, and the Court rejects Qualcomm's self-serving justifications as pretextual.[569]

Judge Koh's reported interpretation of the IRS transcript was preposterous. It was contrary to fact and highly prejudicial to Qualcomm. *Dozens* of pages of the IRS meeting transcript from July 2012 convey Qualcomm's concerns

---

[564] *Id.* at 821.
[565] *Id.* at 756.
[566] *Id.*
[567] *Id.* (emphasis added).
[568] *Id.*
[569] *Id.* at 757–58 (alteration in original) (quoting IRS Transcript, *supra* note 503, at 71:18–23).

about licensing at different levels in the supply chain for mobile devices practicing Qualcomm's cellular SEPs. Mr. Gonell's statement that "licensing only OEMs is more lucrative" followed an antecedent discussion of the doctrine of patent exhaustion and the cognitive dissonance of trying to apply a seemingly high royalty rate to a small royalty base (at the component level).

Judge Koh's interpretation of Mr. Gonell's statements to the IRS was implausible because it assumed away, or was incognizant of, the critical role that the doctrine of patent exhaustion unquestionably played in Qualcomm's refinement of its business model of licensing its patent portfolio. Considering how context can transform one's understanding of the relevance to *FTC v. Qualcomm* of the doctrine of patent exhaustion or the perils of cognitive dissonance in the setting of a patent royalty at a particular level in the chain of production, it is imperative to examine Mr. Gonell's statement to the IRS in the context of the broader set of statements that he and other senior Qualcomm executives made to the IRS concerning patent exhaustion:

> Mr. Reifschneider: [T]o this day [in July 2012], licensees . . . will make those arguments [concerning patent exhaustion] to us in the course of negotiating, . . . license terms or audit findings . . . . Anytime there's an issue about how much money [a licensee] has to pay us, it's one of the things the [licensee is] likely to trot out and argue about [or] threaten us with, to some extent. It remains a very real issue for us.

> Mr. Howell [IRS representative]: Okay. So it sounds like since you can only collect the royalty at one—on one point in this line [that is, either from (1) a rival modem manufacturer, or (2) an OEM—but not both], how it was a business decision to opt to collect it at the handset level, because it was worth a lot more at the time or still is. How—

> Mr. Blecker: Oh, it's more than that, it's more than that. That's an understatement

> Mr. Howell: Okay.

> Mr. Blecker: Because *it had the potential of threatening our entire revenue stream at the handset level.*

> Mr. Howell: Okay.

> Mr. Blecker: Right? There was a potential that depending on how this thing all turned out and courts ruled on [patent exhaustion], et cetera, et cetera, our entire handset revenue stream could have been threatened.

> Mr. Howell: Okay.

> Mr. Blecker: So, . . . the ninety-five percent of our royalty revenues that you guys [at the IRS] gladly take taxes on in the United States could have disappeared, and we could have been left with this chip royalty revenue. That's the real threat.

Mr. Gonell: But having . . . to choose between one or the other then you're right, *obviously the handset is humongously more—*

Mr. Howell: Yeah.

Mr. Gonell: *—lucrative for a bunch of . . . reasons.*

Mr. Howell: Right. So you could come up if you wanted to, just charge—charge the royalty on the chipset but you would be—

Mr. Reifschneider: No. No, practically you can't.

Mr. Howell: —completely out of the handset royalty, is that not right?

Mr. Reifschneider: Oh, yeah. Now, that's the concern.

Mr. Blecker: That's the concern.

Mr. Gonell: Right.

Mr. Howell: But I'm just saying—

Mr. Reifschneider: *So I thought you were saying you could . . . charge the same amount of royalty [to the rival modem manufacturer] that you [charge the OEM]—that would never work.*

Mr. Howell: No, I'm saying if you went after the chipset-only royalty you would have to give up the. . . handset royalty, how you can't do both. And so it was a business. . . decision obviously to—

Mr. Blecker: If you want to call it a decision—

Mr. Howell: —to pursue—no, no, I mean—

Mr. Blecker: —I mean, *it's a no-brainer.*

Mr. Howell: Yeah. Yeah. Right.[570]

Judge Koh appeared to infer that an anticompetitive desire to collect an "unreasonably high" royalty motivated Qualcomm's business practices. Context plainly indicates otherwise. When Mr. Gonell remarked that it was "humongously more lucrative" for Qualcomm to grant exhaustive licenses to its cellular SEPs only to OEMs, he was concurring with Mr. Howell, a representative of the IRS, that, given the choice of licensing its cellular SEPs exhaustively at either the component level or the handset level (but not both)—and threatened by the cognitive dissonance of asking a court to apply a seemingly high royalty rate to a relatively low royalty base—any rational firm would choose the latter strategy.

Thus, Judge Koh's stated reason for finding Mr. Gonell not to be a credible witness—that his trial testimony supposedly contradicted statements

---

[570] IRS Transcript, *supra* note 503, at 70:15–72:23 (emphasis added).

made to the IRS—was implausible in light of substantial evidence in the record.

2. *Why Did Qualcomm Avoid Selling Modems to Unlicensed OEMs and Offering Exhaustive Licenses to Its Cellular SEPs to Rival Modem Manufacturers?*

Mr. Reifschneider, the very first witness whom the FTC called in *FTC v. Qualcomm* (and who testified by deposition), represented in his deposition on February 22, 2018, and February 23, 2018, that the fear of patent exhaustion motivated Qualcomm to avoid both selling modems to unlicensed OEMs and offering exhaustive licenses to its cellular SEPs to rival modem manufacturers. Referring to a slide attached to an email, "titled 'Licensee Disputes/Extensions,' [which said]: 'Issue: Whether to maintain policy of refusing to sell ASICs to unlicensed entities,'"[571] Jennifer Milici of the FTC questioned Mr. Reifschneider about a particular statement on the slide:

> Q [Ms. Milici:] Okay. Under that point, it says: "Such sales [of ASICs] present the risk of a finding of patent exhaustion in a dispute over royalties." Is that what you understand to be the reason for the policy?
>
> A [Mr. Reifschneider:] My understanding was that was the concern for the risk to the licensing business of selling . . . chips to unlicensed customers, the . . . risk of a customer making an argument of patent exhaustion and sort of undercutting the ability to license the patent portfolio. Yes.[572]

Ms. Milici subsequently asked the following clarifying questions of Mr. Reifschneider:

> Q[.] So if I understand the concern, the concern is that if you sell a chip to an unlicensed customer, that you would not be able to get royalties for the IP embodied on the chip and the—and not for any other IP?[573]
>
> A[.] The concern, as I tried to explain before, was that the company we were dealing with would argue, or take the position, that, as a result of patent exhaustion, they did not need to pay royalties at all, or needed to pay less in royalties.[574]

In addition to his testimony that Qualcomm avoided patent exhaustion by selling modems only to licensed OEMs, Mr. Reifschneider testified that

---

[571] Deposition of Eric Reifschneider (Vol. 1), *supra* note 20, at 29:23–30:1.
[572] *Id.* at 30:10–20.
[573] *Id.* at 42:6–10.
[574] *Id.* at 42:13–17.

Qualcomm did not offer exhaustive licenses to its cellular SEPs to rival modem manufacturers:

> [Q.] While you were a general manager of QTL, did Qualcomm have a policy of not granting exhaustive licenses to ASIC manufacturers?
>
> A[.] Well, again, I . . . didn't think of things in terms of policies. But the practice at the time I was general manager was not to seek to license exhaustively other component suppliers.[575]

This testimony by Mr. Reifschneider was substantial evidence that Qualcomm's business model sought to avoid patent exhaustion.

Nevertheless, the lawyer representing the plaintiff class seeking $15 billion in treble damages from Qualcomm, Rio Pierce, who also deposed Mr. Reifschneider, apparently contended that Qualcomm was trying to prevent an OEM from challenging Qualcomm's standard royalty rate. Inquiring about Qualcomm's negotiations with Apple in 2015, Mr. Pierce quoted an email from Mr. Reifschneider to Derek Aberle (then President of QTL) and Mr. Gonell that said: "'We have tried to find compromises and workarounds as they have whittled away, slowly and surely, at every layer of protection of our business model.'"[576]

Mr. Pierce then tried to get an admission from Mr. Reifschneider, but the series of questions fizzled, and Mr. Pierce changed the topic to how an OEM might go about destroying Qualcomm's business model:

> Q[.] So your business model is built to protect against an OEM bringing FRAND litigation; correct?
>
> A[.] No. No. What I think, as I sit here now and look at this, I was referring to . . . the ability to have both a licensing business and a product business—in our case, a chip business—at the same time and be able to generate revenues from both of those businesses at the same time.[577]

Mr. Pierce turned to Qualcomm's concern over patent exhaustion:

> Q[.] And so everyone at Qualcomm understood that in this licensing negotiation with Apple, where Apple wanted a guarantee of chipset supply, the—the return objective was that Qualcomm got legal language that protected them against exhaustion arguments; correct?

---

[575] *Id.* at 53:12–18.

[576] Deposition of Eric Reifschneider (Vol. 2), *supra* note 3, at 315:20–23; *see id.* at 313:7–16 ("[Q.] There's two e-mails—it's three e-mails here—email chain from February 20th, 2015. I'm going to be focusing on the top e-mail, which is an e-mail from you, Eric Reifschneider, to Derek Aberle and Fabian Gonell. A[.] Uh-huh. Q[.] Do you see that? And it says—the subject is regarding 'Mav follow up.' Fair to say that this whole e-mail chain is about Apple negotiations? A[.] Yes. Yes.").

[577] *Id.* at 315:25–316:7.

MR. BORNSTEIN: Object to the form.

A[.] That was an important consideration for us.[578]

Mr. Pierce then switched the topic and asked Mr. Reifschneider about the difference, for purposes of Qualcomm's business model, of its licensing SEPs pursuant to a bilaterally negotiated FRAND royalty versus a judicially imposed FRAND royalty:

> [Q.] But that consideration alone didn't seem to alleviate your concerns about how Apple was attacking your business model. Based on this e-mail, it seems that you had broader concerns that [sic] just exhaustion. You were also concerned about the fact that Apple could disrupt the peaceful relationship by, for example, initiating litigation that resulted in a judicial determination of a FRAND rate for Qualcomm's SEPs.
>
> MR. BORNSTEIN: Is there a question?
>
> [Q.] Isn't that a fair characterization of your—of your comments in this e-mail, where you talk about how they are "whittling away slowly and surely at every layer of protection of our business model"?
>
> A[.] I remember being concerned, based on things they had said they might do if we didn't work out some sort of agreement, that could create serious risks for QTL and for Qualcomm.
>
> Q[.] Is it a serious risk to QTL that a judge could determine a FRAND rate for Qualcomm's portfolio that was different from Qualcomm's proposed FRAND rate?
>
> A[.] At the time I was general manager, I think there were fewer such FRAND decisions than there are now. But generally, I was concerned about that risk.[579]

Then came Mr. Pierce's striking question—upon which I remarked at the very beginning of this article—about how a judge might be persuaded to destroy, by "slash[ing] Qualcomm's royalty rate," much of the value that Qualcomm had methodically created by combining its unique licensing practices with a sustained dynamic capability for inventing and developing commercially successful technologies of foundational significance:

> Q[.] And Qualcomm's—QTL is responsible for a majority of Qualcomm's profits. And so if a judge came along and slashed—slashed Qualcomm's royalty rate, that would destroy a great deal of the value of Qualcomm's business model; correct?

---

[578] *Id.* at 318:9–15.
[579] *Id.* at 318:16–319:15.

A[.] As I said, I was concerned about the possibility of . . . a FRAND determination having an impact on QTL royalty revenue.[580]

Mr. Pierce then appeared to insinuate that Qualcomm's "peaceful relationship"
with OEMs, and the absence of FRAND litigation filed against Qualcomm
by OEMs, was in fact evidence probative of anticompetitive conduct by
Qualcomm:

> Q[.] So Qualcomm's business model has been successful at—apart from
> Apple and Nokia, at preserving a peaceful relationship with cell phone man-
> ufacturers where they don't initiate FRAND litigation; correct?
>
> MR. BORNSTEIN: Object to the form of the question.
>
> A[.] I mean, we worked very hard to maintain peaceful relationships, which
> is why we were . . . always willing to listen and engage in discussion. And . . .
> there was just no shortage of . . . issues that would come up from time to
> time with licensees. But [during] my time as general manager, we were . . .
> able to resolve most of them amicably. And there were some that were
> unresolved when I stepped down. But . . . other than an arbitration with LG
> that was either pending or looming at the time, I don't remember any other
> situation that resulted in litigation.[581]

Mr. Reifschneider's representation to the IRS in 2012—that Qualcomm's
principal motivation for licensing exhaustively only at the device level was
to avoid patent exhaustion—corroborated his videotaped deposition testimony from February 2018, which was played at trial on January 4, 2019. The
vilification of Qualcomm's efforts to maintain peaceful relationships with its
customers, and the insinuation that peaceful supplier relationships would be
evidence probative of anticompetitive conduct, was startling.

It is a generic, commonsense business objective—not unique to
FRAND-committed patents—that a patent holder would prefer to enforce
its patents without putting them at risk of being found unenforceable. For
the FTC to contend otherwise was to mischaracterize the legal constraints
under which Qualcomm operated when modifying its business model for a
completely legitimate business purpose. That purpose was the mitigation
of risk arising from the Supreme Court's evolving explanation of the reach
of the doctrine of patent exhaustion. Risk bearing is costly. Taking precautions to mitigate risk—including the risk from changes in what had previously
appeared to be settled doctrines of judicially made law—is presumptively
efficient all the way up to the point where the marginal cost of reducing
risk equals the expected marginal benefit of doing so. Put differently, for

---

[580] *Id.* at 319:16–23.
[581] *Id.* at 320:13–321:6.

Qualcomm's management not to have taken such precautions to mitigate risk from the Supreme Court's changing interpretation of the law of patent exhaustion would have been inefficient as a matter of economics and negligent as a matter of law.[582]

Nothing about efficient risk mitigation is inherently anticompetitive. But suppose, for sake of argument (but contrary to the evidence) that Qualcomm's mitigation of risk did entail some tradeoff with respect to a marginal diminution in the vitality of the competitive process in the two relevant markets for modems at issue in *FTC v. Qualcomm*. At no time did the FTC show that Qualcomm could have mitigated that risk by some alternative means that was equally efficacious but less threatening with respect to the competitive sensitivities that they imagined.

3. *Did Qualcomm's Business Practice of Not Offering Exhaustive Licenses to Its Cellular SEPs to Rival Modem Manufacturers Affect Judge Koh's Permanent, Worldwide Injunction?*

As we will see in greater detail in Part XX, Judge Koh imposed a permanent, worldwide injunction on Qualcomm composed of five parts. It is worth pausing here to observe that her stated purpose for imposing the first and second components of her permanent, worldwide injunction included Qualcomm's business practices of (1) not selling modems to unlicensed OEMs and (2) not licensing it patents exhaustively to rival modem manufacturers.

The first component of Judge Koh's permanent, worldwide injunction specified that "Qualcomm must not condition the supply of modem chips on a customer's patent license status and Qualcomm must negotiate or renegotiate license terms with customers in good faith under conditions free from the threat of lack of access to or discriminatory provision of modem chip supply or associated technical support or access to software."[583] Her stated purpose for so enjoining Qualcomm was to "address[] Qualcomm's practices of not selling modem chips exhaustively, requiring OEMs to sign a separate license before buying modem chips, and Qualcomm's associated threats to cut off OEMs' chip supply and technical support and to delay or revoke access to software, which the Court held constitute anticompetitive conduct under the Sherman Act."[584] The evolution of the doctrine of patent exhaustion casts doubt on Judge Koh's conclusion that Qualcomm's conduct was anticompetitive. Qualcomm made an intelligent business decision motivated

---

[582] *See* United States v. Carroll Towing Co., 159 F.2d 169, 172 (2ᵈ Cir. 1947) (Hand, J.); United States Fid. & Guar. Co. v. Jadranska Slobodna Plovidba, 683 F.2d 1022, 1026 (7ᵗʰ Cir. 1982) (discussing the Hand Formula for negligence in *Carroll Towing*); *see also* POSNER, ECONOMIC ANALYSIS OF LAW, *supra* note 214, at 191–96.
[583] FTC v. Qualcomm Inc., 411 F. Supp. 3d 658, 820 (N.D. Cal. 2019).
[584] *Id.*

by its need to adapt to the Supreme Court's changing case law that directly affects the economics of patent licensing.

Perhaps most critically, the second component of Judge Koh's permanent, worldwide injunction specified that "Qualcomm must make exhaustive SEP licenses available to modem-chip suppliers on fair, reasonable, and non-discriminatory ('FRAND') terms and to submit, as necessary, to arbitral or judicial dispute resolution to determine such terms."[585] Her stated purpose for so enjoining Qualcomm was to "address[] Qualcomm's refusal to license rival modem chip suppliers on FRAND terms,"[586] which, she said, "the Court held is anticompetitive conduct under the Sherman Act."[587] Judge Koh said, apparently without any regard to the Supreme Court's recent disquisitions on the doctrine of patent exhaustion, that "Qualcomm itself has licensed its SEPs to rival modem chip suppliers."[588] Yet, Judge Koh never mentioned the critical fact that those "licenses" were "to make and sell *but not use*"[589] certain of Qualcomm's claimed inventions.

A different judge might have considered it the wiser exercise of discretion to flag that critical fact and then precisely explain its legal ramifications for the plausibility of the FTC's theory of antitrust liability. Judge Koh instead ignored this highly relevant fact and erroneously implied that Qualcomm had previously licensed its cellular SEPs exhaustively to rival modem manufacturers.

In sum, Judge Koh's findings of fact and conclusions of law, and the permanent, worldwide injunction that she thereupon imposed, materially relied on her incomplete and inaccurate explication of the role that the Supreme Court's doctrine of patent exhaustion had played in the lawful evolution of Qualcomm's business practices over a number of years.

IV. Professor Shapiro's Testimony

Professor Shapiro testified that Qualcomm had monopoly power in the CDMA modem market and in the "premium" LTE modem market and that Qualcomm's licensing practices harmed competition in those two markets.[590] The entirety of his testimony in *FTC v. Qualcomm* depended on the premise that Qualcomm was charging an "unreasonably high" royalty "surcharge" on an exhaustive license to its cellular SEPs that allegedly became a "tax" on the "all-in price" that OEMs paid for rivals' modems. Professor Shapiro even

---

585   *Id.* at 821.
586   *Id.*
587   *Id.*
588   *Id.*
589   IRS Transcript, *supra* note 503, at 23:4 (Marv Blecker (Senior Vice President, Qualcomm Technology Licensing)) (emphasis added).
590   Transcript of Proceedings (Volume 6) at 1119:7–12, FTC v. Qualcomm Inc., No 5:17-cv-00220-LHK (N.D. Cal. Jan. 15, 2019) (Testimony of Carl Shapiro).

admitted on cross examination by Mr. Van Nest that it was "correct" that his testimony, in its entirety, would be "irrelevant" if the evidence did not prove that Qualcomm had charged OEMs an "unreasonably high" royalty for an exhaustive license to its portfolio of cellular SEPs.[591]

It is perplexing then that Professor Shapiro made no attempt to prove the existence of his alleged royalty "surcharge" and modem "tax," much less to quantify them or their economic effects. Instead, he *assumed* the existence of the royalty "surcharge" and the modem "tax," and he stated that he had "*reason to believe* the royalty surcharge was substantial and that ha[d] inevitable consequences."[592] Professor Shapiro also assumed that the alleged royalty "surcharge" harmed competition in his two relevant markets, although he did not examine any empirical evidence to verify that conclusion. He asked the court instead to trust his theoretical bargaining model's predictions, which he admitted contradicted evidence of what had actually occurred in the real world.

Professor Shapiro's reliance on a theoretical bargaining model, which he made no attempt to ground in the facts and data of *FTC v. Qualcomm*, vividly reminds us of Nobel laureate Friedrich Hayek's warning: "The power of abstract ideas rests largely on the very fact that they are not consciously held as theories but are treated by most people as self-evident truths which act as tacit presuppositions."[593] On cross examination, Professor Shapiro did indeed treat his theory as self-evident truth. And when Judge Koh evidently incorporated Professor Shapiro's theory without attribution into her findings of fact and conclusions of law, she tacitly presupposed its verisimilitude.

A. Unredacted Expert Economic Opinions That Professor Shapiro Disclosed in His Reports, and a Summation of His Economic Theory of Harm at Trial

Professor Shapiro's expert opinions disclosed in two expert reports exchanged before trial must be pieced together from the excerpts attached to various redacted filings on the labyrinthine docket in *FTC v. Qualcomm*. Yet, as we shall see, the opinions that Professor Shapiro disclosed before trial, and to

---

[591] *Id.* at 1198:2–1198:25 ("Q. Okay. So point one: if the Court were to determine that the evidence doesn't support the existence of a supra-FRAND royalty, then the rest of your analysis can be ignored; right? It depends on that as a starting point? A. So if the Court were to determine that all this leverage didn't lead to anything in terms of a supra—a royalty surcharge— Q. That's right? A. —then the economic consequences of the surcharge would not come into play. I think that's logical. Q. I think that's what I said. A. I just— Q. Unless the evidence supports the existence of a supra-FRAND royalty, this analysis is irrelevant; right? I think that's what you just said, but— A. I guess I—I'm resisting, I admit a little bit, that irrelevant makes me feel bad. (Laughter.) By Mr. Van Nest: Q. Don't feel bad. A. But I think that, yes, the building block for, for this discussion of effects is that Qualcomm was able to achieve a royalty surcharge by applying the chip leverage. So, yes, that is correct.").

[592] *Id.* at 1210:13–15 (emphasis added).

[593] Friedrich A. Hayek, Law, Legislation and Liberty: Rules and Order 70 (Univ. of Chicago Press 1973).

which he testified on two days at trial, appeared to be the key to understanding why Judge Koh reached substantially all of her conclusions concerning Qualcomm's violations of the Sherman Act. Recall that Professor Shapiro was the only witness to be called to testify twice, and that by a substantial margin he gave more pages of trial testimony than any other witness.[594]

The purpose of an expert witness's report and deposition is to disclose the opinion of the expert witness and the bases for that opinion, but the report and deposition typically are not admitted as evidence at trial. Under Federal Rule of Civil Procedure 26(a)(2), "a party must disclose to the other parties the identity of any [expert] witness it may use at trial to present evidence" and "this disclosure must be accompanied by a written report . . . signed by the witness."[595] Pursuant to Rule 26(a)(2)(B), "[t]he report must contain: (i) a complete statement of all opinions the witness will express and the basis and reasons for them."[596]

The limited information that is available from the docket in *FTC v. Qualcomm* prevents the public from knowing the precise structure of the theoretical bargaining model that motivated Professor Shapiro's trial testimony before Judge Koh. As an aside, it is unclear on what grounds evidence concerning the specification of Professor Shapiro's theoretical bargaining model properly could be redacted from public view—since, by definition, the explanation of a theoretical economic model does not require any disclosure of the confidential business information that one subsequently uses as inputs for the model so that one can generate outputs that are relevant to the facts of the case. Why did scores of pages of Professor Shapiro's reports need to be redacted?

Professor Shapiro submitted two expert economic reports in *FTC v. Qualcomm*, one dated May 24, 2018 and styled as "Expert Report of Carl Shapiro,"[597] and the second dated July 26, 2018 and styled as "Rebuttal Report of Carl Shapiro."[598] Because a complete record of Professor Shapiro's expert reports and deposition testimony are not publicly available, and because Judge Koh did not comment at all on Professor Shapiro's trial testimony in

---

[594] *See supra* note 238 and accompanying text.

[595] Fed. R. Civ. P. 26(a)(2); *accord* Yeti by Molly, Ltd. v. Deckers Outdoor Corp., 259 F.3d 1101, 1106 (9th Cir. 2001).

[596] Fed. R. Civ. P. 26(a)(2)(B). Rule 26(a)(2)(D) provides: "A party must make these disclosures at the times and in the sequence that the court orders." Fed. R. Civ. P. 26(a)(2)(D). Federal Rule of Civil Procedure 37(c)(1) provides: "If a party fails to provide information or identify a witness as required by Rule 26(a) or (e), the party is not allowed to use that information or witness to supply evidence on a motion, at a hearing, or at a trial, unless the failure was substantially justified or is harmless." Fed R. Civ. P. 37(c)(1). "Rule 37 'gives teeth' to Rule 26's disclosure requirements by forbidding the use at trial of any information that is not properly disclosed." Goodman v. Staples the Office Superstore, LLC, 644 F.3d 817, 827 (9th Cir. 2011). Nevertheless, under Rule 37(c)(1), "[t]he information may be introduced if the parties' failure to disclose the required information is substantially justified or harmless." *Yeti by Molly*, 259 F.3d at 1106.

[597] Initial Expert Report of Carl Shapiro in *FTC v. Qualcomm*, *supra* note 115.

[598] Rebuttal Expert Report of Carl Shapiro in *FTC v. Qualcomm*, *supra* note 115.

her findings of fact and conclusions of law in *FTC v. Qualcomm*, the public cannot evaluate whether the FTC properly disclosed all of Professor Shapiro's opinions, and all the bases for those opinions, before trial.

1. Professor Shapiro's Initial Expert Report

Although Professor Shapiro's initial expert report was not admitted into evidence at trial, its (redacted) disclosure pursuant to Rule 26(a)(2), summarizing the opinions that he expected to express in sworn testimony at trial, is instructive.

a. Qualifications and Compensation

In his initial report, Professor Shapiro began by listing his qualifications:

> I have considerable experience with the application of economics for the purpose of enforcing the antitrust laws. I served during 1995–1996 and again during 2009–2011 as the Deputy Assistant Attorney General for Economics in the Antitrust Division of the U.S. Department of Justice. I have also served on several occasions as an expert witness or consultant to the Antitrust Division or the U.S. Federal Trade Commission. I have also consulted or served as an expert witness on numerous antitrust matters for private companies in the technology sector, as well as many other industries. A list of cases in which I have testified during the past four years is attached as Appendix B.[599]

Appendix B to Professor Shapiro's initial expert report appears not to be publicly available.

Professor Shapiro then disclosed his compensation for the case:

> I am being compensated for my work on this case at a rate of $880 per hour. This compensation is unrelated to the outcome of this matter. My work in this case has been supported by Bates White, LLC, an economic consulting firm. I also receive compensation from Bates White based on Bates White's staff billings on this case.[600]

Professor Shapiro's initial expert report left a number of things unsaid. These things were all the standard questions that an experienced trial lawyer would pin down when deposing an expert economic witness in a complex commercial dispute to help understand the witness' incentives and identify possible sources of bias. These questions might not be asked on cross examination in open court during the subsequent trial, but sometimes they are asked in an

---

[599] Initial Expert Report of Carl Shapiro in *FTC v. Qualcomm*, *supra* note 115, at 2.
[600] *Id.*

attempt to impeach the expert witness. Professor Shapiro's deposition is not publicly available in the docket of *FTC v. Qualcomm*, nor is the entirety of his expert reports (including the usual boilerplate at the beginning of an expert report about the terms and scope of the engagement). Yet, none of his trial testimony was redacted on grounds that it discussed confidential business information that was under seal.

Here are some things that an experienced trial lawyer would notice that the publicly available portions of Professor Shapiro's report and his trial testimony before Judge Koh did not say. He did not say why Bates White rather that Charles River Associates was supporting him. He did not say whether $880 per hour was his customary hourly rate for expert economic testimony. (In contrast, as of 2018, many distinguished expert economic witnesses billed private-sector clients in the range of $1200 to $1400 per hour. Professor Edward Snyder, for example, disclosed in June 2018 that he had charged Qualcomm $1,250 per hour for his time as an expert economic witness in *FTC v. Qualcomm*.[601]) Professor Shapiro did not say when he started working on the case, how many hours he worked on the case, and what his total personal billings to the case were. Nor did he say when Bates White started working on the case, how many hour Bates White worked on the case, how many persons at Bates White in total assisted Professor Shapiro, what tasks they performed, what the total fees of Bates White were, and what the amount of compensation was that Bates White directed to Professor Shapiro, whether that compensation was calculated according to Bates White's customary finder's fee, and whether Bates White compensated Charles River Associates in any way for the opportunity to support Professor Shapiro's work in *FTC v. Qualcomm*. Finally, Professor Shapiro did not say how much the FTC (which is to say, American taxpayers) had paid in total for all of the professional services rendered by Professor Shapiro and Bates White in connection with his reports, deposition, assistance to counsel in trial preparation, requests from counsel for assistance in responding to Qualcomm's interrogatories,

---

[601] *See* Expert Report of Edward A. Snyder, Ph.D. at 3, FTC v. Qualcomm Inc., No. 5:17-cv-00220-LHK (N.D. Cal. June 28, 2018), ECF No. 1244 ("I have directed employees of Analysis Group, Inc., an economic research and consulting firm, to assist me in this assignment. I am being compensated at my normal hourly rate of $1,250 for time spent on this matter, and I receive compensation based on the professional fees of Analysis Group. No compensation is contingent on the nature of my findings or on the outcome of this litigation."). Professor Snyder's report was 368 pages long, excluding appendices. *Cf.* Optis Wireless Tech., LLC v. Apple Inc., No. 2:19-cv-00066-JRG, slip op. at 2 (E.D. Tex. July 17, 2020) (Gilstrap, C.J.) ("The Court ORDERS that Apple produce the total composite gross dollar amount billed by each expert for Apple, through any and all counsel for Apple, for all matters in which Apple is or was a named party; . . . The Court further ORDERS that Optis produce the total composite gross dollar amount billed or invoiced by each expert for Optis to Irell & Manella LLP and/or McKool Smith, P.C. and related to litigation in which Apple Inc. is named as a party; . . . All productions of total composite billed or invoiced amounts are to include (1) gross billings during 2019, (2) gross billings year-to-date for 2020, and (3) a composite of all billings (i.e., a total dollar amount billed) over the last five years, from June 1, 2015 through May 31, 2020. Further, these three composite numbers are to be provided individually for each expert in the above-captioned case[.]") (footnote omitted).

and the like. These tasks are all routine for an expert economic witness and his or her backup team to be instructed by counsel to undertake in complex commercial litigation, and they can easily demand thousands of hours of work in a case as complex as *FTC v. Qualcomm*.

b. Assignment

Next, Professor Shapiro described the nature of his assignment:

> I have been asked by the Federal Trade Commission (FTC) to provide an economic analysis of the likely competitive effects of Qualcomm's commercial practices that are the subject of the FTC's complaint in this case. The FTC also asked me to define the relevant markets applicable to the analysis of this conduct and to assess whether Qualcomm possesses monopoly power in any of these markets.[602]

Professor Shapiro then disclosed his opinions.

c. Opinions About Market Definition and Monopoly Power

Professor Shapiro first disclosed his opinion that the CDMA modem market and the "premium" LTE modem market were the two relevant antitrust markets. He disclosed his opinion that Qualcomm had possessed monopoly power in the CDMA modem market from 2006 to 2016:

> There is a relevant antitrust product market for "CDMA Modem Chips." These are modem chips that comply with CDMA standards, that is, with CDMA 2G or 3G capabilities. From the perspective of a manufacturer of handsets purchasing modem chips, a modem chip that does not comply with CDMA standards is not a good substitute for a CDMA Modem Chip. My conclusion that CDMA Modem Chips are a relevant market is based in part on my implementation of the Hypothetical Monopolist Test, the standard method employed by antitrust economists for over 35 years to define relevant antitrust markets. The geographic scope of this product market is worldwide. Qualcomm had monopoly power in the market for CDMA Modem Chips from 2006 through at least 2016. [Redacted]. Customers purchasing CDMA Modem Chips had very limited alternatives to Qualcomm's CMDA Modem Chips during this period of time.[603]

Professor Shapiro next disclosed his opinion that Qualcomm had possessed monopoly power in the "premium" LTE modem market from 2011 to 2016:

---

602 Initial Expert Report of Carl Shapiro in *FTC v. Qualcomm, supra* note 115, at 2.
603 *Id.* at 3.

There is a relevant antitrust market for "Premium LTE Modem Chips." These are modem chips that comply with the LTE standard and are used in premium handsets, as that term is used by Qualcomm. From the perspective of a manufacturer of handsets purchasing modem chips, other modem chips are not good substitutes for Premium LTE Modem Chips. In particular, modem chips with fewer capabilities that are not used in premium handsets are not a good substitute for Premium LTE Modem Chips. My conclusion that Premium LTE Modem Chips are a relevant market is in part based on my implementation of the Hypothetical Monopolist Test. The geographic scope of this product market is worldwide. Qualcomm had monopoly power in the market for Premium LTE Modem Chips from the launch of LTE handsets in 2011 through at least 2016. [Redacted]. Customers purchasing Premium LTE Modem Chips had very limited alternatives to Qualcomm's Premium LTE Modem Chips.[604]

Professor Shapiro thus disclosed that he had implemented the Hypothetical Monopolist Test to conclude that one of his two relevant antitrust markets was the worldwide market for "premium" LTE modems.

d. Opinions About Qualcomm's Licensing Practice

Professor Shapiro then expressed his conclusion that Qualcomm's practice of selling modems only to licensed OEMs enabled Qualcomm to charge an "unreasonably high" (or supra-FRAND) royalty for a license to its cellular SEP portfolio:

Qualcomm has employed a "no-license/no-chips" policy for many years. Under this policy, Qualcomm will not supply its modem chips to a handset manufacturer that has not signed a patent license with Qualcomm covering Qualcomm's cellular standard-essential patents (SEPs). Through use of this policy, Qualcomm has brought its bargaining leverage based on its monopoly power over modem chips to bear on its patent licensing negotiations with handset manufacturers. As a result of Qualcomm's no-license/no-chips policy, Qualcomm has been able to obtain unreasonably high royalties for its cellular SEPs, notwithstanding Qualcomm's commitment to license its cellular SEPs on fair, reasonable, and non-discriminatory (FRAND) terms.[605]

After more than 100 pages of entirely redacted analysis, Professor Shapiro summarized his opinion about the effects of Qualcomm's licensing practice:

[Redacted] . . . this reallocation weakens and excludes Qualcomm's rivals by reducing the demand for their modem chips.

---

[604] *Id.*
[605] *Id.*

The central competition problem is that Qualcomm is using the market power associated with its modem chips to induce OEMs to agree to pay a per-handset royalty in excess of a reasonable level when purchasing modem chips from any of Qualcomm's rivals. This excess per-handset royalty charge (x in my notation) has the effect of raising the cost to the OEM of purchasing a modem chip from Qualcomm's rivals, by exactly the amount of Qualcomm's excess royalties, x. This higher cost in turn depresses the demand for modem chips sold by Qualcomm's rivals. Put simply, an OEM's demand for a rival modem chip is reduced if the OEM must pay the excess royalty x when it uses a rival modem chip.

Equivalently, one can think of the excess royalty x as an extra cost that Qualcomm imposes on its rivals when they sell modem chips. This would literally be true if the rival were the entity paying the SEP royalties directly to Qualcomm. However, the underlying economics are identical, whether the *OEM* pays an extra amount x to Qualcomm when using a rival chip, or whether the *rival* pays that extra amount directly to Qualcomm. In the first case, the license fee is a strict complement to the rival's modem chip. In the second case, the license fee is an unavoidable cost borne by the rival. These are economically equivalent. Qualcomm's no-license/no-chips policy is an example of how a monopolist can use its monopoly power to raise the costs incurred by its rivals, which weakens or excludes them, and thereby fortifies its monopoly position.

This excess royalty is economically equivalent to a "tax" imposed by Qualcomm on the OEM's use of rival modem chips. By raising the cost on rival modem chips, this excess royalty inevitably and predictably raises the all-in price of rival chipsets and reduces the quantity of those chipsets sold, for a given all-in price charged by Qualcomm. This excess royalty also inevitably and predictably reduces the operating income that any rivals can earn from selling chipsets, which can be expected to reduce the investments these rivals make in modem chips. This is turn leads to longer-term anticompetitive effects on innovation.

For all of these reasons, this excess royalty excludes rival modem-chip suppliers. In the short run, that exclusion takes the form of reducing the competitive constraint that the rivals impose on Qualcomm, which leads to reduced output of rival modem chips and a higher all-in price for rival modem chips. This is an example of the general economic principle that when a good is taxed, its price goes up and the quantity of that good sold goes down. In the long run, that exclusion also takes the form of reduced investments by rival modem chip suppliers, leading those rivals to offer lower quality modem chips and/or to have reduced capacity. In time, the excess royalty can induce exit from the market altogether.[606]

In sum, Professor Shapiro disclosed in his initial expert report his opinion that Qualcomm used its alleged market power in two relevant antitrust markets for

---

[606] *Id.* at 114–15 (emphasis in original) (footnotes omitted).

modems to obtain an "unreasonably high" royalty for an exhaustive license to its portfolio of cellular SEPs. That unreasonably high royalty was, in his view, economically equivalent to a modem "tax" because it allegedly raised the costs to OEMs of purchasing rivals' modems and consequently decreased the demand for those modems. Professor Shapiro stated that the alleged modem "tax" reduced the operating income that Qualcomm's rivals could earn from selling modems, thereby constraining the ability of those rivals to invest in research and development and to compete with Qualcomm, both in the short run and in the long run. He did not appear to mention patent exhaustion in connection with his opinion that "Qualcomm's no-license/no-chips policy is an example of how a monopolist can use its monopoly power to raise the costs incurred by its rivals, which weakens or excludes them, and thereby fortifies its monopoly position."[607]

e.   Opinions About Anticompetitive Harm

Professor Shapiro then posited that the observation that certain firms had ceased to sell modems during the time when Qualcomm allegedly had a monopoly supported his conclusion that Qualcomm's licensing practices had harmed rivals:

> While it is difficult to isolate the effect of Qualcomm's conduct on its modem chip rivals, we do know, as discussed above in Section VIII.C, that Texas Instruments, Broadcom, Marvell, Nvidia, and ST-Ericsson all stopped selling modem chips between 2012 and 2015. These companies were unable to make sufficient sales at margins that would justify continuing to make the substantial R&D investments needed to remain competitive in the sale of Premium LTE Modem Chips. There is evidence from the exited rivals that depressed margins in the sale of modem chips contributed to their exit. Broadcom's [Robert] Rango described the margins that Broadcom's modem chip business earned as "not attractive" and below Broadcom's gross margin target of 50%. A Broadcom Board of Directors presentation from 2011 identified the "[a]bility to resource the opportunities" as a key "Risk/Challenge" in the sales of modem chips. With respect to Marvell, former Marvell Vice President Vivek Chhabra testified that Marvell's gross margins were 14% prior to exiting the modem chip business, much lower than Marvell's 40% to 50% gross margin targets. Nvidia likewise earned lower margins on its modem chips than it did on other chips it sold, and the poor return on investment was a factor in Nvidia's decision to wind down its business. Additionally, as MediaTek has attempted to move from lower tiers to the premium tier, it has found that the margins it earns on its

---

[607] *Id.* at 114.

more premium products are unsustainable. MediaTek's [Finbarr] Moynihan [Redacted].[608]

As we shall see, Professor Shapiro failed to examine whether the poor performance of those companies was in any way connected to Qualcomm's licensing practices or instead eventuated because of poor management or other reasons unrelated to Qualcomm. Put differently, it appears that Professor Shapiro made no attempt to demonstrate a causal relationship between Qualcomm's conduct and the mediocre performance of certain other modem manufacturers.

After five more pages of redactions, Professor Shapiro disclosed his opinion concerning the effects of Qualcomm's practice of licensing its cellular SEPs exhaustively to OEMs rather than rival modem manufacturers:

> Qualcomm's refusal to license its modem chip rivals further harms competition *to the extent that rivals' inability to obtain a license from Qualcomm on reasonable terms discourages investment.* For example, in 2011, Samsung and several other companies negotiated to form a joint venture called "Dragonfly" that would have developed and sold modem chips to third parties. One of the key conditions for that joint venture was that it obtain a license from Qualcomm to sell modem chips. [Redacted].[609]

Thus, in Professor Shapiro's view, Qualcomm's refusal to license its cellular SEPs exhaustively to modem manufacturers harmed competition—to the extent that the absence of such a license discouraged investment by Qualcomm's rivals.

Yet, as we shall see, Professor Shapiro admitted at trial that he had not analyzed the extent to which rivals' investment diminished in the counterfactual conditional world that he imagined.[610] Rather, Professor Shapiro conjectured at trial that, even though investment in R&D by rival modem manufacturers might have stayed the same or even increased during the relevant time period, Qualcomm's conduct (pursuant to Professor Shapiro's

---

[608] *Id.* at 115 (second alteration in original) (footnotes omitted).

[609] *Id.* at 121 (emphasis added) (footnote omitted).

[610] Transcript of Proceedings (Volume 6) at 1206:15–1207:13, FTC v. Qualcomm Inc., No. 5:17-cv-00220-LHK (N.D. Cal. Jan. 15, 2019) (Testimony of Carl Shapiro) ("Q. Your path to harm involves a situation—I thought I understood, Professor Shapiro— A. Yep. Q. —in which over . . . time rivals' commitment to research and development would tend to go down. That's what we established earlier with this arrow; right? A. All other things equal, that would be the effect of the royalty surcharge and the reduced margins and volumes. Q. But my point is—my question is, excuse me, you didn't do anything to see whether they actually did go down during the period you're talking about; right? That's all I want to know. A. I don't think—I think you're still continuing to conflate two very different issues. Q. Excuse me? A. What happened to the R&D? Q. Um-hum. A. And the effect of Qualcomm's practices. So I think we need to be clear about the difference. No, I didn't track—I didn't report—I didn't report as part of my analysis the month, the quarterly or annual R&D by Samsung in this area, if that could be broken out. No, I'm not doing that. That is not informative, as far as I'm concerned, about given all what you're talking about, about the effects of the practices here, which my analysis is later focussed on that.").

a priori reasoning) impeded those investments. The redacted version of Professor Shapiro's expert report (and his trial testimony) did not disclose his explanation for how Qualcomm's conduct proximately (or even tenuously) caused harm to competition.

> f.   *The Assumption That Qualcomm's Royalties for an Exhaustive License to Its Portfolio of Cellular SEPs Were "Unreasonably High"*

Professor Shapiro acknowledged in an obscure passage from his expert report that, if Qualcomm had charged OEMs merely a *reasonable* royalty for an exhaustive license to its portfolio of cellular SEPs, then its choice to offer such licenses only to OEMs (rather than to rival modem manufacturers) could not have had any significant effect on competition:

> Beyond these harms, the exclusionary effect of Qualcomm's refusal to license rival modem-chip makers depends on the per-handset royalties that OEMs pay for Qualcomm's SEPs. If OEMs were able to enter into SEP licenses with Qualcomm at the same per-handset royalty of that $\bar{\gamma}$ rivals could obtain in the counterfactual, then the effects of Qualcomm's refusal to license to its modem-chip rivals might be relatively minor. However, as shown above, that is not the case: due to Qualcomm's no-license/no-chips policy, OEMs pay royalties for Qualcomm's SEPs that the [sic] exceed the reasonable per handset royalties of $\bar{\gamma}$.[611]

In other words, Professor Shapiro's conclusion that Qualcomm's refusal to license its cellular SEPs exhaustively to rival modem manufacturers harmed competition evidently was based on his unproven *assumption* that Qualcomm was charging a supra-FRAND royalty for an exhaustive license to its portfolio of cellular SEPs.

> g.   *The Conjecture Why Rival Modem Manufacturers Had Not Resorted to Litigation or Arbitration to Obtain an Exhaustive License to Qualcomm's Portfolio of Cellular SEPs*

Professor Shapiro then disclosed his opinion concerning why rival modem manufacturers had not resorted to litigation or arbitration to obtain an exhaustive license to Qualcomm's portfolio of cellular SEPs:

> Qualcomm's practices have limited the ability and incentives of its modem-chip rivals to counter these harms. I understand that in 2015 the Ninth Circuit held that a manufacturer of standard-compliant products could file a breach-of-contract action to enforce a SEP holder's FRAND

---

[611]   Initial Expert Report of Carl Shapiro in *FTC v. Qualcomm, supra* note 115, at 121.

commitments, whereas the ability to bring such an action had previously been unclear. [Redacted][.] Since 2015, although Qualcomm's modem-chip rivals may now have the *ability* to file actions to compel Qualcomm to comply with its FRAND commitments, Qualcomm's practices have reduced those rivals' *incentive* to file such actions. First, a modem-chip rival may reasonably fear that Qualcomm would retaliate if it took legal action to enforce Qualcomm's obligation to license its SEPs on reasonable terms. As noted above, Qualcomm has informed modem-chip rivals that have sought exhaustive licenses that it does not grant exhaustive licenses to modem-chip suppliers. Qualcomm has informed some rivals that granting an exhaustive [Redacted].[612]

Professor Shapiro did not clarify in that passage what kind of retaliation Qualcomm could have used against rival modem manufacturers to prevent them from enforcing those alleged rights in court.

h. Calculation of Qualcomm's Market Share of "Premium" LTE Modems

The next available excerpt from Professor Shapiro's initial expert report referenced his definition of the "Premium LTE Modem Chips" and his estimate of Qualcomm's market share:

> My alternative method defines Premium LTE Modem Chips based on the uplink and downlink speeds of the chips in the most recently released model of the iPhone (the first model to use LTE was the iPhone 5, released in 2012—all LTE chips sold prior to the first LTE iPhone release in 2012 are assumed to be premium by virtue of the fact that they were the first LTE chips). The cutoff of the uplink and downlink speeds is assumed to be as of the date of handset launch (Q3 in a typical year). Chips at least as fast as those in the most recent iPhone, as of Q3 of the launch year, are considered premium. This approach based on the performance of chips in the Apple iPhone yields market shares that are relatively similar to the approach based on the set of chips in premium handsets as defined by Qualcomm. The Apple iPhone-based definition yields lower volumes, and generally lower Qualcomm shares, as compared to the "premium handset" definition. The shares and volumes from the definition based on the Apple iPhone are shown below in Figure 24.[613]

---

[612] *Id.* (emphasis in original) (footnotes omitted).

[613] Expert Report of Carl Shapiro (Public Version) at E-45, FTC v. Qualcomm Inc., No. 5:17-cv-00220-LHK (N.D. Cal. May 24, 2018), *Exhibit 2 to* Defendant Qualcomm Incorporated's Brief in Opposition to the FTC's Request That the Court Issue an Injunction Without Considering Evidence of Post-Discovery Facts, FTC v. Qualcomm Inc., No. 5:17-cv-00220-LHK (N.D. Cal. Oct. 31, 2018), ECF No. 929-3.

Professor Shapiro's Figure 24, "Premium LTE Annual Volumes and Market Shares: Apple Launch Definition," is redacted.[614]

The remainder of Professor Shapiro's analysis in his initial expert report, which spans at least 121 pages (considering that the last page available is numbered page 121), is also shielded from public scrutiny because of redactions.[615]

2. *Professor Shapiro's Rebuttal Expert Report*

In the single unredacted page of his rebuttal expert report that is publicly available, Professor Shapiro disputed certain opinions of Professor Aviv Nevo:

> The problem arises in Section 6.2 of the Nevo Report. Professor Nevo's analysis there contains a fundamental error in economics, which I explain below. This error then infects and invalidates Professor Nevo's claims in Section 6.3 of the Nevo Report that supra-FRAND royalties have not caused any short-term harm to competition. Those claims rely largely on the erroneous arguments that Professor Nevo makes in Section 6.2 of his report.[616]

Under the caption "VI.H.1. One Cannot Infer a Lack of Anti-Competitive Effects from Evidence of Output Growth and Innovation," Professor Shapiro disclosed an opinion purporting to rebut Professor Nevo. That opinion neatly summarized Professor Shapiro's utopian counterfactual conditional. For convenience, I reproduce Professor Shapiro's rebuttal opinion here:

> As I . . . discuss above in Section III, Professor Nevo appears to believe that because mobile phone sales have increased and prices have fallen, the conduct at issue could not have had any anticompetitive effects. He states:
>
> > In recent years, handset prices have fallen while sales and quality have increased dramatically. There has been significant entry and expansion among OEMs and modem chip makers. As a result, consumers have enjoyed lower prices, higher quality, and increased variety. The evidence shows that the cellular industry is healthy, competitive, and driven by innovation. In this section, I present economic evidence that demonstrates these facts and show that

---

[614] *Id.*

[615] One other page of factual discussion in Professor Shapiro's expert report is publicly available. *See* Reply Exhibit 1 to Federal Trade Commission's Reply in Support of Motion to Exclude Expert Testimony of Dr. Edward A. Snyder, FTC v. Qualcomm Inc., No. 5:17-cv-02200-LHK (N.D. Cal. Oct. 4, 2018), ECF No. 891-2. Other passages of Professor Shapiro's expert report are quoted in the publicly available Expert Report of Edward A. Snyder Ph.D., FTC v. Qualcomm Inc., No. 5:17-cv-02200-LHK (N.D. Cal. June 28, 2018), ECF No. 1244.

[616] Rebuttal Expert Report of Carl Shapiro in *FTC v. Qualcomm*, *supra* note 115, at 92.

they are not consistent with the FTC and Professor Shapiro's claim that the cellular industry suffers from reduced competition and innovation.

Professor Nevo's logic here is transparently faulty. The evidence he puts forward regarding cellular handset prices and quality does not demonstrate an absence of anticompetitive effects. Professor Nevo has not addressed the relevant comparison: *competitive conditions with vs. without Qualcomm's no-license/no-chips policy*. Industries that are growing and where technology is advancing are certainly not immune from antitrust problems. To suggest otherwise is antithetical to a long history of antitrust enforcement in technology-driven industries in the United States, from the *Standard Oil* case in 1911 to the *Microsoft* case 20 years ago. A central danger in such industries is that a powerful incumbent will stifle competition and retard innovation in an effort to protect its position. These effects can arise in the context of ongoing innovation. The current case fits that general pattern.[617]

In other words, Professor Shapiro attempted to reject Professor Nevo's criticism by imagining a utopian counterfactual conditional—a hypothetical state of the world whose measures of economic well-being were uniformly more magnificent than those of the real world. Professor Shapiro said that, although in the real world prices had decreased, output had expanded, and innovation had delivered products of even higher quality, his opinion that Qualcomm had engaged in anticompetitive practices nonetheless was still compelling because he could imagine a more resplendent state of the world.

Yet, to establish the evidentiary relevance of his utopian counterfactual conditional and the supposed reliability of his opinions predicated upon it, Professor Shapiro needed to do more than demand that others credit his reimagined world. Professor Shapiro's redacted rebuttal expert report did not appear to disclose that he had taken these additional steps of analysis and reasoning. His expert report did not indicate that he had performed any analysis to prove that his utopian counterfactual conditional was realistic.

Other than those three paragraphs on page 92 of Professor Shapiro's rebuttal report, none of the analysis in his rebuttal report appears to be available to the public.

3. *Professor Shapiro's Summation of His Economic Theory of Harm in His Live Direct Testimony During Judge Koh's Bench Trial*

Presiding over the bench trial as the finder of fact, Judge Koh would have considered only Professor Shapiro's live testimony (supplemented by his trial demonstratives), but *not* his expert report, because there is no indication

---

[617] *Id.* (emphasis in original) (footnote omitted) (quoting paragraph 25 of Professor Nevo's expert report, which does not appear to be publicly available).

that the FTC moved Professor Shapiro's expert report into evidence at trial. On direct examination by Rajesh James of the FTC on January 15, 2019, the final day of the FTC's case-in-chief, Professor Shapiro began his testimony as the FTC's final in-person witness by summarizing his conclusions about Qualcomm's alleged monopoly power:

> [T]he conclusion has to do with Qualcomm's market power, monopoly power in two markets that we'll talk about, the market for CDMA modem chips and the market for premium LTE modem chips, and it's my view that Qualcomm had monopoly power in those markets through 2016. . . . [T]he CDMA market would be starting in 2006. The premium LTE market doesn't really start until 2011.[618]

Professor Shapiro then testified on the effect that he surmised that Qualcomm's licensing practices had had on competition:

> [W]hat I've done here, is analyz[e] the effects of three different Qualcomm policies that operate in concert: the no license, no chips policy, the incentive payments that Qualcomm makes to OEM's in some of its licensing negotiations, and its refusal to license its standard essential patents to its modem chip rivals. So looking at these three policies working together, it's my view and conclusion that they harmed competition in the markets that I've just—we've just been talking about in those two markets.[619]

Professor Shapiro testified that the combination of three practices— (1) Qualcomm's so-called "no license, no chips policy," which was Qualcomm's practice of selling modems only to licensed OEMs, (2) Qualcomm's policy of licensing its cellular SEPs only to OEMs (but not to rival modem manufacturers), and (3) Qualcomm's grant of incentive payments to certain OEMs, allegedly to achieve exclusivity—harmed competition in his two relevant markets. He then elaborated on his theory of harm when he testified about the effects of each of those three challenged practices. Yet, Professor Shapiro never mentioned in his trial testimony the importance of Qualcomm's avoidance of patent exhaustion in connection with its first two practices.

---

[618] Transcript of Proceedings (Volume 6) at 1119:8–12, 1119:20–22, FTC v. Qualcomm Inc., No. 5:17-cv-00220-LHK (N.D. Cal. Jan. 15, 2019) (Testimony of Carl Shapiro).

[619] *Id.* at 1120:1–10; *see also id.* at 1123:19–21, 1123:25–1124:3 ("I'm referring to the Qualcomm policy that if an OEM does not have a license to Qualcomm's cellular SEPs, then Qualcomm will not sell that OEM their modem chips. . . . So this works together with Qualcomm's refusal to license its cellular standard essential patents to its rivals, and the incentive payments that were used in some cases to induce OEM's to sign licenses.").

a. *Professor Shapiro's Testimony About Qualcomm's Practice of Selling Modems Only to Licensed OEMs*

Professor Shapiro testified that Qualcomm's practice of selling its modems only to licensed OEMs was anticompetitive because it (1) enabled Qualcomm to obtain an "unreasonably high" (or "supra-FRAND") royalty "surcharge" on an exhaustive license to its cellular SEPs, which in turn (2) supposedly became a "tax" (equivalent to the amount of the royalty "surcharge") on the "all-in price" that OEMs paid for rivals' modems, which, in turn, (3) reduced those rivals' sales, squeezed their margins, and constrained their ability to compete with Qualcomm, and increased the prices paid by OEMs for modems and final consumers for handsets. Yet, during Professor Shapiro's testimony at trial, it became evident that his opinions were speculative and lacked any foundation in the facts of the case.

i. *Testimony About Qualcomm's FRAND Royalties*

During his trial testimony, Professor Shapiro first reiterated his opinion that Qualcomm had used its alleged monopoly power in what he considered to be the two relevant markets for modems to obtain an "unreasonably high" (or "supra-FRAND") royalty "surcharge" on an exhaustive license to its cellular SEPs:

> Qualcomm, through these policies, used its monopoly power over modem chips to extract supra-FRAND royalties from OEM's, and I'm going to use three terms probably interchangeably, supra-FRAND royalties, unreasonably high royalties, or getting a royalty surcharge. And what I mean by all of those is simply that Qualcomm was able to get OEM's to pay royalties for Qualcomm standard essential patents that were above the level of reasonable royalties.[620]

Surprisingly, the direct examination of Professor Shapiro by Mr. James glossed over the factual predicate for Professor Shapiro's opinion that Qualcomm was charging supra-FRAND royalties. And, as we shall see in Part IV.E, Professor Shapiro eventually admitted on cross examination during the FTC's rebuttal case that he had never examined Qualcomm's actual royalties and that he had never determined a FRAND royalty for a license to Qualcomm's cellular SEP portfolio. Instead, Professor Shapiro testified, he predicated his conclusions about the reasonableness of Qualcomm's royalties for its cellular SEP portfolio solely on a theoretical bargaining model that had no connection to any empirical data in *FTC v. Qualcomm*.

---

[620] *Id.* at 1120:15–23.

> ## ii. Testimony About the Alleged Royalty "Surcharge" That Supposedly Became a "Tax" on the "All-In Price" That OEMs Paid for Rivals' Modems

Professor Shapiro further testified on direct examination during the FTC's case-in-chief that Qualcomm's allegedly "unreasonably high" (or "supra-FRAND") royalty "surcharge" on an exhaustive license to its cellular SEPs became a "tax" on the "all-in price" that OEMs paid for rivals' modems. That modem "tax" supposedly weakened rivals' ability to compete with Qualcomm in two relevant markets for modems:

> So the fundamental concern that one has here and that I've explored in detail is that Qualcomm is using its market power, its monopoly power over the chips to extract an unreasonably high royalty for the standard essential patents, and that in doing that, that is effectively a tax or raises the cost of its rivals and thereby weakens them as competitors and fortifies Qualcomm's monopoly power. . . . So this tax or this royalty surcharge will have significant adverse, or I'll say anticompetitive effects if Qualcomm is able to achieve that.[621]

Still on direct examination, which permitted Professor Shapiro to lecture at length with the aid of a slide show, he presented a discursive hypothetical example to explain how, in his view, the alleged royalty "surcharge" or modem "tax" affected rival modem manufacturers:

> So in my example—and the numbers are purely illustrative or conceptual to get the concepts. But suppose that the OEM is willing to pay as much as $40 for the chip. In economics we call that willingness to pay. I'll use the term value. $40. And that reflects, you know, how much money they can make with the handset with that chip in it. So that's the value. On the other hand, there are some costs that have to be incurred. The rival, let's assume that the cost of making the chip is $5. And there's a royalty that has to be paid to Qualcomm, the reasonable royalty, assumed to be $10. So that's— if you look on the bar on the right-hand side here, those are the blue, the darker blue. Those are costs that must be incurred if this transaction goes forward. Those costs in total come to $15. That leaves $25 gains from trade. And bargaining, they would bargain over that, and let's just stick with a neutral assumption, they split the gains from trade equally. If that's the case, there's $25 of gains from trade, so they each get [$]12.50 of surplus from this transaction. For the rival, what that means is since—let's suppose, to make simple, that the OEM is writing the check to Qualcomm for the royalty. So the rival, if they're going to get [$]12.50 of margin, they have a $5 chip, they're going to sell the chip for [$]17.50. So that's going to be the chip price.

---

621 *Id.* at 1124:6–16, 1124:21–23.

From the OEM's point of view, they're going to have to pay [$]17.50 for the chip, they're going to pay $10 to Qualcomm, to the all-in price to the OEM is [$]27.50, and they had a $40 value, that they had an all-in price of [$]27.50, so the buyer gets a surplus of [$]12.50. And the same surplus as the seller since we're assuming that they split the gains equally. So this is the baseline with a reasonable royalty. And I'm—you know, the assumption here with my numbers is this is a profitable transaction for both sides and they—and Qualcomm gets its reasonable royalty of $10. So the whole point here is now to compare this to what happens if we add an additional royalty surcharge that Qualcomm gets?[622]

We will return to whether Professor Shapiro's assumption of an equal division of surplus between Qualcomm and the OEM was indeed "neutral," as he represented. Notice, also, that he defined Qualcomm's "reasonable royalty" exogenously—that is, without regard to the surplus created in his hypothetical transaction.[623]

Professor Shapiro then continued with another discursive example:

So that's what the second slide is designed to show Your Honor, to—so let's walk through the numbers here, how the economics of the transaction between Qualcomm and—excuse me—between an OEM and a rival manufacturer change when we add the royalty surcharge. So if you look on the—at the right-hand side here in red we've got the additional royalty surcharge, this is on top of the FRAND royalty itself. So the—now the costs that are associated with this transaction for the two parties are the production costs of $5 for the rival, the reasonable royalty of $10, and the royalty surcharge on top of that of $10. So that's $25 of costs. And, therefore, the gains from trade shrink down to $15. They were previously [$]25. So let's continue to make this simple in that neutral assumption that the gains from trade are split equally. In that case, the $15 of gains from trade are split, each side gets $7.50 of surplus. And by the same logic we had before, what that means is that the price of the modem chip is going to be [$]12.50, that is, the $5 production cost, I said the rival gets a [$]7.50 margin, so the price is [$]12.50. But then from the OEM's point of view, the all-in price is the [$]12.50 they have to pay for the chip, plus the $20 of royalties they have to

622 *Id.* at 1131:3–1132:18.

623 That assumption is debatable. *See* J. Gregory Sidak, *Bargaining Power and Patent Damages*, 19 STAN. TECH. L. REV. 1, 20–25 (2015); J. Gregory Sidak, *What Makes FRAND Fair? The Just Price, Contract Formation, and the Division of Surplus from Voluntary Exchange*, 4 CRITERION J. ON INNOVATION 701, 721–25 (2019); Sidak & Skog, *Hedonic Prices and Patent Royalties*, *supra* note 446, at 661–66; J. Gregory Sidak, *Is a FRAND Royalty a Point or a Range?*, 2 CRITERION J. ON INNOVATION 401, 406–11 (2017); Sidak, *The Meaning of FRAND, Part I: Royalties*, *supra* note 446, at 1042–43; *see also* Airbus Helicopters, S.A.S. v. Bell Helicopter Textron Canada Limitée, 2017 F.C. 170, [99] (Can.), https://decisions.fct-cf.gc.ca/fc-cf/decisions/en/223697/1/document.do (expressly applying the bargaining-range framework for dividing surplus from voluntary exchange explained in Sidak, *Bargaining Power and Patent Damages*, *supra*). A FRAND or RAND royalty is not calculated as an exogenous cost that reduces the surplus. The patent holder is entitled to share in the surplus. Consequently, Professor Shapiro's counterfactual conditional by assumption tilts the analysis to favor the implementer and the rival modem manufacturers over Qualcomm.

pay Qualcomm. So the all-in price is [$]32.50. And compared with the—the key point is to compare this to the previous example with the reasonable royalty. So now *the rival is harmed by $5 because their margin was reduced* from [$]7.50 to [$]12.50. The OEM's costs go up by $5, the all-in price is their cost here, they have to pay the royalties and the chip price, that goes up by $5. So between the two of them, the rival is harmed by $5, the OEM's cost goes up by $5, that splits the $10 surcharge. They've got to cover it somehow if they're going to do this transaction. If they're splitting the gains from trade equally, that's how it's going to go, it's going to be split.[624]

In short, Professor Shapiro argued that the modem "tax" imposed by Qualcomm's allegedly supra-FRAND royalty reduced the "gains from trade" in a transaction between an OEM and a rival modem manufacturer. Consequently, he argued, the cost to an OEM of a modem would increase, and the profit margin that a rival modem manufacturer could attain by selling those modems would decrease. Professor Shapiro elaborated:

> So the effect of the surcharge that Qualcomm was able to achieve . . . has been to impose a burden on transactions between the OEM's and Qualcomm's rivals. . . . And then the consequences, both the buyers and sellers in those transactions are harmed. The OEM is the buyer. They're harmed. The all-in price goes up. The rivals are harmed, they're getting smaller margin [sic]. And the combined harm equals the royalty surcharge if we also include the consumers, okay? So this harm is split in the end between the rival's margins being reduced, the OEM's having their margins reduced somewhat, and consumers picking up some of the tab. . . . The number of transactions will fall because some transactions will not have enough gains from trade to bear the burden of the tax. *So we will also expect to see a reduction in the number of transactions taking place, that is, OEM's purchasing modem chips from Qualcomm's rivals*, and that is going to cause further harm to the rivals, OEM's, and consumers. *The rivals perhaps most clearly because they're selling fewer chips.* They're making lower margins on the chips they sell, and they're selling fewer chips.[625]

Thus, Professor Shapiro testified that the modem "tax" harmed both OEMs and rival modem manufacturers—the former through higher "all-in prices" for modems, and the latter through lower profit margins on the sales of their modems.

Put differently, as an expert economic witness, Professor Shapiro was testifying under oath that these outcomes were his predictions of the competitive effects of the royalty "surcharge" and modem "tax" that he believed

---

[624] Transcript of Proceedings (Volume 6) at 1135:11–1136:20, FTC v. Qualcomm Inc., No. 5:17-cv-00220-LHK (N.D. Cal. Jan. 15, 2019) (Testimony of Carl Shapiro) (emphasis added).

[625] *Id.* at 1137:18–20, 1138:19–1139:1 (emphasis added).

Qualcomm had been charging OEMs. Professor Shapiro's predictions were empirically testable hypotheses. Yet, as we shall see, Professor Shapiro would soon be made to admit on cross examination that he did not attempt to test empirically any of the hypotheses presented in his testimony.

iii. Testimony About the Effects of the Alleged Modem "Tax" on Competition and Modem Prices

Professor Shapiro's direct examination during the FTC's case-in-chief continued with his testimony about how the alleged modem "tax" would supposedly affect rival modem manufacturers in the long run:

> If these rivals have higher costs, they're going to be less effective competitors, meaning they're going to have to pass on those costs to some degree to their—in their prices, and that makes them less effective competitors. So rivals are weakened. This inevitably fortifies Qualcomm's monopoly power. And that has adverse effects on competition in the short run and the long run. The short run, *we're going to end up with higher all-in prices for the chips*, basically higher costs for the OEM's. And in the long run—we're still at the previous run—the long run, I haven't talked about that, but it's inevitable that since the rivals are having their margins squeezed on the chips they're selling, their margins are being reduced and they're selling fewer chips, that the operating profits they can earn from being in this business are reduced and that is going to inevitably reduce their incentives to make R&D investments.[626]

In other words, Professor Shapiro testified that lower profit margins for rival modem manufacturers would necessarily imply that those manufacturers would have fewer resources to invest in R&D, which would impair their ability to compete with Qualcomm in the long run.

Professor Shapiro also testified that the alleged modem "tax" would increase the "all-in price" that OEMs would pay for both Qualcomm modems *and* non-Qualcomm modems, as well as the price that final consumers would pay for handsets:

> And then I want to emphasize that *the higher prices are not just the prices for the rival modem chips, but Qualcomm's prices are also going to go up*, and I haven't made that point yet, so let me explain why. And it's the all-in prices that matter, because that's what affects the OEM's costs. Why will Qualcomm's all-in prices go up? Well, there's two reasons. First, they've got rivals who are weakened and charging higher all-in prices because they're having to pay the surcharge. So as a general rule, when your competitors raise their price, it tends to give a firm incentive to raise his price as well in oligopolies,

---

[626] *Id.* at 1142:13–1143:5 (emphasis added).

and in addition to that, Qualcomm is less keen to compete to win business from its competitors because even when it loses, it gets a royalty surcharge. And so that's another reason why Qualcomm will not be as aggressive in pricing and will tend to raise its all-in prices due to the royalty surcharge. So from the point of view of competition and the cost hers [sic], the OEM's, *I would expect the prediction here would be that the effect of this is to cause all-in modem prices to go up for the Qualcomm modems and the rival modems.* And that in turn is going to get passed through to consumers because this is across the board, this is all the OEM's, and so *we're going to have pass through so the final consumers will be harmed as well.* So when you put all this together, we get really the full panoply of anticompetitive concerns that one has in monopolization cases, weakened rival, fortified monopoly power, tendency to discourage rivals from investing, either pushing them to exit or discourage entry, higher prices for consumers, for direct customers, and harm passed downstream to final consumers. Those are the effects of these three policies working together.[627]

Professor Shapiro thus testified at trial during the FTC's case-in-chief that the alleged royalty "surcharge" and modem "tax" would have led to higher "all-in prices" for modems and higher prices paid by end consumers for smartphones and other devices that used modems. Again, these economic predictions were empirically testable hypotheses about the competitive effects of Qualcomm's challenged business practices.

b. *Professor Shapiro's Testimony About Qualcomm's Policy of Refusing to Offer Exhaustive Licenses to Its Cellular SEPs to Rival Modem Manufacturers*

Professor Shapiro's trial testimony reiterated the opinion that he had disclosed in his expert reports: that Qualcomm's refusal to license its cellular SEPs exhaustively to modem manufacturers harmed competition in what he considered to be the two relevant markets for modems. Yet, he did not testify that he had conducted any empirical analysis of the facts and data of the case to support that conclusion. Professor Shapiro discussed Qualcomm's refusal to license its cellular SEPs exhaustively to rival modem manufacturers mainly in reference to his discussion of his utopian counterfactual conditional. Yet, he testified that he did not conduct any empirical analysis to justifiy his conclusion that Qualcomm's refusal to offer rival modem manufacturers exhaustive licenses to its cellular SEPs was anticompetitive. If anything,

---

[627] *Id.* at 1143:11–1144:18 (emphasis added); *see also id.* at 1124:17–24 ("So I hope it's clear, actually, if a monopolist finds a way to weaken its rivals by raising their cost, then that's going to be a competition concern. The rivals will be disadvantaged and the monopoly power will be greater. So this tax or this royalty surcharge will have significant adverse, or I'll say anticompetitive effects if Qualcomm is able to achieve that, and we're going to talk about how they did that.").

Professor Shapiro's testimony confirmed that, by itself, Qualcomm's decision to license its cellular SEPs exhaustively at the device level of the value chain, rather than the component level, could not have harmed competition.

  i.   *"What the World Would Look Like" Under Professor Shapiro's Counterfactual Conditions*

During the FTC's case-in-chief, Mr. James asked Professor Shapiro on direct examination "what the world would look like" if Qualcomm had licensed its cellular SEPs exhaustively to modem manufacturers.[628] In response, Professor Shapiro began by matter-of-factly rendering the legal opinion that FRAND commitments require the SEP holder to offer exhaustive licenses to cellular SEPs at the component level. He testified:

> So I think the cleanest, maybe easiest way to see that is to first suppose that Qualcomm honored its FRAND commitments and licensed its cellular standard essential patents to its modem chip rivals, how would things have played out if they had offered those licenses? And in that case, I would say the, the rivals and Qualcomm would negotiate a license and, of course, if they couldn't agree on the terms, then Qualcomm could sue the rival for patent infringement and a court, or maybe arbitration, arbitrators would establish the reasonable royalty rate. So bargaining in the shadow of that court determined rate, I would expect—and this is in the counter factual—we would expect and have that Qualcomm would, in fact, license its patents, these cellular standard essential patents to its rivals on reasonable terms. So that's kind of the cleanest first way to view the counter factual. And then the rivals are able to compete against Qualcomm in selling to OEM's the modem chips, bearing the cost of the reasonable royalties, but not bearing any higher costs, not paying some royalty surcharge, just bearing that reasonable royalty cost. And that is the counter factual that we will be comparing the out—the real world to that.[629]

Thus, Professor Shapiro argued that, if Qualcomm had offered to license its cellular SEPs exhaustively to rival modem manufacturers, those manufacturers could have obtained an exhaustive license to Qualcomm's cellular SEPs on FRAND terms.

Recall, however, that Professor Shapiro never showed that the royalties that Qualcomm charged to OEMs for an exhaustive license to its cellular SEPs exceeded the ceiling of the FRAND range. So, for rival modem manufacturers to pay a lower royalty for an exhaustive license to Qualcomm's cellular SEPs in Professor Shapiro's counterfactual conditional world than what OEMs already had been paying, some additional factor would need to come

---

[628] *Id.* at 1124:25–1125:1.
[629] *Id.* at 1125:14–1126:12.

into play. Professor Shapiro did not explain in his testimony what that additional factor might be.

> ii.   *The Amount of Royalties Due Qualcomm Versus the Level in the Chain of Production at Which Qualcomm Chose to License Its Cellular SEPs Exhaustively*

It was central to Professor Shapiro's testimony that a given royalty for an exhaustive license to Qualcomm's cellular SEPs would have had the same economic effect on competition, irrespective of whether that royalty was collected from an OEM or from a modem manufacturer. In his direct examination by Mr. James during the FTC's case-in-chief, Professor Shapiro testified:

> Q. And did you read Mr. Van Nest's [opening] statement [in the trial transcript] about Qualcomm's policy of not licensing rival chip makers?
>
> A. I did.
>
> Q. He said, "it allows chip makers to compete without paying any money to Qualcomm, so the chip makers, are in effect, free riding. They're not taking a license. They're also not paying any royalties." How do you respond to that?
>
> A. I respond badly to that. That is incorrect as a matter of economics. I think you can see that I work through the economic effect of the refusal to license, Qualcomm's refusal to license to the rivals. And the problem—the reason this is incorrect is the OEM—excuse me. When the rivals—they're not paying the license, they're not paying the royalties directly to Qualcomm. But when they sell the chips, their customers have to pay an unreasonably high royalty to Qualcomm. That is economically equivalent to the rivals themselves having to pay that unreasonably high royalty. It doesn't matter which side of the transaction is paying the tax, the economics are exactly the same. . . . They are being harmed, the rivals are being harmed because of the surcharge that their customers have to pay.[630]

According to Professor Shapiro, Qualcomm's charging a supra-FRAND royalty to an OEM would be "economically equivalent" to Qualcomm's charging a supra-FRAND royalty to a modem manufacturer (if Qualcomm were to license its cellular SEPs exhaustively at the component level).

Professor Shapiro's testimony therefore revealed implicitly (if perhaps inadvertently) that he was concerned with the *amount* of Qualcomm's royalties, rather the level within the chain of production at which Qualcomm chose to license its cellular SEPs exhaustively. Indeed, as we have already

---

[630]   *Id.* at 1139:12–1140:7, 1140:9–10.

seen, Professor Shapiro admitted in his initial expert report that, if OEMs could obtain an exhaustive license to Qualcomm's cellular SEPs on FRAND terms, then Qualcomm's refusal to license its cellular SEPs exhaustively to rival modem manufacturers would have had "relatively minor" effects on competition.[631] (Professor Shapiro did not explain why he believed that there would still be "relatively minor" effects on competition rather than *no* effects on competition.)

Professor Shapiro even conceded during his direct examination during the FTC's case-in-chief that it might have been appropriate for Qualcomm to license its cellular SEPs only to OEMs, if Qualcomm's cellular SEPs were practiced at the device level:

> Q. You talked about a counter factual in which Qualcomm would be licensing its modem chip rivals; right?
>
> A. Yes, that's what I was just talking about.
>
> Q. Would that exclude the possibility of Qualcomm entering into licensing arrangements with OEM's as well?
>
> A. No, no. So it seems—we would either—no. So if Qualcomm chose to license to OEM's, perhaps that would be more efficient, and I understand that particularly from Mr. Mollenkopf's testimony, that Qualcomm has some of their cellular standard essential patents read on the device, but not on the chip. So if they found it more efficient to license to the OEM's, that would absolutely be, you know, allowed. There's nothing preventing that from happening. But in that situation, then in the counter factual, Qualcomm would not be allowed to, to use the no license, no chips policy, meaning when an OEM is negotiating with—excuse me. When Qualcomm is negotiating with an OEM, they would not be able to threaten withholding chips as part of that licensing negotiation.[632]

Neither Professor Shapiro nor any other FTC expert appeared to have performed any analysis to rebut the proposition that OEMs practiced Qualcomm's cellular SEPs at the device level. That is, Professor Shapiro acknowledged that Qualcomm's practices might have been efficient under those circumstances, and he acknowledged unrebutted evidence that those circumstances existed; but he then proceeded to ignore the possibility raised by his own testimony, including any quantification of the extent to which

---

[631] Initial Expert Report of Carl Shapiro in *FTC v. Qualcomm, supra* note 115, at 121.

[632] Transcript of Proceedings (Volume 6) at 1126:13–1127:8, FTC v. Qualcomm Inc., No 5:17-cv-00220-LHK (N.D. Cal. Jan. 15, 2019) (Testimony of Carl Shapiro). As we will see in the Conclusion, the FTC well understood that Professor Shapiro's counterfactual conditional was implausible because no OEM would request an exhaustive license from Qualcomm after Judge Koh had enjoined Qualcomm. *See also supra* note 560.

OEMs practiced Qualcomm's cellular SEPs in the handset but not within the modem.

c.   Professor Shapiro's Testimony About Qualcomm's Allegedly Exclusive Agreements with Apple

Professor Shapiro's direct examination during the FTC's case-in-chief also addressed the question of how Qualcomm's 2011 and 2013 agreements with Apple—the Transition Agreement (TA) and First Amended Transition Agreement (FATA), respectively—supposedly harmed competition. Professor Shapiro testified:

> [U]nder these agreements, if Apple had decided to launch devices that contained non-Qualcomm modem chips, Apple would have faced a very large financial penalty in the form of having to forfeit certain payments that Qualcomm would otherwise be making to Apple. . . . I'm not saying the agreements were *de jure* exclusive. I'm studying the economic incentives that the agreements created in the form of this large penalty that Apple would bear if they chose to pick Intel for the iPads. . . . [T]he way the agreements worked was that—and particularly the First Amended Transition Agreement [FATA] which had these provisions—was that Qualcomm would make certain payments to Apple over time, incentive payments, and so long as Apple remained exclusive with Qualcomm, those payments would be made following a certain schedule. But if there came a time when Apple broke from exclusivity and launched a device with a non-Qualcomm modem chip, then there would be significant consequences financially for Apple, really in two forms you could think about it. First, some of the payments that Qualcomm had made by that time would be clawed back by Qualcomm from Apple. And, second, Qualcomm—payments that were scheduled to be made from Qualcomm to Apple in the future would not be made.[633]

Professor Shapiro was ambiguous about whether he considered the agreements between Apple and Qualcomm to be exclusive-in-fact.

Professor Shapiro portrayed Apple as a victim on the rationale that it would forfeit price discounts if it chose to ignore express conditions in the supply agreement with Qualcomm, to which Apple had willingly agreed:

> So the concern with this type of structure, these large payments conditioned on exclusivity, is that they will, as a practical matter, blockade an entrant from getting into the market. So when employed by a monopolist in a situation where there's an entrant who has—who's not in the market really and is trying to get in and this customer is the key route in, then the concern would be that this would block that entry and harm competition because

---

[633] *Id.* at 1163:24–1164:4, 1164:10–13, 1164:15–1165:3.

the entrant, in this case Intel, would—by not getting this, the business that they have a shot at . . . they would be then a weaker—not—let me put it differently. If Intel is able to get this business, this foothold, they will become a stronger competitor in the future. And so blocking that can have competitive effects.[634]

This passage of testimony was breathtaking for two reasons. First, Professor Shapiro made harm to competition synonymous with harm to Intel. He testified that two bilaterally negotiated agreements between Qualcomm and Apple harmed competition, because, in his view, the possibility of Apple's forfeiting the price discounts offered by Qualcomm would deter Apple from willingly abandoning the supply agreement with Qualcomm by purchasing modems from Intel. Professor Shapiro had just subordinated the consumer-welfare standard in American antitrust jurisprudence not merely to a competitor-welfare standard, but more precisely to a standard predicated on advancement of the economic fortunes of a single company: the "Intel-welfare" standard. We will see in Part XVI that Judge Koh embraced that same standard.

Second, Professor Shapiro argued this equivalency of harm-to-competition and harm-to-Intel despite the fact that Intel had suffered *no* harm: Apple willingly abandoned the benefits of its supposedly *de facto* exclusive supply agreement with Qualcomm when it released iPhones in September 2016 equipped with Intel modems. This apparent proposal to replace the consumer-welfare lodestar of antitrust jurisprudence with the "Intel-welfare" standard was perplexing.

Yet, Professor Shapiro's economic reasoning then became ornate. He seemed to testify under oath that Qualcomm was trying to maintain good relations with Apple to keep it from "challeng[ing] Qualcomm's licensing practices."[635] To Professor Shapiro, the *absence* of patent-infringement or breach-of-FRAND litigation between Apple and Qualcomm was suspicious. That is, evidence of harmonious relations between a supplier and its customer was "an additional concern" to Professor Shapiro—even though he acknowledged that "antitrust economists" ordinarily would not see nefarious implications of supply-chain amity in their "standard" analysis of allegedly anticompetitive business practices:

> There's an additional concern here that [sic] that's not the standard one that antitrust economists look at, but it's in play here, namely, that the concern, let's say, from Qualcomm's perspective that if they—if Apple becomes less reliant on Qualcomm for these premium LTE modem chips, that Apple will be in a better position or more likely to challenge Qualcomm's licensing

---

[634] *Id.* at 1166:24–1167:14.
[635] *Id.* at 1167:23–24.

practices and their—ultimately the royalties they've been collecting for their standard essential patents. And that is a strategic benefit to Qualcomm of keeping Apple in their, in their camp, if you will, or having Apple continue to purchase the Qualcomm chips and not move to Intel.[636]

Professor Shapiro argued that Qualcomm granted price discounts to Apple to preserve Qualcomm's market position in the modem industry, because those price discounts dissuaded Apple from switching to other modem suppliers. Yet again, that argument was contrary to fact, considering that Apple began using Intel modems in the iPhone in September 2016 and, by September 2018, was using Intel exclusively for the newly released models of iPhones.

Still, it was Professor Shapiro's sworn testimony that Qualcomm's payments to Apple, in combination with Qualcomm's other licensing practices, harmed competition among modem manufacturers:

> I think the three policies work together, and really the no license, no chips working together with the refusal to license rivals set up a situation where Qualcomm was able to use its chip leverage to bring to bear in negotiations with OEM's to get unreasonably high royalties on its cellular SEPs, and critically so that when an OEM purchased a modem chip from a rival of Qualcomm, they would be paying Qualcomm more than a reasonable amount. And that ultimately leads to a variety of harms to competition. That's the central point about no license, no chips, and then we had this additional much more specific conduct, in particular the contract signed in 2013 with Apple, that further had—caused some additional danger of harm to competition because Intel was trying to get in at that time.[637]

In sum, Professor Shapiro testified that two supply agreements negotiated and executed by Qualcomm and Apple harmed competition among modem manufacturers, because the possibility of Apple's forfeiting price discounts that Qualcomm granted it deterred Apple from purchasing its modems from rival modem manufacturers—particularly, Intel. Yet, Professor Shapiro so testified despite the fact that Apple in fact began relying on Intel for some, and eventually all, of the modems used in the latest models of Apple iPhones. Moreover, as we shall see, Professor Shapiro did not analyze whether those agreements between Apple and Qualcomm foreclosed a sufficient share of the two relevant markets to have had exclusionary effects. Finally, what was stopping other modem manufacturers from offering their own loyalty arrangements to Apple? Professor Shapiro did not venture an opinion.

---

[636] *Id.* at 1167:18–1168:3.
[637] *Id.* at 1175:2–15.

B. Was Professor Shapiro's Testimony Concerning the Supposed Royalty "Surcharge" on an Exhaustive License to Qualcomm's Portfolio of SEPs Specious?

Professor Shapiro never testified about Qualcomm's actual royalties, nor did he perform any analysis to determine a reasonable royalty for an exhaustive license to Qualcomm's portfolio of cellular SEPs (much less Qualcomm's overall patent portfolio). Instead, his testimony about the amount of Qualcomm's royalties for its cellular SEPs was based solely on the predictions arising from his theoretical bargaining model, which appeared to resemble his prior writings concerning "patent holdup." Even then, Professor Shapiro's testimony failed to apply to the facts of *FTC v. Qualcomm* the definition of a FRAND royalty that he had advocated in his prior writings. Consequently, his testimony was not substantial evidence tending to prove the existence of a supposed royalty "surcharge" on an exhaustive license to Qualcomm's portfolio of cellular SEPs.

1. Did Professor Shapiro's Testimony Mask an Accusation of Patent Holdup and Ignore Patent Exhaustion?

Professor Shapiro conspicuously did not invoke the words "patent holdup" to describe Qualcomm's conduct. (The phrase also does not appear anywhere in Judge Koh's findings of fact and conclusions of law.) Yet, the theory on which Professor Shapiro predicated his testimony that Qualcomm's royalties for an exhaustive license to its cellular SEPs were "supra-FRAND," and thus imposed an "unreasonably high" royalty "surcharge" on an exhaustive license to Qualcomm's portfolio of cellular SEPs, resembled the patent hold-up conjecture that Professor Shapiro had been advocating for over a decade. Professor Shapiro did not indicate in his testimony how the three labels that he used interchangeably to describe the price that Qualcomm charged for an exhaustive license to its portfolio of cellular SEPs—"supra-FRAND royalties, unreasonably high royalties, [and] . . . a royalty surcharge"[638]—were distinguishable from the excessive royalty that he predicted in his prior writings would result from "patent holdup," as he had defined that term.

---

[638] Transcript of Proceedings (Volume 6) at 1120:18–19, FTC v. Qualcomm Inc., No 5:17-cv-00220-LHK (N.D. Cal. Jan. 15, 2019) (Testimony of Carl Shapiro).

a. *What Distinguished Professor Shapiro's Testimony About Monopoly in* FTC v. Qualcomm *from His Prior Writings Concerning Patent Holdup?*

The most consequential definition of patent holdup appeared in an article that Professor Shapiro co-authored in 2007 with Mark Lemley of Stanford Law School. The Lemley-Shapiro definition of patent holdup specified how, when negotiating with a potential licensee, a patent holder (not necessarily an SEP holder) could threaten to enjoin the potential licensee's unlicensed use of the patent, thereby enabling the patent holder to negotiate an "excess" price, or "royalty overcharge," for a license to its claimed inventions:

> The threat that a patent holder will obtain an injunction that will force the downstream producer to pull its product from the market can be very powerful. These threats can greatly affect licensing negotiations, especially in cases where the injunction is based on a patent covering one small component of a complex, profitable, and popular product. Injunction threats often involve a strong element of *holdup* in the common circumstance in which the defendant has already invested heavily to design, manufacture, market, and sell the product with the allegedly infringing feature. As we show below, the threat of an injunction can enable a patent holder to negotiate royalties far in excess of the patent holder's true economic contribution. Such *royalty overcharges* act as a *tax* on new products incorporating the patented technology, thereby impeding rather than promoting innovation.[639]

The canonical Lemley-Shapiro definition of patent holdup bore a striking resemblance to, if not a complete identity with, Professor Shapiro's testimony in *FTC v. Qualcomm*. The "royalty overcharge[]" or "tax" that resulted from patent holdup, according to the 2007 Lemley-Shapiro article, appeared to be equivalent to the "unreasonably high" royalty "surcharge" on an exhaustive license to Qualcomm's portfolio of cellular SEPs (which, Professor Shapiro testified in *FTC v. Qualcomm*, allegedly became a "tax" on the "all-in price" that OEMs paid for rivals' modems) that supposedly resulted from Qualcomm's allegedly *anticompetitive* conduct.[640] Note that the Lemley-Shapiro conjec-

---

[639] Lemley & Shapiro, *Patent Holdup and Royalty Stacking, supra* note 118, at 1992–93 (first emphasis in original) (second and third emphases added).

[640] Professor Shapiro and Judge Koh consistently used the word "surcharge" instead of the word "overcharge" to describe Qualcomm's allegedly "unreasonably high" royalty "surcharge." *Cf.* Transcript of Proceedings (Volume 6) at 1194:7–16, FTC v. Qualcomm Inc., No 5:17-cv-00220-LHK (N.D. Cal. Jan. 15, 2019) (Testimony of Carl Shapiro) (declining on cross examination to characterize the royalties that Qualcomm charged as being "excess," despite the fact that the word "excess" appeared 10 times in the public, redacted version of the Initial Expert Report of Carl Shapiro in *FTC v. Qualcomm, supra* note 115, at 114–15).

ture about patent holdup did not assert that the "royalty overcharge" or "tax" constituted an antitrust violation or flowed from anticompetitive behavior.

i. *The Threat of an Injunction or a Supply Interruption*

Under Professor Shapiro's theory of harm in *FTC v. Qualcomm*, Qualcomm allegedly used its monopoly power over two relevant markets for modems to threaten to interrupt the supply of modems to its licensees of cellular SEPs (rather than threaten to seek an injunction, as Shapiro envisioned in his 2007 article with Professor Lemley) so as to extract from its licensees a royalty "surcharge" on an exhaustive license to its cellular SEPs. As in his article on patent holdup with Professor Lemley, Professor Shapiro testified that the threat that Qualcomm might interrupt its supply of modems could have forced an OEM to discontinue manufacturing its products (because the OEM would have had no alternative access to modems); and thus, Professor Shapiro testified, this threat by Qualcomm affected licensing negotiations and enabled Qualcomm to obtain a royalty that exceeded the economic value of an exhaustive license to its cellular SEPs.

ii. *The Royalty "Overcharge" or Royalty "Surcharge" That Supposedly Gave Rise to a Modem "Tax"*

Just as Professor Shapiro had conjectured that the "royalty overcharges" that he predicted would result from patent holdup would "act as a tax on new products incorporating the patented technology," so too he testified in his direct examination during the FTC's case-in-chief in *FTC v. Qualcomm* that the royalty "surcharge" would act as a "naked tax"—this time on the modems sold by Qualcomm's rivals (as opposed to the products of Qualcomm's downstream customers, which in this case were handsets manufactured by OEMs):

> Q. So you've been analyzing Qualcomm's use of modem chip leverage to obtain a royalty surcharge on transactions between rivals and OEM's. Is it material to your analysis that the surcharge takes the form of a royalty as opposed to bearing another label?
>
> A. No, it does not matter. I think one way to see that most clearly is to think of a hypothetical where a monopolist tells its customer, if you want my product, then as a condition, you need to pay me a fee every time you buy a product from my competitors. That would be, I would think, blatantly anticompetitive by raising the costs of the rivals and discouraging customers from purchasing from the rivals. That is economically equivalent to what we've got here with the royalty surcharge because [of] the reasonable royalties Qualcomm is entitled to because of their patents. But the royalty surcharge, that is disconnected from their R&D and inventions—let me

restate that. That is disconnected from the standard essential patents. That's an extra piece. And so it really operates just like this naked tax in my hypothetical to raise rivals' costs and harm competition. *And the fact that it's called a royalty doesn't change those economics.* Because I really want to emphasize, the reasonable royalty, they're totally entitled to those. It's—we're talking about something above and beyond that, and that operates like this naked tax.[641]

Professor Shapiro thus appeared to testify that the particular label used to describe his royalty "surcharge" and modem "tax" theory was inconsequential because the economics did not change on the basis of the label used.

Professor Shapiro's argument was too facile. He implied that Qualcomm was charging a price for an exhaustive license to its cellular SEPs that was the sum of a "reasonable royalty" and a royalty "surcharge" (which supposedly became a "naked tax" on the "all-in price" that OEMs paid for rivals' modems). Yet, it would still be the case if Qualcomm were charging solely a "reasonable royalty," as Professor Shapiro described it in his direct-examination testimony, that Qualcomm would "tell[] its customer, if you want my product [a Qualcomm modem], then as a condition, you need to pay me a fee [a reasonable royalty] every time you buy a product [a rival modem] from my competitors."[642] Professor Shapiro testified that "[t]hat would be . . . blatantly anticompetitive by raising the costs of the rivals and discouraging customers from purchasing from the rivals."[643] That conclusion holds regardless of whether the payment by the OEM to Qualcomm is demagogued as a "naked tax" or benignly called a "reasonable royalty." Yet, that reasoning leads to an absurdity, because Qualcomm's charging a reasonable royalty to every OEM for an exhaustive license to Qualcomm's cellular SEPs could not be anticompetitive.

iii. The Supposed Effect of the Royalty "Surcharge" on Innovation

Finally, just as in his definition of patent holdup, Professor Shapiro conjectured that Qualcomm's royalty "surcharge" "imped[ed] rather than promot[ed] innovation."[644] If his theory of harm was by all appearances identical to his patent-holdup conjecture, why did Professor Shapiro choose not to invoke

---

[641] *Id.* at 1144:19–1145:20 (emphasis added).

[642] *Id.* at 1144:25–1145:3.

[643] *Id.* at 1145:4–6.

[644] *Compare* Lemley & Shapiro, *Patent Holdup and Royalty Stacking, supra* note 118, at 1993, *with* Transcript of Proceedings (Volume 6) at 1196:8–20, FTC v. Qualcomm Inc., No 5:17-cv-00220-LHK (N.D. Cal. Jan. 15, 2019) (Testimony of Carl Shapiro) ("Q. Okay. And then you said when income goes down, that can be expected to reduce rivals' investment in R&D, research and development; right? A. Everything else equal, that—I mean, *it's really the expected future earnings that drive the R&D investment.* So, yes, everything else equal, I think that's a completely uncontroversial economic proposition. Q. And you say that ultimately will lead to harm to competition because innovation will slow down, among other reasons; right? A. Well, that's—exactly. That's the mechanism, and that would be the general—I think the clear prediction all else equal.") (emphasis added).

the conjecture that he had defined a dozen years earlier and had defended in the face of criticisms lodged in the years since?

b.   Is Patent Holdup a Hoax?

Proponents of the patent-holdup conjecture claim that it rests on the holdup theory that the late Nobel laureate Oliver Williamson of Berkeley and other economists advanced in the literature on transaction-cost economics.[645] For example, in 2020 in the *University of Pennsylvania Law Review*, Professors Shapiro and Lemley attributed holdup theory to Williamson and wrote that "[p]atent holdup is a specific application of the general theory of holdup."[646] Similarly, Professors Shapiro and Douglas Melamed wrote in an article on FRAND royalties in the *Yale Law Journal* in 2018: "These implications of lock-in and ex post dealings are well understood: they represent an example of the general concept of lock-in and opportunism developed by Oliver Williamson. Williamson was awarded the Nobel Prize for this work."[647] Even before one sits down to dissect the logic of the patent-holdup conjecture step by step alongside the logic of Williamson's theory of holdup, the extravagance of this claim by Professor Shapiro and his coauthors is called into question by the fact that the Nobel Prize committee's report on the work by Williamson, which explains in detail and at length why he merited sharing the Prize in 2009 with Elinor Ostrom, conspicuously omits any mention of patents or the patent-holdup conjecture.[648]

Professor Shapiro's 2020 article with Professor Lemley and his 2018 article with Professor Melamed ignored that, by 2015 at the latest, economists and legal scholars had already disproven this false representation of the provenance of the patent-holdup conjecture. The many definitions of "patent

---

[645] Joseph Farrell, John Hayes, Carl Shapiro & Theresa Sullivan, *Standard Setting, Patents, and Hold-Up*, 74 ANTITRUST L.J. 603, 604, 607 (2007).

[646] Carl Shapiro & Mark A. Lemley, *The Role of Antitrust in Preventing Patent Holdup*, 168 U. PENN. L. REV. (forthcoming 2020) (manuscript at 7–8, 15).

[647] A. Douglas Melamed & Carl Shapiro, *How Antitrust Law Can Make FRAND Commitments More Effective*, 127 YALE L.J. 2110, 2115 & n.14 (2018) (citing Steven Tadelis & Oliver E. Williamson, *Transaction Cost Economics*, in THE HANDBOOK OF ORGANIZATIONAL ECONOMICS 159 (Robert Gibbons & John Roberts eds., Princeton Univ. Press 2012)). Professor Melamed is today a law professor at Stanford. He was previously senior vice president and general counsel of Intel and, before that, a partner at WilmerHale and Acting Assistant Attorney General at the Antitrust Division of the U.S. Department of Justice. While at Intel, Professor Melamed publicly endorsed, on the company's behalf, the patent-holdup conjecture in congressional testimony and advocated specific policy recommendations based upon it. *See Standard Essential Patent Disputes and Antitrust Law: Hearing Before the Subcomm. on Antitrust, Competition Policy & Consumer Rights of the S. Comm. on the Judiciary*, 113th Cong. 51 (2013) (statement of A. Douglas Melamed, Senior Vice President and Gen. Counsel, Intel Corp.), https://www.intel.com/content/dam/www/public/us/en/documents/corporate-information/melamed-testimony-july-30-2013-statement.pdf.

[648] *See* ECONOMIC SCIENCES PRIZE COMMITTEE OF THE ROYAL SWEDISH ACADEMY OF SCIENCES, SCIENTIFIC BACKGROUND ON THE SVERIGES RIKSBANK PRIZE IN ECONOMIC SCIENCES IN MEMORY OF ALFRED NOBEL 2009: ECONOMIC GOVERNANCE (Oct. 12, 2009), https://www.nobelprize.org/uploads/2018/06/advanced-economicsciences2009.pdf.

holdup" that proponents had introduced since 2007 in fact did *not* track the economic reasoning of Williamson's canonical definition of holdup.

i.   The Key Assumptions of Williamson's Holdup Theory

The term "holdup" has a precise meaning in economics. It is the opportunistic appropriation of another firm's quasi rents.[649] Transaction-cost economics explains that a firm will enter a market if it expects to earn a positive economic rent, which is defined as the firm's expected revenues (R) net of its operating cost (c) and its investment cost (k)—that is, $R - c - k$.[650] Thus, a firm will enter the market if $R - c - k > 0$.

In Williamson's terminology, a "fundamental transformation" in the firm's incentives to remain in the market occurs after the firm has entered and made an investment k that is specific to a transaction with a particular firm.[651] After k is sunk, only the firm's quasi rents—that is, expected revenues net of operating costs ($R - c$)—affect the firm's decision to continue operating.[652] As long as $(R - c) \geq 0$, firm A will choose, in the short run, to remain in the market.[653] Hence, if firm A and firm B negotiate the terms of a transaction *after* firm A has made a relationship-specific (sunk) investment, firm B might opportunistically appropriate part, or all, of firm A's quasi rent.

For holdup to occur, three necessary conditions must be satisfied.[654] First, it is necessary that firm A have made a relationship-specific investment. Second, it is necessary that the contract between firm A and firm B be incomplete. Williamson called this second element the requirement of

---

[649] *See* Oliver E. Williamson, *Transaction-Cost Economics: The Governance of Contractual Relations*, 22 J.L. & Econ. 233, 234 (1979); Benjamin Klein, Robert G. Crawford & Armen A. Alchian, *Vertical Integration, Appropriable Rents, and the Competitive Contracting Process*, 21 J.L. & Econ. 297, 297–98 (1978); Benjamin Klein & Keith Leffler, *The Role of Market Forces in Assuring Contractual Performance*, 89 J. Pol. Econ. 615, 617–18 (1981).

[650] *See, e.g.*, Sidak, *The Meaning of FRAND, Part I: Royalties, supra* note 446, at 977.

[651] Oliver E. Williamson, The Economic Institutions of Capitalism 52–56, 61 (Free Press 1985).

[652] *See, e.g.*, Sidak, *The Meaning of FRAND, Part I: Royalties, supra* note 446, at 977. This difference is often called a firm's "operating profit." When a firm's expected operating profit is negative, the firm minimizes its losses by shutting down production in the short run (and exiting the industry in the long run). *See, e.g.*, N. Gregory Mankiw, Principles of Economics 274 (Cengage Learning 8ᵗʰ ed. 2018) [hereinafter Mankiw, Principles of Economics (8ᵗʰ ed.)]; Carlton & Perloff, Modern Industrial Organization, *supra* note 179, at 59 (defining quasi rents as "[t]he revenues earned in excess of avoidable cost . . . which are the payments above the minimum amount necessary to keep a firm operating in the short run"). Accountants give quasi rent a different name: contribution margin. *See, e.g.*, Charles T. Horngren, Srikant M. Datar & Madhav V. Rajan, Cost Accounting: A Managerial Emphasis 68–70 (Pearson 15ᵗʰ ed. 2014).

[653] The appropriable quasi rent cannot exceed the costs of switching to the next-best alternative. *See* Klein, Crawford & Alchian, *Vertical Integration, Appropriable Rents, and the Competitive Contracting Process, supra* note 649, at 298 ("The quasi-rent value of the asset is the excess of its value over its salvage value, that is, its value in its next best *use* to another renter. The potentially appropriable specialized portion of the quasi rent is that portion, if any, in excess of its value to the second highest-valuing *user*.") (emphasis in original).

[654] Williamson, The Economic Institutions of Capitalism, *supra* note 651, at 56–57.

"uncertainty."[655] Third, it is necessary that firm *B* act opportunistically pursuant to its incomplete contract with firm *A*. Williamson described opportunism as "self-interest seeking with guile."[656]

ii.   Can One Infer the Patent-Holdup Conjecture from Williamson's Holdup Theory?

Economists and legal scholars have shown that the key assumptions of Williamson's holdup theory are missing from the licensing negotiations for SEPs.[657] The claim that the patent-holdup conjecture descends from Williamson's legitimate theory of holdup implies that a larger corpus of economic scholarship supports the conjecture than is remotely the case.

First, the patent-holdup conjecture assumes that implementers of industry standards will systematically make relationship-specific investments before negotiating license terms with a given SEP holder. However, skeptical scholars have explained that it is unreasonable to expect that an SEP holder and an implementer always negotiate license terms for SEPs after the implementer has already made its relationship-specific investment.[658] Second, the critical assumption of "uncertainty" in Williamson's holdup model typically does not hold for SEPs.[659] Third, proponents of the patent-holdup conjecture assume that, once the infringer has made a relationship-specific investment, the SEP holder will, with certainty, act opportunistically toward the implementer by offering a royalty that exceeds the legitimately FRAND range. For example, Professor Fiona Scott Morton of Yale and Charles River Associates testified before Congress that an SEP holder "[has] no reason" to "turn down . . . additional profits" from engaging in behavior that she regards to constitute patent holdup.[660] However, economists have rebutted that assertion by

---

[655] *Id.* at 79–80.

[656] Galetovic & Haber, *The Fallacies of Patent-Holdup Theory, supra* note 164, at 23 (quoting WILLIAMSON, THE ECONOMIC INSTITUTIONS OF CAPITALISM, *supra* note 651, at 47); *see also* WILLIAMSON, THE ECONOMIC INSTITUTIONS OF CAPITALISM, *supra* note 651, at 47 ("[O]pportunism refers to the incomplete or distorted disclosure of information, especially to calculated efforts to mislead, distort, disguise, obfuscate, or otherwise confuse.").

[657] *See, e.g.,* Galetovic & Haber, *The Fallacies of Patent-Holdup Theory, supra* note 164, at 23–26; Alexander Galetovic & Stephen Haber, *Innovation Under Threat? An Assessment of the Evidence for Patent Holdup and Royalty Stacking in SEP-Intensive, IT Industries,* CPI ANTITRUST CHRON., Sept. 2016, at 2; Pierre Larouche & Florian Schuett, *Repeated Interaction in Standard Setting* 1, 2–4 (Tilburg Law Sch. Res. Paper No. 16/2016, 2016); Sidak, *The Meaning of FRAND, Part I: Royalties, supra* note 446, 1029; Damien Geradin & Miguel Rato, *Can Standard-Setting Lead to Exploitative Abuse? A Dissonant View on Patent Hold-Up, Royalty Stacking and the Meaning of FRAND,* 3 EUR. COMPETITION J. 101, 126 (2007).

[658] *See* Sidak, *Is Patent Holdup a Hoax?, supra* note 118, at 414–17; *see also* Richard A. Epstein, F. Scott Kieff & Daniel F. Spulber, *The FTC, IP, and SSOs: Government Hold-Up Replacing Private Coordination,* 8 J. COMPETITION L. & ECON. 1, 18 (2012).

[659] *See* Sidak, *Is Patent Holdup a Hoax?, supra* note 118, at 417–32; *see also* Galetovic & Haber, *The Fallacies of Patent-Holdup Theory, supra* note 164, at 25; Epstein, Kieff & Spulber, *The FTC, IP, and SSOs: Government Hold-Up Replacing Private Coordination, supra* note 658, at 18.

[660] *International Trade Commission (ITC) Patent Litigation: Hearing Before the Subcomm. on Courts, Intellectual Prop., & the Internet of the H. Comm. on the Judiciary,* 114th Cong. 5 (2016) (written testimony of Fiona M.

showing why the SEP holder might find it to be in its greater self-interest to forgo opportunism and offer the implementer a genuinely FRAND royalty.[661]

Thus, one cannot infer the patent-holdup conjecture from Williamson's holdup theory. Consequently, the proponents of the patent-holdup conjecture have never been truly describing Williamsonian holdup all these years; instead, they have been describing a *sui generis* theory in which excessive royalties for SEPs are deemed to exist because those royalties supposedly exceed a legitimately FRAND level.[662] For example, in a moment of remarkable candor captured on camera and preserved for posterity on the Internet, Professor Scott Morton said, in an interview at a conference on SEPs organized by Jean Tirole and held at the Toulouse School of Economics in May 2013, that FRAND "basically means a very low price."[663]

c. Did the Allegedly Supra-FRAND Royalty in FTC v. Qualcomm Result from Patent Holdup or a Monopoly Price?

Was *FTC v. Qualcomm* really a patent-holdup case masquerading as an antitrust case? In *FTC v. Qualcomm*, Professor Shapiro testified that his theoretical bargaining model supported a finding of antitrust liability. In regard to the patent-holdup conjecture, he had similarly developed a theoretical bargaining model that, as applied to the FRAND or RAND commitment, would support a finding of liability based on breach of contract. It appears still to be the case after a number of years that Professor Shapiro has not substantiated either bargaining model empirically.

As a theoretical matter, Professor Shapiro's models were vigorously disputed. Notably, he did not establish necessary or sufficient conditions for his predicted harms to occur. He did not disprove or limit the applicability of alternate models suggesting positive effects from the behaviors that he condemned. At most, Professor Shapiro expanded the universe of theoretically potential outcomes of those behaviors. Yet, he never established why

---

Scott Morton, Professor, Yale University School of Management), https://judiciary.house.gov/wp-content/uploads/2016/04/04.14.16-Scott-Morton-Testimony.pdf.

[661] *See* Sidak, *Is Patent Holdup a Hoax?*, *supra* note 118, at 433–35; *see also* Epstein, Kieff & Spulber, *The FTC, IP, and SSOs: Government Hold-Up Replacing Private Coordination*, *supra* note 658, at 20; Sidak, *Does the International Trade Commission Facilitate Patent Holdup?*, *supra* note 367, at 607–08, 614–15; J. Gregory Sidak, *The Meaning of FRAND, Part II: Injunctions*, 11 J. COMPETITION L. & ECON. 201, 231 (2015).

[662] *See, e.g.*, Jorge L. Contreras, *Much Ado About Hold-Up*, 2019 U. ILL. L. REV. 875, 885 ("Courts adjudicating disputes between patent holders and manufacturers have subsequently adopted streamlined definitions of hold-up such as: '[t]he ability of a holder of [a] SEP to demand more than the value of its patented technology,' and 'when the holder of a SEP demands excessive royalties after companies are locked into using a standard.'") (alterations in original) (first quoting Microsoft Corp. v. Motorola, Inc., No. C10-1823JLR, 2013 WL 2111217, at *10 (W.D. Wash. Apr. 25, 2013) (Robart, J.); and then quoting Ericsson Inc. v. D-Link Sys., Inc., 773 F.3d 1201, 1209 (Fed. Cir. 2014)).

[663] Standard-Essential Patents: A Conference at the Toulouse School of Economics (2013), https://ut-capitole.ubicast.tv/permalink/v12513c68a6d372rccoo/iframe/, at approximately 2:06 (video interview of Fiona Scott Morton).

the outcomes that his models predicted were more likely to occur than alternative outcomes. Where was the daylight between the antitrust theory of liability in *FTC v. Qualcomm* (predicated on an allegedly supra-FRAND price) and the contractual theory of liability (also predicated on an allegedly supra-FRAND price)?

i.   *Disambiguating a Monopoly Price from a Price That Results from Patent Holdup*

Although the FTC and Professor Shapiro (and certainly Judge Koh) did not attempt to distinguish a monopoly price from a FRAND royalty in *FTC v. Qualcomm*, there is no reason to believe that a monopoly price is equivalent to a FRAND royalty, or that a monopoly price exceeds a FRAND royalty. A monopoly price might or might not exceed the ceiling on a range of royalties that are FRAND. A monopoly price also might or might not exceed the price that results from patent holdup.

One could argue that a profit-maximizing, unconstrained, unregulated monopoly price for Qualcomm's portfolio of cellular SEPs will be less than the price for that portfolio that results from patent holdup, if one defines holdup consistently with Williamsonian holdup. The profit-maximizing monopolist does not seek to drive a customer out of business by appropriating its quasi rents. To the contrary, the profit-maximizing monopolist seeks to charge as high a price as it can without losing profit, on the margin. It is not the purpose of that monopoly price to threaten the viability of the customer who has made asset-specific investments in reliance on the continuation of the contractual relationship. Charging a profit-maximizing monopoly price produces a stable equilibrium, because the customer paying the monopoly price can still cover its operating costs *and* replace its capital when it wears out. The predicted result of monopoly is that the customer stays in the market but earns a smaller profit margin.

In contrast, patent holdup does not produce a long-run economic equilibrium, for the reasons that Alexander Galetovic and Stephen Haber have cogently explained.[664] In other words, the price that results from patent holdup is not moderated by the monopolist's desire to avoid driving its customer out of business through the appropriation of the customer's quasi rents. The predicted result of patent holdup is that the customer exits the market not later than when its capital wears out. The customer will expect *not* to recover its capital costs and therefore it will *not* willingly invest to remain in the market in the next period of the game.

---

[664] Galetovic & Haber, *The Fallacies of Patent-Holdup Theory*, *supra* note 164, at 11; *see also* Sidak, *Is Patent Holdup a Hoax?*, *supra* note 118, at 472–74.

Galetovic and Haber also showed that monopoly power is not necessary to induce exit.[665] Only the three Williamsonian conditions need to obtain, and those conditions do not include having monopoly power. How then did the FTC prove, and how did Judge Koh find, that the cause of the instances of "exit" from the modem business was not patent holdup (which requires no monopoly and *does* predict exit by licensees of SEPs)?

ii.   *Patent Holdup and the Exercise of Monopoly Power*

When he cast the problem as one of the exercise of monopoly power, Professor Shapiro advocated a theory of harm that ambiguated his theoretical bargaining model in *FTC v. Qualcomm*. He testified that Qualcomm possessed a monopoly over modems, *not* that Qualcomm possessed a monopoly over cellular SEPs.[666] Of course, it would have been a losing antitrust argument for Professor Shapiro to have testified in *FTC v. Qualcomm* that Qualcomm charged OEMs too much for its patents; that unilateral conduct aimed at customers is not plausibly an antitrust violation. Instead, he testified that Qualcomm's actual monopoly power was over modems, and that the impairment or induced "exit" of rival modem manufacturers was evidence of harm to the competitive process.

One could argue that a price could be below the holdup price but still represent a profit-maximizing monopoly price that does not violate antitrust law, if there were no anticompetitive behavior associated with the acquisition or maintenance of the power to charge that price. Moreover, it is conceivable that that monopoly price in this situation, which does *not* induce the implementer's exit or threaten its viability, is a FRAND-compliant price. When a firm is charging a FRAND-compliant price, that price might be either between the monopoly price and the holdup price, or below the monopoly price.

iii. *Monopoly Power, Patent Holdup, and Exit in* FTC v. Qualcomm

In *FTC v. Qualcomm*, Professor Shapiro predicted that the price that Qualcomm charged for an exhaustive license to its portfolio of cellular SEPs exceeded a FRAND price. He did not appear to specify whether it was his opinion (1) that FRAND is unique point, and that the price that Qualcomm charged for an exhaustive license to its cellular SEPs exceeded that point, or, in the alternative, (2) that FRAND is a range, and that the price that Qualcomm charged for an exhaustive license to its cellular SEPs exceeded the

---

[665]   Galetovic & Haber, *The Fallacies of Patent-Holdup Theory, supra* note 164, at 11.
[666]   Transcript of Proceedings (Volume 6) at 1119:7–12, FTC v. Qualcomm Inc., No 5:17-cv-00220-LHK (N.D. Cal. Jan. 15, 2019) (Testimony of Carl Shapiro).

ceiling of that range. Professor Shapiro's theory holds only if one adopts his own definition of holdup, which is inconsistent with Williamsonian holdup.[667] Did Professor Shapiro believe that the supra-FRAND price was sufficient to induce holdup, and therefore exit by rival modem manufacturers? We shall examine in greater depth in Part XV the supposed "exit" that occurred when a rival modem manufacturer sold its business to a prospective entrant; in particular, we shall ask whether the FTC proved that such "exit" caused any net harm to competition in the two modem markets.

2.   *The 2013 Lemley-Shapiro Definition of a FRAND Royalty as the Result of a Hypothetical Negotiation Before Standard Adoption*

In a 2013 article co-authored with Professor Lemley, Professor Shapiro wrote that "a reasonable royalty should be based on a hypothetical, arms-length negotiation that takes place at the time the SSO is setting the standard."[668] Professor Shapiro further wrote in his 2013 article with Professor Lemley that "the reasonable price is the price [the parties] . . . would negotiate at that point, *not a price that differs for each implementer depending on the happenstance of when that party begins implementing the standard.*"[669] When cross-examined by Mr. Van Nest on January 15, 2019, Professor Shapiro confirmed that he stood by the definition of a FRAND royalty that he had advocated in his prior writings:

> Q. Okay. And you've written before that a FRAND rate would be a reasonable rate for a party's entire portfolio of standard essential patents; correct?
>
> A. That's how it's often discussed.
>
> Q. Okay.
>
> A. And I think I've written that in my papers, yes, that's correct.
>
> Q. Okay. And you've also said the consensus approach to FRAND for SEPs are royalties that would result from hypothetical negotiations over licensing terms before the intellectual property is incorporated into a standard; right?
>
> A. Yes.
>
> Q. And that's something, maybe the only thing, but something that you and Professor Nevo both agree on; right?
>
> A. I think we agree on more than that.

---

[667] *See* Lemley & Shapiro, *Patent Holdup and Royalty Stacking, supra* note 118, at 1992–93; *see also* Sidak, *Is Patent Holdup a Hoax?, supra* note 118, at 407–08.

[668] Lemley & Shapiro, *A Simple Approach to Setting Reasonable Royalties for Standard-Essential Patents, supra* note 118, at 1147.

[669] *Id.* (emphasis added).

Q. Okay.

A. But I'm glad to know he agrees with that.

Q. I hope that's true. And so the consensus view, according to you and to Professor Nevo, is that the royalty reasonable would be one negotiated at arm's length between a buyer and a seller before there's a standard in place, or before the property is incorporated in the standard; correct?

A. Conceptually, that's correct, with the idea being at a time when there would be technologic—a choice between different technologies and therefore different patents that would become standard essential.[670]

Thus, it was Professor Shapiro's sworn testimony that a FRAND royalty for a portfolio of cellular SEPs should be equal to the royalty that an SEP holder and an OEM would have negotiated before the standard's adoption.

3. *The Fallacies of the "*Ex Ante *Incremental Value" Methodology for Calculating a FRAND or RAND Royalty*

I have written extensively why this *"ex ante* incremental value" methodology for calculating a FRAND or RAND royalty not only rests of a number of serious flaws of economic theory, but also will typically be unworkable in practice because the data required to produce empirical results that are relevant to the facts of a given case often will not exist.[671] In particular, I have argued at length that the Lemley-Shapiro definition of a FRAND (or RAND) royalty for an SEP, even if *au courant* among professors in economics departments and law schools, is decidedly *not* the legal rule that courts in fact use to set a FRAND (or RAND) royalty.[672]

The *ex ante* incremental value approach for determining a FRAND or RAND royalty is specious for both theoretical and practical reasons. First, the methodology rests on an incorrect economic understanding of standard setting, and, if used, the methodology would systemically bias the FRAND or RAND royalty in favor of the implementer (over the SEP holder). Second, implementing the *ex ante* incremental value approach would require using hypothetical data that do not exist. It should therefore come as no surprise that, in practice, it appears as of August 2020 that no court has ever used an *ex ante* incremental value approach to determine a FRAND or RAND royalty for SEPs.

---

[670] Transcript of Proceedings (Volume 6) at 1211:6–1212:7, FTC v. Qualcomm Inc., No. 5:17-cv-00220-LHK (N.D. Cal. Jan. 15, 2019) (Testimony of Carl Shapiro).

[671] *See* Sidak, *Misconceptions Concerning the Use of Hedonic Prices to Determine FRAND or RAND Royalties for Standard-Essential Patents, supra* note 446, at 504–15; Sidak, *Is Patent Holdup a Hoax?, supra* note 118, at 448–55; Sidak, *The Meaning of FRAND, Part I: Royalties, supra* note 446, at 968–86; Sidak, *Tournaments and FRAND Royalties, supra* note 446, at 103–07; *see also* sources cited *supra* note 446.

[672] *See* sources cited *supra* note 671.

     a. Why the Ex Ante *Incremental Value Approach for Patent-Infringement Cases Involving SEPs Misapplies the Standard Hypothetical Negotiation Framework*

The *ex ante* incremental value approach modifies the hypothetical negotiation framework used in a typical patent-infringement case—that is, a case concerning non-SEPs—by moving the date of the hypothetical negotiation from the moment immediately before first infringement to the moment immediately before standard adoption. SEPs are complements, not substitutes. One cannot examine the next-best noninfringing alternative to an SEP unless one backdates to the moment of standard adoption the hypothetical negotiation between the patent holder and the implementer (who is notionally represented in that negotiation by the SSO, acting collectively—which is an impermissible assumption for reasons we shall see shortly). The *ex ante* incremental value method does so and then, critically but implicitly, makes the economist's *ceteris paribus* assumption—that all other factors remain the same as one factor is changed.

    But do all other factors really remain the same in the real world? Certainly not. The putative need to undertake a hypothetical bargaining analysis does not grant one authority to include dispositive assumptions, either explicit or implicit, that are either unworldly or unlawful in the extant world.

    The *ex ante* incremental value approach sets an arbitrary point in time at which to consider the hypothetical negotiation, and it neglects the implementer's costs of lawfully acquiring the next-best noninfringing alternative. Moreover, the model upon which the *ex ante* incremental value approach is predicated—a static Bertrand pricing game without capacity constraints—inaccurately portrays how technology becomes incorporated into a standard. Bertrand competition describes a (static) situation in which each competing firm's strategy consists of its choice of the price at which to sell its output.[673] Formally, one can view the degree of product differentiation in a Bertrand pricing game as measuring the incremental value of a technology. As technologies become more differentiated, the incremental value of the best technology over the next-best technology increases, and the Bertrand-equilibrium price approaches the monopolist's price. As technologies become less differentiated, the incremental value of the best technology over the next-best technology decreases, and the Bertrand-equilibrium price approaches the perfectly competitive price.[674]

---

[673] *See, e.g.,* MICHAEL L. KATZ & HARVEY S. ROSEN, MICROECONOMICS 504–08 (McGraw-Hill 3ᵈ ed. 1998); CARLTON & PERLOFF, *supra* note 179, at 171–72.

[674] *See* CARLTON & PERLOFF, *supra* note 179, at 172–74; JEAN TIROLE, THE THEORY OF INDUSTRIAL ORGANIZATION 210–12 (MIT Press 2002) (1988).

The process of developing and setting voluntary standards more closely resembles the structured rivalry observed in a tournament than it does the particular form of rivalry hypothesized in Bertrand competition. Yet, to my knowledge, proponents of the *ex ante* incremental value approach have never explained why the economic literature on tournaments is less instructive than their attempt to use a static Bertrand pricing model to explain the manifestly dynamic phenomenon of competition through innovation.

i. The Mistaken Timing of the Hypothetical Negotiation in the Ex Ante *Incremental Value Approach*

From an economic perspective, the *ex ante* incremental value approach is specious because it is "not *ex ante* enough." I have made this argument repeatedly in the scholarly literature since at least 2013.[675] Seven years on, proponents of the *ex ante* incremental value approach continue to ignore this criticism of a key assumption that is critical to the predictions of their theory.[676]

To be unbiased and intellectually rigorous, the chosen moment of the hypothetical negotiation between the willing licensor and the willing licensee of an SEP must be pushed back in time not merely from the eve of first infringement to the eve of the SSO's standard adoption, but rather all the way back to the moment just before the patent holder decided to monetize his invention within the open standard of the SSO in question by declaring his patent essential (rather than outside the SSO through a proprietary standard or some other business strategy predicated on exclusion rather than open access, as shown in Figure 4).[677]

As Figure 4 shows, the *ex ante* incremental value approach considers the value of the patent holder's technology after the patent holder has already decided to monetize its technology through a standard (Stage 3). In contrast, at the earlier moment (Stage 1), both the patent holder and the implementer still have outside options to the hypothetical negotiation. (If there is a competing standard, another outside option for the patent holder is to

---

[675] *See* Sidak, *The Meaning of FRAND, Part I: Royalties, supra* note 446, at 983; *see also* Sidak, *Is Patent Holdup a Hoax?, supra* note 118, at 452.

[676] *See, e.g.*, PATENT REMEDIES AND COMPLEX PRODUCTS: TOWARD A GLOBAL CONSENSUS (C. Bradford Biddle, Jorge L. Contreras, Brian J. Love & Norman V. Siebrasse eds., Cambridge Univ. Press 2019); Timothy S. Simcoe & Allan L. Shampine, *Economics of Patents and Standardization: Network Effects, Hold-Up, Hold-Out, Stacking, in* THE CAMBRIDGE HANDBOOK OF TECHNICAL STANDARDIZATION LAW: COMPETITION, ANTITRUST, AND PATENTS 100 (Jorge L. Contreras ed., Cambridge Univ. Press 2017); Shapiro & Lemley, *The Role of Antitrust in Preventing Patent Holdup, supra* note 646 (manuscript at 15–16); Mark A. Lemley & Timothy Simcoe, *How Essential Are Standard-Essential Patents?*, 104 CORNELL L. REV. 607 (2019); Melamed & Shapiro, *How Antitrust Law Can Make FRAND Commitments More Effective, supra* note 647, at 2113; William F. Lee & A. Douglas Melamed, *Breaking the Vicious Cycle of Patent Damages*, 101 CORNELL L. REV. 385, 392 (2016).

[677] For a general discussion of the strategic options available to innovators generally (not merely SEP holders), see the classic analysis in Teece, *Profiting from Technological Innovation: Implications for Integration, Collaboration, Licensing and Public Policy, supra* note 431.

commit its patented technology to a different SSO. For ease of exposition, Figure 4 does not depict that possible option.) Both the seller and the buyer of innovative inputs intended for the downstream product still have substitution opportunities. Neither party at that anterior moment is subject to lock-in or holdup. That moment more closely resembles the Rawlsian original position, in which the patent holder and implementer are both still veiled in ignorance of the commercial potential of the technology before them.

Figure 4. The Process by Which a Patent Holder
Can Monetize Proprietary Technology

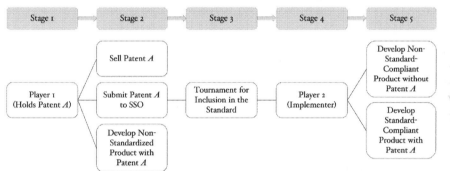

In contrast, the *ex ante* incremental value approach is selective, asymmetric, and therefore inherently biased. It would set a FRAND or RAND rate so as to restore the implementer—but not the patent holder—to his original position. The implementer in the typical academic depiction of the *ex ante* hypothetical negotiation would still have substitution opportunities, but the patent holder would not. That unstated assumption stacks the deck in favor of the implementer in this theoretical bargaining model.

ii. *The Neglected Costs of Acquiring the Next-Best Noninfringing Alternative*

The *ex ante* incremental value approach ignores the implementer's acquisition cost of the next-best noninfringing substitute, and thus it mischaracterizes what a FRAND or RAND royalty commitment represents. So long as the *ex ante* incremental value exceeds the difference in the licensing price for two competing patented technologies, the licensees will purchase the rights to the higher-valued technology at a price up to the incremental value of that patented technology *plus* the price of lawfully acquiring the right to use the less valuable technology. So, even under these relatively weak assumptions, the price for the patent *must* exceed the *ex ante* incremental value in any nontrivial case.

For example, if a Lincoln is worth $4,000 more to me than a Ford, I still must pay, say, $40,000 for the Lincoln—not $4,000—because other buyers have their own private valuations of the Lincoln and have bid up its price. The price I must pay for the Lincoln is still $40,000, and not merely the $4,000 of incremental value that the Lincoln gives me over the Ford.

A second example might help proponents of the *ex ante* incremental value approach to grasp this argument with greater immediacy. Suppose that in a FRAND lawsuit the alleged infringer has the choice of retaining as its expert economic witness a Stanford professor for $1,200 per hour or a Harvard professor for $1,400 per hour. Assume that both economists possess the prerequisites to perform the engagement competently, but that the Harvard professor is more famous. Would a reasonable price for the services of the Harvard professor be $200 per hour, because that amount is the extent of his incremental value to the client over the value of the next-best alternative not chosen—namely, the equally competent but less famous Stanford professor? The fact that patent litigators do not observe Harvard professors charging $200 per hour for their time answers that question.

Granted, in some cases, it might be possible for the implementer to acquire the rights to the next-best noninfringing substitute at zero additional expense, such as if the technology exists in the public domain. But one cannot generalize this condition, and it is fallacious economic reasoning simply to assume (as in my experience expert economic witnesses often do) that the next-best alternative is free. To the contrary, the cost of acquiring the next-best alternative is a fact-specific inquiry that courts would need to determine on a case-by-case basis. Thus, with this unidentified and unsubstantiated assumption, the typical rendition of the *ex ante* incremental value approach cannot ensure that the licensee's incremental profit from using the patent in suit rather than the next-best noninfringing substitute will translate into a high enough royalty to enable the patent holder to recover the sunk costs of having developed the patented technology.

> *iii. The Failure to Disaggregate the Increment of the Implementer's Bargaining Power Attributable to the Implicit But Erroneous Assumption That Implementers May Lawfully Negotiate Collectively as a Monopsonist*

A particularly serious error of economic reasoning inherent in the *ex ante* incremental value thesis is the failure to disaggregate the degree of bargaining power that an individual implementer would wield vis-à-vis an SEP holder from the degree of bargaining power that *all* implementers would collectively wield vis-à-vis the same SEP holder if they could lawfully coordinate their purchases as a monopsonist. If it is to have any economic defensibility at all, the hypothetical negotiation at the time of standard adoption is properly cast as a series of simultaneous, bilateral negotiations between the SEP holder and each of the implementers. It is incorrect to treat that hypothetical negotiation in the FRAND context as a single transaction occurring between one SEP holder and a solitary agent representing all implementers.

The difference between the two versions of the *ex ante* hypothetical negotiation is the increment in bargaining power that implementers gain when they act collectively. It is well understood in economic theory that a monopsonist pays a lower price for an input (and consumes a lower volume of the input) than do competing buyers acting individually.[678] It is no less incorrect to assume implicitly in the *ex ante* hypothetical negotiation that implementers (who are horizontal competitors in the various markets for downstream products) may lawfully exchange information with one another about the prices that they are bilaterally negotiating with the SEP holder, so that implementers can collusively simulate monopsony power.

To equate, without any adjustment for monopsonistic negotiation, the *ex ante* incremental value of a given SEP to its FRAND price is to assume tacitly that implementers may lawfully acquire and exploit monopsony power to suppress the SEP's price. Such an interpretation of the FRAND commitment demands that the SSO must play the role of a buyer's cartel in the purchase of a given technology input. However, the law does not permit implementers to do so.

Section 1 of the Sherman Act forbids horizontal price fixing among buyers as well as sellers.[679] Clearly, the monopsonistic suppression of the competitive price for an exhaustive license to an SEP would exceed the legitimate purpose of the FRAND commitment as an ancillary restraint that increases economic efficiency.[680] At a minimum, this erroneous interpretation of the FRAND commitment would make the contract void at common law for being contrary to the public interest.

---

[678] *See* Sidak, *Patent Holdup and Oligopsonistic Collusion in Standard-Setting Organizations*, *supra* note 446, at 142–46; *see also* MANKIW, PRINCIPLES OF ECONOMICS (8th ed.), *supra* note 652, at 374.

[679] 15 U.S.C. § 1; *see also supra* notes 410–416 and accompanying text.

[680] The doctrine of ancillary restraints originated in the English common law in 1711 in *Mitchel v. Reynolds* and permits two or more firms to restrain competition among themselves if their doing so is essential to their creation of a new market, product, or productive efficiency. (1711) 24 Eng. Rep. 347 (Q.B.). Such cooperation among firms benefits consumers. However, Congress outlawed any contract in restraint of trade when it enacted section 1 of the Sherman Act in 1890. 15 U.S.C. § 1. This language sweeps so broadly that, if taken literally, it would outlaw cooperation among firms that manifestly benefits consumers. It is not surprising, therefore, that within only nine years the Supreme Court qualified the literalism of section 1 when it incorporated the doctrine of ancillary restraints into American antitrust jurisprudence. *Addyston Pipe & Steel Co. v. United States*, 175 U.S. 211 (1899). The Court affirmed the opinion of Judge (later, President and Chief Justice) William Howard Taft for the Sixth Circuit, which held that a covenant "merely ancillary to the main purpose of a lawful contract, and necessary to protect the covenantee in the full enjoyment of the legitimate fruits of the contract" is not unlawful. *United States v. Addyston Pipe & Steel Co.*, 85 F. 271, 282 (6th Cir. 1898).

To advance economic efficiency and increase consumer surplus, the ancillary restraint needs only to ensure that the selection of the standard does not empower the patent holder to charge implementers more than a FRAND royalty after the SSO has selected the patent holder's technology and made the patent covering that technology essential to the standard. To interpret the FRAND price as being the monopsony price goes too far—as a matter of legal analysis, as a matter of economic analysis, and as a matter of common sense. No plausible interpretation of the FRAND contract should conclude that the inventor consented to receiving a royalty suppressed to the monopsony level.

iv. *The Inapplicability to Standard Setting of a Static Bertrand Pricing Game Without Capacity Constraints*

According to the *ex ante* incremental value approach, if two inventors each develop a similar substitute technology, and if the two technologies would generate an equal amount of value to a manufacturer, the manufacturer would need to pay only a nominal FRAND royalty for the technology chosen for adoption into the standard, because the two inventors would compete to sell their respective technologies. Thus, it is conjectured, the two inventors would enable the manufacturer to bid down the FRAND royalty to nearly zero.[681]

The argument that a FRAND royalty is effectively zero implicitly depends on modeling competition between the technologies in the standards development and standards setting process as a static Bertrand pricing game without capacity restraints. However, the argument that a price war between SEP holders would drive down a FRAND royalty nearly to zero requires one to make at least three heroic assumptions: (1) that there is no differentiation between the competing (substitute) technologies, (2) that the inventors lack any outside option for monetizing their technologies, and (3) that each inventor has some ancillary revenue stream generating a positive return to its participation in the SSO, such that the inventor can cover the costs of that participation without licensing its patents.

The standard rendition of the theory of the *ex ante* hypothetical negotiation fails to acknowledge all three of these implicit assumptions. When assumptions (1) and (2) are met, the SEP holder cannot receive a positive

---

[681] For example, in *Innovatio*, Judge James Holderman wrote in 2013 that a respected economist, Dr. Gregory Leonard, "testified that . . . if two patented and equally effective alternatives both cost the same amount, . . . the two patent holders would negotiate the price down to effectively zero." *In re* Innovatio IP Ventures, LLC, No. 11-cv-09308, 2013 WL 5593609, at *20 (N.D. Ill. Oct. 3, 2013). Dr. Leonard declined to defend the "effectively zero" argument in a subsequent article, which goes only so far as to say that, "[i]n competitive markets, the price for a product tends to be lower the greater the number of substitutes for the product, all else equal." Gregory K. Leonard & Mario A. Lopez, *Determining RAND Royalty Rates for Standard-Essential Patents*, 29 ANTITRUST, Fall 2014, at 86, 87.

payoff from any use of its SEPs, nor can the SEP holder recover the cost of its participation in the SSO. Unless the costs of participation in the SSO are zero, the SEP holder will not participate, absent some ancillary revenue stream. That ancillary revenue source could arise from vertical integration or from some other form of multiproduct output that enables the SEP holder to internalize some of the benefits arising from the standard by offering an SEP at a zero royalty. In any case, this ancillary revenue stream is a significant deviation from the traditional assumptions underlying Bertrand competition.

What empirical evidence indicates that an SSO could simultaneously choose from *many* substitute technologies for each and every facet of a standard, and that those substitute technologies are all homogeneous in terms of price and quality? None. If all substitute technologies were homogeneous, then standard setting would essentially be a lottery—and a most peculiar lottery at that, with a winner who receives only a penny for his troubles. The *ex ante* incremental value approach ignores the need to ensure the continued participation of inventors in the current standard and in future standards.

Compared with a static Bertrand pricing game without capacity constraints, a more appropriate model for determining a FRAND royalty is a tournament.[682] Economists have long studied the effects of tournament structures and prizes on effort levels.[683] All things being equal, higher prize levels lead to better performances by the participants, and higher marginal returns to effort cause participants to exert greater effort.[684]

In standard setting, firms invest not only in developing patents, but also in competing to have their technologies adopted into a standard.[685] If the winner of that tournament—whose patented technology the SSO adopts into the standard—is not compensated for that additional investment, how can one expect patent holders to invest in participation in the collective development and setting of open standards? Investment in innovation would flow instead into proprietary standards—of precisely the sort that, if they proved to be commercially successful, fuel titanic disputes over monopolization or abuse of dominance.

The "winner-take-all" nature of standard setting increases the risk to inventors and their investors. Using the *ex ante* incremental value approach

---

[682] *See* Sidak, *Tournaments and FRAND Royalties, supra* note 446.

[683] *See, e.g.*, Edward P. Lazear & Sherwin Rosen, *Rank-Order Tournaments as Optimum Labor Contracts*, 89 J. Pol. Econ. 841 (1981); H. Lorne Carmichael, *The Agents-Agents Problem: Payment by Relative Output*, 1 J. Lab. Econ. 50 (1983); Clive Bull, Andrew Schotter & Keith Weigelt, *Tournaments and Piece Rates: An Experimental Study*, 95 J. Pol. Econ. 1 (1987).

[684] *See* Ronald G. Ehrenberg & Michael L. Bognanno, *Do Tournaments Have Incentive Effects?*, 98 J. Pol. Econ. 1307, 1322 (1990); *see also* Ronald G. Ehrenberg & Michael L. Bognanno, *The Incentive Effects of Tournaments Revisited: Evidence from the European PGA Tour*, 43 Indus. & Lab. Rel. Rev. 74-S (1990).

[685] For a related explanation of the static versus dynamic benefits of standardization, see Jonathan D. Putnam, *Economic Determinations in "Frand Rate"-Setting: A Guide for the Perplexed*, 41 Fordham Int'l L.J. 953 (2018).

and other rent-shifting proposals that view low prices for intellectual property as the sole objective of standard setting fails to compensate inventors and their investors for their risk bearing.[686] In contrast, a tournament-based model would consider that the expected payoff for each participant must satisfy each participant's individual-rationality constraint. Consequently, the aggregate payoff—which in this case equals the FRAND royalty itself—must exceed the sum of the costs of participation *for each participant*.

> ### b.   Do Courts Actually Rely on the Ex Ante *Incremental Value Approach?*

Implementing the *ex ante* incremental value approach would typically require using hypothetical data that do not exist. At best, the *ex ante* incremental value approach would need to rely on data produced before the standard was set—such as data collected by conjoint analysis surveys, sales predictions, or other methods that all would be limited in their reliability by the issues common to any prediction.

Thus, the *ex ante* incremental value approach would require conjecturing about what competing technologies *might have been* available at the time of standard adoption, and then evaluating the degree to which the chosen technology was superior to the (conjectured) next-best competing technology (if any existed) that the SSO did not adopt.[687] Expert economic testimony of that nature would likely be impractical and unreliable. It would contain little serious economic analysis and a good deal of unverifiable prognostication by industry "futurists."

Not surprisingly, courts do not in fact rely on the *ex ante* incremental value approach to calculate a FRAND or RAND royalty in disputes concerning SEPs.[688] Nonetheless, some economists, academics, government agencies, and other commentators misstate that U.S. law *requires* that a FRAND or RAND royalty be calculated on the basis of an *ex ante* hypothetical negotiation

---

[686] *See supra* note 663.

[687] A more promising empirical methodology for calculating a FRAND or RAND royalty using actual transactional data is to estimate hedonic prices for the features enabled by the SEPs in question. *See* Alexander Galetovic, *Hedonic Prices, Patent Royalties, and the Theory of Value and Distribution: A Comment on Sidak and Skog*, 3 Criterion J. on Innovation 59, 64–65 (2018) (discussing Sidak & Skog, *Hedonic Prices and Patent Royalties, supra* note 446) ("It would be difficult to exaggerate the difference between, on the one hand, Sidak's and Skog's approach, which deduces the value of a technology from observed market transactions, and, on the other hand, valuation approaches that are based on unobserved hypotheticals."); *id.* at 70 ("Sidak and Skog make an important contribution, because they link technology valuation with actual and observable market transactions and prices. This sets them apart from authors that argue that courts should compare the new technology with a hypothetical technology that never existed and was seemingly discarded by the standard-setting organization.").

[688] *See* Sidak, *Misconceptions Concerning the Use of Hedonic Prices to Determine FRAND or RAND Royalties for Standard-Essential Patents, supra* note 446, at 511–12; J. Gregory Sidak, *Judge Selna's Errors in* TCL v. Ericsson *Concerning Apportionment, Nondiscrimination, and Royalties Under the FRAND Contract*, 4 Criterion J. on Innovation 101, 131–32 (2019); Sidak, *Is Patent Holdup a Hoax?, supra* note 118, at 448–55; Sidak, *The Meaning of FRAND, Part I: Royalties, supra* note 446, at 968–86.

occurring immediately before the standard is adopted.[689] That proposition is simply incorrect. That misrepresentation of the controlling law has appeared in the literature at least since 2007 and has been exhaustively rebutted.[690]

4. Did Professor Shapiro Fail to Apply His Own Definition of a FRAND Royalty to the Facts of the Case?

Professor Shapiro has written extensively about FRAND royalties and how to define them. Yet, he failed to apply his own definition of a FRAND royalty to the specific facts in *FTC v. Qualcomm* concerning Qualcomm's royalties for an exhaustive license to its cellular SEPs. For purposes of scrutinizing Professor Shapiro's testimony in *FTC v. Qualcomm* regarding his proposed economic definition of a FRAND or RAND royalty, I will temporarily suspend my disbelief in the utility of Professor Shapiro's theoretical construct.

a. Professor Shapiro's Testimony Mistakenly Assumed That None of Qualcomm's Licenses Had Been Negotiated Before Standard Adoption, Which the 2013 Lemley-Shapiro Article Considered Evidence That a Royalty Was FRAND

When Mr. Van Nest informed Professor Shapiro during his cross examination on January 15, 2019 that the royalties specified in some of Qualcomm's license agreements had been negotiated *before* the adoption of the relevant

---

[689] *See* Allan L. Shampine, *Paper Trail: Working Paper and Recent Scholarship*, ANTITRUST SOURCE, Oct. 2017, at 1–2 (review of Sidak & Skog, *Hedonic Prices and Patent Royalties*, *supra* note 446); Oral Argument at 33:29–40, TCL Commc'n Tech. Holdings Ltd. v. Telefonaktiebolaget LM, 943 F.3d 1360 (Fed. Cir. 2019) (No. 2018-1363) ("The test . . . for FRAND is to look at what is the value that's added to the product over other alternatives prior to the establishment of the standard.") (argument of Stephen Korniczky of Sheppard Mullin on behalf of TCL), http://oralarguments.cafc.uscourts.gov/default.aspx?fl=2018-1363. mp3; Leonard & Lopez, *Determining RAND Royalty Rates for Standard-Essential Patents*, *supra* note 681, at 87 ("The definition of RAND can be further refined to be the ex ante incremental value of the SEP, which is the additional value provided by the SEP over the next-best substitute technology."); *see also* Gregory K. Leonard, *Reflections on the Debates Surrounding Standard-Essential Patents*, 14 ANTITRUST SOURCE, Aug. 2015, at 1, 5 ("One element of the SEP debates is whether a 'reasonable' royalty for an SEP under a RAND commitment should be based on a valuation of the SEP before the standard was set, often termed to be an 'ex ante' valuation. Some have pointed out that such a valuation is ex ante only with respect to the implementer's sunk cost investments in developing their products; it is ex post with respect to the inventor's sunk cost investments in developing the patented invention. However, the framework of the U.S. patent system calls for patents to be valued in the ex ante sense defined above."); Lemley & Shapiro, *A Simple Approach to Setting Reasonable Royalties for Standard-Essential Patents*, *supra* note 118, at 1148 ("The hypothetical negotiation needs to take place under conditions where the alternative specifications have been identified, so that the parties are well informed about the best potential non-infringing alternatives to the proposed standard. . . . The key idea here is that a reasonable royalty should reflect what would happen as a result of well-informed ex ante technology competition. The incremental value of the patented technology over and above the next-best alternative serves as an upper bound to the reasonable royalties. To this end, SSO best practice includes maintaining records, such as minutes from SSO meetings, that will inform subsequent negotiators and arbitrators of the ex ante technical alternatives that were feasible or considered, along with their pros and cons.").
[690] *See, e.g.*, Sidak, *Is Patent Holdup a Hoax?*, *supra* note 118, at 448–55; Sidak, *The Meaning of FRAND, Part I: Royalties*, *supra* note 446, at 968–86.

standard, Professor Shapiro seemed to admit that he was unaware of that fact because he had conducted no factual investigation on the topic:

> Q. Professor Shapiro, you know that a number of license agreements that Qualcomm entered into with OEM's were entered into before Qualcomm technology was adopted into a standard? You're aware of that?
>
> A. I guess there are different standards over time. Maybe you should tell me what specific license agreements you mean. I'm really—
>
> Q. Well—
>
> A. There are many different fact patterns. I'm not sure what you're referring to.
>
> Q. Sure. You haven't even attempted to form an opinion on whether Qualcomm's early CDMA licenses, for example, with Nokia, Motorola, or AT&T, are FRAND or not; right?
>
> A. You know, this hasn't even attempted also just—it just—okay. I guess I didn't attempt to do that, that is true.[691]

In other words, Professor Shapiro's testimony that Qualcomm's royalties for its cellular SEPs were "unreasonably high" appeared to assume erroneously that all of Qualcomm's licenses with OEMs had been negotiated *after* standard adoption. Professor Shapiro admitted that he never examined Qualcomm's CDMA license agreements that predated the adoption of that standard.

>   b.   *The Inconsistency Between the 2013 Lemley-Shapiro Article and Professor Shapiro's Testimony That a FRAND Royalty Must Decline Over Time*

Professor Shapiro testified on direct examination on January 28, 2019 during the FTC's rebuttal case that the royalties specified in Qualcomm's early licenses exceeded the FRAND ceiling during the later years (when, he further testified, Qualcomm possessed monopoly power over the two modem markets). The reason why he could so conclude, Professor Shapiro testified, was that Qualcomm's royalties specified in those licenses had not declined over time:

> We have good reasons to suspect and expect that the reasonable rate would decline over this 20, 25 year period. Qualcomm's fundamental patents have expired during this period of time. The handsets have become completely different and, you know, there's a whole different set of functions in them.

---

691   Transcript of Proceedings (Volume 6) at 1214:19–1215:9, FTC v. Qualcomm Inc., No. 5:17-cv-00220-LHK (N.D. Cal. Jan. 15, 2019) (Testimony of Carl Shapiro).

And Qualcomm's share of the cellular standard essential patents has declined.[692]

Earlier, when being cross-examined by Mr. Van Nest during the FTC's case-in-chief on January 15, 2019, Professor Shapiro had similarly testified:

> Q. . . . For standard essential patents, a reasonable royalty should be based on a hypothetical, arm's length negotiation that takes place at the time the standard setting organization is setting the standard. We already covered that and you acknowledged that's your view.
>
> A. Okay.
>
> Q. And Professor Nevo's view as well; correct?
>
> A. Okay. And I believe what we're saying here is if—if a—let me make sure I get the language here right. If an implementer enters the market later, at which time there are fewer choices because the patent is already in the standard, then we don't take that as the time at which a negotiation occurs. We ask about what that implementer would have negotiated earlier before there was the lock in to the standard.
>
> Q. But the—
>
> A. That's the point.
>
> Q. Fair enough. But the implementer also doesn't get a break off the FRAND rate simply because he or she entered later? That's also what you're saying; correct?
>
> A. Well, no, that is not correct actually, because if somebody enters at a point where maybe, for example, suppose that the most [sic] of the portfolio of one licensee, standard essential patent holder has expired, okay? Then the situation is going to change by then.[693]

The questions that Mr. Van Nest posed actually quoted in part from an article that Professor Shapiro co-authored with Professor Lemley in 2013:

> For standard-essential patents, a reasonable royalty should be based on a hypothetical, arms-length negotiation that takes place *at the time the SSO is setting the standard*.[694]

---

[692] Transcript of Proceedings (Volume 10) at 2047:19–25, FTC v. Qualcomm Inc., No. 5:17-cv-00220-LHK (N.D. Cal. Jan. 28, 2019) (Testimony of Carl Shapiro).

[693] Transcript of Proceedings (Volume 6) at 1213:5–1214:5, FTC v. Qualcomm Inc., No. 5:17-cv-00220-LHK (N.D. Cal. Jan. 15, 2019) (Testimony of Carl Shapiro).

[694] Lemley & Shapiro, *A Simple Approach to Setting Reasonable Royalties for Standard-Essential Patents*, *supra* note 118, at 1147 (footnote omitted) (emphasis added).

Thus, to justify his testimony in *FTC v. Qualcomm* that Qualcomm's royalty for its portfolio of cellular SEPs should have decreased over time, Professor Shapiro appeared to retreat from the opinion that he had expressed in his 2013 article with Professor Lemley that every implementer should obtain the *same* royalty irrespective of the time at which it began selling the standard-compliant product.

c. The Inherent Fallacy of Professor Shapiro's Testimony That a FRAND Royalty Must Decline Over Time

Apart from evidently contradicting his 2013 article with Professor Lemley, Professor Shapiro's testimony that Qualcomm's royalties for its cellular SEPs exceeded FRAND because they did not decrease over time was wrong for at least two reasons.

First, whether a portfolio royalty for cellular SEPs shall decrease over time will depend on the specific circumstances of the case. The royalty might decrease if the cellular SEPs that are included in the portfolio expire. Yet, the SEP holder might add new cellular SEPs to the license portfolio, such that the royalty remains constant or even increases over time. The SEP holder could also add non-cellular SEPs and non-SEPs to the portfolio over time, which could further increase the portfolio royalty. Therefore, whether a royalty for a cellular SEP portfolio should decrease, increase, or remain constant is a question of fact that can be answered only by examining the specific changes to a given portfolio. Professor Shapiro was thus incorrect when he testified that as a general proposition a FRAND royalty for an SEP portfolio could only decline over time as cellular SEPs expire, for he ignored that a FRAND royalty for an SEP portfolio could increase over time as new cellular SEPs accrue to the licensor's portfolio.

Second, Professor Shapiro did not give testimony on any economic analysis of the changes to Qualcomm's cellular SEP portfolio to support his conclusion that Qualcomm's royalty for that portfolio should have decreased over time. He did not give testimony on any analysis of how Qualcomm's cellular SEP portfolio changed over time. He did not give testimony on how many of Qualcomm's cellular SEPs had expired and how many new cellular SEPs Qualcomm had added to its portfolio. He did not give testimony on the value of any of Qualcomm's cellular SEPs, let alone the value of its non-cellular SEPs and its non-SEPs. Instead, Professor Shapiro appeared to base his testimony on the arbitrary assumption that a FRAND royalty for a cellular SEP portfolio *must* decrease over time.

d. Summation on Professor Shapiro's Definition of a FRAND Royalty

The definition of a FRAND royalty that Professor Shapiro adopted in his prior writings would support the conclusion that Qualcomm's royalties for its cellular SEPs were FRAND. Yet, in his trial testimony in *FTC v. Qualcomm*, Professor Shapiro backed away from his own definition of a FRAND royalty by testifying that Qualcomm's early license agreements were too old to provide reliable evidence of a FRAND royalty. He even testified that evidence that Qualcomm's royalties had remained constant over time supported his conclusion that those royalties necessarily exceeded the FRAND range, because certain of Qualcomm's cellular SEPs had expired. Yet, Professor Shapiro's testimony conspicuously did not examine whether the growth of Qualcomm's patent portfolio resulting from the addition of cellular SEPs, non-cellular SEPs, and non-SEPs offset any diminution in the value of that portfolio by virtue of the expiration of Qualcomm's older cellular SEPs.

C. Professor Shapiro's Incorrect Conclusions About Qualcomm's Alleged Modem "Tax" That Supposedly Resulted from Qualcomm's Alleged Royalty "Surcharge"

As we have seen, the first fallacy of Professor Shapiro's theoretical bargaining model was that it failed to prove that Qualcomm's royalties for an exhaustive license to its portfolio of cellular SEPs exceeded the ceiling on the range of FRAND royalties. He presented no evidence to support his conjecture that there existed a "surcharge" on Qualcomm's royalty for an exhaustive license to its portfolio of cellular SEPs. He merely asserted that proposition as though it were a fact.

The second fallacy of Professor Shapiro's bargaining model concerned his conclusions about the "tax" on the "all-in price" of modems that supposedly resulted from Qualcomm's alleged royalty "surcharge." Suppose for sake of argument (but contrary to any evidence that Professor Shapiro provided in his testimony) that Qualcomm's royalties for an exhaustive license to its portfolio of cellular SEPs did exceed the ceiling on the range of FRAND royalties. It still would not follow, as Professor Shapiro testified, that those royalties would have harmed competition. His explanation for how such harm would have arisen was illogical and contradicted by his own testimony.

1. Invoking the Nomenclature of Public Finance to Justify Evading the Cost of Consuming a Necessary Input or Factor of Production

In *FTC v. Qualcomm*, Mr. James of the FTC tendered, and Judge Koh certified without objection, Professor Shapiro "as an expert in the field of industrial organization economics and antitrust economics"—but Mr. James did *not* tender Professor Shapiro as an expert in the field of public finance.[695] Professor Shapiro's expert report and trial testimony in *FTC v. Qualcomm* introduced terms of art uncommon to antitrust analysis in support of the FTC's novel theory of liability that Qualcomm's "unreasonably high" royalty for an exhaustive license to its cellular SEPs included a "surcharge" that gave rise to a modem "tax," which was supposedly anticompetitive.

These buzzwords "pad and bedazzle," to borrow a phrase from Judge Posner, but "if one stripped them away one would lay bare a slim and unimpressive substance, the literary counterpart to a shaven Persian cat."[696] Both Professor Shapiro and (as we will see shortly) the FTC were using the terminology of public finance to imply mistakenly that that distinct field of economics was the provenance of the FTC's novel theory of antitrust liability.

2. *Professor Shapiro's Mistaken Tax Analogy*

When Professor Shapiro spoke of the "incidence" of the "tax," he invoked a term of art from public finance,[697] a field in economics distinct from industrial organization and, incidentally, not a specialty that Professor Shapiro claimed when he explained why he considered himself qualified to give expert testimony in *FTC v. Qualcomm*.[698] The incidence or "burden" of a tax answers the question, who ultimately bears the cost of the tax?[699] For example, is a corporate income tax borne by one of the factors of production (such as capital)?[700] In *Fulton Corp. v. Faulkner*, the Supreme Court observed that "[t]he actual incidence of a tax may depend on elasticities of supply and demand, the ability of producers and consumers to substitute one product for another, the structure of the relevant market, the timeframe over which the tax is imposed and evaluated, and so on."[701] Yet, the Court also emphasized

---

[695] Transcript of Proceedings (Volume 6) at 1118:19–21, FTC v. Qualcomm Inc., No. 5:17-cv-00220-LHK (N.D. Cal. Jan. 15, 2019) (Testimony of Carl Shapiro); *see also id.* at 1118:22–24 ("Mr. Van Nest: No objection, Your Honor. The Court: All right. So certified. Go ahead, please.").

[696] Richard A. Posner, *The Constitution as Mirror: Tribe's Constitutional Choices*, 84 MICH. L. REV. 551, 567 (1986) (reviewing LAURENCE H. TRIBE, CONSTITUTIONAL CHOICES (Harvard Univ. Press 1985)).

[697] *See, e.g.*, HARVEY S. ROSEN, PUBLIC FINANCE 274 (Mc-Graw Hill 7th ed. 2005).

[698] *See* Initial Expert Report of Carl Shapiro in *FTC v. Qualcomm*, *supra* note 115, at 2; Transcript of Proceedings (Volume 6) at 1117:5–1118:23, FTC v. Qualcomm Inc., No. 5:17-cv-00220-LHK (N.D. Cal. Jan. 15, 2019) (Testimony of Carl Shapiro).

[699] *See, e.g.*, John B. Shoven, *Tax Incidence, in* 4 THE NEW PALGRAVE: A DICTIONARY OF ECONOMICS, *supra* note 265, at 609, 609 ("Tax incidence analysis is the study of the effects of a particular tax or a tax system on the distribution of economic welfare. The key question is who actually bears the burden of the resources transferred to the government by the tax."); ROSEN, PUBLIC FINANCE, *supra* note 697, at 274 ("The statutory incidence of a tax indicates who is legally responsible for the tax. . . . Because prices may change in response to the tax, knowledge of statutory incidence tells us *essentially nothing* about who really pays the tax. In contrast, the economic incidence of a tax is the change in the distribution of private real income induced by a tax. . . . [T]he forces that determine the extent to which statutory and economic incidence differ [denote] the amount of tax shifting.") (boldface suppressed) (emphasis in original).

[700] *See* Arnold C. Harberger, *The Incidence of the Corporation Income Tax*, 70 J. POL. ECON. 215 (1962).

[701] 516 U.S. 325, 341 (1996) (citing Commonwealth Edison Co. v. Montana, 453 U.S. 609, 619 n.8 (1981)).

that "'courts as institutions are poorly equipped to evaluate with precision the relative burdens of various methods of taxation.'"[702]

Professor Shapiro argued, on the basis of tax incidence theory, that it made no difference whether a "tax" on the "all-in price" of a modem supposedly arising from Qualcomm's royalty "surcharge" was imposed at the component level or the device level, as that cost would still be passed on to the device.[703] The incidence of his conjectured "tax" was the mobile device, he argued. As we shall see in Part V, Judge Koh embraced Professor Shapiro's "tax" theory, even though she did not cite any of his testimony. Instead, she cited page 156 of the seventh edition of *Principles of Microeconomics*, an undergraduate textbook by Professor Gregory Mankiw of Harvard University, published in 2014.[704] Yet, even then, the cited text did not support her conclusions. Quoting Professor Mankiw, Judge Koh found that Qualcomm's supposed modem "tax" (resulting from the alleged royalty "surcharge") "'places a wedge between the price that buyers pay and the price that sellers receive,' and demand for such transactions decreases."[705] "Rivals see lower sales volumes and lower margins," Judge Koh added, no longer quoting Professor Mankiw, "and consumers see less advanced features as competition decreases."[706]

To understand the fallacies of Judge Koh's findings of fact and conclusions of law concerning the "tax" analogy, we should start by scrutinizing what Professor Mankiw actually wrote on page 156 of the seventh edition of his textbook *Principles of Microeconomics*: "When a tax is levied on buyers, the demand curve shifts downward by the size of the tax; when it is levied on sellers, the supply curve shifts upward by that amount. In either case, when the tax is enacted, the price paid by buyers rises, and the price received by sellers falls."[707] Figure 5 replicates the diagram that accompanies this discussion on page 156 in Professor Mankiw's textbook.

Figure 5 shows that, when the government taxes a good, the quantity of the good demanded (and sold) falls. Thus, the size of the market for the good shrinks. Yet, as we shall see, Professor Mankiw's analysis offers no insights for examining the effects that the royalties for an exhaustive license to Qualcomm's cellular SEPs have on the prices of, and demand for, its rivals' modems.

---

[702] *Id.* at 342 (quoting Minneapolis Star & Tribune Co. v. Minn. Comm'r of Revenue, 460 U.S. 575, 589 (1983)).

[703] Transcript of Proceedings (Volume 6) at 1137:18–1138:13, FTC v. Qualcomm Inc., No. 5:17-cv-00220-LHK (N.D. Cal. Jan. 15, 2019) (Testimony of Carl Shapiro).

[704] FTC v. Qualcomm Inc., 411 F. Supp. 3d 658, 792 (N.D. Cal. 2019) (citing N. GREGORY MANKIW, PRINCIPLES OF MICROECONOMICS 156 (Cengage Learning 7th ed. 2014)).

[705] *Id.* (quoting MANKIW, PRINCIPLES OF MICROECONOMICS, *supra* note 704, at 156).

[706] *Id.*

[707] MANKIW, PRINCIPLES OF MICROECONOMICS, *supra* note 704, at 156.

Figure 5. Professor Mankiw's Exposition of the Effects
of a Tax on Page 156 of His Undergraduate
Microeconomics Textbook

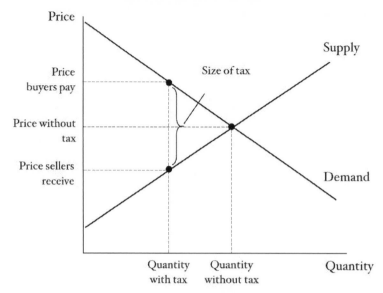

Source: Mankiw, Principles of Microeconomics, *supra* note 704, at 156 fig.8-1.

3. The Supposed "Wedge" Was Incompatible with the Monopolistic Market That the FTC Alleged Existed

Professor Mankiw's explanation of the "wedge" assumes a perfectly competitive market, which is incompatible with the monopolistic market that the FTC alleged, that Professor Shapiro testified existed, and that Judge Koh found as a matter of fact did exist. That distinction between perfect competition and monopoly is substantial. In a monopolistic market, there is no traditional supply curve, as the same textbook by Professor Mankiw later explains on page 308: "a monopoly does not have a supply curve. . . . [W]e never talk about a monopoly's supply curve."[708]

Consequently, Judge Koh's citation of and reliance on Professor Mankiw's discussion of the "wedge," bounded by the supply curve and the demand curve, was nonsensical. Judge Koh's misapplication of Professor Mankiw's discussion on page 156 of the seventh edition of his undergraduate microeconomics textbook reveals that she did not recognize the fallacy of Professor Shapiro's trope of Qualcomm's supposed royalty "surcharge" on an exhaustive license for Qualcomm's cellular SEPs and the supposedly resulting "tax" on the "all-in price" of a rival's sale of its modem to an OEM.

---

[708] *Id.* at 308.

4. *What Was the Probative Value of Professor Shapiro's Testimony on the Supposed Modem "Tax" That He Characterized as a "Wedge"?*

Professor Shapiro's testimony about a "tax" on the "all-in price" of a rival modem manufacturer's sale of a modem to an OEM was needlessly complicated and obscure (particularly in light of the fact that all of the intellectual machinery that he trundled out was then never used to generate an empirical estimate of anything). In the true evidentiary sense, the probative value of this testimony by Professor Shapiro was "substantially outweighed by a danger of . . . confusing the issues."[709] By invoking the nomenclature of public finance, Professor Shapiro gave testimony that might have appeared to Judge Koh to rest on greater intellectual rigor than it did.

We can divide Professor Shapiro's claim of a "tax" on the "all-in price" of a transaction into two different scenarios.

a. *The Supposed "Wedge" Arising from an OEM's Purchase of a Rival's Modem*

In the first scenario, Professor Shapiro cast the OEM as the buyer, the rival modem manufacturer as the seller, and Qualcomm as the analogue to the government tax collector taking what Judge Koh called the "wedge" (which, according to Professor Shapiro, is a modem "tax" that precisely equaled the amount of Qualcomm's royalty "surcharge"). So, in this first scenario, Professor Shapiro envisioned a three-party transaction. When the transaction is characterized as occurring between an OEM and a modem manufacturer, the tax analogy is uninformative: the counterparties to that transaction do not pay the "tax" to a government tax collector. Instead, the "tax" is paid to the supplier of a complementary input—namely, the owner of the cellular SEPs that read on the modem and the mobile device.

If the FTC has not proven by a preponderance of the evidence that the royalty for an exhaustive license to Qualcomm's cellular SEPs exceeds the ceiling on the range of FRAND royalties, then this narrative of course collapses, as Mr. Van Nest established during his devastating cross examination of Professor Shapiro. In that case, the amount of Qualcomm's royalty "surcharge" is zero. Consequently, the amount of the "tax" on the "all-in price" of a modem is also necessarily zero. The "wedge" in that case does not exist. Someone searching for it is like the blind man in a dark room looking for a black cat that is not there.[710]

---

[709] FED. R. EVID. 403.

[710] WILLIAM JAMES, SOME PROBLEMS OF PHILOSOPHY: A BEGINNING OF AN INTRODUCTION TO PHILOSOPHY 9 (Longmans, Green & Co. 1911). Some trace the black cat to Charles Darwin or Confucius or the English jurist Lord Bowen.

If one accepts for sake of argument (but contrary to fact) that the FTC managed to prove by a preponderance of the evidence that Qualcomm's supposed royalty "surcharge" on an exhaustive license to its portfolio of cellular SEPs gave rise to a "tax" on the "all-in price" that OEMs paid for rivals' modems, it was still specious to characterize that royalty "surcharge" and modem "tax" as a "wedge," because the same supposed "tax" applied to *all* modem purchases, including purchases of Qualcomm's modems. That is, invocation of the "wedge" jargon was specious because the supposed "tax" was chip-agnostic. The "tax" would dampen demand for Qualcomm's own modems at the same time that it dampened demand for the modems manufactured by Qualcomm's rivals. That is the nature of complementarity of demand. In Berkeley, a "surcharge" on the price of milk is a "tax" on the espresso used to make a cappuccino in *any* latte bar along Telegraph Avenue.

Does an offhand citation to an introductory microeconomics textbook by a Harvard professor suffice to prove the existence of a specific economic fact in a particular case? It was the FTC's burden of production to put on evidence, and then the agency's burden to prove by a preponderance of the evidence, that the supposed modem "tax" exceeded zero and gave rise to a "wedge" that produced an anticompetitive effect in the FTC's two relevant markets for modems. So, even if the FTC had proved the economic conjecture that the supposed modem "tax" produced a "wedge," it was still the FTC's burden to establish by a preponderance of the evidence that, in the counterfactual conditional universe in which Qualcomm's supposed modem "tax" exceeded zero, output of rivals' modems would have been greater, smartphone prices would have been lower, smartphone performance would been superior, or some other salubrious effect of competition would exist that was necessarily forgone in the real world as a direct result of the "wedge."

Professor Shapiro's conjectural testimony was incapable of proving the existence of the supposed "wedge" in *FTC v. Qualcomm*. Perhaps for that reason Judge Koh never mentioned his testimony in her findings of fact and conclusions of law. Of course we will never know for sure because her findings of fact and conclusions of law were silent on the question. Just as they were silent on the question of how she could have concluded that the remaining evidence in the record—*other than Professor Shapiro's testimony*—was weighty enough to be preponderant proof that the "wedge" existed.

> *b. Did Qualcomm's Exhaustive Licensing of Its Cellular SEPs to OEMs Give Rise to a "Wedge"?*

The second possible scenario for a transaction is one that Professor Shapiro did not explicitly discuss in his testimony. This time, the transaction simply consists of Qualcomm's exhaustive licensing of its cellular SEPs to the OEM. For purposes of Figure 5, Qualcomm is the seller, and the OEM is the buyer.

Professor Shapiro testified on direct examination during the FTC's case-in-chief that "there's a cost that those transaction parties have to pay, you know, much like if the government has a tax, the buyer and seller have to—together, between them, they have to write a check to the government."[711] Of course Qualcomm and the OEM did *not* "have to write a check to the government" to complete their patent-licensing transaction, and the government tax collector therefore did *not* capture any "wedge" between what the OEM paid and what Qualcomm received for an exhaustive license to Qualcomm's cellular SEPs. Thus, to the extent that Professor Shapiro's trial testimony erroneously inserted the government as a tax collector between Qualcomm and the OEM, that testimony was specious: like the black cat, the "tax" collector was nonexistent, such that the "wedge" also was nonexistent.

In this second scenario there is no third party who is the analogue to the imaginary government tax collector. The "all-in price" of an exhaustive license to Qualcomm's cellular SEPs is simply the royalty itself. The "wedge" in this scenario never existed in the first place. It was a phantasm.

c.   Does the "Tax" Jargon Help or Confuse the Fact Finder's Analysis of the Economics of the Demand for Two Complementary Inputs?

Consider a different example, akin to the first scenario, in which a downstream firm assembles a product consisting of two complementary inputs. The owner of a sports bar buys a big screen television so that his patrons, who are avid soccer fans, can watch the World Cup while they drink alcoholic beverages.

The bar owner also needs to subscribe to a sports package that includes the World Cup, which is exclusively offered by a direct broadcast satellite (DBS) provider. Is it helpful or merely confusing for an economist to call the price of the bar owner's subscription to the World Cup sports package a "tax" on his purchase of the big screen television? Does this jargon from public finance add anything to our understanding of the transaction? Does the bar owner seriously expect Target to reduce the price of a big screen television if he explains to the sales clerk that the DBS provider is charging an "unreasonably high" price for World Cup programming, which raises the bar owner's "all-in price" of supplying World Cup programming to his customers, which in turn reduces his expected gains from trade from a transaction with Target for the sale of a big screen television? Do we, the economist's

---

[711] Transcript of Proceedings (Volume 6) at 1137:22–1138:1, FTC v. Qualcomm Inc., No. 5:17-cv-00220-LHK (N.D. Cal. Jan. 15, 2019) (Testimony of Carl Shapiro).

nontechnical audience hearing this narrative, find it the least bit intuitive and illuminating? In the strict evidentiary sense, is this narrative helpful?

Why not simply drop the extraneous nomenclature and say that the big screen television and a satellite subscription to the World Cup programming are complements for assembling a thirsty audience in a sports bar? The bar owner's demand for a big screen television increases as the price of a satellite sports subscription to the World Cup falls, because they are complements in his effort to attract bar customers.

Suppose that an illicit decoder can enable one to receive satellite sports programming without paying for a subscription.[712] To the bar owner using an illicit decoder, the "all-in price" of offering his patrons World Cup programming would decline in magnitude and be the sum of (1) the one-time cost of the decoder and the related hardware (the satellite dish, the wiring, the labor for installation, and so forth), and (2) the price of a big screen television. The bar owner's demand for a big screen television would increase, because the supplier of World Cup programming would no longer be "taxing" the bar owner's "all-in price" of providing World Cup games to his clientele while they consumed alcoholic beverages.

Indeed, to borrow Professor Shapiro's terminology, one might say that the World Cup programming was now being supplied at an "unreasonably *low*" price. Indeed, the price received by the DBS provider for its World Cup programming would be zero whenever a consumer received the satellite transmissions with an illicit decoder.[713] So, instead of there being a royalty "surcharge" on the price of viewing the World Cup at the sports bar, there would be a royalty "credit." That royalty "credit" then would impose a negative "tax" on the "all-in price" of the bar owner's offering of World Cup programming to his clientele. A negative tax is called a "subsidy."

How does this vignette relate to Qualcomm, OEMs, and modem manufacturers? The World Cup programming is Qualcomm's portfolio of cellular SEPs. The decoder box is the unlicensed use of that portfolio. The big screen television, without any content, is the bare modem. The definition of "unreasonably low" is "below the lower bound of the FRAND range." And the subsidy is the extent to which the royalty paid for an exhaustive license

---

[712] My example is not so hypothetical. I was once an expert economic witness for América Móvil in an antitrust case in Puerto Rico that alleged monopolization of the market for multichannel video programming distribution in San Juan. Throughout San Juan, one could readily observe handbills and signs advertising illicit decoder boxes to acquire the multichannel video content of the DBS provider. Thus, one question relevant to market definition and market power was whether the relatively widespread misappropriation of downlinks of satellite programming constrained the pricing of the cable television operator serving San Juan. The district court never reached the question because the First Circuit affirmed dismissal on *Noerr-Pennington* grounds. Puerto Rico Tel. Co. v. San Juan Cable LLC, 874 F.3d 767 (1st Cir. 2017).

[713] For simplicity, I set to one side whether the DBS provider would earn some incrementally higher advertising revenue because his audience size would increase by the number of free riders using illicit decoder boxes.

to Qualcomm's cellular SEPs (by the OEM and the modem manufacturer jointly, in Professor Shapiro's schema) falls below the lower bound of the FRAND range.

Professor Shapiro might try to draw distinctions between the increment of royalties that is "reasonable" and the increment that is "unreasonably high." But characterizing the price of a complement as a "tax" does not turn on such an exercise of line drawing. That overlay of "reasonableness" is completely *ad hoc*. Either the cost that is part of the "all-in price" is the price of a complement, or it is a payment to a third party for some obligation having no connection to the creation of the end product (which is to say, the cost is purely a tax in the colloquial sense of the word as well as the economic sense or legal sense). That is true whether the "all-in" product being examined is a functioning modem for a smartphone, or the World Cup being displayed on a big screen television in a sports bar.

> d. *Did Professor Shapiro's Novel "Tax" Theory Rely on the Seventh Edition of Professor Mankiw's Undergraduate Microeconomics Textbook?*

Did Professor Shapiro cite page 156 of the seventh edition of Professor Mankiw's undergraduate microeconomics textbook? On January 28, 2019, Professor Shapiro testified on direct examination in support of the FTC's rebuttal case:

> Q. Professor Nevo testified that, quote, "if we're worried about raising rivals' costs, it seems counterintuitive to me that we want to solve that by saying we want to have licensing directly to rivals," unquote.
>
> A. This is not—you have the wrong thing up here. Right.
>
> Q. How do you respond to the testimony regarding licensing directly to rivals?
>
> A. So, Your Honor, when I was here last time, I explained how a royalty surcharge acts as a tax on—raises rivals' costs because it is a burden on the transactions between the rival and the OEM and cuts into the gains from trade. That analysis is correct. Whether the royalty surcharge is paid to Qualcomm by the OEM or the rival is immaterial. That's a standard textbook result in economics. *I cited the textbook in my report.* I think I mentioned this last time. *That is just not a matter of debate, it's a matter of economics.*[714]

---

[714] Transcript of Proceedings (Volume 10) at 2056:15–2057:7, FTC v. Qualcomm Inc., No. 5:17-cv-00220-LHK (N.D. Cal. Jan. 28, 2019) (Testimony of Carl Shapiro) (emphasis added).

According to Professor Shapiro, his "tax" theory was correct and could not be criticized, because his theory bore the imposing pedigree of an economic textbook.

Which "standard textbook"? Neither of Professor Shapiro's expert reports had been moved into evidence, and he never identified at trial the textbook that was the basis for this portion of his sworn trial testimony. And it apparently was not obvious, at least to Judge Koh, how Professor Shapiro's "tax" theory could be inferred from basic economic principles, because the single citation to the seventh edition of Professor Mankiw's microeconomics textbook in Judge Koh's findings of fact and conclusions of law in *FTC v. Qualcomm* was erroneous. Professor Shapiro's vague references to the "textbook" from which his "tax" theory supposedly descended were reminiscent of how proponents of the patent-holdup conjecture invoked Williamson's generalized holdup theory as the provenance of their conjecture.[715]

It is telling that Professor Shapiro elsewhere admitted that, at its core, his testimony concerning the effect of Qualcomm's supposed royalty "surcharge" and modem "tax" on rival modem manufacturers "isn't even economics."[716] "This is just arithmetic," he testified.[717]

5. Patent Royalties and Pigouvian Taxes

It is useful to compare Professor Shapiro's and Judge Koh's specious modem "tax" to a true example of a Pigouvian tax, such as an emissions charge imposed on each unit of output of a product that creates pollution in its manufacture or use.[718]

---

[715] See *supra* notes 645–663 and accompanying text; Sidak, *Is Patent Holdup a Hoax?*, *supra* note 118, at 407–11.

[716] Transcript of Proceedings (Volume 10) at 2059:14–15, FTC v. Qualcomm Inc., No. 5:17-cv-00220-LHK (N.D. Cal. Jan. 28, 2019) (Testimony of Carl Shapiro).

[717] *Id.* at 2059:14; *see also id.* at 2059:6–18 ("But what's the effect on Qualcomm? The effect on Qualcomm is no change. Their all-in price has not changed. All we've done is raised the royalty part by $10 and reduce the chip part by $10. So the all-in price is the same. So Qualcomm can neutralize this with no harm to their bottom line at all, their margin basically, when you look at the all-in price, while Intel had to take the full hit of the royalty surcharge to neutralize. This is just arithmetic, by the way. This isn't even economics. So just by arithmetic you can see that the effect of the royalty surcharge is not symmetric as between Intel and Qualcomm in my example.").

[718] For a nontechnical overview of Pigouvian taxes, see Jonathan S. Masur & Eric A. Posner, *Toward a Pigouvian State*, 164 U. Pa. L. Rev. 93, 94–95 (2015) ("According to most economists, the optimal form of regulation of firms that produce negative externalities is a tax known as a Pigouvian tax, named after the English economist, Arthur Pigou. A Pigouvian tax is a tax equal to the harm that the firm imposes on third parties. For example, if a manufacturer pollutes, and the pollution causes a harm of $100 per unit of pollution to people who live in the area, then the firm should pay a tax of $100 per unit of pollution. This ensures that the manufacturer pollutes only if the value of the pollution-generating activities exceeds the harm, such that the social value of those activities is positive.") (citing Agnar Sandmo, *Direct Versus Indirect Pigouvian Taxation*, 7 Eur. Econ. Rev. 337 (1976)).

a.   A Pigouvian Tax on Air Pollutants

Suppose that a factory cannot produce a mobile handset without emitting some air pollutants. Suppose that the government taxes each handset sold to reflect its incremental responsibility for the social cost of the resulting air pollution. In the words of the textbook by Professor Harvey Rosen, a public finance scholar at Princeton University and (like Professor Mankiw) a former chairman of the President's Council of Economic Advisers, a Pigouvian tax would be "a tax levied on each unit of a polluter's output in an amount just equal to the marginal damage it inflicts *at the efficient level of output*."[719] The seventh edition of the microeconomics textbook by Professor Mankiw that Judge Koh cited provides at page 156 a helpful visualization of how a tax, including a Pigouvian tax, affects the demand for the taxed product or service.

A Pigouvian tax on the OEM's pollution would require the OEM to internalize the social cost created by its consumption of clear air.[720] If the OEM did not need to pay this pollution tax, it could pay a lower "all-in price" for the totality of the inputs required to make a handset. To the extent that the OEM passed on that cost decrease to consumers, the OEM would then experience higher demand for, and a higher output of, its handsets. Consumers of smartphones would benefit from the higher output and lower price. In addition, more free cash flow would accrue, which the OEM perhaps could devote to improving its products through greater investment in R&D.

All that would stand in the way of these salutary effects would be the OEM's legal obligation in this example to pay for fouling the air. The OEM is not legally entitled to pollute the air and harm third parties with impunity. Consequently, the claim of static efficiency gains from lower prices and higher sales of handsets (as well as the claims of dynamic efficiency gains from supposedly higher investment in R&D by OEMs that are able to generate marginally greater free cash flow) is at least exaggerated if not illusory, because it comes at the cost of harming others by virtue of the OEM's marginal degradation of the environment.

---

[719] ROSEN, PUBLIC FINANCE, *supra* note 697, at 92 (emphasis in original).
[720] Masur and Posner present the standard rationale for the Pigouvian tax:

> The Pigouvian tax is a tax equal to the amount of money necessary to ensure that the firm produces the socially optimal number of widgets. If the factory [emitting pollutants] must pay a tax equal to the harm that each unit of production causes to the neighbors, then the factory will be forced to take into account the social cost. The harm to the neighbors now plays a role in the factory's profit maximization. To maximize profits, the firm produces up until the marginal benefit equals the marginal cost to the factory plus the social cost to the neighbors. Thus, the factory produces fewer widgets, the number equal to the socially optimal number.

Masur & Posner, *Toward a Pigouvian State*, *supra* note 718, at 101.

b.   Is a Royalty for an Exhaustive License to Qualcomm's Cellular SEPs a "Tax"?

A royalty for an exhaustive license to Qualcomm's portfolio of cellular SEPs is not a "tax" on the OEM's products, let alone a "tax" on the products of rival modem manufacturers. Whether it is paid by the OEM or by the modem manufacturer, what Professor Shapiro (and Judge Koh and the FTC) call a "tax" is simply the wage paid to the owner of intellectual property consumed in the production and use of a smartphone.[721] One can view that intellectual property either as an input (along with the physical components required to manufacture the substrate of the modem) or as a factor of production (like capital or labor—intellectual property being characterized in this sense as a kind of capital stock of inventive knowledge). Under either characterization, the wage paid to intellectual property is no more a "tax" than are the fabrication costs necessary for a contract manufacturer to assemble a single handset in China or the transportation costs necessary to fly that finished handset to the United States by cargo jet.

This "tax" nomenclature of Professor Shapiro (and Judge Koh and the FTC) exemplifies the political use of the English language: who likes to pay a tax?[722] The purpose of Qualcomm's alleged "tax" on the "all-in price" of a modem is of course not to raise general revenues for the government, which would be the case of a real-world lump-sum tax on a product or an *ad valorem* tax (such as an excise tax or a value-added tax (VAT)). Rather, the "tax" on the "all-in price" of a modem that Professor Shapiro described in his sworn testimony would compensate Qualcomm specifically for the consumption of a privately owned resource—namely, Qualcomm's portfolio of cellular SEPs. With equal force, manufacturers of smartphones might call the salaries that they must pay to their engineers in Silicon Valley a noxious "tax." *That* of course was a different lawsuit before Judge Koh, which certain votaries of *FTC v. Qualcomm* might prefer to forget.[723]

---

[721] *Cf.* Jonathan M. Barnett, *The "License as Tax" Fallacy* 3 (USC Gould Sch. of Law Ctr. for Law and Social Sci., Legal Studies Research Papers Series No. 19-35, July 3, 2020), https://papers.ssrn.com/sol3/papers.cfm?abstract_id=3503148 ("While this framework [that an IP license operates as a 'tax'] facilitates the application of standard monopoly pricing models to the IP context, it overstates the market power typically exerted by IP licensors and mischaracterizes the typical function of IP licenses in content and technology markets. More specifically, this framework overlooks the fact that IP licenses generally increase, rather than deplete, economic surplus by overcoming transactional hazards that can otherwise preclude efficient transactions among entities that hold complementary IP and non-IP assets.").

[722] *See* George Orwell, *Politics and the English Language*, 13 Horizon 252 (1946), *reprinted in* The Orwell Reader: Fiction, Essays, and Reportage 355 (Harcourt 1956).

[723] *See* Order Granting Plaintiffs' Motion for Final Approval of Class Action Settlement with Defendants Adobe Systems Incorporated, Apple Inc., Google Inc., and Intel Corporation, *In re* High-Tech Employee Antitrust Litig., No. 11-cv-02509-LHK (N.D. Cal. Sept. 2, 2015) (Koh, J.) (reporting that Apple and Intel were among the companies accused of unlawfully agreeing not to recruit each other's employees in violation of the Sherman Act).

    c.   Did the Supposed Modem "Tax" Reduce Rivals' Modem Sales to OEMs?

In addition, Judge Koh made an unjustified factual leap when she found that the "tax" on the "all-in price" of a modem reduced sales of modems to OEMs by Qualcomm's rivals.[724] The passage from page 156 of the seventh edition of Professor Mankiw's microeconomics textbook, upon which Judge Koh relied in her findings of fact and conclusions of law, does not address how a tax affects the sales or revenue of *competing* products. Rather, the passage solely addresses the situation in which *only* the taxed product is purchased, and its purchaser does not receive another product as a part of that transaction.

    Recall that there is no "wedge" between the royalty that an OEM pays for an exhaustive license to Qualcomm's portfolio of cellular SEPs and the royalty that Qualcomm receives. Nor is there any "wedge" between the price that an OEM pays for a modem and the payment that the manufacturer of that modem receives. Except to the extent that an excise tax of general applicability is already collected by the government on such transactions, in neither instance does the government (or any other third party) capture, by its imposition of a royalty "surcharge" and a "tax" on the "all-in price" of a modem, some portion of the consideration exchanged.

    Nevertheless, to the extent that it was proper to characterize Qualcomm's supposed royalty "surcharge" for an exhaustive license to its portfolio of cellular SEPs as a "tax" on the "all-in price" of rivals' modems that constituted a "wedge," that characterization was specious because the supposed modem "tax" was chip-agnostic. To the contrary, the Ninth Circuit recognized that "Qualcomm's royalties are 'chip-supplier neutral' because Qualcomm collects them from *all* OEMs that license its patents, not just 'rivals' customers."[725] Put differently, Professor Mankiw's analysis on page 156 of the seventh edition of *Principles of Microeconomics* does not support as a matter of law or fact Judge Koh's erroneous conclusion that Qualcomm's modem "tax" reduces the sales or margins of rival modem manufacturers.

    6.   The FTC's Citation of Irrelevant Economic Authority

Repeatedly throughout its prosecution of *FTC v. Qualcomm* the FTC emphasized its mistaken economic analysis of a royalty "surcharge" on an exhaustive license for cellular SEPs that supposedly gave rise to a "tax" on the "all-in price" of a sale of a modem to an OEM. In its opposition to Qualcomm's motion to dismiss, the FTC contended, on May 12, 2017, that "[o]ne kind

---

[724] FTC v. Qualcomm Inc., 411 F. Supp. 3d 658, 762 (N.D. Cal. 2019).
[725] FTC v. Qualcomm Inc., No. 19-16122, 2020 WL 4591476, at *13 (9th Cir. Aug. 11, 2020) (emphasis in original) (quoting FTC Brief to the Ninth Circuit, *supra* note 286, at 77).

of unfavorable term that a monopolist may impose is a penalty or 'tax' that the monopolist's competitors or its customers must pay to the monopolist when they transact with one another."[726] In the footnote immediately following that sentence, the FTC cited pages 125 and 156 of the seventh edition of Professor Mankiw's microeconomics textbook for the proposition that, "[w]hether the tax is paid by a monopolist's rivals or by its customers makes no difference from either a legal or economic perspective."[727]

On December 6, 2018, in its pretrial proposed findings of fact and conclusions of law, the FTC again cited pages 125 and 156 of the seventh edition of Professor Mankiw's microeconomics textbook to support, in a more attenuated manner, the agency's contention that "[a] firm with market or monopoly power may impair the opportunities of competitors by imposing costs on the competitors' customers or by imposing costs directly on the competitors themselves."[728]

And in her closing argument at trial on January 29, 2019, Ms. Milici of the FTC repeated the agency's erroneous understanding of the seventh edition of Professor Mankiw's undergraduate microeconomics textbook: "The royalty surcharge operates as a tax, and that tax reduces what Qualcomm's rivals and their customers can gain by trading with one another. . . . [T]he tax reduces the gains from trade and makes rivals' chips less attractive."[729] Less attractive than what? A modem for which the OEM purchaser can avoid some or all of the costs of an exhaustive license to the cellular SEPs that are necessary components for the modem?

Why did the FTC represent to Judge Koh in multiple court documents that an irrelevant passage from the seventh edition of Professor Mankiw's undergraduate microeconomics textbook was authority legitimating the agency's novel theory that Qualcomm had violated the Sherman Act by supposedly charging a royalty "surcharge" on the exhaustive licensing of its cellular SEPs to OEMs, which in turn supposedly imposed a "tax" on the "all-in price" of a modem purchased by an OEM? One is compelled to ask why nobody spotted this erroneous and irrelevant citation to authority—not the agency's Bureau of Competition, not its Bureau of Economics, not its former commissioners who had authorized the filing of the complaint in *FTC v. Qualcomm*, not its subsequent commissioners who had failed to spot the agency's erroneous advocacy before Judge Koh and seek voluntary dismissal

---

[726] Federal Trade Commission's Opposition to Qualcomm's Motion to Dismiss (Redacted Version) at 9–10, FTC v. Qualcomm Inc., No. 5:17-cv-00220-LHK, 2017 WL 4678946 (N.D. Cal. May 12, 2017), ECF No. 140 [hereinafter FTC's Opposition to Qualcomm's Motion to Dismiss, 2017 WL 4678946] (citing MANKIW, PRINCIPLES OF MICROECONOMICS, *supra* note 704, at 125, 156).

[727] *Id.* at 10 n.6 (citing MANKIW, PRINCIPLES OF MICROECONOMICS, *supra* note 704, at 125, 156).

[728] FTC's Proposed Findings of Fact and Conclusions of Law, *supra* note 485, ¶ 35, at 62 (citing MANKIW, PRINCIPLES OF MICROECONOMICS, *supra* note 704, at 125, 156).

[729] Transcript of Proceedings (Volume 11) at 2127:18–20, 2127:23–24, FTC v. Qualcomm Inc., No. 5:17-cv-00220-LHK (N.D. Cal. Jan. 29, 2019) (closing argument of Jennifer Milici for the FTC).

of this specious claim before trial, and not the outside lawyers and economic experts whom the agency had engaged to support its case. Evidently, none of these persons, all working at taxpayer expense, had mastered undergraduate microeconomics enough to recognize that the FTC was pitching an incoherent theory of antitrust liability to Judge Koh.

Far from discerning that the FTC's royalty "surcharge" and modem "tax" theory of antitrust liability was bunk, Judge Koh embraced it and even cited in her findings of fact and conclusions of law the same page 156 of the seventh edition of Professor Mankiw's microeconomics textbook.[730]

D. Would a Royalty "Surcharge" and Modem "Tax" Harm Competition?

Suppose for sake of argument that one accepted Professor Shapiro's testimony that Qualcomm charged an "unreasonably high" royalty for an exhaustive license to its portfolio of cellular SEPs, and that that royalty had the effect of imposing a "tax" on the "all-in price" of modems. There still would be no basis to conclude that the alleged royalty "surcharge" harmed *competition* among modem manufacturers. A simple numerical example shows why Professor Shapiro's contention that his alleged royalty "surcharge" would reduce the quantity sold of non-Qualcomm modems was nonsensical.

Suppose that a reasonable royalty for Qualcomm's cellular SEP portfolio is $5 per handset (as Professor Shapiro assumed in his numerical example), but that Qualcomm uses its alleged monopoly power (over one or both of Professor Shapiro's two relevant product markets for modems) to coerce OEMs to pay a $9 per handset royalty instead. In this example, the royalty "surcharge" is equal to $4 per handset. An OEM must pay a reasonable royalty of $5 and the "surcharge" of $4, irrespective of whether it uses a Qualcomm modem or a non-Qualcomm modem to build a handset. In Professor Shapiro's view, that "surcharge" harmed competition among modem manufacturers because, when considering which modem to buy, OEMs considered that "all-in price."

But that reasoning is specious. Table 5 shows that the "all-in price" could not have disadvantaged Qualcomm's rivals.

Table 5 shows that the difference between the "all-in price" for a Qualcomm modem and the "all-in price" for a rival modem is merely the difference in the price of the *bare modems themselves*.

---

[730] FTC v. Qualcomm Inc., 411 F. Supp. 3d 658, 792 (N.D. Cal. 2019) (citing MANKIW, PRINCIPLES OF MICROECONOMICS, *supra* note 704, at 156).

Table 5. "All-In Price" Comparison

	"All-In Price" for Qualcomm Modems	"All-In Price" for Non-Qualcomm Modems
Bare Modem Price	$20	$20
Reasonable Royalty for Qualcomm's Cellular SEP Portfolio (Per Handset)	$5	$5
Qualcomm's Alleged "Surcharge" on Its Cellular SEP Portfolio (Per Handset)	$4	$4
Total	$29	$29

Because Qualcomm in fact imposed the same royalty "surcharge" on Qualcomm modems and non-Qualcomm modems, the "surcharge" could not have affected an OEM's selection, on the margin, of a particular brand of modem. An OEM will select the modem available for the lowest quality-adjusted price. (For simplicity, assume that all modems are comparable to Qualcomm's in terms of performance—a generous assumption in favor of Professor Shapiro and the FTC in light of the evidence to the contrary in the trial record.) Therefore, even if Qualcomm's licensing practice did impose a "tax" on the "all-in price" of a modem purchased by an OEM (which the economic evidence did not preponderantly establish), a royalty "surcharge" and a modem "tax" that were "chip-agnostic" could not distort competition. A chip-agnostic modem "tax" would be symmetrically applied to a Qualcomm modem and to a rival manufacturer's modem.

1.   The Omission of Any Analysis of the Doctrine of Patent Exhaustion

Professor Shapiro's testimony in *FTC v. Qualcomm* conspicuously ignored the doctrine of patent exhaustion. He objected to Qualcomm's refusal to offer exhaustive licenses to its cellular SEPs at the component level to rival modem manufacturers. We saw that Qualcomm's doing so would have fully exhausted it patent rights in its cellular SEPs (assuming for ease of exposition that those cellular SEPs were not also practiced outside the modem—that is, elsewhere in the handset or in the infrastructure of the cellular network).

If Qualcomm exhaustively licensed its cellular SEPs at the modem level, it obviously could not license them a second time at the handset level. So, Qualcomm would need to choose the more profitable level in the vertical chain of production at which to license its cellular SEPs, and then license its cellular SEPs *only* at the level, on an *exhaustive* basis. Professor Shapiro omitted from his testimony any mention that the magnitude of the royalty revenue for Qualcomm from licensing its cellular SEPs exhaustively at the modem level would be a small fraction of the royalty revenue that Qualcomm would receive from licensing those same patents exhaustively at the handset level.

Professor Shapiro seemed to imply that the difference between the two amounts of royalty, when computed on a per-handset basis, would equal what he called a "naked tax." A more descriptive name for that differential would be "the incremental returns to Qualcomm's unique business model from lawfully structuring its cellular SEP licenses and related commercial arrangements to mitigate the effects of patent exhaustion."

2.   *Was It Plausible That Modem Manufacturers Relied on Free Cash Flow from Operations to Fund Their Investments in R&D?*

As we shall see in Part XIV, it appeared to be an unresolved question of fact in *FTC v. Qualcomm* whether either Qualcomm or rival modem manufacturers (or both) could plausibly have relied on external sources of funds (rather than free cash flow from operations) to finance their respective R&D investments. Judge Koh did not resolve this economic question of fact, even though the *a priori* conjecture advanced by each party making that argument in favor of its own position was susceptible to empirical attempts at verification or refutation.

On the one hand, the FTC alleged,[731] Professor Shapiro testified,[732] and Judge Koh found[733] that one harm to the competitive process was that *rival* modem manufacturers were incapable of throwing off enough free cash flow

---

[731] *See* FTC Complaint, 2017 WL 242848, *supra* note 28, at 19 ("The incremental royalty that OEMs pay to Qualcomm operates as a 'tax' that raises OEMs' costs of using baseband processors supplied by Qualcomm's competitors, reduces demand for competitors' processors, and reduces the ability and incentive of competitors to invest and innovate."); *id.* at 20 ("Reduced sales and margins resulting from Qualcomm's tax diminish competitors' abilities and incentives to invest and innovate."); *id.* at 29 ("By raising OEMs' all-in costs of using competitors' baseband processors, Qualcomm's conduct has also diminished OEMs' demand for those processors, reduced competitors' sales and margins, and diminished competitors' ability and incentive to invest and innovate.").

[732] *See* Transcript of Proceedings (Volume 6) at 1122:3–12, FTC v. Qualcomm Inc., No. 5:17-cv-00220-LHK (N.D. Cal. Jan. 15, 2019) (Testimony of Carl Shapiro); *id.* at 1244:8–12.

[733] *See* FTC v. *Qualcomm*, 411 F. Supp. 3d at 798–99 ("Even when Qualcomm's licensing practices do not outright eliminate competition, Qualcomm can suppress rivals' sales such that rivals lack revenue to invest in research and development . . . . Reducing rivals' revenue to invest in research and development *gravely harms* rivals because producing modem chips requires very high fixed research and development costs. . . . Accordingly, to cover the costs of research and development, a modem chip supplier must generate a larger customer base.") (emphasis added); *id.* at 800 ("Thus, by suppressing rivals' sales and revenue to invest in research and development for new technology, Qualcomm *ensures that its rivals will lose repeatedly*. Those losses further suppress rivals' sales, and further suppress rivals' ability to fund research and development.") (emphasis added); *id.* at 737 ("Qualcomm's exclusive deals, which delayed Intel's ability to sell modem chips to Apple until September 2016, foreclosed Intel and other rivals from benefits including . . . a revenue boost critical to funding research and development and acquiring technology."); *id.* at 744 ("Qualcomm refused its rival MediaTek's 2008 request for a patent license, and would only enter an agreement that restricted MediaTek's customer base. Qualcomm's refusal suppressed MediaTek's revenues and prevented MediaTek from being able to fund research and development for future generations of modem chips.").

from operations to fund their R&D investment concerning modems. On the other hand, Qualcomm argued that its need to fund its R&D investments in developing fundamental cellular technologies justified the royalties that it collected from exhaustively licensing its cellular SEPs to OEMs.[734] The counterargument to both arguments was that Qualcomm (or its rivals) could have funded its R&D investments externally, through debt or equity raised in the capital markets.

Yet, Qualcomm and the FTC (on behalf of Intel and other rival modem manufacturers) could not necessarily make the free-cash-flow argument with equal plausibility. Consider the following question. As between Qualcomm and Intel (which was Qualcomm's principal rival in the provision of thin modems to Apple at the time of trial in *FTC v. Qualcomm*), which of the two companies more plausibly could have relied on external sources of capital, as opposed to free cash flow, to fund its respective R&D investments?

From testimony at trial, it was clear that Intel (and its outside management consultants at Bain) believed that Qualcomm's productivity of investment in R&D greatly surpassed that of rival modem manufacturers, including— presumably to the considerable embarrassment of its senior management— Intel.[735] If Qualcomm's productivity of R&D investment so fundamentally differed from that of Intel's, that observed difference might suggest that material questions of fact existed that could have provided a principled basis for giving greater credence to the free-cash-flow argument when applied to Qualcomm than when applied to Intel or other rival modem manufacturers.

Professor Shapiro did not appear to distinguish the relative need for or efficiency of internally funding R&D depending on the business model of a given modem manufacturer. And Judge Koh evidently did not even spot the

---

[734] *See* Qualcomm's Motion to Dismiss, 2017 WL 4678941, *supra* note 41, at 6 ("Because Qualcomm receives compensation for its patents exclusively through royalties rather than through the price of its chips, a finding of exhaustion or implied license would enable an unlicensed OEM to practice at least some of Qualcomm's SEPs and non-SEPs for free, and thereby harm Qualcomm's ability to earn a return on its R&D investments in developing cellular technologies.") (citations omitted); *id.* at 24 ("Qualcomm does not wish to facilitate infringement of its patents and jeopardize its ability to recover its extensive investments in R&D regarding fundamental cellular communication technologies.").

[735] Transcript of Proceedings (Volume 3) at 601:22–602:9, FTC v. Qualcomm Inc., No. 5:17-cv-00220-LHK (N.D. Cal. Jan. 8, 2019) (Testimony of Aichatou Evans (Chief Strategy Officer, Intel)) ("Q. . . . [Y]ou agreed at the time in 2015, Ms. Evans, with the statement that Intel and Qualcomm investment in mobile SoC has been on par, but Qualcomm product output is 2 to 3 times Intel; right? A. Yeah, I accepted this statement as fact given the—like the numbers, yes. Q. And that actually was a statement that you agreed with at the time, wasn't it? A. I agreed with the fact. Q. Okay. A. Yes."); *see also* Transcript of Proceedings (Volume 9) at 1842:25–1843:9, FTC v. Qualcomm Inc., No. 5:17-cv-00220-LHK (N.D. Cal. Jan. 25, 2019) (Testimony of Christopher Johnson (Bain)) ("Q. Mr. Johnson, what was Bain's conclusion regarding Intel's overall SoC R&D investment comparable to Qualcomm? A. Specifically on page 3? Q. Yes. And just to be clear, speaking at a high level about the main conclusion so we don't get into sealed information. A. What's written on the page, Intel Overall SoC R&D Investment Comparable to Qualcomm. Q. And what was the conclusion regarding how many more times output Qualcomm had . . . than Intel? A. Three times more output."); Transcript of Proceedings (Volume 10) at 2076:14–21, FTC v. Qualcomm Inc., No. 5:17-cv-00220-LHK (N.D. Cal. Jan. 28, 2019) (Testimony of Carl Shapiro).

issue as being a relevant question of fact, much less one on which there might be material dispute between the FTC and Qualcomm.

For example, one might conjecture that a proven innovator like Qualcomm is more likely to rely on self-funding for its R&D than is a less innovative firm like Intel or another rival modem manufacturer. It seems entirely plausible that some of Qualcomm's innovations have been so far advanced relative to the state of the art that only genuine technological pioneers can competently assess the risk-reward tradeoff of the requisite R&D investment. Put differently, the firm making foundational inventions (such as Qualcomm) has asymmetric information that the capital markets will never be able to replicate over the critical time horizon (since investment bankers are not the people to whom the U.S. Patent and Trademark Office is issuing patents for carrier aggregation, for example). Furthermore, Qualcomm's tutelage of investment bankers could invite free riding, in the sense that investment bankers newly tutored in the newest technology could use that material information all the better to price the risk of the R&D projects of Qualcomm's rivals.

That same informational asymmetry would less likely afflict second movers (such as Intel). The kind of R&D that a second mover (or "fast follower") pursues is likely to be closer to commercial implementation, and therefore it is likely to be more defined and less abstract than the foundational R&D that Qualcomm undertakes as the more innovative first mover. Consequently, external funders could more readily price the risk of supplying capital to the second mover than to the first mover (because the first mover had already proved the commercial worth of the technology in question).

If such an imperfection in the capital markets indeed exists, it might indicate that internal funding from net free cash flow was more efficient for Qualcomm (the leading-edge innovator) than would have been Qualcomm's attempt to educate the capital markets to provide it the requisite debt or equity funding for particular R&D projects. In addition, external financing might require more disclosure by Qualcomm of highly valuable technologies before those technologies were ready to be patented than would be wise from the perspective of IP management; and trade secret law might be an unsatisfactory alternative regime of IP protection in the interim. Hence, Qualcomm might have had good reason to prefer to fund its foundational R&D internally.

Even apart from the preceding conjectures of economic fact, to the extent that pricing imperfections in the capital markets were symmetric across rival modem manufacturers, such that the FTC's and Qualcomm's arguments were in equipoise, why was it proper as a matter of the law of evidence for Judge Koh to make a finding in the FTC's favor predicated on its unproven argument?

3. *Was Qualcomm's Alleged Royalty "Surcharge" or Modem "Tax" Asymmetric?*

Professor Shapiro addressed the criticism raised by Professor Aviv Nevo in his expert report that a chip-agnostic "tax" could not harm competition. Professor Shapiro testified as follows on direct examination by Mr. James for the FTC on January 15, 2019, during the FTC's case-in-chief:

> Q. . . . So Qualcomm has also made an argument that even if they got a royalty surcharge, it would not disadvantage their rivals relative to them. Qualcomm's expert, Professor Nevo, has written "Professor Shapiro's theory is flawed because any alleged tax would not disproportionately affect the demand for Qualcomm's rival's chips relative to the demand for Qualcomm's chip. The tax is chip-agnostic and non-discriminatory. Any tax would apply equally to purchases of Qualcomm's chips and rivals' chips." And how do you respond to that argument?
>
> A. Well, I'm sorry to say this is also incorrect. The—and I think the easiest way to see that, Your Honor, is to go back and look at what I just did and compare it to when Qualcomm sells its chips. So we just went through the surcharge is a burden on transactions between Qualcomm—excuse me—between the OEM and Qualcomm's rivals, and it reduces the gains from trade by the amount of the surcharge. Let's think now about the transactions between Qualcomm and an OEM, okay? Because Professor Nevo is saying that the tax is chip-agnostic, non-discriminatory. *Well, the royalty surcharge does not reduce the gains from trade between Qualcomm and the OEM in the same manner because they're not paying—because Qualcomm is the recipient of the royalties, okay?* It's a fundamental difference. When an OEM buys a chip from a rival, the two of them together have to write a check to Qualcomm. When an OEM buys a chip from Qualcomm, there's no money going out to third parties. *If you want to think about this as Qualcomm's chip division is bearing the cost of those royalties like its rivals are, that's okay. But then there's an equal offsetting benefit or revenue to Qualcomm's licensing division because they're the recipient of the royalty.* So that's just fundamentally different between the two transactions, and that's actually clearest when we think about transactions that expand the market for modem chips. So it's just not correct to say that, that a royalty surcharge is—affects these two types of transactions equally. It's a mistake.[736]

The document containing the passage that Mr. James quoted from Professor Nevo (presumably his expert report or a demonstrative to his direct testimony, yet to be given as of the time of Professor Shapiro's testimony on January 15, 2019) is not publicly available. Consequently, it not possible on

---

[736] Transcript of Proceedings (Volume 6) at 1140:11–1142:1, FTC v. Qualcomm Inc., No. 5:17-cv-00220-LHK (N.D. Cal. Jan. 15, 2019) (Testimony of Carl Shapiro) (emphasis added).

the basis of publicly available documents to give any citation to (or verification of) the quotation attributed to Professor Nevo by Mr. James of the FTC while conducting his direct examination of Professor Shapiro.

We can see from the Professor Shapiro's answer above that he testified on direct examination that even a chip-agnostic and nondiscriminatory "tax" could have harmed competition among modem manufacturers, supposedly because, while it reduced the "gains from trade" in a transaction between an OEM and a rival modem manufacturer, the modem "tax" did not affect in the same way the "gains from trade" in a transaction between an OEM and Qualcomm. Professor Shapiro said that, whereas the modem "tax" would have reduced the revenue that a modem manufacturer could earn by selling its modems to OEMs, the modem "tax" would not have had the same effect on Qualcomm's revenue.

Accompanying Professor Shapiro's direct testimony on January 15, 2019 were demonstratives consisting of a slide presentation. One slide was entitled, "Gains from Trade When an OEM Purchases a Modem Chip from Qualcomm." On it appeared bullet points with these phrases:

- Royalty surcharge does not impose a burden on these transactions

- Royalty surcharge is not a cost to Qualcomm

- Can think of royalty as cost to QCT and equal benefit to QTL

    — Out of one pocket, into another[737]

Professor Shapiro's bullet points confirmed that Professor Nevo's critique was absolutely correct.

It is regrettable that, as we shall see in Part IX, Judge Koh felt compelled to find Professor Nevo too unreliable as an expert economic witness to discuss his opinions seriously; for it appears, from the limited information in the public domain concerning his testimony, that Judge Koh's proper consideration of Professor Nevo's critique would have flipped the outcome of the bench trial in *FTC v. Qualcomm*. If Judge Koh had taken Professor Nevo seriously, she would have had to have rejected the FTC's novel royalty "surcharge" and modem "tax" theory of monopolization as implausible on its face. Put differently, Judge Koh could not have ruled in the FTC's favor on its royalty "surcharge" and modem "tax" theory of monopolization without first disparaging in its entirety the reliability of Professor Nevo's expert testimony and thus finding a reason to ignore every portion of his testimony.

Yet, Professor Shapiro's asymmetry assumption was fallacious for at least four reasons.

---

[737] Shapiro Demonstratives, *supra* note 114, at 32.

a. Professor Shapiro's Incorrect Definition of Cost

First, Professor Shapiro did not realize the fallacy of his testimony that his conjectured "[r]oyalty surcharge [wa]s not a cost to Qualcomm" and that one can regard the payment by Qualcomm as flowing "[o]ut of one pocket, into another."[738] Professor Shapiro implied that the royalty that Qualcomm charged on one of its own modems is a wash—some kind of transfer-pricing exercise having no underlying economic substance or significance.

That proposition was false as a matter of *a priori* economic reasoning because it ignored the logic underlying Armen Alchian's classic definition of cost: "In economics, the cost of an event is the highest-valued opportunity *necessarily* forsaken."[739] In private correspondence circa 1996, Professor Alchian requested that I add emphasis to the word "necessarily" when discussing his definition of cost.[740] I have gladly obliged ever since.[741]

The highest net benefit of all opportunities necessarily forgone is the opportunity cost of an action. In contrast to Alchian's understanding of "cost," Professor Shapiro implied that Qualcomm had a zero opportunity cost of exhaustively licensing its cellular SEPs to QCT for the manufacture of Qualcomm modems. Why would Professor Shapiro think that? Did he believe, myopically, that the (short-run) marginal cost of using extant intellectual property is zero—such that its seemingly "efficient" royalty should be zero?

For whatever reason, Professor Shapiro ignored that Qualcomm could, at any time and at significant financial advantage, securitize and alienate to a third party the revenue stream that QTL could earn from the exhaustive licensing of Qualcomm's cellular SEPs. That thought experiment for identifying Qualcomm's opportunity cost was precisely the kind of economic reasoning one would expect Qualcomm's management to consider if weighing the pros and cons of divesting Qualcomm's QTL licensing business from the company's QCT modem business. And of course, as Judge Koh observed on multiple occasions in her findings of fact and conclusions of law, Qualcomm's management did in fact actively study the feasibility of some such divestiture in 2007 and again in 2015.[742] If Qualcomm were to alienate the revenue

---

[738] *Id.*

[739] Armen A. Alchian, *Cost, in* 3 INTERNATIONAL ENCYCLOPEDIA OF THE SOCIAL SCIENCES 404, 404 (David L. Sills & Robert K. Merton eds., MacMillan Co. & Free Press 1968) (emphasis added).

[740] *See* J. GREGORY SIDAK & DANIEL F. SPULBER, DEREGULATORY TAKINGS AND THE REGULATORY CONTRACT: THE COMPETITIVE TRANSFORMATION OF NETWORK INDUSTRIES IN THE UNITED STATES 101 n.1, 275 n.8 (Cambridge Univ. Press 1997).

[741] Judge Posner has remarked that "[t]he economic concept of cost (opportunity cost) is," after the Law of Demand, "the second fundamental principle of economics." POSNER, ECONOMIC ANALYSIS OF LAW, *supra* note 214, at 6.

[742] *See* FTC v. Qualcomm Inc., 411 F. Supp. 3d 658, 773 (N.D. Cal. 2019) ("Qualcomm first analyzed whether to split QCT and QTL beginning in 2007, in an analysis called Project Berlin."); *id.* at 774 ("In 2015, Qualcomm initiated Project Phoenix, a second analysis of whether to split QCT and QTL.");

stream from its QTL licensing business, the value of that asset would depend on the true economic value of the licensing transactions involved. It would not depend, as Professor Shapiro seemed to imply, on some arbitrary transfer-pricing protocol in which the licensing revenue to QTL and the cost to QCT were offsetting accounting entries of any arbitrarily chosen magnitude.

Furthermore, the need to comply with IRS transfer-pricing regulations might independently cast doubt on the real-world plausibility of Professor Shapiro's assumption that Qualcomm could impose a royalty "surcharge" and "tax" on the "all-in price" of rivals' modems while avoiding the imposition of the same royalty "surcharge" and "tax" on the "all-in price" of QCT's modems. It is striking that, in his redacted testimony and disclosed opinions, Professor Shapiro did not once comment on the relevance of the July 2012 IRS conference transcript, upon which Judge Koh so heavily relied in making her findings of fact and conclusions of law.

> b. *Professor Shapiro's Assumption That Qualcomm Need Not Recoup the Costs of Its Investments*

The second fallacy of economic reasoning in Professor Shapiro's assumption of an asymmetric royalty "surcharge" and modem "tax" was that the assumption contradicted Qualcomm's position that it needed to recoup the cost of its investment to create its extensive portfolio of cellular SEPs practiced in modems in the first place. Professor Shapiro emphasized elsewhere in the redacted versions of his testimony and reports a *rival* modem manufacturer's need to throw off enough free cash flow from its operations to continue funding its R&D activities—which is to say, to generate enough free cash flow to recoup its sunk investments in R&D.[743]

---

id. at 817 ("Further, Qualcomm explicitly considered its potential advantages in 5G during its 2015 Project Phoenix analysis of whether to split QTL and QCT.").

[743] *See* Initial Expert Report of Carl Shapiro in *FTC v. Qualcomm, supra* note 115, at 114–15 ("This excess royalty is economically equivalent to a 'tax' imposed by Qualcomm on the OEM's use of rival modem chips. By raising the cost on rival modem chips, this excess royalty inevitably and predictably raises the all-in price of rival chipsets and reduces the quantity of those chipsets sold, for a given all-in price charged by Qualcomm. This excess royalty also inevitably and predictably reduces the operating income that any rivals can earn from selling chipsets, which can be expected to reduce the investments these rivals make in modem chips. This is turn leads to longer-term anticompetitive effects on innovation."); Transcript of Proceedings (Volume 6) at 1122:3–12, FTC v. Qualcomm Inc., No. 5:17-cv-00220-LHK (N.D. Cal. Jan. 15, 2019) (Testimony of Carl Shapiro) ("And the modem chips, I would say the key thing to keep in mind is this is a market that there's [sic] rapid technological change, of course that's common in the whole semiconductor sector, high tech sector, which means in order for companies to participate and be effective competitors at selling modem chips, they need to engage in very substantial R&D expenditures. And that means that in order for that to pay, they have to have a reasonable prospect of earning margins, sufficient margins and sufficient volumes to recoup those R&D investments."); *id.* at 1244:8–12 ("So we might see a company that was having, was having stable R&D because their market share—they were not selling as many chips as they were hoping to and the margins were being trimmed, and if the margins had been bigger, they would have had rising R&D, they would have had more investment.").

Yet, when it came to Qualcomm and its portfolio of 120,000 patents and pending patent applications as of the time of trial, Professor Shapiro did not treat Qualcomm and rival modem manufacturers symmetrically. He elided any explanation of Qualcomm's need for there to be positive expected returns to its investment in R&D if such investment were to continue to be elicited. Instead, Professor Shapiro treated the existence of the cellular SEPs in question as a black box—just part of the scenery in some exogenously determined state of nature that Professor Shapiro had assumed to pre-exist in his theoretical bargaining model. Are we seriously asked to believe that Qualcomm possessed a priceless trove of cellular SEPs that popped into existence without cost, without toil, without risk?[744]

c. *Could a Reduction in Rivals' Margins and Rivals' Sales Have Harmed Competition?*

Third, Professor Shapiro failed to distinguish the type of conduct that American law prohibits from the type of conduct that American law permits or even encourages. In his second appearance on the witness stand, during his direct examination in the FTC's rebuttal case on January 28, 2019, Professor Shapiro repeated his argument that even a chip-neutral "tax" could harm competition. Mr. James of the FTC asked:

> Q. Professor Nevo testified that any royalty surcharge would be chip neutral as between Qualcomm and its rivals because the OEM pays a surcharge regardless of the modem chip that it uses. What's your reaction to that testimony?
>
> A. So, Your Honor, this is a critical point here so I'm going to dwell on it a little bit. First, of course the rival—*of course the OEM pays the royalty and the surcharge regardless of which chip they buy. That's not in dispute.* But that's not the answer to the economics, so let's go back through this. First, I went through the gains from trade analysis last time and explained that when the—when Qualcomm collects this royalty surcharge on a transaction where an OEM purchases a chip from a rival, that's—that raises the cost there,

---

[744] Judge Koh's reasoning resembled Professor Shapiro's. *See FTC v. Qualcomm*, 411 F. Supp. 3d at 737 ("Qualcomm's exclusive deals, which delayed Intel's ability to sell modem chips to Apple until September 2016, foreclosed Intel and other rivals from benefits including . . . a revenue boost critical to funding research and development and acquiring technology."); *id.* at 744 ("Qualcomm refused its rival MediaTek's 2008 request for a patent license, and would only enter an agreement that restricted MediaTek's customer base. Qualcomm's refusal suppressed MediaTek's revenues and prevented MediaTek from being able to fund research and development for future generations of modem chips."); *id.* at 797 ("Qualcomm's suppression of rivals' sales also forecloses rivals from the revenue necessary to invest in research and development and acquisitions to develop new technology."); *id.* at 799 ("Reducing rivals' revenue to invest in research and development gravely harms rivals because producing modem chips requires very high fixed research and development costs."); *id.* ("Producing premium LTE modem chips is especially sensitive to customer volume because research and development for premium modem chips is more expensive.").

burdens that transaction, and weakens the rival as a competitor. Now, I also pointed out that the impact is not at all the same on a transaction between Qualcomm and the OEM because, yes, sure, the OEM pays the royalty surcharge to Qualcomm, but that's—Qualcomm's the recipient of that. It's in one pocket and out the other. So the gains from trade between the OEM and Qualcomm are not reduced in the same way by the surcharge. It's not going out to third parties. So that basic analysis stands. I just want to remind the Court of that because he did not—he did not show that there's anything wrong with that. Okay?[745]

Professor Shapiro attempted to support this circuitous explanation with a new hypothetical example:

> Another way to see this—this is such a key point in the case—is think about the royalty surcharge. Suppose we have a $10 royalty surcharge. Now, Intel is trying to sell a chip to an OEM. They're like, well, look, the only way to neutralize the effect of that royalty surcharge so the OEM's costs aren't going up, they'd have to cut their chip price by $10. They could mathematically do that. Okay? So they have to cut the chip price by $10, that would cut their margin by $10. Okay. Now, think about Qualcomm—because Professor Nevo is saying this is chip neutral—what would happen—think about a transaction between the OEM and Qualcomm. Now the OEM is paying the extra $10. Qualcomm could also neutralize that so the OEM's total all-in price wouldn't be—they would reduce their chip price by $10. Okay. That would be the same. But what's the effect on Qualcomm? The effect on Qualcomm is no change. Their all-in price has not changed. *All we've done is raised the royalty part by $10 and reduce the chip part by $10.* So the all-in price is the same. So Qualcomm can neutralize this with no harm to their bottom line at all, their margin basically, when you look at the all-in price, while Intel had to take the full hit of the royalty surcharge to neutralize. *This is just arithmetic, by the way. This isn't even economics. So just by arithmetic you can see that the effect of the royalty surcharge is not symmetric as between Intel and Qualcomm in my example.*[746]

In other words, Professor Shapiro shifted his argument and said that even a symmetric royalty "surcharge" and modem "tax" could harm competition among modem manufacturers, because it would reduce the compensation that modem manufacturers could obtain when selling their modems to OEMs, reduce modem manufacturers' total number of sales, or both.[747]

---

[745] Transcript of Proceedings (Volume 10) at 2057:13–2058:15, FTC v. Qualcomm Inc., No. 5:17-cv-00220-LHK (N.D. Cal. Jan. 28, 2019) (Testimony of Carl Shapiro) (emphasis added).

[746] *Id.* at 2058:16–2059:18 (emphasis added).

[747] Transcript of Proceedings (Volume 6) at 1138:5–6, FTC v. Qualcomm Inc., No. 5:17-cv-00220-LHK (N.D. Cal. Jan. 15, 2019) (Testimony of Carl Shapiro) ("The rivals are harmed, they're getting smaller margin [sic]."); *id.* at 1138:19–21 ("The number of transactions will fall because some transactions will not have enough gains from trade to bear the burden of the tax."); *id.* at 1138:22–1139:3 ("So we will also expect

Professor Shapiro evidently ignored that U.S. antitrust law does not require a monopolist to ensure that its competitors earn sufficient margins (or make enough sales) to remain competitive.[748]

Moreover, the "all-in price" would not affect the OEM's choice of a modem, provided that the quality-adjusted price of a bare non-Qualcomm modem was less than or equal to the quality-adjusted price of a bare Qualcomm modem. (Persons familiar with the economic literature on access pricing will immediately recognize the similarity of the competitive analysis here to the analysis motivating the efficient component-pricing rule, also known as "parity pricing."[749]) Unless Qualcomm's modem price was predatory—which the FTC did not allege, and which no evidence in the public record or in Judge Koh's findings of fact and conclusions of law substantiated—Qualcomm's forcing of competitors to reduce their prices for modems to match its own lower price was virtuous rivalry that American antitrust jurisprudence applauds. The Ninth Circuit in *FTC v. Qualcomm* found that,

> not only did the FTC offer no evidence that Qualcomm engaged in predatory pricing, the district court's entire antitrust analysis is premised on the opposite proposition: that Qualcomm "charge[s] monopoly prices on modem chips." Indeed, the district court faulted Qualcomm for lowering its prices only when other companies introduced CDMA modem chips to the market to effectively compete.[750]

As a matter of law, those lower prices could not remotely support a section 2 claim under the Sherman Act after *linkLine*, which we will examine in detail in Parts V.E and XVIII.

In sum, an evidently unstated (or poorly articulated) premise of Professor Shapiro's opinion (and the FTC's advocacy) was that the alleged royalty "surcharge" and modem "tax" enabled Qualcomm to reduce the price attributable to its own modems; to pass on to OEMs the savings from paying the lower "all-in price" of a Qualcomm modem; to cause rival modem manufacturers to lower their "all-in prices" in response; and thereby to reduce the margins and possibly also the unit sales of rival modem manufacturers

---

to see a reduction in the number of transactions taking place, that is, OEM's purchasing modem chips from Qualcomm's rivals, and that is going to cause further harm to the rivals, OEM's, and consumers. The rivals perhaps most clearly because they're selling fewer chips. They're making lower margins on the chips the sell, and they're selling fewer chips.").

[748] *See* Pacific Bell Tel. Co. v. linkLine Commc'ns, Inc., 555 U.S. 438, 450 (2009) ("[I]f a firm has no antitrust duty to deal with its competitors at wholesale, it certainly has no duty to deal under terms and conditions that the rivals find commercially advantageous.").

[749] *See* WILLIAM J. BAUMOL & J. GREGORY SIDAK, TOWARD COMPETITION IN LOCAL TELEPHONY 93–116 (MIT Press & AEI Press 1994); William J. Baumol & J. Gregory Sidak, *The Pricing of Inputs Sold to Competitors*, 11 YALE J. ON REG. 171 (1994); Robert D. Willig, *The Theory of Network Access Pricing, in* ISSUES IN PUBLIC UTILITY REGULATION 109 (H.M. Trebing ed., Michigan State Univ. Public Utility Papers 1979).

[750] FTC v. Qualcomm Inc., No. 19-16122, 2020 WL 4591476, at *18 (9ᵗʰ Cir. Aug. 11, 2020) (alteration in original) (citation omitted) (quoting FTC v. Qualcomm Inc., 411 F. Supp. 3d 658, 800 (N.D. Cal. 2019)).

(depending on the new relative price of Qualcomm modems to the prices of non-Qualcomm modems). (There were further links in Professor Shapiro's chain of causation—rivals supposedly would have had less free cash flow to invest in R&D—but we need not add those additional conjectures here to see the legal fallacy of Professor Shapiro's argument.) Even if his conjectured chain of causation were factually correct, the ultimate finding of fact that would result from it would not support the conclusion of law that Qualcomm's conduct was anticompetitive. That is true because of one simple reason: the Supreme Court of the United States no longer recognizes an antitrust cause of action for a margin squeeze.

d. Would a Modem "Tax" That Raises Prices for OEMs Be Anticompetitive?

Fourth, Professor Shapiro claimed on direct examination during the FTC's rebuttal case on January 28, 2019 that, even if the alleged modem "tax" did not reduce the profits or sales of rival modem manufacturers, it still would be anticompetitive because it would harm final consumers:

> Professor Nevo seems to be saying, you impose this royalty surcharge, it's agnostic, it doesn't really hurt the rivals. I guess that's what chip agnostic means because it's neutral. Well, where's the money coming from? The royalty surcharge is going to get—somebody has got to be paying it. Qualcomm is picking up the money. And I'm saying the rival is going to eat part of that. What I said was the rival ate part of it, the OEM eats part of it, and part of it is passed on to consumers. They're going to split the pain. Professor Nevo seems to be suggesting, well, the rival isn't going to get hurt. I don't think that's right. But if you just follow his own logic, if that were true and the rivals' margins aren't cut, who's paying the surcharge? It would have to be entirely the OEM's, which means basically the final consumers. So as far as I can tell, his defense of this is it would hurt consumers even worse than I have said. That does not strike me as a very strong defense in an antitrust case.[751]

Professor Shapiro did not elaborate on this possible state of the world. Perhaps, he was envisioning a situation in which Qualcomm and rival modem manufacturers would not have reduced their modem prices to "neutralize" Qualcomm's alleged royalty "surcharge" and modem "tax." In the above example summarized in Table 5, both Qualcomm and its rivals would have offered their modems for $20. In that case, the "tax" would have increased the "all-in price" for *all* modems. As we have seen, such an increase in the "all-in

---

[751] Transcript of Proceedings (Volume 10) at 2060:13–2061:6, FTC v. Qualcomm Inc., No. 5:17-cv-00220-LHK (N.D. Cal. Jan. 28, 2019) (Testimony of Carl Shapiro).

price" could not have affected competition *among* modem manufacturers, because an OEM would have had to pay the same "tax" irrespective of whether it would have purchased Qualcomm's modems or non-Qualcomm modems. Professor Shapiro expressly admitted this point on direct examination on January 28, 2019. Yet, Professor Shapiro testified that the "tax" still would have been anticompetitive because it would have harmed final consumers in the form of higher prices.

Suppose instead that all OEMs faced a fuel surcharge on the cost of air cargo shipments of handsets from China to the United States, and suppose further that the fuel surcharge was precisely equal on a per-handset basis to the amount of an exogenous spike in the price of jet fuel. By Professor Shapiro's reasoning, this cost increase borne by all competitors in the market would be anticompetitive. Yet, that reasoning is spurious. Industry output would decline, all other factors being equal, but in a competitive market all producers would pass through the increase in marginal cost in the prices of their products. Professor Shapiro implicitly but speciously equated competition with the amount of aggregate demand for handsets and, derivatively, the aggregate demand for modems as essential inputs in handsets.

As we shall see, Professor Shapiro's testimony that the alleged royalty "surcharge" and modem "tax" would have increased the prices of final goods was factually unsupported, and it did not comport with publicly available information about the substantial price premium that consumers were willing to pay for some smartphone brands. (Professor Shapiro might better protect consumer welfare by asking why various OEMs are evidently able to charge consumers in the United States several hundred dollars per smartphone as a "surcharge" or "tax" for affixing their particular brand names to a handset with a given suite of functionalities that was fabricated by contract manufacturers in Asia.[752]) But even if one were to assume, contrary to the evidence, that Professor Shapiro's predictions about the effects on final consumers of the alleged royalty "surcharge" and modem "tax" were correct, that assumption still would not support the conclusion that the royalty "surcharge" and modem "tax" were anticompetitive. U.S. antitrust law does not condemn high prices unless they harm competition.[753]

---

[752] *See* J. Gregory Sidak & Jeremy O. Skog, *Hedonic Prices for Multicomponent Products*, 4 CRITERION J. ON INNOVATION 301, 301, 333, 346 (2019).

[753] *See* Verizon Commc'ns Inc. v. Law Offices of Curtis V. Trinko, LLP, 540 U.S. 398, 407 (2004) ("The mere possession of monopoly power, and the concomitant charging of monopoly prices, is not only not unlawful; it is an important element of the free-market system. The opportunity to charge monopoly prices—at least for a short period—is what attracts 'business acumen' in the first place; it induces risk taking that produces innovation and economic growth. To safeguard the incentive to innovate, the possession of monopoly power will not be found unlawful unless it is accompanied by an element of anticompetitive *conduct*.") (emphasis in original) (quoting United States v. Grinnell Corp., 384 U.S. 563, 571 (1966)).

4. *Did the FTC's Own Theory of the Royalty "Surcharge" and Modem "Tax" Contradict Professor Shapiro's Actual Trial Testimony?*

The FTC's closing argument at trial on January 29, 2019, raised what appears to have been a disturbing inconsistency between the agency's depiction of Professor Shapiro's trial testimony and what he actually said in his testimony. As we saw, Professor Nevo testified that the royalty "surcharge" and modem "tax" were "chip agnostic" and therefore could not have had an anticompetitive effect on rival modem manufacturers.[754] When Professor Shapiro returned to the stand on January 28, 2019 to testify in the FTC's rebuttal case, he volunteered during his *direct* examination by the FTC's counsel—*not* during cross examination by Qualcomm's counsel—that he agreed with Professor Nevo, such that there was no dispute that the royalty "surcharge" and modem "tax" (if they even existed) would be borne by an OEM purchasing both rival modems and Qualcomm modems alike. As we previously saw, Professor Shapiro made the following highly consequential admission: "First, of course the rival—*of course the OEM pays the royalty and the surcharge regardless of which chip they buy. That's not in dispute.*"[755]

These two sentences form the most significant passage of testimony in the entire trial record of *FTC v. Qualcomm*. Until Professor Shapiro made this admission on the morning of the final day of testimony, January 29, 2019, it certainly would have appeared to anyone hearing the trial witnesses or reading their transcribed testimonies that it *was* a matter of dispute between the FTC and Qualcomm whether, in Professor Shapiro's theoretical bargaining model, the OEM paid the reasonable royalty and the royalty "surcharge" regardless of which brand of chip it bought. And of course Professor Shapiro's admission that there was no dispute on this question of fact was completely ignored by Judge Koh in her findings of fact and conclusions of law, as she never once mentioned Professor Shapiro.

Moreover, Professor Shapiro's insinuation that there never really had been any disagreement on this point did not make sense as a matter of pretrial motions practice. If this material question of fact truly were not disputed by the FTC and Qualcomm, then why was it not so discussed in Judge Koh's order on Qualcomm's motion to dismiss? Barring that, why was this supposed absence of dispute not among the stipulations of fact that Judge Koh listed near the beginning of her findings of fact and conclusions of law?[756]

Professor Shapiro's admission was hugely probative, for it disproved the FTC's royalty "surcharge" and modem "tax" theory of antitrust liability.

---

[754] Transcript of Proceedings (Volume 9) at 1913:3–16, FTC v. Qualcomm Inc., No. 5:17-cv-00220-LHK (N.D. Cal. Jan. 25, 2019) (Testimony of Aviv Nevo).

[755] Transcript of Proceedings (Volume 10) at 2057:19–21, FTC v. Qualcomm Inc., No. 5:17-cv-00220-LHK (N.D. Cal. Jan. 28, 2019) (Testimony of Carl Shapiro) (emphasis added).

[756] FTC v. Qualcomm Inc., 411 F. Supp. 3d 658, 669–71 (N.D. Cal. 2019) ("STIPULATED FACTS").

Without asymmetry in the application of the royalty "surcharge" and modem "tax"—without an absence of "chip agnosticism," to use Professor Nevo's terminology—there could be no anticompetitive effect from the challenged licensing behavior by Qualcomm. And therefore, as Qualcomm observed in its motion to dismiss, in the absence of an asymmetric royalty for Qualcomm's patents,[757] the FTC's claim would collapse to a plain vanilla allegation of margin squeeze, which the Supreme Court stopped recognizing as a cause of action in *linkLine*.

Despite Professor Shapiro's stunning admission on direct examination on January 28, 2019 that Qualcomm's royalty "surcharge" and modem "tax" were symmetric across all modem manufacturers, the very next day in its closing argument at trial the FTC incredibly took the opposite position—now in contradiction to Professor Shapiro's sworn testimony. The FTC's lawyer, Ms. Milici, apparently alluded to a slide from the demonstratives that Professor Shapiro had used on his first day of testimony (on January 15, 2019) and told Judge Koh:

> And as Dr. Shapiro explains on [the] right part of this slide, *Qualcomm's royalty surcharge is not chip neutral.* This is because when an OEM buys Qualcomm chips, the gains from trade are not reduced because the royalty is paid to Qualcomm. Qualcomm is the tax collector.[758]

It might have been true that Professor Shapiro's slide from his demonstratives *from January 15, 2019* said what the FTC represented to Judge Koh that it did; however, when Professor Shapiro returned to the stand *on January 28, 2019*, he conceded, within the sheltering arms of direct examination by the FTC, that there was no asymmetry in the application of his theoretical royalty "surcharge" and modem "tax."

Consequently, this particular slide from Professor Shapiro's demonstratives of January 15, 2019 no longer appeared to reflect accurately his ultimate testimony at trial as of the closing day of evidence, January 28, 2019. Were the *Brady* rule to apply with equal force to a civil prosecution, would it have violated the *Brady* rule for Ms. Milici to represent in her closing argument that the alleged royalty "surcharge" and modem "tax" were *not* "chip neutral," considering that Professor Shapiro admitted under oath the previous day that the royalty "surcharge" and modem "tax" were indeed "chip-agnostic," and that there was no dispute as to that proposition?

Judge Koh apparently did not spot that conflict between Professor Shapiro's testimony on January 28, 2019 and the FTC's closing argument on

---

757 Qualcomm's Motion to Dismiss, 2017 WL 4678941, *supra* note 41, at 12.
758 Transcript of Proceedings (Volume 11) at 2127:25–2128:4, FTC v. Qualcomm Inc., No. 5:17-cv-00220-LHK (N.D. Cal. Jan. 29, 2019) (closing argument of Jennifer Milici for the FTC) (emphasis added).

January 29, 2019. She did not mention it, either in the transcript for closing arguments that day or in her subsequent findings of fact and conclusions of law.

E. Did Professor Shapiro's Theoretical Bargaining Model Include Any Empirical Analysis?

A sophisticated trial lawyer or judge reading the trial transcript in *FTC v. Qualcomm* could conclude that Professor Shapiro made admissions under oath on January 28, 2019 that disproved the FTC's case. As we will see in the following sections, he repeatedly testified that his analysis was "purely illustrative or conceptual" and based solely on assumptions.[759] Professor Shapiro admitted that he had *assumed* that Qualcomm's royalties for an exhaustive license to its portfolio of cellular SEPs exceeded the ceiling on the range of FRAND royalties and that those royalties imposed a royalty "surcharge" that in turn imposed a "tax" on non-Qualcomm modems.[760] Yet, Professor Shapiro never attempted to examine Qualcomm's actual royalties charged for an exhaustive license to its cellular SEPs and thereupon quantify the actual size of the alleged royalty "surcharge."[761] Professor Shapiro also admitted under oath that, although he testified about the effects that the royalty "surcharge" supposedly had on OEMs, modem manufacturers, and final consumers of mobile devices, he never actually examined empirical evidence of any such predicted effects.[762] In other words, Professor Shapiro's testimony confirmed that his opinions relied overwhelmingly, if not exclusively, on the predictions of a theoretical model that he did not connect to the facts of *FTC v. Qualcomm*.

1. Professor Shapiro Did Not Examine Any Empirical Evidence to Determine a FRAND Royalty or a Range of FRAND Royalties for Qualcomm's Cellular SEPs

Professor Shapiro's testimony relied on the assumed existence of a supra-FRAND royalty that Qualcomm had allegedly extracted from OEMs. Yet, he did not calculate a FRAND or RAND royalty, or a FRAND or RAND range, for an exhaustive license to Qualcomm's portfolio of cellular SEPs.

Under cross examination by Mr. Van Nest, Professor Shapiro admitted that he had performed no quantitative analysis of Qualcomm's royalties for its cellular SEPs at all:

---

[759] *See, e.g., id.* at 1131:3–4; *id.* at 1199:5–19; *id.* at 1200:10–23.

[760] *See id.* at 1199:11–16.

[761] *See id.* at 1202:13–20.

[762] *See id.* at 1205:3–17; *id.* at 1206:15–1208:5.

Q. . . . And you are not offering an opinion about either the FRAND rate or the FRAND range as part of your analysis; correct?

A. That's correct.

Q. All right?

A. I'm offering an opinion about the supra—the royalty surcharge, not the level on which it's applied. Not the reasonable royalty base to which it's applied.

Q. Yeah. You're assuming the surcharge and you're working through your analysis here in the tax theory; correct?

A. No, I'm not assuming the surcharge. I explained how it arose.

Q. Okay. But you haven't done any quantitative analysis or economic quantitative analysis to come up with a FRAND rate or a FRAND range; right?

A. Like I said, that's what Mr. Lasinski is doing. I'm testifying about the royalty surcharge.[763]

In other words, although it was Professor Shapiro's sworn testimony that the market power that Qualcomm allegedly had in the two modem markets that he had defined would have permitted Qualcomm to extract from OEMs supra-FRAND royalties for an exhaustive license to Qualcomm's portfolio of cellular SEPs, he had not performed any empirical analysis to determine whether Qualcomm's royalties actually exceeded the ceiling of the FRAND range.

This absence of empirical analysis in Professor Shapiro's testimony in *FTC v. Qualcomm* was consistent with his scholarly writings on patent issues. It appears that as of 2020 Professor Shapiro has authored or co-authored 33 articles, book chapters, working papers, and books that address patent licensing.[764] Of that scholarship, apparently only one article, *Standard Setting*

---

[763] *Id.* at 1197:10–1198:1.

[764] *See* Shapiro & Lemley, *The Role of Antitrust in Preventing Patent Holdup, supra* note 646; Federico, Scott Morton & Shapiro, *Antitrust and Innovation: Welcoming and Protecting Disruption, supra* note 373; Melamed & Shapiro, *How Antitrust Law Can Make FRAND Commitments More Effective, supra* note 675; Stuart Graham, Peter Menell, Carl Shapiro & Tim Simcoe, *Final Report of the Berkeley Center for Law & Technology Patent Damages Workshop*, 25 Tex. Intell. Prop. L.J. 115 (2017); Carl Shapiro, *Patent Remedies*, 106 Am. Econ. Rev.: Papers & Proc. 198 (2016); Scott Morton & Shapiro, *Patent Assertions: Are We Any Closer to Aligning Reward to Contribution?, supra* note 373; Aaron S. Edlin, C. Scott Hemphill, Herbert J. Hovenkamp & Carl Shapiro, *The* Actavis *Inference: Theory and Practice*, 67 Rutgers U. L. Rev. 585 (2015); Scott Morton & Shapiro, *Strategic Patent Acquisitions, supra* note 373; Lemley & Shapiro, *A Simple Approach to Setting Reasonable Royalties for Standard-Essential Patents, supra* note 118; Aaron Edlin, Scott Hemphill, Herbert Hovenkamp & Carl Shapiro, *Activating* Actavis, 28 Antitrust, Fall 2013, at 16; Carl Shapiro, *Injunctions, Hold-Up, and Patent Royalties*, 12 Am. L. & Econ. Rev. 280 (2010); Joseph Farrell & Carl Shapiro, *How Strong Are Weak Patents?*, 98 Am. Econ. Rev. 1347 (2008); Carl Shapiro, *Patent Reform: Aligning Reward and Contribution, in* 8 Innovation Policy and the Economy 111 (Adam B. Jaffe, Josh Lerner & Scott Stern eds., Univ. of Chicago Press 2007); Farrell, Hayes, Shapiro & Sullivan, *Standard Setting, Patents, and Hold-Up, supra* note 645; Mark A. Lemley & Carl Shapiro, *Reply: Patent Holdup and Royalty Stacking*, 85 Tex. L. Rev. 2163 (2007); Lemley & Shapiro, *Patent Holdup and Royalty Stacking, supra* note 118; Mark A. Lemley & Carl Shapiro, *Probabilistic*

in High-Definition Television from 1992, contains an econometric analysis of a testable hypothesis.[765]

Professor Shapiro's lack of empirical investigation in *FTC v. Qualcomm* is striking, though consistent with the paucity of econometric analysis in his many scholarly writings on patent licensing since the 1980s. Instead of undertaking original empirical research in *FTC v. Qualcomm*, Professor Shapiro left the actual calculation of a FRAND rate or a FRAND range—a necessary baseline to determining the existence and magnitude of an allegedly supra-FRAND royalty—to Michael Lasinski, the FTC's patent valuation expert and an accountant by training. On cross examination on January 15, 2019 by Mr. Van Nest during the FTC's case-in-chief, Professor Shapiro testified:

> Q. Well, you understood, when your deposition was taken you said, "Mr. Lasinski is covering that"; right?
>
> A. Yes. He's the one who's offering an opinion about the FRAND rate.[766]

Professor Shapiro's decision to rely on Mr. Lasinski for the key input to Professor Shapiro's theoretical bargaining model was baffling for at least two reasons.

Patents, 19 J. Econ. Persp. 75 (2005); Carl Shapiro, *Patent System Reform: Economic Analysis and Critique*, 19 Berkeley Tech. L.J. 1017 (2004); Hal R. Varian, Joseph Farrell & Carl Shapiro, The Economics of Information Technology: An Introduction (Cambridge Univ. Press 2004); Joseph Farrell & Carl Shapiro, Intellectual Property, Competition, and Information Technology (Univ. of California, Berkeley Competition Pol'y Ctr. Working Paper No. CPC04-45, 2004); Carl Shapiro, *Technology Cross-Licensing Practices: FTC v. Intel (1999)*, in The Antitrust Revolution: Economics, Competition, and Policy 350 (John E. Kwoka, Jr. & Lawrence J. White eds., Oxford Univ. Press 4th ed. 2003); Carl Shapiro, *Antitrust Limits to Patent Settlements*, 34 RAND J. Econ. 391 (2003); Carl Shapiro, *Antitrust Analysis of Patent Settlements Between Rivals*, 17 Antitrust, Summer 2003, at 70; Carl Shapiro, *Setting Compatibility Standards: Cooperation or Collusion?*, in Expanding the Boundaries of Intellectual Property: Innovation Policy for the Knowledge Society 81 (Rochelle Cooper Dreyfuss, Diane Leenheer Zimmerman & Harry First eds., Oxford Univ. Press 2001); Carl Shapiro, *Navigating the Patent Thicket: Cross Licenses, Patent Pools, and Standard Setting*, in 1 Innovation Policy and the Economy 119 (Adam B. Jaffe, Josh Lerner & Scott Stern eds., Univ. of Chicago Press 2000); Richard J. Gilbert & Carl Shapiro, *Unilateral Refusals to License Intellectual Property and International Competition Policy*, in Competition and Trade Policies: Coherence or Conflict 65 (Einar Hope & Per Maeleng eds., Routledge 1998); Richard Gilbert & Carl Shapiro, *Antitrust Issues in the Licensing of Intellectual Property: The Nine No-No's Meet the Nineties*, 1997 Brookings Papers on Econ. Activity: Microecon. 283 (1997); Richard J. Gilbert & Carl Shapiro, *An Economic Analysis of Unilateral Refusals to License Intellectual Property*, 93 Proc. Nat'l Acad. Sci. USA 12,749 (1996); Joseph Farrell & Carl Shapiro, *Standard Setting in High-Definition Television*, 1992 Brookings Papers on Econ. Activity: Microecon. 1, 55–56 (1992); Richard Gilbert & Carl Shapiro, *Optimal Patent Length and Breadth*, 21 RAND J. Econ. 106 (1990); Michael L. Katz & Carl Shapiro, *R&D Rivalry with Licensing or Imitation*, 77 Am. Econ. Rev. 402 (1987); Michael L. Katz & Carl Shapiro, *How to License Intangible Property*, 101 Q.J. Econ. 567 (1986); Michael L. Katz & Carl Shapiro, *On the Licensing of Innovations*, 16 RAND J. Econ. 504 (1985); Carl Shapiro, *Patent Licensing and R&D Rivalry*, 75 Am. Econ. Rev. 25 (1985).

[765] *See* Farrell & Shapiro, *Standard Setting in High-Definition Television*, *supra* note 764, at 55–56 ("To determine the role of network affiliation in determining when a station adopted color, we estimated a hazard rate model using data on adoption dates and network affiliation.").

[766] Transcript of Proceedings (Volume 6) at 1197:6–9, FTC v. Qualcomm Inc., No. 5:17-cv-00220-LHK (N.D. Cal. Jan. 15, 2019) (Testimony of Carl Shapiro).

292 The Criterion Journal on Innovation [Vol. 6:1

First, Mr. Lasinski testified that, although he was a certified public accountant and had testified as an expert in many patent disputes, he did not have formal credentials in economics, much less credentials in antitrust economics or industrial organization. During his cross examination by Mr. Bornstein during the FTC's case-in-chief, Mr. Lasinski was asked the following questions and gave the following answers concerning the extent of his formal training in economics:

> Q. Now, you're not an economist; correct, sir?
>
> A. I'm not a Ph.D. economist, but I use economics every day as it relates to unpacking license agreements and pricing license agreements.
>
> Q. You don't have any degree in economics at all; correct?
>
> A. I do not.
>
> Q. Okay.
>
> A. That is accurate. I should also say I've taken economic classes, but I don't have a degree in economics.
>
> Q. And you're not testifying today as an economist; right?
>
> A. No, I'm not.[767]

Why would the FTC have instructed Professor Shapiro, an internationally recognized antitrust economist with roughly four decades of experience and two stints as the chief economist of the Antitrust Division, to leave such an important economic calculation to an accountant with no comparable experience in antitrust economics or industrial organization?

Second, it was even more perplexing that Professor Shapiro testified under cross examination by Mr. Van Nest during the FTC's case-in-chief on January 15, 2019 that he had *declined* to rely on Mr. Lasinski's calculation of a FRAND royalty for an exhaustive license to Qualcomm's portfolio of cellular SEPs:

> Q. Okay. And you're not offering any opinion as to what the FRAND rate or range of Qualcomm's SEP is; isn't that right?
>
> A. That is correct.
>
> Q. Right. You're relying on Mr. Lasinski for that?
>
> A. No, I'm not relying on him.[768]

Why did Professor Shapiro at trial decline to rely on Mr. Lasinski's determination of a FRAND royalty? Did Professor Shapiro consider Mr. Lasinski's testimony unreliable? Judge Koh stated in her findings of fact and conclusions of law that "the Court does not rely on Lasinski's testimony."[769] If Professor Shapiro did not rely on Mr. Lasinski's testimony about the FRAND rate or the FRAND range for an exhaustive license to Qualcomm's portfolio of cellular SEPs, and if Professor Shapiro did not perform that analysis himself, then what *was* the basis for Professor Shapiro's sworn testimony that the royalties specified in Qualcomm's exhaustive license agreements for its portfolio of cellular SEPs exceeded the ceiling of the FRAND range?

Professor Shapiro did not present any empirical analysis to support his testimony that Qualcomm's royalties for an exhaustive license to its cellular SEPs were supra-FRAND. That failure of evidence is shocking, considering that he subsequently admitted that his entire royalty "surcharge" and modem "tax" theory depended on there being actual economic proof of the existence of a supra-FRAND royalty. We saw earlier that Professor Shapiro admitted on cross examination by Mr. Van Nest during the FTC's case-in-chief on January 15, 2019 that the entirety of his testimony would be irrelevant if Judge Koh did not find that a preponderance of the evidence established that Qualcomm had charged a supra-FRAND royalty for its portfolio of cellular SEPs:

> Q. Okay. So point one: if the Court were to determine that the evidence doesn't support the existence of a supra-FRAND royalty, then the rest of your analysis can be ignored; right? It depends on that as a starting point?
>
> A. So if the Court were to determine that all this leverage didn't lead to anything in terms of a supra—a royalty surcharge—
>
> Q. That's right?
>
> A. —then the economic consequences of the surcharge would not come into play. I think that's logical.
>
> Q. I think that's what I said.
>
> A. I just—
>
> Q. Unless the evidence supports the existence of a supra-FRAND royalty, this analysis is irrelevant; right? I think that's what you just said, but—
>
> A. I guess I—I'm resisting, I admit a little bit, that irrelevant makes me feel bad.
>
> (Laughter.)
>
> By Mr. Van Nest:

---

[769] FTC v. Qualcomm Inc., 411 F. Supp. 3d 658, 790 (N.D. Cal. 2019).

Q. Don't feel bad.

A. But I think that, yes, the building block for, for this discussion of effects is that Qualcomm was able to achieve a royalty surcharge by applying the chip leverage. So, yes, that is correct.[770]

Despite Professor Shapiro's stunning admission on January 15, 2019 that his entire testimony on the supposed royalty "surcharge" and modem "tax" would be irrelevant if the FTC could not prove by a preponderance of the evidence that Qualcomm was charging OEMs a supra-FRAND royalty for an exhaustive license to its cellular SEPs, he also admitted that he had not made any attempt to examine any empirical evidence to determine whether Qualcomm's royalties for an exhaustive license to its portfolio of cellular SEPs actually exceeded the FRAND range.

The star expert economic witness for the FTC, which bore the burden of production on Qualcomm's allegedly anticompetitive conduct, did not calculate a FRAND royalty or a range of FRAND royalties for an exhaustive license to Qualcomm's cellular SEPs. Professor Shapiro did not even rely on the expert testimony of Mr. Lasinski. Instead, Professor Shapiro appeared throughout his sworn testimony to do no more than *assume* that Qualcomm's royalties for an exhaustive license to its cellular SEPs exceeded the FRAND ceiling.

> 2. *Professor Shapiro Conceded Multiple Times During His Testimony That He Had Assumed the Existence of a Royalty "Surcharge" and Modem "Tax" and Testified Merely That He Had "Reason to Believe" That the Royalty "Surcharge" and Modem "Tax" Were "Substantial"*

We have seen that Professor Shapiro never testified what a FRAND royalty or a range of FRAND royalties for an exhaustive license to Qualcomm's cellular SEPs would be. It necessarily follows that he never testified by how much (if at all) Qualcomm's actual royalties for an exhaustive license to its cellular SEPs allegedly exceeded the FRAND ceiling. It further follows that Professor Shapiro never testified whether any royalty "surcharge" and modem "tax" actually arose from Qualcomm's challenged licensing practices. All of Professor Shapiro's testimony was strictly conditional: *if* a royalty "surcharge" and modem "tax" existed, then certain bad things would follow.

In fact, in his cross-examination testimony during the FTC's case-in-chief on January 15, 2019, Professor Shapiro repeatedly emphasized that he had not conducted any empirical analysis of the alleged royalty "surcharge" and modem "tax" and that he had not made any other attempt to quantify it:

---

770 Transcript of Proceedings (Volume 6) at 1198:2–1198:25, FTC v. Qualcomm Inc., No. 5:17-cv-00220-LHK (N.D. Cal. Jan. 15, 2019) (Testimony of Carl Shapiro).

Q. But, again, you haven't done any quantitative analysis to determine how much of the surcharge you're opining about, if any, was caused by chip leverage as opposed to the threat of litigation, the fear of litigation, the fear of injunctions and other factors; right? You haven't done that?

A. I have not quantified the royalty surcharge.

Q. Okay. Now—

A. But I *believe* it's substantial.[771]

What was the basis for Professor Shapiro to testify that he *believed* that the royalty "surcharge" was "substantial"? Mr. Van Nest probed this point:

Q. . . . But it's certainly the case that you haven't quantified the effect on any other chip maker of the Qualcomm supra-FRAND royalty you're assuming, have you?

A. I've said already I have not—I have not quantified the magnitude of the royalty surcharge. I pointed out *strong reasons to believe* that it was substantial.[772]

When he returned to testify during the FTC's rebuttal case on January 28, 2019, Professor Shapiro reiterated on cross examination his belief that Qualcomm had charged a supra-FRAND royalty for an exhaustive license to its portfolio of cellular SEPs:

Q. But you told us last time that you've done no empirical work whatsoever to determine the size of any supra-FRAND royalty you're assuming existed; correct?

A. What I said is I have not quantified it. I explained why we have *good reason to believe* that it was substantial.[773]

In other words, Professor Shapiro *believed* that Qualcomm's allegedly supra-FRAND royalties for an exhaustive license to its portfolio of cellular SEPs were imposing a royalty "surcharge" and a "tax" on the "all-in price" paid by OEMs for modems. Yet, he repeatedly admitted at trial that he had not performed any empirical analysis to substantiate his *belief* that the alleged royalty "surcharge" and modem "tax" actually existed.

When the FTC's lawyer, Rajesh James, asked Professor Shapiro in his redirect examination (during his first day of testimony, during the FTC's

---

[771] *Id.* at 1202:13–20 (emphasis added); *see also id.* at 1202:3–7 ("Q. . . . And you also have not done any quantitative analysis to determine how much of the surcharge, if any, was caused by chip leverage with respect to any OEM; isn't that right? A. I've not done a quantitative measurement there.").

[772] *Id.* at 1203:23–1204:4 (emphasis added).

[773] Transcript of Proceedings (Volume 10) at 2066:10–14, FTC v. Qualcomm Inc., No. 5:17-cv-00220-LHK (N.D. Cal. Jan. 28, 2019) (Testimony of Carl Shapiro) (emphasis added).

case-in-chief on January 15, 2019) how he determined that Qualcomm's royalty "surcharge" and modem "tax" were substantial despite his having made no attempt to quantify it, Professor Shapiro answered as follows:

> Q. Mr. Van Nest asked you if you had quantified the royalty surcharge. Is that right?
>
> A. He did, a number of times.
>
> Q. And you said you hadn't?
>
> A. Correct.
>
> Q. But it's part of your opinion that the surcharge is substantial; right?
>
> A. That is correct.
>
> Q. And how do you know that?
>
> A. So based on the bargaining principles, the ability of Qualcomm to elevate the royalty above the reasonable level by using the threat of a—of not selling chips to an OEM is proportionate to the power of that threat in particular, the cost to the OEM of not being able to obtain access to the Qualcomm chips. And I think there's—I'm relying on OEM testimony here, and beyond that, that that cost was very high for OEM's, and so I would expect, using bargaining theory, that the royalty surcharge that Qualcomm was able to obtain by deploying that threat was also—was substantial.[774]

So, Professor Shapiro testified that he was relying on "OEM testimony" and "bargaining theory" to reach his "reason to believe" that the alleged royalty "surcharge" and modem "tax" were "substantial."

As is evident from his testimony, Professor Shapiro decided to rely on his *belief*, rather than real-world evidence, when discussing the alleged royalty "surcharge" and modem "tax." His sworn testimony in *FTC v. Qualcomm* was not the first time that Professor Shapiro has insisted that his own belief-based opinions should receive more weight than empirical analysis. In 2015, Professor Shapiro seemed to demand that his patent-holdup conjecture simply be excused from scientific scrutiny and that its skeptics be discredited because they were "patent-holdup deniers."[775] It is ironic then that Professor Lemley, Professor Shapiro's co-author of the patent-holdup conjecture, decried in 2015 what he called "faith-based intellectual property," which, Professor Lemley said, "is at its base a religion and not a science because it does not admit the prospect of being proven wrong."[776]

---

[774] Transcript of Proceedings (Volume 6) at 1242:16–1243:11, FTC v. Qualcomm Inc., No. 5:17-cv-00220-LHK (N.D. Cal. Jan. 15, 2019) (Testimony of Carl Shapiro) (emphasis added).

[775] Carl Shapiro, Patent Holdup: Myth or Reality? 19 (Oct. 6, 2015) (unpublished manuscript), https://www.scribd.com/document/319856394/Shapiro-Patent-Holdup-Myth-or-Reality-DRAFT-2015-10-06.

[776] Mark A. Lemley, *Faith-Based Intellectual Property*, 62 UCLA L. Rev. 1328, 1346 (2015).

The effect of Professor Shapiro's denunciation of his critics as "deniers" was to tilt the inquiry by insisting (without merit) that its starting point was a consensus that the conjecture in question was a firmly established scientific truth. Professor Shapiro's defense of the patent-holdup conjecture thus radiated a sense of entitlement rather than a willingness to engage in a genuine intellectual debate over the merits of his theory. The result was something less than a scholar's serious response to scientific criticisms of his research that others had carefully documented and brought to his attention.

Returning to Professor Shapiro's sworn testimony in *FTC v. Qualcomm*, exactly how large were the "significant," belief-based royalty "surcharge" and modem "tax" that he conjectured? According to Professor Shapiro's testimony, he did not quantify the royalty "surcharge" and modem "tax" themselves (for his analysis was purely theoretical), so it would have made no sense for him to attempt to quantify any effects supposedly flowing from the alleged royalty "surcharge" and modem "tax." Consequently, all of the numbers in his bargaining model would have been purely theoretical as well.

Professor Shapiro's sworn testimony was an edifice of assumption. Yet, as we shall see in Part IV.F.4, he criticized Professor Nevo for the high crime of conducting an empirical test that contained an assumption. Did Professor Shapiro believe that only *his own* conjectures, theoretical methodologies, and assumptions had validity?

Professor Shapiro relied on his own theoretical bargaining model to *predict* what he thought would occur, rather than relying on real-world evidence to *observe* what actually had occurred. Consequently, his testimony about Qualcomm's alleged royalty "surcharge" and modem "tax" was subjective and nonfalsifiable. He testified that he "rel[ied] on OEM testimony"[777] in determining that the royalty "surcharge" and modem "tax" were "substantial."[778] Professor Shapiro did not explain how he controlled for the possibility that the testimony of OEM executives might be colored by their self-interest in seeking to pay Qualcomm as low a royalty as possible for an exhaustive license to its cellular SEPs. Yet, other economic theorists no less regarded than Professor Shapiro had written several decades earlier about the need to be skeptical of the testimony of interested parties in adversarial proceedings.[779]

Professor Shapiro's theoretical bargaining model therefore rested on the *assumption* that Qualcomm's position afforded it leverage over OEMs and that this assumed leverage resulted in a "substantial" royalty "surcharge" for an exhaustive license to Qualcomm's portfolio of cellular SEPs. Yet,

---

[777] Transcript of Proceedings (Volume 6) at 1243:7, FTC v. Qualcomm Inc., No. 5:17-cv-00220-LHK (N.D. Cal. Jan. 15, 2019) (Testimony of Carl Shapiro).

[778] *Id.* at 1243:7, 1243:11.

[779] *See* Paul Milgrom & John Roberts, *Relying on the Information of Interested Parties*, 17 RAND J. Econ. 18 (1986).

Professor Shapiro's act of stating an economic conjecture was nothing more than the beginning of the scientific process, not the end; and it certainly does not prove a hypothesis merely to state it as a theoretical possibility and then repeatedly profess one's sincere belief that the hypothesis is true.

One could reasonably question whether *any* jury would find Professor Shapiro's idiosyncratic *belief* to be preponderant evidence for finding Qualcomm liable for anticompetitive conduct. An economic expert's opinion that is completely disconnected from the facts of the case, or is predicated on nothing more than "subjective belief or unsupported speculation,"[780] is typically considered insufficiently reliable to be admitted as evidence in a jury trial.[781] Thus, one could question whether Professor Shapiro's belief-based testimony could have satisfied the FTC's initial burden of producing sufficient *prima facie* evidence that Qualcomm's licensing practices had an actual anticompetitive effect.

3. Professor Shapiro Did Not Quantify Any of the Effects of His Assumed Royalty "Surcharge" and Modem "Tax" on Modem Manufacturers

Not only did Professor Shapiro admit that he made no attempt to prove the existence of the alleged supra-FRAND royalty "surcharge" and modem "tax," much less quantify them, he also made no attempt to measure the effects that his assumed royalty "surcharge" and modem "tax" supposedly had on modem manufacturers.

a. Was Professor Shapiro's Testimony About the Effect That the Royalty "Surcharge" and Modem "Tax" Had on Modem Manufacturers Based Solely on His Own "Illustrative" Examples?

At trial, Professor Shapiro gave testimony predicated on a theoretical bargaining model that supposedly illustrated how a royalty "surcharge" and modem "tax" would affect modem manufacturers. Professor Shapiro testified that his hypothetical royalty "surcharge" and modem "tax" reduced the gains from trade in transactions between OEMs and modem manufacturers,

---

[780] Daubert v. Merrell Dow Pharm., Inc., 509 U.S. 579, 590 (1993) (construing the word "knowledge" in Federal Rule of Evidence 702(a)); *see also* FED. R. EVID. 702(a) (specifying that expert testimony is admissible evidence only if "the expert's scientific, technical, or other specialized *knowledge* will help the trier of fact to understand the evidence or to determine a fact in issue") (emphasis added).

[781] *See* FED. R. EVID. 702(d) (specifying that expert testimony is admissible evidence only if "the expert has reliably applied the principles and methods to the facts of the case"); *Daubert*, 509 U.S. at 590–91; General Elec. Co. v. Joiner, 522 U.S. 136, 142 (1997); Kumho Tire Co. v. Carmichael, 526 U.S. 137, 141 (1999). As we shall see in Part IX.D, even though *FTC v. Qualcomm* was a *bench* trial, not a jury trial, the *Daubert* standard concerning the admissibility of expert testimony as evidence still applied.

which in turn supposedly reduced the profit margins of manufacturers of non-Qualcomm modems.[782]

But again, Professor Shapiro did not examine the *actual* effects on rival modem manufacturers. Instead, he based his testimony on a theoretical example. On cross examination by Mr. Van Nest during the FTC's case-in-chief on January 15, 2019, Professor Shapiro testified:

> Q. . . . So could we have slide 28 from—so here's what you—here's what you showed this morning. I take it this is *purely illustrative*. I think that's what you said.
>
> A. Yes.
>
> Q. That the royalty surcharge there is *hypothetical?*
>
> A. That's correct.
>
> Q. Right? It's not based on any quantitative analysis that you did or Lasinski did or anybody did. *It's just a number you've assumed; right?*
>
> A. *It's illustrative. I thought I was clear on that.*
>
> Q. Okay, good. And the rivals' cost, the chip maker's cost, that $5 number, that's illustrative, too?
>
> A. All the numbers here are.[783]

In fact, Professor Shapiro admitted to Mr. Van Nest on cross examination that none of the numbers that Professor Shapiro had used in his theoretical bargaining model had any basis in reality:

> Q. . . . And also the rivals' cost [of a modem], that hypothetical number is substantially lower than what your report suggests is the rivals' cost on average; right?
>
> A. These are just illustrative numbers. They're not meant to—*it's just a concept.*
>
> Q. Okay. The actual number from your report for rivals' cost is somewhere between $16 and $21, not $5; right?
>
> A. I don't know. The costs change over time and by type of chip. So if you want to show me what that is.
>
> Q. Sure.

---

[782] *See, e.g.,* Transcript of Proceedings (Volume 6) at 1133:8–1137:8, FTC v. Qualcomm Inc., No. 5:17-cv-00220-LHK (N.D. Cal. Jan. 15, 2019) (Testimony of Carl Shapiro).
[783] *Id.* at 1199:5–19 (emphasis added).

A. But, no, you should not think this $5 has anything to do with—it's not meant to be an actual chip cost. It's meant to illustrate the concept.[784]

Thus, Professor Shapiro admitted on cross examination by Mr. Van Nest that the real figures concerning the costs of rival modem manufacturers diverged from his "illustrative" figures, but that Professor Shapiro did not know by how much. Moreover, some of Professor Shapiro's hypothetical examples did not even concern smartphones:

Q. . . . And as we see on the chart here, the products you're listing, those are all limited to—those are iPads, not phones; right?

A: Yes. These are the contestable products at the time that I'm using for the test. Of course, to the extent Intel was kept out of getting into the Apple account at this time, it had some follow-on effects as well.

Q. We'll get to that in a minute.

A: Okay.

Q. I just want to be sure the Court's clear. The products that you're listing here as contestable, in other words, that Intel had a shot to get, those are only iPads, not iPhones; right?

A: That's correct. These—these here are iPads as shown, correct.

Q. And you've done your analysis here on profit sacrifice, et cetera, based only on the iPads, giving no consideration to the iPhones; right?

A. Well, in this primary scenario here, the contestable products do not include any iPhone.[785]

In other words, at least some of Professor Shapiro's "illustrative" figures were so far disconnected from reality that they were not even meant to illustrate how Qualcomm's allegedly anticompetitive conduct supposedly affected handset (iPhone) prices, as opposed to tablet (iPad) prices.

It is evident from these excerpts from Professor Shapiro's testimony that he relied on *hypothetical* prices and *hypothetical* costs in his model to illustrate what he predicted would occur *if* Qualcomm's licensing practices had imposed what he called a royalty "surcharge" and modem "tax" in connection with Qualcomm's exhaustive licensing of its cellular SEPs to OEMs. Yet, as we have just seen, Professor Shapiro never determined what a FRAND royalty for an OEM's exhaustive license to Qualcomm's portfolio of cellular SEPs would have been, and thus he never calculated by how much Qualcomm's royalty supposedly exceeded the ceiling on the FRAND range. It necessarily

---

[784] *Id.* at 1200:10–23 (emphasis added).
[785] *Id.* at 1230:7–1231:2.

follows that the allegedly anticompetitive effects on rival modem manufacturers that Professor Shapiro's theoretical bargaining model predicted would have resulted from his assumption that Qualcomm was charging OEMs a royalty "surcharge" were also "purely illustrative."[786] Also "purely illustrative" were the existence and magnitude of the modem "tax" that Professor Shapiro hypothesized would result from the royalty "surcharge." Professor Shapiro's testimony never connected his prediction of hypothetical competitive effects to what actually occurred in the real world.

> b.   *Professor Shapiro Did Not Examine the Actual Effect That Qualcomm's Alleged Royalty "Surcharge" and Modem "Tax" Had Had on the Operating Profits of Modem Manufacturers*

Professor Shapiro testified that Qualcomm's alleged royalty "surcharge" and modem "tax" had decreased the profit margins of rival modem manufacturers. Yet, he admitted on cross examination during the FTC's case-in-chief that he had not performed any economic analysis of the profits of rival modem manufacturers:

> Q. You didn't analyze the direction up or down or sideways of the operating income of any of the chip maker rivals that you're here claiming were harmed; correct?
>
> A. I've explained why the income would be reduced substantially by a royalty surcharge, and I—but if you're saying did I measure their income and how it went up and down over time because of problems they had in their operations? No, I didn't do that.[787]

Professor Shapiro's testimony about the effect that the alleged royalty "surcharge" and modem "tax" had had on the operating income of rival modem manufacturers was thus unsupported by substantial evidence. The FTC bore the burden of production and the burden of persuasion on this question.

> c.   *Professor Shapiro Did Not Quantify Any of the Effects of His Assumed Royalty "Surcharge" and Modem "Tax" on R&D Investment by Rival Modem Manufacturers*

As we saw in Part IV.A, Professor Shapiro testified that the alleged royalty "surcharge" and modem "tax" constrained the ability of rival modem manufacturers to compete with Qualcomm in the long run. He testified that, by reducing rivals' margins, Qualcomm's royalty "surcharge" and modem "tax"

---

[786] *Id.* at 1131:3–4.
[787] *Id.* at 1205:10–17.

supposedly impaired the ability of Qualcomm's rivals to make investments in R&D that might enable them to develop more technologically advanced modems that could compete with Qualcomm's modems. Professor Shapiro also testified that the alleged royalty "surcharge" and modem "tax" would have resulted in diminished investments in R&D made by OEMs. Yet, as we will see below, he admitted at trial that he had never examined empirical data about investments in R&D by either OEMs or modem manufacturers.

> *i.   Did Professor Shapiro Conduct Any Empirical Analysis on the Effects of Qualcomm's Alleged Royalty "Surcharge" and Modem "Tax" on Rivals' R&D Investments?*

First, during his cross examination by Mr. Van Nest on January 15, 2019, Professor Shapiro admitted that he did not examine how Qualcomm's challenged conduct had affected R&D investments by OEMs:

> Q. Professor Shapiro, just so the Court is clear, you have made no effort to quantify the effect of Qualcomm's policies on any OEM's research and development expenses or their pricing or their market share; right?
>
> A. I have not provided a quantification of those effects.[788]

Mr. Van Nest then elicited from Professor Shapiro a similar admission about his lack of empirical analysis of the R&D investments actually made by any rival modem manufacturer:

> Q. Your path to harm involves a situation—I thought I understood, Professor Shapiro—
>
> A. Yep.
>
> Q. —in which over . . . time rivals' commitment to research and development would tend to go down. That's what we established earlier with this arrow; right?
>
> A. All other things equal, that would be the effect of the royalty surcharge and the reduced margins and volumes.
>
> Q. But my point is—my question is, excuse me, you didn't do anything to see whether they actually did go down during the period you're talking about; right? That's all I want to know.
>
> A. I don't think—I think you're still continuing to conflate two very different issues.
>
> Q. Excuse me?

---

[788] *Id.* at 1250:3–7.

A. What happened to the R&D?

Q. Um-hum.

A. And the effect of Qualcomm's practices. So I think we need to be clear about the difference. No, I didn't track—I didn't report—I didn't report as part of my analysis the month, the quarterly or annual R&D by Samsung in this area, if that could be broken out. No, I'm not doing that. *That is not informative, as far as I'm concerned*, about given all what you're talking about, about the effects of the practices here, which my analysis is later focussed on that.

Q. Okay. But just to complete it—you didn't conduct any analysis of Huawei's R&D spending during this period at all; right?

A. Again, if you mean by analysis, did I do some calculations with their financials and say something about that in my report? No.

Q. Okay. And you didn't do that with Intel?

A. *That is not part of my analysis or methodology or anything I need to do to—under my opinions, no.*

Q. You didn't do it with Samsung, Broadcom, Ericsson or Marvel[l], or any other chip maker, that was operating in this time period; right, Professor Shapiro?

A. Again, performing some type of analysis, you don't really even know what you mean, what that would be. I've explained why it's not relevant *as far as I understand the question*. I did not present any of those analyses as part of my report, no.[789]

Professor Shapiro admitted that he did not examine the R&D of a single one of Qualcomm's rivals during the time when (he testified) Qualcomm had monopoly power.

Professor Shapiro confirmed that admission on cross examination with Mr. Van Nest on January 28, 2019, when Professor Shapiro returned to testify on behalf of the FTC in its rebuttal case:

Q. Similarly, with respect to your tax theory, you've done nothing to analyze the R&D spending of any particular chip making rival to Qualcomm; correct?

A. I have not analyzed—I think if you mean by analyzed, look at exactly why they spent this amount of money or when they did it, I have not got into that, that is correct.

Q. Your tax theory predicts that spending will go down, but you did no testing to determine whether or not that was the case; correct?

---

[789] *Id.* at 1206:15–1208:5 (emphasis added).

A. I did not—look, *I stand by the theory* that if you have a—if your margins are cut and your quantities of units are cut, you're going to have smaller operating income and that's going to be a drag on possible investments. I did not empirically test how that played out with different modem chip suppliers.

Q. In other words, you didn't actually look at anybody's margins or anybody's spending or anybody's research and development, you simply assumed there would be an impact because that's what your tax theory predicts; correct?

A. I did not look at—I did not do the type of analysis Professor Snyder did regarding looking at rival by rival and I explained, I believe, according to my analogy, why I don't think that's a good methodology. That is not an accurate way of determining the effects of Qualcomm's conduct.[790]

Thus, Professor Shapiro predicated his sworn testimony about the effect of the alleged royalty "surcharge" and modem "tax" on R&D investments by rival modem manufacturers solely on the predictions of his theoretical bargaining model. He further based his testimony on an "analogy" that we will examine in detail in Part IV.I. Professor Shapiro admitted that he never examined the available empirical data to test whether those data supported or refuted his theoretical predictions.

>   ii.   *Why Did Professor Shapiro's Rebuttal Report Not Disclose Opinions Purporting to Rebut Dr. Chipty's Empirical Analysis of Rivals' R&D Investments During the Period When Qualcomm's Allegedly Anticompetitive Conduct Assertedly Occurred?*

In contrast, Dr. Tasneem Chipty, opining as an expert economic witness in Qualcomm's defense, did analyze the actual R&D spending of rival modem manufacturers when Qualcomm's allegedly anticompetitive conduct assertedly occurred.[791] On cross examination during the FTC's case-in-chief on January 15, 2019—which was seven days before Dr. Chipty testified in Qualcomm's defense—Professor Shapiro gave the following responses to these questions from Mr. Van Nest concerning this empirical analysis in Dr. Chipty's expert report:

> Q. . . . Dr. Chipty looked at actual real world research and development spending by several chip makers, Qualcomm, Huawei, Intel, MediaTek, Samsung. Do you see that in Exhibit 11?

---

[790] Transcript of Proceedings (Volume 10) at 2073:21–2074:19, FTC v. Qualcomm Inc., No. 5:17-cv-00220-LHK (N.D. Cal. Jan. 28, 2019) (Testimony of Carl Shapiro) (emphasis added).

[791] See, e.g., Transcript of Proceedings (Volume 8) at 1696:19–22, FTC v. Qualcomm Inc., No. 5:17-cv-00220-LHK (N.D. Cal. Jan. 22, 2019) (Testimony of Tasneem Chipty).

A. I do. But this is firm-wide investment. This isn't about modem chips.

Q. And you certainly had a chance to comment on this in your rebuttal report after you had a chance to review it in her report; correct?

A. Certainly, yes, I did have a chance.

Q. And you didn't take issue with it one way or the other, did you?

A. *I didn't feel it was anything that I needed to respond to. I guess I may have had my folks look and see if this was accurate.*[792]

Professor Shapiro thus admitted on cross examination that he had conducted no analysis of his own to determine whether Qualcomm's alleged royalty "surcharge" and modem "tax" had actually had the effects on R&D investment by rival modem manufacturers that his theoretical model predicted.

iii. Did Professor Shapiro Consider Dr. Chipty's Empirical Analysis of Rivals' R&D Investments in the Course of Preparing His Rebuttal Testimony?

But what is perhaps more striking is that Professor Shapiro could not say one way or another whether he or anyone on the team of economists assisting him at the Bates White consultancy had even expended the effort to verify Dr. Chipty's analysis of real-world data on R&D spending by rival modem manufacturers; nor, Professor Shapiro admitted, did he even know whether Dr. Chipty's findings tended to support or refute his own theory of harm to competition.

Recall that Professor Shapiro was already scheduled to return to the stand on January 28, 2019 to testify during the FTC's rebuttal case, on the last day of witness testimony in *FTC v. Qualcomm*. Yet, how could Professor Shapiro purport to rebut Dr. Chipty on January 28 if, on January 15, he had just admitted that he did not even know what she had opined in her expert report? Obviously, the window for disclosure of Professor Shapiro's expert opinions had long since closed.

As of January 15, 2019, after two years of litigation that surely cost many millions of dollars, Professor Shapiro's response to Dr. Chipty's analysis was an *ipse dixit*—a dismissive shrug of the shoulders. His admitted basis for ignoring Dr. Chipty's expert opinions on the question of actual R&D investment by rival modem manufacturers was an idiosyncratic feeling: "I didn't feel it was anything that I needed to respond to."[793]

---

[792] Transcript of Proceedings (Volume 6) at 1209:7–22, FTC v. Qualcomm Inc., No. 5:17-cv-00220-LHK (N.D. Cal. Jan. 15, 2019) (Testimony of Carl Shapiro) (emphasis added).
[793] *Id.* at 1209:20.

    d. *Professor Shapiro Testified That It Was Unnecessary for Him to Examine Empirical Evidence of the Effects That Qualcomm's Alleged Royalty "Surcharge" and Modem "Tax" Had Actually Had on Rival Modem Manufacturers*

As we have just seen, Professor Shapiro testified that his analysis focused on his theoretical predictions of the competitive effects of Qualcomm's business practices, yet he made no attempt to quantify those predicted effects or even to find evidence confirming their existence. During his cross examination on January 15, 2019, during the FTC's case-in-chief, Professor Shapiro testified:

> Q. In any event, Professor Shapiro, it's certainly the case that you have not quantified the effects of Qualcomm's business practices on any other chip maker during this relevant period; correct?
>
> A. I have not quantified that, that is correct. I have reason to believe the royalty surcharge was substantial and that has inevitable consequences. But I have not done the type of financial analysis you've been asking me about.[794]

Again, Professor Shapiro stated that he had "reason to believe the royalty surcharge was substantial" and would harm Qualcomm's competitors, but that evidently he did not feel compelled to do any sort of real-world analysis to defend his belief.

Professor Shapiro even maintained that his hypothetical bargaining model spoke for itself, and that he did not "need" to show how the hypothetical royalty "surcharge" and modem "tax" played out in the real world:

> Q. Let's go back to raising rivals' costs. This is part of your theory, but, in fact, you haven't done any economic analysis of the actual costs in the real world of any other chip maker; right?
>
> A. Are you referring to the royalty costs or other costs when you say the costs?
>
> Q. Other costs in the real world that rivals incur.
>
> A. I have not done an analysis of their production costs. *I don't need to do that.*[795]

Apparently in Professor Shapiro's opinion, the predictions of his theoretical bargaining model alone sufficed to prove that Qualcomm's conduct had had anticompetitive effects.

Despite the evidentiary requirement in Rule 702 that Professor Shapiro tie the predictions of his theoretical model to the specific facts of *FTC v.*

---

[794] *Id.* at 1210:9–16.
[795] *Id.* at 1202:21–1203:4 (emphasis added).

Qualcomm,[796] he testified that he did not need to examine the actual effects of Qualcomm's conduct. To the contrary, Professor Shapiro testified, his examination of the actual effects of Qualcomm's alleged royalty "surcharge" and modem "tax" would have been a "complete waste of time."[797]

This reasoning was more than a condescending *ipse dixit*. Professor Shapiro was essentially invoking the tort doctrine of *res ipsa loquitur* to the task of proving anticompetitive effects in a monopolization case. It was not merely that Professor Shapiro had arbitrarily said that it was so. The thing itself—Professor Shapiro's theoretical prediction—could speak conclusively to its own truthfulness. Of course no such doctrine exists in antitrust law. And for Professor Shapiro to improvise one by declaring that it is unnecessary and a complete waste of time to require the government's expert economic witness to present fact-based testimony confirming actual competitive harm is to alter the allocation of the burden of production and the burden of persuasion so profoundly as to violate a defendant's right to due process of law.

4. *Professor Shapiro Merely Assumed, Rather Than Quantified, Harm to Final Consumers*

Professor Shapiro testified that Qualcomm's alleged royalty "surcharge" and modem "tax" "ultimately harm[ed] final consumers."[798] Specifically, he testified that OEMs would have passed some of the additional cost arising from Qualcomm's alleged royalty "surcharge" and modem "tax" on to consumers, presumably in the form of higher smartphone prices.[799]

Yet, on cross examination by Mr. Van Nest during the FTC's rebuttal case on January 28, 2019, Professor Shapiro admitted that he had not

---

[796] FED. R. EVID. 702; Daubert v. Merrell Dow Pharm., Inc., 509 U.S. 579, 591 (1993); General Elec. Co. v. Joiner, 522 U.S. 136, 152 (1997); Kumho Tire Co. v. Carmichael, 526 U.S. 137, 138 (1999).

[797] Transcript of Proceedings (Volume 6) at 1204:24–25, FTC v. Qualcomm Inc., No. 5:17-cv-00220-LHK (N.D. Cal. Jan. 28, 2019) (Testimony of Carl Shapiro); *see also id.* at 1204:5–1205:2 ("Q. You haven't quantified the effect of this royalty on any other chip maker; right? A. Well, I haven't quantified the royalty surcharge, so—in general, so I haven't quantified it regarding specific chip makers, either. That follows. Q. Okay. And—fair enough. Rivals' income, I think you'd probably give me the same answer, you didn't do anything from a quantitative standpoint to look at what happened to any of these rivals' incomes during this relevant period; right? A. That's right. I'm not—I'm not doing the damages calculation for the rivals who were injured. Q. In other words, rivals' income, like rivals' costs, can go up and down based on lots of factors; correct? A. We're talking again about the non-royalty costs? Q. That's right? A. Certainly. It's a dynamic industry. These things change. Q. They change, and they change weekly, monthly, sometimes daily; right? A. Right. And that's exactly why it would be a complete waste of time to look at all of that, when I can focus on the surcharge, which is the extra cost that's associated with the conduct at issue.").

[798] *Id.* at 1121:4–5.

[799] *Id.* at 1136:21–1137:1 ("Now, the OEM won't necessarily eat that whole $5 extra cost. In general, they will be able to pass some of that on to their customers, particularly if all the other OEM's are experiencing the same cost increase. Pretty—so we would expect that $5 of OEM costs to be split in terms of ultimate incidents [sic] between the OEM and the final consumers.").

examined how Qualcomm's alleged royalty "surcharge" and modem "tax" affected handset prices:

> Q. And again, Professor Shapiro, . . . I just want to be clear, you haven't quantified the effects of Qualcomm's conduct on handset prices at all; right?
>
> A. I think it's the same thing I've already answered. To quantify that would flow from a quantification of the royalty surcharge. I said I have reason to believe it's significant, but I'm not putting a number on it. So then I don't quantify these follow-on [e]ffects.
>
> Q. Can I get a yes or no to my question, please?
>
> A. Maybe you want to—I don't know exactly what it was, so . . .
>
> *Q. You have not quantified the effects of Qualcomm's conduct on handset prices in any market; right?*
>
> *A. That is correct.*[800]

Professor Shapiro merely *assumed* that Qualcomm's alleged royalty "surcharge" and modem "tax" would have increased smartphone prices; and, he admitted, he did not examine evidence about actual prices to determine whether higher smartphone prices actually eventuated during the period of Qualcomm's allegedly anticompetitive conduct.

Professor Shapiro's assumption about harm to final consumers was not only unsupported, but also counterintuitive, if one considers the large premium that consumers pay for some smartphone brands. In 2019, Jeremy Skog and I published an article, *Hedonic Prices for Multicomponent Products*, in which we explained that, although the price of a smartphone likely reflects its functional features that consumers value (such the phone's storage capacity, camera resolution, battery life, display size, and display resolution), econometric analysis enables one to infer that a nontrivial portion of the price is attributable to the smartphone's brand name and its perceived social value.[801] Our hedonic price analysis showed that a smartphone's brand possesses statistically significant explanatory power for a smartphone's price above and beyond the smartphone's functional features. For example, we found that consumers were willing to pay a statistically significant premium for the Apple brand (relative to a benchmark brand, which was HTC in our study) that was between $238.33 and $299.38 per phone.[802]

If real-world data indicated that consumers were already paying close to a $300 premium for a specific brand name, how realistic was Professor Shapiro's prediction that a $10 increase in the price of a modem (which

---

[800] *Id.* at 1218:4–17 (emphasis added).
[801] Sidak & Skog, *Hedonic Prices for Multicomponent Products*, *supra* note 752.
[802] *Id.* at 333.

would correspond to 1.2 percent of the median price of an iPhone[803]) would decrease consumer welfare? Would an increase of a modem price of $10 really have changed the OEM's retail price or would such an increase merely have reduced the brand premium for OEMs? These are relevant questions that one would need to address to estimate the possible harm to final consumers from Qualcomm's alleged royalty "surcharge" and modem "tax." Professor Shapiro did not address, let alone answer, any of those questions.

5.　*Blackboard Economics*

With respect to the testimony that is in the public domain, Professor Shapiro's opinions about how Qualcomm's licensing practices supposedly harmed competition rested on conjectures of a royalty "surcharge" and a "tax" on the "all-in price" that OEMs allegedly paid for modems. Yet, he did not conduct any empirical analysis to confirm the existence of the conjectured royalty "surcharge" and modem "tax" or to quantify that royalty "surcharge" and modem "tax" or their actual effects on OEMs, rival modem manufacturers, or final consumers. Professor Shapiro admitted at trial that the real figures for Qualcomm's royalties for an exhaustive license to its cellular SEPs were significantly different from the "illustrative" figures that he chose to use in his testimony.

Thus, Professor Shapiro's testimony of a conjectured royalty "surcharge" and a conjectured modem "tax" causing anticompetitive harm in *FTC v. Qualcomm* was reminiscent of Ronald Coase's criticism in his Nobel Prize lecture of the lack of an empirical mooring in much modern industrial organization theory: "What is studied is a system which lives in the minds of economists but not on earth. I have called the result 'blackboard economics.'"[804]

---

[803] *See id.* at 311 (finding, using the Strategy Analytics SpecTRAX database, that the median price for Apple iPhones was $812.50 as of December 2018).

[804] Coase, *The Institutional Structure of Production, supra* note 466, at 714. For further explanation of Coase's notion of "blackboard economics," see Harold Demsetz, *Ronald Harry Coase, in* 1 THE NEW PALGRAVE DICTIONARY OF ECONOMICS AND THE LAW, *supra* note 265, at 262, 265. Demsetz elaborated:

> What Coase objects to as blackboard economics is not mathematics but a style of theorizing that is uninformed by and unchecked against actual behavior. Coase believes that blackboard economics runs a serious danger of not reflecting all the important constraints and opportunities that actually guide the actions of persons. The manipulation of symbols, be these verbal, geometric or mathematical, without attention to how people actually behave, *and in the possibly mistaken belief that actual behavior mimics the theorist's manipulation of symbols*, is what Coase means by blackboard economics. Mathematical techniques do not necessarily lead to blackboard economics, but the inherent nature of these techniques, or of the theorists with a proclivity for relying heavily on them, suggests to Coase that this method of theorizing is likely to take on the characteristics of blackboard economics.

Id. (emphasis added).

F.   Professor Shapiro Failed to Examine Evidence About Harm to Competition

As we have seen, Professor Shapiro based his trial testimony on blackboard economics—predictions from an economic model that was both theoretically unsound and detached from the facts of *FTC v. Qualcomm*. Consequently, it should come as no surprise that actual evidence from the modem industry disproved, rather than supported, the predictions of Professor Shapiro's theoretical bargaining model. If Qualcomm had been engaging in anticompetitive conduct, then one would have expected Qualcomm's market share of modem sales to have increased or, at the very least, to have remained constant during the years in which the allegedly anticompetitive conduct occurred.[805] Yet, empirical evidence indicated the opposite. Qualcomm's market share fell, and rival modem manufacturers gained significant market share during that period.

At trial, Professor Shapiro tried to address the inconsistency between the predictions of his theoretical model and the available empirical evidence by testifying that his utopian counterfactual conditional would be even more magnificent. That is, he testified that, in the absence of Qualcomm's challenged conduct, modem prices could have decreased even more, output could have grown even more, and there could have been even more investment in R&D by modem manufacturers.

1.   Predictions About First Derivatives in Professor Shapiro's Testimony on Theoretical Harm to Competition

Although he did not say so in as many words, Professor Shapiro in essence argued that his utopian counterfactual conditional enabled him to testify on the basis of his prediction of the first derivative of price, output, and R&D investment with respect to time, respectively. Time of course is merely a proxy for some other variable that changes over time but might not be directly observable or measurable. This use of time as a proxy is the basis for familiar before-and-after arguments about causation or quantification of injury.

In *FTC v. Qualcomm*, Professor Shapiro testified about the direction and rate of change. The direction of change conveys whether the variable being examined increases or decreases from one period of observation to the next in response to some perturbation (such as the introduction of the allegedly anticompetitive conduct by Qualcomm). The amount that the variable of interest changes within a given increment of time is the rate (or speed or

---

[805] My use of the shorthand phrase "market share" here does not imply that I believe that Professor Shapiro or the FTC or Judge Koh properly defined the relevant market or markets as a matter of antitrust law. I address the errors of market definition in *FTC v. Qualcomm* in Part XI.

velocity) of change in the observed variable. For infinitesimally small increments of time, the rate of change is the first derivative of the observed variable with respect to time. It should matter a great deal to the plausibility of the FTC's theory of harm in *FTC v. Qualcomm* whether the sign on the first derivative of each variable of interest was positive or negative: a positive sign means that the observed variable increased over time in the real world, and a negative sign means that the observed variable decreased over time in the real world.

One would have expected the FTC to supply evidence, in the form of expert economic testimony, to prove that Qualcomm's conduct harmed competition because that conduct caused modem prices to rise (positive first derivative of price with respect to time), output to fall (negative first derivative of output with respect to time), or investment in R&D to fall (negative first derivative of R&D investment with respect to time). Yet, Qualcomm proved that none of those predictions came to pass in the real world. The actual direction of change for each of the three variables with respect to time (negative, positive, and positive, respectively) was the opposite.

Nonetheless, Professor Shapiro had a backup argument: the first derivatives of price, output, and R&D investment would all have been *larger* in absolute value if not for Qualcomm's challenged conduct. But why should a finder of fact believe Professor Shapiro's purely theoretical predictions of the magnitudes of those derivatives to be reliable and probative of the competitive effects of Qualcomm's challenged conduct? How was Qualcomm to disprove the predictions of Professor Shapiro's utopian counterfactual conditional? How would a finder of fact balance any unquantifiable hypothetical harm against procompetitive effects? Professor Shapiro's testimony attempted to salvage the FTC's theory of harm in the face of contradictory facts. However, his theoretical conjectures were properly understood to be irrelevant and unhelpful under the Federal Rules of Evidence.

2. *Did Empirical Evidence Contradict the Predictions of Professor Shapiro's Theoretical Bargaining Model?*

Professor Shapiro testified that he did not conduct any analysis of real-world facts or data to support his utopian counterfactual conditional about (quality-adjusted) prices, output, and R&D spending in the modem industry. His conjecture about the "but-for" state of the world was at all times strictly theoretical. Professor Shapiro was forced to admit that empirical evidence contradicted the most fundamental of his theoretical model's predictions about the supposedly anticompetitive effects of Qualcomm's challenged conduct. Qualcomm's lawyer, Mr. Van Nest, disproved three such predictions in his cross examination of Professor Shapiro on January 28, 2019.

a. *Predicted Market Shares of Modem Manufacturers*

First, Professor Shapiro was forced by Mr. Van Nest on cross examination on January 28, 2019, during the FTC's rebuttal case, to concede that Qualcomm's market share decreased and that the market shares of rival modem manufacturers increased during the time when Qualcomm allegedly engaged in anticompetitive conduct:

> Q. . . . Now, your tax theory predicts that as the all-in price of rival chips goes up, Qualcomm will gain market share at the expense of its rivals; isn't that right?
>
> A. Yes, everything else equal, that is correct.
>
> Q. So using Intel as an example, you actually predicted in your rebuttal report that Qualcomm will gain market share at the expense of Intel; right?
>
> A. Again, everything else equal, that is the *natural and inevitable economic consequence* of the raising rivals' costs. I stand by that.
>
> Q. But, in fact, as you acknowledged two weeks ago here in this courtroom, Qualcomm's market share in what you call the LTE premium market has been declining since 2014; right?
>
> A. It has.
>
> Q. And it's been declining as the shares of competitors, like Samsung and MediaTek, have been growing; right?
>
> A. I think that follows arithmetically, yes.
>
> Q. And, indeed, when you and I spoke about this two weeks ago, you said that in 2017, Qualcomm's market share fell and Intel's market share rose when Intel got in at Apple; correct?
>
> A. That is true.[806]

The FTC bore the burden of production and the burden of persuasion on Professor Shapiro's prediction about market shares. Needless to say, the observed *increase* in rivals' market shares disproved Professor Shapiro's prediction of a decrease.

b. *Predicted "All-In Prices" for Modems*

Second, Mr. Van Nest on the same day forced Professor Shapiro to admit on cross examination that, contrary to the prediction of his theoretical bargaining model, the "all-in price" for modems had decreased, rather than

---

[806] Transcript of Proceedings (Volume 10) at 2063:16–2064:12, FTC v. Qualcomm Inc., No. 5:17-cv-00220-LHK (N.D. Cal. Jan. 28, 2019) (Testimony of Carl Shapiro) (emphasis added).

increased, during the time when Qualcomm allegedly engaged in anticompetitive practices:

> Q. Now, your tax theory also predicts that total demand for modem chips will tend to fall as the all-in prices tend to rise; isn't that correct?
>
> A. Yes, other things equal, that's the normal law of demand, that's correct.
>
> Q. But, in fact, as your own studies show us, the number of premium LTE modems sold has increased dramatically during the period when you allege Qualcomm had market power; right?
>
> A. That's correct. The quality adjusted price of these devices has come down a lot. The operating systems, there's so many features that have led to that. To suggest that that is—that contradicts the theory, the law of demand regarding price of modem chips is incorrect.
>
> Q. Excuse me. But it is the case, as you established last time, that the number of premium LTE modems sold during the period you claim Qualcomm had monopoly power has increased dramatically; right?
>
> A. Yes, I've said the, this is a—
>
> Q. Thank you, Professor Shapiro.[807]

We saw in Part F to the Introduction that, although Professor Shapiro's theoretical bargaining model predicted that Qualcomm's licensing practices (1) would have raised the "all-in price" paid by an OEM for a modem and consequently (2) would have reduced demand for those modems, the data proved that the quality-adjusted price decreased and the demand for modems dramatically increased during the relevant timeframe.

c.   *Predicted R&D Investment by Rival Modem Manufacturers*

Third, Mr. Van Nest forced Professor Shapiro to admit on cross examination that empirical evidence disproved the prediction of his theoretical model that the royalty "surcharge" and modem "tax" would reduce the profit margins of rival modem manufacturers, which would in turn would supposedly decrease their investments in R&D. As we saw earlier, Professor Shapiro confirmed these predictions on cross examination during his first appearance on the stand, as a witness during the FTC's case-in-chief, on January 15, 2019:

> Q. . . . And then you said that when income goes down, that can be expected to reduce rivals' investment in R&D, research and development; right?

---

[807] *Id.* at 2064:13–2065:6.

A. Everything else equal, that—I mean, it's really the expected future earnings that drive the R&D investment. So, yes, everything else equal, I think that's a completely uncontroversial economic proposition.[808]

Yet, when Professor Shapiro returned to the stand on January 28, 2019 to testify in the FTC's rebuttal of Qualcomm's defense, he was forced by Mr. Van Nest to admit on cross examination that the R&D spending of modem manufacturers increased during the time when Qualcomm was allegedly imposing a royalty "surcharge" and a modem "tax" on the "all-in price" that OEMs paid for non-Qualcomm modems:

> Q. . . . [L]et's go to . . . the R&D spending. QDX 9348.001. . . . Now, this shows that during the period when you say your tax theory predicts that R&D spending will go down, firm-wide R&D spending from these chip making rivals either went up or remained constant?
>
> A. Well, I don't know what you're seeing in these lines saying up or constant. I completely reject the notion that looking at Intel and Samsung's firm-wide R&D is a way of telling you anything about their modem chip businesses.
>
> Q. Well, let's take a look at MediaTek. MediaTek, in 2005, was spending about 15 percent . . . of its firm-wide revenue on R&D; correct?
>
> A. I see that.
>
> Q. Look at MediaTek.
>
> A. I see that.
>
> Q. And that went up through the period so that by 2017, they were spending nearly 25 percent of their revenue on R&D; isn't that right?
>
> A. I see that.
>
> Q. And they're one of the success stories in this market?
>
> A. I think they are, yes.
>
> . . . .
>
> Q. Now, you've also heard or read testimony during our trial that some of the rivals spent R&D money inefficiently; right?
>
> A. I have heard that.
>
> Q. For example, Intel commissioned a study from Bain, which was presented in court Friday, [January 25, 2019,] which concluded that although Intel's spending was on par, their output of R&D lagged Qualcomm very significantly; right?

---

[808] Transcript of Proceedings (Volume 6) at 1196:8–14, FTC v. Qualcomm Inc., No. 5:17-cv-00220-LHK (N.D. Cal. Jan. 15, 2019) (Testimony of Carl Shapiro); *see also supra* note 644.

A. I remember that.[809]

As in the case of Professor Shapiro's testimony predicting the effect of Qualcomm's challenged conduct on the market shares of rival modem manufacturers and the "all-in prices" of rivals' modems, Mr. Van Nest again forced Professor Shapiro to admit on cross examination that empirical evidence disproved his testimony predicting that R&D investment by rival modem manufacturers would decline. Again, this factual proposition was the FTC's burden to prove by a preponderance of the evidence. The FTC failed to do so through Professor Shapiro's testimony.

3. Professor Shapiro's Utopian Counterfactual Conditional Was Specious, and He Conducted No Analysis of His "But-For" World

Professor Shapiro tried to explain away the fact that the empirical evidence disproved the predictions of his theoretical bargaining model by imagining a utopian counterfactual conditional more magnificent than the real world. He said that, even though quality-adjusted prices in the modem industry had decreased, even though output had increased, and even though there was increased investment in R&D by rival modem manufacturers, his theoretical bargaining model was still reliable because the market could have performed even better. Yet, Professor Shapiro conceded that he had not conducted any analysis to support the plausibility of his conjecture about his utopian counterfactual conditional universe.

a. Professor Shapiro Testified That the Modem Industry Would Have Grown "a Bit Faster" Absent Qualcomm's Challenged Conduct

On redirect examination by Rajesh James of the FTC during the agency's rebuttal case on January 28, 2019, Professor Shapiro initially tried to diminish the significance of the inconsistency between the empirical evidence and the predictions that he derived from his theoretical bargaining model. Mr. James asked Professor Shapiro a "cleanup" question to enable him to rehabilitate his answers to Mr. Van Nest's cross examination. Professor Shapiro's answer was largely unintelligible:

> Q. Mr. Van Nest asked you about different changes over time in market shares and R&D and in prices. Do those questions cause you to doubt your, quote-unquote, tax theory as Mr. Van Nest called it?

---

[809] Transcript of Proceedings (Volume 10) at 2075:5–2076:2, 2076:14–21, FTC v. Qualcomm Inc., No. 5:17-cv-00220-LHK (N.D. Cal. Jan. 28, 2019) (Testimony of Carl Shapiro).

A. No, and he's not really even challenging the tax theory as such. He's—this whole line that he was asking, and all of their experts have developed, that the markets—you know, the products are getting better, everything has got to be fine, you know, it's—it's not an accurate way to look at what's going on. The royalty surcharge—look, if we're talking about—look, I'm just going to—I don't know exactly what the number is, but if it's dollars per phone, of course the market is going to still grow and worldwide adoption is going to grow. *But it would have grown a bit faster, it would have been cheaper if you take away that tax.* So I just—I just think it's the same—it's not a reliable way to look at the problem. And I think that neither Dr. Chipty or Professor Nevo acknowledged that they can't say—I think Professor Nevo—he can't say the market wouldn't have done better without Qualcomm's conduct or without the surcharge. But he then said, but it did very well. So I just don't think they're engaging on the question, what are the effects of the conduct?[810]

As we have already seen, Professor Shapiro's answers on cross examination made it clear that his analysis fell prey to the Nirvana Fallacy. In Professor Shapiro's utopian counterfactual conditional universe, competition would have improved in the absence of Qualcomm's allegedly anticompetitive conduct. Yet, he made no attempt to prove that contention. Moreover, it appeared that even Professor Shapiro was retreating from the grandiosity of his utopian counterfactual conditional by arguing, in his response to Mr. James above, that, absent Qualcomm's challenged conduct, worldwide adoption of smartphones would have grown only "a bit faster."[811] If so, was the gigantic undertaking of *FTC v. Qualcomm* remotely worth the candle? Professor Shapiro did not express any concern that Judge Koh's use of his theoretical predictions to justify imposing antitrust liability on Qualcomm might risk some unintended consequences.

> b. *Professor Shapiro Conducted No Empirical Analysis to Prove or Disprove the Predictions of His Utopian Counterfactual Conditional*

On January 15, 2019, Mr. Van Nest had already forced Professor Shapiro to admit on cross examination during the FTC's case-in-chief that he had not conducted any analysis to determine what Qualcomm's market shares in his two relevant modem markets would have been had Qualcomm not engaged in the challenged licensing practices:

Q. Now, you also haven't conducted any analysis to determine how market shares would have been different but for Qualcomm's conduct in the but for world; right?

---

[810] *Id.* at 2085:7–2086:5 (emphasis added).
[811] *Id.* at 2085:21.

A. That is true. I'm not offering a but for set of, or counter factual set of market shares.

Q. Okay. That's true for both the CDMA market and the premium LTE market that you defined as well; correct?

A. That is correct.

Q. That's not something that you undertook as part of your report?

A. Correct.[812]

Professor Shapiro also admitted during cross examination on January 15, 2019 that he had not examined whether quality-adjusted prices for modems would have decreased by even more, had Qualcomm not engaged in the challenged practices:

Q. And you haven't conducted any quantitative analysis comparing how pricing would have been in the but for world; right?

A. That's correct, I haven't quantified the surcharge which I think you would need to do to go then try to track the passthrough effects of the surcharge. So, no, I have not quantified those effects.

Q. And you haven't done that for either the CDMA market or the premium LTE market; correct?

A. It's the same answer. I did not quantify the royalty surcharge, so tracing through those effects in either of those markets and quantifying that in terms of impact on consumers, I have not done that quantification.[813]

Professor Shapiro thus testified that, because he had not quantified the royalty "surcharge" and modem "tax," he never quantified how much of the supposed "tax" was split among each of the OEMs purchasing modems, the modem manufacturers selling modems, and the consumers purchasing modem-equipped devices. As we shall see in Part VI, it was clearly the FTC's burden of production to present evidence that Qualcomm's conduct had harmed competition, and it was clearly the FTC's burden of persuasion to prove that proposition by a preponderance of the evidence. Were Professor Shapiro's theoretical predictions evidence probative of anticompetitive harm? It was not and never could be Qualcomm's burden of production to prove the negative. It was not and never could be Qualcomm's burden to prove its innocence.

---

[812] Transcript of Proceedings (Volume 6) at 1210:17–1211:2, FTC v. Qualcomm Inc., No. 5:17-cv-00220-LHK (N.D. Cal. Jan. 15, 2019) (Testimony of Carl Shapiro).
[813] *Id.* at 1217:11–23.

      c. Professor Shapiro Conceded That Real-World Evidence Showed "Great Improvement" in the Modem Industry During the Period of Qualcomm's Allegedly Anticompetitive Conduct

Professor Shapiro's testimony criticizing Qualcomm's economic experts was even more perplexing when one considers that each of Qualcomm's expert economic witnesses expressly relied on real-world data in the modem industry to support his or her testimony. On direct examination during the FTC's rebuttal case on January 28, 2019, Mr. James asked Professor Shapiro:

> Q. Qualcomm's economic experts all assert that the overall performance of the modem chip industry is inconsistent with your conclusion that Qualcomm's conduct harmed competition. What's your reaction to that testimony?
>
> A. As I said at the beginning, we agree that there's been a great improvement in modem chips, as in many other high tech markets. If one were to look at that fact alone and say, oh, there can't be any antitrust problem here, there couldn't be any abuse of monopoly position, that would amount to basically not having antitrust enforcement in the high tech sector. And as an antitrust economist, I think that would be a terrible mistake because in these types of dynamic industries, it's very important that the firms that are leaders, who very often typically got there on the merits, that they don't then engage in conduct that basically trips up or stiff arms competitors who are trying to catch and overtake them.[814]

Professor Shapiro admitted in this answer that, during the period of Qualcomm's allegedly anticompetitive conduct, real-world evidence showed that there had been "great improvement" in the two relevant markets for modems that he defined.[815]

    Yet, he testified that even that "great improvement" did not support the conclusion that Qualcomm's conduct did not harm competition, because, Professor Shapiro evidently reasoned, there was no way to know how much better competition in his two relevant markets could have been in the absence of Qualcomm's conduct. When discussing his utopian counterfactual conditional, Professor Shapiro appeared to devalue the importance of real-world evidence when it contradicted the predictions of his theoretical bargaining model.

    But by what reasoning could Professor Shapiro reliably conclude that his assertion of a utopian counterfactual conditional would constitute preponderant evidence of an anticompetitive effect? For the reasons previously

---

[814] Transcript of Proceedings (Volume 10) at 2037:19–2038:10, FTC v. Qualcomm Inc., No. 5:17-cv-00220-LHK (N.D. Cal. Jan. 28, 2019) (Testimony of Carl Shapiro).

[815] *Id.* at 2037:24.

discussed, that proposition would seem clearly erroneous as a matter of law—not merely the case law interpreting the Sherman Act, but also the Supreme Court's interpretation of the Due Process Clause of the Fifth Amendment in *Mathews v. Eldridge*. In practical terms, Professor Shapiro seemed to insist that the defendant in a government monopolization case bears the burden of production and the burden of persuasion during the government's own case-in-chief to disprove the government's utopian counterfactual conditional that the world could have been a materially better place for consumers and the competitive process if the challenged conduct had never occurred. Put differently, Professor Shapiro seemed to treat his utopian counterfactual conditional as a rebuttable presumption of anticompetitive effect—which is to say, an evidentiary device that shifts onto the defendant the burden of production and the burden of persuasion to prove its innocence by a preponderance of the evidence.

d.   *Professor Shapiro's Change of Message on Recross Examination*

In sum, without citing any specific facts, Professor Shapiro conjectured that the market "would have grown a bit faster" had Qualcomm not engaged in the challenged practices.[816] Rather than rely on data and real-world evidence to support that testimony, Professor Shapiro asked Judge Koh to trust his utopian counterfactual conditional, which he offered as a system of beliefs.

Perhaps sensing the gravity of his admissions on direct examination on January 28, 2019, Professor Shapiro appeared to adopt a different approach by the time that Mr. Van Nest conducted his recross examination:

> Q. Now, Professor Shapiro, you told us that there's no way to know how much better things would have been in this dynamic, growing market but for Qualcomm's conduct; correct?
>
> A. I think it's very difficult to know that, and I have not quantified that.
>
> Q. And that's what I wanted to find out. You've done nothing whatsoever to quantify how prices, market shares, spending, or anything else would have differed in your but for world; right?
>
> A. I have not calculated damages here.
>
> Q. Isn't the answer to my question no?
>
> A. I have not quantified those effects such as one would want to do for damages. I'm talking about the harm to competition that was a result of Qualcomm's conduct.

---

[816]   *Id.* at 2085:21.

Q. In presenting your opinions that the world could have been better, you've done nothing empirical to support that view; right?

A. I've explained how Qualcomm's conduct harmed competition—

Q. Excuse me, Professor Shapiro.

A. —to competition, and—

Q. My question was different. You've done nothing empirical to support that view; right?

A. That is *incorrect*.

Mr. Van Nest: I have nothing further, Your Honor.[817]

After admitting multiple times earlier on the morning of January 28, 2019 that he had not conducted any empirical analysis of his counterfactual "but-for" world, Professor Shapiro pushed back against Mr. Van Nest when asked to confirm that same admission during this final colloquy. Why did Professor Shapiro end this colloquy by appearing to contradict his own prior admission about his counterfactual conditional, having already conceded that point multiple times throughout his cross examination by Mr. Van Nest? Judge Koh remained silent during this colloquy.[818]

Mr. James had no further redirect examination of Professor Shapiro for the FTC.[819] The taking of testimony in *FTC v. Qualcomm* had come to an end. Professor Shapiro had the last word.

4. Professor Shapiro Was Critical of Other Expert Witnesses for Assuming Various Figures, Yet He Admitted That His Entire Testimony Was Built on Assumptions

After having admitted numerous times that his own testimony was purely hypothetical, that it relied on "illustrative" numbers, and that it was not based on any real-world evidence, Professor Shapiro criticized Qualcomm's expert, Professor Aviv Nevo, for conducting expert economic analysis that, in Professor Shapiro's estimation, employed an assumption.

On direct examination during the FTC's rebuttal case on January 28, 2019, Mr. James asked Professor Shapiro the following question and received the following answer:

Q. Let's go through some of those slides presented by Professor Nevo. Mr. Kotarski, can you bring up Professor Nevo's slide number 4, CDMA

---

[817] *Id.* at 2088:17–2089:16 (emphasis added).
[818] *See id.*
[819] *Id.* at 2089:21.

contractual rates. What's your reaction to Professor Nevo's testimony regarding his slide number 4?

A. Okay. So, Your Honor, just to remind you, what he was doing here is you see the grey area towards the right where it says Shapiro alleges CDMA market power, that's starting in 2006. He's comparing that era—excuse me—that time period to prior years when there was no allegation in the case of CDMA market power. So now—he then assumes that Qualcomm had no market power over CDMA chips prior to 2006 so he can do a before and after. Okay. But that doesn't make any sense—well, let me—that's not what I mean. *That assumption is not justified.* The whole test is based on an assumption that there's a before and after, Qualcomm didn't have power and then they did. But he didn't test that. *He just assumed they didn't have power,* market power before 2006. And he's—that just—*that assumption is unjustified,* and he's going to have a very difficult time trying to defend that—well, he didn't defend it. There's evidence to the contrary, and he acknowledged that Qualcomm was, for years, the sole supplier of CDMA chips and was, you know, was the pioneer and out ahead. *So he's got a completely unjustified assumption that is the basis for the entire test.* That's why I'm saying it's not a valid test.[820]

Professor Shapiro's testimony on the modem "tax" theory of antitrust liability was entirely based on his theoretical bargaining model. That model *assumed* that Qualcomm had charged OEMs a supra-FRAND royalty "surcharge," which supposedly imposed a modem "tax" on transactions between OEMs and rival modem manufacturers (although he eventually conceded that the "tax" would apply also to modem transactions between OEMs and Qualcomm). Professor Shapiro admitted that he did not quantify either the "surcharge" or the "tax."

Yet, he criticized Professor Nevo for assuming that Qualcomm's bargaining power was weaker before 2006 than after, even though Professor Nevo (unlike Professor Shapiro) had attempted to use real-world data (drawn from Qualcomm's actual licenses) to construct a meaningful bargaining model. Was it intellectually consistent for Professor Shapiro to fault Professor Nevo for conducting an econometric test that contained an assumption over which reasonable minds could differ? Moreover, notice again that Professor Shapiro's criticism of Professor Nevo would essentially reverse the presumption of innocence by imposing on Qualcomm the evidentiary burden to prove a negative—namely, that Qualcomm did *not* possess market power in the CDMA modem market in the earlier period during which the FTC had

---

[820] *Id.* at 2045:21–2047:2 (emphasis added); *see also id.* at 2049:20–22 ("And [Professor Nevo's] assumption that Qualcomm had no chip leverage based on WCDMA chips, he hasn't analyzed that. *It's an assumption.*") (emphasis added).

not alleged that Qualcomm had engaged in any anticompetitive conduct in any modem market.

When Mr. Van Nest confronted Professor Shapiro on cross examination with the fact that his own analysis was devoid of empiricism, Professor Shapiro again resorted to his *res ipsa loquitur* rationale: his theoretical bargaining model spoke for itself, and any analysis connected to the real world would have been unreliable. Professor Shapiro admitted during his direct examination on January 28, 2019 that, unlike Professor Nevo, he did not even examine the Qualcomm CDMA licenses at issue:

> Q. During his testimony, Professor Nevo criticized you for not attempting empirical analyses along the lines of those that he presented. Why didn't you try those kind of analyses?
>
> A. Look, I wouldn't want to do these type of analyses. I've just explained why they're not reliable and they're poorly done. Another way to put it is presented with hundreds of licenses, complicated licenses, maybe one could tease through that, look through that and construct a data set based on those licenses. I don't see a way to do that reliably. Professor Nevo certainly did not do so.[821]

Professor Shapiro testified that conducting empirical tests as a basis for expert economic testimony in *FTC v. Qualcomm* would have been "very difficult, if not impossible":

> Q. Now, you gave some testimony about Professor Nevo's empirical tests. I take it you've done no testing whatsoever, empirical or otherwise, to determine whether the contract rate or some other rate is economically meaningful; correct?
>
> A. I don't understand the question. *I can tell you whether a rate is economically meaningful once I understand what it measures. That's not an empirical question.*[822]

After receiving this Delphic response from Professor Shapiro, Mr. Van Nest rephrased the question:

> Q. My question, Professor Shapiro, is you did no retesting of Professor Nevo's numbers using some rate other than the contract rate? As you told us in your testimony, you haven't done these sorts of tests at all; right?
>
> A. I have not gone back to his set of contracts and tried to construct an economically meaningful variable. Like I said, I think that would be *very difficult, if not impossible.*

---

[821] *Id.* at 2054:25–2055:11.
[822] *Id.* at 2072:12–20 (emphasis added).

Q. And you haven't done it; right?

A. That's correct.[823]

At other points during his testimony in support of the FTC's rebuttal case on January 28, 2019, Professor Shapiro criticized Professor Nevo's empirical tests for being "not reliable"[824] and "poorly done"[825] and for containing "all these problems."[826] On cross examination, Mr. Van Nest challenged Professor Shapiro on such criticisms:

Q. You're limited to criticizing the empirical work that Professor Nevo did because you haven't done any empirical work of your own; right?

A. I've done—my analysis stands on its own. You're referring to specific rebuttal testimony, so, yeah, I'm responding to what he did and explaining why it's got all these problems.

Q. And you've done no empirical study of Qualcomm's license rates, royalty rates, or upfront payments over the years at all; correct?

A. Again, I looked at the licenses. But if you mean by empirical study trying to take all of these hundreds of licenses and distill them into simple data, I don't think you can do that. So, no, I didn't do it.

Q. And you have not done it?

A. I just said I didn't do it.[827]

Considering that Professor Shapiro appeared to believe sincerely that conducting empirical tests to prove such contentions would have been "very difficult, if not impossible,"[828] and considering that the FTC bore the burden of production and the burden of persuasion, it is difficult to see how Professor Shapiro's testimony during this colloquy with Mr. Van Nest on January 28, 2019 helped to prove either the FTC's case-in-chief or its rebuttal case.

G. *Parallels Between Professor Shapiro's Testimony in* United States v. AT&T *and in* FTC v. Qualcomm

Professor Shapiro's reliance on a theoretical bargaining model in *FTC v. Qualcomm* was problematic. Because the model did not rely on actual data, it did not provide any empirical basis for determining whether, in fact, Qualcomm's licensing practices had harmed competition. At best, Professor

---

[823] *Id.* at 2072:21–2073:4 (emphasis added).
[824] *Id.* at 2055:5.
[825] *Id.* at 2055:5–6.
[826] *Id.* at 2073:10–11.
[827] *Id.* at 2073:5–20.
[828] *Id.* at 2073:2.

Shapiro's model yielded a theoretical conjecture that might or might not have been true. As we saw above, Professor Shapiro insisted on cross examination during the FTC's rebuttal case on January 28, 2019 that his purely theoretical bargaining methodology sufficed for the task at hand: "I can tell you whether a rate is economically meaningful once I understand what it measures. That's not an empirical question."[829]

At the time of the trial in *FTC v. Qualcomm* in January 2019, at least one court had found Professor Shapiro's expert economic testimony based on a theoretical bargaining model to be too speculative to provide reliable evidence of competitive effects in an antitrust case. The decision of the U.S. District Court for the District of Columbia on June 12, 2018 in the litigation over AT&T's acquisition of Time Warner, *United States v. AT&T Inc.*[830]—which was later unanimously affirmed on February 26, 2019 by the D.C. Circuit[831]— voiced concern over Professor Shapiro's reliance on a theoretical bargaining model when analyzing the merger's potential competitive effects.

Others have observed that certain criticisms raised in *United States v. AT&T* apply with equal force to Professor Shapiro's testimony in *FTC v. Qualcomm*. In an article published in March 2019, Judge Douglas Ginsburg and former FTC commissioner Joshua Wright of George Mason University observed that "Dr. Shapiro's model in *Qualcomm* appears to suffer from many of the same flaws that ultimately discredited his model in *AT&T/Time Warner*: It is based upon assumptions that contradict real-world evidence and it does not robustly or persuasively identify anticompetitive effects."[832] They elaborated:

> As complex economic evidence like bargaining models become more common in antitrust litigation, judges must carefully engage with the experts on both sides to determine whether there is direct evidence on the likely competitive effects of the challenged conduct. Where "real-world evidence," as Judge Leon called it, contradicts the predictions of a bargaining model, judges should reject the model rather than the reality.[833]

Many of the D.C. Circuit's criticisms of the theoretical bargaining model that Professor Shapiro used as a basis for testimony in support of the government's challenge to the AT&T-Time Warner merger appeared to apply with equal force to the model that was the centerpiece of his testimony in *FTC v. Qualcomm*. Two salient observations follow.

---

[829] *Id.* at 2072:18–20.

[830] 310 F. Supp. 3d 161, 226 (D.D.C. 2018), *aff'd*, 916 F.3d 1029 (D.C. Cir. 2019).

[831] United States v. AT&T Inc., 916 F.3d 1029 (D.C. Cir. 2019).

[832] Douglas Ginsburg & Joshua Wright, *Use and Abuse of Bargaining Models in Antitrust: AT&T/Time-Warner and FTC v. Qualcomm*, Truth on the Market (Mar. 14, 2019).

[833] *Id.*; *see also* Wright & Yun, *Use and Abuse of Bargaining Models in Antitrust*, *supra* note 205, at 1075–78.

First, on cross examination by Mr. Van Nest in *FTC v. Qualcomm* on January 28, 2019, Professor Shapiro testified that he continued to stand by his theoretical bargaining model, which Judge Leon had criticized in *United States v. AT&T*. Yet, less than one month later, on February 26, 2019, the D.C. Circuit unanimously affirmed Judge Leon's judgment in *United States v. AT&T*, finding that Judge Leon had not erred in concluding that Professor Shapiro's theoretical bargaining model was unreliable. Consequently, to the extent that Professor Shapiro's theoretical bargaining model was substantially similar in each of the two cases, Professor Shapiro chose to double down— and Mr. Van Nest thereupon powerfully impeached Professor Shapiro's testimony concerning the reliability of his royalty "surcharge" and modem "tax" theory of anticompetitive harm in *FTC v. Qualcomm*.

Second, considering that the D.C. Circuit affirmed Judge Leon after the trial in *FTC v. Qualcomm* had concluded, but *before* Judge Koh had issued her findings of fact and conclusions of law on May 21, 2019, it is essential to ask whether Judge Koh discharged her duty to make special findings of fact pursuant to Federal Rule of Civil Procedure 52(a)(1) when she completely omitted from her findings of fact and conclusions of law any discussion of Mr. Van Nest's devastating impeachment of Professor Shapiro and his novel royalty "surcharge" and modem "tax" theory of anticompetitive harm. We shall examine that question in detail in Part V.

1. *The D.C. Circuit's Affirmance of Judge Leon's Finding in* United States v. AT&T *That Professor Shapiro's Theoretical Bargaining Model Lacked Both "Reliability and Factual Credibility"*

Professor Shapiro served as the Antitrust Division's expert economic witness in its challenge to the AT&T-Time Warner merger. Senior Judge Richard Leon of the U.S. District Court for the District of Columbia presided over the case. Fewer than three weeks after Professor Shapiro submitted his initial expert report in *FTC v. Qualcomm*,[834] Judge Leon issued his decision in the bench trial in *United States v. AT&T*, in which he criticized Professor Shapiro's theoretical bargaining model and denied the government's request to enjoin the merger.[835]

---

[834] Initial Expert Report of Carl Shapiro in *FTC v. Qualcomm*, *supra* note 115.
[835] *United States v. AT&T*, 310 F. Supp. 3d at 226.

Figure 6. Timeline of Events Surrounding *FTC v. Qualcomm* and the Licensing Dispute Between Apple and Qualcomm

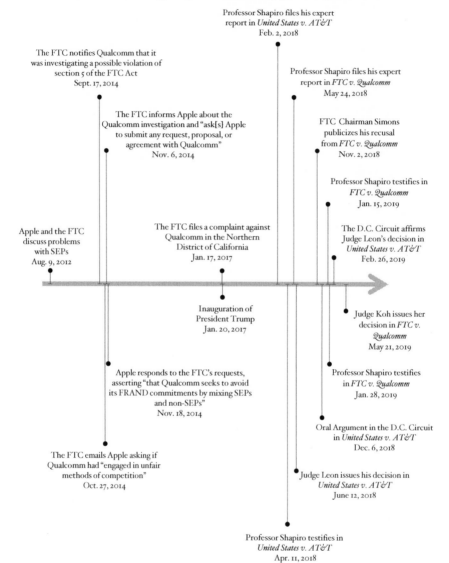

Professor Shapiro files his expert report in *United States v. AT&T*
Feb. 2, 2018

The FTC notifies Qualcomm that it was investigating a possible violation of section 5 of the FTC Act
Sept. 17, 2014

Professor Shapiro files his expert report in *FTC v. Qualcomm*
May 24, 2018

The FTC informs Apple about the Qualcomm investigation and "ask[s] Apple to submit any request, proposal, or agreement with Qualcomm"
Nov. 6, 2014

FTC Chairman Simons publicizes his recusal from *FTC v. Qualcomm*
Nov. 2, 2018

Professor Shapiro testifies in *FTC v. Qualcomm*
Jan. 15, 2019

Apple and the FTC discuss problems with SEPs
Aug. 9, 2012

The FTC files a complaint against Qualcomm in the Northern District of California
Jan. 17, 2017

The D.C. Circuit affirms Judge Leon's decision in *United States v. AT&T*
Feb. 26, 2019

Inauguration of President Trump
Jan. 20, 2017

Judge Koh issues her decision in *FTC v. Qualcomm*
May 21, 2019

Apple responds to the FTC's requests, asserting "that Qualcomm seeks to avoid its FRAND commitments by mixing SEPs and non-SEPs"
Nov. 18, 2014

Professor Shapiro testifies in *FTC v. Qualcomm*
Jan. 28, 2019

Oral Argument in the D.C. Circuit in *United States v. AT&T*
Dec. 6, 2018

The FTC emails Apple asking if Qualcomm had "engaged in unfair methods of competition"
Oct. 27, 2014

Judge Leon issues his decision in *United States v. AT&T*
June 12, 2018

Professor Shapiro testifies in *United States v. AT&T*
Apr. 11, 2018

Sources: Order on Apple's Motion for Summary Judgment, *supra* note 310, at 8–9; FTC Complaint, 2017 WL 242848, *supra* note 28; President Donald J. Trump, Remarks of President Donald J. Trump—As Prepared for Delivery: Inaugural Address, *supra* note 417; Expert Report of Carl Shapiro (Public Version), United States v. AT&T Inc., No. 1:17-cv-02511-RJL (N.D. Cal. Feb. 2, 2018); Transcript of Bench Trial (Morning Session) at 2167:22–2270:20, United States v. AT&T Inc., No. 1:17-cv-02511-RJL (D.D.C. Apr. 11, 2018) (Testimony of Carl Shapiro); Transcript of Bench Trial (Afternoon Session) at 2275:5–2408:13, United States v. AT&T Inc., No. 1:17-cv-02511-RJL (D.D.C. Apr. 11, 2018) (Testimony of Carl Shapiro); Initial Expert Report of Carl Shapiro in *FTC v. Qualcomm*, *supra* note 115; United States v. AT&T Inc., 310 F. Supp. 3d 161, 226 (D.D.C. 2018), *aff'd*, 916 F.3d 1029 (D.C. Cir. 2019); Alexei Alexis, *FTC Chair Simons Recuses from Qualcomm*

Antitrust Case (1), *supra* note 422; Oral Argument, United States v. AT&T Inc., 916 F.3d 1029 (D.C. Cir. 2019) (No. 18-5214), https://www.cadc.uscourts.gov/recordings/recordings2018. nsf/20084E298F4E754B8525835B006ABFB5/$file/18-5214.mp3; Transcript of Proceedings (Volume 6) at 1117:3–1250:8, FTC v. Qualcomm Inc., No. 5:17-cv-00220-LHK (N.D. Cal. Jan. 15, 2019) (Testimony of Carl Shapiro); Transcript of Proceedings (Volume 10) at 2031:6–2089:16, FTC v. Qualcomm Inc., No. 5:17-cv-00220-LHK (N.D. Cal. Jan. 28, 2019) (Testimony of Carl Shapiro); United States v. AT&T Inc., 916 F.3d 1029 (D.C. Cir. 2019); FTC v. Qualcomm Inc., 411 F. Supp. 3d 658 (N.D. Cal. 2019).

The government appealed its loss to the D.C. Circuit, which at oral argument on December 6, 2018 echoed Judge Leon's criticisms of Professor Shapiro's theoretical bargaining methodology.[836] The D.C. Circuit unanimously affirmed Judge Leon's decision.[837] As Judge Leon—and later the D.C. Circuit—concluded, Professor Shapiro's analysis in *United States v. AT&T* was too theoretical and too detached from the real-world evidence presented at trial to provide reliable predictions of the merger's likely competitive effects.[838]

Judge Leon found that "Professor Shapiro constructed a rather complex economic bargaining model" that attempted to predict the competitive effects of the proposed merger.[839] Professor Shapiro testified that the vertical integration of Time Warner (a content creator and programmer) and AT&T (acting as a content distributor) would increase the bargaining power of the new entity. Specifically, he testified that Turner Broadcasting, a Time Warner unit that licenses its networks to third parties, would have increased

[836] *See* Oral Argument, United States v. AT&T Inc., 916 F.3d 1029 (D.C. Cir. 2019) (No. 18-5214), https://www. cadc.uscourts.gov/recordings/recordings2018.nsf/20084E298F4E754B8525835B006ABFB5/$file/18-5214. mp3.

[837] *United States v. AT&T*, 916 F.3d at 1029.

[838] *See* Janusz A. Ordover, J. Gregory Sidak & Robert D. Willig, *Is Professor Salop Right That Judge Leon Bungled* United States v. AT&T?, 3 CRITERION J. ON INNOVATION 249, 250 (2018) ("Judge Leon found that, although Nash bargaining can be a useful approach to evaluating mergers in some cases, the empirical evidence in this case did not support the government's claims, even when viewed through the lens of Nash bargaining. In large part, the problems he identified rested on the inputs to Professor Shapiro's model, not the model itself.").

Professor Shapiro's subsequent expert economic testimony in litigation over another prominent merger (from four firms to three firms) was similarly rejected in February 2020 because it was found to be predicated on insufficiently reliable data. New York v. Deutsche Telekom AG, 439 F. Supp. 3d 179, 238 (S.D.N.Y. 2020) ("The Court hesitates, however, to place too much stock in [Professor Carl] Shapiro's upward pricing pressure analysis given the numerous aspects of the market that it does not capture, as well as the potential that the underlying data may not be sufficiently reliable. Reliance on Shapiro's methodology is further complicated by the theory of consumer harm that Shapiro advances. It essentially asks the Court to assess how slowly or quickly T-Mobile would lower its prices or offer non-price benefits such as high-definition Netflix with or without the merger, regardless of what other competitors do. It is already difficult to assess the competitive effects of a merger in such a rapidly changing industry; asking the Court to assess whether consumers would receive high-definition Netflix in 2020 or 2021 only compounds the necessarily speculative quality of this inquiry."). Elsewhere (but this time on behalf of Sprint), Professor Shapiro in 1997 had reservations whether the entry of a fourth firm into the interexchange (long-distance) market would significantly *increase* competition. *See* Declaration of Carl Shapiro at 8, *In re* Application by BellSouth Corporation, BellSouth Telecommunications, Inc., and BellSouth Long Distance, Inc., for Provision of In-Region, InterLATA Services in South Carolina, Dkt. No. 97-208 (F.C.C. Oct. 1997) (filed on behalf of Sprint Corp. in opposition to BellSouth's section 271 application in South Carolina), https://ecfsapi.fcc.gov/file/1935050004.pdf.

[839] *United States v. AT&T*, 310 F. Supp. 3d at 225.

bargaining leverage in negotiations with AT&T's rival distributors.[840] His bargaining model predicted that, because of that increased bargaining leverage, net prices faced by consumers of video content would increase.[841]

AT&T countered that Professor Shapiro's theoretical bargaining model "lack[ed] a sufficient basis in the trial evidence."[842] Judge Leon observed that Professor Shapiro admitted at trial that "his bargaining model d[id] not 'literally predict[] the price increases that will occur in negotiations in the real world.'"[843] Furthermore, Judge Leon noted, AT&T's expert witness, Professor Dennis Carlton of the University of Chicago, showed that Professor Shapiro's model, when using recent (and accurate) data as inputs, actually predicted that consumers would receive price *reductions*—not price increases—as a result of the merger.[844]

Judge Leon agreed with AT&T. He found that the inputs in Professor Shapiro's theoretical bargaining model were not based on real-world evidence.[845] He also criticized Professor Shapiro's decision to ignore Turner's existing contracts with distributors in his predictive model. Judge Leon noted that "Turner is currently party to long-term affiliate agreements with nearly all of its distributors."[846] Professor Shapiro admitted at trial that those agreements would "prevent [Turner] from raising the fees for some number of years,"[847] but he said that he decided to ignore those agreements in his analysis. He reasoned that including those agreements "would be counterproductive because those agreements [we]re 'temporar[y]' and will 'expire

---

[840] *Id.* at 225.

[841] *Id.* at 199.

[842] *Id.* at 226 (citing Transcript of Bench Trial (Afternoon Session) at 2315:12, United States v. AT&T Inc., No. 1:17-cv-02511-RJL (D.D.C. Apr. 11, 2018) (Testimony of Carl Shapiro)).

[843] *Id.* at 225 (alteration in original) (citing Transcript of Bench Trial (Afternoon Session) at 2294:18–2295:1, United States v. AT&T Inc., No. 1:17-cv-02511-RJL (D.D.C. Apr. 11, 2018) (Testimony of Carl Shapiro)).

[844] *Id.* at 240 ("Not surprisingly, Professor Carlton testified that simply by accounting for all current affiliate agreements and making no other changes to Professor Shapiro's model, the model would generate a predicted net *benefit* to consumers rather than a net harm for the years 2016 and 2017.") (emphasis in original); *see also* Ordover, Sidak & Willig, *Is Professor Salop Right That Judge Leon Bungled* United States v. AT&T?, *supra* note 838, at 250–51 ("The court found that Professor Shapiro employed unreliable estimates of critical inputs, including his estimate of the number of subscribers who would depart from their video content distributors and switch to DirecTV if faced with a loss of Turner content, and his use of outdated and inflated profit margins for AT&T. And, critically, Judge Leon found that small changes in the values of these inputs caused the model's predictions to change dramatically. Indeed, modest changes to the inputs caused the predicted sign for competitive harm to *flip*, so that the government's predicted prices for the programming in question would fall after the merger rather than rise. Moreover, he decided, on the basis of industry testimony, that the long-term blackouts that Professor Shapiro used as the fallback option in his Nash bargaining model are not credible threats. Given these findings, Judge Leon was fully justified in holding that the government had failed to meet its burden to prove that the merger was likely to harm competition and consumers.") (emphasis in original).

[845] *United States v. AT&T*, 310 F. Supp. 3d at 226–27.

[846] *Id.* at 239 (citing Transcript of Bench Trial (Afternoon Session) at 2316:3–18, United States v. AT&T Inc., No. 1:17-cv-02511-RJL (D.D.C. Apr. 11, 2018) (Testimony of Carl Shapiro)).

[847] Transcript of Bench Trial (Morning Session) at 2209:8–9, United States v. AT&T Inc., No. 1:17-cv-02511-RJL (D.D.C. Apr. 11, 2018) (Testimony of Carl Shapiro).

in time.'"[848] Yet, Judge Leon found that, because the available evidence "show[ed] that the real-world effect of Turner's present affiliate agreements will be rather 'significant' until at least 2021,"[849] it was improper for Professor Shapiro to ignore the long-term affiliate agreements.

Judge Leon ultimately refused to rely on Professor Shapiro's theoretical bargaining model:

> [T]he evidence at trial showed that Professor Shapiro's model lacks both "reliability and factual credibility," and thus fails to generate probative predictions of future harm associated with the Government's increased-leverage theory. Accordingly, neither Professor Shapiro's model, nor his testimony based on it, provides me with an adequate basis to conclude that the challenged merger will lead to *any* raised costs on the part of distributors *or* consumers—much less consumer harms that outweigh the conceded $350 million in annual cost savings to AT & T's customers.[850]

Because Professor Shapiro's theoretical bargaining model was detached from actual evidence, Judge Leon found that the model did not reliably predict the effects that a merger would have on competition.

The D.C. Circuit unanimously affirmed Judge Leon's decision less than one month later.[851] In the oral argument for *United States v. AT&T*, the D.C. Circuit shared Judge Leon's concerns with Professor Shapiro's theoretical bargaining model.[852] Judge David B. Sentelle told the government's lawyer during oral argument, "if you are going to rely on an economic model, you have to rely on it with quantification. The bare theorem . . . doesn't prove anything in a particular case. You have to have numbers to make a model work."[853] The D.C. Circuit ultimately rejected the government's appeal, finding no clear error in the district court's decision.[854]

---

[848] *United States v. AT&T*, 310 F. Supp. 3d at 240 (second alteration in original) (first quoting Transcript of Bench Trial (Morning Session) at 2209:11–19, United States v. AT&T Inc., No. 1:17-cv-02511-RJL (D.D.C. Apr. 11, 2018) (Testimony of Carl Shapiro); and then quoting Transcript of Bench Trial (Afternoon Session) at 2320:24–2321:10, United States v. AT&T Inc., No. 1:17-cv-02511-RJL (D.D.C. Apr. 11, 2018) (Testimony of Carl Shapiro)).

[849] *Id.* (quoting Transcript of Bench Trial (Afternoon Session) at 2316:14–18, United States v. AT&T Inc., No. 1:17-cv-02511-RJL (D.D.C. Apr. 11, 2018) (Testimony of Carl Shapiro)).

[850] *Id.* at 241 (emphasis in original) (quoting United States v. Anthem, Inc., 855 F.3d 345, 363 (D.C. Cir. 2017)).

[851] United States v. AT&T Inc., 916 F.3d 1029 (D.C. Cir. 2019).

[852] Oral Argument, United States v. AT&T Inc., 916 F.3d 1029 (D.C. Cir. 2019) (No. 18-5214), https://www.cadc.uscourts.gov/recordings/recordings2018.nsf/20084E298F4E754B8525835B006ABFB5/$file/18-5214.mp3.

[853] *Id.* at 34:58–35:14 (comment of Judge Sentelle).

[854] *United States v. AT&T*, 916 F.3d at 1032.

    2.　*In* FTC v. Qualcomm, *Did Professor Shapiro Stand by His Testimony in* United States v. AT&T *That Judge Leon (and, Later, the D.C. Circuit) Found Unreliable?*

On Professor Shapiro's second day of testimony in *FTC v. Qualcomm*, during the FTC's rebuttal case on January 28, 2019, he confirmed that he knew of Judge Leon's decision in *United States v. AT&T*.[855] Judge Leon issued his decision criticizing Professor Shapiro's methodology in *United States v. AT&T* on June 12, 2018, fewer than three weeks *after* Professor Shapiro had submitted his initial expert report in *FTC v. Qualcomm* on May 24, 2018.[856] Figure 6 presents a timeline of key events concerning Professor Shapiro's respective testimony in *FTC v. Qualcomm* and *United States v. AT&T*, as well as other key dates that preceded the FTC's filing of its complaint against Qualcomm.

    Considering that Judge Leon's criticism of Professor Shapiro's theoretical bargaining model was a matter of public record, it is perplexing that Professor Shapiro would stand by that methodology in *FTC v. Qualcomm*. On January 28, 2019, during Professor Shapiro's second appearance on the stand in *FTC v. Qualcomm*, Mr. Van Nest subjected him to the following line of impeachment questions during cross examination:

> Q. Now, Professor Shapiro, this is not the first time you've been criticized in public for ignoring real-world evidence, is it?
>
> A. Oh, probably not. I've been doing this a long time.
>
> Q. As a matter of fact, you recently testified on behalf of the government as their chief economic expert in the government's challenge to the AT&T/Time Warner merger; right?
>
> Mr. James: Objection. This is outside the scope of the rebuttal testimony.
>
> Mr. Van Nest: Your Honor, this is impeachment. It goes to his reliability and credibility as an expert. And he raised, himself, in his testimony, that he's done this a lot, including for the D.O.J., including in merger contexts, and that's what I want to ask him about.
>
> The Court: It's overruled. Go ahead. You may continue.
>
> Mr. Van Nest: Thank You.
>
> Q. You were the government's chief economic expert in the government's challenge to the AT&T/Time Warner merger; correct?
>
> A. Correct.

---

[855] Transcript of Proceedings (Volume 10) at 2080:15–2082:25, FTC v. Qualcomm Inc., No. 5:17-cv-00220-LHK (N.D. Cal. Jan. 28, 2019) (Testimony of Carl Shapiro).

[856] Initial Expert Report of Carl Shapiro in *FTC v. Qualcomm*, *supra* note 115.

Q. And you testified just last year, in March or April [2018], in that proceeding; right?

A. That is correct.

Q. And you presented a theory of bargaining leverage based on bargaining theory. You said the merger would allow AT&T to exercise too much leverage over content providers in future negotiations; right? Correct?

A. That sounds correct.

Q. Um-hum. And the court there completely rejected your opinion as unreliable, not credible, and completely inconsistent with the real-world evidence; right?

A. I don't—that sounds very strong. Judge Leon had a number of criticisms of mine. If you want to refer to his specific criticisms, let's look at his opinion.[857]

Mr. Van Nest then proceeded to quote excerpts from Judge Leon's opinion in *United States v. AT&T*:

Q. Let's do it. It's in your binder, United States versus AT&T is what the heading says, and it's Judge Leon's opinion of June 12th, 2018. And I'll call your attention to page 113 of that opinion where Judge Leon said, "unfortunately for Professor Shapiro, the facts adduced at trial regarding the real-world operation of affiliate negotiations demonstrated that his testimony 'rests on assumptions' that are 'implausible and inconsistent with record evidence.'" He said that; correct?

A. I see that.

Q. He went on to say, "indeed, this opinion by Professor Shapiro runs contrary to all of the real-world testimony during the trial from those who have actually negotiated on behalf of vertically integrated companies." He said that as well?

A. Where is that?

Q. That's just a little bit below what I just read, same page, 113. "Indeed, this opinion by Professor Shapiro runs contrary to all of the real-world testimony during the trial from those who have actually negotiated on behalf of vertically integrated companies." He said that; right?

A. I see that, yes.

Q. And on the next page he said, page 114, "one was left to wonder why Professor Shapiro turned a blind eye to such extensive real-world experience." He said that as well; right?

---

[857] Transcript of Proceedings (Volume 10) at 2079:23–2081:6, FTC v. Qualcomm Inc., No. 5:17-cv-00220-LHK (N.D. Cal. Jan. 28, 2019) (Testimony of Carl Shapiro).

A. I see that.

Q. And at the end of the day, what he concluded was that your model, your bargaining model, your leverage model, "lacked both 'reliability and factual credibility,' and, thus, failed to generate probative predictions of future harm." That's at page 149. He says that as well; right? That's what he said?

A. 149.

Q. 149. Middle of the page, "by contrast, the evidence at trial showed that Professor Shapiro's model lacks both 'reliability and factual credibility' and thus fails to generate probative predictions of future harm associated with the government's increased-leverage theory." That's what the judge concluded in your opinion regarding the model; correct?

A. I see that.

Mr. Van Nest: Your Honor, I have no further questions, but would like to reserve time for recross.[858]

Mr. James for the FTC began his redirect examination by trying to clean up Mr. Van Nest's impeachment of Professor Shapiro:

Q. Professor Shapiro, have you testified in court apart from the AT&T case that Mr. Van Nest talked about?

A. Yes. Over my career, I think I said about 20 or 25 times.

Q. How does the AT&T case compare to the other experiences you've had?

A. It's just an outlier. I have to say, I—you know, I can explain what I think happened. But I—in my view, my opinions and testimony has been generally very well received by judges and relied upon many times.

Q. Is there anything further you wanted to add to your questioning by Mr. Van Nest about the AT&T matter?

A. Yes, thank you. Your Honor, if you want to go down that road, I would just suggest you look at the D.O.J.'s appeal briefs, and we'll see what the D.C. Circuit does with this.[859]

Professor Shapiro then elaborated that, if Judge Leon's "opinion . . . [were] accepted" by the D.C. Circuit, "it would be contrary I think basically to what all economists would say about bargaining theory."[860] He concluded that the Antitrust Division's "appeal . . . explains where he [Judge Leon] went

---

858 *Id.* at 2081:7–2083:2 (underscore omitted).
859 *Id.* at 2083:22–2084:11.
860 *Id.* at 2084:13–15.

wrong."[861] One month later the D.C. Circuit in fact unanimously affirmed Judge Leon's rejection of Professor Shapiro's theoretical bargaining model.

In sum, as in *United States v. AT&T*, Professor Shapiro's theoretical bargaining model in *FTC v. Qualcomm* lacked factual support. Considering that the FTC bore the burden of production, it was perplexing that the FTC's expert economic witness would (1) assume the existence of the royalty "surcharge" and modem "tax" upon which his entire testimony rested, and (2) decline to apply his theoretical bargaining model to available real-world data. By the end of trial, after Professor Shapiro had conceded on multiple occasions that he had not performed any empirical analysis, his testimony seemed to have become a liability for the FTC's case—just as Judge Leon had observed that Professor Shapiro's testimony seemed to have become a liability for the Antitrust Division's prosecution of the merger between AT&T and Time Warner: "I couldn't help but notice that the more and more questions were raised during the trial about the reliability of Professor Shapiro's theory and model, the more the Government appeared to be minimizing the importance of his analysis."[862]

H. Ignoring Repeated Interactions

From the publicly available portions of Professor Shapiro's expert reports and testimony in *FTC v. Qualcomm*, it appears that his theoretical bargaining model ignored that OEMs and Qualcomm had engaged in repeated interactions. Although Qualcomm and OEMs had executed license agreements as well as modem supply agreements on a repeated basis, Professor Shapiro evidently did not consider how the repeated interaction between the two counterparties would reduce uncertainty about each counterparty's future behavior, which in turn should have affected the predictions of his bargaining model.

1. Professor Shapiro's Prior Writings on the Evolution of Game-Theoretic Responses in Repeated Interactions Between Firms

That conspicuous omission of an examination of repeated interactions is especially perplexing in Professor Shapiro's case because some of his most noted scholarly research since 1980 has relied on theoretical models of how consumer information and seller reputation evolve as experience accretes over time, or on models of how game-theoretic responses evolve in repeated interactions between firms during which learning occurs.[863] Professor Shapiro

---

[861] *Id.* at 2084:21–22.

[862] *See* United States v. AT&T, 310 F. Supp. 3d 161, 220 (D.D.C. 2018).

[863] *See, e.g.*, Carl Shapiro, Consumer Information, Product Quality and Seller Reputation 20 (Oct. 10, 1980) (unpublished Ph.D. dissertation, MIT) (on file with MIT Libraries Document Services, MIT)

wrote in 1982 that "[i]mproved information increases the speed of learning by consumers," which implies that a consumer's expectations can and will develop given the reduction of uncertainty that naturally occurs over time.[864] He also posited in 1983 that, as a general rule, "as buyers learn about [a] product, the demand curve shifts over time," further highlighting the significance of learning in any repeated interaction among economic actors.[865]

With respect to dynamic games, Professor Shapiro wrote that "firms can make lasting commitments so that history matters," such that dynamic games "are *not* simple repetitions of the static competition."[866] In his 1989 chapter on oligopoly in the *Handbook of Industrial Organization*, Professor Shapiro offered the following observation that would seem highly relevant to Qualcomm's ability to engage in repeated rounds of opportunistic or anticompetitive behavior directed at OEMs: "Infinitely repeated games are fundamentally different from finitely repeated ones in that there is always the possibility of retaliation and punishment in the future."[867]

Why was the opportunity to avoid the theorized harm to competition that Professor Shapiro's bargaining model predicted in *FTC v. Qualcomm* not an impetus for OEMs and rival modem manufacturers to work together to reduce the dependence of OEMs on Qualcomm modems, so that Qualcomm would no longer hold this supposed club over the heads of OEMs, to the supposed detriment of rival modem manufacturers? Are we to posit that OEMs and rival modem manufacturers blithely continued, year after year, to sit on their hands?

To assume such docility would ignore how Professor Shapiro has written about firm interactions and rivalries in his prior academic writings spanning four decades. Moreover, that assumption of docility would ignore the intuition, understood since at least the time of Thomas Bayes in the 18th century, that expectations are continuously updated on the basis of observation and experience.[868] Simply put, it is inconceivable that Qualcomm's licensees would allow it to demand "unreasonably high" royalties for an exhaustive license to its cellular SEPs and that, as each year's new smartphone

---

("I argue strongly for <u>adaptive</u> expectations by consumers in response to quality changes by a seller.") (underscore in original).

[864] Carl Shapiro, *Consumer Information, Product Quality, and Seller Reputation*, 13 BELL J. ECON. 20, 34 (1982).

[865] Carl Shapiro, *Optimal Pricing of Experience Goods*, 14 BELL J. ECON. 497, 497 (1983).

[866] Carl Shapiro, *Theories of Oligopoly Behavior*, *in* 1 HANDBOOK OF INDUSTRIAL ORGANIZATION 329, 332 (Richard Schmalensee & Robert D. Willig eds., North-Holland 1989) (emphasis in original).

[867] *Id.* at 362.

[868] *See, e.g.*, MARTIN J. OSBORNE, AN INTRODUCTION TO GAME THEORY 280 (Oxford Univ. Press 2004) ("The eponymous Thomas Bayes (1702–61) first showed how probabilities should be changed in the light of new information."); *see also* KENNETH J. ARROW, *Alternative Approaches to the Theory of Choice in Risk-Taking Situations*, *in* ESSAYS IN THE THEORY OF RISK-BEARING 1, 11 (North-Holland 1974) ("The first systematic study of the inference of probabilities from empirical evidence was the justly famous contribution of Thomas Bayes[.]").

models were developed, handset OEMs would allow Qualcomm to exercise monopoly power over modem sales on an annual basis—all without eliciting a response by OEMs or rival modem manufacturers.

2. *Professor Shapiro's Unsupported Expectations About Qualcomm's Future Practices*

Professor Shapiro testified that Qualcomm's licensing practices could "continue into the future,"[869] but how would he know? He did not perform the necessary analysis to support his prognostication.

Professor Shapiro's theory of harm was based on the assertion that Qualcomm had used the monopoly power that it allegedly possessed in what he had defined as the two relevant modem markets to induce OEMs to pay supra-FRAND royalties for an exhaustive license to Qualcomm's portfolio of cellular SEPs. Professor Shapiro claimed to have examined Qualcomm's market power in those two markets from 2006 until 2016. Yet, he evidently did not examine the market power (if any) that Qualcomm possessed thereafter in either market.

During his cross examination by Mr. Van Nest during the FTC's case-in-chief on January 15, 2019, Professor Shapiro testified:

> Q. And as I think we established earlier today, you don't have an opinion on what market power Qualcomm has today; correct?
>
> A. I'm not offering opinions about their monopoly power in 2019.[870]

Professor Shapiro also said that, from an economic perspective, it would be impossible to analyze markets that would come into existence in the future, such as the putative market for 5G modems:

> Q. Okay. And at the time you formed your opinions and created your report, it was the case that it's not really possible to reliably analyze the market for 5G chips at this time?
>
> A. Well, if you mean by analyze the market, predict market shares, for example, or know exactly which chips or devices will come out at what time, I think that's, that's fair. We do have a pretty good indication that Qualcomm's got some leadership position there, just as they did with 4G. But that would not be a full analysis of the market.
>
> Q. Right. And you said in your report, "it is thus not possible reliably to analyze the market for 5G chips at this time." Right?

---

[869] Transcript of Proceedings (Volume 6) at 1249:15, FTC v. Qualcomm Inc., No. 5:17-cv-00220-LHK (N.D. Cal. Jan. 15, 2019) (Testimony of Carl Shapiro).
[870] *Id.* at 1241:15–19.

A. Could you show me where that is? I want to make sure I understand the context.

Q. Sure. It's in paragraph 113 of your report. Your report is in the first tab of the notebook.

A. Okay.

Q. We can put it up on the screen if that's easier.

A. No. Well, actually, it's not easier for me. But it's up to you.

Q. Let's put it up on the screen, please, paragraph 113.

A. Of my report?

Q. I'm sorry.

A. That doesn't seem right to me.

Q. I apologize. It's your rebuttal report. I apologize. We've got a lot of reports.

A. That's true.

Q. Can we have it up? It's the paragraph that says, 5G-compliant chips are not being incorporated into handsets until 2019. Now I have it. "It is thus not possible reliably to analyze the market for 5[G] chips at this time." You said that in your rebuttal report; correct?

A. Yes. And why don't we read the next sentence then.

Q. You'll get a chance to do that, Professor Shapiro, with your counsel—

A. Okay. So I stand by that.

Q. —If you think it's incomplete. But you stand by the statement that it's not possible to analyze it reliably at this time; right?

A. I stand by this. I just wanted to understand the context.[871]

Thus, although Professor Shapiro testified that Qualcomm had a "leadership position" in the modem market, it was his sworn testimony on January 15, 2019 that it was impossible to predict reliably whether Qualcomm would have monopoly power in the market for 5G modems.

That admission was highly significant, for establishing that Qualcomm would have monopoly power in the market for 5G modems was essential for Professor Shapiro's contention that Qualcomm would continue to engage in what he considered to be anticompetitive conduct. Professor Shapiro admitted on cross examination during the FTC's case-in-chief on January 15, 2019 that, if OEMs could switch to the use of non-Qualcomm modems (which

---

[871] *Id.* at 1180:13–1182:6.

would imply that Qualcomm had little or no market power), then Qualcomm could not extract a supra-FRAND royalty for a license to its 5G cellular SEP portfolio:

> Q. And you have noted in your report that if OEM's had access to chips from other people at a comparable price and with sufficient volume, then Qualcomm's policy of selling chips only to folks with a license could have no effect in elevating the per unit royalty price; right?
>
> A. Can you show me what part of my report you're referring to, please?
>
> Q. Well, let me ask you first. Do you recall concluding that if OEM's had sufficient alternatives and enough volume and at a comparable price, that the policy that you've been so critical of would have no effect in elevating royalties at all?
>
> A. If the cost to an OEM of losing access to Qualcomm's chips were nil, then the no license, no chips policy would have no bite, and, therefore, it would not be able—Qualcomm would not be able to elevate royalties above reasonable levels using that policy alone.[872]

During his redirect examination on January 15, 2019, Professor Shapiro read an excerpt from his expert report (which is evidently not otherwise publicly available) to support his prediction that Qualcomm would continue to engage in anticompetitive conduct:

> 5G-compliant chips are not being incorporated into commercial handsets until 2019. It is thus not possible reliably to analyze the market for 5G chips at this time. *But if* the 5G lead that Qualcomm expects materializes, and OEM's are as reliant on Qualcomm for 5G chips as they have been in the past for CDMA and premium LTE chips, then I would expect the anticompetitive effects of the Qualcomm policies at issue in this case to continue into the future.[873]

It is not clear why Professor Shapiro's conditional predictions about the future of 5G would constitute reliable evidence that was probative of Qualcomm's future market power. Would it not have been more appropriate for Professor Shapiro to consider evidence about subsequent market developments, such as evidence about changes in market shares and market entry? Did Professor Shapiro consider the analysis of actual evidence unnecessary? Despite having examined no information about the availability of non-Qualcomm 5G modems, Professor Shapiro predicted that Qualcomm would be able to

---

[872] *Id.* at 1240:24–1241:14.
[873] *Id.* at 1249:8–15 (emphasis added).

engage in anticompetitive conduct in the future. That prediction appeared to have no foundation.

I.   *Professor Shapiro's Testimony About a Sabotaged Kayak Race*

During his direct examination by Rajesh James of the FTC in its rebuttal case, on the last day of trial before closing arguments, Professor Shapiro analogized rival modem manufacturers to kayaks racing down a river, some sabotaged with surreptitiously placed rocks, which Professor Shapiro analogized to the supposed royalty "surcharge" and modem "tax." Professor Shapiro's "analogy" enchanted journalists,[874] but it did not resemble the real world in any respect, and it was devoid of evidentiary value.

1.   *Analogizing Qualcomm to an Imaginary Saboteur in a Kayak Race*

Mr. James asked Professor Shapiro on direct examination—which is to say, in an assuredly rehearsed manner—how he would "evaluate Professor [Edward] Snyder's methodology" for defending Qualcomm's conduct according to a three-part competitive analysis of the foresight, investment, and execution of rival modem manufacturers (which we will examine in detail in Part IX.B.3).[875] Professor Shapiro responded, "Well, let me do this by way of an analogy."[876]

Professor Shapiro's offer naturally prompted Mr. Van Nest's objection that Professor Shapiro's "analogy" was "outside the scope of [his] rebuttal report" as it concerned Professor Snyder's opinions.[877] Mr. James responded that Professor Shapiro's resort to a previously undisclosed "analogy" was proper because it would help to frame "the issues relating to the dynamism of the industry and the hazards of attempting to ascertain after the fact how specific competitors would have fared absent Qualcomm's challenged practices," which Mr. James claimed had been adequately disclosed because they had "been addressed by Professor Shapiro" in several paragraphs of his rebuttal report.[878]

Considering that fanfare by Mr. James, Judge Koh might have expected that Professor Shapiro had something extraordinarily probative to tell her as the finder of fact. She overruled Qualcomm's objection.[879]

---

[874] *See, e.g.*, Shara Tibken, *FTC's Witness Criticizes Qualcomm's Economics Expert as 'Sloppy,'* CNET, Jan. 28, 2019; Matthew Renda, *Experts Duel in FTC-Qualcomm Licensing Spat*, COURTHOUSE NEWS, Jan. 28, 2019.

[875] Transcript of Proceedings (Volume 10) at 2034:11, FTC v. Qualcomm Inc., No. 5:17-cv-00220-LHK (N.D. Cal. Jan. 28, 2019) (Testimony of Carl Shapiro).

[876] *Id.* at 2034:12.

[877] *Id.* at 2034:14–16.

[878] *Id.* at 2034:24–2035:4.

[879] *Id.* at 2036:1.

a.   The Accusation of Kayak Sabotage

Professor Shapiro thus proceeded to describe his "analogy":

> Think of the market as a flowing river and the firms as kayaks who are trying
> to navigate and race down the river. And it's true, you can look at each kayak
> and see what do they do in terms of foresight? Did they plan ahead about
> the kayaking? What was the investment? Do they have a good quality kayak?
> And did they do their training and how did they execute.[880]

Notwithstanding the variation in foresight, investment, and execution that
the kayakers exhibit, Professor Shapiro supposed that a contestant could win
the race by cheating. Specifically, he assumed that one kayak team is accused
of sabotaging the kayaks of its rivals:

> But now suppose I told you in this race, one of the teams was *accused* of
> hiding rocks in the other team's boats. It really wouldn't make a lot of sense
> to look at the boats go down the river and see, oh, I can explain this boat
> didn't turn right here, and this boat wasn't quite as good as the other, and
> this boat, they didn't know this log was coming. No.[881]

Notice that Professor Shapiro did not assume that a particular contestant
was *confirmed* to have cheated. Rather, he assumed that a contestant could be
merely *accused* of cheating.

Professor Shapiro's imaginary story thus seemed to admit from the start
the possibility that the accusation of sabotage might be entirely false. And,
because Professor Shapiro had not yet introduced his audience to any additional characters in his story, we can only surmise that the accusation of
sabotage would need to come from a rival kayaker, whose veracity—Professor
Shapiro neglected to mention—would itself need to be skeptically scrutinized.
There is, after all, a presumption of innocence in the United States, even with
respect to accusations of cheating in imaginary sporting events. And there
is, further, the danger that serial losers in kayak races, disheartened by their
own mediocrity, might impute their failure not to the legitimate superiority
of the serial winner, but to a scurrilous accusation that the winner cheated.
Exacerbating that danger is the possibility that, to embroider Professor
Shapiro's imaginary story only slightly, serial losers might be tempted to lobby
the Federal Kayak Commission to deploy its considerable public resources to
investigate and prosecute the serial winner on a novel theory of sabotaging
the kayaks of his rivals. Professor Shapiro ignored that the ability to make
false accusations against the serial winner could itself become a competitive

---

[880]   *Id.* at 2036:8–15.
[881]   *Id.* at 2036:16–22 (emphasis added).

weapon of contestants who lacked the requisite skills to compete successfully on meritorious terms.

b. Did the Presence of Rocks Affect the Kayaks?

Professor Shapiro of course analogized the accused cheater to Qualcomm, the rocks with which the accused cheater allegedly sabotaged other kayaks to Qualcomm's supposed royalty "surcharge" and modem "tax," and the allegedly injured kayakers to rival modem manufacturers. He continued:

> The more direct approach would be to say, wait a minute. The rocks— which are analogous to the royalty surcharge—we know rocks weigh down canoes and make them slower—kayaks, make them slower and more likely to capsize. And I've explained how the royalty surcharge acts like a tax on the competitors. So the more sensible approach and the analogy would be to say, let's look and investigate and see if the team accused of placing the rocks did so and whether they were sufficiently heavy to make any difference. Well, the analogy would be, let's look and see whether the conduct created a royalty surcharge, and was it significant? I did that first. And then we can then trace through the effects, how did that affect the market?[882]

The trial transcript indicates that, upon hearing this testimony by Professor Shapiro, Judge Koh said nothing from the bench. For example, she did not ask Professor Shapiro to explain who in his story of the kayaks was analogous to OEMs, or precisely what aspect of his story represented the modem-purchase transaction between the OEM and a rival modem manufacturer that was supposedly subject to a modem "tax."

Although Professor Shapiro did not provide the following level of elaboration, it would appear that his story of the kayaks assumed that a contestant's probability of winning the race was a function of (at least) four variables. (We will see shortly that the probability of winning a whitewater kayak race is likely a function of more than four variables that can be readily identified, but for the time being let us restrict the discussion to the four variables that Professor Shapiro apparently considered.) Consistent with Professor Snyder's model for explaining competitive outcomes, and as a first approximation, a contestant's probability of winning the kayak race increases (1) with a contestant's level of foresight, (2) with its level (or productivity) of investment, and (3) with its level of execution. However, Professor Shapiro posits, the contestant's probability of winning decreases (4) if a rival has cheated by hiding rocks in the contestant's kayak.

---

[882] *Id.* at 2036:22–2037:11.

c. Was It Plausible That the Accused Cheater Repeatedly Escaped Detection?

Yet, before indulging Professor Shapiro's "analogy" a moment further, it is essential to emphasize that the risk to contestants posed by a cheater's "hiding" rocks in the kayaks of rivals is credible only if that act of sabotage can escape detection until *after* the race is run. By the end of the race, the hidden rocks—if they actually exist and are not merely a false accusation— will surely have been discovered. And that revelation will mark the last time that a kayak race involving any of these same contestants (or this same race organizer, or anyone who has heard the account of this act of kayak sabotage) will occur without there being an inspection for hidden rocks conducted *before* the start of any race.

In other words, Professor Shapiro was describing in his testimony an act of cheating that could succeed *at most only once*. This caveat is important at face value, but also because it seems out of character with Professor Shapiro's academic research. Recall that we saw that much of Professor Shapiro's scholarly output since 1980 has studied how information and reputation evolve as experience accretes over time, or how game-theoretic responses evolve in repeated interactions during which learning occurs.[883]

d. The Marginal Effect of the Hidden Rocks on the Contestant's Probability of Winning

Professor Shapiro was implicitly assuming also that the marginal effect of the hidden rocks on the contestant's probability of winning had greater explanatory power (in terms of the magnitude of the effect and the level of confidence with which we would impute proximate causation to it) than would the marginal variations in a given contestant's levels of foresight, investment, and execution relative to the corresponding levels for other contestants. And of course if the accusation of sabotage by a given contestant were falsely made, the only causal factors that properly could be blamed for a given contestant's poor performance would be the contestant's own deficiency in foresight or investment or execution—either independently or in combination with one another.

Finally, any predictive model will contain an error term. We will examine some of the exogenous factors (apart from the cheater's sabotage) whose significance in predicting victory or defeat in a whitewater kayak race might dwarf the predictive power of the four variables discussed above, such that their omission from the model might cause the importance of the error term to increase.

---

[883] *See supra* text accompanying notes 863–867.

e.   Can Analogy Substitute for Economic Analysis?

Professor Shapiro used his "analogy" to condemn Professor Snyder's methodology. In Professor Shapiro's opinion, it was Professor Snyder's burden (which in Professor Shapiro's opinion Professor Snyder failed to carry) to prove that Qualcomm's conduct *did not* proximately cause the failing rival modem manufacturers to fail. According to Professor Shapiro, Professor Snyder's factually based economic methodology was less probative of Qualcomm's possible antitrust liability than was Professor Shapiro's kayak story:

> In the case of the analogy, I certainly would not think it would be very good for the race officials to say, oh, well, they put the rocks in the boats, but, you know, this boat really wasn't very good and they made a mistake on that rapid, so we don't care about the rocks. That would amount to blaming the victims. I just don't think that methodology is reliable.[884]

Elsewhere in his testimony of January 28, 2019, Professor Shapiro reiterated his belief that his kayak analogy adequately explained why he did not need to conduct the sort of analysis that Professor Snyder did and why that analysis supposedly was not "accurate":

> I did not do the type of analysis Professor Snyder did regarding looking at rival by rival and I explained, I believe, *according to my analogy*, why I don't think that's a good methodology. That is not an accurate way of determining the effects of Qualcomm's conduct.[885]

Was it remotely plausible for Professor Shapiro to "believe" that storytelling can refute the serious analysis of an opposing expert economic witness? Analogy cannot substitute for economic analysis. Analogy is not evidence.

2.   Was Professor Shapiro's "Analogy" Coherent?

Professor Shapiro's "analogy" immediately invited his audience to ask embarrassing questions about the conspicuous holes in the plot.

a.   Where in the Sabotaged Kayaks Would the Hidden Rocks Repose, Undetected?

To expose those holes in Professor Shapiro's kayak story, consider the Dagger Katana 10.4 kayak, which is designed for "a wild romp through class III

---

[884] Transcript of Proceedings (Volume 10) at 2037:11–17, FTC v. Qualcomm Inc., No. 5:17-cv-00220-LHK (N.D. Cal. Jan. 28, 2019) (Testimony of Carl Shapiro).

[885] *Id.* at 2074:15–19 (emphasis added).

whitewater."[886] Shown in Figure 7, it weighs 56 pounds and is 10 feet, 4 inches long.[887]

Figure 7. The Dagger Katana 10.4 Kayak

Source: *Dagger Katana 10.4 Kayak*, REI Co-op, https://www.rei.com/product/882562/dagger-katana-104-kayak.

First and foremost, where would a saboteur hide rocks in a kayak? A photograph of the compact Katana kayak indicates that there is little room to hide rocks. Perhaps a saboteur could conceal the rocks in the kayak's deck hatch. But then why would the kayaker not check his deck hatch (if his kayak has one, as the Katana does) when he hears the rocks rattling around? Why would the kayaker not check the cockpit for hidden rocks? And how would the kayaker manage not to notice the unexpected weight that the cheater's hidden rocks had added to the kayak?

Put differently, how could the presence of hidden rocks plausibly escape detection by the intended victims of the kayak sabotage? How could no one in the victim class of rival kayakers notice the added weight when portaging his kayak to the river? Why would none of the victims alert the officials to unsportsmanlike conduct by some person or persons unknown? Did Professor Shapiro expect us to assume that uninvited rocks never spill out and thus reveal to the victimized kayaker, if he is so oblivious as not to have noticed sooner, that he is the target of sabotage? Are we supposed to assume that a typical kayak racer would not notice if he were sitting on rocks while racing his kayak?

---

[886] *Dagger Katana 10.4 Kayak*, REI Co-op, https://www.rei.com/product/882562/dagger-katana-104-kayak.
[887] *Id.*

Professor Shapiro's rocks-in-the-kayak "analogy" had so abstracted away facts from the real world that it no longer resembled actual kayaking, much less Qualcomm's alleged royalty "surcharge" on an exhaustive license to its portfolio of cellular SEPs and the alleged modem "tax."

> b.   *Was Professor Shapiro Correct That Kayaks Weighed Down by Rocks Are Slower and More Likely to Capsize Than Their Unburdened Rivals?*

Beyond suspending belief over the failure of rival kayakers to detect the *presence* of the cumbersome rocks, Professor Shapiro asked that the finder of fact suspend disbelief over the supposed *effect* of the rocks on the racing kayaks. Perhaps the defining characteristic of Professor Shapiro's "analogy" was that "rocks weigh down . . . kayaks [and] make them slower and more likely to capsize."[888] Do facts tend to confirm or refute that hypothesis? The burdened kayaks, Professor Shapiro conjectured, would travel more slowly down the racecourse than their unburdened rival, and for that reason alone the burdened kayaks would lose the race. The burdened kayaks, Professor Shapiro added, would also be more likely to capsize than their unburdened rivals. Yet even a cursory investigation casts serious doubt on those central tenets of his "analogy."

In *Two Years Before the Mast*, Richard Henry Dana wrote of how his ship, "having discharged her cargo and taken in ballast, . . . prepared to get under weigh."[889] Quite possibly, Dana visited the spot in San Diego Bay called Ballast Point—originally named Punta de los Guijarros, or Cobblestone Point— where, in the California of 1840, ships loaded and unloaded cobblestones used for ballast.[890] Taking on cobblestones would lower the ship's center of gravity and improve its stability. In the California of 2019, Professor Shapiro implicitly assumed in his rocks-in-the-kayak "analogy" that the proximate cause of winning the race was speed—which, he hypothesized, the rocks would reduce. Yet, the fact that some kayakers choose to use ballast implies that they would willingly sacrifice some speed for greater stability.[891]

Professor Shapiro's "analogy" could not support his unambiguous conclusion that the rocks impeded the burdened kayaks, because people do in fact use ballast to improve stability. Might a few rocks in the kayak be welcomed

---

[888] Transcript of Proceedings (Volume 10) at 2036:24–25, FTC v. Qualcomm Inc., No. 5:17-cv-00220-LHK (N.D. Cal. Jan. 28, 2019) (Testimony of Carl Shapiro).

[889] RICHARD HENRY DANA, JR., TWO YEARS BEFORE THE MAST ch. XXIII (1840).

[890] GERALD G. KUHN & FRANCIS P. SHEPARD, SEA CLIFFS, BEACHES, AND COASTAL VALLEYS OF SAN DIEGO COUNTY 157 (Univ. of California Press 1984).

[891] *See, e.g.*, Frank Ladd, *Kayak Stability*, TOPKAYAKER.NET, undated, http://www.topkayaker.net/Articles/ Instruction/Balance.html; *Ballast for a Kayak*, PADDLING.COM, https://forums.paddling.com/t/ballast-for-a-kayak/67727. Some kayaks have a skeg for added stability. *See, e.g., Parts of a Kayak: Understanding Your Boat*, REI CO-OP, https://www.rei.com/learn/expert-advice/kayak-parts.html?series=intro-to-kayaking.

ballast for some kayakers? And, if so, was Professor Shapiro's "analogy" too frothy as a matter of kayaking, much less as a matter of antitrust jurisprudence?

c.   *The Parameters of the Metaphorical Race*

What was the *effect* of the hidden rocks on the outcome of Professor Shapiro's imaginary kayak race? Put differently, what factors influence the velocity of a river's current and thus influence a kayak's velocity during a race through river rapids? As a first approximation, at least five factors seem relevant: (1) the slope gradient (the vertical drop in the river's elevation) over the interval in question, (2) the extent to which the river channel narrows, (3) the roughness of the channel, (4) the level of the river channel, which depends on the rate at which water enters the river from its tributaries, and (5) whether the tide is high or low. Put differently, the velocity of the river current and the velocity of the kayak depend on the size and declivity and drag of the channel, and the volume of water being forced through the channel. We observe the greatest velocity where the river channel narrows over smooth rock and has the greatest vertical drop.[892] Likewise, we see a faster river current at flood stage, following a rainstorm or a snow melt, and a slower river current during dry months.

Kayak races along river rapids of course are typically slalom events, not straight-line dashes, and river rocks create a natural obstacle course. Consequently, factors other than a kayak's velocity surely influence a contestant's probability of winning the race. Maneuverability in the face of obstacles is critical to a contestant's performance. A tradeoff exists between velocity and control, particularly because the character of the rapids on a given stretch of river can change substantially under different conditions. For example, the Virginia side of the Little Falls rapid, several miles above Washington, D.C. on the Potomac River, "is a [class] III–IV rapid" that "is harder when the tide is low and/or the river is above 3 ft."[893] Kayakers report that "Little Falls completely changes as a rapid as the water level rises, and takes on an aggressive and chaotic character not found at lower levels."[894]

---

[892] The Great Falls of the Potomac, northwest of Washington, D.C., illustrate an especially dangerous confluence of these factors that has resulted in many drownings:

> The falls consist of cascading rapids and several 20 foot waterfalls, with a total 76-foot drop in elevation over a distance of less than a mile. The Potomac River narrows from nearly 1,000 feet, just above the falls, to between 60 and 100 feet wide as it rushes through Mather Gorge, a short distance below the falls. The Great Falls of the Potomac display the steepest and most spectacular fall line rapids of any eastern river.

Jim Burnett, *"If You Enter the River, You Will Die,"* Nat'l Parks Traveler, May 24, 2010, https://www.nationalparkstraveler.org/2010/05/if-you-enter-river-you-will-die5897.

[893] *See Potomac*, American Whitewater, https://www.americanwhitewater.org/content/River/detail/id/90/.

[894] *Id.*

Professor Shapiro's "analogy" did not appear to contemplate how any of those considerations might better explain a kayaker's performance than his imagined rocks in the kayak could.

d.   Would or Would Not the Rocks Be Kayak Agnostic?

Even more fundamentally, Professor Shapiro's "analogy" was specious on its face because it assumed that Qualcomm was discriminating in its placement of rocks in kayaks: by Professor Shapiro's assumption, nefarious rocks reposed only in non-Qualcomm kayaks. That was akin to his saying that only non-Qualcomm modems were saddled with a royalty "surcharge" and modem "tax." Yet, recall that, on the final day of taking evidence at trial, January 28, 2019, Professor Shapiro admitted that *both* Qualcomm and non-Qualcomm modems would bear the royalty "surcharge" and modem "tax" under his theory of competitive harm. As we saw earlier, in his direct examination he testified that "of course *the OEM pays the royalty and the surcharge regardless of which chip they buy.* That's not in dispute."[895] In other words, Professor Shapiro agreed with Professor Nevo that Qualcomm's licensing policy was "chip agnostic." Any supposed royalty "surcharge" and modem "tax" were therefore symmetric across different brands of modems and could not have been the basis for any kind of anticompetitive discrimination that Qualcomm directed at rival modem manufacturers.

It was difficult to reconcile Professor Shapiro's admission at page 2057 of the trial transcript on January 28, 2019—that Qualcomm's licensing policy was "chip agnostic"—with the predicate of his "analogy," that only *non*-Qualcomm kayaks would be burdened with rocks. Minutes before his admission that Qualcomm's licensing policy was "chip agnostic," Professor Shapiro had testified, at page 2036 of the trial transcript, that in his kayak story "one of the teams was accused of hiding rocks in the *other* team[s'] boats."[896] In her closing argument to Judge Koh, Ms. Milici of the FTC did not try to reconcile that stark discrepancy. Instead, she appeared to disregard Professor Shapiro's contradictory "analogy" altogether when she told Judge Koh that "Qualcomm's royalty surcharge is *not* chip neutral."[897] The question of whether rocks burdened Qualcomm's *own* kayak in Professor Shapiro's analogy appeared to produce a material inconsistency between the FTC's understanding of the case and Professor Shapiro's understanding of the case. Judge Koh did not acknowledge that inconsistency in her findings of fact and conclusions of law.

---

[895] Transcript of Proceedings (Volume 10) at 2057:19–21, FTC v. Qualcomm Inc., No. 5:17-cv-00220-LHK (N.D. Cal. Jan. 28, 2019) (Testimony of Carl Shapiro) (emphasis added).

[896] *Id.* at 2036:16–17 (emphasis added).

[897] Transcript of Proceedings (Volume 11) at 2128:1, FTC v. Qualcomm Inc., No. 5:17-cv-00220-LHK (N.D. Cal. Jan. 29, 2019) (closing argument of Jennifer Milici for the FTC) (emphasis added).

### e.	Did Professor Shapiro's Analogy Presume That Qualcomm Had Engaged in Criminal Misconduct?

The Federal Rules of Evidence do not provide for trial by imagination. Professor Shapiro's kayak "analogy" was lacking in any probative value because his factual predicate preordained the answer to the question that he purported to examine.

When Professor Shapiro imagined the saboteur hiding rocks in his rivals' boats, the saboteur had necessarily committed an intentional tort—perhaps a trespass to chattel or a fraud on the organizers of the race—as well as a misdemeanor, such as reckless endangerment of property,[898] or a felonious crime, such as conspiracy or reckless endangerment to persons.[899] To the extent that sabotage by stowing hidden rocks increased the risk that a kayak would capsize (as Professor Shapiro conjectured), and to the extent that the capsizing of the kayak in powerful river rapids in turn would increase the risk of a kayaker's drowning, could such a depraved indifference to human life foreseeably result in second-degree murder?[900] Separately, if the cheater's sabotage independently constituted a felony, and if the sabotage caused a kayaker's death, could the saboteurs be prosecuted for felony murder?[901]

Simply to posit that a party was cheating in the manner that Professor Shapiro imagined was to presume that the cheater had attempted to rig the competition by criminal means, whether or not the cheater actually managed to win.[902] To the contrary of hiding rocks in a rival's kayak, the development and licensing of a large and valuable portfolio of cellular SEPs is inherently creative and productive, not inherently imitative, envious, or destructive. It

---

[898] *See* N.Y. PENAL CODE § 145.25 (defining misdemeanor reckless endangerment of property: "A person is guilty of reckless endangerment of property when he recklessly engages in conduct which creates a substantial risk of damage to the property of another person in an amount exceeding two hundred fifty dollars. Reckless endangerment of property is a class B misdemeanor."); *id.* § 120.20 (defining misdemeanor reckless endangerment: "A person is guilty of reckless endangerment in the second degree when he recklessly engages in conduct which creates a substantial risk of serious physical injury to another person.").

[899] *See, e.g., id.* § 120.25 (defining felony reckless endangerment: "A person is guilty of reckless endangerment in the first degree when, under circumstances evincing a depraved indifference to human life, he recklessly engages in conduct which creates a grave risk of death to another person.").

[900] *See, e.g., id.* § 125.25 (defining murder in the second degree: "A person is guilty of murder in the second degree when: . . . 2. Under circumstances evincing a depraved indifference to human life, he recklessly engages in conduct which creates a grave risk of death to another person, and thereby causes the death of another person.").

[901] *See, e.g.,* J. Gregory Sidak, *Two Economic Rationales for Felony Murder*, 2016 CORNELL L. REV. ONLINE 51.

[902] For her role in the attack on rival figure skater Nancy Kerrigan at the Olympic trials in Portland, Oregon in 1994, Tonya Harding "pleaded guilty to conspiracy to hinder prosecution," "was sentenced to three years' probation," and was "ordered to pay \$160,000 and . . . do 500 hours of community service." *Figure Skating: Gillooly Sentenced to Two Years in Jail*, N.Y. TIMES, July 14, 1994, at B17. The United States Figure Skating Association barred Harding for life. *Id.* Two of her co-conspirators were sentenced to prison. *Id.* The sentencing judge said: "It is a blot on the city of Portland's reputation that will linger long after the names of [the five conspirators] have vanished from our collective memory. All that will be recalled is a band of thugs from Portland . . . tried to rig the national figure skating association championships and the Olympics by stealth and violence." *Id.*

certainly is not conduct creating a substantial risk of serious physical injury to another person or conduct evincing a depraved indifference to human life, as the malicious sabotage of Professor Shapiro's imaginary cheater would need to manifest for it plausibly to be capable of achieving its intended purpose of rigging the outcome of the kayak race. Put differently, Professor Shapiro's kayak story begins with the heavy-handed assumption that Qualcomm's behavior is analogous to serious criminal conduct.

Professor Shapiro then presumed to argue that it "would amount to *blaming the victims*" "for the race officials to say" that, notwithstanding that the saboteur "put the rocks in the boats, . . . this boat really wasn't very good and they made a mistake on that rapid, so we don't care about the rocks."[903] Professor Shapiro resorted to the ancient logical fallacy of appealing to pity—which in its Latin expression, *argumentum ad misericordiam*, even more vividly expresses the fallacy as an appeal to a pitying heart.[904] Professor Shapiro tempted us to skip a rational inquiry into the proximate cause of a particular kayaker's failure because Professor Shapiro had already cast the kayaker as a victim deserving our pity (much as he had already analogized Qualcomm to a criminal deserving our loathing). If in the eyes of the law pity could so readily displace a dispassionate and reasoned examination of proximate causation, Mrs. Palsgraf never would have lost her lawsuit against the Long Island Railroad.[905]

f.   Was Professor Shapiro's Testimony on His Kayak "Analogy" Evidence Properly Admitted at Trial?

Surely it was not a close call whether Professor Shapiro's kayak "analogy" was evidence admissible at trial. He evidently had not disclosed the kayak "analogy" in his expert rebuttal report,[906] as Federal Rules of Civil Procedure 26(a)(2)(B) and 37(c)(1) require.[907] Nor was there reason to believe that Professor Shapiro's failure to disclose his opinion was substantially

---

[903] Transcript of Proceedings (Volume 10) at 2038:11–16, FTC v. Qualcomm Inc., No. 5:17-cv-00220-LHK (N.D. Cal. Jan. 28, 2019) (Testimony of Carl Shapiro) (emphasis added).

[904] *See* Irving M. Copi & Carl Cohen, Introduction to Logic 129 (Pearson Education 12th ed. 2005); *see also* Trudy Govier, A Practical Study of Argument 170 (Wadsworth 7th ed. 2010). The appeal to pity is said to be a fallacy "when used to gain acceptance for a conclusion without fulfilling the obligation of supporting the conclusion by providing strong and relevant evidence to meet a burden of proof. The emotional appeal is used to disguise the lack of solid evidence for a contention when a fallacy of [this] type[] is perpetrated." Douglas N. Walton, Informal Logic: A Handbook for Critical Argumentation 20 (Cambridge Univ. Press 1989).

[905] Palsgraf v. Long Island R.R., 162 N.E. 99 (N.Y. 1928) (Cardozo, J.).

[906] *See* Transcript of Proceedings (Volume 10) at 2034:11–2036:1, FTC v. Qualcomm Inc., No. 5:17-cv-00220-LHK (N.D. Cal. Jan. 28, 2019) (Testimony of Carl Shapiro).

[907] Fed. R. Civ. P. 26(a)(2)(B) ("The report must contain: (i) a complete statement of all opinions the witness will express and the basis and reasons for them."); Fed R. Civ. P. 37(c)(1) ("If a party fails to provide information or identify a witness as required by Rule 26(a) or (e), the party is not allowed to use that information or witness to supply evidence on a motion, at a hearing, or at a trial, unless the failure was substantially justified or is harmless.").

justified or harmless.[908] Hearing, as ostensibly expert economic testimony, an imaginary story that begins by analogizing Qualcomm to a saboteur engaged in criminal conduct is not harmless. Setting aside those basic procedural deficiencies, are we to believe that Professor Shapiro's kayak story had a "tendency to make a fact more or less probable than it would be without the evidence," *and* that "the fact [wa]s of consequence in determining the action"?[909] Surely not, for any of the multitude of independent reasons analyzed here.

But suppose that we suspend disbelief and accept that Professor Shapiro's kayak "analogy" was somehow relevant as a matter of the law of evidence. Surely this testimony was still inadmissible because "its probative value [wa]s substantially outweighed by a danger of one or more of" "unfair prejudice, confusing the issues, . . . undue delay, [and] wasting time[]."[910] The transcript of Professor Shapiro's testimony during the FTC's rebuttal case on January 28, 2019 indicates that Judge Koh said nothing from the bench about Professor Shapiro's kayak "analogy."[911]

3. Professor Shapiro's Selective Reliance on Deductive Reasoning, Inductive Reasoning, and Analogical Reasoning

At different times in his testimony in *FTC v. Qualcomm*, Professor Shapiro switched between arguments predicated on deductive reasoning and arguments predicated on inductive reasoning. As we have seen, during redirect examination on the last day of trial, January 28, 2019, he introduced a completely new argument, which he claimed was predicated on analogical reasoning. I briefly review the differences between the deductive arguments and the inductive arguments that Professor Shapiro used. After that, I show how he erroneously claimed on the last day of trial that he was making an argument by analogy. Professor Shapiro's elaborate argument by "analogy" about rocks in kayaks was fallacious because it was in fact nothing more than a metaphor. It was inherently nonfalsifiable, and it was devoid of any connection to the facts in *FTC v. Qualcomm*.

a. Distinguishing Deductive Arguments from Inductive Arguments in Professor Shapiro's Testimony

In simplistic terms, a deductive argument tends to proceed from theory, to hypothesis, to observation, to "confirmation" (or, more precisely, attempts at

---

[908] *See id.* 37(c)(1).

[909] FED. R. EVID. 401.

[910] *Id.* 403; *see also id.* 611(a)(2) ("The court should exercise reasonable control over the mode and order of examining witnesses and presenting evidence so as to . . . avoid wasting time.").

[911] *Cf.* CODE OF CONDUCT FOR UNITED STATES JUDGES, *supra* note 65, Canon 3A(2) ("A judge . . . should maintain order . . . in all judicial proceedings.").

refutation or falsification). A simple argument that is deductively valid tends to follow the form, "if *A*, then *B*," such that *B* holds if *A* is true. In contrast, an inductive argument tends to proceed from observation, to identification of a pattern, to hypothesis, to theory. Formally, it can be argued that "deductive arguments are those in which conclusive favorable relevance to the conclusion is attributed to the premises," and inductive arguments are all others.[912]

Professor Shapiro claimed that he did not need to substantiate, as an empirical matter, that Qualcomm's royalty for an exhaustive license to its cellular SEPs exceeded the ceiling of the FRAND range because economic theory alone enabled him to conclude that a royalty "surcharge" existed. That claim resembled an incomplete deductive argument. Professor Shapiro appeared to have in mind a theoretical principle of general applicability, which he then applied to the facts of this case; but he never empirically substantiated or attempted to refute the correctness of that general principle's application.

Professor Shapiro's argument appeared to accord with the following statement: "his economic analysis was relevant *only if* Qualcomm's royalty for its cellular SEPs were found to exceed the FRAND range"—or, equivalently by contraposition, "if Qualcomm's royalty for its cellular SEPs were *not* found to exceed the FRAND range, then his economic analysis would be irrelevant." That is the proposition with which Professor Shapiro explicitly agreed at trial during cross examination by Mr. Van Nest on January 15, 2019.[913] Thus, Professor Shapiro constructed a theory and a hypothesis, which he did not confirm by observation, and he admitted under oath that his hypothesis would be irrelevant if observation (of a FRAND-compliant royalty, as opposed to a supra-FRAND royalty) enabled one to reject his hypothesis.

At other times, and especially in the case of his rocks-in-the-kayaks testimony, Professor Shapiro reasoned inductively, attempting to construct an elaborate general theory of Qualcomm's supposedly anticompetitive conduct from individual scraps of evidence. In particular, Professor Shapiro relied on the presumptively self-interested testimony of rival modem manufacturers and OEMs to identify a supposed pattern—which then served as the predicate for his hypothesis and elaborate theory of harm. Yet, the rocks-in-the-kayaks testimony, as we have seen, was so lacking in verisimilitude as to lack certain defining characteristics of either inductive reasoning or deductive reasoning.

---

[912] George Bowles, *The Deductive/Inductive Distinction*, 16 INFORMAL LOGIC 159, 171 (1994).
[913] Transcript of Proceedings (Volume 6) at 1198:2–1198:25, FTC v. Qualcomm Inc., No 5:17-cv-00220-LHK (N.D. Cal. Jan. 15, 2019) (Testimony of Carl Shapiro).

b.   *Professor Shapiro's Fallacious Reliance on a Mere Metaphor When He Claimed to Be Arguing by Analogy*

An argument by analogy differs from both a deductive argument and an inductive argument.[914] John Stuart Mill said that "no word . . . is used more loosely, or in a greater variety of senses, than Analogy."[915] He argued that, in its common understanding, analogical reasoning resembles inductive reasoning:

> Two things resemble each other in one or more respects; a certain proposition is true of the one; therefore it is true of the other. But we have nothing here by which to discriminate analogy from induction, since this type will serve for all reasoning from experience. In the strictest induction, equally with the faintest analogy, we conclude because A resembles B in one or more properties, that it does so in a certain other property. The difference is, that in the case of a complete induction it has been previously shown, by due comparison of instances, that there is an invariable conjunction between the former property or properties and the latter property; but in what is called analogical reasoning, no such conjunction has been made out.[916]

Mill elaborated:

> [W]e conclude (and that is all which the argument of analogy amounts to) that a fact *m*, known to be true of A, is more likely to be true of B if B agrees with A in some of its properties (even though no connection is known to exist between *m* and those properties), than if no resemblance at all could be traced between B and any other thing known to possess the attribute *m*.[917]

Although Professor Shapiro referred to his rocks-in-the-kayak testimony as an "analogy," his story of the kayaks was not really an analogy to anything at issue in *FTC v. Qualcomm*. He did not compare one real-world phenomenon to a second real-world phenomenon, so as to provide a basis for making conjectures or inferences about the unobserved or unexplained aspects of the second real-world phenomenon.[918] Rather, he imagined a fictitious hypo-

---

[914] *See, e.g.*, Andrew Juthe, *Argument by Analogy*, 19 ARGUMENTATION 1 (2005); William R. Brown, *Two Traditions of Analogy*, 11 INFORMAL LOGIC 161 (1989); *see also* GOVIER, A PRACTICAL STUDY OF ARGUMENT, *supra* note 904, at 339–40 ("Sometimes the analogies on which arguments are based are so loose and far-fetched that it is impossible even to classify them as *a priori* or inductive. It seems as though a gross image of a primary subject is given by the analogue and the unwary audience is supposed to be lulled into a conclusion. Such loose uses of analogy are often discussed as instances of the fallacy of faulty analogy. They involve an appeal to similarities that are highly superficial and give no real support to the conclusion sought."); COPI & COHEN, INTRODUCTION TO LOGIC, *supra* note 904, at 442; WALTON, INFORMAL LOGIC: A HANDBOOK FOR CRITICAL ARGUMENTATION, *supra* note 904, at 258.

[915] JOHN STUART MILL, A SYSTEM OF LOGIC RATIOCINATIVE AND INDUCTIVE ch. XX (Of Analogy), § 1, at 683 [393] (Harper & Bros. 8th ed. 1882) (1843).

[916] *Id.* § 1, at 684 [393–94].

[917] *Id.* § 1, at 684–85 [393–94].

[918] *See Analogy n.*, OXFORD ENGLISH DICTIONARY (3d ed. 2015) ("A comparison made between one thing and another for the purpose of explanation or clarification.").

thetical situation (sabotage at the kayak race) and then asserted that it had pertinent similarities to a real-world phenomenon (Qualcomm's licensing of cellular SEPs), such that the imaginary, fictitious hypothetical supposedly could reliably inform Judge Koh's findings of fact and conclusions of law in the real-world antitrust case of *FTC v. Qualcomm*.

But all the heavy lifting in Professor Shapiro's vignette about the kayaks was performed not by any tight-fitting analogical reasoning but in his mere description of the criminal act of sabotage in his fictitious hypothetical. "Rocks in the kayak" became a *metaphor*, not an analogy.[919] And jurists well understand that the communicative function assigned to a word or a clever turn of phrase can be cause for concern. "Metaphors in law are to be narrowly watched," Justice Benjamin Cardozo warned us, "for starting as devices to liberate thought, they end often by enslaving it."[920] Equating Qualcomm's licensing policies for cellular SEPs to hiding rocks in a competitor's kayak to sabotage him "is well enough if the picturesqueness of the epithets does not lead us to forget" the actual economic substance of the question requiring a sober answer.[921] But, of course, "rocks in the kayak" is an epithet that one might infer Professor Shapiro to have chosen specifically for its hoped-for efficacy in inducing that very forgetfulness in the listener entrusted to make findings of fact and conclusions of law, Judge Koh.[922]

J.   *Professor Shapiro's Specious Analysis of Market Definition*

Professor Shapiro's market definition was incorrect and methodologically flawed, and his demagoguery of "pricing based on value" rather than cost was misplaced. When asked about his application of the hypothetical monopolist

---

[919] *See, e.g.*, Brian Lightbody & Michael Berman, *The Metaphoric Fallacy to a Deductive Inference*, 30 Informal Logic 185 (2010).

[920] Berkey v. Third Avenue Ry. Co., 155 N.E. 58, 61 (N.Y. 1926).

[921] *Id.*

[922] In his canonical essay on legal reasoning, Edward Levi explained how "[t]he movement of concepts into and out of the law makes [Justice Cardozo's] point" about the enslavement of free thought by metaphors. Edward Hirsch Levi, *An Introduction to Legal Reasoning*, 15 U. Chi. L. Rev. 501, 506 (1948). Levi observed:

> If the society has begun to see certain significant similarities or differences, the comparison emerges with a word. When the word is finally accepted, it becomes a legal concept. Its meaning continues to change. But the comparison is not only between the instances which have been included under it and the actual case at hand, but also in terms of hypothetical instances which the word by itself suggests. . . . In the long run a circular motion can be seen. The first stage is the creation of the legal concept which is built up as cases are compared. The period is one in which the court fumbles for a phrase. Several phrases may be tried out; the misuse or misunderstanding of words itself may have an effect. The concept sounds like another, and the jump to the second is made. The second stage is the period when the concept is more or less fixed, although reasoning by example continues to classify items inside and out of the concept. The third stage is the breakdown of the concept, as reasoning by example has moved so far ahead as to make it clear that the suggestive influence of the word is no longer desired.

Id. at 506.

test (HMT), Professor Shapiro testified on direct examination during the FTC's case-in-chief on January 15, 2019 that he applied the HMT by comparing the price difference between a CDMA modem and a UMTS modem:

> Q. Did you also implement the hypothetical monopolist test in another way?
>
> A. I also—yes, I did, through something called the CDMA adder. So Qualcomm's pricing was to add that adder to CDMA chips over equivalent UMTS modem chips, and that was another indication that the price Qualcomm was able to get was significantly higher than a competitive price for CDMA modem chips, essentially pricing based on value rather than more of a cost-based price that competition would tend to push towards. And that also, following the hypothetical monopolist test, led to the conclusion that CDMA modem chips is a relevant product market.[923]

Professor Shapiro testified that that price difference between a CDMA modem and a UMTS modem was evidence probative of Qualcomm's ability to charge a price "significantly higher" than a competitive price for a CDMA modem. Yet, as specified by the antitrust agencies in the Horizontal Merger Guidelines, the hypothetical monopolist test

> requires that a hypothetical profit-maximizing firm, not subject to price regulation, that was the only present and future seller of those products ("hypothetical monopolist") likely would impose at least a small but significant and non-transitory increase in price ("SSNIP") on at least one product in the market.[924]

That is, the hypothetical monopolist test would define the market for CDMA modems to be a relevant antitrust market only if a hypothetical monopolist could profitably impose a SSNIP on at least one of the products in that market.

Professor Shapiro appeared to assume that the proper benchmark price from which one should consider the profitability of a SSNIP was the competitive price for a product. Yet, Professor Shapiro did not testify why the observed price of a *UMTS* modem would serve as a proxy for the competitive price of a *CDMA* modem. Did Professor Shapiro compare the marginal costs of the two types of modems? Did he compare the per-unit incremental cost of developing a CDMA modem versus a UMTS modem? Even if one assumes that comparing the prices of CDMA and UMTS modems was a meaningful

---

[923] Transcript of Proceedings (Volume 6) at 1154:9–21, FTC v. Qualcomm Inc., No. 5:17-cv-00220-LHK (N.D. Cal. Jan. 15, 2019) (Testimony of Carl Shapiro).

[924] U.S. Dep't of Justice & Fed. Trade Comm'n, Horizontal Merger Guidelines 9 (2010), https://www.justice.gov/sites/default/files/atr/legacy/2010/08/19/hmg-2010.pdf.

application of the hypothetical monopolist test, there was no indication from his testimony at trial that Professor Shapiro undertook the analysis necessary to make such a comparison in an economically rigorous and meaningful way.

Moreover, Professor Shapiro's testimony that Qualcomm's "pricing based on value rather than more of a cost-based price . . . . led to the conclusion that CDMA modem chips is a relevant market" ignored established antitrust jurisprudence to the contrary. In 1989 in *A.A. Poultry Farms, Inc. v. Rose Acre Farms, Inc.*, Judge Frank Easterbrook wrote for the Seventh Circuit that "[f]irms need not like their competitors; they need not cheer them on to success; a desire to extinguish one's rivals is entirely consistent with, often is the motive behind, competition."[925] He then famously explained why a defendant's admission in a monopolization case that its prices are based on value (as opposed to cost) is not evidence probative of the alleged monopolist's ability to collect a monopoly price:

> [T]ake Lois Rust's statement that Rose Acre's prices were unrelated to its costs. *Plaintiffs treat this as a smoking gun. Far from it, such a statement reveals Rose Acre to be a price taker.* In perfect competition, firms must sell at the going price, no matter what their own costs are. High costs do not translate to the ability to collect a high price; someone else will sell for less. *Monopolists set price by reference to their costs (to be precise, they set quantity where marginal cost equals marginal revenue, a measure reflecting the shape of the market's demand curve, and charge the price the market will bear at that quantity); competitors set price by reference to the market.* A predator, too, is highly sensitive to its costs of doing business; it calculates how much sacrifice it needs to make (and could bear), and uses that as the basis of its prices. *So the statement that Rose Acre does not pay attention to its own costs when setting price reveals that the firm was acting as a competitor rather than a monopolist. Yet statements of this sort readily may be misunderstood by lawyers and jurors, whose expertise lies in fields other than economics.*[926]

Far from being evidence of monopoly pricing, Judge Easterbrook reasoned, pricing based on value reveals that a firm is acting as a competitor rather than a monopolist.

Finally, Professor Shapiro's conclusion that pricing based on value somehow satisfied the hypothetical monopolist test would imply that any non-commoditized product competes in its own relevant product market and is produced by a monopolist, contrary to Judge Easterbrook's reasoning in *Rose Acre Farms*. Nor is Professor Shapiro's monopolies-for-all test the approach actually articulated in the Horizontal Merger Guidelines, which

---

[925] 881 F.2d 1396, 1402 (7th Cir. 1989) (Easterbrook, J.).
[926] *Id.* (emphasis added).

specify that "[m]arket definition focuses solely on demand substitution factors," indicating the important role of *value* in market definition.[927]

K. *Professor Shapiro's Specious Analysis of Qualcomm's Market Power*

Professor Shapiro's analysis of market shares and barriers to entry was similarly flawed. When questioned about the "premium" LTE modem market during his direct examination on January 15, 2019, Professor Shapiro observed that Qualcomm had high market shares in his defined product market, and he imputed economic significance to those market shares on the basis of what he characterized to be "not easy" entry into that market:

> Q. And under the structural approach, what was your final step with regard to the premium LTE modem chip market?
>
> A. So then we're asking—these market shares are quite high and would tend to indicate significant market power. Are they somehow giving us a false positive in that respect because entry is so easy that there's really no significant power there? And again, I think it's quite clear that entry is not easy into this market. You know, Samsung and Intel have gotten in, and MediaTek, but it takes time. It's not easy to do. And it's the sort of market where the market shares are meaningful following the structural approach, and it's not the case that entry is so easy that we should—that we would brush aside these type of market shares in this structural analysis.[928]

Professor Shapiro's testimony invites criticisms with respect to (1) his reliance on evidence about Qualcomm's market share and (2) his analysis of barriers to entry.

1. *Market Shares*

Professor Shapiro evidently gave considerable weight to evidence about Qualcomm's market share. Yet, as we will see in Part XI.C, in markets where companies compete *for* the market, as is the case in the modem industry, market shares might provide relatively inconsequential information about a firm's market power.

Oddly, Professor Shapiro also emphasized the importance of rapid technological change to the proper analysis of market power in antitrust cases. On direct examination during the FTC's case-in-chief on January 15, 2019, he testified that the modem market was characterized by rapid technological change, which necessitated substantial investment in R&D by competitors:

---

[927] U.S. Dep't of Justice & Fed. Trade Comm'n, Horizontal Merger Guidelines, *supra* note 924, at 9.

[928] Transcript of Proceedings (Volume 6) at 1162:2–15, FTC v. Qualcomm Inc., No. 5:17-cv-00220-LHK (N.D. Cal. Jan. 15, 2019) (Testimony of Carl Shapiro).

Q. Professor Shapiro, before we delve into the details of your analysis, could you provide the Court with the market context in which your analysis takes place?

A. So there are, I believe, two items, I'll say, that we want to keep track of here: the modem chips and the standard essential patents and really how they interact with each other is at the heart of this case and is what makes it interesting to me, but also makes the economics analysis, I don't know, I don't want to say tricky, but that's underlying what's going on. *And the modem chips, I would say the key thing to keep in mind is this is a market that there's rapid technological change, of course that's common in the whole semiconductor sector, high tech sector, which means in order for companies to participate and be effective competitors at selling modem chips, they need to engage in very substantial R&D expenditures. And that means that in order for that to pay, they have to have a reasonable prospect of earning margins, sufficient margins and sufficient volumes to recoup those R&D investments. Now, it's risky. Not everybody will recoup. But that's the way the investment decisions get made.* So that's the context of modems. And because the R&D expenses are so high, there are very substantial scale economies. You really can't operate on a very small level and be in this game because you wouldn't be able to recoup your R&D investments.[929]

Although Professor Shapiro acknowledged that modem markets experience "rapid technological change," he ignored that competition in a technologically dynamic industry is *for* the market.

We shall see in greater detail in Part XI.C that competition among rival modem manufacturers occurs at the *design* stage. Rival modem manufacturers compete in a tournament to win a contract for a particular OEM's business, before that winning modem—or even the handset using that winning modem—has entered production. Consequently, eventual market shares are divorced from the competition that preordains those market shares, sometimes by a matter of years. Subsequently observed market shares indicate the outcome of an anterior tournament among rival modem manufacturers. At the time that the design competition occurs, the market share of each market participant might be zero for the relevant product market that the hypothetical monopolist test will define around the modem that eventually wins the tournament. In such a setting, the traditional structural focus on market shares lacks economic meaning.

2. Barriers to Entry

Although Professor Shapiro testified that his two antitrust product markets were characterized by high barriers to entry, he acknowledged that several firms—including Samsung, Intel, and MediaTek—were able to overcome any

---

[929] *Id.* at 1121:18–1122:19 (emphasis added).

such barriers and enter his product markets.[930] As we shall see, Professor Shapiro also acknowledged that those rival firms gained substantial market share in his markets—an outcome that one would not expect to observe in a market characterized by high barriers to entry.

When Professor Shapiro faced evidence on cross examination that contradicted his analysis of high barriers to entry, he appeared either to confuse his economic analysis or to misunderstand his own relevant product markets:

> Q. Well, Intel bought VIA in 2015 according to your report; isn't that right?
>
> A. I think that's correct.
>
> Q. And by 2016, Intel was selling CDMA chips in the markets we're talking about as you reflected earlier this morning.
>
> A. Okay. When we talk about entry and entry barriers—
>
> Q. Excuse me just a minute.
>
> A. —we're not talking about acquisition.
>
> Q. —Professor Shapiro. Weren't they [Intel] selling chips within a year of purchasing VIA? That's what I asked.
>
> A. Okay. But that doesn't—okay. It's just misleading because if you enter by acquisition, that's not the right question. Of course you can enter a market by acquiring somebody who's already selling that product. That's not the question for entry analysis.[931]

Professor Shapiro acknowledged that after acquiring VIA, Intel began producing modems for Apple. Yet, he characterized entry by acquisition as effectively not constituting entry at all. His analysis was specious in three ways.

First, entry by acquisition in the telecommunications industry does in fact occur. One prominent example of market entry by acquisition occurred when Deutsche Telekom entered the U.S. cellular industry when it acquired the mobile network operator VoiceStream and rebranded it T-Mobile. Deutsche Telekom reported in 2002: "The acquisition of VoiceStream *and*

---

[930] *Id.* at 1160:10–1161:2 ("Q. After defining a relevant market, what was the next step under the structural approach? A. So then we're going to measure market shares in this market, and so this only starts in 2011 because that's when the premium LTE modem chips first get shipped. . . . Qualcomm's market share, they're the—they're the sole supplier of these for a couple years, so 2013. And then their share does decline some, not much in 2014, but more in '15 and '16. It declined to 81 percent in 2015, and then 57 percent in 2016. And the reason is there's a significant piece there of MediaTek, again, probably predominantly in China. But we also see Samsung and Intel coming in in 2016, which is when they're winning some of the iPhone sales by 2016. So—okay. So, but, again, Qualcomm's share is nearly 100 percent for the first several years, then 81 percent, and then 57 percent in 2016.").

[931] *Id.* at 1183:21–1184:11.

*thus the successful entry into the U.S. market—*the largest individual market world-wide for mobile communications—was without doubt the outstanding event for us in 2001."[932] Would Professor Shapiro contend that competition among American mobile network operators did not increase when VoiceStream became T-Mobile?

Second, the reason why entry analysis is relevant in antitrust analysis is that a *potential* entrant could stymie the exercise of market power by an incumbent firm. Whether the "entrant" is a new firm or has entered through its acquisition by an existing competitor is relevant only if one is conducting a structural inquiry into counting firms and market shares—an exercise that economic analysis regards as outdated and misguided.[933] A new entrant, or even a new owner of an existing firm, might be able to constrain the exercise of market power by other firms in a way that the firm it replaced could not (or the ownership and management team that it replaced could not). Yet, Professor Shapiro never appeared to perform the analysis that would suffice to indicate whether a large multinational company like Intel, with decades of experience as a leader in microprocessor development, could be an effective competitor producing "premium" LTE modems.

Third, Professor Shapiro appeared to overlook that he had defined relatively narrow relevant product markets. If Intel entered the CDMA modem market by acquiring VIA, did it not follow that Professor Shapiro believed that VIA was *already* competing in that market? Intel faced a make-or-buy decision concerning entry, and it chose "buy." Did Professor Shapiro correctly measure VIA's market share and correctly evaluate its future potency as a competitor, considering that Intel thought VIA valuable enough to acquire? Was Professor Shapiro's estimate of market shares in the relevant product market therefore inconsistent with his own entry analysis?

L.   *Professor Shapiro's Confusing Discussion of Apple's Allegedly Exclusive Use of Qualcomm Modems*

Professor Shapiro testified at trial that Qualcomm harmed competition among modem manufacturers by executing agreements with Apple, "particularly in 2013, where [Qualcomm] made large payments to Apple in

---

[932] Deutsche Telekom, Modern Teams: The 2001 Financial Year 10 (2002) (emphasis added); *see also* Deutsche Telekom AG, Annual Report for the Fiscal Year Ended December 31, 2001 (SEC Form 20-F), at 13 (filed June 18, 2002).

[933] *Cf.* Louis Kaplow & Carl Shapiro, *Antitrust, in* 2 Handbook of Law and Economics 1073, 1091 (A. Mitchell Polinsky & Steven Shavell eds., North-Holland 2007) ("Courts—and thus lawyers and government agencies—traditionally equate high market shares with a high degree of market power and low shares with a low degree of market power. This association is highly misleading if the market elasticity of demand is ignored, and likewise if rivals' elasticity of supply is not considered.").

exchange for Apple using Qualcomm chips exclusively."[934] Yet, Professor Shapiro's testimony ultimately could not have sufficed to enable Judge Koh to determine whether Qualcomm's agreements with Apple were capable of harming competition among modem manufacturers.

1. Did Professor Shapiro Ever Actually Testify That Qualcomm's Contracts with Apple Were Exclusive?

Professor Shapiro acknowledged on direct examination by Mr. James during the FTC's case-in-chief on January 15, 2019 that the agreements that Qualcomm executed with Apple did not contractually prohibit Apple from using non-Qualcomm modems:

> Q. But you're aware that the agreements doesn't—or rather don't expressly condition Qualcomm's sale of chips to Apple on Apple remaining exclusive; right?
>
> A. I'm aware of that. And, in fact, in 2016, Apple did pick Intel chips for the iPhone. So I'm not saying the agreements were *de jure* exclusive.[935]

It was Professor Shapiro's testimony that, although Apple was permitted to switch to the use of non-Qualcomm modems, Apple would have had no incentive to do so, because it would have had to forfeit substantial payments from Qualcomm.

a. "When I Use a Word, It Means Just What I Choose It to Mean"

Next, Professor Shapiro testified to a highly consequential and revealing proposition about his understanding of the relevant facts and controlling law in *FTC v. Qualcomm*:

> Q. You described the agreements in your summary of conclusions as involving exclusivity. What do you mean by that[?]
>
> A. I mean the following very specific thing: that under these agreements, if Apple had decided to launch devices that contained non-Qualcomm modem chips, Apple would have faced a very large financial penalty in the form of having to forfeit certain payments that Qualcomm would otherwise be making to Apple.[936]

---

[934] Transcript of Proceedings (Volume 6) at 1121:13–15, FTC v. Qualcomm Inc., No. 5:17-cv-00220-LHK (N.D. Cal. Jan. 15, 2019) (Testimony of Carl Shapiro); *see also id.* at 1121:12–16.

[935] *Id.* at 1164:5–10.

[936] *Id.* at 1163:21–1164:4.

When Professor Shapiro uses a word, it means just what he chooses it to mean. Exclusive means nonexclusive. This fallacy of argumentation—an extreme version of the *ipse dixit*—is so notorious in law that it has become a cliché for courts to quote the canonical passage from Lewis Carroll:

> "When *I* use a word," Humpty Dumpty said, in rather a scornful tone, "it means just what I choose it to mean—neither more nor less."
>
> "The question is," said Alice, "whether you *can* make words mean so many different things."
>
> "The question is," said Humpty Dumpty, "which is to be master—that's all."[937]

Professor Shapiro's inversion of the definition of "exclusivity" distorted not only antitrust law, but also basic microeconomics.

b.   Preference and Constraint

Two concepts permeate microeconomic theory: *preference* and *constraint*. For example, in the theory of the household (also known as the theory of the consumer) and in the theory of the firm, economists define an objective function (utility for consumers, profits for the firm), which the consumer or the firm maximizes subject to one or more constraints (such as the consumer's limited budget, or the firm's need to break even or its need to comply with some form of price regulation). In either case, the mechanics of the analysis for drawing conclusions of the resulting behavior of the consumer or the firm is called constrained optimization.[938]

A contractual obligation for Apple to purchase all of its demand for modems from Qualcomm would be a constraint, to which it would have voluntarily agreed by contract. In contrast, Apple might have a preference to purchase all of its demand for modems from Qualcomm because the price and non-price attributes of the modems make them superior to the modems of Qualcomm's competitors. Economic actors respond to incentives, which are commonly expressed in terms of the relative prices of two or more alternatives, in light of the preferences of those economic actors. That is the phenomenon that evidently interested Professor Shapiro when he addressed the TA and FATA supply agreements between Apple and Qualcomm. Yet,

---

[937] Lewis Carroll, Through the Looking Glass, and What Alice Found There 113 (Bloomsbury 2001) (1871) (emphasis in original). For an example of the Supreme Court's invocation of Alice's colloquy with Humpty Dumpty on manipulating the meaning of words, see Lopez v. Gonzales, 549 U.S. 47, 54 & n.5 (2006).

[938] *See, e.g.*, Alpha C. Chiang & Kevin Wainwright, Fundamental Methods of Mathematical Economics 347 (McGraw-Hill 4th ed. 2005).

in effect Professor Shapiro recharacterized Apple's own preference as a constraint, which Qualcomm supposedly had imposed on Apple.

Professor Shapiro elaborated on these themes in his direct examination by Mr. James:

> A. . . . I'm studying the economic incentives that the agreements created in the form of this large penalty that Apple would bear if they chose to pick Intel for the iPads.
>
> Q. And what do you mean by very strong incentives?
>
> A. Well, the way the agreements worked was that—and particularly the First Amended Transition Agreement which had these provisions—was that Qualcomm would make certain payments to Apple over time, incentive payments, and so long as Apple remained exclusive with Qualcomm, those payments would be made following a certain schedule. But if there came a time when Apple broke from exclusivity and launched a device with a non-Qualcomm modem chip, then there would be significant consequences financially for Apple, really in two forms you could think about it. First, some of the payments that Qualcomm had made by that time would be clawed back by Qualcomm from Apple. And, second, Qualcomm—payments that were scheduled to be made from Qualcomm to Apple in the future would not be made. And I use the term "payments at risk" to capture both of those concepts. "Payments at risk" meaning from Apple's point of view, if they launch a device with a non-Qualcomm chip in it, they will lose those payments so they are at risk.[939]

Professor Shapiro testified that Qualcomm's payments to Apple induced Apple to use Qualcomm's modems exclusively. Yet, Professor Shapiro immediately appeared to contradict even that theory in explaining the facts of the case:

> Q. So what does this demonstrative show?
>
> A. Okay. So this—so this shows the magnitude of these payments that Qualcomm made to Apple that were conditioned on exclusivity, and the first row shows the payments under the Transition Agreement signed in 2011, and those are relevant for any analysis because some of those were still at risk after the second agreement was signed in February of 2013, the FATA, as I'll call it, First Amended Transition Agreement, and the second row shows the magnitude of those. The reason there are two columns, Your Honor, is the first column of these numbers is what Apple reported. The second column is what Qualcomm projected. They're somewhat different. My analysis does not hinge on—it applies whichever set of numbers you would use, I would

---

[939] Transcript of Proceedings (Volume 6) at 1164:8–1165:7, FTC v. Qualcomm Inc., No. 5:17-cv-00220-LHK (N.D. Cal. Jan. 15, 2019) (Testimony of Carl Shapiro).

reach the same conclusion, and then there's just a total there. So these are very large sums of money. But I do note, as you mentioned, Your Honor, that while these are the total payments at risk, not all these payments were ultimately made from Qualcomm to Apple because Apple sacrificed a good chunk of them in 2016 when they launched the iPhone 7 using the Intel chips in September 2016.[940]

Professor Shapiro therefore expressly recognized that, despite the existence of its agreements with Qualcomm, Apple chose to forgo Qualcomm's payments and instead launch the iPhone 7 with Intel modems. Clearly the financial payments specified in the agreements between Apple and Qualcomm were not so powerful an incentive for Apple to cause it actually to rely exclusively on Qualcomm to supply modems for new models of iPhones.

2. *Professor Shapiro's Tendentious Nomenclature of "Payments at Risk"*

In his direct examination testimony during the FTC's case-in-chief, Professor Shapiro consistently used terms that disparaged Qualcomm's payments to Apple. He referred to "payments at risk" as evidence that the agreements negotiated between Qualcomm and Apple were exclusive-in-fact. Yet, understood in their proper economic context, "payments at risk" merely connote the opportunity cost to Apple of walking away from its supply agreement with Qualcomm. The alternative available to Apple—of not satisfying the terms on which the rebates from Qualcomm were conditioned—was a real option that Apple held and could exercise anytime at its discretion.

Professor Shapiro's characterization of "payments at risk" made that option sound scary, since risk has inherently pejorative connotations; but such was not the case in reality. In fact, Apple chose to exercise that real option when it chose to procure Intel modems for use in the iPhone 7 in 2016. Apple had executed its supply agreements with Qualcomm willingly and subsequently chose to forgo the discounts that Qualcomm offered Apple. From an economic perspective, it would appear that Apple did so when it viewed such forbearance as more profitable than procuring modems from only Qualcomm.

Apple willingly positioned itself to have the freedom to choose at its convenience either to do business with only Qualcomm on the one hand or to sacrifice certain rebates from Qualcomm by sending some of its modem orders to Intel on the other hand. What Professor Shapiro preferred to call "payments at risk" did not foreclose Apple from procuring modems from Intel or from Qualcomm's other competitors in the least; rather, those contingent payments by Qualcomm facilitated Apple's choice in that regard

---

[940] *Id.* at 1165:25–1166:21.

by helping it to identify its opportunity cost of moving from a single source of modem supply to multiple sources.

It was therefore specious for Professor Shapiro to cast aspersions on Qualcomm for having offered attractive price discounts that Apple chose to forgo, but—one could imagine—would have preferred to retain if doing so did not mean satisfying the conditions precedent for those payments. The TA and the FATA did not create "payments at risk" for Apple; the agreements created commercial flexibility in procurement. That is to say, the TA and the FATA *reduced* risk for Apple.

But at the same time, Apple was not entitled by the TA or the FATA to have its cake and eat it too.

3. *Did Professor Shapiro's Economic Analysis Suffice to Determine Whether or Not Qualcomm's TA and FATA Agreements with Apple Were Capable of Having an Anticompetitive Effect?*

Professor Shapiro failed to perform the necessary economic analysis to determine whether Qualcomm's agreements to supply Apple with modems could harm competition. Exclusive dealing agreements are ubiquitous and often benefit the seller, the buyer, and consumers at large. An exclusive dealing agreement can have anticompetitive effects only when it forecloses rivals from a significant portion of the relevant market.[941] Thus, to determine whether an exclusive dealing agreement can harm competition, it is necessary to examine first whether the agreement forecloses a significant share of the relevant market. As we shall see later, the Supreme Court made this requirement explicit in 1961 in *Tampa Electric*.[942] It is an uncontroversial proposition in antitrust jurisprudence.

Yet, Professor Shapiro never examined what portion of his two relevant markets Qualcomm's modem-supply agreements with Apple allegedly foreclosed. Instead, he said that he performed an "equally efficient competitor test,"[943] but even then Professor Shapiro erroneously focused his analysis only on *Apple's* products, rather than on the entirety of the products supplied in his relevant markets. During his direct examination during the FTC's

---

[941] Tampa Elec. Co. v. Nashville Coal Co., 365 U.S. 320, 328 (1961); *see also* Jefferson Parish Hosp. Dist. No. 2 v. Hyde, 466 U.S. 2, 45 (1984) ("Exclusive dealing is an unreasonable restraint on trade only when a significant fraction of buyers or sellers are frozen out of a market by the exclusive deal."); U.S. Healthcare, Inc. v. Healthsource, Inc., 986 F.2d 589, 597 (1st Cir. 1993) (Boudin, J.) ("The point is that proof of substantial foreclosure and of 'probable immediate and future effects' is the essential basis under *Tampa* for an attack on an exclusivity clause.") (quoting *Tampa Electric*, 365 U.S. at 329); Omega Envtl., Inc. v. Gilbarco, Inc., 127 F.3d 1157, 1162 (9th Cir. 1997) ("Only those arrangements whose 'probable' effect is to 'foreclose competition in a substantial share of the line of commerce affected' violate Section 3 [of the Clayton Act].") (quoting *Tampa Electric*, 365 U.S. at 327).

[942] *Tampa Electric*, 365 U.S. at 328.

[943] Transcript of Proceedings (Volume 6) at 1168:7, FTC v. Qualcomm Inc., No. 5:17-cv-00220-LHK (N.D. Cal. Jan. 15, 2019) (Testimony of Carl Shapiro).

case-in-chief on January 15, 2019, when describing the type of analysis that he performed to assess the effects of Qualcomm's 2013 agreement with Apple, Professor Shapiro relied again on the "Intel-welfare" standard and testified:

> Q. What analysis have you done of the 2013 agreement?
>
> A. So I'm able to look at the 2013 agreement and perform what we call a—excuse me—a profit sacrifice test, also known as an equally efficient competitor test, really to see whether the penalties that Apple faced if they had gone with Intel for the iPads were disproportionate or unreasonably high.
>
> Q. And when you say unreasonably high, what do you mean?
>
> A. So I think the easiest way to see that is to take it from the perspective of the entrant, Intel—this is the equally efficient competitor test—to ask, imagine an entrant, and it's really more abstract, it doesn't have to be Intel, imagine an entrant who's just as efficient as Qualcomm and their entry route to first get a certain quantity of sales that is currently available at Apple? And *I'm going to talk about the iPads as that group.* But whatever that group is, if they could make those sales and earn some margins on those, just like Qualcomm is, would they be able to make money in the face of this agreement? Which means they'd have to compensate Apple for the penalty that Apple would bear for the payments that Apple would lose from Qualcomm. So you're asking if an equally efficient entrant could make a play for these contestable units, contestable sales, which are going to be iPads, given they'd have to buy Apple out of the contract? And that—could they make money doing that? If that would be profitable for an entrant, then the agreement passes muster under the test. If that would be unprofitable for the entrant, then the agreement is going to fail this test. It's very much like price cost test in predatory pricing, but it has this structure of we've got this penalty payment and that—we're attributing that to these sales because the entrant under this methodology would have to compensate the customer for the lost incentive payments.[944]

Professor Shapiro then explained what he believed to be the consequences of these "penalties":

> Q. What are the consequences of a deal of this kind for relationships between Apple and potential entrants?
>
> A. So—I think the record shows that in the presence of this deal, it was not going to be—Apple's view was it was not going to be economically practicable to go to Intel—we can talk about potential entrants generally, but Intel was in the flesh, if you will—to go with them for iPads or for, let's say, a moderate amount of volume. It really means from Apple's point of view, they're either

---

[944] *Id.* at 1168:4–1169:12 (emphasis added).

going to stay with Qualcomm exclusively or they're going to have to go quite big for an entrant to make it worth paying the penalty, and the entrant would have to offer *significantly better prices than Qualcomm* on large volumes in order for it to pay for Apple. And so that's, that was the consequence once the agreements were signed of the situation as between Apple and any potential alternative supplier.[945]

Professor Shapiro testified that, because the payment that Qualcomm made to Apple was conditioned on the exclusive use of Qualcomm's modems, Intel would have been unable to make a sufficiently attractive offer to Apple to enter the market, because doing so would have required Intel "to offer significantly better prices than Qualcomm." (It is unclear whether Professor Shapiro ever considered in his analysis the value, from mitigation of the risk of supply-chain disruption, that Apple would have derived from having a second source of supply.) It was Professor Shapiro's testimony that, if Intel offered sufficiently low prices to compensate Apple for the lost payments from Qualcomm, Intel would not be able to "make money" from selling modems to Apple solely for iPads.[946] It is regrettable that an expert economic witness would use such imprecise and colloquial terminology—Intel's ability to "make money"—to frame his sworn trial testimony about entry and the competitive ramifications of Qualcomm's supply of modems to Apple for the iPhone. If Professor Shapiro believed that "making money" was a necessary condition for Intel's ability to supply modems to Apple, what did that condition entail in precise economic terms? The burden of production and the burden of persuasion were on the FTC. (We will consider later why Professor Shapiro erred in considering only iPads in his analysis of contestable sales, rather than considering the possibility that Intel also would supply modems for at least some iPhones.)

It would seem that, in Professor Shapiro's estimation, the outcome that Intel could not "make money" supplying Apple with modems for iPads would have been detrimental for competition. Yet, Professor Shapiro's testimony was incorrect for four reasons.

a.   Which Test Did Professor Shapiro Perform to Evaluate the Effects That Qualcomm's Agreements with Apple Had on Competition?

First, Professor Shapiro offered confusing testimony regarding the test he performed to evaluate the effects that Qualcomm's agreements with Apple had on competition. He mentioned three different tests—(1) a profit-sacrifice

---

[945] *Id.* at 1169:13–1170:4 (emphasis added).
[946] *Id.* at 1169:3.

test, (2) the equally-efficient-competitor test, and (3) a price-cost test—and he suggested that they were equivalent, although they are not.

A profit-sacrifice test posits that the challenged practice should be considered anticompetitive if it makes no rational sense but for its goal to exclude competitors.[947] The equally-efficient-competitor test focuses on competitors, rather than the profits of the alleged monopolist, and seeks to determine whether the challenged practice is likely to exclude from the market a competitor that is at least as efficient as the incumbent.[948] A price-cost test, which is typically applied in a predatory-pricing case, is again different, because it examines whether a firm has priced its products below an appropriate measure of its own cost (as opposed to the competitor's cost).[949]

On the basis of Professor Shapiro's trial testimony, it appears that he performed a variant of the equally-efficient-competitor test. If Professor Shapiro also performed a profit-sacrifice test or a price-cost test, he did not explain how either of those tests supported his testimony about exclusivity.

b.   Did Professor Shapiro's Equally-Efficient-Competitor Test Enable Him to Identify Whether Qualcomm's Agreements Foreclosed a Significant Portion of the Relevant Market?

Second, according to his trial testimony, Professor Shapiro did not apply his equally-efficient-competitor test in a way that would permit him to opine on whether Qualcomm's agreements foreclosed a significant portion of the relevant market. Professor Shapiro disclosed the following information about his application of the equally-efficient-competitor test during his testimony on direction examination during the FTC's case-in-chief on January 15, 2019:

> Q. How did you implement the test in this case?
>
> A. So I implemented the test by identifying what we call the contestable units, which are the sales that were currently available to Intel, seeing what margin they could earn on those if they were as efficient as Qualcomm, and then seeing whether they could still make money if they had to cover the penalty like I said. Another way to think about it that's economically equivalent, and this would be the profit sacrifice label, is from Qualcomm's point of view, they made sales—they made profits on the iPad sales, the contestable sales, through some margins. But they would have avoided

---

[947] *See, e.g.*, Novell, Inc. v. Microsoft Corp., 731 F.3d 1064, 1076 (10th Cir. 2013) (Gorsuch, J.) ("The point of the profit sacrifice test is to isolate conduct that has *no* possible efficiency justification.") (emphasis in original); *see also* Gregory J. Werden, *Identifying Exclusionary Conduct Under Section 2: The "No Economic Sense" Test*, 73 ANTITRUST L.J. 413, 415–17 (2006); Daniel A. Crane, *Mixed Bundling, Profit Sacrifice, and Consumer Welfare*, 55 EMORY L.J. 423, 448–50 (2006).

[948] *See, e.g.*, RICHARD A. POSNER, ANTITRUST LAW 194–95 (Univ. of Chicago Press 2d ed. 2001) [hereinafter POSNER, ANTITRUST LAW (2d ed.)].

[949] *See, e.g.*, Benjamin Klein & Andres V. Lerner, *Price-Cost Tests in Antitrust Analysis of Single Product Loyalty Contracts*, 80 ANTITRUST L.J. 631, 631–32 (2016).

paying a large amount of money to Apple if Apple had not bought those products. So if we attribute those Qualcomm payments to these products as a cost effectively, as a payout from Qualcomm, was Qualcomm sacrificing profits to make these sales? And so it's exactly the same arithmetic, was Qualcomm sacrificing profits with this attribution of the profits, or would Intel have had to lose money in the first round as part of an entry strategy? So I did that by measuring the margin on those products and the size of the penalty payments that would have applied to the iPad, to the iPad sales.[950]

Professor Shapiro then elaborated on his calculations:

Q. Let's bring up the next demonstrative. Are these your calculations?

A. Yes. So this is—this is really from the profit sacrifice perspective. A comparison of Qualcomm's direct margins on the Apple iPads to the incentive payments that were at risk. So the contestable products here are a series of iPads that Apple ended up launching starting in October 2014, and there's—there's evidence in the record that this was the—a likely plan that Apple was pursuing before they signed the agreements with Qualcomm, to work with Intel on this basis first with the iPads, see how it would go, and then possibly award them iPhones later. So they were in very active discussions with Intel, as you heard from Ms. Evans. I think you heard from Mr. Blevins and [Mr.] Williams as well on this. So these are the contestable products. Then—I'm going to assume all these numbers are confidential. So the incentive payments at risk—oh, and you can see how many units were involved through the period of time I'm able to measure. Then you can see the incentive payments at risk, which is to say if Apple had gone with Intel for these products and launched them in October 2014, at that time, how much—what would [be] the incentive payments at risk under the FATA, and that's the number, the large number in the middle here under A, labeled A. And then we're comparing that to the direct margins that Qualcomm earned on these products, which is B, a smaller number. And since the incentive payments at risk are far in excess of the margins, we see this was profit sacrifice when we do this attribution of the incentive payments to these sales. The other perspective would be for Intel to get in, if they could have earned these same margins shown as B, assuming they're equally efficient, they could make those margins, but they'd have to buy Apple out of the contract. That would cost the amount shown in A. That would be a big loss. And, in fact, neither Apple nor Intel considered that because it was—that was unrealistic, which is an indication of how, how badly the FATA failed this test actually. So that's the finding, that's the result of the test, that this structure of this agreement involved a profit sacrifice by Qualcomm, or would block an equally efficient competitor from making these contestable

---

[950] Transcript of Proceedings (Volume 6) at 1170:5–1171:2, FTC v. Qualcomm Inc., No. 5:17-cv-00220-LHK (N.D. Cal. Jan. 15, 2019) (Testimony of Carl Shapiro).

sales, or would require that competitor to lose a substantial amount of money to get that foothold in the market.[951]

It is clear from Professor Shapiro's testimony that his analysis focused exclusively on *Apple's* products—and even then only a subset of Apple's mobile devices: iPads. Yet, an analysis that focuses exclusively on Apple's products is inconclusive as to whether the agreements foreclosed a significant part of the relevant *market*. Inconclusive evidence is not preponderant evidence.

c.   Did Substantial Evidence Refute Professor Shapiro's Assumption That Intel Was an Equally Efficient Competitor to Qualcomm?

Third, substantial evidence refuted the critical assumption, which Professor Shapiro specifically testified he had made in his "equally-efficient-competitor" test, that the imaginary rival modem manufacturer in his test was in fact an equally efficient competitor to Qualcomm. The rival modem manufacturer of greatest apparent interest to the FTC and Professor Shapiro was obviously Intel. Yet, as we shall see in detail in Parts XIV and XVI, both Aichatou "Aicha" Evans, then Chief Strategy Officer of Intel, and Christopher Johnson, a partner at Bain who had advised Intel on competitive strategy, testified at trial in *FTC v. Qualcomm* that Intel was in fact a substantially *less* efficient competitor than Qualcomm with respect to transforming R&D investment in modems into commercially valuable products—indeed, Bain found that Qualcomm's R&D investment was *three times* more productive than Intel's.[952] Ms. Evans also admitted that Intel's unlicensed "product cost of its modem chips [was] higher than Qualcomm's."[953]

During the FTC's rebuttal case on January 28, 2019, Mr. Van Nest got Professor Shapiro to admit on cross examination that he was aware of the sworn testimony at trial that Bain had found that Intel was a demonstrably less efficient competitor than Qualcomm with respect to R&D investment in modems.[954] To the extent that Professor Shapiro was referring in his own

---

[951] *Id.* at 1171:3–1172:24.

[952] *See supra* note 735.

[953] Transcript of Proceedings (Volume 4) at 655:1–3, FTC v. Qualcomm Inc., No. 5:17-cv-00220-LHK (N.D. Cal. Jan. 11, 2019) (Testimony of Aichatou Evans (Chief Strategy Officer, Intel)) ("Q. Now, Intel has concluded that the product cost of its modem chips is higher than Qualcomm's; right? A. Yes."); *see also id.* at 656:8–657:2 ("Q. . . . [D]oes the Intel column on the left of this table [on slide 3 of QX 95] have projected product costs for Intel modem chips from 2017 through 2019? A. Yes. Q. And does the Qualcomm column on the right have Intel's estimate of Qualcomm's product cost for its slim modems during that same time period? A. Yeah. I mean, our best guesstimate; right? We don't work at Qualcomm, so— Q. Sure. A. Uh-huh. Q. But these are Intel's best estimates of what Qualcomm's product costs are; right? A. Yes. Q. And as shown in QX 95, Intel's product costs are higher than Qualcomm's; right? A. Yeah. It's hard to compete with you guys. With Qualcomm, we have to pick our spots, and we were very clear that first we get the socket, second we get the seat at the table with respect to the strategy, and then we drive to profitability.").

[954] Transcript of Proceedings (Volume 10) at 2076:14–21, FTC v. Qualcomm Inc., No. 5:17-cv-00220-LHK (N.D. Cal. Jan. 28, 2019) (Testimony of Carl Shapiro) ("Q. Now, you've also heard or read testimony

testimony to the equal efficiency of competitors in regard to the *manufacture* of modems (as opposed to the productivity of their investment in R&D), such testimony would have been irrelevant. Both Intel and Qualcomm relied on fabless production for their modems. That is, both firms relied upon contract manufacturers to fabricate their modems, and the cost structure for such manufacturing depended on a third party's fabrication facility overseas.

In short, for purposes of his "equally-efficient-competitor" test, Professor Shapiro assumed the truthfulness of an essential factual proposition—namely, the proposition that Intel was absolutely as efficient a producer of modems as Qualcomm. That proposition was actually refuted in the sworn cross examination testimony of witnesses friendly to the FTC. Yet, proceeding as if that proposition had not already been proven false in open court, Professor Shapiro gave testimony on January 28, 2019 predicting harm to competition that might theoretically eventuate from the "exit" of an *equally efficient* competitor.

This piece of counterfactual testimony was necessarily irrelevant and unreliable as an evidentiary matter because it proceeded from a demonstrably false premise. It displayed the same "blackboard economics" immanent in Professor Shapiro's testimony concerning the royalty "surcharge" and the modem "tax."

d.   Did Professor Shapiro Examine What Portion of the Relevant Markets Qualcomm's Agreements with Apple Foreclosed?

Fourth, even if one assumes for sake of argument that Qualcomm's supply agreement with Apple prevented Intel from supplying Apple, that still would not support the conclusion that the agreement harmed competition. Antitrust law is not concerned with the foreclosure of one customer. The "Intel-welfare" standard is not the law. If Professor Shapiro truly wanted to apply an "equally-efficient-competitor test," he should have examined a different question: whether a competitor as efficient as Qualcomm could have achieved sufficient scale by selling modems to cover the incremental cost of selling *to the rest of OEMs*, despite Qualcomm's agreements with Apple. By focusing his analysis on only one buyer of the products sold in the relevant market (Apple), Professor Shapiro did not perform the "equally-efficient-competitor test," nor did he remotely apply the controlling standard that the Supreme Court articulated in *Tampa Electric*.

One is left to wonder why Professor Shapiro did not examine what portion of the relevant markets Qualcomm's agreements with Apple foreclosed. Was

---

during our trial that some of the rivals spent R&D money inefficiently; right? A. I have heard that. Q. For example, Intel commissioned a study from Bain, which was presented in court Friday, [January 25, 2019,] which concluded that although Intel's spending was on par, their output of R&D lagged Qualcomm very significantly; right? A. I remember that.").

he not aware of the precise questions of fact that an economic expert needs to answer to aid the court in determining pursuant to *Tampa Electric* whether an (allegedly) exclusive dealing agreement violates the Sherman Act? Did the FTC's lawyers fail to instruct Professor Shapiro that he needed to examine the portion of the relevant *market* that Qualcomm's agreements with Apple foreclosed to assist the court in determining whether the agreements were anticompetitive? It is a mystery why the FTC evidently did not direct Professor Shapiro to apply the controlling Supreme Court test for assessing the lawfulness of exclusive dealing agreements.

V. Did Judge Koh Deny Qualcomm Due Process by Omitting Any Findings Concerning Professor Shapiro's Exculpatory Expert Testimony on the FTC's Theory of a Royalty "Surcharge" and a Modem "Tax"?

Following the bench trial in January 2019, Judge Koh issued her findings of fact and conclusions of law on May 21, 2019. To some, Judge Koh might have created the appearance of having resorted to an inquisitorial style of judging that deviates from what Congress created through its enactment of the Federal Rules of Evidence and other provisions of the Judicial Code. Having no more than the limited jurisdiction defined by Congress, the federal courts decide cases or controversies through the adversarial process. No matter how noble a federal judge regards the government's motive when, in the exercise of its executive powers, it prosecutes a private actor accused of having violated a public law, and no matter how ignoble the judge might regard that private actor, the judge's role as adjudicator may not properly merge with the government's role as prosecutor. Congress has additionally chosen to limit the kind of evidence that may permissibly predicate a federal judge's findings that a violation of public law has occurred, and Congress has mandated as well the candid reporting of the basis for the judge's findings of fact and conclusions of law.

Particularly unusual was Judge Koh's treatment of witness testimony. Recall that at least one prominent antitrust economist read Judge Koh to have incorporated Professor Shapiro's "'economic opinions *throughout* the decision'" in *FTC v. Qualcomm*.[955] In addition, the American Antitrust Institute (AAI) nominated Professor Shapiro, on the basis of his testimony in *FTC v. Qualcomm*, for an award for "Outstanding Antitrust Litigation

---

[955] *No License, No Chips? No Dice: Dissecting Judge Koh's Opinion in FTC v. Qualcomm, supra* note 236 (emphasis added) (quoting Professor Fiona Scott Morton of Yale University and Charles River Associates).

Achievement in Economics."[956] Given these plaudits for Professor Shapiro's testimony, it was passing strange that Judge Koh omitted any reference to that testimony, despite the fact that Professor Shapiro was the FTC's star economic witness, that he was the only witness to take the stand twice, and that by a substantial margin he generated more pages of transcribed trial testimony than any other witness.

Judge Koh's decision not to mention Professor Shapiro in her findings of fact and conclusions of law was particularly surprising considering that she devoted an early section of her findings of fact and conclusions of law, entitled "Credibility Determinations," to disparaging the testimony of Qualcomm's company witnesses.[957] To be precise, in her "Credibility Determinations" section, Judge Koh mentioned *only* Qualcomm witnesses, and she did not make credibility determinations for any FTC witness or any third-party witness. In particular, Judge Koh did not make any determination concerning Professor Shapiro's credibility. One could question whether Judge Koh's failure to make any credibility findings about Professor Shapiro's testimony, despite her apparently total reliance on his testimony to address complex economic questions, complied with Rule 52(a)(1) of the Federal Rules of Civil Procedure.

In a bench trial in a monopolization case brought by the FTC, is the judge required under Rule 52(a)(1) to make special findings of fact when the government's expert economic witness has made admissions under oath that would tend to exculpate the defendant? Despite predicting that Qualcomm's licensing practices had had, and would have, dire effects on competition, Professor Shapiro repeatedly admitted on cross examination that he had not examined whether any empirical evidence substantiated his conjectures. Expert economic testimony that is disembodied from any actual facts of the case is a phantom more likely to mislead than inform the finder of fact, even when the finder of fact is a judge presiding over a bench trial.

---

[956] Press Release, American Antitrust Institute, AAI 2019 Antitrust Enforcement Awards Honorees Announced (Oct. 9, 2019), https://www.antitrustinstitute.org/4436-2/. AAI describes itself as follows: "Since its inception, AAI has created and shaped the modern 'progressive antitrust' movement, with a focus on preserving a competitive economy through vigorous public and private enforcement of the antitrust laws." *Mission and History*, American Antitrust Institute, https://www.antitrustinstitute.org/about-us/. AAI contrasts its orientation with that of what it calls the "conservative movement": "By the 1980s, . . . [a]dvocacy by the conservative law and economics movement steered antitrust policy in a non-interventionist direction marked by lax merger control and forbearance from policing monopolistic and other anticompetitive practices. The conservative movement has been, and continues to be, rooted in excessive deference to unsubstantiated efficiencies and pro-business justifications for mergers and abusive conduct." *Id.*

[957] FTC v. Qualcomm Inc., 411 F. Supp. 3d 658, 676–80 (N.D. Cal. 2019).

A. *The Similarities Between Judge Koh's Findings of Fact and Professor Shapiro's Testimony*

Judge Koh's findings of fact corresponded to most of the opinions that Professor Shapiro expressed in his trial testimony, to the extent that one can confirm or infer his opinions from the publicly available documents. For example, as we have seen, Professor Shapiro testified that "Qualcomm had monopoly power" in "the market for CDMA modem chips and the market for Premium LTE modem chips . . . through 2016."[958] Judge Koh either agreed with his assertion or reached the same conclusion without the assistance of expert testimony.[959] Similarly, Professor Shapiro testified that (1) "Qualcomm, through these policies, used its monopoly power over modem chips to extract supra-FRAND royalties from OEMs,"[960] and (2) Qualcomm's "unreasonably high royalty" "raise[d] the cost of its rivals and thereby weaken[ed] them as competitors."[961] As we have seen, Professor Shapiro opined in his expert report:

> This excess royalty is economically equivalent to a "tax" imposed by Qualcomm on the OEM's use of rival modem chips. By raising the cost on rival modem chips, this excess royalty inevitably and predictably raises the all-in price of rival chipsets and reduces the quantity of those chipsets sold, for a given all-in price charged by Qualcomm. This excess royalty also inevitably and predictably reduces the operating income that any rivals can earn from selling chipsets, which can be expected to reduce the investments these rivals make in modem chips. This i[n] turn leads to longer-term anti-competitive effects on innovation.[962]

It is not clear that Judge Koh ever saw Professor Shapiro's expert report (since nothing in the trial transcript indicated that the report was moved

---

[958] Transcript of Proceedings (Volume 6) at 1119:9–12, FTC v. Qualcomm Inc., No. 5:17-cv-00220-LHK (N.D. Cal. Jan. 15, 2019) (Testimony of Carl Shapiro); *accord* Shapiro Demonstratives, *supra* note 114, at 3 ("Qualcomm had monopoly power over CDMA modem chips and over Premium LTE modem chips through 2016").

[959] *FTC v. Qualcomm*, 411 F. Supp. 3d at 685–95.

[960] Transcript of Proceedings (Volume 6) at 1120:15–16, FTC v. Qualcomm Inc., No. 5:17-cv-00220-LHK (N.D. Cal. Jan. 15, 2019) (Testimony of Carl Shapiro); *accord* Shapiro Demonstratives, *supra* note 114, at 3 ("Qualcomm used its monopoly power over modem chips to extract supra-FRAND royalties from OEMs").

[961] Transcript of Proceedings (Volume 6) at 1124:6–12, FTC v. Qualcomm Inc., No. 5:17-cv-00220-LHK (N.D. Cal. Jan. 15, 2019) (Testimony of Carl Shapiro); *accord* Shapiro Demonstratives, *supra* note 114, at 3 ("Qualcomm's royalty surcharge raise[d] the costs of Qualcomm's rivals, weakening them as competitors"); *see also id.* at 30; Transcript of Proceedings (Volume 6) at 1143:18–24, FTC v. Qualcomm Inc., No. 5:17-cv-00220-LHK (N.D. Cal. Jan. 15, 2019) (Testimony of Carl Shapiro) ("First, they've got rivals who are weakened and charging higher all-in prices because they're having to pay the surcharge. So as a general rule, when your competitors raise their price, it tends to give a firm incentive to raise his price as well in oligopolies, and in addition to that, Qualcomm is less keen to compete to win business from its competitors because even when it loses, it gets a royalty surcharge.").

[962] Initial Expert Report of Carl Shapiro in *FTC v. Qualcomm*, *supra* note 115, at 114–15.

into evidence), and the transcript of Professor Shapiro's direct testimony at trial noticeably lacked the concision of the paragraph quoted above from his report.[963] Still, Judge Koh adopted the same conclusions:

> Qualcomm's unreasonably high royalty rates enable Qualcomm to control rivals' prices because Qualcomm receives the royalty even when an OEM uses one of Qualcomm's rival's chips. Thus, the "all-in" price of any modem chip sold by one of Qualcomm's rivals effectively includes two components: (1) the nominal chip price; and (2) Qualcomm's royalty surcharge.[964]

Judge Koh found that, "[b]ecause Qualcomm receives royalties on any handset sale, even when that handset contains a rival's modem chip, Qualcomm's unreasonably high royalty rates impose an artificial and anticompetitive surcharge on the price of rivals' modem chips."[965] She added that "[Qualcomm's royalty] surcharge affects demand for rivals' chips . . . . Rivals see lower sales volumes and lower margins, and consumers see less advanced features as competition decreases."[966] Therefore, Judge Koh agreed with Professor Shapiro (1) that Qualcomm's supposedly "unreasonably high" royalties became a "surcharge" on the "price" of rivals' modems;[967] (2) that because of "surcharge" on the "all-in price," rivals' modems were less attractive to OEMs;[968] and (3) that the royalty "surcharge" reduced rivals' margins and undermined their ability to invest in innovation.[969]

As we have seen, Professor Shapiro also testified that a theoretical bargaining model supported his opinion that "Qualcomm's no-license/no-chips policy together with Qualcomm's refusal to license its standard-essential patents to its modem-chip rivals harmed competition."[970] He testified as well that "a specific arrangement that Qualcomm made with Apple, particularly

---

[963] Judge Posner and I have argued that the reports of expert witnesses *should* routinely be moved into evidence, notwithstanding the usual objection based on hearsay. *See* RICHARD A. POSNER, DIVERGENT PATHS: THE ACADEMY AND THE JUDICIARY 145 (Harvard Univ. Press 2016). As Judge Posner observes, "[w]ith the expert's report excluded from the trial, his effectiveness as a witness may depend more on his congeniality as a storyteller than on the accuracy of his analysis." *Id.*

[964] *FTC v. Qualcomm*, 411 F. Supp. 3d at 791.

[965] *Id.* at 698.

[966] *Id.* at 792.

[967] *Id.* at 698.

[968] *Id.* at 792.

[969] *Id.* at 797.

[970] Shapiro Demonstratives, *supra* note 114, at 3; *see also* Transcript of Proceedings (Volume 6) at 1120:1–10, FTC v. Qualcomm Inc., No. 5:17-cv-00220-LHK (N.D. Cal. Jan. 15, 2019) (Testimony of Carl Shapiro) ("[W]hat I've done here, is analyzing the effects of three different Qualcomm policies that operate in concert: the no license, no chips policy, the incentive payments that Qualcomm makes to OEM's in some of its licensing negotiations, and its refusal to license its standard essential patents to its modem chip rivals. So looking at these three policies working together, it's my view and conclusion that they harmed competition in the markets that I've just—we've just been talking about in those two markets.").

in 2013, where they made large payments to Apple in exchange for Apple using Qualcomm chips exclusively . . . harmed competition as well."[971]

Judge Koh adopted all of those opinions as her own findings, yet without once citing Professor Shapiro's testimony.[972] She said that: (1) "Qualcomm . . . refuses to license rivals in violation of its FRAND commitments,"[973] (2) "Qualcomm's refusal to license its modem chip SEPs to rival modem chip suppliers prevents rivals' entry,"[974] and (3) "[b]y preventing rivals from entering the market and restricting the sales of those rivals that do enter, Qualcomm entrenches its monopoly power, maintains its chip leverage over OEMs, and sustains its unreasonably high royalty rates."[975] Judge Koh also found that "Qualcomm's exclusive deals with Apple . . . violate the Sherman Act," because they arguably "shrunk rivals' sales and foreclosed its rivals from the positive network effects of working with Apple."[976]

In sum, it appears that Judge Koh adopted without attribution much of Professor Shapiro's trial testimony and many of his conclusions as her own findings of fact. Why? How could that expansive omission possibly comply with Rule 52(a)(1) of the Federal Rules of Civil Procedure?

B.   *The Absence of Any Mention of Professor Shapiro's Testimony in Judge Koh's Opinion*

One reasonable interpretation of the omission from Judge Koh's findings of fact and conclusions of law of any mention of Professor Shapiro or his trial testimony is that she found his testimony unhelpful, perhaps even unreliable in the strict evidentiary sense. But if that were the case, why did she not say so explicitly?

In contrast to her silence regarding Professor Shapiro, Judge Koh did make specific findings on the credibility or reliability of Qualcomm's witnesses. She explained for several pages why she found the trial testimony of Qualcomm's executives not to be credible.[977] She also explained why she found Qualcomm's expert economic witnesses not to be reliable.[978] Judge Koh found that "Qualcomm's experts all simply ignored the effects of Qualcomm's own anticompetitive conduct," and she added that, for that reason, she would

---

[971] Transcript of Proceedings (Volume 6) at 1121:12–16, FTC v. Qualcomm Inc., No. 5:17-cv-00220-LHK (N.D. Cal. Jan. 15, 2019) (Testimony of Carl Shapiro); *accord* Shapiro Demonstratives, *supra* note 114, at 3 ("Qualcomm further harmed competition by making large payments to Apple in exchange for exclusivity").

[972] *FTC v. Qualcomm*, 411 F. Supp. 3d at 751, 763.

[973] *Id.* at 795.

[974] *Id.*

[975] *Id.* (citation omitted).

[976] *Id.* at 762.

[977] *Id.* at 676–80.

[978] *Id.* at 805 (finding Professor Edward Snyder, Professor Aviv Nevo, and Dr. Tasneem Chipty to be unreliable).

not rely on their testimony[979] (even though Judge Koh did cite their opinions when she found that they supported her conclusions[980]). In addition, Judge Koh briefly discussed the testimony of the FTC's patent valuation expert, Mr. Lasinski, and said that she would not rely on it because his methodologies were not reliable (although, again, she did cite his testimony to support several of her conclusions that were adverse to Qualcomm).[981]

In other words, Judge Koh did state explicitly whether she found the trial testimony of certain witnesses to be insufficiently credible or reliable. Yet, she did not once mention in her findings of fact and conclusions of law the credibility or reliability of the trial testimony of the FTC's premier expert economic witness, Professor Shapiro. One is left to wonder whether Judge Koh's failure to refer at all to Professor Shapiro's testimony was due to her finding (without mention or elaboration anywhere in her findings of fact

---

[979] *Id.*

[980] *See, e.g., id.* at 686 ("Qualcomm's CDMA adder has been as high as 30% over comparable UMTS chips, as Qualcomm's expert Tasneem Chipty conceded at trial.") (citing Transcript of Proceedings (Volume 8) at 1747:4–10, FTC v. Qualcomm Inc., No. 5:17-cv-00220-LHK (N.D. Cal. Jan. 22, 2019) (Testimony of Tasneem Chipty)); *see id.* at 772 ("In addition, Qualcomm's own expert, Dr. Tasneem Chipty, conceded that Qualcomm's exclusive deals with Apple were not necessary for Qualcomm to realize its target profits on thin modems."); *id.* at 782 ("Likewise, Qualcomm expert Dr. Aviv Nevo testified that handsets have changed dramatically since Qualcomm entered its first license agreements."); *id.* at 819 ("Although Qualcomm argues that Qualcomm could not have used CDMA market power to obtain unreasonably high royalty rates in WCDMA license agreements, Qualcomm's own expert Dr. Aviv Nevo admitted at trial that Qualcomm's WCDMA license agreements often covered sales of CDMA handsets.").

[981] *Id.* at 789 ("Lastly, Michael Lasinski, the FTC's patent valuation expert, also concluded that Qualcomm's royalty rates are unreasonably high. Lasinski's methodologies are not reliable, as he evaluated SEP holders' relative portfolio strength in part by counting SEP holders' approved contributions to standards."). *But see id.* at 780 ("Michael Lasinski, an FTC patent expert, testified that Avanci awards SEP licensors a maximum of [Redacted] points for deemed SEPs, a maximum of [Redacted] points for approved contributions, and a maximum of [Redacted] points for historical licensing revenue. According to Lasinski, 'deemed SEPs' are SEPs that studies have concluded are in fact essential to a standard. According to Lasinski, Qualcomm and Ericsson have comparable SEP portfolios under Avanci's point-scoring system. That is so even though one of the Avanci methods—historical licensing revenue—clearly favors Qualcomm because Qualcomm charges vastly higher royalty rates to OEMs than Ericsson does, as the Court will explain in more detail below. . . . Accordingly, Qualcomm's contributions to standards do not justify Qualcomm's unreasonably high royalty rate.") (first, second, and third alterations in original) (quoting Transcript of Proceedings (Volume 5) at 1016:23, FTC v. Qualcomm Inc., No. 5:17-cv-00220-LHK (N.D. Cal. Jan. 14, 2019) (Testimony of Michael Lasinski)) (citing Transcript of Proceedings (Volume 5) at 1025:21–1026:1, 1016:23–1017:2, 1027:2–13, FTC v. Qualcomm Inc., No. 5:17-cv-00220-LHK (N.D. Cal. Jan. 14, 2019) (Testimony of Michael Lasinski)); *id.* at 782 ("The modem chip also does not drive handset value because handset users can now more easily use Wi-Fi to transmit data. Michael Lasinski, an FTC expert, testified that the use of Wi-Fi to transmit data has increased: '[I]t turns out that significantly more data is being offloaded to Wi-Fi networks.'") (alteration in original) (quoting Transcript of Proceedings (Volume 5) at 1016:2–3, FTC v. Qualcomm Inc., No. 5:17-cv-00220-LHK (N.D. Cal. Jan. 14, 2019) (Testimony of Michael Lasinski)); *id.* at 790 ("However, Lasinski's ultimate conclusions are in line with the documentary evidence that Qualcomm's royalty rates are unreasonably high. . . . The Court notes that Lasinski's calculations are consistent with [Redacted]'s and [Redacted]'s rates. Thus, based on all the foregoing evidence—primarily Qualcomm's own documents—the Court concludes that Qualcomm's royalty rates are unreasonably high.").

and conclusions of law) that his testimony lacked credibility or reliability (or both, as Judge Leon had found in *United States v. AT&T*[982]).

An alternative explanation for Judge Koh's omission of any reference to Professor Shapiro or his trial testimony is that she did find his testimony persuasive and helpful and that she did in fact rely on it in reaching her findings of fact. But if that were the case, then why did Judge Koh not cite Professor Shapiro's testimony to support her findings of fact about complex economic questions? For example, would it not have been proper to cite Professor Shapiro's testimony for her findings about the definition of the relevant product market or the probative value of a theoretical bargaining model that supposedly supported the FTC's assertion that Qualcomm's licensing conduct had produced "unreasonably high" royalties that harmed competition?

In light of Professor Shapiro's unconvincing testimony before Judge Leon in the AT&T-Time Warner merger, one might interpret Judge Koh's lack of any citations to Professor Shapiro's testimony to mean that, although she was persuaded by his testimony, she wanted to spare her own findings of fact any additional vulnerability on appeal from having relied on Professor Shapiro's testimony. Perhaps Judge Koh's findings of fact and conclusions of law in *FTC v. Qualcomm* would be imperiled on appeal if they expressly relied on expert testimony predicated on the same kind of theoretical bargaining model that Judge Leon and the D.C. Circuit had just found to be lacking in reliability and factual credibility in *United States v. AT&T*. The Antitrust Division's loss in that case was so decisive—which is to say, so institutionally humiliating for the Department of Justice—that the Division declined to appeal to the Supreme Court.[983]

As we saw earlier, Judge Leon wrote in *United States v. AT&T* that he "couldn't help but notice that the more and more questions were raised during the trial about the reliability of Professor Shapiro's theory and model, the more the Government appeared to be minimizing the importance of his analysis."[984] Just as the Antitrust Division, according to Judge Leon's account, deemphasized Professor Shapiro's testimony in *United States v. AT&T*, so also might one interpret Judge Koh in *FTC v. Qualcomm* to have deemphasized Professor Shapiro's testimony to the point of making him vanish from her findings of fact and conclusions of law entirely.

---

[982] United States v. AT&T Inc., 310 F. Supp. 3d 161, 241 (D.D.C. 2018), *aff'd*, 916 F.3d 1029 (D.C. Cir. 2019) ("Professor Shapiro's model lacks both 'reliability and factual credibility.'") (quoting United States v. Anthem, Inc., 855 F.3d 345, 363 (D.C. Cir. 2017)).

[983] David Shepardson, *U.S. Justice Department: No Plans to Appeal AT&T Time Warner Ruling*, Reuters, Feb. 26, 2019 ("'We are grateful that the Court of Appeals considered our objections to the District Court opinion. The department has no plans to seek further review,' Justice Department spokesman Jeremy Edwards said in a statement.").

[984] United States v. AT&T Inc., 310 F. Supp. 3d 161, 220 (D.D.C. 2018), *aff'd*, 916 F.3d 1029 (D.C. Cir. 2019).

The Ninth Circuit (should it choose to rehear *FTC v. Qualcomm en banc*) and the Supreme Court might choose to consider *sua sponte* whether it properly lies within a federal judge's discretion during a bench trial to accept and rely upon expert testimony without ever mentioning the expert whose testimony the judge has accepted as true. How does it possibly enhance the quality of justice to cloak a judge's reasoned decision in this kind of mystery?

C. Did Judge Koh's Omission of Any Discussion of Professor Shapiro's Expert Economic Testimony Violate Federal Rule of Civil Procedure 52(a)(1)?

Recall from Part IV.G that Qualcomm and other commentators criticized the robustness of Professor Shapiro's theoretical bargaining model in *United States v. AT&T* and emphasized that actual market evidence contradicted his theory's predictions. That deviation of theory from fact made the government's use of Professor Shapiro's theoretical bargaining model as evidence of an antitrust violation in *United States v. AT&T* unreliable and factually incredible.

Yet, because Judge Koh never cited Professor Shapiro's expert testimony in *FTC v. Qualcomm* to support her findings of fact, she averted the need to make special findings of fact on his theoretical bargaining model and his other lines of expert economic testimony. It necessarily follows that Judge Koh also appears to have averted the need to make special findings of fact concerning the criticisms of Professor Shapiro's model that Qualcomm's expert economic witnesses raised in their trial testimony.[985] And Judge Koh also averted the need to make a special finding of fact on whether Professor Shapiro's theoretical bargaining model—and the economic predictions predicated on it—were relevant, reliable, and sufficiently connected to the facts of the case to support the various conclusions presented in his testimony.

1. Appellate Review of Findings of Fact

By omitting any reference to Professor Shapiro's testimony, Judge Koh's findings of fact and conclusions of law in *FTC v. Qualcomm* also ensured that his theoretical bargaining model (and his testimony that Qualcomm's challenged practices harmed competition) could be expected to escape in the Ninth Circuit the close scrutiny that Professor Shapiro's model had received in the D.C. Circuit's review in *United States v. AT&T*. Federal Rule of Civil Procedure 52(a)(6) provides that "[f]indings of fact, whether based on oral or other evidence, must not be set aside unless clearly erroneous, and the

---

[985]   *See* Transcript of Proceedings (Volume 8) at 1693:6–1775:4, FTC v. Qualcomm Inc., No. 5:17-cv-00220-LHK (N.D. Cal. Jan. 22, 2019) (Testimony of Tasneem Chipty); *id.* at 1775:7–1813:25 (Testimony of Edward Snyder); Transcript of Proceedings (Volume 9) at 1860:7–1966:15, FTC v. Qualcomm Inc., No. 5:17-cv-00220-LHK (N.D. Cal. Jan. 25, 2019) (Testimony of Aviv Nevo).

reviewing court must give due regard to the trial court's opportunity to judge the witnesses' credibility."[986] As the D.C. Circuit emphasized in *United States v. Microsoft*, "[t]here is no *de novo* appellate review of factfindings."[987]

In *Microsoft*, Judge Thomas Penfield Jackson wrote his findings of fact without any citations to the record.[988] Judge Jackson's adroit opinion writing thus boxed in the D.C. Circuit, giving it little choice but to accept his findings of fact at face value, lest it conduct precisely the *de novo* review that it said it may not undertake.

Similarly, because some readers of Judge Koh's May 21, 2019 opinion might understand her to have tacitly presented Professor Shapiro's testimony about economic questions as her own independent findings of *fact*, the Ninth Circuit and the Supreme Court could have been expected to abstain from any meaningful review of the correctness of those findings. In other words, by not acknowledging at all the existence and substance of Professor Shapiro's voluminous expert testimony in *FTC v. Qualcomm*, Judge Koh might appear to some sophisticated jurists and trial lawyers to have impaired the ability of the Ninth Circuit and, in time, the Supreme Court to ascertain whether her

---

[986] Fed. R. Civ. P. 52(a)(6).

[987] United States v. Microsoft Corp., 253 F.3d 34, 117 (D.C. Cir. 2001) (en banc) (per curiam) (citing Fed. R. Civ. P. 52(a)).

[988] *See* United States v. Microsoft Corp., 97 F. Supp. 2d 59, 63 (D.D.C. 2000), *aff'd*, 253 F.3d 34 (D.C. Cir. 2001) (en banc) (per curiam); *see also* Howard A. Shelanski & J. Gregory Sidak, *Antitrust Divestiture in Network Industries*, 68 U. Chi. L. Rev. 1, 73–74 (2001) (commenting on Judge Jackson's omission of any citations to the record). By the time Judge Jackson's decision was on appeal, it had come to light that he "had been giving secret interviews to select reporters before entering final judgment—in some instances long before." *Microsoft*, 253 F.3d at 108. "Concealment of the interviews," the D.C. Circuit found, "suggests knowledge of their impropriety." *Id.* at 112. On the basis of this behavior and other acts, the D.C. Circuit found that Judge Jackson had engaged in judicial misconduct:

> Canon 3A(6) of the Code of Conduct for United States Judges requires federal judges to "avoid public comment on the merits of [] pending or impending" cases. Canon 2 tells judges to "avoid impropriety and the appearance of impropriety in all activities," on the bench and off. Canon 3A(4) forbids judges to initiate or consider *ex parte* communications on the merits of pending or impending proceedings. Section 455(a) of the Judicial Code requires judges to recuse themselves when their "impartiality might reasonably be questioned."
>
> All indications are that the District Judge violated each of these ethical precepts by talking about the case with reporters. The violations were deliberate, repeated, egregious, and flagrant.

Id. at 107 (alteration in original) (first quoting Code of Conduct for United States Judges, *supra* note 65, Canon 3A(6); then quoting Code of Conduct for United States Judges, *supra* note 65, Canon 2A; and then quoting 28 U.S.C. § 455(a)); *see also id.* at 109 ("Reports of the interviews have the District Judge describing Microsoft's conduct, with particular emphasis on what he regarded as the company's prevarication, hubris, and impenitence."). The D.C. Circuit specifically found that Judge Jackson had violated Canon 2A:

> Canon 2A requires federal judges to "respect and comply with the law" and to "act at all times in a manner that promotes public confidence in the integrity and impartiality of the judiciary." The Code of Conduct is the law with respect to the ethical obligations of federal judges, and it is clear the District Judge violated it on multiple occasions in this case. The rampant disregard for the judiciary's ethical obligations that the public witnessed in this case undoubtedly jeopardizes "public confidence in the integrity" of the District Court proceedings.

Id. at 113 (quoting Code of Conduct for United States Judges, *supra* note 65, Canon 2A).

factual findings rested on the application of sound economic theories to the evidence in the case.

2.   Sua Sponte *Examination of Compliance with Rule 52(a)(1)*

The ability of the Ninth Circuit and the Supreme Court to review Judge Koh's nonexistent findings on the reliability or unreliability of Professor Shapiro's theoretical bargaining model and its predictions was potentially determinative in *FTC v. Qualcomm*. A skeptical review of Judge Koh's findings of fact would call into question the legal sufficiency of the FTC's case-in-chief against Qualcomm, if Judge Koh in fact relied on Professor Shapiro's testimony and if the same disqualifying defects that Judge Leon and the D.C. Circuit identified in Professor Shapiro's theoretical bargaining model in *United States v. AT&T* also diminished the reliability and factual credibility of his expert testimony in *FTC v. Qualcomm*. (Recall from Figure 6 that Professor Shapiro formulated his testimony in *FTC v. Qualcomm* before learning that the D.C. Circuit would be unanimously affirming Judge Leon's finding that Professor Shapiro's theoretical bargaining model was unreliable and wanting in factual credibility.)

It is therefore altogether proper for the Ninth Circuit (should it decide to rehear *FTC v. Qualcomm en banc*) and the Supreme Court to ask *sua sponte* whether, by declining to acknowledge the existence of Professor Shapiro's testimony and by failing to explain specifically the evidentiary weight that she had given it in her findings of fact and conclusions of law, Judge Koh violated Federal Rule of Civil Procedure 52(a)(1), which requires that, "[i]n an action tried on the facts without a jury . . . , the court *must* find the facts specially."[989] The Supreme Court emphasized in 1943 in *Kelly v. Everglades Drainage District* that, although Rule 52 does not require the district court to make findings on all matters, the court must make sufficient findings "to indicate the factual basis for the ultimate conclusion."[990] One purpose of Rule 52(a), the Ninth Circuit has said, is "'to aid the appellate court's understanding of the basis of the trial court's decision.'"[991] As Judge Posner wrote for the Seventh Circuit

---

[989] Fed. R. Civ. P. 52(a)(1) (emphasis added).

[990] 319 U.S. 415, 422 (1943).

[991] Simeonoff v. Hiner, 249 F.3d 883, 891 (9th Cir. 2001) (quoting Vance v. Am. Hawaii Cruises, Inc., 789 F.2d 790, 792 (9th Cir. 1986)); *see also* Valsamis v. Gonzalez-Romero, 748 F.3d 61, 62 (1st Cir. 2014) ("Rule 52(a)(1) is designed to ensure not only that the parties are adequately apprised of the district court's findings and rationale but also that a reviewing court will thereafter be able to evaluate the bona fides of the district court's decision."); Garner v. Kennedy, 713 F.3d 237, 242–43 (5th Cir. 2013) ("Rule 52(a)(1) serves three main purposes: '1) aiding the trial court's adjudication process by engendering care by the court in determining the facts; 2) promoting the operation of the doctrines of res judicata and estoppel by judgment; and 3) providing findings explicit enough to enable appellate courts to carry out a meaningful review.'") (quoting Chandler v. City of Dallas, 958 F.2d 85, 88 (5th Cir. 1992) (per curiam)); Bartsh v. Northwest Airlines, Inc., 831 F.2d 1297, 1304 (7th Cir. 1987) ("The purpose of this requirement is twofold: (1) to provide appellate courts with a clear understanding of the basis of the trial court's decision, and (2) to aid the trial court in considering and adjudicating the facts."); Lyles v. United States, 759 F.2d 941, 943 (D.C. Cir. 1985)

in 1982 in *Rucker v. Higher Educational Aids Board*, "[t]his means that 'there must be findings, stated either in the court's opinion or separately, which are sufficient to indicate the factual basis for the ultimate conclusion.' Otherwise the reviewing court has no way of knowing what the facts of the case are."[992]

3. *Remand to a Different District Judge*

When a court fails to make adequate factual findings to permit the appellate court to perform its role of reviewer, the typical remedy is a remand for additional fact finding.[993] In *Rucker*, however, the Seventh Circuit's remedy for the district judge's violation of Rule 52(a)(1) following a bench trial was more emphatic. Judge Posner wrote that the proper remedy was "to remand for a new trial" to "be conducted by a *different* judge."[994]

("One of [the] chief purposes [of Rule 52(a)] is 'to aid the appellate court by affording it a clear understanding of the ground or basis of the decision of the trial court.'") (quoting CHARLES WRIGHT & ARTHUR MILLER, FEDERAL PRACTICE AND PROCEDURE § 2571, at 679 (Thomson Reuters 1971)); Colorado Flying Acad., Inc. v. United States, 724 F.2d 871, 877 (10th Cir. 1984) ("[Federal] Rule [of Civil Procedure 52(a)] is designed to provide the appellate court with a clear understanding of the basis of the trial court's decision and to aid the trial court in considering and adjudicating the facts.").

[992] 669 F.2d 1179, 1183–84 (7th Cir. 1982) (quoting *Everglades Drainage*, 319 U.S. at 422) (citing Denofre v. Transp. Ins. Rating Bureau, 532 F.2d 43, 45 (7th Cir. 1976)). More than three decades later, when reflecting on what makes "[g]ood judicial opinion writing," Judge Posner advised judges: "Brevity is the soul of wit, all right, but be sure you don't leave out of the opinion anything the reader may need in order to understand what the case is about and why you are deciding it as you are. It's remarkable how many judicial opinions are simultaneously overlong and incomplete." POSNER, DIVERGENT PATHS: THE ACADEMY AND THE JUDICIARY, *supra* note 963, at 271. Judge Posner added: "Be candid as well as truthful. Tell the reader the real reason for the outcome." *Id.*

[993] *See, e.g.*, Baldinger v. Ferri, 483 F. App'x 708, 711 (3d Cir. 2012) ("We find that the District Court's explanation for its order is inadequate for us to engage in any meaningful review, and therefore will vacate the District Court's order and remand."); PharMethod, Inc. v. Caserta, 382 F. App'x 214, 218 (3d Cir. 2010) ("Given the paucity of findings of fact and conclusions of law, there is an insufficient basis for meaningful appellate review. We accordingly must remand so that the district court can fulfill its obligations under Rule 52(a)(2)."); Redditt v. Miss. Extended Care Ctr., Inc., 718 F.2d 1381, 1386 (5th Cir. 1983) ("This Court cannot determine whether the district court's finding that plaintiff failed to demonstrate pretext was clearly erroneous when the district court's finding is not expressed with sufficient particularity. It is not the function of this Court to make credibility choices and findings of fact. We are therefore left with no choice but to vacate the judgment of the district court for failure to comply with Fed. R. Civ. P. 52(a) and remand for findings of fact which indicate the factual basis for the district court's conclusion on the issue of pretext."); Lumbermen's Underwriting All. v. Can-Car, Inc., 645 F.2d 17, 18 (9th Cir. 1980) ("These conclusory findings simply do not meet the standards [Rule 52(a) and decisions construing it] enunciated above. We think this case must be remanded for additional and more detailed findings and conclusions."); Parrinello v. Finn, 589 F.2d 100, 101 (2d Cir. 1978) (remanding because "the district court failed to make sufficient findings of fact to enable us adequately to review its decision dismissing the action on the merits").

[994] *Rucker*, 669 F.2d at 1184 (emphasis added); *cf.* O'Shea v. Riverway Towing Co., 677 F.2d 1194, 1201 (7th Cir. 1982) (Posner, J.) ("[C]ompliance with Rule 52(a) of the Federal Rules of Civil Procedure requires that in a bench trial the district judge set out the steps by which he arrived at his award for lost future earnings, in order to assist the appellate court in reviewing the award. The district judge failed to do that here. We do not consider this reversible error, because our own analysis convinces us that the award of damages for lost future wages was reasonable. But for the future we ask the district judges in this circuit to indicate the steps by which they arrive at damage awards for lost future earnings.") (citing *Rucker*, 669 F.2d at 1183–84).

4. The Trial Court's Subsidiary Findings and Analytical Process

The Fifth Circuit's 2019 decision in *Eni US Operating Co. v. Transocean Offshore Deepwater Drilling, Inc.*[995] provided guidance for assessing Judge Koh's compliance with Rule 52(a)(1). On an appeal from a bench trial in which the district judge had made special findings of fact pursuant to Rule 52(a)(1), the Fifth Circuit said:

> The question before us is how detailed those factual findings need to be. Is the district court required to make subsidiary findings? Or can it announce only its ultimate factual conclusion? We long ago answered that question: Rule 52(a) compels a district court to lay out enough subsidiary findings to allow us to understand "the basis of the trial court's decision." Put differently, "the findings . . . must be sufficiently detailed to give us a clear understanding of the analytical process by which [the] ultimate findings were reached and to assure us that the trial court took care in ascertaining the facts."[996]

Were Judge Koh's findings of complex economic facts sufficiently detailed to permit the Ninth Circuit and the Supreme Court to understand the analytical process that she followed in reaching her conclusions?

Some of the inadequate factual findings from a bench trial that have necessitated a remand seem quotidian when compared with the complexity of the factual findings that Judge Koh was obliged to make in *FTC v. Qualcomm*.[997] The Ninth Circuit has said that, although it "ha[d] previously disapproved of the mechanical adoption of findings and conclusions prepared by the victorious party[,] . . . [t]he verbatim adoption of findings suggested by a party is not automatically objectionable, . . . so long as those findings are supported by the record."[998] Yet, we shall see that Judge Koh's conclusions about Qualcomm's market power, Qualcomm's "unreasonably high" royalty rates, the existence of the alleged royalty "surcharge" and modem "tax," and the effects that the alleged royalty "surcharge" and modem "tax" had on the

---

[995] 919 F.3d 931 (5th Cir. 2019).

[996] *Id.* at 935 (alterations in original) (citations omitted) (first quoting Gulf King Shrimp Co. v. Wirtz, 407 F.2d 508, 515 (5th Cir. 1969); and then quoting Golf City, Inc. v. Wilson Sporting Goods, Co., 555 F.2d 426, 433 (5th Cir. 1977)).

[997] *See, e.g.,* King v. United States, 553 F.3d 1156, 1161 (8th Cir. 2009) ("We cannot . . . determine whether . . . Dunfee's alleged statement to Triplett at a retirement party in March or April 2005 . . . is direct evidence of age discrimination because the district court failed to make a factual finding about whether Triplett's testimony about Dunfee's alleged statement was credible . . . . Because this was a bench trial, the district court was required to '"find the facts specially and state separately its conclusions of law."'") (quoting Darst-Webbe Tenant Ass'n Bd. v. St. Louis Hous. Auth., 339 F.3d 702, 711 (8th Cir. 2003) (quoting FED. R. CIV. P. 52(a))).

[998] Unt v. Aerospace Corp., 765 F.2d 1440, 1444–45 (9th Cir. 1985) (first citing Lumbermen's Underwriting All. v. Can-Car, Inc., 645 F.2d 17, 18 (9th Cir. 1980); and then citing United States v. El Paso Nat. Gas Co., 376 U.S. 651, 656 (1964)).

output and profits and investments of Qualcomm's rivals were all findings lacking a cogent explanation in Judge Koh's written opinion.

It is useful to compare Judge Koh's findings of fact with a jury's verdict. In a jury trial, the judge issues jury instructions, which typically ask only for yes-or-no answers and a dollar amount (for the award of damages). The jury is not expected or asked to give a "reasoned decision" for its verdict. The reasoned decision in effect is inferred from the combination of the judge's instructions to the jury and the judge's subsequent ruling on some or all of a motion for judgment as a matter of law, a renewed motion for judgment as a matter of law, and a motion for a new trial, in which the judge typically will specify whether the jury had "substantial evidence" for its finding on a given question.[999]

A recurring problem with Judge Koh's findings of fact from her bench trial in *FTC v. Qualcomm* is that they resembled too much a jury's yes-or-no answers, as if the FTC's proposed conclusions of law were the jury instructions. In contrast, to comply with Federal Rule of Civil Procedure 52(a)(1), Judge Koh's findings of fact should have provided a clear "reasoned decision" for all critical factual propositions upon which she relied in making her conclusions of law.

D. Was Judge Koh Correct in Finding That Qualcomm's Licensing Practices Imposed an Anticompetitive "Surcharge" on the "All-in Price" of Rivals' Modems?

Judge Koh found that "Qualcomm's unreasonably high royalty rates impose[d] a surcharge on rivals' modem chips."[1000] That finding of fact closely corresponded to Professor Shapiro's testimony—although he distinguished the royalty "surcharge" from the modem "tax."[1001] Judge Koh's finding was illogical and contrary to substantial evidence. Her conclusions of law concerning the royalty "surcharge" contradicted controlling antitrust jurisprudence.

Judge Koh also found that Qualcomm charged a higher royalty to OEMs that used non-Qualcomm modems than it charged OEMs that used Qualcomm modems, which in her opinion further harmed Qualcomm's rivals.[1002] Yet, the solitary instance that Judge Koh cited as evidence of a

---

[999] *See* Fed. R. Civ. P. 50, 59.

[1000] FTC v. Qualcomm Inc., 411 F. Supp. 3d 658, 790 (N.D. Cal. 2019).

[1001] *See* Transcript of Proceedings (Volume 6) at 1124:6–12, FTC v. Qualcomm Inc., No. 5:17-cv-00220-LHK (N.D. Cal. Jan. 15, 2019) (Testimony of Carl Shapiro) ("So the fundamental concern that one has here and that I've explored in detail is that Qualcomm is using its market power, its monopoly power over the chips to extract an unreasonably high royalty for the standard essential patents, and that in doing that, that is effectively a tax or raises the cost of its rivals and thereby weakens them as competitors and fortifies Qualcomm's monopoly power."). This opinion was more concisely disclosed in Professor Shapiro's initial report, which was of course not moved into evidence but did closely track his demonstratives supporting his direct examination during the FTC's case-in-chief. *See supra* note 606 and accompanying text.

[1002] *FTC v. Qualcomm*, 411 F. Supp. 3d at 698.

higher royalty of this sort was a license that Qualcomm executed with LGE in 2004.[1003] Qualcomm revised that isolated license in 2007, so as to charge LGE the same royalty irrespective of the brand of modem that LGE used in its mobile devices.[1004] Judge Koh did not explain whether this one extraordinary license had any other distinctive features that might have accounted for why it alone among Qualcomm's many licenses contained an asymmetric royalty rate. Judge Koh did not explain in her findings of fact and conclusions of law why she considered it reliable under the Federal Rules of Evidence to extrapolate a generalized finding of fact—namely, that Qualcomm charged a higher cellular SEP royalty to all OEMs that used non-Qualcomm modems—from a single incident, of limited duration, more than a decade in the past, concerning a single OEM.[1005]

As we shall see in Part VII, although Judge Koh concluded that Qualcomm charged OEMs an "unreasonably high" royalty for an exhaustive license to its portfolio of cellular SEPs, the evidence that she cited in her findings of fact and conclusions of law failed to support her conclusion. Judge Koh did not rely on any economic analysis to determine the value of Qualcomm's portfolio of cellular SEPs. The evidence that she summarized was at best anecdotal. Even if taken at face value, that evidence did not support her conclusion that Qualcomm's royalties for an exhaustive license to its cellular SEPs were "unreasonably high."

Judge Koh should have recognized that the FTC's failure to prove by a preponderance of the evidence that those royalties were "unreasonably high" obliterated Professor Shapiro's theory of the royalty "surcharge" and modem "tax." As we saw in Part IV, Professor Shapiro admitted on cross examination during the FTC's case-in-chief that there would be no harm to competition from Qualcomm's licensing practices if Qualcomm did not charge OEMs "unreasonably high" royalties for an exhaustive license to its portfolio of cellular SEPs.[1006]

Yet, even if one assumes for sake of argument (but contrary to the evidence) that Qualcomm's royalties for an exhaustive license to its cellular SEPs were "unreasonably high," there still would be no support for the conclusion that those royalties harmed competition among modem manufacturers. Judge Koh found that because Qualcomm charged all OEMs a royalty "surcharge" on an exhaustive license to Qualcomm's portfolio of cellular SEPs, including OEMs that used non-Qualcomm modems, the royalty imposed a "tax" on modems manufactured by Qualcomm's rivals.[1007] She reasoned that OEMs

---

[1003] *Id.* at 698–701.

[1004] *Id.* at 701–02.

[1005] *Id.* at 743–44.

[1006] Transcript of Proceedings (Volume 6) at 1198:2–25, FTC v. Qualcomm Inc., No. 5:17-cv-00220-LHK (N.D. Cal. Jan. 15, 2019) (Testimony of Carl Shapiro).

[1007] *FTC v. Qualcomm*, 411 F. Supp. 3d at 790.

considered a modem's "all-in price," which (she said) consisted of (1) the price of a modem and (2) the royalty "surcharge" that the OEM supposedly must pay to Qualcomm for an exhaustive license to its cellular SEPs.[1008]

But Judge Koh's definition of a modem's "all-in price" was erroneous, and she did not explain how a modem's "all-in price" would harm competition. Judge Koh did not present a calculation based on data in evidence in *FTC v. Qualcomm*. She did not present a numerical example (much less an algebraic formula) to explain how she came to find that Qualcomm's licensing practices imposed a "tax" on rivals' modems and how the "all-in price" of rival's modems reduced the sales and margins and investments of those rival modem manufacturers.

Judge Koh's reasoning was obscure. I summarize here her "all-in price" theory of competitive harm as faithfully as possible. I then expose its contradictions.

1.   Did Judge Koh Coherently Define a Modem's "All-In Price"?

To understand Judge Koh's conclusion about a modem's "all-in price," suppose that a reasonable royalty for an exhaustive license to Qualcomm's portfolio of cellular SEPs is $5, but that Qualcomm is able to use its alleged monopoly power (over one or both of Judge Koh's two relevant product markets for modems) to coerce OEMs to pay a $9 royalty instead. In this example, the "surcharge" is equal to $4. An OEM must pay the "surcharge" of $4, irrespective of whether it uses Qualcomm modems or non-Qualcomm modems. In Judge Koh's view (as in Professor Shapiro's view), that royalty "surcharge" harms competition among modem manufacturers because, when considering which modem to buy, OEMs supposedly consider that "all-in price," which includes the cost of an exhaustive license to Qualcomm's cellular SEPs.[1009]

Judge Koh's own definition of the "all-in price" was incoherent because it conspicuously omitted the "reasonable royalty," which is $5 in the example above. She stated in her findings of fact and conclusions of law that "the 'all-in' price of any modem chip sold by one of Qualcomm's rivals effectively includes two components: (1) the nominal chip price; and (2) Qualcomm's royalty surcharge."[1010] By that statement, Judge Koh ignored that every smartphone sold in the United States must be authorized to use the SEPs and non-SEPs that it practices, regardless of whether Qualcomm or one of its rivals makes the modem used in the smartphone. Table 6 compares Judge Koh's incomplete definition of "all-in price" with the correct definition of "all-in price."

[1008]   *Id.* at 791.
[1009]   *Id.* at 790.
[1010]   *Id.* at 791.

Table 6. "All-In Price" Comparison

	Correct "All-In Price"	"All-In Price" as Defined by Judge Koh
Modem Price	$20	$20
Reasonable Royalty for an Exhaustive License to Qualcomm's Portfolio of Cellular SEPs	$5	–
Qualcomm's Alleged Royalty "Surcharge"	$4	$4
Total	$29	$24

Judge Koh's definition of the "all-in price" of a modem was nonsensical because it ignored that it was not in dispute in *FTC v. Qualcomm* that Qualcomm was entitled to earn not less than what Professor Shapiro called a "reasonable royalty" for an OEM's exhaustive license to Qualcomm's portfolio of cellular SEPs when the OEM bought a modem. In other words, Judge Koh's explanation of the "all-in price" of a modem was not even consistent with Professor Shapiro's definition of the "all-in price" during his trial testimony.

2. Would the OEM's Payment of the Modem's "All-In Price" Harm Competition in the Relevant Markets for Modems?

Even if one ignores Judge Koh's incoherent definition of a modem's "all-in price," her theory of harm to competition was still illogical. Judge Koh also did not explain how the alleged royalty "surcharge" and modem "tax"—supposedly embedded into every modem's "all-in price"—reduced the sales and margins of rival modem manufacturers. We shall see that substantial evidence disproved those predictions by Judge Koh.

Judge Koh found that, "[u]nder Qualcomm's patent license agreements with OEMs, Qualcomm charges its unreasonably high royalty rates anytime an OEM sells a handset, even when that handset contains a rival's modem chip."[1011] "Thus," she argued, "Qualcomm imposes an artificial surcharge on all sales of its rivals' modem chips."[1012] Like Professor Shapiro, Judge Koh conjectured that, because of the "surcharge," "[r]ivals see lower sales volumes and lower margins, and consumers see less advanced features as competition decreases."[1013]

[1011] *Id.* at 790.
[1012] *Id.*
[1013] *Id.* at 792.

These findings of fact by Judge Koh's were specious for at least three reasons.

a. Was It Reasonable for Qualcomm to Charge Royalties for Its Cellular SEPs to OEMs That Used Non-Qualcomm Modems?

First, when presenting her royalty "surcharge" theory, Judge Koh did not ask the obvious question: did the OEMs in question practice Qualcomm's cellular SEPs even in their smartphones equipped with non-Qualcomm modems? If so, then the question of which brand of modem an OEM used would be irrelevant to whether that OEM was obliged to compensate Qualcomm for practicing its cellular SEPs in that OEM's smartphone. Regardless of the brand of modem that the OEM used, the OEM would *still* have needed to compensate Qualcomm for exhaustively practicing Qualcomm's portfolio of cellular SEPs.

Far from being an "artificial surcharge," the royalty payment that Qualcomm received from that OEM would simply be the lawful compensation that Qualcomm was entitled to receive for the OEM's implementation of Qualcomm's cellular SEPs. Provided that Qualcomm's royalty for an exhaustive license to its cellular SEPs was reasonable (which the FTC never disproved), there was nothing untoward about Qualcomm's policy of charging every OEM a royalty for its use of Qualcomm's portfolio of cellular SEPs, irrespective of the brand of modem that the OEM chose to use in its smartphones.

But suppose for sake of argument (but contrary to the evidence) that Qualcomm charged OEMs a royalty for an exhaustive license to its cellular SEPs that was indeed "unreasonably high." Judge Koh's finding that Qualcomm's licensing practices for its cellular SEPs imposed a royalty "surcharge" on OEMs that used non-Qualcomm modems still would have relied on faulty economic reasoning. If Qualcomm had been enforcing its cellular SEPs only against OEMs that used non-Qualcomm modems (and not against OEMs that used *Qualcomm's* modems), then Judge Koh would have observed Qualcomm's royalty as an additional cost to the OEM of purchasing a non-Qualcomm modem.

But that is *not* what Judge Koh found from the evidence. Judge Koh actually found: "Under Qualcomm's patent license agreements with OEMs, Qualcomm charges its unreasonably high royalty rates *anytime* an OEM sells a handset, even when that handset contains a rival's modem chip."[1014] Put differently, Judge Koh found that "Qualcomm charges its unreasonably high royalty . . . when that handset contains" a Qualcomm modem. Consequently, Qualcomm's royalty for an exhaustive license to its portfolio of cellular SEPs

---

[1014] *Id.* at 790 (emphasis added).

did *not* asymmetrically raise the effective "all-in price" of modems sold only by Qualcomm's rivals.

  b. The Lack of Synchronization Between the OEM's Contracting for an Exhaustive License to Qualcomm's Cellular SEPs and the OEM's Negotiation for the Purchase of Modems for a Particular Release of Smartphone

Second, to understand the fallacies of Judge Koh's royalty "surcharge" conjecture, it is helpful to consider the difference between (1) the duration of an exhaustive license to Qualcomm's portfolio of cellular SEPs that Qualcomm executes with an individual OEM and (2) the frequency with which that OEM selects a supplier of modems. Qualcomm's portfolio license agreements typically last for a number of years. In 2019, for example, Qualcomm executed a five-year license with LGE.[1015] Similarly, as part of the 2019 agreement by which Apple and Qualcomm settled all of their legal disputes, the parties executed "a six-year license agreement, effective as of April 1, 2019, including a two-year option to extend," which would extend the license duration to eight years.[1016] In 2009, Qualcomm and Samsung executed a 15-year cross license agreement, which the parties extended in 2019.[1017]

  In contrast to entering into an exhaustive license to Qualcomm's portfolio of cellular SEPs lasting 5 to 15 years, a given OEM typically selects modem suppliers on shorter intervals. For example, from 2016 to 2019, Apple revisited its selection of modem suppliers for its next-generation iPhone *each year*. Tony Blevins, Vice President of Procurement at Apple, testified during the FTC's case-in-chief on January 11, 2019 that Apple chose Qualcomm as the sole modem supplier for the iPhone 6,[1018] that Apple chose both Qualcomm and Intel to supply the 2016 iPhone,[1019] that Apple chose Intel exclusively to

---

[1015] *See* Press Release, Qualcomm Inc., Qualcomm and LGE Enter into a New Global Patent License Agreement (Aug. 20, 2019), https://www.qualcomm.com/news/releases/2019/08/20/qualcomm-and-lge-enter-new-global-patent-license-agreement (indicating that the parties executed a 5-year agreement).

[1016] Press Release, Apple Inc., Qualcomm and Apple Agree to Drop All Litigation (Apr. 16, 2019), https://www.apple.com/newsroom/2019/04/qualcomm-and-apple-agree-to-drop-all-litigation/.

[1017] *See* Press Release, Samsung Electronics Inc., Cross License Agreement with Qualcomm (Nov. 6, 2009), https://www.samsung.com/us/news/newsPreviewRead.do?news_seq=15370; Press Release, Qualcomm Inc., Qualcomm and Samsung Amend Long-Term Cross-License Agreement (Jan. 31, 2018), https://www.qualcomm.com/news/releases/2018/01/31/qualcomm-and-samsung-amend-long-term-cross-license-agreement.

[1018] Transcript of Proceedings (Volume 4) at 674:3–11, FTC v. Qualcomm Inc., No. 5:17-cv-00220-LHK (N.D. Cal. Jan. 11, 2019) (Testimony of Tony Blevins (Vice President of Procurement, Apple)) ("Q. When Apple first began buying LTE chips for the 2012 iPhone, which companies were capable of supplying chips that met Apple's needs? A. My recollection is our assessment was that Qualcomm had a superior offering, and so therefore, we narrowed our choice to Qualcomm for that first offering. Q. Did that ever change? A. It changed later. I think around 2016, we sourced with both Qualcomm and Intel.").

[1019] *Id.*

supply the 2018 iPhone,[1020] and that Apple was considering Intel, MediaTek, and Samsung as potential suppliers for the 2019 iPhone.[1021]

The frequency with which an OEM like Apple reevaluates its choice of a modem supplier makes clear that, contrary to Judge Koh's findings of fact, the terms of an exhaustive license to Qualcomm's portfolio of cellular SEPs, including the royalty for that exhaustive license, cannot realistically affect an OEM's selection of a modem supplier. It would be implausible to argue that the license agreement that Qualcomm executed with Apple in 2019 will influence Apple's choice of a modem supplier for the iPhones that Apple will release during the years thereafter: the terms of that portfolio license agreement will remain unchanged, regardless of whether Apple chooses to buy its modems from Qualcomm, MediaTek, or Samsung, and regardless of whether Apple chooses to develop its own modems internally through its acquisition of Intel's modem business in 2019.[1022] Consequently, it was specious for Judge Koh to conjecture, purely as a matter of *a priori* economic reasoning, that the royalty that Qualcomm charged for an exhaustive license to its portfolio of cellular SEPs had the effect of imposing a royalty "surcharge" or a "tax" on the price of modems sold by Qualcomm's rivals.

>   c.   *Did the "All-In Price" Favor Qualcomm Modems Over Non-Qualcomm Modems?*

Third, Judge Koh tried to support her analysis of the supposed royalty "surcharge" by claiming that the "effective price" or "all-in price" of any modem sold by one of Qualcomm's rivals included two components: (1) the nominal modem price and (2) Qualcomm's royalty "surcharge."[1023] However, we saw that her observation was incomplete because it ignored the per-unit cost of the indisputably "reasonable" increment of the royalty that an OEM would need to pay for an exhaustive license to use Qualcomm's portfolio of cellular SEPs.

The "all-in price" of a Qualcomm modem would then properly be defined to consist of (1) Qualcomm's nominal chip price and (2) Qualcomm's *full* royalty consisting of (a) a reasonable royalty for an exhaustive license to Qualcomm's portfolio of cellular SEPs and (b) the allegedly "unreasonably

---

[1020]   *Id.* at 720:2–6 ("Q. Mr. Blevins, as of the date of your deposition in this case, which was March 13th and 14th of 2018, Apple had decided to use Intel as the sole supplier of basebands for the 2018 iPhones, correct? A. That is correct.").

[1021]   *Id.* at 720:19–24 ("Q. As of the date of your deposition, Apple was considering Intel, MediaTek, and Samsung for baseband processors for 2019 iPhones, correct? A. That is correct, because in that period of time we knew that Qualcomm had already withdrawn. So they were no longer a candidate. Your statement is correct.").

[1022]   *See* Press Release, Apple Inc., Apple to Acquire the Majority of Intel's Smartphone Modem Business (July 25, 2019), https://www.apple.com/newsroom/2019/07/apple-to-acquire-the-majority-of-intels-smartphone-modem-business/.

[1023]   FTC v. Qualcomm Inc., 411 F. Supp. 3d 658, 791 (N.D. Cal. 2019).

high" royalty "surcharge." So defined, the "all-in price" of a modem did not favor Qualcomm's modem over non-Qualcomm modems. As noted above, *this* definition of the "all-in price" is the one that Professor Shapiro used in his testimony, which of course Judge Koh did not acknowledge anywhere in her findings of fact and conclusions of law in *FTC v. Qualcomm*.

> 3.   *What Facts Supported Judge Koh's Finding That Qualcomm Charged OEMs That Used Non-Qualcomm Modems a Higher Royalty for an Exhaustive License to Its Portfolio of Cellular SEPs?*

Judge Koh's theory of competitive harm might have been more plausible on a theoretical level if it had alleged that Qualcomm systematically charged OEMs higher royalties for an exhaustive license to its cellular SEPs when OEMs used non-Qualcomm modems. Yet, Judge Koh notably did *not* make such a finding of fact concerning the pricing of Qualcomm's cellular SEPs generally (subject to the one caveat that I discuss below).[1024]

> a.   *Why Did Judge Koh Rely on the Solitary Instance of the 2004 SULA Between LGE and Qualcomm to Find, as a General Matter, That Qualcomm Charged OEMs Higher Royalty Rates for an Exhaustive License to Its Cellular SEPs When OEMs Purchased Rivals' Modems Than When OEMs Purchased Qualcomm's Modems?*

Judge Koh found that, "[a]t times, Qualcomm has even charged OEMs higher royalty rates when OEMs purchase rivals' chips than when OEMs purchase Qualcomm's chips, which further harms rivals."[1025] That finding of fact was tendentious.

The *solitary* piece of evidence that Judge Koh cited to support that finding of fact was the "2004 SULA Amendment" between LGE and Qualcomm, which, according to Judge Koh, provided that "LGE paid Qualcomm a 5% running royalty on handsets containing Qualcomm modem chips and a 5.75% running royalty on handsets containing non-Qualcomm modem chips."[1026] Because the SULA with LGE was filed under seal, the contract's full content is not publicly available. Yet, we know that the full name of the agreement was the Amendment to Infrastructure and Subscriber Unit License and Technical Assistance Agreement.[1027] That lengthy title suggests that the contract's scope might have encompassed something more than solely a license to Qualcomm's portfolio of cellular SEPs.

[1024]   *Id.* at 807–12.
[1025]   *Id.* at 698.
[1026]   *Id.* at 701.
[1027]   *See id.*

If that were the case, then it would have been simplistic and incorrect for Judge Koh to have compared the royalty rate specified in Qualcomm's 2004 agreement with LGE with the royalties specified in Qualcomm's other license agreements.[1028] Instead, one would need to separate the value of Qualcomm's exhaustively licensed portfolio of cellular SEPs from the value of the other consideration exchanged in the agreement to identify the implicit one-way royalty that LGE would pay under different scenarios from which it would have been free to choose.[1029] Judge Koh's findings of fact and conclusions of law did not indicate that she conducted any such analysis of valuation under different contracting scenarios.

> *b.   Why Did Judge Koh's Findings Not Explain the Significance of the Fact That, Following Qualcomm's Voluntary Renegotiation in 2007 of Its 2004 SULA with LGE, the Factual Record Was Devoid of Evidence That Qualcomm's Exhaustive Licensing of Its Portfolio of Cellular SEPs Treated Any OEM Asymmetrically on the Basis of Whether It Also Bought a Qualcomm Modem?*

Furthermore, even when Judge Koh cited this sole piece of evidence of an asymmetric rate having been charged for an exhaustive license to Qualcomm's cellular SEPs when LGE used a rival's modem, she conceded that, by 2007, Qualcomm and LGE had amended the SULA so that Qualcomm would henceforth charge LGE the *same* royalty rate on devices equipped with Qualcomm modems as on devices equipped with non-Qualcomm modems.[1030] So how could Judge Koh possibly have considered Qualcomm's 2004 license with LGE a smoking gun that was highly probative at a monopolization trial 15 years later?

One cannot overstate the importance of this evidentiary exaggeration in Judge Koh's findings of fact: the *sole* instance of Qualcomm's supposedly charging a higher royalty for an exhaustive license to its cellular SEPs when an OEM used non-Qualcomm modems was a 0.75-percentage-point difference, for one OEM, for a three-year period ending a decade before the FTC filed its lawsuit, which Qualcomm agreed with the OEM to discontinue. How Qualcomm's particular licensing practice toward LGE plausibly could have begotten a successful strategy of monopolization encompassing many other OEMs (with whom no contracts having a similarly two-tiered rate provision

---

[1028]   *See, e.g.*, J. Gregory Sidak, *Converting Royalty Payment Structures for Patent Licenses*, 1 CRITERION J. ON INNOVATION 901, 901 (2016) ("To analyze and compare the different royalty payments of . . . [different] licenses, an economic expert or court must convert the royalties to a common structure."); Sidak & Skog, *Hedonic Prices and Patent Royalties, supra* note 446, at 611.

[1029]   *See, e.g.*, J. Gregory Sidak, *Why* Unwired Planet *Might Revolutionize the Resolution of FRAND Licensing Disputes*, 3 CRITERION J. ON INNOVATION 601, 609 (2018).

[1030]   *FTC v. Qualcomm*, 411 F. Supp. 3d at 701.

were mentioned) is a mystery that Judge Koh did not explain in her findings of fact and conclusions of law. Even at the simple level of logic and grammar, this singular anecdote involving LGE did not support Judge Koh's finding of fact that Qualcomm systematically charged OEMs—*plural*—asymmetrically higher royalty rates for an exhaustive license to its cellular SEPs when OEMs used non-Qualcomm modems in their mobile devices.[1031]

Judge Koh also did not say whether all other provisions in the LGE license agreement would have remained constant if LGE had decided to use a non-Qualcomm modem and pay the higher running royalty rate for Qualcomm's cellular SEPs. That is, it appeared from her findings of fact and conclusions of law that Judge Koh was implicitly making the *ceteris paribus* assumption, which we saw is familiar in economic analysis.[1032] Yet, the obvious question to ask is this: Upon a duly diligent examination of the provisions and circumstances of the 2004 SULA Amendment between LGE and Qualcomm, could one plausibly conclude, as Judge Koh evidently concluded from whatever examination of that agreement she undertook (but did not report), that everything else *would have* remained constant when LGE chose to pay Qualcomm the higher royalty for a license to its cellular SEPs?

When Dr. Jacobs, Qualcomm's founder, was cross examined at trial about an email that he received from Steve Altman, Qualcomm's President, on January 8, 2007 concerning the renegotiation of LG's license, Dr. Jacobs in essence posed this very question. He immediately remarked that *other* contractual terms, favorable to LG, might have accompanied the higher royalty rate for Qualcomm cellular SEPs that applied when LG chose to use a non-Qualcomm modem:

> Q. Looking at the first Arabic numeral, Mr. Altman [of Qualcomm] states "they currently pay 5 percent when they use our chip and 5.75 percent when they don't." Now, that accurately states the royalty rate that is [sic] LG paid Qualcomm at this time; right?
>
> A. I believe that's the case.
>
> Q. Now, this royalty rate difference based on whether LG purchased Qualcomm's chipsets or a competitor's chipsets provided LG with an incentive to purchase Qualcomm's chipsets; is that right?
>
> A. *I don't know what all the other terms involved were*, but that by itself would be an incentive.[1033]

[1031] *Id.* ("At *times*, Qualcomm has even charged *OEMs* higher royalty rates when *OEMs* purchase rivals' chips than when *OEMs* purchase Qualcomm's chips.") (emphasis added).

[1032] *See supra* note 277 and accompanying text.

[1033] Transcript of Proceedings (Volume 6) at 1287:19–1288:5, FTC v. Qualcomm Inc., No. 5:17-cv-00220-LHK (N.D. Cal. Jan. 15, 2019) (Testimony of Irwin Jacobs (Co-Founder, Qualcomm)) (emphasis added).

Judge Koh heard this testimony. But, evidently because she found Dr. Jacobs not to be a credible witness, she disregarded in her findings of fact the (highly plausible) possibility that LGE's choice to accept the burden to pay the higher running royalty rate of 5.75 percent would be accompanied by some conditional act or forbearance by Qualcomm that conveyed a greater countervailing amount of incremental value *to* LGE. That outcome, after all, would be the standard prediction of the economic theory of voluntary exchange by rational actors.[1034]

Conversely, Judge Koh did not exclude the (highly plausible) possibility that Qualcomm was willing to charge the lower 5-percent running royalty rate for an exhaustive license to its cellular SEPs when it supplied LGE the modem because of some cost that Qualcomm was thereby able to avoid (which is to say, an economy of scope), such that Qualcomm could share some of that incremental surplus with LGE.

Restated in formal economic terms, Judge Koh did not consider the possibility in her findings of fact and conclusions of law that the 2004 SULA Amendment between LGE and Qualcomm contained, by virtue of its two-tiered royalty structure, what economists call an "optional tariff," a contractual mechanism that economists typically applaud for its salutary effects on economic efficiency and consumer choice.[1035]

c.   *Why Did Judge Koh Rely on Stale Evidence from the Distant Past While Pretending to Be Prescient Years into the Future?*

Perhaps the work of judging requires some element of mystery for its intended audience to take the leap of faith and accept that the expositor of the law has legitimacy. If one embraces an imperative view of law—as much about the trial and much about the findings of fact and conclusions of law in *FTC v. Qualcomm* suggest Judge Koh does—then the legitimacy of law ultimately turns upon who shall exercise the power of imperator. Hence the black robes, the courthouses built to resemble Greek temples, and the Latin phrases that telegraph a secular hunger for something transcendent. Hence, also, the reliance on rhetoric to suspend the reader's disbelief—something that Judge Posner addresses, fittingly, in a chapter on the law of evidence: "Rhetoric, as explained by Aristotle in his treatise on the subject, is the set

---

[1034] The economic principle that voluntary exchange is mutually beneficial is as profound as it is simple, and for that reason economists call it, "The Fundamental Theorem of Exchange." *See, e.g.,* JACK HIRSHLEIFER, AMIHAI GLAZER & DAVID HIRSHLEIFER, PRICE THEORY AND APPLICATIONS: DECISIONS, MARKETS, AND INFORMATION 203 (Cambridge Univ. Press 7th ed. 2005).

[1035] *See, e.g.,* J. Gregory Sidak, *Fair and Unfair Discrimination in Royalties for Standard-Essential Patents Encumbered by a FRAND or RAND Commitment,* 2 CRITERION J. ON INNOVATION 301, 321 (2017); *see also* John C. Panzar & J. Gregory Sidak, *When Does an Optional Tariff Not Lead to a Pareto Improvement? The Ambiguous Effects of Self-Selecting Nonlinear Pricing When Demand Is Interdependent or Firms Do Not Maximize Profit,* 2 J. COMPETITION L. & ECON. 285 (2006).

of techniques for inducing belief in matters involving irremediable uncertainty. An important dimension of effective rhetoric is making the speaker credible."[1036] And the master rhetorician among jurists was, in Judge Posner's assessment, Justice Oliver Wendell Holmes.[1037]

As an example of judicial opinion writing, Judge Koh's findings of fact and conclusions of law in *FTC v. Qualcomm* sorely needed to persuade her readers to suspend disbelief and lend her credibility, yet she offered them no Holmesian trope of rhetoric. It was consequently all the more conspicuous and awkward that Judge Koh seemed to think that no one would notice that she was deciding an antitrust claim in 2019 in one of the most technologically dynamic of all industries—and was thereupon ordering a permanent, worldwide injunction extending until at least 2026—on the basis of findings of fact concerning pricing policies that were 12 to 15 years out of date by the time that *FTC v. Qualcomm* went to trial. Absent additional support, evidence that Qualcomm once executed a license with an OEM in 2004 that appears to have contained an optional tariff regarding the royalty rate, and that the counterparties amended that same license three years later to eliminate the rate disparity, cannot remotely support a finding of fact that Qualcomm *systematically* charged higher royalties for an exhaustive license to its cellular SEPs to OEMs that used modems supplied by Qualcomm's rivals, as Judge Koh implied.[1038]

Moreover, as we shall see, Judge Koh's permanent, worldwide injunction proceeded on the conceit that she possessed the clarity to direct how the global mobile communication industry should evolve. That perspective stands in contrast to the writings of Nobel laureate Friedrich Hayek, who argued that, given the costliness of acquiring information and of centrally gathering and evaluating it, markets are superior institutions to bureaucracies (to which a federal district judge overseeing a permanent, worldwide

---

[1036] POSNER, ECONOMIC ANALYSIS OF LAW, *supra* note 214, at 840.

[1037] Judge Posner considers the foremost example of a judge's mastery of rhetoric to be Justice Holmes' dissent in 1905 in *Lochner*, which famously proclaimed: "The Fourteenth Amendment does not enact Mr. Herbert Spencer's Social Statics." *See* RICHARD A. POSNER, LAW AND LITERATURE: A MISUNDERSTOOD RELATIONSHIP 342 (Harvard Univ. Press 3ᵈ ed. 2009) (1988) (discussing Lochner v. New York, 198 U.S. 45, 75 (1905) (Holmes, J., dissenting)). It is a tribute to the rhetorical power of Justice Holmes' brief dissent that it has succeeded to this day in persuading nearly every law professor in the United States despite its relying on an epistemological fallacy. *See* J. Gregory Sidak, *Capitalism, Socialism, and the Constitution*, 4 CRITERION J. ON INNOVATION 801, 815–19 (2019). What is most immediately striking about the dissent is its premise that majoritarianism can validate an empirical proposition. Justice Holmes chose to ignore the fact that knowledge, revealed through the process of scientific discovery, depends in no way on the operation of some majoritarian mechanism. If Fabian socialism was in 1905 the most extreme alternative to capitalism that Justice Holmes might have observed, it was a cheap gesture for him to say that the Constitution was not predicated on a system of private property and entrepreneurship. As long as socialism was not perceived as a threat to democratic capitalism, socialism would never garner the support of "a majority to embody their opinions in law." *Lochner*, 198 U.S. at 75 (Holmes, J., dissenting). It was therefore costless for Justice Holmes to strike the pose that the Constitution is so open-minded as to be agnostic about the choice between capitalism and forms of government antithetical to it.

[1038] *See supra* note 1031 and accompanying text.

injunction is no exception) for making information-intensive decisions.[1039] The Ninth Circuit in *FTC v. Qualcomm* rejected Judge Koh's conceit when it recognized that "[t]he record suggests that [*FTC v. Qualcomm*] is more like [*Ohio v. American Express*], where a company's novel business practice at first appeared to be anticompetitive, but in fact was disruptive in a manner that was beneficial to consumers in the long run because it forced rival credit card companies to adapt and innovate."[1040]

Even on a modest scale, Judge Koh's findings of fact and conclusions of law in *FTC v. Qualcomm* soon tended to confirm Hayek's thesis. Despite having presided as the finder of fact over a massive government antitrust case featuring informed company witnesses from Apple and Intel who were directly involved in the purchase and sale of modems, Judge Koh still seemed to lack the prescience to realize that Apple would likely acquire Intel's modem business, as Apple indeed did a mere two months after she had issued her findings of fact and conclusions of law.[1041] Yet, Judge Koh considered herself to possess enough foresight to announce a permanent, worldwide injunction that would have her regulate Qualcomm's business for at least the next seven years.

4. Did Qualcomm's Payments to OEMs Result in Discriminatory Royalties?

At times, Judge Koh found that a discount payment that Qualcomm made to an OEM reduced the royalty rate that Qualcomm charged the OEM for an exhaustive license to Qualcomm's portfolio of cellular SEPs. At other times, Judge Koh found that the discount payment reduced the price of Qualcomm's modems. Judge Koh appeared to have no coherent rationale for making one classification rather than the other.

In the former case, Judge Koh called the result "a significantly reduced *effective royalty rate*."[1042] For example, she found that "Qualcomm has engaged in anticompetitive conduct toward Samsung" in part by "reducing the royalty rate if Samsung purchased at least 85% of its chipsets from Qualcomm" and "offering Samsung chip incentive funds if Samsung purchased 100% of its premium chips from Qualcomm."[1043] Judge Koh found that "Qualcomm engaged in anticompetitive conduct toward Huawei by," among other things,

---

[1039] Friedrich A. Hayek, *The Use of Knowledge in Society*, 35 Am. Econ. Rev. 519 (1945).

[1040] FTC v. Qualcomm Inc., No. 19-16122, 2020 WL 4591476, at *19 (9th Cir. Aug. 11, 2020) (citing Ohio v. Am. Express Co., 138 S. Ct. 2274, 2290 (2018)).

[1041] *See* Press Release, Apple Inc., Apple to Acquire the Majority of Intel's Smartphone Modem Business (July 25, 2019), https://www.apple.com/newsroom/2019/07/apple-to-acquire-the-majority-of-intels-smartphone-modem-business/.

[1042] FTC v. Qualcomm Inc., 411 F. Supp. 3d 658, 716 (N.D. Cal. 2019) (emphasis added) (discussing Qualcomm's dealings with Motorola).

[1043] *Id.* at 709.

"giving a drastically reduced royalty rate if Huawei purchased 100% of its chips from Qualcomm."[1044] And "Qualcomm engaged in anticompetitive conduct toward Motorola by," among other things, "offering a significantly reduced effective royalty rate if Motorola purchased 100% of its chips from Qualcomm."[1045]

These findings purportedly established that Qualcomm was charging different royalty rates for an exhaustive license to its portfolio of cellular SEPs to different OEMs rather than charging those OEMs different prices for Qualcomm modems. Yet, Judge Koh reported no evidence that the former was the case. Notably, the FTC itself never alleged that Qualcomm systematically charged higher royalties for its cellular SEPs if the OEM bought non-Qualcomm modems.[1046]

Professor Shapiro's testimony did lament the unremarkable fact that, relative to the nonexistent counterfactual conditional world in which an OEM could *freely* use Qualcomm's portfolio of cellular SEPs without taking a license, an OEM would have perceived rival modems to be more expensive after imputing to them the price that the OEM was obliged to pay for an exhaustive license to Qualcomm's cellular SEPs in conjunction with a non-Qualcomm modem. But it appears from the publicly available records— and it is very significant—that Professor Shapiro never testified at trial that an OEM avoided the cost of paying for an exhaustive license to Qualcomm's portfolio of cellular SEPs *when the OEM bought a Qualcomm modem.*

In sum, Judge Koh did not provide a satisfactory explanation for why Qualcomm's licensing practices would create a royalty "surcharge" that would impose a "tax" on the "all-in price" of non-Qualcomm modems. There was no reason to exempt an OEM from the royalty payment owed to Qualcomm for the use of its cellular SEPs simply because the OEM purchased a non-Qualcomm modem. If an OEM practiced Qualcomm's cellular SEPs, it should have compensated Qualcomm for that use.

The means to do so was to enter into, and pay FRAND or RAND royalties for, an exhaustive license to Qualcomm's portfolio of cellular SEPs. The question of which brand of modem an OEM used in its mobile device was irrelevant to whether Qualcomm was entitled to FRAND or RAND compensation for the OEM's exhaustive use of Qualcomm's cellular SEPs.

[1044] *Id.* at 714.

[1045] *Id.*; *see also id.* at 716.

[1046] FTC Complaint, 2017 WL 242848, *supra* note 28; FTC's Proposed Findings of Fact and Conclusions of Law, *supra* note 485. The FTC also declined to allege that Qualcomm unlawfully tied cellular SEPs to modems or modems to cellular SEPs.

5. *Did Professor Shapiro Err in Assuming in His Theoretical Bargaining Model of Competitive Harm That OEMs Would Not Pay the Same Royalty "Surcharge" and Modem "Tax" on Purchases of Qualcomm Modems, Such That No Asymmetric Harm Would Result, and Why Did Judge Koh Not Acknowledge That the Asymmetry Assumption Was Outcome-Determinative?*

As we have seen, Professor Shapiro confirmed during his direct-examination testimony during the FTC's case-in-chief on January 15, 2019 that his theory of an anticompetitive royalty "surcharge" and modem "tax" was predicated on an unreliable assumption: that QTL (Qualcomm's licensing division) could impose this supposed price increase on rival modem manufacturers without needing to impose the same price increase simultaneously on Qualcomm's own production of modems by its QCT division. In other words, Professor Shapiro seemed to have testified (as of January 15, 2019) that the royalty "surcharge" and modem "tax" were not what I call "symmetric" (and what Professor Nevo, one of Qualcomm's three expert economic witnesses, described in his testimony as being not "chip-agnostic").

One cannot overstate the practical consequences of Professor Shapiro's apparent assumption (which he later repudiated during his direct examination by Rajesh James of the FTC on January 28, 2019) that the royalty "surcharge" and modem "tax" were *asymmetric*. That assumption was determinative in the sense that it was a necessary (but not sufficient) condition for the FTC's central theory of competitive harm to have any shred of real-world plausibility. The assumption of an asymmetric royalty "surcharge" and an asymmetric modem "tax" drove the supposed result in Professor Shapiro's theoretical bargaining model of competitive harm. Yet, that assumption was implausible as a matter of *a priori* economic reasoning—and of course, being never more than an assumption, it was also necessarily unsubstantiated by any facts in evidence.

Even though Judge Koh conspicuously ignored Professor Shapiro's role in *FTC v. Qualcomm* in her findings of fact and conclusions of law, his asymmetry assumption permeated Judge Koh's findings of fact and conclusions of law, perhaps without her recognition and certainly without her explanation. Professor Shapiro's apparent assumption of an asymmetric royalty "surcharge" and an asymmetric modem "tax" was a far subtler economic fallacy to spot than the fallacy underlying the FTC's irrelevant citation to the tax-wedge diagram from the seventh edition of Professor Mankiw's undergraduate microeconomics textbook that we saw in Part IV.C.[1047] If Judge Koh lacked the facility in economics to discern the latter fallacy *sua sponte*, the likelihood

---

[1047] *FTC v. Qualcomm*, 411 F. Supp. 3d at 792 (citing Mankiw, Principles of Microeconomics, *supra* note 704, at 156).

that she could have spotted the former fallacy without the aid of Professor Nevo's opposing expert testimony would seem to be nil. After all, the benefit that the finder of fact can derive from having such additional discernment at the ready is precisely why we bother to insinuate expert economic witnesses into antitrust litigation in the first place.

Without Professor Shapiro's apparent assumption of asymmetry, Judge Koh's findings of fact and conclusions of law on the FTC's royalty "surcharge" and modem "tax" theory of antitrust liability would immediately collapse (independently of any other reversible errors that one might identify in those findings and conclusions). The supposed asymmetry of the royalty "surcharge" and modem "tax" was, in short, the sleight of hand animating *FTC v. Qualcomm.*

Judge Koh's findings of fact and conclusions of law actually made this fallacious argument harder for a reviewing court to detect and evaluate. Not only did she omit any analysis of this outcome-determinative economic assumption underlying the FTC's theory of liability, she also ignored Professor Nevo's concise and accurate criticism of Professor Shapiro's key assumption, since Judge Koh had chosen to discredit as unreliable *everything* to which Professor Nevo testified at trial.[1048] In retrospect, one can starkly see how ill-advised—and outcome-determinative—Judge Koh's exercise of discretion was with respect to her findings that Qualcomm's expert economists were entirely unreliable.

E. If They Did Exist, Would a Royalty "Surcharge" and a Modem "Tax" Be Lawful Under Supreme Court and Ninth Circuit Precedent?

Suppose that we accepted for sake of argument (but contrary to the evidence) Judge Koh's finding that Qualcomm's allegedly "unreasonably high" royalty "surcharge" imposed a "tax" on rivals' modems, thereby reducing the sales and profits of those rivals. It still would not follow as a matter of American antitrust law that such a royalty "surcharge" and modem "tax" were unlawful.

Judge Koh found that "[p]ractices that unfairly suppress sales of competing products 'below the critical level necessary for any rival to pose a real threat' cause anticompetitive harm because they exclude competitors from the marketplace and thereby harm competition in general."[1049] She reasoned that, "[b]ecause the surcharge also raises the market price of rivals' chips, Qualcomm prevents rivals from underbidding Qualcomm," which in turn allegedly permits Qualcomm to maintain its monopoly in the "premium" LTE modem market.[1050] Judge Koh also found that the "surcharge" drove

---

[1048] *Id.* at 805.
[1049] *Id.* at 791 (quoting United States v. Dentsply Int'l, Inc., 399 F.3d 181, 191 (3ᵈ Cir. 2005)).
[1050] *Id.* at 792.

a "wedge" between the price that Qualcomm's rivals received for modems and the price that OEMs paid for those modems, which, she further found, had the effect that "[r]ivals see lower sales volumes and lower margins, and consumers see less advanced features as competition decreases."[1051]

Yet, Judge Koh's conclusion that Qualcomm's licensing strategy was unlawful because it reduced the profit margins of rivals directly violated Supreme Court precedent.

1. *The Controlling Authority of* linkLine

The Supreme Court's 2009 decision in *linkLine* addressed an allegation of margin squeeze involving AT&T, the owner of local-exchange infrastructure and facilities needed to provide (among other services) digital subscriber line (DSL) broadband Internet access service.[1052] AT&T was accused of unlawfully squeezing the profit margins of competing Internet service providers that resold access to AT&T's network. AT&T allegedly did so by "setting a high wholesale price for DSL transport and a low retail price for DSL Internet service."[1053]

The Supreme Court explicitly rejected the proposition that antitrust law protects a rival's profit margins.[1054] The Court emphasized that, "[a]s a general rule, businesses are free to choose the parties with whom they will deal, as well as the prices, terms, and conditions of that dealing."[1055] It also said that a firm "has no obligation to deal under terms and conditions favorable to its competitors."[1056] The Court reasoned that, because "'[c]utting prices in order to increase business often is the very essence of competition,' . . . impos[ing] antitrust liability for prices that are too low . . . [would] 'chill the very conduct the antitrust laws are designed to protect.'"[1057]

The Court consequently concluded that, "[i]f there is no duty to deal at the wholesale level and no predatory pricing at the retail level, then a firm is certainly not required to price *both* of these services in a manner that preserves its rivals' profit margins."[1058] In short, eight years before the

---

[1051] *Id.*

[1052] 555 U.S. 438, 438 (2009). With the late Judge Robert Bork, I urged the Supreme Court to grant *certiorari* in *linkLine* and subsequently (on the merits) to abolish the price squeeze as a theory of antitrust liability under U.S. law. *See* Brief of *Amici Curiae* Professors and Scholars in Law and Economics in Support of the Petitioners, *linkLine*, 555 U.S. 438 (No. 07-512), 2007 WL 4132899; Brief of *Amici Curiae* Professors and Scholars in Law and Economics in Support of the Petitioners, *linkLine*, 555 U.S. 438 (No. 07-512), 2008 WL 4125499; *see also* J. Gregory Sidak, *Abolishing the Price Squeeze as a Theory of Antitrust Liability*, 4 J. COMPETITION L. & ECON. 279 (2008).

[1053] *linkLine*, 555 U.S. at 443.

[1054] *Id.* at 452.

[1055] *Id.* at 448.

[1056] *Id.* at 450–51.

[1057] *Id.* at 451 (quoting Matsushita Elec. Indus. Co. v. Zenith Radio Corp., 475 U.S. 574, 594 (1986)).

[1058] *Id.* at 452 (emphasis in original); *see also* FTC v. Qualcomm Inc., No. 19-16122, 2020 WL 4591476, at *17 (9th Cir. Aug. 11, 2020).

FTC filed its complaint in *FTC v. Qualcomm*, the Supreme Court had explicitly rejected the proposition that a firm's pricing practices might violate the Sherman Act simply because it does not leave an adequate profit margin for its competitors.

2. *The Controlling Authority of* Abbott Labs

The Ninth Circuit applied *linkLine* in *John Doe v. Abbott Laboratories*,[1059] a case whose fact pattern strongly resembled the fact pattern in *FTC v. Qualcomm*. The American medical device and health care company Abbott offered two complementary products: (1) Norvir, a drug used by HIV patients to "boost" the efficacy of protease inhibitors and (2) Kaletra, a protease inhibitor.[1060] Other companies, including Bristol-Myers Squibb and GlaxoSmithKline, competed with Abbott in selling protease inhibitors, but obtained "permission by the FDA to promote Norvir as a booster to be taken along with their own inhibitors."[1061]

After the FDA granted that permission, Abbott reportedly increased the price of Norvir from $1.71 to $8.57 but left the price of its protease inhibitor unchanged. The plaintiff alleged that Abbott's pricing strategy raised "the total cost to the patient of boosted protease inhibitor therapies provided by Abbott's competitors."[1062] The plaintiff also alleged that the strategy enabled Abbott to "leverage[] its Norvir monopoly to attempt to monopolize the boosted market for Kaletra," thereby violating section 2 of the Sherman Act.[1063]

Although the district court denied Abbott's motion for dismissal and summary judgment, the Ninth Circuit reversed, finding that *linkLine* required dismissal of the case.[1064] The Ninth Circuit reasoned:

> [The plaintiffs] try to distance themselves from *[l]ink[L]ine* on the footing that their claim is for monopoly leveraging, not price squeezing, and that Abbott provides products to consumers in both the booster and boosted markets whereas AT & T provided products in retail and wholesale markets. We understand the difference, but it is insubstantial. However labeled, Abbott's conduct is the functional equivalent of the price squeeze the [Supreme] Court found unobjectionable in *[l]ink[L]ine*. Abbott sells Norvir as a standalone inhibitor and as part of a boosted inhibitor instead of selling Norvir to its competitors at a high price for use with their own protease inhibitors while attributing a lower price to the product when used as part

---

[1059] 571 F.3d 930 (9th Cir. 2009).
[1060] *Id.* at 932.
[1061] *Id.*
[1062] *Id.*
[1063] *Id.*
[1064] *Id.* at 934–35.

of its own boosted inhibitor. Either way, the alleged vice is that Abbott is using its monopoly position in the booster market to raise the price of Norvir while selling its own boosted inhibitor at too low a price. And either way, this puts the squeeze on competing producers of protease inhibitors that depend on Norvir for their boosted effectiveness and consumer acceptance.[1065]

The Ninth Circuit found that, "absent an antitrust refusal to deal (or some other exclusionary practice) in the monopoly market or below-cost pricing in the second market," allegations about monopoly leveraging could not violate section 2 of the Sherman Act.[1066] The Ninth Circuit also provided a simple explanation for why one of its district judges could have gone so far astray: "It is understandable that the district court did not follow *[l]ink[L]ine* as at the time it ruled *[l]ink[L]ine* had not yet been decided" in the Supreme Court.[1067] (And of course in *linkLine* the Supreme Court reversed the Ninth Circuit.)

Perhaps tellingly, in its *per curiam* order partially staying Judge Koh's permanent, worldwide injunction on August 23, 2019,[1068] the Ninth Circuit went out of its way to cite *Abbott Labs*, unnecessary though it was for purposes of reaching its ruling on the stay. Citing *Abbott Labs*, the Ninth Circuit observed:

> We are satisfied that Qualcomm has shown, at minimum, the presence of serious questions on the merits of the district court's determination that Qualcomm has an antitrust duty to license its SEPs to rival chip suppliers. Qualcomm likewise has made the requisite showing that its practice of charging OEMs royalties for its patents on a per-handset basis does not violate the antitrust laws.[1069]

In addition, the Ninth Circuit reminded readers in a footnote of a detail conspicuously absent from Judge Koh's findings of fact and conclusions of law:

> Breaking from her standard practice, then-FTC Commissioner Maureen K. Ohlhausen issued a written dissenting statement to express her disagreement with the theory urged in the complaint and adopted by the district

---

[1065] *Id.* at 935.

[1066] *Id.* at 931.

[1067] *Id.* at 931 n.1.

[1068] FTC v. Qualcomm Inc., 935 F.3d 752 (9th Cir. 2019) (per curiam).

[1069] *Id.* at 756 (first citing Lair v. Bullock, 697 F.3d 1200, 1204 (9th Cir. 2012); and then citing John Doe v. Abbott Labs., 571 F.3d 930, 931 (9th Cir. 2009)); *see also id.* (explaining that *Abbott Labs* held "that 'allegations of monopoly leveraging through pricing conduct in two markets' do not 'state a claim under § 2 of the Sherman Act absent an antitrust refusal to deal (or some other exclusionary practice) in the monopoly market or below-cost pricing in the second market'") (quoting *Abbott Labs*, 571 F.3d at 931).

court that Qualcomm's royalty rates operate as an exclusionary tax or surcharge on competitor products.[1070]

Some might have interpreted the Ninth Circuit's *sua sponte* references to *Abbott Labs* and to Commissioner Ohlhausen's dissent to signal that Judge Koh's findings of fact and conclusions of law—and, particularly, her decision to ignore what would appear to be clearly controlling Supreme Court and Ninth Circuit precedent—would engender skepticism on appeal.

3. *Judge Koh's Reliance on Irrelevant Decisions*

Incredibly, Judge Koh's findings of fact and conclusions of law in *FTC v. Qualcomm* did not ever cite the Ninth Circuit's decision in *Doe v. Abbott Labs.* Nor did she cite the case in her order denying Qualcomm's motion to dismiss for failure to state a claim under section 5(a) of the FTC Act,[1071] even though Qualcomm had expressly identified the case in its briefs.[1072] (The FTC likewise did not reference *Abbott Labs* in its brief opposing Qualcomm's motion to dismiss.[1073])

Judge Koh's conclusion about Qualcomm's allegedly anticompetitive royalty "surcharge" and modem "tax" flouted the Supreme Court's holding in *linkLine* and the Ninth Circuit's holding in *Abbott Labs*. Rather than apply these controlling precedents, Judge Koh analogized the facts in *FTC v. Qualcomm* to a Seventh Circuit decision and a federal district court decision from Utah, both of which predated *linkLine* and *Abbott Labs*. Those two decisions could not possibly support her finding of antitrust liability, even if one were to ignore for the moment the obvious point that lower-court decisions and decisions of other circuit courts cannot subordinate the Supreme Court's and the Ninth Circuit's binding authority over the law that will apply in a bench trial in the Northern District of California.

a. *The Irrelevance of* Premier

First, Judge Koh compared the facts in *FTC v. Qualcomm* to the facts presented in the Seventh Circuit's 1987 decision in *Premier Electrical Construction Co. v. National Electrical Contractors Association*, which, in her view,

---

[1070] *Id.* at 756 n.1 (citing Dissenting Statement of Commissioner Maureen K. Ohlhausen at 1–2, *In re* Qualcomm, Inc., File No. 141-0199 (F.T.C. Jan. 17, 2017)). Commissioner Ohlhausen's name, and any mention of the fact that she dissented from the FTC's complaint, do not appear in Judge Koh's findings of fact and conclusions of law. *See supra* note 296 and accompanying text.

[1071] *See* Order Denying Motion to Dismiss, 2017 WL 2774406, *supra* note 49, at *8–9.

[1072] *See* Qualcomm's Motion to Dismiss, 2017 WL 4678941, *supra* note 41, at 13; Defendant Qualcomm Incorporated's Reply Memorandum of Points and Authorities in Support of Motion to Dismiss (Redacted Version) at 9, 10, FTC v. Qualcomm Inc., No. 5:17-cv-00220-LHK, 2017 WL 2417318 (N.D. Cal. June 2, 2017).

[1073] *See* FTC's Opposition to Qualcomm's Motion to Dismiss, 2017 WL 4678946, *supra* note 726.

"demonstrates how a monopolist can use an across-the-board price increase to impose artificial constraints that disproportionally harm the monopolist's competitors."[1074] Judge Koh's interpretation of *Premier* contorted Judge Frank Easterbrook's opinion for a unanimous panel of the Seventh Circuit.

Judge Easterbrook observed that *Premier* concerned price-fixing among horizontal competitors, "a per se violation of the antitrust laws."[1075] In contrast, the restraints in question in *FTC v. Qualcomm* were vertical and were reviewable under the rule of reason. Judge Easterbrook identified the potential benefits of exclusive vertical agreements and, in a sentiment uncharacteristic of Judge Koh's findings of fact and conclusions of law in *FTC v. Qualcomm*, he admonished: "Judges know less than manufacturers about optimal distribution arrangements, so it is unlikely that they could improve the position of consumers by forcing manufacturers to adopt distribution policies manufacturers have not favored voluntarily."[1076]

Premier did *not* concern a monopolist's conduct and, therefore, Judge Koh's citation of the Seventh Circuit's decision shed no light whatsoever on whether Qualcomm's unilateral practices might be anticompetitive.

b. *The Irrelevance of* Caldera

Second, Judge Koh compared Qualcomm's licensing practice to those at issue in a 20-year-old district court case from Utah (located in the Tenth Circuit), *Caldera, Inc. v. Microsoft Corp.*, which concerned Microsoft's licenses for its Windows operating system, which required OEMs to pay Microsoft "'a royalty on every machine the OEM shipped regardless of whether the machine contained [Microsoft's operating system] or another operating system.'"[1077] Judge Koh said that Microsoft's licensing practice "raised the all-in price of Caldera's operating system."[1078] She also said that Microsoft offered discounts "if OEMs entered the license agreements" that required OEMs to pay a royalty on every computer, regardless of the installed operating system, "which induced OEMs to enter agreements that raised the effective price of Caldera's operating system."[1079] Judge Koh then observed that, in *Caldera*, "the district court concluded that a reasonable jury could conclude that Microsoft's license agreements and discounts 'resulted in an agreement

---

[1074] FTC v. Qualcomm Inc., 411 F. Supp. 3d 658, 791 (N.D. Cal. 2019) (citing Premier Elec. Constr. Co. v. Nat'l Elec. Contractors Ass'n, 814 F.2d 358 (7th Cir. 1987)).

[1075] *Premier*, 814 F.2d at 368. The Fourth Circuit had already reviewed the legality of the challenged conduct before the Seventh Circuit's review of *Premier*. *See* National Elec. Contractors Ass'n v. Nat'l Constructors Ass'n, 678 F.2d 492 (4th Cir. 1982). The Seventh Circuit reviewed the finding of liability in its case "with a strong presumption in favor of the Fourth Circuit's disposition." *Premier*, 814 F.2d at 368.

[1076] *Id.* at 369.

[1077] *FTC v. Qualcomm*, 411 F. Supp. at 792 (alteration in original) (quoting Caldera, Inc. v. Microsoft Corp., 87 F. Supp. 2d 1244, 1250 (D. Utah 1999)).

[1078] *Id.* (citing *Caldera*, 87 F. Supp. 2d at 1250).

[1079] *Id.* (citing *Caldera*, 87 F. Supp. 2d at 1250).

with the practical effect of exclusivity' because Microsoft's surcharge increased the effective price of Caldera's operating systems."[1080]

Yet, as Judge Koh noted, the court in *Caldera* was ruling on a summary judgment motion.[1081] That a jury considering another set of facts "could conclude" that Microsoft's license agreements and discounts had "the practical effect of exclusivity" bears no relationship to Judge Koh's findings in the very next sentence of her findings of fact and conclusions of law that "Qualcomm's surcharge increased the effective price of rivals' modem chips and Qualcomm's agreements with OEMs result in exclusivity."[1082]

Judge Koh also ignored that the district court in *Caldera* said that "the standard for determining whether Microsoft's licensing agreements constitute illegal exclusive dealings was established in *Tampa Electric Co. v. Nashville Coal Co.*"[1083] Recall that Judge Koh gave *Tampa Electric* lip service but did not actually apply its framework to assess whether Qualcomm's TA and FATA supply contracts with Apple violated the Sherman Act.

Moreover, the facts of *Caldera* do not resemble those of *FTC v. Qualcomm*. Microsoft was licensing proprietary software,[1084] but a license to that software was not essential to an OEM that had chosen to load onto its computers a competitor's operating system. In contrast, a license to Qualcomm's portfolio of cellular SEPs was strictly essential to every OEM, regardless of the brand of modem that the OEM chose to use in its mobile device.

The Ninth Circuit in *FTC v. Qualcomm* completely rejected Judge Koh's reliance on *Caldera*.[1085] *Caldera* was not pertinent to *FTC v. Qualcomm*. And, even if it had been informative, *Caldera* would have simply directed Judge Koh to do what she ultimately declined to do: apply the Supreme Court's test in *Tampa Electric* in earnest.

4. Did Judge Koh Misapply the Law?

Judge Koh's findings of fact and conclusions of law that Qualcomm imposed a royalty "surcharge" and modem "tax" on its cellular SEPs, which was then supposedly borne by rival modem manufacturers, was specious as a matter of evidence and economic reasoning. But even if her royalty "surcharge" and modem "tax" conjecture were correct as a matter of theory and evidence, it still could not have supported her finding of liability under the controlling antitrust jurisprudence.

[1080] *Id.* (quoting *Caldera*, 87 F. Supp. 2d at 1250).

[1081] *Id.*

[1082] *Id.*

[1083] *Caldera*, 87 F. Supp. 2d at 1250 (citing Tampa Elec. Co. v. Nashville Coal Co., 365 U.S. 320 (1961)).

[1084] *Id.* at 1246.

[1085] FTC v. Qualcomm Inc., No. 19-16122, 2020 WL 4591476, at *17 (9th Cir. Aug. 11, 2020).

The Supreme Court in *linkLine* unambiguously said that a monopolist has no duty to ensure that its pricing will maintain sufficient profit for its rivals to survive. The Ninth Circuit reiterated that holding in *Abbott Labs*. Judge Koh's findings of fact and conclusions of law that Qualcomm reduced the sales or profits of rival modem manufacturers therefore could not have supported her conclusion of law that Qualcomm's conduct was anticompetitive.

Judge Koh oddly treated the Supreme Court's controlling precedent in *linkLine* as having less authority than a pair of older decisions from lower courts that she proceeded to read in an unnatural fashion. And she inexplicably declined to cite, much less apply, the subsequent controlling application of *linkLine* in the Ninth Circuit, *Abbott Labs*.

VI. Did Judge Koh's Peremptory Findings on Harm to Competition Violate the Supreme Court's Burden-Shifting Framework in *American Express*?

Judge Koh's evidentiary presumption of harm to competition in *FTC v. Qualcomm* contravened the Supreme Court's established burden of production and burden of persuasion in antitrust cases. More fundamentally, her evidentiary presumption of harm to competition violated the presumption of innocence embodied in the Due Process Clause of the Fifth Amendment to the Constitution.

A. *The Burden of Production and the Burden of Persuasion in the American Law of Evidence*

Judge Posner has explained (as a general principle of law) that the burden of proof has two separate aspects. The first is the burden of producing (or submitting) evidence to the court. The second is the burden of persuading the court that the party carrying the burden of production ought to win the case.[1086]

[1086] Posner, Economic Analysis of Law, *supra* note 214, at 844. This distinction between the burden of production and the burden of persuasion was not crisply articulated in American law until James Bradley Thayer, A Preliminary Treatise on Evidence at the Common Law 355 (Little, Brown & Co. 1898). Thayer distinguished "[t]he peculiar duty of him who has the risk of any given proposition on which parties are at issue,—who will lose the case if he does not make this proposition out, when all has been said and done" from "the duty of going forward in argument or in producing evidence." *Id.* "Where the parties to a civil action are in dispute over a material issue of fact, then that party who will lose if the trier's mind is in equipoise may be said to bear the risk that the trier will not be affirmatively persuaded or the risk of nonpersuasion upon that issue." Fleming James, Jr. & Geoffrey C. Hazard, Jr., Civil Procedure 241 (Little, Brown & Co. 2ᵈ ed. 1977) (footnote omitted). The expression "the risk of nonpersuasion" is attributed to John Henry Wigmore's treatise. *See id.* (quoting 9 John Henry Wigmore, A Treatise on the Anglo-American System of Evidence in Trials at Common Law § 2485 (Little, Brown & Co. 3ᵈ ed. 1940)).

When a party that has the burden of proof fails to produce the necessary evidence to show the merits of its claim, that party will lose. But even if a party carries its burden of producing evidence, that party will not necessarily prevail.

The party also has the burden of persuasion, which is the burden to prove the merits of its claim according to the applicable quantum or measure of proof—such as the preponderance of the evidence, clear and convincing evidence, or proof beyond a reasonable doubt. In civil cases, a party typically must meet the preponderance-of-the-evidence standard. In other words, the evidence presented by the plaintiff must show, in Judge Posner's words, "that the probability that [the] claim is meritorious exceeds, however slightly, the probability that it is not."[1087]

B. *The Supreme Court's Affirmation in* American Express *of the Burden of Production and the Burden of Persuasion Under Section 2 of the Sherman Act*

The Supreme Court has long recognized the uncontroversial principle that, unless conduct is considered to be unlawful *per se*, the plaintiff in a Sherman Act case bears the burden to prove (pursuant to the rule of reason) that the conduct that it challenges actually harms competition.[1088] This principle applies regardless of whether the challenged conduct is scrutinized under section 1 or section 2 of the Sherman Act.[1089] Liability arising from an agree-

---

[1087] POSNER, ECONOMIC ANALYSIS OF LAW, *supra* note 214, at 845; *see also* JAMES & HAZARD, CIVIL PROCEDURE, *supra* note 1086, at 243 ("The usual formulation of the test in civil cases is that there must be a *preponderance of evidence* in favor of the party having the persuasion burden (the proponent) before he is entitled to a verdict. An alternative phrase often used is *greater weight* of the evidence. The general statement (in either form or both, coupled in the alternative as 'preponderance or greater weight of the evidence') is usually explained as referring not to the number of witnesses or quantity of evidence but to the convincing force of the evidence.") (emphasis in original) (footnotes omitted).

[1088] *See, e.g.,* Ohio v. Am. Express Co., 138 S. Ct. 2274, 2284 (2018); NYNEX Corp. v. Discon, Inc., 525 U.S. 128, 135 (1998) ("We conclude no boycott-related *per se* rule applies and that the *plaintiff* here must allege and prove harm, not just to a single competitor, but to the competitive process, *i.e.,* to competition itself.") (emphasis added); *see also* FTC v. Ind. Fed'n of Dentists, 476 U.S. 447, 457–58 (1986); Arkansas Carpenters Health & Welfare Fund v. Bayer AG, 604 F.3d 98, 104 (2ᵈ Cir. 2010); Worldwide Basketball & Sport Tours, Inc. v. Nat'l Collegiate Athletic Ass'n, 388 F.3d 955, 959 (6ᵗʰ Cir. 2004); United States v. Microsoft Corp., 253 F.3d 34, 59 (D.C. Cir. 2001) (en banc) (per curiam); Tanaka v. Univ. of S. Cal., 252 F.3d 1059, 1063 (9ᵗʰ Cir. 2001); United States v. Brown Univ., 5 F.3d 658, 668 (3ᵈ Cir. 1993).

[1089] *See, e.g., NYNEX,* 525 U.S. at 135 (analyzing section 1 of the Sherman Act); Pacific Bell Tel. Co. v. linkLine Commc'ns, Inc., 555 U.S. 438, 451 (2009) (analyzing section 2 of the Sherman Act). The Supreme Court reiterated in 2018 in *American Express* that "[a] small group of restraints are unreasonable *per se* because they 'always or almost always tend to restrict competition and decrease output,'" such that a court need not evaluate the actual effect on competition of an agreement found to be unlawful *per se*. 138 S. Ct. at 2283 (quoting Business Elecs. Corp. v. Sharp Elecs. Corp., 485 U.S. 717, 723 (1988)); *see also* Leegin Creative Leather Prods., Inc. v. PSKS, Inc., 551 U.S. 877, 886 (2007) ("The *per se* rule, treating categories of restraints as necessarily illegal, eliminates the need to study the reasonableness of an individual restraint in light of the real market forces at work.") (citing *Sharp,* 485 U.S. at 723); *NYNEX,* 525 U.S. at 133 ("[C]ertain kinds of agreements will so often prove so harmful to competition and so rarely prove justified that the antitrust laws do not require proof that an agreement of that kind is, in fact, anticompetitive in the particular circumstances.").

ment or unilateral conduct scrutinized under the rule of reason turns on the *actual* competitive effects of the challenged practice: did the challenged agreement or conduct, on balance, unreasonably restrain competition in the relevant market?[1090]

In scrutinizing an agreement under the rule of reason to determine whether it violates section 1 of the Sherman Act, courts typically employ what has come to be called a "three-step burden-shifting framework."[1091] Again, the same principle applies in cases scrutinizing unilateral conduct under section 2 of the Sherman Act.[1092] The Supreme Court confirmed in 2018 in *American Express* that in *any* case under the rule of reason the plaintiff has the initial burden of production and the burden of persuasion.[1093]

If the plaintiff carries its initial burden of production and proves an anticompetitive effect by a preponderance of the evidence, the burden of production then shifts to the defendant to prove by a preponderance of the evidence that it had a procompetitive rationale for the challenged conduct.[1094] If the defendant carries those burdens of production and persuasion, then the burden of production reverts to the plaintiff to prove by a preponderance of the evidence that the defendant could have achieved the same procompetitive effects by less restrictive means.[1095]

C. Does It Violate American Express *to Make a Defendant Bear the Burden of Production and the Burden of Persuasion to "Construct a Hypothetical Marketplace That Would Have Existed"?*

Qualcomm emphasized in its opening brief to the Ninth Circuit that there was no evidence that it had caused anticompetitive harm.[1096] The FTC and Judge Koh evidently considered such evidence unnecessary. In its rebuttal

---

[1090] *See, e.g., Leegin*, 551 U.S. at 886.

[1091] *American Express*, 138 S. Ct. at 2284; *see also, e.g., Microsoft*, 253 F.3d at 59, 84; King Drug Co. of Florence, Inc. v. Smithkline Beecham Corp., 791 F.3d 388, 412 (3ᵈ Cir. 2015); K.M.B. Warehouse Distribs., Inc. v. Walker Mfg. Co., 61 F.3d 123, 127 (2ᵈ Cir. 1995); Bhan v. NME Hosps., 929 F.2d 1404, 1413 (9ᵗʰ Cir. 1991).

[1092] *See, e.g., Microsoft*, 253 F.3d at 59 ("[T]he plaintiff, on whom the burden of proof of course rests, must demonstrate that the monopolist's conduct indeed has the requisite anticompetitive effect.") (first citing Monsanto Co. v. Spray-Rite Serv. Corp., 465 U.S. 752, 763 (1984); then citing United States v. Arnold, Schwinn & Co., 388 U.S. 365, 374 n.5 (1967), *overruled on other grounds*, Continental T. V., Inc. v. GTE Sylvania Inc., 433 U.S. 36 (1977); and then citing Brooke Grp. Ltd. v. Brown & Williamson Tobacco Corp., 509 U.S. 209, 225–26 (1993)).

[1093] 138 S. Ct. at 2284.

[1094] *See, e.g., id.; see also Microsoft*, 253 F.3d at 59 (citing Eastman Kodak Co. v. Image Tech. Servs., Inc., 504 U.S. 451, 483 (1992)).

[1095] *Microsoft*, 253 F.3d at 59.

[1096] Opening Brief for Appellant Qualcomm Incorporated at 57, FTC v. Qualcomm Inc., No. 19-16122 (9ᵗʰ Cir. Aug. 23, 2019) ("Here, the District Court did not identify any means by which Qualcomm's licensing practices distort ordinary modem chip competition on the merits. Nor did it find that Qualcomm's accused practices—*as distinguished from competitive advantages* conferred by its superior products and technology—in fact caused any 'harm' or 'outcome' in the market.") (emphasis in original) (citing United States v. Grinnell Corp., 384 U.S. 563, 571 (1966)).

closing argument at trial, the FTC argued that the government did not have the burden to "construct a hypothetical marketplace that would have existed" without the challenged practices, and the agency claimed that the D.C. Circuit's decision in *Microsoft* and the Supreme Court's decision in *American Express* supported that interpretation of law.[1097]

That interpretation of law comported with the one that Judge Koh had adopted in her findings of fact and conclusions of law. Relying on *Microsoft*, she said:

> The FTC is not required "to reconstruct the hypothetical marketplace absent a defendant's conduct." Thus, the Court need not conclude that Qualcomm's anticompetitive licensing practices are the sole reason for any particular rival's exit or any particular rival's reduced performance to conclude that Qualcomm's anticompetitive practices harmed competition in the CDMA and premium LTE modem chip markets.[1098]

Judge Koh misread *Microsoft*. It is well established in American antitrust law that the plaintiff, whether a private party or the government, bears the initial burden of production in a rule of reason case to show that the challenged conduct harmed competition. *Microsoft* certainly did not overrule that principle, as Judge Koh's misunderstanding of the decision would require us to believe. To the contrary, the D.C. Circuit stated that, "if a plaintiff successfully establishes a *prima facie* case under § 2 by *demonstrating anticompetitive effect*, then the monopolist may proffer a 'procompetitive justification' for its conduct."[1099]

Venerated though it may be, *Microsoft* is the not the last word. There is a Supreme Court of the United States. And 17 years after *Microsoft*, that Court in 2018 in *American Express* confirmed that, pursuant to the rule of reason in a Sherman Act case, "the plaintiff has the initial burden to prove that the challenged [conduct] has a *substantial* anticompetitive effect that harms consumers in the relevant market."[1100]

Writing in May 2019, Judge Koh had no remotely plausible legal authority with which to excuse the FTC from the evidentiary burden of proving its *prima facie* case against Qualcomm. In *FTC v. Qualcomm*, the FTC offered no evidence that would suffice to satisfy its initial burden of production, much less its burden of persuasion amounting to a preponderance of the evidence. In practical effect, the FTC's failure of proof meant that Judge Koh's finding of liability necessarily was predicated on her having required Qualcomm

---

[1097] Transcript of Proceedings (Volume 11) at 2178:20–2179:4, FTC v. Qualcomm Inc., No. 5:17-cv-00220-LHK (N.D. Cal. Jan. 29, 2019) (rebuttal closing argument of Jennifer Milici for the FTC).

[1098] *FTC v. Qualcomm*, 411 F. Supp. 3d at 805 (quoting *Microsoft*, 253 F.3d at 79).

[1099] *Microsoft*, 253 F.3d at 59 (first emphasis in original) (second emphasis added).

[1100] *See, e.g., American Express*, 138 S. Ct. at 2284 (emphasis added); *see also Microsoft*, 253 F.3d at 59 (citing Eastman Kodak Co. v. Image Tech. Servs., Inc., 504 U.S. 451, 483 (1992)).

to prove the *negative* of the first step in the Supreme Court's three-step burden-sharing framework. That inversion of *American Express* and earlier Supreme Court precedent was a clearly erroneous application of law.

1.   Did Judge Koh's Assumption About Harm to Competition Violate the Presumption of Innocence Protected by the Due Process Clause?

Judge Koh's requirement that *Qualcomm* disprove the FTC's claims about harm to competition in practical effect reversed the presumption of Qualcomm's innocence, which amounted to a deprivation of its liberty or property without due process.[1101] The Supreme Court has recognized that the Due Process Clauses of the Fifth and Fourteenth Amendments extend the presumption of innocence to civil prosecutions as well as criminal prosecutions.[1102]

In *Speiser v. Randall*, Justice William Brennan wrote for the Supreme Court: "Due process commands that no man shall lose his liberty unless the Government has borne the burden of producing the evidence and convincing the factfinder of his guilt."[1103] The case involved the potential infringement of speech, and thus it implicated the familiar overdeterrence rationale in the Court's jurisprudence on free speech that it subsequently extended to its antitrust jurisprudence:[1104]

> The man who knows that he must bring forth proof and persuade another of the lawfulness of his conduct necessarily must steer far wider of the unlawful zone than if the State must bear these burdens. This is especially to be feared when the complexity of the proofs and the generality of the standards applied provide but shifting sands on which the litigant must maintain his position. How can a claimant whose declaration is rejected possibly sustain the burden of proving the negative of these complex factual elements?[1105]

How could Qualcomm prove the negative—that is, the absence of anticompetitive effects—if in fact, as opposed to the FTC's theory, there never were any anticompetitive effects?

Professor Shapiro for one would revert to the Nirvana Fallacy and argue that the absence of discernable anticompetitive effects is not evidence that

---

[1101]   *See* Nelson v. Colorado, 137 S. Ct. 1249, 1255 (2017); *see also* United States v. Gooding, 25 U.S. (12 Wheat.) 460, 471 (1827) (Story, J.) ("[T]he general rule of our jurisprudence is, that the party accused need not establish his innocence, but it is for the government itself to prove his guilt, before it is entitled to a verdict of conviction.").

[1102]   *See, e.g.*, Speiser v. Randall, 357 U.S. 513, 526 (1958) (Brennan, J.) (civil tax proceeding).

[1103]   *Id.*

[1104]   *See* Michael K. Block & J. Gregory Sidak, *The Cost of Antitrust Deterrence: Why Not Hang a Price Fixer Now and Then?*, 68 Geo. L.J. 1131, 1135 (1980) (discussing early antitrust decisions raising the overdeterrence concern); Michael K. Block, Frederick C. Nold & J. Gregory Sidak, *The Deterrent Effect of Antitrust Enforcement*, 89 J. Pol. Econ. 429, 429–30 (1981).

[1105]   *Speiser*, 357 U.S. at 526 (citation omitted).

Qualcomm did not prevent a superior counterfactual conditional world from coming into existence. And the FTC, in its rebuttal closing argument at trial, argued that "construct[ing] a hypothetical marketplace that would have existed without these years of [Qualcomm's allegedly anticompetitive] conduct. . . *would be impossible.*"[1106] How could any antitrust defendant rebut those arguments if it truly were the law that the defendant bore the burden of production and the burden of persuasion to prove the nonexistence of a given professor's or a given enforcement agency's or a given district judge's alternative vision of an imaginary counterfactual conditional state of the world that the plaintiff admits is *impossible* to construct?

2. *Did Judge Koh Disparage the Expert Testimony of Qualcomm's Three Expert Witnesses Because They Did Not Help the FTC Carry Its Initial Burden of Persuasion Pursuant to* American Express?

Judge Koh denounced *Qualcomm's* three expert economic witnesses for not having opined on the anticompetitive effects of Qualcomm' practices. What if the anticompetitive effects did not exist?

Judge Koh found that Professor Edward Snyder "never even considered how Qualcomm's anticompetitive practices affect Qualcomm's rivals."[1107] Judge Koh next found that Professor Aviv Nevo "opined that the modem chip industry is 'thriving,' but made no claim about how Qualcomm's practices might have affected the industry."[1108] Judge Koh then found that Dr. Tasneem Chipty did not question Qualcomm's supposedly anticompetitive practices and that Dr. Chipty "conceded that she conducted no analysis of how Qualcomm's refusal to license rivals, refusal to sell modem chips exhaustively, requirement that an OEM sign a license before purchasing modem chips, and threats to cut off chip supply and other support affected modem chip markets."[1109]

As we shall see in Part IX, Judge Koh also criticized Qualcomm's experts for failing to "rebut" the FTC's (nonexistent) evidence that Qualcomm's royalties were "unreasonably high."[1110] In practical effect, Judge Koh demanded that Qualcomm prove the negative of the key conjecture propelling the FTC's royalty "surcharge" and modem "tax" theory of antitrust liability: that is, Judge Koh expected Qualcomm to bear the burden to prove that, contrary to the FTC's conjecture, Qualcomm's royalty rates on its bilaterally negotiated

---

[1106] Transcript of Proceedings (Volume 11) at 2178:24–2179:1, FTC v. Qualcomm Inc., No. 5:17-cv-00220-LHK (N.D. Cal. Jan. 29, 2019) (rebuttal closing argument of Jennifer Milici for the FTC) (emphasis added).
[1107] FTC v. Qualcomm Inc., 411 F. Supp. 3d 658, 805 (N.D. Cal. 2019).
[1108] *Id.*
[1109] *Id.*
[1110] *Id.* at 780.

license agreements for its portfolio of cellular SEPs were *not* "unreasonably high."[1111]

For these reasons, Judge Koh found all three of Qualcomm's expert economic witnesses to be unreliable.[1112] In other words, Judge Koh gave the expert testimony of these three economists absolutely no evidentiary weight. That evidentiary ruling was preposterous as a matter of antitrust law and disturbing as an exercise of judicial discretion. Judge Koh's reliability findings of Professor Snyder, Dr. Chipty, and Professor Nevo were not only plainly erroneous (because they were nonsensical), but also unjustifiably derogatory and injurious to the professional reputations of these respected economists.

Judge Koh herself acknowledged that it was the *FTC's* initial burden of production, not Qualcomm's, to present evidence that Qualcomm's conduct had an actual anticompetitive effect in a relevant market.[1113] To carry its burden of persuasion, the FTC would need to have proven an anticompetitive effect by a preponderance of the evidence. Yet, Judge Koh disparaged the expert testimony of Qualcomm's three expert witnesses because they did not help the FTC carry its burden of persuasion under the Supreme Court's three-step burden-shifting framework. Judge Koh's conclusions of law on anticompetitive effects consequently were plainly erroneous because they misapplied *American Express.*

D. Did Judge Koh Make Specific Findings Concerning Qualcomm's Procompetitive Rationales?

Following Judge Koh's erroneous finding that the FTC had satisfied its initial burden of production and burden of persuasion pursuant to the rule of reason to prove an anticompetitive effect, the burden of production and the burden of persuasion supposedly shifted to Qualcomm "to show a procompetitive rationale" for its conduct.[1114]

[1111] *Cf.* ResQNet.com, Inc. v. Lansa, Inc., 594 F.3d 860, 872 (Fed. Cir. 2010) (per curiam) ("The district court seems to have been heavily influenced by Lansa's decision to offer no expert testimony to counter Dr. David's opinion. But it was ResQNet's burden, not Lansa's, to persuade the court with legally sufficient evidence regarding an appropriate reasonable royalty. As a matter of simple procedure, Lansa had no obligation to rebut until ResQNet met its burden with reliable and sufficient evidence. This court should not sustain a royalty award based on inapposite licenses simply because Lansa did not proffer an expert to rebut Dr. David.") (first citing Lucent Techs., Inc. v. Gateway, Inc., 580 F.3d 1301, 1329 (Fed. Cir. 2009); and then citing SmithKline Diagnostics, Inc. v. Helena Labs. Corp., 926 F.2d 1161, 1168 (Fed. Cir. 1991)).

[1112] *FTC v. Qualcomm*, 411 F. Supp. 3d at 805.

[1113] *Id.* at 695–96.

[1114] Ohio v. Am. Express Co., 138 S. Ct. 2274, 2284 (2018).

1. Judge Koh's Addition of "Pretextual" as a Gloss on American Express

On nine occasions in her findings of fact and conclusions of law, Judge Koh perfunctorily used the epithet "pretextual" to condemn Qualcomm's procompetitive rationales for each of four practices for which she found that the FTC had met its burden of production to show anticompetitive effects and to do so by the requisite burden of persuasion, a preponderance of the evidence.[1115] Those four practices were (1) Qualcomm's refusal to offer exhaustive licenses to its portfolio of cellular SEPs to rival modem manufacturers,[1116] (2) Qualcomm's practice of selling modems only to licensed OEMs,[1117] (3) Qualcomm's allegedly exclusive supply agreements with Apple,[1118] and (4) Qualcomm's practice of granting chip incentive funds.[1119] Judge Koh directed every instance of her nine findings of a "pretextual" argument or offer of proof at Qualcomm. She did not find any of the FTC's arguments to be "pretextual."

After observing that "[t]he Court has already rejected all of Qualcomm's litigation justifications for its conduct as pretextual,"[1120] Judge Koh then leapfrogged to the pronouncement that, "[e]ven if Qualcomm had shown non-pretextual procompetitive justifications for its conduct, the foregoing anticompetitive harm is so severe that the 'anticompetitive harm outweighs [any] procompetitive benefit' of Qualcomm's conduct."[1121] To be clear, the

---

[1115] *FTC v. Qualcomm*, 411 F. Supp. 3d at 751, 756 (twice), 758, 772 (twice), 778, 795, 806.

[1116] In connection with Qualcomm's practice of licensing its cellular SEPs on an exhaustive basis to OEMs only and never offering an exhaustive license to its cellular SEPs to rival modem manufacturers, Judge Koh "reject[ed] as pretextual Qualcomm's justifications for refusing to license its rivals." *Id.* at 751; *see also id.* at 756 ("Qualcomm's Justifications for its Refusal to License Rivals Are Pretextual."). Judge Koh found that "Qualcomm offers self-serving and pretextual justifications for Qualcomm's refusal to license modem chip suppliers." *Id.* On this point, Judge Koh found that Fabian "Gonell's trial testimony was not credible," and she "reject[ed] Qualcomm's self-serving justifications as pretextual." *Id.* at 758.

[1117] In connection with Qualcomm's practice of selling modems only to licensed OEMs, Judge Koh "reject[ed] Qualcomm's justification as pretextual." *Id.* at 778.

[1118] In connection with the allegations of exclusive dealing, Judge Koh found that certain "Qualcomm documents contradict Qualcomm's claim that its exclusive deals with Apple were necessary to defray 'relationship-specific' costs of working with Apple," and that, "[l]ike Qualcomm's other supposed justifications for its unlawful conduct, this alleged justification is pretextual and contradicted by Qualcomm's own documents." *Id.* at 772. She concluded that "Qualcomm's litigation justification is pretextual and contradicted by Qualcomm's own documents." *Id.*

[1119] In connection with Qualcomm's chip incentive funds, Judge Koh "reject[ed] Qualcomm's procompetitive justification as pretextual." *Id.* at 795.

[1120] *Id.* at 806.

[1121] *Id.* at 806–07 (second alteration in original) (quoting United States v. Microsoft Corp., 253 F.3d 34, 59 (D.C. Cir. 2001) (en banc) (per curiam)). Notwithstanding her addition of the bracketed word "any" to this passage, Judge Koh actually slightly misquoted *Microsoft* at page 59, which specified, in relevant part: "anticompetitive harm *of the conduct* outweighs the procompetitive benefit." *Microsoft*, 253 F.3d at 59 (emphasis added to denote words omitted from Judge Koh's quotation). Judge Koh specified where in her findings of fact and conclusions of law she had reported each of her findings that every one of Qualcomm's procompetitive business justifications was "pretextual": "Section V.C. (refusal to license rivals); Section V.E. (Apple exclusive agreements); Section V.F. (refusal to sell modem chips without a license agreement); Section V.I. (chip incentive funds)." *Id.* at 806.

word "any" in brackets so appears in Judge Koh's findings of fact and conclusions of law.

Judge Koh seemed to say that *American Express* did not require her to weigh Qualcomm's evidence of a "procompetitive rationale" if she could instead peremptorily classify that evidence as "pretextual," which she of course did with respect to every production of evidence that Qualcomm had made in support of its affirmative defense. This interpretation of Judge Koh's ruling implies that she thought that Qualcomm had failed from the outset to carry its burden of production on the affirmative defense (*not* its burden of persuasion) by failing to identify any respectable "procompetitive rationale." In other words, her understanding of "pretextual" implied that the evidence that Qualcomm produced on the question of its "procompetitive rationale" was unworthy of being weighed by the finder of fact—an outlook that we will examine more closely below. Judge Koh portrayed Qualcomm's efficiency defense as relying on frivolous arguments that were beneath the dignity of the court to consider.

But Judge Koh had a backup. She pivoted to making a conclusion of law in the alternative. In the process, she resorted to a quite different line of legal reasoning. Judge Koh purported to do an abbreviated balancing of anticompetitive effects and procompetitive rationales. She concluded in the exiguity of a single sentence that the anticompetitive harm from Qualcomm's alleged conduct was so great that *nothing* that Qualcomm could produce as evidence would suffice to carry its burden of persuasion on the existence of a "procompetitive rationale." Nothing that Qualcomm could prove about any "procompetitive rationale" would suffice to permit the finder of fact to proceed under *American Express* to the third and final question, on which the FTC of course would bear the burden of production and the burden of persuasion: whether a less restrictive means existed for Qualcomm to achieve its procompetitive purpose.

Epistemologically, Judge Koh's holding in the alternative was a much taller claim than her pigeon-holing of Qualcomm's evidence of "procompetitive rationale" as "pretextual." How would Judge Koh possibly know that no possible "procompetitive rationale" was available to Qualcomm that would more than offset the anticompetitive harm that in her opinion had occurred? And, if she were correct, why bother holding a trial? In practical effect, Judge Koh was announcing the rule that Qualcomm's challenged business practices were *per se* illegal. That result would of course be absurd, as we shall see.

2. *What Did Judge Koh Mean When She Condemned Qualcomm's Procompetitive Rationales as "Pretextual"?*

Judge Koh's use of the epithet "pretextual" came from *Microsoft*[1122] (which in turn cited the Supreme Court's 1992 *Kodak* decision[1123]). Judge Koh wrote: "Courts have defined a procompetitive justification as 'a *nonpretextual* claim that [the defendant's] conduct is indeed a form of competition on the merits because it involves, for example, greater efficiency or enhanced consumer appeal.'"[1124] She elaborated that "[a] defendant does not meet its burden with a purported procompetitive justification that is merely pretextual,"[1125] and she quoted the Supreme Court's opinion in *Kodak* for the proposition that "a defendant must show 'valid business reasons' for its actions."[1126] Yet, Judge Koh did not define "pretextual" any more clearly than that.

Scrutiny of Judge Koh's rulings that Qualcomm's business justifications were "pretextual" should proceed on two levels: the law, and the political use of the English language. We begin with the law, since it is so simple, emphatic, and dispositive. The Supreme Court's explanation of its three-part burden-shifting framework in *American Express*—issued 26 years after *Kodak* and 17 years after *Microsoft*—did not contain any chatter about "pretextual" procompetitive rationales. *American Express* instead specified that, "[i]f the plaintiff carries its burden, then the burden shifts to the defendant to show a procompetitive rationale" for the conduct.[1127] *American Express* is the controlling law of the United States, the controlling law of the Ninth Circuit, and the controlling law in Judge Koh's courtroom.

Now, as to the English language. Words matter, as George Orwell famously observed.[1128] And "pretextual" is an uncommonly pompous word. So, we should pause to make sure we understand not only what the dictionary says that it means, but also what Judge Koh seemed to be communicating by her choice of this word rather than a different one that was more plainspoken. What precisely did Judge Koh mean "pretextual" to connote when she used the word to condemn every one of Qualcomm's procompetitive rationales?

"Pretextual" is the literal antonym for "nonpretextual," which is the word that the D.C. Circuit in *Microsoft* used to specify evidence that would not satisfy the defendant's burden of production, such that the burden of

---

[1122] *Microsoft*, 253 F.3d at 59.

[1123] Eastman Kodak Co. v. Image Tech. Servs., Inc., 504 U.S. 451, 483 (1992).

[1124] *FTC v. Qualcomm*, 411 F. Supp. 3d at 697 (alteration in original) (emphasis added) (quoting *Microsoft*, 253 F.3d at 58) (citing *Kodak*, 504 U.S. at 483 (explaining that a defendant must show "valid business reasons" for its actions)).

[1125] *Id.* (first citing *Kodak*, 504 U.S. at 484; and then citing Bhan v. NME Hosps., Inc., 929 F.2d 1404, 1413 (9th Cir. 1991)).

[1126] *Id.* (quoting *Kodak*, 504 U.S. at 483).

[1127] Ohio v. Am. Express Co., 138 S. Ct. 2274, 2284 (2018).

[1128] *See* ORWELL, *Politics and the English Language*, *supra* note 722; *see also supra* note 775.

production would never shift back to the plaintiff to prove by a preponderance of the evidence that any procompetitive benefits proven by the defendant outweighed the anticompetitive harm. But the D.C. Circuit's definition is hardly satisfying. To say that "pretextual" means "not nonpretextual" is uninformative. That circularity of meaning invites the reader to suspect that a court has invoked "pretextual" as an ever-ready *post hoc* rationalization.

The *Oxford English Dictionary* defines "pretext" variously as: "[a] reason put forward to *conceal* one's real purpose or object; a *pretended* motivation for a *selfish* or *criminal* act; an excuse or *pretence*."[1129] Is there a pattern here? Considering that Judge Koh labeled several of Qualcomm's procompetitive rationales to be "self-serving,"[1130] contradicted by Qualcomm's own documents,[1131] or "litigation" justifications[1132] (similar to her condemnation that certain evidence that she received had been made for litigation), perhaps her reason to reject the evidence in question was her apparent belief that none of Qualcomm's procompetitive rationales was the "real purpose" motivating Qualcomm's conduct.

Other areas of U.S. law support this pejorative interpretation of "pretextual." The Supreme Court of the United States uses the word to describe racial profiling in traffic stops by police,[1133] racial discrimination in civil rights law,[1134] age discrimination in employment law,[1135] racial discrimination in peremptory challenges to jurors,[1136] and concealment of the Census Bureau's allegedly xenophobic motive in asking a question in the 2020 Census about

---

[1129] *Pretext n.*, Oxford English Dictionary (3ᵈ ed. 2015) (emphasis added).

[1130] *FTC v. Qualcomm*, 411 F. Supp. 3d at 756, 758.

[1131] *Id.* at 772.

[1132] *Id.*

[1133] *See, e.g.*, Whren v. United States, 517 U.S. 806, 813–14 (1996) (Scalia, J.) (specifying that "the constitutional reasonableness of traffic stops" does not depend "on the actual motivations of the individual officers involved," such that a "pretextual [traffic] stop" would not fall afoul of the Fourth Amendment because "[s]ubjective intentions play no role in ordinary, probable-cause Fourth Amendment analysis").

[1134] *See, e.g.*, Texas Dep't of Cmty. Affairs v. Burdine, 450 U.S. 248, 257–58 (1981), *cited in* Comcast Corp. v. Nat'l Ass'n of African American-Owned Media, 140 S. Ct. 1009, 1019 (2020) (Gorsuch, J.) ("[O]nce a plaintiff establishes a prima facie case of race discrimination through indirect proof, the defendant bears the burden of producing a race-neutral explanation for its action, after which the plaintiff may challenge that explanation as pretextual.").

[1135] *See, e.g.*, Babb v. Wilkie, 140 S. Ct. 1168, 1172 (2020) (Alito, J.) (citing McDonnell Douglas Corp. v. Green, 411 U.S. 792 (1973)); Dupree v. Apple, Inc., No. 16-CV-00289-LHK, 2017 WL 2617978, at *8 (N.D. Cal. June 16, 2017) (Koh, J.) (Order Granting Summary Judgment) ("Under Title VII [of the Civil Rights Act] and [the California Fair Employment and Housing Act], in the absence of direct or circumstantial evidence of discriminatory intent, as here, Plaintiff must establish a disparate treatment discrimination case using the framework outlined in *McDonnell Douglas Corp. v. Green*. If Plaintiff establishes a *prima facie* case, the burden shifts to Defendant to articulate a legitimate, non-discriminatory reason for its action. If Defendant articulates a legitimate, non-discriminatory reason, the burden shifts back to Plaintiff to demonstrate that the employer's stated reason was a pretext for unlawful discrimination.") (citations omitted) (citing *McDonnell Douglas*, 411 U.S. at 792).

[1136] *See, e.g.*, Flowers v. Mississippi, 139 S. Ct. 2228, 2241 (2019) (Kavanaugh, J.) (consistent with the Fourteenth Amendment, and pursuant to *Batson v. Kentucky*, "once a prima facie case of discrimination has been shown by a defendant, the State must provide race-neutral reasons for its peremptory strikes," and "[t]he trial judge must determine whether the prosecutor's stated reasons were the actual reasons or instead were a pretext for discrimination") (citing *Batson*, 476 U.S. 79, 97–98 (1986)).

the respondent's citizenship.[1137] All of these formal uses of the adjective "pretextual" by the Supreme Court were inherently derogatory circa 2019.

These examples indicate that, as used by the Supreme Court of the United States, "pretext" or "pretextual" implies an intent to *deceive* the finder of fact (or some other third party), particularly to advance an invidious objective. One could argue that a "pretextual" legal argument is insincere, factually insubstantial, and *disingenuous*; and that "pretextual" evidence is "put forward to conceal one's real purpose"[1138] or is—simply put—knowingly false. A finding that evidence is "pretextual" indicates not merely that a party is incapable of carrying its burden of persuasion in good faith to show that the evidence satisfies some quantum of proof (in the case of *FTC v. Qualcomm*, the preponderance of the evidence), but rather that the inherent quality of the party's evidence fails to satisfy even its burden of *production*. The evidence is somehow deficient in kind, undeserving of consideration, in a word: unclean. This kind of derision is typically reserved (by the U.S. Courts of Appeals) for frivolous arguments, typically crammed into the last few pages of an appellant's brief. But when a district judge refuses to consider the weight of a genuinely serious argument because he or she deems it "pretextual," there is a clear implication that the judge is calling the party (if not also the party's lawyer) a liar.

When a judge sitting as finder of fact calls evidence "pretextual," such that the evidence has not satisfied a party's burden of production, the judge has provided himself or herself an excuse for not proceeding to determine whether the party bearing the burden of production has satisfied its burden of persuasion. The result resembles a *per se* rule. At a minimum, in an antitrust case like *FTC v. Qualcomm*, this result substantively alters the legal rule that rightfully controls the determination of liability.

3.   Did Judge Koh's Finding That Qualcomm's Procompetitive Rationales Were "Pretextual" Obviate Weighing the Evidence?

Perhaps Judge Koh would have found that Qualcomm failed to show by a preponderance of the evidence that it had a single procompetitive rationale for its supposedly anticompetitive conduct. Put differently, she could have *weighed* the evidence that Qualcomm put before her. Thereupon, she might have found that the *weight* of the evidence of Qualcomm's procompetitive rationales favored the FTC. Judge Koh could have taken seriously Qualcomm's explanation of the paradigm shift in the Supreme Court's jurisprudence on patent exhaustion.

[1137] *See, e.g.*, Department of Commerce v. New York, 139 S. Ct. 2551, 2573–74 (2019) (Roberts, C.J.) (discussing "pretext" in the context of administrative law in connection with questions regarding citizenship to be included in the 2020 Census).

[1138] *Pretext n.*, Oxford English Dictionary (3ᵈ ed. 2015).

But Judge Koh evidently believed that she did not even need to weigh the evidence, because she found that each and every one of Qualcomm's procompetitive rationales could be peremptorily classified as "pretextual" and thus be denied further consideration. Judge Koh's implication appeared to be that each such legal argument deserving disregard was untrue, deceptive, and argued in bad faith. She thereby appeared to have excused herself from the essential task given the finder of fact—to *weigh* evidence. And in the process she excused the FTC from what would have been its burden of production and its burden of persuasion to show: that the anticompetitive harm of Qualcomm's challenged conduct outweighed the procompetitive benefits that Qualcomm had identified in its affirmative defense.

Considering the word's inherently pejorative connotations, the mere invocation of the adjective "pretextual" can be a contrivance and an *ipse dixit*. The characterization of evidence as "pretextual" is a red flag in a bench trial: it suggests that the judge might be about to flout Federal Rule of Civil Procedure 52(a)(1) by declining to make specific findings on some material fact that has turned out to be a pain in the neck for the judge. The denunciation of a defendant's offer of proof as "pretextual" can be a dodge. It is an epithet by which a judge can eschew the obligation of supplying a reasoned decision for a ruling that is consequential, perhaps even dispositive.

In this sense, the finding that a procompetitive rationale, offered by the defendant under the three-step burden-shifting framework of *American Express*, is "pretextual" resembles the finding that a witness's testimony is "not credible" and therefore will receive no evidentiary weight. Judge Koh's finding that all of Qualcomm's procompetitive rationales were "pretextual" seemed to continue not only the peremptory characterization of Qualcomm's witnesses as lacking credibility, but also her casual insinuation on the second day of trial that Qualcomm's lawyers, who supposedly overstaffed their defense of Qualcomm in such a disreputable manner as to "churn" the case,[1139] also made disreputable legal arguments to the court.

E. Did the Ninth Circuit Recognize That Judge Koh Had Erroneously Applied the Three-Part Burden Shifting Framework of American Express?

The Ninth Circuit in *FTC v. Qualcomm* in effect recognized that Judge Koh had erroneously applied the three-part burden-shifting framework of *American Express*. The Ninth Circuit saw that Judge Koh had permitted the FTC, having failed to carry its burden of persuasion on anticompetitive effect, to leapfrog ahead to denigrating Qualcomm's procompetitive rationale for declining to offer exhaustive licenses to its cellular SEPs to rival modem manufacturers:

[1139] *See supra* notes 66–72 and accompanying text.

More critically, this part of the FTC's argument skips ahead to an examination of Qualcomm's procompetitive justifications, failing to recognize that the burden does not shift to Qualcomm to provide such justifications unless and until the FTC meets its initial burden of proving anticompetitive harm. Because the FTC has not met its initial burden under the rule of reason framework, we are less critical of Qualcomm's procompetitive justifications for its OEM-level licensing policy—which, in any case, appear to be reasonable and consistent with current industry practice.[1140]

Consequently, the Ninth Circuit concluded that the FTC had not "met its burden under the rule of reason to show that Qualcomm's practices ha[d] crossed the line to 'conduct which unfairly tends to destroy competition itself.'"[1141]

VII. Did Qualcomm Charge "Unreasonably High" Royalties for Its Cellular SEPs?

On at least 85 occasions in her findings of fact and conclusions of law Judge Koh mentioned Qualcomm's alleged, or supposedly proven, "unreasonably high royalty rate" for its patent portfolio.[1142] Yet she did not rely on *any* economic analysis to support that conclusion. The extent of Judge Koh's repetition of this unproven proposition is reminiscent of Thomas Sowell's observation that "the policy preferences of 'experts' do not become empirical facts by consensual approval or by sheer repetition."[1143]

The facts did not support Judge Koh's finding that Qualcomm (1) charged OEMs an "unreasonably high" royalty for an exhaustive license to its portfolio of cellular SEPs or (2) imposed a royalty "surcharge" and modem "tax" on modems sold by its rivals. Nor did the facts support Judge Koh's finding that the payments that Qualcomm made to Apple (or other OEMs), or that Qualcomm's refusal to offer exhaustive licenses to its cellular SEPs to rival modem manufacturers, increased Qualcomm's supposed ability to charge OEMs "unreasonably high" royalties for an exhaustive license to its cellular SEPs and to impose a modem "tax" on transactions between OEMs and rival modem manufacturers. Judge Koh did not examine the sales or profits of Qualcomm's rivals to determine whether Qualcomm's practices reduced either.

[1140] FTC v. Qualcomm Inc., No. 19-16122, 2020 WL 4591476, at *13 (9th Cir. Aug. 11, 2020).

[1141] *Id.* at *21 (quoting Spectrum Sports, Inc. v. McQuillan, 506 U.S. 447, 458 (1993)).

[1142] *See supra* note 294 and accompanying text.

[1143] Thomas Sowell, Knowledge and Decisions 284 (Basic Books 1980).

A. *Did Qualcomm Charge OEMs "Unreasonably High" Royalties for an Exhaustive License to Its Portfolio of Cellular SEPs?*

Qualcomm emphasized in its motion to dismiss that "the FTC does not plead any facts purporting to show what Qualcomm's royalties should be or by how much they are purportedly 'elevated.'"[1144] Qualcomm added that, "[w]ithout such alleged facts, the key premise of the FTC's theory—that royalties are 'elevated'—is without support."[1145] Judge Koh of course denied that motion. Yet, her bench trial did not produce any empirical evidence to support the FTC's assertion. The FTC's claim that Qualcomm's royalties were "unreasonably high" remained empirically unsupported even after Judge Koh issued her findings of fact and conclusions of law in *FTC v. Qualcomm*.

Judge Koh acknowledged that Qualcomm typically licenses both its SEPs and its non-SEPs.[1146] She also acknowledged that "Qualcomm receives higher royalty rates for portfolio licenses than for SEP-only licenses."[1147] Those portfolio licenses consist of "cellular SEPs, non-cellular SEPs, and non-SEPs."[1148] As we saw in the Part E to the Introduction, Qualcomm has charged a 5-percent royalty for an exhaustive license to its entire patent portfolio (which included non-SEPs) for a multimode device, and a 4-percent royalty for an exhaustive license to its 5G portfolio only, subject also to a cap on the handset's wholesale net selling price for royalty purposes set at $400.[1149] Thus, since January 2018, the maximum royalty per unit that Qualcomm would charge under a SULA for an exhaustive license to its entire patent portfolio for use in a handset sold in the United States has been $20 per handset.[1150] Furthermore, as Judge Koh observed, "Qualcomm SULAs grant rights both to the relevant Qualcomm patents existing at the time of the SULA and additional relevant Qualcomm patents issued during the license term."[1151]

Notwithstanding these nuances in Qualcomm's structure of royalty rates, and without performing any additional analysis of those rates, Judge Koh found that Qualcomm's rates were "unreasonably high." Notably, Judge Koh did not say whether her conclusion about "unreasonably high" royalty rates applied only to Qualcomm's cellular SEPs or also to its non-cellular SEPs and its non-SEPs.

As an aside, it is not even clear why Judge Koh would have had federal jurisdiction to declare that the royalties for non-SEPs are "unreasonably

---

[1144] Qualcomm's Motion to Dismiss, 2017 WL 4678941, *supra* note 41, at 9.
[1145] *Id.*
[1146] *FTC v. Qualcomm*, 411 F. Supp 3d at 672.
[1147] *Id.*
[1148] *Id.*
[1149] *See supra* Table 2 and accompanying text.
[1150] *See supra* Table 2 and accompanying text.
[1151] *FTC v. Qualcomm*, 411 F. Supp 3d at 673.

high." She was not being asked to award Qualcomm damages for patent infringement, she was not setting a compulsory license to Qualcomm's non-SEPs, and the Patent Act certainly does not envision prospective rate-making proceedings for Qualcomm's portfolio of non-SEPs.

B. *Did Judge Koh Identify Expert Economic Testimony to Support Her Finding That Qualcomm's Royalties Were "Unreasonably High"?*

The FTC's patent valuation expert, Michael Lasinski, testified that Qualcomm's royalties were "unreasonably high,"[1152] but it is telling that the FTC chose an accountant to opine on patent valuation when the agency already had at its disposal a world-famous academic industrial organization economist (and two-time chief economist of the Antitrust Division), Professor Shapiro. It typically has been my observation that, in expert testimony predicated on accounting methodologies, the accountant assumes (rather than derives) all the key economic inputs concerning demand or production for purposes of making his discounted cash flow calculations; worse, in many cases I have observed that the accounting expert does not seem to recognize why merely assuming the values of critical variables concerning demand or supply conditions calls into question under Federal Rule of Evidence 702 the reliability and relevance of the supposedly expert opinions he purports to offer.[1153]

It is essential to understand the fundamental methodological difference between expert testimony that rests on accounting conventions and expert testimony that rests on economic reasoning. Accounting and economics are not substitutes for one another. They are different fields that are complementary to one another. Accounting analysis is, in essence, backward-looking. The focus of accounting is to track stocks and flows of assets and liabilities. When examining the actions of a firm in a commercial dispute, accounting conventions can be useful for categorizing the facts as they are. Accounting enables a firm or an outside auditor to track a firm's financial health or its position within an industry, relative to similar firms. Yet, accounting does not reveal anything about causal relationships among the variables it tracks.

[1152] *Id.* at 789. In her opening statement at trial on January 4, 2019, Ms. Milici of the FTC argued that "Mr. Lasinski's expert opinion" was "that Qualcomm's royalty rates [we]re *far above any indicators of fair and reasonable rates*." Transcript of Proceedings (Volume 1) at 23:12–14, FTC v. Qualcomm Inc., No. 5:17-cv-00220-LHK (N.D. Cal. Jan. 4, 2019) (opening statement of Jennifer Milici for the FTC) (emphasis added). Ms. Milici further claimed, "Under no combination of accepted methods or measures are Qualcomm's royalties within the range of rates that a court would consider FRAND." Transcript of Proceedings (Volume 1) at 23:19–21, FTC v. Qualcomm Inc., No. 5:17-cv-00220-LHK (N.D. Cal. Jan. 4, 2019) (opening statement of Jennifer Milici for the FTC). These claims were unpersuasive in light of the testimony that Mr. Lasinski gave at trial several days later.

[1153] *See* J. Gregory Sidak, *Economists as Arbitrators*, 30 EMORY INT'L L. REV. 2105 (2016); *see also* Sidak, *Is Patent Holdup a Hoax?*, *supra* note 118, at 460–61.

Economic analysis, in contrast, can provide intellectually rigorous esti-mations of a rational party's behavior in the but-for world. Economics enables one to investigate the relevant incentives and opportunities that a firm faces when determining its strategic decisions. Economics also enables one to formulate testable hypotheses and subject them to empirical methods that will allow one to accept or reject those hypotheses. In formu-lating those hypotheses, economics relies on an established body of scien-tific knowledge—most notably, price theory. Although accounting methods provide only the facts about which products consumers have purchased, economics can predict changes in consumer behavior in response to a change in consumer preferences, incomes, prices of complements or substitutes, or other factors relevant to consumer demand.

In *FTC v. Qualcomm*, Judge Koh found Mr. Lasinski's methodologies not sufficiently reliable to use in her findings of fact and conclusions of law concerning the reasonableness of Qualcomm's royalty.[1154] She was ambiguous about what royalty rate or rates studied by Mr. Lasinski she was addressing when discussing his testimony. Judge Koh twice spoke of Mr. Lasinski's testi-mony that "Qualcomm's royalty rates are unreasonably high."[1155] Yet, she did so without specifying whether the rates being examined were for Qualcomm's cellular SEPs, its non-cellular SEPs, its non-SEPs, or some combina-tion thereof; nor did she explain whether those rates were single-mode or multimode rates. In the same passage, Judge Koh also spoke of Mr. Lasinski's testimony that "Qualcomm's FRAND royalty rate should be below 1%," but she did not explain, among other things, (1) whether that rate was strictly for Qualcomm's non-cellular SEPs, (2) whether it was a single-mode or multimode rate, (3) what royalty base was being used, and (4) whether the royalty base was subject to a cap.[1156] Considering how many times Judge Koh repeated the proposition that Qualcomm's royalties were "unreasonably high," one would have expected her to have heeded Federal Rule of Civil Procedure 52(a)(1) and to have made special findings of fact that were free of ambiguity on the question of what she precisely meant by "unreasonably high."

Thus, if one takes at face value the findings of fact and conclusions of law in *FTC v. Qualcomm*, one must conclude that Judge Koh did not rely on *either* economic evidence (in the form of Professor Shapiro's expert testimony) or accounting evidence (in the form of Mr. Lasinski's expert testimony) to conclude that Qualcomm charged "unreasonably high" royalty rates for its patents.

[1154] *FTC v. Qualcomm*, 411 F. Supp. 3d at 790.
[1155] *Id.* at 789, 790.
[1156] *Id.* at 790.

C. *Did Judge Koh Rely on Anecdotal Evidence to Support Her Finding That Qualcomm's Royalties Were "Unreasonably High"?*

Instead, Judge Koh relied strictly on anecdotal evidence, including: (1) evidence from Qualcomm's internal documents emphasizing the importance of Qualcomm's modem business for the success of its licensing program, (2) evidence of Qualcomm's conduct in negotiating its license agreements with OEMs, (3) evidence from Qualcomm's internal statements about its contribution to industry standards, and (4) evidence of Qualcomm's practice of using a smartphone's price as the royalty base. Yet, those listed categories of evidence did not remotely carry the FTC's burden of persuasion to establish that the royalties that Qualcomm charged OEMs for an exhaustive license to its portfolio of cellular SEPs were "unreasonably high."[1157]

1. *Statements Contained in Qualcomm's Internal Documents*

Judge Koh found that, "[i]n Qualcomm's own documents, Qualcomm has repeatedly admitted that Qualcomm's monopoly chip market share—not the value of Qualcomm's patents—sustains Qualcomm's royalty rates."[1158] To substantiate that proposition, she cited a 2007 email that Marv Blecker, at that time president of Qualcomm's licensing division (QTL), sent to Qualcomm's CEO, Paul Jacobs.[1159] The email examined the pros and cons of a potential separation of QTL from Qualcomm CDMA Technologies (QCT), Qualcomm's main chip and software business.[1160] Mr. Blecker wrote that, "'[w]ithout chip business, more licensees/potential licensees might fight QTL license demands.'"[1161] Judge Koh also cited a 2008 email that Steve Altman, at the time Qualcomm's President, sent to Paul Jacobs noting that

---

[1157] Besides being unsupported by substantial evidence, Judge Koh's finding that Qualcomm's FRAND (or RAND) royalty was "unreasonably high" would have violated the Seventh Amendment to the U.S. Constitution, had she decided legal (rather than equitable) claims. *See* U.S. CONST. amend. VII ("In Suits at common law, where the value in controversy shall exceed twenty dollars, the right of trial by jury shall be preserved, and no fact tried by a jury, shall be otherwise re-examined in any Court of the United States, than according to the rules of the common law."). On December 5, 2019, the U.S. Court of Appeals for the Federal Circuit reversed Judge James Selna's decision in TCL Commc'n Tech. Holdings Ltd. v. Telefonaktiebolaget LM Ericsson, Nos. SACV 14-341 JVS, CV 15-2370 JVS, 2018 WL 4488286 (C.D. Cal. Sept. 14, 2018), on the grounds that the decision "deprived Ericsson of its Seventh Amendment right to a jury trial by deciding the legal relief of a release payment for past unlicensed sales [of standard-compliant devices] in a bench trial." TCL Commc'n Tech. Holdings Ltd. v. Telefonaktiebolaget LM Ericsson, 943 F.3d 1360, 1375 (Fed. Cir. 2019). Had Judge Koh predicated her rulings concerning the unreasonableness of a FRAND (or RAND) royalty on a *legal* claim in a patent-infringement case (and had Qualcomm reserved its right to a jury trial), the Federal Circuit's decision in *TCL v. Ericsson* implies that Judge Koh's findings of fact in *FTC v. Qualcomm* would have warranted vacatur on grounds that those findings were unconstitutional.

[1158] *FTC v. Qualcomm*, 411 F. Supp. 3d at 773.

[1159] *Id.*

[1160] *Id.*

[1161] *Id.* at 773 (quoting Email from Marv Blecker, President, Qualcomm Technology Licensing, to Paul Jacobs, CEO, Qualcomm (May 2007)).

"the only companies that had attacked Qualcomm bought little or no chips from Qualcomm, so the combination of QCT and QTL greatly enhances QTL's success."[1162]

Judge Koh found that those statements—made more than a decade before the trial in *FTC v. Qualcomm*—proved that Qualcomm could charge OEMs the royalties it did because of its supposed monopoly over (certain categories of) modems, rather than the value of its portfolio of cellular SEPs.[1163] Yet, the statements that Judge Koh cited did not support her conclusion that the royalties that Qualcomm charged OEMs for an exhaustive license to Qualcomm's cellular SEPs were "unreasonably high."

> a. *Did Qualcomm's Large Market Share for Certain Modems Enable It to Charge a Premium on CDMA Modems?*

Judge Koh's statements about the supposed correlation between Qualcomm's market share for (certain) modems and its alleged ability to charge OEMs an "unreasonably high" royalty for an exhaustive license to Qualcomm's portfolio of cellular SEPs were nonsensical from an economic perspective. Demand curves slope downward, not upward. Demand for a firm's product increases as the firm reduces its price. A firm's ability to charge high prices for its products is not an increasing function of its market share, yet Judge Koh embraced this specious causal connection between willingness to pay and market share when she found: "*Due to Qualcomm's large market share* [for certain modems], Qualcomm has been able to charge a premium on CDMA modem chips."[1164]

(Alternatively, if we indulge Judge Koh's economic misconception about the nature and direction of causation from market share to price, what does it then tell us that she refused to give dispositive weight to Qualcomm's falling market share in her market for "premium" LTE modems? Judge Koh should have acknowledged that that fact alone would cause the FTC's case to crumble. And, more to the point, what does it say that Judge Koh refused to consider evidence (in the public domain) following the cutoff of fact discovery that showed that Qualcomm's market share for "premium" LTE modems continued to fall?)

Furthermore, the statements by Qualcomm executives in 2007 and 2008 that Judge Koh cited merely suggested that those executives, more than a decade before trial, viewed the modem business as useful for bringing an unlicensed OEM to the negotiation table and for ensuring that any such OEM execute, in a timely manner, an exhaustive license to use Qualcomm's portfolio of cellular SEPs. That business purpose was then and is still now hardly

---

[1162] *Id.* (citing Email from Steve Altman, President, Qualcomm, to Paul Jacobs, CEO, Qualcomm (Feb. 2008)).

[1163] *Id.* at 775.

[1164] *Id.* at 686 (emphasis added).

surprising. As of August 2020, Qualcomm had a patent portfolio consisting of more than 140,000 patents and patent applications worldwide.[1165] At an earlier point in time when Qualcomm had only 120,000 granted patents and pending applications, approximately 20 percent of that portfolio consisted of cellular SEPs and pending applications.[1166] It is doubtful that Qualcomm could feasibly enforce each of its cellular SEPs against an infringing OEM through litigation, because the transaction costs to do so would be astronomical. If the cost of enforcing a single patent through litigation were merely $1 million (an unrealistically low approximation), Qualcomm would incur a cost of $24 billion to enforce its entire portfolio of cellular SEPs against a single implementer (assuming as a first approximation that all of the pending patent applications resulted in issued patents).

There is an alternative interpretation of this documentary evidence that is far more plausible and far less remarkable than the one that Judge Koh embraced: Qualcomm's executives appeared to believe more than a decade before the trial in *FTC v. Qualcomm* that Qualcomm's modem business was an important tool for confronting unlicensed OEMs implementing Qualcomm's cellular SEPs, for avoiding protracted negotiation or litigation with them, and for obtaining prompt compensation from them for their use of Qualcomm's portfolio of cellular SEPs. As a matter of law, none of those effects was anticompetitive. Each was meritorious. Each provided a compelling "procompetitive rationale" for Qualcomm's licensing practices within the meaning of the Supreme Court's 2018 decision in *American Express*.[1167] Taken together, those procompetitive effects did not and cannot "alchemize" into an antitrust violation any more than the independently lawful pricing policies that Chief Justice Roberts examined in *linkLine*.[1168]

  b. Were Statements in Documents from 2007 and 2008 Evidence Probative of the Reasonableness of Qualcomm's Royalties for an Exhaustive License to Its Cellular SEPs?

Judge Koh then made a logical leap that was both unstated and fallacious. The fact that she construed this documentary evidence from 2007 and 2008 to establish that Qualcomm had used its modem business to induce unlicensed OEMs to negotiate exhaustive patent licenses for Qualcomm's cellular SEPs did not necessarily imply that Qualcomm's royalties for its cellular SEPs were "unreasonably high," as Judge Koh concluded. It was at least equally plausible that, after inducing an unlicensed OEM to negotiate to execute an exhaustive

---

[1165] *See supra* notes 11 and 124–126 and accompanying text.

[1166] Transcript of Proceedings (Volume 7) at 1538:5–15, FTC v. Qualcomm Inc., No. 5:17-cv-00220-LHK (N.D. Cal. Jan. 18, 2019) (Testimony of Liren Chen (Senior Vice President and Legal Counsel, QTL)).

[1167] Ohio v. Am. Express Co., 138 S. Ct. 2274, 2284 (2018).

[1168] Pacific Bell Tel. Co. v. linkLine Commc'ns, Inc., 555 U.S. 438, 457 (2009).

license to Qualcomm's cellular SEPs, Qualcomm still charged the OEM not more than a reasonable royalty (within the precise meaning of the applicable RAND or FRAND commitment).

Even if the modem business permitted Qualcomm to negotiate a higher royalty than it could have negotiated otherwise, Judge Koh did not cite any evidence from which to conclude that Qualcomm's negotiated royalty exceeded the range of reasonable royalties for an OEM to pay for an exhaustive license to Qualcomm's portfolio of cellular SEPs; nor did she cite any evidence that the negotiated royalty unreasonably exceeded the value to a particular OEM of an exhaustive license to Qualcomm's portfolio of cellular SEPs.[1169]

Judge Koh also did not cite any evidence why it would be reasonable for her to *assume*, as she did, that an unlicensed OEM that had been brought to the negotiating table was made to pay a royalty for an exhaustive license to Qualcomm's portfolio of cellular SEPs that would necessarily be "unreasonably high," as that concept is precisely understood in either the contractual interpretation of Qualcomm's FRAND or RAND obligation with a given SSO or the statutory interpretation of Qualcomm's rights under section 284 of the Patent Act. A legitimately FRAND (or RAND) royalty is by definition reasonable—and therefore it cannot be deemed "unreasonably high."

In sum, the statements that Judge Koh cited from Qualcomm's documents from 2007 and 2008 did not support her logical leap that Qualcomm's royalties for an OEM's exhaustive license to Qualcomm's cellular SEPs were "unreasonably high." To the contrary, Judge Koh appeared to have done nothing more than assume her conclusion after having recited some extraneous documentary evidence from more than a decade earlier.

2. *Qualcomm's Licensing Conduct*

The evidence that Judge Koh cited regarding Qualcomm's negotiating conduct did not provide a persuasive factual predicate for her conclusion that Qualcomm charged "unreasonably high" royalties for an exhaustive license to its portfolio of cellular SEPs.

[1169] *Cf.* Certain Wireless Devices with 3G and/or 4G Capabilities and Components Thereof, Inv. No. 337-TA-868, slip op. at 118 (USITC June 13, 2014) (Initial Determination) ("While the possibility or existence of an exclusion order may benefit [the SEP holder] in negotiating a license, and move the license fee in the upper direction on the FRAND scale, there are hundreds of other economic factors that go into the parties finding a royalty or flat amount both can agree on.").

a. *Did Qualcomm's Decision Not to Provide Claim Charts to Potential Licensees Have Any Bearing on the Reasonableness of Its Royalties for an Exhaustive License to Its Cellular SEPs?*

One supposedly objectionable act upon which Judge Koh remarked at least eight times in her findings of fact and conclusions of law was that, supposedly unlike other patent holders, "Qualcomm refuses to provide patent lists and patent claim charts during license negotiations."[1170] Considering that Qualcomm's issued patents number in the tens of thousands (and that its total number of patents and patent applications as of 2020 exceeds 140,000), and considering further that Qualcomm licenses its patents on a portfolio basis, this protestation was disingenuous because it ignored the commercial reality of the licensing negotiations that Judge Koh addressed.

Qualcomm's disinclination to supply so much information in such granular form to so many prospective licensees in light of its recognized eminence as an innovator in mobile communications had a sound basis in the minimization of transaction costs. Judge Koh should have recognized, but did not recognize, that business practices tending to minimize the transaction costs of licensing SEPs amounted, under *American Express*, to Qualcomm's successful carrying of its burden to produce, and its burden to persuade by a preponderance of the evidence, that Qualcomm had a "procompetitive rationale" for declining to supply patent lists and patent claim charts during license negotiations concerning its cellular SEPs.[1171]

Moreover, Qualcomm's decision not to provide claim charts had no bearing on the reasonableness of its royalty for an exhaustive license to a portfolio consisting of tens of thousands of cellular SEPs. Judge Koh's conclusion to the contrary was a *non sequitur*. Suppose, for example, that Qualcomm declined to provide that information and still offered a genuinely FRAND or RAND royalty for an exhaustive license to the cellular SEPs contained in its portfolio. A reasonable royalty can occupy any point along the bargaining range—either as a matter of contractual interpretation of the SEP holder's FRAND or RAND obligation or as a matter of statutory interpretation of the patent holder's rights under section 284 of the Patent Act.[1172]

[1170] FTC v. Qualcomm Inc., 411 F. Supp. 3d 658, 773 (N.D. Cal. 2019); *see also id.* at 698, 710, 713, 714, 743, 776, 810.

[1171] *American Express*, 138 S. Ct. at 2284.

[1172] For an explanation of the complementary economic rationale for this conclusion, see Sidak, *Is a FRAND Royalty a Point or a Range?*, *supra* note 623, at 427; Sidak & Skog, *Hedonic Prices and Patent Royalties*, *supra* note 446, at 601; J. Gregory Sidak, *Apportionment, FRAND Royalties, and Comparable Licenses After Ericsson v. D Link*, 2016 U. Ill. L. Rev. 1809, 1823, 1834. Courts in various jurisdictions have embraced this legal conclusion in FRAND or RAND disputes. In the United States, see TCL Commc'n Tech. Holdings Ltd. v. Telefonaktiebolaget LM Ericsson, Nos. SACV 14-341 JVS, CV 15-2370 JVS, 2018 WL 4488286, at *54 (C.D. Cal. Sept. 14, 2018) (Selna, J.), *vacated and reversed in part on other grounds and remanded*, 943 F.3d 1360 (Fed. Cir. 2019). Although I believe that Judge Selna committed reversible errors in other aspects of his calculation of a FRAND royalty in *TCL v. Ericsson*, I believe that he correctly found that

Consequently, Judge Koh's particular findings of fact concerning patent lists and patent claims charts did not begin to establish a logical connection to her conclusion that Qualcomm's royalties for an exhaustive license to its portfolio of cellular SEPs were "unreasonably high"—and thus higher than the ceiling on the range of reasonable royalties. Again, Judge Koh appeared simply to have assumed her conclusion.

> b. *Did Judge Koh's Finding That Qualcomm Sold Components Other Than Modems on an Exhaustive Basis Support Her Conclusion That Qualcomm's Royalties for an Exhaustive License to Its Portfolio of SEPs Were "Unreasonably High"?*

Judge Koh also said that "Qualcomm sells other components exhaustive-ly,"[1173] which, she found, "further indicates that QCT's monopoly power sustains Qualcomm's unreasonably high royalty rates."[1174] In particular, she found: "When asked at trial whether 'device manufacturers purchasing Wi-Fi components from Qualcomm have to first take a license to Qualcomm's

---

a FRAND royalty may occupy any point along a range. *See* Sidak, *Judge Selna's Errors in* TCL v. Ericsson *Concerning Apportionment, Nondiscrimination, and Royalties Under the FRAND Contract, supra* note 688, at 122. In the United Kingdom, see Unwired Planet Int'l Ltd v. Huawei Techs. Co. [2018] EWCA (Civ) 2344 [121] (Eng.) ("In our judgment it is unreal to suggest that two parties, acting fairly and reasonably, will necessarily arrive at precisely the same set of licence terms as two other parties, also acting fairly and reasonably and faced with the same set of circumstances. To the contrary, the reality is that a number of sets of terms may all be fair and reasonable in a given set of circumstances."), *cited in* Sidak, *Why* Unwired Planet *Might Revolutionize the Resolution of FRAND Licensing Disputes, supra* note 1029, at 662–63. In Germany, see Sisvel v. Haier, Bundesgerichtshof [BGH] [Federal Court of Justice] May 5, 2020, KZR 36/17, ¶ 81 (Ger.), https://www.arnold-ruess.com/fileadmin/user_upload/2020_07_07_FCJ_SisvelvHaier_English. pdf ("What constitutes reasonable and non-discriminatory terms and conditions of a licence agreement in a particular case usually depends on a variety of circumstances. As in other cases of (possible) abuse of a dominant position, the dominant patentee is not in principle obliged to grant licenses in the manner of a 'uniform tariff' which grants equal conditions to all users. Nor does such an obligation arise from the FRAND Declaration of Commitment.") (citation omitted) ("Was im Einzelfall angemessene und nicht-diskriminierende Bedingungen eines Lizenzvertrages sind, hängt regelmäßig von einer Vielzahl von Umständen ab. Wie auch in anderen Fällen eines (möglichen) Missbrauchs einer marktbeherrschenden Stellung ist der marktbeherrschende Patentinhaber nicht grundsätzlich verpflichtet, Lizenzen nach Art eines 'Einheitstarifs' zu vergeben, der allen Nutzern gleiche Bedingungen einräumt. Eine solche Verp-flichtung ergibt sich auch nichtaus der FRAND-Selbstverpflichtungserklärung."). In the Netherlands, see Rechtbank Den Haag 8 februari 2017, ECLI:NL:RBDHA.2017:1025 ¶ 4.3 (Archos S.A./Koninklijke Philips N.V.) (Neth.) ("It is furthermore generally accepted and can in essence also be derived from the system of the *Huawei/ZTE* judgment, that a FRAND license has a certain bandwidth. After all, it was found in the judgment that, first, the SEP-holder makes a FRAND offer and, subsequently, if the SEP-user finds that unacceptable, the user can make a counter-offer that must also be FRAND.") ("Voorts wordt algemeen aangenomen en valt in wezen ook uit het systeem van de Huawei/ZTE-beslissing af te leiden, dat een FRAND-licentie een bepaalde bandbreedte kent. In die beslissing wordt immers overwogen dat eerst de SEP-houder een FRAND-aanbod doet en vervolgens, als de SEP-gebruiker zich daar niet in kan vinden, de gebruiker een tegenaanbod kan doen dat eveneens FRAND dient te zijn.") (citing Case C-170/13, Huawei Techs. Co. v. ZTE Corp., 2015 E.C.R. 477) (footnotes omitted). I understand the Dutch court's use of the word "bandwidth" (*bandbreedte*) in this context to express the same concept as what other courts and I have called the FRAND range. I am not aware of any scholarly literature or any court opinion that has given a different meaning to the FRAND range or the FRAND "bandwidth."

[1173] *FTC v. Qualcomm*, 411 F. Supp. 3d at 777.
[1174] *Id.* at 776.

Wi-Fi standard essential patents,' Fabian Gonell (QTL Legal Counsel and Senior Vice President, Licensing Strategy) testified 'No.'"[1175] Judge Koh further found:

> Qualcomm made the distinction explicit in a Qualcomm slide deck presented to Tony Blevins (Apple Vice President of Procurement). To purchase modem chips, an OEM "[m]ust be a licensee in good standing." For all other components, however, an OEM needs "[n]o separate license," and Qualcomm will sell the component on an exhaustive basis. Thus, Qualcomm only refuses to sell modem chips exhaustively and requires OEMs to sign patent license agreements before purchasing modem chips where Qualcomm has monopoly power.[1176]

Did Judge Koh ever identify what these "other components" were, apart from her vague reference to "Wi-Fi components"? When were these "other components" sold? How did Judge Koh know that Qualcomm did not have monopoly power over any of those "other components"? Did she hear any evidence on the question? How many distinct "other components" were there, and what were their respective sales volumes? To whom did Qualcomm sell them? Were those "other components" also practiced in handsets? What is the product life cycle for each of these "other components"? Are these "other components" commodities, or are they design-win products like modems? Are these "other components" sold in a spot market, or are they supplied for a defined term in a contract akin to a SULA?

How significant is Qualcomm's portfolio of Wi-Fi SEPs and non-SEPs relative to its overall licensing business? Do these "other components" constitute a significant fraction of Qualcomm's total sales of components? Or are they, when measured by revenues, merely a fraction of the fraction that Qualcomm's modem business already represents relative to the revenues generated by the company's licensing business? If so, is it commercially feasible to license the patents in these "other components" exhaustively through bilateral license negotiations rather than by permitting Qualcomm's patents reading on such "other components" to be exhausted by its sale of those "other components" to customers?

What are the transaction costs of negotiating exhaustive licenses with OEMs for the patents practiced in these "other components"? If an OEM takes a license to Qualcomm's entire portfolio of 140,000 patents and pending patent applications, are not these "other components" already explicitly

---

[1175] *Id.* at 727 (quoting Transcript of Proceedings (Volume 7) at 1483:18–21, FTC v. Qualcomm Inc., No. 5:17-cv-00220-LHK (N.D. Cal. Jan. 18, 2019) (Testimony of Fabian Gonell (Legal Counsel and Senior Vice President, Licensing Strategy, Qualcomm Technology Licensing))).

[1176] *Id.* at 776–77 (citations omitted) (quoting CX8261-004 (Qualcomm slide deck presented to Tony Blevins (Vice President of Procurement, Apple))).

licensed under the same business model with which Qualcomm chooses to license its cellular SEPs exhaustively—namely, to the OEM at the device level? Are these "other components" instead pieces of cellular infrastructure? Are they pieces of test equipment for cellular technologies?

Why, as Judge Koh seemed to imply, does antitrust law have anything to say about whether Qualcomm must follow the same business model with respect to the exploitation of any patents that it owns that read on these "other components" as Qualcomm employs with respect to its patented technology practiced in modems and handsets? Did Judge Koh believe that antitrust law compels homogeneity of the business strategy across every product made by a multiproduct firm?

Judge Koh did not ask or answer these questions.

c.   *Were Provisions in Qualcomm's Licenses That Required OEMs to Cross-License Their Own Patents to Qualcomm "Unusual"?*

Judge Koh also criticized Qualcomm for including in its license agreements "unusual provisions that require OEMs to cross-license their patents."[1177] This statement is exceptionally puzzling because there is nothing "unusual" about such provisions.

This peculiar remark suggests that, although Judge Koh had been a U.S. district judge in Silicon Valley for nearly a decade at the time of the trial in *FTC v. Qualcomm*—and although she had presided six years earlier over a high-profile dispute between Apple and Samsung requiring her interpretation of ETSI's IPR Policy and ETSI's FRAND obligation[1178]—she had evidently forgotten in the meantime that cross licensing of patents is commonplace in the context of SEPs. Indeed, cross licensing is so commonplace that section 6.1 of ETSI's IPR Policy explicitly permits an SEP holder to demand reciprocity as a condition of its offer to license its SEPs to an implementer:

[1177] *Id.* at 698.

[1178] *See, e.g.,* Apple, Inc. v. Samsung Elecs. Co., 920 F. Supp. 2d 1116, 1139–40 (N.D. Cal. 2013) (Koh, J.) (Order of January 29, 2013, Granting in Part and Denying in Part Apple's Motion for Judgment as a Matter of Law) ("Finally, Apple argues that Apple is entitled to judgment as a matter of law that Samsung breached the European Telecommunications Standards Institute's ('ETSI's') Intellectual Property Rights ('IPR') Policy, and that in so doing, Samsung violated section 2 of the Sherman Act. . . . Apple and Samsung are both members of ETSI. ETSI has a set of policies concerning the IPRs of its members, including when and how they must be disclosed during the standard-setting process, and what sorts of terms ETSI members must offer for licenses of their IPRs that are necessarily infringed by practicing the standards (so-called 'essential IPRs'). IPRs include patents and patent applications. . . . Samsung . . . made both general and patent-specific declarations that it was prepared to license [certain] standards-essential patents on fair, reasonable, and non-discriminatory ('FRAND') terms."); *id.* at 1140 (analyzing "the disclosure requirement [of] the ETSI IPR Policy").

"The above [FRAND] undertaking may be made subject to the condition that those who seek licences agree to reciprocate."[1179]

Consequently, one routinely observes SEP licenses being structured as two-way licenses with a net balancing payment.[1180] Therefore, the fact that, as an SEP holder subject to ETSI's IPR Policy, Qualcomm had routinely asked licensees to cross-license their SEPs to Qualcomm provided Judge Koh absolutely no evidence that Qualcomm's license agreements were "unusual" or that Qualcomm had charged any licensee (net) royalties that were "unreasonably high."

3. *Qualcomm's Contribution to Industry Standards*

Judge Koh found that "Qualcomm's own documents . . . show that Qualcomm is not the top standards contributor," which in her opinion confirmed that "QCT's monopoly chip market share rather than the value of QTL's patents sustain QTL's unreasonably high royalty rates."[1181] She found that, according to Qualcomm's own statements, "other patent holders like Nokia and Ericsson have made comparable or even greater contributions to cellular standards than Qualcomm,"[1182] yet their royalty rates and licensing revenues were "a fraction of Qualcomm's."[1183]

Judge Koh's findings of fact and conclusions of law also contained multiple references to testimony by executives at various OEMs who complained that Qualcomm's royalty for its portfolio of cellular SEPs exceeded the royalties that other SEP holders charged.[1184] She also said that, "even though Qualcomm's share of SEPs is declining and Qualcomm's SEPs expire with successive standards, Qualcomm still maintains a constant royalty rate" of

---

[1179] European Telecommunications Standards Institute (ETSI), ETSI Intellectual Property Rights Policy, Annex 6, cl. 6.1 (Apr. 3, 2019) [hereinafter ETSI IPR Policy], https://www.etsi.org/images/files/IPR/etsi-ipr-policy.pdf.

[1180] *See* Sidak, *Converting Royalty Payment Structures for Patent Licenses*, *supra* note 1028, at 907 ("Unlike a one-way license, a cross license assigns to each party the right to use the counterparty's patents. Implicit in a cross license is the idea that each party pays to use the counterparty's licensed patents. However, the one-way royalties that the two parties pay each other are not determined separately in the license. Rather, the license specifies only a single balancing royalty—that is, the ultimate royalty that one party (the net payor) must pay to the counterparty (the net payee). Specifying only the balancing royalty payment reduces the license agreement's transaction costs and accounting costs by simultaneously accounting for both parties' royalty payments."); *see also id.* at 907–10, 913–15 (showing the algebraic derivation of a net balancing payment in a cross license).

[1181] *FTC v. Qualcomm*, 411 F. Supp. 3d at 778.

[1182] *Id.*

[1183] *Id.* at 779.

[1184] *See, e.g., id.* at 720 ("John Grubbs (BlackBerry Senior Director of Intellectual Property Transactions) testified that the royalty rates BlackBerry paid Qualcomm were 'significantly higher than any other SEP rate [BlackBerry] paid to anybody else in the industry.'") (alteration in original) (quoting Deposition of John Grubbs at 236:5–7, *attachment to* Federal Trade Commission's Submission of Trial Testimony That Occurred on January 7[, 2019], FTC v. Qualcomm Inc., No. 5:17-cv-00220-LHK (N.D. Cal. Jan. 8, 2019), ECF No. 1185-2) (quoting, on the public record, deposition testimony that had been sealed).

5 percent of the wholesale price of the mobile device,[1185] which in her view constituted further evidence that Qualcomm's royalties were "unreasonably high."[1186]

Judge Koh's reasoning was unpersuasive because it assumed rather than established the necessary factual predicate. Four points deserve examination.

a.   Are SEPs Complements to, or Substitutes for, One Another?

First, it bears repeating that SEPs are complements to one another, not substitutes for one another. Consequently, one SEP portfolio for a given standard is necessarily a complement to another SEP portfolio for that same standard.

One would not be surprised if the royalties on patents practiced by an automobile's engine differed in magnitude from the royalties on patents practiced by its drive train or its telematics control unit (TCU), since the engine and the drive train and the TCU are all complements to one another when used to make an automobile. The license for one of them is not a "comparable" for the others in the (false) sense that the patented technologies are substitutes for one another. Any valuation methodology predicated on one's analysis of "comparable licenses" must keep this key economic distinction clearly in mind when purporting to draw inferences about what a given portfolio of SEPs is worth when it is voluntarily exchanged pursuant to a bilateral negotiation.

b.   Are All Cellular SEP Portfolios Equally Valuable?

Second, by necessity, *some* portfolio of SEPs for mobile devices must be the most valuable one. Would Apple and the other various OEMs testifying in *FTC v. Qualcomm* have moderated their demands for lower royalties one iota if the particularly valuable portfolio of cellular SEPs in question had belonged to some company other than Qualcomm?

c.   Did Judge Koh Analyze the Material Components of Consideration Exchanged in Qualcomm's License Agreements?

Third, Judge Koh did not cite any facts or data concerning (1) the contribution that Qualcomm or other SEP holders had made to various cellular standards, or (2) the royalties that any other SEP holder was charging for a license to its portfolio of cellular SEPs. Without knowing those facts and data, Judge Koh could not have analyzed properly the material components of consideration exchanged in Qualcomm's license agreements. For example, did Judge

---

[1185]   *Id.* at 783.
[1186]   *Id.* at 784.

Koh properly control for the (possibly low) value of cross licenses from other SEP holders to Qualcomm, since for many years Qualcomm has not (and does not now) manufacture handsets (and thus would have no demand for patents that it did not practice in any of its own manufactured products)?

The absence of such analysis from Judge Koh's findings of fact and conclusions of law made her comparison of Qualcomm's royalties to the royalties that other SEP holders charged speculative. Judge Koh merely recited general statements from Qualcomm's internal documents about its contribution to standards (when compared with the contributions of other SEP holders), and she then extrapolated from those statements alone a factual conclusion about the supposed reasonableness of the royalty for an exhaustive license to Qualcomm's portfolio of cellular SEPs.

One needs only to compare the complexity of the discussion of portfolio quality in contemporary SEP disputes—such as *TCL v. Ericsson*[1187] in the United States or *Unwired Planet v. Huawei*[1188] in the United Kingdom—to see how shallow Judge Koh's discussion of portfolio quality was in *FTC v. Qualcomm.*[1189] I can say from my own professional experience that international commercial arbitrations comparable in complexity to *TCL v. Ericsson* and *Unwired Planet* regularly arise and require highly experienced arbitrators, sitting in confidential proceedings, to calculate FRAND or RAND royalties for SEPs with a degree of economic sophistication that puts the level of discourse in Judge Koh's findings of fact and conclusions of law in *FTC v. Qualcomm* to shame.

d. Did Judge Koh Distinguish Qualcomm's Cellular SEP Portfolio from Its Portfolios of Non-Cellular SEPs and Non-SEPs?

Fourth, Judge Koh did not consider the significance of her own observation that Qualcomm has routinely licensed its SEPs (both cellular and non-cellular) as well as implementation patents in a single portfolio.[1190] Although she heard testimony specifically on the subject from Liren Chen (Senior Vice President

---

[1187] TCL Commc'n Tech. Holdings Ltd. v. Telefonaktiebolaget LM Ericsson, No. 14-341, 2018 WL 4488286 (C.D. Cal. Sept. 14, 2018), *vacated and reversed in part on other grounds and remanded*, 943 F.3d 1360 (Fed. Cir. 2019).

[1188] Unwired Planet Int'l Ltd v. Huawei Techs. Co. [2017] EWHC (Pat) 2988 (Birss, J.), *aff'd*, [2018] EWCA (Civ) 2344, *argued*, UKSC 2018/0214 (Eng.).

[1189] *See* Sidak, *Judge Selna's Errors in* TCL v. Ericsson *Concerning Apportionment, Nondiscrimination, and Royalties Under the FRAND Contract*, *supra* note 688, at 173–90; Sidak, *Why* Unwired Planet *Might Revolutionize the Resolution of FRAND Licensing Disputes*, *supra* note 1029, at 632–43.

[1190] *FTC v. Qualcomm*, 411 F. Supp. 3d at 672 ("Qualcomm primarily licenses its patents on a 'portfolio basis,' which means that a licensee pays for and receives rights to all three categories of Qualcomm patents—cellular SEPs, non-cellular SEPs, and non-SEPs.").

and Legal Counsel for QTL),[1191] Judge Koh did not examine the proportion that implementation patents comprise of Qualcomm's portfolio.

Consequently, Judge Koh necessarily did not examine what portion of a reasonable royalty for an exhaustive license to Qualcomm's *entire* patent portfolio would be attributable to Qualcomm's implementation patents rather than its SEPs. (One could repeat this disaggregation with respect to Qualcomm's cellular SEPs and its non-cellular SEPs.) Judge Koh evidently ignored that, although a FRAND or RAND commitment contractually constrains the royalty that an SEP holder may charge for an exhaustive license to an SEP, it does not so constrain the royalty for an exhaustive license to a non-SEP. Nor does the Patent Act impose a regime of compulsory licensing on the non-SEP. A patentee may refuse to offer to license a non-SEP.

For example, Judge Koh heard—but did not comment upon in her findings of fact and conclusions of law—the testimony from Apple at trial that it had taken the position in negotiations with Qualcomm that Apple would refuse to cross license its own intellectual property, including its non-SEPs, to Qualcomm. Tony Blevins, Apple's Vice President of Procurement, testified on January 11, 2019 about Apple's refusal to enter into an outbound patent license with Qualcomm:

> Q. Did Apple enter into a license agreement with Qualcomm?
>
> A. No. To this date, we've not entered into a license agreement with them.
>
> Q. Why not?
>
> A. There have been a number of stumbling blocks. The biggest one is we don't understand why, in order to buy a component from them, we have to enter into a licensing agreement that cross-licenses all of Apple's I.P. back to them. We simply don't understand why that's fair or why it's in anyone's best interest, other than Qualcomm.[1192]

The trial testimony of Mr. Blevins exemplified how the Patent Act neither regulates the royalties that a patent holder may demand for an exhaustive license to a non-SEP nor prohibits the holder of a non-SEP from refusing to license its patent entirely.

In addition, Judge Koh did not examine how the number of Qualcomm's implementation patents has changed over time. If the value of Qualcomm's implementation patents had increased over time—for example, because Qualcomm had added new and valuable patents to its portfolio—one would

---

[1191] Transcript of Proceedings (Volume 7) at 1538:5–15, 1540:14–17, 1552:16–17, FTC v. Qualcomm Inc., No. 5:17-cv-00220-LHK (N.D. Cal. Jan. 18, 2019) (Testimony of Liren Chen (Senior Vice President and Legal Counsel, QTL)).

[1192] Transcript of Proceedings (Volume 4) at 678:11–20, FTC v. Qualcomm Inc., No. 5:17-cv-00220-LHK (N.D. Cal. Jan. 11, 2019) (Testimony of Tony Blevins (Vice President of Procurement, Apple)).

expect the royalty for an exhaustive license to Qualcomm's portfolio to have remained constant or even to have increased over time despite Qualcomm's supposedly decreasing contribution of patents essential to the standard.

Put differently, the recurrent allegation that Qualcomm's patent portfolio has aged out and is not so valuable today relative to the portfolios of other patent licensors is misleading. It ignores the economic significance of the representation about Qualcomm's portfolio that Mr. Van Nest made to Judge Koh in his opening statement for Qualcomm: "Only about 20 percent of the portfolio is in cellular standard essential patents."[1193]

Therefore, evidence that the royalty for Qualcomm's overall portfolio remained constant over time did not provide Judge Koh facts from she could have reliably concluded that Qualcomm's royalty for an exhaustive license to its cellular SEPs was "unreasonably high."

4. Qualcomm's Use of a Royalty Base

Regarding Qualcomm's selection of a royalty base, Judge Koh found that "it is unreasonable for Qualcomm to charge its unreasonably high royalty rates on the sale price of an entire handset, as even Qualcomm's own document recognizes that a modem chip does not drive a cellular handset's value."[1194] She further found that "Qualcomm's use of the handset device as the royalty base is inconsistent with Federal Circuit law on the patent rule of apportionment" and that "Qualcomm is not entitled to a royalty on the entire handset."[1195] She concluded that "Qualcomm's collection of a royalty on the entire handset is inconsistent with . . . Federal Circuit law on the smallest salable patent practicing unit."[1196]

Those statements revealed that Judge Koh misunderstood (and misstated) the relevance of those Federal Circuit precedents for private licensing negotiations. Contrary to what Judge Koh asserted in her findings of fact and conclusions of law, Federal Circuit law does not limit the royalty base that parties may select in their license agreements. Curiously, although Judge Koh was concerned with the Federal Circuit's rules about the use of a royalty base for the purpose of calculating patent damages, she ignored other rules that courts routinely apply for quantifying damages.[1197]

[1193] Transcript of Proceedings (Volume 1) at 31:21–22, FTC v. Qualcomm Inc., No. 5:17-cv-00220-LHK (N.D. Cal. Jan. 4, 2019) (opening statement of Robert Van Nest for Qualcomm).

[1194] *FTC v. Qualcomm*, 411 F. Supp. 3d at 780–81.

[1195] *Id.* at 783.

[1196] *Id.*

[1197] *See, e.g.*, Ericsson, Inc. v. D-Link Sys., Inc., 773 F.3d 1201, 1227–28 (Fed. Cir. 2014); Apple Inc. v. Motorola, Inc., 757 F.3d 1286, 1325–26 (Fed. Cir. 2014); Monsanto Co. v. McFarling, 488 F.3d 973, 978–79 (Fed. Cir. 2007); Nickson Indus., Inc. v. Rol Mfg. Co., 847 F.2d 795, 798 (Fed. Cir. 1988); Georgia-Pacific Corp. v. United States Plywood Corp., 318 F. Supp. 1116, 1120 (S.D.N.Y. 1970).

a. *Did Judge Koh's Discussion of the Proper Royalty Base Erroneously Imply That Qualcomm's Royalties Per Handset Were Vastly Higher Than They Actually Were?*

It is important to recognize that "the sale price of an entire handset" was a misleading shorthand for Judge Koh to use to describe Qualcomm's royalty base. That incorrect description implied that a 5-percent royalty rate on a smartphone whose retail price was $1000 would produce a royalty of $50 per handset.

In actuality, as Judge Koh elsewhere acknowledged in her findings of fact and conclusions of law, "[t]he parties stipulated that in a typical SULA [Subscriber Unit License Agreement], Qualcomm receive[d] consideration in the form of a running royalty rate calculated [(1)] as a percentage of the licensee's *wholesale net selling price of the end-user device* (minus applicable deductions), [and (2)] *subject to royalty caps.*"[1198] She elaborated that Qualcomm "capped the maximum royalty base or net selling price of the handset at $400."[1199] Alex Rogers, President of QTL, testified that, "as of January 2018, the cap was reduced from $500 to $400," such that, "if a device was actually sold on the market for $800, the royalty rate would only be applied up to $400. That would cap the net selling price of the device."[1200] Thus, a 5-percent running royalty rate on *any* handset whose *wholesale* price equaled or exceeded $400—even an iPhone selling at retail for $1000 or more—would be $20.

But even the $20 per unit figure would be misleading if we accept, as Judge Koh observed, that Qualcomm "rebated Apple's royalty payments to a total of $7.50 per handset."[1201] A $50 per-unit royalty on a $1000 iPhone was 6.67 times the $7.50 per-unit royalty that Judge Koh said that Qualcomm actually agreed to accept from Apple.

For these reasons, readers of Judge Koh's discussion of the proper royalty base in her findings of fact and conclusions of law might get a hugely mangled impression of the actual dollar amounts at stake.

[1198] *FTC v. Qualcomm*, 411 F. Supp. 3d at 673 (emphasis added) (citing Joint Stipulation Regarding Undisputed Facts, *supra* note 144, at 10).

[1199] *Id.* (citing Transcript of Proceedings (Volume 9) at 1979:19–23, FTC v. Qualcomm Inc., No. 5:17-cv-00220-LHK (N.D. Cal. Jan. 25, 2019) (Testimony of Alex Rogers (President, Qualcomm Technology Licensing))).

[1200] Transcript of Proceedings (Volume 9) at 1979:22–1980:2, FTC v. Qualcomm Inc., No. 5:17-cv-00220-LHK (N.D. Cal. Jan. 25, 2019) (Testimony of Alex Rogers (President, Qualcomm Technology Licensing)).

[1201] *FTC v. Qualcomm*, 411 F. Supp. 3d at 725. Recall that Apple's Chief Operating Officer, Jeff Williams, testified at trial that Apple's royalty payment to Qualcomm was $7.50 (net of "rebates") per handset at a time when Apple was paying $30 for each (unlicensed) modem sourced solely from Qualcomm. *See supra* note 148.

b.   Was Qualcomm's Selection of a Particular Royalty Base Evidence That Its Royalty Was "Unreasonably High"?

The selection of the royalty base cannot, on its own, reveal whether a royalty for a license to a given patent portfolio is "unreasonably high." Any royalty base could produce a total amount of royalty compensation that correctly reflects the value of the licensed technology, provided that it is combined with an appropriate royalty rate. For example, assume that reasonable compensation for a license to firm *A*'s patent portfolio ranges from $18 to $23. In that case, both a 5-percent royalty rate applied to a royalty base of $400 and a 50-percent royalty rate applied to a royalty base of $40 would produce the same royalty payment, $20, which is within the range of reasonable royalties. By simple arithmetic, both the combinations (1) of a large royalty base with a low royalty rate and (2) a small royalty base with a higher royalty rate can produce reasonable royalty payments. Consequently, there is no reason to conclude, as Judge Koh did, that Qualcomm's use of the handset price (rather than the price of a component used in the handset) as the royalty base would automatically produce an "unreasonably high" royalty.

To determine whether a royalty is reasonable, one would need to evaluate a royalty base in conjunction with the royalty rate. Judge Koh found that Qualcomm applied its "unreasonably high royalty rates" to an inappropriate royalty base.[1202] Yet, Judge Koh did not determine a reasonable royalty for an exhaustive license to Qualcomm's portfolio—or to any subset of that portfolio, such as Qualcomm's cellular SEPs. Therefore, it would have been impossible for her to determine, on the basis of the evidence that she reported in her findings of fact and conclusions of law, whether the combination of Qualcomm's royalty rate and Qualcomm's royalty base produced an "unreasonably high" royalty. Consequently, it was a *non sequitur* for Judge Koh to say that she had found that, because Qualcomm used the handset price as the royalty base, Qualcomm's royalty was "unreasonably high."

c.   Was Qualcomm's Selection of a Particular Royalty Base Unlawful Under Federal Circuit Precedent?

Judge Koh misstated the law when concluding that Qualcomm's selection of the handset price as the royalty base was "inconsistent" with the Federal Circuit's law on apportionment.[1203] The apportionment requirement is essential to determining *damages* for patent infringement.[1204] For more than

---

[1202] *FTC v. Qualcomm*, 411 F. Supp. 3d at 780–81.

[1203] *Id.* at 783 ("Further, Qualcomm's use of the handset device as the royalty base is inconsistent with Federal Circuit law on the patent rule of apportionment.").

[1204] *See, e.g.*, Garretson v. Clark, 111 U.S. 120, 121 (1884); Commonwealth Sci. & Indus. Rsch. Org. v. Cisco Sys., Inc., 809 F.3d 1295, 1301 (Fed. Cir. 2015); Ericsson, Inc. v. D-Link Sys., Inc., 773 F.3d 1201, 1226

130 years, the Supreme Court has emphasized that, when seeking damages for the infringement of a patented technology included in a multicomponent product, a patent holder must "give evidence tending to separate or apportion the defendant's profits and the patentee's damages between the patented feature and the unpatented features[.]"[1205]

Various methodologies permit a finder of fact to disaggregate the value of the patented technology from the value of noninfringing components. For example, one can estimate the patented technology's value by applying a royalty rate to the price of the final product.[1206] One may alternatively apportion the value of the patented technology by applying a (higher) royalty rate to the smaller royalty base corresponding to the price of the smallest salable patent-practicing unit (SSPPU).[1207] It is also possible to analyze comparable licenses covering the relevant technology to determine the value that market participants have attributed to the patented invention in voluntary licensing transactions.[1208] All three methodologies seek to apportion the patent damage award according to the value of "the claimed invention's footprint in the market place."[1209]

The Federal Circuit has expressed skepticism about apportioning patent damages in an infringement case by applying a lesser royalty rate to the entire value of the downstream product rather than a greater royalty rate to the value of the SSPPU.[1210] The court has cautioned that, although one could derive an appropriate royalty by using the entire market value of the downstream product as the royalty base, presenting a jury with the large profits and revenue derived from sales of the downstream product might bias the jury's damages award upward.[1211] The Federal Circuit reasoned that the jury "may be less equipped to understand the extent to which the royalty rate" requires adjustment to reflect the true incremental value of the patented technology.[1212] The Federal Circuit consequently developed an evidentiary principle for jury trials—the entire market value rule (EMVR)—which supports the use of the downstream product as the royalty base only when "the patented feature drives the demand for an entire multicomponent

---

(Fed. Cir. 2014); VirnetX, Inc. v. Cisco Sys., Inc., 767 F.3d 1308, 1329 (Fed. Cir. 2014); LaserDynamics, Inc. v. Quanta Comput., Inc., 694 F.3d 51, 67 (Fed. Cir. 2012).

[1205] *Garretson*, 111 U.S. at 121; *see also* Keystone Mfg. Co. v. Adams, 151 U.S. 139, 148 (1894); City of Elizabeth v. Am. Nicholson Pavement Co., 97 U.S. 126, 138–39 (1877).

[1206] *Ericsson v. D-Link*, 773 F.3d at 1226; *see also* Sidak, *Apportionment, FRAND Royalties, and Comparable Licenses After* Ericsson v. D-Link, *supra* note 1172, at 1829.

[1207] *See* Sidak, *Apportionment, FRAND Royalties, and Comparable Licenses After* Ericsson v. D-Link, *supra* note 1172, at 1829.

[1208] *Id.*

[1209] Uniloc USA, Inc. v. Microsoft Corp., 632 F.3d 1292, 1317 (Fed. Cir. 2011).

[1210] *See, e.g.*, LaserDynamics, Inc. v. Quanta Comput., Inc., 694 F.3d 51, 61 (Fed. Cir. 2012); *Uniloc*, 632 F.3d at 1320.

[1211] *See, e.g.*, *Uniloc*, 632 F.3d at 1320; VirnetX, Inc. v. Cisco Sys., Inc., 767 F.3d 1308, 1333 (Fed. Cir. 2014).

[1212] *Ericsson v. D-Link*, 773 F.3d at 1227.

product."[1213] Conversely, when in a jury trial the weight of the evidence does not establish that the patented feature drove demand for the entire multi-component product, the Federal Circuit favors apportionment of patent damages by using the SSPPU as the royalty base.[1214]

In *FTC v. Qualcomm*, Judge Koh's findings of fact and conclusions of law concerning Qualcomm's selection of a royalty base in its licensing practices referred to Federal Circuit cases discussing the EMVR. In particular, Judge Koh asserted that

> the Federal Circuit held in *LaserDynamics, Inc. v. Quanta Computer, Inc.* that "it is generally required that royalties be based not on the entire product, but instead on the smallest salable patent-practicing unit." *Thus, Qualcomm is not entitled to a royalty on the entire handset.*[1215]

Judge Koh's second sentence in the passage quoted above is a *non sequitur*.

The EMVR is an evidentiary principle applied for determining damages in jury trials; it is not a rule that constrains parties when negotiating licensing agreements outside the courtroom. It is not the purpose of the EMVR to limit the parties' selection of the royalty base to the patented feature that supposedly drives demand for the licensed multicomponent product. Indeed, the Federal Circuit observed in *Ericsson v. D-Link* that real-world licenses typically do *not* resemble the EMVR.[1216] Put more starkly, license agreements commonly use the price of the entire multicomponent product as the royalty base even when there is no evidence that the patented technology drives the demand for that product.[1217] Before engrafting the EMVR onto the Sherman Act, a different judge—one having a greater affinity for the writings of Ronald Coase and other Nobel laureates in economics—might pause upon reading *LaserDynamics* and *Ericsson v. D-Link* to ask the obvious question: does this commonly observed contracting structure in bilaterally negotiated licenses for patents have a "procompetitive rationale"?[1218]

Judge Koh of course did not ask that question. One cannot even say in her defense that she condemned the unfamiliar. Rather, she distorted Federal

---

[1213] *LaserDynamics*, 694 F.3d at 67.

[1214] *Id.* at 67–68; *see also* Cornell Univ. v. Hewlett-Packard Co., 609 F. Supp. 2d 279, 283, 286–87 (N.D.N.Y. 2009); *VirnetX*, 767 F.3d at 1329.

[1215] FTC v. Qualcomm Inc., 411 F. Supp. 3d 658, 783 (N.D. Cal. 2019) (citation omitted) (emphasis added) (quoting *LaserDynamics*, 694 F.3d at 67); *see also id.* ("[T]he Federal Circuit has clarified that '[w]here the smallest salable unit is, in fact, a multi-component product containing several non-infringing features with no relation to the patented features . . . , the patentee must do more to estimate what portion of the value of that product is attributable to the patented technology.'") (second and third alterations in original) (quoting *VirnetX*, 767 F.3d at 1327).

[1216] *Ericsson v. D-Link*, 773 F.3d at 1228 ("As the testimony at trial established, licenses are generally negotiated without consideration of the EMVR[.]").

[1217] *See, e.g.*, Exmark Mfg. Co. v. Briggs & Stratton Power Prod. Grp., LLC, 879 F.3d 1332, 1349 (Fed. Cir. 2018).

[1218] Ohio v. Am. Express Co., 138 S. Ct. 2274, 2284 (2018).

Circuit precedent to the extent that she implied or concluded as a matter of law that Qualcomm's licensing practices were required to mimic the EMVR. To the contrary, the EMVR and the apportionment requirement did not, and do not, constrain Qualcomm's freedom to choose the royalty base that it wishes to use in its licenses for its cellular SEPs or its other patents. Calling Judge Koh's analysis of Qualcomm's chosen royalty base "fundamentally flawed,"[1219] the Ninth Circuit endorsed this same reasoning: "No court has held that the SSPPU concept is a per se rule for 'reasonable royalty' calculations; instead, the concept is used as a tool in jury cases to minimize potential jury confusion when the jury is weighing complex expert testimony about patent damages."[1220] Nor is the SSPPU even a "concept . . . *required* when calculating patent damages."[1221] Consequently, evidence that Qualcomm had used the handset price as a royalty base for pricing its portfolio of cellular SEPs (which was not even factually correct, as we saw above, considering the wholesale price caps for the applicable royalty base and the additional discounts extended) would not support Judge Koh's finding that Qualcomm's royalty rate for its cellular SEPs was "unreasonably high."

d.   *Why Would OEMs Prefer to Compel Qualcomm to Use the Price of the Modem as the Royalty Base for an Exhaustive License to Qualcomm's Portfolio of Cellular SEPs?*

If the selection of the royalty base neither affects the ultimate royalty payment nor violates existing Federal Circuit law concerning the calculation of a reasonable royalty for patent infringement, then why do OEMs bother opposing the use of the (capped) price of the downstream product (the smartphone) as the royalty base for purposes of calculating royalties for an exhaustive license to Qualcomm's portfolio of cellular SEPs (and for calculating royalties for Qualcomm's patents more generally)?

One possible explanation is that OEMs seek to reduce their royalty payments for SEPs by exploiting, for their economic benefit, a potential cognitive bias. Economists define a cognitive bias as "a departure in inference or judgment from objective analysis that leads to a distortion in perception or understanding."[1222] In this particular licensing context, the cognitive

---

[1219]   FTC v. Qualcomm Inc., No. 19-16122, 2020 WL 4591476, at *16 (9th Cir. Aug. 11, 2020).

[1220]   *Id.* (first citing *Ericsson v. D-Link*, 773 F.3d at 1226; then citing *VirnetX*, 767 F.3d at 1327–28; and then citing *LaserDynamics*, 694 F.3d at 68).

[1221]   *Id.* (emphasis in original) (citing Commonwealth Sci. & Indus. Rsch. Org. v. Cisco Sys., Inc., 809 F.3d 1295, 1303 (Fed. Cir. 2015)).

[1222]   Edwin T. Burton & Sunit N. Shah, Behavioral Finance: Understanding the Social, Cognitive, and Economic Debates 135 (John Wiley & Sons 2013). More generally, Nobel laureate Richard Thaler, citing the work of Nobel laureate Herbert Simon, has observed: "The possibility of cognitive error is of obvious importance in light of what Herbert Simon has called *bounded rationality*. Think of the human brain as a personal computer, with a very slow processor and a memory system that is both small and unreliable." Richard H. Thaler, The Winner's Curse: Paradoxes and Anomalies of

bias is the misperception that a FRAND royalty for the exhaustive use of Qualcomm's portfolio of cellular SEPs must be less (and perhaps significantly less) than the price for a "bare" modem. In effect, the OEMs and the manufacturers of modems might argue that the price of the intellectual property could never exceed the price of the substrate on which it is embedded. A moment's consideration confirms why that proposition is nonsense.

Any claim that a modem's price must exceed the per-unit FRAND royalty for an exhaustive license to a portfolio of cellular SEPs would be economic and legal fiction. The story in *Harry Potter* is more valuable than the ink, paper, and glue used to fabricate the book that contains the story.[1223] That is, on a per-device basis, the value of the exhaustive right to use a portfolio of cellular SEPs might exceed the value of a bare modem. Therefore, the proper royalty for an exhaustive license to that portfolio of cellular SEPs would exceed 100 percent of the price of a bare modem, if that is the chosen royalty base.

It might be the case that OEMs, the FTC, or perhaps Judge Koh would hope to force Qualcomm to apply for its entire portfolio the same royalty rate (say, 5 percent) that it applies to the $400 capped price of the smartphone to a different and much smaller royalty base consisting of the price of an unlicensed modem. Yet, that interpretation of law would misrepresent how the royalty rate will change inversely as the royalty base changes.[1224] One can view that misinterpretation of law from an economic perspective as attempting to impose—either naïvely or mendaciously—a *ceteris paribus* assumption in circumstances where everything else clearly would not remain constant.

As a matter of common sense, the incremental value of mobile connectivity is smaller as a percentage of the price of a $400 smartphone, which will include features and software that have value outside their use in mobile devices, than it is as a percentage of the price of a bare modem, which has the primary function of providing mobile connectivity. Consequently, the royalty *rate* for a license to the same technologies practiced by a lower-priced component of a handset would need to be much greater than the royalty rate that would be applied to the price of the handset. (And of course we saw earlier

---

ECONOMIC LIFE 2–3 (Princeton Univ. Press 1992) (emphasis in original); *see also* Herbert A. Simon, *Bounded Rationality*, *in* 1 THE NEW PALGRAVE: A DICTIONARY OF ECONOMICS, *supra* note 265, at 266, 266 ("The term 'bounded rationality' is used to designate rational choice that takes into account the cognitive limitations of the decision-maker—limitations of both knowledge and computational capacity. Bounded rationality is a central theme in the behavioural approach to economics, which is deeply concerned with the ways in which the actual decision-making process influences the decisions that are reached.").

1223 *See* Commonwealth Sci. & Indus. Rsch. Org. v. Cisco Sys., Inc., No. 6:11-cv-00343, 2014 WL 3805817, at *11 (E.D. Tex. July 23, 2014) (Davis, C.J.), *vacated and remanded on other grounds*, 809 F.3d 1295 (Fed. Cir. 2015), *cited in* J. Gregory Sidak, *The Proper Royalty Base for Patent Damages*, 10 J. COMPETITION L. & ECON. 989, 1019 (2014).

1224 *See* Sidak, *The Proper Royalty Base for Patent Damages*, *supra* note 1223, at 1021; Sidak, *Apportionment, FRAND Royalties, and Comparable Licenses After* Ericsson v. D-Link, *supra* note 1172, at 1829.

that "the price of the handset" is, in Qualcomm's case, actually a wholesale price that is capped at $400.)

Correct analysis of the appropriate royalty *rate* must complement any analysis of a particular royalty *base*. The one is meaningless without the other. It was therefore incorrect for Judge Koh to suggest that Qualcomm's use of the handset price as a royalty base could, on its own, constitute evidence that Qualcomm's royalty rate for its portfolio of cellular SEPs was "unreasonably high."

> 5. *Was It Relevant Whether or Not Qualcomm's Royalty Rates for an Exhaustive License to Its Cellular SEPs Had Been "Tested" in Litigation?*

Sophistry is the art of making the lesser argument sound the greater. Judge Koh resorted to sophistry when finding that Qualcomm's royalties were "unreasonably high" because they had not precipitated litigation such that they had been "tested" in court.[1225] She found that "Qualcomm's unreasonably high royalty rates have not been tested by litigation because Qualcomm's chip supply leverage insulates Qualcomm from legal challenges."[1226] For at least five reasons, this argument was specious and eristic.

First, Judge Koh did not cite any evidence that any SSO had ever defined its FRAND or RAND rate in terms of a rate that had been "tested" in litigation and survived. No SSO to my knowledge has such a rule or policy. And understandably so. It is hardly plausible that the intended purpose of a FRAND or RAND commitment is to fuel litigation immediately after parties have executed a license for SEPs; to the contrary, one would expect the objectives of a FRAND or RAND commitment to be more attainable in an environment of patent peace with respect to standardized products.

Second, Judge Koh referred uniformly in her findings of fact and conclusions of law to Qualcomm's "unreasonably high" "royalty rates," but she did not expressly restrict her finding to "royalty rates" paid for an exhaustive license to Qualcomm's cellular SEPs rather than Qualcomm's entire patent portfolio. Judge Koh did not cite any valid economic justification for her apparent insinuation that a royalty for *implementation* patents ought to be condemned as "unreasonably high" simply because no court had yet confirmed its reasonableness through litigation.[1227]

[1225] FTC v. Qualcomm Inc., 411 F. Supp. 3d 658, 786 (N.D. Cal. 2019).

[1226] *Id.*

[1227] *See, e.g., id.* ("Qualcomm's *unreasonably high royalty rates* have not been tested by litigation because Qualcomm's chip supply leverage insulates Qualcomm from legal challenges. Qualcomm's own documents recognize how Qualcomm's monopoly modem chip share prevents litigation, which sustains Qualcomm's *unreasonably high royalty rates*.") (emphasis added); *id.* at 790 ("[T]he Court concludes that *Qualcomm's royalty rates are unreasonably high*. These *unreasonably high royalty rates* raise costs to OEMs, and harm consumers

Third, Judge Koh did not consider any alternative hypotheses that could plausibly explain the absence of litigation over the reasonableness of the royalty for Qualcomm's portfolio of cellular SEPs (or any subset of Qualcomm's larger patent portfolio). Is it not plausible, for example, that an absence of litigation indicates that the extent of genuine dispute over the value of Qualcomm's portfolio of cellular SEPs was too small to justify the cost of litigation?

Fourth, Judge Koh did not explain why, considering her evident skepticism of the value of an exhaustive license to Qualcomm's portfolio of cellular SEPs, any amount of "testing" through litigation of a subset of Qualcomm's cellular SEPs would be enough to convince her that Qualcomm was charging a reasonable royalty for an exhaustive license to the many thousands of other patents in Qualcomm's portfolio of cellular SEPs. Judge Koh did not say, for example, what "testing" would require in terms of statistical sampling methods, considering that litigating tens of thousands of patents, with potentially hundreds of thousands of claims, would plainly be infeasible.

Recall that Alex Rogers, President of QTL, testified on January 25, 2019 that Apple sent Qualcomm an arbitration proposal in April 2016 "that no human being could actually complete, or no sets of arbitrators could actually complete within a reasonable timeframe," because Apple "insisted that every SEP, a claim from every SEP[,] be evaluated for essentiality[,] validity, [and] infringement, on a detailed basis for thousands upon thousands of SEPs."[1228] How in her findings of fact and conclusions of law did Judge Koh address Mr. Rogers' legitimate concern about the intractability of Apple's preferred mode of "testing" the value of Qualcomm's cellular SEPs? Where did Judge Koh consider the transaction costs that would be necessary to compile and evaluate the volume of evidence that Apple's preferred mode of "testing" would require? Where within Judge Koh's explanation of her litigation-testing thesis was there any limiting principle for resolving a dispute over the valuation of a portfolio containing tens of thousands of SEPs, which was the size of Qualcomm's portfolio of cellular SEPs? Her findings of fact and conclusions of law were conspicuously silent on these questions.

Fifth, Judge Koh in effect announced new law: the royalty for an exhaustive license to a portfolio of cellular SEPs (upon which sophisticated corporations, represented by counsel, previously had willingly agreed in an arms-length commercial negotiation) is "unreasonably high" (such that the licensee is thus entitled to the appropriate legal or equitable remedy) *unless* the SEP holder first has successfully sued to establish the reasonableness of that

---

because OEMs pass those costs along to consumers. *Qualcomm's unreasonably high royalty rates* also prevent OEMs from investing in new handset features, which further harms consumers.") (emphasis added).

[1228] Transcript of Proceedings (Volume 9) at 2017:5–7, FTC v. Qualcomm Inc., No. 5:17-cv-00220-LHK (N.D. Cal. Jan. 25, 2019) (Testimony of Alex Rogers (President, Qualcomm Technology Licensing)).

royalty (or, presumably, has been unsuccessfully sued over the alleged unreasonableness of that royalty). That novel legal principle would be hugely costly, for the reasons just discussed. Considering how long it takes to litigate a case alleging patent infringement or breach of a FRAND or RAND contract, we can safely predict that Judge Koh's process of "testing" Qualcomm's cellular SEPs in court would last considerably longer than it took to litigate *FTC v. Qualcomm*.

In an industry as technologically dynamic as mobile communications, the amount of time required to complete the process of price-formation-by-litigation that Judge Koh evidently envisioned could easily exceed the product life cycle of a typical model of smartphone. And of course federal judges are not the only pool of specially trained professionals capable of rendering opinions on the value of intangible assets. There are already standing armies of investment bankers, accountants, economists, management consultants, arbitrators, valuation specialists, consulting engineers, and attorneys willing and able to produce fairness opinions on, or appraisals of, the value of an exhaustive license to a company's portfolio of cellular SEPs. Many of those service providers work on a speedier timetable than several years of litigation in federal court, followed by another year or more of appeals, followed perhaps by a remand for further evidentiary hearings.

D. Was Qualcomm's Supposedly "Unreasonably High" Royalty for an OEM's Exhaustive License to Its Cellular SEPs Evidence Probative of Antitrust Liability?

Even if Judge Koh could have reported a persuasive basis for her finding of fact that Qualcomm had charged OEMs an "unreasonably high" royalty for an exhaustive license to its portfolio of cellular SEPs (or that Qualcomm's "unreasonably high" royalty represented a monopoly price for an exhaustive license to its portfolio of cellular SEPs), as a matter of law that finding by itself could not have supported her finding of *antitrust* liability.

The Supreme Court said in *Trinko* in 2004 that charging a monopoly price "is not only not unlawful; it is an important element of the free-market system."[1229] The Court reasoned that "[t]he opportunity to charge monopoly prices—at least for a short period—is what attracts 'business acumen' in the first place; it induces risk taking that produces innovation and economic growth."[1230] Courts of appeals have reiterated that fundamen-

---

[1229] Verizon Commc'ns Inc. v. Law Offices of Curtis V. Trinko, LLP, 540 U.S. 398, 407 (2004).

[1230] *Id.* (quoting United States v. Grinnell Corp., 384 U.S. 563, 571 (1966)); *see also* Pacific Bell Tel. Co. v. linkLine Commc'ns, Inc., 555 U.S. 438, 448 (2009) ("As a general rule, businesses are free to choose the parties with whom they will deal, as well as the prices, terms, and conditions of that dealing.") (citing United States v. Colgate & Co., 250 U.S. 300, 307 (1919)).

tal principle.[1231] In *Rambus Inc. v. FTC*, for example, the late Judge Stephen Williams wrote for the D.C. Circuit that charging a monopoly price is not an exclusionary practice, because it "has no particular tendency to exclude rivals and thus to diminish competition."[1232] He added that "high prices and constrained output tend to *attract* competitors, not to repel them."[1233]

Put differently, charging OEMs an "unreasonably high" royalty for an exhaustive license to a portfolio of cellular SEPs does not state a claim under section 2 of the Sherman Act.

E. Did the Absence of Substantial Evidence That Qualcomm's Royalty for an Exhaustive License to Its Cellular SEPs Was "Unreasonably High" Invalidate the Theory of the Royalty "Surcharge" and Modem "Tax" That the FTC and Professor Shapiro Advanced?

The absence of substantial evidence that Qualcomm's royalty for an OEM's exhaustive license to its portfolio of cellular SEPs was "unreasonably high" also upended Judge Koh's finding that Qualcomm's licensing practices imposed a royalty "surcharge" on OEMs, which OEMs supposedly viewed as a "tax" on the "all-in prices" paid for rival modems. As we saw in Part IV, Professor Shapiro admitted during trial that, if Qualcomm did not charge OEMs an "unreasonably high" royalty for an exhaustive license to its cellular SEPs, then "the economic consequences of the surcharge would not come into play."[1234]

Judge Koh should have made a finding of fact on this highly relevant admission by Professor Shapiro. It was material—and Judge Koh should have deemed it dispositive—to the outcome of *FTC v. Qualcomm*.

Suppressing any mention of this exculpatory admission given by Professor Shapiro in sworn testimony at trial denied the Ninth Circuit and the Supreme Court a complete picture of the frailty of the facts upon which rested the FTC's novel theory of antitrust liability. Consequently, considering the insubstantiality of the evidence that Judge Koh did cite for the supposed existence of an "unreasonably high" royalty for an exhaustive license to Qualcomm's cellular SEPs, there was no substantial and persuasive evidentiary basis reported in her findings of fact and conclusions of law to find that Qualcomm imposed a modem "tax" on transactions between OEMs and rival modem manufacturers.

[1231] *See, e.g.*, John Doe v. Abbott Labs., 571 F.3d 930, 935 (9th Cir. 2009); ZF Meritor, LLC v. Eaton Corp., 696 F.3d 254, 344 (3d Cir. 2012) (quoting *Trinko*, 540 U.S. at 407).

[1232] 522 F.3d 456, 464 (D.C. Cir. 2008).

[1233] *Id.* at 466 (emphasis added).

[1234] Transcript of Proceedings (Volume 6) at 1198:10–11, FTC v. Qualcomm Inc., No. 5:17-cv-00220-LHK (N.D. Cal. Jan. 15, 2019) (Testimony of Carl Shapiro).

In its opening and closing arguments at trial on January 4, 2019 and January 29, 2019, the FTC sought to minimize the significance of the absence of evidence supporting its claim that Qualcomm's royalty for an exhaustive license to its portfolio of cellular SEPs was unreasonable. "If [it] is true," the FTC argued, that "Qualcomm has valuable patents and has invented technology that is fundamental to cellular communications . . . [,] then Qualcomm should not be afraid to prove the value of its standard essential patents in patent litigation."[1235] Several pages later in the trial transcript, the FTC similarly complained that "Qualcomm will not provide the court with any alternative estimate of what a Court would award in FRAND litigation."[1236] The FTC criticized Qualcomm for having "spent a lot of trial time discussing the scope of its patent portfolio without providing any valuation or valuation methodology to justify its royalties."[1237]

These extravagant arguments by the FTC's counsel, Ms. Milici, would reverse the burden of production. Because of due process of law, a judge may not presume an alleged monopolist to be guilty until it proves its innocence. In *FTC v. Qualcomm*, it was impermissible for Judge Koh or the FTC to presume Qualcomm to be liable under section 2 of the Sherman Act unless it could prove by a preponderance of the evidence that its royalties for an exhaustive license to its cellular SEPs were *"not* unreasonably high."

Yet, the FTC seemed to act like a law enforcement agency that had so lost its way that it cared nothing for the presumption of innocence and due process of law. Instead, Ms. Milici complained in her closing argument for the FTC: "Not one of Qualcomm's witnesses testified about how much Qualcomm's patents are worth. No Qualcomm expert attempted to value Qualcomm's portfolio or proposed a methodology for doing so."[1238]

Why Qualcomm did not need to make such a showing should have been obvious to the FTC: as a matter of due process, it was not Qualcomm's burden to produce evidence proving its innocence under the FTC's novel theory of liability concerning the supposed royalty "surcharge" and modem "tax." It appears from the trial transcripts that Judge Koh never once admonished the FTC, even by the time of Ms. Milici's closing argument, to refrain in her advocacy from inverting the burden of production and the burden of persuasion. Nor did Judge Koh address this deprivation of due process in her findings of fact and conclusions of law.

FTC v. Qualcomm was not a FRAND royalty case. Neither the FTC nor Qualcomm sought a declaratory judgment from Judge Koh of a FRAND or

---

[1235] Transcript of Proceedings (Volume I) at 13:4–9, FTC v. Qualcomm Inc., No. 5:17-cv-00220-LHK (N.D. Cal. Jan. 4, 2019) (opening statement of Jennifer Milici for the FTC).

[1236] *Id.* at 23:24–25.

[1237] Transcript of Proceedings (Volume II) at 2115:1–3, FTC v. Qualcomm Inc., No. 5:17-cv-00220-LHK (N.D. Cal. Jan. 29, 2019) (closing argument of Jennifer Milici for the FTC).

[1238] *Id.* at 2125:15–18.

RAND royalty. If they had, the case would have been vastly more complex than it was, and it would have taken substantially longer to try. The case also would have been tried before a jury unless Qualcomm (improbably) waived its Seventh Amendment right to a jury trial.[1239] Yet, the FTC wanted to have it both ways. The FTC tried to create, as an appendage to its antitrust case, a miniature FRAND royalty determination.

In this movie within a movie, Qualcomm would be cast as the regulated public utility, *FTC v. Qualcomm* would nominally be the ratemaking proceeding, and Judge Koh would play the *de facto* public utilities commissioner from whom Qualcomm would seek advance regulatory approval for its tariffed rate for an OEM's exhaustive license to Qualcomm's cellular SEPs on just, reasonable, and nondiscriminatory terms. It is critical to recall that, in that setting of a regulated public utility, all that is not permitted is forbidden; and the burden of proving the reasonableness of a proposed rate is on the regulated utility.

This absence of pricing freedom is a hugely important distinction between industry-specific regulation and antitrust law. It is specious on both legal and economic grounds lightly to impute a regime of such price regulation to an industry where no legislation has expressly created such a regulator and defined its mandate and powers.

F. *Did Qualcomm's Payments to OEMs Bolster Qualcomm's Supposedly "Unreasonably High" Royalties for an Exhaustive License to Its Cellular SEPs?*

Judge Koh found that Qualcomm's payments to Apple and other OEMs "help[ed] maintain Qualcomm's unreasonably high royalty rates and surcharge on rivals' chips by inducing OEMs to sign license agreements."[1240] In essence, Judge Koh found that Qualcomm's payments persuaded OEMs to enter exclusive dealing agreements with Qualcomm, an outcome that allegedly entrenched Qualcomm's monopoly power over certain kinds of modems and permitted Qualcomm to continue charging what she considered to be "unreasonably high" royalties for exhaustive licenses to its cellular SEPs. Judge Koh also found that Qualcomm's "unreasonably high royalty rates generate the revenue that enable[d] QTL to offer OEMs hundreds of millions (or in the case of Qualcomm's exclusive deals with Apple, billions)" to OEMs.[1241] She further found that "QTL's unreasonably high royalty rates enable QTL to offer OEMs enormous chip incentive funds, which lower the

---

[1239] *See* TCL Commc'n Tech. Holdings Ltd. v. Telefonaktiebolaget LM Ericsson, 943 F.3d 1360, 1371–72 (Fed. Cir. 2019).

[1240] FTC v. Qualcomm Inc., 411 F. Supp. 3d 658, 794 (N.D. Cal. 2019); *see also id.* at 792.

[1241] *Id.* at 792.

relative price of Qualcomm's modem chips, result in exclusivity, and maintain Qualcomm's ability to impose a surcharge on rivals' modem chips."[1242]

Judge Koh's finding that Qualcomm's "unreasonably high royalty rates . . . *lower the relative price* of Qualcomm's modem chips" was unclear or incorrect (or both).[1243] As we saw earlier, it was implausible that the level of Qualcomm's royalties for an exhaustive license to its cellular SEPs affected the relative price of non-Qualcomm modems to Qualcomm modems, because Judge Koh did not cite any evidence that Qualcomm *systematically* charged higher royalties for exhaustive licenses to its cellular SEPs to OEMs purchasing non-Qualcomm modems than to OEMs purchasing Qualcomm modems. Without evidence that Qualcomm systematically charged OEMs asymmetric cellular SEP royalties on the basis of the brand of modem that those OEMs purchased, the FTC's "surcharge" conjecture should have collapsed.

In short, those findings by Judge Koh were unsubstantiated. Because Judge Koh never established that Qualcomm's royalties for an exhaustive license to its cellular SEPs were "unreasonably high," she did not have any factual foundation upon which to conclude that Qualcomm's payments to Apple or any other OEM "bolstered" Qualcomm's ability to charge those allegedly "unreasonably high" royalties.[1244]

Judge Koh's criticism of Qualcomm's payments to Apple and other OEMs boiled down to the allegation that Qualcomm engaged in anticompetitive exclusive dealing. Yet, her analysis of the effects of Qualcomm's payments on competition offered no incremental insight beyond her explicit discussion of exclusive dealing, which we will examine in detail in Part XIII. Judge Koh found that "Qualcomm's exclusive deals with Apple are the most prominent single example of such funds [paid to OEMs], but Qualcomm regularly gave OEMs chip incentives that result in exclusivity and in combination 'severely restrict the market's ambit.'"[1245] Judge Koh then cited several examples in which, between 2004 and 2018, Qualcomm included in its contracts with OEMs (including Blackberry, LGE, Samsung, Lenovo, Motorola, Huawei, and Apple) some form of payment in exchange for some minimum share of the OEM's requirements for modems or some minimum level of unit sales of modems.[1246] She found that those discounts caused exclusivity.[1247]

Yet, Judge Koh did not cite any actual analysis of the *competitive effect* of the exclusivity that she found. As we saw earlier, and as we will examine

---

1242 *Id.* at 795.

1243 *Id.* (emphasis added).

1244 *FTC v. Qualcomm*, 411 F. Supp. 3d at 720.

1245 *Id.* at 792 (quoting United States v. Dentsply Int'l, Inc., 399 F.3d 181, 191 (3ᵈ Cir. 2005)).

1246 *Id.* at 792–95. For example, "QTL offered Lenovo $180 million in chip incentives that were contingent on Lenovo purchasing at least 80 million modem chips from QCT *over two years*." *Id.* at 793 (emphasis added).

1247 *Id.* at 793.

in greater depth in Part XIII, courts and economists believe that exclusive dealing agreements can harm competition *only* when they foreclose competitors from a substantial part of the relevant market. To find competitive harm from a price decrease requires the application of a price-cost test, yet Judge Koh did not conduct one, and she did not identify the facts that would be necessary for others to conduct that test.

G. *Did Qualcomm's Refusal to Offer Exhaustive Licenses to Its Portfolio of Cellular SEPs to Rival Modem Manufacturers Increase Qualcomm's Market Share, Increase Its Royalty Rates, or Generate Exclusivity?*

Judge Koh found that Qualcomm's refusal to offer exhaustive licenses to its cellular SEPs to rival modem manufacturers "prevents rivals' entry, promotes rivals' exit, and hampers Qualcomm's rivals."[1248] She found that Qualcomm's refusal to offer exhaustive licenses to its cellular SEPs to rival modem manufacturers reduced its "rivals' customer base and sales," which in turn supposedly increased Qualcomm's market share (presumably in Judge Koh's two relevant product markets for modems) and royalty rates (presumably for an exhaustive license to its cellular SEPs, as opposed to its non-cellular SEPs or non-SEPs) and increased the likelihood of exclusivity.[1249] Judge Koh did not cite any market analysis or empirical evidence to support those findings of fact. (In fact, she could not: as we saw in Part F to the Introduction, the empirical evidence contradicted her dire predictions.) Judge Koh also did not explain on *a priori* grounds why Qualcomm's practices would produce the economic effects that she predicted.

Judge Koh did not cite any evidence that Qualcomm had ever asserted its intellectual property rights in its cellular SEPs against rival modem manufacturers. We saw in Part III that Qualcomm had never exhaustively licensed its cellular SEPs to rival modem manufacturers, and Judge Koh found that Qualcomm had executed agreements "that permit[ted] rivals to sell modem chips to only 'Authorized Purchasers'—Qualcomm licensees."[1250] Qualcomm's nonexhaustive agreements with rival modem manufacturers are noteworthy: After an OEM had executed an exhaustive license agreement with Qualcomm for its portfolio of cellular SEPs, that OEM was free to choose *any* supplier of modems. An OEM paid the same royalty for an exhaustive license to Qualcomm's cellular SEPs, whether the OEM used that patent portfolio in conjunction with a Qualcomm modem or a non-Qualcomm modem.

[1248] *Id.* at 795.
[1249] *Id.* at 797.
[1250] *Id.* at 795.

Simply put, unless Qualcomm was asserting its intellectual property rights in its cellular SEPs against rival modem manufacturers, which Qualcomm was not doing, Judge Koh's *a priori* reasoning—that Qualcomm's refusal to offer exhaustive licenses to its cellular SEPs directly to rival modem manufacturers excluded those rivals from the market and reduced their sales—was implausible on its face and unsubstantiated as an evidentiary matter.

Again, even if Qualcomm's refusal to offer licenses to its portfolio of cellular SEPs to rival modem manufacturers had had the effect of excluding those rivals and hampering their ability to compete, that evidence by itself would not have sufficed to support Judge Koh's ultimate conclusion that Qualcomm had violated section 2 of the Sherman Act. Irrespective of the effects that a refusal to deal with a rival has on competition (either alone or when combined with other practices), that refusal cannot violate American antitrust law unless it first falls within the limited exception, which the Supreme Court created in *Aspen Skiing*, to the general freedom in American antitrust law not to deal with one's competitors. We shall see in Part XII.B that the evidence that Judge Koh identified and weighed in her findings of fact and conclusions of law did not show that Qualcomm's conduct fit that narrow exception of *Aspen Skiing*.

VIII. Did Evidence of Qualcomm's Supposedly Anticompetitive Intent Obviate Proof of Anticompetitive Effects?

Rather than focus on evidence about harm to competition, Judge Koh focused on Qualcomm's intent. She found that "Qualcomm's own documents show that Qualcomm knew its licensing practices could lead to antitrust liability, knew its licensing practices violate FRAND, and knew its licensing practices harm competition, yet continued anyway."[1251] Judge Koh found that the evidence of Qualcomm's supposedly anticompetitive intent *"confirm[ed]* the Court's conclusion that Qualcomm's licensing practices cause antitrust harm."[1252]

It is important to pause for a moment and emphasize Judge Koh's logic: intent is conclusive evidence of actual competitive harm. If that proposition were in fact the law, plaintiffs would dispense with trying to prove anticompetitive effects altogether, since it would suffice for them merely to prove that the defendant intended to harm the competitive process. That reasoning of course is erroneous as a matter of law.

[1251] *Id.* at 807.
[1252] *Id.* at 812 (emphasis added).

A. *Judge Koh's Misreading of* Aspen Skiing *and* Alcoa *on Specific Intent, General Intent, and Anticompetitive Effect*

To support her conclusion that evidence of anticompetitive intent sufficed to prove that Qualcomm's licensing practices caused competitive harm, Judge Koh quoted *Aspen Skiing*: "'no monopolist monopolizes unconscious of what he is doing.'"[1253] Yet, Judge Koh's reliance on this passage misjudges the Supreme Court's modern jurisprudence on monopolization.

1. *Judge Learned Hand's Analysis of Specific Intent to Monopolize a Market*

The phrase that Judge Koh attributed to *Aspen Skiing* actually comes from Judge Learned Hand's decision for the Second Circuit in *Alcoa*, forty years earlier.[1254] In the phrase that both Judge Koh and *Aspen Skiing* quoted, Judge Hand was making the point that section 2 of the Sherman Act does not require evidence of specific intent. As Judge Robert Bork later observed (and as the Supreme Court quoted in *Aspen Skiing*), "Improper exclusion (exclusion not the result of superior efficiency) is always deliberately intended."[1255] In 1948, the Court endorsed Judge Hand's reasoning in *Alcoa*, stating in *United States v. Griffith* that "[i]t is . . . not always necessary to find a specific intent to restrain trade or to build a monopoly in order to find that the anti-trust laws have been violated."[1256]

Thus, even in the antitrust thinking of 1945, Judge Hand was not reasoning that judicial recognition of a general-intent standard for section 2 obviated a plaintiff's proof of anticompetitive *effects*.[1257] Instead, Judge Hand merely reasoned that, when there is already evidence of anticompetitive effect, the plaintiff need not prove that a monopolist had specific anticompetitive intent.

Judge Hand's memorable turn of phrase from 1945 does not mean—as Judge Koh's interpretation of it 74 years later would imply—that the intent requirement does double duty under section 2 of the Sherman Act. *Alcoa* did not establish that a plaintiff may prove liability for monopolization without proving an anticompetitive effect. Nor in the years since has the Supreme Court erased the requirement under section 2 to prove that the monopolist had an anticompetitive effect.

[1253] *Id.* (quoting Aspen Skiing Co. v. Aspen Highlands Skiing Corp., 472 U.S. 585, 602 (1985)).

[1254] United States v. Aluminum Co. of Am., 148 F.2d 416, 432 (2ᵈ Cir. 1945).

[1255] Robert H. Bork, The Antitrust Paradox: A Policy at War with Itself 160 (Free Press rev. ed. 1993) (1978), *quoted in Aspen Skiing*, 472 U.S. at 602–03.

[1256] 334 U.S. 100, 105 (1948).

[1257] *See, e.g.*, Keith N. Hylton, *The Law and Economics of Monopolization Standards*, in Antitrust Law and Economics 82, 85–86 (Keith N. Hylton ed., Edward Elgar 2010).

2. *The Supreme Court's Respectful Overruling of Judge Learned Hand's Analysis of Margin Squeezes*

More to the point, the Supreme Court in *linkLine* in effect overruled *Alcoa's* jurisprudence on margin squeezes, which is the aspect of *Alcoa* most germane to, but certainly not controlling for, *FTC v. Qualcomm*. Chief Justice Roberts wrote for the Court:

> Like the Court of Appeals, *amici* argue that price-squeeze claims have been recognized by Courts of Appeals for many years, beginning with Judge Hand's opinion in *United States v. Aluminum Co. of America* (*Alcoa*). In that case, the Government alleged that Alcoa was using its monopoly power in the upstream aluminum ingot market to squeeze the profits of downstream aluminum sheet fabricators. The court concluded: "That it was unlawful to set the price of 'sheet' so low and hold the price of ingot so high, seems to us unquestionable, provided, as we have held, that on this record the price of ingot must be regarded as higher than a 'fair price.'" Given developments in economic theory and antitrust jurisprudence since *Alcoa*, we find our recent decisions in *Trinko* and *Brooke Group* more pertinent to the question before us.[1258]

Judge Koh made both an error of omission and an error of commission with respect to *Alcoa*.

Her error of omission was that she ignored the portion of *Alcoa* that the Supreme Court had repudiated a decade earlier in *linkLine*. An appreciation of the basis for that repudiation was necessary if Judge Koh was to have had a proper understanding of how to determine, under the Court's contemporary monopolization decisions, whether Qualcomm's challenged conduct had had an actual anticompetitive effect.

Judge Koh's error of commission was her reliance upon a different passage, originating in *Alcoa* and quoted in *Aspen Skiing*, to rule erroneously that evidence of Qualcomm's general intent to cause an anticompetitive effect could prove that Qualcomm's licensing practices had in fact caused an actual anticompetitive effect.

B. *Did the FTC Introduce Preponderant Evidence That Qualcomm Had Anticompetitive Intent?*

Judge Koh's finding that Qualcomm had anticompetitive intent was not persuasive because substantial evidence contradicted it. Evidence that Qualcomm was concerned that some firms might file an antitrust action

---

[1258] Pacific Bell Tel. Co. v. linkLine Commc'ns, Inc., 555 U.S. 438, 452 n.3 (2009) (citations omitted) (quoting *Alcoa*, 148 F.2d at 438).

against Qualcomm did not prove that Qualcomm believed that its actions were indeed anticompetitive.

Moreover, Judge Koh's finding of anticompetitive intent was substantially predicated on a snippet of a single slide from a draft PowerPoint presentation (Plaintiff Exhibit CX5809), apparently emailed in the middle of the night by a Qualcomm employee who was not among the senior management at Qualcomm. Judge Koh's findings of fact and conclusions of law reproduced that incomplete image of a single draft slide no fewer than four times.

At trial, the FTC did not elicit any testimony concerning the origin or reliability of that draft of a slide. Nor apparently did Judge Koh regard the authority of that partial draft slide with any degree of skepticism. Finally, and most importantly, Exhibit CX5809 was irrelevant as a matter of antitrust law and was not reliable evidence probative of Qualcomm's intent—anticompetitive or otherwise.

1. Is Knowledge of One's Risk of Being Sued on an Antitrust Claim Evidence of One's Own Anticompetitive Intent?

Judge Koh repeatedly found that Qualcomm recognized that its licensing practices could expose Qualcomm to antitrust claims.[1259] For example, she found that Qualcomm understood that conditioning its sale of modems to an OEM on the execution of a license agreement with that OEM could result in antitrust liability.[1260]

It is hardly surprising that antitrust litigation might arise in an industry where technological innovation has succeeded in creating enormous economic surplus that multiple actors seek to appropriate to themselves. Judge Koh's findings of fact and conclusions of law strike an innocent pose, unsuspecting of the possibility that antitrust litigation itself might be exploited to advance the private economic advantage of the companies bringing such claims (or on whose behalf a government enforcement agency has been persuaded to bring such claims at taxpayer expense).[1261]

That Qualcomm expressed concern that a buyer or a competitor might pursue antitrust claims against Qualcomm certainly does not tend to prove

---

[1259] FTC v. Qualcomm Inc., 411 F. Supp. 3d 658, 807 (N.D. Cal. 2019) ("Qualcomm's own documents show that Qualcomm knew its licensing practices could lead to antitrust liability."); *id.* ("Qualcomm admitted in contemporaneous documents that its practices of avoiding patent exhaustion, requiring OEMs to sign a separate license before purchasing modem chips, and threatening to cut off OEMs' chip supply may cause antitrust liability."); *id.* ("For example, in a May 2012 slide deck . . . , Qualcomm admitted that its licensing practices could lead to antitrust claims."); *id.* ("Qualcomm's internal contemporaneous documents repeatedly acknowledge that its licensing practices expose Qualcomm to antitrust claims."); *id.* at 808 ("Thus, Qualcomm repeatedly acknowledged that its licensing practices raise antitrust claims, yet continued the licensing practices anyway.").

[1260] *Id.* at 807.

[1261] *See, e.g.,* William J. Baumol & Janusz A. Ordover, *Use of Antitrust to Subvert Competition*, 28 J.L. & ECON. 247 (1985).

that Qualcomm itself believed that its practices were in fact anticompetitive, much less did it prove that Qualcomm intended to harm competition. On its face, that evidence is consistent with the interpretation that Qualcomm believed that some firms might file (or might threaten to file) antitrust complaints in court or before an enforcement agency, in the United States or a foreign country, to gain bargaining power in their commercial negotiations with Qualcomm over the licensing of its cellular SEPs.

Thus, the evidence that Judge Koh cited fell far short of tending to prove that Qualcomm had anticompetitive intent. To the contrary, such an interpretation of that evidence sounds naïve about the rough and tumble of commerce in a notoriously litigious sector.

2. *Judge Koh's Apparent Smoking Gun*

To support her conclusion that Qualcomm had an anticompetitive intent, Judge Koh cited page 41 of Plaintiff's Exhibit CX5809, which evidently in its entirety was an email with an attached draft of a PowerPoint slide deck for an upcoming Qualcomm pricing presentation in 2009.[1262] This document appeared to be what Judge Koh considered the smoking gun in *FTC v. Qualcomm*, because she cited CX5809 in four separate places, each time embedding an image box of the page into the body of her findings of fact and conclusions of law.[1263] The image box that Judge Koh embedded four times in her findings of fact and conclusions of law is reproduced in Figure 8.

Figure 8. Judge Koh's Expurgated Reproduction
of Page 41 of Plaintiff's Exhibit CX5809

Source: FTC v. Qualcomm, 411 F. Supp. 3d at 745, 761, 799, 811 (all pages citing an expurgated reproduction of CX5809-041).

A nearly identical copy of the same expurgated figure appeared in the slide deck that the FTC displayed during its closing argument:

[1262] Email from Jeremy Blair to Sanjay Mehta, Carbon Copy to Will Wyatt, Sean Zanderson, Marc McCloskey, Peter Rosen, and Carol Blubaugh, Subject: 11/23/09 Draft PRC Minutes (Nov. 24, 2009, 3:56:48 AM), FTC v. Qualcomm Inc., No. 19-16122 (9th Cir. Nov. 22, 2019), ID: 11509360, ECF No. 139-3, 139 SER Vol. 3, at SER0695 [hereinafter Email from Jeremy Blair].

[1263] *FTC v. Qualcomm*, 411 F. Supp. 3d at 745, 761, 799, 811 (all cited pages reproducing an expurgated version of page 41 of CX5809-041).

Figure 9. The FTC's Expurgated Reproduction
of Page 41 of Plaintiff's Exhibit CX5809

CX5809-041

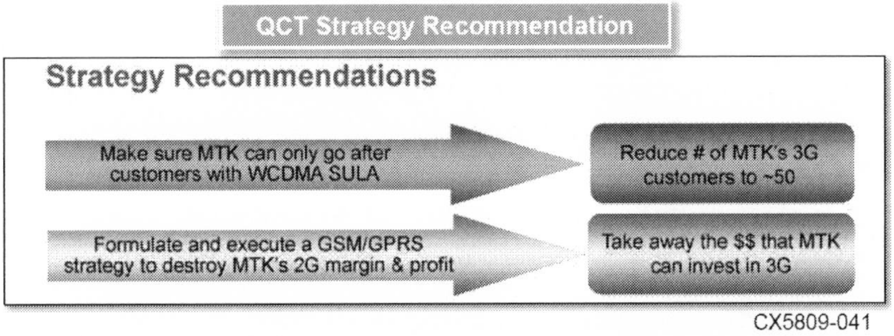

Source: Federal Trade Commission's Closing Argument Slide Presentation (Public Redacted Version) at 44, FTC v. Qualcomm Inc., No. 5:17-cv-00220-LHK (N.D. Cal. Jan. 29, 2019), https://www.ftc.gov/system/files/documents/cases/2019_01_29_ftc_closing_slides_redacted.pdf (citing an expurgated reproduction of CX5809-041).

Close examination of the bottom edge of Judge Koh's image box (in Figure 8) reveals horizontal lines that appear to be the outline of additional images below the bottom (second) horizontal arrow and text bubble, highlighted in green in the original. (Notice that the FTC's version of the image box in Figure 9 does *not* contain the same outline of additional images evident in Figure 8.)

The casual reader of Judge Koh's findings of fact and conclusions of law might not appreciate that she inserted four times into her findings of fact and conclusions of law an *expurgated* version of page 41 of CX5809, which even showed the traces of a cropping line. The complete, unexpurgated version of page 41 of CX5809, which is publicly available in the appellate docket of *FTC v. Qualcomm*, reported *five* strategy recommendations—not two, as Judge Koh's findings of fact and conclusions of law might cause readers to believe.[1264] Figure 10 reproduces the complete, unexpurgated version of Judge Koh's apparent smoking gun.

[1264] Plaintiff's Exhibit CX5809-041, Strategy Recommendations, FTC v. Qualcomm Inc., No. 19-16122 (9th Cir. Nov. 22, 2019), ID: 11509360, ECF No. 139-3, at SER0698 [hereinafter Unexpurgated Version of Plaintiff's Exhibit CX5809-041]. The unexpurgated version of CX5809-041 was publicly disclosed in the appellate docket notwithstanding that it contained a legend stating, "HIGHLY CONFIDENTIAL-ATTORNEYS' EYES ONLY."

Figure 10. Unexpurgated Reproduction
of Page 41 of Plaintiff's Exhibit CX5809

Case: 19-16122, 11/22/2019, ID. 11509360, DktEntry: 139-3, Page 165 of 281

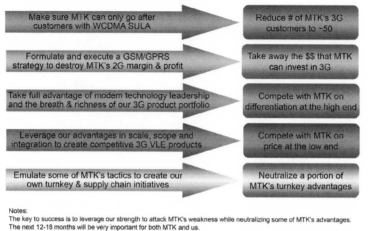

Source: Unexpurgated Version of Plaintiff's Exhibit CX5809-041, *supra* note 1264.

Considering the apparent degree of deliberation by Judge Koh over this slide, why did she choose to reproduce, in four separate places, only a partial, expurgated version of page 41 of CX5809? Why did the FTC also display an expurgated version of page 41 of CX5809 during its closing argument before Judge Koh? Did the remaining three strategy recommendations and accompanying notes on page 41 of CX5809 tend to refute the FTC's allegation, and Judge Koh's conclusion, that this document was evidence that Qualcomm had anticompetitive intent?

3. The Unconfirmed Provenance of Judge Koh's Apparent Smoking Gun

One might expect Judge Koh to have identified in her findings of fact and conclusions of law the author of the email and the PowerPoint slide deck, including page 41 of CX5809. Was it an experienced senior executive? A junior analyst more eager than wise? A management consultant prone to bravado and business school clichés? Judge Koh did not say. No one reading solely Judge Koh's findings of fact and conclusions of law in *FTC v. Qualcomm* would have a clue as to who the author of CX5809 was. Yet, anyone reading the trial transcript in *FTC v. Qualcomm* would immediately know that the sender of the email was identified as someone named Jeremy Blair.

At 10:15 a.m. on Tuesday, January 8, 2019, the FTC's lawyer, Mika Ikeda, began her direct examination of William Wyatt, Qualcomm's Vice President of Finance, during the FTC's case-in-chief.[1265] Although he was called as a witness by the FTC, Mr. Wyatt was of course adverse to the FTC, and thus his direct examination naturally had the tone of cross examination, and his subsequent cross examination by Qualcomm's lawyer had the tone of direct examination.

Relatively early in the 34 minutes that followed (before the court's morning break at 10:49), Ms. Ikeda asked Mr. Wyatt to turn to tab 5 in the binder before him and examine CX5809:

> Q. Turn to tab 5 in your binder. This is CX 5809. This is an e-mail from Jeremy Blair to Sanjay Mehta copying you and some other Qualcomm employees; correct?
>
> A. I don't see that in my binder.
>
> Q. 5809?
>
> A. I don't see that.
>
> Q. I can give you a copy. May I approach?
>
> The Court: Yes, go ahead, please.
>
> By Ms. Ikeda:
>
> Q. This is an e-mail from you to—excuse me, from Jeremy Blair to Sanjay Mehta copying you?
>
> A. Yes.
>
> Ms. Ikeda: Move to admit CX 5809.
>
> The Court: Any objection?
>
> Mr. Even: No objection.
>
> The Court: It's admitted.[1266]

In its entirety, the FTC's direct examination of Mr. Wyatt on this email and CX5809 consisted of the following colloquy:

> Q. And Mr. Blair attaches a PowerPoint presentation entitled PRC Meeting November 23rd, 2009. Do you see that?
>
> A. I do.
>
> Q. PRC refers to Prying [sic: Pricing] Review Committee; correct?

[1265] Transcript of Proceedings (Volume 3) at 427:4, FTC v. Qualcomm Inc., No. 5:17-cv-00220-LHK (N.D. Cal. Jan. 8, 2019) (Testimony of William Wyatt (Vice President of Finance, Qualcomm)).
[1266] *Id.* at 438:22–439:13.

A. Correct.

Q. Directing your attention to page 41 of CX 5809, this is entitled Strategy Recommendations, first strategy recommendations at the top left, make sure MTK can only go after customers with WCDMA SULA. Do you see that?

A. I do.

Q. And from that recommendation there's an arrow pointing to the right to another text box that says reduce number of MTK's 3G customers to around 50; correct?

A. Yes.

Q. And then the next strategy recommendation after that says formulate and execute a GSM/GPRS strategy to destroy MTK's 2G margin and profit. Do you see that?

A. I do.

Q. And from there—there's an arrow pointing to another text box that says take away the dollar sign, dollar sign that MTK can invest in 3G. Do you see that?

A. Yes, I do.

Q. And dollar sign, dollar sign refers to money?

A. Yes.[1267]

The direct examination of Mr. Wyatt by the FTC's lawyer raised many questions, none of which Judge Koh framed or answered. Yet, these unasked and unanswered questions are all ones that would immediately occur to any experienced appellate judge reviewing Judge Koh's findings of fact and conclusions of law in *FTC v. Qualcomm*.

4. *Who Is or Was Jeremy Blair, and Why Were the FTC and Judge Koh So Incurious About Him?*

Who was Mr. Blair and what was his role at Qualcomm at that time? Was he still employed by Qualcomm at the time of trial in *FTC v. Qualcomm*? If so, in what capacity? If not, when and why did Mr. Blair leave the company?

Did a superior request that the PowerPoint presentation be created, or did Mr. Blair take it upon himself to create it? What was the purpose of this presentation? What decisionmaking authority did he have to implement any of the recommendations contained in CX5809?

[1267] *Id.* at 439:17–440:18.

Mr. Blair evidently sent the email to which the PowerPoint presentation was attached, but that apparent fact certainly did not prove that he wrote the presentation. Did Mr. Blair himself in fact *draft* the PowerPoint presentation that was attached to his email? If so, did he draft it in its entirety? Did he have help? If so, when and from whom? If Mr. Blair did not draft the PowerPoint presentation, then who did?

Ms. Ikeda was obviously using Mr. Wyatt's examination as a way for the FTC to introduce CX5809 into evidence. But by having asked Mr. Wyatt to answer questions about a PowerPoint slide that he did not prepare or distribute, the FTC invites us to ask why the agency then stopped short in its questioning of Mr. Wyatt at trial and became so incurious. Why did the FTC decline to ask any questions of Mr. Wyatt concerning the provenance and subsequent use of CX5809? Did the FTC ever depose Mr. Blair? Why did the FTC not call Mr. Blair to explain under oath at trial the precise meaning of the slide that we are asked to believe that he authored in late November of 2009?

What was the precise relevance of CX5809 to either Qualcomm's allegedly anticompetitive intent or to the allegedly anticompetitive effect of its business practices? Did Qualcomm in fact ultimately adopt any of the proposed "Strategy Recommendations" contained in CX5809? Is there any evidence that Qualcomm's management ever relied on any portion of CX5809 in making any decision?

The FTC did not elicit answers to any of those questions at trial. Nor did Judge Koh.

In fact, Judge Koh did not mention Jeremy Blair's name a single time in her findings of fact and conclusions of law, even though Ms. Ikeda of the FTC mentioned his name three times during her examination of Mr. Wyatt at trial.[1268] Thus an observant reader of Judge Koh's findings of fact and conclusions of law, including a jurist on an appellate court, might be left to wonder: who is or was this Jeremy Blair?

A search of "Jeremy Blair" on LinkedIn produced at least 400 search results. One entry that consistently appeared in the top five search results was that of one Jeremy Blair of the "Greater San Diego Area" whose reported experience included a stint as a Senior Finance Manager at Qualcomm from June 2006 to October 2014.[1269] We obviously cannot conclude from a

---

[1268] *Id.* at 438:22–24 ("Q. Turn to tab 5 in your binder. This is CX 5809. This is an e-mail from Jeremy Blair to Sanjay Mehta copying you and some other Qualcomm employees; correct?"); *id.* at 439:7–9 ("Q. This is an e-mail from you to—excuse me, from Jeremy Blair to Sanjay Mehta copying you? A. Yes."); *id.* at 439:17–19 ("Q. And Mr. Blair attaches a PowerPoint presentation entitled PRC Meeting November 23rd, 2009. Do you see that? A. I do.").

[1269] *Jeremy Blair*, LINKEDIN, https://www.linkedin.com/in/jeremy-blair-526821176/ (last visited Aug. 19, 2020). According to LinkedIn, this Jeremy Blair has, since November 2019, been the Franchise Owner and General Manager of NerdsToGo in San Diego. *Id.*

LinkedIn posting that this person is the same Mr. Blair whom Ms. Ikeda mentioned at trial, but we can use commonsense to formulate questions that an experienced trial lawyer or judge might have asked to remove the uncertainty in a reliable manner. Why did Judge Koh not make any findings that would have definitively answered whether this person was the same Jeremy Blair who emailed the PowerPoint presentation that so intrigued Judge Koh that she took pains to reproduce an expurgated image of page 41 of CX5809 four times in her findings of fact and conclusions of law?

Whoever Mr. Blair is or was, Judge Koh evidently understood him to have offered Qualcomm's management "Strategy Recommendations" for reducing MediaTek's customer base and thereby reducing the amount of money that MediaTek supposedly could invest in 3G. Notably, Judge Koh did not say anywhere in her findings of fact and conclusions of law whether Qualcomm's management *accepted* these "Strategy Recommendations" from Mr. Blair and acted upon them. That omission from Judge Koh's decision of May 21, 2019 was surprising, considering the exceptional number of times that she reproduced the same expurgated version of the slide in her findings of fact and conclusions of law.

5. *Was Judge Koh's Apparent Smoking Gun a Mere Draft?*

Mr. Blair's email is available in the public record.[1270] Two days before Thanksgiving of 2009, Mr. Blair sent the following email at 3:56:48 a.m. on November 24, 2009, with the subject line "11/23/09 Draft PRC Minutes" and an apparent attachment titled "PRC MM 112309 DRAFT.pptx," to Sanjay Mehta, with a copy to Will Wyatt, Sean Zanderson, Marc McCloskey, Peter Rosen, and Carol Blubaugh:

> Sanjay – attached are the draft PRC minutes for your review. Per your request, Pete's Inventec Kayak topic has been moved to offline, so this will need to be closed via email or a brief offline session.
>
> Carol – cc'ing you as well given the short work week and quick turnaround required.
>
> Thanks,
> Jeremy[1271]

Mr. Blair's email indicated in at least three places that the attached PowerPoint presentation was a *draft*. Yet, Ms. Ikeda of the FTC conspicuously did not mention during her examination of Mr. Wyatt concerning CX5809 that the file name for the document included, in all caps, the word "DRAFT." Nor did

---

[1270] Email from Jeremy Blair, *supra* note 1262.
[1271] *Id.* The sender's time zone is not indicated on the email, so I presume that it was Pacific time.

she mention that, although Mr. Blair's email mentioned a "quick turnaround required," the "Importance" designation he gave his email was "Normal."[1272]

Did Mr. Mehta in fact review the attached PowerPoint presentation or that particular slide? Did he approve the draft, or did the final version substantially vary from this draft sent shortly before 4:00 a.m. on November 24, 2009? What roles did Mr. Zanderson, Mr. McCloskey, Mr. Rosen, and Ms. Blubaugh play in reviewing this draft presentation? Who received the PowerPoint presentation after Mr. Mehta possibly reviewed it? Did that person or those persons also review it? Did they give other persons instructions to review the PowerPoint presentation in any way?

If a final version of the PowerPoint presentation existed, why did the FTC not introduce the final version as an exhibit instead of a draft? Did the final draft, if it existed, omit Judge Koh's smoking gun? Might Mr. Blair's mention of a "short turnaround time" and the strange time stamp from the predawn hours of November 24, 2009 have indicated that the specific slide in question had been generated hastily—and without the review and approval of Qualcomm's senior management?

Considering all of these obvious questions left unasked and unanswered concerning this piece of documentary evidence, an observant reader of Judge Koh's findings of fact and conclusions of law might reasonably ask, How probative of an anticompetitive intent was her smoking gun in reality? At zero marginal cost, Judge Koh could have reported the extent to which the FTC, which bore the burden of production and the burden of persuasion on both anticompetitive intent and anticompetitive effect, had presented evidence at trial that would supply answers to these questions. And the fact that this greater evidentiary context would have been costless for Judge Koh to have identified in her findings of fact and conclusions of law is relevant to whether she faithfully discharged her duties under Federal Rule of Civil Procedure 52(a)(1) and the Due Process Clause as construed in *Mathews v. Eldridge*.

6. *The Irrelevance of Judge Koh's Apparent Smoking Gun Under Antitrust Law*

Judge Koh ignored that Qualcomm could have *lawfully* achieved the recommendation on page 41 of CX5809—that is, reducing MediaTek's customer base by aggressively engaging in virtuous competition—simply by offering better products at prices that fell consistently from one year to the next. Qualcomm did in fact compete in that virtuous manner. Qualcomm's offering of lower prices and higher product quality would not only decrease MediaTek's expected sales, but also could reduce MediaTek's optimal level

---

[1272] *Id.*

of investment in 3G technology. A single slide by an unidentified author from a 10-year-old draft of a PowerPoint presentation was hardly enough for Judge Koh to conclude that the FTC had carried its burden of persuasion and shown by a preponderance of the evidence that Qualcomm possessed an "intent to harm competition."[1273]

Judge Koh's reliance on documentary evidence to infer Qualcomm's intent, and her corresponding decision to "largely discount[] Qualcomm's trial testimony prepared specifically for this litigation,"[1274] was reminiscent of Judge Posner's longstanding critique (dating to 1976 at least) of the undue reliance of fact finders on evidence of intent in an antitrust case:

> It is extraordinarily difficult to ascertain the intent of a large corporation by the methods of litigation. What juries (and many judges) do not understand is that the availability of evidence of improper intent is often a function of luck and of the defendant's legal sophistication, not of the underlying reality. A firm with executives sensitized to antitrust problems will not leave any documentary trail of improper intent; one whose executives lack this sensitivity will often create rich evidence of such intent simply by the clumsy choice of words to describe innocent behavior. Especially misleading here is the inveterate tendency of sales executives to brag to their superiors about their competitive prowess, often using metaphors of coercion that are compelling evidence of predatory intent to the naïve. Any doctrine that relies upon proof of intent is going to be applied erratically at best.[1275]

Judge Posner made these remarks specifically in the context of discussing predatory pricing, but his observations plainly have broader relevance to proof of intent in connection with other theories of antitrust liability. In 1989 in *Rose Acre Farms*, Judge Easterbrook formally wove this insight into the antitrust jurisprudence of the Seventh Circuit:

> Almost all evidence bearing on "intent" tends to show both greed-driven desire to succeed and glee at a rival's predicament. Take, for example, the statement David Rust made to Phillip Gressell: "We are going to run you out of the egg business. Your days are numbered." Undoubtedly Rust wanted to leave Gressell scratching in the dust, but drive to succeed lies at the core of a rivalrous economy. Firms need not like their competitors; they need not cheer them on to success: a desire to extinguish one's rivals is entirely consistent with, often is the motive behind, competition. . . .

[1273] FTC v. Qualcomm Inc., 411 F. Supp. 3d 658, 811–12 (N.D. Cal. 2019).

[1274] *Id.* at 680.

[1275] RICHARD A. POSNER, ANTITRUST LAW: AN ECONOMIC PERSPECTIVE 189–90 (Univ. of Chicago Press 1976); *see also* General Leaseways, Inc. v. Nat'l Truck Leasing Ass'n, 744 F.2d 588, 595–96 (7th Cir. 1984) (Posner, J.) ("[I]nternal company documents used to show anticompetitive intent . . . cast only a dim light on what ought to be the central question in an antitrust case: actual or probable anticompetitive effect.").

Intent does not help to separate competition from attempted monopolization and invites juries to penalize hard competition. It also complicates litigation. Lawyers rummage through business records seeking to discover tidbits that will sound impressive (or aggressive) when read to a jury. Traipsing through the warehouses of business in search of misleading evidence both increases the costs of litigation and reduces the accuracy of decisions. Stripping intent away brings the real economic questions to the fore at the same time as it streamlines antitrust litigation.[1276]

Quoting Judge Easterbrook's opinion in *Rose Acre*, Justice Brett Kavanaugh likewise observed in 2008 in his dissent from the D.C. Circuit's decision in *Whole Foods*: "'Intent does not help to separate competition from attempted monopolization.'"[1277]

C. *Was Judge Koh's Use of the Existence of Foreign Government Investigations of Qualcomm to Infer Anticompetitive Intent Under American Antitrust Law Relevant, Reliable, and Proper?*

Near the beginning of her findings of fact and conclusions of law in *FTC v. Qualcomm*, Judge Koh inserted two conspicuous sections sounding what would be recurring themes in her findings of fact and conclusions of law. Both cast Qualcomm and its executives in a pejorative light.

We shall see in Part IX.A that one theme concerned the credibility of the trial testimony of Qualcomm's company witnesses, including its founder, Dr. Irwin Jacobs. Judge Koh presented her criticism in a manner that would have the incidental effect of insulating its derogatory portrayal of these persons from any meaningful appellate review, considering the particularly deferential standard of review that Rule 52(a)(6) provides for credibility findings in bench trials.[1278] This section of Judge Koh's findings of fact and conclusions of law had the rhetorical effect of individually discrediting the named executives of Qualcomm.

Nothing more needs to be said about this first theme at this point other than to contrast it with the second, which was Judge Koh's explanation—in a section captioned, "Government Investigations, Findings, and Fines"—that "Qualcomm's licensing practices have been the subject of government investigations . . . in Asia and Europe since at least 2009."[1279] This second section summarized or quoted "descriptions of various government

---

[1276] A.A. Poultry Farms, Inc. v. Rose Acre Farms, Inc., 881 F.2d 1396, 1402 (7th Cir. 1989) (Easterbrook, J.); *cf.* FTC v. Qualcomm Inc., No. 19-16122, 2020 WL 4591476, at *11 (9th Cir. Aug. 11, 2020) ("'Competitors are not required to engage in a lovefest.'") (quoting Aerotec Int'l, Inc. v. Honeywell Int'l, Inc., 836 F.3d 1171, 1184 (9th Cir. 2016)).

[1277] FTC v. Whole Foods Mkt., Inc., 548 F.3d 1028, 1057 (D.C. Cir. 2008) (Kavanaugh, J., dissenting) (quoting *Rose Acre*, 881 F.2d at 1402).

[1278] FED. R. CIV. P. 52(a)(6); *see also supra* note 986 and accompanying text.

[1279] FTC v. Qualcomm Inc., 411 F. Supp. 3d 658, 676 (N.D. Cal. 2019).

investigations and findings . . . from Qualcomm's 2017 10-K filed with the SEC on November 1, 2017,"[1280] as well as "[p]resentation notes from a slide deck that Boston Consulting Group ('BCG') presented to the Qualcomm Board of Directors in 2015."[1281]

This second section in Judge Koh's findings of fact and conclusions of law had the rhetorical effect of discrediting Qualcomm collectively as a corporation in the global economy. Was the reader to believe that Qualcomm was as deplorable a company as its senior executives supposedly were deplorable human beings?

1. *Did Judge Koh's Recitation of Foreign Investigations Flout* American Express *and Reverse the Presumption of Innocence in an American Courtroom?*

It bears repeating that much of Judge Koh's discussion concerned *investigations*, not adjudicated findings of liability. Only a 2017 decision and fine by the Taiwan Fair Trade Commission (TFTC) appeared by negative implication from Judge Koh's discussion to be a final and unappealable adjudication adverse to Qualcomm by the time she issued her findings of fact and conclusions of law.[1282] One adjudicated finding of liability had been stayed by the Tokyo High Court,[1283] and another was on appeal to the Korea Supreme Court.[1284] One investigation "remained ongoing" before the European Commission,[1285] and another had been settled with the National Development and Reform Commission (NDRC) of the People's Republic of China, resulting in a rectification plan.[1286] Moreover, as we saw in Part I.A.6, Alex Rogers testified in

---

[1280] *Id.* at 675; *see also id.* at 675–76 (citing various pages of CX7257, which is presumably the SEC Form 10-K referenced). Although Judge Koh could have taken judicial notice of Qualcomm's SEC filing, Qualcomm's Form 10-K was moved into evidence by the FTC's lawyer, Ms. Milici. Transcript of Proceedings (Volume 4) at 800:15–801:4, FTC v. Qualcomm Inc., No. 5:17-cv-00220-LHK (N.D. Cal. Jan. 11, 2019).

[1281] *FTC v. Qualcomm*, 411 F. Supp. 3d at 676 (citing CX3755-004). The FTC's lawyer, Mr. Matheson, moved, and Judge Koh admitted, the BCG documents into evidence, despite Qualcomm's hearsay objection to the documents. Transcript of Proceedings (Volume 1) at 94:16–95:6, FTC v. Qualcomm Inc., No. 5:17-cv-00220-LHK (N.D. Cal. Jan. 4, 2019).

[1282] *FTC v. Qualcomm*, 411 F. Supp. 3d at 676 (citing CX7257-099).

[1283] *Id.* at 675 (citing CX7257-097).

[1284] *Id.* (citing CX7257-097 to -098).

[1285] *Id.* (citing CX7257-098). The European Commission announced on January 24, 2018 that it had fined Qualcomm €997,439,000. Commission Decision Relating to Proceedings Under Article 102 of the Treaty on the Functioning of the European Union and Article 54 of the Agreement on the European Economic Area ¶ 598, Case No. AT.40220—Qualcomm (Exclusivity Payments), C (2018) 240 final (Jan. 24, 2018). Nearly 2.5 years later, on June 8, 2020, the European Commission published its full prohibition decision. *Id.*; *see also Antitrust/Cartel Cases – 40220 Qualcomm (Exclusivity Payments)*, EUROPEAN COMMISSION, https://ec.europa.eu/competition/elojade/isef/case_details.cfm?proc_code=1_40220. Qualcomm had promptly announced on January 24, 2018 that it would appeal that fine to the General Court of the European Union. Press Release, Qualcomm Inc., Qualcomm to Appeal European Commission Decision Regarding Modem Chip Agreement (Jan. 24, 2018), https://www.qualcomm.com/news/releases/2018/01/24/qualcomm-appeal-european-commission-decision-regarding-modem-chip-agreement.

[1286] *FTC v. Qualcomm*, 411 F. Supp. 3d at 676 (citing CX7257-027).

detail at trial that the NDRC's investigation and rectification plan had no bearing on Qualcomm's choice to (1) license its cellular SEPs exhaustively only to OEMs and (2) sell modems only to licensed purchasers.[1287] Consequently, the NDRC's investigation into Qualcomm in China, and its resulting rectification plan for Qualcomm, in no way supported the FTC's requested relief in *FTC v. Qualcomm* or Judge Koh's findings of fact and conclusions of law, much less the specific provisions of her permanent, worldwide injunction.

Judge Koh's recitation of these foreign investigations not so subtly reversed the presumption of innocence and burdened Qualcomm, from early in her narrative, with proving a negative: that it was not an inveterate antitrust violator whose culpability in *FTC v. Qualcomm* Judge Koh should be permitted to presume.[1288] For the reasons we saw earlier concerning Judge Koh's flawed execution of the Supreme Court's three-part burden-shifting framework under *American Express*, this portion of Judge Koh's findings of fact and conclusions of law in *FTC v. Qualcomm* denied Qualcomm due process of law.

[1287] *See supra* note 361 and accompanying text.

[1288] In two investigations before the International Trade Commission that went to full evidentiary hearings in 2018, before Judge Koh's trial in *FTC v. Qualcomm*, counsel for Apple and Intel (WilmerHale) argued (by means of what were ostensibly cross-examination questions) that these same foreign antitrust investigations and adjudications of Qualcomm were grounds for the ITC to deny Qualcomm its requested exclusion order under section 337 of the Tariff Act of 1930 for Apple's alleged infringement of certain Qualcomm non-SEPs practiced in the iPhone 7, 8, and X. *See* Open Sessions Hearing Transcript (Revised & Corrected) at 1599:21–1600:13, Certain Mobile Electronic Devices and Radio Frequency and Processing Components Thereof, Inv. No. 337-TA-1065 (USITC July 3, 2018) (Testimony of James Thompson (CTO, Qualcomm)) ("[Mr. Joseph Mueller of WilmerHale:] The Korea Fair Trade Commission found Qualcomm to have engaged in anticompetitive behavior; correct? A[.] I think that's been resolved actually but I—I think that's resolved. Q[.] Sir, the Korea Fair Trade Commission reached a decision that found Qualcomm to have engaged in anticompetitive conduct; correct? A[.] I guess I'm not—I don't know, so yeah, sorry. Q[.] European Commission has concluded that Qualcomm has engaged in anticompetitive conduct; correct? A[.] Yes. Q[.] Taiwanese Fair Trade Commission has concluded that Qualcomm has engaged in anticompetitive conduct? A[.] Yes. Q[.] Japanese Fair Trade Commission has concluded that Qualcomm has engaged in anticompetitive conduct? A[.] I'm not familiar with that."); Open Sessions Hearing Transcript (Revised and Corrected) at 1202:15–1204:4, Certain Mobile Electronic Devices and Radio Frequency and Processing Components Thereof (II), Inv. No. 337-TA-1093 (USITC Sept. 20, 2018) (Testimony of Carla Mulhern, Analysis Group (Qualcomm Expert Witness)) ("[Mr. Joseph Mueller of WilmerHale:] . . . You understand of course that Qualcomm has also been the subject of investigations by other antitrust regulators all around the world? A[.] Yes, I recall that. Q[.] For example, the Korea Fair Trade Commission concluded that Qualcomm had violated Korean antitrust law; right? A[.] I think Mr. Cordell mentioned that in his cross-examination of me in the 1065 [Investigation]. Q[.] And it's true; right? A[.] From the materials he showed me, it appears to be true. Q[.] The Taiwanese Fair Trade Commission concluded that Qualcomm had violated the Taiwanese antitrust law through its business practices; correct? A[.] I generally recall that. Q[.] The European Commission has concluded that Qualcomm violated European competition law through its patent licensing and baseband chipset sales practices; right? A[.] I generally recall that. Q[.] And others, the Japanese Fair Trade Commission, I believe, may be another, that has found over the years Qualcomm to have violated Japanese competition law? A[.] I don't remember that one. Q[.] Okay. But we can agree on this, a number of antitrust regulators all around the world have investigated Qualcomm's business practices and concluded they are anticompetitive? A[.] I think some have made conclusions in that regard. I have not looked into it closely because it's not relevant to my analysis for the reasons I described previously. Q[.] We can agree on two things. Various antitrust agencies have concluded that Qualcomm's business practices are anticompetitive; right? A[.] I think there have been some conclusions in that regard, but I hesitate—as I said, I have not looked into those—the specifics of each much those things [sic], so I don't want to render conclusions without bases here.").

2. *Did the Foreign Investigations Apply the Same Substantive Legal Rules on Monopolization and Afford the Same Due Process of Law That Would Guide an American Court?*

If it was Judge Koh's intention to make *FTC v. Qualcomm* a morality play with Qualcomm as its monster, she managed instead to deliver a farce. Her denigration of the company depended, for example, on giving weight to the actions taken by unidentified bureaucrats in the People's Republic of China whose reasoned decision, if one exists, was nowhere scrutinized by Judge Koh in her findings of fact and conclusions of law and whose motives for investigating Qualcomm in the first place were left to speculation.

A skeptic who cares about the Federal Rules of Evidence might ask: Why would a U.S. federal district judge consider such stuff relevant to the findings of fact and conclusions of law to be made in a bench trial being litigated under American antitrust law in an American courtroom? To constitute relevant evidence under Federal Rule of Evidence 401, these details would need to have a "tendency to make a fact" that "is of consequence in determining the action" "more or less probable than it would be without the evidence."[1289]

How are these details of any consequence to determining a violation of the Sherman Act? Because of the close similarity of China's antitrust law to America's jurisprudence on monopolization? Our common heritage of due process? Issue preclusion with respect to the findings of the foreign enforcer or court? Our shared understanding of the rules of evidence and the economic analysis of law?

Starting several decades ago, America urged every nation with running water, and even some without, to enact antitrust laws.[1290] With varying degrees of enthusiasm and competence they all complied. Having won that battle, America lost the war: the new converts to antitrust soon embraced Europe's far more interventionist "best practices," which enforcers surreptitiously use to pursue industrial policy rather than competitive markets. Foreign antitrust law on the topic of monopolization particularly diverges from American doctrine.

A different judge might have considered it the wiser exercise of discretion not to impute significance, and give such pride of place in his or her opinion,[1291] to the findings of foreign agencies or courts operating in jurisdictions where substantive antitrust law is more invasive, the rules of evidence

---

[1289] *See* FED. R. EVID. 401 ("Evidence is relevant if: (a) it has any tendency to make a fact more or less probable than it would be without the evidence; and (b) the fact is of consequence in determining the action."); *id.* 402 ("Irrelevant evidence is not admissible.").

[1290] These remarks extend Sidak, *The Tempting of American Antitrust Law: An Open Letter to President Trump, supra* note 355, at 202.

[1291] Judge Koh repeatedly mentioned enforcement actions or investigations by the KFTC, FTC v. Qualcomm Inc., 411 F. Supp. 3d 658, 675, 709, 714, 750, 774, 815, 822–23 (N.D. Cal. 2019); by the Japan Fair Trade Commission (JFTC), *id.* at 675, 774; by the Taiwan Fair Trade Commission (TFTC), *id.* at 676; by

less precise, and procedural protections anemic or altogether absent. In an American jury trial, to the extent that foreign enforcement actions would be considered even remotely relevant for purposes of deciding whether Qualcomm had violated the Sherman Act—which of course does *not* recognize excessive pricing or margin squeeze as a cause of action under the Supreme Court's jurisprudence—surely any federal judge would exclude such evidence under Federal Rule of Evidence 403 as inadmissible because its prejudicial effect on the jury would substantially outweigh its probative value (if any).[1292] In a bench trial, we should observe the same result, but for a different reason. Although the finder of fact would certainly be less prone than a jury to the sophistry that Federal Rule of Evidence 403 seeks to prevent, that judge's enhanced role as finder fact would not justify his or her consideration of facts that remained irrelevant under Rule 401 on other grounds, including their capacity to cause unfair prejudice or confusion of the issues.

3.   *Does the FTC Want to Trade Due Process of Law and the American Jurisprudence on Monopolization for the Laws of the Foreign Nations Whose Investigations It Cited Approvingly?*

It seems inescapable as a matter of the federal law of evidence in the United States that Judge Koh's discussion of foreign enforcement actions and judicial decisions was irrelevant to the claims pleaded in the complaint in *FTC v. Qualcomm*. Why then did she accentuate the actions of foreign enforcement agencies in her findings of fact and conclusions of law?

The FTC stated in its closing argument at trial that "the legal standard for imposing equitable relief in this case requires the FTC to show that the anti-competitive conduct is ongoing or likely to recur."[1293] The FTC argued that "[t]he evidence easily meets this standard" because "Qualcomm's conduct has been ongoing despite recent law enforcement *actions* by foreign antitrust agencies that led to billions of dollars in fines."[1294]

Apart from being a *non sequitur* and thus incoherent, this argument was troubling if taken at face value. The FTC asserted that the permanent injunction that a federal district judge chooses to issue following a trial in the United States resulting in the imposition of liability for a violation of the Sherman Act should somehow depend on enforcement "actions"—not even convictions or findings of civil liability—undertaken by foreign governments

---

the European Commission (DG Comp), *id.* at 675, 755, 779; and by the NDRC of the People's Republic of China, *id.* at 673, 676, 714, 719, 774.

[1292]   Fed. R. Evid. 403 ("The court may exclude relevant evidence if its probative value is substantially outweighed by a danger of one or more of the following: unfair prejudice, confusing the issues, misleading the jury, undue delay, wasting time, or needlessly presenting cumulative evidence.").

[1293]   Transcript of Proceedings (Volume 11) at 2134:3–5, FTC v. Qualcomm Inc., No. 5:17-cv-00220-LHK (N.D. Cal. Jan. 29, 2019) (closing argument of Jennifer Milici for the FTC).

[1294]   *Id.* at 2134:6, 2134:8–10 (emphasis added).

operating under different substantive antitrust rules, different rules of civil or criminal procedure, different rules of evidence, and different constitutional protections of liberty and property. The FTC's closing argument was a breathtaking prescription for depriving an American company of due process of law in an American courtroom. A fundamental transformation indeed.

IX. Judge Koh's Disparagement of Qualcomm's Witnesses: Credibility, Reliability, and Unjustified Harm to Reputation

Although Judge Koh did not say whether or not Professor Shapiro's testimony was credible, she did discredit the trial testimony of at least seven then-current and former Qualcomm executives, including its founder, Dr. Irwin Jacobs.[1295]

The sweeping nature of Judge Koh's denunciation of Qualcomm's executives[1296] was reminiscent of Judge Jackson's vilification of Bill Gates in *Microsoft*.[1297] Judge Koh also found not to be credible the testimony of Dirk Weiler, Head of Standards Policy at Nokia, whom Qualcomm called to testify in its defense as a percipient witness as to what ETSI had done through its IPR Policy and in response to proposals to amend its IPR Policy to address the calculation of a FRAND royalty.[1298]

[1295] *FTC v. Qualcomm*, 411 F. Supp. 3d at 676–80. They included Cristiano Amon (President, Qualcomm), Steve Mollenkopf (CEO, Qualcomm), Derek Aberle (former President, Qualcomm), Alex Rogers (President, Qualcomm Technology Licensing), Fabian Gonell (Legal Counsel and Senior Vice President, Licensing Strategy, Qualcomm Technology Licensing), Dr. Irwin Jacobs (Co-Founder, Qualcomm), and Dr. James Thompson (CTO, Qualcomm). For Judge Koh's credibility findings concerning Dr. Jacobs, see *id.* at 680.

[1296] *See id.* at 676 ("The Court finds Qualcomm's internal, contemporaneous documents more persuasive than Qualcomm's trial testimony prepared specifically for this antitrust litigation. Specifically, many Qualcomm executives' trial testimony was contradicted by these witnesses' own contemporaneous emails, handwritten notes, and recorded statements to the Internal Revenue Service ('IRS').") (citation omitted) (citing *In re* High-Tech Employee Antitrust Litig., 289 F.R.D. 555, 576 (N.D. Cal. 2013) (Koh, J.)); *id.* at 677 ("[D]espite [Qualcomm President Cristiano] Amon's own handwriting acknowledging 2015 chip supply threats, Amon testified under oath at his deposition and trial that he was unaware of QTL threats to cutoff [sic] chip supply. Furthermore, Cristiano Amon himself approved joint QTL and QCT plans to cut off chip supply during patent licensing disputes."); *id.* ("Likewise, at trial, Steve Mollenkopf (Qualcomm CEO) testified that he was not aware that Qualcomm had ever cut off an OEM's chip supply. . . . Mollenkopf's testimony also was not consistent with his contemporaneous emails."); *id.* at 679 ("The Court does not find [former Qualcomm President Derek] Aberle's prepared for trial testimony credible."); *id.* ("[QTL President Alex] Rogers' testimony was not consistent with his own emails."); *id.* at 680 ("In addition to giving testimony under oath at trial that contradicted their contemporaneous emails, handwritten notes, and recorded statements to the IRS, some Qualcomm witnesses also lacked credibility in other ways. For example, Dr. Irwin Jacobs (Qualcomm Co-Founder), Steve Mollenkopf (Qualcomm CEO), and Dr. James Thompson (Qualcomm CTO) gave such long, fast, and practiced narratives on direct examination that Qualcomm's counsel had to tell the witnesses to slow down. . . . By contrast, when cross-examined by the FTC, each witness was very reluctant and slow to answer, and at times cagey.").

[1297] United States v. Microsoft Corp., 253 F.3d 34, 109–10 (D.C. Cir. 2001) (en banc) (per curiam).

[1298] *FTC v. Qualcomm*, 411 F. Supp. 3d at 756 ("The Court finds that Weiler was not credible.").

Table 7 reports, by order of appearance, the 27 witnesses who testified in person at trial, and the credibility or reliability determinations (if any) that Judge Koh made in regard to each witness.

Table 7. Witnesses Who Testified in Person at the Bench Trial
in *FTC v. Qualcomm* (by Order of Appearance)

Sponsoring Party	Name	Professional Affiliation	Direct Examiner	Cross Examiner	Judge Koh's Credibility or Reliability Determination
FTC	David Wise	Senior Vice President, Qualcomm	Daniel Matheson, FTC	Justina Sessions, Keker	None
FTC	Steven Altman	Former President, Qualcomm	Daniel Matheson, FTC	Gary Bornstein, Cravath	None
FTC	Derek Aberle	Former President, QTL and Qualcomm	Jennifer Milici, FTC	Gary Bornstein, Cravath	Not credible
FTC	John Moynihan	General Manager, MediaTek	Philip Kehl, FTC	Matan Shacham, Keker	None
FTC	William Wyatt	Vice President of Finance, Qualcomm	Mika Ikeda, FTC	Yonatan Even, Cravath	None
FTC	Cristiano Amon	President, Qualcomm	Daniel Matheson, FTC	Justina Sessions, Keker	Testimony "not consistent with his contemporaneous emails and handwritten notes"
FTC	Aichatou Evans	Senior Vice President and Chief Strategy Officer, Intel	Wesley Carson, FTC	Antony Ryan, Cravath	Credible
FTC	Tony Blevins	Vice President of Procurement, Apple	Joseph Baker, FTC	Justina Sessions, Keker	None
FTC	Steve Mollenkopf	CEO, Qualcomm	Jennifer Milici, FTC	Robert Van Nest, Keker	Not credible
FTC	Jeff Williams	COO, Apple	Joseph Baker, FTC	Eugene Paige, Keker	None

Sponsoring Party	Name	Professional Affiliation	Direct Examiner	Cross Examiner	Judge Koh's Credibility or Reliability Determination
FTC	Richard Donaldson	Former Senior Vice President and General Patent Counsel, Texas Instruments	Elizabeth Gillen, FTC	Eugene Paige, Keker	Reliable
FTC	Michael Lasinski	CEO and Managing Director, 284 Partners	Aaron Ross, FTC	Gary Bornstein, Cravath	Not reliable
FTC	Carl Shapiro	Professor, University of California at Berkeley	Rajesh James, FTC	Robert Van Nest, Keker	None
Qualcomm	Irwin Jacobs	Founder, Former Chairman and CEO, Qualcomm	Robert Van Nest, Keker	Daniel Matheson, FTC	Not credible; testimony "inapposite"
Qualcomm	Durga Malladi	Senior Vice President and General Manager of 4G and 5G, Qualcomm	Justina Sessions, Keker	Nathaniel Hopkin, FTC	Testimony "inapposite"
Qualcomm	James Thompson	Executive Vice President of Engineering and CTO, Qualcomm	Eugene Paige, Keker	Philip Kehl, FTC	Not credible
Qualcomm	Fabian Gonell	Senior Vice President of Licensing Strategy and Legal Counsel, QTL	Gary Bornstein, Cravath	Kenneth Merber, FTC	Not credible
Qualcomm	Matthias Sauer	Director of Cellular Systems Architecture, Apple	Eugene Paige, Keker	Wesley Carson, FTC	None
Qualcomm	Liren Chen	Senior Vice President of Engineering and Legal Counsel, QTL	Richard Zembek, Norton Rose	None	Testimony "inapposite"

Sponsoring Party	Name	Professional Affiliation	Direct Examiner	Cross Examiner	Judge Koh's Credibility or Reliability Determination
Qualcomm	Jeffrey Andrews	Professor, University of Texas at Austin	Eric Hall, Norton Rose	Alexander Ansaldo, FTC	Testimony "inapposite"
Qualcomm	Lorenzo Casaccia	Vice President of Technical Standards, Qualcomm	Marc Collier, Norton Rose	Kenneth Merber, FTC	None
Qualcomm	Dirk Weiler	Head of Standards Policy, Nokia	Richard Taffet, Morgan Lewis	Elizabeth Gillen, FTC	Not credible
Qualcomm	Tasneem Chipty	Founder, Managing Principal, Matrix Economics	Yonatan Even, Cravath	Daniel Matheson, FTC	Not reliable
Qualcomm	Edward Snyder	Dean and Professor, Yale School of Management	Matan Shacham, Keker	Mika Ikeda, FTC	Not reliable
Qualcomm	Christopher Johnson	Partner, Bain & Company	Jordan Peterson, Cravath	Nathaniel Hopkin, FTC	None
Qualcomm	Aviv Nevo	Professor, University of Pennsylvania	Gary Bornstein, Cravath	Jennifer Milici, FTC	Not reliable
Qualcomm	Alex Rogers	President, QTL	Robert Van Nest, Keker	Daniel Matheson, FTC	Testimony "not consistent with his own emails"

Of the 27 testifying witnesses, Judge Koh found six witnesses not to be credible and seven witnesses not to be reliable. All of the witnesses found not credible (with the exception of one Nokia executive, Mr. Weiler) were current or former Qualcomm executives. They were Mr. Aberle, Mr. Mollenkopf, Dr. Jacobs, Dr. Thompson, Mr. Gonell, and Mr. Weiler. All of the witnesses found not reliable (with the exception of Mr. Lasinski) were Qualcomm executives or expert witnesses. They were Mr. Amon, Mr. Lasinski, Dr. Malladi, Professor Andrews, Dr. Chipty, Professor Snyder, and Professor Nevo. In addition, Judge Koh specifically stated in her findings of fact and conclusions of law that the testimony concerning Qualcomm's patent portfolio given by Dr. Chen (a Qualcomm executive), Dr. Jacobs, Dr. Malladi (a Qualcomm executive), and Professor Andrews (a Qualcomm expert witness) was "inapposite."[1299] She also found Mr. Rogers' testimony to be "not consistent with his own emails."[1300] In contrast to these adverse findings, Judge Koh specifically found that Ms. Evans (of Intel) was "credible"[1301] and that Mr. Donaldson (an expert witness who testified on behalf of the FTC) was "reliable."[1302]

By my count, of the friendly witnesses that Qualcomm called in its defense, only one—Lorenzo Casaccia—escaped being denigrated by Judge Koh as "not credible" or "not reliable" or "inapposite," or as having given live testimony at trial that was "not consistent" with his past emails. Of the FTC's friendly witnesses called to testify in support of its case-in-chief, only Mr. Lasinski was adversely weighed (as not reliable) by Judge Koh. Professor Shapiro of course was not mentioned at all.

At trial, the parties also replayed by video the deposition designations of 22 other witnesses, whose identities and professional affiliations Table 8 reports. Judge Koh did not appear to make specific credibility or reliability determinations about the witnesses who appeared by videotaped deposition, with one notable exception.

Judge Koh specifically found that "Ericsson's contemporaneous documents and statements contradict[ed] . . . Ericsson's self-serving and made-for-litigation justifications for refusing to license modem chip suppliers."[1303] Yet, she did not then substantiate in that section of her findings of fact and conclusions of law her laconic condemnation of Ericsson and, by implication, Christina Petersson, Ericsson's witness who testified by videotaped deposition. (Ms. Petersson subsequently became Ericsson's Chief Intellectual Property Officer in April 2019.[1304]) Instead, Judge Koh identified statements made by Nokia and its witness Dirk Weiler that induced her to call Mr. Weiler "not credible."

Nokia and Ericsson, of course, are not the same firm. Nevertheless, both companies were by 2019 expected to figure prominently in the "car wars," a worldwide controversy regarding the licensing of standardized mobile communication technology in the telematics applications in smart vehicles. Was it reckless for Judge Koh to imply that Ms. Petersson was not credible, and thereby to impugn her reputation, knowing that Ms. Petersson was actively involved in FRAND litigation of this sort and would likely be appearing again as a witness? Does an unexplained credibility determination

---

[1299] *Id.* at 779–80.
[1300] *Id.* at 679.
[1301] *Id.* at 733.
[1302] *Id.* at 788.
[1303] *Id.* at 755.
[1304] Christina Schulze, *Ericsson Announces Christina Petersson as CIPO*, JUVE PATENT (Apr. 2, 2019), https://www.juve-patent.com/news-and-stories/people-and-business/ericsson-announces-christina-petersson-as-cipo/.

by innuendo satisfy a trial judge's duty as finder of fact in a bench trial, pursuant to Federal Rule of Civil Procedure 52(a)(1)?

Table 8. Witnesses Who Appeared by Videotaped Deposition
in *FTC v. Qualcomm* (by Order of First Appearance)

Called By	Name	Professional Affiliation
FTC & Qualcomm	Eric Reifschneider	QTL
FTC & Qualcomm	Ira Blumberg	Lenovo
FTC	Paul Jacobs	Qualcomm
FTC & Qualcomm	Nanfen Yu	Huawei
FTC & Qualcomm	John Grubbs	BlackBerry
FTC	Scott McGregor	Broadcom
FTC	Andrew Hong	Samsung
FTC	Mark Davis	Intel
FTC & Qualcomm	Injung Lee	Samsung
FTC & Qualcomm	Todd Madderom	Motorola
FTC	Hwi-Jae Cho	LG Electronics
FTC & Qualcomm	Christina Petersson	Ericsson
FTC	Brian Chong	Wistron
FTC	Monica Yang	Pegatron
FTC & Qualcomm	Marvin Blecker	Qualcomm
Qualcomm	Martin Zander	Ericsson
Qualcomm	Stefan Wolff	Intel
Qualcomm	Thomas Lindner	Intel
Qualcomm	Ranae McElvaine	InterDigital
Qualcomm	Ilkka Rahnasto	Nokia
Qualcomm	Seungho Ahn	Samsung
Qualcomm	Yooseok Kim	Samsung

Credibility findings of course offer the trial judge an expedient and effectively unreviewable means to shut down legitimate lines of evidence and to paint disfavored arguments of law or fact not merely as being contrary to the weight of the evidence, but as lacking the character for truthfulness.[1305] Why scrutinize the intellectual merits of the message when one can simply shoot the messenger? Knowing that appellate courts review credibility find-ings with great deference, do some judges endogenously change the nature of their decision making and characterize findings of fact as relating to the credibility of a witness as opposed to the weight of the evidence?

Although a judge has broad discretion in weighing evidence, at least some of Judge Koh's credibility findings and reliability findings conflicted with substantial evidence in the record. One could question whether some of Judge Koh's published statements about Qualcomm's witnesses would be defamatory if written by someone not cloaked in a judge's privileges and immunities. Even though the Ninth Circuit reversed Judge Koh's judgment, that reversal did not erase Judge Koh's acts of disparagement.

A. *Judge Koh's Disparagement of Qualcomm's Founder, Dr. Irwin Jacobs*

Judge Koh accepted at face value the fact testimony of self-interested rivals and customers of Qualcomm while discrediting the fact testimony of most of Qualcomm's witnesses. Of particular note, Judge Koh "largely discount[ed]" the trial testimony given by the co-founder of Qualcomm, Dr. Irwin Jacobs, because, she found, his testimony was "prepared specifically for this litigation"[1306] and was "at times cagey."[1307] Her rationale for making those deci-sions was unconvincing.

As we have seen, Judge Koh found that Dr. Jacobs, who was 85 years old at the time of his trial testimony in *FTC v. Qualcomm*,[1308] was among the Qualcomm witnesses who gave "long, fast, and practiced narratives on direct examination" and "that Qualcomm's counsel had to tell the witness[] to slow down,"[1309] and, "[b]y contrast, when cross-examined by the FTC, . . . was very reluctant and slow to answer, and at times cagey."[1310] This belittling assess-ment of Dr. Jacobs' trial testimony was surprising to hear from an experi-enced trial judge.

[1305] *See* Fed. R. Evid. 608(a).

[1306] *FTC v. Qualcomm*, 411 F. Supp. 3d at 680.

[1307] *Id.* This statement by Judge Koh evidently pertained to a number of Qualcomm witnesses, but it immediately followed her specific criticism of Dr. Jacobs' testimony.

[1308] *See Irwin M. Jacobs*, Wikipedia, https://en.wikipedia.org/wiki/Irwin_M._Jacobs.

[1309] *FTC v. Qualcomm*, 411 F. Supp. 3d at 680 (citing Transcript of Proceedings (Volume 6) at 1259:25–1260:2, FTC v. Qualcomm Inc., No. 5:17-cv-00220-LHK (N.D. Cal. Jan. 15, 2019) (Testimony of Irwin Jacobs (Co-Founder, Qualcomm))).

[1310] *Id.*

1. Did Dr. Jacobs' Rapid Answers to Direct-Examination Questions Believably Support Judge Koh's Disparagement of His Character for Truthfulness?

Judge Koh's impression of the passage in Dr. Jacobs' direct examination at which counsel for Qualcomm asked him to slow down might not square with the impression that others draw from reading the trial transcript. Dr. Jacobs was being questioned about events 30 years in the past, when Qualcomm was struggling to gain industry acceptance for its pathbreaking CDMA technology, which Dr. Jacobs had invented with his colleagues:

> Q [by Mr. Robert Van Nest, Counsel for Qualcomm]. What were the main problems that you had to overcome in making CDMA effective for cellular communications?
>
> A [Dr. Irwin Jacobs]. Well, there were a lot that people had identified and had tried to find solutions. One of the key ones was called power control. Again, if you're speaking to somebody and you're yelling too loud, that would reduce the capability to hear other conversations. It would reduce the capacity. And so you had to adjust it so you're just getting enough power at your receiver to reliably hear that, to reliably receive the digital data, but not so much that you're drowning out others. So the problem is as you drive, you may become inside of a particular base station, move away from it, so signals go up and down fairly rapidly. The question is, how do you control that? We came up with a very powerful approach for doing power control. Another issue with radio signals is they bounce off many buildings, many other areas, you don't get just one copy, you get multiple copies. That reduces the capacity in general. But with CDMA, it has an ability to live with those additional reflections and, in fact, we came up with a scheme where you could receive each one separately and combine them together to get a better result. So that was another major step ahead. Another was how do you do handoffs as you're moving from cell site to cell site, you have to hand off your signal. The more traditional approaches, the TDMA, you drop one base station and look for the next one and connect to it and there's a little bit of a gap and you could have a drop. With CDMA, you could listen to the next one while you were listening to the first one and then gradually transfer more and more attention to the second one. So it was not—it's a soft handoff. And as part of that, in the—again, TDMA so that you would keep down the interference, you couldn't use the same frequencies on neighboring base stations or even on multiple antennas on the same base stations. So you had to divide up the frequency spectrum. You didn't have for any given user the full spectrum, therefore, so that reduced capacity. With CDMA, you could use the same frequencies everywhere.
>
> Q. Once Qualcomm floated this idea of using CDMA, was it welcomed by the industry overall?

A. I don't think I'd put it that way, no.

(Laughter.)

The Witness: There was a lot of negative feelings about—some people had worked on it and had problems, so they didn't believe we had solutions. But the industry, in January of 19—I'll have to keep careful on my years here—in January of 1989 had actually a vote whether to go with either TDMA or FDMA, and it was a very big battle up to that point. TDMA won by a narrow edge. People were tired of fighting about technologies, so people had said, okay, we're going ahead with TDMA.

By Mr. Van Nest:
Q. Did you give up?

A. We, ourselves, had just begun to look at CDMA again. We had to tell [sic] our Omni Tracks [OmniTRACS], the truck communication product first, so we had only started looking at it again in about November of '88. So we didn't go to the industry until '89, and nobody wanted to hear about something new. Our approach then was we had to build a demonstration to show that we had solved the problems, and that you could get both better quality, as well as many more users in the same amount of radio spectrum. So we proceeded to do that.

Q. I'm going to ask you, Dr. Jacobs, to slow down just a little bit. We're trying to take down every word, and I want to be sure we do that.

A. I'm afraid my New England accent doesn't help.

Q. No, you're coming through fine.[1311]

It is reasonable—indeed, it should be easy—for any reader of this transcript, including a judge sitting on an appellate court, to imagine Dr. Jacobs' becoming particularly animated, his speech accelerating as he, now an octogenarian, is being asked to recount the signal accomplishment of his long and distinguished career. Such a demeanor on the witness stand would of course not justify Judge Koh's impugning Dr. Jacobs' character for truthfulness.

Nor can one take seriously Judge Koh's proposition that Dr. Jacobs needed a "practiced narrative" to explain in court the rivalry between CDMA and TDMA technologies for mobile communications circa 1989. On the basis of the trial transcript, Dr. Jacobs' direct testimony reads as being substantially less rehearsed than the direct testimony of the FTC's witnesses. After all, witnesses routinely bring demonstratives, which make their direct testimony quintessentially "practiced." Nowhere in her findings of fact and conclusions of law did Judge Koh disparage any FTC witness (including the unmentioned Professor Shapiro) because he or she came to the stand

---

[1311] Transcript of Proceedings (Volume 6) at 1257:8–1260:4, FTC v. Qualcomm Inc., No. 5:17-cv-00220-LHK (N.D. Cal. Jan. 15, 2019) (Testimony of Irwin Jacobs (Co-Founder, Qualcomm)).

equipped with a PowerPoint presentation to use during direct examination (as Professor Shapiro evidently did with his demonstratives).

But more fundamentally, why would Judge Koh even consider a "practiced narrative" on direct examination to be evidence of a lack of credibility? *Any* well-prepared witness in a case as complex as *FTC v. Qualcomm* is made to understand that the lawyer who will conduct the witness's direct examination will be working within a strict time constraint. Direct examination is not a talk show. Nothing about the procedure of taking direct-examination testimony at trial is intended to promote chatty spontaneity.

If Judge Koh had found in her experience that bench trials produce direct-examination testimony that seems rehearsed, she could have done in *FTC v. Qualcomm* what her fellow judges on the Northern District of California have done in other bench trials: instruct the parties to submit prefiled direct-examination testimony, typically in question-and-answer form.[1312] This procedure is of course routinely used before administrative agencies, regulatory commissions, and Article I courts. The Ninth Circuit has permitted this procedure in bankruptcy court since at least 1992.[1313] The procedure is also routinely used in commercial arbitration.[1314] After being sworn in, the witness adopts the prefiled written testimony, which is then moved into evidence. The witness is then passed for oral cross examination. Oral redirect examination follows. Considering that Judge Koh chose not to avail herself of this procedure already being used by other Northern District judges, she could hardly complain with good grace in *FTC v. Qualcomm* that Dr. Jacobs' "practiced narrative" on direct examination was evidence that he lacked credibility.

2. *Did Dr. Jacobs' Slowness to Answer Cross-Examination Questions Believably Support Judge Koh's Disparagement of His Character for Truthfulness?*

Judge Koh's criticism of Dr. Jacobs' cross examination rings hollow. Testifying in open court is a stressful experience for any witness. It would be unnatural for any witness *not* to respond to cross-examination questions with greater caution than direct-examination questions. Nowhere in her findings of fact and conclusions of law did Judge Koh disparage any FTC witness on the

---

[1312] *See* QUINN EMANUEL URQUHART & SULLIVAN, MAY 2019: TRIAL PRACTICE UPDATE (2019) ("Judges Illston, Orrick, and White in the Northern District of California have guidelines allowing for the use of witness statements presenting direct testimony in bench trials. . . . Over half of the forty-one judges in the District Court for the Southern District of New York (21 of 41) in fact *require* the use of direct witness statements in bench trials unless otherwise ordered.") (emphasis in original).

[1313] *See, e.g., In re* Adair, 965 F.2d 777, 779 (9ᵗʰ Cir. 1992) (per curiam).

[1314] *See* 2 GARY B. BORN, INTERNATIONAL COMMERCIAL ARBITRATION 2284 (Wolters Kluwer 2ᵈ ed. 2014) ("[P]arties will frequently submit written witness statements, often attached to their written submissions, setting forth the direct testimony of the witnesses on whom they rely.") (footnote omitted).

grounds that he or she was "very reluctant and slow to answer" or "at times cagey" during cross examination, despite the fact that the trial transcript contains multiple examples of Qualcomm's counsel struggling with an FTC witness on cross examination.[1315]

Judge Koh did not cite any specific instance in Dr. Jacobs' cross examination that epitomized her highly specific criticism that his testimony was "cagey." Nothing evident in the transcript of Dr. Jacobs' cross examination suggested that his answers were less than forthright.

That an 85-year-old witness was "very reluctant and slow to answer" cross-examination questions intended to paint the company that he had founded as an unlawful monopolist might have struck a different judge as unremarkable. At the beginning of his direct examination, Dr. Jacobs had summarized in one sentence what he called "a very satisfactory career" at Qualcomm: "I was one of the eight founders of the company, very instrumental in being able to select which projects we worked on over the years, had great excitement in growing the company from something small to something very substantial, and in particular, coming up with some initial ideas that became very useful to people worldwide."[1316]

3.   *The Character for Truthfulness and "the Spirit of Innovation"*

The Federal Rules of Evidence define "credibility" as "the witness's reputation for having a character for truthfulness[.]"[1317] A more contemplative judge might have paused to consider the following words of Nobel laureate Edmund Phelps, for in disparaging Dr. Jacobs' character for truthfulness,

---

[1315] *See, e.g.*, Transcript of Proceedings (Volume 3) at 594:21–595:1, 596:9–25, 602:10–22, FTC v. Qualcomm Inc., No. 5:17-cv-00220-LHK (N.D. Cal. Jan. 8, 2019) (Testimony of Aichatou Evans (Chief Strategy Officer, Intel)); Transcript of Proceedings (Volume 5) at 1058:15–1059:23, 1064:20–1065:4, 1078:1–18, FTC v. Qualcomm Inc., No. 5:17-cv-00220-LHK (N.D. Cal. Jan. 14, 2019) (Testimony of Michael Lasinski). Mr. Van Nest's blunt remarks during his closing argument for Qualcomm indicate that his cross-examination of Professor Shapiro was at times contentious:

> They're trying to prove this tax theory, and that's why this is important, what we talked about with Professor Shapiro. They're saying that there was a supra-FRAND tax that he predicts would raise rivals' cost—those are chip makers—he predicts would reduce rivals' income, he predicts would reduce rivals' spending in R&D, he predicts would cause harm. The problem for him is that the time for theories and predictions is pretrial, not trial. You have to prove it. You have to have evidence. He admitted not looking at any one of these factors, Your Honor, for any participant in this market. . . . My point on Professor Shapiro is you don't get past the burden by just telling me what your theory is, and *he repeatedly treated us like idiots* because we [sic] couldn't understand that.

Transcript of Proceedings (Volume 11) at 2155:3–13, 2155:23–2156:1, FTC v. Qualcomm Inc., No. 5:17-cv-00220-LHK (N.D. Cal. Jan. 29, 2019) (closing argument of Robert Van Nest for Qualcomm) (emphasis added).

[1316] Transcript of Proceedings (Volume 6) at 1252:9–15, FTC v. Qualcomm Inc., No. 5:17-cv-00220-LHK (N.D. Cal. Jan. 15, 2019) (Testimony of Irwin Jacobs (Co-Founder, Qualcomm)).

[1317] FED. R. EVID. 608(a).

Judge Koh also impugned countless others who are driven by what Phelps calls "the spirit of innovation":

> Economics has not done enough to define its own premises. A small part of the economics literature addresses the role of entrepreneurs, the risk-takers who, in attempting innovations, choose to face true uncertainty, with the result that outcomes can't be predicted. But it is not only a small group of entrepreneurs who want to take risks and try new things. Adventure and discovery appeal to people in every walk of life.
>
> This consideration allows us to assert the *morality of the marketplace* itself, as opposed to requiring morality *in* the marketplace. Capitalism is the only economic system thus far discovered that allows human beings to realize their nature to innovate, discover, and take risks. Because human freedom is a good thing, capitalism is in this respect a good system. It is good apart from its instrumental function of presenting opportunities for income and consumption.[1318]

Qualcomm was not founded in a freshman house on Harvard Yard. Dr. Jacobs earned his doctorate in 1959 from the Massachusetts Institute of Technology, where he became an assistant professor (and later an associate professor) of electrical engineering.[1319] In 1965, he co-authored *Principles of Communication Engineering*,[1320] the first textbook on digital communications. Dr. Jacobs went on to become professor of computer science and engineering at the University of California, San Diego (UCSD).[1321] He developed CDMA technology and deployed it worldwide through Qualcomm, which he co-founded in 1985.[1322] Dr. Jacobs has received many honors and prizes, including the Marconi Prize.[1323] And he has donated hundreds of millions of dollars to philanthropic endeavors, including gifts to build the Jacobs School of Engineering at UCSD and the Jacobs Medical Center at UCSD.[1324]

A different judge, one perhaps possessing different attitudes toward entrepreneurship and risk taking, might have concluded that the fact that the FTC was seeking to dismantle the business model that Qualcomm had

---

[1318] Edmund Phelps, *Economic Justice and the Spirit of Innovation*, First Things, Oct. 2009 (emphasis in original). Phelps' subsequent book amplifies the themes of his 2009 essay. *See* Edmund Phelps, Mass Flourishing: How Grassroots Innovation Created Jobs, Challenge, and Change (Princeton Univ. Press 2013).

[1319] *See, e.g.*, Alan S. Brown, *Profiles in Leadership #10: Irwin Jacobs: Engineer, Entrepreneur, and Philanthropist*, Bent of Tau Beta Pi, Spring 2017, at 20, 21, https://www.tbp.org/pubs/Features/Sp17Brown.pdf.

[1320] John M. Wozencraft & Irwin Mark Jacobs, Principles of Communication Engineering (John Wiley & Sons 1965).

[1321] Brown, *Profiles in Leadership #10: Irwin Jacobs: Engineer, Entrepreneur, and Philanthropist, supra* note 1319, at 21.

[1322] *Id.* Qualcomm was actually the second successful technology firm that Dr. Jacobs founded. *See* Dave Mock, The Qualcomm Equation: How a Fledgling Telecom Company Forged a New Path to Big Profits and Market Dominance 21–25 (AMACOM 2005).

[1323] *See Irwin Mark Jacobs*, Marconi Society, http://marconisociety.org/fellows/irwin-mark-jacobs/.

[1324] Diane Bell, *A Commitment to Sharing Wealth*, San Diego Union-Tribune, Aug. 14, 2010.

successfully constructed and refined over the course of 34 years could reasonably explain why Dr. Jacobs might have appeared particularly cautious under cross examination. For Dr. Jacobs, who epitomized Phelps' "spirit of innovation," a life well-lived was on trial; but for Judge Koh, Irwin Jacobs was evidently just another person in her courtroom she did not trust to tell the truth.

B. *Judge Koh's Reliability Findings Concerning Qualcomm's Expert Economic Witnesses*

Judge Koh found all three of Qualcomm's expert economic witnesses—Professor Aviv Nevo, Dr. Tasneem Chipty, and Professor Edward Snyder—to be unreliable. In each case, Judge Koh's credibility finding was implausible and capricious.

1. *Professor Aviv Nevo*

Professor Nevo is the George A. Weiss and Lydia Bravo Weiss University Professor at the University of Pennsylvania, the highest professorial rank that exists at Penn. He is the co-editor of *Econometrica*, the world's foremost academic journal on empirical methods in economics. Professor Nevo served as Deputy Assistant Attorney General for Economic Analysis (chief economist) at the Antitrust Division during the Obama administration. He received his Ph.D. from Harvard University.[1325]

We have already seen the immense evidentiary significance of Professor Nevo's testimony rebutting Professor Shapiro's theory of a royalty "surcharge" and a modem "tax." Let us focus here narrowly on Judge Koh's stated reason for her finding that Professor Nevo's testimony was "not reliable."[1326] She reasoned that Professor Nevo "ignored Qualcomm's anticompetitive practices" and "made no claim about how Qualcomm's practices might have affected the industry."[1327] That rationale for Judge Koh's evidentiary ruling conflicted with the trial transcript.

Professor Nevo testified during his direct examination by Mr. Bornstein on January 25, 2019 during Qualcomm's defense case that one of the three parts of his assignment was "to evaluate the FTC's claim that Qualcomm's alleged supra-FRAND rates acts [sic] as a tax that harms competition."[1328] Professor Nevo expressly addressed the supposedly "anticompetitive effects"

[1325] *See Aviv Nevo*, PENN ECON., https://economics.sas.upenn.edu/people/aviv-nevo. My search of the docket did not produce any public version of Professor Nevo's expert report(s).

[1326] FTC v. Qualcomm Inc., 411 F. Supp. 3d 658, 805 (N.D. Cal. 2019).

[1327] *Id.*

[1328] Transcript of Proceedings (Volume 9) at 1863:22–24, FTC v. Qualcomm Inc., No. 5:17-cv-00220-LHK (N.D. Cal. Jan. 25, 2019) (Testimony of Aviv Nevo).

of Qualcomm's allegedly "anticompetitive behavior" during his direct examination. With respect to the FTC's modem "tax" theory of liability, he testified:

> Q. And you were looking at *anticompetitive effects* where?
>
> A. So the *anticompetitive behavior* I was looking for is where they alleged, which is in the chip market. So I was looking at the competition of the *anticompetitive behavior* in the chip market.[1329]

A few questions later, Professor Nevo gave Mr. Bornstein a detailed answer when asked, "What's your starting point for how a royalty would affect competition among chip suppliers?"[1330] Still addressing the FTC's modem "tax" theory, Professor Nevo testified several pages later, "If we want to see or want to study the anticompetitive effect, we have to have a model of competition, which [Professor Shapiro] really did not do."[1331]

Professor Nevo uttered the word "competition" or "competitive" or "anticompetitive" *17* times in his trial testimony.[1332] In light of the evidence in the trial transcript, it is puzzling how Judge Koh possibly could have found that Professor Nevo's refutation of the FTC's royalty "surcharge" and modem "tax" theory ignored "how Qualcomm's practices might have affected the industry."[1333] .

2. *Dr. Tasneem Chipty*

Dr. Tasneem Chipty was the Founder and Managing Principal of Matrix Economics, a boutique consulting firm focused on competition analysis for adversarial proceedings, including antitrust litigation and merger reviews. She received her Ph.D. in economics from MIT and has taught at Ohio State, Brandeis, and MIT.[1334]

[1329] *Id.* at 1889:19–23 (emphasis added).

[1330] *Id.* at 1890:14–15.

[1331] *Id.* at 1893:6–8; *see also id.* at 1896:4–6 ("[I]f we want to have a model explaining an antitrust or anti-competitive effect, we have to have a model of competition.").

[1332] In his trial testimony, Professor Nevo mentioned "competition" eight times. *Id.* at 1863:24, 1889:22, 1890:16, 1893:6, 1893:7, 1895:23, 1896:9, 1896:12. He used the word "competitive" once. *Id.* at 1900:19. He used the word "anticompetitive" eight times. *Id.* at 1889:18, 1889:20, 1889:22, 1893:7, 1896:5, 1896:12, 1897:8, 1914:6.

[1333] FTC v. Qualcomm Inc., 411 F. Supp. 3d 658, 805 (N.D. Cal. 2019).

[1334] *See Curriculum Vitae of Tasneem Chipty*, MATRIX ECON., https://matrixeconomics.com/wp-content/uploads/2020/02/Chipty-CV-Jan-2020.pdf. My search of the docket has not produced any public version of Dr. Chipty's expert report(s). Matrix Economics was acquired by AlixPartners on June 1, 2020. *See* Press Release, AlixPartners, AlixPartners Bolsters Global Economics Consulting Capability with the Acquisition of Leading Independent Boutique Matrix Economics (June 1, 2020), https://www.alixpartners.com/media-center/press-releases/acquisition-of-leading-independent-economics-consulting-boutique-matrix-economics/.

Judge Koh found that Dr. Chipty "acknowledged that her analysis ignored Qualcomm's anticompetitive practices."[1335] Judge Koh gave as examples that "Dr. Chipty conceded that she conducted no analysis of how Qualcomm's refusal to license rivals, refusal to sell modem chips exhaustively, requirement that an OEM sign a license before purchasing modem chips, and threats to cut off chip supply and other support affected modem chip markets."[1336]

Judge Koh's criticisms of Dr. Chipty's testimony were contrived and orthogonal, because her assignment was to address *other* issues in *FTC v. Qualcomm*. On direct examination by Yonatan Even of Cravath, Swaine & Moore during Qualcomm's defense case on January 22, 2019, Dr. Chipty testified:

> Q. Dr. Chipty, . . . what was your assignment in this case?
>
> A. Well, I was asked to evaluate and respond to Professor Shapiro's analyses and opinions with respect to market definition, market power, and the Apple agreements. With respect to the Apple agreements, I evaluated whether they had legitimate business justifications and whether, in fact, *they resulted in harm to competition in his asserted markets.*[1337]

In other words, in apparent contradiction of Judge Koh's representation in her findings of fact and conclusions of law, Dr. Chipty *did* address one alleged source of harm to competition (among rival modem manufacturers) in the relevant product markets that Professor Shapiro (and Judge Koh) had defined for CDMA modems and "premium" LTE modems. Judge Koh's findings to the contrary were mistaken.

The larger fallacy of Judge Koh's reliability finding is that it was of course hardly fair for Judge Koh to impugn the reliability of Dr. Chipty's testimony on the grounds that she did not address certain other economic questions that counsel for Qualcomm had assigned either Professor Nevo or Professor Snyder to address. Qualcomm was entitled to divide its expert economic testimony among three different witnesses. Yet, in a *non sequitur*, Judge Koh ruled that, "because Dr. Chipty failed to consider whether Qualcomm's actual anticompetitive practices harmed rivals, the Court finds that Dr. Chipty's opinions are not reliable."[1338] By negative implication, Judge Koh did *not* rule that Dr. Chipty's testimony was unreliable because of any deficiency in her analysis of the economic questions that Qualcomm had assigned to her to analyze, including whether Qualcomm's supply agreements with Apple

---

[1335] *FTC v. Qualcomm*, 411 F. Supp. 3d at 805.

[1336] *Id.* (citing Transcript of Proceedings (Volume 8) at 1738:3-1739:3, FTC v. Qualcomm Inc., No. 5:17-cv-00220-LHK (N.D. Cal. Jan. 22, 2019) (Testimony of Tasneem Chipty)).

[1337] Transcript of Proceedings (Volume 8) at 1695:10-19, FTC v. Qualcomm Inc., No. 5:17-cv-00220-LHK (N.D. Cal. Jan. 22, 2019) (Testimony of Tasneem Chipty) (emphasis added).

[1338] *FTC v. Qualcomm*, 411 F. Supp. 3d at 805.

actually had an anticompetitive effect on the two relevant markets served by rival modem manufacturers.

3. Professor Edward Snyder

Professor Snyder is the William S. Beinecke Professor of Economics and Management, and the former Dean, at the Yale School of Management. He was previously the Dean and George Shultz Professor of Economics at the University of Chicago Booth School of Business. He received his Ph.D. in economics from the University of Chicago and began his career as an economist in the Antitrust Division.[1339] Professor Snyder's expert report, which is publicly available in redacted form, was 368 pages long (excluding appendices) and contained 1,581 footnotes.[1340]

Although Judge Koh previously had denied the FTC's *Daubert* motion to exclude Professor Snyder's testimony on the grounds that it was unreliable, she nonetheless disparaged the reliability of his trial testimony, which was predicated on the very same report, on the following grounds:

> Dr. Edward Snyder, a Qualcomm economic expert, never even considered how Qualcomm's anticompetitive practices affect Qualcomm's rivals. Dr. Snyder testified that only had he found evidence to contradict his own theory that "independent" factors harmed Qualcomm's rivals "would [he] have gone to the next step to evaluate . . . the FTC's claims about Qualcomm's conduct." Dr. Snyder ignored Qualcomm's conduct even though Dr. Snyder conceded that his "independent" factors are not mutually exclusive with Qualcomm's conduct, and that "anticompetitive conduct by a dominant firm can affect its rivals' investment decisions." Because Dr. Snyder did not even evaluate Qualcomm's conduct, the Court finds that Dr. Snyder's opinions are not reliable.[1341]

This finding by Judge Koh was plainly erroneous and entirely unpersuasive.

I reviewed all 368 pages of the redacted public version of Professor Snyder's expert report. It offered an economist's framework for answering the quintessential question that the Supreme Court posed in *Grinnell*: did the monopolist willfully acquire or maintain its monopoly power by means *other than* "growth or development as a consequence of a superior product, business acumen, or historic accident"?[1342] Rather than quote this familiar

---

[1339] See *Edward A. Snyder*, YALE SCH. MGMT., https://som.yale.edu/faculty/edward-snyder.

[1340] Expert Report of Edward A. Snyder Ph.D., FTC v. Qualcomm Inc., No. 5:17-cv-02200-LHK (N.D. Cal. June 28, 2018), ECF No. 1244.

[1341] *FTC v. Qualcomm*, 411 F. Supp. 3d at 805 (alterations in original) (first quoting Transcript of Proceedings (Volume 8) at 1788:6–8, FTC v. Qualcomm Inc., No. 5:17-cv-00220-LHK (N.D. Cal. Jan. 22, 2019) (Testimony of Edward Snyder); and then quoting *id.* at 1808:24–1809:1).

[1342] United States v. Grinnell Corp., 384 U.S. 563, 571 (1966); *see also supra* notes 270–272 and accompanying text.

phrase and then promptly ignore its practical evidentiary significance for determining liability for monopolization (as so many have done since the Court issued its decision in *Grinnell* in 1966), Professor Snyder in essence took the Court at its word. Accordingly, he asked in effect, What economic facts tend to prove the presence or absence of "a superior product, business acumen, or historic accident"?

Professor Snyder approached the task of answering *Grinnell*'s fundamental question by characterizing the lawful advantage that a monopolist might have acquired over its rivals as having derived meritoriously from three elements: foresight, investment, and execution. He was attempting to assist the finder of fact by analyzing for her benefit the real-world facts and data directly relevant to the Supreme Court's formulation of a controlling statement of law. Professor Snyder's triad of foresight, investment, and execution was obedient to *Grinnell* in the sense that business acumen would seem indisputably to encompass at least foresight and execution. And Professor Snyder also paid homage to *Alcoa* by expressly considering one of Judge Hand's enumerated considerations: foresight.[1343] Professor Snyder's final focus—investment—plainly resonated with later Supreme Court decisions such as *linkLine* and *Trinko*, but it also could be understood to incorporate more immediately and more literally *Alcoa*'s particular attention to "superior skill . . . and industry."[1344]

Professor Snyder's approach to answering *Grinnell*'s fundamental question was innovative. It was directly relevant to, and probative of, the ultimate question of whether Qualcomm was liable for monopolization. We saw in Part I.1.g to the Introduction that the most natural meaning to impart to *Grinnell*'s "business acumen" passage is to conclude that proof of the absence of alternative hypotheses for the monopolist's lawful acquisition or maintenance of its monopoly is the *plaintiff's* burden of production to address as part of its *prima facie* case and the *plaintiff's* burden of persuasion to establish by a preponderance of the evidence.

Yet, an appellate court reading Judge Koh's findings of fact and conclusions of law in isolation—without the benefit of reading Professor Snyder's trial testimony, much less his voluminous expert report (which of course was not moved into evidence at trial)—would have no clue as to the substantial relevance and nuance of his expert economic testimony. That lacuna in Judge Koh's findings of fact and conclusions of law in *FTC v. Qualcomm* resulted directly from her failure to make full and complete factual findings, as Rule 52(a)(1) requires of any federal judge presiding over a bench trial.

Judge Koh did not make and did not report such findings concerning Professor Snyder's testimony. She did not even report that he expressly

---

[1343] United States v. Aluminum Co. of Am., 148 F.2d 416, 430 (2ᵈ Cir. 1945).
[1344] *Id.*

testified that the assignment given him by Qualcomm's counsel was to address the issue of anticompetitive harm (which Judge Koh incongruously found that Professor Snyder did not address):

> Q. Professor Snyder, what were you asked to do in this case?
>
> A. I was asked to assess the FTC's claim that Qualcomm's alleged conduct caused *anticompetitive harms* in the modem chip industry.
>
> Q. Were you also asked to evaluate the opinion of any of the FTC's experts as part of your assignment?
>
> A. Yes. I was asked to evaluate Professor Shapiro's opinions to the effect that Qualcomm's alleged conduct did cause *anticompetitive harms* in the industry.[1345]

Professor Snyder was simply asked whether there was any validity to the FTC's claim that Qualcomm's conduct had caused anticompetitive harm in the modem industry. Relying on his economic expertise, and because he found no evidence to the contrary, Professor Snyder testified that independent factors caused the harm to rival modem manufacturers that Professor Shapiro instead had imputed to allegedly anticompetitive behavior by Qualcomm.

Judge Koh inexplicably found that Professor Snyder did not testify about anticompetitive effects. How she could make that finding in the presence of Professor Snyder's explicit testimony directly on point at page 1778 of the trial transcript is staggering. Judge Koh then proceeded to rule that *all* of Professor Snyder's expert testimony was unreliable. That ruling was capricious and clearly erroneous. Even if Judge Koh had been correct in criticizing the focus and scope of Professor Snyder's testimony, why would those supposed deficiencies in any way diminish the reliability of his expert assessment *of Professor Shapiro's expert testimony?*

C. *Judge Koh's Finding That Testimony Concerning the Technical Achievements of Qualcomm's Patents Was "Inapposite"*

We saw in Part I.1.a to the Introduction that Judge Koh disregarded testimony concerning Qualcomm's foundational technological contributions. She called the testimony of Dr. Chen, Dr. Jacobs, Dr. Malladi, and Professor Andrews "inapposite."[1346] The FTC did not put on testimony rebutting any of these witnesses.

[1345] Transcript of Proceedings (Volume 8) at 1778:6–14, FTC v. Qualcomm Inc., No. 5:17-cv-00220-LHK (N.D. Cal. Jan. 22, 2019) (Testimony of Edward Snyder) (emphasis added).
[1346] *FTC v. Qualcomm*, 411 F. Supp. 3d at 779.

Judge Koh's description of the testimony of Dr. Chen, Dr. Jacobs, Dr. Malladi, and Professor Andrews as "inapposite" was puzzling. The word does not appear in the Federal Rules of Evidence. The *Oxford English Dictionary* defines "inapposite" as meaning "[n]ot apposite, not to the point, out of place; impertinent."[1347] In modern English usage, the word means inappropriate or irrelevant.[1348] So, was Judge Koh saying that the testimony of these four witnesses was "irrelevant," as that word is understood to have special meaning under the Federal Rules of Evidence?[1349]

If so, *why* was their testimony irrelevant? Why would Judge Koh think that the "inapposite" testimony of these four Qualcomm witnesses lacked "any tendency to make a fact more or less probable than it would be without the evidence"?[1350] Why would Judge Koh believe that the facts established in their testimony were not "of consequence in determining the action"?[1351] And why did Judge Koh not simply use some variant of the word "relevant," which the Federal Rules of Evidence plainly do use, and spare us the mystery of decoding her intended meaning?

Perhaps the answer is that Judge Koh saw daylight between "inapposite" and "irrelevant." When lawyers say "inapposite," they are usually discussing the applicability of some putative source of *legal* authority. So, we might read in a brief or an opinion that the 1897 landmark decision of the Freedonia Supreme Court in *Smith v. Jones* is inapposite to the present dispute over the scope of section 9(b) of the Tar Sands Reclamation Act of 1973. One can find an example of that precise usage of "inapposite" in Judge Koh's own findings of fact and conclusions of law in *FTC v. Qualcomm*.[1352]

But, upon hearing *factual* propositions rather than legal propositions, an experienced trial lawyer or judge might find it full of high sentence but a bit obtuse to be told that the testimony of a particular witness is to be discredited or ignored for being "inapposite." Liked a cracked bell, that denunciation does not ring true, precisely because (as noted above) the adjective "inapposite" does not map onto any readily identifiable principle in the law of evidence.

Judge Koh's characterization of a witness' testimony as "inapposite," and thus her decision to cast that testimony into oblivion, resembles her peremptory device of calling the testimony of a fact witness "not credible" or the testimony of an expert economic witness "not reliable" or the factual

---

[1347] *Inapposite adj.*, OXFORD ENGLISH DICTIONARY (3ᵈ ed. 2015).

[1348] *See, e.g.*, BRYAN A. GARNER, GARNER'S MODERN ENGLISH USAGE 496 (Oxford Univ. Press 4ᵗʰ ed. 2016).

[1349] *See* FED. R. EVID. 402 ("Irrelevant evidence is not admissible.").

[1350] *Id.* 401.

[1351] *Id.*

[1352] *See* FTC v. Qualcomm Inc., 411 F. Supp. 3d 658, 690 (N.D. Cal. 2019) ("*Archer-Daniels-Midland* is inapposite.") (citing United States v. Archer-Daniels-Midland Co., 781 F. Supp. 1400 (S.D. Iowa 1991)).

evidence offered to support a procompetitive rationale for Qualcomm's business model "pretextual." These various epithets all point to the same overwhelming question: Sitting as the finder of fact, did Judge Koh refuse to weigh probative evidence introduced by Qualcomm that would have established that the FTC failed to prove its *prima facie* case by a preponderance of the evidence?

D. *Were Judge Koh's Findings That All of Qualcomm's Expert Economic Witnesses Were Unreliable Clearly Reasoned and Persuasively Communicated?*

Judge Koh found that all of Qualcomm's expert economic witnesses were "unreliable." The Federal Rules of Evidence discuss reliability only in Rule 702, which concerns expert testimony. Rule 702 specifies requirements for the admissibility of expert testimony: (1) "the testimony is based upon sufficient facts or data," (2) "the testimony is the product of reliable principles and methods," and (3) "the expert has reliably applied the principles and methods reliably to the facts of the case."[1353] As interpreted by the Supreme Court in *Daubert*,[1354] *Joiner*,[1355] and *Kumho*,[1356] Rule 702 creates a gate for the admissibility of expert economic testimony. Those decisions by the Court emphasize that the trial judge is the gatekeeper to protect the jury from being exposed to unreliable expert testimony, commonly called "junk science."[1357]

1.   *Is* Daubert *Inherent in Due Process?*

Unreliability under Rule 702 means that the expert testimony was based on an unsound methodology, or that the expert testimony failed to apply a sound methodology to the facts and data of the case, or both. At a higher level of abstraction, the Supreme Court said in *Daubert* that expert testimony must be scientific, in the same epistemological sense that philosopher Sir Karl Popper outlined.[1358]

A "conjecture" in the Popperian sense is an *a priori* hypothesis that must survive rigorous attempts at falsification (both theoretical and empirical) before it can be accepted as plausibly true (that is, before it can be regarded as having what Popper called verisimilitude or "truthlikeness").[1359] Strictly speaking, Popper believed that we never really confirm a conjecture; we only

---

[1353] FED. R. EVID. 702.
[1354] Daubert v. Merrell Dow Pharm., Inc., 509 U.S. 579 (1993).
[1355] General Elec. Co. v. Joiner, 522 U.S. 136 (1997).
[1356] Kumho Tire Co. v. Carmichael, 526 U.S. 137 (1999).
[1357] *See Daubert*, 509 U.S. at 589–97; *Joiner*, 522 U.S. at 142; *Kumho*, 526 U.S. at 141.
[1358] *Daubert*, 509 U.S. at 593.
[1359] *See* POPPER, CONJECTURES AND REFUTATIONS: THE GROWTH OF SCIENTIFIC KNOWLEDGE, *supra* note 275; POPPER, OBJECTIVE KNOWLEDGE, *supra* note 275.

fail to refute it. But in the course of repeatedly failing to refute a conjecture, we become more confident that it is true. Popper called the information in which we have such confidence "objective knowledge."

In the same manner, expert testimony must be predicated on a testable hypothesis, which is to say the scientific method. This insight, embraced by the Court in *Daubert*,[1360] would seem relevant whether or not a jury is the finder of fact. This insight implies that *Daubert*'s exclusion of unreliable expert testimony is not a mere rule of evidence enacted by Congress in the Judicial Code, but a necessary element of due process: a straightforward application of *Mathews v. Eldridge* would imply that the expected harm to a party from being subjected to unreliable expert testimony would greatly outweigh the burden to the court of affording such additional process as is necessary to exclude the fact finder's consideration of expert testimony that is unreliable (and therefore necessarily irrelevant and lacking in any probative value).

This interpretation of *Daubert* dovetails with Judge Posner's "search theory" of the law of evidence, which is perfectly symmetric to his law-and-economics restatement of the Due Process Clause of the Fifth Amendment as interpreted by the Supreme Court in *Mathews v. Eldridge*.[1361] Again, the comparison of the marginal cost to the expected marginal benefit associated with the investment in one more increment of "care" or "process" or "evidentiary search" directly extends the economic reasoning that motivated the Hand Formula for negligence in 1947.[1362]

2. *Considering That Judge Koh Was Not Performing a Gatekeeper Function with Respect to a Jury, What Was Her Rationale for Finding That Qualcomm's Expert Economic Witnesses Were Unreliable?*

FTC v. Qualcomm was of course a bench trial. Judge Koh was herself the finder of fact, not merely the gatekeeper for jurors serving as finders of fact. Consequently, in finding Qualcomm's expert witnesses to be unreliable, Judge Koh was necessarily basing her findings on some consideration *other than* the need to shield a lay jury from junk science.

In particular, in its *Daubert* motion to exclude the expert economic testimony of Professor Snyder (which appears from my inspection of the voluminous docket to have been the only *Daubert* motion filed to exclude expert economic testimony in *FTC v. Qualcomm*), the FTC relied on two district

---

[1360] *See Daubert*, 509 U.S. at 593 (quoting POPPER, CONJECTURES AND REFUTATIONS: THE GROWTH OF SCIENTIFIC KNOWLEDGE, *supra* note 275, at 37 ("[T]he criterion of the scientific status of a theory is its falsifiability, or refutability, or testability.") (alteration in original) (emphasis omitted)); *see also* Sidak, *Court-Appointed Neutral Economic Experts, supra* note 276, at 384–86 (tracing the epistemological foundation of *Daubert* and its progeny).

[1361] *See supra* note 214 and accompanying text.

[1362] *See* POSNER, ECONOMIC ANALYSIS OF LAW, *supra* note 214, at 837–39; Richard A. Posner, *An Economic Approach to the Law of Evidence*, 51 STAN. L. REV. 1477, 1481–84 (1999).

court opinions to argue that, in the Ninth Circuit, """the *Daubert* standards governing admissibility of expert testimony must still be met, even during a bench trial.""""[1363] When, on December 17, 2018, Judge Koh denied the FTC's motion to exclude Professor Snyder's testimony, she applied the *Daubert* standard to "reject[] the FTC's arguments that Dr. Snyder's opinion [was] unreliable"[1364] and to conclude that "Dr. Snyder's testimony [was] reliable[.]"[1365] She went so far as to say that, "[h]ere, the Court concludes that Dr. Snyder's testimony is based on a reliable methodology and is not the 'junk science' *Daubert* aims to preclude from jury consideration."[1366]

So, Judge Koh's diametrically opposite conclusion in her findings of fact and conclusion of law on May 21, 2019—that, "[b]ecause Dr. Snyder did not even evaluate Qualcomm's conduct, the Court finds that Dr. Snyder's opinions are not reliable"[1367]—could not have been predicated on the due process understanding of *Daubert* that I outlined above. Rather, Judge Koh seemed to have based her decision to assign no weight to the testimony of Qualcomm's expert witnesses on some other notion of reliability that remains undefined in her findings of fact and conclusions of law.

Judge Koh must not have been *excluding* the testimony of Qualcomm's expert economists. If she had been doing so, she would have expressly ruled on a *Daubert* motion or a motion *in limine* and found the disclosed expert opinions to be inadmissible at trial. There is also no question that Judge Koh certified Qualcomm's expert economist witnesses and permitted them to give testimony at trial that she admitted into evidence. Because Judge Koh did not rule, save for the occasional objection, that any of the testimony of Qualcomm's expert economists was inadmissible (as would be the case in a successful *Daubert* motion), it necessarily follows that her findings on the unreliability of that expert testimony were tantamount to her ruling that the testimony, although admissible, deserved no weight.

[1363] Federal Trade Commission's Notice of Motion and Motion to Exclude Expert Testimony of Dr. Edward A. Snyder, and Memorandum in Support (Redacted Version) at 5, FTC v. Qualcomm Inc., No. 5:17-cv-00220-LHK (N.D. Cal. Aug. 30, 2018), ECF No. 788 (quoting Sierra Club v. Talen Mont. LLC, No. CV 13-32-BLG-DLC-JCL, 2016 WL 11200732, at *3 (D. Mont. Mar. 25, 2016) (quoting Schilder Dairy, LLC v. DeLaval, Inc., No. CV 09-531-REB, 2011 WL 2634251, at *2 (D. Id. July 5, 2011))). Several appellate decisions from outside the Ninth Circuit have explicitly said that *Daubert* applies in a bench trial, or in an adjudication before an administrative law judge. *See, e.g.*, Seaboard Lumber Co. v. United States, 308 F.3d 1283, 1301–02 (Fed. Cir. 2002) (ALJ proceeding); United States v. Brown, 279 F. Supp. 2d 1238, 1243 (S.D. Ala. 2003), *aff'd*, 415 F.3d 1257 (11ᵗʰ Cir. 2005) (bench trial); Bradley v. Brown, 852 F. Supp. 690, 700 (N.D. Ind.), *aff'd*, 42 F.3d 434 (7ᵗʰ Cir. 1994) (bench trial).

[1364] Order Denying the FTC's Motion to Exclude Expert Testimony of Dr. Edward Snyder at 7, FTC v. Qualcomm Inc., No. 17-CV-00220-LHK, 2018 WL 6615050, at *4 (N.D. Cal. Dec. 17, 2018).

[1365] *Id.* at 9, 2018 WL 6615050, at *5.

[1366] *Id.* at 6, 2018 WL 6615050, at *4.

[1367] FTC v. Qualcomm Inc., 411 F. Supp. 3d 658, 805 (N.D. Cal. 2019).

3. *Did Judge Koh Implicitly Announce an Unprecedented Inquisitorial Rule for Assessing the Reliability of Expert Economic Witnesses?*

What, then, was Judge Koh's rationale for giving no weight to Qualcomm's admissible expert economic testimony? Judge Koh seemed to be adopting the audacious rule that the testimony of an expert economic witness may be deemed devoid of probative merit if the witness has not been instructed by counsel to address a particular question on which the judge would prefer to hear expert testimony. Again, one senses a whiff of the inquisitorial in Judge Koh's approach to judging.

In prior writings, I have criticized on the basis of personal observation the practice of eminent international law firms' failing to correct erroneous legal premises on which expert economic witnesses construct their testimony, which then properly would be (but in practice seldom is) recognized to be necessarily unreliable under Rule 702 and *Daubert*.[1368] But that criticism does not apply to, and thus would not justify or excuse, Judge Koh's refusal to give any weight to the testimony of Qualcomm's expert economic witnesses. I found no indication in the trial transcript that counsel for Qualcomm had instructed Qualcomm's three expert economic witnesses to give legally irrelevant testimony or had failed to steer those witnesses back to relevant topics if they happened to stray during their testimony at trial onto an irrelevant tangent.

To the contrary, under Judge Koh's apparent rationale for denying evidentiary weight to expert economic testimony, a properly instructed expert witness who gave entirely reliable testimony on relevant topics *A*, *B*, and *C* could nonetheless be found altogether unreliable because the expert had not been instructed by counsel also to testify on some topic *D*, which might even be a topic on which the party did not bear the burden of production and the burden persuasion. This novel evidentiary rule announced by Judge Koh deprived Qualcomm of its freedom to divide topics of proof among its multiple expert witnesses as Qualcomm's counsel saw fit. Nothing was inherently unreliable about Qualcomm's giving its expert economic witnesses distinct assignments that did not overlap with one another or did not address topics on which Qualcomm chose not to present expert testimony (again, because Qualcomm quite possibly bore no burden of production or persuasion).

The implicit rule announced in Judge Koh's findings of fact and conclusions of law in *FTC v. Qualcomm* was that a judge in a bench trial has the

---

[1368] *See* J. Gregory Sidak, *The FRAND Contract*, 3 CRITERION J. ON INNOVATION 1, 8 (2018) ("Given [the] receptivity of judges to hear expert economic testimony that might assist the court's legal interpretation of the FRAND contract and the fact finder's weighing of the evidence, it is disappointing to observe, in my experience, that some highly credentialed scholars who appear as expert economic witnesses in FRAND litigations or arbitrations misunderstand (or feign ignorance of) the elementary distinction between a contract offer and contract formation.").

discretion to dictate, on grounds of reliability, how a party may structure its presentation of expert economic testimony in support of its defense. But that implicit rule was specious. In effect it would recast reliability findings as *credibility* findings—which, unlike reliability findings, ordinarily would be entitled to elevated deference on appeal under Federal Rule of Evidence 52(a)(6).[1369]

4. *Why Did Judge Koh Not Appoint Her Own Neutral Economic Expert Pursuant to Federal Rule of Evidence 706?*

Judge Koh conspicuously did not avail herself of a ready tool for addressing her recurrent complaint that Qualcomm's expert economic witnesses supposedly did not testify on the question that she wanted them to address: she could have installed her own court-appointed neutral economic expert pursuant to Federal Rule of Evidence 706,[1370] as Justice Stephen Breyer has recommended. In the Supreme Court's 1997 decision in *Joiner*,[1371] Justice Breyer encouraged the use of neutral experts as a way to "overcome the inherent difficulty of making determinations about complicated scientific, or otherwise technical, evidence."[1372] Even though "cases presenting significant science-related issues have increased in number," he noted, "*Daubert*'s gatekeeping requirement will not prove inordinately difficult to implement" when using a neutral expert.[1373] Appointing a neutral expert "will help secure . . . the ascertainment of truth and the just determination of proceedings."[1374]

In contrast to Judge Koh in *FTC v. Qualcomm*, Judge William Alsup embraced Justice Breyer's recommendation and appointed a neutral economic expert in *Oracle America v. Google*, which by now has been litigated in the Northern District of California for a decade.[1375] In denying Oracle's motion to disqualify Professor James Kearl for reappointment as a Rule 706 expert, Judge Alsup discussed the benefits that the court had derived from having used Professor Kearl in that capacity earlier in the litigation and the likely benefits from the court's continued use of Professor Kearl, both before and during trial:

[1369] FED R. CIV. P. 52(a)(6).

[1370] FED. R. EVID. 706; *see also* Sidak, *Court-Appointed Neutral Economic Experts, supra* note 276.

[1371] General Elec. Co. v. Joiner, 522 U.S. 136 (1997).

[1372] *Id.* at 149.

[1373] *Id.* at 149–50.

[1374] *Id.* at 150. Herbert Hovenkamp has endorsed the use of neutral economic experts in antitrust cases and has offered thoughtful suggestions on how a judge might best instruct them. *See* HERBERT HOVENKAMP, THE ANTITRUST ENTERPRISE: PRINCIPLE AND EXECUTION 89–91 (Harvard Univ. Press 2005).

[1375] Order Denying Oracle's Motion to Disqualify Rule 706 Expert, Oracle Am., Inc. v. Google Inc., No. C 10-03561 WHA, 2015 WL 7429277 (N.D. Cal. Nov. 23, 2015) [hereinafter *Oracle v. Google* Rule 706 Expert Order, 2015 WL 7429277] (denying Oracle's motion to disqualify Professor James Kearl as Judge Alsup's court-appointed neutral economic expert).

It is worth recalling here that Oracle's damages expert, Dr. Iain Cockburn, needed three tries before producing a viable damages study, and parts of his third faced successful challenges as well. Thus, the appointment of a Rule 706 expert proved prescient. Dr. Kearl's continued involvement will be useful both in assisting the jury in comprehending the complexity of the question of damages and in assisting the Court in navigating any *Daubert* issues that will arise with the parties' new damages studies. Accordingly, a Rule 706 expert remains appropriate in this case, subject to the remote possibility that after application of *Daubert* the surviving damage theories by both sides will be so uncomplicated that a Rule 706 expert will be unnecessary to assist the jury, a possibility the Court will consider before the trial gets under way.[1376]

There is no reason to believe that the antitrust and FRAND questions presented in *FTC v. Qualcomm* were qualitatively less complicated than the questions of copyright damages presented in *Oracle America v. Google*. The cost of the court-appointed neutral economic expert in *FTC v. Qualcomm* would have been borne by the parties, not the court. Judge Koh could have instructed the neutral expert to give her an objective assessment of the scientific merit of the testimony of the opposing expert economic witnesses, including their testimony on the allegedly anticompetitive effects of Qualcomm's accused conduct.

That is how Judge Posner used me in the two patent infringement cases in which he appointed me the court's neutral economic expert.[1377] In both cases, I filed an expert report evaluating the reports on damages that the opposing party experts had prepared. In the second case, I was also deposed by counsel for the opposing parties. Judge Posner presided over my deposition. Both cases settled within days after either the submission of my report or my deposition.[1378]

[1376] *Id.* at *6.

[1377] *See* Sidak, *Court-Appointed Neutral Economic Experts, supra* note 276; *see also* POSNER, DIVERGENT PATHS: THE ACADEMY AND THE JUDICIARY, *supra* note 963, at 133–35 & n.72.

[1378] It appears that Judge Alsup envisioned using his Rule 706 witness similarly:

> Early on, the Court appointed an expert pursuant to Rule 706 "to testify before the jury at trial . . . and *not* [to serve] as a confidential advisor to the judge" regarding the issues of damages (for copyright and patent claims). A memorandum order detailed the need fo [sic] a Rule 706 expert: "[I]n light of the parties' extremely divergent views on damages and the unusual complexity of the damages aspect of this case, an independent economic expert was needed to aid the jury."

Oracle v. Google Rule 706 Expert Order, *supra* note 1375, 2015 WL 7429277, at *1 (alterations in original) (emphasis in original) (citations omitted) (first quoting Memorandum Opinion Regarding Rule 706 Expert at 3–4, Oracle Am., Inc. v. Google Inc., No. C 10-03561 WHA (N.D. Cal. Nov. 9, 2011), ECF No. 610; and then quoting *id.* at 3).

E. *Did Judge Koh Suppress Exculpatory Evidence When Reporting Her Findings of Fact Concerning Testimony Given by Dirk Weiler and Ilkka Rahnasto in Qualcomm's Defense as Percipient Witnesses on Behalf of Nokia (a Third Party)?*

Judge Koh found that "[Mr.] Weiler was not credible"[1379] because he "conveniently claimed complete ignorance about the specific licenses and licensing discussions of [Mr.] Weiler's employer, Nokia."[1380] But that finding was a *non sequitur*.

The apparent purpose of Mr. Weiler's testimony was not to explain what Nokia's business practices were during a period of time when Nokia did not employ Mr. Weiler. Why would he have had specialized knowledge of *that* subject? Rather, the testimony's apparent purpose was for Mr. Weiler to describe, as a percipient witness, what ETSI had done over the course of many years through its IPR Policy and in response to proposals to amend its IPR Policy to address the calculation of a FRAND royalty. A second Nokia witness, Ilkka Rahnasto, testified at trial by videotaped deposition transcript about Nokia's licensing practices. Judge Koh never mentioned Dr. Rahnasto or his testimony in her findings of fact and conclusions of law.

1. The Relevance of Patent Exhaustion to Nokia—and Ericsson

It is worth pausing momentarily to note the particular relevance of Mr. Weiler's testimony to three important issues.

a. Was Nokia's 2006 Pleading to the European Commission "Diametrically Opposed" to Mr. Weiler's Trial Testimony and Nokia's Position in Its Amicus Brief in FTC v. Qualcomm*?*

First, Judge Koh remarked that Nokia had taken the position *in 2006* before the European Commission that Qualcomm's FRAND commitments obligated Qualcomm to offer "licenses" to its cellular SEPs to rival modem manufacturers.[1381] She elaborated that, "in 2006, Nokia argued before the European Commission that Qualcomm's FRAND commitment to license its SEPs to a modem chip supplier was 'unequivocal.'"[1382] In particular, Judge Koh said that, "[s]pecifically, Nokia 'alleged that Qualcomm's termination of a modem chip license "after having induced SSOs to base . . . standards on

---

[1379] FTC v. Qualcomm Inc., 411 F. Supp. 3d 658, 756 (N.D. Cal. 2019).

[1380] *Id.* at 755.

[1381] *Id.*

[1382] *Id.* (quoting Order Granting FTC's Motion for Partial Summary Judgment on Qualcomm's Contractual Duties Pursuant to the Contracts with ATIS and the TIA, 2018 WL 5848999, *supra* note 52, at *13).

Qualcomm's technology" breached "Qualcomm's duty to license on FRAND terms" based on multiple IPR policies."'[1383]

Judge Koh made two findings of fact concerning Nokia's credibility on the basis of her premise. First, in her order granting the FTC partial summary judgment, she had said that, "[e]ven though Nokia argued that Qualcomm's FRAND commitment to license to a modem chip supplier was 'unequivocal,' Nokia now contends that the FTC's interpretations of Qualcomm's commitments under the TIA and ATIS IPR policies are 'novel and very surprising.'"'[1384] In that order, Judge Koh found that the FTC did "not offer Nokia's filing for the truth of whether Qualcomm breached its FRAND obligations, but rather to demonstrate that Nokia *took the position* that Qualcomm had done so," presumably to impeach the position that Nokia had taken in its *amicus* brief filed in *FTC v. Qualcomm* opposing the FTC's motion for partial summary judgment.[1385] Judge Koh concluded that Nokia's position in 2006 contradicted the position that Nokia had advocated in 2018 as an *amicus* in *FTC v. Qualcomm* that the FTC's proposed interpretation of two RAND commitments made by Qualcomm was novel (and erroneous).[1386]

In her second finding of fact concerning Nokia's credibility, Judge Koh concluded that Mr. Weiler's testimony that "Nokia follows FRAND 'by licensing its patents on the device level'"[1387] was "diametrically opposed to what Nokia represented to the European Commission in 2006."[1388]

Neither of Judge Koh's two conclusions followed from her premise. Wittingly or unwittingly, she was playing a word game. Judge Koh again used the word "license" without specifying whether the "license" that Nokia

---

[1383] *Id.* (quoting Order Granting FTC's Motion for Partial Summary Judgment on Qualcomm's Contractual Duties Pursuant to the Contracts with ATIS and the TIA, 2018 WL 5848999, *supra* note 52, at *13 (alteration in original) (quoting Complaint to the Commission of the European Communities Directorate-General Competition Against Qualcomm Incorporated Submitted by Nokia Oyj Regarding Exclusionary and Exploitative Practices of Qualcomm Infringing Article 82 EC Restricting Competition in the Licensing of CDMA and W-CDMA Standard Technologies and in the Supply of CDMA and W-CDMA Chipsets for Mobile Terminal Equipment at 46 (Feb. 13, 2006), *Reply Exhibit 25 to* FTC's Reply in Support of Partial Summary Judgment, *supra* note 485, ECF No. 893-2)).

[1384] Order Granting FTC's Motion for Partial Summary Judgment on Qualcomm's Contractual Duties Pursuant to the Contracts with ATIS and the TIA, 2018 WL 5848999, *supra* note 52, at *13 (first quoting Complaint to the Commission of the European Communities Directorate-General Competition Against Qualcomm Incorporated Submitted by Nokia Oyj Regarding Exclusionary and Exploitative Practices of Qualcomm Infringing Article 82 EC Restricting Competition in the Licensing of CDMA and W-CDMA Standard Technologies and in the Supply of CDMA and W-CDMA Chipsets for Mobile Terminal Equipment at 46 (Feb. 13, 2006), *Reply Exhibit 25 to* FTC's Reply in Support of Partial Summary Judgment, *supra* note 485; and then quoting Brief of Nokia Technologies Oy *Amicus Curiae* in Support of Defendant Qualcomm Incorporated's Opposition to Motion for Partial Summary Judgment at 2, FTC v. Qualcomm Inc., No. 5:17-cv-00220-LHK (N.D. Cal. Oct. 3, 2018)).

[1385] *Id.* at *13 n.7 (emphasis in original).

[1386] *FTC v. Qualcomm*, 411 F. Supp. 3d at 755 (citing Order Granting FTC's Motion for Partial Summary Judgment on Qualcomm's Contractual Duties Pursuant to the Contracts with ATIS and the TIA, 2018 WL 5848999, *supra* note 52, at *13).

[1387] *Id.* (quoting Transcript of Proceedings (Volume 8) at 1672:4–6, FTC v. Qualcomm Inc., No. 5:17-cv-00220-LHK (N.D. Cal. Jan. 22, 2019) (Testimony of Dirk Weiler (Head of Standards, Nokia))).

[1388] *Id.*

contemplated in 2006, which obviously preceded the decision of the Supreme Court of the United States in 2008 in *Quanta*, was understood to be exhaustive or nonexhaustive. We saw in Part III why the distinction between an exhaustive license and a nonexhaustive "license" before *Quanta* was critical. Judge Koh did not establish that Nokia had argued to the European Commission in 2006 that Qualcomm was required to offer an *exhaustive* license to its SEPs to rival modem manufacturers. The more plausible interpretation—and the interpretation that Judge Koh might not have recognized, considering her apparent admission at trial that patent exhaustion confused her[1389]—is that Nokia's position in 2006 was that rival modem manufacturers were entitled to an offer of a *nonexhaustive* "license," as parties had used that term in commercial agreements before *Quanta*.

That reading would comport with—rather than be "diametrically opposed to"—Nokia's two positions in 2018 and 2019 in *FTC v. Qualcomm* that Judge Koh condemned. First, Nokia took the position in its *amicus* brief that it would be novel and incorrect to interpret two SSO RAND contracts to require the *exhaustive* licensing of cellular SEPs to rival modem manufacturers.[1390] Second, we shall see that Mr. Weiler testified that Nokia's policy is to offer exhaustive licenses only to OEMs.[1391]

Consequently, because Judge Koh's findings of fact and conclusions of law appeared to manifest confusion about the importance of patent exhaustion to *FTC v. Qualcomm*, she never actually established an inconsistency between Nokia's position in 2006 and its position in its *amicus* brief and in testimony in *FTC v. Qualcomm*. Consequently, Judge Koh's findings predicated on that apparent confusion were spurious. She was describing a false conflict.

[1389] *See supra* notes 88–91 and accompanying text.

[1390] Brief of Nokia Technologies Oy *Amicus Curiae* in Support of Defendant Qualcomm Incorporated's Opposition to Motion for Partial Summary Judgment at 7–8, FTC v. Qualcomm Inc., No. 5:17-cv-00220-LHK (N.D. Cal. Oct. 3, 2018) ("[E]nd user product licensing avoids complications that may arise with respect to patent exhaustion claims. If licenses were now to be required at the component level under the ATIS and TIA IPR Policies, potential or existing licensees of relevant SEPs under those policies could argue in license negotiations that certain cellular SEP owners would have to splinter their portfolios and license subsets of their relevant SEP claims to different component suppliers at each level in the value chain. And thereafter, that alleged patent exhaustion or implied rights would alleviate any need for a license to other SEP claims at their point in the value chain. Moreover, specific components may be used beyond a given standard and standards development organization ('SDO') IPR Policy for which the SEP holder made a FRAND commitment (and would normally limit its license to). Under such circumstances, if the requirement were to license applicable SEP claims under a given SDO IPR Policy at the component level, then additional SEP claims may be argued to be exhausted or impliedly licensed at other points in the supply chain such as the end product level.").

[1391] Transcript of Proceedings (Volume 8) at 1679:12–1680:21, FTC v. Qualcomm Inc., No. 5:17-cv-00220-LHK (N.D. Cal. Jan. 22, 2019) (Testimony of Dirk Weiler (Head of Standards, Nokia)).

b. *Was Mr. Weiler's Testimony Concerning ETSI's IPR Policy Relevant for Purposes of Judge Koh's Evaluation of the Credibility of a Witness Representing an Entirely Different Company, Ericsson?*

The second reason that Mr. Weiler's testimony was relevant to interpreting Judge Koh's findings of fact and conclusions of law in *FTC v. Qualcomm* was that Judge Koh applied the same fallacious reasoning to find Ericsson not to be credible. In the same passage in which she disparaged Nokia, Judge Koh summarily impugned Ericsson's credibility, supposedly because Ericsson's explanation for its refusal to offer exhaustive licenses to its SEPs to modem manufacturers were "self-serving and made-for-litigation."[1392]

Judge Koh's conclusion was specious because it was predicated on the same false conflict that she supposedly had identified between Nokia's pleadings and its amicus brief and trial testimony. In other words, she appeared to reason that certain of Ericsson's pleadings from 1998 in litigation against Qualcomm, which specified the word "license," proved that Ericsson had taken a position in litigation in 1998 that was diametrically opposed to the position that it had taken in *FTC v. Qualcomm*. Yet again, Judge Koh used the word "license" without specifying whether the "license" that Ericsson contemplated in 1998—10 years before the Supreme Court's 2008 decision in *Quanta*—was understood to be exhaustive or nonexhaustive. In her findings of fact and conclusions of law, she did not elaborate on her disparagement of Ericsson. Thus, to decipher her finding, one must analyze Judge Koh's order granting the FTC partial summary judgment.

In her order granting the FTC's motion for partial summary judgment, dated November 6, 2018, Judge Koh cited an exhibit that contained a filing from October 1998 in the U.S. District Court for the Eastern District of Texas—in which "Ericsson sued Qualcomm for patent infringement and alleged that Qualcomm products, including two modem chips, infringed Ericsson's SEPs"[1393] that Ericsson alleged were "essential to the IS-95 standard."[1394] Ericsson, Judge Koh explained, accused Qualcomm of patent infringement; Qualcomm responded in its motion for partial summary judgment in 1998 by arguing, according to Judge Koh's paraphrasing, "that

---

[1392] *Id.*

[1393] Order Granting FTC's Motion for Partial Summary Judgment on Qualcomm's Contractual Duties Pursuant to the Contracts with ATIS and the TIA, 2018 WL 5848999, *supra* note 52, at *13 (citing Qualcomm's Motion for Partial Summary Judgment to Limit Ericsson's Requested Relief for the Alleged Infringement of the Patents-in-Suit at 2, Ericsson Inc. v. Qualcomm Inc., No. 2-96-CV183 (E.D. Tex. Oct. 6, 1998), *Reply Exhibit 14 to* FTC's Reply in Support of Partial Summary Judgment, *supra* note 485).

[1394] Qualcomm's Motion for Partial Summary Judgment to Limit Ericsson's Requested Relief for the Alleged Infringement of the Patents-in-Suit at 2, Ericsson Inc. v. Qualcomm Inc., No. 2-96-CV183 (E.D. Tex. Oct. 6, 1998), *Reply Exhibit 14 to* FTC's Reply in Support of Partial Summary Judgment, *supra* note 485; *see also* Plaintiffs' Opening Pre-Trial Brief at 11, Nokia Corp. v. Qualcomm Inc., No. 2330-VCS (Del. Ch. July 15, 2008) ("Ericsson sued Qualcomm for infringement of patents it claimed were essential to the CDMAOne/IS-95 and CDMA2000 standards.").

the TIA IPR [P]olicy . . . requires Ericsson to license *any* patents" that are essential to practice the TIA's standard.[1395] Judge Koh said that, in 1998, "Qualcomm trumpeted the same non-discrimination principles it attempts to reject" in Qualcomm's opposition to the FTC's motion for partial summary judgment, "as Qualcomm argued that the TIA IPR [P]olicy 'ensures that *all* industry participants will be able to develop, manufacture, and sell products compliant with the relevant standard without incurring the risk that patent holders will be able to shut down those operations.'"[1396]

Again, Judge Koh did not establish that Ericsson (or Qualcomm, for that matter) had argued in 1998 that an SEP holder was required to offer an *exhaustive* license to its SEPs to rival modem manufacturers. Again, the more plausible interpretation is that Ericsson's position in 2008 was that rival modem manufacturers were entitled to a *nonexhaustive* "license," as parties used that term in commercial agreements before *Quanta*. Moreover, the statement that she attributed to Qualcomm in 1998 did not appear to manifest any inconsistency with its position in *FTC v. Qualcomm*. To the contrary, that quotation appeared to comport with Qualcomm's position in *FTC v. Qualcomm* that Qualcomm and rival modem manufacturers could achieve freedom to operate through a covenant to sue last (or, before *Quanta*, a nonexhaustive "license"). Simply put, the quotation that Judge Koh attributed to Qualcomm did not establish her premise that Ericsson and Qualcomm had argued in favor of the exhaustive licensing of cellular SEPs at the component level in 1998.

Consequently, Judge Koh's findings concerning Ericsson were predicated on the same kind of false conflict that she attributed to Nokia and Nokia's prior pleadings. Judge Koh did not establish that Ericsson or Qualcomm had argued in a 1998 patent-infringement case that cellular SEP holders are required to offer exhaustive licenses to their cellular SEPs at the component level.

c.   The Exhaustive Licensing of Cellular SEPs at the Component Level and the "Car Wars"

The third reason that Judge Koh's findings concerning Nokia and Ericsson were exceptionally significant was the collateral effect of those findings on future litigation concerning the licensing of cellular SEPs at the component

---

[1395] Order Granting FTC's Motion for Partial Summary Judgment on Qualcomm's Contractual Duties Pursuant to the Contracts with ATIS and the TIA, 2018 WL 5848999, *supra* note 52, at *13 (emphasis in original).

[1396] *Id.* (emphasis in original) (quoting Qualcomm's Motion for Partial Summary Judgment to Limit Ericsson's Requested Relief for the Alleged Infringement of the Patents-in-Suit, Ericsson Inc. v. Qualcomm Inc., No. 2-96-CV183 (E.D. Tex. Oct. 6, 1998), *Reply Exhibit 14 to* FTC's Reply in Support of Partial Summary Judgment, *supra* note 485).

level. Judge Koh's November 6, 2018 order granting the FTC's motion for partial summary judgment that Qualcomm was required to offer exhaustive licenses to its cellular SEPs to rival modem manufacturers,[1397] when combined with her May 21, 2019 findings of fact and conclusion of law that Nokia's position and Ericsson's position about the exhaustive licensing of cellular SEPs were not credible, appeared to prejudge certain issues in another high-profile case then pending before Judge Koh that also concerned the licensing of cellular SEPs, *Continental v. Avanci*.[1398] That dispute is the first American case to be filed in the "car wars."

The car wars are expected to implicate SEP holders, including Ericsson, which became an early participant in the Avanci patent pool, which was created to license cellular SEPs for 5G applications in automobiles, smart meters for electricity, and potentially other devices that will be wirelessly connected in the Internet of Things.[1399] In *Continental v. Avanci*, Nokia is defending against the allegation that it is obligated to offer exhaustive licenses to its SEPs at the component level—which in the automotive context means at the level of the telematics control unit (TCU) rather than the vehicle.[1400] Thus, TCUs are to smart vehicles as modems are to smartphones. This topic is the next chapter in global legal disputes over SEPs and the FRAND contract, and the broader implications of this ruling by Judge Koh will become clearer in Part X.C.

2. *Judge Koh's Trope of "Made-for-Litigation" Evidence*

Judge Koh's criticism that Ericsson's testimony and Nokia's testimony were "made-for-litigation" was tautological. Since at least the writings of Adam Smith, civilization has noticed that human beings tend to act in their economic self-interest.[1401] In what precise sense were the FTC's witnesses—

[1397] Order Granting FTC's Motion for Partial Summary Judgment on Qualcomm's Contractual Duties Pursuant to the Contracts with ATIS and the TIA, 2018 WL 5848999, *supra* note 52.

[1398] Complaint for Breach of FRAND Commitments and Violations of Antitrust and Unfair Competition Laws ¶ 146, at 45–46, Continental Auto. Sys., Inc. v. Avanci, LLC, No. 5:19-cv-02520 (N.D. Cal. May 10, 2019) [hereinafter Complaint, *Continental v. Avanci*].

[1399] *See Vision*, AVANCI, https://www.avanci.com/vision/; *see also Pricing*, AVANCI, https://www.avanci.com/marketplace/#li-pricing ("Royalties will vary from one type of device to the next based on the value the technology brings to the device, not its sales price. For example, the royalty will be different when the licensed product is a vehicle that continuously provides a hotspot, navigation data, streaming entertainment, enhanced safety, warranty services, and remote performance monitoring, rather than a rental bike stand that only sends intermittent signals of bike availability.").

[1400] *See, e.g.*, Karin Matussek & Jan-Patrick Barnert, *Mercedes-Benz May Face German Sales Ban After Nokia Wins Patent Ruling*, BLOOMBERG, Aug. 18, 2020 ("Nokia Oyj won a court ruling in a patent dispute with Daimler AG, giving the Finnish company leverage in a long-running fight over mobile technology in automobiles. Nokia, owner of the Mercedes-Benz brand, violated Nokia's mobile-technology patents, judges in Mannheim, Germany, said Tuesday[, August 18, 2020]. The ruling goes to the heart of how technology must be licensed for mobile-telecommunication systems that are standard features in most modern cars. . . . The court said it had to side with Nokia because Daimler wasn't willing to abide by existing rules for so-called standard essential patents.").

[1401] ADAM SMITH, AN INQUIRY INTO THE NATURE AND CAUSES OF THE WEALTH OF NATIONS bk. 1, ch. 2 (1776) (explaining Smith's theory of enlightened self-interest). As Smith wrote in 1776, "[i]t is not from the

including the company representatives from Apple, Intel, and rival modem manufacturers—*not* giving sworn testimony before Judge Koh that could equally be characterized as self-serving and made-for-litigation? Would anybody who had read Judge Curiel's order denying Apple's motion for summary judgment in *In re Qualcomm Litigation* in March 2019 doubt that self-interest might tinge the testimony of Apple's representatives in *FTC v. Qualcomm*?[1402]

Moreover, the occasion for Ericsson's explanation of its licensing practices for SEPs was deposition testimony by a senior executive based in Sweden. That deposition testimony was specifically intended to substitute, pursuant to Federal Rule of Civil Procedure 32, for in-person testimony to be given under oath before Judge Koh in open court.[1403] Which is to say that the deposition of the senior Ericsson executive consisted of testimonial statements, given under oath and subject to cross examination, that were—not surprisingly—consciously and intentionally "made-for-litigation," just as the Federal Rules provide.

3. *Mr. Weiler's Direct Examination Concerning ETSI's Intellectual Property Rights (IPR) Policy*

Mr. Weiler's testimony cast doubt on the correctness of Judge Koh's order granting the FTC's motion for partial summary judgment that Qualcomm's RAND commitment to two SSOs obligated Qualcomm to offer exhaustive licenses to its cellular SEPs at the component level. Mr. Weiler's testimony also rebutted the testimony of the FTC's expert economic witnesses that Qualcomm had charged a royalty for an exhaustive license to its cellular SEPs that exceeded the FRAND ceiling. I report Mr. Weiler's testimony at some length here because Judge Koh unjustifiably discredited it and disparaged Mr. Weiler's professional reputation.

a. *ETSI's IPR Special Committee*

Mr. Weiler was asked on direct examination by Richard Taffet of Morgan Lewis[1404] during Qualcomm's defense case to explain the creation of ETSI's

---

benevolence of the butcher, the brewer, or the baker, that we expect our dinner, but from their regard to their own interest." *Id.*

[1402] *See supra* notes 310–312 and accompanying text.

[1403] *See* FED. R. CIV. P. 32(a)(1); *see also id.* 32(a)(4)(B) ("A party may use for any purpose the deposition of a witness, whether or not a party, if the court finds . . . that the witness is more than 100 miles from the place of hearing or trial or is outside the United States, unless it appears that the witness's absence was procured by the party offering the deposition[.]").

[1404] It is unclear from Judge Koh's findings of fact and conclusions of law whether she understood that Mr. Taffet, who conducted Mr. Weiler's direct examination, is himself an internationally recognized authority on the formation and governance of ETSI and its IPR Policy. *See, e.g.,* Richard Taffet & Phil Harris, *Standards and Intellectual Property Rights Policies, in* PATENTS AND STANDARDS: PRACTICE, POLICY,

intellectual property rights (IPR) Special Committee and Mr. Weiler's chairmanship of that committee from 2008 to 2018:

> Q. Is there a committee within ETSI that is responsible for the Intellectual Property Policy?
>
> A. Yes. The responsibility for the Policy is within the general assembly. But as the general assembly participants are more from . . . a standard organization only perspective, ETSI has created a special IPR Special Committee where . . . many of the lawyers of our members and others are coming together to discuss potential changes needed for the Policy of ETSI, for the IPR Policy.
>
> Q. That committee is the IPR Special Committee?
>
> A. This is correct.
>
> Q. Have you participated in the IPR SC [Special Committee] at all?
>
> A. Yes, I have participated in that committee from its inception in 2007, and I became the chairman of that committee in 2008, and I have chaired that committee now for ten years until the end of last year.
>
> Q. So as of this time, you're no longer the chair, but you did chair the IPR Special Committee for those ten years?
>
> A. Yes.[1405]

Mr. Weiler then testified about the committee's rule of making decisions by consensus:

> Q. Now, during the time that you were involved with the IPR Special Committee, how were decisions made in the committee?
>
> A. This committee is an advisory committee to the general assembly because the general assembly wants to understand and know [what] . . . the membership view on this topic is. Therefore, I have decided and have done this over these ten years, that all decisions in this committee have to be made by consensus.
>
> Q. And when you use the word "consensus," what do you mean?
>
> A. Consensus means the decision is backed by all stakeholder groups in the membership, so it's absent any sustained opposition of any stakeholder group in order to make sure that everybody who's concerned of [sic] such decisions have [sic] a fair say and is also agreeable to those decisions.

AND ENFORCEMENT ch. 4 (Michael L. Drapkin ed., Bloomberg Law Book Div. 2018), *cited in* HTC Corp. v. Telefonaktiebolaget LM Ericsson, 407 F. Supp. 3d 631, 634 (E.D. Tex. 2019) (Gilstrap, C.J.) (discussing standard essentiality under ETSI's IPR Policy).

[1405] Transcript of Proceedings (Volume 8) at 1668:11–1669:5, FTC v. Qualcomm Inc., No. 5:17-cv-00220-LHK (N.D. Cal. Jan. 22, 2019) (Testimony of Dirk Weiler (Head of Standards, Nokia)).

Q. Does consensus require unanimity of use [sic: views]?

A. No, it does not. So it can't be blocked, any decision, by a single company.

Q. Is it the same as a majority vote, consensus?

A. No, not at all, because when you use majority, so if you have 50 percent, there is a very high likelihood that you miss out complete stakeholder groups. ETSI has a very diverse membership with very diverse interests. We have all the big technology companies in there. So making such decisions by a simple majority would leave out important parts of our members.[1406]

Consequently, Mr. Taffet established that Mr. Weiler had acquired, over the course of more than a decade, substantial experience and expertise in regard to ETSI's IPR Special Committee, which was responsible for deliberating over any potential changes to ETSI's IPR Policy.

b.   ETSI's IPR Policy and FRAND Licensing of SEPs

Mr. Taffet then asked Mr. Weiler which provision of ETSI's IPR Policy most directly concerned FRAND licensing of SEPs:

Q. . . . Mr. Weiler, do you recognize this document [QX2776]?

A. Yes, I do. This is ETSI's intellectual property rights Policy in its current version.

Q. And . . . is there a specific provision in the IPR Policy that most directly addresses FRAND licensing?

A. Yes. If you turn to clause 6.1 of the ETSI IPR Policy, this describes the provisions of FRAND licensing.[1407]

Next, Mr. Taffet asked Mr. Weiler whether ETSI had amended clause 6.1 of its IPR Policy:

Q. Mr. Weiler, has the language of clause 6.1 changed since the time you have been involved with ETSI activities?

A. No.

Q. Now, how does Nokia implement section 6.1?

A. Nokia is implementing its obligation under [clause] 6.1 by licensing its patents on the device level.

Q. And has this been the practice during the entire time you've been employed by Nokia?

[1406] *Id.* at 1669:6–1670:5.
[1407] *Id.* at 1670:6–17.

A. Yes.

Q. Was it also the case during the time that you were employed by Siemens, that they did the same practice?

A. Yes.

Q. And did that practice continue during the time you were employed by the Nokia/Siemens entity that was formed?

A. Also in—also yes.[1408]

Mr. Weiler thus testified that clause 6.1 of the ETSI IPR Policy had not changed since at least 2007 and that various SEP holders implement clause 6.1 by offering exhaustive SEP licenses at the OEM level, rather than at the component level.

> *c.   Clause 6.1 of the ETSI IPR Policy and the Prevalence of Exhaustive Licensing of SEPs to OEMs*

Mr. Taffet then probed how other ETSI members implemented the FRAND obligation arising from clause 6.1 of the ETSI IPR Policy:

> Q. Do you have an understanding, Mr. Weiler, of how other members of ETSI implement clause 6.1?
>
> A. During my time as chairman of this committee, we have discussed the various elements of FRAND and, as I have said, in this committee, all members of ETSI with any interest in licensing have been there and in detail explained over these ten years also how they do the licensing. And as well during this time, I have been participating to [sic] numerous conferences where many member companies in detail have explained their licensing practice. So I'm very well aware of how members, ETSI members are implementing their licensing obligation.[1409]

Mr. Weiler then was asked about the relationship between clause 6.1 of the ETSI IPR Policy and the practice of licensing only at the device level:

> Q. Well, do you have an understanding, sir, of how the other ETSI members implement [clause] 6.1 based upon the foundation that you have just laid?
>
> A. It is my understanding from all this discussion at presentations that I have heard that they all implement the Policy by licensing on the device level.

1408 *Id.* at 1672:1–15.
1409 *Id.* at 1673:6–17.

Q. And let me ask you to just clarify. When you say "device level," what do you mean?

A. The ETSI IPR Policy requires you in [clause] 6.1 to give licenses for equipment, and equipment is defined in ETSI's IPR Policy under clause 15, and in this clause 15, you'll find the definition of equipment under number 4. And that says, "'equipment' shall mean any system or device fully conforming to a standard." And what . . . is my understanding of the industry practice is that in the case of the cellular business, this means that these companies license, for example, the handset and not any subpart of this handset.[1410]

Over the objection of Elizabeth Gillen of the FTC,[1411] Mr. Weiler testified further about why it had long been his understanding (as a percipient witness) that clause 6.1 of ETSI's IPR Policy does not require SEP holders to offer exhaustive licenses to their cellular SEPs at the component level:

Q. Mr. Weiler, what is the basis of your understanding whether device level licensing is consistent with the objectives of clause 6.1?

A. May I turn first to the objectives? ETSI is in the comfortable position to have a policy which is not only the legal text, but also giving the reason why, what are these policy objectives. And this is contained in clause 3 of the ETSI IPR Policy. And these objectives say that ETSI wants the most suitable technology to be implemented in this conduct. They want these technologies to be, and these standards to be able to be implemented by everybody and not be blocked by any patent which is not available. But at the same time, ETSI's objectives in [clause] 3.2 also very explicitly say that the IPR holders should be fairly rewarded for their willingness to contribute their technology into the standard. And these three elements—so best technology, availability to everybody for implementation of this, and thirdly, the fair reward—is then implemented in clause 6.1 where you are asked to give licenses on FRAND terms . . . at least to the equipment device level. And, therefore, in order to achieve the objective to get a fair reward to oblige the patent holder to license on fair and non-discriminatory terms, you have to design a licensing program which fulfills this obligation, and it is obvious that everybody can implement a standard and contribute components of the standard into a device and you then license the device level only, and, therefore, all the implementation going into this device is licensed. And this is why this is fully in line with the policy objectives of ETSI.

Q. Has that been Nokia's understanding since you've been employed by Nokia?

A. Yes.

[1410] *Id.* at 1673:25–1674:17.
[1411] *Id.* at 1674:23–1678:6.

Q. And was it the understanding of Siemens when you were employed by Siemens?

A. Yes.[1412]

Mr. Weiler was then asked whether any member of ETSI's IPR Special Committee had argued that OEM-level licenses contravened clause 6.1 of ETSI's IPR Policy:

Q. And in the ETSI IPR Special Committee, has anyone objected that device level licensing is contrary to [clause] 6.1?

A. There was no single contribution coming into the ETSI IPR committee asking, arguing that this would be inconsistent.

Q. Now, have proposals been made to ETSI's IPR Special Committee to modify clause 6.1 to require component level licensing?

A. No.

Q. And has anyone stated in the Special Committee that by licensing at the device level, that a FRAND commitment is violated?

A. No.[1413]

Thus, Mr. Weiler testified, as a percipient witness, that ETSI's members understood that granting exhaustive SEP licenses to OEMs comports with clause 6.1 of ETSI's IPR Policy.

> d. *Did ETSI's IPR Special Committee Ever Reach Consensus to Change ETSI's IPR Policy to Make a Specific Royalty Base Compulsory in Exhaustive SEP Licenses?*

Mr. Weiler testified that, although certain ETSI members (including Apple) had requested that ETSI change its IPR Policy to specify that the smallest saleable patent-practicing unit serve as the royalty base for any FRAND offer and that there be a specified aggregate royalty, ETSI vigorously debated those proposals:

Q. Now, let me ask you, Mr. Weiler, have proposals been made in the IPR Special Committee to change clause 6.1 so FRAND is more specifically defined?

A. Yes.

Q. When were such proposals made and what were the circumstances?

1412 *Id.* at 1679:12–1680:24.
1413 *Id.* at 1680:25–1681:11.

A. In the end of 2011, ETSI received two letters from Apple and Broadcom requesting ETSI to discuss a change of its IPR Policy to better define FRAND.

Q. [sic: The following two sentences appear to be an answer, not a question.] And as chair of this committee, it is my obligation to see whether I call for [a] meeting of this committee and discuss such topics, and based on my knowledge of the industry discussions, I agreed to call the committee and—with the question, should ETSI discuss potential clarifications, what FRAND means? And so we have discussed this in ETSI during the course of three years.

Q. Now, was one of the proposals that was made to define a common royalty base for calculating a FRAND royalty?

A. Yes.

Q. What was that proposal?

A. The proposal which was submitted by various companies, including Apple, Broadcom, Cisco, Intel and maybe others, [and] this . . . contribution proposed to define the royalty base based on the smallest saleable patent practicing unit, or SSPPU.

Q. And what was the outcome of that proposal?

A. This proposal has been extensively discussed in that committee, and there was no consensus to change the ETSI IPR Policy to include any such provision.

Q. Were other proposals made to the IPR Special Committee to define FRAND as being based on an aggregate royalty or principles of proportionality?

A. Also such a proposal has been made to ETSI and, again, this proposal was intensively discussed. But finally, there was no conclusion and no consensus agreement to implement any of such proposal into the ETSI IPR Policy.[1414]

Consequently, Mr. Weiler testified that, after extensive debate, the ETSI IPR Special Committee considered and declined to accept the proposal—submitted by companies including Apple, Broadcom, Cisco, and Intel—that clause 6.1 of the ETSI IPR Policy be amended to define a common royalty base for calculating a FRAND royalty and to specify an aggregate royalty for exhaustive licenses to SEPs.

[1414] *Id.* at 1681:22–1683:8.

e. *Clause 6.1 of the ETSI IPR Policy and Exhaustive Licensing at the Component Level*

Finally, Mr. Weiler testified during his direct examination by Mr. Taffet that no ETSI member or representative from any U.S. antitrust agency invited to participate in ETSI IPR Special Committee meetings had proposed redefining FRAND to require component-level licensing:

> Q. Okay. Now, have representatives of the United States antitrust agencies participated in ETSI's IPR Special Committee?
>
> A. I have tried to have an all inclusive discussion in this committee, so . . . especially when we started discussing whether FRAND needs to be further defined, I had invited regulators from Japan, from Korea and China, and they all were coming at times. And I also have invited representatives from the U.S. Federal Trade Commission and the Department of Justice, and . . . so the Federal Trade Commission, with Pat Roach, and the Department of Justice with Paul O'Donnell, have regularly participated to [sic] these meetings.
>
> Q. And were these representatives free to make comments or proposals to modify the ETSI IPR Policy?
>
> A. Yes.
>
> . . . .
>
> Q. Did they comment on the proposals you just described?
>
> A. Yes, they commented on the proposals described, and those comments have been captured in the relevant meeting reports of these committees.
>
> Q. And have the meeting reports that you just identified recorded any comments, whether by the U.S. antitrust agencies or anyone else, concerning a request or a proposal to define FRAND as requiring component level licensing?
>
> A. This topic has not been discussed in ETSI.
>
> Mr. Taffet: Thank you, Mr. Weiler. I pass the witness, Your Honor.[1415]

Consequently, Mr. Weiler's testimony indicated his understanding from personal experience that ETSI did not impose, or even consider any request or proposal to impose, the obligation on SEP holders to offer exhaustive licenses to their cellular SEPs at the component level.

[1415] *Id.* at 1683:9–24, 1684:15–25.

4. *Mr. Weiler's Cross Examination*

Judge Koh largely ignored the direct-examination testimony of Mr. Weiler. To the extent that she did not ignore that testimony entirely, she discredited both it and Mr. Weiler. Judge Koh's basis for finding that Mr. Weiler was not credible was Ms. Gillen's cross examination of him for the FTC.

a. *Does Nokia License SEPs?*

Ms. Gillen first established the self-evident proposition that Nokia, a large holder of cellular SEPs and Mr. Weiler's employer, had designated him to be its corporate representative in *FTC v. Qualcomm*:

> Q. Mr. Weiler, you testified earlier that you're employed by Nokia; correct?
>
> A. Yes.
>
> Q. And you were designated as Nokia's corporate representative to testify at a deposition in this case on topics relating to Nokia's understanding of the ETSI IPR Policy; is that right?
>
> A. This is correct.
>
> Q. And Nokia is a licensor; right?
>
> A. Nokia is both licensee and a licensor.
>
> Q. But you'd consider Nokia a *net* licensor; correct?
>
> A. I don't know because I'm not involved in the details of licensing activities of Nokia.
>
> Q. Are you aware that Nokia licenses its standard essential patents to others?
>
> A. I'm aware that Nokia licenses standard essential patents to others, yes.[1416]

Ms. Gillen then asked whether it was more profitable for Nokia to license at the OEM level than at the component level.

Among its other ambiguities, Ms. Gillen's question did not specify *what* Nokia was licensing (cellular SEPs only? Nokia's entire patent portfolio of SEPs and non-SEPs?) and whether the license would be exhaustive or not. Not surprisingly, the question prompted Mr. Taffet's objection:

> Q. And is it more profitable for Nokia to license device makers than component manufacturers?
>
> Mr. Taffet: Objection. Lacks foundation, your honor.
>
> The Court: If you know, you may answer. Go ahead. Overruled.

[1416] *Id.* at 1685:8–1685:24 (emphasis added).

The Witness: As I'm not involved in the licensing activities of my company, I cannot answer the specific question about licensing activities as such.[1417]

Mr. Weiler thus testified that, because he did not participate in Nokia's licensing activities, this question about Nokia's particular licensing strategy was outside his scope of knowledge.

b. Clause 6.1 of ETSI's IPR Policy and the Specific Commercial Terms of Exhaustive SEP Licenses

Ms. Gillen then asked Mr. Weiler about the commercial terms of specific patent licenses:

> Q. You would agree that under the objectives of the ETSI IPR Policy, it would not make sense for one patent holder to charge substantially more royalties than another patent holder who's made a similar amount of contributions; is that right?
>
> A. Well, these are very specific commercial terms between the parties, and ETSI states very clearly that ETSI stays out of these detailed commercial terms. And as my basis of knowledge is with regard to standards and the interface, but not to the specific economic questions and commercial terms of specific patent licenses[,] I don't have a relevant opinion on that.
>
> Q. So at your deposition, on page 145, lines 9 through 19, you testified that the ETSI IPR Policy objectives say there should be fair reward to the contributor of technology. If there's a general agreement that the overall costs for patents cannot be increased unlimited, and for each of the patent holders, this policy objective is true, in a context where you have many patents, there cannot be one patent holder who charges way more than anybody else who has a similar amount of contribution given. Do you stand by that testimony?
>
> A. Yes.[1418]

Ms. Gillen, apparently alluding to testimony given by Lorenzo Casaccia of Qualcomm (given the morning of January 22, 2019, immediately before Mr. Weiler's testimony) that Nokia induces its representatives to 3GPP to increase Nokia's approved contributions,[1419] then probed Mr. Weiler on that same point:

[1417] *Id.* at 1685:25–1686:8.

[1418] *Id.* at 1686:10–1687:6.

[1419] *Id.* at 1643:21–1644:6 (Testimony of Lorenzo Casaccia (Vice President of Technical Standards, Qualcomm)) ("Q. . . . [W]e've discussed issues in the substantive phase and the change control phase with the concept of approved contribution counting. Are there other flaws? A. There are several other flaws. The most important other flaw is that approved contribution counting is subject to manipulation by companies and, in fact, in my experience of several years it has been manipulated by companies. With

Q. Does Nokia offer its 3GPP representatives financial incentives designed to increase the number of approved contributions?

A. To the best of my knowledge, we are not offering financial incentives for increasing the number of contributions.[1420]

Ms. Gillen then asked Mr. Weiler about the specific procedures that ETSI's IPR Special Committee employed to make decisions:

Q. You testified earlier that with respect to making decisions within ETSI, all decisions are usually made by consensus; is that right?

A. This is correct.

Q. And you testified that consensus is the absence of a sustained objection of a materially involved stakeholder group; is that right?

A. Yes.

Q. And Nokia is a materially involved stakeholder group; right?

A. No. Nokia is a part of a stakeholder group. But Nokia alone is a single company and not a complete stakeholder group.

Q. And is Qualcomm a materially involved stakeholder group?

A. Again, Qualcomm is one company. And so this is the difference between unanimity and talking about materially involved stakeholder groups. So you can say, for example, Nokia and Ericsson and Huawei are similar companies who have similar interests, and if all three companies in this example would strongly object to something, then I would say I cannot define here consensus because this is a clear group of stakeholders who would not agree to that.

Q. And you testified that you've never been involved in any licensing discussions at Nokia; right?

A. This is correct, yes.[1421]

Mr. Weiler's answers to Ms. Gillen's questions appeared to indicate that his career had focused on ETSI's IPR Policy, as opposed to specific SEP licensing negotiations between counterparties or the specific commercial terms upon which counterparties had agreed in particular licenses.

Nevertheless, Ms. Gillen continued to interrogate Mr. Weiler about particular commercial terms in patent license agreements involving his prior employer (Siemens) or his current employer (Nokia). On their face, these

---

this, it means that companies have been artificially trying to inflate their numbers of either submitted contributions or approved contributions.").

[1420] *Id.* at 1687:7–11 (Testimony of Dirk Weiler (Head of Standards, Nokia)).

[1421] *Id.* at 1687:12–1688:11.

following questions were not confined to the licensing of cellular SEPs. Ms. Gillen had just established in Mr. Weiler's answer to her immediately preceding question that Mr. Weiler had "never been involved in *any* licensing discussions at Nokia,"[1422] which is to say neither licensing discussions concerning SEPs nor licensing discussions concerning non-SEPs.

So, there was also no hanging implication that Ms. Gillen's next questions for Mr. Weiler were confined to cellular SEPs. And of course Mr. Weiler had explained in considerable detail that the focus of his professional experience had been and continued to be the standardization of cellular technology. Ms. Gillen asked:

> Q. Are you aware that Siemens had a chip level license from Qualcomm in 2000?
>
> A. No.
>
> Q. And so you're not aware whether Nokia has ever granted any exhaustive chip level licenses to Qualcomm?
>
> A. I'm not aware of specific licenses from—inside of Nokia, no.
>
> Q. You testified earlier that Nokia implements licensing practices consistently worldwide; right?
>
> A. This is at least from what I hear, my understanding.[1423]

Considering that Mr. Weiler consistently testified that he was not aware of specific commercial terms in SEP licenses, what was the FTC's intended purpose of continuing to ask questions that Mr. Weiler averred that he could not answer?

c. Does ETSI's IPR Policy Trump the IPR Policies of ATIS and the TIA If the Former Differs in Some Respect from the Latter?

Ms. Gillen asked Mr. Weiler about the ATIS and TIA IPR policies:

> Q. And ATIS and TIA have different IPR policies than ETSI; isn't that right?
>
> A. Well, . . . ATIS and ETSI are from 3GPP, and ATIS, TIA, and ETSI are members of oneM2M. And those organizations have provisions which say that the patent policies of the organizational partners . . . need to be compatible. And so on a level which goes not maybe into very specific legal details, which I'm not qualified to answer here, but there is—it is clear that as they are both members and it has been analyzed that they are compatible.

[1422] *Id.* at 1688:9–1688:11 (emphasis added).
[1423] *Id.* at 1688:12–21.

Q. And is it your position that the ETSI IPR Policy should trump TIA's Policy if those policies are different?

A. If there would be an identification of differences of these policies, then it would need a discussion in 3GPP to see . . . whether those differences are so material that either of the organizations, or those who are changing something in comparison to the others would have to leave.

Q. And you've never held any positions with TIA or ATIS, have you?

A. I've never held any position in ATIS or TIA.

Ms. Gillen: I have no further questions.[1424]

Ms. Gillen posed a hypothetical question: would ETSI's IPR Policy trump the IPR policies of ATIS and the TIA if the former were "different" from the latter? This colloquy was odd for several reasons, not the least of which was that Mr. Weiler confirmed that he had never held any position in ATIS or the TIA, as he had in ETSI. His answer was necessarily the sound of one hand clapping. Moreover, the question lacked foundation. Ms. Gillen had provided no information about the nature of the hypothetical difference in IPR policies. The question invited pure speculation.

Finally, and most improbably, Ms. Gillen was asking Mr. Weiler—who is a physicist by training and does not appear to be a lawyer,[1425] and who emphasized that he was "not qualified to answer" questions about "very specific legal details"[1426]—to render a legal opinion that would necessarily require him to perform contract interpretation and choice-of-law analysis. In keeping with the observation that consistency is the hobgoblin of little minds, Ms. Gillen's parting hypothetical question to Mr. Weiler appeared to contradict her own grounds for an earlier objection, sustained by Judge Koh, that Mr. Weiler should not be permitted to testify about clause 6.1 of ETSI's IPR Policy, lest he stray into legal opinion: "Objection, Your Honor. Mr. Weiler is a fact witness. He's being asked here to testify about his interpretation of a contract provision."[1427] Judge Koh responded that she would sustain Ms. Gillen's objection if Mr. Taffet did not rephrase his question.[1428]

Yet, during cross examination a few minutes later, Judge Koh, hearing no objection from Qualcomm's counsel (understandably, considering Mr. Weiler's earlier testimony on clause 6.1), did not offer any spontaneous remarks or qualifications from the bench concerning the admissibility of

---

[1424] *Id.* at 1685:8–1689:19.

[1425] *See Dirk Weiler*, NOKIA BELL LABS, https://www.bell-labs.com/usr/Dirk.Weiler; *Dirk Weiler*, LINKEDIN, https://www.linkedin.com/in/weilerdirk/ (last visited Aug. 19, 2020).

[1426] Transcript of Proceedings (Volume 8) at 1689:5–6, FTC v. Qualcomm Inc., No. 5:17-cv-00220-LHK (N.D. Cal. Jan. 22, 2019) (Testimony of Dirk Weiler (Head of Standards, Nokia)).

[1427] *Id.* at 1670:21–23.

[1428] *Id.* at 1671:17–22.

what arguably was again legal opinion solicited from a fact witness who lacked any apparent legal training. Ms. Gillen proceeded without interruption to question Mr. Weiler on whether ETSI's IPR Policy would trump the IPR policies of ATIS and the TIA if the former differed from the latter in some unspecified respect.

For a nonlawyer, Mr. Weiler offered a respectable start to answering this hypothetical question, considering the factual vacuum in which Ms. Gillen presented it. In essence, he testified that the first step would be to determine whether the difference between the two sets of IPR policies amounted to a real conflict or merely a false conflict. For him to have said anything more would have been pure speculation. Even this answer of course exceeded the scope of the percipient testimony for which Mr. Weiler had been disclosed as a witness.

5. *Judge Koh's Disparagement of Mr. Weiler*

Judge Koh wrote in her findings of fact and conclusions of law: "The Court finds that Weiler was not credible."[1429] She said that Mr. Weiler "conveniently claimed complete ignorance" of Nokia's commercial agreements.[1430] Consequently, Judge Koh said, "the FTC could not cross-examine Weiler about Nokia's 2006 statements to the European Commission."[1431]

Put differently, it appeared that, because Mr. Weiler had not come to Judge Koh's courtroom prepared to testify about certain of the FTC's preferred topics for his cross examination, Judge Koh refused on credibility grounds to give any weight to his percipient testimony on a completely different topic for which he was eminently qualified to testify—namely, the internal deliberations by consensus on the development of, and proposals to change, clause 6.1 of the ETSI IPR Policy. On *that* question, which was plainly relevant to the merits of *FTC v. Qualcomm*, Mr. Weiler was arguably the world's foremost expert. His percipient testimony was predicated on his unique, first-hand knowledge derived from having chaired ETSI's IPR Special Committee for 10 years.

It might reasonably appear to an experienced trial lawyer or judge reading Judge Koh's findings of fact and conclusions of law that, by publicly calling Mr. Weiler "not credible" because he supposedly had "conveniently claimed complete ignorance" of Nokia's commercial agreements, Judge Koh was saying that Mr. Weiler lied under oath in her courtroom. A different judge might not have disparaged a witness's character for truthfulness with the same nonchalance.

[1429] FTC v. Qualcomm Inc., 411 F. Supp. 3d 658, 756 (N.D. Cal. 2019).
[1430] *Id.* at 755.
[1431] *Id.*

a. Injury to Mr. Weiler and to Nokia

The most plausible message that an experienced trial lawyer or judge could reasonably draw from Judge Koh's findings of fact and conclusions of law concerning Mr. Weiler's credibility is a derogatory one that professionally injures him. Judge Koh's denigration of Mr. Weiler's character for truthfulness surely will be used to impeach his testimony in any future legal proceeding. It is not to be believed that any judge could fail to understand that ramification of such a credibility finding. Such disparagement of a witness by a judge in a bench trial is an imperious ostracism dispensed with impunity.

Judge Koh's censure of Mr. Weiler also will foreseeably injure his employer, Nokia, which of course was not even a party in *FTC v. Qualcomm*. Nokia is, however, a recurring party in disputes that implicate ETSI's FRAND contract, including *Continental v. Avanci*. It is therefore entirely foreseeable that Nokia might have occasion to call Mr. Weiler to testify in the future in light of his unique knowledge of the ETSI IPR Policy and the deliberations of ETSI's IPR Special Committee. It is also entirely foreseeable that Judge Koh's published findings of fact and conclusions of law in *FTC v. Qualcomm* will be cited in other proceedings—whether or not Mr. Weiler is called to testify, and whether or not Nokia is even a party—for purposes of discrediting Mr. Weiler's percipient testimony on the public record regarding the deliberations that occurred during his chairmanship of ETSI's IPR Special Committee concerning the reach of clause 6.1 of the ETSI IPR Policy with respect to the question of the licensing of cellular SEPs at the component level.

For the experienced trial lawyer or judge, Judge Koh's harsh words for Mr. Weiler create the appearance that she disbelieved his sworn testimony that he lacked personal knowledge of the terms of Nokia's commercial agreements. But why? One searches in vain to find anything in Mr. Weiler's cross examination that would remotely justify Judge Koh's disparagement of him.

b. Ilkka Rahnasto's Testimony About Nokia's Licensing Practices

From reading Judge Koh's findings of fact and conclusions of law, an experienced trial lawyer or judge might be led to speculate that Judge Koh drew an adverse inference against Nokia generally and Mr. Weiler personally because Nokia did not send a corporate representative from Finland to testify live at trial who did possess personal knowledge about the terms of particular commercial agreements. But that experienced trial lawyer or judge would be wrong. Notwithstanding Judge Koh's obligation to make specific findings of fact pursuant to Federal Rule of Civil Procedure 52(a)(1), one reading solely her findings of fact and conclusions of law would never realize that a *second* Nokia witness *did* testify at trial by videotaped deposition about Nokia's licensing practices.

That second Nokia executive was Ilkka Rahnasto. Judge Koh never mentioned Dr. Rahnasto or his testimony anywhere in her findings of fact and conclusions of law.

Dr. Rahnasto reportedly held a Ph.D. in law from the University of Helsinki and had served as Senior Vice President of Nokia Technologies, where he "led the company's licensing and patent management efforts globally."[1432] He reportedly held various legal positions at Nokia concerning the licensing of intellectual property rights for 21 years, from 1997 to 2018.[1433] In November of 2018, Dr. Rahnasto left Nokia to become Senior Vice President of Marconi, the parent company of Avanci.[1434] At the time of his videotaped deposition on April 17, 2018, Dr. Rahnasto was still employed by Nokia.

In its defense case, Qualcomm played a portion of Dr. Rahnasto's videotaped deposition testimony on the ninth day of trial, Friday, January 25, 2019, three days after Mr. Weiler had testified.[1435] The excerpt of Dr. Rahnasto's videotaped deposition testimony that Judge Koh received as evidence at trial confirmed that Dr. Rahnasto testified about Nokia's licensing policies. The entirety of that excerpt of testimony, whose existence Judge Koh did not acknowledge in her findings of fact and conclusions of law, is reproduced here:

> MR. TAFFET: I'd like to begin by referring you to a document that's in the pile before you. It is a letter with the Alston & Bird letterhead, and it's been marked previously as CX4321. It should be relatively near the top.[1436]

[1432] Press Release, Marconi, Global IP Leader, Ilkka Rahnasto Joins Marconi as Senior Vice President (Nov. 6, 2018), https://marconi.com/wp-content/uploads/2018/11/Org-ann_Final-Nov-6.pdf.

[1433] *Id.*; *see also Ilkka Rahnasto*, LINKEDIN, https://www.linkedin.com/in/ilkka-rahnasto-7204278/ (last visited Aug. 19, 2020).

[1434] Press Release, Marconi, Global IP Leader, Ilkka Rahnasto Joins Marconi as Senior Vice President (Nov. 6, 2018), https://marconi.com/wp-content/uploads/2018/11/Org-ann_Final-Nov-6.pdf.

[1435] Transcript of Proceedings (Volume 9) at 1968:17–1969:6, FTC v. Qualcomm Inc., No. 5:17-cv-00220-LHK (N.D. Cal. Jan. 25, 2019).

[1436] Videotaped Deposition of Ilkka Rahnasto (Senior Vice President, Nokia) at 8:12–16, FTC v. Qualcomm Inc., No. 5:17-cv-00220-LHK (N.D. Cal. Apr. 17, 2018), *exhibit to* Qualcomm Incorporated's Submission of Deposition Testimony That Was Presented on January 25, 2019 (Trial Day 9), FTC v. Qualcomm Inc., No. 5:17-cv-00220-LHK (N.D. Cal. Jan. 25, 2019), ECF No. 1447-3. The FTC and Qualcomm evidently spliced together certain discontinuous passages of videotaped deposition testimony to produce a continuous video clip to be played in the courtroom at trial, consisting of questions and answers only and omitting any intervening objections and other colloquies among counsel that might have interrupted the questions and answers. *See* FED. R. CIV. P. 32(c) ("Unless the court orders otherwise, a party must provide a transcript of any deposition testimony the party offers, but may provide the court with the testimony in nontranscript form as well."). Consequently, a footnote that appears in the middle of a block quotation of deposition testimony above indicates the precise lines in the deposition transcript to which that quotation corresponds and the fact that a splice occurred there.

Q[.] Now, on page 10, there's a reference to—this is at the bottom of page 10. There's a reference to something that's referred to as a "one point of license practice." Do you see that?

A[.] Yes.

Q[.] Are you familiar with that phrase, "one point of license practice"?

A[.] Yes, I am.

Q[.] Could you explain that to us, please.

A[.] On a general level, it means that *in the value chain of manufacturing products, mobile phones, there's typically one party who is acquiring the relevant patent licenses, and there is also one party in the value chain [to] whom the licenses are being offered.*

Q[.] And with respect to Nokia's use or following of this practice, the one point—is there a specific point in the value chain at which Nokia grants licenses?

A[.] Yes. *We have always the license to the manufacturer of the end product, meaning the manufacturer of the mobile phone, the complete product.*

Q[.] Okay. And has that been Nokia's practice since it first had SEPs?

A[.] Yes.[1437]

Q[.] Then it [CX4321] goes on that Nokia's practice from the very beginning, and that it—meaning the practice—corresponds with industry practice. Do you see that?

A[.] Yes, I can see that.

Q[.] *And is that correct, that Nokia's practice corresponds to industry practice?*[1438]

THE WITNESS: *Based on my experience, that is my understanding.*[1439]

Dr. Rahnasto's testimony tended to establish two facts—(1) that Nokia's practice was to grant exhaustive licenses to its SEPs only to OEMs manufacturing end products including mobile phones, and (2) that it was common industry practice to offer exhaustive SEP licenses only to OEMs manufacturing end products including mobile phones.

In her findings of fact and conclusions of law, Judge Koh suppressed that evidence. Had Judge Koh not suppressed this percipient testimony by Dr. Rahnasto, it would have corroborated both Mr. Weiler's trial testimony and Nokia's position in its 2018 *amicus* brief filed in *FTC v. Qualcomm*.

[1437] *Id.* at 10:24–11:25 (emphasis added).
[1438] *Id.* at 13:15–21 (emphasis added).
[1439] *Id.* at 13:23–24 (emphasis added).

c.   *Was Judge Koh's Apparent Reason for Disparaging Mr. Weiler Believable, Considering Dr. Rahnasto's Testimony About Nokia's Licensing Practices?*

The very existence of Dr. Rahnasto's testimony cast doubt on Judge Koh's apparent reason for finding Mr. Weiler's testimony not to be credible—namely, the fact that Mr. Weiler had come to trial prepared to testify about clause 6.1 of ETSI's IPR Policy and the deliberations of ETSI's IPR Special Committee, instead of the particular terms of Nokia's commercial agreements and its 2006 pleading to the European Commission. Judge Koh's apparent reason for discrediting Mr. Weiler was specious because Nokia made available to the FTC for purposes of cross examination a second company witness whom Nokia actually employed in 2006 in its patent-licensing department. Dr. Rahnasto appeared clearly to be the witness that Nokia had designated to testify about Nokia's licensing practices. Yet, Dr. Rahnasto's testimony, and even his existence, was completely devoid of mention in Judge Koh's findings of fact and conclusions of law.

There is no indication in Judge Koh's findings of fact and conclusions of law that the FTC was unable to call Dr. Rahnasto to testify at trial and to cross examine him on Nokia's particular commercial agreements and its 2006 pleading to the European Commission. Nor is there any indication in Judge Koh's findings of fact and conclusions of law why, in the alternative, the FTC could not have cross examined Dr. Rahnasto on those topics during his deposition and then have designated portions of his videotaped deposition testimony to be replayed at trial, either in the agency's affirmative case or in its rebuttal case. The FTC declined to take either course of action. Why?

A sophisticated trial lawyer or judge might interpret the FTC's failure to take either course of action to indicate instead that the agency had concluded before trial in January 2019 that it was confronting an overwhelming record that Nokia—and, for that matter, every major licensor of cellular SEPs in the industry—had long followed a demonstrable practice of offering exhaustive licenses to cellular SEPs to OEMs only and not to component manufacturers. Is there any doubt that, had the FTC secured *inculpatory* testimony from its cross examination of Dr. Rahnasto at his deposition, the agency would have marshalled that evidence against Qualcomm at trial?

As we shall see in Part X.G.2, Mr. Weiler's testimony and Dr. Rahnasto's testimony both tended to disprove Judge Koh's findings concerning industry practice in her order granting the FTC's motion for partial summary judgment. A finding that it was common industry practice to offer exhaustive cellular SEP licenses to OEMs only would cause the FTC's (and Judge Koh's) theory of antitrust liability in *FTC v. Qualcomm* to crumble, because that theory of antitrust liability was predicated on Judge Koh's erroneous finding that Qualcomm had breached two RAND contracts with two SSOs, ATIS and the TIA. Crediting the testimony of Mr. Weiler and Dr. Rahnasto would be embarrassing to Judge Koh after she had already climbed out on a limb in her partial summary judgment order. There could be no graceful way for her to confess error and climb back. She was halfway through trial.

If Mr. Weiler's supposed prevarication at trial had offended Judge Koh, one might have expected her then to take a keen interest in Dr. Rahnasto's videotaped testimony, which Qualcomm played at trial three days after Mr. Weiler testified. Yet, the trial transcript indicates that Judge Koh did not comment on the substance of Dr. Rahnasto's testimony at trial, and of course his name never appeared in her findings of fact and conclusions of law. Why was there no indication of Judge Koh's particular attentiveness to Dr. Rahnasto's testimony?

Perhaps because two months before trial, in her order granting the FTC partial summary judgment on November 6, 2018, Judge Koh had already climbed out onto the limb where she found herself now perched. She had concluded (erroneously, as we have now seen) that, because Nokia in 2006 had supposedly taken the "diametrically oppos[ite]" position on the exhaustive licensing of cellular SEPs, Nokia's "made-for-litigation" testimony at trial on that topic was mendacious.[1440] To the extent that Judge Koh had prejudged the credibility of Nokia—and even Ericsson and Qualcomm—before trial, that prejudgment was predicated on a spurious premise, because she never established that an inconsistency existed between Nokia's position (and Ericsson's position and Qualcomm's position) on the exhaustive licensing of cellular SEPs in *FTC v. Qualcomm* and in prior litigation. Did Judge Koh decline to acknowledge in her findings of fact and conclusions of law even the existence of Dr. Rahnasto's testimony because she had summarily (but baselessly) concluded before trial that Nokia's testimony was not to be believed?

F.   *What Private Remedy Exists for a Witness Whose Reputation a Judge Has Unjustifiably Impugned?*

According to the *Restatement (Second) of Torts*, "[a] communication is defamatory if it tends so to harm the reputation of another as to lower him in the estimation of the community or to deter third persons from associating or dealing with him."[1441] As we saw earlier, the Federal Rules of Evidence define credibility as a person's "reputation for having a character for truthfulness[.]"[1442] If

---

[1440] FTC v. Qualcomm Inc., 411 F. Supp. 3d 658, 755 (N.D. Cal. 2019) (citing Order Granting FTC's Motion for Partial Summary Judgment on Qualcomm's Contractual Duties Pursuant to the Contracts with ATIS and the TIA, 2018 WL 5848999, *supra* note 52, at *13).

[1441] RESTATEMENT (SECOND) OF TORTS § 559 (AM. LAW INST. 1977).

[1442] FED. R. EVID. 608(a).

untrue and uttered by a private citizen, Judge Koh's derogatory statements that Qualcomm's company witnesses lacked the character for truthfulness in their professions might constitute slander *per se*. The same would be true of Judge Koh's derogatory statements regarding the credibility of Mr. Weiler of Nokia.

It is also possible that Judge Koh's statements that Qualcomm's expert economic witness had produced unreliable testimony might also be slander *per se* if uttered by a private citizen. The *Restatement* provides:

> One who publishes a slander that ascribes to another conduct, character-istics or a condition that would adversely affect his fitness for the proper conduct of his lawful business, trade or profession, or of his public or private office, whether honorary or for profit, is subject to liability without proof of special harm.[1443]

But when a defamatory communication is made by a judge, the legal conse-quences are quite different because several privileges or immunities might or do apply.[1444]

It might surprise nonlawyers to learn, as section 585 of the *Restatement (Second) of Torts* explains: "A judge or other officer performing a judicial func-tion is absolutely privileged to publish defamatory matter in the performance of the function if the publication has some relation to the matter before him."[1445] The *Restatement*'s comments on section 585 elaborate:

> [T]he personal ill will of the judge is immaterial. So too, it is immaterial that he knows the defamatory matter to be false. . . . Abuse of his official position by a judicial officer may subject him to impeachment, recall or removal, but it does not subject him to a civil action for defamation.[1446]

[1443] RESTATEMENT (SECOND) OF TORTS § 573 (AM. LAW INST. 1977).

[1444] *See, e.g.*, Federal Employees Liability Reform and Tort Compensation Act of 1988 (Westfall Act), Pub. L. No. 100-694, 102 Stat. 4563 (codified at 28 U.S.C. §§ 2671, 2674, 2679) (prohibiting federal employees acting within the scope of their employment from being sued for claims arising under state tort law); Federal Tort Claims Act, 28 U.S.C. §§ 1346(b), 2671–80; *id.* § 2680(h) (specifying that the Act's waiver of sovereign immunity does not apply to claims of "libel, slander . . . or interference with contract rights").

[1445] RESTATEMENT (SECOND) OF TORTS § 585 (AM. LAW INST. 1977).

[1446] *Id.* cmt. a; *see also id.* cmt. b ("The rule stated in this Section [585] is applicable to any person acting as a judge of a court, whether of general or limited jurisdiction. . . . Certain governmental agencies whose functions are sometimes said to be quasi-judicial are empowered to exercise a wide discretion in the application of legal principles to varying fact situations, the conclusions reached having the effect of law. While performing these functions, members of these tribunals are protected under the rule stated in this Section."); *id.* cmt. d ("The judicial function is usually exercised in the course of judicial proceedings, that is, after the commencement or institution of the proceedings and before their termination. Thus a judge is protected from liability for any statement of fact or comment that has any connection with a matter before him, whether it concerns the conduct of the parties, witnesses or counsel who are partici-pating in the trial or of a person not so participating."); *id.* cmt. e ("The privilege does not protect a judge who makes a personal attack upon the character of another which has no conceivable reference to the performance of the duties of judicial office. However, the protection is not lost by the mere fact that the

What, then, is a witness' private remedy for being unjustifiably impugned by a judge? It appears to be solely extrajudicial: to exercise one's First Amendment rights of freedom of speech to expose the fallacious reasoning that produced the judge's derogatory publication.

In the Ninth Circuit, although a trial judge's conclusions of law are reviewed *de novo*,[1447] the same judge's findings of fact in a bench trial are reviewed only for clear error.[1448] The latter standard of review has been called "'deferential'"[1449]: the trial judge's findings are accepted unless there is a "definite and firm conviction that a mistake has been committed."[1450] In particular, "[s]pecial deference is paid to a trial court's credibility findings."[1451]

Thus, if a judge in a bench trial wanted to constrict the practical scope of judicial review of his or her findings of fact, he or she could do so by making the outcome in the case appear to turn on one or more credibility findings and the judge's consequent refusal to credit particular trial testimony. The trial testimony so discredited might have presented evidence contradicting the judge's ultimate findings of fact and conclusions of law; and thus that excluded testimony, were it instead considered by the court, would require the judge to expend the additional effort to explain why the weight of the evidence supported his or her ultimate findings of fact and conclusions of law, rather than the findings of fact and conclusions of law that would flow from a well-manicured record from which contradictory testimony had in practical effect been excluded.

This current state of affairs invites the privileged and immunized defamation of witnesses by judges in bench trials. It is regrettable that the Supreme Court has not yet spotted this failing of credibility findings in bench trials and rectified it. The Court should correct this injustice. It should amend Federal Rule of Civil Procedure 52(a)(1). The Court should moderate the degree of deference that is appropriate for a reviewing court to give credibility findings in a bench trial.

The Court should ensure that neither parties *nor witnesses* appearing in federal court are denied liberty or property without due process of law, as it was articulated in *Mathews v. Eldridge*. The Court should clarify that one's loss of reputation at the hands of a judge's privileged and immunized defamatory publication is a liberty interest whose deprivation is protected by the Due Process Clause. So too is a property interest directly implicated.

---

defamatory publication is an indiscretion or a display of personal antagonism on the part of the judge, or that it is not important to the subject of the inquiry if it is not altogether disconnected.").

[1447] O'Bannon v. Nat'l Collegiate Athletic Ass'n, 802 F.3d 1049, 1061 (9th Cir. 2015). Mixed questions of law and fact are also reviewed *de novo*. OneBeacon Ins. Co. v. Haas Indus., Inc., 634 F.3d 1092, 1096 (9th Cir. 2011).

[1448] *O'Bannon*, 802 F.3d at 1061, 1080.

[1449] *Id.* at 1061 (quoting FTC v. BurnLounge, Inc., 753 F.3d 878, 883 (9th Cir. 2014)).

[1450] *Id.* (quoting *BurnLounge*, 753 F.3d at 883).

[1451] Exxon Co. v. Sofec, Inc., 54 F.3d 570, 576 (9th Cir. 1995).

The Court should recognize that the Constitution requires procedural due process when a tangible detriment (such as loss of employment or income or professional standing) results from a judicially inflicted act of privileged and immunized defamation.

In the absence of the Court's recognition of the need for such a remedy, opposing interpretations of fact are no longer considered matters of differing perceptions held in good faith. They are portrayed instead as evidence that one side is ethically deficient. For a federal judge to cast inconvenient testimony as the prevarication of moral lepers is malicious. The Supreme Court and the Courts of Appeals should approach with healthy skepticism the credibility findings in any bench trial that sound like privileged and immunized acts of character assassination.

X. Did Qualcomm Have a Contractual Duty to Offer Exhaustive Licenses to Its Cellular SEPs to Rival Modem Manufacturers?

On November 6, 2018, Judge Koh's pre-trial order in *FTC v. Qualcomm* granting the FTC's motion for partial summary judgment foreshadowed how she would approach the ultimate question of antitrust liability after the bench trial. She found that the RAND contracts between Qualcomm and two SSOs, the Telecommunications Industry Association (TIA) and the Alliance for Telecommunications Industry Solutions (ATIS), obligated Qualcomm to offer exhaustive licenses to its cellular SEPs to rival modem manufacturers.[1452] Judge Koh reiterated that conclusion in her May 21, 2019 findings of fact and conclusions of law, in which she found that Qualcomm's refusal to offer exhaustive licenses to its cellular SEPs to rival modem manufacturers breached the contractual obligations arising from Qualcomm's "FRAND commitments."[1453]

Yet, the evidence that Judge Koh cited in her summary judgment was too insubstantial to support her conclusions. Neither the language in the contracts that Qualcomm executed with ATIS and the TIA nor the other evidence that Judge Koh summarized unambiguously supported her conclusion that Qualcomm is contractually obligated to offer exhaustive licenses to its cellular SEPs to rival modem manufacturers. At the very least, the language of the contracts that Qualcomm executed with the two SSOs was ambiguous. Because genuine disputes of material fact existed as to which of the two conflicting contract interpretations correctly reflected the parties'

[1452] Order Granting FTC's Motion for Partial Summary Judgment on Qualcomm's Contractual Duties Pursuant to the Contracts with ATIS and the TIA, 2018 WL 5848999, *supra* note 52, at *12.

[1453] FTC v. Qualcomm Inc., 411 F. Supp. 3d 658, 752 (N.D. Cal. 2019).

intent, it was not appropriate for Judge Koh to grant the FTC partial summary judgment.[1454]

A. *Did Judge Koh's Findings on Partial Summary Judgment and in Her Findings of Fact and Conclusions of Law Encompass Qualcomm's Contracts with SSOs Other Than ATIS and the TIA?*

Judge Koh's findings were imprecise. Were her findings about Qualcomm's contractual duty to offer exhaustive licenses to its cellular SEPs to rival modem manufacturers limited to the contracts between Qualcomm and each of ATIS and the TIA? Or did her findings sweep so broadly as to encompass Qualcomm's contracts with other SSOs, including ETSI, the Institute of Electrical and Electronics Engineers (IEEE), and the International Telecommunication Union (ITU)? Qualcomm actively participates in about 200 SSOs.[1455] Those SSOs encompass many technologies other that cellular communications, including audio compression and decompression (codec), video codec, memory technology, near field communication, and wireless charging.[1456] One particularly valuable technology is high efficiency video codec (HEVC).[1457]

Judge Koh's partial summary judgment explicitly stated that it "concerns a discrete legal question: whether *two* industry agreements require Qualcomm

---

[1454] *See* United Ass'n Local 38 Pension Tr. Fund v. Aetna Cas. & Sur. Co., 790 F.2d 1428, 1430 (9th Cir. 1986) ("If the interpretation of the language of the contract were the sole issue, the court might be able to resolve the matter on summary judgment for only questions of law would be in controversy.") (citing Beck Park Apartments v. U.S. Dep't of Hous. & Urban Dev., 695 F.2d 366, 369 (9th Cir. 1982)); *id.* ("However, this case cannot be so easily resolved, for where the controversy centers not on interpretation of the contract but on whether the terms of the contract were met the case must be submitted to the trier of fact.").

[1455] Transcript of Proceedings (Volume 7) at 1549:6–12, FTC v. Qualcomm Inc., No. 5:17-cv-00220-LHK (N.D. Cal. Jan. 18, 2019) (Testimony of Liren Chen (Senior Vice President and Legal Counsel, QTL)).

[1456] *Id.* at 1549:22–1550:13.

[1457] *Id.* at 1550:17–1552:9 ("Q. And you mentioned video coding a couple of times. Could you give the Court an example of the type of patents Qualcomm has related to video coding? A. Yes, I can. And before I get into the example here, I do want to explain why video is so important, because generally there's a lot of traffic on the internet and there's over 90 percent of the traffic today on the internet, including mobile internet, . . . driven by video services and video applications. So it's really, really important to be able to transfer a video very highly efficiently and to be able to have the most efficient video codec is critical. So Qualcomm put a lot of effort in inventing video related technology, and one of the really important video standards is called HEVC, . . . high efficiency video codec . . . . So it's able to do really good compression and decompression of the signal while consum[ing] as little power as possible on the mobile device. And Qualcomm is a very active participant, and we are a leading creator of technology that's getting to the HEVC standard. Q. And . . . the HEVC standard, do you make that available to your licensees? A. Yes, we do. Q. And why are they interested in it? A. Because Qualcomm technology offers really significant performance improvement over the competing technologies. So let me give you one example. In the HEVC, there's a Qualcomm invented technology called variable block encoding. What that means is we . . . look at what's on the video, and we . . . also look at how frequent[ly] the video changes frame by frame as the video is transferred, and we . . . pick the most optimized size of the block to encode it. And our technology is at least 50 percent . . . better than the competing technology, and that saves a lot . . . in bandwidth, if you want to deliver the same content of material, which means the carrier can add at least twice as many users on the network for these type of services, or if you want to have the same amount of users supported on the network, you can give them twice as good of services for the same amount of users. And that is very, very significant if you are the network operator or if you're the consumer.").

to license its SEPs to other modem chip suppliers."[1458] Judge Koh's findings of fact and conclusions of law on May 21, 2019 also referred to the two SSOs. On the other hand, some of Judge Koh's statements in her findings of fact and conclusions of law suggested that she had found that such a duty applies more broadly—that is, even to Qualcomm's contracts with other SSOs, including ETSI, the IEEE, and the ITU. For example, one passage stated unconditionally: "Qualcomm's refusal to license rivals violates Qualcomm's FRAND commitments."[1459]

In other words, Judge Koh's May 21, 2019 findings of fact and conclusions of law seemed to imply that her findings about Qualcomm's contractual duty are not limited to the RAND contracts that the company executed with ATIS and the TIA but instead apply generally to FRAND and RAND contracts that Qualcomm has executed with other SSOs. Supporting that interpretation is the fact that the FTC's complaint referred to Qualcomm's commitments made to SSOs more generally, including those made to ETSI, which of course is particularly prominent in standards setting for mobile communications.[1460]

Judge Koh's *assumption* that all FRAND or RAND contracts between Qualcomm and various SSOs created identical contractual obligations was clearly erroneous. The Ninth Circuit failed to recognize the sloppiness of Judge Koh's referring to RAND obligations as FRAND obligations, and it perpetuated the error that the two RAND obligations on which Judge Koh ruled were FRAND obligations.[1461]

The scope of an SEP holder's obligations with respect to a specific SSO depends on both (1) the contract's precise language and (2) the controlling law governing the contract's interpretation.[1462] Because the licensing commit-

---

[1458] Order Granting FTC's Motion for Partial Summary Judgment on Qualcomm's Contractual Duties Pursuant to the Contracts with ATIS and the TIA, 2018 WL 5848999, *supra* note 52, at *1 (emphasis added).

[1459] *FTC v. Qualcomm*, 411 F. Supp. 3d at 751.

[1460] FTC Complaint, 2017 WL 242848, *supra* note 28, at 13; *see also* Transcript of Proceedings (Volume 8) at 1666:5–11, FTC v. Qualcomm Inc., No. 5:17-cv-00220-LHK (N.D. Cal. Jan. 22, 2019) (Testimony of Dirk Weiler (Head of Standards, Nokia)) ("Q. And does ETSI play a particular role in 3GPP? A. Yes. Besides the fact that ETSI was the original source of creating the proposal of creating 3GPP, ETSI also holds the secretariat for 3GPP, [and] a majority of all companies working in 3GPP is coming into 3GPP via the ETSI membership. And also, ETSI provides a repository of declared standard essential patents for all of 3GPP.").

[1461] *See* FTC v. Qualcomm Inc., No. 19-16122, 2020 WL 4591476, at *6 nn.12–13 (9th Cir. Aug. 11, 2020).

[1462] *See, e.g.*, Videotaped Deposition of Ira Blumberg (Vice President, Lenovo) at 131:12–132:10, FTC v. Qualcomm Inc., No. 5:17-cv-00220-LHK (N.D. Cal. Apr. 20, 2018) ("Q. Now, in your view, is there anything improper—improper or inappropriate or contrary to a FRAND obligation for a standard essential patent holder to only license its patents to cellular device makers, rather than to chip makers? MR. KEHL: Object to the form of the question. THE WITNESS: My interpretation of FRAND obligations does suggest that the licensor has an obligation to license any company that requests a license, whether it is a chip company, an end device company, or anything in between. BY MR. HOLTZ: Q. What's that understanding [of FRAND obligations] based on? A. My experience in the industry and my reading of the rules. Q. Which rules? A. The various organizations like ETSI, IEEE, and so on. Q. All right. Do IEEE and ETSI have identical rules with respect to that? A. No, they don't."), *exhibit to* Federal Trade Commission's

ments for SEPs typically contain different language, and because some of the most prominent SSOs involved in mobile communications standards are clearly not governed by the same law, one must examine each individual agreement to identify the particular contractual obligations arising for the SEP holder from that contract. It was error for Judge Koh to assume that all contracts between SEP holders and SSOs are identical.

That error was not harmless. The assumption that all contracts between SEP holders and SSOs are identical might be tolerated in academic writing, when legal concepts are simplified and stylized so that they can be manipulated in the abstract to construct theoretical arguments. But that assumption is indefensible to make in litigation, where a judge must interpret a specific contract between a particular SEP holder and a particular SSO to identify that SEP holder's precise obligations and the precise rights of the specific implementer that claims to be an intended third-party beneficiary of the SEP holder's FRAND or RAND contract.

B.   *Did Judge Koh Improperly Assume That the Verb "License" Denoted "License on an Exhaustive Basis" in the RAND Contracts Between Qualcomm and Each of ATIS and the TIA, Even Though Qualcomm Had Never Granted an Exhaustive License to Any Rival Modem Manufacturer?*

A glaring interpretative omission invalidates the reasoning of Judge Koh's order granting the FTC's motion for partial summary judgment. How could Judge Koh have purported to interpret contracts between Qualcomm and each of ATIS and the TIA when she never performed the essential task of interpreting the word "license"?

1.   Two Alternative Interpretations of the Verb "License"

We saw in Part C.4 to the Introduction and in Part III that the verb "license," as used in commercial agreements before 2008, did not necessarily denote "license on an exhaustive basis," because the Supreme Court in *Quanta* had not yet overturned approximately two decades of Federal Circuit law holding that one may license a patent *nonexhaustively*. And we saw in Part C.4 to the Introduction that Judge Koh appeared to admit at trial that she was "confused" about the *nonexhaustive* "licenses" that Qualcomm had granted to its cellular SEPs to rival modem manufacturers before 2008.

Was it plausible that Qualcomm and each of ATIS and the TIA mutually intended the verb "license" before 2008 specifically to denote "license on an exhaustive basis," as Judge Koh found? Neither of the two RAND

Submission of January 4[, 2019], Testimony By Deposition, FTC v. Qualcomm Inc., No. 5:17-cv-00220-LHK (N.D. Cal. Jan. 7, 2019), ECF No. 1161-2.

contracts between Qualcomm and each of ATIS and the TIA expressly obligated the SEP holder to offer *exhaustive* licenses to its SEPs. Qualcomm had foresight, but it was not clairvoyant. No company is. There is no legitimate basis to conclude that Qualcomm and each of ATIS and the TIA knew that the Supreme Court would redefine the verb "license" in 2008 necessarily to denote "license on an exhaustive basis." So, was it more plausible that Qualcomm and each of ATIS and the TIA thought that a "license" was capable of being nonexhaustive (as the Federal Circuit had held on multiple occasions before 2008)?

Judge Koh did not say. Her omission was material. That material omission was a sufficient, independent basis to vacate Judge Koh's order granting the FTC's motion for partial summary judgment for failure to interpret what was arguably the central word in those contracts.

2. Rejecting the Interpretation That Would Produce an Absurd Economic Result That No Reasonable SEP Holder Would Have Accepted

Even as an economic matter, Judge Koh's ruling that Qualcomm would have agreed in each of two RAND contracts to offer *exhaustive* licenses to its cellular SEPs to rival modem manufacturers was preposterous. And of course one of the most basic principles of contract interpretation is that, "where a contract provision lends itself to two interpretations, a court will not adopt [an] interpretation that leads to unreasonable results, but instead will adopt the construction that is reasonable and that harmonizes the affected contract provisions."[1463] In turn, an unreasonable interpretation is one that "produces an absurd result or one that no reasonable person would have accepted when entering the contract."[1464]

Qualcomm had *never* offered an exhaustive license to its cellular SEPs to rival modem manufacturers. Was it a plausible interpretation of the two RAND contracts that Qualcomm had voluntarily, contractually obligated itself to effectuate the very licensing strategy that it had expressly declined to pursue? Put differently, was it plausible that Qualcomm's management negligently forwent the benefit to its shareholders of earning much greater profit by continuing to offer exhaustive licenses to its cellular SEPs only to OEMs?

[1463] Axis Reinsurance Co. v. HLTH Corp., 993 A.2d 1057, 1063 & n.19 (Del. Super. 2010) (first citing RESTATEMENT (SECOND) OF CONTRACTS § 203 (AM. LAW INST. 1981); then citing Lorillard Tobacco Co. v. Am. Legacy Found., 903 A.2d 728 (Del. 2006); then citing O'Brien v. Progressive N. Ins. Co., 785 A.2d 281, 288 (Del. 2001); and then citing Holland v. Nat'l Auto. Fibres, 194 A.124, 127 (Del. Ch. 1937)).

[1464] Osborn *ex rel.* Osborn v. Kemp, 991 A.2d 1153, 1160 (Del. Super. 2010). For a similar statement applying New York law, see Homeward Residential, Inc. v. Sand Canyon Corp., 298 F.R.D. 116, 129 (S.D.N.Y. 2014) ("[A] court must avoid any [contract] interpretation that would be 'absurd, commercially unreasonable, or contrary to the reasonable expectations of the parties.'") (citations omitted) (quoting Landmark Ventures, Inc. v. Wave Sys. Corp., No. 11 Civ. 8440(PAC), 2012 WL 3822624, at *3 (S.D.N.Y. Sept. 4, 2012)).

Judge Koh did not seem to consider whether her contract interpretation was unreasonable, both because it produced an absurd result, and because no reasonable firm would have accepted such an obligation.

If patent exhaustion confused Judge Koh at trial in January 2019, there is no reason to believe that she understood the critical relevance of patent exhaustion to interpreting the word "license" a few months earlier, when she was drafting her order granting the FTC's motion for partial summary judgment, issued November 6, 2018. Judge Koh evidently imposed the Supreme Court's definition of "license" from 2008—"license on an exhaustive basis"—retroactively upon contracts formed at least several years before 2008.

3. The Optimal Level of Due Process and Judge Koh's Implicit Interpretation of the Verb "License" in Her Partial Summary Judgment Order

Judge Koh appeared not to recognize the massive harm that her partial summary judgment order could cause. Her order was nothing less than a blueprint, as I say in the opening paragraph of this article, for destroying a great deal of the value (and, in the constitutional sense, for taking the private property) not only of Qualcomm, but also of Ericsson, Nokia, and other innovative firms that had declared patents to be essential to either ATIS or the TIA, or both.

Barring vacatur by the appellate courts, Judge Koh's partial summary judgment order already would set in motion the torching of the Palatine Hill. In the span of a few pages of superficial interpretation that completely missed the big issue in the case—the relevance of changes in the case law on the doctrine of patent exhaustion to the meaning of the verb "license"—Judge Koh accomplished what the deposition question of the plaintiff class-action lawyer telegraphed: the imperative to destroy the value of Qualcomm's business model. In that sense, the merits of the ensuing antitrust case were largely irrelevant, save for the claim for $15 billion in treble damages for which Qualcomm would be at risk.

Judge Koh's procedural shortchanging of Qualcomm was unmistakable, because she never interpreted "license" before granting the FTC's motion for partial summary judgment on a pure question of contract interpretation. And it was outrageous from the perspective of due process for Judge Koh to grant a motion for summary judgment and thereby deny Qualcomm the opportunity to give evidence at trial on the question of contract interpretation. Pursuant to Judge Posner's economic analysis of *Mathews v. Eldridge*, which at the least has been the law of the Seventh Circuit since 1982,[1465] the level of

---

[1465] Sutton v. City of Milwaukee, 672 F.2d 644, 645–46 (7th Cir. 1982) (Posner, J.).

process that a party is due increases with the potential harm to that party in the event the incremental procedural protection is denied.

Was Judge Koh's granting of partial summary judgment harmless error? Or did her granting of partial summary judgment amount to a deprivation of due process, considering that granting partial summary judgment (by itself, and even if Judge Koh had found Qualcomm not to be liable on antitrust grounds) was sufficient to create a risk of imminent destruction a substantial amount of value of Qualcomm's cellular SEP portfolio? Judge Koh seemed oblivious to these questions.

C. Did Judge Koh's Findings About Qualcomm's Contractual Duties Apply to All SEPs?

Judge Koh's November 6, 2018 partial summary judgment had important implications not only in the dispute between FTC and Qualcomm, but also in other disputes and in the licensing of SEPs more generally. Some litigants and commentators promptly argued that Judge Koh's reasoning in her partial summary judgment was not limited to Qualcomm's contracts with specific SSOs, but rather applied to *every* FRAND or RAND contract and consequently ought to bind *every* SEP holder in the larger universe of *all* SSOs with respect to the larger universe of *all* implementers.

1. Did Judge Koh's Findings of Fact and Conclusions of Law in FTC v. Qualcomm *Predetermine the Outcome in* Continental v. Avanci?

In *Continental v. Avanci*—an antitrust case filed in the Northern District of California on May 10, 2019[1466] and subsequently assigned on June 17, 2019 to Judge Koh[1467]—the plaintiff, a manufacturer of telematics control units (TCUs) for automobiles, sued Avanci, an agent responsible for licensing 2G, 3G, and 4G SEPs owned by various members of the Avanci SEP-licensing platform.[1468] Continental named as co-defendants Nokia, Conversant, and

---

[1466] Complaint, *Continental v. Avanci, supra* note 1398.

[1467] Order Reassigning Case at 1, Continental Auto. Sys., Inc. v. Avanci, LLC, No. 5:19-cv-02520 (N.D. Cal. June 17, 2019) ("IT IS ORDERED that this case has been reassigned using a proportionate, random and blind system pursuant to General Order No. 44 to the Honorable Lucy H. Koh in the SAN JOSE division for all further proceedings.") (boldface suppressed).

[1468] Complaint, *Continental v. Avanci, supra* note 1398, ¶ 4, at 2–3. On July 29, 2020, one day after the Antitrust Division issued a business review letter favorable to Avanci, Avanci announced that it had launched a new licensing platform to "enable patent owners and IoT and automotive companies to share 5G standard essential wireless patents in a single license." Press Release, Avanci, LLC, Avanci Launches 5G Licensing Platform for the Internet of Things (July 29, 2020), https://www.avanci.com/2020/07/29/avanci-launches-5g-licensing-platform-for-the-internet-of-things/; *see also* Business Review Letter from Hon. Makan Delrahim, Assistant Attorney Gen., U.S. Dep't of Justice, to Mark H. Hamer, Esq., Baker & McKenzie LLP (July 28, 2020), https://www.justice.gov/atr/page/file/1298626/download; Letter from Mark H. Hamer, Esq., Baker & McKenzie LLP, to Hon. Makan Delrahim, Assistant Attorney Gen., U.S. Dep't of Justice (Nov. 21, 2019), https://www.justice.gov/atr/page/file/1298631/download.

PanOptis, which were holders of SEPs that Avanci licensed.[1469] Continental specified seven causes of action, including that the defendants breached their contractual commitments to ETSI, ATIS, and the TIA "by refusing to license to all users of cellular standards"[1470] (or, in the alternative, that the defendants were bound by the doctrine of promissory estoppel to grant such licenses[1471]); that the defendants violated sections 1 and 2 of the Sherman Act on a variety of legal theories of harm;[1472] and that the defendants violated California unfair competition laws.[1473] Continental also sought a declaratory judgment with respect to the FRAND terms and conditions of an exhaustive license to the defendants' SEPs.[1474]

a.   *The Close Relationship Between* FTC v. Qualcomm *and* Continental v. Avanci

Central to Continental's complaint were quotations from Judge Koh's November 6, 2018 partial summary judgment in *FTC v. Qualcomm* to emphasize her finding that "'the TIA and ATIS IPR policies require Qualcomm to license its SEPs to modem chip suppliers.'"[1475] After Judge Koh issued her findings of fact and conclusions of law in *FTC v. Qualcomm* on May 21, 2019, and after *Continental v. Avanci* had by extraordinary luck been randomly assigned to Judge Koh, Continental filed an amended complaint on July 23, 2019, which again (as we shall see) quoted Judge Koh.[1476]

Avanci, which is based in Dallas, asked Judge Koh to transfer the case to the U.S. District Court for the Northern District of Texas, arguing that "the Northern District of California has no connection whatsoever to this dispute or the relevant conduct of the parties."[1477] Although Judge Koh on

---

[1469] Complaint, *Continental v. Avanci*, *supra* note 1398, at 1.

[1470] *Id.* ¶ 146, at 46.

[1471] *Id.* ¶¶ 151–57, at 46–47.

[1472] *Id.* ¶¶ 161–88, at 48–56.

[1473] *Id.* ¶¶ 189–95, at 56–59.

[1474] *Id.* ¶ 160, at 48 ("Continental is entitled to a declaratory judgment with respect to (1) Continental and other suppliers' entitlement to a direct license to Defendants' 2G, 3G, and 4G SEPs on FRAND terms and conditions; (2) a determination that Defendants have not offered Continental a direct license to their alleged 2G, 3G, and 4G SEPs on FRAND terms and conditions; (3) a determination of what constitutes FRAND terms and conditions for a license to Defendants' 2G, 3G, and 4G SEPs, with those terms and conditions being imposed on the parties; and (4) a determination that the FRAND terms and conditions must be consistent with well-established apportionment principles under federal patent law (*i.e.*, the smallest salable patent practicing unit rule).").

[1475] *Id.* ¶ 101, at 27 (quoting Order Granting FTC's Motion for Partial Summary Judgment on Qualcomm's Contractual Duties Pursuant to the Contracts with ATIS and the TIA, 2018 WL 5848999, *supra* note 52, at *10).

[1476] First Amended Complaint for Breach of FRAND Commitments and Violations of Antitrust and Unfair Competition Laws, Continental Auto. Sys., Inc. v. Avanci, LLC, No. 5:19-cv-02520-LHK (N.D. Cal. July 23, 2019), ECF No. 97.

[1477] Defendants' Motion to Transfer Venue to the Northern District of Texas Pursuant to 28 U.S.C. Section 1404(A) at 2, Continental Auto. Sys., Inc. v. Avanci, LLC, No. 5:19-cv-02520-LHK (N.D. Cal. July 31, 2019).

December 11, 2019 granted Avanci's motion to transfer venue of the case to the Northern District of Texas,[1478] her findings of fact and conclusions of law in *FTC v. Qualcomm*—issued 11 days after Continental filed its complaint against Avanci—appeared already to have profound consequences for the defendants in *Continental v. Avanci*.

Judge Koh's findings of fact and conclusions of law in *FTC v. Qualcomm* appeared to be particularly consequential for the ability of Avanci and its fellow defendants eventually to introduce percipient testimony from Nokia's Dirk Weiler that, during his years of direct involvement at ETSI, the SSO never required an SEP holder to offer exhaustive licenses to its cellular SEPs at the component level. Judge Koh had already ruled in *FTC v. Qualcomm* that Mr. Weiler was not a credible witness, and she thereupon ignored his percipient testimony that ETSI had never required the offering of exhaustive component-level licenses to cellular SEPs.

> b.   *Continental's Contention That Exhaustive SEP Licensing Only at the OEM Level Violated the FRAND Obligation and U.S. Antitrust Law*

After filing its amended complaint, Continental filed a motion before Judge Koh on October 8, 2019 seeking a temporary restraining order. Continental's memorandum accompanying its motion cited Judge Koh's findings of fact and conclusions of law in *FTC v. Qualcomm* in connection with Continental's contention that the defendants' request for an injunction to prevent Continental from infringing their patents was "particularly egregious" owing to the defendants' alleged "refusal 'to offer individual fully exhaustive direct FRAND licenses [for SEPs essential to the 2G, 3G, and 4G standards] to suppliers in the automotive supply chain.'"[1479] Continental did not explain in its complaint what the adjective "direct" precisely denoted it its pleadings.

In particular, Continental cited Judge Koh's May 21, 2019 opinion in *FTC v. Qualcomm* to support the contention that Avanci and its co-defendants were "refusing to license at the component level 'because it is more lucrative to license only OEMs'"[1480] and that Judge Koh had found that "Qualcomm's policy of licensing only at the OEM level [was] inconsistent with its FRAND

[1478] Order Granting Motion to Transfer Venue, Continental Auto. Sys., Inc. v. Avanci, LLC, No. 5:19-cv-02520-LHK, 2019 WL 6735604 (N.D. Cal. Dec. 11, 2019) (Koh, J.).

[1479] Continental's Memorandum of Points and Authorities in Support of Its *Ex Parte* Application for Temporary Restraining Order and Order to Show Cause Why a Preliminary Injunction Should Not Issue at 21, Continental Auto. Sys., Inc. v. Avanci, LLC, No. 5:19-cv-02520-LHK (N.D. Cal. Oct. 8, 2019), ECF No. 185-3 [hereinafter Continental's Memorandum of Points and Authorities] (quoting First Amended Complaint for Breach of FRAND Commitments and Violations of Antitrust and Unfair Competition Laws ¶ 171, at 51, Continental Auto. Sys., Inc. v. Avanci, LLC, No. 5:19-cv-02520-LHK (N.D. Cal. July 23, 2019), ECF No. 97).

[1480] Continental's Memorandum of Points and Authorities, *supra* note 1479, at 21 (quoting FTC v. Qualcomm Inc., 411 F. Supp. 3d 658, 753 (N.D. Cal. 2019)). The phrase "because it is more lucrative to

obligation and U.S. antitrust law."[1481] Continental's reasoning was thus incoherent because (like Judge Koh's reasoning) it failed to differentiate among the specific FRAND or RAND contracts, and because it equated U.S. antitrust law with Judge Koh's erroneous interpretation of the law in *FTC v. Qualcomm.* Nevertheless, Continental's reasoning exemplified the apparently preferred interpretation of U.S. antitrust law and the preferred interpretation of the FRAND obligation that some component manufacturers in the automotive industry have advocated since Judge Koh issued her findings of fact and conclusions of law in *FTC v. Qualcomm.*[1482]

      c.   *What Were the Consequences for* Continental v. Avanci *of Judge Koh's Finding of Fact That the Testimony of Nokia's Dirk Weiler in* FTC v. Qualcomm *Was Not Credible?*

A number of Judge Koh's rulings in *FTC v. Qualcomm* were directly relevant to *Continental v. Avanci.* Judge Koh ruled (erroneously, as we shall see) in her partial summary judgment order that an SEP holder who has declared its patents essential to standards of ATIS or the TIA may not refuse to offer exhaustive licenses to those declared SEPs to component manufacturers. That finding on partial summary judgment, taken together with Judge Koh's subsequent finding of fact that the percipient testimony of Dirk Weiler of Nokia concerning ETSI's IPR Policy was not credible, as we saw in Part IX.E, might lead one to expect that Judge Koh likewise would have found in *Continental v. Avanci* that Nokia had no procompetitive rationale under *American Express* for refusing to offer exhaustive licenses to its cellular SEPs on FRAND terms to component manufacturers.

    Even though Judge Koh transferred *Continental v. Avanci* to the Northern District of Texas, she gave Continental (and perhaps other parties adverse to Nokia in other cases) something of exceptional value, particularly in a jury trial: the ability to invoke her determination in *FTC v. Qualcomm* that Mr. Weiler's testimony was not credible, so as to impeach Mr. Weiler or

---

license only OEMs" appears three times in Judge Koh's findings of fact and conclusions of law. *FTC v. Qualcomm,* 411 F. Supp. 3d at 753, 756 (twice).

[1481] Continental's Memorandum of Points and Authorities, *supra* note 1479, at 21 (citing *FTC v. Qualcomm,* 411 F. Supp. 3d at 751–58).

[1482] *See, e.g.,* Dave Djavaherian, President, PacTech Law, P.C., Access to FRAND Licences Under the Contract Laws (2019), https://www.scribd.com/presentation/435185173/19-11-12-Dave-Djavaherian-Presentation; Evelina Kurgonaite, Secretary General, Fair Standards Alliance, Could Judge Koh's Reasoning Be Adopted Under Art. 102 TFEU? (2019), https://de.scribd.com/document/435184753/19-11-12-Evelina-Kurgonaite-Presentation. Mr. Djavaherian has served as an attorney for Continental in its case against Avanci, initially filed before Judge Koh. *See, e.g.,* Declaration of David Djavaherian in Support of Plaintiff Continental Automotive Systems, Inc.'s Opposition to Defendants' Motion to Dismiss First Amended Complaint, Continental Auto. Sys., Inc. v. Avanci, LLC, No. 5:19-cv-02520-LHK (N.D. Cal. Dec. 4, 2019), ECF No. 182-30. Members of the Fair Standards Alliance include Apple, Cisco, Continental, Daimler, and Intel, among others. *See Members,* Fair Standards Alliance, https://fair-standards.org/members/.

any Nokia witness refuting the allegation that Nokia breached its FRAND contract with ETSI by refusing to offer an exhaustive license to its cellular SEPs to Continental, at the component level.

2.   *Do the Specific Provisions of Each FRAND or RAND Contract, Which Are Controlled by Various Bodies of Law, Compel SEP Holders to Offer Exhaustive Licenses to Their Cellular SEPs to Component Manufacturers?*

Some commentators have urged the European Commission to follow Judge Koh's lead and compel every SEP holder to offer exhaustive licenses to its cellular SEPs to component manufacturers (irrespective of whether the SEP holder is a vertically integrated firm, like Qualcomm, which simultaneously competes with those component manufacturers).[1483] Those proposals are legally erroneous.

Regardless of whether one agrees with Judge Koh's conclusion concerning Qualcomm's contractual obligations pursuant to its RAND contracts with ATIS and the TIA, it would be incorrect to assume that Qualcomm's other FRAND or RAND contracts with other SSOs created identical contractual duties. Table 9 compares the language of the RAND commitments of ATIS and the TIA with the language of the FRAND and RAND commitments of the three additional SSOs that the FTC mentioned in its complaint in *FTC v. Qualcomm*—ETSI, the IEEE, and the ITU.[1484] Table 9 also identifies the controlling law for each FRAND or RAND contract.

Table 9 shows that the language of the RAND contracts of ATIS and the TIA differs from the language of the FRAND and RAND contracts that Qualcomm has made to other SSOs. The FRAND and RAND contracts of these five SSOs are also governed by the laws of different jurisdictions. As we will see presently, Judge Koh found that, because the RAND contracts of ATIS and the TIA did not have a choice-of-law provision, California contract law governed. The ITU also does not have a choice-of-law provision. In contrast, the ETSI IPR Policy explicitly provides that French law controls ETSI's FRAND contract, and the IEEE explicitly provides that New York law controls its RAND contract.

[1483] *See supra* note 1482.
[1484] FTC Complaint, 2017 WL 242848, *supra* note 28, at 13.

Table 9. FRAND and RAND Contracts
of the Five SSOs Relevant in *FTC v. Qualcomm*

SSO	Controlling Law (If Specified)	Commitment
TIA	None	"A license under any Essential Patent(s), the license rights which are held by the undersigned Patent Holder, will be made available to all applicants under terms and conditions that are reasonable and non-discriminatory, which may include monetary compensation, and only to the extent necessary for the practice of any or all of the Normative portions for the field of use of practice of the Standard."
ATIS	None	"A license will be made available to applicants under reasonable terms and conditions that are demonstrably free of any unfair discrimination."
ETSI	France	"When an ESSENTIAL IPR relating to a particular STANDARD or TECHNICAL SPECIFICATION is brought to the attention of ETSI, the Director-General of ETSI shall immediately request the owner to give within three months an irrevocable undertaking in writing that it is prepared to grant irrevocable licenses on fair, reasonable, and non-discriminatory ('FRAND') terms and conditions under such IPR to at least the following extent: • MANUFACTURE, including the right to make or have made customized components and sub-systems to the licensee's own design for use in MANUFACTURE; • sell, lease, or otherwise dispose of EQUIPMENT so MANUFAC-TURED; • repair, use, or operate EQUIPMENT; and • use METHODS."
ITU	None	• "[A] patent embodied fully or partly in a Recommendation/Deliverable must be accessible to everybody without undue constraints. To meet this requirement in general is the sole objective of the code of practice. The detailed arrangements arising from patents (licensing, royalties, etc.) are left to the parties concerned, as these arrangements might differ from case to case." • "The patent holder is willing to negotiate licenses with other parties on a non-discriminatory basis on reasonable terms and conditions."
IEEE	New York	"Submitter will make available a license for Essential Patent Claims to an unre-stricted number of Applicants on a worldwide basis without compensation or under Reasonable Rates, with other reasonable terms and conditions that are de-monstrably free of any unfair discrimination to make, have made, use, sell, offer to sell, or import any Compliant Implementation that practices the Essential Patent Claims for use in conforming with the IEEE Standard." (The IEEE Standards Board Bylaws specify that "'*Compliant Implementation*' shall mean any product (e.g., component, sub-assembly, or end product) or service that conforms to any mandatory or optional portion of a normative clause of an IEEE Standard.")

Sources: *Patent Holder Statements*, TIA, https://standards.tiaonline.org/all-standards/procedures/ipr; *IEEE-SA Standards Board Bylaws*, IEEE, https://standards.ieee.org/content/dam/ieee-standards/standards/web/documents/other/sb_bylaws.pdf; *Patent Policy*, ATIS, https://www.atis.org/01_legal/patent-policy/; ETSI IPR Policy, *supra* note 1179, Annex 6, cl. 6.1; *Common Patent Policy for ITU-T/ITU-R/ISO/IEC*, ITU, https://www.itu.int/en/ITU-T/ipr/Pages/policy.aspx; *Policies and Procedures*, IEEE SA, https://standards.ieee.org/about/policies/bylaws/sect6-7.html.

A court cannot ignore those differences when construing an SEP holder's contractual obligations. Even if one assumes for sake of argument that all FRAND contracts and all RAND contracts contain identical language, it is still quite possible that the differences between French contract law and New York contract law—to take only one example—will produce substantively different conclusions about the legal duties that an SEP holder is construed to owe to implementers under the FRAND or RAND contract in question.[1485]

Consequently, there is no basis in law or fact for concluding that Judge Koh's interpretation of the ATIS and TIA RAND contracts correctly identify the contractual obligations arising from the commitments that Qualcomm made to *other* SSOs—including ETSI, the IEEE, and the ITU. Even if one were to assume that Judge Koh's findings in her partial summary judgment are correct (which, we will see shortly, they are not), those findings still would not imply that Qualcomm owes a contractual duty to offer exhaustive licenses to its cellular SEPs (much less a contractual duty to offer exhaustive licenses to its non-cellular SEPs or its non-SEPs) to rival modem manufacturers. Perhaps the FTC understood this point, since it acknowledged (with some degree of self-contradiction) in its motion for partial summary judgment that there was a "need for evidence regarding the meaning of Qualcomm's commitments" to ETSI.[1486]

It would of course be even more unsound to contend that Judge Koh's findings on partial summary judgment concerning Qualcomm's obligations pursuant to its RAND contracts with ATIS and TIA apply to *all* SEPs— including the SEPs in dispute in *Continental v. Avanci*, many of which belong to other SEP holders, are possibly committed to different SSOs than ATIS and TIA, and are exhaustively offered for license to automobile manufac-turers both by a patent pool (Avanci) and by those other SEP holders them-selves through individual bilateral negotiation with each implementer. To the contrary, one must determine the precise obligations arising from each such FRAND or RAND contract on a case-by-case basis.

D. *The FRAND Contract and the RAND Contract*

Any determination of whether an SEP holder has breached its contractual duties pursuant to a commitment that it made to an SSO should start with the determination of whether the commitment creates an enforceable contract. If the contract is enforceable, the determination then should proceed to identify the precise obligations that the contract imposes on the parties as well as on possible intended third-party beneficiaries of that contract.

[1485] *See* J. Gregory Sidak, *Negotiating FRAND Licenses in Good Faith*, 5 Criterion J. on Innovation 1 (2020); Sidak, *The FRAND Contract*, *supra* note 1368.

[1486] FTC's Motion for Partial Summary Judgment, *supra* note 485, at 3.

1. *Is the FRAND or RAND Contract Enforceable?*

Whether an SEP holder's commitment to an SSO is an enforceable contract between them depends on the language of the SEP holder's specific licensing declarations and the applicable law governing the relationship between the SEP holder and the SSO.[1487] Several U.S. courts—applying the contract law of different jurisdictions (including Wisconsin state law, Washington state law, and French law)—have found that the SEP holder's commitment constitutes an enforceable contract with the SSO in question, and that an implementer of the standard is an intended third-party beneficiary of that contract, entitled to enforce the SEP holder's obligations arising from that contract.[1488]

Yet, in at least two reported cases, the SEP holder's commitment to the SSO in question was found to be unenforceable. In two investigations (the 1023 and 1089 Investigations) before the U.S. International Trade Commission, Chief Administrative Law Judge Charles Bullock, in the public versions of two of his Initial Determinations on Violation of Section 337 and Recommended Determinations on Remedy and Bond, found that, on the basis of the specific facts of the case, and pursuant to New York law, the complainant's RAND commitment to the Joint Electron Devices Engineering Council (JEDEC) was too ambiguous to constitute an enforceable contract.[1489] Such a ruling was not possible in *FTC v. Qualcomm* because the parties had stipulated that the commitments that Qualcomm made to ATIS and the TIA were

---

[1487] *See* Apple, Inc. v. Motorola Mobility, Inc., 886 F. Supp. 2d 1061, 1083 (W.D. Wis. 2012) (Crabb, J.) ("In this case, the combination of the policies and bylaws of the standards-setting organizations, Motorola's membership in those organizations and Motorola's assurances that it would license its essential patents on fair, reasonable and nondiscriminatory terms constitute contractual agreements.").

[1488] *See, e.g., id.* at 1085 (applying Wisconsin state law); TCL Commc'n Tech. Holdings Ltd. v. Telefonaktiebolaget LM Ericsson, No. 14-341, 2018 WL 4488286, at *5 (C.D. Cal. Sept. 14, 2018) (Selna, J.) (applying French law), *vacated and reversed in part on other grounds and remanded*, 943 F.3d 1360 (Fed. Cir. 2019); Microsoft Corp. v. Motorola, Inc. (*Microsoft I*), 696 F.3d 872, 878 (9ᵗʰ Cir. 2012) (applying Washington state law). The UK Patents Court has also found that an SEP holder's FRAND commitment to ETSI constitutes an enforceable contract with that SSO, pursuant to French law. *See* Apple Retail UK Ltd. v. Qualcomm (UK) Ltd. [2018] EWHC (Pat) 1188 (Eng.); Unwired Planet Int'l Ltd v. Huawei Techs. Co. [2017] EWHC (Pat) 2988 (Birss, J.), *aff'd*, [2018] EWCA (Civ) 2344, *argued*, UKSC 2018/0214 (Eng.). As of this writing, *Unwired Planet* is on appeal to the Supreme Court of the United Kingdom; however, in April 2020 the parties announced a settlement ending their litigation in the United State and Germany, and it remains unclear whether the appeal to the Supreme Court of the United Kingdom will therefore be dismissed as moot. Mathieu Klos, *Game Over in Unwired Planet and Huawei Dispute in Germany*, JUVE PATENT (Apr. 27, 2020), https://www.juve-patent.com/news-and-stories/cases/game-over-in-unwired-planet-and-huawei-dispute-in-germany/ ("Panoptis, the parent company of Unwired Planet, and Huawei have reached a settlement which ends their litigation in the US and Germany. The battle between the non-practising entity and Huawei has been the root of FRAND discussions across Europe. But the high-stakes patent dispute came to an early end before Germany's highest court could release its decision. The UK Supreme Court is still able to decide on the case.").

[1489] Certain Memory Modules and Components Thereof, and Products Containing Same, Inv. No. 337-TA-1023, slip op. at 195 (USITC Nov. 14, 2017) (Initial Determination—Public Version); Certain Memory Modules and Components Thereof, Inv. No. 337-TA-1089, slip op. at 176 (USITC Oct. 21, 2019) (Initial Determination—Public Version), *reversed in part and vacated in part*, Commission Opinion (Public Version) at 25–29, Certain Memory Modules and Components Thereof, Inv. No. 337-TA-1089 (USITC Apr. 21, 2020). I served as an expert economic witness for the complainant in the 1023 and 1089 Investigations.

enforceable contracts.[1490] Judge Koh's partial summary judgment analysis proceeded on that stipulation.

More generally, however, as of December 2019 the FTC was worried about the possibility that a RAND commitment might not constitute a contract enforceable against the SEP holder. So, on December 11, 2019, the FTC filed with the ITC a statement on the public interest in the 1089 Investigation in which the FTC objected on public policy grounds to Chief Judge Bullock's finding that the RAND contract between JEDEC and Netlist (the complainant) was unenforceable.[1491] The FTC said that it submitted its statement to "explain[] the potential anticompetitive effects of rendering such RAND commitments unenforceable."[1492]

To its credit, the FTC did properly refer to "RAND" commitments rather than "FRAND" commitments. Beyond that, the FTC's comments were unsound because they ignored that contract interpretation requires the application of a specific controlling body of contract law to the precise text of the contract in question. Importantly, the FTC's comments did not contend that Chief Judge Bullock misapplied New York law. Instead, the FTC argued that the ITC should repudiate Chief Judge Bullock's finding for the simple reason that he did not fall in line with the findings of courts applying the law of *other* states to *other* FRAND or RAND contracts, because "courts across the United States have repeatedly concluded that RAND commitments are enforceable."[1493]

The FTC's argument disdained the role of state contract law in the federal system. This specious argument is precisely the one upon which the assembled commissioners of the ITC relied in rejecting as erroneous Chief Judge Bullock's recommended determination that JEDEC's RAND contract was unenforceable:

> The Commission finds that the ALJ erred by not assessing whether the frequent use of "reasonable and nondiscriminatory" terms by standard-setting organizations shows that the phrase is reasonably certain in commercial practice or trade usage, particularly in light of the numerous court cases that have found such agreements enforceable.[1494]

In effect, the FTC advocated—and the ITC endorsed the argument—that a RAND contract's interpretation should depend not on the application of the

---

[1490] Order Granting FTC's Motion for Partial Summary Judgment on Qualcomm's Contractual Duties Pursuant to the Contracts with ATIS and the TIA, 2018 WL 5848999, *supra* note 52, at *9.

[1491] Third Party United States Federal Trade Commission's Statement on the Public Interest, Certain Memory Modules and Components Thereof, Inv. No. 337-TA-1089 (USITC Dec. 11, 2019).

[1492] *Id.* at 1.

[1493] *Id.* at 7.

[1494] Commission Opinion (Public Version) at 26, Certain Memory Modules and Components Thereof, Inv. No. 337-TA-1089 (USITC Apr. 21, 2020).

state law that controls the specific contract—New York law in the case of the 1089 Investigation—but rather on the FTC's generic policy preferences.

Chief Judge Bullock's ruling on the unenforceability of JEDEC's RAND contract under New York law was a question of first impression. So, reasonable minds could understandably differ on how to answer that question. But if Chief Judge Bullock was mistaken as a matter of law, it certainly was not for the feeble reason that the FTC espoused and the ITC embraced.

The ITC is not an Article III court sitting in diversity jurisdiction in Manhattan, much less does the ITC possess the same expertise in New York contract law as do the Justices of the New York Court of Appeals. Yet, the ITC followed the FTC's instruction to ignore the unique content of New York contract jurisprudence on the interpretation of ambiguous contracts controlled by New York law. Instead, following the FTC's instruction, the ITC treated all FRAND and RAND contracts as though they resembled a uniform model statute like the Uniform Commercial Code. It was legally erroneous for the ITC so to contend that the FRAND or RAND contracts of the various SSOs are textually homogenous and are all subject to the same controlling interpretation of the law of a single jurisdiction or to some undefined uniform model code forged by some equally undefined process.

2. *What Obligations Does the FRAND or RAND Contract Impose on the Parties and on Possible Intended Third-Party Beneficiaries?*

A separate question of enforceability concerns the duties that a FRAND or RAND contract creates for an SEP holder and the rights that it confers on the implementers of the corresponding industry standard. American courts have found that an implementer of an industry standard that takes a license to SEPs on FRAND or RAND terms is an intended third-party beneficiary of the FRAND or RAND contract between the SEP holder and the SSO.

It is a basic principle of American contract law that the promisor and the promisee define the scope of the rights of an intended third-party beneficiary.[1495] It necessarily follows that, when the intended third-party beneficiary is an implementer of a voluntary industry standard, the scope of the rights granted to the implementer, including any condition imposed on that grant, is defined by the voluntary exchange between the SEP holder and the SSO. Consequently, the implementer may not invoke the FRAND or RAND contract to claim rights that the SEP holder never agreed with the SSO to grant to an intended third-party beneficiary.

Moreover, only *intended* parties may be third-party beneficiaries of a contract. My prior writings were predicated on the understanding (as the

---

[1495] *See* RESTATEMENT (SECOND) OF CONTRACTS § 309 cmt. b (AM. LAW INST. 1981); *see also* 9 JOSEPH M. PERILLO, CORBIN ON CONTRACTS § 44.7 (Matthew Bender & Co. rev. ed. 2013).

debates over clause 6.1 of the ETSI IPR Policy have confirmed) that component manufacturers seeking an exhaustive license to cellular SEPs at the component level were not *intended* third-party beneficiaries of the ETSI FRAND contract, considering the industry practice of offering exhaustive licenses to cellular SEPs at the device level only.

An SEP holder and an implementer that is an intended third-party beneficiary of that SEP holder's contract with an SSO might disagree about the precise rights that a FRAND or RAND contract grants the implementer. To determine the scope of the implementer's rights as an intended third-party beneficiary, a court must examine (1) the precise terms of the FRAND or RAND contract between the SEP holder and the SSO in question and (2) the controlling law for interpreting that contract, should it be ambiguous and thus need to be construed by a court.

E.   Is a RAND Commitment Legally Equivalent to a FRAND Commitment?

Before examining Judge Koh's findings about Qualcomm's contractual obligations pursuant to its contracts with ATIS and the TIA, two important clarifications are necessary.

First, Judge Koh's definition of a FRAND commitment was legally erroneous. She said that the "*promise to license* SEPs on FRAND terms is generally referred to as a SEP holder's FRAND commitment."[1496] An SEP holder does not promise to ensure contract formation with the implementer on FRAND (or RAND) terms. An SEP holder can make a legitimately FRAND (or RAND) offer to an implementer, but the SEP holder cannot force the implementer to accept that offer, and in that sense the SEP holder cannot plausibly be understood to "promise to license" the implementer, as Judge Koh stated.

Second, both ATIS and the TIA have *RAND* commitments, not FRAND commitments. ATIS requires the SEP holder to commit to offer licenses to its cellular SEPs on "reasonable terms and conditions that are demonstrably free of any unfair discrimination."[1497] The TIA requires an SEP holder to commit to offer licenses "under terms and conditions that are reasonable and non-discriminatory."[1498] Because neither ATIS nor the TIA includes a

---

[1496]   FTC v. Qualcomm Inc., 411 F. Supp. 3d 658, 672 (N.D. Cal. 2019) (emphasis added).

[1497]   ATIS, Operating Procedures for ATIS Forums and Committees 10 (Mar. 1, 2015) [hereinafter ATIS, Operating Procedures for ATIS Forums and Committees], *Exhibit 2 to* FTC's Motion for Partial Summary Judgment, *supra* note 485, *quoted in* Order Granting FTC's Motion for Partial Summary Judgment on Qualcomm's Contractual Duties Pursuant to the Contracts with ATIS and the TIA, 2018 WL 5848999, *supra* note 52, at *3.

[1498]   Telecommunications Industry Association, TIA Intellectual Property Rights Policy (IPR Policy) 9 (3ᵈ ed. Oct. 21, 2016) [hereinafter TIA IPR Policy], *Exhibit 1 to* FTC's Motion for Partial Summary Judgment, *supra* note 485, *quoted in* Order Granting FTC's Motion for Partial Summary Judgment on Qualcomm's Contractual Duties Pursuant to the Contracts with ATIS and the TIA, 2018 WL 5848999, *supra* note 52, at *3.

separate requirement of fairness in its licensing commitment, each of these commitments is properly called a RAND commitment.

Some other SSOs—mainly those based outside of the United States, including ETSI—require the SEP holder to commit to offer licenses to its cellular SEPs on terms that are "fair, reasonable, and nondiscriminatory."[1499] Such an agreement is properly called a FRAND commitment. Despite this well-recognized distinction, Judge Koh consistently misidentified Qualcomm's commitments to ATIS and the TIA as FRAND commitments and, quoting a fleeting remark in a Ninth Circuit decision, asserted that FRAND "is 'legally equivalent' to RAND."[1500]

I have previously explained why the Ninth Circuit's dictum is erroneous and how it is entirely possible for a court to give independent meaning to the fairness requirement of a FRAND commitment.[1501] The opposing argument— that, despite *not* containing the word "fairness" or "fair" or "unfair," a RAND contract is nonetheless equivalent to a FRAND contract—fails as an elementary matter of interpretation because the law strives to give independent meaning to each word in a legal document.[1502] The *Restatement (Second) of Contracts* articulates the general principle in American contract law that "an interpretation which gives a reasonable, lawful, and effective meaning to all the terms is preferred to an interpretation which leaves a part unreasonable, unlawful, or of no effect."[1503] Judge Koh's assertion that FRAND "is 'legally equivalent' to RAND"[1504] violates that principle.

Judge Koh's assertion that RAND is equivalent to FRAND also fails as a matter of economic reasoning. One can view fairness as being an end in itself. Others, myself included, instead propose viewing fairness in this particular context as a means to an end—that end being the successful negotiation of a welfare-enhancing voluntary exchange of patented technology that results in contract formation between the SEP holder and the implementer.[1505]

[1499] *See, e.g.*, ETSI IPR Policy, *supra* note 1179, cl. 6.1.

[1500] Order Granting FTC's Motion for Partial Summary Judgment on Qualcomm's Contractual Duties Pursuant to the Contracts with ATIS and the TIA, 2018 WL 5848999, *supra* note 52, at *2 (quoting *Microsoft I*, 696 F.3d at 877 n.2).

[1501] *See* Sidak, *What Makes FRAND Fair? The Just Price, Contract Formation, and the Division of Surplus from Voluntary Exchange, supra* note 623; Sidak, *Fair and Unfair Discrimination in Royalties for Standard-Essential Patents Encumbered by a FRAND or RAND Commitment, supra* note 1035, at 308–11.

[1502] *See, e.g.*, RESTATEMENT (SECOND) OF CONTRACTS § 203 (AM. LAW INST. 1981); *see also* Warner Commc'ns Inc. v. Chris-Craft Indus., Inc., 583 A.2d 962, 971 (Del. Ch. 1989) ("An interpretation that gives an effect to each term of an agreement, instrument or statute is to be preferred to an interpretation that accounts for some terms as redundant."); Reda v. Eastman Kodak Co., 649 N.Y.S.2d 555, 557 (App. Div. 1996) ("Effect and meaning must be given to every term of the contract.").

[1503] RESTATEMENT (SECOND) OF CONTRACTS § 203 (AM. LAW INST. 1981).

[1504] Order Granting FTC's Motion for Partial Summary Judgment on Qualcomm's Contractual Duties Pursuant to the Contracts with ATIS and the TIA, 2018 WL 5848999, *supra* note 52, at *2 (quoting *Microsoft I*, 696 F.3d at 877 n.2).

[1505] I proposed this interpretation of fairness in the FRAND contract in Sidak, *What Makes FRAND Fair? The Just Price, Contract Formation, and the Division of Surplus from Voluntary Exchange, supra* note 623, at 709, 723–24.

According to this account, the fairness constraint in the FRAND commitment is a lubricant to achieving the economic efficiency inherent in a successful bargain. Requiring fairness in the pricing of SEPs dissuades both the SEP holder and the implementer from (irrationally) walking away from a voluntary, bilateral licensing negotiation that, if successful, would create a positive surplus. In that sense, the fairness constraint in a FRAND contract makes an incremental contribution to constraining the pricing of FRAND-committed SEPs, above and beyond the respective constraints that reasonableness and nondiscrimination impose.

Judge Koh ignored the differences between FRAND contracts and RAND contracts. She even ignored the differences *among* RAND contracts of different SSOs. Rather than examining the precise language of the contracts that Qualcomm had actually executed with ATIS and the TIA, Judge Koh instead relied on the contractual interpretation conducted by other courts of a *different* SSO's RAND contract, which contained *different* language and was executed by a *different* SSO and a *different* SEP holder.

F. Was Summary Judgment Appropriate?

Judge Koh concluded that summary judgment was appropriate in regard to the existence and nature of the contractual duties imposed on Qualcomm pursuant to its contracts with ATIS and the TIA. Considering the strict conditions in the law that a party moving for summary judgment must satisfy, and that a judge ruling on such a motion must obey, did Judge Koh properly grant the FTC's motion?

A different judge might have considered it the wiser exercise of discretion to hear evidence at trial concerning the precise meaning of the specific RAND contracts that Qualcomm executed with ATIS and the TIA.

1. The Standard for Granting a Motion for Summary Judgment

Federal Rule of Civil Procedure 56 specifies a "court shall grant summary judgment if the movant shows that there is no genuine dispute as to any material fact and the movant is entitled to judgment as a matter of law."[1506] A dispute as to a material fact is genuine "if the evidence is such that a reasonable jury could return a verdict for the nonmoving party."[1507] Rule 56 limits to the evidence in the record a court's determination of whether summary judgment is appropriate.[1508]

[1506] FED. R. CIV. P. 56(a).
[1507] Anderson v. Liberty Lobby, Inc., 477 U.S. 242, 248 (1986).
[1508] FED. R. CIV. P. 56(a).

Rule 56 also requires the court to view the evidence in the light most favorable to the nonmoving party.[1509] Yet, the nonmoving party will not avoid summary judgment merely by asserting that the moving party's allegations are factually incorrect. The Supreme Court has emphasized that, "[w]hen the moving party has carried its burden under Rule 56(c), its opponent must do more than simply show that there is some metaphysical doubt as to the material facts."[1510]

However, it is not properly within the judge's discretion when ruling on a motion for summary judgment to make credibility determinations or to weigh conflicting evidence.[1511] The relevant inquiry is whether "the evidence presents a sufficient disagreement to require submission to a jury or whether it is so one-sided that one party must prevail as a matter of law."[1512] A judge shall grant summary judgment when "there can be but one reasonable conclusion as to the verdict,"[1513] such that judgment as a matter of law is proper.[1514] Rule 56 makes no distinction between a jury trial and a bench trial.[1515]

In the partial summary judgment determination in *FTC v. Qualcomm*, the relevant material fact that the parties disputed was whether the contracts that Qualcomm had executed with ATIS and the TIA had created for Qualcomm a duty to offer exhaustive licenses to its cellular SEPs to rival modem manufacturers. The FTC argued that "Qualcomm's contractual commitments to ATIS and TIA to make licenses to relevant SEPs available to 'applicants' on FRAND terms require Qualcomm to make such licenses available to rival modem-chip sellers."[1516] Qualcomm countered that the FTC ignored the qualifying language in the two contracts, which limits the SEP holder's duty to offer an exhaustive license only to an applicant that needs a license to implement or to practice the relevant standard.[1517] Qualcomm argued that, because modems cannot implement or practice a standard, a modem manufacturer cannot be considered an "applicant" for purposes of the contracts that Qualcomm executed with ATIS and the TIA.[1518]

[1509] *Id.* 56(c); *see also* Scott v. Harris, 550 U.S. 372, 379 (2007); Tolan v. Cotton, 572 U.S. 650, 656 (2014).

[1510] Matsushita Elec. Indus. Co. v. Zenith Radio Corp., 475 U.S. 574, 586–87 (1986).

[1511] *Liberty Lobby*, 477 U.S. at 249; *see also* T.W. Elec. Serv. v. Pac. Elec. Contractors Ass'n, 809 F.2d 626, 630 (9th Cir. 1987).

[1512] *Liberty Lobby*, 477 U.S. at 251–52.

[1513] *Id.* at 250.

[1514] *See* Fed. R. Civ. P. 56(a).

[1515] *See, e.g.*, William W. Schwarzer, Alan Hirsch & David J. Barrans, The Analysis and Decision of Summary Judgment Motions: A Monograph on Rule 56 of the Federal Rules of Civil Procedure 39 (Federal Judicial Center 1991) ("[W]hen evidentiary facts are in dispute, when the credibility of witnesses may be in issue, when conflicting evidence must be weighed, a full trial is clearly necessary regardless of whether it is a bench or jury trial.").

[1516] FTC's Motion for Partial Summary Judgment, *supra* note 485, at i.

[1517] Defendant Qualcomm Incorporated's Opposition to Motion for Partial Summary Judgment on Qualcomm's Standard Essential Patent Licensing Commitments at 1–3, FTC v. Qualcomm Inc., No. 5:17-cv-00220-LHK (N.D. Cal. Sept. 25, 2018) [hereinafter Qualcomm's Opposition to FTC's Motion for Partial Summary Judgment]; *see also id.* at 19–20.

[1518] *Id.* at 2.

Judge Koh concluded that there was no genuine dispute as to any material fact, such that the FTC was entitled to judgment as a matter of law.[1519] Yet, the evidence that Judge Koh cited in her findings of fact and conclusions of law indicated that, at the very least, there *was* a genuine dispute as to the material fact of whether or not the RAND contract that Qualcomm had executed with ATIS or with the TIA had created for Qualcomm a contractual duty to offer exhaustive licenses to its cellular SEPs to rival modem manufacturers.

A federal appellate court reviewing an order granting a motion for summary judgment will examine the issue *de novo*.[1520] In other words, the Ninth Circuit will consider whether, "viewing the evidence in the light most favorable to [the nonmoving party], there [was] a genuine dispute of material fact" and, therefore, whether summary judgment was appropriate.[1521]

2. *The Controlling Law for Interpreting the RAND Contracts of ATIS and the TIA*

Judge Koh found that California law controlled Qualcomm's contracts with ATIS and the TIA.[1522] She observed that neither contract included a choice-of-law provision.[1523] Judge Koh found that in such cases section 1646 of the California Civil Code provides that "'[a] contract is to be interpreted according to the law and usage of the place where it is to be performed; or, if it does not indicate a place of performance, according to the law and usage of the place where it is made.'"[1524] She further found, quoting the Ninth Circuit's application of section 1646 in a diversity case, that, "'[w]hen the contract does not expressly specify a place of performance,'" the court should assume that "'the place of performance is the jurisdiction in which the circumstances indicate the parties expected or intended the contract to be performed.'"[1525]

Judge Koh then observed that "Qualcomm was expected to perform its obligations—to provide licenses—from its headquarters in California."[1526] She also observed that Qualcomm's RAND "contracts [with ATIS and the TIA] were formed in California when Qualcomm executed its commitments to comply with the ATIS and TIA IPR policies."[1527] On the basis of that reasoning, Judge Koh concluded and the parties agreed that California law

---

[1519] Order Granting FTC's Motion for Partial Summary Judgment on Qualcomm's Contractual Duties Pursuant to the Contracts with ATIS and the TIA, 2018 WL 5848999, *supra* note 52, at *15.

[1520] *See, e.g.*, Ruiz v. ParadigmWorks Grp., 787 F. App'x 384, 385 (9ᵗʰ Cir. 2019); Fontana v. Haskin, 262 F.3d 871, 876 (9ᵗʰ Cir. 2001); *see also* Eastman Kodak Co. v. Image Tech. Servs., Inc., 504 U.S. 451, 465 (1992).

[1521] *Ruiz*, 787 F. App'x at 386.

[1522] Order Granting FTC's Motion for Partial Summary Judgment on Qualcomm's Contractual Duties Pursuant to the Contracts with ATIS and the TIA, 2018 WL 5848999, *supra* note 52, at *7.

[1523] *Id.*

[1524] *Id.* (alteration in original) (quoting CAL. CIV. CODE § 1646).

[1525] *Id.* (quoting Welles v. Turner Entm't Co., 503 F.3d 728, 738 (9ᵗʰ Cir. 2007)).

[1526] *Id.*

[1527] *Id.*

controlled the RAND contracts that Qualcomm had executed with ATIS and the TIA.[1528]

Judge Koh next outlined the controlling principles of contract interpretation. She said that, "'[u]nder California law, the fundamental goal of contract interpretation is to give effect to the mutual intent of the parties as it existed at the time of contracting.'"[1529] Judge Koh further found that a California court would identify the parties' mutual intent primarily from the language of the contract:

> California's rules of contract interpretation instruct courts that if "[t]he language [of a contract] is clear and explicit, and does not involve an absurdity," the contract language must govern the contract's interpretation. Moreover, "the intention of the parties is to be ascertained from the writing alone, if possible." "Thus, if the meaning a layperson would ascribe to contract language is not ambiguous, [the Court] appl[ies] that meaning." "The whole of a contract is to be taken together, so as to give effect to every part, if reasonably practicable, each clause helping to interpret the other."[1530]

She added that a court might also consider extrinsic evidence to ascertain the parties' intent:

> If a preliminary consideration of that extrinsic evidence demonstrates that the evidence is "(1) 'relevant' to prove (2) 'a meaning to which the language of the instrument is reasonably susceptible,'" the extrinsic evidence is admissible. Relevant extrinsic evidence may "include[] testimony as to the circumstances surrounding the making of the agreement . . . including the object, nature and subject matter of the writing . . . so that the court can place itself in the same situation in which the parties found themselves at the time of contracting."[1531]

However, Judge Koh emphasized, "extrinsic evidence cannot be used to directly contradict an express term of a written contract."[1532]

[1528] *Id.*

[1529] *Id.* (quoting U.S. Cellular Inv. Co. v. GTE Mobilnet, Inc., 281 F.3d 929, 934 (9th Cir. 2002)).

[1530] *Id.* (alterations in original) (citations omitted) (first quoting CAL. CIV. CODE § 1638; then quoting CAL. CIV. CODE § 1639; then quoting AIU Ins. Co. v. Superior Court, 799 P.2d 1253, 1264 (Cal. 1990) (in bank); and then quoting CAL. CIV. CODE § 1641).

[1531] *Id.* at *8 (first quoting *U.S. Cellular*, 281 F.3d at 938 (quoting Pacific Gas & Elec. Co. v. Thomas Drayage & Rigging Co., 442 P.2d 641, 644 (Cal. 1968)); and then quoting *Pacific Gas & Electric*, 442 P.2d at 645 (alterations in original)). *But see* Trident Ctr. v. Conn. Gen. Life Ins. Co., 847 F.2d 564, 568–69 (9th Cir. 1988) ("'Accordingly,' the court stated, 'the exclusion of relevant, extrinsic, evidence to explain the meaning of a written instrument could be justified only if it were feasible to determine the meaning the parties gave to the words from the instrument alone.'") (quoting *Pacific Gas & Electric*, 442 P.2d at 644).

[1532] Order Granting FTC's Motion for Partial Summary Judgment on Qualcomm's Contractual Duties Pursuant to the Contracts with ATIS and the TIA, 2018 WL 5848999, *supra* note 52, at *8 (citing Gerdlund v. Elec. Dispensers Int'l, 235 Cal. Rptr. 279, 282 (Ct. App. 1987)).

Judge Koh ultimately considered both intrinsic and extrinsic evidence to interpret Qualcomm's RAND contracts with ATIS and the TIA. Although she addressed the two contracts together, I will examine them independently. The faulty foundation for Judge Koh's partial summary judgment becomes particularly evident when one examines each RAND contract individually.

G. *Qualcomm's RAND Commitment to ATIS*

Judge Koh found that no genuine dispute of material fact existed as to whether Qualcomm's RAND commitment to ATIS created a contractual duty for Qualcomm to offer exhaustive licenses to its cellular SEPs to rival modem manufacturers.[1533] She observed that, pursuant to the ATIS RAND contract, an SEP holder commits that a license "'will be made available to applicants desiring to utilize the license for the purpose of implementing the standard . . . under reasonable terms and conditions that are demonstrably free of any unfair discrimination.'"[1534] Judge Koh said that "Qualcomm's written assurances to . . . ATIS . . . mirror"[1535] that language and, in particular, that "Qualcomm assured ATIS that Qualcomm would make licenses available 'under reasonable terms and conditions that are demonstrably free of any unfair discrimination to applicants desiring to utilize the license for the purpose of implementing' the relevant standard."[1536]

The FTC and Qualcomm disagreed over the correct interpretation of the requirement to offer licenses to "'applicants desiring to utilize the license for the purpose of implementing' the relevant standard." The FTC argued that any company that requires a license, including a modem manufacturer, should be considered an "applicant" for purposes of the ATIS RAND contract.[1537] In contrast, Qualcomm argued that the FTC incorrectly disregarded the language restricting the universe of relevant "applicants" to those that need a license for purposes of *practicing* an ATIS standard. Qualcomm argued that, because modems cannot implement ATIS standards, manufacturers of those modems are not properly considered "applicants" for purposes of Qualcomm's contract with ATIS. Qualcomm reasoned that ATIS standards "describe the operation of a complete mobile device (*e.g.*, a cellular phone) and the cellular network itself (*e.g.*, the base stations and other infrastructure)," whereas standards "do not describe the operation of modem chips or other components."[1538] In other words, Qualcomm argued that only end-product

---

[1533] *Id.* at *15.
[1534] *Id.* at *3 (alteration in original) (quoting ATIS, Operating Procedures for ATIS Forums and Committees, *supra* note 1497, at 10).
[1535] *Id.* at *9.
[1536] *Id.* (quoting ATIS, Operating Procedures for ATIS Forums and Committees, *supra* note 1497, at 10).
[1537] FTC's Motion for Partial Summary Judgment, *supra* note 485, at 2.
[1538] Qualcomm's Opposition to FTC's Motion for Partial Summary Judgment, *supra* note 1517, at 2.

devices can implement an ATIS standard and, therefore, only manufacturers of those devices are "applicants" that need a license to practice an ATIS standard.

Qualcomm also argued that the FTC's interpretation failed if one considers the recommendations of the American National Standards Institute (ANSI) concerning the patent polices that SSOs should adopt. Specifically, Qualcomm argued that the ATIS Patent Policy adopted verbatim ANSI's Patent Policy and provides that "a license 'will be made available to applicants desiring to utilize the license *for the purpose of implementing the standard* . . . under reasonable terms and conditions that are demonstrably free of any unfair discrimination.'"[1539] Qualcomm emphasized that "ANSI's Executive Standards Council ('ExSC') has expressly determined that its own Patent Policy does *not* require that accredited SDOs [standards development organizations] mandate component-level licensing."[1540] Qualcomm thus disputed that it was reasonable for the FTC to argue that a policy with identical language to ANSI's Patent Policy could impose a materially different licensing obligation—namely, the mandatory offering of component-level exhaustive licenses to cellular SEPs.

The FTC and Qualcomm also disagreed over the correct interpretation of the nondiscrimination requirement of Qualcomm's RAND contract with ATIS. The FTC argued "that Qualcomm's contractual commitments to make licenses available to 'applicants' on non-discriminatory terms require Qualcomm to make such licenses available to competing modem-chip sellers."[1541] Qualcomm countered that its RAND contract with ATIS requires Qualcomm to offer license terms that are free of any unfair discrimination, but that the contract does not "address the antecedent question of whether a license must be made available for any specific purpose or field of use."[1542] In other words, Qualcomm argued that the nondiscrimination requirement in the ATIS RAND contract was irrelevant to determining whether modem manufacturers were "applicants" for purposes of that contract.

Judge Koh dismissed Qualcomm's proposed interpretation of "applicants" and "nondiscrimination."[1543] Yet, as we will see shortly, neither the language of the ATIS RAND commitment nor the extrinsic evidence that Judge Koh cited in her partial summary judgment supported her conclusion.

[1539] *Id.* at 4 (alteration in original) (emphasis in original) (boldface suppressed) (quoting ATIS, Operating Procedures for ATIS Forums and Committees, *supra* note 1497, at 10).

[1540] *Id.* at 7 (emphasis in original) (boldface suppressed).

[1541] FTC's Motion for Partial Summary Judgment, *supra* note 485, at 3.

[1542] Qualcomm's Opposition to FTC's Motion for Partial Summary Judgment, *supra* note 1517, at 2.

[1543] Order Granting FTC's Motion for Partial Summary Judgment on Qualcomm's Contractual Duties Pursuant to the Contracts with ATIS and the TIA, 2018 WL 5848999, *supra* note 52, at *14.

1.   The Language of the ATIS RAND Contract

Judge Koh found that the language of Qualcomm's RAND contract with ATIS contradicted Qualcomm's proposed interpretation. She made three arguments to support her conclusion that summary judgment was proper as a matter of law because there was no genuine dispute of material fact. Each was unpersuasive.

a.   Implementation of Less Than the Whole Standard

First, addressing the ATIS RAND contract and the TIA RAND contract simultaneously, Judge Koh said that, "contrary to Qualcomm's argument, neither IPR policy limits a SEP holder's FRAND commitment to those applicants who themselves 'practice' or 'implement' *whole* standards."[1544] Observing that "[t]he ATIS IPR [P]olicy states that a license must be *'for the purpose* of implementing' a standard,"[1545] she concluded, without explanation, that that statement clearly contradicted Qualcomm's proposed interpretation that only manufacturers of products that comply with an ATIS standard should be considered "applicants."[1546]

That reasoning is unconvincing. The ATIS RAND contract is, at best, silent on whether an "applicant" must comply with the whole standard or merely portions of it. Does the plain language of that contract support Judge Koh's conclusion, to the exclusion of any other possible conclusion, that a firm that implements only a portion of the standard is nonetheless properly considered to be an "applicant"? Even if one were to accept that "applicants" include firms that implement only portions of the standard, is it absolutely clear—is it absolutely unambiguous—that modem manufacturers would satisfy that requirement?

b.   "Complying with" Versus "Implementing" the Standard, and the Relationship of Either to Infringing an SEP

Second, Judge Koh said that Qualcomm's proposed interpretation "violates the non-discrimination obligation, but also makes little sense," because, in her view, modems clearly can implement an ATIS standard.[1547] She reasoned that "Qualcomm's founder conceded[,] and Qualcomm's own documents demonstrate, [that] modem chips may be 'compliant' with

---

[1544]   *Id.* (emphasis added) (quoting Qualcomm's Opposition to FTC's Motion for Partial Summary Judgment, *supra* note 1517, at 17).

[1545]   *Id.* (emphasis in original) (quoting ATIS, Operating Procedures for ATIS Forums and Committees, *supra* note 1497, at 10).

[1546]   *Id.*

[1547]   *Id.*

cellular standards."[1548] Judge Koh did not explain whether she considered an item's being "compliant" with a cellular standard to be equivalent to an item's "implementing" that standard, or whether the distinction between "compliant" and "implementing" would have been absolutely obvious to any lay jury for purposes of granting the FTC's motion for partial summary judgment in *FTC v. Qualcomm*. She further said that Qualcomm conceded that some of its SEPs "are infringed by typical modem chips."[1549] In addition, Judge Koh found that "undisputed evidence in Qualcomm's own documents demonstrates that a modem chip is a core component of the cellular handset, which only underscores how a SEP license to supply modem chips is for the purpose of practicing or implementing cellular standards and why Qualcomm cannot discriminate against modem chip suppliers."[1550]

But this reasoning does not support Judge Koh's grant of summary judgment. Whether or not a modem practices an ATIS standard is a question of fact. To answer that question typically requires (in patent-infringement litigation in federal court or at the ITC) the fact finder's examination of technical evidence, usually assisted by expert testimony of an electrical engineer. Whether a modem infringes an SEP that is essential to practice a standard, or whether the modem is a core component of a smartphone, does not answer the factual question of whether that modem practices an ATIS standard. Judge Koh evidently thought that a modem's infringement of a single SEP would suffice to answer the factual question of whether the modem practices an ATIS standard, for she reasoned that "*any* SEP is by definition necessary to practice or for the purpose of implementing a standard."[1551] That reasoning is unsound. Evidence that an input infringes a single SEP (or, to drive the point closer to what typically transpires in real-world patent litigation, merely one *claim* of a single SEP), cannot by itself support the factual conclusion that the input necessarily implements a portion of a standard, let alone the entire standard.

[1548] *Id.* (quoting Videotaped Deposition of Irwin Mark Jacobs (Co-Founder, Qualcomm) (Vol. 1) at 117:25–118:3, FTC v. Qualcomm Inc., No. 5:17-cv-00220-LHK (N.D. Cal. Mar. 2, 2018) [hereinafter Deposition of Irwin Mark Jacobs (Vol. 1)], *Reply Exhibit 1 to* FTC's Reply in Support of Partial Summary Judgment, *supra* note 485, ECF No. 893-2). Judge Koh's conclusion was based on Dr. Jacobs' one-word answer to a single question posed during his deposition. *See* Deposition of Irwin Mark Jacobs (Vol. 1), *supra*, at 117:25–118:3 ("Q. Did you consider in 1998—did you consider Qualcomm ASICs to be compliant with IS-95 standards? A. Yes."); *see also* FTC v. Qualcomm Inc., 411 F. Supp. 3d 658, 670–71 (N.D. Cal. 2019) ("2G cellular standards include the Global System for Mobile ('GSM') and cdmaOne (also sometimes called 'TIA/EIA/IS-95' or 'IS-95'). . . . TIA adopted cdmaOne as a cellular standard. TIA also adopted IS-95A and IS-95B as improvements to cdmaOne. These are considered 2G standards. . . . cdmaOne uses code division multiple access ('CDMA') technology.").

[1549] Order Granting FTC's Motion for Partial Summary Judgment on Qualcomm's Contractual Duties Pursuant to the Contracts with ATIS and the TIA, 2018 WL 5848999, *supra* note 52, at *14.

[1550] *Id.*

[1551] *Id.* (emphasis added).

c.   Precatory Statements by ATIS About Benefit to the Public and Respect for Intellectual Property Rights

Third, to support her rejection of Qualcomm's proposed interpretation of its RAND contract with ATIS, Judge Koh quoted the ATIS Patent Policy for its statement that it aims "'to benefit the public while respecting the legitimate rights of intellectual property owners.'"[1552] She found that that statement, when combined with other evidence, supported her conclusion that the ATIS RAND commitment obligated Qualcomm to offer exhaustive licenses to its cellular SEPs to rival modem manufacturers.[1553] The intermediate steps in Judge Koh's reasoning were left unstated.

Contrary to Judge Koh's finding, the language that she quoted from the ATIS RAND commitment did not show that Qualcomm's proposed interpretation was nonsensical. Nor did it contradict the language of the ATIS RAND contract.

Thus, contrary to Judge Koh's findings on partial summary judgment, the plain language of the RAND contract between Qualcomm and ATIS did not contradict Qualcomm's proposed interpretation of its contractual duties to ATIS. At the very least, the language was ambiguous, such that there existed, contrary to Judge Koh's findings, a genuine dispute of material fact as to whether Qualcomm's RAND contract with ATIS had imposed on Qualcomm a duty to offer exhaustive licenses to its cellular SEPs to rival modem manufacturers.

2.   Evidence Probative of Existing Industry Practice

Judge Koh rejected Qualcomm's argument that evidence probative of existing industry practice actually contradicted the FTC's own proposed interpretation of the RAND contract that Qualcomm had executed with ATIS. In particular, on the basis of evidence of (1) Qualcomm's outbound SEP "licenses" and (2) Qualcomm's inbound patent licenses, Judge Koh rejected Qualcomm's argument that other SEP holders commonly offered exhaustive cellular SEP licenses only to OEMs and not to rival modem manufacturers.

a.   One Outbound SEP "License" from Qualcomm to an Unidentified Rival Modem Manufacturer

First, Qualcomm cited evidence of the licensing practices of SEP holders such as Nokia, Ericsson, and InterDigital to support its contention that it was a common industry practice "to make licenses available for the manufacture

---

[1552]   *Id.* at *12 (quoting ATIS, Operating Procedures for ATIS Forums and Committees, *supra* note 1497, at 8).

[1553]   *Id.* at *10.

and sale of end-user devices, but not for the manufacture and sale of components such as modem chips."[1554] Judge Koh did not directly dismiss that
evidence.

Instead, she rejected Qualcomm's argument because, she reasoned,
Qualcomm's own licensing practices confirmed that the ATIS RAND
commitment had obligated Qualcomm to offer exhaustive licenses to its
cellular SEPs to rival modem manufacturers.[1555] In particular, Judge Koh found
that Qualcomm conceded that at least one other modem manufacturer had
received an outbound "license" from Qualcomm to Qualcomm's SEPs.[1556]

It is astonishing that Judge Koh did not identify any facts concerning the
Qualcomm "license" with a rival modem manufacturer to which she referred.
She did not identify the party with which Qualcomm executed that "license"
or the year in which that "license" was executed. Judge Koh did not indicate
whether the "license" was exhaustive or merely a "license" to a nonexhaustive subset of Qualcomm's rights in its cellular SEPs. She did not indicate the

---

[1554] Qualcomm's Opposition to FTC's Motion for Partial Summary Judgment, *supra* note 1517, at 8.
The FTC claimed in its closing argument at trial that "Qualcomm's refusal to license rivals is not . . .
common in the industry." Transcript of Proceedings (Volume 11) at 2119:1–2, FTC v. Qualcomm Inc.,
No. 5:17-cv-00220-LHK (N.D. Cal. Jan. 29, 2019) (closing argument of Jennifer Milici for the FTC).
This claim was contradicted in the sense that the deposition testimony of witnesses from Ericsson,
Nokia, and InterDigital established that the common industry practice of SEP holders was to license to
OEMs rather than component manufacturers (which was the relevant distinction to be made concerning
Qualcomm's "rivals" in this claim by the FTC). *See* Videotaped Deposition of Christina Petersson (Vice
President, Ericsson) at 25:5–17, FTC v. Qualcomm Inc., No. 5:17-cv-00220-LHK (N.D. Cal. Apr. 20, 2018)
("Q. And in this value chain when you are granting licenses to Ericsson's SEP, cellular SEP portfolio, who
would you be granting a license to? A. We would be licensing the company putting its name on the fully
compliant equipment and selling that on the market. So it would be Apple, Samsung and those type
of companies. Q. These were the companies that you identified as the OEM? A. Yes. Q. And this has
been Ericsson's practice since you've been involved in the licensing? A. It has, yes."), *exhibit to* Qualcomm
Incorporated's Submission of Deposition Testimony That Was Presented on January 25, 2019 (Trial
Day 9), FTC v. Qualcomm Inc., No. 5:17-cv-00220-LHK (N.D. Cal. Jan. 25, 2019), ECF No. 1447-1;
Videotaped Deposition of Ilkka Rahnasto (Senior Vice President, Nokia) at 11:15–25, 13:15–21, 13:23–24,
FTC v. Qualcomm Inc., No. 5:17-cv-00220-LHK (N.D. Cal. Apr. 17, 2018) ("Q[.] And with respect to
Nokia's use or following of this practice, the one point—is there a specific point in the value chain at
which Nokia grants licenses? A[.] Yes. We have always [granted] the license to the manufacturer of the
end product, meaning the manufacturer of the mobile phone, the complete product. Q[.] Okay. And has
that been Nokia's practice since it first had SEPs? A[.] Yes. . . . Q[.] Then [CX4321] goes on, that Nokia's
practice from the very beginning, and that it—meaning the practice—corresponds with industry practice.
Do you see that? A[.] Yes, I can see that. Q[.] And is that correct, that Nokia's practice corresponds to
industry practice? . . . [A.] Based on my experience, that is my understanding."), *exhibit to* Qualcomm
Incorporated's Submission of Deposition Testimony That Was Presented on January 25, 2019 (Trial Day 9),
FTC v. Qualcomm Inc., No. 5:17-cv-00220-LHK (N.D. Cal. Jan. 25, 2019), ECF No. 1447-3; Videotaped
Deposition of Ranae McElvaine (Vice President, InterDigital) at 30:19–31:15, FTC v. Qualcomm Inc.,
No. 5:17-cv-00220-LHK (N.D. Cal. Apr. 3, 2018) ("Q. . . . 'As a result, InterDigital does not, as a practical
matter, enter into stand-alone patent license agreements with chip manufacturers. Rather, InterDigital
follows industry practice and conducts its licensing business at the handset or other terminal unit level,
and that has been InterDigital's practice for more than 20 years.' So the first question is does what I just
read accurately reflect InterDigital's understanding and business practices? A. Yes."), *exhibit to* Qualcomm
Incorporated's Submission of Deposition Testimony That Was Presented on January 25, 2019 (Trial Day 9),
FTC v. Qualcomm Inc., No. 5:17-cv-00220-LHK (N.D. Cal. Jan. 25, 2019), ECF No. 1447-2.

[1555] Order Granting FTC's Motion for Partial Summary Judgment on Qualcomm's Contractual Duties
Pursuant to the Contracts with ATIS and the TIA, 2018 WL 5848999, *supra* note 52, at *12.

[1556] *Id.*

context in which Qualcomm executed that "license." Judge Koh did not even state whether the "license" included SEPs that Qualcomm had committed *to ATIS standards*.

b. *Qualcomm's Receipt of SEP "Licenses"*

Second, Judge Koh concluded that "Qualcomm's own extensive receipt of SEP licenses to supply modem chips rebuts any argument that a contrary industry practice is so 'certain, uniform, . . . or generally known and notorious' as to be 'regarded as part of the contract.'"[1557] Judge Koh's reasoning was faulty.

Judge Koh did not mention that, until 2000, Qualcomm had its own mobile handset business, which it subsequently sold to Kyocera.[1558] It was therefore ambiguous whether the Qualcomm "licenses" to which Judge Koh referred were outbound licenses of Qualcomm's cellular SEPs to rival modem manufacturers or inbound licenses of patents for Qualcomm's use in its own manufacture of mobile handsets. As we saw earlier, ETSI's IPR Policy provides that its FRAND commitment "is made subject to the condition that those who seek licenses agree to reciprocate."[1559] It was therefore ambiguous from Judge Koh's partial summary judgment order whether the inbound licenses to which she referred were merely instances in which Qualcomm had exercised its right as a licensor under ETSI's FRAND commitment to condition its grant of an outbound license to its own portfolio of ETSI cellular SEPs on the licensee's reciprocal grant-back of a license of its own portfolio of ETSI cellular SEPs to Qualcomm on FRAND terms.

Furthermore, that some modem manufacturers might have received a license to cellular SEPs did not contradict Qualcomm's argument that it was a common industry practice to license cellular SEPs exhaustively only to end-product manufacturers. Dozens of press releases support Qualcomm's understanding of the prevailing industry practice: most, if not all, OEMs

---

[1557] *Id.* at *13 (alteration in original) (quoting Webster v. Klassen, 241 P.2d 302, 306 (Cal. Ct. App. 1952)).

[1558] Qualcomm Inc., Annual Report for the Fiscal Year Ended September 24, 2000 (SEC Form 10-K), at 3 (filed Nov. 3, 2000) [hereinafter 2000 Qualcomm 10-K] ("In February 2000, the Company sold its terrestrial-based CDMA wireless consumer phone business, including its phone inventory, manufacturing equipment and customer commitments, to Kyocera Wireless (Kyocera)."); *see also* Qualcomm Inc., Annual Report for the Fiscal Year Ended September 26, 1999 (SEC Form 10-K), at 11 (filed Nov. 17, 1999) [hereinafter 1999 Qualcomm 10-K] ("QCP [Qualcomm Consumer Products Segment] produces a range of CDMA digital wireless phones, including the Thin Phone and the pdQ smartphone."); Mock, The Qualcomm Equation: How a Fledgling Telecom Company Forged a New Path to Big Profits and Market Dominance, *supra* note 1322, at 147–48.

[1559] ETSI IPR Policy, *supra* note 1179, cl. 6.1.

of mobile devices, have taken a license for Qualcomm's cellular SEPs.[1560] In contrast, I found no evidence in the public domain of a press

---

[1560] *See* Press Release, Qualcomm Inc., Qualcomm and LGE Enter into a New Global Patent License Agreement (Aug. 20, 2019), https://www.qualcomm.com/news/releases/2019/08/20/qualcomm-and-lge-enter-new-global-patent-license-agreement; Press Release, Ericsson, Inc., Ericsson and OPPO Sign Initial Patent License Agreement (Feb. 19, 2019), https://www.ericsson.com/en/press-releases/2019/2/ericsson-and-oppo-sign-initial-patent-license-agreement; Press Release, InterDigital, Inc., Hillcrest Labs and LG Renew License for Smart TV Technology (Feb. 19, 2019), http://ir.interdigital.com/file/Index?KeyFile=396798647; Press Release, InterDigital, Inc., InterDigital Extends Term of Joint Venture and Enters into Patent License Agreement with Sony Corporation of America (Dec. 24, 2018), http://ir.interdigital.com/file/Index?KeyFile=396200896; Press Release, Nokia Corp., Nokia and China's OPPO Sign Patent License Agreement (Nov. 26, 2018), https://www.nokia.com/about-us/news/releases/2018/11/26/nokia-and-chinas-oppo-sign-patent-license-agreement/; Press Release, Nokia Corp, Nokia and Samsung Extend Their Patent License Agreement (Oct. 25, 2018), https://www.nokia.com/about-us/news/releases/2018/10/25/nokia-and-samsung-extend-their-patent-license-agreement/; Press Release, Ericsson, Inc., Ericsson and LG Electronics Sign Global Patent License Agreement (July 30, 2018), https://www.ericsson.com/en/press-releases/2018/7/ericsson-and-lg-electronics-sign-global-patent-license-agreement; Press Release, InterDigital, Inc., InterDigital and Fujitsu Connected Technologies Limited Agree to Worldwide Patent License Agreement for Terminal Units (July 5, 2018), http://ir.interdigital.com/file/Index?KeyFile=394125311; Press Release, Qualcomm Inc., Qualcomm and Samsung Amend Long-Term Cross-License Agreement (Jan. 31, 2018), https://www.qualcomm.com/news/releases/2018/01/31/qualcomm-and-samsung-amend-long-term-cross-license-agreement; Press Release, Nokia Corp., Nokia and Huawei Sign Patent License Agreement (Dec. 21, 2017), https://www.nokia.com/about-us/news/releases/2017/12/21/nokia-and-huawei-sign-patent-license-agreement/; Press Release, InterDigital, Inc., InterDigital and LG Electronics, Inc. Sign Multi-Year Patent License Agreement (Dec. 4, 2017), http://ir.interdigital.com/file/Index?KeyFile=391325057; Press Release, Nokia Corp., Nokia and Xiaomi Sign Business Cooperation and Patent Agreements (July 5, 2017), https://www.nokia.com/about-us/news/releases/2017/07/05/nokia-and-xiaomi-sign-business-cooperation-and-patent-agreements/; Press Release, InterDigital, Inc., InterDigital and Panasonic Mobile Communications Renew Their 4G Patent License (June 7, 2017), http://ir.interdigital.com/file/Index?KeyFile=2000919744; Press Release, InterDigital, Inc., InterDigital Announces Patent License Agreement with Apple (Dec. 15, 2016), http://ir.interdigital.com/file/Index?KeyFile=37131404; Press Release, Qualcomm Inc., Qualcomm Signs 3G/4G China Patent License Agreement with vivo (Aug. 7, 2016), https://www.qualcomm.com/news/releases/2016/08/07/qualcomm-signs-3g4g-china-patent-license-agreement-vivo; Press Release, Qualcomm Inc., Qualcomm Signs 3G/4G China Patent License Agreement with OPPO (July 31, 2016), https://www.qualcomm.com/news/releases/2016/07/31/qualcomm-signs-3g-4g-china-patent-license-agreement-oppo; Press Release, Qualcomm Inc., Qualcomm Signs 3G/4G Chinese Patent License Agreement with Hisense (Apr. 20, 2016), https://www.qualcomm.com/news/releases/2016/04/20/qualcomm-signs-3g4g-chinese-patent-license-agreement-hisense; Press Release, Qualcomm Inc., Qualcomm and Lenovo Sign 3G/4G China Patent License Agreement (Feb. 18, 2016), https://www.qualcomm.com/news/releases/2016/02/18/qualcomm-and-lenovo-sign-3g4g-china-patent-license-agreement; Press Release, Ericsson, Inc., Ericsson and Apple Sign Global Patent License Agreement, Settle Litigation (Dec. 21, 2015), https://www.ericsson.com/en/press-releases/2015/12/ericsson-and-apple-sign-global-patent-license-agreement-settle-litigation; Press Release, Qualcomm Inc., Qualcomm and Xiaomi Sign 3G/4G License Agreement (Dec. 2, 2015), https://www.qualcomm.com/news/releases/2015/12/02/qualcomm-and-xiaomi-sign-3g4g-license-agreement; Press Release, Qualcomm Inc., Qualcomm and Huizhou TCL Mobile Communication Co., Ltd Sign 3G/4G Chinese Patent License Agreement (Nov. 5, 2015), https://www.qualcomm.com/news/releases/2015/11/05/qualcomm-and-huizhou-tcl-mobile-communication-co-ltd-sign-3g4g-chinese; Press Release, Qualcomm Inc., Qualcomm and ZTE Sign New 3G/4G License, Strengthening Long-Term Partnership (Nov. 2, 2015), https://www.qualcomm.com/news/releases/2015/11/02/qualcomm-and-zte-sign-new-3g4g-license-strengthening-long-term-partnership; Press Release, Nokia Corp., LG Electronics and Nokia Technologies Agree on Smartphone Patent License (June 16, 2015), https://www.nokia.com/about-us/news/releases/2015/06/16/lg-electronics-and-nokia-technologies-agree-on-smartphone-patent-license/; Press Release, Qualcomm Inc., Qualcomm and Semp Toshiba Sign 3G/4G License Agreement (Oct. 10, 2012), https://www.qualcomm.com/news/releases/2012/10/10/qualcomm-and-semp-toshiba-sign-3g4g-license-agreement; Press Release, Nokia Corp., Nokia Enters into Patent License Agreement with Apple (June 14, 2011), https://www.nokia.com/about-us/news/releases/2011/06/14/nokia-enters-into-patent-license-agreement-with-apple/; Press Release, Qualcomm Inc., Qualcomm and Lenovo Mobile Enter into WCDMA Subscriber Unit License Agreement (May 7, 2007), https://www.qualcomm.com/news/

release announcing a license between Qualcomm and a rival modem manufacturer (which was not also a handset manufacturer, like Samsung). Many of Qualcomm's license agreements with OEMs of mobile devices predate the FTC's filing of its complaint in *FTC v. Qualcomm* on January 17, 2017. Therefore, a mountain of substantial evidence readily available in the public domain at the time of Judge Koh's partial summary judgment on November 6, 2018 confuted her rejection of Qualcomm's argument that it was a common industry practice to offer exhaustive licenses to cellular SEPs only to OEMs.

3.   *The Indiscretion of Summary Judgment on Component-Level Licensing Under the ATIS RAND Contract*

Rather than dismiss Qualcomm's argument at the summary judgment stage, Judge Koh would have more wisely exercised her discretion by examining evidence at trial concerning the existing industry practice in licensing patents

releases/2007/05/07/qualcomm-and-lenovo-mobile-enter-wcdma-subscriber-unit-license-agreement; Press Release, Qualcomm Inc., Qualcomm and Inventec Appliances Sign 3G Subscriber Unit and Modem Card License Agreement (Mar. 23, 2006), https://www.qualcomm.com/news/releases/2006/03/23/qualcomm-and-inventec-appliances-sign-3g-subscriber-unit-and-modem-card; Press Release, Qualcomm Inc., Qualcomm Signs 3G Worldwide Subscriber Unit License Agreement with Casio (Jan. 26, 2006), https://www.qualcomm.com/news/releases/2006/01/26/qualcomm-signs-3g-worldwide-subscriber-unit-license-agreement-casio; Press Release, Qualcomm Inc., Qualcomm Provides Global QPoint™ License to ZTE Corporation (Apr. 25, 2005), https://www.qualcomm.com/news/releases/2005/04/25/qualcomm-provides-global-qpoint-license-zte-corporation; Press Release, Qualcomm Inc., Qualcomm and Amoi Mobile Sign Worldwide Subscriber License Agreement (Sept. 1, 2004), https://www.qualcomm.com/news/releases/2004/09/01/qualcomm-and-amoi-mobile-sign-worldwide-subscriber-license-agreement; Press Release, Qualcomm Inc., Qualcomm Announces Commercial Agreements to License Qtv, Qcamcorder and Qvideophone to Leading Wireless Handset Manufacturers (Nov. 11, 2003), https://www.qualcomm.com/news/releases/2003/11/11/qualcomm-announces-commercial-agreements-license-qtv-qcamcorder-and; Press Release, Qualcomm Inc., Qualcomm Enters into CDMA Subscriber Unit and Infrastructure License Agreements with 11 Chinese Manufacturers (Jan. 23, 2002), https://www.qualcomm.com/news/releases/2002/01/23/qualcomm-enters-cdma-subscriber-unit-and-infrastructure-license-agreements; Press Release, Qualcomm Inc., Qualcomm Enters into CDMA Subscriber Unit License Agreement with Hisense Group (Nov. 28, 2001), https://www.qualcomm.com/news/releases/2001/11/28/qualcomm-enters-cdma-subscriber-unit-license-agreement-hisense-group; Press Release, Qualcomm Inc., Nokia and Qualcomm Expand License Agreement (July 3, 2001), https://www.qualcomm.com/news/releases/2001/07/03/nokia-and-qualcomm-expand-license-agreement; Press Release, Qualcomm Inc., Qualcomm Enters into CDMA Subscriber Unit License Agreement with ZTE Corporation (July 2, 2001), https://www.qualcomm.com/news/releases/2001/07/02/qualcomm-enters-cdma-subscriber-unit-license-agreement-zte-corporation; Press Release, Qualcomm Inc., Qualcomm Announces Signing of Commercial License for CDMA Network Products with ZTE Corporation (May 21, 2001), https://www.qualcomm.com/news/releases/2001/05/21/qualcomm-announces-signing-commercial-license-cdma-network-products-zte; Press Release, Qualcomm Inc., Qualcomm Expands Matsushita Communication Industrial's CDMA License Agreement (May 9, 2001), https://www.qualcomm.com/news/releases/2001/05/09/qualcomm-expands-matsushita-communication-industrials-cdma-license; Press Release, Qualcomm Inc., Qualcomm Signs CDMA Modem Card License Agreement with Matsushita Electronic Components (Jan. 19, 2001), https://www.qualcomm.com/news/releases/2001/01/19/qualcomm-signs-cdma-modem-card-license-agreement-matsushita-electronic; Press Release, Qualcomm Inc., ERICSSON and Qualcomm Reach Global CDMA Resolution (Mar. 25, 1999), https://www.qualcomm.com/news/releases/1999/03/25/ericsson-and-qualcomm-reach-global-cdma-resolution; Press Release, Qualcomm Inc., Qualcomm and Philips Enter into License Agreement (Mar. 30, 1998), https://www.qualcomm.com/news/releases/1998/03/30/qualcomm-and-philips-enter-license-agreement; Press Release, Qualcomm Inc., Qualcomm Signs CDMA Subscriber Equipment License with Siemens Wireless Terminals (July 17, 1996), https://www.qualcomm.com/news/releases/1996/07/17/qualcomm-signs-cdma-subscriber-equipment-license-siemens-wireless-terminals.

that have been declared essential to ATIS standards. A court may use the custom or usage of trade to "ascertain and explain the meaning and intention of the parties to a contract, whether written or in parol, which could not be done without the aid of this extrinsic evidence."[1561] Hearing more evidence of industry practice at trial would have given Judge Koh a clearer understanding of whether, by executing the ATIS RAND contract, Qualcomm and ATIS intended to limit Qualcomm's freedom to choose the level of the supply chain at which to offer exhaustive licenses to its cellular SEPs.

Judge Koh evidently also did not distinguish the case in which an SEP holder, as a matter of preference, *voluntarily* decides to license its cellular SEPs exhaustively to a component manufacturer from the case in which the SEP holder, as a matter of constraint, has a preexisting contractual duty to do so. In other words, exhaustive licenses with component manufacturers would exist if the SEP holder voluntarily decided to enter into such agreements; but the existence of such licenses would not constitute evidence that an SEP holder had a contractual *duty* to offer licenses exhaustively to its cellular SEPs at the component level. As we saw earlier, preference and constraint are powerful concepts in microeconomic theory; but evidently they are concepts that do not immediately resonate with some trained in other disciplines, including law.

In sum, both the evidence from existing industry practice and the evidence from Qualcomm's own license agreements did not support Judge Koh's conclusion that the ATIS RAND commitment restricts the SEP holder's freedom to choose the level of the supply chain at which to offer exhaustive licenses to its cellular SEPs.

4. *Previous Court Decisions*

Judge Koh cited two Ninth Circuit decisions that, in her view, "establish[ed] that Qualcomm's FRAND commitments include an obligation to license to all comers, including competing modem chip suppliers."[1562] She relied on the 2012 decision in *Microsoft v. Motorola* (*Microsoft I*),[1563] in which the Ninth Circuit found that the SEP holder's RAND commitment to the ITU required "'members who hold IP rights in standard-essential patents to agree to license those patents to *all comers* on terms that are "reasonable and nondiscriminatory," or "RAND.""[1564] Judge Koh said that the Ninth

---

[1561]	Barnard v. Kellogg, 77 U.S. (10 Wall.) 383, 390 (1870).

[1562]	Order Granting FTC's Motion for Partial Summary Judgment on Qualcomm's Contractual Duties Pursuant to the Contracts with ATIS and the TIA, 2018 WL 5848999, *supra* note 52, at *10.

[1563]	*Microsoft I*, 696 F.3d 872.

[1564]	Order Granting FTC's Motion for Partial Summary Judgment on Qualcomm's Contractual Duties Pursuant to the Contracts with ATIS and the TIA, 2018 WL 5848999, *supra* note 52, at *2 (emphasis added by Judge Koh) (quoting *Microsoft I*, 696 F.3d at 876 (quoting Mark A. Lemley, *Intellectual Property Rights and Standard-Setting Organizations*, 90 CALIF. L. REV. 1889, 1906 (2002))).

Circuit reiterated that principle in its 2015 decision in *Microsoft v. Motorola* (*Microsoft II*), when it said that the "'SEP holder *cannot refuse* a license to a manufacturer who commits to paying the RAND rate.'"[1565]

Qualcomm argued that these two Ninth Circuit decisions were irrelevant to interpreting Qualcomm's contract with ATIS because they did "not address the proper interpretation of the ATIS or TIA IPR Policies."[1566] Judge Koh rejected that argument, but her reliance on *Microsoft I* and *Microsoft II* was misplaced for at least two reasons.

a.   Did Judge Koh Treat Ninth Circuit Dicta as Controlling Precedent?

First, the Ninth Circuit never considered, let alone answered, the question of whether an SEP holder has a contractual duty to offer exhaustive licenses to its cellular SEPs to rival modem manufacturers, rather than OEMs of mobile devices.

i.   Why the Ninth Circuit's Dicta Are Not Authoritative

The Ninth Circuit's statements about the duty to offer licenses to SEPs at the component level were mere dicta—"a remark, an aside, concerning some rule of law or legal proposition that is not necessarily essential to the decision and lacks the authority of adjudication."[1567] To use the definition of "dicta" that Judge Posner restated for the Seventh Circuit in 1986, each of these statements by the Ninth Circuit "could have been deleted without seriously impairing the analytical foundations of the holding," and, "being peripheral," each of these statements "may not have received the full and careful consideration of the court that uttered it."[1568] Two years later, Judge Posner added the elegant insight on behalf of the Seventh Circuit that a dictum by a *federal* court necessarily lacks the force of law because it is inessential to the reasoning required to resolve the case or controversy that gave the court its limited jurisdiction to act, pursuant to Article III of the Constitution.[1569]

[1565]   *Id.* at *10 (quoting Microsoft Corp. v. Motorola, Inc. (*Microsoft II*), 795 F.3d 1024, 1031 (9ᵗʰ Cir. 2015) (emphasis added by Judge Koh)).

[1566]   Qualcomm's Opposition to FTC's Motion for Partial Summary Judgment, *supra* note 1517, at 14.

[1567]   United States v. Crawley, 837 F.2d 291, 292 (7ᵗʰ Cir. 1988) (Posner, J.) (quoting Stover v. Stover, 60 Md. App. 470, 476 (1984)).

[1568]   Sarnoff v. Am. Home Prods. Corp., 798 F.2d 1075, 1084 (7ᵗʰ Cir. 1986).

[1569]   Judge Posner recommended in *United States v. Crawley* that, rather than try to supply an abstract definition of "dictum," one reframe the question inductively:

> An alternative to definition is to ask what is at stake in the definition. What is at stake in distinguishing holding from dictum is that a dictum is not authoritative. It is the part of an opinion that a later court, even if it is an inferior court, is free to reject. So instead of asking what the word "dictum" means we can ask what reasons there are against a court's giving weight to a passage found in a previous opinion. There are many. One is that the passage was unnecessary to the outcome of the earlier case and therefore perhaps not as fully considered as it would have been if it were essential to the outcome. A closely related reason is that the

Judge Posner could have been describing Judge Koh's "all comers" phrase, which does not follow from any interpretation by her of any contractual text. Instead, the phrase comes from a passage in *Microsoft I* in which the Ninth Circuit—citing as authority Professor Mark Lemley's well-known article from 2002 on SSOs—was not discussing the duty to offer component-level licenses to cellular SEPs at all, but rather was attributing the existence of the RAND commitment (in general) to the supposed fear that SSOs (in general) had of patent holdup: "Many SSOs try to mitigate the threat of patent holdup by requiring members who hold IP rights in standard-essential patents to agree to license those patents to all comers on terms that are 'reasonable and nondiscriminatory,' or 'RAND.'"[1570]

> ii. *What Professor Lemley Actually Wrote Did Not Support Either the Ninth Circuit's Reasoning in* Microsoft I *or Judge Koh's Reasoning in Her Partial Summary Judgment*

Immediately after this sentence the Ninth Circuit cited as authority Professor Lemley's article. However, the two pages cited certainly do not say anything about offering exhaustive component-level licenses to cellular SEPs or even that, as of 2002, there was any consensus on whether a duty to offer exhaustive licenses to such SEPs to "all comers" existed under the observed RAND (or FRAND) commitments that Professor Lemley found among the 36 SSOs he studied.[1571] To the contrary, Professor Lemley concluded: "What is most striking about the data is the significant variation in policies among the different SSOs."[1572]

Professor Lemley found that this significant variation in contracting was present as well in the individual formulations of the RAND commitment across SSOs:

> While "reasonable and nondiscriminatory licensing" thus appears to be the majority rule among SSOs with a patent policy, relatively few SSOs

---

passage was not an integral part of the earlier opinion—it can be sloughed off without damaging the analytical structure of the opinion, and so it was a redundant part of that opinion and, again, may not have been fully considered. Still another reason is that the passage was not grounded in the facts of the case and the judges may therefore have lacked an adequate experiential basis for it; another, that the issue addressed in the passage was not presented as an issue, hence was not refined by the fires of adversary presentation. All these are reasons for thinking that a particular passage was not a fully measured judicial pronouncement, that it was not likely to be relied on by readers, and indeed that it may not have been part of the decision that resolved the case or controversy on which the court's jurisdiction depended (if a federal court).

837 F.2d at 292–93.

[1570] *Microsoft I*, 696 F.3d at 876 (quoting Lemley, *Intellectual Property Rights and Standard-Setting Organizations, supra* note 1564).

[1571] *Id.* (citing Lemley, *Intellectual Property Rights and Standard-Setting Organizations, supra* note 1564, at 1902, 1906).

[1572] Lemley, *Intellectual Property Rights and Standard-Setting Organizations, supra* note 1563, at 1904.

gave much explanation of what those terms mean or how licensing disputes would be resolved. Only two SSOs specifically provided that the licensing obligation compels a member to license to everyone in the world using the standard, not just to license to other members. It does not necessarily follow that the remaining SSOs intended to restrict the licensing obligation; rather, it appears that they simply had not addressed the issue in their policies. Four SSOs either gave content to the obligation by specifying what a "reasonable" term means, or provided a mechanism for the SSO to resolve disputes about license terms and fees. And one SSO required not only that a license term be reasonable and nondiscriminatory, but also that it not constitute "monopolistic abuse" of a patent. In short, while IP owners at many SSOs were required to license their rights on reasonable and nondiscriminatory terms, it isn't clear what those obligations mean in practice.[1573]

On page 1902 of Professor Lemley's article on SSOs, which the Ninth Circuit also cited, there is again absolutely no discussion of exhaustive component-level licensing of cellular SEPs:

> I study a number of SSO IP policies and find both open and closed groups. Importantly, however, most SSOs that I study fall into neither category. Rather, these SSOs occupy a middle ground between open and closed standards. They permit their members to own IP rights, but require those members to commit in advance to licensing those rights on specified terms and to forgo injunctive relief altogether. These standards are open in the sense that no one can be prohibited from using them. But they are also proprietary; those who would use the standard must pay royalties to the IP owner.[1574]

Professor Lemley's statement that the voluntary standards of SSOs "are open in the sense that no one can be prohibited from using them" must be read in light of the fact that the grant of rights to the intended third-party beneficiaries of an SEP holder's FRAND or RAND commitment is a matter of contract, subject to all the possible transactional diversity among SSOs that Professor Lemley identified in his article. Thus, the grant of rights to the implementer as an intended third-party beneficiary is only as broad and unconditional as the SEP holder and the SSO in question agreed to make it.

The variation that Professor Lemley documented in the meaning and specificity of the RAND commitment across SSOs circa 2002 means that Judge Koh's approach to interpreting the ATIS RAND contract (and, for that matter, the TIA RAND contract) was precarious at best. Professor Lemley further observed in his study on SSOs:

[1573] *Id.* at 1906.
[1574] *Id.* at 1902.

The fact that different SSOs have different rules governing IP rights (or no rules at all) means that it is very difficult for IP owners to know ex ante what rules will govern their rights. Because there is no standard set of rules, companies must investigate the bylaws of each SSO they join in order to understand the implications of joining. While this doesn't seem too onerous a burden in the abstract, a number of practical considerations indicate that companies are unlikely to be fully informed about their IP position.[1575]

One implication of this diversity, Professor Lemley concluded, was that "technology companies don't merely have to figure out what rules apply to them, but they also face a labyrinth of different SSOs with overlapping subject matter concerns, each with its own set of rules."[1576]

Apart from relying on *Microsoft I*, Judge Koh twice cited on her own this same article by Professor Lemley in her partial summary judgment.[1577] Yet, when doing so, Judge Koh did not mention the relevance of the article's noteworthy empirical finding—that "[w]hat is most striking about the data is the significant variation in policies among the different SSOs."[1578] Nor did that singular discovery by Professor Lemley appear to influence in any way Judge Koh's reported reasoning for granting the FTC's motion for partial summary judgment.

iii. *Judge Koh's Misplaced Reliance on* Microsoft II, *in Which the Ninth Circuit in Dicta Erroneously Equated a RAND Contract to a FRAND Contract*

Judge Koh's reliance on *Microsoft II* was no more convincing. The passage that Judge Koh quoted from *Microsoft II* immediately follows the Ninth Circuit's discussion of the patent-holdup conjecture, which cites as one authority the seminal article on that subject by Professors Lemley and Shapiro from 2007.[1579] The Ninth Circuit wrote:

> To mitigate the risk that a SEP holder will extract more than the fair value of its patented technology, many SSOs require SEP holders to agree to license their patents on "reasonable and nondiscriminatory" or "RAND" terms. Under these agreements, an SEP holder cannot refuse a license to a manufacturer who commits to paying the RAND rate.[1580]

[1575] *Id.* at 1906–07.

[1576] *Id.* at 1907.

[1577] Order Granting FTC's Motion for Partial Summary Judgment on Qualcomm's Contractual Duties Pursuant to the Contracts with ATIS and the TIA, 2018 WL 5848999, *supra* note 52, at *10, *12.

[1578] Lemley, *Intellectual Property Rights and Standard-Setting Organizations*, *supra* note 1564, at 1904.

[1579] *Microsoft II*, 795 F.3d at 1031 (citing Lemley & Shapiro, *Patent Holdup and Royalty Stacking*, *supra* note 118, at 2010–13).

[1580] *Id.* (footnote omitted).

In a footnote to the first sentence quoted above, the Ninth Circuit added: "The parallel terms of some SEP licensing agreements require fair, reasonable, and nondiscriminatory, or 'FRAND' rates. FRAND and RAND have the same meaning in the world of SEP licensing and in this opinion."[1581]

The Ninth Circuit did not cite any authority for these assertions of fact and law, which were necessarily dicta because the court was construing a RAND contract, not a FRAND contract, and therefore had no need to expound on the similarity or difference between the two. Three paragraphs earlier in *Microsoft II*, the Ninth Circuit *did* cite as authority the same article on SSOs by Professor Lemley that it cited in *Microsoft I*,[1582] but the Ninth Circuit did not seem to recognize that it was contradicting in *Microsoft II* what Professor Lemley concluded about the "striking" heterogeneity of contract terms observed in the FRAND and RAND commitments that he examined in his study of 36 SSOs.[1583] And needless to say, *Microsoft II*—like *Microsoft I*—certainly did not present the question of whether the RAND commitment obligated the SEP holder to offer exhaustive licenses to its cellular SEPs at the component level.

b.   Was the Ninth Circuit Interpreting Contracts with Different Language That Were Governed by Different Laws?

The second reason that Judge Koh's reliance on *Microsoft I* and *Microsoft II* was misplaced is that the Ninth Circuit examined an SEP holder's contractual obligations to an entirely *different SSO*. Judge Koh dismissed those differences as irrelevant, reasoning that "the Ninth Circuit . . . was interpreting a SSO IPR policy with almost identical language as the TIA and ATIS IPR policies."[1584] That reasoning was unsound for the reasons that we saw above and that Professor Lemley observed in his 2002 article.

In both *Microsoft I* and *Microsoft II*, the Ninth Circuit examined the ITU's RAND commitment, which materially differs from the RAND commitment that Qualcomm made to ATIS. The Ninth Circuit observed in *Microsoft I* that "[t]he ITU's Common Patent Policy (the 'ITU Policy') provides that 'a patent embodied fully or partly in a [standard] must be accessible to everybody without undue constraints.'"[1585] The ATIS Patent Policy, in contrast, requires only that "[a] license will be made available to applicants under reasonable terms and conditions that are demonstrably free of any unfair

---

[1581]   *Id.* at 1031 n.2.

[1582]   *Id.* at 1030 (citing Lemley, *Intellectual Property Rights and Standard-Setting Organizations*, *supra* note 1564).

[1583]   Lemley, *Intellectual Property Rights and Standard-Setting Organizations*, *supra* note 1564, at 1904.

[1584]   Order Granting FTC's Motion for Partial Summary Judgment on Qualcomm's Contractual Duties Pursuant to the Contracts with ATIS and the TIA, 2018 WL 5848999, *supra* note 52, at *11.

[1585]   *Microsoft I*, 696 F.3d at 876 (second alteration in original) (quoting *Common Patent Policy for ITU-T/ITU-R/ISO/IEC*, ITU, https://www.itu.int/en/ITU-T/ipr/Pages/policy.aspx).

discrimination."[1586] The ATIS Patent Policy does not include the requirement that the SEP holder offer exhaustive licenses to "everybody without undue constraints." Because the ITU RAND commitment more strictly constrains the SEP holder than does the ATIS Patent Policy, it was legal error for Judge Koh to declare the ATIS RAND Policy "almost identical" to the ITU RAND commitment and thereupon treat as reliable extrinsic evidence in *FTC v. Qualcomm* the Ninth Circuit's analysis of the ITU RAND commitment in *Microsoft I* and *Microsoft II*.[1587]

Judge Koh also ignored that, unlike Qualcomm's contract with ATIS, the SEP holder's contracts with the ITU and the IEEE were not governed by California law. New York law governs the IEEE RAND contract.[1588] The ITU RAND contract does not contain a choice-of-law provision; because Microsoft sued Motorola in the U.S. District Court for the Western District of Washington, the court applied Washington law to resolve questions concerning contract formation and the rights of intended third-party beneficiaries.[1589]

In other words, the relevant contract examined in *Microsoft I* and *Microsoft II* not only contained different language, but also was governed by different law. Therefore, it was clearly erroneous for Judge Koh to use the Ninth Circuit's discussions of the ITU's RAND commitment in *Microsoft I* and *Microsoft II* as reliable extrinsic evidence from which to infer the meaning that either Qualcomm or ATIS ascribed to the language of the ATIS RAND commitment.

H. *Qualcomm's RAND Commitment to the TIA*

Judge Koh found that no material dispute of fact existed as to whether Qualcomm's contract with the TIA had created a duty to offer exhaustive licenses to modem manufacturers.[1590] She observed that the TIA IPR Policy provides that the TIA will consider the implementation of a patented technology in its standards only if the patent holder makes a RAND commitment.[1591]

[1586] *Patent Policy*, ATIS, https://www.atis.org/01_legal/patent-policy/; *see also* Alliance for Telecommunications Industry Solutions (ATIS) Patent Holder Statement (Mar. 2015), https://www.atis.org/01_legal/docs/ATIS%20Patent%20Assurance%20Form.pdf ("An irrevocable license will be made available under reasonable terms and conditions that are demonstrably free of any unfair discrimination, with compensation, to applicants desiring to utilize the license for the purpose of implementing the American National Standard or other ATIS Deliverable.").

[1587] Order Granting FTC's Motion for Partial Summary Judgment on Qualcomm's Contractual Duties Pursuant to the Contracts with ATIS and the TIA, 2018 WL 5848999, *supra* note 52, at *11.

[1588] *See* IEEE, IEEE-SA Standards Boards Bylaws § 3 (Mar. 2019), https://standards.ieee.org/content/dam/ieee-standards/standards/web/documents/other/sb_bylaws.pdf.

[1589] *See* Microsoft Corp. v. Motorola, Inc., 864 F. Supp. 2d 1023, 1031 (W.D. Wash. 2012).

[1590] Order Granting FTC's Motion for Partial Summary Judgment on Qualcomm's Contractual Duties Pursuant to the Contracts with ATIS and the TIA, 2018 WL 5848999, *supra* note 52, at *10.

[1591] *Id.* at *8.

Specifically, Judge Koh observed that the TIA IPR Policy requires a patent holder to commit that

> "[a] license under any Essential Patent(s), the license rights which are held by the undersigned Patent Holder, will be made available to all applicants under terms and conditions that are reasonable and non-discriminatory . . . and only to the extent necessary for the practice of any or all of the Normative portions for the field of use of practice of the Standard."[1592]

Judge Koh found that Qualcomm's RAND commitment "parrot[s] the language of the TIA . . . IPR polic[y]."[1593]

The FTC and Qualcomm again materially disputed the proper interpretation of the terms "applicants" and "non-discriminatory" that appeared in Qualcomm's contract with the TIA. The FTC argued that Qualcomm had "promised to make licenses available to 'applicants' and 'all applicants' that wish to 'practice' TIA standards, without unfair 'discrimination,'"[1594] and that "[n]o language in the TIA IPR Policy suggests the term 'applicants' is limited to applicants selling a particular type of product or occupying a particular level of the supply chain."[1595] Qualcomm argued, to the contrary, that only a smartphone can practice a TIA standard and that a modem manufacturer therefore cannot be considered an "applicant" for purposes of the TIA RAND contract.[1596]

When scrutinizing Qualcomm's RAND contract with the TIA, Judge Koh examined (1) the language of the TIA RAND commitment (or, more specifically, the language of the TIA IPR Policy that, according to Judge Koh, mirrored the language of Qualcomm's RAND commitment to the TIA) and (2) the TIA IPR Guidelines.[1597] On the basis of that evidence, as well other extrinsic evidence that she considered, Judge Koh concluded that the TIA RAND contract was "'unambiguous,'"[1598] and that it required Qualcomm to offer (exhaustive) licenses to its cellular SEPs to rival modem manufacturers.[1599]

Judge Koh's finding was not persuasive because the evidence that she cited in fact confirmed that a genuine dispute of material fact did in fact exist between Qualcomm and the FTC.

[1592] *Id.* (second alteration in original) (quoting TIA IPR Policy, *supra* note 1498, at 8).

[1593] *Id.* at *9.

[1594] FTC's Motion for Partial Summary Judgment, *supra* note 485, at 18 (quoting TIA IPR Policy, *supra* note 1498, at 8–9).

[1595] *Id.*

[1596] Qualcomm's Opposition to FTC's Motion for Partial Summary Judgment, *supra* note 1517, at 15.

[1597] Order Granting FTC's Motion for Partial Summary Judgment on Qualcomm's Contractual Duties Pursuant to the Contracts with ATIS and the TIA, 2018 WL 5848999, *supra* note 52, at *8, *11–12.

[1598] *Id.* at *15 (quoting Miller v. Glenn Miller Prods., Inc., 454 F.3d 975, 990 (9th Cir. 2006) (per curiam)).

[1599] *Id.* at *10.

1.   The Language of the TIA RAND Contract

Judge Koh found that the language of Qualcomm's RAND contract with the TIA did not support Qualcomm's proposed interpretation. As in the case of Qualcomm's contract with ATIS, she reasoned that the TIA IPR policy is not limited to applicants that practice the whole standard.[1600] Judge Koh found that "the TIA IPR [P]olicy requires that the applicant desire to use the license 'to the extent *necessary* for the practice of any or all of the Normative *portions* for the field use [sic] of use of practice of the Standard.'"[1601] She further reasoned that "[t]he TIA IPR [P]olicy expressly contemplates that a TIA standard may have 'portions' or 'elements,' and that an applicant may receive a license as necessary to practice 'any' portion of a TIA standard."[1602] Yet, those contractual provisions did not contradict Qualcomm's proposed interpretation.

The phrase that a RAND license will be made available "to all applicants . . . to the extent [that a license is] necessary for the practice of any or all of the Normative portions for the field of use of practice of the Standard"[1603] plainly is material in this sentence, but its meaning is ambiguous. Are manufacturers of modems among "all applicants" that need an exhaustive license to Qualcomm's cellular SEPs for the "practice of any or all of the Normative portions for the field of use of practice of the [TIA] Standard"? The TIA IPR Policy does not define "applicants." The TIA IPR Policy also does not define "Normative portions." It does define "Normative (alternate) elements" as "those elements of a Standard, any one or more of which may be complied with in order to claim conformity with the Standard."[1604] Elsewhere, the TIA IPR Policy defines "Normative (mandatory) elements" as "those elements of a Standard which always must be complied with in order to claim conformity with the Standard" and "Normative (optional) elements" as "those elements of a Standard which may be selected in order to claim conformity with the Standard and which, if selected, must be implemented as specified in the Standard."[1605] However, the TIA IPR Policy does not explain how normative "elements" relate to normative "portions," and Judge Koh did not address the question.

The language of the TIA RAND contract also does not say which products may practice normative portions of a TIA standard. In particular, Qualcomm's RAND contract with the TIA does not say whether a modem

---

[1600] *Id.* at *14.
[1601] *Id.* (emphasis added by Judge Koh) (quoting TIA IPR Policy, *supra* note 1498, at 8). Judge Koh errantly added an extra "use" when quoting the TIA IPR Policy in her order.
[1602] *Id.* (quoting TIA, TIA IPR Policy, *supra* note 1498, at 8).
[1603] TIA IPR Policy, *supra* note 1498, at 8.
[1604] *Id.* at 7.
[1605] *Id.*

manufacturer is an applicant that needs an exhaustive license "for the practice of any or all of the Normative portions for the field of use of practice of the Standard."[1606] Judge Koh evidently predicated her findings on lack of ambiguity on the proposition that any product that infringes a Qualcomm cellular SEP (or perhaps even only a single claim contained in a single Qualcomm cellular SEP) should be considered a product that practices (or implements) a portion of a TIA standard. But the evidence that Judge Koh cited in her findings of fact and conclusions of law did not support her conclusion.

To support her rejection of Qualcomm's proposed interpretation of the TIA RAND contract, Judge Koh also found that the TIA IPR Policy includes a statement of purpose in which it emphasized that "[t]he TIA IPR Policy is designed 'to encourage[] holders of intellectual property to contribute their technology to TIA's standardization efforts and enable competing implementations that benefit manufacturers and ultimately consumers.'"[1607] Yet, that precatory statement did not provide any useful information or guidance for interpreting the materially disputed terms of the TIA RAND contract.

In sum, the language of Qualcomm's RAND contract with the TIA was ambiguous as to whether it had obligated Qualcomm to offer exhaustive licenses to its cellular SEPs to rival modem manufacturers. That this disputed question has quickly gained global importance, yet evidently was not expressly addressed by the parties when drafting their contract, is substantial evidence since the time of Judge Koh's partial summary judgment that the TIA RAND contract is, at the least, ambiguous with respect to whether the phrase "all applicants" obligates an SEP holder to offer exhaustive licenses to its cellular SEPs at whatever level of the supply chain the implementer demands. Considering that evident ambiguity, a different judge might have considered it the wiser exercise of discretion to permit the parties to introduce evidence at trial as to which interpretation of the TIA RAND contract was the more plausible.

2. *The TIA Guidelines*

To support her interpretation of Qualcomm's duties pursuant to the TIA RAND contract, Judge Koh relied on the TIA Guidelines. She observed that California law "'has long abandoned a rule that would limit the interpretation of a written instrument to its four corners.'"[1608] She added that, "[u]nder California contract law, the Court *must* provisionally consider

---

[1606] Order Granting FTC's Motion for Partial Summary Judgment on Qualcomm's Contractual Duties Pursuant to the Contracts with ATIS and the TIA, 2018 WL 5848999, *supra* note 52, at *8 (quoting TIA IPR Policy, *supra* note 1498, at 8).

[1607] *Id.* at *12 (second alteration in original) (quoting TIA IPR Policy, *supra* note 1498, at 6).

[1608] *Id.* at *8 (quoting First Nat'l Mortg. Co. v. Fed. Realty Inv. Trust, 631 F.3d 1058, 1066 (9th Cir. 2011) (construing California law)).

extrinsic evidence that 'is relevant to show whether the contractual language is reasonably susceptible to a particular meaning.'"[1609] Judge Koh then found the TIA Guidelines to be relevant extrinsic evidence of the parties' intent, the substance of which was, in her opinion, to obligate Qualcomm to offer exhaustive licenses to its cellular SEPs to rival modem manufacturers.[1610]

Judge Koh found that "the TIA Guidelines specifically identify 'a willingness to license all applicants except for competitors of the licensor' as an example of discriminatory conduct under the TIA IPR [P]olicy."[1611] (As we saw above, however, neither the TIA IPR Policy nor the TIA Guidelines defines "all applicants.") Judge Koh also found that "[t]he TIA Guidelines specifically explain that a SEP holder's FRAND commitment 'prevents the inclusion of patented technology [in a standard] from resulting in a patent holder securing a monopoly in *any market* as a result of the standardization process.'"[1612]

Judge Koh further found that, "[i]f a SEP holder could discriminate against modem chip suppliers, a SEP holder could embed its technology into a cellular standard and then prevent other modem chip suppliers from selling modem chips to cellular handset producers."[1613] To support that finding, Judge Koh reasoned, quoting Professor Lemley's 2002 article on SSOs, that "a company with a SEP 'will effectively control the standard; its patent gives it the right to enjoin anyone else from using the standard.'"[1614] Judge Koh found that "[s]uch discrimination would enable the SEP holder to achieve a monopoly in the modem chip market and limit competing implementations of those components, which directly contradicts the TIA IPR [P]olicy's stated purpose to 'enable competing implementations that benefit manufacturers and ultimately consumers.'"[1615]

Judge Koh's reasoning was unpersuasive for at least five reasons.

First, contrary to Judge Koh's conclusions, the TIA Guidelines do not say anything about whether, by virtue of executing a RAND contract, the parties intended to obligate the SEP holder to offer exhaustive licenses to modem manufacturers. In particular, the Guidelines do not define "applicants" or other relevant terms contained in the TIA IPR Policy.

[1609] *Id.* at *11 (emphasis added) (quoting Adams v. MHC Colony Park, L.P., 169 Cal. Rptr. 3d 146, 161 (Ct. App. 2014)).

[1610] *Id.*

[1611] *Id.* at *12 (quoting TIA, Guidelines to the Intellectual Property Rights Policy of the Telecommunications Industry Association 5 (1st ed. Mar. 2005) [hereinafter TIA IPR Guidelines (1st ed. Mar. 2005)], *Exhibit 30 to* FTC's Motion for Partial Summary Judgment, FTC v. Qualcomm Inc., No. 5:17-cv-00220-LHK (N.D. Cal. Aug. 30, 2018), ECF No. 792-2).

[1612] *Id.* (second alteration in original) (emphasis added by Judge Koh) (quoting TIA IPR Guidelines (1st ed. Mar. 2005), *supra* note 1611, at 1).

[1613] *Id.*

[1614] *Id.* (quoting Lemley, *Intellectual Property Rights and Standard-Setting Organizations*, *supra* note 1564, at 1902).

[1615] *Id.* (citation omitted) (quoting TIA IPR Policy, *supra* note 1498, at 6).

Second, the Guidelines' statement about instances in which an SEP holder "prevents the inclusion of patented technology" to monopolize a market does not help to answer the question of how to interpret the ambiguous term "all applicants." Qualcomm did not prevent a rival modem manufacturer from including a patented technology into its products. Consequently, Judge Koh's citation of evidence that the TIA was concerned that the SEP holder might "prevent[] the inclusion of patented technology" was irrelevant to identifying whether Qualcomm owed a specific contractual duty, pursuant to its RAND contract with the TIA, to offer exhaustive licenses to its cellular SEPs to rival modem manufacturers.

Third, Judge Koh's citation to Professor Lemley's argument that an SEP holder might control access to the standard through exclusionary remedies was a *non sequitur*. Perhaps some found that argument plausible in 2002, when Professor Lemley published his article; but the argument lost any currency that it might have had by 2006, when the Supreme Court's decision in *eBay* greatly restricted a patent holder's ability to obtain an injunction against an infringer.[1616] Similarly, as of August 2020, no SEP holder has been able to enforce an injunction or an ITC exclusion order against an infringer of SEPs in the United States.[1617] Therefore, it is fanciful to argue that at any time from 2006 onward Qualcomm could have excluded rival modem manufacturers from the U.S. market by asserting patents against them.

This third point introduces a closely related fourth point. Judge Koh's references to the risk of monopolization were malapropos. An SEP holder cannot exclude a rival, much less use its cellular SEPs to monopolize the market in which that rival competes, unless the SEP holder *enforces* its cellular SEPs against that rival. The FTC did not allege that Qualcomm ever did so. Rather, the evidence that Judge Koh cited in her findings of fact and conclusions of law on May 21, 2019 indicated that Qualcomm had an "'unwritten policy of *not* going after chip manufacturers.'"[1618] An SEP holder's decision

---

[1616] *See* eBay Inc. v. MercExchange, L.L.C., 547 U.S. 388 (2006). I have repeatedly made this point since 2009. *See* Sidak, *Is Patent Holdup a Hoax?*, *supra* note 118, at 44; Sidak, *Does the International Trade Commission Facilitate Patent Holdup?*, *supra* note 367, at 602; Sidak, *The Meaning of FRAND, Part II: Injunctions*, *supra* note 661, at 224–30; Sidak, *Patent Holdup and Oligopsonistic Collusion in Standard Setting Organizations*, *supra* note 446, at 139–41.

[1617] In an ITC investigation in 2019, Chief Administrative Law Judge Charles Bullock proposed the issuance of an exclusion order on imports into the United States of SK hynix products that he found had infringed Netlist's SEPs subject to JEDEC's RAND commitment. Certain Memory Modules and Components Thereof, Inv. No. 337-TA-1089, slip op. at 168 (USITC Oct. 21, 2019) (Initial Determination—Public Version). In April 2020, however, the commissioners of the ITC reversed in part and vacated in part Chief Judge Bullock's initial determination on violation of section 337 of the Tariff Act of 1930. Notice of the Commission's Final Determination Finding No Violation of Section 337; Termination of the Investigation at 3, Certain Memory Modules and Components Thereof, Inv. No. 337-TA-1089 (USITC Apr. 7, 2020).

[1618] FTC v. Qualcomm Inc., 411 F. Supp. 3d 658, 750 (N.D. Cal. 2019) (emphasis added) (quoting Deposition of Andrew Hong (Legal Counsel, Samsung Intellectual Property Center) at 161:24–25, FTC v. Qualcomm Inc., No. 5:17-cv-00220-LHK (N.D. Cal. Mar. 7, 2018), *exhibit to* Federal Trade

to license its cellular SEPs exhaustively at a lower level of the supply chain, without more, cannot harm competition at a higher level of the supply chain in which that rival operates. Therefore, statements in the TIA Guidelines about the risk of monopolization do not shed light on whether, at the time Qualcomm and the TIA executed the TIA RAND contract, they intended the term "all applicants" to include modem manufacturers. Indeed, the FTC's theory in *FTC v. Qualcomm* was that monopoly power in particular markets for modems *already existed*; the FTC did not contend that Qualcomm had used standardization to acquire monopoly power in a relevant market for modems.[1619]

Fifth, Judge Koh ignored that most SEP holders do *not* manufacture modems. Some SEP holders focus on manufacturing network equipment (such as base stations), others focus on manufacturing terminal devices for end consumers (such as smartphones). Still other SEP holders focus on investing in research and development, without manufacturing any product; instead, they monetize their investments by licensing their patents to others for implementation. Judge Koh's interpretation of the TIA's nondiscrimination requirement would compel an absurd outcome: SEP holders would have the duty to offer exhaustive licenses to their cellular SEPs at different levels of the vertical chain of production, depending on whether the SEP holder manufactures a product that is used at a given level in that chain; moreover, that duty would mutate over time as the SEP holder added or deleted product offerings. Such a duty would invite confusion and high transaction costs, particularly when the ownership of SEPs shifted from a transferor that operates at a different level of the supply chain from that of the transferee. It was unrealistic to presume, as Judge Koh appeared tacitly to presume, that the SEP holder and the TIA both intended to open this Pandora's box by virtue of executing their RAND contract.

Commission's Submission of Trial Testimony That Occurred on January 8[, 2019], FTC v. Qualcomm Inc., No. 5:17-cv-00220-LHK (N.D. Cal. Jan. 11, 2019), ECF No. 1253-3).

[1619] FTC Complaint, 2017 WL 242848, *supra* note 28, at 28 ("Qualcomm has monopoly and market power with respect to CDMA baseband processors and premium LTE baseband processors. Direct evidence of this power includes evidence of Qualcomm's ability to use threatened loss of access to baseband processors to raise the all-in prices of baseband processors, prices that include both nominal processor prices and license fees. . . . Qualcomm has maintained dominant shares of the CDMA and premium LTE baseband processor markets. Each year from at least 2006 through September 2015, Qualcomm's worldwide share of CDMA baseband processor sales exceeded 80%. From at least 2012 through September 2015, Qualcomm's annual share of worldwide premium LTE baseband processor sales has also exceeded 80%.").

I. The Consequences of Judge Koh's Order Granting the FTC Partial Summary Judgment for the Exhaustive Licensing of Cellular SEPs at the Component Level

Whether an SEP holder has a contractual duty to offer exhaustive licenses to its cellular SEPs to implementers at the component level is, as of August 2020, the greatest controversy concerning SEPs. That is because of the implications that this question has for the licensing of the next wave of devices that will harness 5G technologies in a myriad of devices in the Internet of Things, starting most obviously with smart automobiles. The stakeholders are still in the early stages of license negotiation, litigation, intellectual advocacy, and government investigation.

For both SEP holders and implementers, it is possible that the best legal arguments, and the best arguments from a technical or an economic perspective, have yet to be heard. However, it is not too soon to conjecture that, if appellate courts do eventually recognize an SEP holder's contractual duty to offer exhaustive licenses to cellular SEPs at the component level, they will do so on the basis of reasoning more rigorous and nuanced than what one can find in Judge Koh's partial summary judgment order in *FTC v. Qualcomm*.

XI. Did Qualcomm Have Monopoly Power?

Monopoly power, the Supreme Court said in *United States v. Grinnell Corp.*, is the "the power to control prices or exclude competition."[1620] Both the FTC and Professor Shapiro asserted that Qualcomm had monopoly power in the CDMA modem market and in the "premium" LTE modem market.[1621] Judge Koh agreed. She found that Qualcomm had monopoly power (1) in the "global market for CDMA modem chips" between 2006 and 2015[1622] and (2) in the "global market for premium LTE modem chips" from 2011 to 2016.[1623]

Yet, in reaching her conclusion, Judge Koh did not cite any of Professor Shapiro's testimony. She also did not rely on well-established economic methodologies for either defining the relevant market or analyzing a firm's market power in that market. The evidence that she did identify did not imply that Qualcomm had monopoly power. Substantial evidence indicated that Qualcomm lacked monopoly power.

[1620] 384 U.S. 563, 571 (1966).

[1621] FTC Complaint, 2017 WL 242848, *supra* note 28, at 9–12; *see also id.* at 28–29; Transcript of Proceedings (Volume 6) at 1119:7–12, FTC v. Qualcomm Inc., No. 5:17-cv-00220-LHK (N.D. Cal. Jan. 15, 2019) (Testimony of Carl Shapiro); Initial Expert Report of Carl Shapiro in *FTC v. Qualcomm, supra* note 115, at 3.

[1622] FTC v. Qualcomm Inc., 411 F. Supp. 3d 658, 685 (N.D. Cal. 2019).

[1623] *Id.* at 691.

Qualcomm did not appeal Judge Koh's findings on market power.[1624] Consequently, the Ninth Circuit cursorily accepted, in a single conclusory sentence, that Judge Koh had "correctly defined the relevant markets as 'the market for CDMA modem chips and the market for premium LTE modem chips.'"[1625] Perhaps Qualcomm's decision not to appeal Judge Koh's findings on market definition and market power simply reflected the possibility that, considering the limited number of pages in an appellate brief, Qualcomm saw an easier path to reversal in the Ninth Circuit. The fact that Qualcomm did not appeal Judge Koh's findings on market power is obviously no assurance that she applied the controlling precedent correctly. Indeed, she did not.

Why is proof of market power essential to a finding of liability in a monopolization case? In his first antitrust opinion, Judge Posner explained:

> A firm that has no market power is unlikely to adopt policies that disserve its consumers; it cannot afford to. And if it blunders and does adopt such a policy, market retribution will be swift. Thus its mistakes do not seriously threaten consumer welfare, which is the objective that we are told should guide us in interpreting the Sherman Act.[1626]

Judge Koh's findings of fact and conclusions of law in *FTC v. Qualcomm* proceed without a clear understanding that market power is the first filter for separating a possibly meritorious theory of antitrust liability from a fatuous one.

It is a telltale sign of that deficiency that Judge Koh did not recognize and act upon the Supreme Court's most recent teaching on market power in *American Express* in 2018.[1627] Although Judge Koh did cite *American Express* in her findings of fact and conclusions of law, her abbreviated discussion of it suggested that she overlooked the direct implications of the Court's reasoning on assessing market power when a distinctive attribute of the industry is the complementarity of demand among separate but interrelated products— as is plainly the situation in *FTC v. Qualcomm* with respect to cellular SEPs and modems in the mobile communications industry. The Ninth Circuit (should it choose to rehear *FTC v. Qualcomm en banc*)—and, later, the Supreme Court if necessary—should therefore review *sua sponte* Judge Koh's findings concerning market power because of their clear deviation from the Court's recent teaching in *American Express*. As we shall see, even if one assumes *arguendo* that Judge Koh correctly defined her two relevant antitrust product markets,

---

[1624] *See* Qualcomm Incorporated's Pre-Trial Brief, FTC v. Qualcomm Inc., No. 5:17-cv-00220-LHK (N.D. Cal. Jan. 4, 2019).

[1625] FTC v. Qualcomm Inc., No. 19-16122, 2020 WL 4591476, at *10 (9th Cir. Aug. 11, 2020) (quoting *FTC v. Qualcomm*, 411 F. Supp. 3d at 683).

[1626] Valley Liquors, Inc. v. Renfield Imps., Ltd., 678 F.2d 742, 745 (7th Cir. 1982) (Posner, J.) (citing Reiter v. Sonotone Corp., 442 U.S. 330, 343 (1979)).

[1627] Ohio v. Am. Express Co., 138 S. Ct. 2274 (2018).

it necessarily follows, as the Ninth Circuit held, that there is no assurance that the alleged harm to competition occurred in those two markets.

In the following pages, I examine the main errors in Judge Koh's analysis of Qualcomm's market power. Although for brevity I focus on Judge Koh's analysis of Qualcomm's market power in the market for "premium" LTE modems, many of my criticisms apply with equal force to Judge Koh's conclusions regarding Qualcomm's market power in the market for CDMA modems.

A. *"Direct" and "Indirect" Evidence of Market Power*

A firm possesses market power to the extent that it can raise its price above the price that it would charge in a competitive market.[1628] In the scholarly literature on antitrust law and economics, Professor William Landes and then-Professor Richard Posner provided the canonical definition of market power in their 1981 article in the *Harvard Law Review*: "the ability of a firm (or a group of firms, acting jointly) to raise price above the competitive level without losing so many sales so rapidly that the price increase is unprofitable and must be rescinded."[1629]

Landes and Posner explained that "it is the response of the firm's output to a change in its price that determines the degree to which it has market power."[1630] Put differently, a firm's market power depends on the firm's own-price elasticity of demand for its product. If the demand for a firm's product is highly price-elastic, more substitutes exist for that product. Consequently, the firm has a limited ability to raise prices profitably. That is, the firm has limited market power.[1631] By similar reasoning, the less price-elastic demand is for a firm's product, the greater is the firm's market power.

Landes and Posner expressed this inverse relationship between a firm's market power and the firm's own-price elasticity of demand in a formal mathematical model, which begins with the familiar Lerner Index:

$$L_i = (P_i - C_i) / P_i = 1 / e_i, \tag{1}$$

[1628] *See* NCAA v. Bd. of Regents of Univ. of Okla., 468 U.S. 85, 109 n.38 (1984) (first citing Jefferson Parish Hosp. Dist. No. 2 v. Hyde, 466 U.S. 2, 27 (1984); then citing U.S. Steel Corp. v. Fortner Enters., 429 U.S. 610, 620 (1977); and then citing United States v. E.I. du Pont de Nemours & Co., 351 U.S. 377, 391 (1956)).

[1629] William M. Landes & Richard A. Posner, *Market Power in Antitrust Cases*, 94 Harv. L. Rev. 937, 937 (1981); *see also* Posner, Antitrust Law (2ᵈ ed.), *supra* note 948, at 124 (discussing market power as the ability of a firm to maintain a price above the competitive level). The 1981 article by Landes and Posner is the second most cited law review article in antitrust law. *See* Fred R. Shapiro & Michelle Pearse, *The Most-Cited Law Review Articles of All Time*, 110 Mich. L. Rev. 1483, 1498 tbl.IV (2012).

[1630] Landes & Posner, *Market Power in Antitrust Cases*, *supra* note 1629, at 941 n.8.

[1631] *Id.* at 941 ("[T]he higher the elasticity of demand for the firm's product at the firm's profit-maximizing price, the closer that price will be to the competitive price, and the less, therefore, the monopoly overcharge will be.").

where L_i is the Lerner Index for firm i, P_i is the price at firm i's profit-maximizing output, C_i is the marginal cost at firm i's profit-maximizing output, and e_i is firm i's own-price elasticity of demand.[1632] At the profit-maximizing level of output, a higher Lerner Index denotes greater market power because demand is less price-elastic.[1633] Similarly, at the profit-maximizing level of output, a lower Lerner Index denotes less market power because demand is more price-elastic. However, a high Lerner Index will not accurately reflect market power when the firm in question faces high fixed costs.[1634]

Although in principle one could use Equation 1 to estimate a firm's market power, a firm's own-price elasticity of demand often is unknown. Landes and Posner explained that, in those cases, one can express a firm's market power as a function of three variables: (1) the firm's market share, (2) the market's own-price elasticity of demand, and (3) the price elasticity of supply of the firm's competitors.[1635] Equation 2 expresses that relationship:

$$L_i = S_i / (e_d + [e_s \times (1 - S_i)]), \qquad (2)$$

where L_i is the Lerner index for firm i, S_i is firm i's market share, e_d is the market's own-price elasticity of demand, and e_s is the price elasticity of supply of competing firms.[1636] Thus, to measure a firm's market power, one needs to analyze the firm's market share in conjunction with the market's own-price elasticity of demand and the price elasticity of supply of the firm's competitors.

[1632] *Id.* at 939–40. In Equation 1, e_i is treated as a positive number.

[1633] *See id.* at 941–42.

[1634] *See id.* at 939 ("[T]he fact of market power must be distinguished from the amount of market power. When the deviation of price from marginal cost is trivial, or simply reflects certain fixed costs, there is no occasion for antitrust concern."); *see also id.* at 957; Kenneth G. Elzinga & David E. Mills, *The Lerner Index of Monopoly Power: Origins and Uses*, 101 AM. ECON. ASS'N PAPERS & PROC. 558, 559–60 (2011) ("Departures of price and marginal cost are equally attributable to the absence or infeasibility of arrangements to secure subsidies from buyers to bridge the gap between firms' AC [average cost] and MC [marginal cost] when efficient production requires increasing returns. . . . The cost structure of firms in many technology-driven industries (e.g., software, pharmaceuticals) is markedly front-loaded. Marginal cost pricing in these industries is neither feasible nor desirable."); Robert S. Pindyck, *The Measurement of Monopoly Power in Dynamic Markets*, 28 J.L. & ECON. 193, 219 (1985) ("[S]tatic measures of monopoly and monopsony power can be inadequate and possibly misleading when applied to dynamic markets. . . . The application of these measures to a number of examples has shown how a firm's (or cartel's) degree of monopoly power is affected by various forms of intertemporal constraints, including those associated with resource depletion, learning-by-doing, and dynamic adjustment of demand."); Robert H. Bork & J. Gregory Sidak, *The Misuse of Profit Margins to Infer Market Power*, 3 J. COMPETITION L. & ECON. 511, 512 (2013) ("Supracompetitive profits may result from a factor other than market power, such as superior management. Furthermore, in industries with high sunk investment, high profit margins are consistent with a dynamically competitive market.").

[1635] Landes & Posner, *Market Power in Antitrust Cases*, *supra* note 1629, at 941.

[1636] *See id.* at 944–45.

For more than 30 years, the federal courts (including the Ninth Circuit) have considered the Landes-Posner analysis authoritative.[1637] Yet, it appeared from Judge Koh's findings of fact and conclusions of law in *FTC v. Qualcomm* that she was unfamiliar with this established method for evaluating market power.

To analyze whether a firm has market power in a relevant market, a court might examine both direct and indirect evidence of market power. Direct evidence of market power might include firm-specific evidence, such as a firm's profits, profit margins, own-price elasticity of demand, and other indicators that the firm can profitably sustain supracompetitive prices for its products.[1638] Direct evidence of market power is sufficient to establish market power. "If we knew the elasticity of demand facing a group of sellers," then-Professor Posner wrote in 1976 (before his 1981 article with Landes and before William Baxter's revision of the Antitrust Division's Horizontal Merger Guidelines shortly thereafter[1639]), "it would be redundant to ask whether the group constituted an economically meaningful market."[1640] Professor Posner observed that "[i]t is only because we lack confidence in our ability to measure elasticities, or perhaps because we do not think of adopting so explicitly economic an approach, that we have to define markets instead."[1641]

[1637] *See, e.g.*, Ball Mem'l Hosp., Inc. v. Mut. Hosp. Ins., Inc., 784 F.2d 1325, 1331 (7th Cir. 1986) (Easterbrook, J.) (formulating market power as "the ability to raise price significantly higher than the competitive level by restricting output") (citing Landes & Posner, *Market Power in Antitrust Cases*, *supra* note 1629); Reazin v. Blue Cross & Blue Shield of Kan., Inc., 899 F.2d 951, 967 (10th Cir. 1990) ("Market share is relevant to the determination of the existence of market or monopoly power, but 'market share alone is insufficient to establish market power.' It may or may not reflect *actual* power to control price or exclude competition.") (emphasis in original) (citations omitted) (quoting Bright v. Moss Ambulance Serv., Inc., 824 F.2d 819, 824 (10th Cir. 1987)) (first citing Colorado Interstate Gas Co. v. Nat. Gas Pipeline Co., 885 F.2d 683, 695 (10th Cir. 1989); then citing Shoppin' Bag of Pueblo, Inc. v. Dillon Cos., Inc., 783 F.2d 159, 162 (10th Cir. 1986); and then citing Landes & Posner, *Market Power in Antitrust Cases*, *supra* note 1629, at 947); Midwestern Mach. Co. v. Nw. Airlines, Inc., 392 F.3d 265, 274 (8th Cir. 2004) ("Market power is defined as 'the ability of a firm . . . to raise price above the competitive level without losing so many sales so rapidly that the price increase is unprofitable and must be rescinded.'") (alteration in original) (quoting Landes & Posner, *Market Power in Antitrust Cases*, *supra* note 1629, at 937); United States v. LSL Biotechnologies, 379 F.3d 672, 696–97 (9th Cir. 2004) ("Market power is the seller's ability to raise and sustain a price increase without losing so many sales that it must rescind the increase.") (citing Landes & Posner, *Market Power in Antitrust Cases*, *supra* note 1629, at 939).

[1638] *See* Landes & Posner, *Market Power in Antitrust Cases*, *supra* note 1629, at 939–41. If one is forgoing calculus, a product's own-price elasticity of demand is calculated as the percentage change in quantity demanded (that a price change causes) divided by the percentage change in price. If the percentage change in demand exceeds the percentage change in price (in absolute value), then demand for the product is said to be price-elastic. If the percentage change in demand is less than the percentage change in price (in absolute value), then demand for the product is said to be price-inelastic. MANKIW, PRINCIPLES OF ECONOMICS (8th ed.), *supra* note 652, at 90–92.

[1639] *See* Richard A. Posner, *Introduction to Baxter Symposium*, 51 STAN. L. REV. 1007, 1008–09 (1999); Richard Schmalensee, *Bill Baxter in the Antitrust Arena: An Economist's Appreciation*, 51 STAN. L. REV. 1317, 1327–29 (1999).

[1640] POSNER, ANTITRUST LAW: AN ECONOMIC PERSPECTIVE, *supra* note 1275, at 125.

[1641] *Id.*

In 1982, the newly appointed Judge Posner wrote for the Seventh Circuit that, "[s]ince market power can rarely be measured directly by the methods of litigation, it is normally inferred from possession of a substantial percentage of the sales in a market carefully defined in terms of both product and geography."[1642] When direct evidence is unavailable, characteristics of the market—such as market share, barriers to entry, and switching costs—can provide indirect evidence of whether a firm possesses market power.[1643] To infer market power, a firm's market share in the relevant market must be both substantial *and* durable.[1644]

As the Sixth Circuit observed in 1999, "[m]arket share is only a starting point for determining whether monopoly power exists, and the inference of monopoly power does not automatically follow from the possession of a commanding market share."[1645] Likewise, economists have long warned that evidence of high market share is, on its own, insufficient to establish market power.[1646] Professor Shapiro is one of them.[1647] Consequently, when direct evidence of market power is unobservable, a court must evaluate a

---

[1642] Valley Liquors, Inc. v. Renfield Imps., Ltd., 678 F.2d 742, 745 (7th Cir. 1982).

[1643] *See* Landes & Posner, *Market Power in Antitrust Cases, supra* note 1629, at 939–41; *see also* Bork & Sidak, *The Misuse of Profit Margins to Infer Market Power, supra* note 1629, at 512.

[1644] Matsushita Elec. Indus. Co. v. Zenith Radio Corp., 475 U.S. 574, 591 n.15 (1986) ("[W]ithout barriers to entry it would presumably be impossible to maintain supracompetitive prices for an extended time.").

[1645] American Council of Certified Podiatric Physicians & Surgeons v. Am. Bd. of Podiatric Surgery, Inc., 185 F.3d 606, 623 (6th Cir. 1999) (citing Byars v. Bluff City News Co., 609 F.2d 843, 850–51 (6th Cir. 1979)).

[1646] *See, e.g.,* Landes & Posner, *Market Power in Antitrust Cases, supra* note 1629, at 947 ("Since market share is only one . . . factor[] . . . that determine[s] market power, inferences of power from share alone can be misleading. In fact, if market share alone is used to infer power, the market share measure . . . . will be the wrong measure."); CARLTON & PERLOFF, MODERN INDUSTRIAL ORGANIZATION, *supra* note 179, at 644 ("Market shares are imperfect indicators of market power, so additional analysis of the economic conditions is necessary before one can reach a conclusion about market power."); KEITH N. HYLTON, ANTITRUST LAW: ECONOMIC THEORY AND COMMON LAW EVOLUTION 236 (Cambridge Univ. Press 2003) ("[T]here may be cases in which market share is great, but because demand- and supply-side substitutability is also great, the firm's market power is negligible."). Herbert Hovenkamp has observed that "[m]arket multi-sidedness can make traditional market share measures much less valuable as well." Herbert Hovenkamp, *Antitrust and Information Technologies*, 68 FLA. L. REV. 419, 432 (2016)).

[1647] Professor Shapiro has written, with Professor Louis Kaplow of Harvard Law School:

> Courts—and thus lawyers and government agencies—traditionally equate high market shares with a high degree of market power and low shares with a low degree of market power. This association is highly misleading if the market elasticity of demand is ignored, and likewise if rivals' elasticity of supply is not considered.

Kaplow & Shapiro, *Antitrust, supra* note 933, at 1091. Professors Kaplow and Shapiro explain at length how this insight reveals the weaknesses in relying on Judge Learned Hand's famous analysis of market shares and monopoly power in *Alcoa*:

> The central legal question is how much market power is denoted by 'monopoly power.' . . .
> Most famous is the pronouncement in *Alcoa* that a ninety percent share (in the market for aluminum) 'is enough to constitute a monopoly; it is doubtful whether sixty or sixty-four percent would be enough; and certainly thirty-three percent is not.' The difficulty in interpreting this statement is that two distinct issues are conflated: how much market power was thought to exist in that case (a fact question distinctive to that industry under the then-existing conditions), and how much market power is deemed sufficient to constitute monopoly power (a legal/policy

firm's market share in conjunction with other structural indicators of market power, such as the presence or absence of barriers to entry and of switching costs.[1648]

B. Did Judge Koh Examine Direct Evidence of Qualcomm's Market Power?

Judge Koh did not identify any analysis of direct evidence of Qualcomm's market power, such as the profitability of Qualcomm's modem business, or the own-price elasticity of demand for Qualcomm's products. She said instead that "*[l]icensing* is very profitable for Qualcomm."[1649] She also said that licensing "'comprises a very substantial portion of the company's revenue and profit.'"[1650]

Yet, Judge Koh did not rigorously analyze the profit that Qualcomm generated from selling *modems*—the products over which she found Qualcomm to possess a monopoly in two relevant markets. She mentioned that Qualcomm sacrificed profit in the modem business to become Apple's exclusive supplier[1651] and that selling modems to Apple would be profitable for Qualcomm even in the absence of exclusivity.[1652] Judge Koh also observed that, according to Qualcomm's 2016 strategic plan, "Qualcomm earn[ed] its highest margins—ranging from 47-49%—on premium LTE modem chips."[1653] Besides making those limited findings, she did not analyze the profitability of Qualcomm's modem business. In other words, Judge Koh evidently did not

---

question, the answer to which may be entirely independent of the particular case or, if not, its dependence requires specification that was not offered). . . .

This ambiguity is fundamental because in future cases, not in the aluminum industry (under the conditions prevailing at the time of *Alcoa*), a given share, whether 33%, 90%, or some other figure, may convey much more or significantly less power than did a similar share in *Alcoa*. But we know neither how much power over price *Alcoa* required nor how much power was thought to exist for any given share in that industry. Hence, even if both parties' experts in a subsequent case agree that, say, the sustainable margin was 16%, there is no way to tell from *Alcoa* which side wins on the element of monopoly power.

The same opacity characterizes all statements that a given market share is or is not adequate under any market power test—that is, unless one accepts that a given share in a properly defined market conveys the same market power, regardless of the market. But this supposition is emphatically false. . . . Thus, in addition to the market share . . . , both the market elasticity of demand . . . and the elasticity of supply response . . . are important, and we have seen that it is quite possible for a high share to be associated with low market power and a modest share to be associated with substantial market power.

Id. at 1187–88 (footnotes omitted) (quoting United States v. Aluminum Co. of Am., 148 F.2d 416, 424 (2ᵈ Cir. 1945) (Hand, J.)); *see also* Joseph Farrell & Carl Shapiro, *Antitrust Evaluation of Horizontal Mergers: An Economic Alternative to Market Definition*, 10 B.E. J. Theoretical Econ. 1, 3 (2010) ("In recent decades, . . . industrial organization scholars and the courts have been more apt to stress that high concentration can be compatible with vigorous competition and efficient market performance.").

[1648] *See, e.g.*, J. Gregory Sidak, *Memorandum: Will the International Trade Commission or the Antitrust Division Set Policy on Monopoly and Innovation?*, 3 Criterion J. on Innovation 701, 703–05 (2018).

[1649] FTC v. Qualcomm Inc., 411 F. Supp. 3d 658, 674 (N.D. Cal. 2019) (emphasis added).

[1650] *Id.* at 748 (quoting CX7580-001 (email from Steve Altman)); *see also id.* at 754, 761.

[1651] *Id.* at 732; *see also id.* at 734.

[1652] *Id.* at 772.

[1653] *Id.* at 692 (citing CX5551-013 (2016 Strategic Plan, Qualcomm CDMA Technologies)).

consider Qualcomm's profits earned *from its modem business* to be evidence directly probative of Qualcomm's market power.

Judge Koh also did not make any findings about the own-price elasticity of demand for Qualcomm's modems. It has long been recognized among economists and antitrust scholars, as then-Professor Posner wrote in 1976, that "the monopolist will always operate in the elastic portion of his demand curve."[1654] This observation should have led Judge Koh to a simple but profound testable hypothesis in *FTC v. Qualcomm*: was demand price-elastic?

Since Judge Koh found that Qualcomm possessed a monopoly over two different kinds of modems, Judge Posner's observation invites one to ask, what evidence did the FTC—staffed with a legion of economists in its Bureau of Economics, and assisted by Professor Shapiro as the agency's expert economic witness—present that proved by a preponderance of the evidence that the price elasticity of demand for each of those two kinds of Qualcomm modems exceeded 1 in absolute value? Considering that Judge Koh's findings of fact and conclusions of law mention the word "elasticity" only once (and then only when the word appears in a quotation taken from the Supreme Court's decision in *Brown Shoe*[1655]), it appears that the FTC did not proffer any such evidence on Qualcomm's own-price elasticity of demand for each of the two kinds of modems.

Remarkably, the word "elasticity" (or any variation on the word) does not appear once in the 11 redacted, publicly available volumes of the trial transcript in *FTC v. Qualcomm*. In other words, no witness for the FTC gave testimony under oath at trial concerning the own-price elasticity of demand for either of the two kinds of modems, either at the firm (Qualcomm) level or at the market level. What explains this dereliction by the government's lawyers and economists in such a high-profile monopolization case? The FTC's failure to carry even its burden of *production* on this highly probative piece of evidence critical to the agency's *prima facie* case deserves the close scrutiny of the Ninth Circuit (should it choose to rehear *FTC v. Qualcomm en banc*) and the Supreme Court.

Judge Koh appeared not to recognize that the Lerner Index provides direct evidence of market power. If she had evidence of Qualcomm's price of the pertinent modems, along with a proxy for their marginal cost, she could have calculated the Lerner Index for those modems.[1656] A high Lerner Index is a necessary condition for a finding of market power, though not a sufficient condition if the firm has large fixed (or sunk) costs, which of course

---

[1654] Posner, Antitrust Law: An Economic Perspective, *supra* note 1275, at 10.

[1655] *FTC v. Qualcomm*, 411 F. Supp. 3d at 684 ("The boundaries of an antitrust product market 'are determined by the reasonable interchangeability of use or the cross-elasticity of demand between the product itself and substitutes for it.'") (quoting Brown Shoe Co. v. United States, 370 U.S. 294, 325–26 (1962)).

[1656] *See, e.g.*, Elzinga & Mills, *The Lerner Index of Monopoly Power: Origins and Uses*, *supra* note 1629, at 558.

would be a question of fact on which Judge Koh would want to take evidence. Yet, Judge Koh's findings of fact and conclusions of law do not report or even suggest that she performed any analysis of this sort.

C. Did Judge Koh Correctly Examine Indirect Evidence of Market Power?

To assess market power, Judge Koh relied instead solely on indirect evidence of market power.[1657] She first set out to define the relevant markets. Adopting the FTC's contentions, she found that "the CDMA modem chip market" and the "premium LTE modem chip market" (which she defined as "LTE-compliant [modem chips] used in premium handsets"[1658]) were the relevant antitrust product markets.[1659] Yet, as we shall see, Judge Koh did not use any rigorous economic methodology to support that conclusion, which in turn produced an incorrectly narrow market definition.

Relying on a document internal to Qualcomm, Judge Koh then found that Qualcomm held an 89-percent share of the market for "premium" LTE modems in 2014 and an 85-percent market share in 2015.[1660] On the basis of that same document, Judge Koh observed that Qualcomm predicted that its market share would fall to 77 percent in 2016 and 64 percent in 2017.[1661] Judge Koh found that that evidence concerning Qualcomm's market share, in combination with evidence about barriers to entry and expansion, supported her conclusion that Qualcomm possessed monopoly power in the market for "premium" LTE modems between 2011 and 2016 (although she never discussed Qualcomm's market share for "premium" LTE modems before 2014).[1662] These findings were not persuasive.

[1657] *FTC v. Qualcomm*, 411 F. Supp. 3d at 696 (citing Ohio v. Am. Express Co., 138 S. Ct. 2274, 2284 (2018)).

[1658] *Id.* at 691 (quoting Federal Trade Commission's Pretrial Brief at 7, FTC v. Qualcomm Inc., No. 5:17-cv-00220-LHK (N.D. Cal. Dec. 28, 2018), ECF No. 1053).

[1659] *Id.* at 687, 694.

[1660] *Id.* at 694 (citing CX5551-010 (2016 Strategic Plan, Qualcomm CDMA Technologies)).

[1661] *Id.* (citing CX5551-010 (2016 Strategic Plan, Qualcomm CDMA Technologies)).

[1662] *Id.* at 695. As we saw earlier, Professor Shapiro reached the same conclusion by applying a similar methodology. He examined Qualcomm's market share and stated that "it's quite clear that entry is not easy into this market." Transcript of Proceedings (Volume 6) at 1162:9–10, FTC v. Qualcomm Inc., No. 5:17-cv-00220-LHK (N.D. Cal. Jan. 15, 2019) (Testimony of Carl Shapiro). He elaborated on direct examination during the FTC's case-in-chief:

> [T]hese market shares are quite high and would tend to indicate significant market power. Are they somehow giving us a false positive in that respect because entry is so easy that there's really no significant power there? And again, I think it's quite clear that entry is not easy into this market. You know, Samsung and Intel have gotten in, and MediaTek, but it takes time. It's not easy to do. And it's the sort of market where the market shares are meaningful following the structural approach, and it's not the case that entry is so easy that we should—that we would brush aside these type of market shares in this structural analysis.

Id. at 1162:4–15.

1. Did Judge Koh Correctly Apply the Hypothetical Monopolist Test (HMT) to Define the Relevant Product Market?

When defining the relevant market in an antitrust case, a court typically applies the hypothetical monopolist test (HMT). Judge Koh correctly explained that, "[u]nder the [HMT], the court asks 'whether a monopolist in the proposed market could profitably impose a small but significant and nontransitory price increase'" (SSNIP).[1663] If a hypothetical monopolist can profitably impose a SSNIP, then the product market is determined to be sufficiently inclusive. Conversely, Judge Koh explained, "[i]f after the monopolist imposed a SSNIP, customers would purchase products outside the proposed market, the proposed antitrust market definition is too narrow" and should also include products to which consumers would switch in response to a SSNIP.[1664] (In the context of Judge Koh's relevant market for "premium" LTE modems, the "consumers" are the OEMs that purchase such modems to insert into their mobile devices. The "consumers" in this context are not considered the end users who buy those finished mobile devices.)

Judge Koh went through the motions of describing the mechanics of the HMT, but then she set it aside. She did not actually apply the HMT to determine the relevant product market (at least not when defining the "premium" LTE modem market).

Instead, Judge Koh first cited Qualcomm's internal documents and testimony from Qualcomm and Apple executives, which indicated that Qualcomm and OEMs informally categorize LTE modems into different tiers, including a "premium" tier.[1665] Next, she listed more documents and testimony from Qualcomm to support her conclusion that the tier of a smartphone generally matches the tier of the modem that reposes in the smartphone.[1666] Judge Koh also cited the decisions in *FTC v. Whole Foods Market, Inc.* and *United States v. Gillette Co.* for the proposition that courts have deemed a "premium" product market to be a distinct antitrust market.[1667] However, Judge Koh did not mention that the dissenter in *Whole Foods*, Justice Brett Kavanaugh, now sits on the Supreme Court—which might shorten the shelf life of the majority opinion in that D.C. Circuit decision.[1668] Finally, Judge Koh invoked the testimony of Tony Blevins (Apple's Vice President of Procurement), Todd Madderom (Motorola's Director of Procurement), and Finbarr Moynihan

---

[1663] *FTC v. Qualcomm*, 411 F. Supp. 3d at 685 (quoting Theme Promotions, Inc. v. News Am. Mktg. FSI, 546 F.3d 991, 1002 (9th Cir. 2008)).

[1664] *Id.* (citing Saint Alphonsus Med. Center-Nampa Inc. v. St. Luke's Health Sys., Ltd., 778 F.3d 775, 784 (9th Cir. 2015)).

[1665] *Id.* at 691.

[1666] *Id.* at 692.

[1667] *Id.* at 692–93 (first citing FTC v. Whole Foods Mkt., Inc., 548 F.3d 1029 (D.C. Cir. 2008); and then citing United States v. Gillette Co., 828 F. Supp. 78 (D.D.C. 1993)).

[1668] *Whole Foods*, 548 F.3d at 1051 (Kavanaugh, J., dissenting).

(MediaTek's General Manager of Customer Sales and Business Development) to support her opinion that "a non-premium LTE modem chip is not an 'available substitute' for a premium LTE modem chip."[1669]

The dog's breakfast of evidence that Judge Koh reported was a *non sequitur*. It did not enable her to perform the HMT. It did not give Judge Koh a sound evidentiary basis to conclude that consumers of LTE modems would decline to switch to alternative products (such as *non*-"premium" LTE modems) in response to the imposition of a SSNIP for "premium" LTE modems.

a. Did Judge Koh Correctly Define "Premium" LTE Modems?

Judge Koh's definition of a "premium" LTE modem is at best unhelpful for the proper use of the HMT. At worst, it is unscientific and contradicted by the evidence that she herself cited in her findings of fact and conclusions of law.

On the basis of her definition of "premium" LTE modems being "LTE-compliant [modem chips] used in premium handsets,"[1670] any modem, regardless of its features, should be considered a "premium" modem, provided that it reposes in a "premium" smartphone. By that circular reasoning, the proposition that the market for "premium" LTE modems is the relevant antitrust market is nonfalsifiable, because *any* potential substitute to which a manufacturer of "premium" smartphones switches immediately becomes, by definition, a "premium" LTE modem. It is telling that Judge Koh's definition perfectly matched Professor Shapiro's trial testimony during the FTC's case-in-chief: "[P]remium LTE modem chips are modem chips that went into premium handsets."[1671]

Judge Koh's definition of "premium" LTE modems also contradicted the trial testimony that she cited in her findings of fact and conclusions of law. For example, Mr. Blevins of Apple testified that "premium modem chips are distinct from lower tier modem chips in terms of *features* like speed, uplink and downlink performance, quality, miniaturization, and power consumption."[1672] Similarly, Will Wyatt of Qualcomm (QTI's Vice President of Finance) agreed that "'premium tier chipsets typically have a higher product cost and *more*

[1669] *FTC v. Qualcomm*, 411 F. Supp. 3d at 694 (quoting United States v. Microsoft Corp., 253 F.3d 34, 54 (D.C. Cir. 2001) (en banc) (per curiam)).

[1670] *Id.* at 691 (citing Federal Trade Commission's Pretrial Brief at 7, FTC v. Qualcomm Inc., No. 5:17-cv-00220-LHK (N.D. Cal. Dec. 28, 2018), ECF No. 1053).

[1671] Transcript of Proceedings (Volume 6) at 1157:13–14, FTC v. Qualcomm Inc., No. 5:17-cv-00220-LHK (N.D. Cal. Jan. 15, 2019) (Testimony of Carl Shapiro).

[1672] *FTC v. Qualcomm*, 411 F. Supp. 3d at 691 (emphasis added) (citing Transcript of Proceedings (Volume 4) at 673:3–17, FTC v. Qualcomm Inc., No. 5:17-cv-00220-LHK (N.D. Cal. Jan. 11, 2019) (Testimony of Tony Blevins (Vice President of Procurement, Apple))).

functionality.'"[1673] Thus, in trial testimony industry participants at companies adverse to one another both defined a "premium" LTE modem on the basis of the modem's technical *features*, rather than on the basis of the end device in which the modem is implemented, as Judge Koh did in her findings of fact and conclusions of law.

b.   Did the Reported Evidence Support Judge Koh's Definition of the Relevant Product Market?

Even if one ignores Judge Koh's (and Professor Shapiro's) circular definition of a "premium" LTE modem, for at least five reasons there was not substantial evidence for Judge Koh's finding that the "premium" LTE modem market was the relevant product market.

i.   Industry Taxonomy Does Not Trump Consumer Preferences

First, evidence that industry participants classify products into "premium" and non-"premium" tiers does not automatically support the conclusion as a matter of economic analysis that a hypothetical monopolist could profitably impose a SSNIP.

Consider, for example, a hypothetical market for coffee. Coffee sold in supermarkets might be divided into three tiers: low-end, mid-range, and premium. Coffee suppliers, supermarkets, and end consumers might agree with such a classification. Yet, it does not necessarily follow from that taxonomy that a hypothetical monopolist supplying "premium" coffee could profitably increase the price of "premium" coffee by, say, 5 percent. In response to a 5-percent price increase for "premium" coffee, some consumers might switch to drinking mid-range coffee or perhaps to drinking "premium" tea. If we observe such consumer substitution, then both mid-range coffee and high-end tea might be part of the relevant market, because both products constrain the pricing behavior of suppliers of "premium" coffee.

The same logic applies in the LTE modem industry. Judge Koh's reference to the tier classification of modems does not shed light on whether consumers would switch to non-"premium" products in response to Qualcomm's SSNIP. Consequently, evidence that industry participants classify modems into "premium" and non-"premium" tiers does not support the conclusion that "premium" LTE modems constitute the relevant product market.[1674]

[1673] *Id.* (emphasis added) (quoting Transcript of Proceedings (Volume 3) at 434:5–7, FTC v. Qualcomm Inc., No. 5:17-cv-00220-LHK (N.D. Cal. Jan. 8, 2019) (Testimony of Will Wyatt (Vice President of Finance, Qualcomm Technology Licensing))).

[1674] *Cf.* FTC v. Whole Foods Mkt., Inc., 548 F.3d 1028, 1057 (D.C. Cir. 2008) (Kavanaugh, J., dissenting) ("Even if [Whole Foods CEO John] Mackey's comments were directed only to Wild Oats, that would not be evidence that Whole Foods and Wild Oats are in their own product market separate from all other supermarkets. It just as readily suggests that Whole Foods and Wild Oats are two supermarkets that have

ii. *Court Decisions Recognizing "Premium" Product Markets in Entirely Unrelated Industries Reveal Nothing About Consumer Demand for Supposedly "Premium" Modems*

Second, Judge Koh's citation to decisions in which a court deemed the "premium" product market to be a distinct antitrust market is similarly uninformative.[1675] A "premium" product market sometimes might be the relevant product market, but the important question is whether the specific facts of *FTC v. Qualcomm* support the conclusion that "premium" LTE modems constitute the *entire* relevant product market.

As Judge Koh acknowledged in her findings of fact and conclusions of law, the courts in both *Whole Foods* and *Gillette* performed an HMT and analyzed evidence to show that the premium products in question were in fact non-substitutable.[1676] In *Whole Foods*, Whole Foods' internal documents showed that "the majority (in some cases nearly all)" of the relevant customers would stay in the premium market.[1677] In contrast, Judge Koh relied on no economic analysis whatsoever and instead cited merely the testimony of (presumably self-interested) executives from only three companies—including MediaTek, which is not even a "consumer" for antitrust purposes (because it is not a smartphone OEM that buys modems).[1678]

In addition, the relevant product market in *Whole Foods* was *not* predicated solely on price, as in the case of Judge Koh's own arbitrary market-definition classification of a "premium" modem as any modem contained in a smartphone selling for more than $400. By her own words, Judge Koh acknowledged that, relative to other grocery stores, Whole Foods and Wild Oats grocery stores had both higher quality and a differentiated product:

> The FTC proffered undisputed evidence that Whole Foods and Wild Oats "provide *higher levels of customer service* than conventional supermarkets, a 'unique environment,' and a particular focus on the 'core values'" that certain customers espoused. Whole Foods and Wild Oats also sold *more natural and organic products than conventional supermarkets as a proportion of inventory*.[1679]

---

similarly differentiated themselves from the rest of the market, such that Mackey would be especially pleased to see that competitor vanish. Beating the competition from similarly differentiated competitors in a product market is ordinarily an entirely permissible competitive goal. Saying as much, as Mackey did here, does not mean that the similarly differentiated competitor is the only relevant competition in the marketplace."); *see also id.* at 1056 ("'For antitrust purposes, we apply the differentiated label to products that are distinguishable in the minds of buyers but not so different as to belong in separate markets.'") (quoting 2B Phillip E. Areeda & Herbert Hovenkamp, Antitrust Law ¶ 563(a), at 385 (Aspen 3d ed. 2007)).

[1675] *FTC v. Qualcomm*, 411 F. Supp. 3d at 692–94.
[1676] *Id.*
[1677] *Whole Foods*, 548 F.3d at 1040.
[1678] *FTC v. Qualcomm*, 411 F. Supp. 3d at 693–94.
[1679] *Id.* at 692–93 (emphasis added) (quoting *Whole Foods*, 548 F.3d at 1039).

Moreover, Judge Koh did not attempt to disentangle the causation issue posed by the fact that the higher prices at Whole Foods and Wild Oats stores were evidently colinear with the product differentiation and the higher perceived quality of those stores—just as the superior performance of "premium" LTE modems was evidently colinear with their higher prices.

Judge Koh's reliance on *Gillette* was similarly misplaced. She herself quoted the district court's observation that fountain pens priced up to $400 tended to have "'image, prestige, and status'" but lacked the capacity to be "'collectors items or "jewelry" pieces.'"[1680] Again, that recognition by Judge Koh should have indicated to her that certain products are differentiated by their superior quality over some germane dimension of performance and that their prices are consequently higher. But it would not have followed from that recognition for Judge Koh to have concluded that price rather than quality is what has propelled consumer demand for those products.

iii. *Judge Koh's Erroneous Reliance on an Implicit Theory of Veblen Goods to Define Relevant Markets in Antitrust Law*

Third, economists generally believe that demand curves slope downward, not upward. A typical product is not a Veblen good, for which demand "is increased because it bears a higher rather than a lower price."[1681] Economist and sociologist Thorstein Veblen introduced the concept of "conspicuous consumption" in his 1899 book, *The Theory of the Leisure Class.*[1682] A freak of consumer demand theory, a Veblen good "derives its value[] not from the intrinsic worth of what is consumed but from the fact that it permits people to set themselves apart from others by [its] consumption."[1683] Economists today regard Veblen goods as products that "wealthy individuals . . . consume . . . to advertise their wealth, thereby achieving greater social status," and "'Veblen effects' are said to exist when consumers exhibit *a willingness to pay a higher price for a functionally equivalent good.*"[1684]

[1680] *Id.* at 693 (quoting United States v. Gillette Co., 828 F. Supp. 78, 82 (D.D.C. 1993)).

[1681] Harvey Liebenstein, *Bandwagon, Snob, and Veblen Effects in the Theory of Consumers' Demand*, 64 Q.J. ECON. 183, 189 (1950).

[1682] THORSTEIN VEBLEN, THE THEORY OF THE LEISURE CLASS ch. 4 (Martha Banta ed., Oxford Univ. Press 2009) (1899).

[1683] Curtis Eaton & Mukesh Eswaran, *Well-Being and Affluence in the Presence of a Veblen Good*, 119 ECON. J. 1088, 1088 (2009); *see also id.* at 1090 ("The Veblen good is valued only in so far as it affects the consumer's own *relative* consumption of the good[.]") (emphasis in original).

[1684] Laurie Simon Bagwell & B. Douglas Bernheim, *Veblen Effects in a Theory of Conspicuous Consumption*, 85 AM. ECON. REV. 349, 349 (1996) (emphasis added); *see also id.* ("'[A] BMW in every driveway might thrill investors in the short run but ultimately could dissipate the prestige that lures buyers to these luxury cars.'") (quoting Timothy Aeppel, *BMW, Despite Success, Is Acting Like It's Under Siege*, WALL ST. J., Feb. 19, 1992, at B4). Veblen goods are sometimes regarded as a type of "positional good"—that is, a good "whose value depends relatively strongly on how [it] compare[s] with things owned by others." Robert H. Frank, *The Demand for Unobservable and Other Nonpositional Goods*, 75 AM. ECON. REV. 101, 101 (1985).

None of this theoretical apparatus about the anomaly of Veblen goods, which is what would be required to give Judge Koh's reasoning some semblance of deductive economic rigor, sounds remotely like a plausible account of how OEMs in the real world come to demand one modem rather than another to use in a smartphone. Much less does it sound useful or even replicable from an evidentiary perspective. And note, importantly, that the "consumer" in the market-definition exercise in both *Whole Foods* and *Gillette* was the *ultimate* consumer (or "household," in economic jargon), whereas in *FTC v. Qualcomm* the "consumer" is an OEM like Apple or Samsung, purchasing inputs to make its own product to be sold to the ultimate consumer.

An OEM is exceedingly unlikely to behave collectively as a firm according to the predictions of what, in the theory of Veblen goods, is already an exceptional depiction of demand theory manifested at the level of the individual end-consumer. A theory of anomalous demand behavior is an inauspicious foundation on which to improvise a novel methodology for courts to use to define relevant product markets in antitrust cases.

iv. OEM Testimony Tended to Contradict Rather Than Confirm Judge Koh's Theory of Market Definition Predicated on Price Tiers

Fourth, the trial testimony on which Judge Koh relied to support her conclusion that OEMs would not switch to the use of non-"premium" LTE modems was weak.

For example, publicly available information contradicted the testimony that Motorola requires a "premium" LTE modem chip for its "premium" handsets.[1685] Motorola's moto z³ smartphone, which sold for $480 at release and thus would be considered a "premium" smartphone on the basis of Judge Koh's finding that smartphones priced above $400 are "premium" handsets, uses Qualcomm's Snapdragon 800 series "premium" chips.[1686] Yet, more expensive models of Motorola smartphones, such as the moto z⁴ and the moto z³ play, use Qualcomm's *non-"premium"* Snapdragon 600 series chips.[1687]

[1685] *See FTC v. Qualcomm*, 411 F. Supp. 3d at 693–94 (quoting Videotaped Deposition of Todd Madderom (Director of Procurement, Motorola) at 140:13–18, FTC v. Qualcomm Inc., No. 5:17-cv-00220-LHK (N.D. Cal. Mar. 16, 2018) ("Q[.] And how would it impact Motorola's business if it used a nonpremium-tier cellular modem in a premium-tier handset? A[.] We've never considered that because I don't think that's a viable approach. I think that equates to not being able to sell in a product."), *exhibit to* Federal Trade Commission's Submission of Trial Testimony That Occurred on January 11[, 2019], FTC v. Qualcomm Inc., No. 5:17-cv-00220-LHK (N.D. Cal. Jan. 12, 2019), ECF No. 1272-3 [hereinafter Deposition of Todd Madderom]).

[1686] *Moto Z3*, Motorola, https://www.motorola.com/us/products/moto-z-gen-3. Judge Koh cited evidence that Qualcomm's Snapdragon 800 chip series is in the "premium tier." *FTC v. Qualcomm*, 411 F. Supp. 3d at 691. Judge Koh also cited testimony and documents from Qualcomm purporting to show that smartphones priced above $400 are deemed to be "premium" handsets. *Id.* at 692.

[1687] *Moto Z4*, Motorola, https://www.motorola.com/us/products/moto-z-gen-4-unlocked; Matt Swider, *Moto Z Play Review*, Techradar (Sept. 20, 2017), https://www.techradar.com/reviews/phones/

Similarly, Mr. Blevins, Apple's Vice President of Procurement, despite testifying about the importance to Apple of having the "best" components in iPhones, did not explicitly answer how Apple would react to the imposition of a SSNIP on Qualcomm's "premium" LTE modems.[1688]

In short, the statements that Judge Koh cited did not provide substantial evidence that a sufficient share of buyers of "premium" LTE modems would decline to switch to alternative products, such that a hypothetical monopolist could profitably impose a SSNIP on "premium" LTE modems.

v. The Closeness of Demand Substitutes When the Functionalities of Branded Products Advance Over Time

Fifth, Judge Koh's HMT did not consider a simple but important question for defining the relevant product market: For end users (by which we now mean individual consumers or households), which is the closer substitute for the current "premium" smartphone of an OEM—that same OEM's older-generation models or the "premium" smartphone of a rival OEM?

The demand for a modem is derived from the end-user demand for the device that uses that modem. Derived demand is demand for an intermediate good that exists as a result of the demand for another intermediate or final good.[1689] The effect of a SSNIP on demand for a modem (the particular input) depends on the SSNIP's effect on the price that end users pay for the smartphone (the downstream product) and the reactions of smartphone consumers to that change in price. In response to a SSNIP on a "premium" smartphone, an individual consumer might switch to an older-generation model produced by the same OEM (such as an older model of the iPhone), as opposed to a "premium" smartphone produced by a different OEM (such as a Samsung Galaxy). In that case, the SSNIP on a "premium" smartphone increases the first OEM's demand for modems that were considered "premium" when first used in those older smartphones but are now considered non-"premium."

Thus, the salient economic question that Judge Koh ignored is: Would an increase in the price of a "premium" modem used in a "premium" smartphone increase demand for a non-"premium" modem used in an older model of smartphone manufactured by the same OEM? The answer to *that* question would help determine whether the HMT would indicate whether "premium"

---

mobile-phones/moto-z-play-1327411/review/2. Judge Koh implied that Qualcomm's Snapdragon 600 series occupies a lower tier than its Snapdragon 800 series. *See FTC v. Qualcomm*, 411 F. Supp. 3d at 692.

[1688] *FTC v. Qualcomm*, 411 F. Supp. 3d at 693 (citing Transcript of Proceedings (Volume 4) at 673:24–674:2, FTC v. Qualcomm Inc., No. 5:17-cv-00220-LHK (N.D. Cal. Jan. 11, 2019) (Testimony of Tony Blevins (Vice President of Procurement, Apple))). Judge Koh mistakenly cited pages 674–75 of the transcript instead.

[1689] *See, e.g.,* Mankiw, Principles of Economics (8th ed.), *supra* note 652, at 362 ("The demand for a factor of production is a *derived demand*. That is, a firm's demand for a factor of production is derived from its decision to supply a good in another market.") (emphasis in original).

modems and non-"premium" modems belong to the same relevant product market for antitrust purposes.

c. How Does One Define a Relevant Product Market When Competition Occurs at the Design Stage of Product Development?

Competition among modem manufacturers occurs at the modem-design stage. When an OEM like Apple or Samsung is designing a smartphone that it will release at some future date (perhaps one or two years after the modem-design stage), that OEM is evaluating different candidate modems for use in its particular consumer product.[1690]

i. Competition as a Tournament When an OEM Awards a Supply Contract for Modems on the Basis of a "Design Win"

After a modem manufacturer secures a "design win" from the OEM, but before the launch of the new consumer product, both the modem manufacturer and the OEM will work together to design products that serve the joint needs of the two parties.[1691] At the time that competition occurs among modem manufacturers to achieve a design win, the modem that those rivals seek to supply to an OEM as an input might not yet exist. Indeed, even the production capacity of the modem manufacturer might be uncertain, because some modem manufacturers employ "fabless" production and need to contract with a manufacturer to secure production capacity. In short, *competition occurs at a point in time when each competitor is effectively a potential entrant*, and market shares for the losing firms are (and will be) zero for products that are never fully developed or brought to market.

Competition in a design-win market resembles a tournament. The prize might be structured as "winner take all" in the sense of the resulting supply contract being exclusive. Or the design-win tournament might envision multiple suppliers, as in the case of Apple's dual sourcing of modems for the iPhone 7, 8, and X from Qualcomm and Intel. Obviously, the decision of how many suppliers an OEM will use in a design-win market is solely within the OEM's discretion. It is a question of market design.

We have already seen how Judge Koh improperly applied the HMT to identify the modem markets in which Qualcomm competed. Although the winner of a design competition might thereafter have a 100-percent share of sales to a specific OEM or for a specific downstream device, one must examine how a SSNIP at the *component* level is passed on to consumers of the downstream device and how the changes in consumer behavior increase

---

[1690] *See, e.g.,* Transcript of Proceedings (Volume 5) at 889:14–16, FTC v. Qualcomm Inc., No. 5:17-cv-00220-LHK (N.D. Cal. Jan. 14, 2019) (Testimony of Jeff Williams (COO, Apple)).

[1691] *See, e.g., id.* at 890:13–891:9.

and decrease the derived demand for different components used in different downstream devices.

After a manufacturer achieves a design win, that manufacturer and the OEM might continue to negotiate over prices and other non-price terms of a supply agreement. Those agreements will typically span a period of years. The HMT asks whether a hypothetical manufacturer of some set of products could profitably impose a SSNIP over at least one product within the potential market.[1692] If one considers the profitability of imposing a SSNIP (for example, a 5-percent increase to negotiated prices), the hypothetical monopolist notionally would have the freedom to impose a price increase that would likely breach the modem manufacturer's supply contract with the OEM. In other words, the price provisions in the supply contract already would constrain the modem manufacturer's ability to increase its price.

At least one U.S. Court of Appeals has held that, when defining a product market, private contracts must *not* be considered when applying the HMT.[1693] That view is misguided as a matter of economic analysis. If the supply contracts do not affect that market definition exercise, it is conceivable that every product might itself might be found to constitute an antitrust market, and that every design winner (even if supplying only a subset of components to an OEM) would be deemed to have a market share of 100 percent. That finding would be paradoxical and ultimately uninformative. In such a setting, what is the probative value of performing the HMT to define a relevant antitrust product market?

ii. How the Horizontal Merger Guidelines Would Analyze Competition from "Rapid Entrants" in Design-Win Markets

The Horizontal Merger Guidelines contemplate assigning market shares to firms that are not currently producing substitute products, so as to consider those firms to be market participants for analytical purposes. The agencies consider all firms earning revenue in the defined relevant product market to be market participants.[1694] The agencies also include firms that have indicated an intent to enter a market but are not yet earning revenue in the market.[1695] The agencies also consider some firms to be market participants that do not produce a product within the relevant product market and have not committed to enter the market but would likely enter in response to a SSNIP.

[1692] U.S. Dep't of Justice & Fed. Trade Comm'n, Horizontal Merger Guidelines, *supra* note 924, at 9.

[1693] *See* Queen City Pizza, Inc. v. Domino's Pizza, Inc., 124 F.3d 430, 438–39 (3ᵈ Cir. 1997).

[1694] U.S. Dep't of Justice & Fed. Trade Comm'n, Horizontal Merger Guidelines, *supra* note 924, at 15.

[1695] *Id.* The Horizontal Merger Guidelines included as market participants firms that are vertically integrated and are of "competitive significance" in the market, although it is unclear under what circumstances those firms would not also be included under one of the other criteria for inclusion.

One group of likely (but not committed) entrants that the agencies include as market participants is "rapid entrants." They are firms that would likely "provide rapid supply responses with direct competitive impact . . . without incurring significant sunk costs" in response to a SSNIP.[1696] Examples of rapid entrants might include firms operating in nearby geographic markets or firms with idle capacity that could "swing" that capacity into a relevant market in response to a SSNIP.[1697]

At the design stage of product development, each potential manufacturer is in a role similar to the intended entrant or the rapid entrant. How then does one analyze the competitive significance of those potential entrants? Would five competing manufacturers each have a hypothetical 20-percent market share? Would the predicted price be the outcome of a five-player differentiated-products pricing game? Are the sales of the winning manufacturer completely contestable at the design stage, and are per-unit prices equal to the per-unit long-run incremental costs of the product to be developed?

To my knowledge, economic theory and antitrust jurisprudence are both silent on these questions. Yet, Judge Koh's findings of fact and conclusions of law in *FTC v. Qualcomm* underscore why the issues posed by design-win rivalry can be profoundly significant in a market subject characterized by dynamic competition. It is evident that the standard application of the HMT in markets for highly customized products that compete at the design stage is uninformative on both legal and economic grounds. It would be unsound for a court to apply a demonstrably deficient methodology to answering a question simply because the methodology that would yield the correct answer might be hard to identify. It was unreliable and erroneous for Judge Koh to do so in *FTC v. Qualcomm*.

2. Did Judge Koh Correctly Analyze Evidence of Qualcomm's Market Power in the Relevant Market?

Also lacking substantial evidence was Judge Koh's analysis of Qualcomm's market power in what she considered to be the relevant markets. She found that Qualcomm had a large market share in what she defined as the market for "premium" LTE modems.[1698] She relied on no economic analysis whatsoever to support that conclusion.

Instead, Judge Koh merely cited an internal 2016 Qualcomm document estimating and predicting Qualcomm's "premium" LTE modem chip market share (without identifying whether in that document Qualcomm had defined "premium LTE modem chips" the same way that Judge Koh defined them in

---

[1696] *Id.* at 15–16.
[1697] *Id.* at 16.
[1698] FTC v. Qualcomm Inc., 411 F. Supp. 3d 658, 694 (N.D. Cal. 2019).

her findings of fact and conclusions of law) as 89 percent in 2014, 85 percent in 2015, 77 percent in 2016, and 64 percent in 2017.[1699] Judge Koh's conclusion about Qualcomm's market power was unreliable.

a.   Did Qualcomm "Own" a Market Share?

At the outset, it is worth noting that Judge Koh repeatedly defined the required showing for proving monopoly power in terms of whether Qualcomm "owned" a particular market share for CDMA modems or "premium" LTE modems.[1700] This recurring assertion by Judge Koh was imprecise and unscientific; it was also pejorative and factually unfounded in the sense that it implied that Qualcomm's shares of Judge Koh's relevant markets were immune from diminution by the force of competition. Obviously, no firm "owns" a market share in any intellectually rigorous legal sense of the word.

The Supreme Court has explained that the ownership of a thing consists of a bundle of rights that notably includes the right to exclude. When the Court in *Loretto v. Teleprompter* was addressing "[p]roperty rights in a physical thing" in 1982, it said that "'[t]he power to exclude has traditionally been considered one of the most treasured strands in an owner's bundle of property rights.'"[1701] But a market share is not a physical thing, much less a form of property suffused with the treasured right to exclude.

It was therefore erroneous and misleading for Judge Koh even to suggest that the ownership of property is a relevant and useful analogy for understanding the competitive significance of the factual observation that a particular firm has accounted for a particular share of sales in a particular market over a particular number of years. The Supreme Court held unambiguously in *Independent Ink* in 2006 that the grant of a patent—which unquestionably *is* a thing that a person can "own" and exclude others from using—does not necessarily confer market power for purposes of antitrust analysis.[1702] Nor is there any intellectually rigorous economic concept in the field of industrial organization positing that a firm "owns" a given market share.

[1699] *Id.*

[1700] *Id.* at 687 ("To show monopoly power, the FTC must demonstrate that Qualcomm owned a dominant share of the market[.]"); *id.* at 694 ("To show monopoly power, the FTC must demonstrate that Qualcomm owned a dominant share of the market[.]"); *id.* at 690 ("Qualcomm has owned a dominant share of the CDMA modem chip market[.]"); *id.* at 695 ("Qualcomm has owned a dominant share of the premium LTE modem chip market[.]").

[1701] Loretto v. Teleprompter Manhattan CATV Corp., 458 U.S. 419, 435 (1982) (quoting Kaiser Aetna v. United States, 444 U.S. 164, 179–80 (1979)).

[1702] Illinois Tool Works Inc. v. Indep. Ink, Inc., 547 U.S. 28, 45–46 (2006) (8-0 decision) ("Congress, the antitrust enforcement agencies, and most economists have all reached the conclusion that a patent does not necessarily confer market power upon the patentee. Today, we reach the same conclusion, and therefore hold that, in all cases involving a tying arrangement, the plaintiff must prove that the defendant has market power in the tying product.").

If an expert economic witness had disclosed an intention to opine in a jury trial that a firm "owns" a particular market share, a judge, performing his or her duty as the evidentiary gatekeeper, would have good cause to exclude, in response to a motion *in limine*, any testimony to such effect on *Daubert* grounds,[1703] as well as on the grounds that the danger that such terminology might confuse the jury would outweigh its probative value (which would be nil).[1704]

b. *Judge Koh's Findings of High Market Share Ignored Design-Win Competition to Supply the Market*

Besides using pejorative and legally irrelevant nomenclature to describe the economic concept of market power, Judge Koh's analysis of Qualcomm's market share was cursory and detached from basic principles of antitrust economics. It is questionable whether her measure of Qualcomm's market share provided any reliable information, considering that she adopted an artificially narrow definition of the relevant market that found no support in the evidence summarized in her findings of fact and conclusions of law. In addition, Judge Koh's own reference to the internal Qualcomm document showed that Qualcomm's market share had actually *decreased* every year from 2014 to 2017.[1705]

More important, a design win exemplifies what economists call "competition *for* the market," a concept that the D.C. Circuit well understood and applied in *United States v. Microsoft*[1706] and properly credited to

---

[1703] Daubert v. Merrell Dow Pharm., Inc., 509 U.S. 579, 597 (1993) (construing FED. R. EVID. 702).

[1704] FED. R. EVID. 403 ("The court may exclude relevant evidence if its probative value is substantially outweighed by a danger of . . . confusing the issues[.]"). By comparison, courts have stricken testimony in patent-infringement cases that would have referred to the patent holder as a "patent troll." *See, e.g.*, Order on Motions *in Limine* at 2, Core Wireless Licensing S.A.R.L. v. LG Elecs. Inc., No. 2:14-CV-00912-JRG (E.D. Tex. Feb. 15, 2019); Order on Pretrial Motions and Motions *in Limine* at 4, Polaris PowerLED LLC v. Samsung Elecs. Inc., No. 2:17-CV-00715-JRG (E.D. Tex. June 7, 2019); Edward Lee, *Patent Trolls: Moral Panics, Motions in Limine, and Patent Reform*, 19 STAN. TECH. L. REV. 113 (2015); *see also* Memorandum Order ¶ 3, at 3, Pacific Biosciences of Cal., Inc. v. Oxford Nanopore Techs., Inc., Nos. 17-275-LPS-CJB, 17-1353-LPS-CJB (D. Del. Feb. 27, 2020) (Stark, C.J.) (granting patent holder's motion *in limine* "to prevent [the alleged infringer] from using 'pejorative' terms (such as 'non-practicing entity,' 'NPE,' and 'paper patents')"); Order on Motions *in Limine* at 4, Finjan, Inc. v. Cisco Sys. Inc., No. 5:17-cv-00072-BLF (N.D. Cal. May 22, 2020) (Labson Freeman, J.) (finding that, in regard to "the use of the terms 'patent troll,' 'patent assertion entity,' 'PAE,' 'non-practicing entity,' and 'NPE[,]' . . . the Court is now of the opinion that such projective labels are irrelevant, unhelpful to the jury, and in some instances carry negative connotations").

[1705] *FTC v. Qualcomm*, 411 F. Supp. 3d at 694.

[1706] Quoting my own scholarship with Professor Howard Shelanski, the D.C. Circuit observed in *United States v. Microsoft* that "[r]apid technological change leads to markets in which 'firms compete through innovation for temporary market dominance, from which they may be displaced by the next wave of product advancements.'" United States v. Microsoft Corp., 253 F.3d 34, 49 (D.C. Cir. 2001) (en banc) (per curiam) (quoting Shelanski & Sidak, *Antitrust Divestitures in Network Industries*, *supra* note 988, at 11–12). Again, quoting the same article from the *University of Chicago Law Review*, the D.C. Circuit said that this "Schumpeterian competition . . . proceeds 'sequentially over time rather than simultaneously across a market.'" *Id.* at 50 (quoting Shelanski & Sidak, *Antitrust Divestitures in Network Industries*,

economist Harold Demsetz.[1707] As applied to technologically dynamic industries, Demsetz's insight about competition for the market dovetails with
Joseph Schumpeter's famous account of "creative destruction."[1708] Judge
Koh's findings of fact and conclusions of law in *FTC v. Qualcomm* place front
and center an important question of law for the Ninth Circuit (if it chooses
to rehear the case *en banc*) and the Supreme Court to consider: In a market
characterized by successive waves of design wins, does a supplier's design
win at any one point in time create market power? Does the high share of
sales that the winning modem manufacturer necessarily obtains mean that it
possesses market power? Of course not.

i. The Unreliable Inference of Market Power from Market Share Alone in Technologically Dynamic Industries

Measures of market share might reveal little if any reliable information about
a company's actual market power in industries where manufacturers compete
episodically *for* the market in the Demsetzian sense rather than continuously
for individual sales *in* the market. In an industry where there is competition
for a market, firms often compete to be the sole supplier of a good or service
to a given customer by means of a long-term supply contract with that
customer. As the existing contract approaches its expiration, another round
of competition commences among firms to win the next supply contract.
Thus, competition for the market is most vigorous during the contracting
stage. Afterwards, there might not be anything resembling a spot market for
the specially designed product.

Consequently, a high market share can be consistent with an innovative,
competitive market.[1709] An industry in which patents and voluntary standards
figure prominently, as they do with respect to modems and smartphones, is

supra note 988, at 11–12). Professor Shelanski subsequently served as Director of the FTC's Bureau of
Economics from 2012 to 2013.

    Assistant Attorney General Makan Delrahim reiterated the salience of this same passage from
Microsoft in a speech delivered on December 7, 2018, in which he said that Joseph Schumpeter's insight
about creative destruction "was enshrined into antitrust law in the D.C. Circuit's opinion in *United States
v. Microsoft*. The court explained there that 'Schumpeterian competition . . . proceeds sequentially over
time rather than simultaneously across a market' and that '[c]ompetition in [technologically dynamic]
industries is "for the field" rather than "within the field."'" Makan Delrahim, Assistant Attorney Gen.,
Antitrust Div., U.S. Dep't of Justice, Remarks at the 19th Annual Berkeley-Stanford Advanced Patent Law
Institute: "Telegraph Road": Incentivizing Innovation at the Intersection of Patent and Antitrust Law 4
(Dec. 7, 2018), https://www.justice.gov/opa/speech/file/1117686/download (alterations in original) (first
quoting *Microsoft*, 253 F.3d at 49–50 (quoting therein without attribution Shelanski & Sidak, *Antitrust
Divestitures in Network Industries*, *supra* note 988, at 11–12); and then quoting Harold Demsetz, *Why
Regulate Utilities?*, 11 J.L. & ECON. 55, 57 & n.7 (1968)).

   [1707] *See* Demsetz, *Why Regulate Utilities?*, *supra* note 1706, at 55–57 & n.7.

   [1708] SCHUMPETER, CAPITALISM, SOCIALISM AND DEMOCRACY, *supra* note 4, at 81.

   [1709] *See* J. Gregory Sidak & Daniel F. Spulber, *Deregulation and Managed Competition in Network Industries*,
15 YALE J. ON REG. 117, 136–38 (1998); Shelanski & Sidak, *Antitrust Divestiture in Network Industries*,
supra note 988, at 11–12; J. Gregory Sidak & David J. Teece, *Dynamic Competition in Antitrust Law*, 5 J.
COMPETITION L. & ECON. 581, 592–96 (2009).

necessarily a market in which dynamic competition is critical and will likely deliver great gains in consumer welfare. Dynamic competition is a style of competition that relies on innovation to produce new products and processes and concomitant quality-adjusted price reductions of substantial magnitude.

ii. *Dynamic Competition Among Modem Manufacturers to Supply OEMs*

The evidence in *FTC v. Qualcomm* confirmed that there existed dynamic competition among modem manufacturers to supply OEMs. Mr. Madderom, Motorola's Director of Chipset Procurement, testified by videotaped deposition that competition among modem manufacturers for a "socket" on a handset is a design-win form of rivalry that ends once the OEM has chosen a specific design:

> Q[.] Is it viable to seek alternative modems once a socket has already been awarded and designed?
>
> A[.] No. It takes many months of engineering work to design in a replacement solution, if there is even a viable one on the market that supports the need. And there are significant certification costs to obtain the approvals to ship that product in the market.[1710]

The economic implication of this testimony is that the market shares upon which Judge Koh relied actually conveyed no useful information about the truly consequential competition that had already occurred among modem manufacturers to win the contract to supply Motorola's handsets.

Mr. Madderom's testimony confirmed that the market for modems is unquestionably one in which manufacturers compete *for* the market. One of the distinguishing characteristics of the smartphone is that its performance has steadily and dramatically advanced over a relatively short period of time, so much so that a smartphone's standardized technology is expressly recognized by suppliers and consumers alike to coalesce around successive "generations" of discontinuous rather than smoothly continuous advancements in performance. Even within a given generation of a mobile communication standard, the opportunity to supply a firm like Apple is segmented into contracts for particular releases of the iPhone, and Apple's COO, Mr. Williams, expressly called those contracts "design wins."[1711]

[1710] Deposition of Todd Madderom, *supra* note 1685, at 148:4–11.

[1711] *See, e.g., FTC v. Qualcomm*, 411 F. Supp. 3d at 738 ("'Qualcomm has continued to ship us product on the design wins that they have and had at the time. And so they have continued to sell us chips. We have been unable to get them to support us on new design wins past that time, and this has been a challenge.'") (quoting Transcript of Proceedings (Volume 5) at 890:13–17, FTC v. Qualcomm Inc., No. 5:17-cv-00220-LHK (N.D. Cal. Jan. 14, 2019) (Testimony of Jeff Williams (COO, Apple))); *accord id.* at 814.

Multiple manufacturers compete for an agreement to supply LTE modems for each iteration of Apple's smartphones. The manufacturer of LTE modems that wins the competition for the supply contract for a particular generation of Apple's smartphones will necessarily have a large share of modem sales to Apple over the duration of that contract, simply because transactions in that market manifest themselves in episodic, high-volume contracts. It is reasonable to infer that the winner of the supply contract offered Apple the best quality-adjusted price of those modem manufacturers that chose to compete for the business.

iii. Did Judge Koh Ignore the Antitrust Significance of Dynamic or "Schumpeterian" Competition?

A manufacturer's high market share during the term of that supply contract is not evidence that the manufacturer faced an absence of competition when winning that contract. Even a manufacturer with a high market share might face vigorous competition at the contracting stage, such that that manufacturer lacks control over output or prices—and such control is precisely what the Ninth Circuit in *Rebel Oil Co. v. Atlantic Richfield Co.* called "the essence of market power."[1712]

Thus, a high market share in the market for LTE modems is not necessarily evidence of a lack of competition or innovation or gains in consumer surplus. Nor is it necessarily evidence of market power. Even a company with a 90-percent market share might be powerless to raise the price of its modems above competitive levels. Judge Koh ignored those salient features of the market for modems, and that omission made unreliable her inferences of market power drawn from market shares after OEMs had already awarded supply contracts to particular modem manufacturers.

3. Potential Competition and Barriers to Entry

The Ninth Circuit said in *Rebel Oil* that, to prove market power, "[t]he plaintiff must show that new rivals are barred from entering the market and show that existing competitors lack the capacity to expand their output to challenge the . . . high price."[1713] Judge Koh recognized that controlling legal principle in her findings of fact and conclusions of law.[1714] Yet, she then proceeded to ignore the evidence of the competition that Qualcomm faced from other existing suppliers and potential suppliers of "premium" LTE modems.

[1712] 51 F.3d 1421, 1441 (9ᵗʰ Cir. 1995).

[1713] *Id.* at 1439.

[1714] *FTC v. Qualcomm*, 411 F. Supp. 3d at 687.

a. *Rival Suppliers of "Premium" LTE Modems*

Judge Koh found that, although other firms offered "premium" LTE modems, those firms did not constrain Qualcomm's ability to raise prices for its "premium" LTE modems.[1715] Her conclusion finds no support in any evidence that she cited in her findings of fact and conclusions of law.

Judge Koh acknowledged that firms other than Qualcomm manufactured "premium" LTE modems. For example, she found that Intel supplied "premium" LTE modems, but she emphasized that Intel supplied only "thin modems" (the type of modem that only Apple uses in its smartphones).[1716] She acknowledged that, "after Intel won Apple's business, other OEMs reached out about Intel's modem chips."[1717] Judge Koh portrayed the glass as half empty despite the fact that implicit in this finding was her recognition that Intel was indeed actively rivalrous with Qualcomm in supplying "premium" LTE modems to Apple, the leading seller of smartphones in the United States. Judge Koh also found that Exynos, Samsung's modem chip division, made "premium" LTE modem chips and that Samsung was using those modems in its smartphones.[1718] In other words, Judge Koh's own findings confirmed that Qualcomm faced competition (1) from Exynos in supplying "premium" LTE modems to Samsung and (2) from Intel in supplying "premium" LTE modems to Apple. Together, Apple and Samsung accounted for the lion's share of all smartphone sales in the United States.

Judge Koh did not analyze the economic implications of her factual findings—that is, that Qualcomm faced competition in supplying "premium" LTE modems to OEMs that were producing the vast majority of all "premium" smartphones sold. In particular, she ignored that, according to her own definition that a "premium" smartphone is any smartphone priced above $400[1719]—precisely the same break point in price to which Professor Shapiro testified in his product-market definition[1720]—Samsung and Apple were the two largest suppliers of "premium" smartphones in the United States and in the world between 2011 and 2016.

Data from the market-research firm International Data Corporation (IDC)[1721] showed that, in 2011, Apple and Samsung jointly sold 59.2 percent of the "premium" smartphones (defined by Judge Koh as all smartphones priced

---

[1715] *Id.* at 695.
[1716] *Id.* at 694 ("Intel supplies only premium LTE thin modems.").
[1717] *Id.* at 736.
[1718] *Id.* at 694.
[1719] *Id.* at 692.
[1720] Transcript of Proceedings (Volume 6) at 1157:16–17, FTC v. Qualcomm Inc., No. 5:17-cv-00220-LHK (N.D. Cal. Jan. 15, 2019) (Testimony of Carl Shapiro) ("Premium handsets I'm defining to be handsets that cost at least $400 dollars [sic][.]").
[1721] *About IDC*, IDC, https://www.idc.com/about.

above $400) sold in the United States.[1722] The combined share for Apple and Samsung consistently exceeded 80 percent between 2012 and 2015, and it increased to 92.8 percent in 2016.[1723] Using IDC data, Figure 11 shows the shares of "premium" smartphones sold in the United States by manufacturer between 2011 and 2016.

Figure 11. Share of "Premium" Smartphones
Sold in the United States, by Manufacturer, 2011–2016

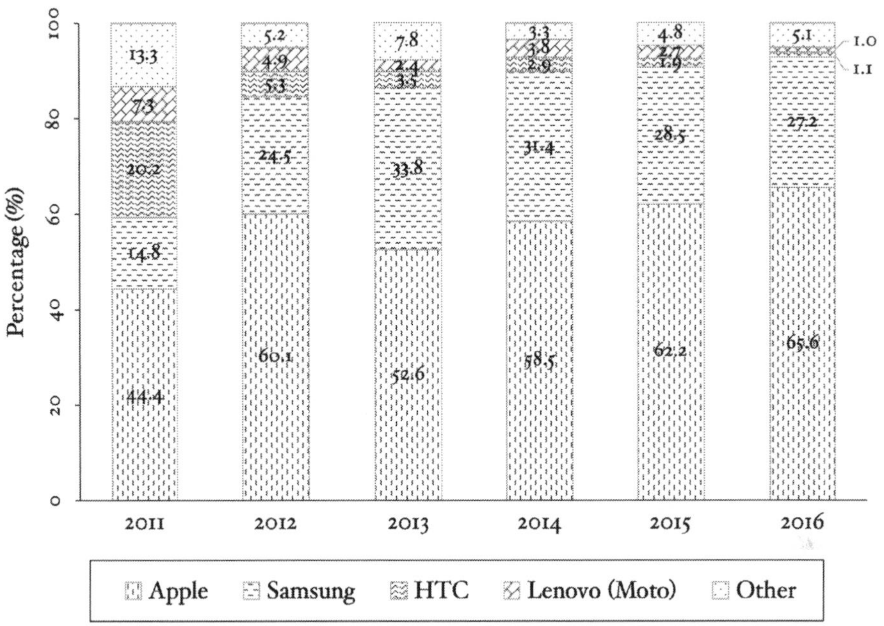

Source: Int'l Data Corp., IDC Quarterly Mobile Phone Tracker: 2017Q4 Historical Release, *supra* note 1722.

Figure 11 shows that, between 2011 and 2016, Apple and Samsung together annually sold between 59.2 percent and 92.8 percent of all "premium" smartphones sold in the United States.

Therefore, between 2011 and 2016, Qualcomm faced competition in supplying "premium" LTE modems to OEMs that sold the majority of "premium" smartphones in the United States. Samsung started using its Exynos LTE modems in its Galaxy Note 4,[1724] which Samsung publicly announced in September 2014.[1725] Samsung's internal decision to use its

---

[1722] Int'l Data Corp., IDC Quarterly Mobile Phone Tracker: 2017Q4 Historical Release (Feb. 9, 2018).

[1723] *Id.*

[1724] *Exynos Modem 303*, Samsung, https://www.samsung.com/semiconductor/minisite/exynos/products/modemrf/exynos-modem-303/.

[1725] Ben Fox Rubin & Shara Tibken, *Samsung Unveils Galaxy Note 4, Note Edge*, CNet, Sept. 3, 2014.

Exynos LTE modems of course must have occurred even earlier, during the product-design stage. (Judge Koh found that, "[b]ecause the OEM must integrate the modem chip into the OEM's handset design process, OEMs may engage with potential modem chip suppliers as many as two years before the OEM plans to commercialize the handset."[1726]) Similarly, in 2014, Apple reportedly discussed plans internally to work with Intel on 4G modems to exert competitive pressure on Qualcomm.[1727] Thus, at least between 2014 and 2016, substantial evidence indicated that Qualcomm *did* face competition from both Samsung and Intel when seeking to supply modems to the manufacturers of the vast majority of "premium" smartphones sold in the United States.

The same conclusion applies if one focuses instead on the *global* "premium" smartphone market. IDC's data show that Samsung and Apple were the top two "premium" smartphone manufacturers that jointly sold the vast majority of "premium" smartphones worldwide from 2011 to 2016.[1728] Huawei became the third largest "premium" smartphone manufacturer in 2016.[1729] As Judge Koh acknowledged, Huawei's subsidiary, HiSilicon, supplies LTE modems to Huawei.[1730] Huawei has used HiSilicon LTE modems in its smartphones since 2012, when the Huawei Ascend D quad smartphone adopted as its SoC the HiSilicon K3V2, which in turn incorporated Huawei's Balong 710 LTE modem.[1731]

Figure 12 shows the shares of "premium" smartphones sold worldwide by manufacturer between 2011 and 2016.

Figure 12 shows that Apple, Samsung, and Huawei together annually sold between 54.8 percent and 89.1 percent of all "premium" smartphones sold worldwide from 2011 to 2016. Therefore, Qualcomm also faced competition when seeking to supply modems to the manufacturers of the vast majority of "premium" smartphones sold globally between 2014 and 2016.

In short, Judge Koh's findings on Qualcomm's market power were contrary to substantial evidence of the competition that Qualcomm actually faced from existing rivals—including Intel, Samsung, and Huawei—when seeking to win supply contracts for forthcoming models of "premium" smartphones.

[1726] FTC v. Qualcomm Inc., 411 F. Supp. 3d 658, 674 (N.D. Cal. 2019).

[1727] *See* Shara Tibken, *Apple Allegedly 'Plotted' to Hurt Qualcomm Years Before It Sued the Company*, CNET, Apr. 24, 2019.

[1728] INT'L DATA CORP., IDC QUARTERLY MOBILE PHONE TRACKER: 2017Q4 HISTORICAL RELEASE, *supra* note 1722.

[1729] *Id.*

[1730] *FTC v. Qualcomm*, 411 F. Supp. 3d at 748.

[1731] Press Release, HiSilicon Co., HiSilicon Releases Leading LTE Multi-Mode Chipset (Feb. 27, 2012), http://www.hisilicon.com/en/Media-Center/News/20120227_HiSilicon.

Figure 12. Share of "Premium" Smartphones
Sold Worldwide, by Manufacturer, 2011–2016

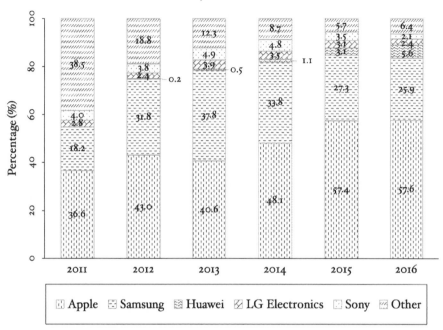

Source: Int'l Data Corp., IDC Quarterly Mobile Phone Tracker: 2017Q4 Historical Release, *supra* note 1722.

b. Were Competitors Unable to Increase Their Output?

Judge Koh found that Qualcomm's existing competitors were "unable to quickly increase their output" of "premium" LTE modems,[1732] but she offered no factual support for that finding, which substantial evidence contradicted. Judge Koh did not examine the number of modems supplied by each manufacturer over time. She did not examine each manufacturer's production capacity. Judge Koh did not explain why large multinational companies like Samsung, Intel, and Huawei would have any difficulty expanding their production of LTE modems. On the basis of her own findings, Qualcomm's market share for "premium" LTE modems in 2017 was 25 percentage points lower than its market share in 2014.[1733] Evidence establishing Qualcomm's decreasing market share disproved Judge Koh's finding that Qualcomm's competitors could not increase their output expeditiously. Total demand for "premium" LTE modems certainly did not fall over the relevant time period.

[1732] *FTC v. Qualcomm*, 411 F. Supp. 3d at 694.
[1733] *Id.* (citing CX5551-010 (2016 Strategic Plan, Qualcomm CDMA Technologies)).

To support her conclusion that competitors could not expand output quickly, Judge Koh merely referred to Qualcomm's alleged "ability to charge monopoly prices on premium LTE modem chips over an extended period."[1734] Even then, Judge Koh did not actually analyze the price for "premium" LTE modems to support her conclusion. Instead, she relied on a statement that Cristiano Amon, Qualcomm's President, made to Apple in November 2013 that "'LTE was not a commodity and would therefore have to be priced "upon value—not cost."'"[1735]

It was clearly erroneous for Judge Koh to equate that statement by Mr. Amon with the proposition that Qualcomm charged monopoly prices for "premium" LTE modems. Mr. Amon's statement communicated the most elementary of all principles of economics: that the price for *any* good depends on the interaction of demand (which encompasses the value that the good creates for consumers) and supply (which encompasses the producer's cost of providing the good). It was clearly erroneous for Judge Koh to equate value-based prices to *monopoly* prices. That specious reasoning would impute monopoly power to *every* seller, including the proverbial wheat farmer in Kansas.

A firm's ability to increase output, and the pace at which it can do so, are inherently factual questions. The answers depend on factors such as manufacturing capacity and raw input availability. Judge Koh did not attempt to weigh such facts. At a minimum, considering the presence of "fabless" manufacturers of modems (including Qualcomm's modems), any decrease in demand for Qualcomm's modems would necessarily free a concomitant amount of capacity (and raw inputs) in the facilities used to manufacture Qualcomm modems, which are called "foundries."[1736]

Fabian Gonell, QTL's Legal Counsel and Senior Vice President for Licensing Strategy, testified at trial: "Qualcomm doesn't actually manufacture any of its own chips. It contracts the manufacturer [sic] of its chips out to

---

[1734] *Id.* at 695 (citing Rebel Oil Co. v. Atlantic Richfield Co., 51 F.3d 1421, 1434 (9th Cir. 1995)).

[1735] *Id.* (quoting CX0597-001).

[1736] Transcript of Proceedings (Volume 7) at 1443:8–13, 1443:18, FTC v. Qualcomm Inc., No. 5:17-cv-00220-LHK (N.D. Cal. Jan. 18, 2019) (Testimony of Fabian Gonell (Legal Counsel and Senior Vice President, Licensing Strategy, Qualcomm Technology Licensing)) ("[A] foundry is a big plant that basically makes chips, makes little ASIC chips, and they're very expensive and very high tech. And people that have foundries very often use them to not only make chips for themselves, make their own chips, but also to make chips for other people. . . . And so Samsung has foundries and has a foundry business.").

people that have foundries and they actually physically make the chips."[1737] The extent to which Qualcomm is able to charge a price for "premium" LTE modems that exceeds its costs is a function of the demand for its modems. With differentiated products, which are not commodities like wheat or crude oil, price itself does not establish how quickly competitors can increase their output.

Judge Koh did not acknowledge that her findings concerning the supposed inability of Qualcomm's rivals to increase their output of "premium" LTE modems were empirically disproven by substantial evidence from the modem industry. Table 10 reports manufacturers' actual unit sales of LTE modems sold globally from 2011 through 2016.

Table 10 shows that, from 2011 to 2016, other major LTE modem suppliers such as Intel, Samsung, MediaTek, and Spreadtrum increased their output. In particular, Samsung, Intel, and HiSilicon significantly increased their production. Judge Koh noted that "Intel supplies only premium LTE thin modems" and that "Exynos, Samsung's modem chip division (also known as Samsung LSI), has a premium LTE modem chip."[1738]

Although Judge Koh did not explicitly acknowledge that HiSilicon, owned by Huawei, supplied "premium" LTE modems, she did list HiSilicon as a current supplier of modems[1739] and indicated that HiSilicon could have potentially "becom[e] a competitor for business from OEMs other than Huawei" had Qualcomm not refused to license HiSilicon.[1740] Meanwhile, Huawei of course has grown to be one of the largest "premium" smartphone suppliers in the world. Consequently, it was clearly erroneous for Judge Koh not to classify HiSilicon LTE modems used in Huawei's "premium" smartphones as "premium" LTE modems, since such a finding of fact would necessarily follow directly from her own definition of a "premium" LTE modem.

In sum, substantial evidence empirically disproved Judge Koh's conclusion that Qualcomm's existing rivals lacked the capacity to expand their output in a timely manner and therefore supposedly lacked the ability to constrain Qualcomm's power to charge high "all-in prices" for its modems. Substantial evidence indicated that Qualcomm's existing rivals demonstrably *did* expand their output of LTE modems from 2011 to 2016.

[1737] *Id.* at 1443:14–17. Mr. Gonell further testified how the phenomenon of fabless chip production implicates the negotiation of patent rights:

> So when you're negotiating patent rights, or some kind of patent rights with a company that has a foundry business, it's common, it's what you do, to make sure that you're distinguishing between the rights you're granting that apply to the company's products, in which case in this case it's Samsung's products, and the rights that may or may not apply to products that they are making for other people as part of their foundry business.

Id. at 1443:19–1444:1.

[1738] *FTC v. Qualcomm*, 411 F. Supp. 3d at 694.

[1739] *Id.* at 675.

[1740] *Id.* at 749.

Table 10. Manufacturers' Unit Sales of LTE
Modems Sold Globally, 2011–2016 (Millions of Units)

Manufacturer	2011	2012	2013	2014	2015	2016
Qualcomm	10.5	131.2	296.4	518.3	707.9	763.8
MediaTek	–	–	–	32.1	163.0	353.9
Samsung	6.0	8.7	10.7	13.4	87.8	118.5
Spreadtrum	–	0.0	0.1	2.9	15.0	90.7
Intel	–	–	3.2	12.4	15.3	60.9
HiSilicon	0.0	0.0	1.4	23.2	40.0	70.5
Altair	0.0	0.0	1.0	3.7	4.7	4.4
Sequans	0.0	0.0	0.2	1.4	2.6	3.7
Leadcore	–	–	–	0.1	20.4	2.1
GCT	1.0	1.7	2.4	1.3	0.9	0.6
Marvell	–	–	0.7	28.7	31.6	3.1
Others	2.3	4.7	1.0	2.3	0.2	0.1
Total	19.8	146.3	317.1	639.8	1089.4	1472.3

Source: Strategy Analytics, Baseband Market Share Tracker 2017: Intel, HiSilicon and Samsung Register Double-Digit LTE Shipment Growth, *supra* sources cited in Figure 1, tab 4e ("LTE").

Note: Table 10 reports the top 11 manufacturers that had the highest average unit sales of LTE modems from 2011 through 2016.

c. *Did Judge Koh Correctly Examine Potential Competition?*

The extent of a firm's market power depends not only on whether there is a lack of actual competition, but also on whether there is a lack of *potential* competition. That is, market power requires the presence of barriers to entry that would impede potential competitors from entering the market and undercutting supracompetitive prices.[1741] The Supreme Court said in 1964 in *Penn-Olin* and again in 1973 in *Falstaff* that "'[t]he existence of an aggressive, well equipped and well financed corporation engaged in the same or related lines of commerce waiting anxiously to enter an oligopolistic market [is] a

---

[1741] *See, e.g.*, Bork, The Antitrust Paradox: A Policy at War with Itself, *supra* note 1255, at 195–96.

substantial incentive to competition which cannot be underestimated.'"[1742] Judge Koh recognized that a company has monopoly power only when "'barriers to entry' protect the dominant firm's ability to control prices," but she did not explain thereafter whether potential competition had in fact constrained Qualcomm's prices for "premium" LTE modems.[1743]

d.   Did Judge Koh Correctly Identify Barriers to Entry?

To define barriers to entry, Judge Koh relied on *United States v. Syufy Enterprises*, a 1990 decision in which she described the Ninth Circuit as having "held that industries that require 'onerous front-end investments that might deter competition from all but the hardiest and most financially secure investors' are characterized by structural entry barriers."[1744] Her reliance on *Syufy* was surprising and unpersuasive.

i.   Did Incumbents Also Face "Onerous Front-End Investments"?

In *Syufy*, the government conceded the *absence* of barriers to entry (as Judge Koh acknowledged), such that the Ninth Circuit's discussion of entry barriers plainly constituted dicta rather than a holding.[1745] In addition, the particular definition of a barrier to entry that Judge Koh quoted is in fact part of a long list of pieces of evidence that the Antitrust Division failed to present to establish the existence of entry barriers in *Syufy*.[1746]

Five years later, in *Rebel Oil*, the Ninth Circuit stated that the existence of barriers to entry will depend on multiple factors:

> The main sources of entry barriers are: (1) legal license requirements; (2) control of an essential or superior resource; (3) entrenched buyer preferences for established brands; (4) capital market evaluations imposing higher capital costs on new entrants; and, in some situations, (5) economies of scale.[1747]

[1742]   United States v. Falstaff Brewing Corp., 410 U.S. 526, 559 (1973) (quoting United States v. Penn-Olin Chem. Co., 378 U.S. 158, 174 (1964)).

[1743]   *FTC v. Qualcomm*, 411 F. Supp. 3d at 684 (quoting Oahu Gas Serv., Inc. v. Pac. Res. Inc., 838 F.2d 360, 366 (9th Cir. 1988)).

[1744]   *Id.* at 688 (quoting United States v. Syufy Enters., 903 F.2d 659, 667 (9th Cir. 1990)).

[1745]   *Syufy*, 903 F.2d at 666–67; *see also FTC v. Qualcomm*, 411 F. Supp. 3d at 690.

[1746]   *Syufy*, 903 F.2d at 666–67.

[1747]   Rebel Oil Co. v. Atlantic Richfield Co., 51 F.3d 1421, 1439 (9th Cir. 1995). Other circuit courts of appeal also recognize that the existence of barriers to entry will depend on multiple factors. *See, e.g.*, United States v. Microsoft Corp., 253 F.3d 34, 55 (D.C. Cir. 2001) (en banc) (per curiam); Buccaneer Energy (USA) Inc. v. Gunnison Energy Corp., 846 F.3d 1297, 1317 (10th Cir. 2017).

In contrast to this list of possible factors, Judge Koh focused her analysis of barriers to entry exclusively on what she (and the Ninth Circuit in *Syufy*) called "'onerous front-end investments.'"[1748]

Notably, Judge Posner has observed, to the contrary, that "[t]he amount of capital required for entry is not a barrier to entry . . . ; presumably it is no greater for the new entrant than for the firms in the market."[1749] Judge Koh's understanding of a barrier to entry corresponded to what Judge Posner has called "a meaningless usage" of that term.[1750]

Even when focusing on "onerous front-end investments," Judge Koh did not conduct any actual analysis of what the nature and magnitude of those investments were, much less any analysis of what supposedly made them distinctly "onerous." When examining barriers to entry in the "CDMA modem chip market," she focused on the deposition testimony of Scott McGregor, Broadcom's former CEO, who testified to the unremarkable proposition that research and development (R&D) for new products requires up-front investment.[1751]

ii. Delayed Entry Is Still Entry

Judge Koh also cited two examples of actual, but "delayed," entry (by MediaTek on a greenfield basis and by Intel through its acquisition of VIA) to support her conclusion that the investments required to develop modems pose structural entry barriers.[1752] These two examples were again unremarkably quotidian. Delayed entry is of course still entry, and Judge Koh did not explain as a matter of law why delayed entry constitutes evidence that "onerous front-end investments" are *barriers* to entry.[1753] If entry is subject to delay—as countless events, grand and prosaic, routinely are in all the works and days of commerce—then prudence dictates that would-be entrants ought to exercise due care to plan for that entirely foreseeable contingency.

[1748] *FTC v. Qualcomm*, 411 F. Supp. 3d at 688 (quoting *Syufy*, 903 F.2d at 667).

[1749] POSNER, ANTITRUST LAW: AN ECONOMIC PERSPECTIVE, *supra* note 1275, at 92.

[1750] *Id.* at 59 ("A barrier to entry is commonly used in a quite literal sense to mean anything which a new entrant must overcome in order to gain a foothold in the market, such as the capital costs of entering the market on an efficient scale. This is a meaningless usage, since it is obvious that a new entrant must incur costs to enter the market, just as his predecessors, the firms now occupying the market, did previously.").

[1751] *FTC v. Qualcomm*, 411 F. Supp. 3d at 688 ("Scott McGregor (former Broadcom CEO) testified at trial that 'the economics of being in the cellular baseband business are very sensitive to volume of customers' because of the front-end investments necessary to fund research and development.") (quoting Videotaped Deposition of Scott McGregor (Former CEO, Broadcom) at 174:19–21, FTC v. Qualcomm Inc., No. 5:17-cv-00220-LHK (N.D. Cal. Mar. 28, 2018), *exhibit to* Federal Trade Commission's Submission of Trial Testimony That Occurred on January 8[, 2019], FTC v. Qualcomm Inc., No. 5:17-cv-00220-LHK (N.D. Cal. Jan. 11, 2019), ECF No. 1253-2 [hereinafter Deposition of Scott McGregor]).

[1752] *Id.* at 688–89.

[1753] *See id.* at 688–91 (discussing barriers to entry in the market for CDMA modems, but not explaining the economic and legal significance of delayed entry); *id.* at 694–95 (discussing barriers to entry in the market for "premium" LTE modems, but not explaining the economic and legal significance of delayed entry).

But, again, the fact that entry *might* entail delay is no reason to presume that, in some systematic manner, the delay asymmetrically impeded second movers yet spared first movers that hardship. Incumbents and entrants alike must wait for the paint to dry and the bread to rise.

iii. Ongoing R&D Investments Are Not Barriers to Entry

For her "premium" LTE modem chips market, Judge Koh relied on the testimony of Finbarr Moynihan, MediaTek's General Manager of Customer Sales and Business Development, and Aicha Evans, Intel's Chief Strategy Officer, who both testified that "premium" LTE modems require more investment in R&D than do CDMA modems.[1754] That proposition, even if assumed to be true, was not evidence that there existed barriers to entry owing to the need for "onerous front-end investments."

Judge Koh's ostensible evidence of "onerous front-end investments" did not consist of any statements that actually concerned *entry*. Instead, Judge Koh relied entirely on statements concerning *ongoing* R&D investments that existing manufacturers of modems, already incumbent competitors in the market, were required to make to maintain their competitive standing to

---

[1754] *Id.* at 695 (first citing Transcript of Proceedings (Volume 3) at 565:5–6, FTC v. Qualcomm Inc., No. 5:17-cv-00220-LHK (N.D. Cal. Jan. 8, 2019) (Testimony of Aichatou Evans (Chief Strategy Officer, Intel)); and then citing Transcript of Proceedings (Volume 3) at 324:25–325:2, 378:2–3, 378:18–20, FTC v. Qualcomm Inc., No. 5:17-cv-00220-LHK (N.D. Cal. Jan. 8, 2019) (Testimony of Finbarr Moynihan (General Manager of Corporate Sales and Business Development, MediaTek))).

Ms. Evans testified about the amount that Intel invested in the modem chipset industry after it acquired Infineon in 2011. Transcript of Proceedings (Volume 3) at 565:3–15, FTC v. Qualcomm Inc., No. 5:17-cv-00220-LHK (N.D. Cal. Jan. 8, 2019) (Testimony of Aichatou Evans (Chief Strategy Officer, Intel)) ("Q. So [after Intel acquired Infineon] what kind of investment did it take for Intel to move Infineon up from a fast follower [to attain a leadership position in the modem chipset industry]? A. Oh. Lots of money, billions of dollars, and an army of engineers worldwide. And then a lot of focus. Q. You mentioned a billion dollars. Where does all that money go? A. It goes to pay the engineers. These are very expensive, specialized engineers. Hopefully they'll forgive me for saying that if they know that I've said that. And the test equipment and the equipment itself. So basically the majority, I would say a good 90 percent of it, goes to the R&D."); *see also* Open Sessions Hearing Transcript (Revised and Corrected) at 1424:6–14, Certain Mobile Electronic Devices and Radio Frequency and Processing Components Thereof (II), Inv. No. 337-TA-1093 (USITC Sept. 21, 2018) (McNamara, ALJ) (Testimony of Aichatou Evans (Chief Strategy Officer, Intel)) ("Q. What are the challenges to becoming a supplier of premium baseband chipsets? A. It's a labor of love, for sure. Lots of money. You have to be willing to invest on average a billion dollars annually for a while. By the time you enter and start developing, it takes at least a couple of years to get to—to get to at least the product that's acceptable. And then you have to have another one in development and another one in definition.").

Finbarr Moynihan also testified about the amount of investment required to develop modem chipsets. Transcript of Proceedings (Volume 2) at 324:24–325:2, FTC v. Qualcomm Inc., No. 5:17-cv-00220-LHK (N.D. Cal. Jan. 7, 2019) (Testimony of Finbarr Moynihan (General Manager of Corporate Sales and Business Development, MediaTek)) ("Q. Where has MediaTek been successful? A. We haven't really penetrated ever what I would call the premier tiers in the market, the high tiers, the highest tiers of the market."); *id.* at 378:2–3 (testifying under seal that MediaTek "decided to focus [its] limited R&D in other places" than "premium" LTE modem chips), *quoted on the public record in FTC v. Qualcomm*, 411 F. Supp. 3d at 695; *id.* at 378:18–20 ("You'd certainly like to see that the higher tiers generate higher profit, higher margins, yeah. It takes more R&D to develop those products.") (testifying under seal), *quoted on the public record in FTC v. Qualcomm*, 411 F. Supp. 3d at 695 & 799.

supply modems for a new generation of mobile devices. That critical distinction was absent from Judge Koh's findings of fact and conclusions of law in *FTC v. Qualcomm*, yet it matters in economics and in antitrust jurisprudence.

iv. *Stiglerian Barriers to Entry*

Investments that both new entrants and the incumbent face, such as R&D investments, are not barriers to entry. Nobel laureate George Stigler defined a barrier to entry as "a cost of producing . . . which must be borne by a firm which seeks to enter an industry but is not borne by firms already in the industry."[1755] Stigler was accordingly skeptical of the significance of barriers to entry. He wrote, "If the discussion of entry barriers suggests that there are effective permanent obstacles to entry in many industries, it is misleading."[1756] Instead, Stigler argued, "entry is basically a question of rate."[1757] What matters is "the pace of entry."[1758]

How might a firm slow the rate of entry into its market? One method is not to charge the monopoly price:

> [I]f one does not seize the entire profits that could be obtained in the absence of entry, entry itself may be retarded, because the prospective entrant is better able to judge existing profits than maximum possible profits. This is the rationale of the traditional belief that potential competition is a significant limitation on the power of a monopolist or group of oligopolists.[1759]

Judge Posner, whose scholarship and judicial opinions on antitrust law show Stigler's heavy influence,[1760] similarly has described a barrier to entry as "a condition that makes the long-run costs of a new entrant higher than those

---

[1755] GEORGE J. STIGLER, THE ORGANIZATION OF INDUSTRY 67 (Univ. of Chicago Press 1968); *see also* CARLTON & PERLOFF, MODERN INDUSTRIAL ORGANIZATION, *supra* note 179, at 77 (defining long-run barriers to entry as "a cost that must be incurred by a new entrant that incumbents do not (or have not had to) bear"). One theoretical variant on Stigler's definition of a barrier to entry would require the additional demonstration that the cost differential reduces economic welfare. C.C. von Weizäcker, *A Welfare Analysis of Barriers to Entry*, 11 BELL J. ECON. 399, 400 (1980) ("We . . . define barriers to entry in the following way, building on Stigler's definition: a barrier to entry is a cost of producing which must be borne by a firm which seeks to enter an industry but is not borne by firms already in the industry *and which implies a distortion in the allocation of resources from the social point of view*.") (emphasis added).

[1756] GEORGE J. STIGLER, THE THEORY OF PRICE 209 (Macmillan 4th ed. 1987) (1946).

[1757] *Id.*

[1758] *Id.*

[1759] *Id.*

[1760] In 1976, five years before he was confirmed for the Seventh Circuit, Judge Posner wrote: "My ideas on antitrust have been greatly influenced over the years by Aaron Director and George J. Stigler. I want to take this opportunity once again to acknowledge my intellectual debts to them while absolving them from responsibility for my conclusions and recommendations, with which they may disagree." POSNER, ANTITRUST LAW: AN ECONOMIC PERSPECTIVE, *supra* note 1275, at x. To my knowledge, neither Director nor Stigler ever lodged such disagreement.

of the existing firms."[1761] Of particular relevance to the claims of entry barriers tossed about in *FTC v. Qualcomm* is Judge Posner's observation that "[e]conomies of scale do not create a barrier to entry; they only dictate the level of output that the new entrant must achieve in order to minimize his costs."[1762]

An investment that entrants and incumbents alike must make is not a barrier to entry in the Stiglerian sense. As Daniel Spulber and I argued in our 1997 book, "The need to sink costs in a *new* technology falls evenly on the incumbent and entrant and thus cannot constitute a barrier to entry."[1763] R&D costs are not unique to entrants to the modem industry. Elsewhere in her findings of fact and conclusions of law, Judge Koh observed—evidently without realizing the contradiction that she was creating—that Qualcomm must make the very same R&D investments that she found constituted barriers to entry for Qualcomm's rivals: "Qualcomm's own documents and testimony recognize that *research and development is necessary to win the race to market.*"[1764]

[1761] POSNER, ECONOMIC ANALYSIS OF LAW, *supra* note 214, at 381. Here, Judge Posner's analysis suggests the influence of Harold Demsetz, *Barriers to Entry*, 72 AM. ECON. REV. 47 (1982). Demsetz argued: "Information costs are the more fundamental barrier to entry." *Id.* at 50. Information about the firm that is valuable to the customer is revealed over time and thus might appear to be colinear with one or more other observed phenomena, such as economies of scale or cost of capital. Demsetz reasoned: "A reputable history is an asset to the firm possessing it and to the buyer who relies on it because information is not free." *Id.* at 51. He argued that is misleading to "view[] advertising expenditures, capital requirements, and scale economies as if they were the basic sources of barriers rather than the cost of information." *Id.* Demsetz's insight about information has a strong flavor of a Stiglerian survivorship model: "New firms and recent entrants by virtue of their shorter histories or absence of specific investments (in particular, product lines) may not be able to impart to consumers, without some compensating effort, the same confidence as has already been secured by older firms through past investments in good performance." *Id.* at 50. Viewed in these terms, we can see the particular value in a technologically dynamic industry of Qualcomm's unique reputation as a serial innovator. Demsetz's colleague at UCLA, Armen Alchian, similarly viewed barriers to entry through the lens of information costs:

> Superior ability, proven talents, large initial investments in equipment, and consumer knowledge of reliable suppliers are created or paid for by incumbent successful firms. To call these "barriers" rather than "filters" is to suggest that they are undesirable and should be reduced. They can be reduced, but only at the cost of destroying valuable assets of the incumbents, assets whose values reflect their value to consumers in permitting lower costs of production and greater confidence and reliability of service without expensive repetitive search and experimentation. Surely it would be wonderful if that information or ability could be achieved without those initial costs, but so would it be desirable if refined copper sprung from the ground without refining.

ARMEN A. ALCHIAN, *Words: Musical or Meaningful?* (1979), *in* 1 THE COLLECTED WORKS OF ARMEN A. ALCHIAN: CHOICE AND COST UNDER UNCERTAINTY 549, 584–85 (Daniel K. Benjamin ed., Liberty Fund 2006).

[1762] POSNER, ANTITRUST LAW: AN ECONOMIC PERSPECTIVE, *supra* note 1275, at 92.

[1763] SIDAK & SPULBER, DEREGULATORY TAKINGS AND THE REGULATORY CONTRACT: THE COMPETITIVE TRANSFORMATION OF NETWORK INDUSTRIES IN THE UNITED STATES, *supra* note 740, at 82 (emphasis in original).

[1764] FTC v. Qualcomm Inc., 411 F. Supp. 3d 658, 799 (N.D. Cal. 2019) (emphasis added); *see also id.* at 767 ("As the 2012 Qualcomm presentation recognizes, sales are critical to investment in research and development."); *id.* at 800 ("Qualcomm can 'take risk and invest in new areas before our competition, so

It was both clearly erroneous and contrary to substantial evidence for Judge Koh to find that investment in R&D is a barrier to entry in her relevant product markets.

v.   *Salvageable R&D Investment Is Not a Barrier to Entry*

Salvageable R&D investments by definition cannot impose a barrier to entry at all, because they are not sunk. If a firm's investment in R&D is salvageable, then those R&D costs are not really sunk, and the firm's cost of exit is lower than it otherwise would be, since the firm will not sacrifice recoupment of its sunk investment upon exiting the market.[1765] As William Baumol eloquently explained in his work on contestable markets, a barrier to exit from an industry also functions *ex ante* as a barrier to entry into that industry.[1766] To the extent that a firm recognizes *ex ante* that it can lower its cost of exiting a market by salvaging the investments that it must necessarily make as a condition of entry, the firm will perceive the true opportunity cost of its entry to be commensurately lower.

Baumol's insight on the relationship between barriers to entry and the cost of exit leads us to an important corollary: barriers to entry are inextricably and inversely related to the degree of asset specificity. Asset specificity informs the degree to which an asset's cost is sunk.[1767] Paul Milgrom and John Roberts of Stanford have defined an asset's degree of specificity as the "fraction of [the asset's] value that would be lost if it were excluded from its major use."[1768]

It is highly significant, both as a matter of law and as a matter of probative economic evidence, that Judge Koh rejected Qualcomm's argument that modem development costs were relationship-specific, which is one example of how an asset can have specific value when optimally deployed.[1769] (That finding by Judge Koh, incidentally, is inconsistent with the extensive testimony, which we saw earlier, documenting the design-win character of an OEM's procurement decision for modems.) For example, Judge Koh found that, for at least one of Qualcomm's thin LTE modems—the

---

we often have a green field to create new intellectual property,' as Paul Jacobs (Qualcomm CEO) stated in a July 2012 letter to the Qualcomm Board of Directors.") (quoting CX6974-017).

[1765] *See, e.g.*, J. Gregory Sidak, *Why Should the Postal Service Deter Amazon's Competitive Entry into Last-Mile Parcel Delivery?*, 2 Criterion J. on Innovation 101, 129 (2017).

[1766] *See* William J. Baumol, John C. Panzar & Robert D. Willig, Contestable Markets and the Theory of Industry Structure 6–7 (Harcourt Brace Jovanovich rev. ed. 1988) (1982); William J. Baumol, *Contestable Markets: An Uprising in the Theory of Industry Structure*, 72 Am. Econ. Rev. 1, 3–4 (1982) (stating that absolute freedom of exit is one way to guarantee freedom of entry into a market).

[1767] *See, e.g.*, J. Gregory Sidak, *An Economic Theory of Censorship Revisited*, 5 Criterion J. on Innovation 701, 721–25 (2020).

[1768] Paul Milgrom & John Roberts, Economics, Organization and Management 307 (Prentice Hall 1992).

[1769] *FTC v. Qualcomm*, 411 F. Supp. 3d at 772.

MDM 9x15—Qualcomm could have achieved its desired minimum return on investment without selling any modems to Apple.[1770] Judge Koh found that "Qualcomm documents contradict Qualcomm's claim that its exclusive deals with Apple were necessary to defray 'relationship-specific' costs of working with Apple."[1771]

Yet, if R&D investments are in fact *not* unique to a particular product or customer, then it is more likely that they can be salvaged by being redeployed to serve the needs of a different product or customer. In other words, Judge Koh's own reasoning in this particular part of her findings of fact and conclusions of law in *FTC v. Qualcomm* directly undermined her conclusion elsewhere in that decision that R&D costs for modems constituted barriers to entry in her relevant product markets.

vi. *Actual Entry Absolutely Refutes the Contention That Barriers to Entry Exist*

Finally, several companies have entered the LTE modem industry since 2011 and have been able to attract a significant share of sales, both in the United States and globally. That occurrence of actual entry during the relevant timeframe disproves Judge Koh's prediction that entry could not occur because of barriers to entry.

Evidence that actual entry occurred necessarily and conclusively confirms that the costs of entry were low enough for entrants to overcome them. Judge Koh did not make any finding of this sort. Her failure to do so was clearly erroneous.

e. *Did Judge Koh Correctly Examine the Competitive Constraints That Qualcomm Faced in Her Relevant Markets?*

Even if one were to accept for sake of argument Judge Koh's finding that Qualcomm's ongoing investment in R&D to develop "premium" LTE modems erected a barrier to entry, that finding did not prove that potential competitors failed to constrain Qualcomm's pricing of its modems. Recall that one must ask how difficult it was for potential entrants to overcome that supposed barrier. Judge Posner explained in 1976 how existing small firms in a market properly obviate debate over barriers to entry in antitrust analysis:

[1770] *Id.*

[1771] *Id.* (quoting Defendant Qualcomm Incorporated's Proposed Findings of Fact and Conclusions of Law at 130, FTC v. Qualcomm Inc., No. 5:17-cv-00220-LHK (N.D. Cal. Dec. 6, 2018) [hereinafter Qualcomm's Proposed Findings of Fact and Conclusions of Law]). Judge Koh found that "Dr. Chipty conceded that to realize [its] target payback ratio for certain thin modems, Qualcomm did not need to sell any thin modems to Apple." *Id.*

By viewing the existing small firms in the market as the equivalent of potential entrants, which they are, and asking what "barriers" they face to growing, we can legitimately elide the question of nonrecurring costs of entry. Those costs are irrelevant if there are small firms in the market that can grow to be large firms, for they will do so if the leading firms charge a price above the competitive level.[1772]

Judge Posner's insight is particularly salient to the facts of *FTC v. Qualcomm* because, as Judge Koh acknowledged, "Qualcomm is a 'fabless' modem chip supplier, which means that QCT outsources the actual fabrication of QCT modem chips to third parties."[1773] But, while Judge Koh was evaluating Qualcomm's alleged market power, she was not mindful of the economic significance of fabless production of modems for her analysis of barriers to entry. (Later in her findings of fact and conclusions of law, Judge Koh also failed to grasp the economic salience of fabless production of modems to her analysis of an antitrust duty to deal under the *Aspen Skiing* exception.)

For example, Judge Koh did not ask whether Samsung and HiSilicon, as potential competitors of Qualcomm, could constrain its pricing of "premium" LTE modems sold to third-party OEMs. Samsung and HiSilicon already supplied LTE modems to themselves, and that capability surely reduced any market power that Qualcomm had with respect to its sales of modems to Samsung or Huawei.

Having supplied "premium" LTE modems to their own downstream smartphone businesses, Samsung and Huawei demonstrated that they had considerable knowledge and expertise with which to supply modems to third-party OEMs as well. It would contradict observed fact to assert that Samsung and Huawei, having acquired the *ability* to supply modems to third-party OEMs, for some reason lacked the *incentive* to do so. In 2016, Samsung in fact supplied its Exynos 8890 SoC modem to the Chinese OEM Meizu for use in its Pro 6 Plus smartphone.[1774] Judge Koh ignored these facts and did not examine how Samsung's or Huawei's ability to supply third-party OEMs constrained any market power that Qualcomm might allegedly possess with respect to "premium" LTE modems.

By the time of the trial in *FTC v. Qualcomm*, Apple was another obvious potential entrant and competitor facing Qualcomm. Apple was already using its own application processors in its mobile phones, and Apple did in fact soon vertically integrate into the baseband processor modem business. Indeed, press speculation about such vertical integration was occurring in

---

[1772] POSNER, ANTITRUST LAW: AN ECONOMIC PERSPECTIVE, *supra* note 1275, at 92.

[1773] *FTC v. Qualcomm*, 411 F. Supp. 3d at 674 (quoting CX7257-013).

[1774] *See INTERVIEW: Meizu Explains Why Exynos Powers Its Flagship Device*, SAMSUNG, Dec. 16, 2016, http://www.samsung.com/semiconductor/minisite/exynos/newsroom/blog/interview-meizu-explains-why-exynos-powers-its-flagship-device/.

December 2018, a month before the trial in *FTC v. Qualcomm* commenced.[1775] On July 25, 2019, barely two months after Judge Koh issued her findings of fact and conclusions of law in *FTC v. Qualcomm*, Apple announced that it would purchase the majority of Intel's modem business by the fourth quarter of 2019.[1776] Considering that Apple had cash holdings of $225.4 billion as of March 30, 2019,[1777] it would be laughable to assert that the capital requirements for it to invest in R&D for "premium" LTE modems would be so high as to bar Apple's entry.

Judge Koh did not examine whether potential competition from a vertically integrated smartphone OEM, particularly Apple, constrained whatever quantum of market power she believed Qualcomm to possess. Apple's announcement of its intention to acquire Intel's modem business was an embarrassing confirmation that Judge Koh's findings on entry and potential competition were neither reliable nor prescient. Even before Apple announced its intention to acquire Intel's modem business, substantial evidence from the LTE modem industry had disproven Judge Koh's conclusion that her relevant markets for modems exhibited high barriers to entry. Thus, Judge Koh's analysis of entry barriers exemplifies how, to borrow a phrase from Judge Posner, her May 21, 2019 opinion in *FTC v. Qualcomm* "repeatedly ventures predictions that events falsify."[1778]

4. *When Assessing Market Power, Did Judge Koh Consider How Complementarity of Demand Constrains the Profit-Maximizing Price for a Modem Because Qualcomm Is a Multiproduct Firm That Also Exhaustively Licenses a Portfolio of Cellular SEPs to OEMs?*

Judge Koh's analysis of Qualcomm's market power was analytically flawed for another reason. It ignored both the economic and legal principles for assessing the market power of a firm that, like Qualcomm, offers to sell complementary products and services.

When a firm sells complementary products, one cannot conclusively infer market power (much less infer allegedly anticompetitive effects) from

---

[1775] Chaim Gartenberg, *Looks Like Apple's Making Its Own Modem to Compete with Qualcomm*, VERGE, Dec. 12, 2018.

[1776] Press Release, Apple Inc., Apple to Acquire the Majority of Intel's Smartphone Modem Business (July 25, 2019), https://www.apple.com/newsroom/2019/07/apple-to-acquire-the-majority-of-intels-smartphone-modem-business/.

[1777] Apple Inc., Quarterly Report for the Quarterly Period Ended March 30, 2019 (SEC Form 10-Q), at 9 (filed May 1, 2019); *see also* Brittany De Lea, *These Tech Giants Have the Largest Cash Stockpiles*, FOX BUS., Nov. 27, 2018 ("Apple's [cash] holdings alone are larger than totals in any sector, with the exception of technology.").

[1778] RICHARD A. POSNER, PUBLIC INTELLECTUALS: A STUDY OF DECLINE 141 (Harvard Univ. Press 2001).

an analysis of the firm's market power over a single product in isolation.[1779] When two products are complements, an increase in the price of one will reduce the demand for the other, all other things being equal.[1780] Because of the interrelated demand for complementary products, a firm's incentive to raise the price of one product is moderated by its understanding that doing so would decrease demand for the firm's second product. Judge Posner has asked "why a firm with a monopoly of one product would want to monopolize a complementary product as well."[1781] The harm to competition in one market would reduce the profit generated by its complementary product. So, anticompetitive intent is implausible to infer.

Consider the demand for Qualcomm's complementary products. If Qualcomm were to raise the price of its "premium" LTE modems, then (to the extent that smartphone manufacturers were to pass along that increment of additional cost to end consumers) the demand for smartphones that use "premium" LTE modems would fall. The resulting decrease in demand for smartphones would, in turn, cause the derived demand for Qualcomm's cellular SEPs practiced in handsets to fall. Consequently, Qualcomm's profit from exhaustively licensing its portfolio of cellular SEPs to OEMs would also fall. The fewer smartphones sold, the lower the royalty revenues (and profits) that Qualcomm could obtain from exhaustively licensing its cellular SEP portfolio to OEMs.

On balance, the prospect of forgoing profits from cellular SEP royalties would moderate the incentive that would exist in isolation for Qualcomm to increase the price of its modems, so that the *combined* sale of a modem and an exhaustive license to an OEM would not become incrementally less profitable on balance for Qualcomm. Therefore, because the demand for Qualcomm's complementary products is interconnected, market forces diminish Qualcomm's incentive to raise the price of each of its individual products.

Stated in more explicitly economic terms, "demand interdependence and multi-market participation can serve to place natural limits on the exercise of significant market power."[1782] Hence, when a firm participates in complementary markets, giving too much weight to evidence about the firm's market share in one of the markets might lead a court mistakenly to infer the existence of significant market power, even though market forces actually

---

[1779] *See* Timothy J. Tardiff & Dennis L. Weisman, *The Dominant Firm Revisited*, 5 J. COMPETITION L. & ECON. 517, 524 (2009); Dennis L. Weisman, *Assessing Market Power: The Trade-Off Between Market Concentration and Multi-Market Participation*, 1 J. COMPETITION L. & ECON. 339, 340 (2005).

[1780] *See, e.g.,* Weisman, *Assessing Market Power: The Trade-Off Between Market Concentration and Multi-Market Participation, supra* note 1779, at 340.

[1781] POSNER, ANTITRUST LAW (2ᵈ ed.), *supra* note 948, at 198–99.

[1782] *See* Tardiff & Weisman, *The Dominant Firm Revisited, supra* note 1779, at 535.

discipline the firm's pricing behavior.[1783] That is, failure to consider demand interdependence between a firm's complementary products is likely to cause a court to overstate that firm's market power in a given market.[1784]

In 2018, the Supreme Court recognized the need to account for demand interdependence in *American Express*.[1785] The principal question in *American Express* was whether a court can properly assess a firm's conduct in a two-sided market if it ignores (1) the effect of that conduct on each of the two sides of the market and (2) the interaction between both sides of the market.[1786] The Court said no. It recognized that a company that competes in a two-sided market must optimally balance prices for each side of the market, such that the firm achieves an optimal aggregate price posture.[1787] The Court then found that "evidence of a price increase on one side of a two-sided transaction platform cannot, by itself, demonstrate an anticompetitive exercise of market power."[1788]

[1783] *Id.* ("The market share of the provider in the particular market is frequently used by regulators to draw inferences about dominance. In telecommunications markets, in particular, where demand complementarities, multi-market participation, and high price/cost margins are the norm, traditional, single-market measures of market power are likely to seriously overstate extant market power.").

[1784] *Id.* at 519, 521.

[1785] Ohio v. Am. Express Co., 138 S. Ct. 2274 (2018).

[1786] *See* J. Gregory Sidak & Robert D. Willig, *Two-Sided Market Definition and Competitive Effects for Credit Cards After* United States v. American Express, 1 CRITERION J. ON INNOVATION 1301, 1303–05 (2016). The arguments in the Sidak-Willig article are based on an amicus brief to the Second Circuit and concern the proper analysis of market definition and market power in two-sided markets for credit cards. *See* Brief for *Amici Curiae* J. Gregory Sidak, Robert D. Willig, David J. Teece, and Keith N. Hylton Scholars and Experts in Antitrust Economics in Support of Defendants-Appellants and Supporting Reversal, United States v. American Express Co., 838 F.3d 179 (2ᵈ Cir. 2016) (No. 15-1672), 2015 WL 4873717 [hereinafter Brief for *Amici Curiae* J. Gregory Sidak *et al.*]. The Second Circuit adopted the position of the amicus brief (and quoted the amicus brief extensively, though not consistently with attribution). *See* United States v. American Express Co., 838 F.3d 179, 202 (2ᵈ Cir. 2016) ("[I]ncreases in merchant fees are a concomitant of a successful investment in creating output and value.") (quoting without citation Brief for *Amici Curiae*, J. Gregory Sidak *et al.*, *supra*, at 9 ("[I]ncreases in merchant discounts are a concomitant of a successful investment in creating output and value.")); *id.* at 203 ("There is no meaningful economic difference between 'dropping American Express' . . . and a decision not to accept American Express in the first place.") (quoting Brief for *Amici Curiae*, J. Gregory Sidak *et al.*, *supra*, at 7 ("There is no meaningful economic difference between 'dropping American Express'—which the district court said would not happen and which indicates market power—and a decision not to accept American Express in the first place.")); *id.* ("A merchant chooses whether or not to accept a particular credit card based on an individualized assessment of the various costs and benefits associated with accepting that card.") (quoting without citation Brief for *Amici Curiae*, J. Gregory Sidak *et al.*, *supra*, at 7 ("A merchant chooses whether or not to accept a card based on its assessment of the costs and benefits of doing so.")). The Supreme Court affirmed the Second Circuit's disposition and reasoning. *American Express*, 138 S. Ct. at 2284.

[1787] *American Express*, 138 S. Ct. at 2281 ("To ensure sufficient participation, two-sided platforms [such as credit cards] must be sensitive to the prices that they charge each side."); *see also id.* at 2277 ("[S]triking the optimal balance of the prices charged on each side of the platform is essential for two-sided platforms to maximize the value of their services and to compete with their rivals."); *id.* at 2286 ("To optimize sales, the network must find the balance of pricing that encourages the greatest number of matches between cardholders and merchants. Because they cannot make a sale unless both sides of the platform simultaneously agree to use their services, two-sided transaction platforms exhibit more pronounced indirect network effects and interconnected pricing and demand.").

[1788] *Id.* at 2287.

The Court's analysis of "interconnected pricing and demand"[1789] in *American Express* provides important guiding principles for assessing Qualcomm's market power. Two-sided markets and indirect network effects are but two examples of demand interdependence. As Justice Stephen Breyer noted even while dissenting in *American Express*, the demand interdependence between a firm's complementary products of course does not imply that the two products (in Qualcomm's case, a modem and an exhaustive license to a portfolio of cellular SEPs) should be considered to be part of the same product market.[1790] Ignoring that Qualcomm sells complementary products would necessarily overstate Qualcomm's market power in the markets where its individual products compete.

Yet, Judge Koh did just that. She ignored the demand interdependence between Qualcomm's modems and its cellular SEPs when she assessed Qualcomm's supposed market power with respect to modems.

5. Did Judge Koh Incorrectly Reject Qualcomm's Claims About Buyers' Power?

Judge Koh rejected Qualcomm's argument that "Qualcomm lacked market power because large OEMs 'could easily retaliate in the much larger non-CDMA segments against any effort by Qualcomm to exercise monopoly power in the far smaller CDMA segment.'"[1791] Although she recognized that buyer power might be relevant in assessing a seller's market power, Judge Koh said that "Qualcomm identifie[d] no evidence that OEMs organized to attempt to force down Qualcomm's prices."[1792] Perhaps (remarkably) Qualcomm identified no such evidence, but that failure to offer proof (if it really occurred) does not mean that such evidence did not readily exist and was not open and notorious in the public square, such that Judge Koh could have taken judicial notice of it after a few moments spent visiting the Antitrust Division's website.

Judge Koh appeared to be unaware of the intense public controversy over the IEEE's 2015 bylaw amendments, which changed how RAND royalties for SEPs would be calculated for SEPs committed to IEEE standards. In a January 28, 2015 letter to Renata Hesse, the Acting Assistant Attorney General in charge of the Antitrust Division, I expressed my concern that the

---

[1789] *Id.* at 2286.

[1790] *See id.* at 2294 (Breyer, J., dissenting) ("But while the market includes substitutes, it does not include what economists call complements: goods or services that are used together with the restrained product, but that cannot be substituted for that product.") (first citing 2B PHILLIP E. AREEDA & HERBERT HOVENKAMP, ANTITRUST LAW ¶ 565(a), at 429 (Wolters Kluwer 4th ed. 2013); and then citing Eastman Kodak Co. v. Image Tech. Servs., Inc., 504 U.S. 451, 463 (1992)).

[1791] FTC v. Qualcomm Inc., 411 F. Supp. 3d 658, 689 (N.D. Cal. 2019) (quoting Qualcomm's Proposed Findings of Fact and Conclusions of Law, *supra* note 1771, at 105–06).

[1792] *Id.* at 690.

IEEE's then-proposed bylaw amendments posed a serious risk of violating section 1 of the Sherman Act by facilitating tacit or explicit collusion among implementers to suppress the royalties they pay for exhaustive licenses to cellular SEPs.[1793]

Companies that were major contributors of technology to the IEEE's standards expressed similar concerns. Ericsson told the IEEE that the proposed amendments "constitute[d] the collective establishment of mandatory, uniform license terms . . . akin to a buyer's-side cartel."[1794] Other major holders of patents essential to IEEE standards, including Qualcomm and Nokia, echoed Ericsson's concern.[1795]

Even if implementers did not collude to decrease royalties for cellular SEPs, powerful buyers acting *unilaterally* still might deter the exercise of any market power over modems possessed by Qualcomm. Judge Koh evidently ignored that a large buyer, such as Apple or Samsung, might be able to constrain Qualcomm's putative market power over modems even without resorting to collusion with other buyers.

XII. DID QUALCOMM WILLFULLY ACQUIRE OR MAINTAIN MONOPOLY POWER?

Suppose for sake of argument that Judge Koh was correct to find Qualcomm a monopolist with respect to her two product markets for modems. That finding alone would not suffice to establish that Qualcomm had violated section 2 of the Sherman Act, which of course does not prohibit the mere possession of monopoly power.[1796] To prove liability under section 2, one must also show that the monopolist engaged in conduct that "harm[s] the competitive *process* and thereby harm[s] consumers."[1797]

Judge Koh found that Qualcomm engaged in several forms of conduct that harmed competition in her relevant markets.[1798] Specifically, she found that Qualcomm (1) engaged in anticompetitive conduct against OEMs, (2) refused to offer exhaustive licenses to its cellular SEPs to rival modem manufacturers, and (3) executed exclusive supply agreements with Apple. She

---

[1793] Sidak's Letter to Hesse, *supra* note 402. The analysis leading me to have this concern over a possible buyer cartel for SEPs appeared in 2009 in Sidak, *Patent Holdup and Oligopsonistic Collusion in Standard Setting Organizations, supra* note 446. For my further criticism of the Obama Antitrust Division's handling of the business review letter concerning the IEEE's bylaw amendment, see Sidak, *The Antitrust Division's Devaluation of Standard-Essential Patents, supra* note 326.

[1794] IEEE-SA Patent Policy: Draft Comments, Second Round, *supra* note 382, cmt. 38 (comment of Dina Kallay (Director for IP and Competition, Ericsson)).

[1795] *See id.* cmt. 13 (comment of Daniel Hermele (Senior Director and Legal Counsel, Qualcomm)); *id.* cmt. 61 (comment of Jari Vaario (Legal Counsel, Nokia)).

[1796] Verizon Commc'ns Inc. v. Law Offices of Curtis V. Trinko, LLP, 540 U.S. 398, 407 (2004).

[1797] United States v. Microsoft Corp., 253 F.3d 34, 58 (D.C. Cir. 2001) (en banc) (per curiam) (emphasis in original).

[1798] FTC v. Qualcomm Inc., 411 F. Supp. 3d 658, 697–98 (N.D. Cal. 2019).

found that those practices collectively (1) led to "unreasonably high" rates for an exhaustive license to Qualcomm's cellular SEP portfolio, (2) imposed a royalty "surcharge" and a modem "tax" on the sale of modems by Qualcomm's rivals, and (3) foreclosed those rivals from the market. We will now examine why the evidence that Judge Koh summarized in her findings of fact and conclusions of law did not support her conclusion that these practices by Qualcomm were anticompetitive.

A. Did Qualcomm Engage in Anticompetitive Conduct Against OEMs?

Judge Koh found that Qualcomm "used its monopoly power in the CDMA and premium LTE modem chip markets to engage in a wide variety of anticompetitive acts against OEMs."[1799] She devoted approximately 46 of the 167 pages of her findings of fact and conclusions of law to reciting facts that supposedly established Qualcomm's "anticompetitive practices in patent license negotiations around Qualcomm's conduct toward the following OEMs: (1) LGE, (2) Sony, (3) Samsung, (4) Huawei, (5) Motorola, (6) Lenovo, (7) BlackBerry, (8) Curitel, (9) BenQ, (10) Apple, (11) VIVO, (12) Wistron, (13) Pegatron, (14) ZTE, (15) Nokia, and (16) smaller Chinese OEMs."[1800]

Judge Koh's rote recitations were formulaic and conclusory, reminiscent of a complaint that a court would dismiss on *Twombly* grounds.[1801] At times, Judge Koh even referred to facts that occurred a dozen years before Qualcomm allegedly had any monopoly power (and over 26 years before Judge Koh issued her findings of fact and conclusions of law), such that it was not clear how those facts could be relevant to determining whether Qualcomm had used its alleged monopoly power against OEMs.[1802]

[1799] *Id.* at 697.

[1800] *Id.* at 698. Judge Koh's recitation of these facts spans page 698 through page 743 of her findings of fact and conclusions of law.

[1801] Bell Atl. Corp. v. Twombly, 550 U.S. 544, 555 (2007) ("[A] formulaic recitation of the elements of a cause of action will not do.").

[1802] *FTC v. Qualcomm*, 411 F. Supp. 3d at 706 ("On September 3, 1993, Samsung and Qualcomm entered into an Infrastructure and Subscriber Unit License and Technical Assistance Agreement.") (citing Joint Stipulation Regarding Undisputed Facts, *supra* note 144, at 8). Judge Koh's findings of fact and conclusions of law in *FTC v. Qualcomm* do not mention any applicable statute of limitations under either the Sherman Act or the FTC Act that might circumscribe her issuance of a permanent, worldwide injunction. In contrast, claims for various forms of monetary relief under the Sherman Act are barred after four years, 15 U.S.C. § 15b, although the "continuing violation" doctrine can make the statute of limitations for damages elastic and thus ambiguous. *See* Hanover Shoe, Inc. v. United Shoe Mach. Corp., 392 U.S. 481, 502 n.15 (1968) (section 2 monopolization case); Zenith Radio Corp. v. Hazeltine Rsch., Inc., 401 U.S. 321, 338 (1971) (section 1 price-fixing case); *see also* Klehr v. A.O. Smith Corp., 521 U.S. 179, 189 (1997) ("Antitrust law provides that, in the case of a 'continuing violation,' say, a price-fixing conspiracy that brings about a series of unlawfully high priced sales over a period of years, 'each overt act that is part of the violation and that injures the plaintiff,' *e.g.*, each sale to the plaintiff, 'starts the statutory period running again[.]'") (quoting 2 Areeda & Hovenkamp, Antitrust Law, *supra* note 413, ¶ 338(b), at 145) (RICO case); Oliver v. SD-3C LLC, 751 F.3d 1081, 1086 (9ᵗʰ Cir. 2014) (applying *Klehr*, 521 U.S. 179). Considering that a class action sought $15 billion in treble damages from Qualcomm on the same theories of liability as those that the FTC litigated in *FTC v. Qualcomm*, *see supra* note 2, and considering the likelihood that the class would have sought to piggyback as a matter of issue preclusion on as many of Judge Koh's findings of fact and

Yet, even if one accepts all of Judge Koh's findings about Qualcomm's licensing practices against OEMs as true, those findings still would not support her conclusion that Qualcomm engaged in anticompetitive conduct. In a monopolization case, Qualcomm cannot be found to have engaged in anticompetitive conduct toward companies with which it does not compete.[1803] And *FTC v. Qualcomm* is a monopolization case, and Qualcomm is not a smartphone OEM.

1.   *Can Qualcomm Engage in Anticompetitive Conduct Against OEMs?*

In a typical instance, Judge Koh summarized some facts about a licensing dispute, with particular solicitude for the complaints of the senior management of the OEM in question. She then explained the dispute's subsequent resolution through Qualcomm's execution of a new or revised patent-licensing agreement with that OEM and the beginning or continuation of Qualcomm's shipments of modems to that exhaustively licensed OEM (or, in some cases, the beginning or continuation of a rival modem manufacturer's shipment of modems to that exhaustively licensed OEM). Judge Koh also typically found that, notwithstanding the execution of the licensing agreement with the OEM in question and the shipment of modems to that OEM, the circumstances of the licensing dispute and its subsequent resolution constituted evidence of Qualcomm's anticompetitive conduct.

Judge Koh found that "Qualcomm refuses to sell modem chips to an OEM until the OEM signs a separate patent license agreement" for Qualcomm's patents (including both SEPs and non-SEPs).[1804] Quoting *Quanta*, she observed that, "[u]nder the doctrine of patent exhaustion, 'the initial authorized sale of a patented item terminates all patent rights to that item.'"[1805] In other words, upon selling a modem to an OEM, Qualcomm could not subsequently ask the OEM to pay royalties for the patented technologies practiced within that modem. Judge Koh found that, to avoid patent exhaustion, "Qualcomm wields its chip monopoly power to coerce OEMs to sign patent

---

conclusions of law as possible, one can imagine that thorny questions concerning the applicable statute of limitations might have arisen in that class action litigation. *See* Class Action Complaint for Violations of Federal and State Antitrust Laws, State Unfair Competition Laws, and the Common Law of Unjust Enrichment at 26–28, Stromberg v. Qualcomm Inc., No. 5:17-cv-00304 (N.D. Cal. Jan. 20, 2017).

[1803] *See, e.g.*, Intergraph Corp. v. Intel Corp., 195 F.3d 1346, 1353 (Fed. Cir. 1999) ("The prohibited conduct must be directed towards competitors and must be intended to injure competition.") (citing Spectrum Sports, Inc. v. McQuillan, 506 U.S. 447, 458 (1993)). The Ninth Circuit's three-judge panel in *FTC v. Qualcomm* properly recognized this reasoning. *See* FTC v. Qualcomm Inc., No. 19-16122, 2020 WL 4591476, at *4 (9th Cir. Aug. 11, 2020) ("Qualcomm does not manufacture and sell cellphones and other end-use products (like smart cars) that consumers purchase and use. Thus, it does not 'compete'—in the antitrust sense—against OEMs like Apple and Samsung in these product markets. Instead, these OEMs are Qualcomm's *customers*.") (emphasis in original).

[1804] *FTC v. Qualcomm*, 411 F. Supp. 3d at 698.

[1805] *Id.* (quoting Quanta Comput., Inc. v. LG Elecs., Inc., 553 U.S. 617, 625 (2008)).

license agreements [before purchasing modems]."[1806] She also found that, to ensure that OEMs execute a license agreement before buying modems, "Qualcomm has cut off OEMs' chip supply, threatened OEMs' chip supply, withheld sample chips, delayed software and threatened to require the return of software, withheld technical support, and refused to share patent claim charts or patent lists."[1807]

In contrast, Derek Aberle, Qualcomm's former president, testified that Qualcomm had *never* shipped commercial quantities of chips to a company without a license.[1808] He also testified under oath that the risk that an unlicensed OEM would claim patent exhaustion if Qualcomm sold one of its modems to the OEM was not merely theoretical.[1809]

Judge Koh then found that Qualcomm's licensing practices permitted it to "generate and sustain Qualcomm's unreasonably high royalty rates" and other unfavorable license terms.[1810] (As we saw in Part IV, Professor Shapiro expressed the same opinion in his testimony.[1811]) After purporting to analyze the license agreements between Qualcomm and various OEMs, Judge Koh concluded that Qualcomm's conduct toward OEMs was anticompetitive.[1812] However, Judge Koh's finding that Qualcomm engaged in exclusionary conduct by using its alleged monopoly power over certain modems to extract from OEMs "unreasonably high" royalties for an exhaustive license to Qualcomm's cellular SEPs was neither factually supported by substantial evidence nor legally sound.

As we saw in Part VII, Judge Koh did not identify preponderant evidence to support her conclusion that OEMs paid "unreasonably high" royalties for an exhaustive license to Qualcomm's cellular SEPs. Yet, even if one assumes for sake of argument (but contrary to fact) that Qualcomm used its supposed monopoly power over certain modems to obtain from OEMs "unreasonably high" royalties for an exhaustive license to its cellular SEPs, that result still

---

[1806] *Id.*

[1807] *Id.* at 743.

[1808] Transcript of Proceedings (Volume 2) at 306:1–8, FTC v. Qualcomm Inc., No. 5:17-cv-00220-LHK (N.D. Cal. Jan. 7, 2019) (Testimony of Derek Aberle (former President, Qualcomm)) ("Q. [CX6522 (email from Derek Aberle to Enrico Salvatori and others)] says 'To my knowledge, we [Qualcomm] have never shipped commercial quantities of chips to a company without a license.' Do you see that? A. Yes. Q. And you said at this point that was a correct statement. Has, following this e-mail, Qualcomm ever shipped commercial quantities of chips to a company without a license? A. I don't believe so.").

[1809] *Id.* at 307:23–308:1 (Testimony of Derek Aberle (former President, Qualcomm)) ("Q. Why did you make the point to Mr. Mollenkopf that Huawei had been claiming patent exhaustion? A. I was trying to emphasize that it wasn't a theoretical risk . . . if we shipped [modems] to them.").

[1810] *FTC v. Qualcomm*, 411 F. Supp. 3d at 698.

[1811] Transcript of Proceedings (Volume 6) at 1120:15–16, FTC v. Qualcomm Inc., No. 5:17-cv-00220-LHK (N.D. Cal. Jan. 15, 2019) (Testimony of Carl Shapiro) ("Qualcomm . . . used its monopoly power over modem chips to extract supra-FRAND royalties from OEM's[.]"); *accord* Shapiro Demonstratives, *supra* note 114, at 3 ("Qualcomm used its monopoly power over modem chips to extract supra-FRAND royalties from OEMs[.]").

[1812] *FTC v. Qualcomm*, 411 F. Supp. 3d at 697.

would not support Judge Koh's finding of anticompetitive conduct as a matter of law.

For conduct to be anticompetitive (or exclusionary), it must "harm the competitive process,"[1813] which in *FTC v. Qualcomm* means that the conduct must have enabled Qualcomm unlawfully to acquire or maintain monopoly power. Yet, neither charging an OEM a high royalty for an exhaustive license to cellular SEPs nor imposing other unfavorable license terms on an OEM harms competition in markets for *modems*—which are the only markets that the FTC alleged, and Judge Koh found, Qualcomm to have monopolized. It necessarily follows that Qualcomm's challenged practices—allegedly directed at OEMs in a *different* market, which Judge Koh never defined—could not have increased Qualcomm's market power with respect to the two kinds of modems that Judge Koh found constituted the two relevant markets in the case. Thus, it was clearly erroneous as a matter of law for Judge Koh to have found that Qualcomm engaged in anticompetitive practices *directed at OEMs*.[1814]

2. Did Qualcomm Need to Justify Its Licensing Practice to Avoid Antitrust Liability?

In her closing argument at trial, Ms. Milici of the FTC remarkably asserted:

> [W]hether Qualcomm actually cut off chip supply is . . . just beside the point. No part of the FTC's case depends on an actual cutoff of chip supply. Qualcomm refused to sell chips to a company before it signed a license and its policy that was written into its contract and communicated to customers was to cut off supply if the customer breached or became unlicensed.[1815]

At the same time, and even more astonishingly, Ms. Milici argued that "[t]he fact that [Qualcomm] generally did not have to cut off chip supply is proof of its market power."[1816]

[1813]   United States v. Microsoft Corp., 253 F.3d 34, 58 (D.C. Cir. 2001) (en banc) (per curiam).

[1814]   The FTC did not plead a tying claim. But in its opening argument at trial the agency nonetheless attacked what it called Qualcomm's "process of tieing [sic] the sale of chips to licensing." Transcript of Proceedings (Volume 1) at 16:23, FTC v. Qualcomm Inc., No. 5:17-cv-00220-LHK (N.D. Cal. Jan. 4, 2019) (opening statement of Jennifer Milici for the FTC). Elsewhere, the FTC told Judge Koh that "Qualcomm will not sell modem chips to a customer unless the customer takes a separate license to Qualcomm's standard essential pat[ent]s." *Id.* at 7:3–5. And in its closing argument at trial the FTC again said that Qualcomm was "tying chips and licenses." Transcript of Proceedings (Volume 11) at 2103:23–24, FTC v. Qualcomm Inc., No. 5:17-cv-00220-LHK (N.D. Cal. Jan. 29, 2019) (closing argument of Jennifer Milici for the FTC). Judge Koh did not address in her findings of fact and conclusions of law whether Qualcomm's licensing practices satisfied the elements necessary to prove unlawful tying.

[1815]   Transcript of Proceedings (Volume 11) at 2112:10–15, FTC v. Qualcomm Inc., No. 5:17-cv-00220-LHK (N.D. Cal. Jan. 29, 2019) (closing argument of Jennifer Milici for the FTC).

[1816]   *Id.* at 2112:16–17.

The net effect of this interpretation of law by the FTC, if taken seriously, would be radical. It would make *per se* unlawful Qualcomm's practice of requiring an OEM to secure an exhaustive license to Qualcomm's cellular SEPs before purchasing Qualcomm modems. Under the FTC's interpretation of the law, there was *no* evidence that Qualcomm could proffer to prove its innocence. *Actually* cutting off an OEM's supply to Qualcomm modems—something that was never Qualcomm's licensing policy—would be, in Ms. Milici's words, "just beside the point." Yet, *not* cutting off an OEM's supply to Qualcomm modems would be proof of Qualcomm's market power, according to the FTC. Needless to say, if Qualcomm did anything more than breathe once it had been deemed to possess market power, the FTC would surely argue that Qualcomm had unlawfully acquired or maintained a monopoly and harmed competition.

The FTC's argument was erroneous for multiple reasons, but the most fundamental reason was the agency's implicit premise that Qualcomm bore the burden to prove its innocence. The practical effect of the FTC's theory, which Judge Koh embraced in her findings of fact and conclusions of law, would be to reverse the burden of production and the burden persuasion—and thus reverse the presumption of innocence. That outcome would of course defy many Supreme Court cases that emphasize that *per se* illegality in antitrust law is reserved for familiar forms of anticompetitive conduct, like horizontal price fixing, that the courts, by their experience over an extended period of time, have safely concluded injure consumers and do not possibly offer an offsetting procompetitive business justification.[1817] Yet, even Ms. Milici, when discussing Qualcomm's licensing model in her closing argument for the FTC, said that "it bears repeating that this policy is *unique*."[1818]

A unique business model is not an antitrust violation. Nor are conformity and reversion to the mean plausibly the virtues manifesting the "business acumen" that the Supreme Court extolled in *Grinnell* and *Trinko*. The herd does not reify "creative destruction." Judge Koh's finding of fact—casting suspicion as it did on Qualcomm because of its uniqueness—was clearly erroneous.

B. Did Qualcomm Violate Antitrust Law by Refusing to Offer Exhaustive Licenses to Its Cellular SEPs to Rival Modem Manufacturers?

Judge Koh found that "another element of Qualcomm's anticompetitive conduct" was "Qualcomm's practice of refusing to license its cellular SEPs to

---

[1817] *See, e.g.*, Broadcast Music, Inc. v. Columbia Broad. Sys., Inc., 441 U.S. 1, 1 (1979); NCAA v. Bd. of Regents of Univ. of Okla., 468 U.S. 85, 98 (1984); Northwest Wholesale Stationers, Inc. v. Pac. Stationery & Printing Co., 472 U.S. 284, 289 (1985); FTC v. Ind. Fed'n of Dentists, 476 U.S. 447, 458–59 (1986).

[1818] Transcript of Proceedings (Volume 11) at 2114:15, FTC v. Qualcomm Inc., No. 5:17-cv-00220-LHK (N.D. Cal. Jan. 29, 2019) (closing argument of Jennifer Milici for the FTC) (emphasis added).

rival modem chip suppliers."[1819] Again, as we saw in Part IV, Professor Shapiro similarly testified that "the no license, no chips working together with the refusal to license rivals set up a situation where Qualcomm was able to use its chip leverage to bring to bear in negotiations with OEM's to get unreasonably high royalties on its cellular SEPs, and critically so that when an OEM purchased a modem chip from a rival of Qualcomm, they would be paying Qualcomm more than a reasonable amount."[1820]

Judge Koh found that "Qualcomm has previously licensed its modem chip SEPs to rivals,"[1821] but that it stopped doing so because it "determined that it was far more lucrative to license only OEMs."[1822] As we saw earlier, Judge Koh was failing to acknowledge that a "license" to Qualcomm's cellular SEPs meant something quite different after the Supreme Court had begun a decade of overturning Federal Circuit decisions on patent exhaustion. A "license" thereafter could convey only an exhaustive grant of the rights that inhere in Qualcomm's cellular SEPs. Ignoring the economic significance of the Supreme Court's gutting of Federal Circuit precedent on the doctrine of patent exhaustion, Judge Koh found that, because Qualcomm terminated what she assumed was a profitable course of dealing, and because such a decision by Qualcomm was in her assessment motivated by "anticompetitive malice," Qualcomm's refusal to offer exhaustive licenses to its cellular SEPs to rival modem manufacturers fell within the exception to a monopolist's general right to refuse to deal with rivals that the Supreme Court recognized in *Aspen Skiing*.[1823]

To the contrary, the Ninth Circuit in *FTC v. Qualcomm* observed that Judge Koh's "conclusion that Qualcomm's refusal to provide exhaustive SEP licenses to rival chip suppliers meets the *Aspen Skiing* exception ignores critical differences between Qualcomm's business practices and the conduct at issue in *Aspen Skiing*, and it ignores the Supreme Court's subsequent warning in *Trinko* that the *Aspen Skiing* exception should be applied only in

---

[1819] *FTC v. Qualcomm*, 411 F. Supp. 3d at 744.

[1820] Transcript of Proceedings (Volume 6) at 1175:2–9, FTC v. Qualcomm Inc., No. 5:17-cv-00220-LHK (N.D. Cal. Jan. 15, 2019) (Testimony of Carl Shapiro); *accord* Shapiro Demonstratives, *supra* note 114, at 3 ("Qualcomm's no-license/no-chips policy together with Qualcomm's refusal to license its standard-essential patents to its modem-chip rivals harmed competition[.]"); *see also* Transcript of Proceedings (Volume 6) at 1139:21–23, 1140:1–7, 1140:9–10, FTC v. Qualcomm Inc., No. 5:17-cv-00220-LHK (N.D. Cal. Jan. 15, 2019) (Testimony of Carl Shapiro) ("I think you can see that I work through the economic effect of the refusal to license, Qualcomm's refusal to license to the rivals. . . . When the rivals—they're not paying the license, they're not paying the royalties directly to Qualcomm. But when they sell the chips, their customers have to pay an unreasonably high royalty to Qualcomm. That is economically equivalent to the rivals themselves having to pay that unreasonably high royalty. It doesn't matter which side of the transaction is paying the tax, the economics are exactly the same. . . . They are being harmed, the rivals are being harmed because of the surcharge that their customers have to pay.").

[1821] *FTC v. Qualcomm*, 411 F. Supp. 3d at 752.

[1822] *Id.* at 753.

[1823] *Id.* at 760–62 (construing Aspen Skiing Co. v. Aspen Highlands Skiing Corp., 472 U.S. 585, 602 (1985)).

rare circumstances."[1824] Apart from failing to recognize the supervening legal and economic relevance of the Supreme Court's recent decisions on patent exhaustion, Judge Koh badly misinterpreted the gradient in the Court's antitrust jurisprudence on monopolization. *Aspen Skiing*'s star is setting, not rising. For Judge Koh's reasoning on Qualcomm's supposed antitrust duty to deal to withstand appellate review, the Supreme Court would need to construe the *Aspen Skiing* exception to swallow the rule of *Trinko*[1825] and *linkLine*[1826] on unilateral refusals to deal. That outcome seems remote.

Furthermore, as we shall see below, the salient facts in *FTC v. Qualcomm* differed significantly from the facts in *Aspen Skiing* and did not support Judge Koh's departure from the Supreme Court's general rule that a firm may freely choose with whom to do business. Judge Koh's conclusion about Qualcomm's supposed antitrust duty to offer exhaustive licenses to its cellular SEPs to rival modem manufacturers misread controlling precedent of both the Supreme Court and the Ninth Circuit. No wonder the FTC disavowed before the Ninth Circuit Judge Koh's imposition of liability on the basis of *Aspen Skiing*.

1.   Does a Patent Holder's Refusal to Offer an Exhaustive License to a Competitor Violate Antitrust Law?

The Sherman Act does not obligate a firm, even a firm possessing monopoly power, to deal with its competitors. "As a general rule," the Supreme Court said in *linkLine*, "businesses are free to choose the parties with whom they will deal, as well as the prices, terms, and conditions of that dealing."[1827] In *Trinko*, the Court considered whether a vertically integrated incumbent local exchange carrier (ILEC) had violated section 2 of the Sherman Act by refusing to provide its downstream competitors access to its network infrastructure, over which the ILEC was deemed to have a monopoly. The Court reiterated its 1919 ruling in *Colgate* that the Sherman Act "'does not restrict the long recognized right of [a] trader or manufacturer . . . to exercise his own independent discretion as to parties with whom he will deal.'"[1828] The Court in *Trinko* reasoned:

> Firms may acquire monopoly power by establishing an infrastructure that renders them uniquely suited to serve their customers. Compelling such firms to share the source of their advantage is in some tension with the underlying purpose of antitrust law, since it may lessen the incentive for

---

[1824] FTC v. Qualcomm Inc., No. 19-16122, 2020 WL 4591476, at *12 (9th Cir. Aug. 11, 2020).

[1825] Verizon Commc'ns Inc. v. Law Offices of Curtis V. Trinko, LLP, 540 U.S. 398, 407–08 (2004).

[1826] Pacific Bell Tel. Co. v. linkLine Commc'ns, Inc., 555 U.S. 438, 448 (2009).

[1827] *Id.*; *see also In re* Adderall XR Antitrust Litig., 754 F.3d 128, 134 (2d Cir. 2014).

[1828] *Trinko*, 540 U.S. at 408 (first alteration in original) (quoting United States v. Colgate & Co., 250 U.S. 300, 307 (1919)).

the monopolist, the rival, or both to invest in those economically beneficial facilities.[1829]

Indeed, a firm's ability to profit from advantages obtained through costly investment in R&D (or in other risky deployments of sunk assets) is essential to competition. That ability motivates firms to make risky investments in innovation in the first place.[1830] Thus, subject to a caveat that we will examine presently in Part XII.B.2, a monopolist may refuse to deal with its competitors without facing the risk that an American court will condemn that refusal as anticompetitive.[1831]

This same principle applies with even greater force when a company's refusal to deal with a competitor concerns a patent right. The Patent Act expressly gives a patent holder the right to make exclusive use of its patented invention.[1832] The Act specifies that a refusal to offer an exhaustive patent license does not constitute patent misuse or an illegal extension of the patent right.[1833] Considering a refusal to offer an exhaustive patent license to be unlawful merely because it addresses a competitor would undermine the Patent Act's purpose.[1834] Basic economics teaches that forcing a firm to share its patented technologies with its rivals would facilitate free riding, reduce incentives to invest in innovation, and in the long run decrease rather than increase competition in technologically dynamic industries.[1835] Consequently, in the words of the Areeda-Hovenkamp antitrust treatise, American courts "have almost uniformly held that a refusal to license [a patent] cannot be an antitrust violation."[1836]

[1829] *Id.* at 407–08.

[1830] *See* Kenneth J. Arrow, *Economic Welfare and the Allocation of Resources for Invention, in* The Rate and Direction of Inventive Activity: Economic and Social Factors 609, 616–17 (Richard R. Nelson ed., Princeton Univ. Press 1962).

[1831] *See, e.g.,* Aerotec Int'l, Inc. v. Honeywell Int'l, Inc., 836 F.3d 1171, 1184 (9th Cir. 2016); Four Corners Nephrology Assocs., P.C. v. Mercy Med. Ctr., 582 F.3d 1216, 1226 (10th Cir. 2009) (Gorsuch, J.).

[1832] *See* 35 U.S.C. § 271(a) ("[W]hoever *without authority* makes, uses, offers to sell, or sells any patented invention, within the United States or imports into the United States any patented invention during the term of the patent therefor, infringes the patent.") (emphasis added).

[1833] *Id.* § 271(d)(4) ("No patent owner . . . shall be denied relief or deemed guilty of misuse or illegal extension of the patent right by reason of his having . . . refused to license or use any rights to the patent.").

[1834] *See, e.g.,* 3 Areeda & Hovenkamp, Antitrust Law, *supra* note 416, ¶ 709(b)(1) ("To interpret the highly general and older language of the Sherman Act or the Clayton Act inconsistently with the highly specific and newer language of the Patent Act would frustrate Congress's intentions to protect the refusal to license.").

[1835] *See, e.g.,* Samuelson & Nordhaus, Economics, *supra* note 169, at 277 ("The purpose [of intellectual property rights] is to give the owner special protection against the material's being copied and used by others without compensation to the owner or original creator."); Robert S. Pindyck & Daniel L. Rubinfeld, Microeconomics 668 (Pearson 9th ed. 2018) (recognizing that the inability to prevent free riding produces a socially suboptimal level of investment).

[1836] 3 Areeda & Hovenkamp, Antitrust Law, *supra* note 416, ¶ 709(b)(1). *But see* Image Tech. Servs., Inc. v. Eastman Kodak Co., 125 F.3d 1195, 1219–20 (9th Cir. 1997) (finding that Kodak's desire to protect its patent rights "was a presumptively legitimate business justification" for a refusal to sell photocopier and micrographic components to individual service operators (ISOs)—which compete with Kodak in the market for repair services—but that evidence rebutted that presumption). In finding that evidence

2. *The* Aspen Skiing *Exception*

In 1985, the Supreme Court created in *Aspen Skiing* an exception to the rule that a firm has no antitrust duty to deal with its competitors, finding that a monopolist violated the Sherman Act by refusing to continue a profitable course of dealing with a competitor.[1837] In 1962, three independent operators of skiing facilities in Aspen, Colorado started offering an interchangeable admission ticket that enabled skiers to visit any of the three facilities at the Aspen resort.[1838] By 1967, Ski Co., one of the operators, had acquired one of the competing facilities and opened another facility, such that it operated three of the four skiing facilities in Aspen.[1839] Ski Co. continued to offer interchangeable tickets until 1978, when it ceased the practice and refused to include its remaining competitor, Highlands, in Ski Co.'s advertising campaigns.[1840]

Highland successfully sued Ski Co. under section 2 of the Sherman Act.[1841] After the Tenth Circuit affirmed, the Supreme Court granted *certiorari* to decide this question: whether "a firm with monopoly power has a duty to cooperate with its smaller rivals in a marketing arrangement in order to avoid violating § 2 of the Sherman Act."[1842] The Supreme Court affirmed.

The Court reasoned that Ski Co. "did not merely reject a novel offer to participate in a cooperative venture that had been proposed by a competitor," but rather "elected to make an important change in a pattern of distribution that had originated in a competitive market[.]"[1843] The Court emphasized that "[s]uch a decision is not necessarily anticompetitive."[1844] Yet, the Court observed that the jury found no business justification for Ski Co.'s decision to discontinue interchangeable tickets. Considering that finding of fact, the Court said that "[t]he jury *may well have concluded* that Ski Co. elected to forgo these short-run benefits [resulting from the cooperation with its smaller

---

rebutted Kodak's procompetitive rationale, the Ninth Circuit observed in *Kodak*, to the contrary of the evidence in *FTC v. Qualcomm*, that "the district court commented that Kodak was not actually motivated by protecting its intellectual property rights." *Id.* at 1219. The Department of Justice and the FTC criticized the Ninth Circuit's reasoning in *Kodak* because of the practical difficulties associated with adopting the court's subjective motivation standard, and the agencies distanced themselves from the decision a dozen years before Judge Koh's decision in *FTC v. Qualcomm*. *See* U.S. Dep't of Justice & Fed. Trade Comm'n, Antitrust Enforcement and Intellectual Property Rights: Promoting Innovation and Competition 17 (2007).

[1837] Aspen Skiing Co. v. Aspen Highlands Skiing Corp., 472 U.S. 585, 611 (1985). For a detailed discussion of the business practices being challenged in *Aspen Skiing*, as well as the questionable finding of monopoly power in the case (which was not part of the appeal to the Supreme Court), see Abbott B. Lipsky, Jr. & J. Gregory Sidak, *Essential Facilities*, 51 Stan. L. Rev. 1187, 1207–11 (1999).

[1838] *Aspen Skiing*, 472 U.S. at 589.

[1839] *Id.* at 589–90.

[1840] *Id.* at 590.

[1841] *Id.* at 595.

[1842] *Id.* at 587.

[1843] *Id.* at 603.

[1844] *Id.* at 604.

rival] because it was more interested in reducing competition in the Aspen market over the long run by harming its smaller competitor."[1845] The Court later observed in *Trinko* that Ski Co.'s "unwillingness to renew the ticket *even if compensated at retail price* revealed a distinctly anticompetitive bent."[1846]

Thus, in *Aspen Skiing*, the Court carved out an exception to the general rule that there is no antitrust duty to deal with a competitor. Two necessary (but not sufficient) requirements for conduct to fall under *Aspen Skiing*'s exception to a monopolist's right to refuse to deal with a competitor are (1) evidence that a monopolist ended a presumably profitable existing course of dealing with a competitor and (2) evidence, as the Court later explained in *Trinko*, of a monopolist's "willingness to forsake short-term profits to achieve an anticompetitive end."[1847]

It bears emphasis, however, that the Court said in *Trinko* in 2004 that "*Aspen* is at or near the outer boundary of § 2 liability."[1848] Several courts, including the Ninth Circuit,[1849] have since found *Aspen Skiing*'s exception to apply only if the decision to end an existing cooperative arrangement has *no* reasonable explanation other than to harm competition.[1850] Most significantly, in *Novell v. Microsoft*, Justice Neil Gorsuch, then a Circuit Judge on the Tenth Circuit, wrote for that court that, to establish the existence of an antitrust duty to deal, the plaintiff must present both evidence that a change in conduct sacrificed short-term profit and that the conduct is "irrational but for its anticompetitive effect."[1851] Similarly, in *Aerotec v. Honeywell*, Judge Margaret McKeown wrote for the Ninth Circuit in 2016 that an antitrust duty to deal with a competitor might arise if "the *only* conceivable rationale [for] or purpose [of ending a preexisting course of cooperation] is 'to sacrifice short-term benefits in order to obtain higher profits in the long run from the exclusion of competition.'"[1852] Other courts have also required evidence that the preexisting cooperation with the monopolist is essential for the smaller rival to compete in the market. A year after the Supreme Court's decision in *Aspen Skiing*, Judge Posner wrote for the Seventh Circuit in *Olympia Equipment Leasing Co. v. Western Union Telegraph Co.* that, if *Aspen Skiing* "stands for any principle that goes beyond its unusual facts, it is that a monopolist may be guilty of monopolization if it refuses to cooperate with a

---

[1845] *Id.* at 608 (emphasis added).

[1846] Verizon Commc'ns Inc. v. Law Offices of Curtis V. Trinko, LLP, 540 U.S. 398, 409 (2004) (emphasis in original).

[1847] *Id.* at 399; *see also* Novell, Inc. v. Microsoft Corp., 731 F.3d 1064, 1075 (10th Cir. 2013) (Gorsuch, J.).

[1848] *Trinko*, 540 U.S. at 399; *see also In re* Adderall XR Antitrust Litig., 754 F.3d 128, 134 (2d Cir. 2014).

[1849] Aerotec Int'l, Inc. v. Honeywell Int'l, Inc., 836 F.3d 1171, 1184 (9th Cir. 2016) (quoting MetroNet Servs. Corp. v. Qwest Corp., 383 F.3d 1124, 1132 (9th Cir. 2004)); *see also* Trendsettah USA, Inc. v. Swisher Int'l, Inc., 761 F. App'x 714, 716 (9th Cir. 2019).

[1850] *See* Brief for the United States as Amicus Curiae in Support of Neither Party at 17, Viamedia, Inc. v. Comcast Corp., No. 18-2852 (7th Cir. Nov. 8, 2018).

[1851] *Novell*, 731 F.3d at 1075 (Gorsuch, J.).

[1852] *Aerotec*, 836 F.3d at 1184 (emphasis added) (quoting *MetroNet*, 383 F.3d at 1132).

competitor in circumstances where some cooperation is *indispensable* to effective competition."[1853]

In sum, at the time that Judge Koh issued her findings of fact and conclusions of law in *FTC v. Qualcomm* in May 2019, it had long been established by the Supreme Court, the Ninth Circuit, and other Circuits that the reasoning of *Aspen Skiing* applies only in *exceptional* cases.

3.   Did Qualcomm's Conduct Fit the Aspen Skiing Exception?

Judge Koh found that Qualcomm refused to offer exhaustive licenses to its cellular SEPs to rival modem manufacturers on several occasions. Yet, she did not consistently say in her findings of fact and conclusions of law whether a particular rival modem manufacturer on a particular occasion sought an *exhaustive* license to Qualcomm's cellular SEPs. We can infer, pursuant to the analysis in Part III, that every request for a "license" from Qualcomm in or after 2008 was necessarily a request for an exhaustive license. The *single* request for a "license" that preceded 2008 that Judge Koh identified in her findings of fact and conclusions of law was a request by Intel in 2004, and she specifically noted that Intel's request in 2004 was for an *exhaustive* license.[1854]

Although Judge Koh did not consistently say whether the noun "license," when used before 2008, denoted a *nonexhaustive* "license" or an exhaustive license, for purposes of precision, let us observe that distinction throughout this part. A similar distinction must be made when "license" is used as a verb. When Judge Koh referred to Qualcomm's having "licensed" its cellular SEPs to a rival modem manufacturer, I enclose "license," "licensed," and "licensing" in quotation marks to denote that such "licenses" preceded 2008 and thus were thought to be nonexhaustive in light of the then-controlling Federal Circuit case law on exhaustion.

Judge Koh found the following:

1.   In 2004 and 2009, Qualcomm refused to offer an exhaustive license to its cellular SEPs to Intel.[1855]

2.   In 2008, Qualcomm refused to offer an exhaustive license to its cellular SEPs to MediaTek.[1856]

3.   In 2009, Qualcomm refused to offer an exhaustive license to its cellular SEPs to HiSilicon.[1857]

[1853] Olympia Equip. Leasing Co. v. W. Union Tel. Co., 797 F.2d 370, 379 (7th Cir. 1986) (emphasis added).

[1854] *See* FTC v. Qualcomm Inc., 411 F. Supp. 3d 658, 748 (N.D. Cal. 2019) ("Thus, [Steve] Altman acknowledged that *Qualcomm could not agree to patent exhaustion* because doing so would reduce QTL's licensing revenues, which comprised 'a very substantial portion of the company's revenue and profit.'") (emphasis added) (quoting CX7580-001 (email from Steve Altman)).

[1855] *Id.* at 747–48.

[1856] *Id.* at 744–45.

[1857] *Id.* at 748–49.

4. In 2011, Qualcomm refused to offer an exhaustive license to its cellular SEPs to Project Dragonfly, a joint venture that⁾ NTT DoCoMo, several Japanese OEMs, and Samsung formed "to design, develop, and sell modem chips."[1858]

5. In 2011 and 2017, Qualcomm refused to offer an exhaustive license to its cellular SEPs to Samsung.[1859]

6. In 2015, Qualcomm refused to offer an exhaustive license to its cellular SEPs to LGE, an OEM that was not manufacturing modems but, according to Judge Koh, nonetheless "wanted a license just in case."[1860]

7. At some unidentified point or points in time, Qualcomm refused to offer a license to its cellular SEPs to Broadcom and Texas Instruments.[1861] Because Judge Koh did not report the date(s) of this refusal (or these refusals) to license by Qualcomm, one cannot tell from her findings of fact and conclusions of law whether the refusal(s) occurred before or after the Supreme Court began revisiting the doctrine of patent exhaustion in 2008.

8. At some unidentified point in time, Qualcomm refused to offer a license to its cellular SEPs to VIA (although it is not clear from Judge Koh's findings of fact and conclusions of law whether VIA ever requested such a license).[1862] Again, because Judge Koh did not report the date of this refusal to license by Qualcomm, one cannot tell from her findings of fact and conclusions of law whether the refusal occurred before or after the Supreme Court began revisiting the doctrine of patent exhaustion in 2008.

Judge Koh found that Qualcomm's refusal to offer exhaustive licenses to its cellular SEPs to rival modem manufacturers fit within *Aspen Skiing*'s exception to a firm's unilateral right to refuse to deal with a competitor.[1863] Yet, for at least the seven reasons discussed below, the evidence that Judge Koh cited in her findings of fact and conclusions of law was not probative and persuasive.

[1858] *Id.* at 745.

[1859] *Id.* at 746; *id.* at 750–51. Judge Koh was presumably referring to Samsung's modem business, as she recognized elsewhere in her findings of fact and conclusions of law that Qualcomm had executed license agreements with Samsung in its capacity as an OEM for its use of Qualcomm's cellular SEPs in Samsung's handsets. *See, e.g., id.* at 705–10.

[1860] *Id.* at 750.

[1861] *Id.* at 749.

[1862] *Id.* at 746–47.

[1863] *Id.* at 758.

a. Did Qualcomm Change Its Licensing Practice?

First, Judge Koh relied heavily on the record of Qualcomm's meeting in July 2012 with the Internal Revenue Service (IRS) to support her conclusion of law that Qualcomm's refusal to offer exhaustive licenses to its cellular SEPs to rival modem manufacturers fit the *Aspen Skiing* exception. Recall that Part III showed how Judge Koh repeatedly cited the record of Qualcomm's meeting with the IRS to support her finding that, in the past, Qualcomm had "licensed" its cellular SEPs to rival modem manufacturers, but that it subsequently stopped doing so.[1864]

Judge Koh's implication was that Qualcomm's alleged change in its practice of offering "licenses" to its cellular SEPs to rival modem manufacturers was comparable to the conduct that the Supreme Court condemned in *Aspen Skiing*. That implication was specious. In actuality, the IRS meeting record materially tends to exculpate Qualcomm—something that Judge Koh evidently did not understand and certainly did not explain in her findings of fact and conclusions of law in *FTC v. Qualcomm*.

As we saw in Part III, the FTC admitted that Qualcomm had *never* licensed its cellular SEPs exhaustively to rival modem manufacturers.[1865] Instead, Qualcomm had always licensed its cellular SEPs exhaustively only to OEMs. Licenses with OEMs historically generated the substantial majority of Qualcomm's licensing revenues. At some point in the past, Qualcomm also offered to rival modem manufacturers what were thought at the time of their

---

[1864] *See, e.g., id.* at 753 ("'The standard form for ASICs was a license, and royalties were charged. That was a limited license, but royalties were charged, and that changed some years ago so that it is now no longer a license and there are no royalties charged.'") (quoting IRS Transcript, *supra* note 503, at 22:18–22 (Fabian Gonell (Legal Counsel and Senior Vice President, Licensing Strategy, Qualcomm Technology Licensing))); *id.* at 756 ("However, Qualcomm's own recorded statements to the IRS show that Qualcomm used to license rival modem chip suppliers, and that Qualcomm stopped licensing rivals because it is more lucrative to license only OEMs."); *id.* at 753 ("Moreover, in a 1999 email, Steve Altman (then a Qualcomm lawyer, later Qualcomm President) stated to Marv Blecker (QTL Senior Vice President) that Qualcomm had licensed modem chip suppliers: 'ASIC licensees pay royalties to QUALCOMM at 3% with no minimum dollar amount.'") (quoting CX8177-001 (email from Steve Altman)); *id.* at 760 ("Qualcomm previously licensed its rivals, as its FRAND commitments require. For example, Fabian Gonell (now QTL Legal Counsel and Senior Vice President, Licensing Strategy) told the IRS that Qualcomm had licensed rival modem chip suppliers: 'The standard form for ASICs was a license, and royalties were charged.' ASIC is another term for modem chip.") (quoting IRS Transcript, *supra* note 503, at 22:18–22 (Fabian Gonell (Legal Counsel and Senior Vice President, Licensing Strategy, Qualcomm Technology Licensing))); *id.* at 762 ("For example, in the 2012 IRS meeting, Qualcomm admitted that Qualcomm has licensed its SEPs to modem chip suppliers for royalties. Fabian Gonell (now QTL Legal Counsel and Senior Vice President, Licensing Strategy) told the IRS that Qualcomm had licensed modem chip rivals and 'royalties were charged.'") (quoting IRS Transcript, *supra* note 503, at 22:18–22 (Fabian Gonell (Legal Counsel and Senior Vice President, Licensing Strategy, Qualcomm Technology Licensing))); *id.* at 821 ("Although Qualcomm claims such a remedy is inconsistent with industry practice, Qualcomm conceded to the IRS in 2012 that Qualcomm licensed modem chip suppliers only until Qualcomm decided that licensing OEMs at the handset level instead was 'humongously more lucrative.' Thus, Qualcomm itself has licensed its SEPs to rival modem chip suppliers.") (quoting IRS Transcript, *supra* note 503, at 71:18–23 (Fabian Gonell (Legal Counsel and Senior Vice President, Licensing Strategy, Qualcomm Technology Licensing))).

[1865] *See supra* note 485 and accompanying text.

execution to be nonexhaustive "licenses to make and sell *but not use*"[1866] certain of Qualcomm's claimed inventions to achieve mutual freedom to operate (and in exchange for a modest royalty). Around the time that the Supreme Court began to revisit the patent exhaustion doctrine in 2008, Qualcomm continued licensing its cellular SEPs exhaustively only to OEMs, but it revised its agreements with rival modem manufacturers so as to preserve the mutual freedom to operate but to reduce the risk that such agreements might be found to exhaust Qualcomm's patent rights.[1867]

Although Judge Koh acknowledged that the "license" agreements that Qualcomm executed with rival modem manufacturers were "limited," she evidently failed to recognize the considerable legal significance of the fact that those "licenses" preceding 2008 were understood at the time of their execution to be nonexhaustive.[1868] She observed that, "when Qualcomm licensed rival modem chip suppliers, revenue from those licenses amounted to only a tiny fraction of Qualcomm's handset royalty revenues."[1869] Approximately 95 percent of Qualcomm's licensing revenue flowed from royalties collected from OEMs.[1870] In addition, Judge Koh acknowledged that "Eric Reifschneider (QTL Senior Vice President and General Manager) told the IRS that if Qualcomm continued to license rival modem chip suppliers, a rival's modem chip sale to an OEM could prevent Qualcomm from collecting royalties from the OEM."[1871]

Despite making these statements in her findings of fact and conclusions of law, Judge Koh evidently did not comprehend the considerable relevance of those statements. Instead, she evidently concluded that the change in the nature of the agreements that Qualcomm executed with rival modem manufacturers was comparable to the termination of the cooperative marketing agreement that the jury in *Aspen Skiing* found to be anticompetitive. However, that analogy would be mistaken, because at no point in the past had Qualcomm ever offered an exhaustive license to its cellular SEPs to any rival modem manufacturer.

[1866] IRS Transcript, *supra* note 503, at 23:4 (Marv Blecker (Senior Vice President, Qualcomm Technology Licensing)) (emphasis added).

[1867] Deposition of Scott McGregor, *supra* note 1751, at 156:16–25 ("Q[.] At some point did Broadcom acquire a license to Qualcomm's standard essential patents? A[.] No, but yes. And so I don't think it's a license. I think it's a mutual non-assert, but anyway, I've read a lot of legal documents in my life but the Broadcom Qualcomm contract between us is the most complex by far of any document I have ever seen. So I will—I will try not to characterize exactly what it is but I think it's more like a non-assert than a license.").

[1868] *FTC v. Qualcomm*, 411 F. Supp. 3d at 753 (quoting IRS Transcript, *supra* note 503, at 22:18–22 (Fabian Gonell (Legal Counsel and Senior Vice President, Licensing Strategy, Qualcomm Technology Licensing))).

[1869] *Id.*

[1870] *Id.*

[1871] *Id.* at 754.

Consequently, Judge Koh's finding that Qualcomm's conduct violated *Aspen Skiing* was not only legally unfounded, but also contrary to the evidence that she herself cited in her findings of fact and conclusions of law.

b.   *The Absence of Evidence of an Existing Course of Dealing Between Qualcomm and Any of the Firms That Judge Koh Identified*

The second deficiency in Judge Koh's conclusion that Qualcomm's conduct satisfied the *Aspen Skiing* exception was that she did not establish a single instance in which Qualcomm terminated an *existing* course of dealing with any of the rival modem manufacturers that I listed at the beginning of this section (because Judge Koh had specifically listed them in her findings of fact and conclusions of law).[1872] Judge Koh did find that "Qualcomm told the IRS in 2012 that Qualcomm [had] previously licensed its modem chips to rival modem chip suppliers," by which we can only presume that she meant that Qualcomm had previously "licensed" its cellular SEPs nonexhaustively to rival modem chip suppliers.[1873] But Judge Koh did not identify *any* of those previously "licensed" rivals. She also cited in her findings of fact and conclusions of law a 1999 email from Steve Altman (then a Qualcomm lawyer and later Qualcomm President) to Marv Blecker (QTL Senior Vice President) as evidence that Qualcomm had "licensed" modem chip suppliers.[1874] But, again, Judge Koh did not identify a single one of those previously "licensed" rivals.

The evidence that Judge Koh cited suggested that, at some indeterminate point in the past before 1999, Qualcomm had executed "license" agreements with some unidentified manufacturer or manufacturers of modems. Yet, it did not follow from anything that Judge Koh reported in her findings of fact and conclusions of law in *FTC v. Qualcomm* that Qualcomm had executed a "license" agreement with MediaTek, Samsung, HiSilicon, VIA, LGE, Broadcom, Intel, Project Dragonfly, or Texas Instruments. Because Judge Koh did not establish that Qualcomm had an existing course of dealing with any of *those* companies, she failed to identify any factual nexus from which to conclude that Qualcomm's refusal to offer an exhaustive license to its cellular SEPs to any of *those* companies terminated an existing course of dealing. This deficiency in Judge Koh's findings of fact and conclusions of law was yet another example of her failure to make special findings of highly material facts, as Federal Rule of Civil Procedure 52(a)(1) required her to do following the bench trial in *FTC v. Qualcomm*.

Judge Koh should have recognized as a matter of antitrust law that this failure of proof would invalidate her reliance on *Aspen Skiing*. The Supreme

---

[1872]   *See supra* notes 1855–1862 and accompanying text.
[1873]   *FTC v. Qualcomm*, 411 F. Supp. 3d at 752–53.
[1874]   *Id.* at 754.

Court emphasized in *Trinko* that in *Aspen Skiing* it had "found significance in the defendant's decision to *cease participation* in a cooperative venture."[1875] Indeed, lower courts have interpreted *Aspen Skiing* to require proof that the monopolist ended an existing cooperative arrangement with a rival.[1876] In 2013 in *Novell v. Microsoft*, Justice Neil Gorsuch, then sitting on the Tenth Circuit, wrote for his court:

> To be sure, requiring a preexisting course of dealing as a precondition to antitrust liability risks the possibility that monopolists might be dissuaded from cooperating with rivals even in procompetitive joint venture arrangements—for fear that, once in them, they can never get out. Inversely, this condition risks deterring the termination of joint ventures when they no longer make economic sense. But the requirement at least advances the larger principle that unadulterated unilateral conduct—situations in which no course of dealing ever existed—won't trigger antitrust scrutiny. It keeps courts, too, out of the business of initiating collusion and helps address, at least to some degree, administrability concerns—presumably profitable terms already agreed to by the parties may suggest terms a court can use to fashion a remedial order without having to cook them up on its own.[1877]

The Ninth Circuit adopted a similar approach eight months after the Supreme Court decided *Trinko* in 2004. As Judge Koh acknowledged, in *MetroNet* the Ninth Circuit identified the existence of the "'unilateral *termination* of a voluntary and profitable course of dealing'"[1878] as one of the three factors that were "'significant for creating antitrust liability' in *Aspen Skiing*."[1879]

In sum, that a monopolist ended a presumably profitable existing course of dealing with the specific competitor in question is a necessary (but not sufficient) condition for the *Aspen Skiing* exception to apply. It is a proposition that is inherently factual. In most instances, it should give rise to a simple yes-or-no conclusion, which in turn should also be simple for the judge or jury to communicate in findings of fact or a jury verdict. The presence or absence of sufficient evidence establishing that proposition should also be simple for a judge to document in any findings of fact and conclusions of law. In contrast, the evidence that Judge Koh purported to weigh in *FTC v.*

[1875] Verizon Commc'ns Inc. v. Law Offices of Curtis V. Trinko, LLP, 540 U.S. 398, 409 (2004) (emphasis added).

[1876] Novell, Inc. v. Microsoft Corp., 731 F.3d 1064, 1074 (10th Cir. 2013) (Gorsuch, J.) ("To invoke *Aspen's* limited exception, the Supreme Court and we have explained, at least two features present in *Aspen* must be present in the case at hand. First, as in *Aspen*, there must be a preexisting voluntary and presumably profitable course of dealing between the monopolist and rival.").

[1877] *Id.* at 1074–75 (citations omitted) (first citing Dennis W. Carlton, *A General Analysis of Exclusionary Conduct and Refusals to Deal—Why* Aspen *and* Kodak *Are Misguided*, 68 ANTITRUST L.J. 659, 677 (2001); and then citing *Trinko*, 540 U.S. at 407).

[1878] *FTC v. Qualcomm*, 411 F. Supp. 3d at 759 (emphasis added) (quoting MetroNet Servs. Corp. v. Qwest Corp., 383 F.3d 1124, 1132 (9th Cir. 2004)).

[1879] *Id.* (quoting *MetroNet*, 383 F.3d at 1131).

Qualcomm—that at some unidentified time in the past Qualcomm had nonexhaustively "licensed" some unidentified companies that operated in the same industry—was far too vague to satisfy this requirement.

c. The Absence of Evidence That Qualcomm Would Earn Economic Profit by Adopting a Strategy of Licensing Its Cellular SEPs Exhaustively to Rival Modem Manufacturers

The third reason that the *Aspen Skiing* exception did not properly apply to the facts of *FTC v. Qualcomm* was that Judge Koh did not identify and weigh any evidence to support her finding that Qualcomm's practice of "licensing" its portfolio of cellular SEPs to rival modem manufacturers (had it existed on an exhaustive basis) had been profitable for Qualcomm in the past, let alone that it would be profitable for Qualcomm in the future. Recall that, to fit within the *Aspen Skiing* exception, a monopolist must end a presumably *profitable* course of cooperation. As the Supreme Court explained in *Trinko*, "[t]he unilateral termination of a voluntary *(and thus presumably profitable)* course of dealing suggested a willingness to forsake short-term profits to achieve an anticompetitive end."[1880]

Judge Koh found that Qualcomm's practice of "licensing" its patents to rival modem manufacturers (nonexhaustively) was profitable, "as Qualcomm received royalties on patent licenses to modem chip suppliers."[1881] Yet, simply receiving compensation for a "license" does not ensure that the compensation is profitable. The most elementary principles of economics teach that economic profit is measured as total revenue minus total economic costs, including all opportunity costs.[1882]

Judge Koh did not establish that Qualcomm would have earned economic profits if it licensed its portfolio of cellular SEPs exhaustively to rival modem manufacturers. Rather, the evidence that Judge Koh identified and weighed in her findings of fact and conclusions of law disproved that proposition and revealed that she was acting on mere assumption. Indeed, Judge Koh quoted a statement from Qualcomm's July 2012 meeting with the IRS in which Mr. Blecker explained to the IRS that Qualcomm earned 95 percent of its royalties from OEMs and "well less than one percent came from component suppliers."[1883] Yet, Judge Koh did not seem to recognize the economic significance of that evidence, which of course predated the trial in *FTC v. Qualcomm*

[1880] *Trinko*, 540 U.S. at 409 (emphasis in original).

[1881] *FTC v. Qualcomm*, 411 F. Supp. 3d at 760.

[1882] Mankiw, Principles of Economics (8th ed.), *supra* note 652, at 250 ("An economist measures a firm's economic profit as the firm's total revenue minus all the opportunity costs (explicit and implicit) of producing the goods and services sold.") (boldface suppressed).

[1883] *FTC v. Qualcomm*, 411 F. Supp. 3d at 753 (quoting IRS Transcript, *supra* note 503, at 32:9–10 (Marv Blecker (Senior Vice President, Qualcomm Technology Licensing))).

by nearly seven years and therefore could not possibly deserve Judge Koh's epithet of having been "made-for-litigation" testimony. Considering the import of Mr. Blecker's statement to the IRS in July 2012, it was clearly erroneous for Judge Koh to assume that Qualcomm could continue to earn economic profit from licensing its cellular SEPs exhaustively at the modem level.

Furthermore, suppose (notwithstanding Judge Koh's failure to identify and weigh any corroborating facts in evidence) that Qualcomm's practice of nonexhaustively "licensing" its cellular SEPs to unidentified rival modem manufacturers could have been profitable in the late 1990s, when Qualcomm voluntarily executed those (nonexhaustive) "license" agreements. There still would be no reason to assume, as Judge Koh implicitly did, that the same practice of "licensing" its cellular SEPs on a *nonexhaustive* basis to rival modem manufacturers would continue to be profitable thereafter (assuming for sake of argument, but contrary to fact after 2008, that it was still permissible for parties to enter into a nonexhaustive "license" in light the Supreme Court's new decisions on patent exhaustion).

Qualcomm's investments in R&D increased significantly over the two decades following the late 1990s. Figure 13 compares, using constant 2016 dollars, Qualcomm's annual investment in R&D between 1999 and 2018, as disclosed in Qualcomm's annual reports. Figure 13 shows that Qualcomm's inflation-adjusted annual investment in R&D increased by more than 850 percent from 1999 to 2018.

It is questionable whether Qualcomm's revenue from nonexhaustively "licensing" rival modem manufacturers could have grown by the same rate as Qualcomm's real R&D expenditures actually grew. Judge Koh certainly did not state in her findings of fact and conclusions of law that she had made that assumption, much less that she had any basis for concluding it to be true. At the same time, Judge Koh confirmed that the revenue that Qualcomm had collected from nonexhaustive "licenses" with modem manufacturers "amounted to only a tiny fraction of Qualcomm's handset royalty revenues."[1884]

Consequently, it appears that Judge Koh had no basis to assume, much less to conclude as a factual matter, that forcing Qualcomm to offer exhaustive licenses to its portfolio of cellular SEP to rival modem manufacturers, rather than solely to OEMs, would have maintained the profitability of Qualcomm's licensing business and would have sustained its ability to make the far greater levels of R&D investment actually observed between 1999 and 2018.

[1884] *Id.*

Figure 13. Qualcomm's R&D Expenditure, Fiscal
Years 1999–2018 (in Constant 2016 Dollars)

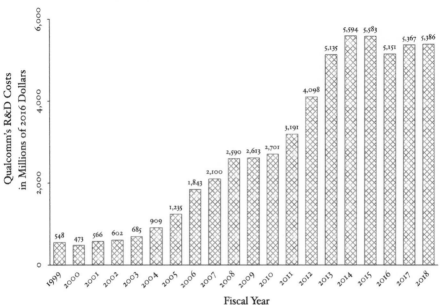

Sources: 1999 Qualcomm 10-K, *supra* note 1558; 2000 Qualcomm 10-K, *supra* note 1558; Qualcomm Inc., Annual Report for the Fiscal Year Ended September 30, 2001 (SEC Form 10-K) (filed Nov. 9, 2001); Qualcomm Inc., Annual Report for the Fiscal Year Ended September 29, 2002 (SEC Form 10-K) (filed Nov. 26, 2002); Qualcomm Inc., Annual Report for the Fiscal Year Ended September 28, 2003 (SEC Form 10-K) (filed Nov. 5, 2003); Qualcomm Inc., Annual Report for the Fiscal Year Ended September 26, 2004 (SEC Form 10-K) (filed Nov. 3, 2004); Qualcomm Inc., Annual Report for the Fiscal Year Ended September 25, 2005 (SEC Form 10-K) (filed Nov. 2, 2005) [hereinafter 2005 Qualcomm 10-K]; Qualcomm Inc., Annual Report for the Fiscal Year Ended September 24, 2006 (SEC Form 10-K) (filed Nov. 2, 2006); Qualcomm Inc., Annual Report for the Fiscal Year Ended September 30, 2007 (SEC Form 10-K) (filed Nov. 8, 2007); Qualcomm Inc., Annual Report for the Fiscal Year Ended September 28, 2008 (SEC Form 10-K) (filed Nov. 6, 2008); Qualcomm Inc., Annual Report for the Fiscal Year Ended September 27, 2009 (SEC Form 10-K) (filed Nov. 5, 2009); Qualcomm Inc., Annual Report for the Fiscal Year Ended September 26, 2010 (SEC Form 10-K) (filed Nov. 3, 2010); Qualcomm Inc., Annual Report for the Fiscal Year Ended September 25, 2011 (SEC Form 10-K) (filed Nov. 2, 2011); Qualcomm Inc., Annual Report for the Fiscal Year Ended September 30, 2012 (SEC Form 10-K) (filed Nov. 7, 2012); Qualcomm Inc., Annual Report for the Fiscal Year Ended September 29, 2013 (SEC Form 10-K) (filed Nov. 6, 2013); Qualcomm Inc., Annual Report for the Fiscal Year Ended September 28, 2014 (SEC Form 10-K) (filed Nov. 5, 2014) [hereinafter 2014 Qualcomm 10-K]; 2015 Qualcomm 10-K, sources cited *supra* Figure 3; Qualcomm Inc., Annual Report for the Fiscal Year Ended September 25, 2016 (SEC Form 10-K) (filed Nov. 2, 2016); 2017 Qualcomm 10-K, sources cited *supra* Figure 3; 2018 Qualcomm 10-K, *supra* note 297; *Consumer Price Index for All Urban Consumers: All Items (CPIAUCSL)*, FRED Economic Data, https://fred.stlouisfed.org/series/CPIAUCSL.

Notes: The R&D expenditures in 2009 and 2010 are the values adjusted for discontinued operations from Qualcomm's 2011 Annual Report. For convenience, I use 2016 as the reference base year, and I convert the R&D expenditures to 2016 dollars using the Consumer Price Index (CPI) for November of each year included in the graph. I use the November observations because that is the month in which Qualcomm released each of its annual reports between 1999 and 2018.

    d. The Absence of Evidence of Qualcomm's Willingness to Forsake Short-Term Profits to Achieve an Anticompetitive End

Suppose, for sake of argument (but contrary to fact), that Qualcomm had "changed" its licensing practices. In other words, suppose (contrary to fact) that Judge Koh correctly found that Qualcomm had previously offered a specific rival modem manufacturer an exhaustive license to its cellular SEPs and thereafter had terminated and refused to renew that exhaustive license with that specific rival.

The fourth reason that Judge Koh's reliance on the *Aspen Skiing* exception was erroneous was that she reported no evidence that a willingness to forsake short-term profits to achieve an anticompetitive end motivated Qualcomm's supposed change in its licensing practices. In *Aspen Skiing*, the Supreme Court found the "most significant" evidence that might support a jury's finding of anticompetitive conduct to be the absence of "any normal business purpose" for discontinuing a profitable course of dealing with a rival.[1885]

It is not immediately clear, either as matter of economic reasoning or as a matter of legal reasoning, what a "normal" business purpose is supposed to be. Lawful, to be sure. But beyond that, what? Any "normal" distribution will have outliers, several standard deviations above and below the mean. Was the Court in *Aspen* endorsing some principle that business practices should regress to the mean to avoid antitrust liability? That interpretation would be perverse, for it would penalize what is new, innovative, unique. But it would be consistent with Judge Koh's apparent anti-Coasean hostility in *FTC v. Qualcomm* toward anything that is unfamiliar about a given firm's institutional structure of production. Might that interpretation of "normal" thus explain Judge Koh's affinity for *Aspen Skiing*, notwithstanding the FTC's representation to the Ninth Circuit at oral argument that it never made *Aspen Skiing* the basis for any of its theories of liability in *FTC v. Qualcomm*?

As we saw above, courts have interpreted *Aspen Skiing* as requiring evidence that a monopolist's refusal to deal with a rival sacrificed short-term profit and that the conduct was, in the words of Justice Gorsuch, "irrational but for its anticompetitive effect."[1886] The Ninth Circuit emphasized in its decision in *FTC v. Qualcomm*:

> Throughout its analysis, the district court conflated the desire to maximize profits with an intent to "destroy competition itself." . . . [T]he goal of antitrust law is not to force businesses to forego profits or even "[t]he opportunity to charge monopoly prices," which is "what attracts 'business

---

[1885] Aspen Skiing Co. v. Aspen Highlands Skiing Corp., 472 U.S. 585, 608 (1985) ("Perhaps most significant . . . is the evidence relating to Ski Co. itself, for Ski Co. did not persuade the jury that its conduct was justified by any normal business purpose.").

[1886] Novell, Inc. v. Microsoft Corp., 731 F.3d 1064, 1075 (10th Cir. 2013) (Gorsuch, J.).

acumen' in the first place." Here, Qualcomm's desire to maximize profits both in the short-term *and* the long-term undermines, rather than supports, the district court's finding of anticompetitive conduct under § 2.[1887]

It is telling that Judge Koh did not find that Qualcomm's supposed change in its licensing practice sacrificed short-term profit, nor did she find that Qualcomm's supposed change was irrational but for its allegedly anticompetitive goal.

To the contrary, Judge Koh emphasized that Qualcomm supposedly changed its licensing practice because exhaustively licensing its cellular SEPs only to OEMs was, in the words of Mr. Gonell of QTL, "'humongously more . . . lucrative'" than exhaustively licensing those same cellular SEPs to rival modem manufacturers.[1888] Judge Koh even found that, in 2004, Qualcomm told Intel that it would not offer an exhaustive license to its cellular SEPs to Intel because doing so "would *reduce* QTL's licensing revenues."[1889] Judge Koh did not seem to recognize that her own findings of fact on this point discredited her reliance on the *Aspen Skiing* exception and consequently obligated her to rule in Qualcomm's favor on the antitrust duty-to-deal claim that she evidently believed that the FTC was trying to prove.

Qualcomm's desire to increase its licensing revenue (the first step toward increasing its *profits* from licensing) provided no information from which Judge Koh could have inferred that Qualcomm had an anticompetitive intent toward rival modem manufacturers. The desire to maintain or increase profit, all else equal, is the goal of *every* firm. In the words of *Aspen Skiing*, it is an entirely "normal business purpose."[1890] By itself, evidence that Qualcomm was pursuing a strategy of profit maximization did not provide Judge Koh any evidence that Qualcomm had an anticompetitive intent.

Furthermore, Judge Koh made the breathtaking observation that "other SEP licensors like Nokia and Ericsson have concluded that licensing only OEMs is more lucrative."[1891] Evidence that even SEP holders (such as Nokia

---

[1887] FTC v. Qualcomm Inc., No. 19-16122, 2020 WL 4591476, at *12 n.15 (9ᵗʰ Cir. Aug. 11, 2020) (third alteration in original) (emphasis in original) (citations omitted) (first quoting Spectrum Sports, Inc. v. McQuillan, 506 U.S. 447, 458 (1993); and then quoting Verizon Commc'ns Inc. v. Law Offices of Curtis V. Trinko, LLP, 540 U.S. 398, 407 (2004)).

[1888] FTC v. Qualcomm, 411 F. Supp. 3d at 751 (quoting IRS Transcript, *supra* note 503, at 71:20–22 (Fabian Gonell, Legal Counsel and Senior Vice President, Licensing Strategy, Qualcomm Technology Licensing)); *see also id.* at 753 ("Qualcomm later stopped licensing rivals because Qualcomm decided that it was more lucrative to license only OEMs.").

[1889] *Id.* at 748 (emphasis added) (citing CX7580-001 (email from Steve Altman)); *see also id.* at 754, 757–58, 797, 821. Unless Qualcomm incrementally avoided a greater amount of cost than the licensing revenue it would lose (which seems unlikely, considering the economies of scale and scope associated with Qualcomm's sunk investments in R&D), Qualcomm was in essence telling Intel in 2004 that exhaustively licensing cellular SEPs to Intel would be incrementally unprofitable for Qualcomm.

[1890] *Aspen Skiing*, 472 U.S. at 608.

[1891] *FTC v. Qualcomm*, 411 F. Supp. 3d at 754–55. Judge Koh asserted that Nokia and Ericsson were "[f]ollowing Qualcomm's lead." *Id.* at 754. But she did not elaborate on what she inferred from that finding of fact.

and Ericsson) that did not compete with modem manufacturers chose to license their SEPs exhaustively only to handset OEMs upended Judge Koh's reasoning that an anticompetitive intent must have motivated Qualcomm's supposed change in its licensing practices.

We have already seen how Judge Koh ignored that the law is dynamic, and that businesses routinely respond to refinements in the law through legitimate and lawful business innovation—in Qualcomm's case, business innovation in the structure of its contracting to avoid patent exhaustion. She also ignored that the modem industry is technologically dynamic and thus might compel companies to revise their business practices.

In comparison, the industry involved in *Aspen Skiing* was not particularly technologically dynamic. It concerned the provision of the infrastructure necessary to enable people to ride flat strips of smoothly laminated material down snow-covered mountainsides for amusement. Over time, better boots, skis, and snowboards have been introduced, and ski resorts have luxuriated their services and accommodations compared with the relatively Spartan quality of the early ski runs in the western United States. But the fundamental interaction between snow, an incline, and the force of gravity has not changed, and thus the quiddity of the product has remained relatively constant.

In contrast, the ability to compete for a design win for the modem to be used in a new smartphone requires a substantial and continuous investment in R&D. Yet, Judge Koh's findings of fact and conclusions of law in *FTC v. Qualcomm* ignored technological change and implicitly assumed that the supposed change in Qualcomm's licensing practices could have had no other rationale than the desire to exclude its rivals from the modem business.

> e. *The Absence of Evidence of Qualcomm's Refusal to Deal Even If Compensated at the Retail Price: Judge Koh's Focus on the Wrong Opportunity Cost of Exhaustive Licensing of Qualcomm's SEPs*

A fifth reason that the *Aspen Skiing* exception was irrelevant to *FTC v. Qualcomm* is that Judge Koh's findings of fact and conclusions of law did not cite any evidence to support her conclusion that Qualcomm refused to license its portfolio of cellular SEPs exhaustively to modem manufacturers "even if compensated at retail price."[1892] It is unclear what "retail price" Judge Koh envisioned, and her more extensive remarks quickly devolved into handwaving about what kind of economic analysis supposedly would be relevant to employ:

[1892] *Id.* at 760 (citing *Trinko*, 540 U.S. at 409 (quoting *Aspen Skiing*, 472 U.S. at 608)).

> In *Trinko*, the United States Supreme Court observed that the defendant's refusal to deal in *Aspen Skiing* "revealed a distinctly anticompetitive bent" because the defendant would not renew the joint lift ticket even if compensated at retail price. Here, Qualcomm's refusal to deal with its rivals reveals *similar anticompetitive malice*.[1893]

Why should Qualcomm's practices "reveal[] similar anticompetitive malice"? The comment is a *non sequitur* because the economic circumstances of *Aspen Skiing* are dissimilar to those of *FTC v. Qualcomm*. Judge Koh did not discern and clearly explain a subtle but important distinction regarding the relevance of this passage from *Aspen Skiing* to Qualcomm's licensing practices: Whether Qualcomm exhaustively licenses its cellular SEPs at the device level or at the component level is a different question from whether, at a given level in the vertical chain of production, the owner of the bottleneck facility is compensated by the access seeker at the retail price rather than the wholesale price for the access seeker's use of that bottleneck facility (including the access seeker's resulting displacement of a retail sale that would have been made in the downstream market by the vertically integrated owner of the bottleneck facility).

An OEM of smartphones and other mobile devices needs to be licensed to use Qualcomm's cellular SEPs whether or not the OEM buys Qualcomm's modem. That legal obligation flows from the simple fact that every standard-compliant modem necessarily practices one or more claims contained in one or more of hundreds or thousands of Qualcomm's cellular SEPs. Therefore, the relevant question is not (as Judge Koh's quotation of the language of *Aspen Skiing* might superficially suggest) whether Qualcomm would exhaustively license its cellular SEPs at the component level if it could collect a royalty equal to the entire retail price of the rival's modem.

Rather, the relevant question is whether Qualcomm would refuse to license its cellular SEPs exhaustively to a rival modem manufacturer if Qualcomm could receive the same royalty as it receives *when it licenses those same cellular SEPs exhaustively to an OEM. That* amount of royalty revenue (minus Qualcomm's transaction costs of licensing) is the relevant opportunity cost facing Qualcomm when it chooses at what level in the vertical chain of production it will exhaustively license its cellular SEPs.[1894]

Suppose, for example, that the effective royalty that a given OEM pays for an exhaustive license to Qualcomm's portfolio of cellular SEPs is $12 per handset. Would Qualcomm be willing to offer an exhaustive license to its cellular SEPs to a rival modem manufacturer if that rival agreed to pay

---

[1893] *Id.* (quoting *Trinko*, 540 U.S. at 409) (emphasis added).

[1894] Again, this analysis is analogous in its reasoning to the efficient component-pricing rule. *See supra* note 749 and accompanying text.

Qualcomm a royalty of $12 per licensed modem? It is both remarkable and conspicuous that Judge Koh dodged this fundamental question.

Instead, Judge Koh invoked some obtuse arithmetic. She referred to Qualcomm's practice of licensing its cellular SEPs to both OEMs and modem manufacturers "'at 3% with no minimum dollar amount.'"[1895] But 3 percent of *what*? A 3-percent running royalty applied to a smartphone selling for (or capped for royalty purposes at) $400 produces a much higher royalty payment (that is, $12) than does a 3-percent running royalty applied to a modem selling for $18[1896] (that is, $0.54). In this numerical example, the royalty payment to the SEP holder by the OEM is 22 times the size of the royalty payment by the rival modem manufacturer.

That difference is enormous and is easily demagogued by those who would benefit from obscuring the correct economic analysis of the matter at hand. That enormous difference also invites one to ask, was Judge Koh assuming that the scope of the component-level "license" is identical to the scope of an exhaustive device-level license? Did she understand that SEP holders have good cause to read Supreme Court decisions beginning with *Quanta* as foreclosing the possibility of an SEP holder's simultaneous grant of a nonexhaustive "license" at the component level and an exhaustive license at the device level?

As a first approximation using plausible parameter values for the smartphone industry, the SEP holder would earn roughly 20 times as much royalty revenue from licensing exhaustively at the device level as it would from licensing exhaustively at the component level. The magnitude of that difference was the key insight to be gleaned from the transcript of Qualcomm's July 2012 meeting with the IRS, yet Judge Koh seemed to have missed that point. Judge Koh did indeed find the IRS transcript probative—but for the wrong reasons. Whether Qualcomm refused to license its cellular SEPs exhaustively to rival modem manufacturers "even if compensated at [the] retail price"[1897] *of a modem* is a question irrelevant to the economic rationality, the superior profitability, and the lawfulness under American antitrust law of Qualcomm's policy of exhaustively licensing its cellular SEPs solely at the device level rather than licensing them also (or exclusively) at the component level.

[1895] *FTC v. Qualcomm*, 411 F. Supp. 3d at 753 (quoting CX7580-001 (email from Steve Altman)).

[1896] *Id.* at 688 ("'When first introduced CBP6 to US market, the price of QSC6055 [a Qualcomm chip] was $18.'") (alteration in original) (quoting CX1770-002 (April 2009 Presentation by Mark Davis, former Vice President and Chief Technical Officer, VIA)).

[1897] *See, e.g., id.* at 759.

    f. Would Aspen Skiing *Require at Most That Qualcomm Deal with "Smaller Rivals"?*

A sixth reason that the *Aspen Skiing* exception properly did not apply in *FTC v. Qualcomm* is that Judge Koh ignored a limiting principle to that exception that one finds in the very language of the Supreme Court's opinion. The Court noted at the outset of its opinion that it granted *certiorari* in *Aspen Skiing* specifically to address the effect that imposing an antitrust duty to deal would have on "smaller rivals."[1898] Thereafter in its relatively short opinion, the Court referred to the monopolist's "smaller rival" or "smaller competitor" four times.[1899] Therefore, the most faithful reading of *Aspen Skiing* is that its circumscription of the general freedom to choose one's customers is available only to minnows. The Ninth Circuit recognized in *FTC v. Qualccom* that, "in *Aspen Skiing*, the defendant refused to sell its lift tickets to a smaller, rival ski resort even as it sold the same lift tickets to any other willing buyer (including any *other* ski resort); moreover, this refusal was designed specifically to put the smaller, nearby rival out of business."[1900] Yet, Judge Koh would make the *Aspen Skiing* exception available to every corporate whale.

    Qualcomm's rivals in the modem industry include very large multinational firms, such as Intel, Samsung, Huawei, and others. And of course Judge Curiel found that it was a triable question of fact for the jury whether the provenance of the FTC's complaint against Qualcomm was the lobbying of that enforcement agency by Apple from 2012 onward.[1901] In August 2018, nine months before Judge Koh issued her findings of fact and conclusions of law in *FTC v. Qualcomm*, Apple became America's first corporation to amass a market value exceeding $1 trillion.[1902] And two months after Judge Koh issued her findings of fact and conclusions of law, Apple became an actual competitor (rather than merely a potential competitor) of Qualcomm by announcing its intention to enter the modem industry through the acquisition of Intel's modem business.[1903] If Qualcomm's prior rivals in the modem industry had been whales for the most part, Apple was now the Leviathan.

    If one must read *Aspen Skiing*—if applicable—to benefit only rival modem manufacturers that are *smaller* than Qualcomm, then what facts did Judge Koh need to find to conclude as a matter of law that a given seeker of an exhaustive license to Qualcomm's cellular SEPs was a suitably "smaller rival" within

---

[1898] Aspen Skiing Co. v. Aspen Highlands Skiing Corp., 472 U.S. 585, 587 (1985).

[1899] *Id.* at 605 ("smaller rival"), 608 ("smaller competitor"), 610 ("smaller rival"), 611 ("smaller rival").

[1900] FTC v. Qualcomm Inc., No. 19-16122, 2020 WL 4591476, at *13 (9th Cir. Aug. 11, 2020) (emphasis in original) (citing *Aspen Skiing*, 472 U.S. at 593–94).

[1901] *See supra* notes 310–312 and accompanying text.

[1902] *See* Matt Phillips, *Apple's $1 Trillion Milestone Reflects Rise of Powerful Megacompanies*, N.Y. Times, Aug. 2, 2018. Two years later, Apple's market value exceeded $2 trillion. *See* Amrith Ramkumar, *Apple Surges to $2 Trillion Market Value*, Wall St. J., Aug. 19, 2020.

[1903] *See supra* note 1022 and accompanying text.

the Supreme Court's meaning? Judge Koh did not ask that question, much less answer it. Instead, she implicitly struck the "smaller rivals" language from the Supreme Court's opinion in *Aspen Skiing* and incorrectly read the case to impose on Qualcomm a duty to deal with modem manufacturers larger than itself, including Intel and such national champions as Samsung and Huawei. And now of course America's new national champion, Apple.

g.   Does Aspen Skiing *Encompass Intellectual Property?*

A seventh reason that the *Aspen Skiing* exception was inapplicable to *FTC v. Qualcomm* is that a patent is not a mountain. Nothing in the Supreme Court's decision implies that an antitrust duty to deal arises from the ownership of intellectual property as opposed to the ownership of a physical asset, such as the developed ski slopes on a Colorado mountainside, to which competitor access was sought in *Aspen Skiing*. Qualcomm itself is a *fabless* manufacturer of modems. It has no physical facility that is a bottleneck to which rivals need access to compete. Judge Koh was therefore imposing a duty to deal under *Aspen Skiing* with respect to a valuable asset that consists solely of Qualcomm's intellectual property.

In 1999, Tad Lipsky and I warned that such an extension of the essential facilities doctrine (to the extent that the Supreme Court even acknowledges that the doctrine legitimately exists) is the least justified and the most susceptible to unintended consequences.[1904] The FTC of course was not so naïve as to plead a claim predicated on the essential facilities doctrine in *FTC v. Qualcomm* when it already had the infinitely malleable standard of section 5 of the FTC Act at its disposal. Still, the warning that Lipsky and I sounded in 1999 concerning the possible extension of the essential facilities doctrine to pure intellectual property applies with equal force to attempts to achieve the same result by expanding the application of the *Aspen Skiing* exception through the auspices of section 5 of the FTC Act.

h.   *The Uncertain Virtue of Forced Sharing*

The evidence that Judge Koh reported in her findings of fact and conclusions of law did not support her conclusion that Qualcomm's refusal to offer exhaustive licenses to its cellular SEPs to rival modem manufacturers fell within *Aspen Skiing*'s narrow exception to the general rule that a firm (even a monopolist) is free under the Sherman Act to refuse to deal with any other firm, including a competitor. She did not cite any evidence that Qualcomm had ever granted an exhaustive license to its cellular SEPs to any of the companies that nowadays operates in the modem industry. Nor did

---

[1904]   *See* Lipsky & Sidak, *Essential Facilities, supra* note 1837, at 1219–20.

Judge Koh cite any evidence that forcing Qualcomm to license its cellular SEPs exhaustively to rival modem manufacturers (rather than solely OEMs) would hold constant the profitability of Qualcomm's licensing business. Nor did Judge Koh cite any evidence that "anticompetitive malice" motivated Qualcomm to change a licensing policy that it had adopted in the late 1990s.

A week after Judge Koh issued her findings of fact and conclusions of law, FTC Commissioner Christine Wilson wrote in the *Wall Street Journal* that the decision "radically expanded a company's legal obligation to help its competitors."[1905] Judge Koh evidently dismissed the economic argument that forcing a company to share the fruits of its costly investments in risky R&D with competitors will ultimately harm innovation and consumers. Judge Koh's findings of fact and conclusions of law in *FTC v. Qualcomm* flouted the Supreme Court's admonition in *Trinko* that courts be "very cautious" in recognizing exceptions to a monopolist's right to refuse to cooperate with a rival "because of the uncertain virtue of forced sharing."[1906]

4. *Did a FRAND or RAND Contract Impose an Antitrust Duty on Qualcomm to Offer Exhaustive Licenses to Its Cellular SEPs to Rival Modem Manufacturers?*

We saw that, in its brief submitted on appeal to the Ninth Circuit, the FTC maintained that at trial it did "not argue that Qualcomm has a duty to deal with its rivals under the heightened *Aspen/Trinko* standard."[1907] Instead, the FTC said that Qualcomm harmed competition *by violating its voluntary (contractual) RAND commitment* to offer an exhaustive license to its cellular SEPs to rival modem manufacturers. Although the FTC acknowledged that a breach of a RAND commitment does not necessarily violate the Sherman Act, it nonetheless argued that "Section 2 liability is appropriate when, as here, a monopolist SEP holder commits to license its rivals on FRAND terms, and then implements a blanket policy of refusing to license those rivals on any terms, with the effect of substantially contributing to the acquisition or maintenance of monopoly power in the relevant market."[1908]

Maybe the FTC was intellectually consistent before both Judge Koh and the Ninth Circuit when purporting to dress up its allegations about

---

[1905] Christine Wilson, *A Court's Dangerous Antitrust Overreach*, WALL ST. J., May 28, 2019.

[1906] Verizon Commc'ns Inc. v. Law Offices of Curtis V. Trinko, LLP, 540 U.S. 398, 408 (2004). For empirical evidence on "the uncertain virtue of forced sharing" of telecommunications infrastructure, see Jerry A. Hausman & J. Gregory Sidak, *Did Mandatory Unbundling Achieve Its Purpose? Empirical Evidence from Five Countries*, 1 J. COMPETITION L. & ECON. 173 (2005).

[1907] FTC Brief to the Ninth Circuit, *supra* note 286, at 30. This section expands the discussion of the antitrust duty to deal appearing in J. Gregory Sidak & Urška Petrovčič, *Did* FTC v. Qualcomm *Create an Antitrust Duty to License Standard-Essential Patents?*, CPI ANTITRUST CHRON., Mar. 2020, at 1.

[1908] FTC Brief to the Ninth Circuit, *supra* note 286, at 69.

Qualcomm's putative antitrust duty to license in a new and stylish theory of antitrust liability, rather than tattered garb of *Aspen Skiing*. But maybe not.

In its proposed findings of fact and conclusions of law submitted to Judge Koh, the FTC appeared still to be trying to have its cake and eat it too, as the FTC twice cited *Aspen Skiing* as controlling authority. The FTC first cited *Aspen Skiing* to support this proposition: "Conduct that raises a competitor's costs or otherwise tends to impair the opportunities of competitors and either does not further competition on the merits or does so in an unnecessarily restrictive way is anticompetitive under the Sherman Act."[1909] *Aspen Skiing* supposedly supported this second proposition as well: "Qualcomm's refusal to make SEP licenses available to competitors in breach of its voluntary commitments to standard-setting organizations is anticompetitive conduct. By failing to comply with its FRAND commitments, it has altered a voluntary course of dealing with anticompetitive malice."[1910]

The FTC's double reliance on *Aspen Skiing* before Judge Koh was not the most persuasive foundation for the agency's subsequent representation to the Ninth Circuit that the agency did "not argue that Qualcomm has a duty to deal with its rivals under the heightened *Aspen/Trinko* standard."[1911] One can appreciate why the FTC would have thought it advisable to send in Mr. Fletcher as its appellate barrister to thread the needle.

Perhaps the FTC and Judge Koh had been talking past one another all along, as she never addressed in her findings of fact and conclusions of law the FTC's novel theory that Qualcomm's FRAND commitment created an antitrust duty (rather than, at most, a contractual duty) to offer exhaustive licenses to its cellular SEPs to rival modem manufacturers. Recall that we saw in Part X how Judge Koh held on summary judgment that, as a matter of contract law, Qualcomm's RAND commitments to ATIS and the TIA "require Qualcomm to license its SEPs to modem chip suppliers."[1912] Judge Koh found that Qualcomm's failure to offer exhaustive licenses to its cellular SEPs to rival modem manufacturers violated its contractual obligations pursuant to its "FRAND [sic] commitments" to ATIS and the TIA.[1913]

But Judge Koh never explained the implication of that contractual (private law) interpretation for her conclusion of law that Qualcomm had

---

[1909] FTC's Proposed Findings of Fact and Conclusions of Law, *supra* note 485, ¶ 33, at 62 (first citing Cascade Health Sols. v. PeaceHealth, 515 F.3d 883, 894 (9th Cir. 2008) (citing Aspen Skiing Co. v. Aspen Highlands Skiing Corp., 472 U.S. 585, 605 n.32 (1985)); and then citing Order Denying Motion to Dismiss, 2017 WL 2774406, *supra* note 49, at *15).

[1910] *Id.* ¶ 40, at 63 (first citing *Aspen Skiing*, 472 U.S. at 610; then citing MetroNet Servs. Corp. v. Qwest Corp., 383 F.3d 1124, 1131 (9th Cir. 2004); and then citing Order Denying Motion to Dismiss, 2017 WL 2774406, *supra* note 49, at *20).

[1911] FTC Brief to the Ninth Circuit, *supra* note 286, at 30.

[1912] Order Granting FTC's Motion for Partial Summary Judgment on Qualcomm's Contractual Duties Pursuant to the Contracts with ATIS and the TIA, 2018 WL 5848999, *supra* note 52, at *15.

[1913] *Id.* at *12.

an *antitrust* (public law) duty to offer exhaustive licenses to its cellular SEPs to rival modem manufacturers. In other words, she never addressed—and certainly did not make conclusions of law embracing—the FTC's contention that Qualcomm's refusal to offer exhaustive licenses to its cellular SEPs to rival modem manufacturers was anticompetitive because that refusal contravened Qualcomm's voluntary RAND commitment. If the FTC truly pleaded and argued this theory of antitrust liability, then Federal Rule of Civil Procedure 52(a)(1) obligated Judge Koh to make special findings of fact on this theory of liability and announce whether those facts constituted preponderant evidence of a violation of the Sherman Act. No such determinations appear in Judge Koh's findings of fact and conclusions of law in *FTC v. Qualcomm*.

Even if Judge Koh had addressed the FTC's novel argument that a breach of contract by Qualcomm can metamorphose into an antitrust violation, there still would be scant support for her to have concluded that Qualcomm's refusal to offer exhaustive licenses to its cellular SEPs to rival modem manufacturers was anticompetitive. We have already seen in Part X why Judge Koh's order granting the FTC's motion for partial summary judgment was erroneous. Judge Koh's order does not suddenly become believable and free from legal error because the FTC needs to use the order as its predicate for constructing a new theory of antitrust liability.

Even if Judge Koh's findings about Qualcomm's contractual duties to ATIS and the TIA had been correct, those findings still would not have sufficed for her to conclude that Qualcomm owed a duty under American antitrust law to offer rival modem manufacturers exhaustive licenses to its portfolio of cellular SEPs. The Supreme Court addressed a similar question in *Trinko*. Although regulations promulgated by the Federal Communications Commission (FCC)[1914] to implement sections 251 and 252[1915] of the Telecommunications Act of 1996[1916] obligated Verizon to provide unbundled access to its network infrastructure to downstream competitors on "'just, reasonable, and non-discriminatory' [JRAND] terms,"[1917] the Court found that Verizon had no *antitrust* duty to deal with such competitors.[1918] The Court reasoned that the FCC's regulations did "not create new claims

---

[1914] Implementation of the Local Competition Provisions in the Telecommunications Act of 1996 and Interconnection Between Local Exchange Carriers and Commercial Mobile Radio Service Providers, First Report and Order, CC Dkt. Nos. 96–98, 95–185, 11 F.C.C. Rcd. 115, 499 (1996); *see also* Jerry A. Hausman & J. Gregory Sidak, *A Consumer-Welfare Approach to the Mandatory Unbundling of Telecommunications Networks*, 109 YALE L.J. 417, 429 (1999); J. Gregory Sidak & Daniel F. Spulber, *The Tragedy of the Telecommons: Government Pricing of Unbundled Network Elements Under the Telecommunications Act of 1996*, 97 COLUM. L. REV. 1081, 1083 (1997).

[1915] 47 U.S.C. §§ 251–52

[1916] Pub. L. No. 104–104, 110 Stat. 56.

[1917] Verizon Commc'ns Inc. v. Law Offices of Curtis V. Trinko, LLP, 540 U.S. 398, 405–06 (2004) (quoting 47 U.S.C. § 251(c)(3)).

[1918] *Id.* at 410.

that go beyond existing antitrust standards."[1919] "That Congress created these duties [to deal]," the Court emphasized, "does not automatically lead to the conclusion that they can be enforced by means of an antitrust claim."[1920] In other words, although Verizon had a duty to grant competitors access to its facilities on JRAND terms, the duty arose from the mandatory unbundling provisions of the Telecommunications Act of 1996 and not from anything in antitrust law.[1921]

From the Court's reasoning in *Trinko*, it is clear that, even if Qualcomm had a contractual duty to offer exhaustive licenses to its cellular SEPs to rival modem manufacturers, that contractual duty would not impose on Qualcomm any new *antitrust* duty beyond what already exists in American antitrust jurisprudence.[1922] Put differently, Qualcomm's violation of a contractual duty is not automatically an antitrust violation. Makan Delrahim, the Assistant Attorney General of the Antitrust Division of the Department of Justice, reiterated this reasoning in September 2018: "A unilateral violation of a FRAND commitment should not give rise to a cause of action under Section 2 of the Sherman Act[.]"[1923]

XIII. Did Qualcomm Engage in Unlawful Exclusive Dealing?

In an exclusive dealing agreement, one firm agrees to transact exclusively with a given supplier or retailer. In exchange for receiving that exclusivity, the supplier or retailer typically offers a discount, a payment, or some other valuable consideration to the counterparty. Judge Koh found two contracts between Qualcomm and Apple to be anticompetitive exclusive dealing agreements: the 2011 Transition Agreement (TA) and the 2013 First

---

[1919] *Id.* at 407.

[1920] *Id.* at 406.

[1921] *Id.* at 410.

[1922] *See, e.g.*, City of Vernon v. S. Calif. Edison Co., 955 F.2d 1361, 1368 (9ᵗʰ Cir. 1992) ("It is certainly true that a claimed breach of contract by unreasonable conduct, standing alone, should not give rise to antitrust liability."); *see also In re* Adderall XR Antitrust Litig., 754 F.3d 128, 135 (2ᵈ Cir. 2014) ("The mere existence of a contractual duty to supply goods does not by itself give rise to an antitrust 'duty to deal.'") (quoting Pacific Bell Tel. Co. v. linkLine Commc'ns, Inc., 555 U.S. 438, 450 (2009)); Gregory J. Werden & Luke M. Froeb, *Why Patent Hold-Up Does Not Violate Antitrust Law*, 27 Tex. Intell. Prop. L.J. 1, 11 (2019) (arguing that, to violate U.S. antitrust law, an SEP holder's conduct must harm the competitive process).

[1923] Makan Delrahim, Assistant Attorney Gen., Antitrust Div., U.S. Dep't of Justice, Remarks Delivered at the IAM's Patent Licensing Conference: Antitrust Law and Patent Licensing in the New Wild West 5 (Sept. 18, 2018), https://www.justice.gov/opa/speech/file/1095011/download; *see also* Makan Delrahim, Assistant Attorney Gen., Antitrust Div., U.S. Dep't of Justice, Remarks at USC Gould School of Law, Take It to the Limit: Respecting Innovation Incentives in the Application of Antitrust Law 8 (Nov. 10, 2017), https://www.justice.gov/opa/speech/file/1010746/download ("If a patent holder is alleged to have violated a commitment to a standard setting organization, that action may have some impact on competition. But, I respectfully submit, that does not mean the heavy hand of antitrust necessarily is the appropriate remedy for the would-be licensee—or the enforcement agency. There are perfectly adequate and more appropriate common law and statutory remedies available to the SSO or its members.") (footnote omitted).

Amendment to Transition Agreement (FATA).[1924] The Ninth Circuit in *FTC v. Qualcomm* concluded, to the contrary, that these two agreements did not have "the actual or practical effect of substantially foreclosing competition in the CDMA modem chip market, or that injunctive relief [wa]s warranted."[1925]

As paraphrased by Judge Koh, the two agreements specified that Qualcomm would make payments to Apple if "Apple purchased substantial volumes of Qualcomm modem chips" and complied with other conditions.[1926] Under the TA, Qualcomm agreed "to pay Apple up to $1 billion . . . from 2011 to 2015."[1927] To receive those payments, Apple committed to "launch a handset with a Qualcomm UMTS modem chip by March 2012"[1928] and to "purchase[] at least 80 million Qualcomm modem chips each year."[1929] In addition, if Apple sold any "'product commercially that incorporate[d] a non-Qualcomm cellular baseband modem,'" the TA would automatically terminate, and Apple would need to reimburse Qualcomm for any payments that Qualcomm had made to Apple pursuant to the TA.[1930] The FATA contained similar provisions that (in Judge Koh's words, paraphrasing the agreement) specified that Qualcomm would pay Apple "hundreds of millions . . . conditioned on Apple's purchase of at least 100 million Qualcomm modem chips in both 2015 and 2016."[1931]

Judge Koh found that the TA and the FATA were "de facto exclusive deals."[1932] Although she acknowledged that some exclusive dealing agreements are procompetitive,[1933] Judge Koh found that, because the TA and the FATA shrank sales of Qualcomm's rivals and foreclosed rivals from "the positive network effects of working with Apple," the two agreements enabled Qualcomm to maintain monopoly power unlawfully in the respective markets that she had defined for CDMA and "premium" LTE modems.[1934]

Professor Shapiro likewise stated in the demonstratives supporting his direct testimony during the FTC's case-in-chief that "Qualcomm . . . harmed competition by making large payments to Apple in exchange for exclusivity."[1935] And, as we saw earlier, at trial Professor Shapiro testified:

> [T]hese large payments conditioned on exclusivity . . . will, as a practical matter, blockade an entrant from getting into the market. So when employed

---

[1924] FTC v. Qualcomm Inc., 411 F. Supp. 3d 658, 762 (N.D. Cal. 2019).
[1925] FTC v. Qualcomm Inc., No. 19-16122, 2020 WL 4591476, at *20 (9th Cir. Aug. 11, 2020).
[1926] *FTC v. Qualcomm*, 411 F. Supp. 3d at 763.
[1927] *Id.* at 728.
[1928] *Id.*
[1929] *Id.* at 763.
[1930] *Id.* (quoting JX0057-004).
[1931] *Id.* at 732.
[1932] *Id.* at 763.
[1933] *Id.* at 766.
[1934] *Id.* at 762.
[1935] Shapiro Demonstratives, *supra* note 114, at 3.

by a monopolist in a situation where there's an entrant who has—who's not in the market really and is trying to get in and this customer is the key route in, then the concern would be that this would block that entry and harm competition because the entrant, in this case Intel, would—by not getting this, the business that they have a shot at, that is currently available, the iPad business I'm talking about here, that they would be then a weaker—not—let me put it differently. If Intel is able to get this business, this foothold, they will become a stronger competitor in the future. And so blocking that can have competitive effects.[1936]

Professor Shapiro was essentially making the infant-industry argument for the FTC to attack Qualcomm's price cuts to Apple for the greater good of nurturing Intel. Professor Shapiro further testified:

> [T]his structure of [the FATA] involved a profit sacrifice by Qualcomm, or would block an equally efficient competitor from making these contestable sales, or would require that competitor to lose a substantial amount of money to get that foothold in the market.[1937]

Subsequent events had already disproven Professors Shapiro's predictions by the time he testified at trial in January 2019. Notwithstanding the supposedly anticompetitive effects of the TA and the FATA, Intel had already managed to win the exclusive contract to supply modems for Apple's new release of iPhones in September 2018, completely displacing Qualcomm.[1938]

Professor Shapiro's courtroom predictions soon were made to look even sillier. Two months after Judge Koh issued her findings of fact and conclusions of law in *FTC v. Qualcomm*, Apple announced that it would acquire Intel's modem business.[1939] That news confuted Professor Shapiro's predictions of the anticompetitive effects of the TA and the FATA. Intel had not merely managed to get "a shot at"[1940] more business with Apple, or a "foothold"[1941] with Apple, such that Intel "will become a stronger competitor in the future."[1942] Apple had just declared that it would vertically integrate into the market by acquiring Intel's modem operations. Apple's entry by acquisition into the modem industry would ensure Intel's former modem

---

[1936] Transcript of Proceedings (Volume 6) at 1166:24–1167:14, FTC v. Qualcomm Inc., No. 5:17-cv-00220-LHK (N.D. Cal. Jan. 15, 2019) (Testimony of Carl Shapiro); *see also supra* text accompanying note 634.

[1937] *Id.* at 1172:20–24.

[1938] *See supra* note 1776 and accompanying text. Nick Statt, *Apple Will Exclusively Use Intel Modems in 2018 iPhones, According to Qualcomm*, VERGE, July 25, 2018; *see also* Stephen Nellis, *As New iPhones Go on Sale, Studies Reveal Chips from Intel and Toshiba*, REUTERS, Sept. 21, 2018.

[1939] *See supra* note 1776 and accompanying text.

[1940] Transcript of Proceedings (Volume 6) at 1167:9, FTC v. Qualcomm Inc., No. 5:17-cv-00220-LHK (N.D. Cal. Jan. 15, 2019) (Testimony of Carl Shapiro).

[1941] *Id.* at 1167:12.

[1942] *Id.* at 1167:13.

division a steady stream of business from its new parent, the largest seller of smartphones in the United States.

Like Professor Shapiro's myopic predictions about the need for Judge Koh to punish Qualcomm's price discounts to protect Intel, Judge Koh's own findings concerning the competitive effects of the TA and the FATA also were incorrect, incomplete, and unpersuasive. Her conclusions of law applied incorrect legal standards—and, in some instances, no legal standard at all—supposedly to evaluate the competitive effects of the two agreements. Judge Koh's findings of fact appeared to rely solely on snippets of anecdotal evidence to support her conclusion that the TA and the FATA were anticompetitive. In short, Judge Koh did not identify substantial evidence to support her conclusion that the TA and the FATA harmed competition in what she defined as the relevant markets.

A. *When Are Exclusive Dealing Contracts Unlawful?*

Judge Koh acknowledged as a general proposition that exclusive agreements are not necessarily anticompetitive,[1943] and the FTC itself states on its website: "*Most* exclusive dealing contracts are beneficial because they encourage marketing support for the manufacturer's brand."[1944] If antitrust concerns ever can arise, it is only when the exclusive dealing arrangement forecloses competition in a substantial share of the relevant market.

The Supreme Court's 1961 decision in *Tampa Electric* analyzed exclusive dealing contracts under the rule of reason by requiring the finder of fact to balance the transaction's procompetitive effects against its anticompetitive effects.[1945] An exclusive dealing agreement is unlawful only if the latter outweigh the former.[1946] *Tampa Electric* and its progeny thus remain consistent with the Supreme Court's recent explication of the rule of reason generally.

In its motion to dismiss, Qualcomm criticized the FTC's complaint for failing to "indicate what portion of the purported market was allegedly foreclosed by the Apple agreements, or which competitors were purportedly excluded from that market."[1947] Notwithstanding the controlling authority of

---

[1943] FTC v. Qualcomm Inc., 411 F. Supp. 3d 658, 766 (N.D. Cal. 2019).

[1944] *Exclusive Dealing or Requirements Contracts*, Fed. Trade Comm'n, https://www.ftc.gov/tips-advice/competition-guidance/guide-antitrust-laws/dealings-supply-chain/exclusive-dealing-or (emphasis added); *see also* Eastern Food Servs., Inc. v. Pontifical Catholic Univ. Servs. Ass'n, 357 F.3d 1, 8 (1st Cir. 2004) (emphasizing that exclusive dealing agreements "may be highly efficient—to assure supply, price stability, outlets, investment, best efforts or the like—and pose no competitive threat at all").

[1945] Tampa Elec. Co. v. Nashville Coal Co., 365 U.S. 320, 327 (1961); *see also* Feitelson v. Google Inc., 80 F. Supp. 3d 1019, 1030 (N.D. Cal. 2015).

[1946] *Tampa Electric*, 365 U.S. at 327; *see also* Allied Orthopedic Appliances Inc. v. Tyco Health Care Grp. LP, 592 F.3d 991, 996 (9th Cir. 2010) ("Under the antitrust rule of reason, an exclusive dealing arrangement violates Section 1 only if its effect is to 'foreclose competition in a substantial share of the line of commerce affected.'") (quoting Omega Envtl., Inc. v. Gilbarco, Inc., 127 F.3d 1157, 1162 (9th Cir. 1997) (quoting *Tampa Electric*, 365 U.S. at 327)).

[1947] Qualcomm's Motion to Dismiss, 2017 WL 4678941, *supra* note 41, at 18.

Tampa Electric (and Qualcomm's explicit reference to that controlling author-ity in its motion to dismiss),[1948] Judge Koh did not conduct a rigorous balanc-ing of the actual anticompetitive effects and procompetitive effects of the TA and the FATA.

Did Qualcomm's and Apple's alleged exclusivity enhance product quality? Did it foreclose rivals from accessing a substantial share of the relevant market? Did the alleged exclusivity prevent a rival from achieving minimum efficient scale? Did it harm consumers of modems or downstream mobile devices? Under *Tampa Electric*, a court would need to answer such questions to determine the competitive effects of the alleged exclusivity attending the TA and the FATA. Judge Koh did not ask, much less answer, any of those questions.

B.   *Did the TA and the FATA Have Anticompetitive Effects?*

Judge Koh found that the TA and the FATA were *de facto* exclusive dealing agreements. Quoting *Tampa Electric*, she said that "agreements that condition benefits to the buyer on exclusivity may be *de facto* exclusive dealing contracts if the 'practical effect' is 'to prevent . . . a buyer from using the products of the competitor of the . . . seller.'"[1949] Judge Koh also said that the Ninth Circuit, in its 2016 decision in *Aerotec v. Honeywell*, emphasized that "'discounts and rebates conditioned on a promise of exclusivity or on purchase of a specified quantity or market share of the seller's goods or services may be understood as "de facto" exclusive dealing contracts because they coerce buyers into purchasing a substantial amount of their needs from the seller.'"[1950] Again quoting *Aerotec*, Judge Koh then said that she "easily conclude[d] that both the TA and FATA were de facto exclusive deals because both coerced '[Apple] into purchasing a substantial amount of their needs from [Qualcomm].'"[1951]

It would be a misunderstanding and misstatement of fact to say that Qualcomm's two agreements with Apple *required* exclusivity. The TA and the FATA offered payments to Apple as a reward for exclusivity, and the agreements would terminate if Apple sold a product using a non-Qualcomm modem.[1952] Apple was not obligated to accept those benefits. It remained free to use modems manufactured by other suppliers if it wished to do so.[1953]

[1948] *Id.* at 19.
[1949] FTC v. Qualcomm Inc., 411 F. Supp. 3d 658, 762–63 (N.D. Cal. 2019) (alterations in original) (quoting *Tampa Electric*, 365 U.S. at 326).
[1950] *Id.* at 763 (quoting Aerotec Int'l, Inc. v. Honeywell Int'l, Inc., 836 F.3d 1171, 1182 (9th Cir. 2016)).
[1951] *Id.* (alterations in original) (quoting *Aerotec*, 836 F.3d at 1182).
[1952] *Id.*
[1953] *Id.* at 769.

1. *What Evidence of Allegedly Exclusive Dealing Did Judge Koh Identify and Weigh?*

Judge Koh based her finding of a coercive relationship on the *magnitude* of the payments that Qualcomm offered to Apple through the TA and the FATA. She found that, "[u]nder both the TA and FATA, Apple received hundreds of millions in incentives from Qualcomm only if Apple purchased substantial volumes of Qualcomm modem chips."[1954] Judge Koh also noted that the termination and clawback provisions in the TA and the FATA would require Apple to forfeit future payments and return past payments if it purchased modem chips from a supplier other than Qualcomm.[1955] Quoting Tony Blevins, Apple's Vice President of Procurement, Judge Koh found that the provisions of the TA and the FATA "effectively prevented Apple from buying modem chips from any supplier other than Qualcomm."[1956] In other words, she found that, even though the two agreements permitted Apple to procure modems from other suppliers, Apple in practice would have an incentive not to do so.[1957] Judge Koh reasoned that, to induce Apple to switch from Qualcomm and to forfeit the receipt of payments from Qualcomm that were conditioned on Apple's use of only Qualcomm's modems, a rival supplier would need to offer an excessive discount on the prices of its modems sold to Apple.[1958]

Judge Koh thus found that the TA and the FATA were *de facto* exclusive dealing agreements, each using price as the predominant mechanism to maintain Apple's alleged exclusivity.[1959] Put simply, Judge Koh found that Qualcomm secured Apple's loyalty by lowering the price of Qualcomm modems. However, the FTC did not allege and Judge Koh did not find that Qualcomm had ever engaged in predatory pricing with respect to its sales of modems to Apple under the TA or the FATA.

2. *Upon What Legal Authority Did Judge Koh Rely to Find That the TA and the FATA Were* De Facto *Exclusive Dealing Agreements?*

It is curious that Judge Koh quoted the Ninth Circuit's 2016 decision in *Aerotec* to support her conclusion that the TA and the FATA were *de facto* exclusive dealing agreements, because that Ninth Circuit decision clearly did not apply to the allegations in *FTC v. Qualcomm*. In *Aerotec*, the Ninth Circuit specifically did not reach a conclusion on recognizing a *de facto* exclusive

---

[1954] *Id.* at 763.
[1955] *Id.*
[1956] *Id.*
[1957] *Id.* at 763–64.
[1958] *Id.* at 763.
[1959] *Id.*

dealing theory of anticompetitive harm. Quoting Justice Stephen Breyer's opinion in *Barry Wright v. ITT Grinnell* when he still sat on the First Circuit, the Ninth Circuit said:

> Although we have not explicitly recognized a "de facto" exclusive dealing theory . . . , we need not reach the issue here because, at bottom, a plaintiff must still show that contracts that were induced were exclusive rather than run-of-the-mill contracts, which inevitably "'foreclose[]' or 'exclude[]' alternative sellers from *some* portion of the market, namely the portion consisting of what was bought."[1960]

Judge Koh turned the Ninth Circuit's language—and its reliance on Justice Breyer's reasoning in *Barry Wright*—on its head.

As we saw above, Judge Koh conceded that not every exclusive dealing agreement is anticompetitive. Yet, leaning heavily on the Third Circuit's decision in *ZF Meritor, LLC v. Eaton Corp.*[1961] to support her finding that the TA and the FATA were anticompetitive, she conspicuously ignored that, in *ZF Meritor*, the Third Circuit said that "the price-cost test may be utilized as a specific application of the 'rule of reason' when the plaintiff alleges that price is the vehicle of exclusion."[1962] Considering that Judge Koh emphatically found that price was Qualcomm's predominant mechanism in the TA and the FATA for achieving exclusion, one would naturally have expected her then to apply the price-cost test. As the Supreme Court explained in 1993 in *Brooke Group*, in a price-cost test the plaintiff must prove "that the [defendant's] prices . . . are below an appropriate measure of [the defendant's] costs."[1963] Yet, Judge Koh did not apply any price-cost test to determine whether the TA and the FATA were capable of harming competition in the relevant markets.

Instead, Judge Koh compared the TA and the FATA with the agreements between truck OEMs and a transmission manufacturer, Eaton, that the Third Circuit found to be anticompetitive in *ZF Meritor*.[1964] She observed that, in *ZF Meritor*, the Third Circuit found the agreements to be unlawful because (1) they excluded Eaton's competitors from 85 percent of the market, (2) the exclusive deals were at least five years in length, and the termination clauses in the agreements were not commercially feasible, and (3) the agreements included additional anticompetitive indicia.[1965] Judge Koh found that those (and other) factors supported her conclusion that the TA and the FATA were

---

[1960] Aerotec Int'l, Inc. v. Honeywell Int'l, Inc., 836 F.3d 1171, 1182 (9th Cir. 2016) (second and third alterations in original) (emphasis added by Ninth Circuit) (citations omitted) (quoting Barry Wright Corp. v. ITT Grinnell Corp., 724 F.2d 227, 236 (1st Cir. 1983) (Breyer, J.)).

[1961] 696 F.3d 254 (3d Cir. 2012).

[1962] *Id.* at 273 (internal citation omitted); *see also id.* at 274 n.11 ("[T]he price-cost test applies to market-share or volume rebates offered by suppliers within a single-product market.").

[1963] Brooke Grp. Ltd. v. Brown & Williamson Tobacco Corp., 509 U.S. 209, 222 (1993).

[1964] *FTC v. Qualcomm*, 411 F. Supp. 3d at 764–75 (citing *ZF Meritor*, 696 F.3d at 271).

[1965] *Id.*

anticompetitive. Yet, as we will see, proper analysis of each of those factors—as well as other factors that Judge Koh considered—in fact indicates that the TA and the FATA were not anticompetitive.

3. Did Qualcomm Achieve "Substantial Foreclosure"?

Economic scholarship explains that an exclusive dealing agreement that affects only a small portion of the relevant market cannot harm competition.[1966] Even with such an agreement in place, the supplier's rivals can compete for a significant share of the market by dealing with other buyers. That an exclusive dealing agreement forecloses a significant share of the relevant market is a necessary (but insufficient) condition for that agreement to have an anticompetitive effect. American courts have embraced this economic insight and have emphasized that evidence of "'[s]ubstantial foreclosure' continues to be a requirement for exclusive dealing to run afoul of the antitrust statutes."[1967]

To determine how much of the market an exclusive dealing agreement has foreclosed, one first must identify the relevant market, including its geographic scope. Judge Koh found that "the geographic boundaries of the CDMA modem chip market are worldwide, a conclusion that Qualcomm does not contest."[1968] Likewise, she found that "the geographic boundaries of the premium LTE modem chip market are worldwide, a conclusion that Qualcomm does not contest."[1969] Before trial, Professor Shapiro similarly had disclosed his opinion that each of these two relevant product markets was worldwide in its geographic scope.[1970] Yet, it does not appear that he testified on the question of geographic market definition at trial, presumably because Qualcomm did not dispute that each of the two alleged product markets was worldwide.

Despite having defined the relevant product markets and their geographic scope, Judge Koh strangely did not proceed to identify the share of the relevant market that the TA and the FATA had foreclosed. Consequently, on the basis of the evidence that she reported and weighed in her findings of

---

[1966] *See, e.g.,* J. Mark Ramseyer & Eric B. Rasmusen, *Exclusive Dealing: Before, Bork, and Beyond,* 57 J.L. & ECON. S145, S153 (2014) (explaining that exclusive dealing might be anticompetitive "only if [the] supplier . . . can foreclose a large enough fraction of the market to deny competitors the minimum efficient scale").

[1967] McWane, Inc. v. FTC, 783 F.3d 814, 837 (11th Cir. 2015) (citing no source in particular for the quoted phrase "substantial foreclosure"); *see also* Tampa Elec. Co. v. Nashville Coal Co., 365 U.S. 320, 328 (1961) ("[T]he competition foreclosed by the contract must be found to constitute a substantial share of the relevant market."); Morales-Villalobos v. Garcia-Llorens, 316 F.3d 51, 55 (1st Cir. 2003) ("[S]ubstantial foreclosure is ordinarily a requirement for a seller arguing that she or he has been unreasonably excluded from opportunities to sell.").

[1968] *FTC v. Qualcomm,* 411 F. Supp. 3d at 685.

[1969] *Id.* at 691.

[1970] Initial Expert Report of Carl Shapiro in *FTC v. Qualcomm, supra* note 115, at 3.

fact and conclusions of law, Judge Koh could not have determined whether Qualcomm's two agreements with Apple foreclosed a substantial share of the market.

If anything, the available evidence more supported the opposite conclusion. Eaton's contracts in *ZF Meritor* were found to have excluded competitors from 85 percent of the market. In contrast, as Figure 12 in Part XI.C.3.a reported, Apple's share of worldwide "premium" smartphone sales (smartphones priced above $400) was 36.6 percent in 2011, when the parties executed the TA, and 40.6 percent in 2013, when they executed the FATA.[1971] Judge Koh did not cite any evidence that Qualcomm's competitors or consumers were harmed by the foreclosure of less than half of what she identified to be the relevant market.

Instead of identifying and weighing objective economic analysis of actual competitive *effects*, Judge Koh emphasized the *subjective expectations* of Qualcomm's management. She found that Qualcomm believed that Apple's exclusivity could "eliminate competition in modem chip markets."[1972] To support that conclusion, she cited a Qualcomm internal email from 2010 in which Steve Mollenkopf, QCT President, wrote that, if Qualcomm entered into an exclusive agreement with Apple, there would likely not be enough demand for thin modems to support another thin modem competitor.[1973] Mr. Mollenkopf's prediction of course turned out to be wrong: Intel in fact eventually became that second supplier of thin modems for Apple's iPhone 7, 8, and X.

Yet, even if one were to accept—implausibly, but for sake of argument—that Qualcomm's subjective expectations were perfectly able to predict actual anticompetitive effects, this line of reasoning by Judge Koh would collapse as a factual matter for a separate reason that she did not acknowledge.

When read in context, Mr. Mollenkopf's email specifically and exclusively described competition for *thin* modems, which necessarily comprised only a subset of the products sold in what Judge Koh had defined as the relevant markets.[1974] Mr. Mollenkopf's phrase "standalone modem volume" is most reasonably understood to connote solely the output of (or demand for) *thin* modems, since he was specifically discussing Apple, which used (and

---

[1971] INT'L DATA CORP., IDC QUARTERLY MOBILE PHONE TRACKER: 2017Q4 HISTORICAL RELEASE, *supra* note 1722.

[1972] *FTC v. Qualcomm*, 411 F. Supp. 3d at 766.

[1973] *Id.* ("For example, in an August 2010 email, Steve Mollenkopf (QCT President) told Paul Jacobs (Qualcomm CEO), Derek Aberle (QTL President), and Steve Altman (Qualcomm President) that if Qualcomm secured Apple exclusivity in the TA, Qualcomm could eliminate any competition from modem chip markets: '[T]here are significant strategic benefits as it is unlikely that there will be enough standalone modem volume to sustain a viable competitor without that slot.'") (alteration in original) (quoting CX5348-001).

[1974] *Id.*

currently still uses) only thin modems.[1975] LTE modems of course include both thin modems and systems on a chip (SoCs), yet Mr. Mollenkopf's email plainly did not concern SoCs.

Consequently, the most evidentiary significance that Judge Koh could plausibly have imputed to this Qualcomm email is the proposition that the TA and the FATA could have eliminated competition in a *subset* of her chosen relevant markets. Mr. Mollenkopf's email did not say anything about overall competition in what Judge Koh found to be the relevant market. Because Judge Koh never identified what portion of "premium" LTE modems thin modems comprise, it was impossible for her to determine on the evidence that she identified and weighed what portion of her relevant market the TA and the FATA actually affected.

The inconsistency between Judge Koh's conclusion and the evidence that she reported and weighed arose because she erroneously omitted all actual analysis of the alleged harm from the TA and the FATA. Had Judge Koh attempted to quantify the percentage of her preferred relevant market that the TA and the FATA had actually foreclosed, she could not have escaped noticing that her conclusion that "substantial foreclosure" had occurred was lacking any factual foundation and thus necessarily led to a conspicuous error of law.

4. Did the Lost Benefits of Working with Apple That Rival Modem Manufacturers Supposedly Experienced Constitute Injuries-in-Fact?

Judge Koh said that the TA and the FATA also denied Qualcomm's rivals the benefits of working with Apple.[1976] Yet, the benefits that Judge Koh cited, some of which were speculative or vague, were actually evidence of the efficiency justifications for Qualcomm and Apple to have entered into those agreements rather than evidence that the TA and the FATA had anticompetitive effects on rival modem manufacturers. Specifically, Judge Koh found:

> Qualcomm's exclusive deals with Apple foreclosed Qualcomm's rivals from: (1) a revenue boost critical to funding research and development and acquisitions; (2) exposure to Apple's "best-in-class" engineering resources; (3) a foothold at Apple for future handsets; (4) opportunities to field test new products with Apple; (5) business opportunities from other OEMs; (6) enhanced standing in SSOs; and (7) opportunities to conduct early field testing and prototyping with network vendors and operators.[1977]

[1975] *See id.* at 674 ("'Thin modems' are standalone modem chips that provide only the core cellular functionality.") (quoting Transcript of Proceedings (Volume 7) at 1378:14, FTC v. Qualcomm Inc., No 5:17-cv-00220-LHK (N.D. Cal. Jan. 18, 2019) (Testimony of James Thompson (CTO, Qualcomm))).

[1976] *Id.* at 766–69.

[1977] *Id.* at 766.

Evidence of "foreclosed revenue" provided no information about the supposedly anticompetitive effects of the TA and the FATA. That argument was a well-known tautology. *Any* exclusive agreement forecloses competitors from the revenue resulting from that agreement. As noted earlier, Justice Breyer observed in *Barry Wright* that "virtually every contract to buy 'forecloses' or 'excludes' alternative sellers from *some* portion of the market, namely the portion consisting of what was bought."[1978]

It was also specious as a matter of elementary financial economics for Judge Koh to reason that Qualcomm's competitors could fund their R&D expenditures only from the free cash flow that would be generated from their modem sales to Apple. Implicit in Judge Koh's reasoning was a theory of corporate finance that a firm's intended use of funds dictates the firm's source of funds. Judge Koh did not further articulate that theory. She did not apply that theory symmetrically to consider the source of Qualcomm's funding of its R&D investment. Nor did she identify and weigh any evidence that would tend to prove her theory's validity and its relevance to the facts of *FTC v. Qualcomm*.

Similarly, exposure to the purchaser's resources, having a "foothold" on which to base future sales, increased business opportunities with the purchaser's other vendors, and field testing the products subject to the allegedly exclusive agreement all would be at least partially foreclosed to rivals from *any* exclusive agreement, including procompetitive exclusive agreements. In other words, these manifestations of foreclosure, even if factually proven to be observed effects rather than mere conjectures, still would not suffice to establish that the TA and the FATA were anticompetitive. Evidence of such effects would confirm at most that the two agreements produced benefits for Qualcomm, which is what any contract is expected to accomplish for each of its counterparties.

It was also tautological for Judge Koh to assert that an exclusive contract with Apple would be anticompetitive because it would deprive Qualcomm's competitors of the benefits of selling to Apple. Unless doing business with Apple was a necessary requirement for modem manufacturers to participate in the relevant markets, there could be no harm to competition from the TA and the FATA. There was in fact substantial evidence that doing business with Apple was *not* such a requirement. Jeff Williams, Apple's COO, testified at trial:

[1978] Barry Wright Corp. v. ITT Grinnell Corp., 724 F.2d 227, 236 (1st Cir. 1983) (Breyer, J.) (emphasis in original); *see also* Fishman v. Estate of Wirtz, 807 F.2d 520, 565 (7th Cir. 1986) (Easterbrook, J., dissenting) ("Every contract ends one form of competition and may create another. . . . So to observe that there has been a suppression of some competition . . . is to state rather than answer the antitrust question.").

Q. . . . [W]hen Apple first released the iPhone, it sourced the baseband processors from Infineon only; correct?

A. Correct.[1979]

Mr. Williams further explained:

Q. . . . After Intel bought Infineon, Apple switched over to sourcing baseband processors for new models from Qualcomm only; correct?

A. Correct, for a period of time.

Q. All right. And now Apple is sourcing baseband processors for the iPhone model it first released in 2018 from Intel only; correct?

A. Reluctantly because Qualcomm will not sell us their new technology.[1980]

Thus, Judge Koh's conjecture about the benefits derived from dealing with Apple was unpersuasive because two compelling pieces of evidence contradicted it: (1) *before* Apple and Qualcomm had agreed upon the TA and the FATA, Apple had purchased modems from Infineon, not Qualcomm; and (2) even before the second of those two agreements had expired at the end of 2016, Apple had begun to purchase modems from Intel. In neither case was a preexisting supply arrangement with Apple a prerequisite for the modem supplier to win Apple's future business. In both cases, a firm *not* currently supplying modems to Apple successfully competed in Judge Koh's relevant product markets. Doing business with Apple was not a prerequisite to participate in the market, much less to compete *for* the market—which is the more consequential manifestation of competition that Judge Koh should have evaluated but instead ignored.

5. *Did Qualcomm Coerce Apple Through the Duration or Termination Provisions of the TA and the FATA?*

Judge Koh did not report a reasoned finding that the TA and the FATA lasted so long as to be capable of harming competition in the relevant markets. She did acknowledge that exclusive dealing contracts that are of short duration or that are easily terminable are unlikely to foreclose competition.[1981] She then compared the length of the TA and the FATA, each allegedly having "a five-year duration," to the exclusive dealing agreements in *ZF Meritor*, which the Third Circuit found to be unlawful because they lasted at least five years

---

[1979] Transcript of Proceedings (Volume 5) at 902:24–903:1, FTC v. Qualcomm Inc., No. 5:17-cv-00220-LHK (N.D. Cal. Jan. 14, 2019) (Testimony of Jeff Williams (COO, Apple)).

[1980] *Id.* at 903:2–10.

[1981] *FTC v. Qualcomm*, 411 F. Supp. 3d at 770.

and were found not to be easily terminable.[1982] Yet, Judge Koh's comparison of the durations of the TA and the FATA to the durations of the exclusive agreements in *ZF Meritor* was fatuous.

a. *Was Judge Koh's Analysis of the Duration of the TA and the FATA Inconclusive?*

In regard to the TA and the FATA, Qualcomm's supposed "coercion" of Apple was limited to a price discount to which Apple agreed before executing the two contracts. However, when the parties executed the TA in 2011, Apple did not yet rely upon Qualcomm for any portion of its modems, because, as Mr. Williams' testimony quoted above confirmed, Apple at that time was using exclusively Infineon modems.[1983]

Consequently, Judge Koh had no factual basis for concluding that Apple had been coerced into using Qualcomm's modems exclusively at the beginning of the contract term owing to the potential clawback of rebates that Qualcomm was prepared to pay (but had not yet begun to pay) to Apple. In 2011, the past rebates that Apple would need to refund to Qualcomm if Apple were to breach the supposed exclusivity provision of the TA were $0.

In other words, Judge Koh's theory of coercion could not possibly begin to have any bite until some later point during the term of the TA, when Qualcomm's cumulative rebates to Apple had become so large as supposedly to "force" Apple to perform on its promise to buy a supposedly exclusive amount of its modem requirements from Qualcomm. The same reasoning applied to the FATA. For however long it took for the TA and the FATA to acquire some capacity for "coercion" (a question of fact that Judge Koh conspicuously did *not* identify and analyze), the two agreements could not have been *de facto* exclusive.

Therefore, although the TA and the FATA each lasted five years, the duration of the interval of *de facto* exclusive dealing of those two agreements was necessarily shorter than five years. Judge Koh did not recognize the need to ask as a factual matter how much shorter. Consequently, she did not determine how much time remained on the TA and the FATA after each agreement supposedly had become *de facto* exclusive in character within the reasoning of *ZF Meritor*. Consequently, her analysis of the duration of the TA and the FATA was incomplete and necessarily inconclusive. Judge Koh did not report that she had been able to identify and weigh reliable evidence to support her findings of fact and conclusions of law on the supposedly anticompetitive effects of the TA and the FATA owing to their duration.

[1982] *Id.*
[1983] *See supra* note 1979 and accompanying text.

b.   *Was It Commercially Feasible for Apple to End the TA and the FATA with Qualcomm?*

Judge Koh did not examine whether it was commercially feasible for Apple to end the TA and the FATA with Qualcomm. In *ZF Meritor*, Eaton was found to be a necessary supplier to truck OEMs. The Third Circuit had found that the OEMs needed to purchase some share of their transmissions from Eaton regardless of whether they purchased all of their transmissions from Eaton.[1984] The Third Circuit thereupon concluded that "Eaton leveraged its position as a supplier of necessary products to coerce the OEMs into entering into the [agreements]."[1985] In addition, Eaton was found to have included other terms in its agreements that implied that a buyer that did not use Eaton's products exclusively could potentially have lost Eaton entirely as a supplier.[1986]

Apple's situation with Qualcomm was entirely different. Recall that, before entering into the TA with Qualcomm in 2011, Apple purchased all of its modems from Infineon; and Apple purchased all of its modems for new models of iPhones introduced in 2018 from Intel. Those facts confirm that Qualcomm was not, in actuality, a necessary supplier to Apple. Both before and after the TA and the FATA, Apple conclusively demonstrated that it was willing and able to forgo buying Qualcomm modems. Because Qualcomm modems were demonstrably not necessary to Apple, Qualcomm could not leverage a position as a "necessary" supplier to Apple to coerce Apple into executing an exclusive agreement with Qualcomm for the supply of modems.

Therefore, the only limit to the commercial feasibility of Apple's power to terminate the TA and the FATA was the implicit cost to Apple of refunding past rebates that it had received on its purchases of modems from Qualcomm. In other words, the only thing "coercing" Apple was its need to refund price discounts on its cumulative purchases of modems from Qualcomm, discounts which of course Apple would have been entitled by contract to keep only if it had performed its end of the bargain. Apple at all times held the option to walk away from the TA or the FATA by refunding the discounts that it had received but not earned under the terms of the supply contract in question.

As with the duration of the *de facto* exclusive portion of the TA and the FATA, the portion of the contract term for the TA or the FATA during which Apple's power to terminate was not commercially feasible was surely shorter than either agreement's full duration. Therefore, Judge Koh's analysis of the feasibility of Apple's terminating the TA and the FATA was, again, conspicuously incomplete and provided no reliable evidence that supported her findings on the supposedly anticompetitive effects of the TA and the FATA.

[1984]   ZF Meritor, LLC v. Eaton Corp., 696 F.3d 254, 263 (3ᵈ Cir. 2012).
[1985]   *Id.* at 285.
[1986]   *Id.*

6. *Were Judge Koh's Additional Anticompetitive Indicia in the TA and the FATA Legally Irrelevant Because They Did Not Concern Markets in Which She Had Found Qualcomm to Possess Monopoly Power?*

Judge Koh cited other elements of the TA and the FATA that, in her view, supported the conclusion that the agreements were anticompetitive. She found that Qualcomm identified that the agreements prevented Apple from (1) working with Intel on an upcoming iPad model and (2) initiating patent litigation against Qualcomm.[1987] Yet, contrary to *ZF Meritor*, both of those examples—which Judge Koh did not independently analyze as a factual matter to determine whether each was actually anticompetitive—occurred *outside* the relevant product markets in which Judge Koh had found that Qualcomm possessed market power.

That is, Judge Koh condemned these additional terms of the TA and the FATA as anticompetitive without ever establishing as a factual matter that Qualcomm was capable of harming competition in the relevant product markets that *those* terms allegedly affected. Moreover, Judge Koh ignored that avoiding litigation is not an anticompetitive effect.

7. *Did Qualcomm's Agreements with Other OEMs Compound the Supposedly Anticompetitive Effects of the TA and the FATA?*

Judge Koh found that Qualcomm's allegedly exclusive agreements with other manufacturers compounded the supposedly anticompetitive effects of the TA and the FATA.[1988] For example, she found that, in 2016, Qualcomm gave LGE "chip incentive funds if LGE purchased at least 85% of its chips from Qualcomm" (although she did not say whether those chips were "premium" LTE modems or non-"premium" modems).[1989] Judge Koh also found that, in 2003, Qualcomm and Huawei executed a license agreement in which "Huawei agreed to purchase 100% of its CDMA chips for handsets sold in China from Qualcomm in exchange for a reduced royalty rate of 2.65%."[1990] Similarly, she found that, in 2013, Qualcomm executed a license agreement with Lenovo, in which Qualcomm agreed to offer Lenovo a rebate, provided that Lenovo commit "'to purchase at least 30M Snapdragon chips from QTI during the first 18 months . . . and at least 50M Snapdragon chips from QTI during the last 12 months.'"[1991]

[1987] *FTC v. Qualcomm*, 411 F. Supp. 3d at 769–70.

[1988] *Id.* at 770–72.

[1989] *Id.* at 699.

[1990] *Id.* at 710. In connection with the "royalty rate of 2.65%," Judge Koh did not specify the applicable royalty base or the scope of the intellectual property rights exchanged for that royalty.

[1991] *Id.* at 718 (quoting Email from Eric Reifschneider, Senior Vice President and General Manager, Qualcomm Technology Licensing (Nov. 19, 2013) (emphasis omitted by Judge Koh)).

Because Judge Koh did not make any findings based on actual analysis of the competitive effects of the TA and the FATA in her relevant markets, she necessarily did not make any findings based on actual analysis to support her conclusion that Qualcomm's agreements with *other* OEMs compounded those competitive effects arising from the TA and the FATA. Judge Koh merely said that "[t]he cumulative impact of Qualcomm's pattern of exclusive deals is to suppress the OEM sales available to rival modem chip suppliers and to substantially foreclose the market available to rivals."[1992]

As in her analysis of the TA and the FATA, Judge Koh did not identify which portion of her relevant markets Qualcomm supposedly had "foreclosed." Nor did Judge Koh say how much of those markets was contestable, or whether Qualcomm's rivals were able to achieve minimum efficient scale, or even whether the sales supposedly "foreclosed" from Qualcomm's rivals were within her relevant product markets. Without conducting any analysis of the actual magnitude of the alleged foreclosure or the economic effects of the supposedly *de facto* exclusivity of the TA and the FATA, Judge Koh found that Qualcomm violated the Sherman Act because those two agreements supposedly foreclosed "a 'substantial share' of the *modem chip market*"—which of course did not literally match any relevant product market that Judge Koh had defined in *FTC v. Qualcomm*.[1993]

C. Did Qualcomm "Coerce" Apple to Accept Lower Prices for Modems?

Judge Koh's conclusion that Apple was "coerced" to accept Qualcomm's payments was implausible. Basic economic principles teach that Apple—a sophisticated buyer of modems—would not have had any economic incentive to execute an agreement that would have enabled Qualcomm to monopolize the market for modems and subsequently exert monopoly power over Apple.

Judge Posner has explained that a buyer "assumes a big risk" by entering into an exclusive dealing agreement for the supply of an input.[1994] Once the supplier achieves a monopoly, the buyer will pay monopoly prices.[1995] Since at least 1976, Judge Posner has presented a simple example, inspired by the famous *United Shoe Machinery* monopolization case,[1996] to explain this economic insight:

> Suppose a manufacturer of shoe machinery offers to lease a machine for $10,000 a year under a lease terminable at will, while United offers to lease a similar machine for $9,000 a year but insists on a ten-year lease designed

---

[1992] *Id.* at 771.

[1993] *Id.* (emphasis added) (quoting Tampa Elec. Co. v. Nashville Coal Co., 365 U.S. 320, 327 (1961)).

[1994] POSNER, ANTITRUST LAW (2ᵈ ed.), *supra* note 948, at 230.

[1995] *Id.*

[1996] United States v. United Shoe Mach. Corp., 110 F. Supp. 295 (D. Mass.), *aff'd per curiam*, 347 U.S. 521 (1953).

to destroy competing producers and enable United to raise its price to $20,000 at the end of the term. The $9,000 price is no bargain to the shoe manufacturers. The deal offered by United imposes an additional cost on the purchaser measured by the present value of the higher price in the future. If that value is, say, $2,000 a year, United's offer is tantamount to charging the lessee $11,000.[1997]

Judge Posner's example illustrates that it would be irrational for a shoe manufacturer to enter into an agreement that, despite providing the shoe manufacturer a short-term discount on the price of an input (the shoe machinery), would facilitate the shoe machinery manufacturer's monopolization of the upstream market for that input.

It would have been similarly irrational for Apple to have executed the 2011 TA and the 2013 FATA if a foreseeable result of the supposed exclusivity attendant to each contract would have been that Qualcomm thereby could eliminate rival modem manufacturers. For years, Apple's management has publicly disclosed to investors that it is wary that "a number of components are currently obtained from single or limited sources, which subjects [Apple] to significant supply and pricing risks."[1998] It is not plausible that Apple would have executed the TA or the FATA in the belief that those agreements posed a risk that Qualcomm could monopolize the modem industry. It is not plausible—because it would not be rational—for a large, sophisticated company like Apple to buy from a supplier on terms that might enable the supplier to emerge subsequently as a monopolist by virtue of Apple's own voluntary conduct.

Professor Shapiro conceded this very point in cross examination during the FTC's case-in-chief in *FTC v. Qualcomm*:

> Q. . . . Apple wouldn't enter into any agreement that is against its own interests; right?
>
> A. So as an antitrust economist, my standing assumption is companies act in their own interests and try to maximize profit, and that would certainly apply to Apple.
>
> Q. All right. And you certainly wouldn't use the word "coerced" to describe the agreements that Qualcomm signed with Apple; right?

[1997] POSNER, ANTITRUST LAW (2ᵈ ed.), *supra* note 948, at 231. The same example appeared virtually verbatim in the original edition Judge Posner's antitrust book in 1976 and has become part of the canon of the Chicago School of antitrust analysis. *See* POSNER, ANTITRUST LAW: AN ECONOMIC PERSPECTIVE, *supra* note 1275, at 203–04.

[1998] Apple Inc., Annual Report for the Fiscal Year Ended September 29, 2012 (SEC Form 10-K), at 7 (filed Oct. 31, 2012) [hereinafter 2012 Apple 10-K]; *see also* Apple Inc., Annual Report for the Fiscal Year Ended September 29, 2018 (SEC Form 10-K), at 10 (filed Nov. 5, 2018) [hereinafter 2018 Apple 10-K].

A. I don't generally use the word "coerced" as an antitrust economist. I know people use it, business people use it, lawyers use it. I just—it's not a word that I tend to use.

Q. Well, but in fact you testified that in particular, you wouldn't use it here; right?

A. That is true. I don't use it in general, and I don't use it here.

Q. And you didn't use it in connection with the Apple agreement with Qualcomm; correct?

A. I did not.

Q. Instead, you said the Apple representatives negotiating the agreements were big boys and girls; right?

A. That sounds like me.

(Laughter.)

By Mr. Van Nest:

Q. And indeed it was.[1999]

Professor Shapiro recognized that it was implausible that the "big boys and girls" at a company as sophisticated as Apple would have executed supply agreements that were contrary to its own interest.

Judge Koh evidently did not consider that what she found to be an anticompetitive discount that Qualcomm gave Apple instead might have been the result of *Apple's own exercise of bargaining power* in its relationship with Qualcomm.[2000] It is routine for courts or antitrust enforcement agencies to consider the economic effects of powerful buyers in competitive analysis. For example, in the Horizontal Merger Guidelines, published jointly by the

---

[1999] Transcript of Proceedings (Volume 6) at 1220:15–1221:14, FTC v. Qualcomm Inc., No. 5:17-cv-00220-LHK (N.D. Cal. Jan. 15, 2019) (Testimony of Carl Shapiro). Curiously, when Professor Shapiro returned to the stand 13 days later to testify during the FTC's rebuttal case, he did speak of "coercion." Transcript of Proceedings (Volume 10) at 2068:23–2069:2, FTC v. Qualcomm Inc., No. 5:17-cv-00220-LHK (N.D. Cal. Jan. 28, 2019) (Testimony of Carl Shapiro) ("Q. This order [issued by the Japan Fair Trade Commission (JFTC) following its investigation of Qualcomm] has nothing to do whatsoever with using chip leverage to influence royalty rates, does it? A. I believe that—I don't know—I do not know, without checking my report more carefully, which I can do, exactly what the nature of the coercion was.").

[2000] Armen Alchian proposed a concise and penetrating definition of bargaining power: "If the highest price a person would be willing to pay for some item exceeds the price he is asked to pay by a large amount, one can choose to say he has great bargaining power. Thus, one *could* define bargaining power as the ratio of (a) the value of [the] good to some person to (b) what he must pay to get it. If (a) does not exceed (b), he has zero bargaining power." ALCHIAN, *Words: Musical or Meaningful?*, *supra* note 1761, at 562 (emphasis in original). My own approach to defining bargaining power in patent licensing resembles Alchian's. *See* Sidak, *Bargaining Power and Patent Damages*, *supra* note 623, at 10–17. However, I focus on the percentage of the surplus from a voluntary exchange that a party gets. Thus, my approach considers more than the ratio of the buyer's willingness to pay to the bargained-for price; it also considers (1) the seller's minimum willingness to accept and (2) the division of surplus between the buyer and the seller. *See* Sidak, *What Makes FRAND Fair? The Just Price, Contract Formation, and the Division of Surplus from Voluntary Exchange*, *supra* note 623, at 702–03.

Antitrust Division and the FTC, the agencies noted that powerful buyers "may constrain the ability of the merging parties to raise prices."[2001]

Yet, throughout her analysis of the TA and the FATA, Judge Koh portrayed Apple as the hapless victim of those agreements, rather than a willing party to them.

D. Did the TA and the FATA Have Procompetitive Effects?

Although Judge Koh did not perform any rigorous analysis of the effects of the TA and the FATA, she nonetheless "conclude[d] that because Qualcomm's exclusive deals with Apple foreclosed a 'substantial share' of the modem chip market, Qualcomm's exclusive deals violated the Sherman Act."[2002] She then rejected Qualcomm's efficiency justification for entering into the two agreements. Judge Koh's exiguous findings on the procompetitive rationale for the TA and the FATA were neither intellectually rigorous nor faithful to controlling precedent.

1. The Benefits of Low Prices

Judge Koh sometimes characterized Qualcomm's payments to OEMs as a *reduced royalty* for an exhaustive license to Qualcomm's portfolio of cellular SEPs.[2003] At other times, she characterized those payments as a *rebate on the*

[2001] U.S. DEP'T OF JUSTICE & FED. TRADE COMM'N, HORIZONTAL MERGER GUIDELINES, *supra* note 924, at 27.

[2002] FTC v. Qualcomm Inc., 411 F. Supp. 3d 658, 771–72 (N.D. Cal. 2019) (quoting Tampa Elec. Co. v. Nashville Coal Co., 365 U.S. 320, 327 (1961)).

[2003] *Id.* at 771 ("In 2016, QTL offered Motorola a chip incentive fund that Motorola concluded would reduce Motorola's effective royalty rate to 3.8% only if Motorola purchased 100% of its modem chips from Qualcomm."); *id.* at 793 (reiterating that, "[i]n 2016, QTL offered Motorola a chip incentive fund that Motorola concluded would reduce Motorola's effective royalty rate to 3.8% only if Motorola purchased 100% of its modem chips from Qualcomm"); *id.* at 716 (discussing a "significantly reduced effective royalty rate" for Motorola); *id.* at 702 ("In 2016, Qualcomm again used chip incentive funds to lower LGE's effective royalty rates on Qualcomm chips only. On or about December 11, 2015, LGE filed a Request for Arbitration with the International Chamber of Commerce in a matter captioned *LG Electronics Inc. v. Qualcomm Inc.* According to Hwi-Jae Cho (Director of LGE Intellectual Property Center), LGE argued in the arbitration that Qualcomm had not reduced its royalty rate even though Qualcomm's patents had become fully paid up under LGE's existing SULA. '[T]here was no royalty rate adjustment even after the fully paid up rights matured.' Under a fully paid up agreement, the licensee's royalty obligations may expire after a certain term. On or about February 18, 2016, Qualcomm filed a response to LGE's Request for Arbitration." (citations omitted) (quoting Redacted Cho Document, Annex B, Witness-Examination Questionnaire to Employee Designated by LG Electronics, Inc. with Knowledge of LGE's Patent License Negotiations with Qualcomm (Mar. 30, 2018) ¶ 195, FTC v. Qualcomm Inc., No. 5:17-cv-00220-LHK (N.D. Cal. Jan. 11, 2019), ECF No. 1246) (citing Joint Stipulation Regarding Undisputed Facts, *supra* note 144, at 8); *id.* at 705 ("Qualcomm has engaged in anticompetitive conduct toward Samsung by threatening Samsung's chip supply, reducing the royalty rate if Samsung purchased at least 85% of its chipsets from Qualcomm."); *id.* at 709 (reiterating that "Qualcomm has engaged in anticompetitive conduct toward Samsung by threatening Samsung's chip supply, reducing the royalty rate if Samsung purchased at least 85% of its chipsets from Qualcomm"); *id.* at 710 ("In the 2003 CDMA SULA, Huawei agreed to purchase 100% of its CDMA chips for handsets sold in China from Qualcomm in exchange for a reduced royalty rate of 2.65%. JX0022-010, -012. However, if Huawei purchased chips from another supplier, or if Huawei sold handsets outside of China, Huawei owed a 5–7% royalty rate on those handsets.") (citations omitted) It is not clear

price of the modem.[2004] Both conclusions are internally inconsistent with findings that Judge Koh made elsewhere in her findings of fact and conclusions of law, where she said that Qualcomm charged a monopoly price for *both* its modems and an exhaustive license to its portfolio of cellular SEPs.[2005]

a.   *Was Apple "Free to Choose" Its Modem Supplier?*

In her discussion of the allegedly exclusive dealing in the TA and the FATA, Judge Koh never used the phrase "royalty rebate" or "royalty rebates,"[2006] although in other parts of her findings of fact and conclusions of law she said that Qualcomm offered Apple a royalty rebate in exchange for supposed exclusivity.[2007] Regardless of whether Judge Koh considered Qualcomm's payment to Apple to be a reduction in the price of a Qualcomm modem or a royalty rebate for an exhaustive license to Qualcomm's portfolio of cellular SEPs, she did not consider the benefits of reduced prices on competition in her relevant markets.

Instead, Judge Koh cited the trial testimony of Tony Blevins, Apple's vice president of procurement, on "how the FATA prevented Apple from choosing the most competitive modem chip" in 2014.[2008] Mr. Blevins testified:

> [W]e'd entered into agreements that offered Apple very significant sums of money for using their [Qualcomm's] chipsets exclusively. So it wasn't the kind of free market that would give us freedom to choose whomever we might want based on a level playing field.[2009]

---

from any findings that Judge Koh made whether Huawei actually paid a higher royalty on devices that used non-Qualcomm modems than on devices that used Qualcomm modems. *See id.* at 710, 714 (giving Huawei "a drastically reduced royalty rate").

[2004] *Id.* at 770 ("For example, in 2010, Qualcomm gave BlackBerry [Redacted] million in chip incentives, which BlackBerry received as rebates on QCT modem chips. . . . Grubbs [referring to John Grubbs, BlackBerry Senior Director of Intellectual Property Transactions] testified that because Qualcomm did not reduce BlackBerry's overall royalty burden, the chip incentive fund reduced the effective price of only Qualcomm modem chips[.]"); *id.* at 702 ("According to a May 2007 Qualcomm accounting memo, Qualcomm offered LGE a 'Strategic Fund,' under which Qualcomm rebated LGE 3–4% of the purchase price on each Qualcomm CDMA or WCDMA modem chip that LGE purchased from 2007 to 2014.") (quoting CX7556-002); *id.* at 718 ("In a November 19, 2013 email, Eric Reifschneider (Senior Vice President and General Manager, Qualcomm Technology Licensing) proposed that Qualcomm would rebate Lenovo $5 for every Qualcomm modem chip Lenovo purchased, up to a total of $180 million.").

[2005] *Id.* at 800.

[2006] *See id.* at 762–72.

[2007] *Id.* at 728 ("[D]uring the TA negotiations, . . . Qualcomm was focused on using Apple's desire for royalty rate rebates to secure exclusivity."); *id.* at 730 ("In 2013, Qualcomm again gave Apple royalty rate rebates in exchange for Apple's effective commitment to purchase modem chips exclusively from Qualcomm."); *id.* at 729 (referring to Tony Blevins' statement that "there would be large rebates associated with the nominal royalty payments if we [Apple] were to use Qualcomm chips exclusively") (citing Transcript of Proceedings (Volume 4) at 689:7–9, FTC v. Qualcomm Inc., No. 5:17-cv-00220-LHK (N.D. Cal. Jan. 11, 2019) (Testimony of Tony Blevins (Vice President of Procurement, Apple))).

[2008] *Id.* at 735–36.

[2009] *Id.* at 736 (first alteration in original) (quoting Transcript of Proceedings (Volume 4) at 701:21–25, FTC v. Qualcomm Inc., No. 5:17-cv-00220-LHK (N.D. Cal. Jan. 11, 2019) (Testimony of Tony Blevins (Vice President of Procurement, Apple))).

Judge Koh did not disparage Mr. Blevins' credibility, so she evidently found that his testimony truthfully conveyed his knowledge and beliefs. Perhaps a different judge would have found it implausible that a "free market" and "a level playing field" had been upended, and that Apple had been denied its "freedom to choose," all because Apple—having entered into an (allegedly) exclusive supply contract for modems, pursuant to which Qualcomm had paid Apple "very significant sums of money" to lower its effective modem price—thereafter felt entitled to the same choices of modem supply as if Qualcomm and Apple had never executed the FATA and Qualcomm had never paid Apple those "very significant sums of money."

> *b.   Intel's Cost Disadvantage Relative to Qualcomm in Modem Supply to Apple*

Moreover, Judge Koh ignored admissions by Aicha Evans, Intel's Chief Strategy Officer, that Intel understood as of May 2017 that the cost to Intel of producing an unlicensed thin modem exceeded the cost to Qualcomm of producing an unlicensed thin modem. In her cross examination during the FTC's case-in-chief, Ms. Evans testified about a slide deck, entitled "Multi Generational LTE Pricing Proposal" and bearing the exhibit number QX95, which "the Apple sales team at Intel" attached to an email dated May 30, 2017 that Ms. Evans had received.[2010]

Ms. Evans admitted that Intel's unlicensed "product cost of its modem chips [was] higher than Qualcomm's."[2011] She further admitted that, as of May 2017, Intel's "projected product costs for Intel modem chips from 2017 through 2019" exceeded "Intel's best estimates of what Qualcomm's product costs" were:

> Q. . . . [D]oes the Intel column on the left of this table [on slide 3 of QX95] have projected product costs for Intel modem chips from 2017 through 2019?
>
> A. Yes.
>
> Q. And does the Qualcomm column on the right have Intel's estimate of Qualcomm's product cost for its slim modems during that same time period?
>
> A. Yeah. I mean, our best guesstimate; right? We don't work at Qualcomm, so—

[2010] Transcript of Proceedings (Volume 4) at 655:4–15, FTC v. Qualcomm Inc., No. 5:17-cv-00220-LHK (N.D. Cal. Jan. 11, 2019) (Testimony of Aichatou Evans (Chief Strategy Officer, Intel)).

[2011] *Id.* at 655:1–3 ("Q. . . . Intel has concluded that the product cost of its modem chips is higher than Qualcomm's; right? A. Yes."); *see also id.* at 657:3–9 ("Q. And these are chip product costs without any license royalties included; right? A. We, we never know with Qualcomm. We assume. I mean, we don't work there and we don't know how the shifting happens. Q. So as far as you know, all the data shown there on QX 95, slide 3, are chip product costs with no license rights; right? A. We assume so.").

Q. Sure.

A. Uh-huh.

Q. But these are Intel's best estimates of what Qualcomm's product costs are; right?

A. Yes.

Q. And as shown in QX 95, Intel's product costs are higher than Qualcomm's; right?

A. Yeah. It's hard to compete with you guys. With Qualcomm, we have to pick our spots, and we were very clear that first we get the socket, second we get the seat at the table with respect to the strategy, and then we drive to profitability.[2012]

In addition, Intel projected that the "product cost gap" between Intel modems and Qualcomm's modems was "worsening" between 2017 and 2019.[2013] Judge Koh's findings of fact and conclusions of law did not mention any of these material admissions by Ms. Evans, and Judge Koh thus ignored the relevance of this testimony to Apple's choice to purchase Qualcomm's thin modems or Intel's thin modems.

c.   The Misapplication of Monopolization Principles

By failing to consider the positive effects that low prices have for consumers and for the competitive process, Judge Koh flouted the most fundamental principle of 130 years of American antitrust jurisprudence. Judge Koh found that "Qualcomm's billion-dollar exclusive deals with Apple are the most prominent single example of Qualcomm *eliminating* chip price competition for OEM business."[2014] This astonishing finding by Judge Koh epitomized the Supreme Court's concern in cases like *linkLine* and *Brooke Group* that a misapplication of monopolization principles could punish, and thus deter, beneficial price competition.

   Low prices are the very essence of competition. The Court emphasized in *Brooke Group* that "[l]ow prices benefit consumers regardless of how those prices are set, and so long as they are above predatory levels, they do not threaten competition. . . . We have adhered to this principle regardless of the type of antitrust claim involved."[2015]

   In *linkLine*, the Court further said that, because "[c]utting prices in order to increase business often is the very essence of competition . . . , [i]n cases

---

[2012]   *Id.* at 656:8–657:2.

[2013]   *Id.* at 656:4–7 ("Q. . . . [D]o you see on the right-hand side of this slide a table headed product cost gap worsening? A. Yes.").

[2014]   *FTC v. Qualcomm*, 411 F. Supp. 3d at 793–94 (emphasis added).

[2015]   Brooke Grp. Ltd. v. Brown & Williamson Tobacco Corp., 509 U.S. 209, 223 (1993).

seeking to impose antitrust liability for prices that are too low, mistaken inferences are 'especially costly, because they chill the very conduct that antitrust laws are designed to protect.'"[2016] The logic of *linkLine* applies with equal force to exclusive dealing contracts when the firm seeking the exclusivity cuts its prices or offers other financial inducements to secure the exclusive contract. Judge Koh did not consider that principle in her analysis of Qualcomm's payments to Apple. She did not perform the necessary analysis to determine whether Qualcomm's payments could harm competition, and she rejected arguments about the procompetitive effects that would predictably flow from Qualcomm's offering of low prices.

Judge Koh did not see that Qualcomm's discounts to Apple reified the price competition that the Supreme Court extolled in *Brooke Group* and *linkLine*. She also did not recognize that the design-win tournament among Qualcomm and other modem manufacturers to win a contract to supply Apple with thin modems for a new version of the iPhone exemplified dynamic competition. Simply put, sellers will offer per-unit discounts to win an exclusive contract with a downstream buyer. Judge Koh did not recognize that competition *for* the market is more consequential for innovation and consumer welfare in a technologically dynamic industry than is competition *within* the market at any given moment in time. Consequently, she did not consider the benefits to competition from the TA and the FATA when analyzing their effects in her relevant markets.

2. The Potential Benefits of the TA and the FATA

When cooperation between two parties requires one party to make a significant relationship-specific investment, which is defined as a sunk investment made in support of a specific transaction that has no salvage value in an alternative use if the transaction prematurely ends, the parties might best be served by negotiating the terms of their cooperation *ex ante* rather than engaging in repeated bargaining after the party in question has incurred the relationship-specific costs.[2017] The late Nobel laureate Oliver Williamson explained that the risk of opportunistic behavior lurks once one party has made a relationship-specific investment.[2018] This potential for opportunism

---

[2016] Pacific Bell Tel. Co. v. linkLine Commc'ns, Inc., 555 U.S. 438, 451 (2009) (quoting Matsushita Elec. Indus. Co. v. Zenith Radio Corp., 475 U.S. 574, 594 (1986)).

[2017] *See* WILLIAMSON, THE ECONOMIC INSTITUTIONS OF CAPITALISM, *supra* note 651, at 52–56, 61; *see also* Oliver E. Williamson, *Transaction-Cost Economics: The Governance of Contractual Relations, supra* note 649, at 234; Klein, Crawford & Alchian, *Vertical Integration, Appropriable Rents, and the Competitive Contracting Process, supra* note 649, at 298.

[2018] *See* WILLIAMSON, THE ECONOMIC INSTITUTIONS OF CAPITALISM, *supra* note 651, at 61. For a survey of this literature as it pertains to the licensing of SEPs, see Sidak, *Is Patent Holdup a Hoax?, supra* note 118, at 414–17.

presents the classic problem of "holdup."[2019] Williamson explained how rational actors will anticipate the risk of holdup and take countermeasures to mitigate it. To the extent that Judge Koh properly attempted to view the TA and the FATA through the lens of Williamsonian transaction-cost economics, her analysis was flawed and incomplete.

a.   *The TA and the FATA as Mechanisms for Qualcomm's Recovery of Its Relationship-Specific Investment to Design Thin Modems for Apple*

An agreement that stimulates loyalty among the parties, such as an exclusive dealing agreement, can promote investment by memorializing the terms of a repeated transaction, reducing the risk of *ex post* opportunism, and enabling a party to recover its relationship-specific investment.[2020] The 2011 TA and the 2013 FATA between Qualcomm and Apple, which encouraged and memorialized Apple's intended loyalty to Qualcomm, protected Qualcomm's ability to recoup its relationship-specific investments undertaken to develop thin LTE modems for use specifically in Apple's products. Without the 2011 TA and the 2013 FATA in place, Qualcomm would have had a diminished incentive to invest in the development of the thin LTE modem that Apple required, because no other OEMs used thin modems in smartphones.

Judge Koh denigrated the specificity of the risk bearing that Qualcomm undertook when it willingly invested in the development of thin modems to accommodate the unique architecture that Apple had chosen for its iPhone. Because the 2011 TA and the 2013 FATA reduced Apple's incentive to switch modem suppliers, the two agreements decreased the risk that Apple would enjoy the benefits of Qualcomm's development of thin modems without compensating Qualcomm fully for the relationship-specific investment that had been necessary for Qualcomm to develop such modems. When the risk of opportunism threatens a firm's ability to recoup its relationship-specific investments, the firm faces an incentive to redirect its investments to less valuable innovations.

By mitigating the risk of opportunism, loyalty incentives can aid the development of high-quality products.[2021] Thus, by reducing the perceived risk that Apple would engage in opportunism, the 2011 TA and the 2013

[2019]   *See* Klein, Crawford & Alchian, *Vertical Integration, Appropriable Rents, and the Competitive Contracting Process*, *supra* note 649, at 298–99.

[2020]   *See* Paul L. Joskow, *Contract Duration and Relationship-Specific Investments: Empirical Evidence from Coal Markets*, 77 Am. Econ. Rev. 168, 168–69 (1987).

[2021]   *See, e.g.*, Daniel A. Crane, *Bargaining Over Loyalty*, 92 Tex. L. Rev. 253, 298–99 (2013) ("[A] wide business-management literature stresses the benefits to buyers of entering into long-term monogamous or semimonogamous relationships with suppliers—of pursuing loyal relationships. Among the frequently cited benefits of buyer-seller loyalty is . . . contributing to product-quality improvement by securing the seller's attention to the buyer's needs.").

FATA enabled Qualcomm to focus on developing high-quality products for Apple, which benefited Qualcomm, Apple, and U.S. consumers. Judge Koh did not consider that possibility.

> b. *Qualcomm's Lawsuit in November 2017 Alleging That Apple Had Misappropriated Trade Secrets Concerning Qualcomm's Modems and Had Given That Confidential Information to Intel to Assist Its Development of Competing Modems*

The relationship between Apple and Qualcomm badly deteriorated. In November 2017, Qualcomm sued Apple in state court in California for allegedly disclosing Qualcomm's trade secrets related to its modems to Intel.[2022] In its amended complaint filed by Quinn Emanuel, Jones Day, and Cravath, Swaine & Moore in September 2018, Qualcomm alleged in relevant part:

> Apple has engaged in a years-long campaign of false promises, stealth, and subterfuge designed to steal Qualcomm's confidential information and trade secrets for the purpose of improving the performance and accelerating time to market of lower-quality modem chipsets, including those developed by Intel Corporation ("Intel"), a competitor of Qualcomm, to render such chipsets useable in Apple iPhones and other devices, with the ultimate goal of diverting Qualcomm's Apple-based business to Intel. Apple has wrongfully acquired, failed to protect, wrongfully used, wrongfully disclosed, and outright stolen Qualcomm's confidential information and trade secrets, and Apple used that stolen technology to divert Qualcomm's Apple-based business to Intel.[2023]

These statements of course were allegations in a complaint, not proven facts. Still, they illustrated why parties might have considered it necessary and proper to resort to exclusive dealing to mitigate the risk of possible freeriding, of which the misappropriation of trade secrets would be but one manifestation—though potentially a substantially more serious manifestation of freeriding than merely not being paid for one's supply of a specialized product to a customer.

These allegations in California state court were publicly reported by Reuters in September 2018, well before the trial in *FTC v. Qualcomm*.[2024] In her findings of fact and conclusions of law in *FTC v. Qualcomm* Judge Koh

---

[2022] Complaint for Breach of Contract, Qualcomm Inc. v. Apple Inc., No. 37-2017-00041389 (Cal. Super. Ct. Nov. 1, 2017).

[2023] First Amended Complaint for Breach of Contract and Trade Secret Misappropriation (Civil Code § 3426, *et seq.*) ¶ 3, at 2, Qualcomm Inc. v. Apple Inc., No. 37-2017-00041389 (Cal. Super. Ct. Sept. 24, 2018).

[2024] Stephen Nellis, *Qualcomm Accuses Apple of Stealing Its Secrets to Help Intel*, Reuters, Sept. 28, 2018.

could have taken judicial notice of the existence of that ongoing litigation by Qualcomm alleging trade secret misappropriation by Apple for the benefit of Intel. But she did not.

c. Taking Seriously the Transaction Costs Savings of Achieving Customer Loyalty

On the topic of loyalty rebates paid by a seller to a buyer, Judge Posner has offered a startling conjecture: "Still another possibility is that loyalty rebates are intended to induce—loyalty. Another name for that might be low transaction costs and customer inertia, which might be another name for economizing on transaction costs."[2025]

By encouraging Apple's loyalty, the 2011 TA and the 2013 FATA reduced, on the margin, the risk that rival modem manufacturers could appropriate the benefits of Qualcomm's investments specifically undertaken to serve Apple's particular commercial needs, considering its exclusive use among smartphone manufacturers of thin modems instead of SoCs in handsets. If, in retrospect, evidence revealed that the TA and the FATA had failed to prevent opportunistic behavior—as Qualcomm's November 2017 lawsuit in California state court implied, if one were to assume those allegations to be true for sake of argument (as, for example, a court would so assume in a motion to dismiss)—then that conclusion regarding the incomplete efficacy of the TA and the FATA would indicate that even their alleged exclusivity was not sufficient to avert Apple's contractual opportunism.

That conclusion of incomplete efficacy certainly would not be evidence that, as Judge Koh eventually found, the alleged exclusivity attendant to the TA and the FATA lacked a procompetitive rationale. However, such evidence of the incomplete efficacy of the loyalty provisions in the TA and the FATA *would* be highly probative evidence that no less restrictive alternative existed that would have been equally or more efficacious in achieving Qualcomm's procompetitive objective of recovering its relationship-specific investment to supply Apple with modems. Put differently, the loyalty provisions in the TA and the FATA turned out to be necessary but obviously not sufficient, considering that the commercial relationship so disintegrated that Qualcomm and Apple were suing one another in multiple fora for breach of contract, among other causes of action. That failure of contracting should have prompted Judge Koh to ask, what contractual provisions in the TA and the FATA would have been both necessary *and* sufficient to achieve Qualcomm's procompetitive objective?

[2025] Richard A. Posner, *Vertical Restraints and Antitrust Policy*, 72 U. Chi. L. Rev. 229, 240 (2005).

3. Was Exclusivity Necessary to Support Qualcomm's Relationship-Specific Investment?

Judge Koh rejected as unreliable the testimony of every one of Qualcomm's expert economic witnesses.[2026] Consequently, the only proffered efficiency justification that she considered as an affirmative defense in her analysis of the TA and the FATA was whether the economic value to Qualcomm of Apple's exclusivity, when evaluated on a *retrospective* basis rather than a prospective basis, was necessary to support the relationship-specific investments that Qualcomm had made to develop thin modems that Apple could use in its mobile devices.[2027]

a. Investment Without Uncertainty

Judge Koh's analysis of Qualcomm's efficiency justification was incoherent as a matter of law and as a matter of economics. It ignored and contradicted Judge Easterbrook's insights concerning the consequences of legal rules for future economic behavior.[2028]

Judge Koh inappropriately used an *ex post* analysis where the circumstances obviously called for an *ex ante* analysis. Consequently, the conclusions that she drew from her analysis of Qualcomm's procompetitive rationale for its (supposed) exclusivity in the TA and the FATA were necessarily unreliable. Judge Koh was inventing a new but specious economic concept: investment without uncertainty.

b. Judge Koh's Ex Post Reinterpretation of Qualcomm's Ex Ante "Target Payback Ratio" for Investment in Modems

With perfect hindsight, Judge Koh found that, as it turned out, Qualcomm did not need to sell any of its MDM 9x15 modems to Apple to achieve its minimum desired rate of return on investment on those modems, which Qualcomm had called its "target payback ratio."[2029] Yet, in yet another apparent violation of Federal Rule of Civil Procedure 52(a)(1), she did not specify what companies besides Apple were buying thin modems, such that sales to Apple would not be necessary for Qualcomm to recoup its cost of designing thin modems.

[2026] FTC v. Qualcomm Inc., 411 F. Supp. 3d 658, 805 (N.D. Cal. 2019) ("[T]he Court finds that Dr. [Edward] Snyder's opinions are not reliable."); *id.* ("[T]he Court finds that Dr. [Aviv] Nevo's opinions are not reliable."); *id.* ("[T]he Court finds that Dr. [Tasneem] Chipty's opinions are not reliable.").

[2027] *Id.* at 772.

[2028] *See supra* text accompanying notes 257–262.

[2029] FTC v. Qualcomm, 411 F. Supp. 3d at 772 (citing Transcript of Proceedings (Volume 8) at 1753:2–5, FTC v. Qualcomm Inc., No. 5:17-cv-00220-LHK (N.D. Cal. Jan. 22, 2019) (Testimony of Tasneem Chipty)).

Judge Koh, though she did not find Dr. Chipty to be a reliable expert economic witness for Qualcomm, nonetheless relied on Dr. Chipty's testimony "that Qualcomm generally targets a payback ratio of three, such that a product's gross margin should triple the upfront research and development investment."[2030] Similarly, Judge Koh, again relying on the testimony of Dr. Chipty, found that, to achieve its target payback ratio of 3 on a different modem, the MDM 9x25, Qualcomm needed to sell some MDM 9x25 modems to Apple, but not 100 percent of the modems that it actually ended up selling to Apple.[2031]

That is, Judge Koh found that, when one viewed *ex post* Qualcomm's investments in modems to supply to Apple, Qualcomm could have attained its target payback ratio with respect to its MDM 9x25 modems even if Apple had not purchased its modems exclusively from Qualcomm. With the benefit of this perfect hindsight, Judge Koh found that Qualcomm did not really need exclusivity with Apple to recover its investments in developing those modems and that, in the specific case of its MDM 9x15 modem, Qualcomm ended up not needing any sales at all to Apple to justify that investment internally.[2032]

Judge Koh then concluded that those findings of fact contradicted Qualcomm's claims, in its proposed findings of fact and conclusions of law, that (on an *ex ante* basis) exclusive supply agreements with Apple "were necessary to defray 'relationship-specific' costs" of designing thin modems for Apple.[2033] Judge Koh found Qualcomm's efficiency defense predicated on the recovery of relationship-specific investment to be—let us guess the adjective—"pretextual."[2034]

Because the only economic authority that Judge Koh cited in her findings of fact and conclusions of law was an undergraduate microeconomics textbook, it is unclear whether she had ever read the writings of the late Nobel laureate Oliver Williamson on the topic of relationship-specific investment. If she had not, perhaps Judge Koh believed that Qualcomm's unreliable expert economic witness simply made up, as a pretext, the concern over Qualcomm's recovery of its relationship-specific investment with respect to its development of thin modems for Apple.

[2030] *Id.* (citing Transcript of Proceedings (Volume 8) at 1752:10–13, FTC v. Qualcomm Inc., No. 5:17-cv-00220-LHK (N.D. Cal. Jan. 22, 2019) (Testimony of Tasneem Chipty)).

[2031] *Id.* (citing Transcript of Proceedings (Volume 8) at 1753:13–16, FTC v. Qualcomm Inc., No. 5:17-cv-00220-LHK (N.D. Cal. Jan. 22, 2019) (Testimony of Tasneem Chipty)).

[2032] *Id.*

[2033] *Id.* (quoting Qualcomm's Proposed Findings of Fact and Conclusions of Law, *supra* note 1771, at 130).

[2034] *Id.*

c. *Judge Koh's Imposition of a Retroactive Prudency Review of Qualcomm's Sunk Investment in Risky Innovation*

Did Judge Koh even ask a coherent question when examining on a retrospective basis whether exclusivity was necessary to achieve Qualcomm's target payback ratio? Judge Koh did not identify any antitrust decision holding that the rule of reason requires the defendant to calculate the expected or required rate of return on contractual exclusivity to prove the lawfulness of exclusivity as an ancillary restraint in a supply agreement. Nor did Judge Koh identify any court decision holding that such an analysis is properly done on an *ex post* basis rather than an *ex ante* basis. (As we saw earlier, Judge Easterbrook ably explained why we properly would expect to search in vain for such a judicial opinion.) Judge Koh did not cite any case holding that evidence that the exclusivity is necessary to achieve some target rate of return on investment is, in turn, necessary for the defendant to prove that an exclusive dealing provision advances a procompetitive rationale that is essential to the commercial success of the overall agreement.

Moreover, even if antitrust jurisprudence had clearly established that the expected rate of return on investment was a necessary data point for the court to examine, the inquiry surely should focus on whether exclusivity was believed to be necessary *at the time of contracting*, not whether exclusivity was retrospectively confirmed to have been necessary in fact, after market uncertainties had lifted. Judge Koh's focus on retrospective necessity-in-fact was not even consistent with her own (errant) focus on Qualcomm's intent rather than the competitive effects of Qualcomm's actions. To the extent that Judge Koh examined whether Qualcomm's procompetitive rationale was valid as a function of some targeted rate of return on its relationship-specific investment, she seemed to be treating Qualcomm as a regulated public utility subject to cost-of-service rate-of-return regulation. Obviously, that approach was fundamentally in conflict with an antitrust inquiry into an unregulated firm's making of risky investments in innovative activity.[2035]

It is of course a familiar theme in the economics of regulation that interest groups and regulators alternate between *ex ante* policies and *ex post* policies concerning the allowable recovery of the costs of long-lived assets as doing so suits their short-term economic objectives.[2036] So, for example, there

---

[2035] *See* Easterbrook, *The Supreme Court 1983 Term-Foreword: The Court and the Economic System*, *supra* note 257, at 10–11.

[2036] *See, e.g.*, SIDAK & SPULBER, DEREGULATORY TAKINGS AND THE REGULATORY CONTRACT: THE COMPETITIVE TRANSFORMATION OF NETWORK INDUSTRIES IN THE UNITED STATES, *supra* note 740, at 102–13; JEAN-JACQUES LAFFONT & JEAN TIROLE, A THEORY OF INCENTIVES IN PROCUREMENT AND REGULATION 53–127 (MIT Press 1993); Victor P. Goldberg, *Regulation and Administered Contracts*, 7 BELL J. ECON. 426 (1976); William J. Baumol & J. Gregory Sidak, *Stranded Costs*, 18 HARV. J.L. & PUB. POL'Y 835 (1995); *see also* Stow Mun. Elec. Dep't v. Dep't of Pub. Utils., 688 N.E.2d 1337, 1346 (Mass. 1997) ("Permitting utilities to recover their prudently incurred stranded costs promotes fair and effective competition in

have been waves of litigation over the past century over whether a utility's allowed return must be predicated on its historic costs or its forward-looking (replacement) costs.[2037] Rarely has principle stood in the way of expediency. Regulators vacillated, depending on whether reproduction costs were rising or falling, perhaps for no other reason than whether they lived in inflationary or deflationary times. Another example of intertemporal expediency in public utility regulation is the retroactive prudency review. Not only did the utility's sunk investment (in electrical generation capacity, for instance) need to be prudent on an *ex ante* basis when made; it would also need to survive being second-guessed *ex post* as to whether, with the benefit of perfect hindsight, the specialized investment in question turned out to have been "used and useful" in the provision of regulated service and in that sense to have been prudent in fact.[2038]

These kinds of policies truncate the positive tail on the distribution of returns to investment and elevate the regulated firm's cost of capital. It is hard to imagine a more misguided and destructive economic policy to impose onto Qualcomm's ability to monetize its risky R&D investment in foundational technologies for cellular communications than what are essentially the tenets of an antiquated corpus of public utility regulation. Yet, in essence that is what Judge Koh did.

> d. *Judge Koh's Failure to Compare the Marginal Revenue That Qualcomm Gained from Apple's Exclusivity with the Marginal Cost to Qualcomm of Making the Relationship-Specific Increment of Investment Necessary to Support Its Supply Relationship with Apple*

Judge Koh's analysis of Qualcomm's relationship-specific investment in support of the TA and the FATA with Apple rested on yet another strand of economic misconception. To consider properly whether Qualcomm needed Apple's exclusivity for Qualcomm to achieve its "target payback ratio," the minimum rate of return on investment that Qualcomm required to justify the investment, Judge Koh would have needed to compare (1) the marginal revenue that Qualcomm gained *from Apple's exclusivity* with (2) the marginal cost to Qualcomm of making the relationship-specific increment of investment necessary to support its supply relationship with Apple. The revenue to

---

the electric industry.") (citing WILLIAM J. BAUMOL & J. GREGORY SIDAK, TRANSMISSION PRICING AND STRANDED COSTS IN THE ELECTRIC POWER INDUSTRY (AEI Press 1995)).

[2037] *Compare* Smyth v. Ames, 169 U.S. 466 (1898), *with* FPC v. Nat. Gas Pipeline, 315 U.S. 575 (1941).

[2038] *See, e.g.,* SIDAK & SPULBER, DEREGULATORY TAKINGS AND THE REGULATORY CONTRACT: THE COMPETITIVE TRANSFORMATION OF NETWORK INDUSTRIES IN THE UNITED STATES, *supra* note 740, at 487–93; William J. Baumol & J. Gregory Sidak, *The Pig in the Python: Is Lumpy Capacity Investment Used and Useful?*, 23 ENERGY L.J. 383 (2002).

Qualcomm from a product might depend on one or both of those measures, but that level of product revenue in no way would indicate the *relative* magnitudes of this particular marginal revenue and this particular marginal cost.

Judge Koh did not make any attempt to quantify either amount. It necessarily follows that she could not and did not evaluate the relative value of one to the other.

That Qualcomm achieved *some* positive rate of return on its modem sales to firms other than Apple did not in any way address the magnitude of Qualcomm's relationship-specific investments that resulted from its relationship *with Apple*. Judge Koh did not consider that it might be the case that a product proves *ex post* to be profitable as a whole, but that it is still not profitable *ex ante* to develop that product *further* to meet the idiosyncratic needs of a specific potential customer.

Apple had long been the *only* major smartphone manufacturer to use a thin modem rather than an SoC.[2039] Consequently, the marginal cost to Qualcomm of making its specialized investment to serve Apple's idiosyncratic need for thin modems might not have been expected to create—and might not have created in fact—any residual value for Qualcomm with respect to its supply of SoCs to different smartphone manufacturers (which, by definition, consisted of all major smartphone manufacturers other than Apple). The extent to which such marginal expenditures by Qualcomm indeed were, or were expected to have been, relationship-specific to Apple was an empirical question. Judge Koh did not ask that question, much less answer it.

4. Did Qualcomm Sacrifice Short-Term Profit and Thereby Harm Competition?

Judge Koh found that Qualcomm's rebates to Apple in 2015 and 2016 represented a short-term profit sacrifice that contradicted Qualcomm's claims about recovering its relationship-specific investments.[2040] She characterized the discounts as a 20-percent short-term profit-margin decrease for Qualcomm.[2041] Yet, if Qualcomm truly had possessed market power in the relevant markets over particular modems, why would it need to cut its profit margins by 20 percent to achieve exclusivity?

Judge Koh emphasized that Qualcomm claimed, in "a Qualcomm slide deck presented to the Qualcomm Board of Directors in 2013," that the discount was necessary to achieve an "'Apple modem design-win.'"[2042] Judge

---

[2039] Wayne Lam, *Qualcomm Extends LTE-A Pro Leadership with Snapdragon X20 Modem*, IHS Markit (Feb. 24, 2017), https://technology.ihs.com/589076/qualcomm-extends-lte-a-pro-leadership-with-snapdragon-x20-modem.

[2040] FTC v. Qualcomm Inc., 411 F. Supp. 3d 658, 772 (N.D. Cal. 2019).

[2041] *Id.*

[2042] *Id.* (quoting CX5527-029).

Koh seemed not to recognize that this evidence emphatically confirmed that Qualcomm was forced to compete on price for Apple's business. In other words, the evidence was exculpatory. Judge Koh did not recognize it to be so.

Judge Koh identified a 20-percent decrease in *profit margin*. She did not explain how she computed that percentage. If Judge Koh was referring to profits as a percentage of revenue, then it is possible that, although Qualcomm's profit *margin* decreased, its *total* profits increased as its total revenue also increased. Any price cut that is profitable for a firm overall is likely to decrease its per-unit profit margins. Judge Koh's findings on Qualcomm's profit margin were vague, if not also unreliable as a matter of economic reasoning.

If Qualcomm had engaged in anticompetitive monopolization, one would predict either monopoly pricing or some other comparable behavior. *United States v. Microsoft*[2043] exemplified a similar absence of proof of monopoly pricing. After that case had concluded, economists Chris Hall and Robert Hall published an article arguing that, although (according to their calculations) Microsoft's unconstrained monopoly price for a copy of the Windows operating system loaded onto a personal computer would have been $813, Microsoft instead charged only $60 so as to effect a strategy of limit pricing.[2044] Hall and Hall argued that Microsoft had charged the price that made it just barely unprofitable for an OEM of personal computers to vertically integrate into designing and supplying its own operating system.[2045]

For a very simple reason the FTC could not have similarly accused Qualcomm of undertaking limit pricing to discourage vertical entry by smartphone OEMs into modem production: vertical entry by some of those OEMs into the manufacture of modems had *already* occurred. The FTC did not accuse Qualcomm of charging a monopolist's price for its modems, nor did the agency accuse Qualcomm of charging a low (but nonpredatory) limit price for its modems with the intention of deterring vertical entry. Instead, the FTC accused Qualcomm of using its alleged monopoly over particular modems to increase prices for another product—an exhaustive license to a

---

[2043]   United States v. Microsoft Corp., 253 F.3d 34 (D.C. Cir. 2001) (en banc) (per curiam).

[2044]   Chris E. Hall & Robert E. Hall, *Toward a Quantification of the Effects of Microsoft's Conduct*, 90 AM. ECON. ASS'N PAPERS & PROC. 188, 189 (2000). An extended version is Robert E. Hall, Optimal Contracts to Defend Upstream Monopoly (Jan. 25, 2000) (unpublished manuscript) (on file with the Hoover Institution and Department of Economics, Stanford University). Hall's analysis yielded results consistent with the finding of Professor Richard Schmalensee in his expert economic testimony for Microsoft that, in Hall's words, "the potential availability of alternatives to Windows accounted for its $65 price to computer makers, when the full monopoly price would be more than $1000." *Id.* at 1. Hall's findings "support[ed] the view that potential substitutes constrain the price of an upstream product even when the substitutes are only potential." *Id.*

[2045]   Hall & Hall, *Toward a Quantification of the Effects of Microsoft's Conduct, supra* note 2044, at 189.

portfolio of cellular SEPs—which by definition had (and has) *no* substitutes and was used in fixed proportion to modems.[2046]

Judge Koh herself cited evidence that, although dated, suggested the extent to which the demand for Qualcomm's modems was price-elastic. She examined the effect of entry by VIA Telecom into the supply of CDMA modems:

> Although VIA lagged in the market, when VIA introduced a CDMA modem chip in a segment where Qualcomm had already introduced a CDMA modem chip, Qualcomm's prices would fall. An April 2009 presentation created by Mark Davis (former VIA Vice President and Chief Technical Officer) stated, "Q and V prices are similar, where comparable products exist," but that "Q's margins are vastly higher in segments where V provides no similar product." The presentation gave a specific example of how Qualcomm only reduced its prices once VIA introduced a chip: *"When first introduced CBP6 to US market, the price of QSC6055 [a Qualcomm chip] was $18." Within weeks, "the QSC6055 price was reduced to $10."*[2047]

Judge Koh evidently did not recognize the exculpatory ramifications of this documentary evidence, which she chose to emphasize. She observed that the price for a particular Qualcomm CDMA modem fell *44 percent* "within weeks" of a single firm's entry.[2048] And, as Judge Koh also noted, where VIA could not so constrain Qualcomm's pricing, VIA's ineffectuality resulted from the fact that it offered a modem that OEMs considered inferior to Qualcomm's.[2049] It was specious for Judge Koh to have concluded from this evidence that "Qualcomm's rivals lacked the ability to increase their output in the short term and discipline Qualcomm's CDMA [pricing]."[2050]

Judge Koh did not make findings of fact about any own-price elasticities of demand. As we saw earlier, the only time the word "elasticity" appeared in Judge Koh's findings of fact and conclusions of law in *FTC v. Qualcomm* was when she quoted a passage from *Brown Shoe* on defining the relevant product market.[2051] Considering the more plausible relationship between the own-price elasticities of demand for Qualcomm's respective products, any

---

[2046] FTC's Proposed Findings of Fact and Conclusions of Law, *supra* note 485, ¶ 343, at 47; *accord FTC v. Qualcomm*, 411 F. Supp. 3d at 778.

[2047] *FTC v. Qualcomm*, 411 F. Supp. 3d at 688 (alteration in original) (emphasis added) (citations omitted) (first quoting CX1770-002; then quoting CX1770-004; and then quoting *id.*). The two sources that Judge Koh cited did not appear to have been docketed. The testimony of Mr. Madderom of Motorola concerning Qualcomm's $4 "adder" for CDMA functionality also confirmed anecdotally Motorola's perception that the demand for Qualcomm CDMA chipsets was own-price-*elastic*. Deposition of Todd Madderom, *supra* note 1685, at 158:18–20 ("Q[.] And so once MediaTek introduced a CDMA chipset, Qualcomm's CDMA prices declined significantly? A[.] Yes, they did. Yes, they did.").

[2048] *FTC v. Qualcomm*, 411 F. Supp. 3d at 688.

[2049] *Id.*

[2050] *Id.*

[2051] *Id.* at 684; *see supra* note 1655.

kind of leveraging narrative, to have had a scintilla of plausibility, would have needed to flow in the opposite direction, such that Qualcomm supposedly would have been using it monopoly over exhaustive licenses to its cellular SEPs to try to monopolize Judge Koh's particular markets for modems.

But *that* theory of course was decidedly *not* what the FTC had alleged, *not* what Professor Shapiro evidently had espoused, and certainly *not* what Judge Koh ultimately found.

E. Summation: Did a Preponderance of the Evidence Support Judge Koh's Conclusion That the TA and FATA Were Anticompetitive Exclusive Dealing Agreements?

The evidence that Judge Koh identified and weighed did not come close to supporting her conclusion that the FTC had carried the burden of persuasion to prove that the TA and FATA were anticompetitive exclusive dealing agreements. Judge Koh's findings of fact emphasized her (highly questionable) inferences about the subjective expectations of Qualcomm's management rather than any hard evidence of actual competitive effects.

Judge Koh found that the TA and FATA were *de facto* exclusive because they supposedly coerced Apple to purchase modems exclusively from Qualcomm. That finding was ridiculous. Apple was a large, sophisticated buyer of modems. What Judge Koh found to be an anticompetitive discount by Qualcomm more plausibly was simply the result of Apple's exercise of bargaining power as the largest seller of smartphones in the United States. Consequently, her findings of fact and conclusions of law lacked substantial evidence for her finding that the TA and the FATA were anticompetitive.

Judge Koh also did not conduct a rigorous analysis of the actual anticompetitive effects and the actual procompetitive effects of the TA and the FATA. Exclusive dealing agreements can mitigate the risks of contractual holdup, free riding, and other potentially opportunistic behavior. That mitigation of risk encourages a firm like Qualcomm to make the kinds of specialized investments that have enabled it to produce the high-quality thin modems that Apple alone among OEMs designed its smartphones to use. Returning to her distinctive epithet, Judge Koh dismissed those potential benefits of the TA and the FATA as "pretextual."[2052] That denunciation was unconvincing. To borrow a phrase from Judge Robert Bork's opinion for the D.C. Circuit in *Rothery*, in the absence of evidence of substantial foreclosure, it would be more appropriate to conclude that Qualcomm's modem-supply agreements with Apple "produce[d] none of the evils of monopoly but enhance[d] consumer welfare by creating efficiency."[2053]

[2052] *FTC v. Qualcomm*, 411 F. Supp. 3d at 751.
[2053] Rothery Storage & Van Co. v. Atlas Van Lines, Inc., 792 F.2d 210, 223 (D.C. Cir. 1986) (Bork, J.).

Finally, as a matter of law, Judge Koh inexplicably never managed to apply *Tampa Electric*. That controlling Supreme Court decision requires that, to be exclusionary, an exclusive dealing agreement must foreclose competition from a substantial part of the relevant market. Making coherent findings of fact on substantial foreclosure requires market analysis, which Judge Koh never conducted.

XIV. Did Qualcomm Harm Investment in R&D?

Judge Koh did not identify or weigh any economic evidence of anticompetitive harm, either in her two relevant product markets for modems or in the downstream markets in which OEMs purchasing those modems sold their mobile devices to end consumers. Instead, she ultimately said that she could find anticompetitive harm to have arisen from Qualcomm's actions because rival modem manufacturers invested less in R&D and consequently produced less innovation. An important unstated assumption by Judge Koh was that rival modem manufacturers funded their investment in R&D exclusively from their free cash flow from operations.

A. The Productivity of Investment in R&D Achieved by Qualcomm and by Rival Modem Manufacturers

Judge Koh's finding of diminished investment in R&D by Qualcomm's rivals was an inherently factual proposition, yet this finding of hers lacked any factual substantiation—much less did it result from Judge Koh's identification and weighing of a body of substantial evidence that was credible and preponderant on this question, for which the FTC plainly bore the burden of production and the burden of persuasion. Judge Koh did not identify any analysis of the level or type of investment in R&D that Qualcomm's rivals made, much less any analysis tending to support her conjecture that the observed level of R&D fell at all, much less that it fell as a direct and proximate result of Qualcomm's challenged conduct.

Judge Koh's unsubstantiated conjecture about competitive harm arising from less R&D investment and less innovation was also predicated on incorrect economic reasoning about the productivity of investment in R&D by Qualcomm and by rival modem manufacturers, respectively. Judge Koh implicitly but erroneously assumed that all dollars of investment are equally productive, regardless of who is making the investment decisions. She assumed that the productivity of investment is the same across different modem manufacturers, and that a marginal change in R&D inputs (that is, an incremental dollar of investment) is proportional to a change in R&D

outputs (that is, the incremental increase in commercially valuable innovation). That assumption was unreliable for at least two reasons.

First, substantial evidence in the record showed that Qualcomm had been more successful than its rivals at turning its R&D investment into commercially successful products.

Second, a firm's investment in a new technology will tend to have a greater effect on innovation than its rival's subsequent investment to commercialize an existing technology after the new technology has already been shown to be commercially successful. Simply put, Qualcomm's investments in developing new technologies contributed more to long-run innovation rates and positive externalities than the investments of rivals who were trying to design their own modems to practice Qualcomm's foundational technologies. Qualcomm's innovations as a first mover allowed its rivals to attempt to imitate Qualcomm's products and exploit a second-mover advantage.[2054]

1. *Did Qualcomm or Rival Modem Manufacturers Have the Stronger Claim to the Need to Finance R&D Investment with Net Free Cash Flows from Operations?*

Ultimately, Qualcomm and the FTC made an identical argument about a direct causal nexus between a firm's free cash flow from operations, its investments in R&D, and its returns on innovation. Qualcomm argued that the free cash flows from its operations fueled its investment in R&D, which in turn yielded new foundational innovations that translated to commercial applications creating significant new value for consumers.

In effect, the proof of Qualcomm's business justification for its licensing practices was manifest in the bounty flowing from those practices: the evidence indicated that Qualcomm was simply better than other firms in creating commercially valuable technologies that generated exceptional licensing revenue, about 20 percent of which Qualcomm committed to plowing continuously into further R&D, year after year.[2055] The FTC seemed

---

[2054] By implementing technologies developed by Qualcomm, second movers can focus investment on product development and will, when they can avail themselves of regulated prices calculated to assist second movers, reduce the incentive for the first mover to invest in the basic research necessary to develop fundamentally new technologies. This effect is analogous to the mandatory unbundling of network elements at regulated prices under the FCC's attempts to implement sections 251 and 252 of the Telecommunications Act of 1996. *See, e.g.*, Hausman & Sidak, *A Consumer-Welfare Approach to the Mandatory Unbundling of Telecommunications Networks, supra* note 1914; Thomas M. Jorde, J. Gregory Sidak & David J. Teece, *Innovation, Investment, and Unbundling*, 17 YALE J. ON REG. 1, 21 (2000).

[2055] *See, e.g.*, Transcript of Proceedings (Volume 6) at 1254:3–6, FTC v. Qualcomm Inc., No. 5:17-cv-00220-LHK (N.D. Cal. Jan. 15, 2019) (Testimony of Irwin Jacobs (Co-Founder, Qualcomm)); Transcript of Proceedings (Volume 6) at 1304:24–1305:1, FTC v. Qualcomm Inc., No. 5:17-cv-00220-LHK (N.D. Cal. Jan. 15, 2019) (Testimony of Durga Malladi (Senior Vice President, Qualcomm)); Transcript of Proceedings (Volume 7) at 1352:1–5, FTC v. Qualcomm Inc., No. 5:17-cv-00220-LHK (N.D. Cal. Jan. 18, 2019) (Testimony of James Thompson (CTO, Qualcomm)); Transcript of Proceedings (Volume 7) at 1539:2–10, FTC v. Qualcomm Inc., No. 5:17-cv-00220-LHK (N.D. Cal. Jan. 18, 2019) (Testimony of Liren Chen

to argue that, despite the failure of rival modem manufacturers to match Qualcomm's record of success in investment in R&D, Judge Koh should nonetheless consider those firms for antitrust purposes to be equally capable of creating and benefiting from the same virtuous cycle of innovation.[2056]

Judge Koh accepted the FTC's argument and discredited Qualcomm's.[2057] Why? How could Judge Koh's findings of fact and conclusions of law in *FTC v. Qualcomm* possibly explain why Qualcomm's reliance on the same reasoning to justify its business conduct was unconvincing?

2. Did Judge Koh Ignore Substantial Evidence That Qualcomm's R&D Investment Was More Productive Than the R&D Investment of Rival Modem Manufacturers?

Judge Koh cited evidence consistent with the conclusion that rival modem manufacturers (including Intel) had a lower productivity of investment than Qualcomm's. She found that "MediaTek has not been able to develop into a competitor in premium LTE modem chips."[2058] Similarly, Judge Koh found that, although Intel had invested "'[l]ots of money, billions of dollars, and an army of engineers worldwide,'"[2059] it had "never met its target margins" and its "sales of modem chips to Apple ha[d] not yet been profitable" as of January 2019.[2060]

That is, even as second movers, Qualcomm's rivals were not effective in their attempts to imitate Qualcomm's innovations. The fact that one investor in R&D (Qualcomm) had cultivated a portfolio of 140,000 patents and patent applications—and had become the dominant supplier of modems— evidently was irrelevant in Judge Koh's view. In her schema, it appeared that each new dollar of investment in R&D was like any other marble drawn randomly from the urn, whose probability of being a particular color was independent of the marbles previously drawn.

The fallacy of that perspective was in its failure to appreciate that the probability of success in making a given investment in R&D might not be independent of the probability of success in a prior investment or a prior progression of investments. Put differently, Judge Koh's view of the

---

(Senior Vice President and Legal Counsel, QTL)); Transcript of Proceedings (Volume 8) at 1798:1–15, FTC v. Qualcomm Inc., No. 5:17-cv-00220-LHK (N.D. Cal. Jan. 22, 2019) (Testimony of Edward Snyder).

[2056] *See* FTC v. Qualcomm Inc., 411 F. Supp. 3d 658, 803–04 (N.D. Cal. 2019).

[2057] *See id.* at 803–06.

[2058] *Id.* at 695 (N.D. Cal. 2019) (citing Sealed Testimony of Finbarr Moynihan (MediaTek General Manager of Corporate Sales and Business Development) at 378:18–20, FTC v. Qualcomm Inc., No. 5:17-cv-00220-LHK (N.D. Cal. Jan. 7, 2019)).

[2059] *Id.* (quoting Transcript of Proceedings (Volume 3) at 565:4–5, FTC v. Qualcomm Inc., No. 5:17-cv-00220-LHK (N.D. Cal. Jan. 8, 2019) (Testimony of Aichatou Evans (Chief Strategy Officer, Intel))).

[2060] *Id.* (citing Transcript of Proceedings (Volume 3) at 587:12–22, FTC v. Qualcomm Inc., No. 5:17-cv-0022-LHK (N.D. Cal. Jan. 8, 2019) (Testimony of Aichatou Evans (Chief Strategy Officer, Intel))).

productivity of investment in R&D excluded any possibility that, through the accretion of knowledge and human capital over some extended period of such investments, Qualcomm and its rivals would make Bayesian updates of the expected probabilities of succeeding at their respective investments in R&D.

But then Judge Koh turned on a dime. It is especially telling that, when fashioning her permanent, worldwide injunction, she seemed resigned to the prospect that Qualcomm *would* continue to be qualitatively superior and more consistent in achieving a high productivity of investment in R&D. (And *that* outcome was supposedly a bad thing, which evidently disheartened Judge Koh.) Judge Koh was doing her own Bayesian updating. She specifically conjectured that Qualcomm would likely be a successful innovator in the transition to 5G mobile technologies and would "likely . . . replicate its market dominance during the transition to 5G."[2061] Judge Koh added that "OEMs and rival modem chip suppliers have also recognized that Qualcomm is likely to have a 5G chip lead."[2062] To justify her decision to issue a permanent, worldwide injunction agaainst Qualcomm that would extend seven years into the future, Judge Koh cited a January 2018 letter to Qualcomm shareholders in which Qualcomm's CEO, Steve Mollenkopf, stated: "'Qualcomm is 12-24 months ahead of our merchant competitors in the transition to 5G—a result of our innovation and technological advancements.'"[2063]

The fact that Qualcomm was positioned to innovate rapidly during the transition to 5G, and the further fact that Qualcomm had similarly surpassed its rivals in previous generations of mobile standards, was substantial evidence indicating the high productivity of Qualcomm's R&D investments relative to that of its rivals. Qualcomm demonstrated itself to be not only a willing first mover in the implementation of next-generation technologies, but also a *capable* first mover possessing the "business acumen" that the Supreme Court lauded in *Grinnell.*[2064]

B. Did Judge Koh Recognize That Investment in Developing New Technologies Increases Dynamic Efficiency More Than Does Investment in Commercializing Existing Technologies?

Most of the evidence concerning investment in R&D to which Judge Koh referred in various parts of her findings of fact and conclusions of law

---

[2061] *Id.* at 816.
[2062] *Id.* at 817.
[2063] *Id.* at 816 (quoting CX8198-004).
[2064] United States v. Grinnell Corp., 384 U.S. 563, 571 (1966); *see also* United States v. Aluminum Co. of Am., 148 F.2d 416, 430 (2ᵈ Cir. 1945).

was firm-specific investment related to bringing products to market.[2065] Firm-specific investment will tend to create fewer positive externalities than will investment in developing foundational new technologies. Because a firm can internalize the returns to firm-specific investment, the benefits of that investment will primarily accrue to its investors.

Although Qualcomm did make firm-specific investments, it also was notably engaged in the development of foundational technologies, as exemplified by lead in developing 5G products and its active role in standards development. When Qualcomm offers those technologies, which are the fruits of its successful R&D for use in standards, it offers benefits to rival modem manufacturers, OEMs, network operators, and retail consumers. Although firm-specific investment might be relevant for issues of entry and static efficiency, it is less likely to affect long-run growth rates owing to technical change. As noted above, Judge Koh essentially ignored that Qualcomm's investment of billions of dollars to develop a new foundational technology makes a greater contribution to dynamic efficiency than does Intel's investing billions of dollars to try to reverse engineer one of Qualcomm's modems.[2066]

[2065] *See, e.g., FTC v. Qualcomm*, 411 F. Supp. 3d at 695 ("Likewise, Aicha Evans (Intel Chief Strategy Officer) testified that when Intel purchased Infineon in 2011 and aimed to develop a premium LTE modem chip from scratch, Intel had to invest heavily: 'Lots of money, billions of dollars, and an army of engineers worldwide.'") (quoting Transcript of Proceedings (Volume 3) at 565:4–5, FTC v. Qualcomm Inc., No. 5:17-cv-00220-LHK (N.D. Cal. Jan. 8, 2019) (Testimony of Aichatou Evans (Chief Strategy Officer, Intel))); *id.* at 767 ("Similarly, Scott McGregor (former Broadcom CEO) testified that 'the economics of being in the cellular baseband business are very sensitive to volume of customers' because of the investments necessary to fund research and development.") (quoting Deposition of Scott McGregor, *supra* note 1751, at 174:19–21); *id.* at 799 ("Finbarr Moynihan (MediaTek General Manager of Corporate Sales and Business Development) testified that premium LTE modem chips require more upfront investment and require higher margin to support that investment."); *id.* at 806 ("According to a 2014 Qualcomm presentation shared with Will Wyatt (QTI Vice President, Finance), the former modem chip supplier Freescale exited the market in 2008 due to 'customer concentration and the need for significant investment in scale to supply customers.'") (quoting CX8292-006).

[2066] In June 2018, I was asked this question during cross examination in the 1065 Investigation before the ITC between Qualcomm and Apple. *See* Open Sessions Hearing Transcript (Revised & Corrected) at 500:19–501:4, 501:12–16, 501:18–23, Certain Mobile Electronic Devices and Radio Frequency and Processing Components Thereof, Inv. No. 337-TA-1065 (USITC June 19, 2018) (Testimony of J. Gregory Sidak) ("[MS. MURRAY]: So is it fair to say that logically, the U.S. would be less of a leader in the area of 5G than it was before Intel's exit, if such an exit did occur? A[.] I think that that's getting speculative, because it's assuming that every dollar invested in the development of 5G technologies is equally productive, regardless of who is making the investment. So if Intel has struggled up to this point to develop its business in mobile devices and chipsets for mobile devices, maybe a dollar that it invests in 5G is not going to be as productive as a dollar invested by some other company. . . . So I think you would have to qualify your conclusion by asking how likely it is that each dollar invested by a number of different companies would be equally productive in terms of generating useful R&D. . . . Q[.] So it is speculative, as you say, as any exclusion order public interest analysis is necessarily speculative, but is it your opinion that a dollar invested by Intel in 5G is less productive than a dollar invested by another company? A[.] Yes."). Little did I know at the time that I testified in the 1065 Investigation that a presentation that Intel received in 2012 from Bain & Company, the management consulting firm that had advised Intel since roughly 2007, had concluded that Qualcomm's productivity of R&D investment on SoCs was three times that of Intel's, as Christopher Johnson of Bain testified at trial. *See* Transcript of Proceedings (Volume 9) at 1842:3–12, 1842:25–1843:9, FTC v. Qualcomm Inc., No. 5:17-cv-00220-LHK (N.D. Cal. Jan. 25, 2019) (Testimony of Christopher Johnson (Bain)).

Liren Chen, Senior Vice President and Legal Counsel for QTL, testified at trial that Qualcomm's SEPs tended to be early and foundational:

> Q. Are there any common characteristics in Qualcomm's standard essential patents?
>
> A. Yes. . . . [A]t the highest level, Qualcomm's standard essential patent[s] generally have earlier priority dates and they tend to cover more, many different foundational, important features of the standard. And our patents are generally filed fairly extensively in terms of jurisdictions, as well as technology areas.[2067]

Mr. Chen also dispelled the misconception that different generations of technology are strictly sequential. Instead, he explained, they overlap:

> [S]ometimes people have the misperception to say you develop one generation technology and then you close the development, you move on to the next one. That's just not how it works, because in the cellular space . . . multiple generational technolog[ies] . . . are in use at the same time. So that's why a lot of phones support multiple modes of different generational technology. . . . [With 3G and 4G technologies], for example, that timeline overlaps because Qualcomm keep[s] on creating new technologies and . . . add[s] those technologies into . . . different generational standards, and not only the next generation[.] . . . [W]e also try to improve the current generational technology standard because it's very important for the carrier, [which] . . . has spent . . . a lot of money deploying the network, so [the carrier] want[s] a longer runway of the network investment before [it] can import the next generation. So we keep on introducing technology in parallel into existing generational technology, as well as into the next one[.][2068]

Judge Koh did not acknowledge in her findings of fact and conclusions of law the relevance of that testimony to the question of Qualcomm's superior productivity of investment in R&D.

Qualcomm's success in its R&D investment allows rival modem manufacturers the opportunity to compete with a second-mover advantage, which lowers their long-run costs and gives them a real option to implement only the successful technologies that Qualcomm has demonstrated are commercially feasible to implement. That is, Qualcomm's investment grants its competitors the valuable "real option" to wait until Qualcomm has proven the commercial feasibility of a foundational technology before investing

---

[2067] Transcript of Proceedings (Volume 7) at 1541:20–1542:2, FTC v. Qualcomm Inc., No. 5:17-cv-00220-LHK (N.D. Cal. Jan. 18, 2019) (Testimony of Liren Chen (Senior Vice President and Legal Counsel, QTL)).
[2068] *Id.* at 1542:18–1542:12.

to develop applications complementary to that technology.[2069] That real option for Qualcomm's rivals reduces their costs and thus can benefit downstream firms and consumers. With this real option, a rival of Qualcomm can select the amount, the timing, and the duration of its access to Qualcomm's technologies.

Put differently, one can view the rights of rivals to access the fruits of Qualcomm's investments in standard-essential technologies as a perpetual call option at a fair, reasonable, and nondiscriminatory price.[2070] When one considers the value of the real option that Qualcomm creates for rival modem manufacturers, its investments in innovation are seen to be more valuable to the rest of the vertical supply chain than are the imitative investments of Qualcomm's rivals.

C. Did Judge Koh Recognize That Qualcomm's Innovation Epitomized the "Business Acumen" That the Supreme Court Said May Lawfully Create and Sustain a Monopoly?

Judge Koh's assumption that all investments are equally productive in creating commercially valuable goods is of course specious on economic grounds and unsound as a matter of legal reasoning. Successful and superior investment in R&D is clearly one possible manifestation of *Grinnell's* "business acumen."[2071] That Qualcomm has been more productive in developing and commercializing new technologies is substantial evidence of business acumen. So also is it substantial evidence of business acumen that Qualcomm appeared to Judge Koh to be likely to be more productive than its rivals with its investments in R&D during the transition to 5G. Qualcomm's past success demonstrated that it had created and configured intellectual property and human capital in a way that yielded insights into how to bring successful products to market ahead of its rivals. In the literature on management strategy, a discipline adjacent but not identical to the field of industrial organization,

---

[2069] The seminal work on real options is AVINASH K. DIXIT & ROBERT S. PINDYCK, INVESTMENT UNDER UNCERTAINTY 6–7 (Princeton Univ. Press 1994). Dixit and Pindyck extended the insights derived from the literature on the pricing of financial options. *See* Fisher Black & Myron Scholes, *The Pricing of Options and Corporate Liabilities*, 81 J. POL. ECON. 637 (1973). Investors routinely value and trade stock options using financial option pricing methodologies such as the Black-Scholes model. *See, e.g.*, ZVI BODIE, ALEX KANE & ALAN J. MARCUS, INVESTMENTS 737–58 (McGraw-Hill 10th ed. 2014). Similarly, the theory of real options yields insights concerning the value of investments in other asset classes, including patents. *See* J. Gregory Sidak, *How Relevant Is Justice Cardozo's "Book of Wisdom" to Patent Damages?*, 16 COLUM. SCI. & TECH. L. REV. 246, 282–83 (2016); Jerry A. Hausman, Gregory K. Leonard & J. Gregory Sidak, *Patent Damages and Real Options: How Judicial Characterization of Noninfringing Alternatives Reduces Incentives to Innovate*, 22 BERKELEY TECH. L.J. 825, 839–46 (2007).

[2070] DIXIT & PINDYCK, *supra* note 2069, at 137.

[2071] United States v. Grinnell Corp., 384 U.S. 563, 571 (1966); *see also supra* notes 270–272 and notes 1343–1344 and accompanying text.

this interpretation of business acumen is captured in the concept of dynamic capabilities, which is particularly associated with the scholarship of David Teece.[2072]

Perhaps Judge Koh found it repugnant that one would attribute Qualcomm's successes and its rivals' failures to an unequal distribution of business acumen. When purporting to analyze harm to competition, she did not differentiate between the value that Qualcomm's investments in R&D created and the value that its rivals' investments in R&D created. Judge Koh ignored whether unique intellectual property or human capital had accreted over time, creating dynamic capabilities that enabled a particular firm (Qualcomm) to achieve superior results with respect to its investment in R&D.

In finding harm to competition, Judge Koh implicitly equated the productivity of investment in R&D by Qualcomm's rivals with Qualcomm's own productivity of investment in R&D. Her finding ignored substantial evidence that Qualcomm's past investments had in fact been substantially more successful and more efficient and more productive than the past investments of its competitors. Judge Koh confused inputs (that is, levels of investment in R&D) with outputs (that is, levels of proven innovation and new products). And she ignored the difference between investment by second movers to bring rival products to market (which will primarily affect static efficiency) and investment by first movers to develop new foundational technologies (which will primarily affect dynamic efficiency).

D. The Role of Bain & Company in Advising Intel on Competitive Strategy vis-à-vis Qualcomm

During its defense, Qualcomm called as a percipient witness Christopher Johnson, a partner at Bain & Company, which had provided management consulting advice to Intel since roughly 2007.[2073] His testimony answered the question: How did Intel and Qualcomm compare in terms of the productivity of R&D investment in their respective modem businesses?

[2072] *See* David J. Teece, Dynamic Capabilities and Strategic Management: Organizing for Innovation and Growth (Oxford Univ. Press 2009).

[2073] Transcript of Proceedings (Volume 9) at 1834:3–5, FTC v. Qualcomm Inc., No. 5:17-cv-00220-LHK (N.D. Cal. Jan. 25, 2019) (Testimony of Christopher Johnson (Bain)); *see also id.* at 1834:18–1835:5 ("Q. And you were deposed in this action on March 28th, 2018; correct? A. I don't remember the exact date, but that sounds right. Q. And as of the date of your deposition, Intel had been a Bain client for about 11 years; is that correct? A. Correct. Q. And you personally provided consulting services to Intel from early 2010 until mid-2011; correct? A. Correct. Q. And then again you provided consulting services to Intel from the summer of 2014 until at least the date of your deposition; correct? A. Correct.").

1. Was Mr. Johnson a Hostile Witness?

The direct examination of Mr. Johnson by Qualcomm's lawyer, Jordan Peterson, was such that Mr. Peterson asked Judge Koh's permission to treat Mr. Johnson as a hostile witness on the grounds that Mr. Johnson had "just testified that he has done consulting work for Intel, which is a competitor of Qualcomm."[2074] Were Judge Koh to rule Mr. Johnson a hostile witness, adverse to Qualcomm, Mr. Peterson could proceed to ask Mr. Johnson leading questions during his direct examination (as would be routinely permissible on cross examination) under Federal Rule of Evidence 611,[2075] in an attempt to impeach him.[2076]

The FTC's lawyer, Nathaniel Hopkin, insisted improbably that, as a witness, Mr. Johnson was perfectly friendly to Qualcomm: "Your Honor, Bain & Company isn't a party opponent. They're not a party in this case. They're not adverse. And Mr. Johnson has never worked for Intel as far as we know."[2077]

Judge Koh did not appear ever to rule on Mr. Peterson's request to treat Mr. Johnson as a hostile witness. Mr. Hopkin thereafter repeatedly objected to Mr. Peterson's interrogation of Mr. Johnson on the ground that Mr. Peterson was asking Mr. Johnson leading questions. Judge Koh often sustained those objections (which would seem to confirm that she had not in fact granted Mr. Peterson's request to designate Mr. Johnson a hostile witness), or Judge Koh asked Mr. Peterson, who was operating under a tight time constraint, to rephrase his question in a nonleading manner.[2078] Judging from the transcript, the interrogation of Mr. Johnson oddly appeared to have been one of the most contentious witness examinations during the entire 10 days of trial.[2079]

[2074] *Id.* at 1835:25–1836:2; *id.* at 1836:11–12 ("Mr. Peterson: To be clear, Your Honor, the witness also moved to quash the subpoena, so he's not here voluntarily.").

[2075] FED. R. EVID. 611(c) ("Leading questions should not be used on direct examination except as necessary to develop the witness's testimony. Ordinarily, the court should allow leading questions . . . on cross-examination . . . and when a party calls a hostile witness, an adverse party, or a witness identified with an adverse party.").

[2076] *See id.* 607 ("Any party, including the party that called the witness, may attack the witness's credibility.").

[2077] Transcript of Proceedings (Volume 9) at 1836:4–7, FTC v. Qualcomm Inc., No. 5:17-cv-00220-LHK (N.D. Cal. Jan. 25, 2019) (Testimony of Christopher Johnson (Bain)).

[2078] *Id.* at 1835:25–1836:2; *see, e.g., id.* at 1837:1–6 ("Q. Now, at various times during the course of Bain's engagement with Intel, it's correct that Bain has done benchmarking comparing Intel's Mobile Wireless business with its competitors? Mr. Hopkin: Objection. Leading. The Court: Sustained.").

[2079] *See, e.g., id.* at 1839:3–15 ("Q. Do you recognize this document? A. I recognize it from my preparation. Q. It's a document Bain prepared? A. Bain, in conjunction with our client. There was probably input from both parties. Intel, that would be. Q. And this reflects the facts that Bain collected and opinions that Bain formed in the regular course of providing consulting services to Intel; correct? Mr. Hopkin: Objection, leading. Mr. Peterson: Your Honor, for the purposes of establishing foundation, I think a leading question is appropriate here. The Court: That's fine. Overruled.").

2. Bain's Competitive Strategy Engagements for Intel

Mr. Peterson began his unfriendly direct examination of Mr. Johnson by asking him to confirm Bain's mode of working on Intel's competitive strategy engagements:

Q. Now, Bain provides outside advice for management teams; correct?

A. Could you be more specific for "outside advice"?

Q. . . . Bain provides an outside perspective, an uncolored position on topics for management teams; correct?

A. That's the goal, yes.

Q. And in the regular course of providing consulting services to its clients, Bain uses a data driven approach; correct?

A. Correct.

Q. And Bain's written work product reflects the facts that Bain collected and the opinions that Bain formed in the course of its work; correct?

A. It does within the scope of what the project is and the data available to us, yes.[2080]

Mr. Peterson questioned Mr. Johnson about Bain's particular work for Intel in connection with its "Mobile Wireless business":

Q. Has Bain done benchmarking between Intel's Mobile Wireless business and its competitors?

A. We have.

Q. Did that benchmarking include Mobile Wireless head counts?

A. Yes.

Q. And do you understand "head count" to mean the number of full-time employees and part-time employees at the Intel Mobile Wireless business unit?

A. It'll depend on the specific exercise. But that could be one way we'd do it, and that would probably be the most usual case. Most usually that's how we would look at it, full-time employees and if you had two part-time employees, that would count as one full-time employee potentially.

Q. And has Bain also looked at Intel Mobile Wireless's R&D spending?

A. In conjunction with our client, yes.[2081]

[2080] *Id.* at 1835:6–19.
[2081] *Id.* at 1837:8–24.

Mr. Johnson proceeded to testify about the substance of Bain's management advice to Intel.

a. *Bain's Evaluation of the Respective Productivity of R&D Investment of Intel and Qualcomm*

Answering questions about a July 2015 Bain presentation prepared for Intel entitled, "Mobile R&D Benchmarking,"[2082] Mr. Johnson explained how, in the presentation, Bain had evaluated the respective abilities of Intel and Qualcomm to create additional products—known as "stock keeping units," or SKUs—as a result of their investments in R&D:

> Q. If you could turn to slide 2.
>
> A. Yes.
>
> Q. This slide correctly shows the findings that you reached as a part of this study; correct?
>
> A. To the best of knowledge, it's a summary of the findings of the study.
>
> Q. And what was the conclusion Bain reached regarding Intel over all mobile productivity?
>
> A. Productivity in terms of product's output, you need SKU output. I think here we're saying that Qualcomm was producing two to three times as many SKUs as Intel.
>
> Q. And the slide contains other conclusions that Bain reached; correct? For example, I'm looking at the second to last bullet, there's additional conclusions there that Bain reached, correct, regarding productivity? What was that conclusion?
>
> A. I believe it's the same conclusion, just inverting the 2 to 3X and saying that Intel product activity lagged Qualcomm by 50 percent.
>
> Q. And if you could turn to slide 4 in that same deck.
>
> A. Okay.
>
> Q. And this slide also illustrates the same principle we were just talking about, that Intel was lagging in product output; correct?
>
> A. That Intel was producing fewer SKUs than Qualcomm.[2083]

Thus, Mr. Johnson testified that, with respect to SKUs, Qualcomm outperformed Intel, even though the two companies made comparable investments

---

[2082] *Id.* at 1844:18–1845:9 (discussing QX123, QX123A).
[2083] *Id.* at 1846:7–1847:6 (discussing QX123A).

in R&D. Judge Koh did not mention this part of Mr. Johnson's testimony in her findings of fact and conclusions of law in *FTC v. Qualcomm*.

>   b.   *Bain's Conclusion That Qualcomm's Productivity of R&D Investment in SoCs Was Three Times That of Intel's*

Mr. Peterson also asked Mr. Johnson what Bain concluded about the level of Intel's Mobile Wireless R&D spending with respect to the comparable R&D spending of its rivals:

> Q. . . . What did Bain conclude . . . with respect to Intel's wireless R&D spending with respect to the total volume of spending?
>
> A. With respect to the total volume of spending?
>
> Q. Correct.
>
> A. Volume of what?
>
> Q. Of dollars spent.
>
> A. I think we—if I understand the question correctly, I think we looked at their total spend, we understood the dollar amount and the head count, and we compared that to other companies, and we found them to be at roughly similar levels. I'm not sure we drew a conclusion as to whether that was right or wrong.[2084]

Mr. Johnson thus testified that Bain had concluded that Intel's level of investment in R&D on "wireless" products was roughly the same as such investment in R&D by other firms.

Mr. Peterson then asked Mr. Johnson specifically about a presentation that he had prepared for Intel concerning Qualcomm:

> Q. Do you recognize this document?
>
> A. I recognize it from my preparation.
>
> Q. It's a document Bain prepared?
>
> A. Bain, in conjunction with our client. There was probably input from both parties. Intel, that would be.
>
> . . . .
>
> Q. And this presentation is titled QCOMM Benchmark Presentation 2012; correct?
>
> A. Are [sic] that's correct.

[2084] *Id.* at 1838:11–23.

Q. And it's dated December 20th, 2012; correct?

A. Correct.

Q. This document was constructed over a period of time leading up to that date as Bain collected these facts and formed these opinions; correct?

A. Again, as Bain did, in conjunction with our client. I think the client had input here.[2085]

Mr. Peterson focused his next questions on the conclusions that Bain had reached about Intel's R&D investment for systems on a chip (SoCs) relative to Qualcomm's R&D investment for SoCs:

Q. Mr. Johnson, do you recognize the term "system" on a chip?

A. I do.

Q. Is that also sometimes referred as to [sic] SoC?

A. It is.

Q. And in the mobile wireless industry, what does that most commonly refer to?

A. A chip that's being used in cell phones where the applications processor, which does the computing, is integrated with the baseband, which does the cellular connectivity. So they're on the same die.

. . . .

Q. Mr. Johnson, what was Bain's conclusion regarding Intel's overall SoC R&D investment comparable to Qualcomm?

A. Specifically on page 3?

Q. Yes. And just to be clear, speaking at a high level about the main conclusion so we don't get into sealed information.

A. What's written on the page, Intel Overall SoC R&D Investment Comparable to Qualcomm.

Q. And what was the conclusion regarding how many more times output Qualcomm had . . . than Intel?

A. Three times more output.[2086]

In other words, it appeared from Mr. Johnson's testimony that Bain had found, in work product undertaken for Intel, that, although Intel's overall investment in R&D on SoCs was comparable to Qualcomm's overall

---

[2085] *Id.* at 1839:3–7, 1839:25–1840:9 (discussing QX122, QX122A).
[2086] *Id.* at 1842:3–12, 1842:25–1843:9.

investment in R&D on SoCs, Qualcomm's productivity of R&D investment on SoCs was three times that of Intel's.

3. Did Judge Koh Cite Mr. Johnson for the Asymmetry Between Qualcomm's and Intel's Productivity of R&D Investment in SoCs?

In her findings of fact and conclusions of law, Judge Koh ignored Mr. Johnson's testimony concerning Intel's inferior productivity of investment in SoCs. She instead twice quoted the same passage of Mr. Johnson's testimony to support the following unremarkable proposition:

> Winning business with an OEM generates deep engagement with that OEM's engineering teams. That engagement both sharpens a modem chip supplier's products and leads to opportunities to customize modem chips for that OEM, as Christopher Johnson (Bain & Co. Partner), who consulted for Intel, testified: "[B]y working with a customer and having access to their products and their engineering teams, you can customize your products and basically improve your pace of innovation in the features you're bringing out."[2087]

Why did Judge Koh credit that seemingly extraneous testimony yet ignore Mr. Johnson's critical admission that Intel's productivity of investment in SoCs lagged by a substantial amount Qualcomm's productivity of investment in SoCs? Mr. Johnson's testimony cast serious doubt on the correctness of Judge Koh's finding that Qualcomm harmed investment in R&D.

XV. The Meaning of Exit

Did Judge Koh use the word "exit" in the correct economic sense? Economics textbooks say little about "exit," yet the concept was critical to Judge Koh's analysis of harm to competition in *FTC v. Qualcomm*. I therefore propose here a critical distinction between two possible economic definitions of "exit." That distinction casts doubt on Judge Koh's apparent interpretation of trial testimony given by representatives of Intel and other rival modem

---

[2087] FTC v. Qualcomm Inc., 411 F. Supp. 3d 658, 801 (N.D. Cal. 2019) (alteration in original) (quoting Transcript of Proceedings (Volume 9) at 1854:16–23, FTC v. Qualcomm Inc., No. 5:17-cv-00220-LHK (N.D. Cal. Jan. 25, 2019) (Testimony of Christopher Johnson (Bain))); *see also id.* at 768 ("Christopher Johnson (Bain & Co. Partner), who consulted for Intel, testified that engineering engagement with an OEM like Apple sharpens a modem chip supplier's products and leads to opportunities to customize products for that OEM: '[B]y working with a customer and having access to their products and their engineering teams, you can customize your products and basically improve your pace of innovation in the features you're bringing out.'") (alteration in original) (quoting Transcript of Proceedings (Volume 9) at 1854:16–23, FTC v. Qualcomm Inc., No. 5:17-cv-00220-LHK (N.D. Cal. Jan. 25, 2019) (Testimony of Christopher Johnson (Bain))).

manufacturers, and therefore on Judge Koh's own conclusions concerning "exit" in her findings of fact and conclusions of law.

A. Transcendent "Exit" Versus Existential "Exit"

The English word "exit" derives from the third-person singular present indicative of the Latin verb *exire*, meaning "to go out."[2088] In Latin, *exit* literally means "he (or she or it) goes out." By William Shakespeare's lifetime, the English language had fashioned from the verb "to exit" a new noun meaning "departure."[2089] I call this first economic meaning of "exit" *transcendent* because it connotes the surpassing of one's existing limits or circumstances as the direct result of one's conscious action: the transfer or conveyance of control, the redeployment of a resource to its highest-valued use, and the salvaging of something still possessing value. Transcendent exit connotes movement, transport, or metamorphosis.

In time, the noun "exit" became broad enough to connote in some circumstances a quite different idea: the end of the existence of a person or thing.[2090] I call this second economic meaning of "exit" *existential* because it connotes the destruction or death or extinguishment of being and consciousness. When a firm "exits" an industry in the existential sense, its productive assets vanish.

To the contrary of *existential* "exit," *transcendent* "exit" implies the salvaging of a thing still possessing value—exit is the path to that thing's preservation or deliverance from ruin. It is that thing's salvation.[2091] So, in an economic sense, does "exit" mean death or deliverance? It cannot be both simultaneously in a given circumstance.

When one uses "exit" to describe the behavior of a firm in a market without specifying whether "exit" has the transcendent connotation or the existential connotation, the analysis that follows will tend to be incomplete as a matter of economic reasoning for two reasons. First, the word "exit," without more, contains no explanation for *why* the firm has decided, or is compelled, to leave the industry. Second, the word "exit" might conflate the *firm's* departure from the industry and the disposition of the firm's dynamic capabilities[2092] and productive assets (including its intellectual property and human capital), which the "exiting" firm no longer will need and employ once it has ceased operating in that industry.

[2088] *Exit v.1*, OXFORD ENGLISH DICTIONARY (3ᵈ ed. 2015).

[2089] *Exit v.2*, OXFORD ENGLISH DICTIONARY (3ᵈ ed. 2015).

[2090] *Id.*

[2091] *Salvation n.*, OXFORD ENGLISH DICTIONARY (3ᵈ ed. 2015) ("The action of saving or delivering; the state or fact of being saved.").

[2092] *See* TEECE, DYNAMIC CAPABILITIES AND STRATEGIC MANAGEMENT: ORGANIZING FOR INNOVATION AND GROWTH, *supra* note 2072.

B. Did Judge Koh Distinguish Between Transcendent "Exit" and Existential "Exit"?

In *FTC v. Qualcomm*, Judge Koh claimed, without any supporting analysis, that the "exit" from the industry of Broadcom and Texas Instruments was "promoted" by Qualcomm's refusal to grant exhaustive licenses to its cellular SEPs to its rivals.[2093] She later identified the "exit" of Broadcom, Freescale, ST-Ericsson, and Texas Instruments each for reasons of decreasing sales or insufficient scale to justify continued operations.[2094] In Broadcom's case, Judge Koh specifically observed that Broadcom's scale did not suffice to support its R&D expenditures.[2095]

Regardless of the reason for a firm's "exit," Judge Koh never differentiated between *existential* "exit" and *transcendent* "exit"—or, in other words, (1) a firm's business decision to discontinue producing a product and (2) a firm's disposition of the assets necessary to make that product. The latter will typically determine the competitive effect of a firm's "exit" decision, but Judge Koh focused exclusively on the former.

C. Exit and the Shutdown Decision

Judge Koh's analysis of Broadcom's "exit" decision contained an elementary fallacy of economic reasoning. Although sunk costs (such as R&D investment) do affect a firm's *entry* decision,[2096] sunk costs do *not* affect the firm's *exit* decision. A manufacturer will not exit the market merely because it

---

[2093] FTC v. Qualcomm Inc., 411 F. Supp. 3d 658, 749 (N.D. Cal. 2019).

[2094] *Id.* at 805–06.

[2095] *Id.*

[2096] *See, e.g.*, CARLTON & PERLOFF, MODERN INDUSTRIAL ORGANIZATION, *supra* note 179, at 80 ("If large *sunk* costs are associated with entry and if entry is unsuccessful, the entrant's losses are large. . . . In such a case, the need for large-scale investment that involves large sunk costs could well provide a disincentive for a potential entrant because it would have so much to lose.") (emphasis in original); PINDYCK & RUBINFELD, MICROECONOMICS, *supra* note 1835, at 218 ("Now consider a *prospective* sunk cost. . . . A prospective sunk cost is an *investment*. Here the firm must decide whether that investment in specialized equipment is *economical*—i.e., whether it will lead to a flow of revenues large enough to justify its cost.") (emphasis in original); *see also* WILLIAMSON, THE ECONOMIC INSTITUTIONS OF CAPITALISM, *supra* note 651, at 169 n.6 (defining sunk costs as "the nonsalvageable part of an advance commitment"). Not surprisingly this analysis resembles parts of the analysis relevant to Williamsonian holdup. *Compare* text accompanying *supra* notes 649–653, *with* SIDAK & SPULBER, DEREGULATORY TAKINGS AND THE REGULATORY CONTRACT: THE COMPETITIVE TRANSFORMATION OF NETWORK INDUSTRIES IN THE UNITED STATES, *supra* note 740, at 423 ("Suppose that to carry out production a firm must invest k dollars. Suppose that the investment k is irreversible, so that k represents sunk costs. The firm has operating costs c and expects to earn revenues R. The firm's economic rent is defined as revenues net of operating cost and investment cost, $R - c - k$. Economic rent provides the incentive for entry. The firm's economic quasi rent is defined as net revenue, $R - c$. The quasi rent provides incentives to stay in the industry after entry costs have been sunk. Having sunk k, the firm decides whether or not to produce on the basis of its comparison of R and c only. It would manifest the fallacy of sunk costs for the firm to base the production decision on the magnitude of k. Thus, after k is sunk, only quasi rents—not economic rents—affect the firm's decision whether or not to produce the good."); *see also* WILLIAMSON, THE ECONOMIC INSTITUTIONS OF CAPITALISM, *supra* note 651, at 169 n.6 (defining sunk costs as "the nonsalvageable part of an advance commitment").

cannot "recoup" its sunk investment. To predict that course of action is to fall prey to the classic "sunk cost fallacy," taught to every student in Econ 1.[2097]

A firm (including one of Qualcomm's rival modem manufacturers) will decide to exit a market because its revenue cannot cover its total variable cost (or, as a proxy in a multiproduct firm, its total decremental cost, which denotes the costs avoided by exiting a market for that product).[2098] This insight is called "the shutdown decision," and its explication also appears in any introductory economics textbook.[2099] Yet, Judge Koh ignored the shutdown decision in her discussion of "exit" in her findings of fact and conclusions of law in *FTC v. Qualcomm*.

Sunk costs might affect a firm's shutdown decision only if one redefines the economic question—which Judge Koh certainly did not do in her findings of fact and conclusions of law—to address *successive waves of sunk investment* made across new generations of technology.[2100] That analysis would describe "exit" within a framework of dynamic competition, in which a firm makes an incremental sunk investment in each period. It would then be a question of fact to identify the degree to which subsequent generations of a product

---

[2097] *See, e.g.*, Sidak & Spulber, Deregulatory Takings and the Regulatory Contract: The Competitive Transformation of Network Industries in the United States, *supra* note 740, at 28 ("Ordinarily, sunk costs do not affect business decisions, which are only concerned with available benefits and avoidable costs. To base future decisions on those costs is known as *the fallacy of sunk costs*.") (emphasis in original); Pindyck & Rubinfeld, Microeconomics, *supra* note 1835, at 218 ("Because a sunk cost cannot be recovered, it should not influence the firm's decisions."); Carlton & Perloff, Modern Industrial Organization, *supra* note 179, at 29 ("A sunk cost is like spilled milk: Once it is sunk, there is no use worrying about it, and it should not affect any subsequent decisions.").

[2098] This distinction explains why, for a multiproduct firm, incremental cost does not equal decremental cost when are sunk costs are present. The level of sunk costs and the relevant production decision affect the magnitude of long-run average-incremental cost. To see why, notice that one might construct the incremental cost of product X by using either of two different measures of the cost of producing all but product X. The first measure would be the cost of producing all but X for a firm that had never produced X. The second measure would use the cost of producing all but X for a firm that initially produced all products and subsequently ceased production of X. Any sunk, irreversible costs that the firm must incur to produce X would be part of the incremental cost of X using the first measure, but not the second measure. *See, e.g.*, David E.M. Sappington & J. Gregory Sidak, *Competition Law for State-Owned Enterprises*, 71 Antitrust L.J. 479, 491 (2003); J. Gregory Sidak, *Maximizing the U.S. Postal Service's Profits from Competitive Products*, 11 J. Competition L. & Econ. 617, 628 (2015) ("A firm may incur sunk costs in adding a product to its line—for example, costs associated with advertising that product's launch—which it cannot recover by ceasing to produce that product.") (citing N. Gregory Mankiw, Principles of Economics 286 (Cengage Learning 7th ed. 2015)); *see also* Mankiw, Principles of Economics (8th ed.), *supra* note 652, at 274.

[2099] *See, e.g.*, Carlton & Perloff, Modern Industrial Organization, *supra* note 179, at 59 ("A firm produces only if doing so is more profitable than not producing. It produces only if the revenues from producing exceed avoidable costs: the costs that are not incurred if a firm ceases production. . . . Thus, the rule for deciding whether to remain in business is: Produce and sell only if revenues are at least as great as total variable costs. [T]he firm should produce and sell at price p only if p equals or exceeds average variable cost.").

[2100] *See, e.g.*, Sidak, *Patent Holdup and Oligopsonistic Collusion in Standard Setting Organizations*, *supra* note 446, at 156 ("Researchers therefore continue to improve upon the previous design, and those sequential stages of R&D require the input of more capital in each successive period such that fixed costs of investment are incurred not in a single period but repeatedly throughout the existence of the market."); J. Gregory Sidak & Daniel F. Spulber, *Givings, Takings, and the Fallacy of Forward-Looking Costs*, 72 N.Y.U. L. Rev. 1068, 1142–43 (1997).

are properly identified as being situated within the same relevant product market, and the degree to which a firm's "exit" is merely a decision not to enter the *next* technological iteration of the "market" rather than a decision to "exit" the market in which a firm currently competes.

Notice, incidentally, that an *incumbent* firm's need to make these kinds of sequential sunk investments so that it can compete in future design-win contests is powerful evidence tending to disprove that sunk investment in R&D constitutes a Stiglerian barrier to entry in the industry. And notice as well that, if the product in question is subject to technological obsolescence, and if the firm declines to update its own product to the next generation of technological performance, demand for its product will fall, all other factors held constant; one could say in that case that the firm has not exited the market, but rather that the firm has allowed the market to pass it by.

Judge Koh's findings of fact and conclusions of law were devoid of any analysis of exit within a framework of dynamic competition. Without having rigorously addressed why Broadcom, Freescale, ST-Ericsson, and Texas Instruments "exited" the modem business, Judge Koh had no factual basis for blaming Qualcomm for supposedly having "promoted" the decisions of those firms to "exit" the modem business. Consequently, her factual findings on "exit" were arbitrary and devoid of substantial evidence.

D. Exit, Dynamic Capabilities, and the Mobility of Complementary Factors of Production

Upon deciding to shut down production and exit an industry, a firm must decide how to dispose of the dynamic capabilities and productive assets that it previously used to compete in that industry. A firm might be able to recover its R&D costs by means other than manufacturing modems, including selling its business or licensing its intellectual property. As we have seen, if a firm's capital investment in R&D is salvageable, then those R&D costs are not really sunk, and the firm's cost of exit is lower than it otherwise would be, because the firm will not sacrifice a sunk investment upon exiting the market.[2101] Low costs of exit facilitate entry, including vertical entry by a supplier or customer of the exiting firm.[2102]

[2101] *See, e.g.*, Sidak, *Why Should the Postal Service Deter Amazon's Competitive Entry into Last-Mile Parcel Delivery?*, *supra* note 1765, at 129.

[2102] *See* BAUMOL, PANZAR & WILLIG, CONTESTABLE MARKETS AND THE THEORY OF INDUSTRY STRUCTURE, *supra* note 1766, at 6–7; Baumol, *Contestable Markets: An Uprising in the Theory of Industry Structure*, *supra* note 1766, at 3–4.

1.   *Will an Exiting Firm Redeploy Capital to Reduce Its Costs of Exit?*

To understand why a firm's assets do not completely disappear upon exit, consider the options available to a firm that decides to shut down its modem business. Even if a manufacturer were to choose to stop the development and production of modems—such as when Intel announced in April 2019 that it would "exit" the "5G smartphone modem business"[2103] (despite never actually having produced such a product for commercial sale)—that manufacturer would seek to salvage or redeploy capital to reduce its costs of exit. I so testified on the public record on June 19, 2018 in the 1065 Investigation at the ITC, 10 months before Intel announced the sale of its modem business to Apple:

> [I]f Intel were to exit the thin modem business, it presumably would sell—well, it *would* sell that business to somebody else. It's not just going to abandon the business if it has some economic value. And so some other company that's interested in developing that product and the future technologies associated with the product will continue.[2104]

Even if all of the firm's assets were liquidated, the underlying technologies that those assets practiced would still remain. The knowledge would not be lost.

Moreover, Qualcomm uses "fabless" manufacturing, as do some other modem manufacturers. For those manufacturers, the capital investment necessary to produce modems consists largely of intellectual property. Unless the dynamic capabilities enabled by the creation of specialized human capital and intellectual property are somehow destroyed, they will also remain available for use by a subsequent entrant into the market.

So, it should have surprised no one that Intel was able to sell its smartphone modem business to Apple in July 2019[2105]—contrary to the dire prediction at trial in *FTC v. Qualcomm* in January 2019 by Aicha Evans, Intel's Chief Strategy Officer and a member of Intel's Management Committee, who testified that Intel's modem business might "exit" and thus "die" or "step out of the [modem] business."[2106] It should have been obvious to Intel's senior

---

[2103] Press Release, Intel Corp., Intel to Exit 5G Smartphone Modem Business, Focus 5G Efforts on Network Infrastructure and Other Data-Centric Opportunities (Apr. 16, 2019), https://newsroom.intel.com/news-releases/intel-modem-statement/#gs.ufi1ur.

[2104] *See* Open Sessions Hearing Transcript (Revised & Corrected) at 498:16–22, Certain Mobile Electronic Devices and Radio Frequency and Processing Components Thereof, Inv. No. 337-TA-1065 (USITC June 19, 2018) (Testimony of J. Gregory Sidak) (emphasis added).

[2105] Press Release, Apple Inc., Apple to Acquire the Majority of Intel's Smartphone Modem Business (July 25, 2019), https://www.apple.com/newsroom/2019/07/apple-to-acquire-the-majority-of-intels-smartphone-modem-business/.

[2106] Transcript of Proceedings (Volume 4) at 665:12–13, FTC v. Qualcomm Inc., No. 5:17-cv-00220-LHK (N.D. Cal. Jan. 11, 2019) (Testimony of Aichatou Evans (Chief Strategy Officer, Intel)).

management in January 2019 that one strategic option available to Intel was to sell its thin modem business to its only substantial customer, Apple.

Apple's eventual acquisition of Intel's smartphone modem business included the transfer of approximately 2,200 Intel employees to Apple as well as transfers of intellectual property, equipment, and leases.[2107] So, Intel's "exit" from the modem business certainly did not in any sense cause that business unit to "die." To the contrary, Intel conveyed its right to the ownership and control of those dynamic capabilities to the largest supplier of smartphones in the United States.

2. Is It Credible That Intel Had Failed, by the Time of Trial, to Discern the Possibility of Selling Its Modem Business to Apple?

Ms. Evans' testimony in *FTC v. Qualcomm* that Intel's modem business, if it were to exit the modem industry, would "die" or "step out of the business"[2108] was consistent with the existential variant of "exit," as opposed to the transcendent variant of "exit." Ms. Evans' choice of words connoted the end of a thing's existence, or the end of its being and consciousness, as opposed to the salvaging and redeployment of its productive assets.

a. Was It Reasonably Foreseeable in January 2019 That Apple Might Purchase Intel's Modem Business If Intel Chose to "Exit" the Modem Industry?

Why, at the time of her trial testimony in *FTC v. Qualcomm* in January 2019, had Ms. Evans apparently not already thoroughly considered that one "exit" strategy for Intel's modem business would be its acquisition by Apple? In this scenario of transcendent "exit," the modem market would not lose a competitor at all; rather, ownership and control of Intel's modem business would simply change hands from the party who valued those assets less to the party who valued those assets more. Apple would affix its logo to the buildings in Santa Clara housing the 2,200 former Intel employees, and this producer of

---

[2107] Press Release, Apple Inc., Apple to Acquire the Majority of Intel's Smartphone Modem Business (July 25, 2019), https://www.apple.com/newsroom/2019/07/apple-to-acquire-the-majority-of-intels-smartphone-modem-business/. Finbarr Moynihan of MediaTek testified at trial that MediaTek similarly had relied on entry by acquisition into the modem industry. Transcript of Proceedings (Volume 2) at 323:2–14, FTC v. Qualcomm Inc., No. 5:17-cv-00220-LHK (N.D. Cal. Jan. 7, 2019) (Testimony of Finbarr Moynihan (General Manager of Corporate Sales and Business Development, MediaTek)) ("Q. And what's Analog Devices? A. It's another semiconductor company, U.S. company headquartered in Massachusetts. Q. Was Analog Devices acquired by MediaTek? A. More accurately, the business unit, the wireless business unit that I worked for was acquired by MediaTek. Not the whole company. Q. What is your understanding of the rationale for the MediaTek acquisition of the wireless Analog Devices? A. What was explained to us at the time was MediaTek was looking to acquire a footprint, R&D teams, sales and business development teams, in the U.S. and Europe predominantly with a focus of going after more tier 1 wireless business.").

[2108] Transcript of Proceedings (Volume 4) at 665:12–13, FTC v. Qualcomm Inc., No. 5:17-cv-00220-LHK (N.D. Cal. Jan. 11, 2019) (Testimony of Aichatou Evans (Chief Strategy Officer, Intel)).

thin modems then would continue operating just as it did before the sale—except for one major difference. Now, this business unit for making modems would operate under the management and control of a company capitalized at more than a trillion dollars. That scenario sounds more like reincarnation than death for Intel's modem business.

Ms. Evans rose to the position of Chief Strategy Officer at Intel along a career trajectory that began in computer engineering, rather than economics or business. Even if Intel's chief strategist did not seem to communicate her strategic insights in precise economic terms, surely at least some of the partners among Intel's outside management consultants at Bain would have understood the concept of backward vertical integration, which the standard competitive strategy course in the MBA curriculum addresses.[2109] What, then, explains Intel's apparent failure as late as Ms. Evans' testimony in *FTC v. Qualcomm* on January 8 and 11, 2019 to discern the possibility that the company might be able to sell its modem business to Apple? How soon after January 11, 2019 did Intel begin negotiating the sale of its modem business to Apple?

By January 14, 2019, an autonomous vehicle startup named Zoox had announced that Ms. Evans was leaving Intel to become the startup's new CEO.[2110] Amazon announced 17 months later, on June 26, 2020, that it would acquire Zoox, reportedly for $1.3 billion in cash, and reportedly in part because of the high quality of Zoox's patent portfolio relating to autonomous vehicles.[2111]

[2109] *See, e.g.*, David Besanko, David Dranove, Mark Shanley & Scott Schaefer, Economics of Strategy 133 (Wiley 6th ed. 2013) ("*Backward Integration*: Firm 2 owns the assets of firm 1 (i.e., firm 2 backward integrates into the function performed by firm 1 by purchasing control over firm 1's assets)."); *see also* U.S. Dep't of Justice & Fed. Trade Comm'n, Draft Vertical Merger Guidelines 9 (Jan. 10, 2020), https://www.justice.gov/opa/press-release/file/1233741/download ("Because vertical mergers combine complementary economic functions and eliminate contracting frictions, they have the potential to create cognizable efficiencies that benefit competition and consumers. Vertical mergers bring together assets used at different levels in the supply chain to make a final product. A single firm able to coordinate how these assets are used may be able to streamline production, inventory management, or distribution, or create innovative products in ways that would have been hard to achieve th[r]ough arm's length contracts.").

[2110] *See* Alan Ohnsman, *Robo-Taxi Startup Zoox Hires Intel Exec Aicha Evans as New CEO*, Forbes, Jan. 14, 2019 ("Zoox, a well-funded Silicon Valley-based autonomous vehicle startup that fired its visionary cofounder and chief executive last year, is hiring Intel's former chief strategy officer to run the company as it races to commercialize its technology."); Tim Higgins, *Autonomous Vehicle Startup Zoox Names Intel Executive Aicha Evans as CEO*, Wall St. J., Jan. 14, 2019.

[2111] *See* Tim Higgins & Matt Grossman, *Amazon to Acquire Self-Driving Startup Zoox*, Wall St. J., June 26, 2020; Louis Columbus, *Using Patent Analytics to See Why Amazon Bought Zoox*, Forbes, July 12, 2020; Stephen Nellis & Jane Lanhee Lee, *Exclusive: Amazon Plans at Least $100 Million to Keep Zoox Talent After $1.3 Billion Deal*, Reuters, July 9, 2020 ("Zoox Chief Executive Aicha Evans got a $3.4 million cash bonus, according to the [deal] documents.").

  b. The Representation by Intel's CEO That Intel Sold Its Modem Business Because It Could Not Achieve "Attractive Returns" from Selling Modems to Its Single Customer, Apple

Intel appointed a new CEO, Robert Swan, on January 31, 2019.[2112] He quickly redefined the company's strategy and, by April 16, 2019, had announced that Intel would exit the modem business.[2113]

  In a videotaped interview with CNBC dated August 1, 2019, Mr. Swan revealed Intel's motivations for selling its modem business to Apple. He said that Intel sold its modem business in part because it could not achieve "attractive returns" from selling a 5G modem to its single customer, Apple:

> Mr. Swan: For 5G in particular, the biggest opportunity for us has always been what we call the cloudification of the network. So we believe in a 5G world that more and more compute will move from the cloud or from the data centers into the network. And that is what we've been investing in, and we see that as significant opportunities. Secondly, for the smartphone modem, . . . the criteria we use when we make these investments is: is it a real technology that's going to differentiate growth for the industry? [For] 5G Network, the answer is yes. [For] 5G smartphone modem, not so much in terms of driving growth for the industry. The second criteria we use is: is it an opportunity for us to play . . . a bigger role in the success of our customers? For the 5G smartphone modem, we really only had one customer [Apple]. And the third criteria is: can we actually make money and generate a good return? We had concluded along the way with only one customer for the 5G smartphone modem we didn't really see a way to get attractive returns for our investors. So we doubled down on 5G Network, where we think there's [sic] real opportunities. And last week we announced the sale of the 5G smartphone modem . . . to Apple. But we also retained access to the technologies in the event that we need a 5G modem for non-smartphone applications, like a PC or an automobile, where we can meet the three criteria: differentiated technology with attractive growth, play a larger role in our customers' success, and generate attractive returns for our shareholders. Those are the three screens we use. 5G is a big investment for us, but it's more the network where we think we can meet all three of those criteria.
>
> Interviewer: So you don't feel like you've been blocked out of a potential growth area as more and more companies begin to release 5G-capable phones?

[2112] *See* Press Release, Intel Corp., Intel Names Robert Swan CEO (Jan. 31, 2019), https://newsroom.intel.com/news-releases/intel-names-robert-swan-ceo/; *see also* Press Release, Intel Corp., Intel CEO Brian Krzanich Resigns; Board Appoints Bob Swan as Interim CEO (June 21, 2018), https://newsroom.intel.com/news-releases/intel-ceo-brian-krzanich-resigns-board-appoints-bob-swan-interim-ceo/.

[2113] *See* Press Release, Intel Corp., Intel to Exit 5G Smartphone Modem Business, Focus 5G Efforts on Network Infrastructure and Other Data-Centric Opportunities (Apr. 16, 2019), https://newsroom.intel.com/news-releases/intel-modem-statement/.

Mr. Swan: No, . . . I don't think we have been blocked out of an area that is a real attractive growth prospect that allows us to play a bigger role in our customers' success and generate attractive returns. I think . . . in the smartphone arena there's quite a bit of concentration with a few big players, and those big players have a tendency to . . . build their own silicon today. So the one left was our customer; we didn't really see prospects for decent returns.[2114]

Mr. Swan said that Intel would continue, after selling its modem business to Apple, to make a "big investment" in 5G that was focused "on the network" where Intel expected to meet its three investment criteria— (1) "differentiated technology with attractive growth," (2) "play a large[] role in [Intel's] customers' success," and (3) "generate attractive returns for [Intel's] shareholders." At a minimum, Mr. Swan confirmed that Intel's modem business did not satisfy the third criterion, because Intel "didn't really see prospects for decent returns" on its modem business; and presumably the modem business also did not satisfy the first criterion, because Apple was Intel's only customer.

c. Did Mr. Swan's Statements About the Sale of Intel's Modem Business to Apple Comport with Ms. Evans' Testimony About Existential "Exit"?

Mr. Swan's remarks of August 2019 indicated that his strategic outlook in regard to Intel's modem business differed from the sworn testimony that Ms. Evans had given in 2018 in two ITC investigations predicting the "death" of Intel's modem business and the imperiling of Intel's investment in 5G development if it were to divest its modem business. In particular, Administrative Law Judge Thomas Pender, who presided over the ITC's 1065 Investigation, found—in a redacted public order issued on October 29, 2018—Ms. Evans' testimony to be "unrebutted, unequivocal, uniquely credible, and highly logical."[2115] He found Ms. Evans' testimony "to be decisive on all matters upon which she offered her testimony concerning Intel's intentions and plans."[2116]

On the basis of Ms. Evans' supposedly "decisive" and "highly logical" testimony, Judge Pender concluded that, "[s]ince the premium base band chip is a 'gateway' product, Intel will disengage from 5G development and supply efforts related to this kind of product" if Intel were no longer to sell modems.[2117] Judge Pender did not explain why Ms. Evans' testimony impressed him as being "uniquely credible" and otherwise worthy of his effusive praise.

[2114] CNBC International TV, *Intel CEO: Why We Sold the Smartphone Modem Business to Apple*, YouTube (Aug. 1, 2019), https://www.youtube.com/watch?v=hWbWbokL2mA.

[2115] 337-TA-1065 Redacted Final Initial Determination, *supra* note 368, at 191.

[2116] *Id.*

[2117] *Id.*

Judge Pender's conjecture was of course revealed by Mr. Swan's August 2019 interview on CNBC to have been erroneous.

In contrast, presiding over the 1093 Investigation (whose fact pattern was identical in regard to the public interest issues under section 337 as the fact pattern in the 1065 Investigation), Administrative Law Judge MaryJoan McNamara reached a conclusion diametrically opposed to Judge Pender's concerning the testimony of Ms. Evans in a redacted public order issued on April 16, 2019. Judge McNamara concluded that "Apple's and Intel's arguments about the effects of an exclusion order rest upon the also *speculative testimony that Intel will withdraw from the chipset market and from 5G development 'with near certainty'*" if the ITC were to grant Qualcomm relief for infringement of certain of its non-SEPs by three models of Apple iPhones.[2118]

Mr. Swan's remarks of August 1, 2019 subsequently confirmed that, to the contrary of Ms. Evans' testimony to the ITC, Intel's sale of its modem business to Apple would *not* impede Intel's expected investment in 5G technologies. Mr. Swan's remarks also confirmed that my own testimony on the public record in the 1065 Investigation concerning Intel's investment in 5G was correct:

Q. You were asked, Mr. Sidak, about 5G.

A. Yes.

Q. And the potential exit of Intel from 5G activities. Do you have a viewpoint or an opinion as to whether it is economically plausible that Intel would abandon its efforts to develop 5G technologies in the event of an exclusion order?

[2118] 337-TA-1093 Redacted Public Interest Findings, *supra* note 369, at 6 (emphasis added) (quoting a passage of sworn testimony by Ms. Evans that apparently is not otherwise publicly available). Ms. Evans was the only witness from Intel to testify at the hearing in the 1093 Investigation. *See* Open Sessions Hearing Transcript (Revised and Corrected) at 302, Certain Mobile Electronic Devices and Radio Frequency and Processing Components Thereof (II), Inv. No. 337-TA-1093 (USITC Sept. 17, 2018); Open Sessions Hearing Transcript (Revised and Corrected) at 587, Certain Mobile Electronic Devices and Radio Frequency and Processing Components Thereof (II), Inv. No. 337-TA-1093 (USITC Sept. 18, 2018); Open Sessions Hearing Transcript (Revised and Corrected) at 900, Certain Mobile Electronic Devices and Radio Frequency and Processing Components Thereof (II), Inv. No. 337-TA-1093 (USITC Sept. 19, 2018); Open Sessions Hearing Transcript (Revised and Corrected) at 1248, Certain Mobile Electronic Devices and Radio Frequency and Processing Components Thereof (II), Inv. No. 337-TA-1093 (USITC Sept. 20, 2018); Open Sessions Hearing Transcript (Revised and Corrected) at 1645, Certain Mobile Electronic Devices and Radio Frequency and Processing Components Thereof (II), Inv. No. 337-TA-1093 (USITC Sept. 21, 2018); Open Sessions Hearing Transcript (Revised and Corrected) at 1955, Certain Mobile Electronic Devices and Radio Frequency and Processing Components Thereof (II), Inv. No. 337-TA-1093 (USITC Sept. 24, 2018); Open Sessions Hearing Transcript (Revised and Corrected) at 2251, Certain Mobile Electronic Devices and Radio Frequency and Processing Components Thereof (II), Inv. No. 337-TA-1093 (USITC Sept. 25, 2018).

A. I don't think it's credible. They would be passing up too great an opportunity, quite apart from the smartphone business.[2119]

Mr. Swan's remarks thus corroborated Judge McNamara's conclusion that Ms. Evans' testimony that Intel would cease to invest in 5G was "speculative."

Judge Koh did not suggest anywhere in her findings of fact and conclusions of law that Ms. Evans' testimony for Intel was "made for litigation" or was "pretextual" or "speculative." To the contrary, Judge Koh—like Judge Pender of the ITC—found Ms. Evans' testimony credible and specifically mentioned that determination.[2120] In fact, Ms. Evans was the only witness of the 27 who testified at trial whom Judge Koh specifically reported in her findings of fact and conclusions of law to be credible.

3. Do Firms Spontaneously Combust When They "Exit"?

A firm's expertise, its intellectual property, its technologies, and even its aggregation of human capital together identify its dynamic capabilities, which are unlikely to disappear entirely upon a firm's decision to shut down. Instead, the firm might simply convey those dynamic capabilities intact to another firm that values them more highly (because it believes that it can manage those dynamic capabilities more productively).

The sale of a modem manufacturer to a smartphone OEM need not harm the competitive landscape for modems; the sale could simply result in a new owner of a manufacturer's productive assets. The buyer might have greater business acumen than the seller. Can one seriously doubt that Apple's acquisition of Intel's modem business will produce a stronger competitor than the former Intel business unit that Intel's CEO said "really only had one customer"?[2121] Judge Koh never addressed that likelihood because she never acknowledged that Apple's acquisition of Intel's modem business was reasonably foreseeable, which of course it was.

Nor did Judge Koh ask what happened to the employees, equipment, and intellectual property of Broadcom, Freescale, ST-Ericsson, and Texas Instruments upon the "exit" of each of those firms from the modem industry. Did they spontaneously combust? Without having asked and answered those questions, Judge Koh could not have made reliable inferences of fact as to whether there had even been an "exit" from the relevant market, as that term would have meaning in antitrust economics. And it necessarily follows that,

---

[2119] Open Sessions Hearing Transcript (Revised & Corrected) at 507:4–13, Certain Mobile Electronic Devices and Radio Frequency and Processing Components Thereof, Inv. No. 337-TA-1065 (USITC June 19, 2018) (Testimony of J. Gregory Sidak).

[2120] FTC v. Qualcomm Inc., 411 F. Supp. 3d 658, 733 (N.D. Cal. 2019) ("The Court finds credible the testimony of Aicha Evans.").

[2121] CNBC International TV, *Intel CEO: Why We Sold the Smartphone Modem Business to Apple*, *supra* note 2114.

if such an "exit" did occur, Judge Koh could not have made reliable inferences of fact as to whether that "exit" had caused any incremental harm to the competitive process.

XVI. Judge Koh and Proximate Causation

Emphasizing proximate causation as part of a section 2 claim, the Ninth Circuit in *FTC v. Qualcomm* quoted *Somers v. Apple*, which expressly required a showing of ""causal antitrust injury""[2122] for purposes of the *prima facie* case for a section 2 violation. It was legal error for Judge Koh to reject the proposition that the FTC bore the burden of production and the burden of persuasion to prove a reasonably proximate causal nexus between Qualcomm's supposedly anticompetitive acts and the supposed harm that its rivals experienced.

In its motion to dismiss filed on April 3, 2017, Qualcomm argued that the FTC's complaint had failed "to plead facts to support . . . that Qualcomm's practice has caused *actual* competitive harm in any modem chip market."[2123] Two years after Qualcomm had filed its motion to dismiss, and after Qualcomm had spent hundreds of millions of dollars on *FTC v. Qualcomm* and concurrent litigation to similar effect,[2124] evidence of harm to competition remained elusive.

Quoting the Supreme Court's decision in *Spectrum Sports*, Judge Koh found, ominously, that Qualcomm's challenged practices "'tend[] to destroy competition itself.'"[2125] She found that those practices "deprive[] rivals of revenues to invest in research and development and acquisitions; foreclose[] rivals from establishing technical and business relationships with OEMs; prevent[] rivals from field testing with OEMs, network vendors, and operators; and ensure[] that Qualcomm retains influence in SSOs, so that Qualcomm can maintain its time-to-market advantage and its unlawful monopoly."[2126] Those findings closely tracked the outcomes that Professor Shapiro, evidently relying on his theoretical bargaining model, predicted would eventuate.[2127]

[2122] FTC v. Qualcomm Inc., No. 19-16122, 2020 WL 4591476, at *8 (9th Cir. Aug. 11, 2020) (quoting Somers v. Apple, Inc., 729 F.3d 953, 963 (9th Cir. 2013) (quoting Allied Orthopedic Appliances Inc. v. Tyco Health Care Grp. LP, 592 F.3d 991, 998 (9th Cir. 2010))). Elsewhere the Ninth Circuit in *FTC v. Qualcomm* said that "courts have also held that the [causation] element of a § 2 claim . . . may be inferred." *Id.* at *10 (citing United States v. Microsoft Corp., 253 F.3d 34, 79 (D.C. Cir. 2001) (en banc) (per curiam)).

[2123] Qualcomm's Motion to Dismiss, 2017 WL 4678941, *supra* note 41, at 8 (emphasis in original); *see id.* at 2 ("[T]he Complaint does not allege a single instance in which a competing chip supplier failed to make a sale, changed its pricing, or suffered any other consequence because of Qualcomm's patent royalties.").

[2124] *See supra* note 297.

[2125] *FTC v. Qualcomm*, 411 F. Supp. 3d at 803 (alteration in original) (quoting Spectrum Sports, Inc. v. McQuillan, 506 U.S. 447, 458 (1993)).

[2126] *Id.*

[2127] Transcript of Proceedings (Volume 6) at 1142:24–1143:5, FTC v. Qualcomm Inc., No. 5:17-cv-00220-LHK (N.D. Cal. Jan. 15, 2019) (Testimony of Carl Shapiro) ("[I]t's inevitable that since the rivals are having their margins squeezed on the chips they're selling, their margins are being reduced and they're selling

Judge Koh, quoting *Microsoft*, said that, *"[b]ecause* Qualcomm's practices *all* reduce rivals' ability to become and remain viable competitors, . . . the practices 'reasonably appear[] capable' of maintaining Qualcomm's monopoly power."[2128] Her use of the word "because" appeared to indicate some ill-defined causal connection between "all" of Qualcomm's practices and a reduction in its rivals' abilities to compete. Judge Koh found that "[t]he modem chip market"—she did not distinguish between the two relevant product markets that she had identified—"reflects the cumulative anticompetitive harm of Qualcomm's practices."[2129] She considered that harm principally to have manifested itself in the fact that "[m]any of Qualcomm's rivals have exited, and those rivals that remain are hobbled by Qualcomm's anticompetitive harms."[2130]

Suppose that one accepts at face value the factual accuracy of Judge Koh's findings regarding the episodes of entry or "exit" by rival modem manufacturers. How did Judge Koh thereafter reason her way to her ultimate conclusion that an anticompetitive effect resulted at the hands of Qualcomm?

We already saw in Part F to the Introduction that Judge Koh did not examine the evidence necessary to substantiate empirically the theoretical conjecture that Qualcomm's practices had produced "exit" or more attenuated effects that supposedly harmed competition. Instead, she willingly accepted that conjecture as true solely on *a priori* grounds. She credulously relied upon self-interested statements made by executives in firms competing against Qualcomm in the modem industry.

Absent from each of Judge Koh's tragedies of "exit" was a reasonably proximate causal nexus between Qualcomm's challenged conduct and the supposedly anticompetitive effect. Antitrust law does not permit such laxity of causation when a party is proving damages, and there is no reason to condone it when a party is proving liability.[2131]

---

fewer chips, that the operating profits they can earn from being in this business are reduced and that is going to inevitably reduce their incentives to make R&D investments."). Notice that Professor Shapiro spoke of the incentive—not the ability—of rival modem manufacturers to make R&D investments. In contrast, Judge Koh was ambiguous as to whether she was addressing the incentive or the ability of rival modem manufacturers to make R&D investments, or whether she was addressing both, or whether she did not recognize the difference between the two for purposes of reporting her findings of fact and conclusions of law.

[2128] *FTC v. Qualcomm*, 411 F. Supp. 3d at 803 (emphasis added) (alteration in original) (quoting United States v. Microsoft Corp., 253 F.3d 34, 59 (D.C. Cir. 2001) (en banc) (per curiam)). Here, Judge Koh spoke of the ability of rival modem manufacturers, not their incentive.

[2129] *Id.*

[2130] *Id.*

[2131] *Cf.* Lotes Co. v. Hon Hai Precision Indus. Co., 753 F.3d 395, 409–13 (2ᵈ Cir. 2014) (discussing the requirement of "a reasonably proximate causal nexus" in proving a Sherman Act claim based on foreign conduct under the Foreign Trade Antitrust Improvements Act, 15 U.S.C. § 6a) (quoting Minn-Chem, Inc. v. Agrium, Inc., 683 F.3d 845, 857 (7ᵗʰ Cir. 2012) (quoting Makan Delrahim, *Drawing the Boundaries of the Sherman Act: Recent Developments in the Application of the Antitrust Laws to Foreign Conduct*, 61 N.Y.U. ANN. SURV. AM. L. 415, 430 (2005))).

A. *Did the FTC Prove Proximate Causation?*

Judge Koh found that "Qualcomm's practice of refusing to license its cellular SEPs to rival modem chip suppliers" was anticompetitive because "[t]his practice . . . promoted rivals' exit from the market, prevented rivals' entry, and delayed or hampered the entry and success of other rivals."[2132] Yet, Judge Koh rejected the proposition that, to establish antitrust liability, it was necessary for the FTC to "show 'a causal link between the challenged conduct and the actual, significant competitive harm.'"[2133] She found that, "even if Qualcomm's rivals have contributed to their own failings, the Court need not conclude that Qualcomm's conduct is the sole reason for its rivals' exits or impaired status to conclude that Qualcomm's practices harmed competition and consumers."[2134]

That interpretation of law was misguided. As we saw in Part I to the Introduction, Judge Koh's approach to proximate causation in a monopolization case was unreliable—particularly in light of the fact that the remedy that the FTC sought in *FTC v. Qualcomm* was of course not damages (which could be confined to antitrust injury and further winnowed down on the basis of proximate causation[2135]), but rather a permanent, worldwide injunction that would upend Qualcomm's entire business model for the exhaustive licensing of cellular SEPs (as well as the business models of Ericsson and Nokia at the same time).

[2132] *FTC v. Qualcomm*, 411 F. Supp. 3d at 744.

[2133] *Id.* at 696 (quoting Qualcomm Incorporated's Pre-Trial Brief at 13, FTC v. Qualcomm Inc., No. 5:17-cv-00220-LHK (N.D. Cal. Dec. 28, 2018), ECF No. 1051).

[2134] *Id.* at 804.

[2135] *See, e.g.*, Holmes v. Secs. Inv'r Prot. Corp., 503 U.S. 258, 267 (1992); Supreme Auto Transp., LLC v. Arcelor Mittal USA, Inc., 902 F.3d 735, 743 (7th Cir. 2018) ("Proximate causation is an essential element that plaintiffs must prove in order to succeed on any of their claims. The purpose of the proximate causation requirement—in both antitrust and tort law—is to avoid speculative recovery by requiring a direct relation between the plaintiff's injury and the defendant's behavior.") (citing *Holmes*, 503 U.S. at 268); *id.* ("[T]he proximate causation requirement in the past has been termed 'antitrust standing,' even though it has nothing to do with a plaintiff's standing to sue under Article III of the U.S. Constitution[.]") (quoting Greater Rockford Energy & Tech. Corp. v. Shell Oil Co., 998 F.2d 391, 395 & n.7 (7th Cir. 1993)); M. Sean Royall, *Disaggregation of Antitrust Damages*, 65 ANTITRUST L.J. 311 (1997); J. Gregory Sidak, Note, *Rethinking Antitrust Damages*, 33 STAN. L. REV. 329 (1981) (proposing the harmonization of antitrust damages principles and antitrust liability principles though the economic analysis of proximate causation inherently required, circa 1980, by the doctrine of antitrust injury). As I explained in 1981, "[c]ourts have treated section 4" of the Clayton Act, 15 U.S.C. § 15, which authorizes private damages for antitrust violations, "as a kind of tort remedy." *Id.* at 335 (first citing Story Parchment Co. v. Paterson Parchment Paper Co., 282 U.S. 555, 563 (1931); and then citing Solomon v. Houston Corrugated Box Co., 526 F.2d 389, 392 n.4 (5th Cir. 1976) ("An antitrust action is in the nature of a tort action[.]")).

1. Judge Koh's Use of the Word "Promote" Apparently to Signal a Diminution of the Burden of Production and the Burden of Persuasion on Proximate Causation with Respect to the "Exit" of Rivals

Judge Koh found that "[m]any of Qualcomm's rivals" had "exited the market,"[2136] and she repeatedly said that Qualcomm had "promoted" those rivals' "exit." She used the word "promote" or "promoted" eight times in her findings of fact and conclusions of law, apparently to denote the causation standard that she applied to establish that the "exit" of certain modem suppliers resulted in some manner, however tenuous, from Qualcomm's allegedly anticompetitive conduct.[2137]

Judge Koh was similarly murky about causation concerning failed attempts at entry. With respect to Samsung's Project Dragonfly joint venture to build a new modem with NTT DoCoMo and Japanese OEMs, Judge Koh found that, in 2011, "Qualcomm's refusal to license Project Dragonfly *contributed to* Project Dragonfly's inability to enter the market."[2138] In one mention of her "promotive" standard of attenuated causation, presumably in a slip of the quill, Judge Koh wrote that "Qualcomm's practice has . . . promoted rivals' *entry*."[2139] Of course, her findings of fact and conclusions of law crumble to the extent that the evidence proved that rivals in fact had entered Judge Koh's two relevant product markets.

By her eight uses of the word "promote" or "promoted," Judge Koh appeared to indicate that the FTC had not proved at trial that Qualcomm had actually "caused," let alone "proximately caused," the instances of rivals' "exit" that she identified in her findings of fact and conclusions of law. Instead, the FTC apparently had proved merely the "promotion" of "exit." Yet, Judge Koh did not cite any legal precedent to substantiate her novel "promotive" standard of attenuated causation.

Judge Koh's renunciation of proximate causation in favor of her "promotive" standard of attenuated causation was spurious because it signaled a diminution of the burden of production. In Judge Koh's courtroom, the FTC apparently did not need to produce evidence of a reasonably proximate

---

[2136] *FTC v. Qualcomm*, 411 F. Supp. 3d at 805.

[2137] *Id.* at 744 ("Qualcomm's practice of refusing to license its cellular SEPs to rival modem chip suppliers. . . has *promoted* rivals' exit from the market[.]") (emphasis added); *id.* at 749 ("Qualcomm's refusal to license has also *promoted* rivals' exit from the modem chip business.") (emphasis added); *id.* ("Qualcomm's failure to license Broadcom *promoted* Broadcom's exit from the market.") (emphasis added); *id.* ("Qualcomm also refused to license its SEPs to rival modem chip supplier Texas Instruments ('TI'), which *promoted* TI's exit from the market.") (emphasis added); *id.* at 751 ("In sum, Qualcomm's refusal to license has . . . *promoted* rivals' exit[.]") (emphasis added); *id.* at 795 ("Qualcomm's refusal to license its modem chip SEPs to rival modem chip suppliers . . . *promotes* rivals' exit[.]") (emphasis added); *id.* at 797 ("Thus, Qualcomm's refusal to license rivals . . . *promotes* exit[.]") (emphasis added).

[2138] *Id.* at 746 (emphasis added). I served from 2002 to 2006 on the U.S. advisory board of NTT DoCoMo, Japan's largest mobile network operator, and in that capacity advised its chairman on regulatory and antitrust trends relevant to mobile communications. I had no involvement in Project Dragonfly.

[2139] *Id.* at 744.

causal nexus between Qualcomm's supposedly anticompetitive acts and each supposed instance of a rival's having "exited."

In addition, Judge Koh's *ad hoc* "promotive" standard of attenuated causation possibly signaled a reduction in the burden of persuasion. It necessarily was less restrictive than the proximate causation standard. That is, her "promotive" standard of attenuated causation enabled the FTC to evade the more stringent proximate causation standard for purposes of proving causation, so as to establish a connection between Qualcomm's actions and the existence of a supposedly anticompetitive injury. (At no time did Judge Koh assert that she was making findings of fact and conclusions of law pursuant to a lesser "incipiency" standard of liability.) Did Judge Koh require the FTC to produce *preponderant* evidence to satisfy her "promotive" standard of attenuated causation, or did she apply some lower burden of persuasion, such as "reasonable suspicion" or "probable cause"? She did not say.

2. *Was Judge Koh Correct That the FTC Did Not Need to Prove Proximate Causation?*

In 1977, the Supreme Court held in *Brunswick Corp. v. Pueblo Bowl-O-Mat, Inc.*[2140] that antitrust injury is "injury of the type the antitrust laws were intended to prevent and that flows from that which makes defendants' acts unlawful."[2141] *Brunswick* applies to equitable relief as well as damages.[2142] Though *Brunswick* is the canonical explanation of "antitrust injury," it is more fundamentally a reaffirmation of the need to establish proximate causation in any antitrust case.

Brunswick directly repudiates the reasoning that Judge Koh embraced when ruling that the FTC need not "show 'a causal link between the challenged conduct and the actual, significant competitive harm.'"[2143] Without that causal link, there can be no legitimate claim that the injury perceived to have occurred flowed proximately from what *Spectrum Sports* expressly calls "conduct which unfairly tends to destroy competition itself."[2144]

[2140]   429 U.S. 477 (1977).

[2141]   *Id.* at 489 (emphasis omitted). For similar statements of the Supreme Court following, or foreshadowing, the *Brunswick* articulation of "antitrust injury," see Atlantic Richfield Co. v. USA Petroleum Co., 495 U.S. 328, 338–39 (1990); Cargill, Inc. v. Monfort of Colo., Inc., 479 U.S. 104, 116–17 (1986); Associated Gen. Contractors v. Cal. State Council of Carpenters, 459 U.S. 519, 539–40 (1983); Blue Shield of Va. v. McCready, 457 U.S. 465, 483 n.19 (1982); J. Truett Payne Co. v. Chrysler Motors Corp., 451 U.S. 557, 562 (1981); Brown Shoe Co. v. United States, 370 U.S. 294, 320 (1962).

[2142]   *See Monfort*, 479 U.S. at 112 ("It would be anomalous . . . to read [section 16 of] the Clayton Act to authorize a private plaintiff to secure an injunction against a threatened injury for which he would not be entitled to compensation if the injury actually occurred.") (construing 15 U.S.C. § 26).

[2143]   *FTC v. Qualcomm*, 411 F. Supp. 3d at 696 (quoting Qualcomm Incorporated's Pre-Trial Brief at 13, FTC v. Qualcomm Inc., No. 5:17-cv-00220-LHK (N.D. Cal. Dec. 28, 2018), ECF No. 1051).

[2144]   Spectrum Sports, Inc. v. McQuillan, 506 U.S. 447, 458 (1993).

Judge Koh of course invoked this same phrase from *Spectrum Sports* five times in her findings of fact and conclusions of law in *FTC v. Qualcomm*.[2145] But, considering the reasoning displayed in her discussion of the requisite standard of causation for proving anticompetitive harm, it seems doubtful that Judge Koh properly understood what the Supreme Court meant by that phrase in *Spectrum Sports*.

B. Did Preponderant Evidence Establish the Superiority of Qualcomm's Modems?

Substantial evidence before Judge Koh supported the conclusion that Qualcomm achieved and maintained its competitive position in the modem industry because of its superior products. Yet, Judge Koh ignored any possibly procompetitive explanation for Qualcomm's superior market position.

Judge Koh paid lip service to the principle articulated in *Grinnell* and *Microsoft* that it is not an antitrust violation for Qualcomm's superior products, business acumen, or luck to reduce the ability of its rivals to "become and remain"[2146] viable competitors.[2147] Yet, she then seemed to ignore that principle when identifying and weighing the salient facts concerning the burden of production and the burden of persuasion on causation in *FTC v. Qualcomm*. In particular, she appeared to repudiate *Grinnell's* requirement that the FTC prove as part of the *prima facie* case that business acumen, among other benign factors or virtuous attributes, was *not* the proximate cause of the alleged harm to a competitor.

Procompetitive conduct, such as selling modems to OEMs at a lower price or at a higher level of quality, would have harmed Qualcomm's rivals. Such meritorious conduct would decrease the sales of Qualcomm's rivals and deprive them of revenue, which they might have wished to invest in R&D. But the adversity visited upon rivals by that competitive effect would not constitute harm to the competitive process.

1. Evidence Establishing the Superiority of Qualcomm's Modems

Qualcomm presented evidence indicating that the proximate cause of the poor financial performance of some of its rivals was that their products were of lower quality than Qualcomm's. For example, James Thompson, Qualcomm's chief technology officer, testified on the public record in September 2018

[2145] *FTC v. Qualcomm*, 411 F. Supp. 3d at 682, 696, 791, 803, 812.

[2146] *Id.* at 803.

[2147] *Id.* at 696 ("It is not enough for conduct to harm a competitor. Nor is maintenance of monopoly power alone sufficient, if that advantage is 'a consequence of a superior product, business acumen, or historic accident.'") (quoting United States v. Grinnell Corp., 384 U.S. 563, 571 (1966)) (citing United States v. Microsoft Corp., 253 F.3d 34, 58 (D.C. Cir. 2001) (en banc) (per curiam)).

in the 1093 Investigation before the ITC that Apple "deprecated" certain features of the 2017 and 2018 iPhones equipped with Qualcomm modems so that the performance of a Qualcomm-equipped iPhone would not be superior to the performance of the Intel-equipped version of the same model of iPhone:

> [I]f you look at [Qualcomm's] chipset[, it] supported certain features—like . . . 4 by 4 MIMO [multiple input multiple output antenna array]. 4 by 4 MIMO is a way of getting double the bandwidth or double the data rate into a particular channel. And Intel['s chipsets used in the iPhone] didn't support that [feature]. So Apple then deprecated that feature from [Qualcomm's] chipset. So [Qualcomm] supported [4 by 4 MIMO] with all of [Qualcomm's] other customers but [Apple] deprecated that feature. There's also something called license assisted access. Same thing happened there. There was a four-way diversity for phone calls. That was another feature that was deprecated by Apple. It really came down to Apple—or Intel did not support those features, so Apple deprecated those features from [Qualcomm's] chipset, even though the competitors [to Apple] were supporting that [feature]. And the networks—or all the operators had deployed the networks to support that [feature] as well.[2148]

Thus, there was substantial evidence, in the form of sworn testimony on the public record, given four months before the trial in *FTC v. Qualcomm*, that would have supported the finding that Judge Koh rejected—namely, that the proximate cause of Intel's misfortunes as a modem manufacturer was *not* Qualcomm's allegedly anticompetitive conduct, but rather Intel's own shortcomings.

2. *Adverse Testimony Conceding the Superiority of Qualcomm's Modems*

Other witnesses similarly testified about the superiority of Qualcomm's products. Todd Madderom, Director of Chipset Procurement at Motorola, testified that, as an OEM, Motorola believed as recently as June 2015 that Samsung had less skill and business acumen as a supplier of modems than Qualcomm to support Motorola's needs for its next release of smartphones bearing the code name "Janus."[2149] Qualcomm also argued that, according to

---

[2148] Open Sessions Hearing Transcript (Revised and Corrected) at 196:7–23, Certain Mobile Electronic Devices and Radio Frequency and Processing Components Thereof (II), Inv. No. 337-TA-1093 (USITC Sept. 17, 2018) (McNamara, ALJ) (Testimony of Dr. James Thompson (CTO, Qualcomm)).

[2149] Deposition of Todd Madderom, *supra* note 1685, at 187:16–188:18 ("Q[.] And the second bullet reads 'Samsung,' and goes on to write, 'We have concluded that Samsung is not ready to support Janus. There are many operational and design support concerns, that is, Samsung's processes are very immature and underdeveloped as it relates to designing a product of an OEM such as Motorola or Lenovo.' Do you see that? A[.] Yes, I do. Q[.] Did you write that language I just read from CX 2018? A[.] Yes, I did. Q[.] What did you mean by that? A[.] In our opinion, Samsung had a strong technical solution, but we were concerned because they had never worked with a customer such as Motorola to support our engineering

Apple's own statements, rivals such as ST-Ericsson and Broadcom "exited" the modem business because their products were not technically advanced enough to meet Apple's needs.[2150]

That "exit" was evidence that competition was working, separating the wheat from the chaff. That outcome understandably might have sorely disappointed the management and shareholders of ST-Ericsson and Broadcom, but their resentment over having failed is not credible and preponderant evidence that the competitive process was in any way disabled from serving its salubrious purpose. And it is decidedly not the purpose of antitrust law to mitigate the risk of one's commercial failure. Every race has its losers.

3. *Judge Koh's Findings Conceding the Superiority of Qualcomm's Modems*

Judge Koh herself repeatedly found in her findings of fact and conclusions of law that Qualcomm's products were superior to the products of its competitors. She noted that John Grubbs, BlackBerry's Senior Director of Intellectual Property Transactions, had testified in 2011 that "'the other chipset manufacturers were at least two years behind [Qualcomm] on LTE.'"[2151] Judge Koh also cited the testimony of Mr. Madderom of Motorola that, although VIA also offered a CDMA modem, OEMs "'didn't feel it was capable or competitive'" compared with Qualcomm's CDMA modems.[2152] And Judge Koh noted that Ira Blumberg, Lenovo's Vice President of Intellectual Property, testified that, "'at least with respect to high-end phones, at the time that we're talking about [between 2013 and 2016], Qualcomm had the best chipset available and . . . it would be difficult to convince consumers and carriers to spend for a high-end phone if it did not have . . . the features, functions, and . . . performance that the Qualcomm chip provided.'"[2153]

---

development work, just how do we manage bug fixes that needed to be, you know, solved during the product development phase. You know, how do they support us from an engineering perspective? We had a sense that they had a strong solution and they may know how to work with their sister division of Samsung Electronics bringing Exynos chipsets to market, but we were very reluctant that they had the staff, the support infrastructure, maybe even the IT systems to really support an engineering design effort with our team.").

[2150] *FTC v. Qualcomm*, 411 F. Supp. 3d at 803 ("For example, Qualcomm presents evidence that Apple viewed both Broadcom and ST Ericsson—rivals that have exited the market—as technically not capable to supply modem chips for a 2013 Apple handset.").

[2151] *Id.* at 694 (quoting Redacted Deposition of John Grubbs (Senior Director of Intellectual Property Transactions, Blackberry) (Volume 1) at 215:22–23, FTC v. Qualcomm Inc., No. 5:17-cv-00220-LHK (N.D. Cal. Mar. 1, 2018), *exhibit to* Federal Trade Commission's Submission of Trial Testimony That Occurred on January 7[, 2019], FTC v. Qualcomm Inc., No. 5:17-cv-00220-LHK (N.D. Cal. Jan. 8, 2019), ECF No. 1185-2).

[2152] *Id.* at 688 (quoting Sealed Deposition of Todd Madderom (Director of Procurement, Motorola) at 157:21–23).

[2153] *Id.* at 717 (quoting Deposition of Ira Blumberg (Vice President of Intellectual Property, Lenovo) (Volume 1) at 71:20–72:1, FTC v. Qualcomm Inc., No. 5:17-cv-00220-LHK (N.D. Cal. Apr. 20, 2018), *exhibit to* Federal Trade Commission's Submission of January 4[, 2019,] Testimony by Deposition, FTC v. Qualcomm Inc., No. 5:17-cv-00220-LHK (N.D. Cal. Jan. 7, 2019), ECF No. 1161-2).

C.   *Did Qualcomm's Refusal to Offer Exhaustive Licenses to Its Cellular SEPs to Rival Modem Manufacturers Cause Them to "Exit" the Modem Industry?*

Did the FTC establish proximate causation for purposes of proving antitrust injury arising from the supposed "exit" of its rivals? In various passages of her findings of fact and conclusions of law, Judge Koh was murky about the evidentiary basis for her findings of fact concerning causation when attributing anticompetitive harm to Qualcomm's policy of refusing to offer exhaustive licenses to its cellular SEPs to rival modem manufacturers.

  1.   *Did Judge Koh Make Findings of Fact That Each Modem Manufacturer Whose "Exit" She Attributed to Qualcomm's Actions in Fact Competed in Her Relevant Product Markets?*

As a preliminary matter, Judge Koh did not make any finding that any of the modem manufacturers that supposedly "exited" the industry was either an actual competitor or a potential competitor of Qualcomm in either of her relevant product markets during the relevant time periods. Although she found that the firms that "exited" the industry had supplied modems,[2154] Judge Koh never actually found that those four firms were manufacturing CDMA modems or "premium" LTE modems when they "exited." Because she failed to establish and report the critical subsidiary finding of fact that those firms competed with Qualcomm in her two relevant product markets, Judge Koh never established that those firms "exited" her relevant product markets.

   If in fact the modem manufacturers that "exited" were not competitors of Qualcomm in Judge Koh's two relevant markets, then their poor performance in, and their "exit" from, the modem industry could not possibly have resulted from Qualcomm's practices in the two product markets that Judge Koh defined.

  2.   *Were the Statements by Executives of Rival Modem Manufacturers Credible and Preponderant Evidence That Qualcomm Had Proximately Caused Those Manufacturers to "Exit" or to Experience Other Attenuated Harms?*

The evidence on which Judge Koh relied to find "promotive," attenuated causation concerning "exit" consisted principally of the lamentations on direct examination of senior executives from Qualcomm's supposedly vanquished competitors. That self-serving testimony repeatedly failed to establish that the precipitating conduct by which Qualcomm supposedly had

---

[2154] *Id.* at 675.

caused a given rival's "exit" was anything that violated the Sherman Act. Judge Koh consistently concluded otherwise.

She cited (1) the deposition testimony of Scott McGregor, the former CEO of Broadcom,[2155] (2) "a 2014 Qualcomm presentation shared with Will Wyatt," Qualcomm's Vice President, which discussed the "exit" from the industry of modem manufacturers Freescale, Ericsson, and Texas Instruments,[2156] and the trial testimony of (3) Finbarr Moynihan of MediaTek[2157] and (4) Aicha Evans, Intel's erstwhile Chief Strategy Officer.[2158] Yet, none of the documentary or testimonial evidence that Judge Koh cited supported her conclusion that Qualcomm's licensing practices had harmed competition. To the contrary, her findings were credulous and conclusory recitals of allegations, devoid of any intellectually rigorous explanation of proximate causation.

Judge Koh's findings were distinctive for their lack of skepticism, curiosity, and inquiry. They were also incognizant of what elementary economic principles have to say about the necessary conditions for a firm to exit an industry that we saw in Part XV, as well as the consequences of that exit for competition.

The concise comeback to all of Judge Koh's reported episodes of "exit" is, and should have been recognized at trial to have been, this: It was altogether lawful for Qualcomm to structure or restructure its exhaustive patent licenses with OEMs for cellular SEPs and its covenants with rival modem manufacturers in whatever manner Qualcomm might have expected would maximize its profits from its licensing and its own use of its portfolio of cellular SEPs in the new legal environment that the Supreme Court had defined by virtue of its disruptive restatement of the doctrine of patent exhaustion.

a. *Broadcom's "Exit"*

Judge Koh took at face value the testimony of Scott McGregor, the former CEO of Broadcom, who testified "that remaining in the modem chip market was not 'economically viable' for Broadcom because Broadcom did not generate the scale 'sufficient to cover the R&D and other costs required to create those chips.'"[2159] She found that "Broadcom exited the modem chip

---

[2155] *Id.* at 805–06 (quoting Deposition of Scott McGregor, *supra* note 1751, at 12:14–17).

[2156] *Id.* at 806 (citing CX8292-006).

[2157] *Id.* (quoting Transcript of Proceedings (Volume 2) at 365:12–13, FTC v. Qualcomm Inc., No. 5:17-cv-00220-LHK (N.D. Cal. Jan. 7, 2019) (Testimony of Finbarr Moynihan (General Manager of Corporate Sales and Business Development, MediaTek))).

[2158] *Id.* (citing Transcript of Proceedings (Volume 3) at 587:12–22, FTC v. Qualcomm Inc., No. 5:17-cv-00220-LHK (N.D. Cal. Jan. 8, 2019) (Testimony of Aichatou Evans (Chief Strategy Officer, Intel))); *see also* Transcript of Proceedings (Volume 3) at 587:23–588:1, FTC v. Qualcomm Inc., No. 5:17-cv-00220-LHK (N.D. Cal. Jan. 8, 2019) (Testimony of Aichatou Evans (Chief Strategy Officer, Intel)).

[2159] *Id.* at 805–06 (quoting Deposition of Scott McGregor, *supra* note 1751, at 12:14–17).

market in July 2014,"[2160] but she did not report when precisely the conduct that supposedly "promoted" Broadcom's "exit" occurred. Mr. McGregor's statements merely invite the question that Judge Koh did not consider: *why* could Broadcom not manage to sell enough modems to cover its costs?[2161]

Judge Koh did not indicate in her findings of fact, for example, the extent to which Mr. McGregor testified that he and other Broadcom executives might bear some degree of responsibility for their company's operating results. The statements that Judge Koh cited did not indicate that Qualcomm proximately caused Broadcom's inability to generate enough sales of modems to remain an economically viable supplier of those products.

b.   The "Exit" of Freescale, ST-Ericsson, and Texas Instruments

Similarly, Judge Koh found that, "[a]ccording to a 2014 Qualcomm presentation shared with Will Wyatt (QTI Vice President, Finance), the former modem chip supplier Freescale exited the market in 2008 due to 'customer concentration and the need for significant investment in scale to supply customers.'"[2162] Judge Koh added that, "[a]ccording to the same 2014 Qualcomm presentation, ST-Ericsson left the market in 2013 due to reduced purchase volumes from two OEM customers, and Texas Instruments also left the market in 2012 due to a reduced customer base."[2163] She did not report when the conduct supposedly had occurred that promoted ST-Ericsson's "exit" and Texas Instruments' "exit".

The FTC's lawyer, Mika Ikeda, moved this document into evidence as an admission of a party-opponent,[2164] which would be admissible despite its being hearsay.[2165] Yet, Ms. Ikeda did not ask, much less answer, the deeper economic question of relevance and probative value: how did the unidentified author of a Qualcomm presentation that was shown to Mr. Wyatt in 2014 know as a fact the subjective intent that motivated a decision, taken years earlier by the management of Qualcomm's supposed rivals, to "exit" or "leave" the modem business? In her findings of fact and conclusions of law, Judge Koh did not ask or answer that question either.

And, furthermore, why would that subjective intent of the senior management of Qualcomm's rivals circa 2008, 2012, and 2013—if it could be ascertained with certainty—even constitute evidence that would have "any

---

[2160] *Id.* at 749.

[2161] Recall the insight of Demsetz that supposed barriers to entry fundamentally pose questions about how easily buyers can acquire information about the seller's reputation for good performance. *See* Demsetz, *Barriers to Entry, supra* note 1761, at 51.

[2162] *FTC v. Qualcomm*, 411 F. Supp. 3d at 806 (quoting CX8292-006).

[2163] *Id.* (citing CX8292-006).

[2164] Transcript of Proceedings (Volume 3) at 443:17–24, FTC v. Qualcomm Inc., No. 5:17-cv-00220-LHK (N.D. Cal. Jan. 8, 2019) (Testimony of Will Wyatt (Vice President, QTI)).

[2165] *See* FED. R. EVID. 801(d)(2).

tendency to make a fact" concerning harm to competition "more or less probable than it would be without the evidence"?[2166] Judge Koh's written decision skipped many subsidiary factual steps in reporting the reasoning underlying her findings of fact as required by Federal Rule of Civil Procedure 52(a)(1).[2167]

In regard to Freescale, what, precisely, did Judge Koh understand "customer concentration" and "the need for significant investment in scale to supply customers" to mean? With all due respect to the author of that presentation shared with Mr. Wyatt, those statements were gobbledygook. "Customer concentration" might have meant a trend toward oligopsony among OEMs—or maybe the author intended some entirely different meaning. And, regardless of what the unidentified author might have meant, did that intended meaning jibe with subsequently observed empirical facts? Similarly, "the need for significant investment in scale to supply customers" could not have come as a rude surprise to Freescale or any other modem manufacturer that willingly chose to enter the industry. And, in any event, that attribute of the industry was not something that Qualcomm had created.

Moreover, the prosaic reasons that Judge Koh cited for the "exit" of both Freescale and ST-Ericsson from the modem industry seemed to bear no relationship to Qualcomm's challenged conduct. She found that "Freescale exited the market in 2008 due to 'customer concentration' and the need for significant investment in scale to supply customers.'"[2168] And Judge Koh found that "ST-Ericsson left the market in 2013 due to reduced purchase volumes from two OEM customers[.]"[2169] She did not explain *why* the demand for the modems of Freescale and ST-Ericsson fell.

Did Judge Koh identify *any* evidence in her findings of fact and conclusions of law that Qualcomm's senior management actually relied on the 2014 presentation to make a single decision that resulted in there being a reasonably proximate causal nexus between some challenged action by Qualcomm and the supposedly anticompetitive effect of Freescale's "exit"? No.

c.   *MediaTek's Inadequate Investment and Slow Modem Deployment*

Judge Koh also said that, according to the trial testimony of Finbarr Moynihan, MediaTek's General Manager of Corporate Sales and Business Development, "MediaTek ha[d] not 'been able to invest enough I think in the modem technology and deploy it fast enough to market.'"[2170] Again, did this statement on

---

[2166] *Id.* 401; *see also id.* 403 ("The court may exclude relevant evidence if its probative value is substantially outweighed by a danger of . . . confusing the issues[.]").

[2167] *See* Fed. R. Civ. P. 52(a)(1).

[2168] *FTC v. Qualcomm*, 411 F. Supp. 3d at 806 (quoting CX8292-006).

[2169] *Id.*

[2170] *Id.* (quoting Transcript of Proceedings (Volume 2) at 365:12–13, FTC v. Qualcomm Inc., No. 5:17-cv-00220-LHK (N.D. Cal. Jan. 7, 2019) (Testimony of Finbarr Moynihan (General Manager of Corporate Sales and Business Development, MediaTek))).

its face not prompt Judge Koh to wonder whether MediaTek's management might have borne a smidgen of responsibility for not investing enough and not being nimble enough to be a viable competitor? Mr. Moynihan's statement gives absolutely *no* indication that Qualcomm proximately caused MediaTek's difficulties.

The supposed harm that Judge Koh identified with respect to MediaTek was of course far more attenuated than the "exit" to which Judge Koh found other modem manufacturers to have resorted to undertaking. In December 2018, one month before the trial in *FTC v. Qualcomm*, MediaTek announced its 5G modem.[2171] MediaTek said that its "first 5G baseband chipset Helio M70 was unveiled to the domestic [Chinese] market following its initial launch mid-year [2018]. The Helio M70 is among the industry's first wave of 5G multi-mode integrated baseband chipsets, cementing MediaTek's status as a leader in the 5G era."[2172]

That development alone casts serious doubt on whether Judge Koh's finding of fact had a credible and preponderant basis in evidence for the statement that MediaTek had been "hobbled by Qualcomm's practices."[2173] MediaTek was so "hobbled" that it proceeded to design and introduce a 5G modem?

d. Did Qualcomm's Refusal to License Its Patents Exhaustively to Huawei's HiSilicon Modem Subsidiary Harm Competition?

The fallacies of Judge Koh's analysis of harm to competition become particularly evident when one examines her reference to the harm that Qualcomm allegedly caused to HiSilicon, Huawei's modem subsidiary.

Judge Koh observed that HiSilicon sought an "exhaustive license from Qualcomm," but Qualcomm refused and instead supposedly offered only a covenant whose substance Judge Koh did not explain.[2174] Judge Koh's findings of fact and conclusions of law did not report the date when HiSilicon made its request. Nor did she report who at Qualcomm communicated the offer of a covenant to HiSilicon, what the substance and wording of the offer were, when Qualcomm made it, and what the substance and wording of HiSilicon's response were.

[2171] *See* Press Release, MediaTek Inc., First Look at MediaTek's Helio M70 5G Baseband Chipset (Dec. 6, 2018), https://www.mediatek.com/news-events/press-releases/first-look-at-mediateks-helio-m70-5g-baseband-chipset.

[2172] *Id.*

[2173] *FTC v. Qualcomm*, 411 F. Supp. 3d at 806. Judge Koh used the word "hobbled" or "hobbling" five times in her findings of fact and conclusions of law to describe the competitive effect of Qualcomm's conduct on other firms. *See id.* at 803 (three times), 804, 806.

[2174] *Id.* at 748 (quoting Deposition of Nanfen Yu (General Counsel, Huawei) at 133:14–15, 133:20–21, FTC v. Qualcomm Inc., No. 5:17-cv-00220-LHK (N.D. Cal. Mar. 14, 2018), *attachment to* Federal Trade Commission's Submission of Trial Testimony That Occurred on January 7[, 2019], FTC v. Qualcomm Inc., No. 5:17-cv-00220-LHK (N.D. Cal. Jan. 8, 2019), ECF No. 1185-1).

All that Judge Koh reported on the matter was that—after the fact, in what Judge Koh might have called made-for-litigation testimony—"Nanfen Yu (Huawei Senior Legal Counsel) testified that Huawei refused to enter the draft agreement because of the onerous reporting requirements, and the requirement that Huawei promise not to assert its patents against Qualcomm."[2175] From these scant facts, Judge Koh found: "*Thus*, Qualcomm's refusal to license HiSilicon has prevented HiSilicon from becoming a competitor for business from OEMs other than Huawei."[2176] The adverb "thus" connotes causation. The *Oxford English Dictionary* defines "thus" as: "In accordance with this; accordingly, and so; consequently; therefore."[2177] In other words, Judge Koh found that the proximate cause of the failure of HiSilicon—a subsidiary of Huawei, the national champion of China—to supply other OEMs with modems was Qualcomm's refusal to license its cellular SEPs exhaustively to Huawei's modem subsidiary at the component level.

Judge Koh did not report any finding on whether or not HiSilicon actually entered into an ASIC Patent Agreement with Qualcomm. She merely implied that HiSilicon did not do so because it objected to the terms of Qualcomm's offer. My analysis therefore proceeds on the assumption that HiSilicon did not enter into an ASIC Patent Agreement with Qualcomm. If, to the contrary, HiSilicon did in fact enter into an ASIC Patent Agreement, then of course this portion of Judge Koh's findings of fact and conclusions of law would be a tempest in a teapot that we should ignore.

Judge Koh's finding that Qualcomm "prevented HiSilicon from becoming a competitor for business from OEMs other than Huawei" is hard to credit. Whatever effect Qualcomm's refusal to license its cellular SEPs exhaustively to Huawei's in-house modem business might have had, it did not appear to have impaired Huawei's ability to sell smartphones, either in the United States or globally. As Figure 12 in Part XI.C.3.a showed, Huawei's share of "premium" smartphones was 5.6 percent in 2016 and had quintupled since 2014, such that Huawei by 2016 had become the world's third largest "premium" smartphone manufacturer.[2178] By January 2020, Huawei was reportedly "the world's No. 1 telecom [equipment] supplier and No. 2 phone manufacturer."[2179] As Huawei's share of "premium" smartphones has risen, so has its opportunity to supply its own modems for those smartphones.

[2175] *Id.* at 748 (citing Deposition of Nanfen Yu (General Counsel, Huawei) at 132:13–20, FTC v. Qualcomm Inc., No. 5:17-cv-00220-LHK (N.D. Cal. Mar. 14, 2018), *attachment to* Federal Trade Commission's Submission of Trial Testimony That Occurred on January 7[, 2019], FTC v. Qualcomm Inc., No. 5:17-cv-00220-LHK (N.D. Cal. Jan. 8, 2019), ECF No. 1185-1).

[2176] *Id.* (emphasis added).

[2177] *Thus adv.*, Oxford English Dictionary (3ᵈ ed. 2015).

[2178] *See supra* note 1729 and accompanying text.

[2179] Sean Keane, *Huawei Ban Timeline: NATO Head Supports UK Review of Chinese Firm's Role in 5G Rollout*, CNet, June 10, 2020.

Judge Koh did not ask the obvious question of whether Huawei's supposed failure to supply other OEMs with modems might have reflected the priorities of Huawei's own competitive strategy, the details of which Judge Koh's findings of fact and conclusions of law did not report. Judge Koh also did not ask the obvious question of whether the willingness of other OEMs to buy modems from HiSilicon might have been diminished by the national security concerns of the U.S. military regarding not only Huawei's network infrastructure technology, but also the technology of its handsets containing HiSilicon modems. The U.S. Department of Defense banned Huawei smartphones in May 2018 from being sold on U.S. military bases.[2180]

Of course, the fact that Huawei phones were banned from sale on U.S. military bases—including, obviously, bases on U.S. soil—meant that Huawei somehow had managed to sell Huawei smartphones (presumably containing a HiSilicon modem) that practiced Qualcomm's cellular SEPs in the United States. Huawei managed to do so notwithstanding Qualcomm's refusal to license its cellular SEPs to HiSilicon exhaustively, as Judge Koh reported in her findings of fact and conclusions of law in *FTC v. Qualcomm*. In other words, Huawei in fact demonstrated that it was perfectly willing to enter into an exhaustive license to Qualcomm's cellular SEPs at the device level for the right to sell Huawei smartphones lawfully in the United States.

Finally, if the exhaustive licensing of Qualcomm's cellular SEPs at the component level were really as critical to Huawei's competitive success in the modem business as Judge Koh found, then why, as Alex Rogers of Qualcomm testified, did the NDRC's rectification plan with Qualcomm notably decline to impose that licensing obligation on Qualcomm?[2181] Surely, Judge Koh did not think that Qualcomm had the power to push around China's antitrust enforcers.

3. Summation: Judge Koh's Findings of Fact Concerning "Exit" or Other Attenuated Harms

Despite many embarrassing gaps in the reliability and probative value of the evidence that Judge Koh identified and weighed in her findings of fact and conclusions of law, she still concluded that, "[g]iven the fragile state of Qualcomm's rivals, the exits of several other rivals, and Qualcomm's continued dominance, the Court concludes that there is *plentiful* 'evidence that the challenged restraint harms competition.'"[2182] Evidence that various manufacturers experienced low sales or low profitability certainly did not prove that Qualcomm proximately caused the poor performance of those firms.

[2180] Katie Collins, *Pentagon Bans Sale of Huawei, ZTE Phones on US Military Bases*, CNET, May 2, 2018.

[2181] *See supra* note 361 and accompanying text.

[2182] FTC v. Qualcomm Inc., 411 F. Supp. 3d 658, 806 (N.D. Cal. 2019) (emphasis added) (quoting Ohio v. Am. Express Co., 138 S. Ct. 2274, 2284 (2018)).

Even if Broadcom, Freescale, ST-Ericsson, and MediaTek were competing with Qualcomm in one or both of Judge Koh's two relevant product markets, the statements by the executives of rival modem manufacturers that she cited did not support the conclusion that Qualcomm's licensing practices proximately caused those firms to "exit" the market between 2006 and 2016.[2183] Considering the vituperation with which Judge Koh denounced as self-serving and "cagey" much of the testimony by Qualcomm's executives,[2184] and considering how she denounced the "self-serving and made-for-litigation" testimony of Qualcomm's witnesses generally,[2185] it is striking that Judge Koh so credulously accepted at face value the testimony of executives from Qualcomm's rivals.

D. *Judge Koh's "Intel-Welfare" Standard*

Judge Koh's "promotive" standard of attenuated causation was incapable of supplying a coherent limiting principle for purposes of proving antitrust injury or supporting the imposition of a remedy because it so expanded judicial discretion as to protect individual competitors instead of the competitive process. The clearest example in *FTC v. Qualcomm* of the application to a rival of that attenuated and indeterminate causal principle was Intel. Judge Koh concluded that it was proper to find Qualcomm liable for the unsatisfactory results that Intel's modem business had experienced, even though substantial evidence indicated that Qualcomm's modem business surpassed Intel's modem business on virtually every relevant competitive dimension.

Two witnesses in particular confirmed that the strategy and execution of Intel's modem business was precarious. First, Ms. Evans, Intel's Chief Strategy Officer, admitted at trial that Intel's modem business had never been profitable, and she conceded that she could not say one way or another whether Intel would benefit from having an exhaustive license at the component level to Qualcomm's cellular SEPs. Those admissions were critically important because they disproved the FTC's theory and Judge Koh's finding that Qualcomm proximately caused anticompetitive harm to Intel's modem business.

Second, Christopher Johnson, a partner at Bain & Company, which as we saw had provided management consulting advice to Intel since roughly 2007, seemed to be unaware at trial of the significance of key legal and economic

---

[2183] *See id.* at 675.

[2184] *See supra* note 1307 and accompanying text.

[2185] *FTC v. Qualcomm*, 411 F. Supp. 3d at 755 (criticizing "Nokia's and Ericsson's self-serving and made-for-litigation justifications"); *id.* at 756 ("Second, Gonell's own recorded statements to the IRS, a U.S. government agency, contradict Gonell's prepared for trial testimony."); *id.* at 779 ("Qualcomm tried to refute its own documents and statements with trial testimony and expert opinion prepared for litigation[.]").

forces informing Qualcomm's licensing practices, including the Supreme Court's revisitation of the doctrine of patent exhaustion and the meaning of the FRAND obligation. In addition, Mr. Johnson appeared to be uncertain of the distinction between modem types, despite the fact that that distinction was critical to Intel's strategy of supplying thin modems to Apple (as opposed to supplying SOCs to Apple or other smartphone OEMs). Intel had made the strategic decision to constrain itself to produce only thin modems for sale almost exclusively to Apple, despite the fact that most OEMs equip their smartphones with SoCs, which are not integrated with the smartphone's application processor. The effect of Intel's strategic decision was to bind its fate to the procurement decisions of a single potential or actual customer—Apple. Mr. Johnson's testimony seemed incognizant of that strategic reality.

The Ninth Circuit in *FTC v. Qualcomm* appeared to acknowledge the peculiarity of the "Intel-welfare" standard that Judge Koh appeared to have applied. When explaining its finding that the 2011 TA and the 2013 FATA between Qualcomm and Apple "did not have the actual or practical effect of substantially foreclosing competition in the CDMA modem chip market,"[2186] the Ninth Circuit remarked, with apparent consternation:

> During the relevant time period (2011–2015), the record suggests that the only serious competition Qualcomm faced with respect to the Apple contracts was from Intel, a company from whom Apple had considered purchasing modem chips prior to signing the 2013 agreement with Qualcomm. The district court made no finding that any other specific competitor or potential competitor was affected by either of Qualcomm's agreements with Apple, and it is undisputed that Intel won Apple's business *the very next year*, in 2014, when Apple's engineering team unanimously recommended that the company select Intel as an alternative supplier of modem chips. The district court found that "Qualcomm's exclusive deals . . . delayed Intel's ability to sell modem chips to Apple until September 2016." There is no indication in the record, however, that Intel was a viable competitor to Qualcomm prior to 2014–2015, or that the 2013 agreement delayed Apple's transition to Intel by any more than one year.[2187]

How could Judge Koh say that Intel's own shortcomings in the modem business were not more determinative than whatever anticompetitive effect the FTC alleged existed (assuming, for purposes of argument, that such an effect did exist)? How did Judge Koh conclude that the apparent deficit of business

---

[2186] FTC v. Qualcomm Inc., No. 19-16122, 2020 WL 4591476, at *21 (9ᵗʰ Cir. Aug. 11, 2020).

[2187] *Id.* (alteration in original) (emphasis in original) (citation omitted) (quoting *FTC v. Qualcomm*, 411 F. Supp. 3d at 737); *see also id.* at *21 n.25 ("[A]t trial, the FTC itself only contended 'that the [2013] agreement foreclosed Intel from supplying chips for a mere five iPad models released over three years and "perhaps" delayed Intel's ability to sell chips for the iPhone by one year[.]'") (second alteration in original) (quoting Opening Brief for Appellant Qualcomm Incorporated at 110, FTC v. Qualcomm Inc., No. 19-16122 (9ᵗʰ Cir. Aug. 23, 2019)).

acumen at Intel's modem operations, revealed in the sworn trial testimony of Ms. Evans and Mr. Johnson, was less causally significant than Qualcomm's challenged conduct? This particularly salient example of Judge Koh's "Intel-welfare" standard demonstrated the infeasibility of her "promotive" standard of attenuated causation.

    1. Ms. Evans' Testimony That Intel's Sales of Modems to Apple Had Never Been Profitable

Judge Koh observed that "Aicha Evans (Intel Chief Strategy Officer) testified that Intel has never met its target margins [for modems] and that Intel's sales of modem chips to Apple have not yet been profitable."[2188]

    a. Intel's Margins on Sales of Modems to Apple

At trial, Ms. Evans testified:

> Q. So when Intel first won Apple's business for the 2016 product, was Intel meeting those margin targets [of 40 percent to 50 percent] at Apple?
>
> A. No.
>
> Q. And what about in the 2017 Apple launch?
>
> A. No.
>
> Q. Has Intel ever achieved these target margins in its supply to Apple?
>
> A. Not yet.
>
> Q. So has Intel's supply of modem chips to Apple been profitable up to this point?
>
> A. No.[2189]

Ms. Evans' testimony suggested that Intel had target margins of 40 to 50 percent, and yet she testified that Intel's sales of modems to Apple had never been *profitable*. Her testimony implied that Intel's actual margins were zero or negative.

[2188] *FTC v. Qualcomm*, 411 F. Supp. 3d at 806 (citing Transcript of Proceedings (Volume 3) at 587:12–22, FTC v. Qualcomm Inc., No. 5:17-cv-00220-LHK (N.D. Cal. Jan. 8, 2019) (Testimony of Aichatou Evans (Chief Strategy Officer, Intel))).

[2189] Transcript of Proceedings (Volume 3) at 587:12–22, FTC v. Qualcomm Inc., No. 5:17-cv-00220-LHK (N.D. Cal. Jan. 8, 2019) (Testimony of Aichatou Evans (Chief Strategy Officer, Intel)); *see also id.* at 587:23–588:1 ("Q. So as of margins that Intel was achieving [on modems] in March 2018, would those margins be sustainable to justify Intel's investment in the industry long term? A. No.").

 b. *Ms. Evans' Admission to the FTC When Testifying Under Oath in September 2016 That She Could Not Answer One Way or the Other Whether Intel Would Benefit from Receiving an Exhaustive License to Qualcomm's Cellular SEPs*

Judge Koh never acknowledged that Ms. Evans, when testifying under oath in an investigatory meeting with the FTC in September 2016 (four months before the FTC filed its complaint against Qualcomm), could not answer one way or the other whether Intel would benefit from receiving an exhaustive license to Qualcomm's cellular SEPs at the component level. That remarkable admission was directly contrary to what Ms. Evans said 28 months later in sworn "made-for-litigation" testimony given during Judge Koh's bench trial.

 On January 11, 2019, during Ms. Evans' cross examination by Antony Ryan during the FTC's case-in-chief, she testified:

> Q. . . . Now, you testified on Tuesday [January 8, 2019] that Qualcomm's licensing practices, in your view, create an unfair playing field; right?
>
> A. That is correct.
>
> Q. And you also testified that solving that problem would require Intel, in your view, to have a license for Qualcomm; right?
>
> A. Assuming it's fair and reasonable.
>
> Q. Okay. Now, do you recall that you met with the FTC staff in September of 2016 without any lawyers from Qualcomm present and that you gave testimony under oath in the investigation of this matter?
>
> A. *If you say so, yeah. I've met with a lot of you all, yeah.*
>
> Q. Do you recall that the FTC asked you if having a license to Qualcomm's standard essential patents would benefit Intel and you testified that you couldn't answer yes or no? Do you recall that?
>
> A. *I—I don't recall. Three years is a long time in my life.*[2190]

Nothing in the trial transcript indicates that Judge Koh at this point admonished Ms. Evans to refrain from making flippant remarks and instead to give direct answers to questions asked of her on cross-examination. Similarly, no discussion appears in Judge Koh's findings of fact and conclusions of law describing Ms. Evans' testimony on cross examination as cagey or reporting that Ms. Evans lacked credibility. To the contrary, as Table 7 documented,

---

[2190] Transcript of Proceedings (Volume 4) at 657:10–658:4, FTC v. Qualcomm Inc., No. 5:17-cv-00220-LHK (N.D. Cal. Jan. 11, 2019) (Testimony of Aichatou Evans (Chief Strategy Officer, Intel)) (emphasis added).

Ms. Evans was the only one of the 27 witnesses who testified at trial in *FTC v. Qualcomm* whom Judge Koh specifically said was "credible."[2191]

Judge Koh also did not make findings on the highly probative nature of Ms. Evans' testimony at trial regarding her earlier sworn testimony to the FTC in September 2016. Notwithstanding Intel's professed need to take an exhaustive license to Qualcomm's portfolio of cellular SEPs at the component level, it was not even clear from the sworn cross-examination testimony of Intel's chief strategist in *FTC v. Qualcomm* that Intel believed that it would benefit from receiving such a license from Qualcomm.

It is staggering that Judge Koh's findings of fact and conclusions of law in *FTC v. Qualcomm* failed to report this apparent inconsistency in Ms. Evans' testimony, for the inconsistency called into question whether, contrary to the FTC's claim (and Professor Shapiro's testimony), Qualcomm's licensing practices concerning its cellular SEPs could have caused any anticompetitive effect with respect to Intel. Recognition by Judge Koh of the apparent inconsistency between Ms. Evans' sworn testimony to the FTC in September 2016 and Ms. Evans' sworn cross-examination testimony at trial on January 11, 2019 would have materially exculpated Qualcomm. Despite her reporting obligations under Rule 52(a)(1), Judge Koh did not report for the benefit of the Ninth Circuit and the Supreme Court any findings of fact concerning this apparent inconsistency across two sets of sworn testimony given by Intel's chief strategist.

2. Bain's Understanding of the Strategic Ramifications of Qualcomm's Licensing Practices

Mr. Johnson's understanding of the strategic ramifications of Qualcomm's licensing practices appeared to be predicated on certain factual assumptions about operative legal principles and critical institutional details that would appear to be less than completely accurate and reliable. One might reasonably infer that that was why Qualcomm, not the FTC, had called Mr. Johnson to the stand in the first place.

a. Bain's Understanding of Customers of Thin Modems and SoCs

Mr. Johnson surprisingly appeared not to know which OEMs and which products were actual or potential customers of Intel's modem business. He seemed to be uncertain of whether Intel produced and sold exclusively thin modems:

[2191] *FTC v. Qualcomm*, 411 F. Supp. 3d at 733.

Q. Are you familiar with the term "discrete" or "thin modem" as used in the wireless industry?

A. I am.

Q. And based on your experience, who are the customers for discrete modems? What categories of companies?

A. In the smartphone space, it tends to be the premium segment. *Some* iPhone uses a discrete modem. I believe *some or all* of the Samsung Galaxy flagships use it. And then there are applications in autonomous driving and internet of things where you don't necessarily need the apps process part of an SoC. You just want the connectivity.[2192]

Contrary to Mr. Johnson's response, it was common knowledge within the wireless industry as of the time of trial in January 2019, as well as at the time of Judge Koh's discovery cutoff in March 2018, that every then-currently available model of Apple's iPhone used a thin modem.[2193] Mr. Johnson's answer that "some" iPhones use a thin modem suggested by negative implication that other iPhones did not, which in fact was not the case as of the time of his testimony in January 2019. The latter category was the null set.

On redirect examination of Mr. Johnson, Mr. Peterson followed up on the extent of Intel's supply of modems for any OEM other than Apple:

Q. Did part of . . . Bain's work for Intel involve looking at Intel's customers?

A. In various parts of their business, yes.

Q. And who were Intel's customers for thin modems as of March 2018?

Mr. Hopkin: Objection. Foundation.

The Court: Overruled.

The Witness: I know Apple was a major customer. I know that at least back in 2014 they had a design win with Samsung. Beyond that, I would defer to Intel for their customer list.

By Mr. Peterson:

Q. Was the design win with Samsung a thin modem?

A. I believe so for their Galaxy Note 5, if I recall correctly.[2194]

2192   Transcript of Proceedings (Volume 9) at 1853:5–15, FTC v. Qualcomm Inc., No. 5:17-cv-00220-LHK (N.D. Cal. Jan. 25, 2019) (Testimony of Christopher Johnson (Bain)) (emphasis added).

2193   *See, e.g.*, Wayne Lam, *In a Mobile SoC World, What's Left for Thin Modems?*, Informa Tech, Jan. 18, 2017 ("There has been only one major OEM which has consistently used a thin modem design in their flagship handsets from 2012 through 2016. While Apple may have diversified its modem supply base it has yet to incorporate the cellular baseband and application processor functions into an SoC[.]").

2194   Transcript of Proceedings (Volume 9) at 1857:25–1858:15, FTC v. Qualcomm Inc., No. 5:17-cv-00220-LHK (N.D. Cal. Jan. 25, 2019) (Testimony of Christopher Johnson (Bain)).

Mr. Johnson's belief that "some or all of the Samsung Galaxy flagships use" a thin modem was at variance with the facts. In addition, his testimony that the Samsung Galaxy Note 5 had a thin modem appeared to be erroneous because Samsung's specification sheet indicated that the Galaxy Note 5 came equipped with an SoC: Samsung's Exynos 7420.[2195]

Table 11 reports the apparent types of modems offered in major Apple smartphones, by model of smartphone, in chronological order by release date.

Table 11. Apple's "Flagship" Smartphones
and Corresponding Modems

Release Date	Phone Model	Modem Model(s)	Modem Type
June 2007	Apple iPhone	Infineon PMB8876	Thin
July 2008	Apple iPhone 3G	Infineon PMB8878	Thin
June 2009	Apple iPhone 3GS	Infineon PMB8878	Thin
June 2010	Apple iPhone 4	Infineon PMB9800, Qualcomm MDM6600	Thin, Thin
Oct. 2011	Apple iPhone 4S	Qualcomm MDM6610	Thin
Sept. 2012	Apple iPhone 5	Qualcomm MDM9615M	Thin
Sept. 2013	Apple iPhone 5C	Qualcomm MDM9615M	Thin
Sept. 2013	Apple iPhone 5S	Qualcomm MDM9615M	Thin
Sept. 2014	Apple iPhone 6	Qualcomm MDM9625M	Thin
Sept. 2014	Apple iPhone 6 Plus	Qualcomm MDM9625M	Thin
Sept. 2015	Apple iPhone 6S	Qualcomm MDM9635M	Thin
Sept. 2015	Apple iPhone 6S Plus	Qualcomm MDM9635M	Thin
Mar. 2016	Apple iPhone SE	Qualcomm MDM9625M	Thin
Sept. 2016	Apple iPhone 7	Qualcomm MDM9625M	Thin
Sept. 2016	Apple iPhone 7 Plus	Qualcomm MDM9625M	Thin

[2195] *See Galaxy Note5*, SAMSUNG, https://www.samsung.com/global/galaxy/galaxy-note5/#!/spec.

Release Date	Phone Model	Modem Model(s)	Modem Type
Sept. 2017	Apple iPhone 8	Qualcomm MDM9645M, Intel XMM7360	Thin, Thin
Sept. 2017	Apple iPhone 8 Plus	Qualcomm MDM9645M, Intel XMM7360	Thin, Thin
Sept. 2017	Apple iPhone X	Qualcomm MDM9655, Intel XMM7480	Thin, Thin
Sept. 2018	Apple iPhone XS	Intel MM7560 Modem	Thin
Sept. 2018	Apple iPhone XS Max	Intel MM7560 Modem	Thin
Sept. 2018	Apple iPhone XR	Intel XMM 7560 Modem	Thin
Sept. 2019	Apple iPhone 11	Intel XMM 7660 Modem (*Unconfirmed*)	Thin
Sept. 2019	Apple iPhone 11 Pro	Intel XMM 7660 Modem (*Unconfirmed*)	Thin
Sept. 2019	Apple iPhone 11 Pro Max	Intel XMM 7660 Modem (*Unconfirmed*)	Thin

Sources: *iPhone 1ˢᵗ Generation Teardown,* iFɪxɪᴛ.ᴄᴏᴍ, https://www.iFixit.com/Teardown/ iPhone+1st+Generation+Teardown/599; *Apple iPhone 3GS 16GB – Interactive Control,* EʟᴇᴄᴛʀᴏɴɪᴄPʀᴏᴅᴜᴄᴛs.ᴄᴏᴍ, http://www2.electronicproducts.com/Apple_iPhone_3GS_16GB- whatsinside_text-82.aspx; *iPhone 4S Shows Key Design and Component Changes,* Iɴғᴏʀᴍᴀ, https:// technology.informa.com/389402/iphone-4s-shows-key-design-and-component-changes; *Apple iPhone 4S Teardown,* TᴇᴄʜIɴsɪɢʜᴛs.ᴄᴏᴍ, https://www.techinsights.com/blog/apple-iphone-4s-teardown; *iPhone 5 Teardown,* IFɪxɪᴛ.ᴄᴏᴍ, https://www.iFixit.com/Teardown/iPhone+5+Teardown/10525; *iPhone 5c Teardown,* IFɪxɪᴛ.ᴄᴏᴍ, https://www.iFixit.com/Teardown/iPhone+5c+Teardown/17382; *iPhone 5S Teardown,* IFɪxɪᴛ.ᴄᴏᴍ, https://www.iFixit.com/Teardown/iPhone+5s+Teardown/17383; *iPhone 6 Teardown,* IFɪxɪᴛ.ᴄᴏᴍ, https://www.iFixit.com/Teardown/iPhone+6+Teardown/29213; *iPhone 6S Plus Teardown,* IFɪxɪᴛ.ᴄᴏᴍ, https:// www.iFixit.com/Teardown/iPhone+6+Plus+Teardown/29206; *iPhone SE Teardown,* IFɪxɪᴛ.ᴄᴏᴍ, https:// www.iFixit.com/Teardown/iPhone+SE+Teardown/60902; *iPhone 7 Teardown,* IFɪxɪᴛ.ᴄᴏᴍ, https://www. iFixit.com/Teardown/iPhone+7+Teardown/67382; *iPhone 7 Plus Teardown,* IFɪxɪᴛ.ᴄᴏᴍ, https://www.iFixit. com/Teardown/iPhone+7+Plus+Teardown/67384; *iPhone X Teardown,* IFɪxɪᴛ.ᴄᴏᴍ, https://www.iFixit.com/ Teardown/iPhone+X+Teardown/98975; *iPhone XS and XS Max Teardown,* IFɪxɪᴛ.ᴄᴏᴍ, https://www.ifixit. com/Teardown/iPhone+XS+and+XS+Max+Teardown/113021; *iPhone 8 Teardown,* IFɪxɪᴛ.ᴄᴏᴍ, https://www. ifixit.com/Teardown/iPhone+8+Teardown/97481; *iPhone 8 Plus Teardown,* IFɪxɪᴛ.ᴄᴏᴍ, https://www.ifixit. com/Teardown/iPhone+8+Plus+Teardown/97482; *iPhone XR Teardown,* IFɪxɪᴛ.ᴄᴏᴍ, https://www.ifixit. com/Teardown/iPhone+XR+Teardown/114123; *iPhone 11 Teardown,* IFɪxɪᴛ.ᴄᴏᴍ, https://www.ifixit.com/ News/33016/iphone-11-teardown; *iPhone 11 Pro Teardown,* IFɪxɪᴛ.ᴄᴏᴍ, https://www.ifixit.com/Teardown/ iPhone+11+Pro+Teardown/129687; *iPhone 11 Pro Max Teardown,* IFɪxɪᴛ.ᴄᴏᴍ, https://www.ifixit.com/Teardown/ iPhone+11+Pro+Max+Teardown/126000.

Table 12 reports the apparent types of modems offered in major Samsung smartphones, by model of smartphone, in chronological order by release date.

Table 12. Samsung's "Flagship" Smartphones
and Corresponding Modems

Release Date	Phone Model	Modem Model(s)	Modem Type
June 2010	Samsung Galaxy S	Samsung Exynos 3110	SoC
April 2011	Samsung Galaxy S II i9100	Samsung Exynos 4210	SoC
July 2011	Samsung Galaxy S Plus	Qualcomm Snapdragon S2	SoC
Oct. 2011	Samsung Galaxy S II i9100G	TI-OMAP 4430	SoC
Dec. 2011	Samsung Galaxy S II i9210 HD	Qualcomm Snapdragon S3	SoC
Apr. 2012	Samsung Galaxy S Advance	ST-Ericsson NovaThor	SoC
May 2012	Samsung Galaxy S III i9300	Samsung Exynos 4412	SoC
Sept. 2012	Samsung Galaxy S Duos	Qualcomm Snapdragon S1	SoC
Sept. 2012	Samsung Galaxy S III i9305	Samsung Exynos 4412	SoC
Dec. 2012	Samsung Galaxy S III Mini	ST-Ericsson NovaThor	SoC
Feb. 2013	Samsung Galaxy S II Plus	Broadcom BC28155	SoC
Apr. 2013	Samsung Galaxy S4 i9505	Qualcomm Snapdragon 500	SoC
Apr. 2013	Samsung Galaxy S4 i9500	Samsung Exynos 5410	SoC
June 2013	Samsung Galaxy S4 Active	Qualcomm Snapdragon 600	SoC
July 2013	Samsung Galaxy S4 Zoom	Pega-Dual +XMM6262	SoC
July 2013	Samsung Galaxy S4 Mini	Qualcomm Snapdragon 400	SoC
Dec. 2013	Samsung Galaxy S Duos 2	Broadcom BCM21664	SoC
Mar. 2014	Samsung Galaxy S III Mini VE	Marvell PXA986	SoC
Mar. 2014	Samsung Galaxy S III Slim G3812B	Marvell PXA1088	SoC

Release Date	Phone Model	Modem Model(s)	Modem Type
Apr. 2014	Samsung Galaxy S III NEO i9300l	Qualcomm Snapdragon 400	SoC
Apr. 2014	Samsung Galaxy S5 SM-G900F	Qualcomm Snapdragon 801	SoC
Apr. 2014	Samsung Galaxy S5 SM-G900H	Samsung Exynos 5422	SoC
June 2014	Samsung Galaxy S Duos 3	Broadcom BCM21663	SoC
June 2014	Samsung Galaxy S5 Active	Qualcomm Snapdragon 801	SoC
June 2014	Samsung Galaxy S5 LTE-A	Qualcomm Snapdragon 805	SoC
June 2014	Samsung Galaxy S III NEO i9301l	Qualcomm Snapdragon 400	SoC
July 2014	Samsung Galaxy S5 Mini	Samsung Exynos 3470	SoC
Apr. 2015	Samsung Galaxy S6	Samsung Exynos 7420	SoC
Apr. 2015	Samsung Galaxy S6	Samsung Exynos 7420	SoC
July 2015	Samsung Galaxy S6 Active	Samsung Exynos 7420	SoC
Aug. 2015	Samsung Galaxy S6 Edge +	Samsung Exynos 7420	SoC
Mar. 2016	Samsung Galaxy S7	Qualcomm Snapdragon 820, Samsung Exynos 8890	SoC, SoC
Mar. 2016	Samsung Galaxy S7 Edge	Qualcomm Snapdragon 820, Samsung Exynos 8890	SoC, SoC
June 2016	Samsung Galaxy S7 Active	Qualcomm Snapdragon 820	SoC
Apr. 2017	Samsung Galaxy S8	Qualcomm Snapdragon 835, Samsung Exynos 8895	SoC, SoC
Apr. 2017	Samsung Galaxy S8 Plus	Qualcomm Snapdragon 835, Samsung Exynos 8895	SoC, SoC

Release Date	Phone Model	Modem Model(s)	Modem Type
Aug. 2017	Samsung Galaxy S8 Active	Qualcomm Snapdragon 835	SoC
Mar. 2018	Samsung Galaxy S9	Qualcomm Snapdragon 845, Samsung Exynos 9810	SoC, SoC
Mar. 2018	Samsung Galaxy S9 Plus	Qualcomm Snapdragon 845, Samsung Exynos 9810	SoC, SoC
Mar. 2019	Samsung Galaxy S10e	Qualcomm Snapdragon 855, Samsung Exynos 9820	SoC, SoC
Mar. 2019	Samsung Galaxy S10	Qualcomm Snapdragon 855, Samsung Exynos 9820	SoC, SoC
Mar. 2019	Samsung Galaxy S10 Plus	Qualcomm Snapdragon 855, Samsung Exynos 9820	SoC, SoC
Apr. 2019	Samsung Galaxy S10 5G	Qualcomm Snapdragon 855, Samsung Exynos 9820	SoC, SoC
Feb. 2020	Samsung Galaxy S10 Lite	Qualcomm Snapdragon 855	SoC

Sources: *Samsung i9000 Galaxy S*, GSMArena.com, https://www.gsmarena.com/samsung_i9000_galaxy_s-3115. php; *Samsung i9001 Galaxy S Plus*, GSMArena.com, https://www.gsmarena.com/samsung_i9001_galaxy_s_ plus-3908.php; *Samsung i9070 Galaxy S Advance*, GSMArena.com, https://www.gsmarena.com/samsung_ i9070_galaxy_s_advance-4469.php; *Samsung Galaxy S Duos S7562*, GSMArena.com, https://www.gsmarena. com/samsung_galaxy_s_duos_s7562-4883.php; *Samsung Galaxy S Duos 2 S7582*, GSMArena.com, https:// www.gsmarena.com/samsung_galaxy_s_duos_2_s7582-5876.php; *Samsung Galaxy S Duos 3*, GSMArena.com, https://www.gsmarena.com/samsung_galaxy_s_duos_3-6662.php; *Samsung i9100 Galaxy S II*, GSMArena. com, https://www.gsmarena.com/samsung_i9100_galaxy_s_ii-3621.php; *Samsung i9100G Galaxy S II*, https:// www.gsmarena.com/samsung_i9100g_galaxy_s_ii-4327.php; *Samsung i9105 Galaxy S II Plus*, GSMArena. com, https://www.gsmarena.com/samsung_i9105_galaxy_s_ii_plus-5213.php; *Samsung Galaxy S II HD LTE*, GSMArena.com, https://www.gsmarena.com/samsung_galaxy_s_ii_hd_lte-4198.php; *Samsung i8190 Galaxy S III Mini*, GSMArena.com, https://www.gsmarena.com/samsung_i8190_galaxy_s_iii-mini-5033. php; *Samsung i8200 Galaxy S III Mini VE*, GSMArena.com, https://www.gsmarena.com/samsung_i8200_ galaxy_s_iii_mini-ve-6190.php; *Samsung G3812B Galaxy S3 Slim*, GSMArena.com, https://www.gsmarena. com/samsung_g3812b_galaxy_s3_slim-6209.php; *Samsung i9300 Galaxy S III*, GSMArena.com, https:// www.gsmarena.com/samsung_i9300_galaxy_s_iii-4238.php; *Samsung i9305 Galaxy S III*, GSMArena. com, https://www.gsmarena.com/samsung_i9305_galaxy_s_iii-5001.php; *Samsung i9300i Galaxy S3 Neo*, GSMArena.com, https://www.gsmarena.com/samsung_i9300i_galaxy_s3_neo-6289.php; *Samsung i9301i Galaxy S3 Neo*, GSMArena.com, https://www.gsmarena.com/samsung_i9301i_galaxy_s3_neo-6433.php; *Samsung Galaxy S4 Zoom*, GSMArena.com, https://www.gsmarena.com/samsung_galaxy_s4_zoom-5447. php; *Samsung i9190 Galaxy S4 Mini*, GSMArena.com, https://www.gsmarena.com/samsung_i9190_galaxy_ s4_mini-5375.php; *Samsung Galaxy i9295 Galaxy S4 Active*, GSMArena.com, https://www.gsmarena.com/ samsung_i9295_galaxy_s4_active-5446.php; *Samsung i9505 Galaxy S4*, GSMArena.com, https://www. gsmarena.com/samsung_i9505_galaxy_s4-5371.php; *Samsung i9500 Galaxy S4*, GSMArena.com, https://www. gsmarena.com/samsung_i9500_galaxy_s4-5125.php; *Samsung SM-G800F Galaxy S5 Dx LTE-A / Galaxy S5 Mini (Samsung Atlantic)*, PhoneDB.net, http://phonedb.net/index.php?m=device&id=6033&c=samsung_

sm-g800f_galaxy_s5_dx_lte-a__galaxy_s5_mini__samsung_atlantic; *Samsung SM-G870A Galaxy S5 Active LTE-A*, PhoneDB.net, http://phonedb.net/index.php?m=device&id=6260&c=samsung_sm-g870a_galaxy_s5_active_lte-a; *Samsung SM-G906S Galaxy S5 LTE-A (Samsung Lentis)*, PhoneDB.net, http://phonedb.net/index.php?m=device&id=6040&c=samsung_sm-g906s_galaxy_s5_lte-a__samsung_lentis; *Samsung SM-G900F Galaxy S5 LTE-A 16GB*, PhoneDB.net, http://phonedb.net/index.php?m=device&id=5837&c=samsung_sm-g900f_galaxy_s5_lte-a_16gb__samsung_pacific; *Samsung SM-G900H Galaxy S5 HSPA 16GB (Samsung Pacific)*, PhoneDB.net, http://phonedb.net/index.php?m=device&id=5884&c=samsung_sm-g900h_galaxy_s5_hspa_16gb__samsung_pacific; *Samsung SM-G925F Galaxy S6 Edge LTE-A 64 GB (Samsung Zero)*, PhoneDB.net, http://phonedb.net/index.php?m=device&id=7781&c=samsung_sm-g925f_galaxy_s6_edge_lte-a_64gb__samsung_zero; *Samsung G890A Galaxy S6 Active LTE-A*, PhoneDB.net, http://phonedb.net/index.php?m=device&id=7853&c=samsung_sm-g890a_galaxy_s6_active_lte-a; *Samsung SM-G930F Galaxy S7 TD-LTE (Samsung Hero)*, PhoneDB.net, http://phonedb.net/index.php?m=device&id=9334&c=samsung_sm-g930f_galaxy_s7_td-lte__samsung_hero; *Samsung SM-G935 Galaxy S7 Edge TD-LTE (Samsung Hero 2)*, PhoneDB.net, http://phonedb.net/index.php?m=device&id=9792&c=samsung_sm-g935f_galaxy_s7_edge_td-lte__samsung_hero_2; *Samsung SM-G950F Galaxy S8 TD-LTE (Samsung Dream)*, PhoneDB.net, http://phonedb.net/index.php?m=device&id=11118&c=samsung_sm-g950f_galaxy_s8_td-lte__samsung_dream; *Samsung SM-G955F Galaxy S8+ TD-LTE / Galaxy S8 Plus (Samsung Dream 2)*, PhoneDB.net, http://phonedb.net/index.php?m=device&id=11161&c=samsung_sm-g955f_galaxy_s8plus_td-lte__galaxy_s8_plus__samsung_dream_2; *Samsung SM-G892A Galaxy S8 Active TD-LTE*, PhoneDB.net, http://phonedb.net/index.php?m=Device&id=11600&c=samsung_sm-g892a_galaxy_s8_active_td-lte; *Samsung SM-660U1 Galaxy S9 TD-LTE US 256 GB (Samsung Star)*, PhoneDB.net, http://phonedb.net/index.php?m=device&id=13353&c=samsung_sm-g960u1_galaxy_s9_td-lte_us_256gb__samsung_star; *Samsung SM-G965U Galaxy S9+ TD-LTE US (Samsung Star 2)*, PhoneDB.net, http://phonedb.net/index.php?m=device&id=12975&c=samsung_sm-g965u_galaxy_s9plus_td-lte_us__samsung_star_2; *Samsung SM-G970U Galaxy S10E TD-LTE US 128 GB (Samsung Beyond 0)*, PhoneDB.net, http://phonedb.net/index.php?m=device&id=14851&c=samsung_sm-g970u_galaxy_s10e_td-lte_us_128gb__samsung_beyond_0; *Samsung SM-G973W Galaxy S10 TD-LTE CA 512GB (Samsung Beyond 1)*, PhoneDB.net, http://phonedb.net/index.php?m=device&id=15494&c=samsung_sm-g973w_galaxy_s10_td-lte_ca_512gb__samsung_beyond_1; *Samsung SM-G975F/DS Galaxy S10+ Global Dual SIM TD-LTE 128GB (Samsung Beyond 2)*, PhoneDB.net, http://phonedb.net/index.php?m=device&id=15498&c=samsung_sm-g975fds_galaxy_s10plus_global_dual_sim_td-lte_128gb__samsung_beyond_2; *Samsung SM-G977U Galaxy S10 5G TD-LTE US 256 GB / SM-G977V (Samsung Beyond X)*, PhoneDB.net, http://phonedb.net/index.php?m=device&id=15511&c=samsung_sm-g977u_galaxy_s10_5g_td-lte_us_256gb__sm-g977v__samsung_beyond_x; *Samsung SM-G770F/DSM Galaxy S10 Lite Dual SIM TD-LTE IN 512 GB (Samsung G770)*, PhoneDB.net, http://phonedb.net/index.php?m=device&id=16631&c=samsung_sm-g770fdsm_galaxy_s10_lite_dual_sim_td-lte_in_512gb__samsung_g770.

Did Judge Koh recognize that a Bain partner who had advised Intel for a period of years on competitive strategy concerning the wireless industry appeared to be uncertain when testifying under oath, in January 2019, about these facts? Did Judge Koh understand that one could reasonably expect that these facts about the use of thin modems and SoCs would have been pertinent pieces of information in a strategic analysis that a management consulting firm would have undertaken on the nature of rivalry between Intel and Qualcomm?

Judge Koh's findings of fact and conclusions of law did not comment on this aspect of Mr. Johnson's testimony. Nor did she report any findings on Mr. Johnson's credibility or reliability as a witness, despite the fact that, as we saw in Part XIV.D, Qualcomm's lawyer had asked Judge Koh to designate Mr. Johnson a hostile witness.

The trial transcript during Mr. Johnson's testimony does not contain any interruption by Judge Koh to probe the credibility, reliability, or relevance of his testimony. If Judge Koh realized that she was hearing testimony that diverged from the facts regarding the actual use of thin modems by Apple and the actual absence of use of thin modems by Samsung, she kept that realization to herself, both at trial and in her subsequent findings of fact and conclusions of law.

b. *Bain's Understanding of the Strategic Implications of Patent Exhaustion and the FRAND Contract for Qualcomm's Licensing Practices*

The FTC's cross examination of Mr. Johnson was friendly because Mr. Johnson was hostile (or at least adverse) to Qualcomm. Mr. Hopkin's friendly cross examination of Mr. Johnson for the FTC soon turned to a highly revealing line of testimony that suggested the apparent limits of Bain's understanding of the procompetitive rationale for Qualcomm's licensing practices in light of the Supreme Court's evolving jurisprudence on patent exhaustion.

Mr. Johnson had not been questioned at the start of his testimony about his professional training, including whether he had any legal education. Mr. Johnson's page on Bain's website indicates that he "holds a JD from Harvard Law School and a degree in economics from Yale University."[2196]

Mr. Hopkin first directed Mr. Johnson to testify about a slide presentation concerning Qualcomm's competitive strategy:

Q. And now if you could please turn in the binder that counsel for Qualcomm handed you to tab for QX 0121A.

A. Okay.

Q. This is the August 12, [apparently 2011] Qualcomm CSD Presentation; is that right?

A. That's right.

Q. Could you flip to slide 9 using the internal pagination.

A. So also this is a slide entitled Qualcomm Successfully Employs Multiple IPR Valuation Strategies. Do you see that?[2197]

A. Value generation strategies, yes.

Q. So what is the chart on the left-hand side of the slide regarding global patent licensing revenue depicting?

A. It's depicting that by these estimates, in 2011, there was about $21 billion in patent licensing within the scope, and it shows for various I.P. blocks, baseband, Wi-Fi, Bluetooth, who were the players in the industry who were collecting that revenue.

Q. And what was the percentage of revenue that Qualcomm accounted for according to this chart for WWAN [acronym undefined] licensing revenue?

[2196] *Chris Johnson*, BAIN, https://www.bain.com/our-team/christopher-johnson/.
[2197] The transcript here appears to be garbled. What the transcript identifies as Mr. Johnson's answer appears instead to be a continuation of Mr. Hopkin's foundation for his question.

A. That would be the column, the box in red on the bottom left corner. It looks like 50 to 55 percent.[2198]

Mr. Johnson proceeded to be questioned, and to give testimony, on what he considered to be the strategic implications of Qualcomm's licensing practices, on the meaning of the FRAND contract, and on the economic significance of the fact that Qualcomm refrained from litigation as a means to enforce its cellular SEPs. As we shall next see, this testimony was noteworthy because it stated an inaccurate factual premise about the legal constraints facing Qualcomm.

i.   *Bain's Apparently Erroneous Strategic Assessment of the Legal Constraints Facing Qualcomm*

Mr. Johnson conjectured as to what would be Qualcomm's optimal competitive strategy subject to the legal constraints that Qualcomm faced:

> Q. And if I could direct your attention to the right-hand side of the slide under the blue box labeled Qualcomm WWAN IPR Strategies?
>
> A. Um-hum.
>
> Q. What was Bain intending to convey here about Qualcomm's licensing practices?
>
> A. I think we drew a few conclusions at the time. *This probably wasn't something that we looked at in depth or had the expertise to fully understand.* That said, the conclusions we were drawing were, first, that at the time *we were observing a two-tiered licensing scheme, meaning that they [Qualcomm] were collecting licensing revenue both from other chip providers, as well as from the end OEM customers.* Another observation here is that *royalties were being negotiated out of court to maintain an undefined nature of fair and reasonable within the FRAND construct.* There's a point around aggressively litigating when necessary, and a point around pro-activity and defense licensing to protect against competitor actions.
>
> . . . .
>
> Q. . . . To the extent you know, what was the intended significance—moving back to QX 121A, slide 9—of the fact from Bain's perspective that royalties were negotiated out of court as mentioned in the second bullet point?

[2198] Transcript of Proceedings (Volume 9) at 1854:5–1855:2, FTC v. Qualcomm Inc., No. 5:17-cv-00220-LHK (N.D. Cal. Jan. 25, 2019) (Testimony of Christopher Johnson (Bain)).

A. *Frankly, it seemed strange to me*, the fact that—if the intent was to maintain undefined nature [sic]. *I didn't author this, but the intent seemed strange.*

Q. Fair enough. No further questions.[2199]

On unfriendly redirect examination of Mr. Johnson, Mr. Peterson followed up on the extent of Mr. Peterson's expertise on the meaning of FRAND:

Q. Mr. Johnson, do you hold yourself out as an expert on FRAND obligations?

A. I do not.[2200]

Mr. Johnson admitted that he personally was not an expert on FRAND obligations, and that Bain did not have the expertise to understand Qualcomm's licensing practices,[2201] such that its conclusions (evidently communicated to Intel) concerning Qualcomm's licensing practices were necessarily inexpert opinions. Bain of course does not appear to be a law firm or to render legal advice or representation to its clients.

Mr. Johnson's trial testimony appeared to indicate that he did not correctly understand that patent exhaustion prevented Qualcomm from collecting royalties at both the modem level and the device level. Substantial evidence in *FTC v. Qualcomm* proved that Mr. Johnson's testimony on Qualcomm's supposedly two-tiered "licensing" scheme was erroneous. Judge Koh did not remark on the erroneous (and necessarily unreliable) nature of that testimony—either at trial, while Mr. Johnson was giving his testimony, or later, when Judge Koh issued her subsequent findings of fact and conclusions of law.

Mr. Johnson also testified twice that Qualcomm's practice of relying on negotiation rather than litigation to license its SEPs "seemed strange."[2202] Why did Bain evidently conclude in its advice to Intel that it was "strange" for an SEP holder to negotiate licenses rather than litigate over FRAND royalties? Suspicion of the unfamiliar uniqueness and innovation of Qualcomm's business model was not a legitimate reason to cast aspersions on Qualcomm's licensing practices.

[2199] *Id.* at 1854:5–1855:22, 1856:10–17 (emphasis added) (discussing QX121A). Mr. Johnson could not recall what the abbreviation CSD meant. *Id.* at 1850:25–1851:1, 1851:8–11 ("Q. Mr. Johnson, if you could turn in your binder to QX 121. Could you tell me what a CSD is? . . . The Witness: I don't remember exactly what the acronym stands for. But it's effectively an internal project to look at a specific topic and then present it out to members of the Intel leadership team.").

[2200] *Id.* at 1858:16–18.

[2201] *Id.* at 1855:9–11 ("This probably wasn't something that we . . . had the expertise to fully understand.").

[2202] *Id.* at 1856:14, 1856:16.

ii.   *Bain's Understanding of Qualcomm's Collection of Royalties*

Substantial evidence in *FTC v. Qualcomm* showed that Qualcomm had ceased to collect any royalty from any modem manufacturer after Qualcomm had ceased to grant nonexhaustive "licenses" in favor of covenants, so as to avoid the risk of patent exhaustion. Mr. Johnson appeared to be unfamiliar with this fact—which, as we have seen, is absolutely essential to understanding *FTC v. Qualcomm*:

> Q. And do you know if Intel and other chip makers pay royalties to Qualcomm?
>
> A. Today or in the past?
>
> Q. As of March 2018.
>
> A. At March 2018—
>
> Q. Looking backwards, yeah.
>
> A. My understanding, and again, *we're at the edge of my knowledge*, was that at the time some of these documents were authored in the 2010, 2012 timeframe, SoC providers were paying royalties to Qualcomm. My understanding is that is not the case today.
>
> Q. And what's your basis for that knowledge?
>
> A. *Good question. It's kind of a blur.* I don't think I came across that—*well, one is the two-tiered licensing scheme that we spoke about a moment ago from both OEM's and SoC vendors, so that made it sound like they're charging SoC vendors.* My personal understanding of Qualcomm's licensing structure is a bit different just from what I've read and what I've been told in conversations.
>
> Mr. Peterson: Thank you. No further questions.[2203]

Mr. Johnson's testimony appeared to manifest confusion. His testimony that Qualcomm was receiving patent royalties from both OEMs and rival manufacturers of SoCs was of course incorrect for the reasons explained earlier. Even Judge Koh acknowledged that Qualcomm had never offered an exhaustive license to its cellular SEPs to rival modem manufacturers and had on various specific occasions declined to offer such a license to MediaTek, a joint venture named Project Dragonfly (involving Samsung, NTT, and two other Japanese companies), Samsung, VIA, Intel, HiSilicon, Broadcom, Texas Instruments, and LGE.[2204]

2203 *Id.* at 1857:25–1859:14 (emphasis added).
2204 FTC v. Qualcomm Inc., 411 F. Supp. 3d 658, 744–51 (N.D. Cal. 2019).

c.   Summation Concerning Bain's Apparent Factual Foundation for Its Strategic Advice to Intel

Mr. Johnson's testimony indicated that he had some misunderstanding about basic factual premises that would be relevant to the management consulting advice that his employer, Bain, evidently might have given Intel over what then was a span of 11 years. If his sworn testimony is an accurate indicator of the depth and breadth of his knowledge, and, by extension, of Bain's management advice to Intel, Mr. Johnson seemed not to understand the implications for competitive strategy of the legal constraints that had arisen from the Supreme Court's revisitation of the doctrine of patent exhaustion, or from the proper contractual interpretation of Qualcomm's FRAND and RAND obligations, or from the proper economic analysis for calculating a royalty for Qualcomm's cellular SEPs under those obligations.

Mr. Johnson claimed no expertise on patent exhaustion or the meaning of the FRAND obligation. Notwithstanding his legal education, Mr. Johnson appeared on the basis of his sworn testimony to treat such details of legal principles and institutions as a black box, rather than factors whose significance would be necessary to understand rigorously in economic terms before one could formulate a firm's competitive strategy in the modem industry. Judge Koh's findings of fact and conclusions of law did not comment on any of those problematic aspects of Mr. Johnson's testimony.

Considering the highly probative testimony of Ms. Evans and Mr. Johnson, was it believable that Judge Koh could have concluded on the facts that Qualcomm proximately caused any supposed harm to Intel? Or was it more reasonable to conclude from those facts that there existed a reasonably proximate causal nexus between the apparently inferior business acumen of Intel's modem operations and its admitted failure ever to have been profitable as of March 2018?

E.   Which Kind of "Competition" Does Antitrust Law Seek to Protect?

What is the understanding of the "competition" that antitrust law seeks to protect? Implicit in Judge Koh's findings of fact and conclusions of law was some benchmark by which she somehow purported to intuit what the optimal velocity of entry into and "exit" from the modem industry should be to achieve some equally unstated societal goal.

Were Judge Koh's findings regarding that supposedly optimal velocity of entry into and "exit" from the modem industry predicated on some vision of the vitality of the competitive *process* that antitrust law seeks to protect, or did she instead rely on some alternative understanding of what

American antitrust jurisprudence means when it speaks precisely of protecting competition?

1. The Competitor-Protection View of Antitrust Law

Judge Koh's assessment of entrants in the modem industry more closely resembled what Judge Posner, writing 36 years earlier, called even then the "older, competitor-protection view" of antitrust law.[2205] To dust off Judge Posner's observation from 1983 and apply it to *FTC v. Qualcomm*, the relevant analysis should have been whether "either the exclusion of an individual [modem manufacturer] . . . or the possible effect of that exclusion on the competitive behavior of other aspirants . . . could result in a higher price or lower quality of [service]" in the relevant geographic market.[2206]

To paraphrase Judge Posner again from 1983, "there is a question to what extent, with their emphasis on the welfare of competitors rather than consumers," the theories of harm advanced by the FTC and accepted by Judge Koh "can survive the consumer-oriented view of antitrust that prevails today."[2207] And to paraphrase Judge Posner in *University Life*, that the business plan of any one modem manufacturer might not be viable unless Qualcomm stopped offering discounts on its sale of its modems and started licensing its cellular SEPs exhaustively at the component level "would have no appreciable effect on competition, viewed as a state in which consumer interests are well served rather than as a process of rivalry that is diminished by the elimination of even one tiny rival."[2208] "That 'there's a special providence in the fall of a sparrow,'" wrote Judge Posner, "is not the contemporary philosophy of antitrust."[2209]

2. Consumer Welfare

Modern antitrust law considers consumer welfare its guiding principle. In a series of decisions for the Seventh Circuit in the early 1980s, Judge Posner explained the connection between competition and consumer welfare: "Competition is the allocation of resources in which economic welfare (consumer welfare, to oversimplify slightly) is maximized; it is not rivalry per se, or a particular form of rivalry, or some minimum number of competitors."[2210] Judge Easterbrook similarly reasoned in his dissent in 1986 in *Fishman v. Estate of Wirtz* that "to know whether a given restraint is an

---

2205 Marrese v. Am. Acad. of Orthopaedic Surgeons, 706 F.2d 1488, 1497 (7th Cir. 1983).

2206 *Id.*

2207 *Id.* at 1495–96.

2208 University Life Ins. Co. of Am. v. Unimarc Ltd., 699 F.2d 846, 853 (7th Cir. 1983).

2209 *Id.* (quoting WILLIAM SHAKESPEARE, HAMLET, act 5, sc. 2, l. 232).

2210 Roland Mach. Co. v. Dresser Indus., Inc., 749 F.2d 380, 395 (7th Cir. 1984) (citing Products Liab. Ins. Agency v. Crum & Forster Ins. Cos., 682 F.2d 660, 663-65 (7th Cir. 1982) (Posner, J.)).

antitrust problem we must identify the potential effects of that restraint on consumers' welfare and allocative efficiency."[2211] The Ninth Circuit, citing *Microsoft*, said in *FTC v. Qualcomm* that, "in order to make out a § 2 violation, the anticompetitive harm identified must be to *competition itself*, not merely to competitors," and the court found that the FTC had "identifie[d] no such harm to competition."[2212]

In a 1983 decision, *Marrese v. American Academy of Orthopaedic Surgeons*, Judge Posner wrote that

> though there is a sense in which the exclusion of any competitor reduces competition, it is not the sense of competition that is relevant to antitrust law. The policy of competition is designed for the ultimate benefit of consumers rather than of individual competitors, and a consumer has no interest in the preservation of a fixed number of competitors greater than the number required to assure his being able to buy at the competitive price.[2213]

In *Products Liability Insurance Agency v. Crum & Forster*, Judge Posner wrote in 1982: "The consumer does not care how many sellers of a particular good or service there are; he cares only that there be enough to assure him a competitive price and quality."[2214] In another antitrust decision in 1983, *University Life Insurance v. Unimarc Life Insurance*, Judge Posner wrote that "competition in the antitrust sense signifies not the preservation of all existing competitors but the maintenance of a sufficient number to assure that consumers get the best possible quality of product at the lowest possible price."[2215]

This understanding of competition long ago transcended the Chicago School of antitrust law. Justice (then Judge) Breyer wrote for the First Circuit in 1987: "'Anticompetitive' [in antitrust law] has a special meaning: it refers not to actions that merely injure individual competitors, but rather to actions that harm the competitive process, a process that aims to bring consumers the benefits of lower prices, better products, and more efficient production

---

[2211] 807 F.2d 520, 567 (7th Cir. 1986) (Easterbrook, J., dissenting) (emphasis in original).

[2212] FTC v. Qualcomm Inc., No. 19-16122, 2020 WL 4591476, at *13 (9th Cir. Aug. 11, 2020) (citing United States v. Microsoft Corp., 253 F.3d 34, 58 (D.C. Cir. 2001) (en banc) (per curiam)).

[2213] 706 F.2d at 1497 (first citing *Products Liab.*, 682 F.2d at 663–64; and then citing *University Life*, 699 F.2d at 853). Perhaps purely for sentimental reasons, I find Judge Posner's original phrasing in *Products Liability Insurance Agency v. Crum & Forster* to be the more axiomatic and lyrical, as befits what was one of the two antitrust opinions that he wrote during his first few months on the Seventh Circuit: "Now there is a sense in which eliminating even a single competitor reduces competition. But it is not the sense that is relevant in deciding whether the antitrust laws have been violated." *Products Liab.*, 682 F.2d at 663. Judge Posner anchored that statement of law in Reiter v. Sonotone Corp., 442 U.S. 330, 343 (1979), and the various accounts of the primacy of consumer welfare "told by the Supreme Court repeatedly in recent years." *Products Liab.*, 682 F.2d at 663.

[2214] *Products Liab.*, 682 F.2d at 664.

[2215] *University Life*, 699 F.2d at 852 (citing *Products Liab.*, 682 F.2d at 663–64).

methods."[2216] And of course what is more authoritative than these Court of Appeals decisions by Judge Posner, Judge Easterbrook, and then-Judge Breyer is the fact that the Supreme Court in time repeatedly embraced precisely this line of reasoning.

In 1993, for example, Justice Byron White wrote for a unanimous Court in *Spectrum Sports*:

> The purpose of the [Sherman] Act is not to protect businesses from the working of the market; it is to protect the public from the failure of the market. The law directs itself not against conduct which is competitive, *even severely so*, but against conduct which unfairly tends to destroy competition itself. It does so not out of solicitude for private concerns but out of concern for the public interest.[2217]

We have seen that Judge Koh repeatedly quoted a portion of this passage in her findings of fact and conclusions of law in *FTC v. Qualcomm*. But her favored excerpt is best understood when read within the full context of the sentences that surround it. This principle in antitrust law dovetails with *Brunswick*, which, as we saw, demands a proximate causation standard when proving antitrust injury.

F. Does the Sherman Act Arrest in Time the Institutional Structure of Production?

If meritorious competition by Qualcomm, manifested in a structure of contracting that it continuously redesigned to navigate the Supreme Court's latest pronouncements on patent exhaustion, caused rival modem manufacturers to "exit" the industry, then such competition from Qualcomm did so *lawfully*. Yet, Judge Koh's findings of fact and conclusions of law in *FTC v. Qualcomm* seemed unaware of that possibility.

Her decision seemed to question Qualcomm's lawful right to modify its business model on demand to avert the harm that Qualcomm's management evidently believed—and explicitly explained in July 2012 to the IRS in the recorded conference upon which Judge Koh so heavily relied in reaching her findings of fact and conclusions of law—that the Supreme Court's new decisions concerning patent exhaustion would have on the profitability of Qualcomm's patent licensing activities, were Qualcomm to license its portfolio of cellular SEPs exhaustively to rival modem manufacturers, as Judge Koh reported that those rivals repeatedly asked Qualcomm to do. Put differently, Judge Koh's view of section 2 of Sherman Act would prevent the continued

---

[2216] Interface Grp., Inc. v. Mass. Port Auth., 816 F.2d 9, 10 (1ˢᵗ Cir. 1987) (citation omitted) (citing Brown Shoe Co. v. United States, 370 U.S. 294, 320 (1962)).

[2217] Spectrum Sports, Inc. v. McQuillan, 506 U.S. 447, 458 (1993) (emphasis added).

evolution of the Coasean nature of the firm, and of the institutional structure of production that Coase described.

In the face of Qualcomm's lawful adaptation of its business model
to the Supreme Court's newly revealed understanding of the doctrine of
patent exhaustion, Judge Koh's findings of fact and conclusions of law in
FTC v. Qualcomm seemed to treat each instance of a rival's "exit" from the
modem business as another piece of evidence of unlawful monopolization
by Qualcomm. Her equating of "exit" to anticompetitive harm was unsound.
The Sherman Act does not seal a firm's business model in a time capsule, nor
does it make the lawfully innovating monopolist his brother's keeper.

XVII. Did Qualcomm Kill WiMAX?

Judge Koh faulted Qualcomm for executing another agreement with Apple:
the 2007 Marketing Incentive Agreement (MIA), which in Judge Koh's
words "lowered Apple's royalty payments to Qualcomm through a rebate
structure."[2218] She found that "[f]rom Qualcomm's perspective, giving Apple
royalty rate rebates was justified because Qualcomm used the MIA to eliminate WiMAX, a competing cellular standard supported by Intel."[2219] Yet,
Judge Koh's findings of fact and conclusions of law regarding the WiMAX
standard were baffling. They were so superficial as to call into question her
respect for the sophistication of the likely readers of her findings of fact and
conclusions of law.

Judge Koh reported in the span of 425 words (which is slightly over one
book page set in 11-point font) that, in 2007, "Qualcomm used its monopoly power against Apple to eliminate WiMAX, a competing cellular standard
supported by Intel"[2220]—*"not because WCDMA,"* which Qualcomm supported,
"was a superior technology, but because Qualcomm's rival was supporting
WiMAX and Qualcomm was not."[2221] Judge Koh returned to this WiMAX
issue much later in her findings of fact and conclusions of law, but by that
point she did little more than restate her earlier finding in these words: "Thus,
Qualcomm eliminated a competing cellular standard supported by Intel *not
because WiMax was inferior,* but to eliminate competition."[2222] That discussion added nothing new, as she had already announced her conclusion—that
Qualcomm killed WiMAX—in the first passage of 425 words.

The superficiality of Judge Koh's explanation for her finding of fact that
Qualcomm "used its monopoly power . . . to eliminate WiMax"[2223] violated

---

[2218] FTC v. Qualcomm Inc., 411 F. Supp. 3d 658, 724 (N.D. Cal. 2019).
[2219] *Id.* at 725.
[2220] *Id.* at 724.
[2221] *Id.* at 726 (emphasis added).
[2222] *Id.* at 798 (emphasis added).
[2223] *Id.* at 724.

Federal Rule of Civil Procedure 52(a)(1). Her error was not harmless error, because Judge Koh appeared to use this particular finding of fact—either independently or supposedly in conjunction with the totality of the circumstances, which we shall examine in Part XVIII—to support her conclusion of law that Qualcomm had violated the Sherman Act. This conclusion, that Judge Koh violated Rule 52(a)(1) when announcing her conclusions of law, follows from the fact that she mentioned the demise of WiMAX again when summarizing her findings concerning Qualcomm's supposedly anticompetitive behavior with respect to Apple: "In sum, Qualcomm engaged in anticompetitive conduct with respect to Apple by . . . eliminating a competing standard supported by Intel[.]"[2224] Two sets of facts in evidence exposed why Judge Koh's findings of fact concerning WiMAX were clearly erroneous.

A. Was Judge Koh's Characterization of the Testimony of Dr. Jacobs Faithful to a Plain Reading of His Words?

First, the evidence that Judge Koh cited three times to support her conclusion about the WiMAX standard was a neatly trimmed snippet of the cross-examination testimony of Qualcomm's founder, Dr. Irwin Jacobs. Yet, Judge Koh's editing of this passage obscured the salient point to which Dr. Jacobs had testified concerning Qualcomm's assessment of WiMAX at least 12 years before the date of trial.

1.   Why Did Qualcomm Decide Not to Pursue WiMAX?

Judge Koh wrote, in three separate but identical passages of her findings of fact and conclusions of law:

> Irwin Jacobs (Qualcomm Co-Founder and former Qualcomm CEO) testified at trial that Qualcomm would have been behind in supplying WiMax chips had WiMax become the 3G standard:
>
>> Q: It's accurate to state, sir, that if WiMax had ended up as the standard, Qualcomm would have been far behind; is that right?
>>
>> A: That's fine.[2225]

This question-and-answer couplet could easily mislead even a sophisticated judge or trial lawyer reading Judge Koh's findings of fact and conclusions of

---

[2224] *Id.* at 738.

[2225] *Id.* at 726 (quoting Transcript of Proceedings (Volume 6) at 1284:10–13, FTC v. Qualcomm Inc., No. 5:17-cv-00220-LHK (N.D. Cal. Jan. 15, 2019) (Testimony of Irwin Jacobs (Co-Founder, Qualcomm))). The identical quotation appears in two subsequent locations in Judge Koh's findings of fact and conclusions of law. *See id.* at 798; *id.* at 811.

law if that reader did not independently scrutinize the trial transcript of the sworn testimony that Dr. Jacobs gave on this issue.

Judge Koh's grooming of this passage from the trial transcript suppressed the fact that, immediately before Dr. Jacobs gave this answer, he had unequivocally testified on cross examination that Qualcomm had decided not to pursue WiMAX because at the time (in 2007) he had concluded that the standard was "an inferior technology" to WCDMA, not because—as Judge Koh found—Qualcomm was seeking to put Intel at a competitive disadvantage:

> Q. Now, you recall that WiMAX was at one point a proposed next generation standard led by Intel; right?
>
> A. That's correct.
>
> Q. And if WiMAX had ended up as the standard, Qualcomm would have been far behind in its ability to provide chips; is that right?
>
> A. *We did not pursue WiMAX because I thought it was an inferior technology.* And so, yes, if that became the worldwide standard, we certainly would have pursued it. But we could have been later.[2226]

Then, the FTC's lawyer, Mr. Matheson, attempted to impeach Dr. Jacobs because, in his deposition in 2018, Dr. Jacobs had said that Qualcomm "*would have been far behind*" (in contrast to his testimony at trial that Qualcomm "*could* have been later") had WiMAX become the next-generation cellular standard around 2007.[2227]

But there was nothing profoundly probative about getting Dr. Jacobs to admit that Qualcomm *would* have had a disadvantage rather than that it merely *could* have had a disadvantage had WiMAX—*in some ill-defined, counterfactual conditional state of the world*—experienced widespread adoption. That proposition was obvious on its face. This line of impeachment was of no practical evidentiary consequence. It surely provided no legitimate basis for Judge Koh to impugn Dr. Jacobs' credibility.

This line of impeachment might even strike some sophisticated readers of the trial transcript as nothing more than the FTC's attempt to humiliate an 85-year-old witness by subjecting him to a memory test about his choice of a single verb in a single answer to an entirely hypothetical question regarding imaginary events that might have occurred in 2007, in a deposition conducted months earlier. Considering that Dr. Jacobs' entire cross examination lasted

---

[2226] Transcript of Proceedings (Volume 6) at 1283:7–16, FTC v. Qualcomm Inc., No. 5:17-cv-00220-LHK (N.D. Cal. Jan. 15, 2019) (Testimony of Irwin Jacobs (Co-Founder, Qualcomm)) (emphasis added).

[2227] *Id.* at 1283:17–25 ("Q. And if you would turn your attention, sir, to your deposition transcript at 124, lines 17 to 25. You did previously testify that Qualcomm would have been far behind in its ability to provide chips; is that right? Mr. Van Nest: Objection, Your Honor. That's not impeaching. That's what the witness just said. Mr. Matheson: I heard could have rather than would have, Your Honor. That's the distinction I was trying to draw. The Court: All right. Go ahead, please.").

only 25 minutes,[2228] it is puzzling why the FTC wanted to burn up time on a question so lacking in relevance and probative value to the FTC's central theory of antitrust liability in *FTC v. Qualcomm*.

What *was* of considerable consequence to Judge Koh's findings of fact was that her selective quotation of Dr. Jacobs' testimony about WiMAX inverted his meaning. Dr. Jacobs' cross-examination testimony contradicted Judge Koh's finding that "Qualcomm eliminated a competing cellular standard supported by Intel *not because WiMax was inferior*, but to eliminate competition."[2229] Judge Koh could plausibly have made that finding of fact only by ascribing zero weight to Dr. Jacobs' actual trial testimony to the contrary—that Qualcomm in 2007 "did not pursue WiMAX *because [Dr. Jacobs] thought it was an inferior technology*"[2230]—on the questionable grounds that his trial testimony about events occurring in or before 2007 was not credible. Judge Koh then relied on her inverted interpretation of Dr. Jacobs' testimony as the essential piece of this particular finding of fact that in 2007 "Qualcomm used its monopoly power against Apple to eliminate WiMax."[2231]

2.   *Was Judge Koh's Depiction of Dr. Jacobs' Testimony Complete?*

Judge Koh's stilted depiction of Dr. Jacobs' testimony on WiMAX was materially incomplete. Without inspecting the trial transcript, even a sophisticated judge or trial lawyer reading Judge Koh's findings of fact and conclusions of law would have no idea that Dr. Jacobs actually testified that his assessment of the technological inferiority of the WiMAX standard (in or before 2007) was the proximate cause for him personally (and Qualcomm institutionally) to disfavor industry adoption of WiMAX. When fairly read in its actual context, Dr. Jacobs' full testimony on the failure of the WiMAX standard contradicted Judge Koh's reporting of this particular finding of fact.

Judge Koh's incomplete reporting of these facts concerning Dr. Jacobs' actual testimony violated Federal Rule of Civil Procedure 52(a)(1) and suppressed information that would have tended to exculpate Qualcomm. Moreover, to the extent that this passage from Dr. Jacobs' brief cross examination also contributed to Judge Koh's finding that Dr. Jacobs was a "cagey" witness who lacked credibility,[2232] we can see that it is doubtful that any reasonable person having the full context of that cross-examination colloquy would draw the same unfavorable conclusion concerning Dr. Jacobs' credibility that Judge Koh reported in her findings of fact and conclusions of law.

[2228] Dr. Jacobs' cross examination began at 2:38 p.m. and ended by 3:03 p.m. *Id.* at 1279:7, 1296:15.

[2229] *FTC v. Qualcomm*, 411 F. Supp. 3d at 798 (emphasis added).

[2230] Transcript of Proceedings (Volume 6) at 1283:13–14, FTC v. Qualcomm Inc., No. 5:17-cv-00220-LHK (N.D. Cal. Jan. 15, 2019) (Testimony of Irwin Jacobs (Co-Founder, Qualcomm)) (emphasis added).

[2231] *FTC v. Qualcomm*, 411 F. Supp. 3d at 724.

[2232] *Id.* at 680.

B. *Was Judge Koh's Cursory Conclusion About the Cause of the Demise of WiMAX Disproven by the Expert Engineering Testimony of Professor Andrews?*

A second sets of facts in evidence exposed why Judge Koh's findings of fact concerning WiMAX were clearly erroneous. Evidence in the record appeared to contradict Judge Koh's conclusions about the WiMAX standard. WiMAX was mentioned 32 times in the public redacted trial transcript in *FTC v. Qualcomm*.[2233] At least some of the trial testimony contradicted Judge Koh's conclusion that the failure of the WiMAX standard was attributable to Qualcomm's agreement with Apple.

Particularly probative were the opinions of Jeffrey Andrews, a professor of electrical engineering at the University of Texas at Austin who had

---

[2233] *See* Transcript of Proceedings (Volume 3) at 594:13–15, FTC v. Qualcomm Inc., No. 5:17-cv-00220-LHK (N.D. Cal. Jan. 8, 2019) (Testimony of Aichatou Evans (Chief Strategy Officer, Intel)) ("Q. But it was Intel that picked WiMAX and then bought a company that didn't have LTE; isn't that right? A. Wow. I'm—no, that's not right."); *id.* at 596:3–8 ("Q. And then down at the bottom of the first page of QX 76, three lines from the bottom of the page do you see you wrote, 'we picked WiMAX and then bought a company that did not have LTE.' Right? A. Yes."); Transcript of Proceedings (Volume 5) at 872:7–14, FTC v. Qualcomm Inc., No. 5:17-cv-00220-LHK (N.D. Cal. Jan. 14, 2019) (Testimony of Jeff Williams (COO, Apple)) ("Q. In negotiating the 2007 marketing incentive agreement, did Qualcomm demand anything from Apple in exchange for the royalty rebates down to $7.50? A. They did. Q. What did they demand? A. That we not ship any WiMAX products. They also asked us to make a statement saying that we were [using] GSM and not WiMAX for the future."); *id.* at 873:6–24 ("Q. Mr. Williams, if you look in paragraph 2 much this exhibit, Mr. Blecker writes to you [sic]? A. 'Motivating Apple to select WCDMA to the exclusion of WiMAX is our primary motivation for entering into this agreement. Otherwise, we would not be doing it.' [Q.] What was WiMAX? A. WiMAX was a competing standard to CDMA and GSM. I don't know all the details about it. It was emerging at the time. I know Intel was supporting it. I know Steve [Jobs] was interested in it. I don't know a ton about it. Q. Did Qualcomm say it wanted Apple to renounce WiMAX? A. No. Q. In the 2007 Marketing Incentive Agreement, did Apple agree to Qualcomm's demand relating to WiMAX? A. We did. Q. And following the execution of that agreement, did Apple pursue WiMAX further? A. No. In essence, it was killed in the cradle for us. We did not."); Transcript of Proceedings (Volume 6) at 1283:7–16, FTC v. Qualcomm Inc., No. 5:17-cv-00220-LHK (N.D. Cal. Jan. 15, 2019) (Testimony of Irwin Jacobs (Co-Founder, Qualcomm)) ("Q. Now, you recall that WiMAX was at one point a proposed next generation standard led by Intel; right? A. That's correct. Q. And if WiMAX had ended up as the standard, Qualcomm would have been far behind in its ability to provide chips; is that right? A. We did not pursue WiMAX because I thought it was an inferior technology. And so, yes, if that became the worldwide standard, we certainly would have pursued it. But we could have been later."); *id.* at 1284:4–1285:2 ("Q. Can you turn your attention to that page of the deposition transcript? A. Which page? Q. Page 124, lines 17 to 25. A. Oh, it's here. WiMAX— Q. It's accurate to state, sir, that if WiMAX had ended up as the standard, Qualcomm would have been far behind; is that right? A. That's fine. Q. And in late 2006, it's fair to say that Qualcomm was interested in getting Apple to make a public commitment to not pursue WiMAX in its next generation of phones; right? A. What year was that? Q. 2006. A. I retired in 2005 as CTO—as CEO. If that was 2006, I'm not sure I was in the middle of those details. But I would imagine that we would be interested in gaining support for LTE. Q. Do you recall one way or the other whether the— A. I do not recall. Q. Do you recall one way or the other whether the original 2007 agreement between Qualcomm and Apple required Apple to not launch products containing WiMAX compatible chips? A. I do not recall."). WiMAX is mentioned another 15 times in the transcript of Professor Jeffrey Andrews' testimony, which I discuss below. *See* Transcript of Proceedings (Volume 8) at 1591 (once), 1611 (four times), 1612 (seven times), 1613 (five times), FTC v. Qualcomm Inc., No. 5:17-cv-00220-LHK (N.D. Cal. Jan. 22, 2019) (Testimony of Jeffrey Andrews (Professor, Electrical Engineering, The University of Texas at Austin)).

written the textbook *Fundamentals of WiMAX*,[2234] who gave the following direct-examination testimony as an expert witness called by Qualcomm in its defense case:

> Q. What happened to mobile WiMAX?
>
> A. Well, . . . it caused a lot of excitement at the time, but eventually . . . early deployments didn't work all that great, and most of the cellular operators and vendors waited for LTE, which solved a lot of those problems, to come along.
>
> Q. As the person who I guess literally wrote the book on WiMAX, can you give us some technical reasons for why . . . that happened to WiMAX?
>
> A. Yeah. I mean, one big one that we saw back then was that the overhead channels in . . . WiMAX . . . were not very efficient. They were really overde-signed. And so they consumed a lot of the resources, so there was . . . a lot less left for data. It was so bad, in fact, that many so [sic] of the people I talked to . . . they just turned off a lot of these advanced control features and just did a very simple option in WiMAX. So this was a major deficiency, the control channels and the overhead procedure. And then . . . another was it used OFDMA [Orthogonal Frequency-Division Multiple Access] in both directions, and as we discussed earlier, the SC-FDMA [Single-Carrier Frequency-Division Multiple Access] which Qualcomm invented had a big impact on the uplink efficiency and range for LTE. And then a third is that WiMAX was a clean slate standard, from a totally new standards body, so it didn't offer backwards compatibility, like LTE offered considerably more backwards compatibility with earlier standards.
>
> Q. So how then did WiMAX compare to LTE?
>
> A. I think . . . once LTE came out, it became clear that LTE was superior to WiMAX for cellular technology on a technical level in basically every way.[2235]

Judge Koh made absolutely no reference in her findings of fact and conclusions of law to Professor Andrews' expert engineering testimony at trial on how these three technical limitations impaired the commercial success

---

[2234] Transcript of Proceedings (Volume 8) at 1591:1–3, FTC v. Qualcomm Inc., No. 5:17-cv-00220-LHK (N.D. Cal. Jan. 22, 2019) (Testimony of Jeffrey Andrews (Professor, Electrical Engineering, The University of Texas at Austin)) ("Q. Have you written any books? A. Yes, I've written two textbooks on 4G cellular standards, and one on LTE, and one on WiMAX."); *id.* at 1611:16–18 ("A. Well, the first book I wrote was on WiMAX, which was an early 4G standard, and then the second book I wrote was on LTE shortly after LTE came out."); *see also id.* at 1590:2–6, 1592:2–4. The two books are JEFFREY ANDREWS, FUNDAMENTALS OF LTE (Prentice Hall 2010), and JEFFREY ANDREWS, FUNDAMENTALS OF WiMAX: UNDERSTANDING BROADBAND WIRELESS NETWORKING (Prentice Hall 2007).

[2235] Transcript of Proceedings (Volume 8) at 1612:1–1613:6, FTC v. Qualcomm Inc., No. 5:17-cv-00220-LHK (N.D. Cal. Jan. 22, 2019) (Testimony of Jeffrey Andrews (Professor, Electrical Engineering, The University of Texas at Austin)).

of WiMAX as a standard. Instead, as we saw in Part IX.C, she found, unpersuasively, that the testimony of Professor Andrews was "inapposite."[2236]

C. *Judge Koh's Incidental Adjudication, in 425 Words, of the Alleged Antitrust Issues Surrounding the Commercial and Technical Failure of WiMAX*

Judge Koh's finding that WiMAX failed to win commercial adoption because Qualcomm supposedly engaged in anticompetitive conduct would be grist for a titanic monopolization case unto itself. But such a case could proceed to discovery only if Judge Koh's theory of antitrust liability, premised on the commercial rejection of WiMAX, had facial plausibility. It did not. It was utterly frivolous. How did this extravagant claim about the supposed cause of the demise of WiMAX ever escape dismissal on a *Twombly* motion?[2237]

Judge Koh did not report in her findings of fact and conclusions of law any findings confirming that the FTC had actually carried its burden of production on this question as part of its case-in-chief, and that the agency had carried its burden of persuasion by proving this claim by a preponderance of the evidence. (And the FTC evidently was not cross examining Dr. Jacobs on WiMAX solely in an attempt to impeach his credibility, since Judge Koh went on to make explicit findings of fact as to how Qualcomm's reaction to the possible commercial adoption of the WiMAX standard, as expressed in Dr. Jacobs' cross examination testimony at trial, was anticompetitive.) Judge Koh's findings of fact and conclusions of law seemed to criticize Qualcomm for failing to rebut, to her satisfaction, an unproven assertion on which the FTC bore the burden of production and the burden of persuasion. Yet, Judge Koh did not report in her findings of fact and conclusions of law that the FTC ever managed to carry either burden.

Finally, why would Judge Koh think that any sophisticated judge or trial lawyer reading her findings of fact and conclusions of law would remotely believe that in the span of 425 words she could incidentally adjudicate the alleged antitrust issues surrounding the commercial and technical failure of WiMAX, an issue which received virtually no attention at trial as part of the FTC's case-in-chief in *FTC v. Qualcomm* or in the FTC's proposed findings of fact and conclusions of law?[2238] Why would Judge Koh think it remotely

---

[2236] *FTC v. Qualcomm*, 411 F. Supp. 3d at 779–80.

[2237] *See* Bell Atl. Corp. v. Twombly, 550 U.S. 544, 557–58 (2007); *see also* Ashcroft v. Iqbal, 556 U.S. 662, 678–79 (2009).

[2238] *See* FTC's Proposed Findings of Fact and Conclusions of Law, *supra* note 485, ¶ 264, at 35 ("Under a 2007 Marketing Incentive Agreement ('MIA'), Qualcomm agreed to rebate to Apple royalties that Qualcomm received from Apple's contract manufacturers in excess of a specified per-handset cap. Qualcomm's payment obligations were conditioned upon, among other things, Apple not selling or licensing a handset implementing the WiMAX standard, a prospective 4G cellular standard."); *id.* ¶ 269–71, at 36 ("In 2007, the WiMAX standard was a prospective next-generation cellular standard, with a low-cost royalty model, championed by Intel and opposed by Qualcomm. In 2007, Qualcomm was

plausible that her readers would believe that, by entering into its 2007 rebate agreement with Apple, Qualcomm killed the WiMAX standard and thereby violated antitrust law?

XVIII. Judge Koh's Invention of Combinatorial Liability: Were Qualcomm's Individually Lawful Practices "Collectively" Unlawful?

One might argue that, even if none of Qualcomm's individual practices was unlawful on its own, those practices, when combined, harmed competition and therefore violated the Sherman Act. This reasoning is specious, yet it appeared to be the underlying rationale of the FTC's complaint,[2239] of Professor Shapiro's testimony,[2240] and ultimately of Judge Koh's finding that Qualcomm's licensing practices "[c]ollectively" harmed competition and were therefore unlawful.[2241]

A. *Ignoring* linkLine *to Fashion a Consolation-Prize Theory of Antitrust Liability*

That reasoning would announce a consolation-prize theory of antitrust liability that would be both factually unsupported by the evidence in *FTC v. Qualcomm* and contrary to controlling Supreme Court precedent.

Chief Justice Roberts, writing for the Court in *linkLine*, made clear a decade before Judge Koh issued her findings of fact and conclusions of law that two lawful acts taken together cannot produce an antitrust violation: "If there is no duty to deal at the wholesale level and no predatory pricing at the retail level, then a firm is certainly not required to price *both* of these services in a manner that preserves its rivals' profit margins."[2242]

---

behind in developing WiMAX modem chips. Qualcomm wanted the industry to know that Apple would not pursue [Redacted].").

[2239] FTC Complaint, 2017 WL 242848, *supra* note 28, at *2 ("Qualcomm has excluded competitors and harmed competition through a set of interrelated policies and practices."); *see also id.* at *31 ("Qualcomm's course of conduct—including (i) conditioning the supply of baseband processors on licenses to FRAND-encumbered patents on Qualcomm's preferred terms; (ii) paying OEMs to accept license terms that impose added costs on OEMs' use of non-Qualcomm baseband processors; (iii) refusing to license FRAND-encumbered patents to baseband processor competitors; and (iv) exclusive dealing with Apple— is anticompetitive and constitutes an unfair method of competition, in violation of Section 5(a) of the FTC Act, 15 U.S.C. § 45(a)."); *id.* ("Qualcomm's license agreements with OEMs, together with terms of its supply and strategic/market-development agreements linked to those license agreements, result from an exercise of Qualcomm's monopoly and market power and are unreasonable restraints of trade.").

[2240] Transcript of Proceedings (Volume 6) at 1120:7–8, FTC v. Qualcomm Inc., No. 5:17-cv-00220 (N.D. Cal. Jan. 15, 2019) (Testimony of Carl Shapiro) ("So looking at these three policies working together, it's my view and conclusion that they harmed competition[.]").

[2241] *FTC v. Qualcomm*, 411 F. Supp. 3d at 797.

[2242] Pacific Bell Tel. Co. v. linkLine Commc'ns, Inc., 555 U.S. 438, 452 (2009) (emphasis in original).

Chief Justice Roberts similarly reasoned that stitching together two specious antitrust claims cannot yield one valid claim. In rejecting the claim of margin squeeze in *linkLine*, he wrote for the Court:

> In this case, plaintiffs have not stated a duty-to-deal claim under *Trinko* and have not stated a predatory pricing claim under *Brooke Group*. They have nonetheless tried to join a wholesale claim that cannot succeed with a retail claim that cannot succeed, and alchemize them into a new form of antitrust liability never before recognized by this Court. We decline the invitation to recognize such claims. *Two wrong claims do not make one that is right.*[2243]

The principle that Chief Justice Roberts outlined for the Court in *linkLine* applies with equal force to the FTC's claims against Qualcomm.

If none of Qualcomm's challenged practices individually violated the Sherman Act, then Judge Koh had no authority to "alchemize" some combination of two or more of those lawful practices into a novel violation of the Sherman Act. Adding more specious theories to the patchwork quilt, as Judge Koh did in *FTC v. Qualcomm*, does not change that conclusion. American antitrust jurisprudence does not recognize a doctrine of "combinatorial liability."

B. *Judge Koh's Invention of Combinatorial Liability*

Judge Koh found that Qualcomm used its monopoly power in her relevant markets for modems to coerce OEMs to accept an "unreasonably high" royalty for Qualcomm's portfolio of cellular SEPs:

> Qualcomm's unreasonably high royalty rates impose a surcharge on rivals' modem chips. Under Qualcomm's patent license agreements with OEMs, Qualcomm charges its unreasonably high royalty rates anytime an OEM sells a handset, even when that handset contains a rival's modem chip. Thus, Qualcomm imposes an artificial surcharge on all sales of its rivals' modem chips. The surcharge increases the effective price of rivals' modem chips, reduces rivals' margins, and results in exclusivity.[2244]

Judge Koh added that, when purchasing modems, OEMs consider the "all-in price," which includes (1) the price of a modem and (2) the royalty "surcharge" that the OEM must pay to Qualcomm.[2245] She also found that,

---

[2243] *Id.* at 457 (emphasis added) (first citing Verizon Commc'ns Inc. v. Law Offices of Curtis V. Trinko, LLP, 540 U.S. 398, 409–10 (2004); and then citing Brooke Grp. Ltd. v. Brown & Williamson Tobacco Corp., 509 U.S. 209, 222–24 (1993)).

[2244] *FTC v. Qualcomm*, 411 F. Supp. 3d at 790.

[2245] *Id.* at 791 ("Thus, the 'all-in' price of any modem chip sold by one of Qualcomm's rivals effectively includes two components: (1) the nominal chip price; and (2) Qualcomm's royalty surcharge."). Recall that we saw earlier that this statement was incoherent. Judge Koh overlooked in this formula the obvious

"[t]o Qualcomm, the surcharge represents 'higher profits,' both because the surcharge brings additional revenue to Qualcomm, and 'because the reduction in competition enable[s]' Qualcomm 'to capture more of the [modem chip] market.'"[2246]

Judge Koh said that the payments that Qualcomm made to win business from Apple and other OEMs "exacerbate[d] the effect of Qualcomm's surcharge on rivals' chips" by lowering the price of Qualcomm's modems (although at times she said instead that those payments lowered the royalty for an exhaustive license to Qualcomm's cellular SEPs).[2247] In her view, the payment "also help[ed] maintain Qualcomm's unreasonably high royalty rates and surcharge on rivals' chips by inducing OEMs to sign license agreements" specifying an unreasonably high royalty for an exhaustive license to Qualcomm's cellular SEPs.[2248] Judge Koh also found that Qualcomm's refusal to offer exhaustive licenses to its cellular SEPs to rival modem manufacturers "preserve[d] Qualcomm's ability to demand unreasonably high royalty rates from OEMs."[2249] She concluded that, "[c]ollectively, the harms caused by Qualcomm's anticompetitive practices take repeated aim at the elements necessary for a rival modem chip supplier to compete in the market."[2250]

Even if one were to assume for sake of argument (but contrary to fact) that Judge Koh's findings about the combined effects of Qualcomm's practices were correct, her findings still would not support her conclusion of law that Qualcomm's interrelated practices violated the Sherman Act. Her conclusions of law were predicated on Ninth Circuit precedent that preceded the Supreme Court's decision in *linkLine* and improperly embraced a totality-of-the-circumstances test.

1. *Can the Combined Effects of Interrelated Practices That Are Individually Lawful Give Rise "Collectively" to Sherman Act Liability?*

To support her conclusion that Qualcomm's practices were "collectively" unlawful, Judge Koh quoted the Ninth Circuit's decision in 2008 in *Cascade Health Solutions*, stating that "'[a]nticompetitive conduct is behavior that tends to impair the opportunities of rivals and either does not further

---

third component: the reasonable royalty for a license to the cellular SEPs. *See supra* notes 1009–1010 and accompanying text. Put differently, the reasonable royalty for a portfolio of cellular SEPs surely is not zero, which it would need to be for Judge Koh's formulation of the "all-in price" not to be nonsense.

2246 *FTC v. Qualcomm*, 411 F. Supp. 3d at 791 (second and third alterations in original) (quoting Premier Elec. Const. Co. v. Nat'l Elec. Contractors Ass'n, 814 F.2d 358, 368 (7ᵗʰ Cir. 1987)).

2247 *Id.* at 792; *cf. id.* at 708.

2248 *Id.* at 794; *see also id.* at 795 ("Thus, QTL's unreasonably high royalty rates enable QTL to offer OEMs enormous chip incentive funds, which lower the relative price of Qualcomm's modem chips, result in exclusivity, and maintain Qualcomm's ability to impose a surcharge on rivals' modem chips.").

2249 *Id.* at 796.

2250 *Id.* at 797 (emphasis added).

competition on the merits or does so in an unnecessarily restrictive way.'"[2251] Quoting *Microsoft*, Judge Koh then added:

> Qualcomm's *interrelated practices* create insurmountable and artificial barriers for Qualcomm's rivals, and thus do not further competition on the merits. Qualcomm's practices all reduce rivals' sales. Qualcomm's chip incentive funds for OEMs lower the effective price of Qualcomm's modem chips, result in exclusivity, and restrict the OEM customer base available to Qualcomm's rivals. . . . The surcharge on rivals' modem chips imposed by Qualcomm's unreasonably high royalty rates increases the cost of rivals' chips, which reduces demand for rivals' chips and reduces rivals' margins. By attacking all facets of rivals' businesses and preventing competition on the merits, these practices "harm the competitive process and thereby harm consumers."[2252]

To support the proposition "a court should consider the *combined* anticompetitive effects" of a defendant's "interrelated practices," Judge Koh quoted the Ninth Circuit's statement in its 1992 price-squeeze decision in *City of Anaheim v. Southern California Edison* that "it would not be proper to focus on specific individual acts of an accused monopolist while refusing to consider their overall combined effect."[2253] That statement predated by 17 years the Supreme Court's decision in *linkLine* abolishing the price squeeze.

Judge Koh's reliance on *City of Anaheim* was precarious, especially in light of the fact that she did not pause to explain why *linkLine* had not implicitly overruled *City of Anaheim* in 2009. Whatever supposedly controlling principle *City of Anaheim* might have embodied before the Supreme Court decided *linkLine*, that Ninth Circuit decision could not possibly have given Judge Koh *carte blanche* in 2019 to do what Chief Justice Roberts in 2009 had told us in *linkLine* no court may do.

2. *The Perils of the Theory of Anticompetitive Harm Based on the Totality of the Circumstances*

Judge Koh essentially embraced a totality-of-the-circumstances test, in which she ignored existing Supreme Court precedent and instead supposedly examined all the circumstances that she considered relevant to determine whether Qualcomm's licensing conduct violated the Sherman Act. A jurist with a different outlook, Justice Antonin Scalia, famously decried

---

[2251] *Id.* (quoting Cascade Health Sols. v. PeaceHealth, 515 F.3d 883, 894 (9th Cir. 2008)).

[2252] *Id.* (emphasis added) (quoting United States v. Microsoft Corp., 253 F.3d 34, 58 (D.C. Cir. 2001) (en banc) (per curiam) (emphasis omitted by Judge Koh)).

[2253] *Id.* at 696 (quoting City of Anaheim v. S. Cal. Edison Co., 955 F.2d 1373, 1378 (9th Cir. 1992)).

the totality-of-the-circumstances test wherever it reared its head.[2254] He urged that such an approach to judicial decision making "be avoided where possible,"[2255] and he instead praised the product that follows from "a clear, general principle of decision: predictability."[2256]

At the opposite end of the Court's political spectrum, Justices William Brennan and Thurgood Marshall opposed for similar reasons the use of a totality-of-the-circumstances test to review searches and seizures under the Fourth Amendment.[2257] Commenting in 1981 on a topic directly relevant years later to *FTC v. Qualcomm*, Judge Frank Easterbrook wrote that the view that a court in a monopolization case should "examine the totality of the circumstances" and base its findings on that examination without further intellectual structure of law or economics is an "approach that eschews rules altogether."[2258]

C. The FTC's Advocacy at Trial Concerning Combinatorial Liability

In her closing argument for the FTC on January 29, 2019, Jennifer Milici told Judge Koh that Qualcomm had thrown up "roadblocks that made it hard for rivals to catch up."[2259] Roadblocks![2260] Roadblocks,[2261] roadblocks,[2262] roadblocks![2263] Ms. Milici exclaimed in one last paroxysm of mixed metaphors: "the *entire marketplace was infected* by these roadblocks"![2264]

Meanwhile, any concern over false positives evidently had fallen from grace among the antitrust nomenklatura. Ms. Milici seemed unfazed that perfectly legitimate business practices, such as offering lower prices or

---

[2254] *See* Antonin Scalia, *The Rule of Law as a Law of Rules*, 56 U. Chi. L.Rev. 1175, 1179 (1989) (stating that adopting a totality of circumstances test "is effectively to conclude that uniformity [in applying law] is not a particularly important objective with respect to the legal question at issue"); *id.* at 1180–81 ("[W]hen an appellate judge comes up with nothing better than a totality of the circumstances test to explain his decision, he is not so much pronouncing the law in the normal sense as engaging in the less exalted function of fact-finding.").

[2255] *Id.* at 1187 ("We will have totality of the circumstances tests and balancing modes of analysis with us forever—and for my sins, I will probably write some of the opinions that use them. All I urge is that those modes of analysis be avoided where possible; that the *Rule* of Law, the law of *rules,* be extended as far as the nature of the question allows; and that, to foster a correct attitude toward the matter, we appellate judges bear in mind that when we have finally reached the point where we can do no more than consult the totality of the circumstances, we are acting more as factfinders than as expositors of the law.").

[2256] *Id.* at 1179.

[2257] Illinois v. Gates, 462 U.S. 213, 291 (1983) (Brennan, J. Marshall, J., dissenting).

[2258] Frank H. Easterbrook, *Predatory Strategies and Counterstrategies*, 48 U. Chi. L. Rev. 263, 263 (1981).

[2259] Transcript of Proceedings (Volume 11) at 2102:11–12, FTC v. Qualcomm Inc., No. 5:17-cv-00220-LHK (N.D. Cal. Jan. 29, 2019) (closing argument of Jennifer Milici for the FTC).

[2260] *Id.* at 2109:22–23 ("Qualcomm . . . put up roadblocks that inhibited the ability of others to catch up.").

[2261] *Id.* at 2110:1 ("It [Qualcomm] put up roadblocks for competitors.").

[2262] *Id.* at 2134:25–2135:1 ("Qualcomm will have a time to market advantage and will use that advantage and the corporate policies challenged here to put up roadblocks that slows its competitors down.").

[2263] *Id.* at 2178:8–10 (closing rebuttal argument of Jennifer Milici for the FTC) ("The issue, the antitrust issue in this case is that once it [Qualcomm] had that dominant position, it threw up roadblocks that prevented other folks from catching up.").

[2264] *Id.* at 2178:15–16 (emphasis added).

more technologically advanced products, by their very nature also create roadblocks for competitors. For decades, the Ninth Circuit has lauded rather than condemned those virtuous practices.[2265] And even *Cascade Health Solutions*, upon which Judge Koh heavily relied to justify her theory of combinatorial liability, said unmistakably that "antitrust laws' prohibitions focus on protecting the competitive process and not on the success or failure of individual competitors."[2266]

D. Was Judge Koh's Imposition of Liability on the Basis of the Totality of the Circumstances and Her Theory of Combinatorial Liability Unconstitutionally Vague?

The totality-of-the-circumstances test that animated Judge Koh theory of combinatorial liability was unwise for an even more fundamental reason than the fact that it is hard to administer. Even if conscientiously administered, it remains hopelessly vague as a matter of due process.

Sections 1 and 2 of the Sherman Act, and section 5 of the FTC Act, are already broad statutes that give minimal direction to a court; for the court then to say that those statutes permit a totality-of-the-evidence test giving rise to a legally cognizable theory of combinatorial liability is to magnify judicial discretion and make the law's command opaque. Judge Easterbrook observed in his *Limits of Antitrust* that "[o]f course judges cannot do what such open-ended formulas require. *When everything is relevant, nothing is dispositive.*"[2267] And the loss of predictability that Justice Scalia emphasized will arise when one relies on the totality-of-the-circumstances test merges, in the limit, into the question of fair notice that Justice George Sutherland famously articulated for the Supreme Court in 1926 in *Connally v. General Construction Co.*:

> That the terms of a penal statute creating a new offense must be sufficiently explicit to inform those who are subject to it what conduct on their part will render them liable to its penalties is a well-recognized requirement, consonant alike with ordinary notions of fair play and the settled rules of law; and a statute which either forbids or requires the doing of an act in

---

[2265] *See, e.g.*, California Comput. Prods., Inc. v. Int'l Bus. Machs. Corp., 613 F.2d 727, 744 (9th Cir. 1979) ("IBM, assuming it was a monopolist, had the right to redesign its products to make them more attractive to buyers whether by reason of lower manufacturing cost and price or improved performance. It was under no duty to help CalComp or other peripheral equipment manufacturers survive or expand."); *see also* J. Gregory Sidak, *Debunking Predatory Innovation*, 83 Colum. L. Rev. 1121 (1983) (analyzing the law and economics of the IBM peripherals litigation and the then-novel theory of technological tie-ins).

[2266] Cascade Health Sols. v. PeaceHealth, 515 F.3d 883, 902 (9th Cir. 2008) ("[A]ntitrust laws' prohibitions focus on protecting the competitive process and not on the success or failure of individual competitors"); *see also* Cascade Cabinet Co. v. W. Cabinet & Millwork Inc., 710 F.2d 1366, 1373 (9th Cir. 1983) ("Although Cascade complains of its business losses, economic injury to a competitor does not equal injury to competition.").

[2267] Frank H. Easterbrook, *Limits of Antitrust*, 63 Tex. L. Rev. 1, 12 (1984) (emphasis added).

terms so vague that men of common intelligence must necessarily guess at its meaning and differ as to its application violates the first essential of due process of law.[2268]

Although the Court was addressing a penal statute in *Connally*, nothing about the Court's logic confines its relevance to criminal rather than civil statutes, or to monetary rather than injunctive relief. The consequences of the FTC's litigation for Qualcomm's shareholders are measured in the billions of dollars. As we saw earlier, Qualcomm's litigation costs in fiscal year 2018 alone exceeded $1.5 million per day,[2269] and the follow-on class action against Qualcomm seeks $15 billion in treble damages.[2270]

One way to recognize the impermissible vagueness of the totality-of-the-circumstances test and the theory of combinatorial liability that Judge Koh used is to take a decremental approach. Suppose that Judge Koh made n factual findings that constituted, in her view, the "circumstances" of the case. Suppose that the Ninth Circuit then reverses r of those findings as being contrary to substantial evidence. How do we know whether the new subset of the original "totality" of the facts, $n - r$, would still suffice to establish Qualcomm's liability, which of course is itself a binary decision rather than something measured by a continuous (scalar) variable? Would tossing out consideration of 1 percent of Judge Koh's "totality" of factual findings cause Qualcomm to prevail on liability? Would tossing out 10 percent? Would tossing out 51 percent? It is hard to imagine that every possible subset of Judge Koh's original "totality" of the facts would be necessary and sufficient to find Qualcomm liable by a preponderance of the evidence.

Judges of course rarely enumerate all of the items that constitute the totality of the circumstances. Enumerating the causal factors would defeat the purpose of resorting to this evidentiary crutch. Instead, judges typically narrate a story. And of course the question that one must ask about the decremental sustainability of Judge Koh's story of combinatorial liability implicitly assumes, strictly for ease of exposition, that all of the n itemized findings of fact have equal probative value, which surely would not be true in a real case, including *FTC v. Qualcomm*.

Seen in these terms, Judge Koh's conclusions of law predicated on the totality of the circumstances were void for vagueness. That conclusion should not be difficult to reach, considering that the FTC was already advocating

---

[2268] 269 U.S. 385, 391 (1926). In 2012, the Court stated that, "[e]ven when speech is not at issue, the void for vagueness doctrine addresses at least two connected but discrete due process concerns: first, that regulated parties should know what is required of them so they may act accordingly; second, precision and guidance are necessary so that those enforcing the law do not act in an arbitrary or discriminatory way." FCC v. Fox Television Stations, Inc., 567 U.S. 239, 253 (2012) (citing Grayned v. City of Rockford, 408 U.S. 104, 108–09 (1972)).

[2269] *See supra* note 297.

[2270] *See supra* note 2 and accompanying text.

what the Ninth Circuit called a possibly "trailblazing application of the antitrust laws"[2271] that the Antitrust Division adamantly opposed.[2272] It is a bad sign for due process of law when two federal antitrust enforcement agencies of common intelligence dispute the law's meaning and differ as to the law's proper application.

XIX. Does the Market for Corporate Control Make Judge Koh's Findings of Competitive Harm Unbelievable?

The allegation that Qualcomm competitively harmed rival modem manufacturers (including Intel) and OEMs (including Apple) fails a reality check. It ignores that there exists the market for corporate control, which broadly speaking encompasses for a given target corporation any market (or transaction) by which one can acquire ownership of enough voting shares to exercise control over the management decisions of that corporation.

A rational firm would never permit itself to be exploited by a supplier's anticompetitive practices if the harm from the supplier's exercise of monopoly power exceeded the costs of acquiring corporate control of that supplier. If the monopolist is a publicly traded company, the harm from monopolization can be mitigated, if not eliminated entirely, through an unsolicited acquisition in the market for corporate control. In other words, the market for corporate control constrains a supplier's ability to exercise monopoly power in a given product market whenever that supplier is a publicly traded corporation.

This insight is so simple, yet its implications so profound for the plausibility of many theories of competitive harm, that it is hard to understand how it has, to my knowledge at least, eluded American courts in their explication of antitrust jurisprudence.[2273] It strains credulity past the breaking point to accept Judge Koh's findings that Qualcomm was bullying large OEMs— including Apple, which Judge Curiel identified as plausibly being powerful enough to have instigated the investigation leading to the FTC's filing of its complaint in *FTC v. Qualcomm*.[2274] If the competitive harms that Qualcomm

---

[2271] FTC v. Qualcomm Inc., 935 F.3d 752, 757 (9th Cir. 2019) (per curiam) (granting Qualcomm's motion to stay in part Judge Koh's injunction).

[2272] *See* Statement of Interest of the United States Concerning Remedies, *supra* note 182; United States' Statement of Interest Concerning Partial Stay, 2019 WL 3306496, *supra* note 205, at *12; Declaration of Under Secretary of Defense for Acquisition and Sustainment Ellen M. Lord at 2, FTC v. Qualcomm Inc., No. 19-16122 (9th Cir. July 15, 2019) [hereinafter Declaration of Under Secretary of Defense].

[2273] I first publicly explained this insight in Sidak, *Is Patent Holdup a Hoax?*, *supra* note 118, at 461–64, yet the proposition first occurred to me in 2008, when I was engaged as a consulting and testifying economic expert in an international commercial arbitration in which antitrust counterclaims arose in response to an alleged breach of contract concerning the licensing of intellectual property.

[2274] *See supra* notes 310–312 and accompanying text.

was alleged to have caused were genuinely palpable, Apple or other OEMs or modem manufacturers could have acquired control of Qualcomm and eliminated the alleged injury to competition from Qualcomm's supposed exploitation of monopoly power. The market for corporate control offered a ready mechanism to mitigate the risk of such injury.

Judge Koh's findings of fact and conclusions of law in *FTC v. Qualcomm* did not spot this line of reasoning and therefore necessarily offered no response to it. But that oversight of course would not prevent either the Ninth Circuit (should it choose to rehear the case *en banc*) or the Supreme Court from taking judicial notice of the insight and addressing *sua sponte* its relevance as a matter of law to the plausibility of each of the FTC's theories of liability in *FTC v. Qualcomm*.

A. The Market for Corporate Control as a Means to Resolve Commercial Disputes, Including Allegations of Monopolization

The analysis of how corporate control transactions can mitigate antitrust injury is but one application of a prominent theme in the law and economics literature.[2275] When the owners of a firm choose to organize their enterprise as a publicly traded corporation, one thing that they implicitly and incidentally do is to consent to resolve any future dispute with a third party through acquisition of corporate control if less invasive means of dispute resolution do not suffice.

To understand how the market for corporate control works, suppose that both parties to a dispute are publicly traded corporations, as is the case for Apple and Qualcomm. In any dispute or negotiation between two publicly traded corporations, each party has the outside option to resolve the dispute by buying control of the other, either in a consensual sale or in an unsolicited control transaction, such as a hostile tender offer. A strategic acquisition aligns incentives between the previously antagonistic corporation and the party buying a controlling interest.

Thus, among publicly traded corporations the market for corporate control always provides an alternative means of dispute resolution by placing the disputants under common ownership and control and thus mooting their dispute. Vertical integration is of course a familiar and accepted method of resolving Williamsonian holdup disputes.[2276] Indeed, the Nobel Prize committee said in its summary of Oliver Williamson's work that his *"**main**

[2275] *See* Henry G. Manne, *Mergers and the Market for Corporate Control*, 73 J. Pol. Econ. 110, 119 (1965); Eugene F. Fama & Michael C. Jensen, *Separation of Ownership and Control*, 26 J.L. & Econ. 301 (1983); Michael C. Jensen & William H. Meckling, *Theory of the Firm: Managerial Behavior, Agency Costs and Ownership Structure*, 3 J. Fin. Econ. 305 (1976).

[2276] *See, e.g.*, Klein, Crawford & Alchian, *Vertical Integration, Appropriable Rents, and the Competitive Contracting Process*, *supra* note 649.

contribution was to formulate a theory of vertical integration."[2277] The market for corporate control provides Qualcomm, OEMs that implement its cellular SEPs, and rival modem manufacturers a method for resolving disputes—including but not limited to disputes over patent infringement, alleged patent holdup, breach of contract, misappropriation of trade secrets, intentional business torts, and the acquisition or maintenance (or, for that matter, the entirely lawful exploitation) of monopoly power.[2278]

1.   *Transaction Costs and Acquisition of Corporate Control*

Lurking of course behind the insights of corporate governance applied here is the deeper insight of the Coase Theorem.[2279] The key Coasean insight is that the gains from dispute resolution quite conceivably exceed the transaction costs of an unsolicited control transaction by orders of magnitude. Thus, although transaction costs are not zero as in the stylized version of the Coase Theorem, they are still small relative to the gains from trade that are attainable from achieving dispute resolution by means of the market for corporate control.

For present purposes, consider how one corporation can acquire a controlling interest in a second corporation, so as to resolve an interfirm dispute arising from the second corporation's monopolization of a given market, which has allegedly injured (or will injure) the first corporation. At a minimum, the potential harm from the act of monopolization is bounded by the victim's costs of acquiring corporate control of the corporation that is exercising monopoly power. If equity markets are efficient, the victim's cost of acquiring a controlling interest in a corporation causing the competitive harm should be offset by the underlying value created by the business operations of the acquired corporation. In that case, the net cost to the victim of acquiring that controlling interest is limited to the transaction costs in the market for corporate control. In some cases, the acquisition of corporate control might be even less costly—and vastly more expeditious—than alternative means of stopping the threat of monopolization, such as spending hundreds of millions of dollars litigating the dispute in courts or before arbitral panels.

Generally, one need not acquire 100 percent of the corporation causing or threatening competitive harm to stop its injurious behavior. A victim of monopolization need purchase only enough equity to exert control over the managerial decision making of the offending corporation. The actual share

---

2277 ECONOMIC SCIENCES PRIZE COMMITTEE OF THE ROYAL SWEDISH ACADEMY OF SCIENCES, SCIENTIFIC BACKGROUND ON THE SVERIGES RIKSBANK PRIZE IN ECONOMIC SCIENCES IN MEMORY OF ALFRED NOBEL 2009: ECONOMIC GOVERNANCE, *supra* note 648, at 7 (19) (emphasis added).
2278 *See* Sidak, *Is Patent Holdup a Hoax?*, *supra* note 118, at 461–62.
2279 *See* R. H. Coase, *The Problem of Social Cost*, 3 J.L. & ECON. 1 (1960).

of voting stock required to exercise control over a publicly traded corporation will depend on the distribution of shares of that corporation and its corporate governance structure (including its voting rules and antitakeover provisions (if any)). In a widely held corporation, ownership of substantially less than 50 percent of voting shares might suffice to exercise control. A firm that buys a controlling equity stake in the monopolist can then direct that the monopolist's harmful business practices cease and thereby eliminate the costs being imposed by the monopolist.

In the stylized case, the shareholders in a publicly traded corporation are anonymous. Susan Woodward and I have argued that this anonymity of shareholders, coupled with limited liability, is efficient in the sense that it enhances liquidity.[2280] With limited liability, one need not expend resources to ascertain the wealth of fellow shareholders in a public corporation to evaluate the extent of one's own potential responsibility for the firm's liabilities. The efficient level of such search is zero, such that complete anonymity of shareholders (as expressed in the appellation *société anonyme*, or *S.A.*) is efficient.

2. *Institutional Investors and Corporate Control*

In practice, however, the presence of institutional investors means that we are in fact able routinely to observe the identities of persons (that is, institutions) controlling large holdings of the outstanding shares of a publicly traded corporation. In particular, as of August 2020, institutional investors held 76.04 percent of Qualcomm's common stock.[2281] Table 13 identifies the 10 largest institutional investors in Qualcomm.

Table 13 reports that, as of August 2020, the 10 largest institutional investors in Qualcomm held approximately 36.4 percent of Qualcomm's common stock.[2282] The three largest institutional investors in Qualcomm (Vanguard, BlackRock, and FMR) collectively held 21 percent of Qualcomm's common stock.[2283]

For present purposes, this observability offers its own countervailing efficiency of a different kind: it lowers the victim's transaction costs of organizing investors in the offending corporation who might support a change in corporate control to end the dispute between the victim and the offending corporation over conduct giving rise to the allegations of monopolization.

[2280] *See* J. Gregory Sidak & Susan E. Woodward, *Corporate Takeovers, the Commerce Clause, and the Efficient Anonymity of Shareholders*, 84 Nw. U. L. Rev. 1092 (1990). Dr. Woodward and I were colleagues at the Council of Economic Advisers in the Executive Office of the President. She served as the chief economist of the Securities and Exchange Commission shortly after we published our article on the efficient anonymity of shareholders.

[2281] *QUALCOMM Incorporated Common Stock (QCOM) Institutional Holdings*, NASDAQ (Aug. 19, 2020), https://www.nasdaq.com/market-activity/stocks/qcom/institutional-holdings.

[2282] *Id.*

[2283] *Id.*

The victim might not need to undertake a control transaction all by itself, and thus it might not need to bear all the risk of possible failure in its stratagem of risk mitigation. Consequently, the costs to resorting to the market for corporate control as a mechanism for dispute resolution between corporations like Apple and Qualcomm might be considerably lower than first appears, if the victim can persuade institutional investors to support the proposed change in control.

Table 13. The 10 Largest Institutional Investors in
Qualcomm's Common Stock as of August 2020

Owner Name	Shares Held	Percentage Ownership of Qualcomm's Common Stock
Vanguard Group Inc.	104,166,567	9.23%
Blackrock Inc.	77,338,447	6.85%
FMR LLC	51,333,949	4.55%
State Street Corp.	47,442,606	4.20%
Price T Rowe Associates Inc. /MD/	41,075,231	3.64%
PRIMECAP Management Co/CA	21,184,833	1.88%
Invesco Ltd.	17,952,409	1.59%
Bank of New York Mellon Corp.	17,663,310	1.57%
Geode Capital Management, LLC	16,911,050	1.50%
Northern Trust Corp.	15,131,907	1.34%

Source: *QUALCOMM Incorporated Common Stock (QCOM) Institutional Holdings*, NASDAQ, *supra* note 2281.
Note: Percentages reported in the column labeled "Percentage Ownership of Qualcomm's Common Stock" are produced by (1) dividing the number of shares that Nasdaq reports are held by the institutional investor by the total number of institutional shares in Qualcomm (857,950,071) and then (2) multiplying that quotient by the percentage of common stock that Nasdaq reports institutional investors own (76.04%).

3. *The Imposition of Incentive Compatibility Through Corporate Control*

When a firm is a publicly traded corporation, any commercial dispute that arises from harm that it arguably causes another can be mitigated by the victim's resort to an unsolicited control transaction in the market for corporate control. When monopolization threatens economic efficiency, as the FTC accused Qualcomm of doing, the firms located upstream and downstream from the monopolist could use the market for corporate control to eliminate that harm. If, for example, monopolization by a component manufacturer slowed technological development of cellular standards or increased the prices of mobile devices, a network operator (such as AT&T or Verizon) or an OEM (such as Apple, Samsung, or Google) would have the incentive to acquire control of the monopolist, replace its management, and impose incentive compatibility so as to stop the anticompetitive actions generating that inefficiency.

B. *The Significance of Apple's Massive Cash Holdings to Its Ready Ability to Use the Market for Corporate Control as a Mechanism to Defeat Anticompetitive Behavior*

The ready opportunity for alternative dispute resolution through the market for corporate control exposes why the theory that Qualcomm coerced Apple to accept unreasonable licensing terms was fatuous.

Qualcomm's alleged monopolization of the two kinds of modems, even if fully reflected in the market price of Qualcomm's stock, would increase the incentives for an OEM (such as Apple) to acquire Qualcomm. For a number of years Apple has had the immediate financial means to acquire *absolute* control of Qualcomm, as opposed to merely the minimum equity stake needed to transfer voting control to Apple. Figure 14 shows Apple's publicly reported cash holdings and Qualcomm's market capitalization from 2011 through 2019, which includes the period (2011 through 2016) during which, Judge Koh found, Qualcomm had effectively forced Apple into a pair of anticompetitive exclusive dealing agreements, the TA and the FATA.

Figure 14 shows that, over virtually the entire period that Qualcomm was allegedly exercising market power in its sales of modems to Apple, Apple had cash holdings that exceeded Qualcomm's entire market capitalization. Apple of course would not necessarily choose to pay all cash to acquire a target firm, nor of course would it need to acquire 100-percent ownership of Qualcomm to acquire managerial control. Fifty-one percent ownership of voting stock typically is sufficient but not necessary to give an acquirer control over a publicly traded corporation.

Figure 14. Comparison of Apple's Cash,
Cash Equivalents, and Marketable Securities,
with Qualcomm's Market Capitalization, 2011–2019

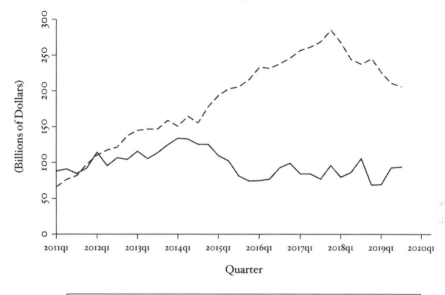

——— Qualcomm's Market Capitalization

– – – – Apple's Cash, Cash Equivalents, and Marketable Securities

Sources: Apple Inc., Quarterly Report for the Quarterly Period Ended December 25, 2010 (SEC Form 10-Q), at 29 (filed Jan. 19, 2011); Apple Inc., Quarterly Report for the Quarterly Period Ended March 26, 2011 (SEC Form 10-Q), at 31 (filed Apr. 21, 2011); Apple Inc., Quarterly Report for the Quarterly Period Ended June 25, 2011 (SEC Form 10-Q), at 33 (filed July 20, 2011); Apple Inc., Annual Report for the Fiscal Year Ended September 24, 2011 (SEC Form 10-K), at 37 (filed Oct. 26, 2011); Apple Inc., Quarterly Report for the Quarterly Period Ended December 31, 2011 (SEC Form 10-Q), at 29 (filed Jan. 25, 2012); Apple Inc., Quarterly Report for the Quarterly Period Ended March 31, 2012 (SEC Form 10-Q), at 32 (filed Apr. 25, 2012); Apple Inc., Quarterly Report for the Quarterly Period Ended June 30, 2012 (SEC Form 10-Q), at 32 (filed July 25, 2012); 2012 Apple 10-K, *supra* note 1998, at 37; Apple Inc., Quarterly Report for the Quarterly Period Ended December 29, 2012 (SEC Form 10-Q), at 31 (filed Jan. 24, 2013); Apple Inc., Quarterly Report for the Quarterly Period Ended March 30, 2013 (SEC Form 10-Q), at 31 (filed Apr. 24, 2013); Apple Inc., Quarterly Report for the Quarterly Period Ended June 29, 2013 (SEC Form 10-Q), at 32 (filed July 24, 2013); Apple Inc., Annual Report for the Fiscal Year Ended September 28, 2013 (SEC Form 10-K), at 35 (filed Oct. 30, 2013); Apple Inc., Quarterly Report for the Quarterly Period Ended December 28, 2013 (SEC Form 10-Q), at 33 (filed Jan. 28, 2014); Apple Inc., Quarterly Report for the Quarterly Period Ended March 29, 2014 (SEC Form 10-Q), at 32 (filed Apr. 24, 2014); Apple Inc., Quarterly Report for the Quarterly Period Ended June 28, 2014 (SEC Form 10-Q), at 34 (filed July 23, 2014); Apple Inc., Annual Report for the Fiscal Year Ended September 27, 2014 (SEC Form 10-K), at 35 (filed Oct. 27, 2014); Apple Inc., Quarterly Report for the Quarterly Period Ended December 27, 2014 (SEC Form 10-Q), at 32 (filed Jan. 28, 2015); Apple Inc., Quarterly Report for the Quarterly Period Ended March 28, 2015 (SEC Form 10-Q), at 31 (filed Apr. 28, 2015); Apple Inc., Quarterly Report for the Quarterly Period Ended June 27, 2015 (SEC Form 10-Q), at 31 (filed July 22, 2015); Apple Inc., Annual Report for the Fiscal Year Ended September 26, 2015 (SEC Form 10-K), at 30 (filed Oct. 28, 2015); Apple Inc., Quarterly Report for the Quarterly Period Ended December 26, 2015 (SEC Form 10-Q), at 29 (filed

Jan. 27, 2016); Apple Inc., Quarterly Report for the Quarterly Period Ended March 26, 2016 (SEC Form 10-Q), at 30 (filed Apr. 27, 2016); Apple Inc., Quarterly Report for the Quarterly Period Ended June 25, 2016 (SEC Form 10-Q), at 31 (filed July 27, 2016); Apple Inc., Annual Report for the Fiscal Year Ended September 24, 2016 (SEC Form 10-K), at 29 (filed Oct. 26, 2016); Apple Inc., Quarterly Report for the Quarterly Period Ended December 31, 2016 (SEC Form 10-Q), at 29 (filed Feb. 1, 2017); Apple Inc., Quarterly Report for the Quarterly Period Ended April 1, 2017 (SEC Form 10-Q), at 29 (filed May 3 2017); Apple Inc., Quarterly Report for the Quarterly Period Ended July 1, 2017 (SEC Form 10-Q), at 30 (filed Aug. 2, 2017); Apple Inc., Annual Report for the Fiscal Year Ended September 30, 2017 (SEC Form 10-K), at 30 (filed Nov. 3, 2017); Apple Inc., Quarterly Report for the Quarterly Period Ended December 30, 2017 (SEC Form 10-Q), at 29 (filed Feb. 2, 2018); Apple Inc., Quarterly Report for the Quarterly Period Ended March 31, 2018 (SEC Form 10-Q), at 30 (filed May 2, 2018); Apple Inc., Quarterly Report for the Quarterly Period Ended June 30, 2018 (SEC Form 10-Q), at 31 (filed Aug. 1, 2018); 2018 Apple 10-K, *supra* note 1998, at 30 (filed Nov. 5, 2018); Apple Inc., Quarterly Report for the Quarterly Period Ended December 29, 2018 (SEC Form 10-Q), at 30 (filed Jan. 30, 2019); Apple Inc., Quarterly Report for the Quarterly Period Ended March 30, 2019 (SEC Form 10-Q), at 31 (filed May 1, 2019); Apple Inc., Quarterly Report for the Quarterly Period Ended June 29, 2019 (SEC Form 10-Q), at 31 (filed July 31, 2019); Apple Inc., Annual Report for the Fiscal Year Ended September 28, 2019 (SEC Form 10-K), at 30 (filed Oct. 30, 2019).

C. *The Corporate Control Premium*

The corporate control premium reflects the additional value—beyond the *pro rata* right to a firm's net cash flows—that attaches to gaining managerial control over the firm. The control premium is the amount that a buyer is willing to pay over the pre-bid market price of a publicly traded corporation so that the buyer may control the target's management decisions. That premium reflects the expectation that the acquirer will be able to increase the value of the target. The acquirer essentially pays a premium for the opportunity to reap a variety of potential benefits from the acquisition: economies of scale and scope, elimination of double marginalization, diversification, improved productivity, and so forth.

A survey by George Alexandridis, Kathleen P. Fuller, Lars Terhaar, and Nickolaos G. Travlos in 2013 found an average takeover premium of 38 percent for larger firms and 54 percent for smaller firms.[2284] Considering the substantial amount of Apple's holdings of cash, cash equivalents, and marketable securities (not to mention its other sources of financing) from 2011 to 2019, Apple surely could have paid a corporate control premium to acquire Qualcomm and immediately direct its management to desist from

---

[2284] George Alexandridis, Kathleen P. Fuller, Lars Terhaar & Nickolaos G. Travlos, *Deal Size, Acquisition Premia and Shareholder Gains*, 20 J. CORP. FIN. 1, 9 (2013). Earlier studies identified a control premium ranging from approximately 30 to 50 percent above the target's pre-bid share price. *See* Bernard S. Black & Joseph A. Grundfest, *Shareholder Gains from Takeovers and Restructurings Between 1981 and 1986*, 5 J. APPLIED CORP. FIN. 109 (1988). Studies and surveys have established a widely accepted premium of 30 percent. *See* Roberta Romano, *A Guide to Takeovers: Theory, Evidence, and Regulation*, 9 YALE J. ON REG. 120 (1992); Gregg A. Jarrell, James A. Brickley & Jeffry M. Netter, *The Market for Corporate Control: The Empirical Evidence Since 1980*, 2 J. ECON. PERSP., Winter 1988, at 49; *see also* Gregor Andrade, Mark Mitchell & Erik Stafford, *New Evidence and Perspectives on Mergers*, 15 J. ECON. PERSP., Spring 2001, at 103, 106 tbl.1.

the actions that the FTC alleged were violations of the Sherman Act. Put differently, through the market for corporate control Apple could have privately imposed on Qualcomm's management the same injunction that Judge Koh publicly imposed in *FTC v. Qualcomm*. Moreover, Apple could have achieved that result in a fraction of the time that it took the FTC to decide to prosecute Qualcomm and litigate *FTC v. Qualcomm*.

D. *The Expiration of Qualcomm's Poison Pill*

Qualcomm had a poison pill in effect from 1995 until 2015, but it is unlikely that that antitakeover provision could have prevented Apple's acquisition of corporate control of Qualcomm. On September 26, 1995, Qualcomm adopted a Preferred Share Purchase Rights Agreement, "to protect stockholders' interests in the event of a proposed takeover of the [c]ompany,"[2285] which Qualcomm amended in December 2006.[2286] In relevant part, the Rights Agreement specified that the Rights would be "exercisable only if a person or group (an Acquiring Person) acquires beneficial ownership of 20% or more of the Company's outstanding shares of common stock without approval of the Board of Directors."[2287] The amended Rights Agreement also provided that Qualcomm "may at any time prior to such time as any Person becomes an Acquiring Person amend this [Rights] Agreement to (a) lower the thresholds [for corporate control] from 20% to any percentage which is (i) greater than the largest percentage of the outstanding Common Shares then known by the Company to be beneficially owned by any person [with certain exceptions] . . . and (ii) *not less than 10%* or (b) increase the Purchase Price for each one one-thousandth of a Preferred Share[.]"[2288] The amended Rights Agreement also specified that it would expire on September 25, 2015.[2289]

    After September 2015, and as of August 2020, Qualcomm's management had not renewed its poison pill. All potential acquirers of Qualcomm would thus have been well-advised by their investment bankers of the expiration of Qualcomm's poison pill. In practical effect, Qualcomm's nonrenewal of its poison pill in 2015 made the company available for acquisition by any buyer willing to pay Qualcomm's shareholders a control premium.

[2285] 2014 Qualcomm 10-K, sources cited *supra* Figure 13, at F-19.

[2286] Qualcomm Inc., Amendment to Amended and Restated Rights Agreement (Dec. 7, 2006), https://www.sec.gov/Archives/edgar/data/804328/000093639206001106/a25743exv99w1.htm, *Exhibit 99.1 to* Qualcomm Inc., Current Report of December 7, 2006 (SEC Form 8-K) (filed Dec. 12, 2006).

[2287] 2014 Qualcomm 10-K, sources cited *supra* Figure 13, at F-19.

[2288] Qualcomm Inc., Amendment to Amended and Restated Rights Agreement 1.3 (Dec. 7, 2006), https://www.sec.gov/Archives/edgar/data/804328/000093639206001106/a25743exv99w1.htm (emphasis added), *Exhibit 99.1 to* Qualcomm Inc., Current Report of December 7, 2006 (SEC Form 8-K) (filed Dec. 12, 2006).

[2289] 2005 Qualcomm 10-K, sources cited *supra* Figure 13, at F-23.

E.   *Was the Absence of a Corporate Control Transaction for Qualcomm by Apple Evidence of the Nonexistence of Qualcomm's Alleged Monopolization?*

If a monopoly in a particular industry causes anticompetitive effects, one would expect to observe evidence of an acquisition of corporate control so as to reverse those effects. The major implementers of industry standards and participants in the mobile communications industry did not avail themselves of that solution with respect to Qualcomm, even though many had ample cash reserves and the ready ability to raise external funding. That failure to mitigate risk would be consistent with those implementers' not genuinely believing that Qualcomm threatened their businesses with anticompetitive harm.

Judge Koh portrayed Qualcomm as charging OEMs "unreasonably high" royalties for an exhaustive license to its portfolio of cellular SEPs. Yet, no large OEM used an unsolicited tender offer to acquire, or even to attempt to acquire, corporate control of Qualcomm. The nonoccurrence of that event calls into question the plausibility of Judge Koh's findings, because one of the most obvious predictions that would follow if Qualcomm had been monopolizing markets for modems did not come to pass.

Occam's razor implies that the best explanation for why we did not observe a hostile takeover of Qualcomm by an OEM is that the charging of allegedly "unreasonably high" royalties for an exhaustive licenses to Qualcomm's cellular SEPs never occurred. Why would a large OEM like Apple passively endure the supposed harm from Qualcomm when that OEM could have stopped that harm in short order through a transaction in the market for corporate control? Apple's acquisition of Qualcomm would have posed no great challenge for antitrust authorities to clear. At most, antitrust agencies would require that the merged firm continue to sell Qualcomm modems to Apple's competitors for some period of time.

The key insight is that, if Qualcomm's actions truly harmed competition or innovation or economic efficiency, the list of firms with both an economic incentive to eliminate that behavior and the financial means to do so included not only an OEM like Apple, but also network operators (like AT&T and Verizon) and software developers (like Google and Microsoft). Each of those firms was (and is) based in the United States and was therefore unlikely to have had its proposed acquisition of Qualcomm blocked by the U.S. government on national security grounds, as Broadcom found its proposed purchase of Qualcomm blocked (as we will examine below). And looking to the future, it is inconceivable that each of those American firms would have allowed Qualcomm, a much smaller corporation, to exercise market power to harm innovation as the cellular industry was transitioning to 5G technologies.

*F.   What Can One Infer About Qualcomm's Alleged Monopoly from Broadcom's
     Unsuccessful Attempt to Acquire Qualcomm and from Apple's Acquisition of
     Intel's Modem Business?*

On November 6, 2017, Broadcom offered to buy Qualcomm for $105 billion.[2290]
By that time, Qualcomm had sued Apple for patent infringement and refusal
to pay royalties that it owed Qualcomm.[2291] Press reports speculated that
Apple's actions had suppressed Qualcomm's share price,[2292] which in turn
had put Qualcomm into play as a target for a corporate takeover. Qualcomm
rejected Broadcom's offer of about $70 per share.[2293] The *New York Times*
conjectured that Broadcom sought to change Qualcomm's licensing practices.[2294] On February 5, 2018, Broadcom raised its offer to $121 billion.[2295]

Broadcom's management did not explain how it would be able to lower
Qualcomm's royalties for exhaustive licenses to its cellular SEPs without
reducing the net free cash flow that Qualcomm had used to fund its R&D
investment. The Committee on Foreign Investment in the United States
(CFIUS) was concerned about the proposed takeover. Broadcom at the
time was a Singaporean corporation, and CFIUS considered Qualcomm
"the current leading company in 5G technology development and standard setting."[2296] CFIUS advised President Trump to block the takeover on
grounds of national security, which he did by executive order on March 12,
2018.[2297]

Broadcom's attempted takeover was evidence that a profitable opportunity appeared to exist for a third party to acquire corporate control
of Qualcomm, particularly at a share price that appeared to have been

---

[2290] *See* Michael J. de la Merced, *Broadcom Targets Qualcomm in Largest-Ever Tech Deal*, N.Y. Times,
Nov. 6, 2017.

[2291] *Id.*

[2292] *Id.* ("Qualcomm believes . . . [that] either a victory over or a settlement with Apple would lift its
stock price."); *id.* ("Qualcomm . . . has been grappling with a sagging stock price and investor wariness that
the Apple fight will continue for some time.").

[2293] *Id.* ("The biggest issue may simply be that Qualcomm believes the current offer, worth about $70
a share, is too low. Qualcomm's trove of patents—among the most formidable in the world of wireless
networking—remains a hugely valuable asset."); *see also* Don Clark & Michael J. de la Merced, *Broadcom
Proposes Unseating Qualcomm Board as Takeover Fight Escalates*, N.Y. Times, Dec. 4, 2017 ("Qualcomm has
argued that the current bid was too low even as a starting point for negotiations[.]"); *id.* ("Broadcom
contends its offer was the most significant catalyst for Qualcomm's stock price in nearly a year. Its shares
had traded below $60 a share for most of the year before Broadcom announced its offer.").

[2294] Clark & de la Merced, *Broadcom Proposes Unseating Qualcomm Board as Takeover Fight Escalates*,
supra note 2293 ("Hock E. Tan, Broadcom's chief executive, is likely to argue that it is time to change
Qualcomm's patent-licensing practices.").

[2295] *See* Michael J. de la Merced & Don Clark, *Broadcom Raises Its Qualcomm Offer to $121 Billion*,
N.Y. Times, Feb. 5, 2018.

[2296] Letter from Aimen N. Mir, Committee on Foreign Investment in the United States, to Mark
Plotkin, Covington & Burling LLP, and Theodore Kassinger, O'Melveny & Myers LLP 2 (Mar. 5, 2018).

[2297] Exec. Order No. 2018-05479, Regarding the Proposed Takeover of Qualcomm Incorporated by
Broadcom Limited, 83 Fed. Reg. 11,631, 11,631 (Mar. 12, 2018) ("The proposed takeover of Qualcomm by
[Broadcom] is prohibited.").

depressed by the FTC's case and Qualcomm's various disputes with Apple. Broadcom's unsuccessful takeover invited the obvious question: Why, with nearly $269 billion in cash on hand in the fall of 2017, did Apple not buy Qualcomm, a company with a market capitalization at that time of approximately $76 billion?[2298] Apple could have acquired ownership and control of not only Qualcomm's modem business, but also its entire portfolio of 140,000 patents and pending applications. And CFIUS of course could not thwart Apple's acquisition of Qualcomm on grounds of national security.

Instead, Apple announced in July 2019 its intention to acquire the modem business of Qualcomm's competitor Intel for the price of only $1 billion.[2299] That announcement obviously proved that Apple was indeed willing and able to invest in developing its own modems at least by acquisition. The purchase price appeared to be roughly two orders of magnitude below the cost of acquiring complete ownership and control of Qualcomm. That disparity provides an informative reference point regarding the market's valuation of Qualcomm's dynamic capabilities for innovation in cellular communications versus Intel's.

Despite its having claimed in multiple proceedings before federal district courts and the ITC that it had been or would be harmed by Qualcomm's exploitation of monopoly power over CDMA and "premium" LTE modems, Apple never resorted to the most obvious form of risk mitigation. Apple never launched a hostile tender offer to acquire corporate control of Qualcomm. Apple's inaction was telling. It was the dog that did not bark in the night. The simplest hypothesis to explain why Apple did not use the market for corporate control to defend itself from Qualcomm is that Qualcomm never caused Apple any anticompetitive harm.

XX. Was Judge Koh's Permanent, Worldwide Injunction Unlawful?

Having found in *FTC v. Qualcomm* that Qualcomm had engaged in anticompetitive conduct, Judge Koh issued a permanent, worldwide injunction against Qualcomm composed of five parts.[2300] Most notably, she ordered

---

[2298] On September 30, 2017, Apple had $268.9 billion in cash and cash equivalents. Apple Inc., Quarterly Report for the Quarterly Period Ended December 30, 2017 (SEC Form 10-Q), at 29 (filed Feb. 2, 2018). As of September 29, 2017, the last trading day of the third quarter of 2017, Qualcomm's market capitalization was $76.57 billion. *QUALCOMM Market Cap 2006–2020 | QCOM*, Macrotrends, https://www.macrotrends.net/stocks/charts/QCOM/qualcomm/market-cap.

[2299] Press Release, Apple Inc., Apple to Acquire the Majority of Intel's Smartphone Modem Business (July 25, 2019), https://www.apple.com/newsroom/2019/07/apple-to-acquire-the-majority-of-intels-smartphone-modem-business/. Intel's acquisition of VIA in 2015 confirmed that, even before Apple's announcement in July 2019 that it would acquire Intel's modem business, the market for corporate control had been a vehicle used to influence competition in the modem industry.

[2300] FTC v. Qualcomm Inc., 411 F. Supp. 3d 658, 820–24 (N.D. Cal. 2019).

that Qualcomm (1) "must not condition the supply of modem chips on a customer's patent license status,"[2301] (2) "must negotiate or renegotiate license terms with customers in good faith under conditions free from the threat of lack of access to or discriminatory provision of modem chip supply or associated technical support or access to software,"[2302] and (3) "must make exhaustive SEP licenses available to modem-chip suppliers on fair, reasonable, and non-discriminatory ('FRAND') terms."[2303]

On July 8, 2019, Qualcomm moved that the Ninth Circuit stay the permanent, worldwide injunction pending appeal. Qualcomm argued that enforcement of Judge Koh's permanent, worldwide injunction would cause the company several kinds of irreparable harm:

> The design of the relevant provisions of the injunction is to change the very structure of Qualcomm's business and to irreversibly reduce Qualcomm's licensing revenue. It requires Qualcomm to renegotiate numerous long-term license agreements with its customers. Further, and in conflict with settled industry practice, it compels Qualcomm to provide exhaustive patent licenses directly to other modem chip suppliers. It thus disrupts the long-standing practice of licensing only the makers of cell phones that incorporate those chips, thereby creating substantial inefficiencies, forcing upon Qualcomm potential patent exhaustion issues and severely undermining Qualcomm's ability to fully protect and recover the value of its patent portfolio.[2304]

Qualcomm additionally argued that, because Judge Koh's permanent, worldwide injunction "rested on flawed antitrust theories that raise serious legal questions on appeal,"[2305] it would likely succeed on the merits in its appeal. In addition, Qualcomm argued that the public interest weighed in favor of staying the permanent, worldwide injunction.[2306]

Several government agencies, including the Antitrust Division and the Department of Defense (DOD), intervened in support of Qualcomm.[2307]

[2301] *Id.* at 820.

[2302] *Id.*

[2303] *Id.* at 821. In addition, Judge Koh ordered that "Qualcomm may not enter express or de facto exclusive dealing agreements for the supply of modem chips." *Id.* at 822. She further prohibited Qualcomm from "interfer[ing] with the ability of any customer to communicate with a government agency about a potential law enforcement or regulatory matter." *Id.* She also ordered Qualcomm "to submit to compliance and monitoring procedures for a period of seven (7) years." *Id.* at 824.

[2304] Motion for Partial Stay of Injunction Pending Appeal at 2–3, FTC v. Qualcomm Inc., No. 19-16122 (9th Cir. July 8, 2019) (footnote omitted).

[2305] Reply in Support of Motion for Partial Stay of Injunction Pending Appeal at 1, FTC v. Qualcomm Inc., No. 19-16122 (9th Cir. July 25, 2019).

[2306] Motion for Partial Stay of Injunction Pending Appeal at 27–28, FTC v. Qualcomm Inc., No. 19-16122 (9th Cir. July 8, 2019).

[2307] United States' Statement of Interest Concerning Partial Stay, 2019 WL 3306496, *supra* note 205; Declaration of Under Secretary of Defense, *supra* note 2272, at 2; Statement of Interest of the United States Concerning Remedies, *supra* note 182.

They argued that Judge Koh's permanent, worldwide injunction would impair Qualcomm's ability to invest in R&D, which in turn would retard American innovation in mobile communications technology, undermine U.S. leadership in 5G technologies, and threaten U.S. national security.[2308] In an order issued on August 23, 2019, the Ninth Circuit accepted Qualcomm's arguments and partially stayed Judge Koh's permanent, worldwide injunction.[2309] On August 11, 2020, the Ninth Circuit's three-judge panel vacated Judge Koh's permanent, worldwide injunction.[2310]

Judge Koh's permanent, worldwide injunction disregarded two salient questions of law. First, Judge Koh refused to consider all of the traditional equitable factors for issuing injunctions when she entered a permanent, worldwide injunction against Qualcomm. She reasoned that, "by its very nature, the determination that a monopolist has violated the Sherman Act and that 'the wrongs are ongoing or likely to recur' is a finding that an injunction is in the public interest because it will restrain the defendant from further anticompetitive conduct."[2311]

Second, Judge Koh did not hold a separate hearing on remedies, as the Antitrust Division had requested. She also refused to consider post-discovery evidence—that is, evidence of market developments that occurred after the cutoff of fact discovery in March 2018—when issuing her permanent, worldwide injunction.[2312] Judge Koh said that there is "no legal requirement that a plaintiff show future market power."[2313] Because she found that Qualcomm's conduct was ongoing and that there was a significant risk that Qualcomm would dominate 5G modems, she found it sufficiently likely that

---

[2308] *See* United States' Statement of Interest Concerning Partial Stay, 2019 WL 3306496, *supra* note 205, at *12 ("In the view of the Executive Branch, diminishment of Qualcomm's competitiveness in 5G innovation and standard-setting would significantly impact U.S. national security."); Declaration of Under Secretary of Defense, *supra* note 2272, at 2 ("DoD firmly believes that any measure that inappropriately limits Qualcomm's technological leadership, ability to invest in research and development (R&D), and market competitiveness, even in the short-term, could harm national security. The risks to national security include the disruption of DoD's supply chain and unsure U.S. leadership in 5G.").

[2309] FTC v. Qualcomm Inc., 935 F.3d 752, 755–57 (9th Cir. 2019) (per curiam) (granting Qualcomm's motion to stay in part Judge Koh's injunction).

[2310] FTC v. Qualcomm Inc., No. 19-16122, 2020 WL 4591476, at *22 (9th Cir. Aug. 11, 2020).

[2311] FTC v. Qualcomm Inc., 411 F. Supp. 3d 658, 813 (N.D. Cal. 2019) (quoting FTC v. Evans Prods. Co., 775 F.2d 1084, 1087 (9th Cir. 1985)).

[2312] *Id.* at 812 ("The Court has already rejected Qualcomm's pre-trial argument that a court must consider 'post-discovery evidence of current market power' before issuing an injunction.") (quoting Order Denying Qualcomm's Request to Introduce Evidence of Post-Discovery Events at 6, FTC v. Qualcomm Inc., No. 5:17-cv-00220-LHK (N.D. Cal. Dec. 13, 2018), ECF No. 997).

[2313] *Id.* at 816.

an antitrust violation would recur[2314] and, therefore, that her issuance of a permanent, worldwide injunction lasting until at least 2026 was appropriate.[2315]

Judge Koh's ruling that equitable considerations were irrelevant for her issuance of a permanent, worldwide injunction, and her refusal to hold a separate hearing on remedies, were improvident and legally erroneous. Had the Ninth Circuit's three-judge panel not reversed Judge Koh's judgment and vacated her permanent, worldwide injunction on August 11, 2020, the Ninth Circuit would have reviewed Judge Koh's grant of a permanent, worldwide injunction for abuse of discretion and application of correct legal principles.[2316] The Ninth Circuit would also have reviewed *de novo* questions of law relating to the injunction.[2317]

A. Did Judge Koh's Permanent, Worldwide Antitrust Injunction Violate eBay?

Judge Koh's decision to issue a permanent, worldwide injunction without examining each of the four traditional equitable factors disregarded the controlling precedent of the Supreme Court's 2006 decision in *eBay*:

> According to well-established principles of equity, a plaintiff seeking a permanent injunction must satisfy a four-factor test before a court may grant such relief. A plaintiff must demonstrate: (1) that it has suffered an irreparable injury; (2) that remedies available at law, such as monetary damages, are inadequate to compensate for that injury; (3) that, considering the balance of hardships between the plaintiff and defendant, a remedy in equity is warranted; and (4) that the public interest would not be disserved by a permanent injunction.[2318]

The Court said that those general principles "apply with equal force to disputes arising under the Patent Act."[2319] Quoting its decision in *Romero-Barcelo*, the Court emphasized that "'a major departure from the long tradition of equity practice should not be lightly implied.'"[2320] "Nothing in the Patent Act

---

[2314] *Id.* ("Qualcomm's internal documents and public statements show that Qualcomm is likely to replicate its market dominance during the transition to 5G, the next generation of modem chips. Here, in both internal documents and public statements, Qualcomm has consistently stated that it is ahead of rival modem chip suppliers in developing 5G modem chips."); *id.* at 818 ("Therefore, because Qualcomm's unlawful practices continue and there is a significant risk that Qualcomm will be dominant in 5G, the Court concludes that the unlawful conduct is likely to recur and that a permanent injunction is warranted.").

[2315] *Id.* at 824 ("In order to ensure Qualcomm's compliance with the above remedies, the Court orders Qualcomm to submit to compliance and monitoring procedures for a period of seven (7) years. Specifically, Qualcomm shall report to the FTC on an annual basis Qualcomm's compliance with the above remedies ordered by the Court.").

[2316] Fortyune v. Am. Multi-Cinema, Inc., 364 F.3d 1075, 1079 (9th Cir. 2004).

[2317] United States v. Hovsepian, 359 F.3d 1144, 1155 (9th Cir. 2004).

[2318] eBay Inc. v. MercExchange, L.L.C., 547 U.S. 388, 391 (2006).

[2319] *Id.*

[2320] *Id.* (quoting Weinberger v. Romero-Barcelo, 456 U.S. 305, 320 (1982)).

indicates that Congress intended such a departure,"[2321] the Court said, and it then concluded that, in cases involving a violation of the Patent Act, no extraordinary rule favors the issuance of a permanent injunction.

By the same reasoning that the Court employed in *eBay*, nothing in the FTC Act permitted Judge Koh to deviate from the long tradition of equity practice when she granted the FTC's request for a permanent, worldwide injunction in *FTC v. Qualcomm*.

1. Was Judge Koh Authorized to Deviate from Established Equitable Practice?

To support her decision, Judge Koh cited the Ninth Circuit's 1985 decision in *FTC v. Evans Products Co.*,[2322] which of course predated *eBay* by 21 years. She began by faulting Qualcomm. In essence, Judge Koh complained that Qualcomm had not shown why the FTC is *not* entitled to its own special rule on permanent injunctions: "Qualcomm cites *no FTC Act case* in which a court considered those equitable factors at the permanent injunction stage."[2323]

But why would Qualcomm ever need to make that showing? Why limit the possible sources of controlling authority to FTC Act cases when the general applicability of the Supreme Court's reasoning in *eBay* was obvious? "Regardless, by its very nature," Judge Koh continued, "the determination that a monopolist has violated the Sherman Act and that 'the wrongs are ongoing or likely to recur' is a finding that an injunction is in the public interest because it will restrain the defendant from further anticompetitive conduct."[2324] Burning the defendant's 5G laboratory to the ground and salting the earth beneath it also would restrain the defendant from further anticompetitive conduct. But of course we do not observe such a wasteful rule. Countervailing considerations typically exist, if one cares to look hard enough for them. For good reason, the name given those countervailing considerations is "the equities." The particular propriety expected of a court sitting in equity counsels moderation and judgment in granting a permanent injunction.

Judge Koh's reasoning in *FTC v. Qualcomm* was unpersuasive because it manifested the same fallacy that the Supreme Court rejected in *eBay*. One could just as easily argue that "the wrongs" from an adjudicated patent infringement "are ongoing or likely to recur" in the absence of a permanent injunction, such that the conclusion that a permanent injunction is in the public interest necessarily follows from the court's anterior finding that a

---

[2321] *Id.* at 391–92.

[2322] FTC v. Qualcomm Inc., 411 F. Supp. 3d 658, 813 (N.D. Cal. 2019) (citing FTC v. Evans Prods. Co., 775 F.2d 1084, 1087 (9th Cir. 1985)).

[2323] *Id.* (emphasis added).

[2324] *Id.* (quoting *Evans Prods.*, 775 F.2d at 1087).

patent has been infringed and the patent holder is entitled by statute to some kind of relief.

As in the case of the Patent Act in *eBay*, Congress did not create by statute an extraordinary rule favoring the issuance of a permanent injunction in cases uniquely involving a violation of the FTC Act. Section 13(b)(2) of the FTC Act provides that "in proper cases the Commission may seek, and after proper proof, the court may issue, a permanent injunction."[2325] That is not saying much. Nothing in that statutory language authorizes a court to deviate from the traditional four-part equitable standard when issuing a permanent injunction.

Judge Koh's findings of fact and conclusions of law to the contrary mistakenly proceed as though Congress created a presumption that a permanent injunction serves the public interest whenever a court has found a violation of the FTC Act. That interpretation of section 13(b)(2) lacks any foundation in the language of the FTC Act. And it is contradicted by the Supreme Court's reasoning in *eBay*, which stressed that departures from the general principles of equity, including the creation of a presumption in favor of issuing a permanent injunction, "'should not be lightly implied.'"[2326]

2. *Does Proving Irreparable Harm Require Proving a "Strong Causal Nexus" Between the Allegedly Unlawful Act and the Alleged Harm?*

The Supreme Court said in *eBay* that there is nothing special about permanent injunctions in patent cases: they must conform to the same principles of equity as a permanent injunction in any run-of-the-mill civil case in federal court. Naturally, there is no presumption of irreparable harm in a patent case.

The Federal Circuit, affirming Judge Koh in *Apple v. Samsung* in 2012 and 2013, has held that to prove irreparable harm in patent litigation so as to satisfy *eBay*'s first equitable factor requires proof of a "sufficiently strong causal nexus relat[ing] the alleged harm to the alleged infringement."[2327] The Federal Circuit clarified in 2015 (in another appeal in *Apple v. Samsung*) that "[t]he causal nexus requirement ensures that an injunction is only entered

---

[2325] 15 U.S.C. § 53(b)(2); *cf.* Bearden v. Ballad Health, No. 20-5047, 2020 WL 4218305, at *4 (6th Cir. July 23, 2020) (Thapar, J.) ("[T]he [Clayton] Act provides for injunctive relief only 'under the same conditions and principles as injunctive relief against threatened conduct that will cause loss or damage is granted by courts of equity.' That language hardly suggests an effort to overhaul the case-or-controversy requirement. And in fact, courts have typically understood antitrust law as imposing a 'more onerous' standard than traditional standing analysis (though this heightened showing goes to the merits, not our subject-matter jurisdiction).") (first quoting 15 U.S.C. § 26; and then quoting Static Control Components, Inc. v. Lexmark Int'l, Inc., 697 F.3d 387, 402 (6th Cir. 2012)).

[2326] *eBay*, 547 U.S. at 391 (quoting Weinberger v. Romero-Barcelo, 456 U.S. 305, 320 (1982)).

[2327] Apple, Inc. v. Samsung Elecs. Co., 695 F.3d 1370, 1374 (Fed. Cir. 2012); *accord* Apple Inc. v. Samsung Elecs. Co., 735 F.3d 1352, 1361 (Fed. Cir. 2013) ("To satisfy the irreparable injury factor, a patentee must establish (1) that absent an injunction it will suffer irreparable injury and (2) that a sufficiently strong causal nexus relates the injury to the infringement.").

against a defendant on account of a harm resulting from the defendant's wrongful conduct, not some other reason" such as "'irreparable harm caused by otherwise lawful competition.'"[2328]

It might be tempting for the FTC to argue that the requirement of a causal nexus in the showing of irreparable harm when the plaintiff seeks a permanent injunction in a patent infringement case is *sui generis* and thus not relevant to the permanent injunction that Judge Koh issued in *FTC v. Qualcomm*. But that reasoning would be specious. It would turn *eBay* on its head. Why should patent litigation uniquely demand a showing of a causal nexus as part of the proof of irreparable harm? To the contrary, it is more plausible to read *eBay* to imply in *FTC v. Qualcomm* that the requirement of proximate causation exists for *any* permanent injunction, including any permanent injunction sought by the FTC for a violation of the Sherman Act.

In *FTC v. Qualcomm*, Judge Koh did not follow even her own reasoning (affirmed by the Federal Circuit) that irreparable harm requires a showing of proximate cause linking the unlawful acts to the observed harm. We saw in Part XVI the "promotive" standard of attenuated causation that Judge Koh appeared to apply to establish that certain rival modem manufacturers "exited" because of Qualcomm's allegedly anticompetitive conduct. Applying the "promotive" standard of attenuated causation, she appeared to concede that the FTC did not prove the existence of a causal nexus between conduct and effect because the record established that there were demonstrably lawful sources of competitive harm to rival modem manufacturers that fully sufficed to explain the failings of those rivals in the marketplace. Hence, in *FTC v. Qualcomm* Judge Koh did not find a sufficiently strong causal nexus between any of the challenged conduct and the claimed harm to rival modem manufacturers.

That absence of a sufficiently strong causal nexus was relevant not only to reviewing for error Judge Koh's findings of fact and conclusions of law on liability, but also her fashioning of a permanent, worldwide injunction (assuming for sake of argument but contrary to fact) that violations of antitrust law did occur. If there was no "strong causal nexus" between an act violating the Sherman Act and a proven anticompetitive effect, Judge Koh could not have properly found irreparable harm and therefore could not have properly issued her permanent, worldwide injunction.

[2328] Apple Inc. v. Samsung Elecs. Co., 809 F.3d 633, 640 (Fed. Cir. 2015) (quoting *Apple v. Samsung*, 735 F.3d at 1361).

3. *Did Judge Koh Erroneously Invoke the Less Demanding Standard for Granting the FTC a Preliminary Injunction, Pursuant to Section 13(b)(2) of the FTC Act?*

Even if (implausibly) *eBay* did not constrain Judge Koh's power to issue a permanent injunction in *FTC v. Qualcomm*, her reliance on the Ninth Circuit's 1985 decision in *FTC v. Evans Products*[2329] as authority was legally erroneous because *Evans* concerned a statutory modification of the rules for issuance of a *preliminary* injunction, not a permanent injunction.

To be sure, Congress did create in section 13(b)(2) of the FTC Act a special rule that a judge must obey when considering whether to grant a motion brought by the FTC for a preliminary injunction. Yet, the FTC Act does not contain any similar rule that relaxes the FTC's required showing when it seeks a *permanent* injunction, as section 13(b)(2) also empowers the agency to do "in proper cases."[2330] Because Judge Koh was issuing a permanent injunction, section 13(b)(2)'s provision concerning the issuance of a preliminary injunction was irrelevant. Yet, Judge Koh would impute to that statutory silence the same relaxation of the FTC's required proof that Congress chose, in a different remedial context, to grant explicitly to the agency—and Judge Koh would purport to claim that authority from the very same paragraph of the statute.

Even if one focuses on the standard that the FTC Act imposes on a judge when issuing a preliminary injunction, Judge Koh's decision to disregard the generally applied equitable considerations fails. In 1981 in *FTC v. Weyerhaeuser Co.*, Justice Ruth Bader Ginsburg, then still a Circuit Judge on the U.S. Court of Appeals for the D.C. Circuit, explained for the majority the proper standard for a trial judge to apply when determining whether to issue a preliminary injunction for a violation of the FTC Act.[2331] In rejecting the argument that the FTC had the automatic right to receive a preliminary injunction, Justice Ginsburg analyzed the derivation and purpose of section 13(b)(2) of the FTC Act.

Justice Ginsburg noted that, before 1973, when Congress amended the FTC Act, courts had already imposed on government agencies seeking interim relief for purposes of enforcing a federal statute a lower standard than the standard applicable to such relief in cases between private parties.[2332] The FTC typically was not required to prove irreparable harm to obtain a preliminary injunction.[2333] The purpose of that statutory amendment to the

---

[2329] *FTC v. Qualcomm*, 411 F. Supp. 3d at 813 (citing *Evans Prods.*, 755 F.2d at 1087).

[2330] 15 U.S.C. § 53(b)(2).

[2331] 665 F.2d 1072, 1081 (D.C. Cir. 1981) (R.B. Ginsburg, J.).

[2332] *Id.* at 1082.

[2333] *Id.* ("[T]he case law lightened the agency's burden by eliminating the need to show irreparable harm.").

FTC Act, Justice Ginsburg explained, was to codify the standard that the case law had already adopted.[2334] She quoted at length the conference report accompanying that statutory amendment:

> "[Section 13(b)] relates to the standard of proof to be met by the Federal Trade Commission for the issuance of a temporary restraining order or a preliminary injunction. It is not intended in any way to impose a totally new standard of proof different from that which is now required of the Commission. The intent is to maintain the statutory or 'public interest' standard which is now applicable, and *not* to impose the traditional 'equity' standard of irreparable damage, probability of success on the merits, and that the balance of equities favors the petitioner. This latter standard derives from common law and is appropriate for litigation between private parties. It is not, however, appropriate for the implementation of a Federal statute by an independent regulatory agency where the standards of the public interest measure the propriety and the need for injunctive relief.
>
> "The inclusion of this new language is to define the duty of the courts to exercise independent judgment on the propriety of issuance of a temporary restraining order or a preliminary injunction. This new language is intended to codify the decisional law of [two cases] and [other] similar cases which have defined the judicial role to include the exercise of such independent judgment. The Conferees did not intend, nor do they consider it appropriate, to burden the Commission with the requirements imposed by the traditional equity standard which the common law applies to private litigants."[2335]

Although this legislative history substantiated the proposition that the FTC did not need to prove irreparable harm to obtain a preliminary injunction, Justice Ginsburg nonetheless emphasized that it would be inappropriate to construe section 13(b)(2) as granting the FTC an *automatic* right to receive a preliminary injunction:

> The case law Congress codified removes irreparable damage as an essential element of the preliminary injunction proponent's case and permits the judge to presume from a likelihood of success showing that the public interest will be served by interim relief. However, the judge remains obligated "to exercise independent judgment on the propriety of issuance of a temporary restraining order or a preliminary injunction." Independent judgment is not exercised when a court responds automatically to the agency's threshold showings. To exercise such judgment, the court must take genuine account of "the equities."[2336]

[2334] *Id.*

[2335] *Id.* at 1081–82 (emphasis in original) (citations omitted) (quoting H.R. Rep. No. 93-624, at 31 (1973) (first citing FTC v. Nat'l Health Aids, Inc., 108 F. Supp. 340 (D. Md. 1952); and then citing FTC v. Sterling Drug, Inc., 317 F.2d 669 (2ᵈ Cir. 1963))).

[2336] *Id.* at 1082 (quoting H.R. Rep. No. 93-624, at 31).

Justice Ginsburg explained that, even though Congress has allowed the FTC to satisfy a lower standard than a private litigant to obtain a preliminary injunction, a district judge still must weigh (the remaining) equitable factors when determining whether granting the FTC's request for a preliminary injunction would be appropriate:

> The Commission urges that there is no equity to weigh here other than the one it advances—the public interest in effective antitrust enforcement. Once the Commission shows a likelihood of ultimate success and a prospect of interim harm if a merger goes unchecked, then, according to the FTC, a preliminary injunction barring the acquisition should issue without further ado. Our reading of the statute and its legislative history does not accord with the Commission's. We find that Congress had in view equities other than antitrust enforcement and a role for the court less mechanical than the one the FTC describes.[2337]

Put differently, Justice Ginsburg's 1981 opinion for the D.C. Circuit in *Weyerhaeuser* concerning the FTC's statutory right to a looser standard for getting a preliminary injunction accurately anticipated *eBay*, 25 years later, by emphasizing that the issuance of such a preliminary injunction was not automatic or "mechanical." To the contrary, it required the exercise of "judgment." Other circuits, including the Ninth Circuit, have applied reasoning that resembles Justice Ginsburg's interpretation of section 13(b)(2) in *Weyerhaeuser*.[2338]

Therefore, even if one were to focus on the standard that courts apply to grant the FTC a *preliminary* injunction, Judge Koh's "mechanical" conclusion that the FTC has an automatic right to receive a permanent, worldwide injunction would still be legal error. The larger point of course is that the Supreme Court's decision in *eBay* is the precedent that Judge Koh should have followed when ruling on the FTC's request for a *permanent* injunction in *FTC v. Qualcomm*.

[2337] *Id.* at 1081.

[2338] *See, e.g.*, FTC v. Consumer Def., LLC, 926 F.3d 1208, 1212 (9th Cir. 2019) ("The FTC counters that in a case involving statutory enforcement where the governing statute authorizes injunctive relief, irreparable harm is presumed, and a court need only weigh the equities and consider the likelihood of success on the merits. The FTC's position is supported by our precedent.") (citing FTC v. World Wide Factors, Ltd., 882 F.2d 344, 346–46 (9th Cir. 1989)); *World Wide Factors*, 882 F.2d at 347 (addressing the district court's weighing of public and private interests); *see also* FTC v. H.N. Singer, Inc., 668 F.2d 1107, 1111 (9th Cir. 1982); FTC v. Penn State Hershey Med. Ctr., 838 F.3d 327, 352 (3d Cir. 2016); FTC v. Univ. Health, Inc., 938 F.2d 1206, 1218 (11th Cir. 1991); FTC v. World Travel Vacation Brokers, Inc., 861 F.2d 1020, 1028–29 (7th Cir. 1988); FTC v. Food Town Stores, Inc., 539 F.2d 1339, 1343 (4th Cir. 1976).

B.   *Did Judge Koh Erroneously Exclude Post-Discovery Evidence of Qualcomm's Alleged Market Power?*

Did Judge Koh err in denying Qualcomm a separate hearing on remedies, as the Antitrust Division urged her to provide? In designing her permanent, worldwide injunction, Judge Koh refused to consider even evidence that had become available in the public domain after the cut-off date for fact discovery in March 2018, 15 months *before* she issued her findings of fact and conclusions of law. At least two important events after the close of fact discovery critically altered any thoughtful assessment of Qualcomm's market power and, therefore, any thoughtful assessment of Qualcomm's ability to benefit from continuing to engage in the allegedly anticompetitive conduct.

With each of these developments it became increasingly imprudent for Judge Koh to order a permanent, worldwide injunction without an evidentiary hearing to address the proper scope and probable impact of that permanent, worldwide injunction. Once again, the framework of *Mathews v. Eldridge*[2339] invites one to ask whether Judge Koh denied Qualcomm due process. The marginal cost to the parties and the court of considering post-discovery evidence was small. Meanwhile, the expected loss (of liberty or property) to Qualcomm in the absence of the court's consideration of such post-discovery evidence was enormous, considering that Judge Koh had ordered a permanent, worldwide injunction that would run at least seven years into the future in a technologically dynamic industry.

1.   *Judge Koh's Refusal to Hear Exculpatory Evidence on Qualcomm's Materially Diminished Share of LTE Modem Sales in 2018*

The first development of obvious importance that Judge Koh's permanent, worldwide injunction ignored was Qualcomm's sharply declining share of modem sales. The Ninth Circuit observed that, "[a]round 2015, . . . Qualcomm's dominant position in the modem chip markets began to recede, as competitors like Intel and MediaTek found ways to successfully compete," and that, "[b]ased on projections from 2017 to 2018, Qualcomm maintains approximately a 79% share of the CDMA modem chip market and a 64% share of the premium LTE modem chip market."[2340] Judge Koh found that Qualcomm had monopoly power in the global market for "premium" LTE modems from 2011 to 2016.[2341] In reaching that conclusion, she relied on

---

[2339]   424 U.S. 319 (1976).

[2340]   FTC v. Qualcomm Inc., No. 19-16122, 2020 WL 4591476, at *3 (9ᵗʰ Cir. Aug. 11, 2020); *see also id.* at *3 n.4 ("According to Qualcomm, its market share in premium LTE modem chips dropped below 50% in 2017.") (citing Opening Brief for Appellant Qualcomm Incorporated at 118, FTC v. Qualcomm Inc., No. 19-16122 (9ᵗʰ Cir. Aug. 23, 2019)).

[2341]   FTC v. Qualcomm Inc., 411 F. Supp. 3d 658, 691–95 (N.D. Cal. 2019).

an internal Qualcomm document identifying (and predicting) Qualcomm's market shares, as well as her own analysis of barriers to entry.[2342]

We saw the errors of Judge Koh's market power analysis in Part XI. Yet, even if one takes at face value Judge Koh's conclusion that Qualcomm had market power between 2011 and 2016 in her relevant market, it would not have followed that Qualcomm still had market power in May 2019, when Judge Koh issued her permanent, worldwide injunction. Qualcomm's market share decreased after 2016, especially when Apple decided to use only Intel's modems for the 2018 release of new iPhones.[2343] Strategy Analytics reported that Qualcomm's share of LTE modem sales dropped to 49 percent in 2018,[2344] and Bloomberg subsequently noted (citing a report by Strategy Analytics) that Qualcomm's share was 43 percent in the second quarter of 2019.[2345]

American courts of course have typically refused to infer market power in antitrust cases where a firm's market share is below 50 percent.[2346] Judge Posner wrote for the Seventh Circuit in 1995 that "[f]ifty percent is below any accepted benchmark for inferring monopoly power from market share."[2347] And the Ninth Circuit the same year stated in *Rebel Oil* that, in cases of actual (rather than attempted) monopolization, "a market share of less than 50 percent is presumptively insufficient to establish market power."[2348]

Consequently, it was legal error for Judge Koh simply to assume when issuing her findings of fact and conclusions of law in May 2019 that Qualcomm still had market power and that it would likely have significant market power over the duration of her permanent, worldwide injunction. By refusing to hear evidence on Qualcomm's actual market share of LTE modems in 2018,

---

[2342] *Id.* at 694–95.

[2343] *See, e.g.,* STRATEGY ANALYTICS, BASEBAND MARKET SHARE TRACKER Q2 2018: MEDIATEK SHOWS SIGNS OF RECOVERY tab 4e ("LTE") (2018) (reporting that Qualcomm's market share of LTE modems dropped from 51.9% in 2016, to 46.9% in 2017, and that Qualcomm's provisional market share of LTE baseband processor was 45.4% in 2018); *see also* Sravan Kundojjala, *Intel Gives Up on 5G Modems While Qualcomm Scores Big with Apple,* STRATEGY ANALYTICS (Apr. 18, 2019) ("[In 2018,] Qualcomm (49%), MediaTek (14%), HiSilicon (13%), Samsung LSI (13%) and Intel (8%) were the top-five baseband players, in terms of revenue.").

[2344] STRATEGY ANALYTICS, BASEBAND MARKET SHARE TRACKER Q2 2018: MEDIATEK SHOWS SIGNS OF RECOVERY tab 4e ("LTE"), *supra* note 2343; *see also* Kundojjala, *Intel Gives Up on 5G Modems While Qualcomm Scores Big with Apple, supra* note 2343.

[2345] *Strategy Analytics—2Q 2019 Baseband Market Share: Qualcomm and Samsung Emerge as Early 5G Contenders,* BLOOMBERG, Oct. 15, 2019.

[2346] *See, e.g.,* Bailey v. Allgas, Inc., 284 F.3d 1237, 1250 (11th Cir. 2002) ("[M]arket share at or less than 50% is inadequate as a matter of law to constitute monopoly power.").

[2347] Blue Cross & Blue Shield United of Wis. v. Marshfield Clinic, 65 F.3d 1406, 1411 (7th Cir. 1995) (Posner, J.).

[2348] Rebel Oil Co. v. Atlantic Richfield Co., 51 F.3d 1421, 1438 (9th Cir. 1995). When defending Intel against the FTC's monopolization lawsuit in 2009, WilmerHale argued that, although Intel possessed a unit share of certain microprocessors that exceeded 85 percent, Intel did not possess monopoly power in the relevant antitrust product market. WilmerHale wrote: "Intel admits that its unit share of x86 microprocessors (but not all CPUs) has been between 70% and 85% since 1999, and that its share of revenues from such sales has generally been above 80% during that time period." Answer of Respondent Intel Corporation at 9, Intel Corp., No. 9341 (F.T.C. Dec. 31, 2009). Yet, WilmerHale argued to the FTC that Intel did *not* "possess[] monopoly power in the market for CPUs." *Id.*

Judge Koh suppressed evidence undermining the logic of her permanent, worldwide injunction. Had Judge Koh considered such evidence, it seems likely that the FTC would have been unable to prove—for any of its section 2 theories of liability—that Qualcomm still possessed market power over LTE modems (of which "premium" LTE modems would be a subset) in 2018. The rationale for Judge Koh's permanent, worldwide injunction would then collapse.

> 2. *Apple's Announcement in July 2019 That It Would Acquire Intel's Modem Business Was Substantial Evidence That Qualcomm's Market Power, to the Extent That It Was Proven or Assumed at Trial Ever to Have Existed, Had Materially Diminished*

A second development occurring after Judge Koh's cut-off date for fact discovery had enormous implications for her assumption that Qualcomm still had market power with respect to modems and would continue to have market power in the future. That development was Apple's announcement on July 25, 2019 that it would acquire Intel's modem business.[2349] Vertical integration by Apple, one of the world's largest buyers of modems, will likely affect competition in the modem market in a significant way. Judge Koh herself emphasized in her findings of fact and conclusions of law Apple's importance to modem manufacturers because of its "scale, engineering support, and prestige."[2350]

Judge Koh's reasoning—that her issuance of a permanent, worldwide injunction did not require evidence that Qualcomm would maintain market power—was misguided. The FTC's theory of harm was based on the conjecture that Qualcomm had used its market power in two relevant antitrust markets for modems to charge OEMs "unreasonably high" royalties for an exhaustive license to its portfolio of cellular SEPs—a practice that in turn allegedly imposed a royalty "surcharge" and "tax" on rivals' modems. It necessarily follows that, if Qualcomm no longer has market power in any of Judge Koh's relevant markets, it will be incapable (as Professor Shapiro admitted) of charging OEMs "unreasonably high" royalties for an exhaustive license to its cellular SEPs; in that case, Qualcomm will be incapable of imposing the alleged royalty "surcharge" and modem "tax."

Typically in the American system of justice, we subject a person to a civil sanction only for some past act or omission that violated a legal duty that the person owed to another. It is the exception rather than the rule that courts engage in anticipatory punishment of civil violations of public laws that have

---

[2349] Press Release, Apple Inc., Apple to Acquire the Majority of Intel's Smartphone Modem Business (July 25, 2019), https://www.apple.com/newsroom/2019/07/apple-to-acquire-the-majority-of-intels-smartphone-modem-business/.

[2350] FTC v. Qualcomm Inc., 411 F. Supp. 3d 658, 731 (N.D. Cal. 2019).

not yet occurred. It could not be otherwise if due process of law and the presumption of innocence are to have meaning.

In *FTC v. Qualcomm*, evidence of Qualcomm's current market power is directly relevant for testing the plausibility of Judge Koh's findings of fact and conclusions of law that Qualcomm would engage in future violations unless subjected to the anticipatory punishment of her permanent, worldwide injunction. Apple's decision to acquire Intel's modem division and to integrate vertically into modem manufacturing quickly confuted Professor Shapiro's testimony at trial that entry by acquisition was not relevant economic evidence in a monopolization case.[2351]

Judge Koh herself conceded that a likelihood of future violations by Qualcomm would be essential to determining that her issuance of an injunction would be appropriate.[2352] Yet, the facts that have accrued since the close of discovery in *FTC v. Qualcomm* have disproven Judge Koh's prediction of Qualcomm's continuing market power, and thus those facts establish the impropriety of her permanent, worldwide injunction.

CONCLUSION

If the imperative to destroy awaits the persevering innovator who, succeeding where others have failed, invents something of insight, originality, and enduring value, we will condemn our children to lives impoverished by the resulting deficit of creativity, risk taking, and discovery. How did the imperative to destroy ultimately manifest itself in the FTC's advocacy in *FTC v. Qualcomm*? It took form in the answer to the following question: Would any OEM take an exhaustive license to Qualcomm's cellular SEPs at the device level once Judge Koh's permanent, worldwide injunction had imposed exhaustive compulsory licensing of Qualcomm's cellular SEPs at the component level? The FTC let the cat out of the bag during its closing argument at trial on January 29, 2019.

The FTC's lawyer, Jennifer Milici, expressed doubt "that Qualcomm has valid patents that would not be exhausted by the chip sale" envisioned by the FTC's requested permanent, worldwide injunction.[2353] She explained her basis for that expectation in the course of disputing Qualcomm's argument that multi-level licensing would inefficiently increase transaction costs. In essence, Ms. Milici told Judge Koh that Qualcomm would not incur greater

---

[2351] *See supra* note 932 and accompanying text.

[2352] *FTC v. Qualcomm*, 411 F. Supp. 3d at 816; *see also* United States v. W. T. Grant Co., 345 U.S. 629, 633 (1953); FTC v. Shire ViroPharma, Inc., 917 F.3d 147, 160 (3ᵈ Cir. 2019); FTC v. AbbVie Inc., 329 F. Supp. 3d 98, 145 (E.D. Pa. 2018); FTC v. Amazon.com, Inc., No. C14-1038, 2016 WL 10654030, at *4–6 (W.D. Wash. July 22, 2016); FTC v. Merch. Servs. Direct, LLC, No. 13–CV–0279, 2013 WL 4094394, at *3 (E.D. Wash. Aug. 13, 2013).

[2353] Transcript of Proceedings (Volume 11) at 2133:11–12, FTC v. Qualcomm Inc., No. 5:17-cv-00220-LHK (N.D. Cal. Jan. 29, 2019) (closing argument of Jennifer Milici for the FTC).

transaction costs from OEM-level licensing of its cellular SEPs because Qualcomm would have no OEM licensees left:

> Qualcomm has asserted that if it had to license its competitors, it would still have to license to OEM's. . . . *[I]t isn't obvious that this is true.* In the IRS audio, Mr. Blecker confirmed that all of Qualcomm's standard essential patents were practiced by chips. And Qualcomm has not introduced any evidence that its device level patents are valid and infringed by any handsets.[2354]

"This case," Ms. Milici assured Judge Koh a few moments later, "is all about promoting fair market based negotiations."[2355]

*   *   *

On May 21, 2019, Judge Lucy Koh of the U.S. District Court for the Northern District of California issued her findings of fact and conclusions of law in the Federal Trade Commission's monopolization case against Qualcomm, a leading U.S contributor to cellular standards and a leading developer and supplier of modems used in smartphones and other mobile devices. Judge Koh found that Qualcomm had engaged in a series of interrelated practices between 2006 and 2016 that collectively harmed competition in what she defined as two relevant antitrust markets for different versions of such modems.

Upon finding a violation of both section 1 and section 2 of the Sherman Act, Judge Koh ordered Qualcomm to submit to a permanent, worldwide injunction that would require, among other things, that the company renegotiate its patent-license agreements (which number in the hundreds and span several decades) and offer exhaustive licenses to its portfolio of cellular SEPs to rival modem manufacturers (rather than solely OEMs, which make mobile devices such as smartphones). Judge Koh also prohibited Qualcomm from limiting the sale of its modems only to OEMs that have first taken a license to Qualcomm's cellular SEPs. Judge Koh's permanent, worldwide injunction would run at least seven years. Yet, even if one assumes for sake of argument

---

[2354] *Id.* at 2133:4–10 (emphasis added).

[2355] *Id.* at 2133:23–24. The Ninth Circuit's three-judge panel properly recognized that, "[d]ue to patent exhaustion, if Qualcomm licensed its SEPs further 'upstream' in the manufacturing process to competing chip suppliers, then its patent rights would be exhausted when these rivals sold their products to OEMs," and that "OEMs would then have little incentive to pay Qualcomm for patent licenses, as they could instead become 'downstream' recipients of the already exhausted patents embodied in these rivals' products." FTC v. Qualcomm Inc., No. 19-16122, 2020 WL 4591476, at *3 (9th Cir. Aug. 11, 2020). Ms. Milici's closing argument notably contradicted Professor Shapiro's testimony to the contrary concerning the counterfactual conditional inhering in his theoretical bargaining model. In that counterfactual conditional, Qualcomm supposedly could continue to grant exhaustive licenses to its cellular SEPs to OEMs after Qualcomm had begun—pursuant to Judge Koh's permanent, worldwide injunction—to grant exhaustive licenses to its cellular SEPs to rival modem manufacturers. *See supra* notes 560 and 632.

(but contrary to fact) that the FTC's theories of liability were well founded, Judge Koh's findings of fact and conclusions of law did not support her imposition of a permanent, worldwide injunction.

In broad terms, three substantive errors invalidated Judge Koh's findings of fact and conclusions of law. Those errors necessarily invalidated the reasoning for the permanent, worldwide injunction that she imposed on Qualcomm.

First, Judge Koh's exercise of discretion over fact finding in the bench trial in *FTC v. Qualcomm* denied Qualcomm due process of law. Judge Koh seemed to adopt, without attribution, the opinions of the FTC's expert economic witness, Professor Carl Shapiro. He testified at trial that Qualcomm had market power in two relevant antitrust markets and that a theoretical bargaining model revealed how Qualcomm's challenged practices supposedly harmed the competitive process. By presenting answers to complex economic questions as being based solely on her own (undefined) analysis (rather than having been influenced in any way by the voluminous expert testimony of Professor Shapiro), Judge Koh avoided having to analyze any of Professor Shapiro's testimony in her findings of fact and conclusions of law. Most significantly, Judge Koh avoided the duty to reconcile her findings and conclusions with the testimony of Professor Shapiro that materially tended to exculpate Qualcomm because his testimony was shown on cross examination to expose the implausibility of the FTC's theory of competitive harm. Consequently, Judge Koh also impaired the ability of the Ninth Circuit and the Supreme Court to examine complex questions of economic fact addressed in Professor Shapiro's testimony. In violation of Rule 52(a)(1) of the Federal Rules of Civil Procedure, Judge Koh failed to make specific findings of fact—in particular, findings concerning the plausibility or implausibility of Professor Shapiro's theoretical bargaining model, which appeared, from his public testimony and from the portions of his expert reports that are in the public domain, to resemble the model upon which he had predicated testimony that the D.C. Circuit had found unreliable several months earlier in *United States v. AT&T*. Finally, Judge Koh gave no weight to the testimony of many of Qualcomm's witnesses (including *all* of its expert economic witnesses), yet her reasons for doing so were unpersuasive and at times contradicted by substantial evidence in the record.

Second, Judge Koh's findings of fact (irrespective of whether they were based on a complete or truncated evidentiary record) had virtually no support in the evidence that she identified. Judge Koh's findings of fact that Qualcomm was charging OEMs "unreasonably high" royalties for an exhaustive license to its cellular SEPs, that Qualcomm squeezed its rivals' margins on modems, and that Qualcomm's practices reduced the sales of those rivals all lacked a factual foundation. She chose to place heavy weight on documentary evidence from the past and discount trial testimony (particularly when Qualcomm witnesses testified). Yet, the recurring problem with Judge Koh's analysis of documentary evidence was her failure to comprehend, and then explain in her findings of fact and conclusions of law, the proper context for interpreting that documentary evidence. Judge Koh misconstrued the transcript of Qualcomm's meeting with the Internal Revenue Service in July 2012. She also misconstrued the evolution of the doctrine of patent exhaustion in the Federal Circuit and the Supreme Court since the 2000s. She did not ask basic questions about the provenance and use of an expurgated slide from November 2009 containing draft strategy recommendations emailed by a non-executive-level Qualcomm employee. Of Qualcomm's hundreds of patent-licensing agreements, Judge Koh focused on a single agreement, between Qualcomm and LGE in 2004, in which Qualcomm had charged asymmetric royalties for devices equipped with Qualcomm modems versus non-Qualcomm modems. Yet, she made that solitary occurrence the ostensible rule rather than the exception for Qualcomm's supposed course of dealing with OEMs. Judge Koh rejected as "pretextual" that Qualcomm made relationship-specific investments to design and supply thin modems for Apple, yet she concluded that an entry barrier exists in the modem industry because of the need for entrants to make large sunk investments. From her specious analysis of these key pieces of evidence, which she repeatedly emphasized, Judge Koh inferred anticompetitive intent, disparaged Qualcomm witnesses, and made legally erroneous findings concerning patent exhaustion, among other issues. Judge Koh's conclusion that Qualcomm's licensing practices had harmed the competitive process was not a proven fact; it was, instead, strictly her *a priori* conjecture that violated established economic principles used by courts in antitrust cases to analyze markets and competition. Judge Koh never analyzed actual empirical evidence about competition in what she defined as the two relevant product markets for modems. Publicly available evidence contradicted her conclusion that Qualcomm's conduct had harmed competition in those product markets. Judge Koh also rejected the proposition that the FTC bore the burden of production and the burden of persuasion to prove a reasonably proximate causal nexus between Qualcomm's supposedly anticompetitive acts and the supposed harm that its rivals experienced. She disregarded preponderant evidence establishing the technical superiority of Qualcomm's modems and relied instead on the self-interested testimony of rival modem manufacturers to conclude that Qualcomm's acts "promoted" the "exit" of certain rivals from the industry or produced some other supposedly anticompetitive effect. Judge Koh's findings of fact and conclusions of law enforced what is best termed the "Intel-welfare standard" instead of the consumer-welfare standard for interpreting the Sherman Act. In short, Judge

Koh's findings of fact were unsupported by substantial evidence and in many instances were demonstrably incorrect.

Third, Judge Koh misapplied or ignored controlling Supreme Court precedent. She found Qualcomm's practices unlawful because they reduced rivals' margins, even though the Supreme Court held in *linkLine* that a firm has no duty to price its products so as to preserve its rivals' profit margins. Judge Koh ignored the Supreme Court's call for caution in condemning low prices when she concluded that the reduction in the price of modems that Qualcomm offered to Apple in exchange for (alleged) exclusivity was anticompetitive. She reached that conclusion without performing any of the analysis that *Tampa Electric* requires to determine whether Qualcomm's payments to customers (which is to say, Qualcomm's price reductions to Apple and other smartphone manufacturers) foreclosed so many sales within the relevant market for modems in question as to be capable of harming competition—as opposed to harming merely individual modem manufacturers that failed to make the sale. And Judge Koh implausibly turned *Aspen Skiing* from an ugly duckling into a swan. What was by the Supreme Court's own description a narrow exception to the rule that even a monopolist may decline to deal with its smaller competitors was transformed by Judge Koh into an expansive rule of compulsory licensing available to every corporate giant, including Apple, the largest seller of smartphones in the United States and the new owner of Intel's former modem business. Judge Koh's error was highlighted by the FTC, which disavowed her findings of fact and conclusions of law regarding *Aspen Skiing* during oral argument in Qualcomm's appeal of *FTC v. Qualcomm* to the Ninth Circuit.

*   *   *

The quality of justice manifested in Judge Koh's bench trial in *FTC v. Qualcomm* invites concern for the following reasons, which are distinct from the three specific grounds that I have identified above for reversing her judgment and vacating her permanent, worldwide injunction and her grant to the FTC of partial summary judgment:

1. As noted above, Judge Koh adjudicated a claim, predicated on *Aspen Skiing*, that the FTC claims it never argued. Article III judges may not issue advisory opinions. They are not inquisitors.

2. Judge Koh revealed by her courtroom remarks during trial that she inadequately understood how the doctrine of patent exhaustion informed the antitrust questions presented. Consequently, she also was incognizant of the enormous relevance of the evolution

of that doctrine in the Supreme Court to her earlier order granting the FTC's motion for partial summary judgment, in which she had found that Qualcomm owed contractual duties to two SSOs to offer exhaustive licenses to its cellular SEPs at the component level. If Judge Koh did not understand patent exhaustion at trial, she certainly did not understand patent exhaustion two months earlier, when she granted the FTC's motion for partial summary judgment.

3. Judge Koh impugned the integrity of Qualcomm's founder and executives, its outside counsel, and its expert economic witnesses (as well as executives from Ericsson and Nokia whom Qualcomm called as percipient witnesses to testify in its defense). Yet, she credulously accepted as truthful, reliable, and relevant the self-interested testimony of competitors or customers, who might be expected to benefit from a permanent, worldwide injunction that would destroy a large portion of the value of Qualcomm's uniquely innovative, successful, and productive business model.

4. Judge Koh suppressed all findings of fact concerning the testimony of the FTC's expert economic witness, Professor Carl Shapiro. Most notably, she suppressed his admissions that would have materially exculpated Qualcomm under the FTC's theory of liability positing a royalty "surcharge" and modem "tax" levied by Qualcomm for an exhaustive license to its cellular SEPs. This judicial conduct by Judge Koh violated Federal Rule of Civil Procedure 52(a)(1) and the Due Process Clause of the Fifth Amendment as interpreted by the Supreme Court in *Mathews v. Eldridge*. The Supreme Court should make clear that due process of law requires that a judge in a bench trial faithfully discharge the obligation, akin to the duty that the *Brady* rule imposes on prosecutors, to report materially exculpatory evidence in the judge's findings of fact.

5. Judge Koh displayed naïveté about economics in the most important government monopolization case since *Microsoft*. Her findings of fact and conclusions of law misapplied undergraduate economics. Judge Koh could have avoided that embarrassment if she had either weighed the opposing expert economic testimony from the parties or exercised her prerogative under Federal Rule of Evidence 706 to appoint her own economic expert. Similarly, Judge Koh could have accepted the Antitrust Division's recommendation that she hold an evidentiary hearing on remedies before issuing her permanent, worldwide injunction.

6. Judge Koh seemed not to comprehend the economic consequences of *FTC v. Qualcomm*, either for Qualcomm or for other innovative firms. Because Judge Koh appeared not to understand what was at stake, she necessarily appeared not to understand the tradeoff to be made on the margin between the cost of, and the expected benefit from, her allowance of additional increments of procedural safeguards. To paraphrase Judge Posner's explanation of the economic logic of *Mathews v. Eldridge*,[2356] in giving Qualcomm the amount of process that it was due under the Fifth Amendment in the face of the government's attempt to deprive the company of a large portion of the value of its business model, Judge Koh should have considered the value of Qualcomm's property at risk of deprivation, the probability of erroneous deprivation if particular procedural safeguards were withheld, and the cost of supplying those additional safeguards. In various ways documented in detail in this article, Judge Koh denied Qualcomm procedural safeguards whose marginal cost of provision would have been minimal or nil. Two conspicuous examples were proper adherence to Federal Rule of Civil Procedure 52(a)(1) and to the controlling burden of production and burden of persuasion under *American Express*. The expected marginal benefit to Qualcomm from Judge Koh's provision of these (denied) procedural safeguards was enormous. The expected marginal benefit to Qualcomm from preventing the improvident imposition of Judge Koh's permanent, worldwide injunction amounted to nothing less than averting the destruction of a large portion of Qualcomm's uniquely innovative, successful, and productive business model. That destruction would be measured in the tens of billions of dollars. The additional increments of process necessary on the margin to reduce the probability of the government's erroneous deprivation of Qualcomm's property would have a cost many orders of magnitude less than the harm to be averted. That probability of erroneous deprivation of property was obviously dangerously high: after all, the Ninth Circuit unanimously reversed Judge Koh's findings of law.

The Ninth Circuit's three-judge panel hearing Qualcomm's appeal in *FTC v. Qualcomm* properly reversed Judge Koh's judgment, vacated her permanent, worldwide injunction, and vacated her grant to the FTC of partial summary judgment. But the panel might not have recognized, because it did not conduct a *de novo* review of Judge Koh's findings of fact, that her decision in *FTC v. Qualcomm* also was deficient in its respect for those appearing in her

---

[2356] *See supra* note 214 and accompanying text.

courtroom, in its sophistication about the proper application of economic analysis to complex commercial litigation in technologically dynamic industries, and in its fidelity to due process of law.